CONCISE
BIBLE
COMMENTARY

DON FLEMING

CONCISE BIBLE COMMENTARY

AMG Publishers

Concise Bible Commentary

Copyright © 1988, 1994 by Don Fleming
Published by AMG Publishers
6815 Shallowford Rd.
Chattanooga, Tennessee 37421

The *Concise Bible Commentary* edition is published with the permission of the author and Bridgeway Publications, GPO Box 2547, Brisbane 4001, Australia.

ISBN 0–89957–672–9

Cover design by Market Street Design, Chattanooga, Tennessee

Printed in Canada
11 10 09 08 07 06 05 –T– 9 8 7 6 5 4 3

Contents

Preface

The origins of this commentary go back to my missionary years in Thailand, when I began writing a few books in the Thai language to help local people understand the Scriptures. The result, after many years, was a series of fifteen mini-commentaries on the Thai Bible.

Although the success of the books in Thai was due largely to the lack of available alternatives, news of the books spread, and it was suggested that I prepare an English equivalent for use in other countries. Over some years the fifteen-volume series was produced in English, but by this time I had written several other books and their production was scattered over a variety of countries.

When Bridgeway Publications in Australia undertook a project to republish all these books in a new format, the fifteen volumes were revised and reissued in eight volumes under the series title of *Bridge Bible Handbooks*. Those eight books are now combined into the present one-volume *Bridge Bible Commentary*, which is a companion in size, style and format to the *Bridge Bible Directory*, an A to Z of biblical information.

The eight *Handbooks* were dedicated to people who, in different ways, had a significant influence in my life and ministry. Since the present volume is not a new work but a reformatted (and in parts revised) version of the eight *Handbooks*, no new dedication attaches to it. Instead I am pleased to acknowledge again my indebtedness to those to whom the earlier editions were dedicated.

Book 1	Philip and Pat Juler
Book 2	Chun Kertyoo
Book 3	Reg and Marjorie Vines
Book 4	David Clines
Book 5	John and Grace Robertson
Book 6	Bob and Vic McCallum
Book 7	Chue Petnamngern
Book 8	Vic and Jean Fleming

In the present book, as in my other books, my aim is to provide biblical reference material that bridges two gaps at the same time. First, I want to bridge the gap in time and culture between the world of the Bible and the world of today. Second, I want to bridge the gap between the technical reference works and the non-technical reader. Above all, my desire is to produce books that will encourage people to read the Bible.

Though labelled a commentary, this volume is not a word-by-word or verse-by-verse technical reference book. But neither is it a survey that flies over the top of the various biblical books without touching the text. Perhaps 'running commentary' would be a more appropriate description.

My suggestion is that instead of trying to 'dig deep' or 'squeeze lessons' from the Bible, we relax a little, try to understand what each book is saying, and then let the Bible do whatever it wants to do. 'Let the Bible speak for itself' — which is the title of a practical handbook I have written on how we might teach the Bible in plain language. The aim of such teaching, like the aim of this commentary, is not to exhaust the meaning of the text, nor to force the text to fit our schemes of interpretation, but to provide enough background and comment to enable people to read with understanding.

The Bible has its own power as God's Word, and is an authoritative standard for teaching truth, correcting error, and instructing in right living. It is living and active, and has its own way of making its message relevant to us as readers, but it can do so only if first we understand it. This commentary is designed to help us understand what the biblical writers might have meant, and to do so in such a way that we might readily see the relevance of the ancient Word to present-day living. And once we have the understanding, we have an obligation to act upon it.

Don Fleming

Genesis

INTRODUCTION

The name Genesis means 'origin' or 'beginning' and is a suitable name for the book of the Bible that speaks of the origins of the universe, of the human race, of human sin and of God's way of salvation. Though it stands at the beginning of our Bibles as an individual book, it was originally part of a much larger book commonly called the Pentateuch.

The Pentateuch

Hebrew, the mother tongue of the Israelite people, was the original language of the Old Testament. During the third century BC this Hebrew Old Testament was translated into Greek, the translation being known as the Septuagint (often written LXX), after 'the seventy' who translated it. From these translators we have borrowed the word Pentateuch as a name for the first five books of the Bible (from two Greek words, *penta*, meaning 'five', and *teuchos*, meaning 'a volume').

Originally the five books were one, but they were put into their present five-volume form so that they could fit conveniently on to five scrolls. The Hebrews referred to the whole Pentateuch simply as 'the law' (2 Chron 17:9; Neh 8:1-3,18; Matt 5:17-19; 11:13; 12:5; Luke 24:44).

Age-old tradition, both Hebrew and Christian, recognizes Moses as the author of the Pentateuch (2 Chron 35:12; Neh 8:1; 13:1; Dan 9:11; Mark 12:26; Luke 16:29-31; Acts 15:21), though the Pentateuch itself does not say who wrote it. Nevertheless, it mentions Moses' literary activity. He wrote down the law that God gave to Israel (Exod 24:4; 34:27; Deut 31:9,24), he kept records of Israel's history (Exod 17:14; Num 33:2) and he wrote poems and songs (Exod 15:1; Deut 1:22,30).

As leader of the nation, Moses was no doubt familiar with the family records, traditional stories and ancient songs that people of former generations had preserved and handed down, whether by word of mouth or in written form (cf. Gen 5:1; 6:9; 10:1; 11:10,27). Like other writers, he would have used material from various sources, especially in writing about places and events outside his own experience (Gen 26:33; 35:19-20; 47:26; Num 21:14). In addition he had direct contact with God and received divine revelations (Exod 3:4-6; 33:9-11; Deut 34:10). Under the guiding hand of God, all this material was put together to produce what we call the five books of Moses.

People who study biblical documents have at times suggested that the Pentateuch reached its final form much later than the time of Moses. They base their ideas on the similarities and contrasts they see in such things as narrative accounts, the names used for God, usage of certain words and phrases, and details of Israel's religious system. Some even see a number of independent documents that were later combined into one.

Amid all the discussion that has taken place concerning these matters, people have sometimes forgotten that the important issue is not how the Pentateuch was written, but what it means. And in both the Hebrew and Christian Bibles it stands as a book whose unity is clear and whose message is the living Word of God (Neh 8:8,14; 9:3; John 5:39,46; Acts 28:23).

The book of Genesis

Those who gave the name 'Genesis' to the first book of the Bible were the translators of the Pentateuch. The ancient Hebrews called the book by its opening words, 'In the beginning'. The book's chief concern, however, is not with physical origins, but with the relationship God desires to have with the people who inhabit his earth.

Adam and Eve, though sinless when created, fell into sin, and the evil consequences of their sin passed on to the human race descended from them. Rebellious humanity deserved, and received, God's judgment, but that judgment was always mixed with mercy. God did not destroy the human life he had created. Rather he worked through it to provide a way of salvation available to all. His way was to choose one man (Abraham), from whom he would build a nation (Israel), through which he would make his will known and eventually produce the Saviour of the world (Jesus).

The book of Genesis shows how human beings rebelled against God and fell under his judgment, but it shows also how God began to carry out his plan for their salvation. After recording his promises to make from Abraham a nation and to give that nation a homeland in Canaan, it shows how the promises concerning both the land and the people began to be fulfilled.

OUTLINE

1:1-2:3 THE STORY OF CREATION

The Bible and science

Modern science has revealed so much about the wonders and the size of the physical universe that human beings may seem almost to be nothing. The Bible takes a different view. Human beings are its main concern, for they alone are made in God's image. The story of creation is but an introduction to the story of God's dealings with the human race. The Bible demonstrates this order of importance from the outset by fitting the story of creation into a mere week, into the opening page of a 1,000-page Bible.

The Bible was never intended to be a scientific textbook. It is not concerned with the sort of investigation that modern science is concerned with. If its language were that of modern science, people in former ages would not have understood it, and people in future ages would find it out of date. The purpose of the Genesis account of creation was not to teach scientific theories, but to give a short simple account of the beginning of things in language that people of any age would understand.

Language of the Bible

As with the rest of the Bible, the book of Genesis was written in the everyday language of the people of the time. For example, the Bible speaks of the four corners of the earth (Isa 11:12) and of the pillars, bases and cornerstone of the earth (Job 9:6; 38:4-6); but if people use those statements to deny that the earth is a globe, they misuse the Bible. They show a misunderstanding of the nature of the Bible's language.

Yet such misunderstandings occur. Centuries ago people thought that the sun moved round the earth, but when one scientist suggested that the earth moved round the sun, he was condemned for not believing the Bible. The argument his accusers used was that the Bible says the earth remains still and the sun rises and sets upon it (1 Chron 16:30; Eccles 1:5).

The Bible speaks of the heavens and the earth as ordinary people see them from their standpoint on earth. The scientist may speak of the sun as the centre of the solar system, with the earth a minor planet of the sun, and the moon a small satellite of the earth. But to people of ancient times, and even to us today, the earth where people live is the centre of their world. The sun is merely the 'greater light to rule the day', and the moon the 'lesser light to rule the night'.

In reading the Bible we must understand not only what the Bible says but also what it means. When it says that God 'sits above the circle of the earth' (Isa 40:22), it does not mean that he sits in space somewhere above the horizon, but that he is the sovereign Lord of the universe. Likewise when it says that God 'made man from the dust of the earth' (Gen 2:7), it does not mean that he took in his hands a ball of clay and formed it into a human shape as a baker makes a gingerbread man, but that he made man out of common chemicals. Even we ourselves, who came by natural processes of birth, are said to be formed out of clay and made from the dust of the earth (Job 10:9; Eccles 3:20).

The Creator at work

God is pleased when people study his creation and learn its wonders (Ps. 111:2). The Bible tells us that God is the Creator, and it reveals something of his purposes in creation, but if people want to find out how the physical creation functions, they must do so by hard work as God has appointed (Gen 3:19). God does not give such knowledge by direct revelation. How the various organs of the human body function, for example, is a problem for medical science to solve, not the Bible. The same principle applies in other fields of science.

Science may tell us more about God's creation, but it does so from a viewpoint that is different from that of the Bible. The Bible tells us that God is the one who did these things, and the scientist tells how he might have done them.

When the Bible says 'God did this' or 'God created that', it does not mean that he must have done so instantaneously or 'magically'. We pray, 'Give us this day our daily bread' (Matt 6:11), but we do not expect God to work instantaneously and drop food from heaven on to our plates. We expect him to work through the normal processes of nature in producing the crops from which we get our food by hard work. Yet we still thank God, for we know that he is the provider of all things. Believers and unbelievers might agree on how nature provides humankind with food, but believers add something extra, because they see God working through nature. The 'laws of nature' are God's laws. Science may investigate the physical world and suggest how something happened, but it cannot say who made it happen. Believers can, for 'by faith we understand that the world was created by the word of God' (Heb 11:3).

Believers may therefore hesitate to dismiss a scientific theory simply by saying, 'But I believe God did it', because the theory may have been the way God has done it. When the scientist tells us how rains falls or how grass grows, we do not contradict him by saying, 'But the Bible says God makes the rain fall, God makes the grass grow' (Matt 5:45; 6:30). We accept both as true.

Plan of the Genesis account

As we might have expected, the Genesis account of creation is from the viewpoint of the ordinary person. The story is recorded as if someone were describing creation, not from somewhere in outer space, but from his dwelling place on earth. The earth is only a very small part of God's creation, but the creation story in the Bible is concerned mainly with the earth and mentions other features only in relation to the earth.

The Genesis account is concerned with showing that God made everything out of nothing, that he worked from the formless to the formed, from the simple to the complex. It outlines how he brought the universe through various stages till his creative activity reached its climax in Adam and Eve. Its basic design is to divide the creation story into two groups of three days each. The first group shows how God created the basic spheres of operation (light and dark; sea and sky; fertile land), the second how he created the features within each of those spheres (lights of day and night; creatures of sea and sky; creatures of the land).

This simple creation story, though not intended to be a scientific account, is not in conflict with science. The following notes suggest one way in which scientific knowledge, far from causing us to doubt the Genesis creation story, may in fact give us a more meaningful view of it.

The creation (1:1-2:3)

Countless years ago God, by his sovereign power and will, created the universe. At first the earth was featureless and in darkness because of the mass of surrounding water, but as the thick clouds of water vapour began to lose their density, a hazy light came by day from the invisible sun (1:1-5; first day). As they lost further density, the surrounding clouds of vapour gradually rose from the earth, producing a clear distinction between the ocean's surface below and the ceiling of heavy cloud overhead (6-8; second day). Meanwhile the earth was drying and land became visible. Simpler forms of life then began to appear. Various kinds of soils and climatic conditions produced various kinds of plants, which were so created as to continue producing further plants of their own kind (9-13; third day).

The heavy cloud overhead, which had been becoming thinner and thinner, finally broke. The sun, moon and stars, previously hidden, now became clearly visible. Their effect upon the earth helped to produce a variety of weather and a pattern of annual seasons (14-19; fourth day).

As God's creative activity moved on, animal life began to appear, with creatures in the sea and creatures in the air, all of them suited to their environment (20-23; fifth day). The land also experienced this development of animal life, till it too became full of all kinds of creatures. Finally came the first human couple, who together represented the peak of God's creation. Like the other animals, they were so made that they could feed themselves from what grew on the earth and reproduce their own kind. But they were different from all other animals and were given power over them; for they alone, of all God's creatures, were made in God's image (24-31; sixth day). (See 'The image of God' below.)

God's rest after the creation of the first human couple signified not that he had become tired or inactive (for he continues to care for what he has created), but that he had brought his work to its goal. Having prepared the natural creation for human life, God now desired humankind to enjoy that creation with him (2:1-3; seventh day).

The image of God

Being made in God's image, human beings are unique in God's creation. Somehow they are like God in a way that nothing else is. This does not mean simply that certain 'parts' of human beings such as their spiritual, moral or mental capacities reflect the divine nature. The whole person is in God's image. Because of this expression of God within them, men and women are in a sense God's representatives upon earth. He has appointed them rulers over the earthly creation (see 1:27-28).

Without the image of God within them, people would not (according to the biblical definition) be human. Even if they had the physical appearance of human beings, they would be no more than creatures of the animal world.

An animal's 'animality' is in itself; a person's humanity is not. It depends for its existence upon God. That is why human beings, in spite of the dignity and status given them by God, cannot exist independently of God. They may want to, and may bring disaster upon themselves as a result (as seen in the story of their original disobedience; see notes on 2:8-17, 3:1-24 below), but they cannot destroy the image of God. The image of God within them is what makes them human.

2:4-4:26 EARLY HUMAN LIFE

Life in the Garden of Eden (2:4-25)

From this point on, the story concentrates on the people God made, rather than on other features of the created universe. Again the Bible states that the world was not always as it is now, but was prepared stage by stage till it was suitable for human habitation. God created Adam (meaning 'man' or 'mankind') not out of nothing, but out of materials he had previously created. Like the other animals, Adam had his physical origins in the common chemicals of the earth, but his life existed in a special relationship with God that no other animal could share (4-7).

This status of existing in God's image brought with it the responsibility to respond to God's purposes. God therefore placed Adam in a chosen locality, a beautiful parkland, for his training and testing. This parkland was part of a well watered territory known as Eden, situated somewhere in the region of Mesopotamia (8-14).

With a variety of foods available and a variety of tasks to be carried out to maintain the garden, Adam had plenty of opportunity to develop in mind and body. He could mature through making choices and learning new skills. God's instructions showed that he wanted the people of his creation to enjoy the fulness of their unique life (to eat of the tree of life), but they had to do so in submission to him. Their creation in the image of God meant they could not be independent of God. They did not have the unlimited right to do as they pleased, to be the sole judge of right and wrong (to eat of the tree of knowledge of good and evil) (15-17).

Whether we see the two trees as metaphorical or literal, their meaning is the same. The emphasis in the story is not that the trees were magical, but that they presented Adam with a choice of either submitting to God or trying to be independent of him. Growth in devotion to God involves self-denial (Heb 5:8). Maturity comes through choosing the good and refusing the evil (Heb 5:14), and each victory over temptation would have helped Adam grow from a state of childlike innocence into one of adult maturity. His fellowship with God would have deepened, and his understanding of God's purposes increased.

Because human life alone existed in God's image, none of the other creatures could share this life in any satisfying way. God therefore gave Adam one of his own kind, but of the opposite sex, to be his companion. The man and the woman were equal in status as being made in God's image (cf. 1:27) and were harmoniously united, to the exclusion of all others (18-25). The woman was later given the name Eve, meaning 'life' or 'living', because she was the one through whom future human life would come (see 3:20).

Human disobedience (3:1-24)

Since human beings were made in God's image, and since God was unlimited, the first human couple soon showed that they too wanted to be unlimited. They had to remember, however, that they were not God; they were only creatures made in the image of God. Just as the image of the moon on the water could not exist independently of the moon, so they could not exist independently of God. Their relationship with God contained an element of dependence, or limitation, and consequently God limited their freedom. He told them not to eat of the tree of the knowledge of good and evil.

Satan, the opponent of God and chief of the evil angels, set out to spoil the relationship between God and those created in his image. His evil work was to tempt them to go beyond the limit God had set, to be independent of God, to put themselves in the place of God, to make their own decisions, to rule their own lives, to be the independent judges of right and wrong. The root sin was pride – the desire people have to be their own god – and through this, Satan successfully tempted them to rebel against God (3:1-7). (For the identification of the snake with Satan see Revelation 12:9.)

In a sense the man and the woman gained a knowledge of good and evil, but from the standpoint of guilty sinners, not from the standpoint of a holy God. They knew evil through doing it, and the result was a feeling of shame (8-13).

14

As for the deceiver Satan, his humiliation would be symbolized in the snake's wriggling in the dirt. Henceforth, the human race (the descendants of Eve) would be in constant conflict with Satan. Yet God promised them victory over Satan. A snake might injure a man by biting his heel, but a man can kill a snake by crushing its head. Humankind had been successfully attacked by Satan, but through Jesus Christ humankind would eventually conquer Satan, though the conquest would involve suffering (14-15).

The disorder created by human sin brought with it suffering for the whole human race. From this time on, people could live in God's world and reproduce their own kind only through suffering. Conflict entered human relationships, and even the harmony between husband and wife became spoiled through domination (16-21).

No longer were human beings at peace with God. They had rejected eternal life, and therefore God withheld it from them. They had wanted to be independent of God, and therefore God sent them away from his presence. They had wanted to determine good and evil for themselves, and therefore God drove them into a world where they would learn good and evil only through the sorrow and hardship created by their own mistakes (22-24).

Sin and human death

According to the Bible, human death is a result of sin (Rom 5:12). Yet it would seem from the nature of the human body that physical death is inevitable, whether sin is present or not. Is there a solution to this problem?

Adam was warned that on the day that he sinned he would die (see 2:17). When he sinned, he passed out of a condition where life dominated into one where death dominated. His whole being was affected, so that spiritually he was cut off from eternal life and physically he was certain to die (Rom 5:12-17). The saving work of Christ reverses the effects of sin, bringing victory over death in both its spiritual and physical aspects (Rom 6:23; 8:10-11; 1 Cor 15:21-22). Christ restores people, in the totality of their being, to the life that is proper to them, eternal life.

Some may argue that since human beings are creatures of the natural world, their lives are controlled by the laws of nature and therefore they must die as other animals do (Eccles 3:19-20). But the Bible shows that human beings are not simply creatures of the natural world. They are related to God in a way that makes them different from all other creatures.

It has been suggested that before Adam sinned, the spiritual life within him was so dominant that it prevented those natural processes towards bodily decay that we might normally expect. Sin so changed the situation that bodily decay could no longer be prevented and death became inevitable. If this was the case, physical death became at the same time a completely natural process and completely a result of sin. Where the spirit had complete control over the body death could not occur, but once it rebelled against God it lost control over the body and death resulted.

We need not imagine the chaos of an over-populated world had sin and death not entered, with people being born but never dying. It is *death* that is the enemy, not the termination of earthly existence. Death has its 'sting' because of sin, but there may be some way of departing this world that has no such sting (1 Cor 15:26,55-56; cf. Gen 5:24; 2 Kings 2:11; 1 Cor 15:51-52; Heb 11:5).

Results of sin in the natural world

Concerning the death of other forms of life before the entrance of sin through Adam, we need not try to picture a world in which death never occurred. It is *human* death that is the consequence of sin. Even in the ideal conditions of the Garden of Eden, fruit and leaves died as they were separated from the trees they grew on (see 2:15-16). Wild creatures existed before Adam sinned (see 3:1). Tigers, sharks and ant-eaters no doubt fed on other animals and helped then, as they do now, to keep the balance of nature.

God did not create the world as one great paradise, nor did he intend human beings to spend their days in lazy idleness. It seems, in fact, that most of the world was untamed and awaited the arrival of the human race to enter its full glory (Rom 8:19-23). The duty of Adam and his descendants was to bring the earth under human control, something they would gradually achieve as their numbers increased and people moved out from Eden into the world beyond (see 1:28). But instead of being the means of God's blessing to nature, they themselves fell into disorder.

The ideal conditions of paradise existed only in the Garden of Eden, where God placed the first human couple for their training and testing. When they sinned, they were driven from this garden into the untamed world outside. But because they had lost the spiritual life that God had given them, the physical creation that God intended for their development became the means of their torment. Physical effort and bodily functions that should have brought pleasure brought instead pain and hardship (see 3:16-19).

Cain and Abel (4:1-16)

Adam and Eve's first two sons, Cain and Abel, maintained a belief in God and presented offerings to him. Abel offered the best of his flock in humble faith and God accepted him. Cain's attitude was arrogant and his life ungodly, and therefore God rejected him (4:1-5; cf. Heb 11:4; 1 John 3:12). Since the attitude and conduct of the offerer were more important than his gifts, God told Cain that if he wanted God to accept him, he would have to overcome the sin that threatened to destroy him. That sin was like a wild beast crouching at the door, waiting to attack its victim (6-7).

Cain failed to overcome his sin and in jealous anger he killed Abel. His taking of Abel's life called out for revenge from the one who had given that life. God therefore drove Cain into the barren countryside, away from the place where people, though sinners, at least still worshipped God. Although Cain remained unrepentant, God in his mercy protected him from any possible revenge killing (8-16).

Cain's followers and Seth's (4:17-26)

Difficult though this new way of life was, the ungodly Cain was no doubt relieved to be free from the influence of God. The human population had been growing constantly, so in a plan to make himself secure Cain established his own independent settlement (17-18).

The beginnings of settled life were marked by both good and evil. People made some progress in the raising of sheep and cattle, and developed skills in various arts and crafts, but morally they became worse. Lamech not only murdered a boy who had done no more than slightly injure him, but wrote a song to celebrate his crime. Cain had at least looked for, and received, God's protection against revenge killing, but Lamech was so arrogant and defiant that he challenged anyone to take action against him (19-24).

Cain's descendants now disappear from the story. From this point on the story will be concerned with the descendants of another of Adam's sons, Seth, for these were the ones who continued to worship God (25-26). Adam and Eve produced many sons and daughters (see 5:4), since part of their responsibility was to help populate the earth (see 1:28). Over a long period different racial groups emerged, as people settled in various regions and multiplied.

The Bible story, however, deals with the history of only a small portion of the human race, namely, that which produced the Semitic people, of whom the Hebrews were a part. This was the one line of descent through which people maintained a belief in the one true God (cf. Rom 1:20-23).

5:1-32 GENEALOGY FROM ADAM TO NOAH

As the human race expanded, the minority of people who remained faithful to God became smaller and smaller. The purpose of the genealogy recorded in this chapter is to trace from Adam to Noah that thin line of believers who kept alive the knowledge of God.

The genealogy does not name every descendant in the line from Adam to Noah, but selects ten important people to form an overall framework. Selective genealogies such as this, being easy to remember, were common in the ancient world. In Genesis 11:10-26 another selective genealogy, also based on ten names, carries on from this one to cover the time from Noah to Abram. (The genealogy of Jesus in Matthew 1:1-17 is also selective, omitting several names to produce a simple arrangement of three sets of fourteen.)

Genealogies, particularly selective genealogies, cannot be used to measure the age of the human race. The word 'son' may simply mean descendant, and the word 'father' may simply mean ancestor (e.g. Matt 1:1,8). The ten men named in the genealogy of this chapter are the ten most prominent men of the era. The list notes also the age of each man when he produced the son who became the first link in the chain between him and the next-named person. Death, as usual, demonstrated the results of sin (5:1-20).

The exceptional case of Enoch, however, might have encouraged the faithful to believe that death was not all-powerful. It would not always have power over those who pleased God (21-24; cf. Heb 11:5). The father of Noah expressed the hope that the ground also would be freed from the curse that human sin had brought (25-32).

Different weather and living conditions may have been part of the reason for the unusually long life spans of that time. (Non-biblical records also speak of unusually long life spans among ancient races in the Mesopotamian region.) Whatever the cause, it was no doubt a gracious provision by God in view of the need for people to spread out and bring more of the untamed world under their control (see 1:28). Such tasks were not easy when the human race was small in numbers and lacking in technical knowledge.

6:1-9:29 REBELLION AND JUDGMENT

The wickedness of human society (6:1-8)

As the population grew and societies developed, people again showed the tendency to want to exist independently of God. Like their original ancestors, they wanted to be as God and live for ever (cf. 3:5,22).

It seems that certain angels (the probable meaning of 'sons of God' in this story; cf. Job 1:6; 38:7; Dan 3:25) had, in rebellion against God, taken human form and co-operated with ambitious people in trying to produce a race of 'super-humans' who would be unconquerable and immortal. In response God reminded his human creatures that they were mortal, kept alive only by his spirit within them. In punishment he reduced the human life span from its former length to approximately 120 years (6:1-4). (God's punishment of the angels is possibly referred to in 1 Peter 3:19-20 and Jude 6.)

People, however, did not heed God's warning. Their wickedness continued to increase, till God decided that the only thing to do was to destroy them (5-8).

The flood (6:9-8:19)

Amid the corruption, there was one man, Noah, who remained faithful to God. Therefore, God promised to preserve Noah, along with his family, so that when the former evil race had been destroyed, he could use Noah and his family to build a new people (9-12; cf. Heb 11:7; 2 Peter 2:4-5).

God's means of destruction was a great flood. Besides preserving Noah and his family, God preserved a pair of each kind of animals in the region, thereby helping to maintain the balance between people and animals.

All the people and animals to be preserved were housed in a huge box-like structure called an ark, which was designed to float on the floodwaters. The ark was about 133 metres long, 22 metres wide and 13 metres high. It had a door in the side, and a light and ventilation opening, almost half a metre deep, running around the top of the wall just below the roof overhang. Horizontally it was divided into three decks and vertically it was divided into a number of rooms. These divisions helped to separate the animals and brace the whole structure (13-22). Noah took additional clean animals into the ark, possibly to use later for food and sacrifices (7:1-10; cf. 8:20; 9:2-3).

It seems that, in addition to the forty days' constant downpour of heavy rain, there was a break in the earth's crust that sent the waters from the sea pouring into the Mesopotamian valley (11-16). Even when the rain stopped and the earth's crust and sea bed settled again, the floodwaters took many months to go down (17-24).

Almost four months after the rain stopped, the ark came to rest somewhere in the Ararat Range (8:1-4). Noah had difficulty seeing anything out of the ark, but he managed to notice a number of hilltops when they later became visible (5). By sending out firstly a raven and then a dove, he found out whether the land was drying out in the lower regions that he could not see (6-12). When at last he removed the ark's covering, he saw clearly that the land had now dried out completely. Nevertheless, he had to wait further till grass and plants had grown sufficiently to support animal life. Finally, more than seven months after the ark had been grounded, Noah, his family and all the animals came out of the ark (13-19).

As we have come to expect, the Bible describes the flood from the viewpoint of an ordinary person who might have seen it (e.g. Noah). As far as Noah was concerned, the flood was universal, as it covered the whole area which he could see or about which he could get information. It probably concerned the area of the world that the Bible story has been concerned with in the previous chapters. It was a total judgment on that ungodly world.

Expressions of universality such as 'all the earth', 'all people', 'every nation under heaven', etc. are used frequently in the Bible with a purely local meaning. They do not necessarily refer to the whole world as we know it today (e.g. Gen 41:57; Deut 2:25; 1 Kings 4:34; 18:10; Dan 4:22; 5:19; Acts 2:5; 11:28; Col 1:23).

A new beginning (8:20-9:7)

On returning to the earth now cleansed from sin, Noah first offered sacrifices to God. God's promise not to destroy the earth by a flood again was not because he expected people to improve. He knew they would be as sinful as ever. If God always dealt with people as they deserved, such floods would occur constantly. But in his mercy God would allow sinful people to continue to live on his earth (20-22).

With this new beginning, God gave Noah the same sorts of commands as he had given Adam. People were still God's representatives over the earth, but they still did not have the right to act independently of God. Even in killing an animal for food, they had to realize that they had no independent right to take its life. By not using the animal's blood (representing its life) for their own benefit, they acknowledged that God was the true owner of that life. Human life was even more precious to God than animal life, because human beings were made in God's image. Therefore, any person who killed another without God's approval was no longer worthy to enjoy God's gift of life and had to be put to death (9:1-7).

God's covenant with Noah (9:8-17)

A covenant was an agreement between two parties that carried with it obligations and possibly benefits or punishments, depending on whether a person kept or broke the covenant. Covenants to which God was a party, however, differed from covenants between people in that they were not agreements between equals. God was always the giver and the other person the receiver. The covenant promises originated in the grace of God and were guaranteed solely by him.

Earlier God had made a covenant promise to Noah to save him and his family (see 6:18). After the flood God made another covenant promise, and, like the first, it originated entirely in God's grace. The covenant was made not with Noah as an individual but with all earthly life through him. God would never again destroy earthly life by a flood (8-11). God pointed Noah to the rainbow as his sign to all generations that the covenant depended entirely upon him for its fulfilment (12-17).

Noah and his sons (9:18-29)

On one occasion Noah brought shame upon himself through becoming drunk. But God's condemnation was concerned more with Noah's son Ham, and particularly his grandson Canaan who tried to add to Noah's disgrace (18-23). God announced a curse on the descendants of Ham who would come through Canaan, though not on Ham's other descendants. The descendants of Canaan would have their land taken from them by the descendants of Shem (the nation Israel) and they themselves would be made to serve Israel (24-26; see Josh 9:23; Judg 1:28; 1 Kings 9:21).

The descendants of Japheth, who spread to the north and west through Asia Minor and Greece, were promised a share in the blessings of Shem. This was fulfilled when the New Testament church spread through this region and multitudes of Gentiles believed. As a result they enjoyed the blessings of God's people that formerly had been limited largely to Israelites (27-29; see Gal 3:14; Eph 3:6).

10:1-11:26 GENEALOGIES FROM NOAH TO ABRAM

Nations descended from Noah (10:1-32)

This genealogy must have been written hundreds of years after the time of Noah, when his descendants had multiplied and moved to many places. By that time differences in language, race and culture were noticeable. The purpose of the listing here is to trace the origin of these groups, not to name every single descendant of Noah.

Again the genealogy is simplified, being based on a selection of seventy descendants. Most likely the names in the genealogy were originally the names of individuals, but later were applied to the peoples descended from them and, in some cases, to the territories or towns inhabited by those peoples. The record concerns only the sons of Noah, and says nothing about peoples in the more distant parts of the world who may not have been affected by the flood.

Japheth's descendants settled mainly in the regions north and north-west of Palestine, spreading across Asia Minor to Greece (10:1-5). The Hamites occupied Canaan (until the Israelites took it from them) and parts of Mesopotamia to the east, while in the south they spread to Egypt and the areas on the western side of the Red Sea (6-20). The descendants of Shem (Semites) also occupied parts of Mesopotamia, and spread south from there across Arabia. The particular part of the Semite family that produced the Israelites (that of Peleg) is merely mentioned here, being treated more fully in the next chapter (21-32).

Sometimes the same name appears in more than one list, since there was much inter-marriage, migration and conquest among the various peoples. Also, it should be noted that the territory of Canaan, later to be occupied by the Israelites, contained many tribal groups (see 15:18-20; 23:17-20; 34:2,30), and sometimes the name of one of these tribal groups may have been used to refer to Canaanites in general (cf. 12:6; 15:16).

Rebellion against God at Babel (11:1-9)

Babel was one of the cities founded by Nimrod in the land of Shinar, ancient Babylonia (see 10:8-12). The people of this region, proud of the society they had established, displayed the same anti-God spirit as had brought about God's judgment through the flood. They joined together to build for themselves a new city that would make them famous and give them complete security. They decided to crown their city with what they considered to be a skyscraper, as a symbol of their advanced civilization and complete self-sufficiency (11:1-4).

Their skyscraper may have been a fortress, or it could have been a temple, but whatever it was God saw it as a symbol of rebellion. The more people progressed, the more they tried to use their collective abilities to build for themselves a society that would make them independent of God. God therefore smashed their unholy union decisively (5-9).

Preparation for Abram (11:10-26)

During the period between Noah and Abram, the earth's population increased greatly. People migrated to various regions, and many tribal groups, even nations, were established (see 10:1-32). It appears from this that there must have been more than ten generations between Noah and Abram. In that case, the genealogy recorded here has been simplified, the ten names listed being those of ten leading men of that period. (See notes on 5:1-32.)

The genealogy from Shem to Eber repeats what has been given in Chapter 10 (10-15; cf. 10:21-24). The genealogy from Eber onwards differs from that in Chapter 10. It traces the line through Eber's elder son Peleg (since that was the line that produced Abram), whereas the genealogy in Chapter 10 traced the line through Eber's younger son Joktan (a line that produced many of the Arab tribes) (16-26; cf. 10:25-31). The genealogy shows also that the human life span was shortening, as God had previously announced (see 6:3).

Note: It seems that the name Eber is the source of the word 'Hebrew'. Although in theory all the descendants of Eber could be called Hebrews, in practice the name became limited to those of the line of descent that passed through Abraham, Isaac and Jacob (14:13; 39:17; 40:15; 43:32). In time it became simply another name for Israelites (Exod 2:6,11; 3:18; 1 Sam 4:6; Jer 34:9; Acts 6:1; Phil 3:5).

11:27-15:21 ABRAM'S ENTRY INTO THE PROMISED LAND

Abram obeys God's call (11:27-12:9)

From the nations of the world God now chose one man through whom he would build a new nation, which, in turn, would be the means of bringing his blessing to the whole world (see 12:2-3). God's chosen man, Abram (later called Abraham), lived originally in the idolatrous city of Ur in ancient Babylonia. Although others in his family worshipped idols (Josh 24:2), Abram worshipped the one true God and obeyed him when told to move out of Ur.

With his wife Sarai (later called Sarah), his father Terah, and his nephew Lot, he travelled north-west through the Mesopotamian valley to the town of Haran, where he settled temporarily (11:27-32; Acts 7:2-4).

Some time later Abram and Sarai, along with Lot, moved at God's direction south into Canaan. Abram believed that God would give him a better dwelling place, even though he did not know exactly where he was to go. He believed also that God would make him the father of a great nation, even though his wife had not been able to have children (12:1-5; Heb 11:8-12). At that time the Canaanites lived in the land, but Abram firmly believed that one day his descendants would live there instead. He openly expressed his faith in God by building altars in the very places where the Canaanites were then living (6-9).

Journey to Egypt and return (12:10-13:18)

A long drought in Canaan must have caused Abram to wonder just how reliable this promised land was. In the end he journeyed to Egypt in search of better pastures (10).

Fearing that the Egyptians would kill him in order to take his beautiful wife, he preserved himself by saying she was his sister. This was half true, because Sarai was a daughter of Terah by another wife (see 20:12); but Abram and Sarai did wrong in telling only half the truth in order to hide the full truth (11-16). Even the Egyptian king whom Abram had deceived was more open and straightforward than Abram. Without delay he drove Abram from Egypt in disgrace (17-20).

Abram and his household returned to Canaan (13:1). Throughout these events he and Lot had preserved their flocks and herds, and even increased their wealth (cf. 12:5,16). In fact, they owned so many animals that the place they had moved to (near the northern tip of the Dead Sea) was not able to support them both and trouble arose between them (2-7).

In contrast to his behaviour in Egypt, Abram acted with generosity and faith. He allowed Lot first choice of the pasture lands available, agreeing to accept for himself whatever remained. No doubt he trusted God to look after him in the land God had promised him. Lot chose the fertile lands east of the Dead Sea (8-13).

God responded to Abram's faith by renewing his promise to make Abram's descendants into a great nation and give them Canaan for a homeland. Abram then moved to the pasture lands west of the Dead Sea and settled at Hebron (14-18).

Abram meets Melchizedek (14:1-24)

Lot's selfish choice brought him unexpected trouble. In the Dead Sea region where Lot lived, a group of city-states rebelled against their Mesopotamian overlords and brought war upon themselves. Lot was captured and his possessions plundered (14:1-12). Abram was in no danger but he was concerned

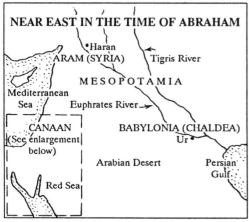

NEAR EAST IN THE TIME OF ABRAHAM

for Lot. With a fighting force of over three hundred from his large household, along with others from neighbouring households, he pursued the invaders. He overpowered the enemy in a surprise night attack, rescued Lot and recovered all the plunder (13-16).

On his return, Abram was met by the king of Sodom, whose goods Abram had recovered. He was met also by Melchizedek, king of the Canaanite city-state of Salem (probably the place later called Jerusalem), who, like Abram, was a worshipper of the Most High God. More than that, Melchizedek was God's priest. He therefore blessed Abram, reminding him that God, and no other, was the true owner of heaven and earth. God was the one who had given Abram this victory. Abram acknowledged this, firstly by making a costly offering to God's priest, and secondly by refusing to accept any reward from the king of Sodom. God alone controlled Abram's affairs in Canaan. Nevertheless, Abram gladly allowed his neighbours to be rewarded (17-24; cf. Heb 7:1-10).

God's covenant with Abram (15:1-21)

Earlier God had promised Abram a people and a land (see 12:2; 13:15). Abram's faith concerning the promised land had been tested through drought and conflict, and his faith concerning the promised people was constantly being tested through his wife's

inability to have children. According to a custom of the time, a childless couple could adopt a person and make him heir to the family property. Abram therefore decided to adopt his trusted slave Eliezer. But God persuaded him not to, reassuring him that he would have a son and, through that son, countless descendants. Abram believed God, and on the basis of his faith God accepted him as righteous (15:1-6; cf. Rom 4:1-5,13-22).

God then confirmed his promise to Abram of a people and a land in a traditional covenant-making ceremony. Normally in such ceremonies sacrificial animals were cut in halves, after which the two parties to the covenant walked between the halves, calling down the fate of the slaughtered animals upon themselves should they break the covenant. God therefore commanded Abram to prepare the animals (7-11; cf. Jer 34:18).

In this case, however, God alone (symbolized by a smoking fire-pot and a flaming torch) passed between the pieces of the slaughtered animals, because he alone took the responsibility to fulfil the covenant promises. All was by God's grace, and was received by Abram through faith. Yet Abram felt a terrifying darkness upon him, for the covenant would be fulfilled amid opposition, bondage, judgment and oppression over a period of hundreds of years. God would be patient with the peoples of

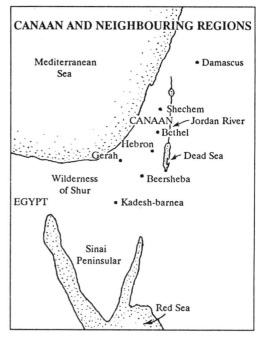

CANAAN AND NEIGHBOURING REGIONS

Canaan and give them ample opportunity to repent. Only when their wickedness had reached uncontrollable limits would he allow Israel to destroy them and possess their land (12-21).

The reason God established the descendants of Abram as the nation Israel was chiefly to use Israel to produce Jesus the Saviour. God's promise of worldwide blessing through Abram was fulfilled in Jesus Christ, through whom people of all nations may receive God's salvation. Jesus Christ was, in a special sense, the promised descendant of Abram (see 12:2-3; Luke 1:54-55,72-73; Gal 3:16). When believers become Christ's people, they become, through him, Abram's descendants also, and so share in the blessings promised to Abram (Rom 4:16-17; Gal 3:6-9,14,29; Eph 3:6). The permanent rest God gives them is more than a dwelling place in Canaan; it is salvation through Jesus Christ (Heb 4:6-10).

16:1-25:18 ABRAM AND THE PROMISED HEIR

Birth of Ishmael (16:1-16)

When Abram earlier suggested adopting his slave as his heir, God reassured him that his heir would be a son of his own (see 15:2-4). But after ten years in Canaan, Sarai was still childless. Weakened in faith, she suggested that Abram obtain his son through their slave-girl Hagar. This was not God's way, but it followed an accepted custom among the people of the region. All legal rights over the child belonged to the wife, not to the slave-girl, though the wife had no right to expel the slave-girl. However, when jealousy arose between Sarai and Hagar, Sarai enforced her rights with such bitterness that Hagar fled (16:1-6).

Hagar was probably heading for her home country Egypt when she was met by the angel of the Lord. Through the angel God told Hagar to return and submit to Sarai, adding that the son to be born to her would himself become the father of a great people. He would be named Ishmael and would grow into a tough, fiercely independent desert-dweller (7-12; cf. 17:20; 21:13). Hagar was so amazed to think she had seen God and lived, that she addressed God by a special name in acknowledgment of her extraordinary experience (13-16).

Note: In the early books of the Old Testament the angel of God appears almost to be the same as God himself. This is possibly because the angel is so closely identified with God as his messenger that when he speaks, God speaks. The temporary physical appearance of the angel is interpreted as the temporary physical appearance of God. (See also 21:17-18; 22:15-17; Exod 3:2-6.)

The covenant sealed (17:1-27)

As Abram and Sarai grew older, God told them again that he would be faithful to his promises. He revealed himself to them in a new name of power (God Almighty) and gave them each new names (Abraham and Sarah) to emphasize that he would make them parents of a multitude (17:1-6,15-16). The Almighty had made a covenant to be God to Abraham and his descendants, and he would give them Canaan to be their homeland (7-8).

To reassure Abraham that he would keep his covenant promises, God told him to make a permanent distinguishing mark in his body. This mark, circumcision, was a symbol of God's faithfulness to his covenant and a sign that Abraham believed God's promises and obeyed his commands. Circumcision sealed Abraham's faith and at the same time demonstrated his obedience (Rom 4:9-12; cf. Acts 7:8). Others in Abraham's household, and all his male descendants throughout the generations to come, were likewise to be circumcised if they wished to be God's people under the covenant. The covenant originated with God, but people had to respond to God's grace with faithful obedience if they were to participate in the blessings of the covenant (9-14).

When God promised Abraham that Sarah would have a son, Abraham felt, in view of his and Sarah's old age, that this was almost too much to expect. It seemed to him more reasonable to expect God to make Ishmael (now an impressive thirteen-year-old youth; see 16:16; 17:1) heir to the covenant promises. God told Abraham that Ishmael would certainly have a notable line of descendants, but God's covenant people would be established through the son yet to be born, Isaac (15-22). Abraham believed God's covenant promises, and gave expression to his faith by carrying out God's covenant commands (23-27).

Messengers from God (18:1-33)

A short time later three men visited Abraham (who was still living at Hebron; see 13:18; 14:13; 18:1.) Abraham welcomed them, not realizing at first that they were God's special representatives. This was another appearance of the angel of the Lord (18:1-8; see also v. 22; 19:1; Heb 13:2). Apparently Abraham had not been able to convince Sarah that she would have a child, so God sent his messenger to her direct. She had to share Abraham's faith (9-15).

21

Because Abraham had an important part in God's plan, not only for the nation Israel but for the whole world, God decided to tell Abraham what he intended to do to the wicked city of Sodom (16-21). Therefore, while two of the messengers went on to Sodom, the third stayed behind with Abraham. Abraham's plea to God not to destroy Sodom showed a good understanding of the righteousness and mercy of God, but it showed also that Abraham did not realize how bad Sodom was (22-33).

Sodom and Gomorrah (19:1-38)

Meanwhile the two messengers arrived in Sodom. Lot, knowing the danger that strangers faced in the streets of Sodom at night, welcomed them into his house (19:1-3). Although Lot did not agree with the immoral practices of Sodom (2 Peter 2:7-8), he apparently did not have the courage to oppose them. He was even prepared to allow the sexual perverts of the city to rape his daughters, in order to protect his two guests from homosexual assault. In a blinding judgment, God showed his hatred of sexual violence and perversion (4-11; cf. Lev 18:22; 20:13; Rom 1:26-27; 1 Cor 6:9-10; 1 Tim 1:10).

God's messengers then told Lot and his family to escape, because Sodom was about to be destroyed (12-14). Yet Lot had become so much at home in Sodom that God's messengers had almost to drag him from the city. Even then he asked a special favour from God that would allow him to carry on his former way of life in another city (15-22).

The region around the Dead Sea where Sodom and Gomorrah were situated contained tar pits, sulphur and natural gases (cf. 14:10). A combination of an earthquake and lightning could have caused an explosion similar to that of a volcano, resulting in burning sulphur raining down over the cities (and over Lot's wife). At the same time it was a direct judgment by God, happening at the time and in the place God had announced (23-29).

So horrifying was the destruction, that Lot decided he could no longer live in safety inside the city. So he took his family out to the hills and lived in a cave. But his two daughters, still affected by the evil influences of Sodom, forced their father into immoral sexual relations with them. The two children that were born through this immorality produced respectively the Ammonites and the Moabites, peoples who later became a source of trouble to Israel (30-38).

Abraham deceives Abimelech (20:1-18)

From Hebron Abraham moved into the territory of the Philistine king Abimelech. As a result of Abraham's deceit concerning Sarah, Abimelech took Sarah as a wife and brought God's threat of death upon him (20:1-7). Upon discovering the truth, Abimelech acted quickly and honourably. He restored Sarah's honour in the eyes of the people, gave gifts to Abraham, and invited Abraham to settle in his land (8-16). Humbled by these events, Abraham turned again in faith to God and asked his blessings on Abimelech and his people (17-18).

The failure of Abraham and Sarah at a time so close to the birth of Isaac showed once more that the fulfilment of God's covenant promise of an heir depended on divine grace, not on human merit.

Birth of Isaac (21:1-21)

When Isaac was born, Abraham circumcised him as commanded. In this way he demonstrated that Isaac was heir to God's covenant promises (21:1-7; cf. 17:9-14).

Ishmael made fun of the covenant family, as Sarah had feared. Being the son of a slave-girl, Ishmael had the right to inherit some of Abraham's wealth, but he could surrender this right in exchange for the freedom of himself and his mother. Sarah, determined that her son should be the sole heir, tried to persuade Abraham to force freedom upon Hagar and Ishmael by expelling them. Abraham hesitated to do this, because they had full rights to remain in his household. But God supported Sarah's suggestion. He promised to look after Hagar and Ishmael, and to make of Ishmael a great people; but his covenant was with Isaac (8-21).

Treaty with Abimelech (21:22-34)

Abraham had settled in the south of Canaan in Abimelech's territory and at Abimelech's invitation (see 20:15). Abimelech, however, was still wary of Abraham and fearful of the God whom Abraham worshipped. He suggested that Abraham and he make a treaty that would guarantee good relations between them (22-24). Abraham agreed to this, but at the same time he forced Abimelech to agree to return to him a well that Abimelech's herdsmen claimed as theirs. Abimelech publicly bound himself to the agreement by accepting from Abraham seven lambs as a witness (25-34). The place where the well was located became known as Beersheba, and Abraham later settled there (see 22:19).

The offering of Isaac (22:1-19)

Although Abraham probably knew that certain peoples of the ancient world at times sacrificed children to the gods, he was no doubt shocked when God told him to sacrifice Isaac. It tested not only his obedience but also his faith, because once Isaac was dead, God could no longer fulfil his covenant promise of giving Isaac a multitude of descendants. A conflict existed between obedience to God's command and faith in his promise. Nevertheless, Abraham obeyed, believing that God would provide the solution to this difficulty, even if it meant raising the sacrificed son back to life (22:1-8; cf. Heb 11:17-19).

Abraham passed God's test: his obedience proved his faith. He did, in fact, sacrifice Isaac, though he did not kill him. God provided an innocent substitute, and Isaac's life was given back, as it were, from the dead (9-14; cf. Heb 11:19; James 2:21-24). God pointed out how these events proved that obedience was the way to blessing. He then reassured Abraham of a multitude of descendants through Isaac (15-19).

Further expressions of faith (22:20-23:20)

While Abraham was establishing his family in Canaan, the family of his brother Nahor in Mesopotamia was growing. The writer records this growth to introduce Rebekah, the future wife of Isaac (20-24).

Back in Canaan, Abraham moved from Beersheba to Hebron, and there Sarah died (23:1-2). Though God had promised the whole of Canaan to Abraham and his descendants, Abraham still owned no land there. The death of Sarah gave him an opportunity to buy a piece of land which, besides being a burial place, symbolized his permanent ownership of Canaan (3-18). By being buried in Canaan, Abraham and his family expressed their faith that this was their homeland, and one day their descendants would live there permanently (19-20; cf. 25:8-10; 49:29-32; 50:13,25; Heb 11:13,22).

A wife for Isaac (24:1-67)

Since Isaac would succeed Abraham as heir to the land of Canaan and ancestor of the promised nation, Abraham required two things concerning him. First, he was not to leave Canaan; second, he was not to marry one of the Canaanites, as they were under God's judgment. Abraham therefore sent his chief servant (possibly Eliezer; see 15:2) on a long journey to Paddan-aram in north-western Mesopotamia to find a wife for Isaac among Abraham's relatives there (24:1-9).

The servant prayed for God's special guidance (10-14) and, on finding that God had led him to the grand-daughter of Abraham's brother, praised God for answering his prayer. The girl's name was Rebekah (15-27). The servant then explained to Rebekah's father Bethuel and her brother Laban why he believed she was God's chosen wife for Isaac (28-49). When all parties agreed that Rebekah should go and marry Isaac, Abraham's servant gave gifts to Rebekah's family as the bride price, and Rebekah's family gave servants to her as a wedding gift (50-61). The large party then journeyed to Canaan, where Rebekah met and married Isaac (62-67).

Abraham's other descendants (25:1-18)

Before continuing the story of Isaac, the writer concludes the story of Abraham with a summary of his other descendants. Besides having a relationship with Hagar, Abraham had taken a minor wife, Keturah (1 Chron 1:28,32). But since Isaac was the promised heir, only he could remain in Canaan and receive Abraham's inheritance. Abraham therefore gave gifts to his minor wives and their children and sent them off to establish independent lives elsewhere. They became ancestors of various Arab tribes (25:1-6).

There was a brief reunion between Ishmael and Isaac at the burial of Abraham (7-11), but Ishmael and his family remained largely outside Canaan. The promises given earlier to Ishmael were fulfilled in the many Arab tribes descended from him (12-18).

25:19-28:9 ISAAC PASSES ON THE INHERITANCE

Isaac's two sons (25:19-34)

After being childless for twenty years, Isaac and Rebekah had twin sons. The characters of the two sons proved to be opposites, and this was later reflected in the two nations that were descended from them. God appointed that the elder, Esau, should serve the younger, Jacob (19-26). But that did not excuse the worthlessness of Esau in selling his right as the eldest son (cf. Heb 12:16-17). Nor did it excuse the ruthlessness of Jacob in gaining the birthright (27-34).

The right of the firstborn was to become family head and receive a double share of the inheritance. In the wider view of the covenant promises given to Abraham, the inheritance involved headship of the nation Israel and possession of the land of Canaan.

Isaac and Abimelech (26:1-33)

When a famine created hardship in Canaan, Isaac proved his faith and obedience by refusing to leave the land. He remained in the Palestine region on the south coast of Canaan, believing that God would provide for him and his household in the land God

23

promised him. But he lacked the faith to trust God to protect him from violence and, like his father, he lied to protect himself (26:1-11; cf. 12:10-20, 20:1-18).

God blessed Isaac as he had promised, but Isaac's farming successes stirred up the envy of the Philistines. He and his men were forced to flee from place to place as the Philistines either seized their wells or filled them in (12-22). Gradually he was pushed out of the best Philistine pastures, but God was still with him. Though he was forced back eventually to Beersheba, God reassured him of his presence and encouraged him to persevere (23-25).

The Philistine king, fearful of the power of Isaac's God, thought it wise to renew the treaty made previously with Abraham. In spite of the Philistines' hostility and arrogance, Isaac renewed the treaty (26-31; cf. 21:22-24). That same day Isaac's men found water, having redug Abraham's well that the Philistines had apparently filled in (32-33; cf. 21:25-34).

Note: Abimelech (meaning 'father-king') was not a person's name, but a Philistine royal title (cf. the Egyptian royal title, Pharaoh). The Abimelech of Abraham's day was a different Abimelech from the one of Isaac's day. The Abimelech of David's day was named Achish (cf. the title of Ps 34 with 1 Sam 21:10-15). Likewise Phicol was not a person's name, but the title of the army commander (cf. 21:32; 26:26).

Jacob receives Isaac's blessing (26:34-28:9)

The custom in ancient times was for the father of the household to confirm the birthright on his firstborn son by giving his special blessing just before he died. People considered this blessing to be more than just a promise; they saw it as a prophecy that carried God's favour. Isaac knew that God's will was for Jacob, not Esau, to receive the firstborn's blessing (see 25:23). Yet he was determined to give the blessing to Esau, even though Esau, by taking wives from among the Canaanites, confirmed his own position as being outside God's covenant blessings (26:34-27:4).

Rebekah and Jacob were also at fault, because of their deceit and lack of trust in God (5-24). In spite of these failures, Jacob received the blessing that God intended for him. He was to be the head of God's promised people, who would live in a prosperous land and have victory over their enemies (25-29).

On finding that his scheme had not worked, Isaac accepted the fact that God's will for the

blessing of Jacob could not be changed (30-37). The only blessing Isaac could give Esau was the promise that he too would be father of a nation (to be known as Edom; cf. 25:30); but that nation would live in a barren region where it would be in constant conflict with its neighbours, particularly Israel (38-40; cf. Num 24:18; 1 Sam 14:47; 2 Sam 8:13-14; 1 Kings 11:15-16; 2 Kings 8:20-22; 14:7,22).

In bitterness Esau planned to kill Jacob, so Rebekah decided to send Jacob to her brother Laban for safety (41-45). However, knowing Isaac's feeling concerning Jacob's deceit, she gave Isaac a different reason for sending Jacob away. Jacob needed a wife, and Rebekah knew that Isaac would not want a third Canaanite daughter-in-law, as Esau's existing Canaanite wives created enough trouble (46; cf. 26:34-35). Isaac therefore agreed to Rebekah's suggestion to send Jacob north to find a wife among Rebekah's relatives. He sent Jacob off with the blessing of the covenant, this time giving his blessing knowingly and willingly. As for Rebekah, she gained what she wanted, but as far as we know she never saw her favourite son again (28:1-5).

When Esau learnt that his parents did not approve of his Canaanite wives, he married again, this time to one of Ishmael's daughters. By such a marriage, Esau gave further confirmation that he was outside God's covenant blessings (6-9).

28:10-36:43 JACOB ESTABLISHES THE FAMILY

Jacob's marriages (28:10-29:30)

Before Jacob left Canaan, God appeared to him in a dream. In spite of Jacob's shameful behaviour, God repeated to him the covenant promises given earlier to Abraham and Isaac, promising also to bring him back safely to Canaan (10-15; cf. 12:1-3; 26:24). In return for God's favour to him, Jacob promised to be loyal in his devotion and generous in his offerings. He named the place where he met God, Bethel (16-22).

From Bethel Jacob journeyed on and finally reached Haran. He first met his cousin Rachel at a well, and she took him home to her father Laban (29:1-14). Laban was as deceitful with Jacob as Jacob had been with Isaac. When Jacob had worked for Laban seven years as payment of the bride price for Rachel, Laban gave him the older daughter Leah instead. After the week-long wedding celebrations for Jacob and Leah were over, Laban gave Rachel to Jacob as a second wife, but only on the condition that Jacob worked an additional seven years as payment of the second bride price. According to custom, each wife received a slave-girl as a wedding gift (15-30; cf. 24:59).

Children born in Haran (29:31-30:24)

Jacob's coolness to Leah created unhappiness in his household. Leah's desire for Jacob's love is seen in the names she gave her first four sons (31-35). Rachel, feeling ashamed that she had not yet produced a child herself, gave her slave-girl to Jacob so that the slave-girl might produce a son whom Rachel could adopt as her own. The result was two sons (30:1-8; cf. 16:1-4). Leah, believing she was not able to have any more children, did the same, and soon Jacob had two more sons (9-13).

When Leah obtained some mandrakes (plants used to make a medicine that people believed helped a woman become pregnant), Rachel bought them from her at the price of giving her a night with Jacob. Rachel's bitterness increased when she found that the mandrakes did not help her, whereas Leah had another son. Leah soon afterwards had yet another son (her sixth) and then a daughter (14-21). Finally Rachel had a son, Jacob's eleventh (22-24).

Jacob tricks Laban (30:25-43)

After Rachel had borne him a son, Jacob decided to return to Canaan. Laban asked Jacob what wages he would like, since much of Laban's prosperity had resulted from Jacob's farming ability (25-30). Jacob claimed as wages all the part-coloured animals in the flock, plus all the black sheep. As these were relatively few in number, Laban agreed, though he then attempted to lessen Jacob's profit by removing from the flocks all the part-coloured animals and black sheep he could find (31-36).

But Jacob was not to be beaten. He decided not to return to Canaan immediately, and spent the next few years carefully breeding Laban's animals. He cross-bred the best of the animals to produce more and more sheep and goats that were healthy and of a colour that advantaged him, while the number of all-black goats and all-white sheep (Laban's share) steadily decreased, in both quality and quantity. Like others of his time, Jacob thought that if an animal when breeding was startled by the sight of something spotted or striped, its offspring would be spotted or striped. His success was due rather to his wise selection of animals, and especially to the overruling activity of God (37-43; cf. 31:8-9).

Jacob flees from Laban (31:1-55)

As Laban and his sons became increasingly hostile to him, Jacob prepared to leave for Canaan without delay (31:1-13). Leah and Rachel agreed, for they too were angry with Laban. He had used them to make himself rich, but apparently had no intention of giving them a share in the inheritance (14-16). Therefore, when they fled, Rachel stole her father's household idols, for according to Mesopotamian custom possession of these gave her some right to the inheritance (17-21).

Laban was upset to find that Jacob and his family had escaped, but was particularly upset that they had taken his idols with them. However, when he caught up with Jacob he was unable to find his idols (22-35). Jacob could bear Laban's persecution no longer, and accused him of heartless ingratitude in view of Jacob's twenty years hard work for him (36-42).

Jacob and Laban, equally suspicious of each other, then made an agreement to prevent one from attacking the other. They set up a stone as witness to their agreement and, by eating a sacrificial meal together, bound themselves to their word (43-55).

Preparing to meet Esau (32:1-32)

During the twenty years that Jacob had been in Mesopotamia, Esau had established his household in territory to the south near the Dead Sea. Jacob knew that if he was to live in peace in Canaan, he would first have to put things right with Esau. With much fear and anxiety he sent news to Esau that he was coming to meet him (32:1-8).

Jacob had by now learnt a humility before God that was lacking the previous time he met Esau. He thanked God for his remarkable blessings in the past, and prayed that God's promises for the future would guarantee protection for him against his brother (9-12). At the same time he thought it wise to send Esau a series of gifts, with the aim of winning his favour (13-21).

Still moving south, Jacob sent his family across the river Jabbok, while he remained behind by himself (22-24a). That night he met God, who appeared to him in the form of a man wrestling with him. As they wrestled, Jacob realized that this 'man' had superhuman strength and the power to bless. As in previous conflicts, Jacob was determined to win, but now he had to learn that against God he could never win. His proud self-confidence was at last defeated. Yet in another sense Jacob did win, for he demanded, and received, a special blessing of God's power that would ensure victory in the future. Though defeated and humbled, he did not lose his persistence or fighting spirit. The old determination was still there, but Jacob the cheat now became

Israel, God's champion (24b-29). By giving him a permanent limp, God never allowed Jacob to forget that the only way he triumphed was through defeat (30-32).

Meeting with Esau (33:1-17)

Jacob may have had a dramatic spiritual experience with God, but he still had to face Esau the next day. He took precautions to protect his family against any possible hostility, then went ahead to meet Esau personally (33:1-3). Esau showed a generous spirit of forgiveness, with the result that the dreaded meeting proved to be a happy reunion. Jacob had gained Esau's birthright and blessing by cunning and deceit,

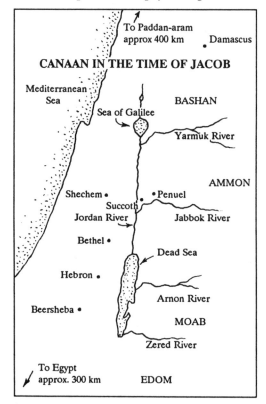

CANAAN IN THE TIME OF JACOB

but he was not allowed to enjoy them fully till he humbled himself before Esau, and Esau acknowledged that he had no claim against Jacob. Esau did this by accepting Jacob's gift (4-11).

Esau asked Jacob to follow him to Edom, but Jacob thought it better not to go immediately. He had a large family and large flocks and herds, and decided to settle for the time being at the town of Succoth nearby (12-17).

Back in Canaan (33:18-35:15)

From Succoth Jacob later moved with his household across the Jordan River into Canaan itself and settled in Shechem. By buying a piece of land, he gained permanent possession of part of the land God had promised to him and his descendants (18-20; cf. 23:1-20; 28:1-5).

When the son of a local headman raped Jacob's daughter Dinah, the headman suggested to Jacob that his son marry Dinah, and that Jacob's sons marry the local Canaanite women (34:1-12). Jacob's sons agreed to the intermarriage provided the men of Shechem were first circumcised (13-17). The Shechemites agreed, for they saw the opportunity for economic profit through intermarriage with Jacob's household (18-24).

But Jacob's sons deceived the Shechemites. As soon as the Shechemite men were circumcised and not physically in a condition to defend themselves, Jacob's sons attacked the town, killing the men and plundering their households (25-29). By going too far in taking revenge for the rape of their sister, Jacob's sons opened the way for further violence (30-31).

God then told Jacob to go to Bethel, where God had appeared to him at the time of his departure from Canaan many years earlier (35:1; cf. 28:11-22; 31:13). First, however, all those with Jacob were to get rid of any idols they had brought with them from Mesopotamia (2-4). In view of the hostility against Jacob and his household after the massacre at Shechem, God gave them his special protection as they travelled (5-8).

At Bethel God renewed his covenant promises to Jacob. The significance of God's reassurance at this time was that Jacob was now back in the land God had given him, and he had with him the family through whom God's promises would be fulfilled (9-15; cf. 13:14-16; 17:2).

Further details of Jacob's family (35:16-29)

This section of the history of Israel closes by recording the birth of Jacob's last son (16-18), the death of Rachel (19-21), the sin of Reuben because of which he lost the birthright (22; cf. 49:4; 1 Chron 5:1), the names of Jacob's twelve sons, who are listed in legal order according to their mothers (23-26), and the death of Isaac (27-29).

Descendants of Esau (36:1-43)

The story is now about to move on from Jacob to his family, but first the record of Esau is brought to a close. The covenant family (Jacob's) had settled in Canaan, while the non-covenant family (Esau's) had settled in Edom. There, over many years, Esau's descendants grew into a large nation (36:1-19; cf. 27:39-40). As the Edomites grew, the original inhabitants of the land, the Horites, were either forced to move elsewhere or absorbed into Edom (20-30; cf. 14:6; Deut 2:12). The record lists the early Edomite kings (31-39) and the main Edomite tribal divisions (40-43).

37:1-50:26 FAMILY GROWTH AND THE MOVE TO EGYPT

Joseph taken to Egypt (37:1-36)

God had told Abraham that his descendants would become slaves in a foreign land, and would remain there till Canaan was ready for judgment. Then they would destroy the Canaanites and possess their land (see 15:13-16). The long story of Joseph shows how God was directing events according to his pre-announced purposes.

Being the father's favourite, Joseph was not popular with his ten older brothers. He was even less popular when he told them about his dreams, which suggested that one day he would have authority over them (37:1-11). When a suitable opportunity arose, his brothers tried to kill him, but Reuben saved his life (12-24). The brothers then sold Joseph to some traders who took him to Egypt, where he became a slave in the house of Potiphar, one of Pharaoh's chief officers (25-36).

Judah and his descendants (38:1-30)

Back in Canaan, Jacob's family had further troubles. Judah, Jacob's fourth eldest son, had three sons, the eldest of whom had married. When this son died childless, Judah, according to the custom of the time, asked his next son Onan to have a temporary sexual relationship with the widow Tamar, with the hope that by him Tamar might produce a child. Legally, this child would be considered son of the dead man and so would carry on the family name and inheritance. But Onan refused, for he wanted any children he fathered to be his own. Because of his refusal to carry out his family obligation, God killed him (38:1-10).

Thinking that he had already lost two sons because of Tamar, Judah hesitated to give his last son to her in case that son died too. Even when the son was old enough to marry, Judah would not give him to her. Tamar therefore thought of a plan to force Judah himself to have intercourse with her, so that she might produce an heir. She disguised herself as a prostitute and succeeded in seducing Judah (11-19). When Judah later found that his

daughter-in-law was pregnant, he saw a welcome opportunity to be rid of her once and for all. Tamar saved herself and shamed Judah by revealing that he was the cause of her pregnancy (20-26).

Tamar gave birth to twins, the elder of whom began that line of descent from Judah which led to David and finally produced Jesus the Messiah (27-30; cf. Matt 1:3,6,16; Luke 3:23,31,33).

Joseph's rise to power (39:1-41:57)

In contrast to Judah, Joseph was blameless in his behaviour in Egypt. Soon he was placed in charge of Potiphar's household (39:1-6). When he rejected the immoral invitations of Potiphar's wife, she turned against him bitterly and had him thrown into prison (7-20). Again his behaviour was blameless, and soon he was given a position of responsibility over the other prisoners (21-23).

Among the prisoners who later joined Joseph were two of Pharaoh's palace officials (40:1-4). One night they both had unusual dreams and, believing the dreams foretold something, told their dreams to Joseph. Joseph predicted that within three days one of the officials would be restored to his former position and the other executed (5-19). The predictions came true, but the restored official failed to do as Joseph requested and bring Joseph's case to Pharaoh's attention (20-23; cf. v. 14-15).

Two years later, when Pharaoh described some puzzling dreams to his palace advisers, the restored official for the first time told the king about Joseph (41:1-13). As a result Pharaoh sent for Joseph, who interpreted the dreams as meaning that Egypt would have seven years of plenty followed by seven years of famine (14-32). Joseph added a recommendation of his own that would ensure a constant food supply throughout the fourteen years (33-36).

Pharaoh was so impressed with Joseph that he made him not only administrator of the program but governor of all Egypt (37-44). The thirteen years Joseph spent as a slave and a prisoner (cf. v. 46 with 37:2) taught him much about practical wisdom and dependence on God, qualities that would now help him considerably in his government of Egypt. He married an Egyptian and had two sons by her (45-52). When the famine came, Egypt alone was prepared for it, and people travelled there from other countries to buy food (53-57).

Joseph and his brothers (42:1-45:28)

When Joseph's brothers came to Egypt to buy grain, Joseph recognized them but they did not recognize him (42:1-8). Rather than make himself known to them immediately, Joseph decided to test them to see if they had experienced any change of heart over the years. Joseph was not looking for revenge. His apparently harsh treatment of them, mixed with kindness, was designed to stir their consciences. They realized they were being punished for their unjust treatment of their younger brother (9-24). Further events impressed upon them that God was dealing with them (25-28).

Joseph's brothers returned to Canaan with a genuine desire to do what was right. But when they told Jacob what the Egyptian governor required of them, they could not persuade him to cooperate (29-38).

After resisting for some time, Jacob eventually realized that he had to allow his sons to return to Egypt, this time taking Benjamin with them. A new spirit of unity and self-sacrifice now appeared among the sons of Jacob (43:1-14). They were still fearful of Joseph (15-23), whose remarkable knowledge gave them the uneasy feeling that they could hide nothing from him (24-34).

The greatest test of the brothers came when Joseph placed them in a situation similar to that of many years earlier when they had sold him. He accused them of a theft by Benjamin, and then gave them the chance to save themselves at Benjamin's expense (44:1-17). The brothers could easily have escaped by sacrificing Benjamin, but instead one of them offered to bear the punishment in his place, so that he, the favourite son, could return to his father (18-34).

Joseph's plan had succeeded. His brothers, accepting the consequences of their past guilt, were now changed men, both in their attitudes and in their behaviour. Therefore, when Joseph told them who he was, he had no need to accuse them of their misdeeds. Instead he pointed out that God had arranged for him to come to Egypt so that the covenant family could be kept alive during the famine (45:1-8). He told them that, since the famine would last another five years, they should bring Jacob and their families to Egypt where he could look after them (9-15).

Pharaoh confirmed Joseph's invitation and provided his family with transport for the move (16-20). Loaded with provisions, the brothers then returned home and told their father all that had happened (21-28).

The migration to Egypt (46:1-47:12)

As they were leaving Canaan for Egypt, Jacob and his family stopped to worship God at Beersheba, the last town in Canaan. Here God told Jacob that, though he would die in Egypt, his descendants would one day return and possess the land (46:1-4). Jacob's family, at the time of the move to Egypt, numbered about seventy people (5-27).

Knowing that Egyptians did not like to live alongside people who kept sheep or cattle, Joseph told his brothers to tell Pharaoh that they were keepers of both sheep and cattle and that they had brought their flocks and herds with them. This would ensure that Pharaoh gave them a territory separate from the Egyptians, where they could live together and multiply without their culture and religion being too easily corrupted by the Egyptians (28-34). Joseph's plan again succeeded, and the family settled in the fertile land of Goshen near the mouth of the river Nile (47:1-12).

Joseph's economic policy (47:13-26)

If Joseph had not planned wisely, the seven-year famine would have ruined Egypt and Canaan. He gave the people food in return for their money (13-15), then, when they had no money, in return for their animals (16-17), then, when they had no animals, in return for their land and even themselves (18-19). In the end all the land belonged to the government and everybody worked for the government, but in return Joseph gave the people land and seed for farming (20-24).

Joseph's policy may have appeared to be hard-hearted at first, but in time the people discovered that it saved them from disaster. Soon they were producing good crops again, though they had to pay the usual tax to the government (25-26).

Words for Joseph and his sons (47:27-48:22)

By insisting that Joseph bury him at Machpelah, Jacob showed his faith in God's promises. He knew that Canaan would become the land of his people (27-31; cf. 23:17-20; 35:12; 46:4).

Joseph's two sons, Ephraim and Manasseh, were by now about twenty years old (see 41:50; 45:6; 47:28), and Joseph wanted his father to bless them before he died. This blessing was more than an expression of good wishes; it was an announcement believed to carry with it the power to make the blessing come true. Jacob blessed Ephraim and Manasseh, raising them to the status of sons. This gave Joseph the birthright that Reuben had lost, for now Joseph, through his two sons, would receive twice the inheritance of Jacob's other sons (48:1-7; 1 Chron 5:1-2).

Both of Joseph's sons would become heads of tribes in Israel, though the tribe of the younger son

Ephraim would be greater than that of Manasseh (8-20). Jacob also gave to Joseph his plot of ground near Shechem, which was the one piece of land he owned in Canaan (21-22; cf. 33:19; 34:26-29; John 4:5).

Blessings on Jacob's twelve sons (49:1-28)

The last words of Jacob to his sons found their fulfilment in the history of Israel's twelve tribes (49:1-2). First Jacob dealt with the six sons of Leah (see v. 3-15), then with the four sons of the minor wives (see v. 16-21), and finally with the two sons of Rachel (see v. 22-27).

Reuben should have been strong, but through lack of self-control he lost the leadership of the nation (3-4; cf. 35:22). Simeon and Levi had been

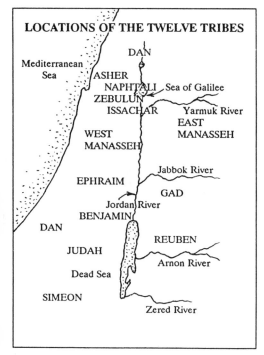

LOCATIONS OF THE TWELVE TRIBES

violent, and their tribes were scattered in Israel (5-7; cf. 34:25-26). Simeon lost its separate tribal identity and was absorbed into Judah (Josh 19:1,9). Levi, however, had a more honourable scattering because of its zeal against idolatry. It had no separate tribal inheritance of its own, but was given cities in all the other tribes (Exod 32:26-29; Num 35:2-8).

Judah was the leading tribe, fierce and powerful in conquering its enemies and ruling over the other tribes. From this tribe came the royal family of

David, whose greatest king, the Messiah, would rule universally in an age of unimaginable prosperity (8-12; cf. Judg 1:2; 2 Sam 7:16; Rev 5:5).

The tribe of Zebulun, which settled near the Mediterranean coast, was enriched through the trade that passed through its territory to the sea (13; cf. Deut 33:18-19). Issachar gained some prosperity from the good farming country it inhabited, but too often it submitted to the powerful Canaanites who controlled much of the region (14-15).

Though pushed out of its original territory on the coast, Dan believed it had the same right to exist as any other tribe. It gained a new dwelling place in the far north, but only by treachery and cruelty (16-18; cf. Judg 18:1-31). Gad, on the east of Jordan, was more open to attack than the western tribes, but its men were fierce fighters who drove back the invaders (19; cf. Deut 33:20).

Asher, bordering the northern coast, lived in rich farming lands whose olive orchards produced the best oil in Palestine (20; cf. Deut 33:24). The neighbouring tribe of Naphtali spread across the highland pasture lands to the Sea of Galilee (21; cf. Deut 33:23).

At the time of Jacob's prophecy, Joseph was at the height of his power. He may have been treacherously attacked in the past, but God had strengthened and blessed him (22-24). The two tribes descended from Joseph were likewise blessed. They were large in number, and the regions they occupied were among the best in the land (25-26; cf. Josh 17:17-18). The final tribe, Benjamin, was too warlike for its own good, and brought such trouble upon itself that it was almost wiped out (27-28; cf. Judg 19:1-21:25).

Deaths of Jacob and Joseph (49:29-50:26)

Again Jacob insisted that he be buried at Machpelah, as a final witness that he died having the same faith as Abraham and Isaac (29-33; cf. 47:29-31). When Jacob died, Pharaoh declared an official time of mourning for him of seventy days. Pharaoh also sent a large group of officials and servants to Canaan with Jacob's family to provide all necessary help and protection (50:1-9). The Canaanites were amazed that Egyptians should come all the way to Canaan to bury someone who was obviously a very important person (10-14).

After seventeen years in Egypt (see 47:28), Joseph's brothers still had feelings of guilt and fear because of their treatment of Joseph in his youth. Joseph was saddened that they should think he might yet try to take revenge on them. He repeated that he would look after them in the future as he had in the past, for God had overruled their evil to preserve the family (15-21; cf. 45:7).

Joseph lived for at least another fifty years after the death of his father (22; cf. 41:46; 45:6; 47:28). Like his father he saw his family grow, and he died with the same assurance that his descendants would inhabit the promised land. As an expression of that faith, he left instructions that when the covenant people moved to Canaan they take his remains with them (23-26; cf. Heb 11:22). His faith was not disappointed (Exod 13:19; Josh 24:32).

APPENDIX

Line of descent from Abraham to the nation Israel

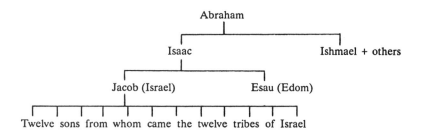

Chronology from Abraham to the Exodus (dates only approximate)

1925 BC	Abraham and Sarah enter Canaan	Abraham aged 76	Gen 16:3,16
1915	Ishmael born	Abraham aged 86	Gen 16:16
1901	Isaac born	Abraham aged 100	Gen 21:5
1841	Jacob born	Isaac aged 60	Gen 25:26
1826	Abraham dies aged 175		Gen 25:7
1751	Joseph born	Jacob aged 90	Gen 41:46; 45:6; 47:9
1721	Joseph enters Pharaoh's service	Joseph aged 30	Gen 41:46
1721	Isaac dies aged 180		Gen 35:28
1711	Jacob's family migrates to Egypt	Joseph aged 40; Jacob aged 130	Gen 41:46; 45:6; 47:9
1694	Jacob dies aged 147		Gen 47:28
1641	Joseph dies aged 110		Gen 50:22
1280	Moses leads Israel out of Egypt	Moses aged 80	Exod 12:41; Acts 7:23,30

Exodus

BACKGROUND

As with Genesis, Exodus takes its name from the Septuagint (abbreviated as LXX), the first Greek translation of the Old Testament. The name means 'a going out', and refers to the central event of the book, Israel's escape from Egypt.

The Genesis story concluded with the family of Jacob (Israel) firmly settled in Egypt. Exodus takes up the story approximately four hundred years later (Gen 15:13-14; Exod 12:41), by which time the descendants of Israel had multiplied till they were a nation in their own right, even though still in Egypt. The book shows how God delivered his people from slavery in Egypt, led them to Mount Sinai, and there formally confirmed the covenant made with Abraham, so that Israel might become in reality a people who would belong to and live for God. God then gave the people, through Moses, the principles by which they were to live and the religious order which they were to maintain if they were to enjoy the blessings of the covenant.

Revelation of God's character

Apart from its value in recording the historical facts on which Israel's national and religious life was built, Exodus is important in revealing much of the character of the one who was Israel's God. Above all, he was a God who redeems. The people of Israel were always to remember him as the one who brought them 'out of the land of Egypt, out of the house of bondage' (Exod 6:3-8; 20:2).

Israelites were to see their history not just as a collection of stories, but as a revelation to them of who God was, how he operated, and what he expected from them. God was involved in every aspect of Israel's life: victories were his saving acts, disasters were his judgments. The preservation and growth of the nation was God's doing (Exod 1:21; 14:21-22,31; 32:35). Israel's God was holy, which meant that the people also had to be holy. They were to be set apart for God and were to keep his commandments (Exod 19:5).

Yet this God, who was different from and separate from his sinful creatures (Exod 19:12-13), also wanted to dwell among them (Exod 25:8; 33:14). The one whose holiness and justice required the punishment of the sinner (Exod 32:33) was the same one who graciously provided the way whereby repentant sinners could come to him, have their sins forgiven and be brought into living fellowship with the holy God (Exod 29:10-14; 34:6-7).

OUTLINE

1:1-4:31	Preparation of Moses
5:1-15:21	Deliverance from Egypt
15:22-18:27	Journey to Sinai
19:1-24:18	Making of the covenant
25:1-31:18	The tabernacle and the priesthood
32:1-34:35	Covenant broken and renewed
35:1-40:38	Construction of the tabernacle

1:1-4:31 PREPARATION OF MOSES

Egypt's oppression of Israel (1:1-22)

The small community of Israelites who first settled in Egypt were all members of one family, the family of Jacob, and their early days were ones of happiness and prosperity (Gen 46:1-7; 47:11-12). God had promised they would grow into a nation, and over the following centuries they increased in numbers and influence till they dominated the whole of the north-east corner of Egypt (1:1-7; cf. Gen 13:16; 17:2; 47:27).

By this time the Egyptian rulers no longer showed friendship to the Israelites (or Hebrews, as the Egyptians called them). Pharaoh feared that if an enemy invaded from the north-east, the Israelites might join them, so he decided to act. He took control of the Israelites and forced them into slavery, using them to build fortified cities where he could keep supplies for his army (8-14). Pharaoh also tried to control the Hebrews' population growth by introducing a policy of child slaughter. But his plan failed, largely because of the courage of the Hebrew midwives, who feared God more than they feared him. Through it all God was at work, preserving his people according to his covenant promise (15-22).

Preparation of Moses (2:1-25)

Moses was the person God chose to save his people and lead them out of Egypt. He was born of godly

Hebrew parents, who no doubt taught him that the true and living God was the only legitimate object of human worship, and this God had chosen Israel to be his people. At the same time Moses grew up in the Egyptian palace, where he was trained in the best learning and culture available at that time (2:1-10; see Acts 7:22; Heb 11:23).

By the time he was forty years of age, Moses believed that God had chosen him to deliver Israel from oppression in Egypt. But when in a burst of anger he killed an Egyptian who was beating a Hebrew, he showed that he was not yet ready for the task God had for him. Neither were his people ready to recognize him as their deliverer. To save his life Moses fled Egypt, and in so doing he rejected, willingly and decisively, his Egyptian status (11-15; see Acts 7:23-29; Heb 11:24-25).

Midian, the place to which Moses escaped, was a semi-desert region to the east, believed to be somewhere in the Sinai peninsular. (The Midianites were descended from Abraham through one of his lesser wives, Keturah, and so were distant relatives of the Hebrews; Gen 25:2-4.) Moses lived for many years in the house of a Midianite chief, Jethro (also known as Reuel), whose daughter Moses married. Here Moses no doubt learnt much about desert life and tribal administration, experience that later proved useful in his leadership of Israel on the journey to Canaan (16-22).

For forty years Moses remained in Midian (Acts 7:30). During this time the Hebrews back in Egypt were suffering increasingly cruel persecution, but at the same time God was preparing Moses to save them. God was teaching Moses those qualities of discipline, toughness, obedience and trust that were necessary if Moses was to rescue God's people from slavery in Egypt and bring them safely to their new homeland (23-25).

God calls Moses (3:1-12)

While Moses was minding sheep at Mount Sinai (also called Mount Horeb, after the range in which it was situated), the unseen God, who for eighty years had silently guided his life, made himself known to him. The revelation of God in the burning bush showed that though this God was unapproachably holy, he could dwell among earthly things without destroying them (3:1-6).

God was now going to use Moses to deliver his people from bondage in Egypt and bring them into a new homeland in Canaan. Moses was hesitant when he saw the task that lay ahead, but God assured him of divine help. Once Moses had led

the Israelites out of Egypt and brought them to Mount Sinai, he would know with assurance that Israel would conquer all enemies and possess the promised land (7-12).

The God of Israel (3:13-22)

If Moses was to present himself to the people of Israel as the one who would lead them out of Egypt, he would need to convince them that he knew God's purposes for them. But he doubted whether they would understand, since they did not know the character of him whom they vaguely called the God of their ancestors. In asking God for help in explaining his purposes to them, Moses was wanting to know not simply the name of God, but the character of the God who owned that name (13).

On certain occasions when God gave a fresh revelation of himself, he revealed a new title for himself that summarized the revelation in one or two words. The name that God announced to Moses on this occasion was 'I am'.

The name 'I am' and the few words of divine explanation that accompanied it were deliberately mysterious, for God's concern was not to satisfy curiosity, but to make himself known to those who wished to know him. His name indicated a character that would be revealed in the triumphant events to come. The eternal, unchangeable, ever-present, ever-active God would prove himself to be always dependable and completely able to meet every need of his people. He would be whatever he would choose to prove himself to be in the varied circumstances Israel would meet (14-17).

Although Moses would eventually be accepted by the Israelites, he would meet only stubbornness in the Egyptian king. He would have an early demonstration of the character of his opponent in Pharaoh's refusal to allow the Israelites' reasonable request to offer sacrifices in a place that was not offensive to the Egyptians (cf. 8:26-27). So great would be the display of God's power in overcoming such stubbornness, that the Egyptians would gladly give their riches to the Israelites (a debt they owed after so many years of slave labour) in order to be rid of them (18-22; see 12:33-36).

The name of God

Israel's ancestors knew God as 'the LORD', Yahweh (or Jehovah) (Gen 2:4; 12:1; 26:2; 28:21; 49:18), but the name meant little to the Israelites of Moses' time. God's revelation to Moses in the 'I am' statement of Exodus 3:14 was an explanation of what the name Yahweh should have meant to God's people.

In the Hebrew language the word translated 'I am' is related to the name Yahweh. Originally, Hebrew was written with consonants only, and the readers put in the vowels as they read. It is believed that 'Yahweh' is the correct pronunciation of the word YHWH (the name of Israel's God), though absolute certainty is not possible, as there are no Hebrew records old enough to preserve the original pronunciation. By the time it had become the practice to add the vowels in written Hebrew, the Jews no longer spoke the name YHWH. They claimed this showed their reverence for the holy name of God, but for many it was more a super-stition. Whatever the reason, the practice developed that when Jews read the Scriptures, instead of speaking the word YHWH, they substituted the word *adonai*, meaning 'lord' or 'master'.

When the Hebrew Bible added vowels to the consonants for the first time (about 300 BC), it put the vowels of *adonai* to the consonants YHWH. This produced a new word, Jehovah, though Jews continued to substitute *adonai* for YHWH when speaking. Translators of English versions of the Bible usually avoid the pronunciation problem by using the expression 'the LORD' (in capital letters) as the substitute for YHWH.

God gives his power to Moses (4:1-17)

In reply to Moses' further complaints that the people of Israel would not believe God had sent him, God enabled Moses to perform three startling signs. The Israelites had no doubt seen magicians in Egypt and such signs would impress them. But they would see that what Moses demonstrated was more than mere magic (4:1-9).

At times Moses himself showed a tendency towards the same disbelief as he suspected in his fellow Israelites. Whether his claim to be unskilled in speech was true or not, his attitude showed a lack of faith. He was merely making excuses and this displeased God. The outcome of his complaint was that God appointed his older brother Aaron to be his spokesman (10-17).

Moses returns to Egypt (4:18-31)

After meeting God, Moses returned to Jethro and then set out with his wife and sons for Egypt. God warned Moses of the stubbornness he could expect to meet in Pharaoh and of the disaster this would bring upon the Egyptian people (18-23). However, Moses could hardly instruct Israel to obey God when he himself had neglected the first requirement of the covenant, the circumcision of his son (cf. Gen. 17:10,14). God sent Moses a near-fatal illness or

accident to awaken him to his responsibilities. As Moses was unable to perform the operation, his wife did so instead. Consequently, she saved Moses' life and so received her husband back when she thought she had lost him for ever (24-26).

Aaron came to meet Moses at Horeb and the two then moved on to Egypt. As Moses expected, the Israelites were unbelieving at first, but they changed their minds when they saw the divinely directed signs (27-31).

The hardening of Pharaoh's heart

In considering the biblical language concerning the hardening of Pharaoh's heart, we must bear in mind that to the godly Hebrew, God was the first cause of everything. Language that to us seems strange would not appear strange to the writer of this story. He would see no inconsistency in saying that God hardened Pharaoh's heart, that Pharaoh hardened his own heart, or that Pharaoh's heart was hardened. They were different ways of saying the same thing.

Certainly, we must not imagine that God hardened Pharaoh's heart against his will, then punished him for having hardness of heart. Before Moses had returned to Egypt, Pharaoh's heart was filled with pride and rebellion against the God of Israel. This was clearly shown in his treatment of the Israelites, and was confirmed by his challenge to God when Moses first met him (5:1-2). His heart was already hardened by his own choice. He was determined to resist God at all costs, in spite of repeated opportunities to reverse this attitude (7:13; 8:32). By confirming Pharaoh in this hardness, God showed both the greatness of Pharaoh's sin and the justice with which it was punished (9:12; cf. Rom 9:14-18).

5:1-15:21 DELIVERANCE FROM EGYPT

Moses' first meeting with Pharaoh (5:1-6:27)

In the eyes of the Israelites, Moses' first meeting with Pharaoh was a disaster. Pharaoh had no fear of Yahweh and no concern for Yahweh's people. In fact, when Moses asked to take his people into the wilderness to offer sacrifices to Yahweh, Pharaoh responded by accusing the Israelites of laziness and making their work harder (5:1-14). This not only increased the suffering of the Israelites but also caused them to turn against Moses. Their great deliverer had done nothing but add to their troubles (15-21)!

Moses was bitterly disappointed at what was happening. It seemed to him that God had failed to keep his promise. In desperation he turned to God and was reassured (22-6:1).

God told Moses that the full significance of his character as Yahweh, the Saviour and Redeemer of his covenant people, would now be revealed to these oppressed slaves in a way that the great men of former times had never seen. Those men, Israel's ancestors, knew that God was the Almighty, the one who created and controls all things and who is fully able to fulfil all his promises; but they had never experienced his character as the covenant Redeemer, the one who would save them from slavery according to the promise given to Abraham (Gen 15:13-14).

In the days of the ancestors, the nation Israel did not exist; it was but a promise of something future. As a result the significance of Yahweh as Saviour-Redeemer had gradually been forgotten. But now the full significance of that name would be dramatically revealed. The Israelites would learn not just the name of their God, but the character indicated by that name. Yahweh was a God of redemption (2-8).

When Moses tried to explain all this to the disheartened Israelites, they were not interested enough to listen. This in turn caused Moses to become disheartened, but God strengthened and encouraged him (9-13).

A selective genealogy shows how God had been working through Israel's history to produce Moses and Aaron at this time. They were prepared and appointed by him to carry out his work of delivering Israel from Egypt. The two men belonged to the tribe of Levi (14-27).

Forecast of coming judgment (6:28-7:13)

Before Moses approached Pharaoh to give him a final opportunity to release Israel, God reminded Moses that not just Pharaoh but the whole Egyptian nation was under the threat of judgment. People and king alike were stubbornly opposed to Yahweh and were devoted followers of Yahweh's enemies, the Egyptian gods (6:28-7:7; cf. 9:27; 12:12).

These were gods of nature and were therefore connected with the river Nile, on which Egypt depended entirely for its water and for the fertile soil washed down at flood time each year. According to the Egyptians' belief, their gods brought them fruitfulness and prosperity. The plagues that God sent were therefore a judgment on these gods, bringing devastation to the Nile valley and creating widespread ruin and disease. Because these plagues had a religious significance, the Bible calls them 'signs' (see 10:2).

God gave Pharaoh one last chance to release the Israelites before the plagues began. But when his magicians used their skills to imitate the miracle performed by Moses and Aaron, Pharaoh arrogantly dismissed the Israelite leaders (8-13).

Nine plagues (7:14-10:29)

The timing, intensity and extent of these plagues show clearly that they were sent by God. It also seems fairly clear that God used the physical characteristics of the Nile valley to produce them.

When the first plague struck, it polluted all the water in the Nile and in the irrigation canals and reservoirs connected with it, resulting in all the fish dying. As the dead fish floated to the banks they would force the frogs out of the water, thereby producing the second plague. Egypt's magicians were able to copy Moses in these two plagues, though in view of the abundance of red water and frogs, their achievements were hardly impressive. They would have helped Pharaoh more by removing the plagues. God alone was in control, and Moses proved this to Pharaoh by removing the plagues at the time he had announced (7:14-8:15).

As God intensified his display of power in the successive plagues, the Egyptian magicians were forced to admit defeat. They saw that Moses and Aaron were not just a couple of sorcerers or magicians who could foresee events then perform tricks to make it appear they had produced the events. This was the direct activity of God, and the protection of Israel through the plagues confirmed the fact. The favourable breeding conditions created by the first two plagues may have been the causes God used to produce successive plagues of gnats and flies (8:16-32).

With piles of dead frogs rotting in the sun and swarms of flies spreading the germs, there was soon a deadly plague of cattle disease throughout the land (Israel's cattle excepted). This was followed by an outbreak of painful skin diseases among the Egyptian people (9:1-12).

Before he announced the seventh plague, God reminded Pharaoh of his mercy towards him in the previous plagues. God could have destroyed him and his people in one mighty plague, but instead he sent these lesser plagues, each time giving Pharaoh an opportunity to repent. The longer Pharaoh delayed, the greater would be his downfall, and the greater would be God's glory when he finally overthrew him. God gave good warning before the coming destruction by hail and lightning, so that people could escape the judgment if they wished. Many of Pharaoh's courtiers, fearful of Israel's God, heeded

Moses' warnings and so were not affected by the disaster (9:13-35).

A clear division now existed among Pharaoh's courtiers. Some stubbornly supported Pharaoh but others tried to persuade him to release the Israelites. Pharaoh offered Moses a compromise that was unacceptable and disaster struck again. Only the flax and barley had been destroyed in the seventh plague. The wheat, which grew up later in the season, was now destroyed by locusts in the eighth plague (10:1-20).

The ninth plague was probably a dust storm so intense that the sun was blotted out and the land left as dark as night. So thick was the dust that the darkness could literally be felt. Pharaoh would still not release the Israelites unconditionally. Moses saw that the time for reasoning with Pharaoh had come to an end (10:21-29).

Final plague announced (11:1-10)

Although God gave Pharaoh full warning of the final plague, he stated no time. However, the Israelites had to make preparation for departure from Egypt, for this plague would bring more than judgment on Egypt; it would bring redemption for God's people (11:1-3; for v. 2-3 see notes on 3:21-22). The plague, some form of physical affliction, would prove fatal to the firstborn of people and animals throughout Egypt. It would fulfil the warning given earlier to Pharaoh (4-10; see 4:22-23).

The Passover (12:1-36)

Until now the Israelites had escaped the judgment of the plagues without having to do anything, but now their safety depended on their carrying out God's commands. Redemption involves faith and obedience.

Each family would be delivered from judgment only by killing a sacrificial animal as substitute for it, and sprinkling the animal's blood on the door of the house where the family lived. The sprinkled blood indicated to those outside that a substitutionary sacrifice had been made; the life of an animal had been taken instead of the life of the firstborn. The Lord's executioner would then 'pass over' that house and no one inside would be killed.

The Passover feast that followed was to be prepared with a minimum of delay. For this reason, the animal was not to be cut up or boiled, but roasted whole over an open fire, and the bread was to be baked without yeast (leaven) to save time waiting for it to rise. The meal was to be simple and the people were to eat it in haste, fully dressed ready for their departure in the morning. They were not to save any of the uneaten meat for the next day, possibly to avoid spoiling, and possibly to prevent people from keeping it as a sort of magic charm. The simplicity and solemnity of the meal no doubt kept them from any feelings of self-glory (12:1-14).

For the next week the people would have no time to bake their bread leavened. They therefore had to carry their dough and baking pans with them, baking as they went. Throughout its future history, Israel was never to forget its hasty departure from Egypt. A symbolic re-enactment of the Passover along with a Feast of Unleavened Bread was to be held as an annual festival, to remind the people of Israel of their deliverance from bondage (15-36; cf. Mark 14:1).

The Israelites leave Egypt (12:37-51)

Approximately 430 years after Jacob entered Egypt with his family, his nation of descendants departed (cf. Gen 15:13; 46:6-7). A sizable group of non-Israelite people, including Egyptians and others who had intermarried or mingled with the Israelites, went with them (37-42). The Israelites were not to send these people back, but neither were they to lessen God's requirements for joining in religious festivals simply to suit these foreigners. Rather they were to encourage the foreigners to carry out the covenant requirements and join with them as worshippers of Yahweh, the only true God (43-51).

Dedication of the firstborn (13:1-16)

Since God had spared the firstborn of Israel's people and animals in the Passover judgment, these rightly belonged to him. The people were to acknowledge this by dedicating, or setting apart, their firstborn to God in an act of thankful worship (13:1-2; see also v. 15). This act also symbolized the consecration (or dedication) of the entire redeemed nation to God, since Israel as a whole was God's firstborn (see 4:22). The people were reminded again to keep the Feast of Passover and Unleavened Bread, for the event that the feast commemorated was the reason for the dedication of the firstborn (3-10).

Animals considered ceremonially clean, such as sheep and cattle, were dedicated to God by means of sacrifice. Animals considered ceremonially unclean and therefore unfit to be offered as sacrifices, such as donkeys, had to be redeemed. That is, they had to be bought back from God, and this was done by the payment of a clean animal in the place of the unclean. If an animal was not redeemed, it had to be destroyed. Human sacrifice, however, was forbidden. Instead the parents ceremonially presented their firstborn to God, and then redeemed the child by a payment of money (11-16; cf. Num 18:15-16).

Note: The instruction in 13:9,16, which speaks of the necessity for true religion in one's inner life and outward behaviour, is in figurative language that Jews of later generations understood literally. This resulted in the creation of phylacteries. These were small boxes containing strips of cloth on which people wrote selected teachings from the law of God. The Jews usually wore phylacteries on their arms or foreheads (see Matt 23:5).

Final triumph over Egypt (13:17-14:31)

When they left Egypt, the Israelites did not go by way of the Mediterranean coast, as this was well defended by the Egyptians and war would certainly have resulted. Instead they went east towards the Red Sea (17-18). (A literal translation for the name of this stretch of water is Sea of Reeds. It was not the 200 kilometre wide sea that we today call the Red Sea, but probably an extension of the Red Sea's north-western arm, the Gulf of Suez. It seems to have been a large shallow expanse of water near the line of the present-day Suez Canal.)

Guided by the symbols of God's presence, the Israelites headed for Canaan. They took with them the embalmed body of Joseph, in accordance with Joseph's earlier request whereby he expressed his faith that one day his people would return to the promised land (19-22; cf. Gen 50:25; Heb 11:22).

The Israelites, by contrast, showed no faith at all when they found they had been led into a dead end. With an impassable stretch of water in front of them, Egyptian soldiers in pursuit behind them, and difficult country on both sides, escape seemed impossible (14:1-12). Moses, however, saw that God was in control. God had drawn Pharaoh out, and now he would be glorified in a final demonstration of power that would overthrow Egypt and bring complete deliverance to his people (13-18).

By nightfall the Egyptians had almost caught up to the Israelites, but the fiery cloud that symbolized God's presence came between the two, and so prevented the Egyptians from advancing farther (19-20). The Israelites received further assistance from the wind, which blew at gale force all night and dried up enough of the sea to form a passage for them to cross to the other side. Just before daybreak, when all the Israelites had crossed over, the Egyptians tried to follow. But by then the wind had dropped and the sea waters began to return to normal, bringing firstly confusion, then panic, and finally destruction to the Egyptian chariot force (21-29). God's intervention had defeated the enemy

and at the same time humbled Israel to a new attitude of faith and reverence (30-31).

Moses' victory song (15:1-21)

The song that Moses and the people sang was more than just a song of rejoicing over a fallen enemy. It was above all a song of praise to God, whose character the people had come to know better in the events of their deliverance from Egypt. He was a God of power who saved his people and overthrew their enemies, a God of terrible majesty and holiness

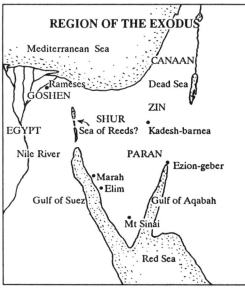

REGION OF THE EXODUS

Mediterranean Sea
CANAAN
Rameses
Dead Sea
GOSHEN
ZIN
SHUR
EGYPT
Sea of Reeds?
Kadesh-barnea
Nile River
PARAN
Ezion-geber
Marah
Elim
Gulf of Suez
Gulf of Aqabah
Mt Sinai
Red Sea

who so directed the forces of nature that arrogant, rebellious people were destroyed (15:1-10). Yahweh executed his judgment on Egypt's gods and proved to his people that he was the only God. Moreover, he was their covenant Redeemer, and was faithful to his promises (11-13; cf. 6:6; 12:12).

In addition the victory gave Israel confidence for the future. As God overthrew mighty Egypt, so he would overthrow less powerful nations that Israel would meet on the journey ahead. Having redeemed his people from bondage, God would surely bring them into the land he had promised them (14-18). Miriam then led the women in a victory celebration of music, dancing and singing (19-21).

15:22-18:27 JOURNEY TO SINAI

Complaints about water (15:22-27)

Having spent all their lives in Egypt, the Israelite people were not prepared for the hardships of life in the barren wilderness regions. Their joyous feelings of faith, so confidently displayed in their song of victory at the Red Sea, did not last long. When, after three days thirsty travel, they found that the only water available was undrinkable, they complained bitterly (22-24).

God had to teach the people that his presence among them did not mean they would be free of the problems of daily living. Nevertheless, if they lived each day in obedience to him, he would help them survive in the desert amid hardship and disease. He could teach them bushcraft so that undrinkable water could be made drinkable; or he could guide their journeyings so that they came to places where good water was available (25-27).

Complaints about food (16:1-36)

The people soon forgot God's goodness to them in giving them water, and complained against him again. This time their complaint was that they had no food (16:1-3). Once more God lovingly gave his people what they needed. From this time on till they entered Canaan, their regular food would be a flake-like substance that they had never seen before. They called the food manna (meaning 'What is it?'), because they did not know what else to call it (4; see v. 15).

God supplied the manna every morning and the people had to eat it that day. The only exceptions concerned the Sabbath, their weekly day of rest. On Saturday mornings God gave no manna, but on Fridays he gave two days supply, half of which the people kept for use on Saturday. The manna spoiled quickly, so the people preserved the extra amount for Saturday by baking or boiling it beforehand (5-7; see v. 23). The night before the first supply of manna, God gave the people additional food in the form of an abundance of birds which, apparently being tired after a long flight, were easily caught and cooked for supper (8-13). Concerning the collection and distribution of the manna in the morning, Moses gave instructions to ensure that no one had either too much or too little (14-18).

Through the command that prohibited keeping the manna overnight, God gave his people the opportunity to prove their obedience. Through the promise that ensured rest on the Sabbath because of the double supply of manna each Friday, God presented them with a way to demonstrate their faith. But in both matters they failed (19-30).

Moses was commanded to put part of the manna in a jar and keep it as a memorial of how God fed his people in the wilderness. The jar was later placed in the ark of the covenant together with

Aaron's rod and the stone tablets on which the law was written (31-36; see Heb 9:4).

Events at Rephidim (17:1-16)

When the people arrived at Rephidim and found no water, they again complained against God and against Moses. Once more Moses prayed for them and once more God miraculously provided. The names by which the place became known, Massah and Meribah, reminded the people of how they 'tested' God (Massah) and 'argued with' Moses (Meribah) (17:1-7).

The Amalekites, a race of wild desert nomads descended from Esau (see Gen 36:12,16), saw the migration of the Israelites to their region as a threat to their security. They attacked Israel but, again in response to Moses' prayer, God gave Israel a notable victory (8-13). Israel could expect further trouble from the Amalekites in the future. For the benefit of future leaders, Moses recorded that God would fight for Israel until Amalek was entirely wiped out (14-16; cf. Deut 25:17-19; 1 Sam 15:2-23; 1 Chron 4:41-43).

On looking back over the weeks since Israel left the Red Sea, we can see how God proved that he could meet all his people's needs. He had preserved them through all dangers and hardships, whether from thirst, disease, hunger or war.

Organizing the administration (18:1-27)

As the Israelites approached Sinai, Moses' wife and children joined him. (He had apparently sent them back to Midian for safety during the time of his conflict with Pharaoh.) With them came Moses' father-in-law Jethro, now a believer in the God of Israel (18:1-12).

Moses had a heavy responsibility in leading the people and dealing with their troubles, and Jethro soon saw that it was wearing him out. Up till then, the people brought all their disputes to Moses, and they accepted his decisions as the laws of God. Jethro suggested that the time had come for a more organized system of administration, with responsible men appointed to assist Moses. These could look after the simple everyday cases, leaving only the more difficult cases for Moses. This would relieve the pressure on Moses and at the same time benefit the people, for they too were becoming worn out because of the long delays in waiting for cases to be heard (13-23). Moses saw the worth of Jethro's advice and put it into practice. Meanwhile Jethro returned home (24-27).

Now that others were to assist Moses in judging the people, a set of laws became necessary. The judges needed some recognized standard if they were to give fair judgments. God therefore gave ten commandments (Chapter 20) as the basic principles that were to underlie the whole law. These were probably the principles that Moses had used as his unwritten standard all the time. The miscellaneous laws that follow (Chapters 21-23, known as the Book of the Covenant) were based on these principles. They were probably taken from cases that Moses had already judged and were now confirmed as being acceptable laws for the future.

19:1-24:18 MAKING OF THE COVENANT

Israel at Mount Sinai (19:1-25)

The arrival of the people at Mount Sinai marked the fulfilment of the promise God made to Moses on the occasion of the burning bush (see 3:12). The journey from Egypt took three months and was accomplished solely by God's power and care. Long before the nation of Israel existed, God chose it to be his people and he confirmed this choice in a covenant made with Abraham. He then guided the history of Abraham's descendants to bring his covenant promises to fulfilment (see Gen 12:2; 15:7-21; Exod 2:24; 4:22; 6:6-8; 15:13). (For the meaning of 'covenant' see note on Genesis 9:8-17.) The blessings of this covenant meant that the people of Israel were to belong to God and, as priests, worship and serve him. As God's chosen people, Israel was to represent him to the nations of the world (19:1-6).

Although the covenant was established solely by God's grace, the covenant's central blessing of communion with God could become a reality only as the people were holy in life and devoted to him; and this could be so only as they understood God's requirements and were obedient to them. The people acknowledged this and solemnly pledged themselves to carry out God's commands. Thus, although the covenant originated in divine grace and was not conditional upon human works (see Gal 3:17-18), the people were still required to keep their part of the covenant if they were to enjoy its blessings (7-9).

Before receiving the detailed requirements of the covenant, the people were reminded of the holiness of the God who initiated the covenant. So holy was he that the people had to carry out symbolic acts of cleansing over the next two days before they were allowed even to look on the mountain while God was speaking there with Moses. A boundary was drawn around the mountain to emphasize the distance between this holy God and his sinful people (10-15). The people were then given a brief view of the awesome power of the one to whom they had submitted themselves. He was not be treated lightly. Any, except those specially invited, who crossed the boundary around the mountain, whether out of idle curiosity or misguided zeal, would be struck with certain death (16-25).

Basic principles of the covenant (20:1-17)

The form of the covenant God made with Israel followed a pattern that was common in the ancient world when an overlord made a covenant with his subjects. God introduced himself to his people by declaring his name and status as Yahweh the sovereign Lord, and recounting to his people what he had graciously done for them. He reminded them that their God was living and active, and that the words they were about to hear were a revelation direct from him (20:1-2).

After the introduction came the basic covenant obligations, summarized in ten easily remembered commandments. These were not laws in the legal sense, for they carried no penalties. Rather they were the principles on which the nation's laws would be built and by which the nation should live.

The first three commandments were concerned mainly with attitudes to God. He alone was the true God; there was room for no other (3). No image of any kind was to be an object of worship, whether used as a symbol of the true God or as the representation of some other (false) god. God would act in righteous judgment against those who rebelled in this way, and against those of succeeding generations who followed the bad example of their ancestors. The sins of one generation would affect the next. But to those who remained faithful, God would prove himself faithful (4-6).

Yahweh's people were not to misuse his name, either in swearing to a statement that was not true or in swearing to a vow that was not kept. They were also to be careful not to use his name irreverently, such as when cursing in anger (7; cf. Lev 24:16).

In the fourth commandment God showed that people could combine an attitude of reverence towards him with an attitude of care for their own needs. The weekly Sabbath encouraged people to worship God, since the day was set apart to him as holy, but at the same time it benefited them by making sure they had adequate rest from their regular work (8-11).

The remaining six commandments dealt with people's duties in the community. They were to be faithful to their family responsibilities, and in doing so would help towards a healthy stable society and ensure for themselves a long and happy life. They were to act with love and consideration towards others by refraining from murder, maintaining purity in sexual relationships, respecting other people's rights to their possessions, refusing to make false accusations, and avoiding the desire for anything belonging to another person (12-17).

Correct attitudes in worship (20:18-26)

Moses was satisfied when he saw that the people, having witnessed the frightening events connected with God's coming to Mount Sinai, were suitably humbled. They became aware of their shortcomings and at the same time developed a greater fear of God (18-21).

People were to show a similarly humble attitude when they built altars at places of God's special revelation (e.g. 17:14-16). Because Israel was a wandering people, such altars were not to be permanent; because Israel was a sinful people, the altars were not to be lavish. They were to consist of simply a mound of earth or a heap of loose rocks, depending on which material was available in the region. The altars were not to be so high that they required steps, in order to avoid any immodesty that might occur if people lifted up their robes while climbing the steps (22-26; cf. 28:42-43).

Characteristics of Hebrew laws

Hebrew laws were mainly of two kinds. The first kind we have met in the Ten Commandments. These were absolute standards, usually in the negative (e.g. 'You shall not steal'). The second kind, which we shall meet repeatedly in the next three chapters, consisted of laws that probably resulted from cases where Moses or his assistants had given judgments, and those judgments now became standards for use in future cases (e.g. 'If a man borrows anything from his neighbour, and it is hurt or dies . . . he shall make full restitution'). Laws of the first kind may be considered basic principles; those of the second kind, the application of those principles to specific circumstances.

When reading the Hebrew law code, we should remember that it was designed to suit the cultural and social habits of the time. It's purpose was to maintain order and administer justice among a people whose way of life was already established. For example, it did not immediately outlaw slavery, for the social, economic and political order of the age was so constructed that slavery could not be instantly abolished. But Hebrew law introduced attitudes of consideration for the welfare of others

that were unknown in most other ancient cultures, and so began the process that eventually brought an end to slavery.

Hebrew law was in some ways similar to other law codes of the ancient world, but it also had some important differences. A fundamental requirement was that the punishment had to fit the crime. There was not the brutality found in some ancient nations, where punishments were out of all proportion to the crime (21:22-25; Deut 25:3). Also, justice was the same for everyone, regardless of status. Laws did not favour the upper classes, but guaranteed a fair hearing for all (23:3,6; Lev 19:15).

In particular the Hebrew law code protected the rights of the defenceless and disadvantaged, such as the poor (23:6), foreigners (23:9), widows and orphans (22:22), debtors who sold themselves into slavery (21:1-11) and even those who were born slaves (23:12).

The basic reason for these differences was no doubt that the Hebrew law came from God, a fact that is stated repeatedly. Legal, moral and religious matters were not separated as in some law codes, for in the community of God's people all areas of life were relevant to each other. The people viewed everything in the light of their understanding of God and their relation to him.

Laws concerning slavery (21:1-11)

Among the Hebrews a slave had rights. Any person, man or woman, who became the slave of another Hebrew, could not be held as a slave for more than six years (21:1-2; Deut 15:12). If a man took his wife with him into slavery, he also took her with him when he was released. If he was unmarried when he became a slave, then later was given a wife by his master, he did not take his wife and children with him when released. They remained with the master. However, if he chose to continue working for the master, he could keep his wife and family (3-6).

The case of a female slave who had become a wife or concubine of the master was different. She was not freed after six years like other slaves, but neither could her master sell her to a foreigner if he no longer wanted her. She had to be bought either by her parents or by some other close relative. If no one bought her, the husband-master had to continue to look after her in accordance with her rights as his wife. If the husband failed to do this, he had to free her without payment (7-11).

Concerning violence and injury (21:12-27)

Death was the penalty for wilful murder, violence to parents and kidnapping for slavery. Israelite law did not allow the widespread ancient practice of a murderer trying to escape punishment by clinging to the horns of the altar and pleading for mercy. But cases of manslaughter were different. When the Israelites settled in their new homeland, they were to appoint certain places as cities of refuge, where a person guilty of manslaughter could find safety (12-17; Num 35:9-15; Deut 19:1-6).

A person had to pay compensation for injuries done to others, the amount paid depending on the nature of the injury and the loss or inconvenience it caused (18-19). A master could not treat a slave brutally and could not beat him to death. If he did, he was punished. If there was no proof that the slave's death was the result of the beating, the master was not punished; but neither could he replace the slave. He had to bear the cost of the loss (20-21).

The basic principle of justice was 'an eye for an eye and a tooth for a tooth'; that is, the punishment had to fit the crime. A heavy penalty was required for a major offence, a light penalty for a minor offence. This principle also restricted vengeance, as people often take revenge far in excess of the wrong done to them (22-25). If a slave suffered serious injury through cruel treatment, he was compensated by being freed unconditionally (26-27).

Jesus, in his reference to 'an eye for an eye and a tooth for a tooth' (see Matthew 5:38-42), did not contradict the principle of fair punishment for wrongdoing, a principle that is a basic element in civil government. Jesus was not laying down laws for civil administrators as was the case with Moses, but was reminding his disciples that they must not always stand on their rights. In personal relationships they must be guided by a spirit of forgiveness, self-denial and active love towards the offender. The spirit ruling in the hearts of Christians is not the same as that which rules in the code of legal justice.

Injuries caused by animals (21:28-36)

Laws were laid down both to protect and to punish the owners of animals that injured or killed people. In determining how much the owner was at fault and what compensation he should pay, the main consideration was how much he could be held responsible for control of the animal. If the person killed by the animal was a slave, compensation was paid to the master, since he owned the slave. But the slave was acknowledged as a human being, not treated as a mere 'thing', and the animal that killed him was destroyed as in the case of an animal that killed a free person. This destruction of the animal was a recognition of the sanctity of human life (28-32).

The principles for assessing responsibility and compensation for injury to animals were similar to those outlined above for injury to people. All parties received fair treatment (33-36).

Laws about repayment (22:1-17)

A convicted thief had to return stolen goods and pay a fine in the form of an additional compensation to the owner. The more serious the crime, the heavier the fine. If the thief could not make the payment, he himself became the payment by becoming the slave of the one whose goods he had stolen. It was not lawful to kill a thief caught in the act, unless at night, when self-defence could make such action excusable. Normally the thief was to be captured and brought before the judges (22:1-4).

Compensation had to be made for damage caused by cattle or fire (5-6). A person who had goods left in his care could become the centre of a dispute if those goods were lost or damaged. If he could satisfy the judges, either through making a statement on oath or by producing evidence, that he was not responsible, he was not required to pay compensation. But if a suspicion of dishonesty existed, or if two parties claimed possession of the same thing, the judges had some means of deciding who was wrong (7-15).

When a man, through misbehaviour, caused a young woman to lose her virginity, he had to pay compensation to the woman's father. This payment was required whether the father allowed the man to marry his daughter or not, because the father now had no chance of obtaining the bride price he could normally expect for a virgin daughter (16-17).

Miscellaneous matters (22:18-23:19)

Israelite law prohibited pagan customs and religious practices that threatened the nation's spiritual life. The penalty for such offences was usually death (18-20). The Israelite people were to remember their own bitter experiences in Egypt and show mercy to the disadvantaged. The law against charging interest on a loan was designed to encourage the rich to help the poor instead of exploiting them (21-27). (For the contrast between lending that is greedy exploitation and lending that is a legitimate investment see Luke 6:34; 19:23.) Being part of a nation dedicated to God, the people were to be respectful and generous towards him, and keep themselves pure from all uncleanness (28-31).

Officials had to administer strict justice at all times. They were not to favour either the rich or the poor, nor were they to allow popular opinion to influence justice. Yet to follow strictly the letter of the law was not enough. People were to be kind to others, even to enemies and foreigners. They were also to be kind to animals (23:1-9).

Every seventh year the people had to rest the land from farming. Any produce that grew of itself during that year was to be left for the poor. God would give extra produce in the sixth year so that there would be no shortage the following year. Every seventh day was to be a rest day for all, masters, workers and animals (10-13; see Lev 25:18-22).

There were three main festivals each year that at least all male adults were to attend. The first of these was Passover-Unleavened Bread, which commemorated the deliverance from Egypt. The second was Pentecost-Harvest Firstfruits, which was celebrated fifty days later and marked the end of the wheat harvest. The third was Tabernacles-Ingathering (GNB: Festival of Shelters), which came at the end of the agricultural year (14-17; for details see Lev 23:1-44).

One superstitious heathen practice that Israel's law prohibited was the keeping of part of a sacrifice as a good luck charm. Another was the boiling of a young goat in its mother's milk, in the hope that this would give increase in the flocks (18-19).

Promises and instructions (23:20-33)

The covenant document, which began in Chapter 20 and which has laid down God's requirements for his people, concludes with a number of promises and warnings. This again follows the well known form of ancient covenant documents. The specific promises for God's people were protection on their journey to the promised land, victory over enemies, health and prosperity in Canaan, and national expansion till they filled their allotted territory. These blessings, however, were conditional upon their obedience and complete loyalty to God (20-33).

The covenant sealed (24:1-18)

When Moses recounted the covenant demands to them, the people once more declared their willingness to obey (cf. 19:8). In ancient times covenants were usually sealed by blood (see notes on Gen 15:7-21), and at Sinai too God and his people were joined in a blood ritual. Half of the blood was thrown against the altar (representing God) and half was sprinkled on the people. This blood ritual, though having its usual significance in covenant ceremonies, may have had added meaning in view of Israel's recent experience in the events of the Passover. On that occasion sacrificial blood was

evidence of life laid down to release a person under condemnation of death. The blood that sealed the covenant at Sinai seems to have had a similar significance. It spoke of Israel's release from the penalty of past sin so that the nation entered the covenant as a people who were holy and dedicated to God (24:1-8; cf. 19:5-6). (For details of the various sacrificial offerings see notes on Leviticus 1:1-7:38.)

To emphasize the closeness of this covenant relation with God, the representatives of Israel went up into the mountain, where they saw the glory of God (without being struck dead, the writer notes) and ate the meal of the peace offering in fellowship together (9-11). On returning to the camp, Moses appointed Aaron and Hur to govern the people in his absence while he and Joshua returned to the mountain. Joshua went only part of the way, but Moses, when invited, entered the very presence of God. He was there about six weeks, during which he received God's directions concerning the building of the tabernacle and the establishment of the priesthood, as recorded in Chapters 25-31 (12-18).

25:1-31:18 THE TABERNACLE AND THE PRIESTHOOD

Purpose of the tabernacle

The cloud on the mountain was only a temporary sign of God's presence with his people. Now that Israel was beginning a new era, God gave the people a tabernacle, or tent, as a permanent sign that he dwelt among them and was part of them. He was the very centre of their national life. This tabernacle was known as the tent of meeting (39:32), for it was the place where God met with his people. It was also called the tent of the testimony (38:21), to remind the people that within it, in the ark, was the testimony of God, the law, that was to guide and control their lives.

Yet while God dwelt among his people, he also, in a sense, dwelt apart from them, for they were sinful and he was holy. They could not come to God directly. They had to come first to the priests and offer sacrifices, then the priests approached God on their behalf. The contrasts between the limitations of this old covenant and the perfections of the new covenant through Jesus Christ are presented in the New Testament book of Hebrews. But until God's purposes were fulfilled in the life, death and resurrection of Jesus, the laws and ceremonies of the old covenant helped people to understand God and to understand themselves.

God did not design these laws and ceremonies as a means by which people might earn salvation. Rather they were part of the developing plan of God that showed people, stage by stage, how he was able to forgive those who trusted in him, yet be just in doing so. This revelation reached its climax in Jesus Christ, and on the basis of his death God could forgive all who had faith in him, even those who lived in Old Testament times (Rom 3:25-26; Heb 9:15).

Then, as now, people were saved only by faith in the sovereign God who in his mercy forgave them and accepted them. Faith, not understanding, was the requirement for salvation. A person's understanding of how God's work of salvation operated depended on how far the divine revelation had progressed in its movement towards completion in Jesus Christ. But in any era the repentant sinner who turned in faith to God could be forgiven.

Design of the tabernacle

The tabernacle was designed so that it could be easily put together, taken apart and transported, for the people of Israel took it with them on their journey to Canaan and set it up at camps along the way.

Simply described, the tabernacle consisted of a wooden box-like frame covered with a cloth and protected from the weather by a tent that covered the whole. In outward appearance it was a tent (which is the meaning of the word 'tabernacle'). The timber framed structure hidden under this tent consisted of two rooms. The front room, which was entered through a curtain, was called the Holy Place and contained three pieces of furniture — a table, a lampstand and an altar for burning incense. A second curtain separated the Holy Place from the smaller rear room, which was called the Most Holy Place or Holy of Holies. This room was the symbolic dwelling place of God and contained the ark of the covenant.

This tabernacle-tent was set in a large court surrounded by a fence. In this enclosure were two articles, the most important of which was an altar on which all the animal and food sacrifices were offered. The other article was a laver, or large basin, in which the priests washed. The tabernacle complex was in the centre of the camp, with the people's tents pitched in an orderly arrangement around it (see Num 2:1-31; 3:21-38).

As a structure, the tabernacle was entirely suited to Israel's circumstances. A tent over a pre-fabricated frame was suitable for a travelling people, and its construction could withstand the desert winds. Many of its articles of furniture were fitted at the corners with rings, through which poles were placed to make the articles easy to carry. The wood to be used was plentiful in the region, did not warp or rot easily and was light, which helped further towards easy transport. Metals were of the kind that would not rust. Timber was overlaid with metal, bronze being used to cover articles in the open courtyard, and gold those inside the tabernacle-tent. Cloth hangings were suitable for the entrances and partitions of a tent.

The brilliance of the metals and the richness of the cloth hangings increased as one moved from the outer court, through the Holy Place to the Most Holy Place. This helped emphasize the glory and majesty of Yahweh, the King of Israel (cf. 28:2).

Materials given by the people (25:1-9)

All the building materials used in the tabernacle came from the voluntary offerings of the people, who at the time were enjoying a degree of prosperity because of their recent gains from the Egyptians and the Amalekites (25:1-7; see 12:36; 17:13). The people gave so generously that Moses had more than he needed and asked them not to bring any more (see 36:5-7). In order that the visible (symbolic) dwelling place of God might be a help and not a hindrance to the people's spiritual growth, everything had to be built according to God's instructions. The people were not to try to 'improve' God's plan by introducing ideas they may have got from similar kinds of structures they had seen in Egypt (8-9).

Ark of the covenant (25:10-22)

The ark (GNB: covenant box) was a gold covered wooden box, two and a half cubits long, one and a half cubits wide, and one and a half cubits high. (A cubit was about forty-four centimetres or eighteen inches.) It was the only piece of furniture in the Most Holy Place (see 26:34). Inside the ark were the two stone tablets on which the law was written, as a constant reminder to the people of Israel that the God who dwelt among them was also their law-giver (10-16; Deut 10:1-5). (Later Aaron's rod and the golden pot of manna were also placed in the ark; see Heb 9:4.)

A specially sacred part of the ark was its richly ornamented lid, called the mercy seat. The two cherubim (GNB: winged creatures) attached to the top of the mercy seat apparently symbolized divine protection of the seat, the ark and the contents (17-21). This mercy seat appears to have been a visible throne for the invisible God. It was the place where God spoke with Moses and where the high

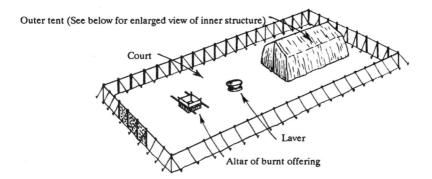

Outer tent (See below for enlarged view of inner structure)

Court

Laver

Altar of burnt offering

ABOVE: THE TABERNACLE AND ITS COURT

BELOW: ENLARGED CUTAWAY OF INNER STRUCTURE

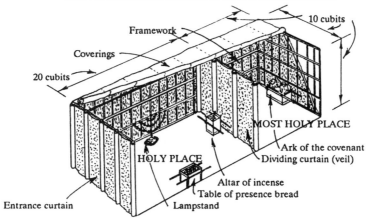

Framework

10 cubits

Coverings

20 cubits

MOST HOLY PLACE

Ark of the covenant

HOLY PLACE

Dividing curtain (veil)

Altar of incense

Table of presence bread

Entrance curtain

Lampstand

THE TABERNACLE

priest made atonement for the sins of the people when he entered the Most Holy Place once a year (Lev 16:1-19,29-31; Heb 9:7). The name mercy seat emphasized to the people of Israel that when they finally reached the heart of their religion they were still sinners, dependent entirely upon the mercy of God for their salvation (22).

The table and the lampstand (25:23-40)

These two pieces of furniture were placed opposite each other against the side walls of the Holy Place (see 26:35). The table was made of wood overlaid with gold, and the vessels associated with it (used in the ceremonies of the Holy Place) were all made of gold (23-29). On the table were twelve small loaves of bread (called 'presence bread') arranged in two rows of six. Each Sabbath the priests placed twelve fresh loaves on the table and ate the old loaves (Lev 24:5-9). The symbolism of the presence bread is not explained. Possibly it was a reminder that the whole of Israel, in its twelve tribes, lived constantly in the presence of God. God was their provider, and the bread was a fitting and constant acknowledgment of this before him (30).

No dimensions are given for the lampstand. It weighed about thirty-five kilograms, held seven lamps, was made of one piece of gold, and was richly ornamented. Its trays and other utensils were also of gold. This seven-headed lamp provided continual light in the otherwise dark Holy Place, and was tended by the priests morning and evening (31-40; cf. 27:20-21).

43

Curtains, coverings and framework (26:1-37)

Probably the easiest way to picture the two-roomed structure under the tent is as a huge open box with a cloth draped over it. This cloth was a multi-coloured, richly embroidered linen covering that formed a ceiling and hung over the four sides but did not quite reach the ground. It consisted of two sets of five curtain strips sewn along their length and then tied together to form one huge covering (26:1-6).

Over this multi-coloured linen covering was draped a second covering, this one of black goats' hair. It was cut and sewn in similar fashion to the inner linen covering but was bigger all round so that it reached to the ground, thereby protecting the inner covering (7-13).

Pitched over this covered box-like structure was a two-layer tent made of animal skins. This provided the entire structure inside with protection against the weather (14).

The two sides and rear of the structure under the tent were made of wooden frames overlaid with gold and fitted vertically. This produced a structure thirty cubits long, ten cubits wide and ten cubits high. The wooden frames were inserted into metal bases and held firm by five horizontal bars in each wall (15-30).

A richly embroidered multi-coloured curtain was hung from pillars to form a partition between the two rooms of this rectangular structure. This curtain is usually called the veil, to distinguish it from another curtain that hung from another set of pillars to form the front wall and entrance to the structure (31-37). The pillars were fitted into metal bases and were probably held firm at the top by a connecting horizontal bar. Their tops were richly ornamented (see 36:38).

Altar of burnt offering (27:1-8)

All animal sacrifices were offered on what has become known as the brazen altar (though the metal referred to in older English versions as brass was probably bronze or, less likely, copper). The altar was made of timber overlaid with bronze and was hollow inside. Its utensils also were made of bronze (27:1-3).

The instructions do not tell us how sacrifices were burnt on this altar. Either the altar was filled with earth to form a mound on which the sacrifices were burnt, or it had an internal grid for the same purpose. Halfway up the altar on the outside was a horizontal ledge supported by a grating. The priest may have stood on this ledge while offering the sacrifices, to avoid treading in the blood of

the sacrificial animals that was poured out at the base (4-8).

Tabernacle court; oil for the lamp (27:9-21)

Around the perimeter of the tabernacle courtyard (GNB: enclosure) was a fence, which separated the tabernacle sufficiently from the camp to create a feeling of reverence towards the symbolic dwelling place of God. This fence gave protection against desert winds and was high enough to prevent people outside from watching the rituals out of idle curiosity.

The fence was made of cloth attached to posts, which were fitted into metal bases in the ground and held firm by ropes tied to ground pegs (see 35:17-18). A silver band at the tops of the posts may have been a decoration, or it may have been a means of connecting the tops of all the posts to give the fence added stability. As with the tabernacle-tent, the court faced east and had a curtain entrance in its eastern side (9-19).

Light from the seven-headed lamp was the only light in the tabernacle. The ordinary people supplied the oil for the lamp, and the priests tended the lamp morning and evening to keep it burning continually (20-21).

The priesthood

Having outlined his plans for the tabernacle as the central place of worship for his people, God now provided further for that worship by establishing a priesthood. The priests were responsible for the proper functioning of all matters connected with the tabernacle and its services.

Until now Moses had been not only the leader of the people but also the go-between, or mediator, between the people and God. In the ordered religious life of the nation that was now being established, this function of people's representative in religious affairs was given to Aaron (who was appointed high priest) and his sons (who were the ordinary priests that assisted him). In future only direct male descendants of Aaron could be priests. It was further revealed (see notes on 32:25-29 below) that only those of the same tribe as Aaron, the tribe of Levi, could assist in the practical affairs of the tabernacle such as its erection, maintenance and transport (cf. 6:16-25; 29:9; Num 3:9-10).

Priests were required to offer sacrifices on behalf of those who brought them (Heb 8:3). They therefore served as mediators between the people and God. They also carried out daily functions connected with the overall tabernacle rituals, such as ensuring that a sacrifice was burning on the altar continually (29:38-42; Lev 6:12), keeping the lamp burning in the Holy Place (27:20-21) and offering incense on the golden altar (30:7-8). They were also to teach the law of God to the people and serve as moral guides to the nation (Deut 31:9-13; 33:10; Mal 2:7).

Only priests could enter the Holy Place and only the high priest the Most Holy Place. Even then he could do so only once a year, on the Day of Atonement (Lev 16:1-19,29-31; Heb 9:6-7).

Clothing for the priests (28:1-43)

All priests wore special clothing that gave them a dignity and honour suited to their office. The high priest's clothing was especially striking, but more importantly its various pieces helped the people understand the sacredness of his functions before God (28:1-3).

The most colourful piece of clothing worn by the high priest was the ephod (GNB: sacred vest), a short linen garment of the same material as the tabernacle curtains but with gold thread worked into the cloth (see 39:2-3). It was held in place by two shoulder straps and bound at the waist by a band (RSV: girdle; GNB: sash) of the same material. Attached to the shoulder straps were two stones, one to each shoulder, engraved with the names of the tribes of Israel (4-14).

Positioned centrally over the high priest's chest was a piece of richly embroidered cloth, doubled to form a square flat pouch. This was called the breastplate or breastpiece. Fixed to the outside of it were twelve precious stones, again symbolic of Israel's twelve tribes. The breastplate was tied over the ephod with gold chains attached to rings at the four corners. Inside it were the Urim and Thummim, generally thought to be two small objects which, when drawn out of the pouch, would indicate 'yes' or 'no' to a suitably put question (15-30; cf. Num 27:21; 1 Sam 14:41; 28:6).

Directly beneath the ephod was a blue robe. From the bottom of this robe hung bells and pomegranates, so that when the high priest moved from place to place inside the tabernacle, the people outside, on hearing the bells, could follow him in their thoughts and prayers. The sound of the bells would reassure them, letting them know that the high priest had not been struck dead. Their offering had been accepted (31-35).

On his head the high priest wore a turban, fixed to the front of which was a gold plate engraved with the words 'Holy to the Lord'. This declared to all that holiness was essential to every part of Israelite worship (36-38). The remaining garments of the high priest (that is, those worn under his blue robe) were the same as those for ordinary priests, namely, a full length long-sleeved white linen garment (GNB: embroidered shirt), along with undergarments and other accessories (39-43).

Several features of the high priest's clothing reminded him constantly that he was acting not as an individual, but as the representative of the people. First there were the engraved stones bearing the names of the twelve tribes on his shoulder pieces

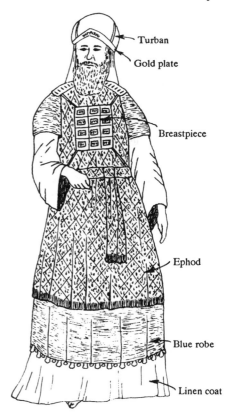

Turban

Gold plate

Breastpiece

Ephod

Blue robe

Linen coat

HIGH PRIEST

and breastplate (v. 12,21). Second there were the objects known as the Urim and Thummim, through which he sought God's will in judging the people (v. 30). And third there was the gold plate on his turban to symbolize that he bore their guilt before the holy God who alone could pardon them (v. 38).

Dedication of the priests (29:1-37)

One purpose of this dedication ceremony was to impress upon priests and people alike that those

45

who served God had to do so with purity and reverence. The priests were washed, symbolizing purification, then clothed and anointed, symbolizing appointment to their position (29:1-9).

Since they themselves were not free from sin, the priests had to offer sacrifices for their own sins before they could act on behalf of others. First they offered a bull as a sin offering. By laying their hands on its head, they identified themselves with the animal. As their representative it died the death that they, because of their sins, should have died. The blood placed on the horns of the altar was evidence of life laid down. The offering of the best parts of the animal on the altar signified the priests' devotion to God, and the burning of its remains outside the camp their hatred of sin (10-14).

Once sin had been justly dealt with, the priests offered a burnt offering. By burning the entire animal on the altar they pledged total dedication to God and his service (15-18).

After this the priests offered a second ram, called the ram of ordination (GNB: dedication). The unusual procedure in placing blood on the ear, thumb, toe and clothing of the priests probably symbolized the dedication of their whole life and service to God (19-21). Another way the priests demonstrated their dedication was by taking the most valued parts of the animal, along with certain cereal foods, waving them up and down in symbolic offering to God, then sacrificing them on the altar (22-25).

God showed his acceptance of the priests' offering and his fellowship with them by giving them, as their special portion, certain other parts of the sacrificial animal. Again, however, the offerers first waved these portions before God to acknowledge that all rightly belonged to him (26-28). Finally, the priests came together to eat the remainder of the animal in a meal, thereby expressing fellowship with one another and with God (29-34).

This whole ceremony was repeated seven days. This gave the priests time to think carefully about the importance of the ritual and the life of service that lay ahead (35-37).

The daily offerings (29:38-46)

As an expression of Israel's constant devotion to God, an offering of consecration was kept burning on the altar continually. The priests renewed the offering morning and evening, arranging the parts of the sacrificial animal on the altar in such a way as to ensure that the fire never went out (38-42; see Lev 6:8-13). God reminded Moses that his purpose in giving Israel the tabernacle and the priesthood

was that he might dwell among his people and that they might know and serve him (43-46).

Altar of incense; tabernacle tax (30:1-16)

The altar of incense was made of wood overlaid with gold. It was much smaller than the altar of burnt offering, was located in a different place and was designed for a different purpose. It was not used for sacrifices, but only for the burning of incense, offered each morning and evening. Incense was a substance produced by grinding and blending certain spices (see v. 34-38 below), and when burnt gave off thick white smoke and a strong smell. Its ceremonial burning seems to have symbolized the offering of prayers and homage to God (30:1-10).

Whenever there was a national census, the people were to pay a special tax, which was then used for the maintenance of the tabernacle. This tax was equal for all, but small enough for even the poorest to pay, indicating that before God the rich had no advantage over the poor. The lives of all were preserved on the same basis, the mercy of God. All had an equal share in the maintenance of the tabernacle and its services (11-16).

Bronze laver (30:17-21)

The laver was a large basin in which the priests washed their hands and feet before either entering the Holy Place or administering the sacrifices. No doubt they needed to wash again after offering the sacrifices (cf. 2 Chron 4:6). Such washing, apart from its practical benefits, had symbolic significance, since cleansing from all uncleanness was necessary for acceptable service for God (17-21).

No details are given concerning the shape or size of the laver, though it was large enough to require a firm base or stand (see v. 17). It was made from polished bronze mirrors that many of the women gave as their contribution to the construction the tabernacle (see 38:8).

Anointing oil; incense (30:22-38)

Oil had special significance when used to anoint people or things. Anointing, in its highest sense, meant that holy oil was poured over, or otherwise applied to, people or things to signify that they were set apart for the service of God. The art of preparing oils, perfumes and incenses was well known in Egypt and Arabia, and the Israelites apparently learnt such skills from these people. But the formula given to Moses for the anointing oil was to be used only for the oil of the tabernacle rituals (22-33).

Likewise the incense for the tabernacle was to be made according to an exclusive formula. This incense was to burn 'before the testimony', that is, on the golden altar that stood in front of the ark of the testimony (the covenant box) but separated from it by a curtain (34-38).

Craftsmen for the work (31:1-11)

In building the tabernacle, the craftsmen were to follow strictly the God-given plan, but they still had plenty of opportunity to use their creative abilities. The power of God's Spirit worked through human intelligence and ability. At the same time people had to remember that natural ability was not enough for the service of God. His Spirit was necessary in guiding the craftsmen so that everything might be in accordance with his purposes (31:1-6)

This combination of obedience and initiative in the work of the craftsmen applied not just to the tabernacle itself. It applied also to the priests' clothing, the anointing oil and the incense (7-11).

The tabernacle and its services were similar enough to other ancient structures and religious practices for the Israelite people to understand them readily. Yet they were different enough to impress upon them the uniqueness of Yahweh and the faith by which they served him.

The weekly day of rest (31:12-18)

People might have thought that, because the tabernacle was a sacred structure, they could work on it on the Sabbath day. God reminded them to keep the weekly Sabbath as a holy day of rest. This rest was part of God's plan for preserving the holiness of his people (12-17).

God then gave Moses the ten basic commandments of the covenant engraved on stone as he had promised (see 24:12; cf. Deut 10:4). Having received God's instructions for his people, Moses went down from the mountain to put them into practice (18).

32:1-34:35 COVENANT BROKEN AND RENEWED

The golden bull (32:1-35)

Although they were God's people and had been delivered by his mighty power from slavery in Egypt, the Israelites were still very much Egyptian in their feelings, thinking and habits. They made an animal idol as a visible symbol of their unseen God, then developed a ritual to go with it, complete with priest, altar, sacrifices and feasting. And, as often happened with the pagan religions, drunkenness and immoral sex-play accompanied their idolatry (32:1-6).

This all happened while Moses was still on the mountain. God told Moses what was happening

during his absence, adding that the people, because of their sin, deserved to be wiped out. God could then start afresh to build a people for himself, using Moses as the father of his new people just as previously he had used Abraham and, through him, Jacob (7-10).

Moses, thinking more of God's honour than his own, successfully pleaded with God not to destroy Israel, for the Egyptians would surely misunderstand his actions and accuse him of deceiving his people. Moses based his plea on God's mighty acts of deliverance in the past and his promises to Israel's ancestors. God heard Moses' prayer and as a result Israel was saved from destruction (11-14).

Reassured by God's response but still angry with the people, Moses returned to the camp. By breaking the stone tablets on which the law was engraved, he demonstrated graphically to the people that they had broken God's law. By grinding the idol to powder, mixing it with water and making the people drink it, he forced them to admit their sin and accept its consequences (15-20). At the same time he held Aaron responsible, because as leader of the people Aaron should have opposed the idolaters. Instead he followed them (21-24).

God did not wipe out the nation, but neither could he overlook sin. Men of the tribe of Levi, who had remained faithful to God amid the rebellion, carried out God's judgment and for their zeal were rewarded. Once the tabernacle was constructed and in use, only those of this tribe would be servants of God in the general duties connected with it (25-29; cf. Num 1:47-53; Deut 33:8-11). Note: The family of Aaron was one family within the tribe of Levi (see 4:14), and God had already given them the sole rights to the specialized work of the priesthood (see 28:1; 29:9). The Israelite priesthood is therefore referred to sometimes as the Aaronic priesthood, sometimes as the Levitical priesthood.

In a display of genuine love for the unbelieving people, Moses offered to die on their behalf and so be punished for them. But God would not accept the death of one person for another, for all were sinners, though the extent of their sin varied. God would hold each person responsible for his or her actions. He would show mercy on the unfaithful nation, but he would punish individuals who rebelled against him (30-35).

Assurance of God's presence (33:1-23)

Because of his mercy God allowed the people to continue their journey to the land he had promised their ancestors, but because of their sin he could not go with them lest he destroy them. However, he promised to send a heavenly representative to go before them into Canaan. He also required the people to give a clear outward sign of mourning for their past sin and the loss of fellowship with God that resulted from it (33:1-6).

God's refusal to go with Israel troubled Moses. He therefore came to God with yet another request on behalf of the rebellious people. In introducing this prayer, the writer gives us a picture of how the people of Israel worshipped during the time before they built the tabernacle. Moses met and talked with God in a tent outside the main camp, while the people stood at their tent doors facing Moses' tent and worshipping in spirit with him. Moses' chief assistant, Joshua, acted as guardian of this sacred meeting place (7-11; cf. 24:13).

Moses then put his question to God. If God would not dwell among the people lest he destroy them, and if his special representative was not to dwell among them but go ahead of them, who then *would* dwell among them? The people may have been rebellious, but Moses did not want God to remove himself from them completely. He asked God for some clear indication of his plans. God replied by promising Moses his presence. This reassured Moses, for he saw no purpose in Israel's entering Canaan as God's people if his presence was not among them (12-16).

God's reply encouraged Moses to ask even more. He wanted a greater spiritual understanding of the nature of God. In answer God revealed to Moses something more of his glory. The vision was not to satisfy curiosity about God's appearance, but to reveal the goodness, mercy and glory of him who was Israel's God, Yahweh (17-23). (This vision took place a little later, when Moses returned to the mountain; see 34:4-7.)

The covenant re-established (34:1-35)

When the people first swore their faithfulness to the covenant, they promised to keep all its requirements (see 24:3-8), but in practice they failed badly. God in his grace would renew the covenant, and to this end he called Moses back up the mountain. His fresh revelation to Moses therefore emphasized his love and mercy, but it also reminded the people of his righteous justice. Moses, painfully aware of the Israelites' weakness, appealed to the grace of God, asking that he would still dwell among them and own them as his people in spite of their stubbornness (34:1-9).

God then renewed his covenant, promising Israel provision and protection. He would cause the world to be amazed at the greatness of his power as he drove out nation after nation to give his people the land he had promised them (10-11). He sternly warned his people against copying, or even tolerating, heathen religious practices in their new land. This warning was particularly appropriate in view of recent events in the worship of the golden idol. To forsake God and follow other religious ideas would be spiritual adultery, compared to the unfaithfulness of a woman who leaves her husband for another man (12-17).

Accompanying the renewal of the covenant was a command to the people never to forget their deliverance from Egypt. Therefore, they were to keep the Feast of Unleavened Bread and maintain the practice of redeeming their firstborn (18-20; see 12:15-36; 13:1-16). Also specifically mentioned was the obligation to keep the weekly Sabbath and the annual festivals (21-24; see 23:12-17). Additional reminders concerned requirements for sacrifices and firstfruits (25-26; see 23:18-19).

God then made a declaration that the covenant Israel had broken was now re-established. Though the account is brief, Moses was with God on the mountain for about six weeks, as on the previous occasion (27-28; cf. 24:18).

Moses' appearance was so changed through his meeting with God, that he covered his face with a cloth when speaking to the people. The man who met God was unaware of his glory till others told him of it; by contrast, the people who had easily fallen into sin were afraid when they met one who appeared to them as a shining messenger from God (29-35; cf. 2 Cor 3:7-18).

35:1-40:38 CONSTRUCTION OF THE TABERNACLE

This section largely repeats the instruction given on the mountain in Chapters 25-31. It emphasizes that the people had to do God's work according to his covenant requirements. Therefore, they were to keep the Sabbath (35:1-3; cf. 31:16). If they wanted God to accept their offerings for the building of the tabernacle, they had to present those offerings in a spirit of joy and willingness (35:4-29). Though all could give offerings, only those with the God-given ability and the right motivation were to do the work (35:30-36:1). The people responded so generously in bringing materials for the work, that Moses asked them to stop giving (36:2-7).

The workmen then started on the tabernacle, making the double layer of inner coverings and the double layer outer tent (36:8-19), the wooden framework, the pillars and the curtains (36:20-38), the ark and the mercy seat (37:1-9), and the table, lampstand and altar of incense (37:10-29). They also made the articles for the court area, namely, the altar of burnt offering (38:1-7), the laver (38:8) and the fence that surrounded the court (38:9-20). Then follows a list of the offerings (38:21-31) and an account of the priests' clothing (39:1-31).

With much satisfaction and thanks, Moses inspected the completed, but as yet unassembled, parts of the tabernacle (39:32-43). He then supervised the erection of the entire complex, and dedicated the tabernacle and the priests as God had instructed him (40:1-33).

Exactly one year after leaving Egypt, or nine months after arriving at Sinai, the Israelites set up the newly made tabernacle (see 12:2; 19:1; 40:17). The cloud then rested on it as the visible evidence of God's dwelling among his people as the centre of their life and the object of their worship. This same cloud guided them on their journey through the wilderness to Canaan. Whether they camped or travelled, Yahweh, their covenant Redeemer, was with them (40:34-38).

Leviticus

BACKGROUND

In accordance with his promise to Abraham, God had brought the people of Israel out of Egypt and set them on their way to Canaan. After three months they arrived at Mount Sinai, where they remained for about a year while they organized themselves for the new life that lay ahead (Exod 19:1; Num 10:11). The book of Leviticus contains some of the teaching God gave to his people during the year they were camped at Sinai.

Religious system for a covenant people

The people of Israel knew that God had freely chosen them to be his people and in his grace had freed them from slavery in Egypt. They therefore responded fittingly by promising to do whatever he required of them (Gen 12:2; 15:7-21; Exod 2:24; 4:22; 6:6-8; 19:4-9; 20:2). God then joined himself to Israel in a covenant ceremony in which he laid down certain basic principles and detailed commandments, and the people in reply promised unconditional obedience (Exod 20:1-24:18).

God went on to show his people the plans he had for the religious life of the nation. He would provide them with a central place of worship, a priesthood to officiate in religious matters, and a sacrificial system by which they could demonstrate their faith towards him (Exod 25:1-Lev 7:38). To this he added a body of laws to ensure that priests and people alike were holy and pure in their relations with him and with one another (Lev 8:1-27:34).

This brief summary of the contents of Exodus and Leviticus shows that there is no break between the two books (cf. Exod 40:17; Lev 1:1; 27:34). It shows also that readers need to be familiar with the tabernacle and the priesthood in the second half of Exodus in order to understand the sacrificial system in the opening chapters of Leviticus. (Concerning the artificial division that produced the first five books of the Bible, see the introductory notes to Genesis, sub-heading 'The Pentateuch'.)

Although the book is entitled Leviticus, it contains little instruction for the Levites as a whole. (This instruction is given mainly in the next book, Numbers.) Almost the whole of the instruction in Leviticus is for the priests, who were only one family (the family of Aaron) within the tribe of Levi (Exod 29:9; Num 3:9-10). However, Israel's religious system in general is commonly called the Levitical system, and the Aaronic priesthood is sometimes called the Levitical priesthood.

Christianity is not part of the Israelite religious system, and Christians are not under Israel's law (Rom 6:14; Gal 5:1-4). But Christians can learn much from Leviticus as they understand those universal and timeless principles that underlie the specific laws given to one nation for a particular period (Rom 8:3-4; Gal 5:14,18). Also, since the Bible repeatedly refers to the sacrifices, festivals, rituals and ceremonies of the Levitical system, an understanding of Leviticus will help readers understand the rest of the Bible better.

OUTLINE

1:1-7:38	The offerings
8:1-10:20	The priesthood established
11:1-15:33	Cleanness and uncleanness
16:1-17:16	The blood of atonement
18:1-22:33	Practical holiness
23:1-27:34	Special occasions

ISRAEL'S SACRIFICIAL SYSTEM

Offerers and their attitudes

From earliest times, offerings and sacrifices were a means by which people expressed their devotion to God. Some sacrifices were like gifts, the worshippers offering the best of their crops or animals to God in thanks for his goodness (Gen 4:4; 8:20). Other sacrifices emphasized fellowship, the offerers eating part of the sacrifice in a meal with their relatives and friends in the presence of God (Gen 31:54). Others were for the forgiveness of sins, where a slaughtered animal bore the penalty that the offerers, because of their sins, should have borne (Job 42:8). Features of these early sacrifices were later developed in the sacrificial system of Israel.

In any era or nation, the heart attitude of the worshippers was more important than their gifts. Abel offered the best of his flock in humble faith and God accepted his offering. Cain's attitude was arrogant and his life ungodly, and therefore God rejected his offering (Gen 4:2-5; Heb 11:4; 1 John 3:12). The Bible does not say that Abel's offering was more acceptable than Cain's because it involved the shedding of blood. Not till the time of Noah did God reveal the special significance of blood (Gen 9:3-6), and not till the time of Moses did he show clearly the value of blood for atonement (Lev 17:11).

God progressively revealed his ways as people were able to understand them, but the acceptance of offerings always depended on the spiritual condition of the offerers. The sacrificial system developed under Moses in no way ignored this principle; on the contrary, it had this principle as its basis. But troubles arose when people carried out the rituals mechanically, without genuine faith and uprightness. The prophets of God condemned such religion, not because of any fault in the sacrificial system, but because of the way people misused it (Isa 1:13-20; Amos 5:21-24; Micah 6:6-8).

Significance of blood

The Passover was an important event in the development of Israel's sacrificial system, for there the people saw the significance of blood more clearly. Since blood was a symbol of life, shed blood was a symbol of death — not death through natural causes but death through killing (Gen 9:3-6; Num 35:19,33). The blood of the Passover lamb was important not because of any special quality in the blood itself, but because it represented the animal's death, by which the firstborn was saved from judgment. The animal's death was the important thing; the blood sprinkled around the door was but a visible sign that the animal's life had been taken instead of the life of a person (Exod 12:13).

In Israel's sacrificial system God gave this shed blood of animals to guilty sinners to make atonement for their sin (Lev 17:11). All were guilty before God, and the penalty was death. They were cut off from God and had no way of bringing themselves back to God. Sinners who sought God's forgiveness realized there could be no forgiveness for sin, no releasing them from its consequences, apart from death. God therefore gave the blood of a guiltless substitute to bring cleansing and release from sin. Pardon was not something people had to squeeze from an unwilling God, but was the merciful gift of a God who wanted to forgive. The escaping of God's punishment was not something they brought about, but was due to God himself.

The animal that died in sacrifice suffered the penalty of sin so that sinners could be forgiven; for without such shedding of blood there could be no forgiveness (Heb 9:22). The blood of these animal sacrifices did not take away sins (Heb 10:4), but it did provide a way whereby people could see that God was acting justly in dealing with their sins. The only blood able to cleanse sins is the blood of Jesus Christ — his death on the cross — and in view of his death God could 'pass over', temporarily, the sins of believers in former ages. They were forgiven, one might say, on credit, because sin could not be actually removed till Christ died (Rom 3:25-26; Heb 9:15).

Sacrifice and salvation

It should always be remembered that the law, or the old covenant (to which the law belonged), was never meant to be permanent. Its purpose was to prepare the way for Jesus Christ, whose death did all that the Israelite sacrifices could not do. If, then, these sacrifices could not bring salvation, how, it may be asked, could those who lived under the old covenant be saved?

The answer is that people living under the old covenant were saved the same way as people are today — by the grace of God; and they received that salvation by faith (Eph 2:8). No people have ever been able to boast that they have achieved God's salvation by their own works (Eph 2:9).

Abraham lived hundreds of years before the introduction of the old covenant at Sinai, but he was saved by faith (Rom 4:13,16,22; Gal 3:17-18). The law was given at Sinai not as a means of saving people, but as a means of showing them the sort of life that a holy God required of them. In itself it was good, and it was intended to benefit those who were under it (Lev 18:5; Rom 7:10,12). But sinful human nature stirs people up to rebel against God, with the result that the law, though intended for people's good, in reality showed up their sin (Rom 7:7-13).

The benefit of the law in relation to salvation was that it showed people their sinfulness, so that they could then turn in faith to God and ask for his mercy and forgiveness (Rom 3:19-20; Gal 3:19). The law could teach, but it could not save. It could train, but it could not bring perfection. It could only prepare the way for Christ, who did all that the law could not do (Rom 8:3-4; Gal 3:23-25).

Although God in his grace forgave those who in faith turned to him, the sacrificial system and other religious practices detailed in the law were a God-given way by which people could express that faith. The instructions for the rituals provided a way by which they could demonstrate their obedience. The entire sacrificial system was a means by which

God taught people what atonement involved. It was a further stage in the development of his plan of salvation, a plan that reached its fulfilment in Jesus Christ (Rom 3:21; Heb 9:23-26).

Whether people in Old Testament times knew it or not, Jesus Christ was the means by which God forgave those who turned to him in faith (Rom 3:25-26). The basis of salvation was always faith, not knowledge, and certainly not works (Rom 4:1-8).

Content of the sacrifices

The details of the sacrificial rituals taught the people that though God forgave sin freely, he did not treat sin lightly. He was a just God, and the sacrifices helped to teach people the meaning of atonement.

Whatever animal a person offered, it had to be without defects, symbolizing perfection. It was not, so to speak, under condemnation itself and so was fit to be the guiltless substitute for the guilty sinner (Lev 1:3,10). Normally the offerings, whether animal sacrifices such as bulls, goats, sheep, doves and pigeons, or food offerings such as cereals, flour, oil and wine, had to be the property of those who offered them. They were things that people had worked for and were in some way identified with personally. Wild animals and fish, though they could be eaten, could not be offered as sacrifices. Whatever people offered had to cost them something; they were things people sacrificed. They were offerings, things people gave (cf. 2 Sam 24:24). God did not want to drive anyone into poverty, nor did he delight in the death of animals; but he had to impress upon people that sin was a serious matter, and its removal was costly.

God's consideration for the people is seen in the alternatives he provided. People could offer the kinds of animals that they could afford and that were in keeping with their status in the community (Lev 1:3,10,14; 5:7-13).

No matter what status people enjoyed or what kinds of sacrifices they offered, the offerings always had to be the best available. Animals usually had to be males, which were more costly than females. To ensure that offerings were as near perfect as possible, salt was added to preserve them, and leaven (yeast) was forbidden to avoid spoiling (Lev 2:11,13).

The procedure followed

Much detail is given concerning the preparation and offering of the sacrifices, again emphasizing the orderly thoroughness that God required. The overall pattern was similar for most of the offerings. When the offerer brought the animal he laid his hands on its head, indicating that it was bearing his guilt and that he desired God to accept it on his behalf (Lev 1:4). He then killed it. He had to do this himself, an action that impressed upon him the horror that had resulted from his sin (Lev 1:11).

The animal was killed not on the altar but in the court of the tabernacle on the north side of the altar. The priest collected the blood in a basin to apply in various places, as a visible sign that a life had been taken to bear the penalty of sin. In some cases the priest splashed the blood against the sides of the altar of sacrifice; in others he took the blood into the tent to apply to the altar of incense or the mercy seat, then returned and poured out the remainder on the ground beside the altar (Lev 1:11; 4:7; 16:14). In the case of bird offerings, the amount of blood was not sufficient for all this ritual, and was usually drained out beside the altar (Lev 1:15; cf. 14:15).

With each kind of sacrifice, some of it was burnt, though the amount that was burnt and the place in which it was burnt varied. The portions that were not burnt were eaten, sometimes by the priests and worshippers, sometimes by the priests and their families, and sometimes by the priests alone.

There were five main offerings. Directions concerning those who brought the offerings are given in Leviticus 1:1-6:7, and further details of procedure for the priests are given in Leviticus 6:8-7:38. The following notes combine details from the two sections to help towards a clearer understanding of the five different offerings.

1:1-7:38 THE OFFERINGS

The burnt offering (1:1-17)

Of all the offerings, the burnt offering was the most ancient. It had been in general use among God's people long before Moses set out laws to regulate it. The offerings of Noah, Abraham and the Israelites in Egypt were all earlier forms of this sacrifice (Gen 8:20; 22:2; Exod 10:25). It was called the burnt offering because all the flesh was burnt upon the altar. None of it was eaten.

Thanksgiving, devotion and atonement were all in some way symbolized in this sacrifice, but by far the outstanding characteristic was that of dedication or consecration. The burning of the whole animal on the altar symbolized the complete devotion and dedication of the offerers (cf. Rom 12:1). Before the burning, however, a blood ritual reminded the offerers that, without atonement, they could have no relation with God. They had to deal with sin first (1:1-5). The washing of the animal's internal organs before burning may have suggested the need for inner cleansing before offering oneself to God. The sacrifice went up to God as something specially pleasing to him (6-9).

The law did not specify a particular kind of animal for the burnt offering. The choice of animal depended largely on the family circumstances and financial capacity of the offerers. Although the initial regulations were for more expensive animals such as cattle, similar regulations were set out for less expensive animals such as sheep and goats (10-13). There were even regulations for birds, which were the only animals that some poor people could afford (14-17).

An additional point found in 'the law of the burnt offering' in Chapter 6 is that the fire on the altar was never to go out. As a continual expression of devotion to God, an offering of consecration was kept burning on the altar continually. It was renewed each morning and evening (cf. Exod 29:38-42). When burning the evening sacrifice, the priests were to arrange the pieces of the sacrifice so that they fed the fire all night. The priests tended the fire and removed the ashes at the time of the morning sacrifice. The fire had little chance of going out during the day, because individuals would offer sacrifices constantly (6:8-13).

The cereal offering (2:1-16)

Products offered in the cereal offering (GNB: grain offering) came from the common food of the people. These offerings were the people's acknowledgment to God that they received their daily provisions from him. The products offered were therefore both a gift and a thanksgiving. The wine offering, sometimes called the drink offering, had similar significance (see 23:13,18,37).

It seems that cereal offerings and wine offerings were never offered alone, but always with burnt offerings and peace offerings (Num 15:1-10). This showed that consecration to God (as pictured in the burnt offering) and fellowship with God (as pictured in the peace offering) were not separate from the ordinary affairs of life. In the ritual of the cereal offering the priest burnt a handful of the food with the sacrifice; in the wine offering he poured some of the wine over the sacrifice. Any food that remained belonged to the priests (2:1-10).

Leaven and honey, because of their tendency to spoil, were not to be offered on the altar. However, like grain and other fruit, they could be offered as firstfruits in thanks to God for his provision of the produce of the land (11-16).

'The law of the cereal offering' emphasized that the priests had to be in a state of ceremonial holiness when they ate the portion of the sacrifice that was not burnt on the altar (6:14-18). Just as there was a continual burnt offering, so there was a continual cereal offering, which the priests took from their own food and offered morning and evening. The priests, as well as the people, had to acknowledge that God was their daily provider (6:19-2", Exod 29:38-42).

The peace offering (3:1-17)

Among Israelites in general, the most popular of the offerings was the peace offering (GNB: fellowship offering). The characteristic feature of this offering was the feast for the worshippers that followed the sacrifice (1 Sam 9:12-13). First, however, the animal was sacrificed with blood ritual the same as that of the burnt offering. Then the Lord's portion, consisting of the richest and most vital parts of the animal, was burnt upon the altar, probably to indicate consecration, as in the burnt offering (3:1-5; 7:22-27). This procedure, which was outlined first for cattle, applied also to sheep and goats (6-17).

Only when the offerers had completed these two steps of atonement and dedication could they go ahead with the feast. Even then they had first to provide the priest with his portion, which the priest, before eating, symbolically offered to God by the ritual of waving it up and down (7:28-36; cf. Exod 29:26-28).

The offerers and their guests then joined in a joyous feast where they ate the remainder of the sacrifice. No offerer could eat alone, because the offering was to express peace, and this was indicated in the fellowship of people eating together. This in turn pictured the higher fellowship with God. The offering also encouraged people to be generous and hospitable, for they were to share their meal not only with friends and relatives, but also with the poor and needy (Deut 12:5-7,12-13).

Meat for the feast came from the sacrificial animal, but other food items, such as cakes and biscuits, came from the daily food of the people. Though the host did not offer these additional food products on the altar, he still had to present a portion to God. He did this by giving a portion to the priest together with the priest's portion of the sacrificial animal (7:11-14).

A time limit was set for this feast, possibly to ensure that the food did not spoil in the hot climate. If the offering was a thanksgiving, a person would very likely invite a good number of friends to join and celebrate with him; as a result the food could all be conveniently eaten in one day. But if the offering was for a vow or was a personal freewill offering, the ceremony would be more private and the number of people invited would be much smaller. The food could not all be eaten in one day, so the time limit was extended to two days (7:15-18).

People had to remember at all times that the happiness of the feast did not lessen its holiness. Therefore, all who joined in had to be ceremonially clean (7:19-21).

The sin offering: regulations (4:1-35)

Burnt offerings, cereal offerings and peace offerings were not compulsory; people made them voluntarily to express their devotion. The sin offering, however, was compulsory whenever people realized they had committed some (accidental) sin that broke their fellowship with God. In the other offerings there was an element of atonement (for sin affects everything that people do), but in the sin offering, atonement was the central issue.

The animal was killed in the usual manner and again the richest and most vital parts were burnt on the altar as God's portion. The special feature of the sin offering was the treatment of the blood and the carcass. In the case of sin of the high priest (4:1-12) or of the whole nation (13-21), some blood from the sacrifice was poured out on the altar and some was taken into the Holy Place, where it was sprinkled in front of the veil and placed on the horns of the altar of incense. This was to show that approach to God, previously hindered through sin, was possible again, because atonement had been made. After this the carcass was burnt outside the camp. When people saw this being done, they knew that the ritual was over: sin had been judged and fellowship with God was restored.

In the case of a private person (in contrast to the case of the high priest or the whole nation), the animal's blood and carcass were treated differently. The place where the priest met with God, and where the nation met with God through him, was in the Holy Place at the veil that hung between the altar of incense and the ark of the covenant. Therefore, the blood was applied there, to symbolize that through the blood of atonement access to God was possible again (see v. 6-7). But for ordinary people, the place of meeting with God was the altar in the court where they offered their sacrifices. The blood was therefore applied to this altar, to symbolize atonement and renewal of fellowship with God (22-35).

No blood from the sin offering of a private person was taken into the Holy Place, and the carcass, instead of being destroyed outside the camp, was eaten solemnly by the priests. The worshipper would have assurance that God was satisfied and fellowship restored when he saw the same priest who offered the sacrifice on his behalf eating part of it in the presence of God. The priest was allowed to eat the sacrificial meat in this case, because the sin offering was not for his own sin. He could not do so when the sin offering was for his own sin or for the sin of the nation of which he was a member (6:24-29).

A simple rule summarized the procedure for the treatment of the carcass and the blood. In those cases where the blood was brought into the Holy Place, the carcass had to be burnt, not eaten. In those cases where the blood was not brought into the Holy Place, the carcass had to be eaten, not burnt (6:30; 10:18).

The sin offering: its uses (5:1-13)

Sin offerings could be offered only for those sins that people committed unintentionally, such as through carelessness, haste, accident or weakness. When people realized they were guilty of such sins, they had to make confession and bring a sin offering (5:1-6; cf. 4:13,22,27). No sacrifice was available for deliberate or premeditated sins (Num 15:30). The sin offering therefore showed up the weakness of the sacrificial system. It provided only for those sins that people might have thought excusable, but provided no way of dealing with the sins that troubled them most. (See further comment below: 'Limitations of the offerings'.)

There were grades in the offerings made by various classes of people. The sin offering for a priest or for the whole nation had to be a young bull (4:3,14); for a ruler, a male goat (4:23); and for the common people, either a female goat (4:28), a female lamb (4:32), two birds (5:7), or cereal (5:11), depending on the financial ability of the offerer. In each of the above cases there was a sin offering for atonement and the miniature burnt offering, usually referred to as the Lord's portion. In the case of the sin offering for a private citizen, there was also a sacrificial meal for the priests.

In the special offering available for the poor, two birds were offered instead of one. The reason for this was that one bird was not large enough to divide between the two parts of the ritual. The first bird provided the blood for the atonement ritual (the sin offering), and the second was wholly burnt on the altar (the Lord's portion, or miniature burnt offering) (7-10).

A bloodless offering (flour) was available for those who were virtually destitute. It had to be offered humbly and plainly, so that offerers might understand clearly that their atonement did not depend on any trimmings they might add, but on the sacrificial blood with which the offering was mixed when placed on the altar (11-13).

The guilt offering (5:14-6:7)

Regulations concerning the guilt offering (GNB: repayment offering) were similar to those for the sin offering made by non-priestly individuals, except that no gradations were allowed (7:1-10; see notes on 4:22-35).

Like the sin offering, the guilt offering was offered when people realized they had committed sin unknowingly. But the guilt offering differed from the sin offering in that it was offered in cases where the wrongdoing involved money or things of monetary value and therefore could be measured. For example, people may have forgotten to present firstlings or tithes, things that rightly belonged to God. In such cases they had to pay the money or goods to the priests (God's representatives) along with an additional twenty percent as a fine, before presenting the guilt offering (5:14-19).

A similar rule applied in cases where people unintentionally caused others to suffer some loss of money, goods or property. The full loss had to be paid back, along with a fine amounting to one fifth of its value. This fine compensated the owner and punished the offender (6:1-7).

The law of the offerings (6:8-7:38)

In the section known as 'the law of the offerings', the additional regulations were mainly for the benefit of the officiating priests. These regulations have already been dealt with in the discussion on the preceding chapters. Although the present chapters list the offerings in a slightly different order from the earlier chapters, the same five categories are dealt with: the burnt offering (6:8-13; see notes on 1:1-17), the cereal offering (6:14-23; see notes on 2:1-16), the sin offering (6:24-30; see notes on 4:1-5:13), the guilt offering (7:1-10; see notes on 5:14-6:7) and the peace offering (7:11-38; see notes on 3:1-17).

Limitations of the offerings

If the sin offering and the guilt offering were only for sins committed unknowingly, what were people to do when they had knowingly done wrong and later been sorry for it? The sacrificial system showed up sin in all its horror and taught people how serious a matter sin was, but it also showed that it had no complete solution to the problem. None of the five categories of sacrifice was designed to provide a way for wilful, guilty, yet repentant sinners to find acceptance with God. Guilty sinners had no *right* to forgiveness. They were left with nowhere to turn except to God himself; they could do nothing but cast themselves upon God's mercy.

This does not mean that repentant sinners could ignore the sacrifices, as if they were of no use. The sacrifices had been given by God and they all contained symbolic acts of atonement. In addition, a sacrifice was offered on the Day of Atonement for the cleansing of all the sins of the people (see 16:30). Repentant sinners could by faith cry out for mercy, realizing that God provided a way of approach to him through these sacrifices. But the sacrifices would have defeated their purpose if people could use them to gain automatic forgiveness without thinking of God or their own desperate spiritual need. The sacrifices pointed beyond themselves to the mercy of God, which in every age is the only hope for sinners (Ps 51:1-2,16-17).

Believers of Old Testament times may not have seen clearly that full cleansing could come only through the perfect sacrifice of Jesus Christ, but they had no doubt that their salvation depended solely on God's grace. And on the basis of Christ's sacrifice (which the Levitical sacrifices foreshadowed), God exercised mercy while at the same time being righteous in forgiving those who had faith in him (Rom 3:21-26; Heb 9:23-10:4).

8:1-10:20 THE PRIESTHOOD ESTABLISHED

Ordination of the priests (8:1-36)

After giving instruction concerning the sacrifices, Moses put into practice God's commands for the ordination (or dedication) of the priests. (For the details and meaning of this ordination ceremony see notes on Exodus 29:1-37.)

First Moses washed the priests, symbolizing cleansing, then clothed and anointed them, symbolizing their appointment to office (8:1-13). (For the significance of the priests' clothing see notes on Exodus 28:1-43.) Since the priests themselves were not free from sin, they had to carry out acts of atonement for themselves before they could act on behalf of others. They offered a bull as a sin offering, according to the laws laid down in the previous chapters (14-17). Once cleansed from sin, they offered a ram as a burnt offering, dedicating themselves to God's service (18-21).

The priests then offered a second ram in a special offering of ordination. This offering was not listed in Chapters 1-7, as it was used only in the ceremony for ordination of the priests. Blood was applied to the ears, hands, feet and clothing of the priests, to indicate the consecration to God of all that they were and all that they did. They gave further demonstration of their dedication to God by taking the most valued parts of the animal and other sacrificial food, waving them up and down in symbolic offering to God, and then sacrificing them to him by burning them on the altar. Since Moses was acting as officiating priest in this service, he also received his portion (22-30).

After the presentations to God and Moses, the priests received their portions, which they ate in holy fellowship with one another and with God, as in the peace offering. The whole ceremony was repeated seven days, giving time to think calmly and solemnly on its importance and on the life of priestly service that lay ahead (31-36).

The priests begin their duties (9:1-24)

Immediately after the seven-day ordination period, Aaron and his sons began their duties. Before acting as the representatives of others, they offered a sin offering for their own cleansing and a burnt offering for their own dedication (9:1-14). After this they offered four sacrifices on behalf of Israel: a sin offering, to indicate that the people were cleansed from sin; a burnt offering, to indicate that they were dedicated to God; a cereal offering, to indicate that the people were thankful for his provision; and a peace offering, to indicate that they were in close fellowship with him (15-21).

Moses then took Aaron into the tabernacle, probably to hand over to him the responsibility for the duties to be carried on inside the tent. God showed publicly his approval of the dedication ceremony, and the people responded by showing their humble submission to God (22-24).

Sin of Nadab and Abihu (10:1-20)

Although Aaron and his four sons had a special place in the Israelite community, they had no right to act independently of God. When the two older sons offered fire upon the altar of incense contrary to the way they had been instructed, they were punished with instant death (10:1-4). (Apparently the only fire allowed on the altar of incense was that which came from the altar of burnt offering; see 16:12; Num 16:46.)

God demanded obedience and holiness in all matters connected with the service of the tabernacle.

This truth was impressed upon the people when they saw the two offenders, along with their priestly clothes, buried outside the camp. Moses allowed no mourning for them by the other priests, as their death was an act of God's judgment (5-7).

Under no circumstances were God's priests to carry out his service carelessly or in an unfit state of mind, body or spirit (8-11). They were also to note carefully which parts of the offerings belonged to them and how they were to eat them (12-15).

In view of these instructions, Moses was angry when he found that the portion of the people's sin offering that the priests should have eaten had been burnt instead (cf. 6:26; 9:3,15). Aaron replied that because of the terrible happenings that day, his two younger sons thought it would be more acceptable to God for them to burn their portion in sorrow than to eat it in joy. Their action was wrong but it came from good motives. Moses, with great sympathy and understanding, saw this and said no more. No doubt God also saw that the attitude of heart of these two brothers was vastly different from that of the former two. They were therefore pardoned, whereas the former two were punished (16-20).

11:1-15:33 CLEANNESS AND UNCLEANNESS

Since Israel's God was holy, Israel itself had to be holy (11:44-45). One duty of the priests was to distinguish between what was holy and unholy, clean and unclean (10:10). This holiness was to extend to every part of the people's lives, including the food they ate and their bodily cleanliness. Those who broke any of the laws of cleanliness were considered unclean and had to be ceremonially cleansed before they could join again in the full religious life of the nation. The whole system of ritual cleanness and uncleanness was an object lesson in sin, its results and its cleansing.

Besides having a religious purpose, the laws ensured that the nation as a whole would be as physically healthy as possible. The laws prevented people from eating foods that could be harmful, ensured that diseases received proper attention, and limited the chances of infectious diseases spreading through the camp. The laws also prevented Israelites from mixing too freely with people of surrounding nations, and thereby helped preserve the purity of Israel's religion.

Concerning animals (11:1-47)

In reading these laws, we should remember that they were given to a people few in number, living in a hot and very small country, in an age when scientific knowledge as we know it today was not possible. The laws were not meant to govern the lives of all people in every country or every age (Acts 10:13-15; Rom 14:14,20; 1 Cor 10:31; 1 Tim 4:4).

Groupings of animals as those that 'chew the cud', 'have divided hoofs', 'have fins and scales', etc. were not intended to be scientific classifications. Rather they were a simple means of identifying the various kinds of animals to be met in the region where Israel lived. Most of the animals here called unclean lived in places or fed on foods likely to contain germs. They could easily pass diseases on to any who ate their flesh (11:1-23).

Any person who touched the dead body of an animal was considered unclean till evening. In other words the person was quarantined till cleansed of possible disease-carrying germs (24-28; cf. Num 19:11-22).

In the case of lifeless objects that came in contact with anything dead, the treatment depended on how readily those objects could be washed or otherwise cleansed. If full cleansing was not possible, such as with earthenware pots, the object had to be destroyed (29-33). People had to be particularly careful concerning drinking water that was kept in earthenware pots, but a spring or well was usually considered safe since it had a constant supply of fresh water (34-40).

The section concludes with a reminder that these laws, though they brought obvious health benefits, were concerned basically with keeping the people holy before God. The covenant people of God were to be disciplined in what they ate and how they lived. They had to learn to choose the good and refuse the bad, if they were to maintain their lives in a right relation with him (41-47).

Concerning childbirth (12:1-8)

One consequence of Eve's sin that affected women in general was the trouble and pain of childbirth (Gen 3:16). The process of conceiving and giving birth was affected by sin from the beginning (Ps 51:5), which is probably the reason why Israelite law required the mother to be ceremonially cleansed after childbirth.

If the child born was a boy, the mother was cut off from physical contact with members of her family for seven days, and from all things religious for forty days. If the child born was a girl, the time of uncleanness in each case was doubled. This also was probably related to the consequences of Eve's sin on those of her sex. Boys were circumcised when eight

days old (12:1-5; for the significance of circumcision see Gen 17:9-14).

When the time of her ceremonial uncleanness was over, the mother indicated her dedication to God by offering a burnt offering, and her cleansing and restoration by offering a sin offering. If she could not afford the animal that was normally required for the burnt offering, she could offer a bird instead (6-8; cf. Luke 2:21-24).

Detection of leprosy (13:1-59)

Biblical scholars and medical scientists alike have shown that the leprosy the Old Testament speaks of was not always the disease that we know as leprosy today. The word had a broad meaning that covered a number of infectious skin diseases, some of which were curable. It applied even to fungus or mildew on clothes and buildings.

Laws laid down in these chapters concerned two main things. Firstly, because such disease was symbolic of sin, it made people ceremonially unclean and unable to join in the religious activities of the community till they were healed and ceremonially cleansed. Secondly, the public health had to be protected by separating infected people from the camp and destroying anything that might carry the disease to others.

These chapters are not concerned with the treatment of the disease. Instructions outlined here were for priests, not for doctors. Priests had the responsibility to see that holiness was maintained in the camp, and this holiness was inseparable from ordinary health and cleanliness. These laws helped the priests detect the disease in its early stages and so prevent infection from spreading.

People were to report any suspicious looking skin infection to the priests, who then quarantined the patient till they were sure whether the disease was dangerous. If it proved to be leprosy, the person was not merely quarantined but was put out of the camp (13:1-11; see v. 45-46). Cases may have arisen where a person could have appeared to be getting leprosy, but the suspected disease later proved to be something else. In fact, it may even have healed itself (12-17). Any boil or inflammation had to be investigated (18-28); also any itches, skin spots or falling out of the hair (29-44). If someone was found to be carrying an infectious disease, the person was excluded from the camp (45-46).

Mildew was often a problem in damp or humid weather, and the law of Moses set out regulations to counter its harmful effects. Any clothing found to contain mildew had to be brought to the priests for

57

examination (47-49). Affected clothing had to be washed, and if that did not remove the problem, it had to be destroyed (50-59).

Restoration after healing (14:1-32)

A lengthy ritual was laid down for the restoration of a cleansed leper or any other person who had been healed of an infectious skin disease. The ritual lasted more than a week, and began at the place where the person was temporarily living outside the camp (14:1-3; cf. v. 10).

The cleansed person, previously 'dead' through his disease, symbolized his 'death' by killing a bird, symbolized his cleansing by draining the bird's blood into a bowl of pure water, and symbolized his new life of freedom by releasing a second bird, which had been stained with the blood of the first. The priest then sprinkled some of the blood seven times on the cleansed person, using a brush made of hyssop bound to a cedarwood handle with red cord. One reason why the bird's blood was dropped into the bowl of water was to 'expand' it, because the amount of blood from one bird was not by itself enough for all the ritual (4-7).

Washing and shaving completed the cleansing ritual for the first day. The person was then allowed to return to the camp, but not yet to visit his own tent (8-9).

After waiting outside his tent for a week, the cleansed person offered sacrifices at the tabernacle and was re-admitted to the full fellowship of Israel. Since he had not been able to fulfil his religious responsibilities during the time of his isolation from the tabernacle, he first offered a guilt offering in repayment. The priest then applied some of the sacrificial blood, along with holy oil, to the person's head, hand and foot, symbolizing the person's total rededication to the service of God (10-18). This was followed by the presentation of a sin offering, a burnt offering and a cereal offering (19-20). The person who was too poor to afford animals for the sin offering and burnt offering could offer birds instead, though the cleansing ritual itself followed the usual pattern (21-32).

Mildew in houses (14:33-57)

Instructions were also given concerning what people were to do when, upon settling in Canaan, they lived in houses where mildew and fungus on the walls attracted disease-carrying germs. First they were to arrange for the priest to make a thorough inspection (33-36). If, after a week's quarantine, the trouble persisted, the owners of the house were to remove and replace infected plaster and stones (37-42). If this did not cure the trouble, they had to demolish the house (43-47). The ritual for the rededication of a cleansed house was similar to that for the rededication of a cleansed person (48-57).

Discharges from sexual organs (15:1-33)

Strict precautions were to be taken when a man was found to have venereal disease or some other infection connected with his sexual organs, to prevent the infection spreading to others (15:1-12). After apparent healing, the man had to wait a further week to ensure he was fully healed. He then carried out cleansing rites, offering a sin offering and a burnt offering (13-15).

After sexual intercourse, ceremonial uncleanness remained only till evening and was removed by bathing (16-18). A woman was ceremonially unclean for seven days during her normal menstruation, and again it seems that the uncleanness was removed by bathing (19-24). If she suffered from abnormal or lengthy discharge, she was not ceremonially clean till seven days after her return to normal health. In this case a sin offering and a burnt offering were also required (25-33).

16:1-17:16 THE BLOOD OF ATONEMENT

Day of Atonement: introduction (16:1-10)

God's dramatic judgment on Aaron's two sons (see 10:1-7) showed clearly that the priests needed to act with care and reverence in everything they did, especially inside the tabernacle (that is, in the Holy Place). This chapter goes on to explain that only the high priest could enter the inner sanctuary (the Most Holy Place), and then only once a year, on the Day of Atonement.

Although the regular rituals dealt with sin in various ways, the people were still not perfect and their sacrifices not fully effective. Even the best offerings did not enable the offerers to come into the presence of their God, not even through their representative, the high priest. Therefore, on this one day of the year when entrance into God's presence was available, all the sins of the previous year were brought before God for his forgiveness and removal, so that the people, through their priestly representative, could enter his presence unhindered.

But the priests also were sinners, and had to make atonement for themselves before they could make it on behalf of others (cf. Heb 9:7). The regulations for the day's proceedings begin by specifying the animals needed (16:1-5) and outlining the main offerings, namely, a sin offering for the priests (6; explained in detail in v. 11-14), and a two-part sin offering for the people (7-10; explained in detail in v. 15-22).

Day of Atonement: sacrifices (16:11-22)

Aaron sacrificed the priests' sin offering at the altar in the tabernacle courtyard, then took fire from this altar along with blood from the sacrifice into the tabernacle (that is, into the tent). He used the fire to burn incense on the golden altar that stood in the Holy Place against the curtain dividing the Holy Place from the Most Holy Place. As he drew back this curtain to enter the Most Holy Place, incense from the altar floated through the open curtain and covered the mercy seat (the lid of the ark, the covenant box), the symbolic dwelling place of God. Aaron then sprinkled the blood of the sacrificial animal on and in front of the mercy seat (11-14).

This sprinkling of the blood on the mercy seat reminded the Israelites that mercy, God's mercy, was their only hope for salvation. In spite of all their sacrifices and other rituals, when they at last reached the climax of their highest religious exercise, they could do nothing but acknowledge that they were helpless sinners, dependent entirely on God's mercy for their forgiveness.

After completing the ritual for the priests' sin offering, Aaron came out of the tabernacle-tent into the open courtyard. He offered the people's sin offering on the altar of sacrifice, and returned into the Most Holy Place with the sacrificial blood to repeat the ritual at the mercy seat. Since everything that human beings have contact with is affected by their sin, the blood of the people's sin offering was used also to make atonement for all parts of the tabernacle that any person had touched (15-19; cf. Heb 9:21-22).

The people's sin offering consisted of not one goat but two. After sacrificing the first goat and applying its blood inside the tabernacle-tent, Aaron returned to the courtyard to carry out the ritual with the second goat. He laid his hands on its head, confessed over it the sins of the people, and sent it far away into the wilderness to a place from which it could not return. This was apparently a further picture to the people that their sins had been laid on an innocent victim and taken far away from them (20-22).

Although the blood ritual of the annual Day of Atonement had meaning to the Israelite people of Old Testament times, it was still only a shadow or outline of the reality that was to come through Jesus Christ (Heb 7:19; 10:1). For the way in which it pictured the sacrificial death of Christ, and for the contrast between its limitations and the perfection of the atoning work of Christ, see Hebrews 9:6-14,23-28.

Day of Atonement: other details (16:23-34)

Until now the high priest was clothed in the plain white clothes of the ordinary priests (see v. 4). This may have been to emphasize to him the need for humility and the importance of purity in all his representative actions in the ritual of sin-cleansing. Now that atonement for sin had been made, he bathed himself, put on his normal high priestly clothes and offered burnt offerings of consecration, first for the priests, then for the people. All others whose duties brought them into contact with the sin offering during the ritual had likewise to cleanse themselves (23-28).

As for the Israelite people as a whole, they were to participate in this solemn act of confession and atonement in a fitting spirit of shame and humility. It seems that on that day they were to do no work and eat no food (29-34).

Sacredness of blood (17:1-16)

The blood ritual of the Day of Atonement shows the importance of animal blood in God's sight. The blood of the animal signified the death of the animal. Therefore, when Israelites wanted to kill animals from their flocks or herds to obtain meat, they were not to slaughter the animals thoughtlessly, but bring them to the tabernacle altar and kill them as peace offering. Thus, besides getting their meat, they acknowledged God in an act of worship. An additional benefit of this regulation was that it prevented the killing of animals in the open fields, where the Israelites might be tempted to follow the Egyptian custom of offering animals to satyrs (goat-like demons) (17:1-7).

When Israelites killed animals not for meat but solely as religious sacrifices, they could carry out the killing only at the tabernacle altar (8-9). Later, when they settled in Canaan, the laws concerning killing animals for meat were adjusted to suit the new circumstances (see notes on Deut 12:15-28).

God gave animal flesh to humankind as food, but in taking animal life people had to acknowledge God as the rightful owner of that life. Because an animal's shed blood represented its life that had been taken, people were not to eat or drink it (cf. Gen 9:3-4). They were to pour the blood out either at the altar (in the case of animals suitable for sacrifice) or on the ground (in the case of animals not suitable for sacrifice). This was an act of sacrificial thanks to God for the benefit he allowed at the cost of the animal's life. Yet so amazing is the grace of God that, having forbidden people to use the shed blood of animals in any way for their own benefit, God gave that blood to them as a means of making atonement for their sins (10-14).

On occasions people may have eaten, perhaps unknowingly, of flesh from which the blood had not been properly drained. In such cases they were considered unclean for the rest of the day, but they suffered no other penalty, provided they carried out the required cleansing ritual (15-16).

18:1-22:33 PRACTICAL HOLINESS

Sexual relationships (18:1-30)

Moral standards in the ancient world were low, a fact well illustrated by the list of sexual perversions given in this chapter. In Egypt the Israelites had seen these things practised all around them, and in Canaan, to which they were travelling, the moral filth was even greater; so great, in fact, that it was incurable. As at the time of the Flood, God saw that the only solution was to destroy the entire population (18:1-5).

The sexual unions (RSV: 'the uncovering of the nakedness') forbidden here are contrary to the decent relationships expected in a family. Sexual unions between parents and children, brothers and sisters, in-laws and in-laws, could result only from unnatural and uncontrolled lust. If allowed to go unchecked, such behaviour would eventually ruin marriage, family and society (6-18).

Other perversions were also forbidden, such as homosexuality, sexual unions between humans and animals, and the offering of one's children either as burnt sacrifices or as religious prostitutes (19-23). (Molech was an Ammonite god to whom people sometimes offered children as burnt sacrifices; see 1 Kings 11:5-7; 2 Chron 28:1-3; Jer 7:31; 32:35.) The opening warning concerning the destruction of all who practise such things is repeated, with an added reminder to the Israelites that they would suffer the fate of the Canaanites if they ignored God's moral instruction (24-30).

Miscellaneous matters (19:1-37)

Probably the miscellaneous laws collected here were decisions or warnings given by Moses in cases where there was some doubt about what was right or wrong. Often all that was needed was a reminder of existing laws; for example, those concerning respect for parents, Sabbath-keeping, worship of idols and eating of sacrificial food (19:1-8).

When harvesting, farmers were always to leave something for the poor (9-10). Employers had to pay wages promptly, and judges had to be impartial and free of corruption. People in general were to avoid stealing, lying, and exploiting the disadvantaged (11-15). They were to love each other, avoid gossip and exercise forgiveness (16-18).

Israelites were warned not to copy superstitious customs concerning cattle-breeding, farming and weaving that the heathen believed would increase productivity. They were to follow God and trust his ordering of nature (19). A man could not treat a slave-girl as if she had no rights, and if he took advantage of her he was to be punished (20-22). Farmers were to use wise farming methods to obtain the best possible results, but they were still required to offer the firstfruits to God before enjoying the produce themselves (23-25).

Another short list outlaws further superstitious practices that the heathen thought brought good luck. These included the cutting of the hair or beard into certain shapes and the making of cuttings or tattoos on the body (26-28; cf. 1 Kings 18:28). All forms of prostitution, fortune-telling and witchcraft were forbidden (29-31; cf. 2 Kings 21:6). People were to respect the elderly, help foreign travellers and refugees, and be honest in all their business dealings (32-37; cf. Amos 8:4-6).

Penalties for wrongdoing (20:1-27)

The law now sets out penalties for the more serious offences outlined in Chapters 18 and 19. People who offered their children to the gods were to be stoned to death (20:1-5; for Molech see note on 18:21). Those who looked for guidance through witchcraft were guilty of rebellion against God and were to be punished by being cut off from the life of the community. A person who consulted the spirits of the dead was to be killed (6-9,27).

Most of the perverse sexual unions mentioned in Chapter 18 were also punishable by death (10-21). The Israelites had to be holy before God, and this meant they had to separate themselves from the sinful practices of the Canaanites. If they failed in this, God would destroy them as he would the Canaanites (22-27).

Rules concerning priests (21:1-22:16)

Priests carried a heavy responsibility in acting on the people's behalf in offering their sacrifices, and therefore they had to guard against ceremonial uncleanness. They were to have nothing to do with the burial of the dead, except in the case of close relatives, and were not to make public show of their sorrow by disfiguring themselves. They and their families were to be blameless in all things moral (21:1-9).

Rules for the high priest were even stricter than those for the ordinary priests. He was not to touch any dead body at all, nor to show the most ordinary signs of mourning. In fact, he was not even to cease his duties temporarily to show respect for the dead (10-15).

A priest with any physical defects could not act as the people's representative in offering sacrifices. However, since the defects were not the result of his own doing, he was still allowed to enjoy the benefits of the sacrifices (16-24).

If a priest became ceremonially unclean by any means whatever, he was not to have contact with the holy things of God till he had been ceremonially cleansed (22:1-9). The part of the sacrificial food that became the priest's portion was to be eaten only by the priest's immediate family and those slaves who were considered permanent members of his household. Visitors, neighbours, hired workers and any of his children who married and set up house elsewhere were not allowed to eat the sacrificial food. Should a person eat such food unknowingly, he had to replace it, adding a fifth to it as a fine for his mistake (10-16).

Animals for sacrifice (22:17-33)

All animals offered in sacrifice to God had to be the best available. The only exception concerned the freewill offering, for in that case the state of the animal was an indication of the offerer's state of heart (17-25).

Sacrificial animals had to be at least a week old, to ensure that they were normal and healthy. When people made sacrifices, they were to have sympathy for the innocent animals that lost their lives. For this reason a mother animal was not to be killed on the same day as her young (26-30). As always, the Israelites' behaviour was to reflect the holiness of the God who had redeemed them and now dwelt among them (31-33).

23:1-27:34 SPECIAL OCCASIONS

God's holy days (23:1-3)

There were three main feasts, or festivals, of the Israelite religious year: Passover-Unleavened Bread and Pentecost-Harvest Firstfruits at the beginning of the year, and Tabernacles-Ingathering half way

through the year. On these three occasions all the men of Israel were to assemble at the central place of worship (Exod 23:14-17). People participated in these feasts with a mixture of solemnity and joy. They were humbled before God, yet thankful to him for his merciful salvation and never-failing provision (23:1-2).

Before God gave his people the details of these festivals, he reminded them that the most basic of all their special religious days was the weekly Sabbath of holy rest. In the excitement of the annual festivals, the people were not to forget their regular weekly obligations (3).

Feasts at the beginning of the year (23:4-22)

The Israelite religious year began with the month that celebrated the Passover and the escape from Egypt (Exod 12:2). This was the season of spring in Israel and corresponds with March-April on our calendar. (It seems that Israelites also had a secular calendar, which differed from the religious calendar by six months. This means that the first month of the religious calendar was the seventh month of the secular calendar, and the beginning of the seventh month of the religious calendar was New Year on the secular calendar.)

On the fourteenth day of the first month was the Passover, which commemorated God's act of 'passing over' the houses of Israel when the firstborn throughout Egypt were killed (4-5; see notes on Exod 12:1-14). Immediately after the Passover was the seven-day Feast of Unleavened Bread. This was in remembrance of the people's hurried departure from Egypt, when they had no time to bake their bread leavened but carried their dough and baking pans with them, baking as they went (6-8; see notes on Exod 12:15-36).

At this time the barley was ripe and ready to harvest. (The wheat was not ready till a few weeks later.) Therefore, on the day after the first day of the Feast of Unleavened Bread, a sheaf of the firstfruits of the barley harvest was presented to the priests and waved up and down in offering to God. This was the people's acknowledgment to God that he had given the harvest that they were about to reap (9-11).

On the same day as they presented the sheaf offering, the people also presented animal sacrifices. They sought forgiveness for their sins through a sin offering, and in gratitude to God for his gifts they consecrated themselves to him afresh through a burnt offering. They also acknowledged his care and provision in general by presenting a cereal offering and a wine offering taken from their daily household food (12-13; Num 28:16-25). Only after they acknowledged the whole harvest as belonging to God were they allowed to gain benefit from it for themselves (14).

During the next six weeks people were busy harvesting, first the barley and then the wheat. At the end of the wheat harvest they offered to God two loaves of bread such as they ate in their normal meals, as an expression of gratitude to him for their daily food. They also sacrificed a sin offering and a burnt offering as at the time of the barley firstfruits, and, in addition, a peace offering. Because this was a harvest festival, the holy worship was accompanied by much rejoicing (15-21; Num 28:26-31).

This festival was known by different names. Falling as it did on the fiftieth day after Passover, it was sometimes called the Feast of Pentecost ('pentecost' meaning 'fiftieth'). It was also called the Feast of Weeks (being a week of weeks after the offering of the barley firstfruits), the Feast of Firstfruits and the Feast of Harvest.

Since this festival marked the end of the harvest season, a reminder was given not to be selfish when reaping, but to leave some grain for the poor (22; cf. Deut 16:9-12).

Mid-year festival season (23:23-44)

The first day of the seventh month (somewhere during September-October on our calendar) was the Day of Trumpets. On this occasion the people were called together for a religious ceremony by the blowing of trumpets, the purpose of the ceremony being to prepare the people for the solemn cleansing of sin that followed ten days later on the Day of Atonement (23-32; see notes on 16:1-34).

A further five days later, on the fifteenth day of the month, was the start of the week-long Feast of Tabernacles (RSV: Feast of Booths; GNB: Festival of Shelters). On this occasion the people lived in booths (huts or shelters) made of branches of trees and palm leaves in memory of their time in the wilderness. This feast was also called the Feast of Ingathering, for it marked the end of the agricultural year, when all the grapes, olives, dates, figs and other produce of the land had been gathered in. It was a joyous festival, as all Israel rejoiced in thanksgiving before God for his blessing on all their farming activity (33-44; Deut 16:13-15; for details see Num 29:12-38).

The people were now well stocked with food for the winter months that lay ahead. During winter the

rains came, and soon the people began sowing and planting for the next annual cycle.

Reverence for God (24:1-23)

Further instructions are given to remind the Israelites of their daily and weekly responsibilities in relation to the Holy Place. To begin with the people had to supply the oil so that the priests could keep the lamp burning continually (24:1-4). The priests also had to make sure that twelve cakes of 'presence bread', renewed weekly, were on the table before the Lord continually. This was possibly to symbolize that the nation Israel, which consisted of twelve tribes, lived continually in the presence of God and received its provision from him (5-9; cf. Exod 25:23-30).

A quarrel that arose in the camp resulted in one of the parties cursing the holy name of God. This was not merely bad language, but speech that showed an irreverent and rebellious spirit towards God, possibly influenced by attitudes brought from Egypt. Moses did not act hastily in punishing the offender, but waited for God to show him what to do (10-12).

God's judgment was that any person, regardless of nationality, who was heard cursing his name should be stoned to death. The public participation of the accusers in the execution would impress upon them that they could not make accusations lightly. They had to be absolutely certain that the person was guilty (13-16).

The principle that God laid down as the basis of judgment, in civil as in religious offences, was that the punishment had to be in proportion to the crime. It was never to take the form of revenge and was never to be in excess of the wrong that had been done (17-23; see notes on Exod 21:22-27).

Sabbatical and jubilee years (25:1-34)

When the Israelites conquered Canaan and divided it among their tribes and families, they were not to be selfish or greedy in their use of the land. Just as people and their working animals were to rest one day in seven, so the land was to rest one year in seven. The lack of cultivation during this seventh or sabbatical year gave people the opportunity to recognize in a special way that God was the rightful owner of the land. At the same time it gave the land the opportunity to renew its powers of reproduction (25:1-7; cf. Exod 23:10-11).

After seven lots of seven years there was an additional sabbath year called the jubilee, or fiftieth year (GNB: the Year of Restoration). In this year all land that had been sold or otherwise changed hands during the previous fifty years returned to the original owner. This helped maintain the fairness of the original distribution of the land. It prevented the poor from losing their family property permanently, and prevented the rich from gaining control of the whole land (8-12).

In view of the return of all land to the original owner in the fiftieth year, the sale price had to be reduced from its original value, so that it was proportionate to the number of years that remained till the fiftieth year. People were to be honest in their buying and selling of land, and not cheat each other (13-17).

People had no reason to fear a shortage of food during the sabbatical and jubilee years. Whatever grew of itself during the 'rest' years was sufficient for the poor and for the flocks and herds (see v. 6,7,12; Exod 23:10-11). In addition God would bless every sixth year with double, and the forty-eighth year with triple, the normal produce. This would ensure enough food throughout the sabbatical and jubilee years (18-22). The people were not to act as if they owned the land and could do as they liked with it. God was the owner; they were merely tenants (23-24).

If people needed money they could sell their land, but as soon as possible either they or a close relative had to buy it back (redeem it). The price again depended on how many years remained till the next jubilee, when normally they would receive all their land back free (25-28).

These laws for the return of land in the year of jubilee applied to all land in the country regions, such as farm and pastoral land, country villages, and districts where the Levites lived and kept their flocks. The only place where they did not apply was in the walled cities, where houses were close together and occupied very little land. The interests of such people were usually commercial and had nothing to do with the cultivation of the land and its 'rest' years (29-34; cf. v. 15-16).

Sympathetic treatment of others (25:35-55)

Because all Israel existed in a special relation to God, Israelites were not to take advantage of each other. They could lend money to those in need, but were not to charge interest (35-38). They could give employment to those who wished to work for them to repay debts, but they could not make such people permanent slaves as they could foreigners (39-46).

When Israelites sold themselves as slaves to resident foreigners to repay debts, their relatives had to make every effort to buy them back. They were to do so fairly by paying the equivalent of a labourer's wages for the period from the day of the transaction to the year of jubilee, when normally slaves would be released. Masters were to consider their slaves' well-being and not treat them harshly (47-55).

Promises and warnings (26:1-46)

God reminded the people to put into practice all they had been taught concerning him, his sabbaths and his sanctuary (26:1-2). Obedience would bring agricultural prosperity, social contentment, victory over enemies, and a comforting sense of God's presence (3-13). Disobedience would bring widespread disease, defeat by enemies, drought and destruction, till they awoke to their sin and turned again to God (14-20).

If the people failed to respond, God would increase their disasters, sending against them fierce enemies who would starve them to death, butcher them with the sword, devastate their cities and take them captive into other countries (21-33). If the people refused to rest the land every seventh year, God would force them to rest it by allowing foreign invaders to carry them into exile. Their land would then lie desolate and waste (34-39; cf. 2 Chron 36:20-21; Jer 34:13-22). When finally they turned in confession to God, he would bring them back to their land according to the covenant he made with them (40-46).

Valuations for things vowed (27:1-34)

People often vowed things to God out of gratitude for his goodness to them, usually in some crisis they had met. If the offering vowed was a person, this person was not to be offered in sacrifice but was to be redeemed, or bought back, by the payment of money to the sanctuary. The amount to be paid was estimated by the priests according to the usefulness of the person offered. The priests were to give special consideration to a poor person who could not pay the amount estimated (27:1-8).

Concerning the vowing of animals to God, if a person vowed a clean animal (that is, an animal eligible for sacrifice), he could not redeem it. He had either to offer the animal in sacrifice or give it to the priests, who could either keep it or sell it. All money from sales went into the sanctuary treasury. If any person, after vowing one thing, tried to offer something else instead, he lost both (9-10).

When a person vowed an unclean animal (that is, an animal not eligible for sacrifice, such as a camel or an ass), he had to give it to the priests, who again could either put it to work or sell it. Alternatively, the person who vowed it could buy it back at an estimated price, but he had to add a fine of one fifth of the animal's value, because he kept for himself something he had vowed to God (11-13). Similar laws applied in the case of a vowed house (14-15).

Arrangements for a person who vowed land were much the same. If he wished to buy it back, the value depended on the number of years to the year of jubilee, when normally all land would return to the original owner. If the person who vowed the land did not buy it back, or if he sold it after vowing it, it did not return to him in the year of jubilee. It became the permanent property of the sanctuary (16-21). If the land a person vowed was not his originally and was not bought back by him after he vowed it, it returned to the original owner at the year of jubilee (22-25).

Firstlings of clean animals could not be vowed to God, since they were his already (Exod 13:2). Firstlings of unclean animals could be vowed, then either bought back by the offerer or sold by the priests as in normal cases (26-27). Anything that was devoted to God for destruction could not be vowed, redeemed or sold (28-29).

The tithe (i.e. one tenth) of all produce and animals belonged to God. It could be kept for personal use only by payment of its value to the sanctuary, along with the usual fine (30-34).

Numbers

BACKGROUND

At the point where the book of Numbers opens, the people of Israel had been camped at Mount Sinai almost one year. During that time God had been preparing them for the life ahead by instructing them in the kind of religious, moral and social order he required of them as his covenant people. (For details see introductory notes to Leviticus.) The time had now come for the people to leave Sinai and head for the promised land, Canaan. The book of Numbers details the preparations for the journey, outlines certain regulations that the people had to follow, and describes significant events that occurred along the way.

A nation in the wilderness

On two occasions between the people of Israel's departure from Egypt and entrance into Canaan, Moses conducted an official counting, or census, of the nation. These two census are recorded in the book of Numbers, and from them the book takes its name.

The first census, at the beginning of the book, helped Israel prepare an army for the conquest of Canaan. Although the journey to Canaan should have taken only a few weeks, it actually took about forty years. The reason for this was that the people rebelled against God by refusing to trust him for victory, whereupon God left them in the wilderness till that generation died off and a new generation grew up. The second census, which is towards the end of the book, was therefore forty years after the first, its purpose being to organize the new generation for the conquest of Canaan.

Since the two census represent only a small portion of the book, the English title 'Numbers' does not give a true indication of the book's contents. The Hebrew title 'In the Wilderness' is probably more suitable, as the book covers the journey from Sinai to the borders of Canaan, and much of this journey was through wilderness country. Most of the stories recorded in Numbers are concerned with this journey. The book gives very little information concerning the forty wasted years when Israel was not journeying, but 'wandering', in the wilderness (Num 32:13).

OUTLINE

1:1-10:10 PREPARATIONS FOR THE JOURNEY

A military census (1:1-54)

Before leaving Sinai, Moses took a census of the number of men available for military service, so that he could plan and prepare for the battles that lay ahead. Twelve of Israel's leading men, one from each tribe, helped him carry out the work (1:1-16). The census was no doubt carried out over several weeks, and was finished twenty days before the people left Sinai (17-46; cf. 10:11).

The Levites were not included in this census, as they were not required for military service. Their duty was to transport and look after the tabernacle, setting it up when the people camped and taking it down when they were ready to move on. For this reason, the Levites camped around the tabernacle, and the other twelve tribes camped farther out according to the plan described in the following chapters (47-54).

Plans for camping and marching (2:1-34)

In setting up a camp, the Israelites arranged themselves in four groups of three, one group on each of the four sides of the tabernacle. Each of these four groups had a flag bearing the name of the senior tribe in the group. The group on the eastern side was under the flag of Judah, and when the people journeyed this group went first (2:1-9). The group on the southern side was under the flag of Reuben, and this group had second place in the procession (10-16).

Next in the march came Levi, carrying the tabernacle. The tabernacle and the tribe that looked after it were therefore central in the march just as they were central in the camp, emphasizing that God was always in the midst of his people (17). The group under Ephraim, which camped on the west side of the tabernacle, came behind the tabernacle in the procession (18-24), and the group under Dan,

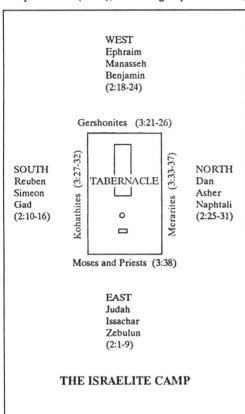

WEST
Ephraim
Manasseh
Benjamin
(2:18-24)

Gershonites (3:21-26)

Kohathites (3:27-32)

TABERNACLE

Merarites (3:33-37)

SOUTH
Reuben
Simeon
Gad
(2:10-16)

NORTH
Dan
Asher
Naphtali
(2:25-31)

Moses and Priests (3:38)

EAST
Judah
Issachar
Zebulun
(2:1-9)

THE ISRAELITE CAMP

which camped on the north side of the tabernacle, came last (25-31). There were special arrangements for the Levites (32-34; see 3:14-39).

The importance of the Levites (3:1-51)

Details are now given concerning the position of the Levites in the camp and the duties given to them. Although all Levites were God's special servants, the only Levites who were priests were those descended from Aaron. The writer therefore gives details of Aaron's family (3:1-4). The Levites maintained the tabernacle and helped the priests in the religious ceremonies, but only Aaron and his sons did the priestly work itself (5-10; cf. 1 Chron 23:3-5,24-32).

Because God preserved Israel's firstborn during the Passover judgment in Egypt, those firstborn became his special possession. But for the service of the tabernacle, God took the whole tribe of Levi as

his special possession instead of those who had been spared in the Passover judgment (11-13).

In counting the Levites, Moses divided them into three sections according to the three families descended from Levi's three sons, Gershon, Kohath and Merari (14-20; cf. Exod 6:16). The Levites camped on the four sides of the tabernacle in the area between the tabernacle and the other tribes (see 1:53).

The Gershon group camped on the west side of the tabernacle and looked after most of the curtains and hangings (21-26). The Kohath group camped on the south side and had care of the tabernacle's most sacred objects — the furniture, the vessels and the curtain (or veil) that separated the Holy Place from the Most Holy Place (27-32). The Merari group camped on the north side and had responsibility for all the timber and metal parts belonging to the tabernacle framework and the fence that surrounded the court (33-37). Moses, Aaron and the priests camped on the east side of the tabernacle in front of the entrance and had responsibility for all the ceremonies (38-39).

From the census Moses learnt that there were 22,273 firstborn but only 22,000 Levites. Since the firstborn were replaced by Levites on a one-for-one basis, this meant that 273 firstborn still had not been replaced. They still belonged to God. They therefore had to be bought back from God, or redeemed, by a payment of money to God's representatives, the priests (40-51).

Some duties of the Levites (4:1-49)

Moses then took a special census of Levites, but this time counted only those aged between thirty and fifty, for only those in this age group did the actual work (4:1-3). The work detailed here concerned taking down the tabernacle and packing it for transport. (Further details are given in 7:1-11.)

The priests themselves packed the furniture and other sacred articles, for not even the Kohathites who carried them were allowed to see or touch them. A covering of soft cloth protected the articles from scratching, and a further covering of animal skin protected them from the weather. All articles were carried on either poles or boards. The ark had a special outer covering of blue so that all could see it prominently in the procession (4-20).

After the furniture and vessels were removed from the tabernacle, the curtains and hangings were taken down. These were carried by the Gershonites (21-28). The framework and foundations were then taken apart and packed ready for carrying by the Merarites (29-33).

Aaron's eldest surviving son Eleazar, who was in charge of all the Levites, supervised the whole work. He took direct control of the Kohathites, since they carried the most holy things. His younger brother Ithamar controlled the Gershonites and Merarites (see 3:32; 4:16,28,33). The writer then records the number of working men in the three Levitical groups (34-49).

Laws for uncleanness and repayment (5:1-10)

The laws grouped together in Chapter 5 deal with problems likely to arise where people lived close to each other in a community such as Israel's. People who were ceremonially unclean, whether through disease or any other cause, were put outside the camp. The religious significance of this was that it demonstrated that defilement could not be tolerated in a community where the holy God dwelt. The practical benefit was that it helped prevent the spread of infectious disease (5:1-4; see notes on Lev 13:1-15:33).

When people through carelessness caused harm or loss to others, they had to confess their wrong, present a sin offering and pay back the loss, together with a fine amounting to one fifth of its value. If the wronged person or a near relative could not be found, the offender had to make the repayment and the fine to the priests instead (5-10; see notes on Lev 5:14-6:7).

Suspicion of adultery (5:11-31)

If a man suspected his wife of having sexual relations with another man but he had no evidence, he had to bring her to the priest, along with a small sin offering, to determine whether she was guilty (11-15; cf. Lev 5:11). The test that the priest conducted was known as a trial by ordeal.

The priest announced the curse that rested on an unfaithful wife, wrote this curse down in ink, then washed the ink into a bowl of holy water that also contained dust taken from the tabernacle floor. The woman acknowledged the curse by taking the sin offering in her hands and swearing an oath. Then the priest offered the offering, after which the woman drank the water (16-26).

Such a ritual must have had great emotional effect, for by drinking the water the woman was taking into herself symbols of God's holy presence (dust from the tabernacle floor) and his curse on sin (the ink). But the innocent had nothing to fear, because the water was only slightly dirty and would not normally cause any illness. If, however, the woman was suddenly attacked by violent pains, it showed she was guilty (27-31).

Many ancient peoples (including, it seems, Israel) used trials by ordeal to determine guilt or innocence for a variety of offences. God took this well known custom, purified it from the idolatry and injustice that usually characterized it, and used it to impress upon his people the purity and faithfulness he required in the marriage bond. Heathen trials by ordeal were mostly cruel and certain to bring a verdict of guilt unless the most unlikely happened. By contrast, the Israelite trial described here was physically harmless and in no way biased against the accused.

Nazirite vows (6:1-21)

The name Nazirite is not to be confused with Nazarene (the name for a citizen of Nazareth). It comes from the Hebrew word *nazir*, whose meaning indicates that a Nazirite vow was one of separation. People could make such a vow if they wanted to declare openly that they had set themselves apart to God for a certain period to do some particular service (6:1-2).

Nazirites expressed their commitment to their vow by submitting to three specific requirements. By refusing wine and anything likely to produce it, they showed their temporary refusal of the enjoyments of life. At the same time they ensured they would not lose control of themselves through drunkenness. By letting their hair grow, they made it clear to the general public that they were living under the conditions of the vow. By not touching anything dead, they emphasized to themselves and others the holiness that their service for God required (3-8).

No remedy was available for those who broke a vow deliberately. If they accidentally touched a dead body they could ask forgiveness through a ceremony in which they offered two birds (the usual offering for ceremonial uncleanness; Lev 15:13-15) and a lamb (an additional guilt offering; Lev 5:6). But the time they had observed the vow was lost and they had to begin all over again (9-12).

At the end of the period of their vow, Nazirites offered sacrifices and shaved all hair from the head. They were no longer bound by the three specific conditions of the Nazirite vow (13-20). As for the thing vowed, they must have done what they had promised. Their sincerity would be indicated by the voluntary offering of any additional sacrifices they could afford (21).

The priestly blessing (6:22-27)

When the priests blessed the people, the blessing they pronounced was a reminder that God alone provided Israel with health, prosperity, protection and safety. In his grace and mercy he would be patient with their failures, correct their weaknesses and give them the full enjoyment of his unlimited blessings. They were God's own people (22-27).

Offerings from Israel's leaders (7:1-88)

The story returns briefly to the ceremony of the dedication of the tabernacle that had taken place a month or so previously (7:1; see Exod 40:17; Num 1:1). At this ceremony the leaders of the twelve tribes brought their gifts to the altar and offered them to God. The event is recorded here probably because it gives information about the wagons and oxen to be used in transporting the tabernacle. Two wagons and four oxen were for the Gershonites, who carried the tabernacle's curtains and hangings. Four wagons and eight oxen were for the Merarites, who carried the larger and heavier load of the frames and foundation materials. The Kohathites, who carried the furniture and sacred vessels, received no wagons or oxen, because they carried their loads on shoulder poles (2-11).

All twelve tribal leaders donated the same amount. They shared the cost of the wagons and oxen equally, and brought identical offerings of vessels, cereals, oil, incense and animals required for the sacrificial rituals of the tabernacle. The writer's purpose in repeating the details of the identical offerings is perhaps to emphasize that all tribes had an equal share in the maintenance of the tabernacle and its services (12-88).

More about the tabernacle (7:89-8:4)

A short note mentions how Moses received God's messages in the Most Holy Place. Normally, no one except the high priest could enter the Most Holy Place, but Moses'-position was unique (89; cf. 12:7-8; Deut 34:10-12). Moses passed on instructions to Aaron to ensure that when the lamps were placed on the lampstand, they were positioned to throw light forward towards the opposite wall, and so give good light in the Holy Place (8:1-4).

Dedication of the Levites (8:5-26)

The ceremony described here parallels that for the dedication of the priests that has already been described in Leviticus 8:1-36. The washing, shaving, and offering of a sin offering indicated cleansing from sin; the offering of a burnt offering indicated dedication to God's service. The action of the twelve tribal leaders (acting on behalf of the whole people) in laying their hands on the heads of the Levites was the people's acknowledgment of the Levites as their representatives. By the symbolic action of waving his arms up and down, Aaron presented the Levites to God for his service (5-13). God then gave them back to Aaron to help him and the other priests in their work (14-19). Everything was done according to God's instructions (20-22).

Twenty-five is given here as the minimum age for Levitical service, compared with thirty stated earlier (see 4:3). Perhaps there was an initial training period of five years. Levites ceased from their main duties when they became fifty years of age, but could still help in various ways (23-26).

Feast of Passover (9:1-14)

Before leaving Sinai, Israel kept the Passover in remembrance of the deliverance from Egypt. (For details of the Passover feast see notes on Exodus 12:1-36.) All Israelites were to keep the Passover, but a problem arose when some men thought they should not, because they were ceremonially unclean through handling a dead body. They asked Moses what to do and Moses asked God (9:1-8).

God's instruction was that a second Passover feast was to be held, a month after the first, for those who missed the official feast through being either ceremonially unclean or away on a journey at the time. But all others had to join in the regular feast, and any who broke this law were to be expelled from the camp. Even non-Israelites who lived among them were to keep the Passover, provided they were circumcised (9-14; cf. Exod 12:43-49).

God's guidance (9:15-10:10)

From the Red Sea to Sinai a cloud had guided Israel as a visible sign that God dwelt among and led his people (Exod 13:21-22). This cloud covered the completed tabernacle, indicating clearly to all that God accepted it. God was the centre of their life and the object of their worship (Exod 40:34-38). Through the cloud God would continue to guide them, and they had to respond to his commands with prompt obedience (15-23).

When Moses wanted to pass God's commands on to the people, he called a meeting by blowing two trumpets. If he blew only one trumpet, it meant he was calling only the tribal leaders. If the movement of the cloud showed that the time had come to break camp, a series of distinctive short blasts (called alarms) told the various tribes when to begin marching (10:1-8). Once Israel settled in Canaan, the trumpets were to be blown in times of war and at the annual feasts, as a symbolic request to God to remember his people (9-10).

10:11-14:45 FROM SINAI TO KADESH

The procession moves off (10:11-36)

Almost one year after they arrived at Mount Sinai, the people of Israel, led by Judah, moved off on the journey to Canaan (11-16; see Exod 19:1). The Gershonites and Merarites went in advance of the Kohathites, probably so that they could set up the tabernacle, ready for placement of the furniture when the Kohathites arrived (17-28).

Although the cloud guided Israel, the leaders still needed to know local conditions. For this reason Moses asked his brother-in-law Hobab to go with them, as Hobab had grown up in the region (29-32). Apparently the ark went in front of the whole procession, symbolizing, as Moses' prayer indicated, the leadership of God in overcoming obstacles and making a way for his people. When the people set up a new camp (in this case, after three days' journey) Moses prayed again, inviting God to dwell among them (33-36).

Moses' heavy burden (11:1-35)

The people had travelled only a short time when they began to complain against God, with the result that God punished them (11:1-3). Among those who journeyed with the Israelites from Egypt were some foreigners who had mixed with the Israelites in Egypt (Exod 12:38). These people complained that they were tired of having the same food every day, even though it was miraculously supplied by God. They wanted some of the food they had been used to in Egypt (4-9). (For the origin of manna see Exodus 16:1-36.)

Soon the discontent spread throughout the camp. Moses complained to God that the responsibility of looking after this complaining multitude was a burden greater than he could bear. In addition he knew of no way to provide such a crowd of people with the food they wanted (10-15).

God did not rebuke Moses for his outburst. He understood Moses' troubles and helped him through them. God commanded Moses to bring seventy of the leading elders of Israel to the tabernacle, where he gave them a share of the same spirit as he had given Moses, so that they could help Moses in the government of the people. God responded to Moses' second complaint by promising a supply of meat that would give the people more than they asked for. In their greed for meat they would eat so much that they would become sick (16-23).

When the seventy leaders received this spirit from God they prophesied. Two of their number for some reason had not attended the ceremony at the tabernacle, but the spirit came upon them where they were in the camp and they prophesied there. Joshua, one of Moses' assistants, was concerned about this and asked Moses to silence the men. He apparently felt that if the people saw these men doing what previously only Moses did, they might give them the sort of respect that previously they gave solely to Moses. Moses rebuked Joshua. He was not jealous if others became more honoured in the eyes of the people; in fact, he wished that all the people might have God's Spirit upon them (24-30).

God gave the people the meat they wanted, but it brought an outbreak of disease that caused many deaths. The meat came from countless birds which, being tired after a long flight where they battled heavy winds, were easily caught only a few feet above the ground (31-35).

Miriam and Aaron's jealousy (12:1-16)

Apparently Moses' first wife had died and he had remarried. His new wife was not an Israelite, and Miriam and Aaron used this as an excuse to criticize him. The real reason for their attack, however, was their jealousy of Moses' status as supreme leader of Israel. Moses, being a humble man, did not defend himself, because he knew that God was the only true judge; and God's judgment was that although Aaron, Miriam and the seventy had a part in the leadership of Israel, Moses' position was unique. God spoke with him directly and entrusted him with supreme authority over his people (12:1-8).

Miriam apparently had taken the lead against Moses and so was the more severely punished, though Aaron shared her shame and sorrow. Moses' humble spirit was again shown when he asked God to forgive Miriam. God did, but just as a daughter who had been publicly rebuked by her father had to spend seven days in shame, so did Miriam. She had been rebuked by God with leprosy and, though now cleansed, she still had to spend seven days in isolation the same as other cleansed lepers (9-16; cf. Lev 14:8).

The twelve spies (13:1-33)

Israel pushed on towards the promised land. The long and tiresome journey through the wilderness of Paran was relieved by stoppages at various points where the people set up camp for a few days (see 10:12; 11:35; 12:16; 13:3). As they moved nearer to Canaan, Moses sent twelve spies, one from each tribe, to see what they could find out about the country — its terrain, its people, its defences and its productivity (13:1-20). The spies probably split up, going in different directions to search out the required information. They covered the land from south to north, west to east (21-24).

Meanwhile the people had journeyed closer to Canaan and set up camp at Kadesh, in the north of the wilderness of Paran. There the spies rejoined the camp after their forty days fact-finding mission (25-26). In brief, their report was that the land was very fruitful but its inhabitants were fearsome. For ten of the spies, this observation about the local inhabitants was sufficient reason to cancel all plans for the invasion of Canaan, and they persuaded the people to agree with them. Only two spies, Joshua and Caleb, suggested Israel go ahead as planned and occupy the land (27-33; 14:6).

Israel's refusal to enter Canaan (14:1-45)

Only a year earlier the Israelites had experienced the power of God in giving them victory over the mighty Egyptians, but now they had no faith to believe that he would lead them to victory over the less powerful Canaanites. They rebelled against God and his leaders by deciding to appoint a new leader instead of Moses and go back to Egypt. God therefore told Moses that he would destroy Israel and build a new nation for himself through Moses (14:1-12).

Again the humility of Moses showed itself. He asked God not to destroy his rebellious people, lest other nations mock him, saying he was weak, unable to finish what he began. Moses appealed to God to be merciful to his people and forgive them as he had done in the past (13-19).

God answered Moses' prayer and did not destroy the people, but neither did he ignore their rebellion. Although they had experienced God's mighty power in the past, they now said they would rather die in the wilderness than trust him for victory over the Canaanites. God's punishment was that they would have their wish: they would die in the wilderness (20-25; see v. 2).

The people had complained that they were concerned about the future of their children (v. 3). God assured them he would look after the children and bring them into Canaan, but the rebellious adults would die in the wilderness. All who were at that time twenty years of age or over (except Joshua and Caleb) would die during the next forty years. Only when they were dead and a new generation had grown up would Israel enter the promised land. The ten rebellious spies died immediately (26-38).

Because the people feared the enemy and refused to enter the promised land, God turned them back into the wilderness (v. 25). But on hearing of their punishment, they then tried to attack the enemies whom previously they feared. This again was a rebellion against God. They had lost their opportunity to enter Canaan, and God's will for them now was to remain in the wilderness for the next forty years. But the people stubbornly persisted. Earlier they refused to go into Canaan with God; now they tried to conquer the land without him. They were defeated, as they themselves had forecast when they heard the spies' report. With God there would be victory, without him defeat (39-45; cf. 13:31-33).

15:1-19:22 LESSONS AT KADESH

Miscellaneous regulations (15:1-41)

Animal sacrifices that were wholly or partly burnt on the altar had to be accompanied by cereal offerings and drink offerings. The amounts of flour, oil and wine to be offered increased with the size of the animal (15:1-16; for details see notes on Lev 2:1-16). Another sort of offering was a cake made from the first lot of grain threshed after harvest. It was an acknowledgment that all grain came from God (17-21).

Should the people as a whole be guilty of sin through carelessness, they could ask God's forgiveness by offering the required sacrifices (22-26). A similar provision was available for the individual who sinned through carelessness, but no provision was available for the person who sinned deliberately in bold defiance of God (27-31; for details see notes on Lev. 4:1-5:13).

An example is then given of a person who defied God by deliberately breaking his law. The man was swiftly punished (32-36). Moses told the people that in future they were to wear cords and tassels on the corners of their clothes to remind them to keep God's law (37-41; cf. Matt 9:20; 23:5).

Korah, Dathan and Abiram (16:1-50)

In the events recorded in this chapter, two groups combined to rebel against the leadership of Moses and Aaron. One was a group of 250 prominent Levites under the leadership of Korah, who were envious that only Aaron and his family were allowed to be priests. The other was a group headed by two Reubenites, Dathan and Abiram, who were envious and critical of Moses' leadership of the nation (16:1-3).

Moses again allowed God to be the judge. He asked both groups to appear before God with him to see who was right. The Reubenites refused but the Levites went, taking a crowd from the camp with them in support (4-15). The Levites were to burn incense in firepans, or censers (which, as a rule, only Aaron and his sons were allowed to do), so that God might show his approval or otherwise (16-19).

God threatened to destroy the whole camp, and although Moses and Aaron knew he had the right to do so, they begged him not to (20-24). He responded to their prayer by destroying only those who actually took part in the rebellion. Korah, Dathan, Abiram and some of their chief supporters were swallowed up by the earth in the sight of the camp, but the 250 Levites suffered a different fate. They had wanted to burn incense before God; now they were burnt by fire from God (25-35).

Neither the fire nor the firepans used by the rebellious Levites could be used again. Eleazar the priest emptied the firepans and had them beaten into a bronze plate to cover the altar, where it was a constant reminder that only the family of Aaron could burn incense before God (36-40).

The people blamed Moses and Aaron for the death of the rebels and gathered at the tabernacle in a hostile demonstration against the leaders (41). Again God threatened to destroy the people (42-45), and again Moses and Aaron begged him not to. But God's judgment in the form of a deadly plague had already begun, and it was stopped only when Aaron made atonement for them by burning incense. This emphasized once more that only the priests could take fire from the altar and offer it with incense before the Lord (46-50).

Aaron's rod (17:1-13)

The two Reubenites, Dathan and Abiram, had challenged the right of Moses (a Levite) to lead the country; the Levite, Korah, had challenged the right of Aaron's family to be the sole priestly family in the Levitical tribe. Having destroyed the rebels, God now gave clear proof that the tribe of Levi was his specially chosen tribe, and the family of Aaron his specially chosen family within that tribe. He did this by miraculously changing the rod identified with the tribe Levi and the priest Aaron (17:1-8).

From that time on, Moses was to keep Aaron's rod in front of the ark, as a reminder of the divinely chosen positions of Levi and Aaron in Israel (9-11). (The rod was later placed inside the ark; Heb 9:4.) The people understood God's message and feared even to go near the tabernacle (12-13).

Support of priests and Levites (18:1-32)

In view of the recent rebellion, God gave further instruction concerning the separate responsibilities of priests and Levites. The Levites were to help the priests and were under their direction, but they were not to do any priestly work in the sanctuary (i.e. the tabernacle-tent). Only the priests could enter the sanctuary, and in so doing they took the risks on behalf of the people for any wrongdoing in relation to God's holy dwelling (18:1-7).

Since the priests had no time to earn a living like others, they had to be supported in other ways. Their food supplies — meat, oil, wine, grain, fruit, etc. — came partly from offerings that required a portion to be set aside for the priests, and partly from firstfruits and other offerings given to the tabernacle (8-14). When the firstborn of all living things were offered to God, they became, in part, the property of the priests, God's representatives. When people or animals were redeemed, the priests received the payment (the redemption price). When a firstborn animal was sacrificed, the priest received a portion. The contributions from all these offerings helped compensate the priests for not being allowed to own land (15-20).

Details are then given for the support of the Levites. Like the priests they did religious service for the people, on whose behalf they ran the risk of doing wrong in matters relating to the tabernacle and its ceremonies. In return for this they received the people's tithes. This constant income from the tithes was also compensation for their not receiving a separate tribal area in Canaan (21-24).

Having received tithes, the Levites themselves then paid tithes. Though the tithe of their income was the produce of other people's fields and vineyards, God accepted it as being their own. Likewise what remained was reckoned to be their own, and they were free to use it accordingly. The tithes of the Levites helped support the priests (25-32).

More laws about cleansing (19:1-22)

God had told the people earlier that any who came in contact with a dead body were to be considered ceremonially unclean. They had to be ceremonially cleansed with water before they could again mix in the community or join in public worship. (For the significance of the laws of cleansing see introductory notes to Leviticus 11:1-15:33.)

Israel now received instructions concerning the preparation of the water to be used in the cleansing ritual. First of all a healthy young cow was killed, after which its blood was ritually sprinkled. The meaning was that the animal, symbolically perfect, bore the consequences of sin and uncleanness. Its carcass was then burnt and its ashes were kept in a special place to be mixed with pure water (v. 17) to form the water of cleansing. All who took part in the killing and burning of the animal were themselves ceremonially unclean for the remainder of the day (19:1-10).

The water of cleansing gained its symbolic power from the ashes of the sacrificial animal mixed with it. The ashes were proof of the animal's death, by which the curse of sin was removed. In the cleansing ritual, the priest sprinkled the water over the person being cleansed (11-13). The tent of a dead person, along with its contents, was unclean, and the cleansing ritual again included sprinkling with the water of cleansing. Objects likely to contain some impurity, such as uncovered containers and even graves, made any person who contacted them unclean (14-19).

Uncleanness spread to anyone or anything that the unclean person touched. This was further reason for people to make sure they obeyed all the laws relating to cleanness and uncleanness (20-22).

The cleansing ritual may have been useful in teaching that sin and death kept people from God's presence, but it was unable to bring more than ceremonial cleansing. It cleansed externally in the sense that it removed the results of physical contact with unclean things, but it could not cleanse the conscience or remove the results of sin. Only the death of Jesus Christ could do that (Heb 9:13-14; 10:22; 1 Peter 1:2).

20:1-22:1 FROM KADESH TO THE PLAINS OF MOAB

Moses' sin at Meribah (20:1-13)

Kadesh-barnea, or Kadesh, on the northern edge of the wilderness of Paran, appears to have been the Israelites' centre during their years of wandering in the wilderness. On one occasion just after the people returned to Kadesh, Miriam died (20:1).

Again there was a shortage of water and again the people complained. (See Exodus 17:1-7 for a similar story.) When Moses and Aaron told God of the people's complaint, God told Moses to speak to the rocky hill beside which they were camped, and water would flow out (2-9).

Moses was angry with the people for their rebellious spirit. Instead of humbly doing as God told him and showing them that God was providing for them, Moses disobeyed God's command and misrepresented him before the people. Instead of accepting God's directions in faith and speaking to the rock, Moses acted according to his own feelings. In anger he struck the rock, called the people rebels, and rebuked them for their constant demands on him as their leader. In so doing, he disobeyed God,

spoke rashly to the people, and took personal credit for the miracle instead of giving honour to God. God's punishment was to prevent Moses (and Aaron who had supported him) from entering the promised land (10-13; cf. 20:24; 27:12-14; Deut 3:26-27; Ps 106:32-33).

The long detour (20:14-21:20)

A well used trade route called the King's Highway ran from Ezion-geber on the Red Sea through the kingdoms of Edom and Moab into Syria. Moses

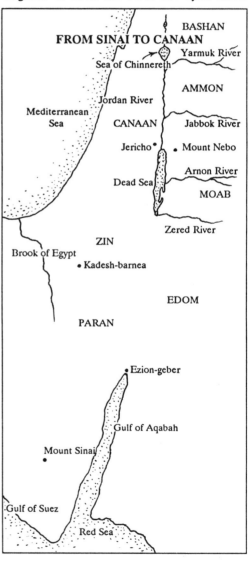

FROM SINAI TO CANAAN

decided to use this route for Israel's entrance into Canaan. He therefore asked the Edomite king for permission to pass through his territory, promising not to damage Edom's fields or use its water. If, in an emergency, the Israelites needed to use Edom's water, they would pay for it. Moses expected a favourable reply, because Israel and Edom were brother nations (Edom being descended from Esau, Israel from Jacob), but the king of Edom refused (14-21).

Israel changed route and soon came to Mount Hor. There Aaron died, his death being God's judgment for his sin at Meribah. God announced his death in advance, so that a ceremony could be held to appoint Eleazar, Aaron's oldest surviving son, as the replacement high priest before Aaron died (22-29).

When one of the Canaanite kings heard that Israel was heading towards Canaan, he launched an attack and took some of the people captive. Israel responded promptly, and with God's help destroyed the attackers. It was the first step towards Israel's conquest of Canaan (21:1-3; cf. Deut 20:16-18).

The long detour that the Edomites forced upon the Israelites caused the people to become impatient and complaining again. God punished them with a plague of snakes whose bite produced burning pains and even death. Moses prayed for the people, and God replied by promising to heal all who stopped complaining and trusted in him (4-9).

Moving forward again, the Israelites journeyed around the fortified areas of Moab, crossed the Zered River, and headed north across the tableland region east of the Dead Sea. The writer mentions two significant events in the brief account of the journey across the tableland. One was the crossing of the Arnon River, which marked the boundary between Moabite and Amorite territory; the other was the discovery of water in one particularly dry region. The people celebrated the events by singing well known songs (10-20).

Territory seized east of Jordan (21:21-22:1)

Although Israel had not attacked its brother nation Edom when the king of Edom refused a request to pass through his territory, it did not hesitate to go to war with the Amorite king Sihon who refused a similar request. The Amorites started the fighting, but Israel crushed their army, conquered their chief city Heshbon, and overran their territory (21-25). The victory was especially pleasing to Israel, because the Amorites had only recently gained this territory from the Moabites. The Amorites had written a victory song to celebrate their conquest of Moab

(along with its national god Chemosh), but now they themselves were conquered (26-30). As a result of this victory, Israel now controlled an area on Canaan's eastern border that extended from the Arnon River north to the Jabbok River (31-32).

Israel expanded even farther north with its conquest of Og, another Amorite king, who ruled over the rich pasture land of Bashan. This gave Israel control of the whole region east of the Jordan River (33-35). The Israelites set up their main camp on the plains of Moab, east of Jordan opposite Jericho (22:1).

22:2-32:42 EVENTS ON THE PLAINS OF MOAB

Balak sends for Balaam (22:2-35)

The victories of the advancing Israelites put fear into the Moabite king, Balak. After gaining the assurance of Midianite support, he sent for Balaam, a non-Israelite soothsayer who knew something of Israel's God. Balak believed that Balaam had supernatural power, by which he could put a curse on Israel that would ensure its defeat (2-6).

Although the messengers from Moab and Midian promised to reward Balaam richly, Balaam refused to go, for God had shown him that Israel was not to be cursed. But Balaam weakened when the messengers returned with a renewed request and a more tempting offer. Balaam clearly knew God's will, but he sent to ask God again. He was tempted by the offered reward and hoped that somehow God would allow him to go. In the end God allowed him to go so that he might teach him a lesson (7-20; cf. 2 Peter 2:15; Jude 11).

God was angry with Balaam for his stubbornness in going to Balak and showed him that only divine mercy had stopped him from being destroyed. Then, when Balaam offered to turn back, God forced him to go on, though he would not get the reward he wanted and would speak only what God wanted him to speak (21-35).

Balaam's announcements (22:36-24:25)

Balak welcomed Balaam and took him to a high place where he could see the vastness of the Israelite camp. Balak no doubt hoped that Balaam, on seeing this, would be convinced that the Israelites were a serious threat and would put a destructive curse upon them (36-41). But Balaam announced God's approval of the Israelites. Their vast number, their place in history and their present migration were according to God's will. Balaam comforted himself with the thought that if Balak killed him for giving

73

a blessing instead of a curse, he would at least die for doing right (23:1-12).

Not giving in easily, Balak tried again to get Balaam to curse Israel, hoping that a change of place might bring a different result. As on the previous occasion, Balaam foresaw no misfortune or trouble for Israel, because God was on Israel's side. God had saved the people from Egypt and he would give them victory over other enemies (13-24).

Angrily, Balak told Balaam that even if he would not curse the Israelites, he had no need to bless them (25-26)! For a third time Balak looked for a way to make Balaam curse them. This time, apparently in an effort to please Balak, Balaam did not look for omens as he had done previously, but just looked out over Israel and waited to see what words came to him. But God's Spirit came upon him. The sight of Israel's vast camp spreading over the countryside prompted Balaam to prophesy a prosperous and victorious future for the nation (23:27-24:9).

In bitterness Balak dismissed Balaam, saying that if Balaam was disappointed at not receiving the offered reward, he had only God to blame (10-11). Balaam replied with his fourth and final announcement, prophesying Israel's conquest of Moab. In addition the Edomites, Amalekites, Kenites and Assyrians (Asshur) would be destroyed, but Israel would progress (12-25).

Balaam makes Israel sin (25:1-18)

The failure of Balaam to curse Israel meant he did not receive the reward Balak offered. Apparently he still wanted to please Balak and gain the reward, so he decided on a plan of his own that had nothing to do with prophesying good or evil but might succeed in destroying Israel. Balaam encouraged the people of Israel to mix with the people of Moab and Midian, and encouraged the Moabite and Midianite women to seduce the Israelite men and invite them to join in the heathen festivals. Balaam thought his plan was succeeding when God sent a plague that killed thousands in Israel because of their immoral and idolatrous behaviour (see 31:16; 2 Peter 2:14-15; Rev 2:14).

Only swift action by Moses and Phinehas saved Israel from destruction. Moses punished the leaders of the rebellion in a mass public execution (25:1-5). Then, while the people were gathering at the tabernacle to express their sorrow and repentance, a leader of the tribe of Simeon openly defied Moses by taking a Midianite woman into his tent. The young priest Phinehas, interested only in the honour of God and the preservation of God's people, killed the man and the woman. For this he was rewarded with the promise that his descendants would be Israel's chief priestly family (6-18).

Another census (26:1-27:11)

About forty years previously Moses had taken a census of those available for military service (see 1:1-54). But all who at the time of that census were twenty years of age or older had since died (except Joshua and Caleb) and a new generation had grown up. A new census was now taken for the double purpose of determining the military strength for the attack on Canaan and making arrangements for the division of the land (26:1-51).

The area of land to be given to each tribe was to be in proportion to the population of the tribe, but the locality of each tribe within Canaan was to be decided by drawing lots (52-56). The Levites were numbered separately. Males were counted from one month old, not from twenty years old as in the case of the other tribes, because the Levites did not do military service and did not have a tribal area as the other tribes (57-62). The new census confirmed that all the adults whose names were listed in the first census were now dead (63-65).

Each tribal area was divided among the families of the tribe according to the male descendants. A case arose where five sisters were left with no family inheritance (i.e. portion of land), because their father had died and they had no brothers whose inheritance they could share (27:1-4). Moses brought the case to God and received the instruction that where a man had no son, his inheritance could pass to his daughters. If he had no children at all, it could pass to his nearest living relative (5-11).

Joshua chosen as Moses' successor (27:12-23)

Although God would not allow Moses to enter the promised land, he would allow him to see it from a mountain on the other side of the river before he died (12-14). (The place of his death would be Mount Nebo in the Moabite hill country of Abarim; Deut 32:49-50.) Moses showed no bitterness when reminded of this divine judgment upon him; he was concerned only that Israel have the leader of God's choice to replace him. God's choice was Joshua, though Joshua would not have the absolute authority that Moses had. Moses spoke to God face to face, but from now on the civil leadership and the religious leadership would be separated. Joshua would receive God's instructions through the high priest (15-23).

It was, in fact, some weeks before Moses died (see Deut 32:48-52; 34:1-8), and in the meantime he had much instruction to pass on to Israel. This is recorded in the remaining chapters of Numbers and in Deuteronomy.

Amounts for the yearly offerings (28:1-29:40)

As the time drew near for the Israelites to settle in their new land, Moses stressed the need for constant devotion to God through the various sacrifices and festivals. First there were to be daily burnt offerings and cereal offerings, morning and evening. The fire on the altar was never to go out (28:1-8; see notes on Lev 6:8-13,19-23).

Besides this daily offering there was an identical weekly offering every Sabbath (9-10). Also there was an offering at the beginning of each month, when a sin offering was added to the usual burnt offering and cereal offering (11-15). These daily, weekly and monthly sacrifices emphasized the importance of regular communication with God, in whose presence the people dwelt. They were not to restrict their religious exercises to the annual festivals.

Even in the annual festivals, sacrifices had a prominent place. (For details of the annual festivals see Leviticus 23:1-44.) Again, these sacrifices were in addition to the usual daily, weekly and monthly sacrifices. The new year festival of Passover, since it had its own sacrificial ritual, did not include any of the standard sacrifices, but the Feast of Unleavened Bread that followed had daily sacrifices (16-25). Identical sacrifices were offered at the Feast of Harvest Firstfruits seven weeks later (26-31).

Quantities are then given for the sacrifices offered at the mid-year festivals. First came the Day of Trumpets (29:1-6). Ten days later was the Day of Atonement (7-11), and a further five days later the Feast of Tabernacles (GNB: Festival of Shelters). The number of sacrifices at this feast was greater than at any other, though the number decreased a little each day (12-38).

All these requirements were concerned solely with the official religious services. Individuals could voluntarily make additional sacrifices as expressions of their devotion (39-40).

Concerning vows (30:1-16)

A vow was a pledge that a person made, whether to God or to a fellow human being, to carry out some specifically stated action. The vow usually involved swearing an oath in the name of God.

When a man made a vow, he could not change his vow once he had sworn it (30:1-2). But when a woman made a vow it could be cancelled by her father (in the case of a single woman) (3-5), or by her husband (in the case of a married woman) (6-9),

provided the man expressed his disapproval on the day he heard her vow. Silence meant approval. If he at first allowed the vow but later changed his mind and stopped the woman fulfilling it, then he, not the woman, was held guilty for the broken vow (10-16).

Judgment on Midian (31:1-54)

God now sent Israel to carry out his judgment on the Midianites (and Balaam with them) for the evil they did to Israel at Peor (see 25:1-9,14-17). Since it was a 'holy' war, the person who led the Israelite forces was not the army general Joshua, but the priest Phinehas (see 25:10-13). The Israelites were to destroy the Midianite fighting forces and burn their settlements. All captives and goods seized in battle were to be given to God, represented by the high priest, Eleazar (31:1-12). When Moses saw that the Israelites spared the Midianite women he was angry, for these women were the ones who caused Israel to sin. He therefore gave orders to execute all the women except the virgins (13-18).

Since the war was a holy judgment by God, the Israelites had to remove whatever uncleanness had resulted from their contact with the enemy. Those who handled dead bodies needed to be ceremonially cleansed (as detailed in Chapter 19). Articles of clothing were purified by washing. Metal articles were purified by passing them through fire and then washing them (19-24).

The goods seized in battle were divided equally between soldiers and non-soldiers. But whereas the soldiers gave only one five-hundredth of their goods to share among the priests, the non-soldiers gave one fiftieth of their goods to share among the Levites (who were far more numerous than priests) (25-47). When the soldiers found they had not lost one man in battle, they made an additional offering to express their thanks to God. The offering was placed in the tabernacle treasury (48-54).

Land for two and a half tribes (32:1-42)

Two and a half tribes (Reuben, Gad and half of Manasseh) asked permission not to cross Jordan and settle in Canaan with the rest of Israel, but to settle in the good pasture lands that Israel had taken control of east of Jordan (32:1-5,33; see notes on 21:21-22:1). Moses replied that the loss of two and a half tribes from Israel's fighting force might discourage the people from attacking Canaan. It would be a repetition of what happened almost forty years previously. On that occasion lack of faith prevented Israel from taking the promised land, with the result that the whole adult population was destroyed in the wilderness (6-15).

The two and a half tribes responded by putting a compromise plan to Moses. They would leave their families and flocks east of Jordan, but their fighting men would go with the rest of Israel to conquer Canaan. When the conquest was over, they would return to settle east of Jordan (16-19). Moses agreed to the plan, but warned of the consequences if they did not keep their promise (20-32). Some of the Manasseh group seized additional territory to that which Israel had already won (33-42).

Later, when the time arrived to cross Jordan and conquer Canaan, the two and a half tribes kept their promise (Josh 22:1-34). Their land was one of the finest parts of the region and was an enrichment to Israel (Song of Songs 4:1; Jer 8:22; Micah 7:14). But it was without natural frontiers, and the other tribes often had to rescue it from enemy invaders (1 Sam 11:1-11; 1 Kings 22:1-4; 2 Kings 8:28). When Israel was eventually conquered by Assyria, the territories of the eastern tribes were among the first to fall, and their inhabitants among the first to be taken into captivity (2 Kings 15:29).

33:1-36:13 PREPARATION FOR ENTRANCE INTO CANAAN

Summary of the journey from Egypt (33:1-49)

Moses kept a record of places where Israel set up camps on the journey from Egypt to the plains of Moab. He records eleven camps between Egypt and Mount Sinai (33:1-15). After the year-long camp at Sinai, the people moved through twenty camps to Ezion-geber. From there they came to Kadesh-barnea, from where their long wanderings of almost forty years began. The book records no movements during this time (16-36). In the fortieth year Israel left Kadesh-barnea and moved through nine camps to the plains of Moab (37-49).

Plans for the division of Canaan (33:50-34:29)

As Canaan was to become the land of Yahweh's people, all the former inhabitants and all trace of their religion had to be removed. Failure to do this would bring trouble for Israel (50-56).

Moses then gave the boundaries of the land that Israel was to occupy. The southern boundary went from the Dead Sea through Kadesh-barnea to the Brook of Egypt, which it followed to the coast. The western boundary followed the coast along the Mediterranean Sea. The northern boundary went from the coast through Mount Hor (not the Mount Hor where Aaron died) to Hazarenan, a place somewhere near the source of the Jordan River. The eastern boundary went from there down through the Sea of Chinnereth (the Lake of Galilee) along the Jordan River to the Dead Sea (34:1-12).

Representatives were appointed to divide this area among nine and a half tribes. (The other two and a half tribes had already been allotted their territory east of Jordan.) Everything was to be under the direction of Joshua and Eleazar (13-29).

Israel under Joshua conquered Canaan, and some of Israel's kings spread their power over neighbouring countries, but Israel never enjoyed sole possession of Canaan and never fully occupied the area marked out here.

Cities for the Levites (35:1-34)

Levi had no tribal area of its own, but received cities, with surrounding pasture lands, in each of the other tribes. There were forty-eight Levitical cities, the number in each tribe being in proportion to the size of the tribe. This ensured that those responsible for teaching God's law to the people were evenly scattered throughout Israel (35:1-8).

Among these forty-eight cities were six cities of refuge, three west of Jordan and three east. These were cities where a person who killed another could flee for safety till he was lawfully judged (9-15). If he was guilty of murder he was executed, but if he had caused the death by accident, he could live in the city of refuge under the chief priest's protection as long as that priest lived. This placed a restriction on his freedom, but at least he was safe from the revenge of the dead man's family (16-28).

A person could not be condemned to death for murder unless at least two people had witnessed his crime, but once found guilty he had to die. No one could buy his freedom. His murderous deed made the land unclean, and that uncleanness could be removed only by his own death (29-34).

A question about tribal land (36:1-13)

Concerning the issue raised earlier by the daughters of Zelophehad, the decision was that where a man died without sons, his inheritance could pass to his daughters (see 27:1-11). Leaders of Manasseh, the tribe to which these women belonged, feared that the land they had just won (see 32:39-42) might be lost to other tribes if the daughters of Zelophehad married men from other tribes (36:1-4). To prevent such a transfer of land, Moses introduced a law to ensure that if, in such a case, a woman married, she had to marry within her own tribe (5-13).

Deuteronomy

BACKGROUND

After receiving the law at Mount Sinai, Israel spent about forty years in the wilderness region between Sinai and Canaan. During this time those who were adults when Israel left Sinai died and a new generation grew up (Num 14:28-35). Moses therefore repeated and explained the law for the people of this new generation before they entered Canaan. This instruction was given during the last two weeks of Moses' life, while Israel was camped on the plains of Moab making preparations to conquer Canaan (Num 22:1; 35:1; Deut 1:1-5).

Because this instruction involved a repetition of the law given at Sinai, the book that records it is known as Deuteronomy (from two Greek words, *deuteros*, meaning 'second', and *nomos*, meaning 'law'). This was not the original title, but was given by the translators of the Septuagint, the first Greek version of the Old Testament. Also Deuteronomy was not originally an individual book, but was part of one long book that has for convenience been divided into five parts, together known as the Pentateuch. (Concerning the Pentateuch and the Septuagint see introductory notes to Genesis.)

Restating the law; renewing the covenant

The book of Deuteronomy is, however, much more than a mere repetition of the law; it is also an exposition. It restates the commandments of the law but with a different emphasis. The laws recorded in Exodus, Leviticus and Numbers gave the clearcut legal requirements; Deuteronomy, though it does not lessen those requirements, adds that Israel's religion must have more than legal correctness. It must have spiritual warmth.

Deuteronomy's style is that of the preacher rather than the lawgiver, and its audience the people as a whole rather than the priests and judges (Deut 8:5-6; 10:12-13). Its emphasis is that the people should keep God's law because they want to know and love him better, not merely because they are required to do so by the covenant (Deut 6:3,5-9; 7:7-8,11).

The covenant is the basis of Deuteronomy, but the relationship between God and his people within that covenant should be one of love. The sovereign love of God towards his people should produce a response of obedient love towards him (Deut 5:6-7; 6:1-3). (For the meaning of the word 'covenant' see notes on Genesis 9:8-17. For the specific meaning of the covenant between Yahweh and Israel see notes on Exodus 19:1-9.)

In his grace God chose Israel to be his people and promised to give them Canaan as their national homeland (Deut 7:6-7; 8:1; 9:4-5). But if the people were to enjoy the blessings of the covenant in loving fellowship with God, they had to know his law and keep it. The previous generation swore covenant loyalty to God at Sinai (Exod 24:7-8), but failed him badly. Now that the new generation was about to enter Canaan, the covenant was renewed. Moses repeated the law and the people gave a fresh pledge of obedience (Deut 26:17-18).

Ancient covenant documents

The form of Deuteronomy is similar to that of the usual covenant document of the ancient Near East, by which a sovereign overlord made a covenant, or treaty, with his subject peoples. Such a treaty was not a negotiated agreement, but a statement by the overlord declaring his sovereignty over the people and laying down the order of life he required of them. The people had no alternative but to accept the overlord's terms.

Usually the document began with an historical introduction where the overlord announced himself and recounted all he had done for his people. Then followed a list of covenant obligations that he placed on the people. Their underlying duty at all times was to be loyal to him and not to act treacherously by forming alliances with foreign powers. After the basic requirements came detailed laws that dealt with specific local issues.

The treaty usually named witnesses. It also contained details of the benefits that would follow the people's obedience and the punishments that would follow their disobedience. The document was then lodged for safekeeping in the sanctuary of the subject people. It provided, however, for periodic public readings and for updating of the details from time to time. It may have concluded with a summary of the covenant's main requirements or a guarantee to continue the covenant as long as the people remained faithful to their obligations.

In relation to the covenant between God and Israel, most of these features can be seen in the accounts given in Exodus, Deuteronomy and Joshua. In the case of Deuteronomy, not only are the above features obvious, but the entire book seems to have been written in the form of a treaty document.

OUTLINE

1:1-4:43 HISTORICAL INTRODUCTION

In style similar to that of ancient treaty documents, Deuteronomy opens by recounting all that Yahweh, Israel's covenant God, has done for his people. It reminds them of his gracious acts on their behalf and calls from them a fitting response of covenant loyalty. The section summarizes events recorded in greater detail in Numbers 10:11-32:42.

From Sinai to Kadesh (1:1-46)

It was only eleven days' journey from Mount Sinai to Kadesh-barnea, and about the same from Kadesh to the plains of Moab where the people now were, but they had taken forty years to get there. Moses began his recollections of the journey by reminding the people that their coming possession of Canaan was solely because of God's grace, not because of any virtue in them (1:1-8).

Only through God's mercy had they grown into a strong and contented people who enjoyed the blessing (rare among ancient races) of just, impartial and humanitarian government (9-18). They would have further proof of God's unfailing goodness when they saw the rich land God was giving them. God had cared for them throughout the long and weary journey from Mount Sinai (Horeb), 'carrying' them as a father carries his young son who has become too tired to walk. Yet they complained against him and refused to go with him into the land he had chosen for them (19-33).

The constant stubbornness of the people was the reason why they were not allowed to enter Canaan. More than that, it was the cause of Moses' not being allowed. He lost patience with them and in so doing brought God's punishment upon himself (34-40; see Num 20:2-13). Still stubborn and disobedient, the people who would not go into Canaan

with God then tried to conquer the country without him. Not surprisingly, they were defeated and driven back into the wilderness (41-46).

From Kadesh to Jordan (2:1-3:29)

God told the Israelites that if they went through the land of Edom, they were not to seize any territory. This was partly because Edom was Israel's brother nation (being descended from Esau), and partly because the Edomites' territory, formerly possessed by the Horites, had been given them by God (2:1-7). Similar restrictions applied to Israel's relations with the nations of Moab and Ammon, both of which were also related to Israel (being descended from Lot). Their territories, formerly the possession of the Rephaim, had also been given them by God (8-23). In like manner the land of the Amorites would be given Israel by God (24-25).

Although the kings of Edom and Moab refused to sell food or water to the Israelites and denied them passage through their lands (Num 20:14-21; 21:10-20), some of the Edomites and Moabites in outlying regions apparently did sell to them as they detoured around the boundaries. But the Amorite king Sihon not only refused all aid, he brought out his army against Israel (26-32). Israel responded by destroying his army and taking possession of his land (33-37). Moving further north, the Israelites conquered Og, another Amorite king, and took possession of the rich pasture land of Bashan that Og formerly controlled (3:1-11).

All the region east of the Jordan River was now under the control of Israel. It was divided between the tribes of Reuben, Gad and half-Manasseh (12-17), but these tribes had to help the other tribes conquer the region west of Jordan (i.e. Canaan) before they could settle down in their newly won territory (18-22). As the great day drew near when Israel would occupy the land that God had centuries before promised to Abraham, Moses longed to cross Jordan and see it. God refused him permission, but allowed him to view the land from a mountain near Israel's camp (23-29).

Warning to be obedient (4:1-43)

The reason Moses outlined Israel's history was to show on the one hand that God's promises did not fail, and on the other that his judgment on disobedience was certain. In view of this, the people were to keep all God's laws and commandments without altering them to suit themselves. If they modelled their national life in Canaan on these laws, they would benefit themselves and be an example to others (4:1-8).

In order that Israel might not forget his laws, God had written them down and commanded Moses to teach them. Moses now passed this command on to the new generation by instructing the people to teach these same laws to their children, and to make sure that the children passed them on to future generations. These laws represented Israel's obligations under the covenant. Moses reminded the people also of the holiness of God and of the reverence that sinful people must exercise when approaching him (9-14).

Since they had not seen any form of God, the people could not make an image of him. Neither were they to use natural objects such as the sun, moon or stars as visible substitutes for him. To worship any of these things would be idolatry and would break one of the basic laws of the covenant (15-24). Such idolatry would bring national disaster, but God would be faithful to his covenant and save those who were sorry for their sin and returned to him (25-31).

Not only was Yahweh the invisible God, he was the only God. He chose Israel as his people and saved them by his miraculous power, not because of anything they had done but solely because of his love for them. Moses therefore urged the people to love him in return. This would guarantee a long and satisfying occupancy of the land that they were about to enter (32-40).

Moses then established three cities of refuge in the area already settled east of Jordan. Three more cities would later be established west of Jordan, after the conquest of Canaan (41-43; see notes on Num 35:9-34).

4:44-11:32 BASIC REQUIREMENTS OF THE COVENANT

In the address just concluded, Moses outlined God's dealings with Israel in the past, and on the basis of this urged Israel to be obedient in the future. He now called a second meeting, this time to 'renew' the covenant, not in the ceremonial sense but in the practical sense. That is, he reawakened the people to their responsibilities under the covenant. He recalled the events when the covenant was made at Sinai (4:44-5:5), he repeated the basic covenant commandments, which were the principles by which the nation was to live (5:6-11:32), and he gave detailed applications of those principles as they affected the daily lives and religious exercises of the people (12:1-26:19).

According to ancient custom, when covenants were renewed, adjustments could be made to bring the laws up to date. On this occasion Moses made frequent adjustments and explanations in view of the new way of life that the Israelites were about to enter. They were no longer a vast crowd of travellers moving through the wilderness, but were about to become a nation of permanent settlers in an agriculturally prosperous country.

These amendments to Israel's laws did not mean that the religion given to them at Sinai was in any way changed. The principles remained the same, but their application was adjusted to suit the different conditions of Canaan.

Ten commandments (4:44-5:33)

The renewal of the covenant began in the style of ancient covenant documents by naming the two parties to the covenant and outlining the relation between them. It also stated the location and time of Moses' announcement. Many of the people gathered there were youths when the covenant was made at Sinai, and could recall the terrifying events of that time (4:44-5:5).

Moses then repeated the ten commandments that Israel had promised to keep as their part of the covenant. These commandments were the basis of all Israel's subsequent laws (6-22; see notes on Exod 20:1-17). Ten short commandments were enough to convince the people that they were sinners who could not remain in the presence of a holy God and live. They therefore asked Moses to receive God's instructions on their behalf, and promised that they would do all that God said (23-33).

The power of love (6:1-25)

No matter how strong their determination to do right, the people would be unable to keep God's law unless they first had a strong and genuine love for God himself. Love for him would give them the inner power to walk in his ways (6:1-5). As well as keeping God's commandments themselves, they had to teach their children to do likewise. Their family life was to be guided by the knowledge of God's law. Their house was to be known as a place where people loved God's law and lived by it (6-9).

Yahweh was the only God. He loved Israel as his specially chosen people and he wanted them to love him in return. God, on his part, would feel pain and grief if in their prosperity they forgot him or if they turned away from him to follow other gods. The people, on their part, would find their full satisfaction through walking humbly before their God and keeping his law (10-19). God's mighty acts on behalf of the Israelite people in the past were for their good, and his desire for them to keep his law in the future was likewise for their good (20-25).

The promised land (7:1-8:20)

Israel's responsibility was to destroy the people of Canaan along with everything connected with their religion, so that nothing would remain in the land that might corrupt God's people (7:1-5). Israel's favoured place as God's chosen people was not an excuse for them to do as they liked, but a reason for them to avoid corruption and be holy. If they were disobedient, they would surely be punished (6-11). But if they were obedient, they would enjoy the blessings of national growth, agricultural prosperity and good health (12-16).

God would lead his people to victory over enemies in the future as he had in the past (17-21), but for the present he would give them only that amount of territory that they could capably control. As their numbers and needs increased, he would lead them to further conquest and expansion. But at all times they had to conduct their wars according to God's laws of holiness (22-26).

The varied experiences of life in the wilderness had taught Israel that life depends on more than the food people eat. It depends upon spiritual forces that are found only in God (8:1-4). The Israelites were to keep this in mind when they settled in Canaan, a land they would find to be rich in natural resources. They were to fear God and thank him for his gifts, not take everything for granted (5-10). If in their prosperity they forgot God and ignored his law, he would punish them as he had punished the Canaanites before them (11-20).

Warning against stubbornness (9:1-10:11)

Moses warned the Israelites not to boast about their coming victories. The conquest of Canaan was by God's power, not theirs. It was because of the wickedness of the Canaanites, not because of any goodness in the Israelites (9:1-5).

Israel, in fact, was a stubborn people, who deserved none of God's good gifts. Moses reminded them of their rebellion at Sinai, how they promised to obey God's law, but broke it before it was even written down (6-21; see notes on Exod 32:1-35). There were other occasions when they rebelled against God's commands (22-24; see Exod 17:1-7; Num 11:1-3,31-34; 14:1-12), but the rebellion at Sinai was a defiance of the freshly made covenant. Only Moses' prayers saved the nation from being wiped out (25-29; see Exod 32:7-14).

God in his grace renewed the covenant (10:1-5; see Exod 34:1-35). He showed his forgiveness of

Aaron by allowing his son to be high priest after him (6-7; see Num 20:22-29), rewarded the Levites for opposing idolatry at the time of the golden calf (8-9; see Exod 32:25-29), and forgave the people, allowing them to journey on to the land he had promised them (10-11; see Exod 34:1-11).

What God demands of Israel (10:12-11:32)

In summary, Moses' instruction to Israel as a people was that they were to fear, obey, love and serve God, in the assurance that he desired only their good (12-13). He had chosen them in mercy, and he wanted them likewise to show mercy to others. They were to have humble purity of heart and genuine love, both in their relations with him and in their relations with others (14-20). They were not to be arrogant or boastful, but were to remember their humble beginnings as a group of aliens in Egypt (21-22).

God's activity in the past, whether in saving his people from their enemies or in punishing them for their rebellion, should have meant something to them. At least it should have prompted them to love God and keep his commandments (11:1-7).

The land the people were going to was not like the land they had come from. Egypt was a flat country. The climate did not favour agriculture and the farmer had to pedal a waterwheel pump to irrigate his crops. But Canaan was a land of hills and valleys with a good rainfall (8-12). This natural blessing, however, could turn into a curse if the people were rebellious. The God who blessed his people with good crops could also punish them with famine (13-17).

In view of all that lay before them in Canaan, the people were to be the more diligent in obeying God's law and teaching it to their children (18-25; see notes on Exod 13:9,16). If they were obedient they would enjoy God's blessing, but if they were disobedient they would fall under his curse. This would be impressed upon them when they entered Canaan and gathered at the mountains Gerizim and Ebal on either side of the town of Shechem. There, as they heard the blessings announced from one side and the curses from the other, they would realize what was involved in pledging themselves to keep the covenant (26-32; see 27:1-26).

12:1-26:19 DETAILED REGULATIONS

In keeping with the pattern of ancient covenant documents, the basic requirements and principles of the covenant (Chapters 5-11) are now followed by the detailed regulations (Chapters 12-26). However,

Moses does not lay down these requirements with the harshness or impersonality of a formal law code. He announces them rather in the pastoral spirit of a preacher, appealing to God's covenant family to respond to God's grace with lives of loyalty to him and justice to others.

The central place of worship (12:1-28)

God's covenant with Israel required the people to worship him only. Therefore, when they entered Canaan they were to remove all trace of foreign religion. In particular they were to destroy the local Canaanite holy places, lest they be tempted to use them in the worship of Yahweh (12:1-4).

The Israelites were to carry out their religious exercises only at the place where the tabernacle (or later the temple) was set up. This centralized worship would help preserve the unity of the people and the purity of their worship (5-7). In contrast to their current circumstances, life in Canaan was to be orderly. There would not be the disorganization at present being experienced because of recent battles and the rushed settlement program for the two and a half tribes east of Jordan (8-14).

During the journey through the wilderness, there had been a simple law concerning the killing of animals for meat. In the case of an animal unsuitable for sacrifice, the people could kill it and eat it anywhere, but in the case of an animal suitable for sacrifice, they could kill it only as a sacrifice at the altar and eat it only as a peace offering (Lev 17:1-7). That was a workable rule as long as the people were all camped close to the tabernacle, but once they were scattered throughout Canaan they would find it impractical to have to take their animals long distances to the tabernacle just to kill them for meat. Moses therefore adjusted the law to suit the new circumstances.

The new law was that, once the people had settled in Canaan, animals suitable for sacrifice could be killed for meat locally the same as animals not suitable for sacrifice, such as gazelles and deer. Killing for sacrifice, however, along with certain other ceremonial practices, had to be carried out at the central place of worship as formerly taught. As usual, the people were not to eat or drink the blood (15-28; see Lev 17:8-16).

Warnings against idolatry (12:29-13:18)

In Canaan the Israelites would meet many new temptations. Moses therefore warned them not to be curious about the religious practices of the former inhabitants, lest they copy them and corrupt their own religion (29-32). They were also to beware of the person who could apparently perform miracles and predict events. The test of the genuineness of the person was not whether his predictions came true, but whether he led people in the ways of God (13:1-5).

Another danger was one that could arise in the family circle when a person developed wrong ideas about God and tried to lead others in the household astray. Like the false prophet he had to be stoned to death. As usual, the person making the accusation had to throw the first stone (6-11).

A danger with much wider consequences could come from open enemies of God who set out deliberately to turn a whole community against him. If careful investigation proved that they had been successful, they and their followers had to be executed, and all trace of their evil removed (12-18).

Cleanness and uncleanness (14:1-21)

God's people were not to follow the superstitious practices of the heathen (14:1-2; see notes on Lev 19:26-28). They were to be 'holy to the Lord', which meant they had to be careful concerning even the food they ate (3-20; see notes on Lev 11:1-23). An animal that died of itself probably contained blood and therefore Israelites were not allowed to eat it; but non-Israelites, to whom blood did not have the same ritual significance, were allowed. Boiling a young animal in its mother's milk was a superstitious practice to be avoided (21; cf. Exod 23:19).

Tithes (14:22-29)

All Israelite families had to pay an annual tithe, amounting to one tenth of all their produce and animals, for the support of the Levites (see notes on Num 18:21-32). This tithe was at the same time an offering to God. The offerer therefore took it to the central place of worship where he presented it to God (and to the Levites) in a ceremonial meal. If the offerer lived so far from the tabernacle (or later the temple) that transporting his goods was a problem, he could sell his tithes locally and take the money instead. The Levites joined in the ceremonial meal, and so too did the offerer's family and slaves (22-27; see also 12:5-7,17-19).

Every third year this tithe, or possibly an additional tithe, was to be distributed in the family's own locality, so that local poor people could benefit from it as well as the Levites. In this case the offerer, after he had distributed his tithes, had to go to the central place of worship and declare before God that he had fulfilled his obligations according to God's command (28-29; see also 26:12-15).

The year of release (15:1-18)

At the end of every seven years all Israelites were to forgive any debts that other Israelites owed them. They were to consider themselves one big family where no one should be driven into poverty or refused a loan in time of hardship, even if the year of release was approaching. God would reward those Israelites who were generous to their fellow Israelites. This law of release did not affect debts owed by foreigners. In those cases normal business procedures applied (15:1-11). (For further details concerning this seventh or sabbatical year see Lev 25:1-7,18-24.)

An Israelite could not keep another Israelite as a slave for more than six years. If the slave wished, he could give himself to his master for lifelong service. If he preferred to go free, his master had to give him enough goods to enable him to begin his new life satisfactorily. The master had no cause for complaint in giving this aid, as he had benefited from the slave's cheap labour for the previous six years (12-18; see also Exod 21:1-11).

If the Israelites ignored these and other laws concerning the sabbatical year, God would punish them by driving them out of their land and into foreign captivity. This would release those they had kept in their power, and give the land rest during their absence (Lev 26:34-43; 2 Chron 36:20-21; Jer 34:13-22).

Firstborn animals (15:19-23)

Since the firstborn of all animals belonged to God, people could not use them for their personal benefit (see notes on Exod 13:1-16). Every firstborn clean animal was sacrificed to God and then eaten by the priests, unless it had some defect. In that case it was used as ordinary meat (19-23; see also Num 18:17-18).

Three annual festivals (16:1-17)

Each year all the male adults in Israel were to gather at the central place of worship for the three great annual festivals: Passover-Unleavened Bread at the beginning of the year (16:1-8; see notes on Exod 12:1-51; Lev 23:4-14); Firstfruits-Weeks, or Harvest Festival, seven weeks after Passover (9-12; see notes on Lev 23:15-22); and Tabernacles-Ingathering, or Festival of Shelters, six months after Passover (13-17; see notes on Lev 23:33-44).

Justice and government (16:18-17:20)

A collection of miscellaneous laws deals with a variety of civil and religious matters. The courts had to administer justice impartially (18-20); the worship of Yahweh was not to involve any symbols or sacred objects taken from other religions (21-22); people were not to offer sick or lame animals in sacrifice (17:1); the testimony of at least two witnesses had to be in agreement before an accused person could be punished (2-7); and when local judges found a case too difficult to decide, they had to take it to the central place of worship where a higher court of judges and priests could decide it (8-13).

God foresaw that the people would later want a king like other nations, so he gave them in advance some of the qualifications and duties of an Israelite king (14-17). The man who became king was to make his own copy of God's law and study it constantly, so that he might govern the people according to God's standards (18-20).

Spiritual guides, good and bad (18:1-22)

Further information is given concerning the support of priests (18:1-5; see notes on Num 18:8-20). If a Levite from the country sold his local possessions to move to the central place of worship, he could retain the money from the sale of his goods and still be financially supported by the people, the same as other Levites (6-8; see notes on Num 18:21-32).

Israel's law prohibited all forms of witchcraft and magic, whether cruel practices in which children were burnt on the altar or made to walk through fire, or common everyday practices such as fortune-telling (9-13). Israelites would have no need to look for help and guidance from those who practised soothsaying, used spells and charms, or consulted the spirits of the dead. God would give the people his specially sent messengers, or prophets, to make his will known to them just as Moses had done (14-19). He would punish those who were not sent by him but set themselves up as prophets (20-22; see also 13:1-5).

Jesus Christ was the supreme prophet, the perfect messenger of God, whose life and ministry gave full meaning to the promise given here (cf. v. 18-19 with Acts 3:22-23; 7:37).

Justice for the accused (19:1-21)

Three cities of refuge had already been established east of Jordan (see 4:41-43), and three more were to be established west of Jordan (19:1-2). In each of these two regions one city was to be in the north, one in the centre and one in the south, so that a city of refuge was within easy reach of every person in the land, no matter where he lived. All six cities had to have well marked roads leading to them so that the refugee could reach safety quickly (3-7; see also Num 35:9-34). The Israelites could add more cities later as their territory expanded beyond its original borders (8-13).

While dealing with matters of land allocation, Moses warned land-owners not to shift boundary markers that they had already agreed upon. Such action was clearly a case of stealing a neighbour's property (14).

In legal matters, because agreement between two or three witnesses was necessary in order to bring a conviction, a person might be tempted to lie so as to ensure an opponent's defeat. If the witness's honesty was in doubt, the case had to be brought before the higher court of priests and judges. If they found that the witness had made a false confession, he was to suffer the punishment he had tried to bring upon his opponent (15-20). The basis of justice was that the punishment had to fit the crime (21). (For other relevant details see the comments before and after the notes on Exodus 21:1-27.)

Rules for war (20:1-20)

God's people were to have confidence in the wars that lay before them, knowing that God was on their side. That did not mean they could be half-hearted or inefficient in the way they planned and fought. All had to give themselves fully to the task before them. Nevertheless, the law temporarily excused some people from military service, such as those who had recently committed themselves to something that could be ruined if they were suddenly called away to the battlefield (20:1-7). If people were cowardly or too afraid to fight, they were to be sent home (8-9).

Israel was not to act with the brutality that characterized other nations. Though they were to destroy the people of Canaan and their cities (for this was God's judgment on the wicked Canaanites), Israel's soldiers were not to destroy non-Canaanite cities unless the people refused Israel's terms of peace. They were to attack only when all else failed; but even then they were to attack only the soldiers, not the women and children (10-18). Also they were to be careful in choosing which trees to cut down for building siegeworks, to avoid destroying the orchards and forests (19-20).

Respect for human life (21:1-23)

Murder made the land unclean, and the uncleanness could be removed only by the execution of the murderer (see Num 35:29-34). Where the murderer could not be found, the elders of the town nearest the place of the murder had to go to an unpolluted stream nearby and carry out the ritual slaughter of a young cow instead of the unknown murderer. The blood of the cow washed away in the stream symbolized the removal of uncleanness caused by the unlawful bloodshed (21:1-9).

An Israelite had to treat with respect any woman taken captive in war. If he wanted to marry her, he had to realize that, because she had just been suddenly removed from her former home, he had to treat her with special consideration. Therefore, he could not take her as a wife till enough time had passed for her to mourn her parents and adjust to the new way of life. Neither could he sell her as a slave if he later decided he did not want her. He had to let her go free (10-14).

In the case of a man who had several wives, the firstborn son was always the heir, whether he was son of the favourite wife or not. This protected the rights of the firstborn against family jealousies and prejudices (15-17).

Where both parents agreed that their son was so uncontrollable as to be criminally dangerous, they could take him to the rulers for a legal judgment on what to do with him. If the rulers judged the young man to be a danger to the community, he was to be stoned to death (18-21). The body of a person stoned to death was hanged on a tree till evening as a mark of disgrace (22-23).

Laws of love and purity (22:1-30)

A collection of miscellaneous laws reminds the people of some everyday responsibilities. They had to go out of their way to help others (22:1-4); they were not to dress in a way that would encourage immorality (5); they were to be thoughtful for the safety of others, birds and animals as well as people (6-8); and they were not to restrict the productivity of their crops through wrong practices, or shorten the lives of their working animals through cruelty (9-11). They were to wear tassels on their clothes to remind them to keep God's commandments (12; see Num 15:37-41).

If a man tried to find an excuse for divorcing his wife by accusing her (falsely) of unchastity before marriage, he was to be whipped and fined for his cruel accusation and prevented from divorcing her (13-19). If, however, a woman *had* been guilty of unchastity before marriage, she had to suffer the penalty, which was death by stoning (20-21). The engaged as well as the married were considered adulterers if they had sexual relations with third parties, and had to be stoned to death. The one exception was the case of a woman who had been raped (22-27). People not engaged who had sexual relations were to marry each other, but the man was to be fined for his folly and had to pay the bride price to the young lady's father (28-30; see Exod 22:16-17).

A holy nation (23:1-25)

Various laws prohibited foreigners, eunuchs and people born through immorality from joining fully in Israel's public worship. This discouraged Israelites from copying heathen practices or marrying heathen people. At the same time it impressed upon them the holiness God required (23:1-8). Holiness also demanded high standards of cleanliness in the camp, particularly in matters concerning discharges from sexual organs and treatment of human excrement (9-14).

Other features of life in surrounding nations that the Israelites were not to follow were the practice of sending back runaway slaves for the sake of gaining a reward, and religious-sexual fertility rights with temple prostitutes (15-18). God's people were to be faithful to him by doing what they promised and by loving one another, such as in helping the needy with money and food (19-25; see notes on Exod 22:21-31; Lev 25:35-46).

Protection for the disadvantaged (24:1-25:4)

Various laws guaranteed protection for defenceless people who might otherwise be exploited. A woman who had been divorced was free from interference by her previous husband. He had to respect the decency of marriage, and had no right to send her away then take her back as he pleased (24:1-4; cf. Matt 5:32; 19:3-9). A newly married man could not be forced into the army till at least one year after marriage (5; cf. 20:7). A poor person who borrowed money could not be forced to give his creditor a millstone as guarantee for the debt, as he would be left with no means of providing flour for his family's food (6).

There was to be no mercy for a kidnapper (7) and no relaxation of the laws concerning leprosy, no matter how important the infected person was (8). However, people were to show mercy to debtors and not to trample on the rights of the poor. Clothing taken as guarantee for a debt had to be returned by evening, so that the person would not have to sleep in the cold (9-13). Employers were to be considerate to their employees, and pay wages daily to those who had no reserve savings (14-15).

Justice was not to favour the rich and powerful. At all times Israelites were to be merciful to the oppressed, remembering how they felt when they were oppressed in Egypt (16-18). When farmers harvested their cereals and fruit, whatever they missed at the first reaping or picking was to be left for the poor (19-22).

Whipping was never to be used to force confessions from suspected lawbreakers, but only to punish those who had been proved guilty. The number of lashes was to be in proportion to the offence and was never to exceed forty (25:1-3). Farmers were to be kind to their animals and allow them to eat as they worked (4).

Family and business relationships (25:5-19)

If a man died having no son, his brother was to have a temporary marital relation with the widow for the purpose of helping her produce a son. Legally, this son would be considered son of the dead man and so would receive his inheritance and carry on his name. If the brother refused to cooperate, he was to be publicly disgraced for allowing the dead man's name to die out (5-10). (If, however, there were surviving daughters, they could receive the father's inheritance; see Num 27:1-11.) This desire to protect even the closest of relatives was no excuse for indecency, and the person guilty of indecency had to be punished (11-12).

People were not to act dishonestly in business dealings, such as through using undersized measures when selling grain and extra heavy weights when weighing the buyer's money (13-16). In commanding Israel to destroy the Amalekites, God showed that he would surely punish those who brutally attacked the weak and defenceless (17-19).

Declarations by Israel and by God (26:1-19)

The first harvest season after the Israelites settled in Canaan would be of particular importance, bringing to a climax the fulfilment of God's promise to Israel of a permanent homeland (26:1-4). The harvest first-fruits offered to God on this occasion would have special significance as the people recalled their humble beginnings, their slavery in Egypt, and the miraculous release that allowed them to possess the land God had prepared for them (5-11).

Besides offering the firstfruits to God, the people had to make an annual offering of tithes. Every third year this tithe (or an additional tithe) was not taken to the central place of worship, but was given to the Levites and the poor in the offerer's own locality (see 14:28-29). This meant that the distribution of this tithe was not under the general supervision of the priests. The law therefore laid down a special requirement to prevent dishonesty and ensure that people kept in mind the religious nature of the offering. According to this require-ment, the offerer, after distributing his tithe, had to go to the central place of worship and declare before God that he had carried out his responsibilities fully (12-15).

Moses had now finished his instruction on the covenant's detailed requirements. The two parties to the covenant then made declarations that bound them together. The people declared that Yahweh was their God and they would keep his commandments, and God declared that they were his people and he would exalt them above all nations (16-19; see also 29:10-15).

27:1-30:20 CONDITIONS OF THE COVENANT

The listing of blessings and curses at the end of the covenant document is again in keeping with the form of ancient Near Eastern treaties. God in his sovereign grace had chosen Israel as his people and preserved them. In gratitude the people were to be obedient to God's commands, and in doing so they would enjoy fellowship with him and blessing in their national life. Disobedience, on the other hand, would bring his judgment upon them, so that they might see their sin, change their ways, and return to him in renewed covenant loyalty.

Blessings and curses (27:1-26)

After the Israelites moved into Canaan, they were to go to the valley between Mt Gerizim and Mt Ebal to declare their loyalty to the covenant. There also they were to write the law on plastered stones and display it publicly where people could read it, and so be reminded constantly of their covenant obligations (27:1-10).

Six tribes were to gather on each of the two mountains, while the Levitical priests, who read the blessings and curses, gathered in the valley between. As the priests read each blessing, the tribes on Mt Gerizim would give their acknowledgment by answering 'Amen'. In the same way the tribes on Mt Ebal would answer 'Amen' after each curse, acknowledging the justice of God's punishment if his people broke his law (11-14; see Josh 8:30-35).

For some reason only the curses are listed here, though the corresponding blessings were in fact read when Joshua later carried out the ceremony (Josh 8:34). The curses mainly concerned sins done in secret, emphasizing that no area of life was hidden from the watchful eye of God. The accursed sins included idolatry (15), disrespect (16), cheating (17), lack of sympathy (18), social injustice (19), sexual perversion (20-23), murder (24), plotting (25) and defiance of God's law in general (26).

Obedience and disobedience (28:1-68)

Further blessings and curses are now listed. These were connected more with the life of the people as a whole and were directly dependent on the people's obedience or disobedience. The blessings mainly concerned agricultural prosperity, family happiness, victory over enemies and honour in the eyes of other nations (28:1-10). God's assurance that he would supply their needs was linked to a warning. They were not to look for family increase or agricultural productivity by worshipping the Canaanite nature gods (11-14).

Corresponding to the blessings for obedience were the curses for disobedience. In general these would take the form of diseases and plagues upon their families, flocks, herds and crops (15-24) and repeated defeat in war (25-35). Finally, the nation that God had chosen to be the leader of all nations would go into humiliating captivity (36-46).

The cruelty of foreign invaders and the horrors of siege warfare are vividly described. People would be so desperate for food that they would eat even their own children (47-57; cf. 2 Kings 6:25-29; Lam 2:19-22; 4:4-10). Eventually, the nation would be destroyed and the people taken captive into foreign countries. There they would be treated worse than animals and meet horrible deaths. Many would be shipped as slaves to Egypt, where they would so flood the slave market that no one would want to buy them (58-68).

The covenant renewed (29:1-30:20)

Israel's lack of understanding of God and his ways meant that the people needed constant reminders of the covenant's purpose, meaning and requirements. Moses gave them such a reminder in this his farewell address to the nation, acting as God's representative in the renewal of the covenant as he had done at the establishment of the covenant at Sinai (Horeb) (29:1-9). The renewed oath of allegiance that the people swore before entering Canaan was binding on future generations (10-15).

If, after they had seen the greatness of Yahweh and the worthlessness of idols, the people stubbornly rejected Yahweh and worshipped other gods, the whole nation ('moist and dry alike') would be in danger of destruction (16-21). In judgment for their breaking the covenant, the land would be devastated and they would be driven from it in shame (22-28).

No person knows everything, but each person must be obedient to whatever knowledge he or she has. The Israelites did not know all that God would do in the future, but they had his revealed will for them in the present in the form of the covenant law, and they had to be obedient to that (29).

Although God might punish his people, in his grace he would forgive them and bring them back to their land if they repented of their sins and turned to him with all their hearts. He would cleanse their hearts and give them the desire to love him afresh. In response to their renewed obedience, he would bless them with renewed prosperity (30:1-10). The command to obey God was not something difficult to hear or understand, but was clear and simple. The people had to act upon it (11-14). Love and obedience would lead to true life and prosperity; self-will and disobedience would lead to disaster and death (15-20).

31:1-34:12 MOSES' LAST DAYS

Arrangements for the future (31:1-29)

Knowing he had only a few more days to live, Moses handed over the leadership of Israel to his divinely appointed successor, Joshua. He reminded both Joshua and the people that fearless commitment to the task ahead, combined with total trust in God, would guarantee victory over the Canaanites and possession of the promised land (31:1-8,14-15,23; see notes on Num 27:12-23).

Moses then made three separate arrangements to ensure that people did not forget their covenant obligations. First, he commanded the priests and leaders to make sure that the entire law was read publicly every seven years (9-15). Second, he himself wrote a song that would stick in people's minds as a constant warning and reminder (16-23. The song is recorded in Chapter 32). Third, he put his own written record of the law in a safe place beside the ark, as a witness against the people when they turned away from it. This copy of the law beside the ark was an absolute standard of reference in all matters of life and conduct (24-29).

These arrangements were again consistent with ancient practices concerning a covenant between an overlord and his subject people. The covenant document was kept in the people's sanctuary, and the leaders conducted periodic public readings to remind the people of their covenant obligations.

The song of Moses (31:30-32:47)

Being aware of the people's tendency to rebellion against God (see v. 29), Moses left with them a song that he wanted everyone to take notice of (30). The song reminded the people of God's loving care for them and of the need for faithfulness on their part towards him. It dealt with the future as well as the past, and reminded the people that in justice God would punish them and in mercy he would forgive them.

As rain benefits young grass, so Moses' words should benefit Israel (32:1-3). Like a rock, God gave Israel (Jeshurun) protection and stability; as their Father, he gave them an honoured place among the nations and a land for an inheritance; but through stubborn selfishness they ruined themselves and disgraced their Father (4-9). God cared for Israel with love and tenderness, giving his people all they needed for a life of contentment; but instead of being thankful, they treated him with contempt. Instead of worshipping him, they worshipped other gods (10-18). Therefore, in his righteous anger, God punished them (19-25).

However, God would not allow the nation to be completely destroyed, lest people thought that they, and not God, controlled Israel's destiny. If they had any understanding, these nations would realize that they could have no victory at all over Israel unless Israel's God allowed it (26-30). Israel's God was just and mighty; the enemies' gods were wicked, immoral and cruel (31-33).

Yahweh was still the supreme ruler. Even when he used other nations to punish his people, he would also punish those nations, along with their gods, for their own wickedness. Then Israel too would see the uselessness of false gods. They would return to Yahweh, and he would heal them (34-43).

The people were to memorize and sing this song, so that it would remind them to keep God's law and warn them of what would happen if they ignored it. God gave the law for their good, and by keeping it they would enjoy life in the land he had given them (44-47).

The blessing of Moses (32:48-33:29)

As God had announced earlier, the time for Moses to die had come (48-52; see Num 27:12-14). The prophetic blessings that he gave Israel before he died foresaw the favours that God would give the various tribes. But first Moses recalled the giving of the law at Sinai. God appeared in flaming majesty, bursting forth in glory brighter than the rising sun. Accompanying him were multitudes of heavenly servants who carry out God's purposes in the lives of individuals and nations. This one, Israel's King, was the one who gave his law to his assembled people (33:1-5).

The tribe of Reuben, though it had lost the rights of the firstborn, was not to allow itself to become weak (6; cf. 1 Chron 5:1). Judah was the most powerful tribe, but besides protecting itself from enemies, it was to help other tribes when they were in trouble. (Simeon, not mentioned here, became absorbed into the tribe of Judah) (7). Levi, the tribe to which Moses and Aaron belonged, had responsibility for religious services and the teaching of the law. Men of this tribe had passed God's test at Massah and proved their covenant faithfulness at Sinai, but had rebelled at Meribah (8-11; cf. Exod 17:1-7; 32:25-29; Num 20:10-13). (For the Urim and Thummim see notes on Exod 28:15-30.)

Benjamin had its special blessing when the temple in Jerusalem was later built in its territory, though the rest of Jerusalem was in Judah's territory (12). The Joseph tribes, Ephraim and Manasseh, were to inherit the best part of Canaan. The God who once appeared in the burning bush would give them special power, so that they would become the leading tribes in the northern kingdom (13-17).

Zebulun and Issachar would prosper through the commercial activity and agricultural richness that characterized their region (18-19). The people of Gad chose their land east of Jordan, but they kept their promise to help other tribes conquer Canaan. They were fierce fighters (20-21). Dan would prove to be a treacherous tribe (e.g. Judg 18:1-31), but Naphtali would be content with a quiet life in the fertile highlands around the Lake of Galilee. Asher would live in a well protected fertile area that would become famous for its olives and the high quality oil they produced (22-25). Protected and blessed by God, all Israel would enjoy victory, prosperity and happiness (26-29).

Death of Moses (34:1-12)

Before Moses died, God allowed him to climb to the peak (Pisgah) of Mount Nebo in the Abarim Range (near the Israelite camp on the plains of Moab) and view the full extent of the magnificent land his people were soon to possess (34:1-4).

The editor responsible for this final chapter adds the note that the exact location of Moses' grave was unknown (5-8). Joshua was the new leader, but neither he nor any who came after him had the unique experience of Moses, who met God face to face, who knew his thoughts and who performed his mighty works (9-12).

Joshua

BACKGROUND

The book of Joshua is concerned largely with Israel's conquest of Canaan and the division of the land among its tribes. As early as the time of Abraham God promised that this land would belong to Israel (Gen 13:14-17), but several hundred years passed before Israel was large enough to conquer and occupy it.

Most of Israel's population growth took place in Egypt, and when God's time arrived Moses led the people out of Egypt towards Canaan (Exod 3:7-10; 12:40-41). However, when the people were close enough to Canaan to prepare for attack, they became fearful of the Canaanites and rebellious against God. Except for two of their tribal leaders, Joshua and Caleb, the people stubbornly refused to trust God and advance into Canaan. In punishment God left them in the wilderness, till the whole adult generation (except Joshua and Caleb) died and a new generation grew up (Num 14:28-35). Now, forty years after their parents left Egypt, the people of this new generation were about to enter Canaan. They were camped on the plains east of the Jordan River opposite Jericho (Num 22:1), Moses had just died (Deut 34:1-5), and Joshua was now the nation's new leader (Deut 34:9; Josh 1:1-2).

Israel's new leader

Joshua had grown up as a slave in Egypt, but the years of hardship helped him develop a strength of character and a faith in God that would one day make him an important national figure. When the Israelites at last escaped from Egypt, Joshua soon showed his leadership qualities by quickly organizing a fighting force and driving off an Amalekite attack (Exod 17:8-16). By the time Israel reached Mt Sinai, Joshua was Moses' chief assistant. He alone went with Moses up into the mountain and kept watch while Moses entered the presence of God (Exod 24:13). Likewise he kept watch outside the tent where Moses met with God (Exod 33:11; cf. Num 11:28).

On the occasion of Israel's rebellion against God in the wilderness, Joshua demonstrated his faith and his courage when he and Caleb stood firm against them (Num 14:6-9). His faith in God gave him patience and kept him from selfish ambition. He showed no jealousy of Moses as Israel's leader, and even tried to defend him against any action that might have appeared to threaten his exalted position (Num 11:26-30).

God chose Joshua to succeed Moses as leader, but he made it clear that Joshua would not exercise the absolute authority that Moses had exercised. Moses' position was unique, and he spoke to God face to face. But after his death the civil leadership and the religious leadership were separated. From that time on the usual procedure was for the civil leader to receive God's instructions through the high priest (Num 27:18-23). Nevertheless, Joshua was a person who understood God. His experience as a spiritual guide, a civil administrator and a military leader fitted him well to lead the people of Israel into the new land and the new era that lay before them (Deut 31:7,14,23; 34:9).

Style of the book

The book of Joshua takes its name from the leading person in the story, but it does not record who wrote it. The writer may have based his material partly on what Joshua himself wrote (Josh 24:25-26), partly on other historical books of the era (Josh 10:13), and partly on various national and tribal records relating to places, families and events (Josh 18:8-9).

Although the book outlines the conquest of Canaan, it does not provide a detailed historical account of events. The battle for Canaan lasted a long time (Josh 11:18), at least five years (Josh 14:7,10), but the writer passes over some of the longer battles in only a few verses. By contrast, he describes events of little military importance in considerable detail.

The reason for this unevenness in the story is that the writer's chief concern is not to provide a detailed military or political record, but to show what God was doing with his people. The writer is more a preacher than a keeper of statistics; more a prophet than a historian.

To the Israelites, a prophet was not primarily a person who predicted the future, but a person who revealed God's will to his people (Isa 1:18-20; Jer 1:7,9; Amos 3:7-8; cf. Exod 4:10-16; 7:1-2). They viewed their history as a revelation of what God was doing, and for this reason most of the biblical books that we call historical, they called prophetical. Many of Israel's historians were prophets (1 Chron 29:29; 2 Chron 9:29; 12:15).

The Israelites divided their prophetical books into two sections, which they called the Former Prophets (Joshua, Judges, Samuel and Kings) and the Latter Prophets (Isaiah, Jeremiah, Ezekiel and the twelve so-called Minor Prophets). In the Former Prophets God revealed his purposes through the history of Israel, showing how the affairs of Israel, and in fact all nations, were under his control. In the Latter Prophets he revealed his purposes through the words of his spokesmen.

Because of this distinctively Israelite way of viewing history, the writer of Joshua has made no attempt to record everything that happened during the era. Neither has he recorded events in strict chronological order. Rather he has selected and arranged his material according to his prophetic purpose. He wants to lead his readers to a greater knowledge of God, through writing about those matters that are of greater significance in God's dealings with his people.

OUTLINE

1:1-5:15 ENTRY INTO CANAAN

Preparations (1:1-2:24)

God's command to Joshua was brief and straightforward: he was to take the land of Canaan. (The region in which Canaan was situated was occupied by various tribal peoples, the most important of whom were the Hittites and the Amorites.) Israel would not win the land without a fight, but the people had God's assurance that wherever they advanced they would gain possession (1:1-5). As leader of the people, Joshua had the assurance of God's presence, but he still needed personal courage and wisdom. These would also be his as he devoted himself to the task of understanding and obeying God's law (6-9).

Joshua then instructed his officials to prepare the people for departure in a few days time (10-11). The two and a half tribes who had asked for and received their inheritance on the eastern side of the Jordan River did not forget the promise they had made earlier to Moses. They were ready to cross Jordan and help their fellow Israelites conquer the western area. After that they would return and settle down to enjoy their own inheritance (12-18; cf. Num 32:1-33).

The first city that the Israelites had to conquer was Jericho, for it blocked their passage through the mountain pass to the land beyond. Joshua sent two men ahead to spy out Jericho, and although their presence in the city was discovered, they received protection from a prostitute named Rahab (2:1-7).

Rahab told the spies that the people of Jericho were terrified of the Israelites; but she herself had heard sufficient of the God of Israel to believe in his power and mercy to save her. By protecting the Israelite spies, she won from them a guarantee that she and her household would be safe from any violence when Israel attacked (8-14; cf. Heb. 11:31). The spies warned her, however, that she would have to remain faithful and follow their instructions if she and her family were to be spared (15-21; cf. James 2:25). The spies' safe return to Israel's camp reassured them that God was in full control and Israel was certain of victory (22-24).

Crossing the Jordan River (3:1-5:1)

Israel's conquest of Jericho was more than just a military exercise. It had religious meaning. The Israelites were to cleanse themselves before God, because he was the one who would lead them against their enemies. His presence was symbolized in the ark of the covenant (GNB: covenant box), which the priests carried ahead of the procession in full view of the people (3:1-6).

As God had worked through Moses, so he would work through Joshua. Just as the waters of the Red Sea had miraculously dried up to allow the former generation to escape from Egypt, so the waters of the Jordan would miraculously dry up to allow the new generation to enter Canaan (7-13).

It seems that the way God stopped the Jordan was by a collapse of its banks at the town of Adam (twenty-five kilometres upstream) that dammed the river. God was controlling events according to his perfectly timed plan, so that the waters at the river crossing dried up just as the priests arrived there. The priests then stood in the middle of the dry river bed until all the people crossed over (14-17).

Twelve men, one from each tribe, were then sent back to take twelve stones from the river bed, to be set up at the place where the people camped that night as a memorial of the great event (4:1-8). Joshua set up another memorial of twelve stones in the middle of the river itself, before the river broke through the earth dam upstream and returned to its normal flow. These remarkable events caused the people to give Joshua the same honour and respect as previously they had given Moses (9-18; cf. 3:7).

Once the people had established their camp at Gilgal, Joshua took the twelve stones that the men had brought from the river and set up the memorial (19-24). When the Canaanites heard about the Israelites' miraculous crossing of the Jordan, they were filled with fear (5:1).

Camp at Gilgal (5:2-15)

Israel's camp at Gilgal became the centre for the battle campaign that was to follow. But before the people could receive the land God promised them in the covenant, they had to renew their covenant relation with him.

During the previous forty years, the people of Israel had brought shame upon themselves through consistently being disobedient and unbelieving. They had even neglected the first requirement of the covenant, which was the circumcision of all new-born male children. Circumcision was the sign of the covenant. Therefore, just as there had been a general circumcision for all males in Abraham's household when the covenant was sealed (see Gen 17:9-14), so again there was a general circumcision in Joshua's time for all who were still uncircumcised. The ceremony sealed them as God's people who were to inherit the land promised to Abraham in the covenant (2-9; see Gen 17:5-8).

With the completion of the circumcision, the people could celebrate the Passover (something that an uncircumcised person was not allowed to do; see Exod 12:47-49). The journey from Egypt to Canaan was now officially over, and therefore the miraculous daily supply of manna ceased (10-12; cf. Exod 16:35).

God's special messenger appeared to Joshua to remind him that God was the commander of Israel's army. This messenger was so closely identified with God that Joshua fell at his feet and worshipped. To him it appeared that God had temporarily taken human form (13-15).

6:1-12:24 CONQUEST OF THE LAND

Destruction of the Canaanites

The following chapters show that the Israelites' conquest of Canaan was well planned. First they won control of the central region (Chapters 6-9). This created a division between the northern and

southern regions, and so prevented Canaanite tribes throughout the country from joining forces. Israel then had a much easier task in conquering the rest of Canaan, first the south (Chapter 10), then the north (Chapter 11).

Israel's destruction of the people of Canaan was not merely for political or material gain. It had a religious and moral purpose in God's plan. He had given the Canaanites time to repent, and the case of Rahab shows that any who turned from their sins

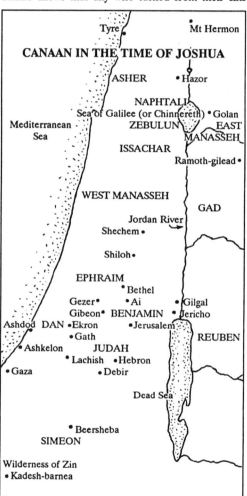

CANAAN IN THE TIME OF JOSHUA

and believed in the God of Israel could be saved. But for the Canaanites as a whole, their wickedness was now so great that the time for judgment had come (Gen 15:16; Deut 7:1-5). In the case of Sodom and Gomorrah, God had used the forces of nature to bring destruction; in the case of the Canaanites, he used his people Israel.

Apart from certain specified exceptions, the Israelites were to spare nothing and keep nothing (Deut 7:1-5; 20:16-18). The judgment had a religious significance, and everything was to be devoted to God for destruction. It was 'devoted', or 'holy', not in the sense of being morally pure, but in the sense of being forbidden to humans. People could not use devoted things for themselves. By destroying them, they were, in effect, presenting them to God and then carrying out God's judgment upon them (see 6:17-18; Lev 27:28-29; Deut 13:17). Concerning the destruction of the Canaanites' possessions, precious metals were excepted. These were added to Israel's treasury, probably after they were ceremonially purified by being passed through fire and washed in water (see 6:19; Num 31:21-23).

One result of moral filth is physical disease. Therefore, the destruction of the Canaanites (in some cases together with their sheep and cattle) ensured the removal of deadly diseases that could have threatened Israel's existence. The absence of Canaanite religious practices would also be a help to Israel's religious life and moral well-being.

Defeat of Jericho (6:1-27)

The destruction of Jericho demonstrated the kind of warfare that Israel was engaged in. God's unusual directions for the conquest of Jericho showed clearly that this was a religious judgment and Israel was his instrument. This was demonstrated in the important role of the priests, the prominence of the ark of the covenant, and the repeated use of the number seven in the battle preparations (6:1-7). Over the next six days the Israelites marched around Jericho once each day, and then returned to the camp at Gilgal (8-14).

On the seventh day the Israelites were to march around the city seven times. When the walls of the city fell, they were to destroy all the people except Rahab and those in her house, and all the goods except the precious metals. The Israelites were to keep nothing for themselves (15-19).

If earthquake activity had caused the collapse of the Jordan's banks, the same earthquake activity may have weakened the foundations of Jericho's walls. Nevertheless, the collapse of the walls at the exact moment God planned showed that victory came through the power of God, in response to the faith of his people (20-25; Heb 11:30). God intended Jericho to remain in ruins, as a permanent memorial that it had been destroyed by his curse. If any person rebuilt the city, the curse would pass on to

him, and as a consequence he would suffer the loss of his own sons (26-27; cf. 1 Kings 16:34).

Achan's sin (7:1-26)

God was angry that Israel had not been fully obedient to him in the conquest of Jericho. One of the people, Achan, secretly kept for himself what he should have destroyed (7:1). Therefore, when the Israelites moved on to attack the much smaller town of Ai, God allowed them to be driven back and to suffer losses (2-5). Joshua was distressed, not just because Israel had been defeated, but because their defeat would encourage the Canaanites. If all the Canaanites joined forces, Israel could be destroyed (6-9).

In response to Joshua's desperate prayer, God told him the reason for Israel's defeat. One person's sin concerning the devoted things of Jericho was enough to break the agreement that the whole nation had made with God, and so bring disaster upon it. God's curse on the devoted things passed on automatically to those associated with them. The person who kept the devoted things was now himself devoted to destruction, and through him Israel was also (see 6:18). The nation could be saved only by destroying the devoted things and all persons and things connected with them (10-15). Through the ritual of drawing lots, Joshua discovered that Achan was the guilty person. Achan's confession confirmed that the choice was correct (16-21). He and all that was his were then destroyed (22-26).

Victory in central Canaan (8:1-9:27)

Now that the Israelites had removed the cause of their defeat, God promised Joshua victory over Ai. He added that on this occasion the Israelites could keep the plunder for themselves (8:1-2).

Even with God's assurance of victory, Joshua planned the attack thoroughly. One company of soldiers was to draw the men of Ai out of the city to fight, then a second company would come out of hiding to attack Ai from the rear (3-9). The plan worked perfectly. When the first Israelite company drew the enemy out, Ai was left defenceless (10-17). The second Israelite company then captured the city (18-19). The men of Ai, caught between the two companies, were wiped out (20-23). The Israelites killed the people trapped inside Ai, after which they plundered the city and burnt it (24-29).

Having now cleared the way, Joshua led his people to Shechem, about thirty kilometres farther on. God had earlier instructed the people through Moses that, as soon as possible after entry into Canaan, they were to go to Shechem to promise their obedience to the covenant. First of all Joshua built an altar, on which the people offered sacrifices that expressed dedication and fellowship. Joshua also wrote the law of God on plastered stones, which he set up in Shechem to remind the people of the rule of life that God laid down for them in their new land (30-32; Deut 27:1-8).

The people gathered at the mountains Gerizim and Ebal, on either side of Shechem, to collectively declare their loyalty to the covenant. The six tribes who gathered at Mt Gerizim answered 'Amen' as the blessings of the law were read. The six tribes who gathered at Mt Ebal answered 'Amen' as the curses for disobedience were read (33-35; cf. Deut 27:11-14).

As Israel's fame spread, certain Canaanite tribes joined forces to resist any further advances (9:1-2). However, the people of Gibeon and three other towns in the central highlands thought of a different way to protect themselves. Knowing that Israel would destroy all the inhabitants of Canaan, they tricked Israel's leaders into agreeing not to kill them. They did this by pretending that they were not from Canaan at all, but were from a distant country (3-15). The Israelites were angry when they discovered the truth, but the leaders would not break their promise. They allowed the Gibeonites to live, but put them to work for Israel (16-21). The Gibeonites were grateful to be alive and willingly submitted to Israel's rule (22-27).

Victory in southern Canaan (10:1-43)

The five kings who between them controlled much of southern Canaan saw Joshua's control of Gibeon as a threat to their security. They decided to conquer Gibeon and so stop any further move south by Israel (10:1-5).

Joshua faced his biggest battle thus far. He knew that it would be a life-or-death struggle, but God encouraged him with the assurance of victory (6-8). God then helped make victory possible by causing some unusual changes in the weather that were favourable to Israel but fatal to the enemy (9-15). The enemy armies were almost destroyed, though some people found refuge in the fortified Canaanite cities (16-21). The five kings were then killed in a public execution, which included symbolic actions to reassure Israel's military leaders that no enemy could stand before them (22-27).

Encouraged by the victory, Joshua led his forces farther into the southern regions of Canaan, where he conquered the key cities. These included cities in the foothills leading down to the coast, such as Libnah, Lachish, Gezer and Eglon (28-35), and more

elevated cities in the central tableland such as Hebron and Debir (36-39). The conquest continued till it reached as far south as Kadesh-barnea and as far west as Gaza on the Mediterranean coast. Israel now controlled almost the whole of southern Canaan (40-43).

Victory in northern Canaan (11:1-15)

Alarmed by Israel's victories in the south, the kings of the north organized the largest, strongest and best equipped army that Israel had yet faced (11:1-5). Again God encouraged Joshua, and again Joshua launched a devastating surprise attack. He defeated the combined northern forces, making sure that he destroyed all their horses and chariots. This was apparently to prevent the Israelites from being tempted to use the horses and chariots themselves instead of trusting wholly upon God (6-9). Joshua captured all the key cities and destroyed the chief city, Hazor. All of northern Canaan was soon in the hands of Israel (10-15).

Summary of Israel's conquests (11:16-12:24)

Now that Israel controlled all the territory that was to become its homeland, the writer summarizes the entire conquest. First he summarizes Joshua's conquest of all the area west of Jordan (i.e. Canaan itself), where nine and a half tribes were to receive their inheritance (16-23). Then he summarizes the former conquest in the time of Moses, when Israel gained control of the territory east of Jordan, where two and a half tribes had already been allotted their inheritance (12:1-6; cf. Num 21:21-35; 32:33). Finally he lists the kings of the Canaanite city-states whom the Israelites had defeated (7-24).

The record of Joshua's conquest of Canaan is now complete. It has dealt only with the main events and has emphasized the decisiveness of Israel's victory. Actually the war lasted a long time, at least five years (cf. 11:18; 14:7,10).

Once Israel had won control of the land as a whole, Israel's leaders began the task of dividing it among the tribes. Throughout the country, however, there were many areas that the Canaanites still occupied, usually because they had either escaped the Israelites or proved too difficult to conquer. Many of these areas were in valleys or plains, where the Canaanites maintained control because of their large forces of chariots (cf. 17:16-18). The individual Israelite tribes were now to clear the Canaanites out of these areas and so enjoy full possession of their inheritance (see 13:1; 14:12). But the people were tired of battle, and the Canaanites whom they failed to destroy later became a source of much trouble to Israel (cf. 15:63; 16:10; 17:12). This is well demonstrated in the book of Judges.

13:1-22:34 DIVISION OF THE LAND

All the land that Israel had conquered was now divided among the twelve tribes. The list of tribal boundaries may not make very interesting reading today, but it was necessary for Israel as a permanent and lawful record to which people could refer if any disagreement arose. It also told the tribes of the enemies that had yet to be destroyed, both within their own tribal areas and in lands round about.

Overall plan for the division (13:1-14:5)

The area west of Jordan, which still contained many areas occupied by Canaanites, was to be divided between nine and a half tribes (13:1-7; for details of the separate tribal areas see 14:6-19:51). The area east of Jordan was to be occupied by two and a half tribes, in accordance with the arrangements that Moses made earlier (8-13; for details see 13:15-33). Cities for the Levites were to be allotted in all the tribes, since Levi had no tribal area of its own (14; Num 18:24; for details see 21:1-42).

Reuben was the most southern of the three eastern tribes, and occupied territory that Israel took from the Amorite king Sihon (15-23). Gad settled in the central section east of Jordan, and occupied much of the region commonly known as Gilead (24-28). The half tribe of Manasseh occupied the northern section east of Jordan, which included part of Gilead along with part of the rich pasture land of Bashan (29-31). The settlement of two and a half tribes east of Jordan instead of in Canaan itself had been approved by Moses (32-33).

Localities for the nine and a half western tribes were decided by drawing lots, but the area of land that each tribe received was in proportion to the population of the tribe (14:1-2; cf. Num 26:54-56; 33:54). In spite of the omission of Levi, the number of tribes among whom Israel's territory was divided (i.e. land on both sides of Jordan) was still twelve. This was because the son who received the birthright received twice the inheritance of the other sons, which in this case meant he received an additional tribe. As a consequence Joseph, who received the firstborn's inheritance instead of Reuben, received two tribes in Israel. The tribes were descended from his two sons, Manasseh and Ephraim (3-5; cf. Gen 48:5-6; 1 Chron 5:1-2).

The tribe of Judah (14:6-15:63)

By far the largest portions of Canaan went to the chief tribes, those of Judah and Joseph (cf. Gen 49:8-12,22-26). Judah received almost the whole of southern Canaan, and Joseph received almost the whole of central Canaan.

Caleb received his special inheritance within the area given to his tribe, Judah. Here he proved that his expression of faith made forty-five years earlier was not mere words. At that time he and Joshua alone in Israel believed that the Israelites could destroy the fearsome people of Anak whom they saw in Canaan. Now Caleb was prepared to do it (6-12; cf. Num 13:25-33; 14:24). Joshua gladly gave him permission to go ahead (13-15).

Judah was allotted southern Palestine between the Dead Sea and the Mediterranean Sea, as far south as the Wilderness of Zin and the Brook of Egypt (15:1-12). Within this territory Caleb then conquered the people of Anak. His courage and faith helped to develop the boldness of others, especially Othniel, who received Caleb's daughter as a reward for his bravery. Caleb also gave the young couple a piece of land as a wedding gift, but because the region was very dry he gave them an additional piece of land containing two springs of water (13-19; Judg 1:11-15; 3:9).

The cities of Judah were grouped in various regions: the dry southern region known as the Negeb (20-32); the low foothills region known as the Shephelah (33-44); the coastal plain territory of the Philistines (45-47); the central highland country (48-60); and the semi-desert region near the Dead Sea (61-62). The prize city of Jerusalem, however, remained unconquered (63).

The Joseph tribes (16:1-17:18)

Ephraim and the western half of Manasseh together occupied most of the central portion of Canaan between the Jordan River and the Mediterranean Sea (16:1-4). The southern part of this territory belonged to Ephraim (5-10), the northern part to Manasseh (17:1). (The other half of Manasseh had already received its allotment east of Jordan.)

Western Manasseh was divided between six major family groups. No details are given concerning portions received by five of these groups, but the remaining portion was subdivided into five smaller portions, which were given to the five daughters of Zelophehad. This was in accordance with the special law which directed that where a man had no son, his inheritance could pass to his daughters (2-6; see Num 27:1-11). Manasseh also took towns from the smaller tribes to its north, apparently claiming it could drive out the Canaanites from these towns. It failed to remove the Canaanites, but still kept the territory for itself (7-13).

Although the Joseph tribes received the best part of Canaan, they were still not satisfied. They wanted more land, but they did not want to work for it or fight for it. Joshua told them that if they cleared the forests and drove out the Canaanites, they would find that they had plenty of land within the territory already allotted to them (14-18).

The seven smaller tribes (18:1-19:51)

Allotments were now finished for two and a half tribes on the east of Jordan (Reuben, Gad and half of Manasseh) and two and a half tribes on the west (Judah, Ephraim and the other half of Manasseh). The next task was to settle the seven smaller tribes that remained. For this purpose the camp, including the tabernacle, was shifted from Gilgal to a more central location at Shiloh (18:1-2; cf. 5:10; 10:6,15,43; 14:6; 19:51; 22:9,12).

Many of the people had by now become lazy and were not willing to fight or work. Joshua stirred them up to finish the job. He sent off men to survey the remainder of the land and divide it into seven portions. He then drew lots to decide which area each tribe would receive (3-10).

Benjamin received a small area between the powerful tribes of Judah and Ephraim. A number of important towns of the central highlands were located in Benjamin, among them Jerusalem, which was just inside Benjamin's southern border (11-28). Simeon was settled in part of the tribal area of Judah (since Judah's area was too large for it), in the dry southern region known as the Negeb. As a result Simeon soon lost its separate tribal identity and was absorbed into the more powerful Judah (19:1-9; cf. Gen 49:5-7).

The next four tribes in the list occupied Galilee and neighbouring regions in the north of Canaan. Zebulun's territory was in the fertile hill country that rose from the coastal plain to the mountains of southern Galilee (10-16). Issachar, which bordered Zebulun, occupied the Valley of Jezreel to the south of the Sea of Galilee. The area was strategically important and agriculturally rich (17-23). Asher was allotted the coastal plain from Mt Carmel north to the Phoenician cities of Tyre and Sidon. But it never gained full control of the area, and had to be content with the region around Mt Carmel and the neighbouring hill country (24-31; Judg 1:31-32). Naphtali was given the Galilean hills and the Jordan Valley north of the Sea of Galilee (32-39).

Dan's original position was on the Philistine coast between the tribes of Judah and Ephraim. Squeezed between Israel's two most powerful tribes, and pushed back from the coast by the Philistines and the Amorites, the tribe of Dan later moved and settled in the far north (40-48; Judg 1:34; 18:1-31). Finally, Joshua received his special inheritance, which, by God's command, he himself chose. It was in the area of his own tribe, Ephraim (49-51).

Cities for the Levites (20:1-21:45)

The Levites were given forty-eight cities throughout Israel, along with surrounding pasture lands for their cattle (see 21:41-42; Num 35:1-8). Among these cities were six cities of refuge (Num 35:6). These were cities where a person who had killed another could flee for safety until he had been lawfully judged (Exod 21:12-14). If he was found guilty of murder he was to be executed, but if he was found to have caused the death accidentally, he could live in the city of refuge under the protection of the chief priest as long as that priest lived. This limited his freedom, but at the same time it ensured that he was safe from the revenge of the dead person's family (20:1-6; Num 35:9-34).

Three of the cities of refuge were west of Jordan and three east. In both the western and eastern regions one city was in the northern section, one in the central and one in the southern (7-9; Num 35:14-15).

Levi had three sons, Kohath, Gershon and Merari. Aaron was of the family of Kohath, and all Aaron's descendants, and no others, were priests (Exod 6:16,18,20; Num 3:10). The forty-eight cities of the Levites were therefore divided into four groups, which corresponded to the four divisions of the Levitical tribe: the priestly Kohathites, the non-priestly Kohathites, the Gershonites and the Merarites (21:1-7).

The drawing of lots decided the allocation of the cities (8), but God controlled the outcome so that the cities given to the priestly Kohathites were all within easy reach of Jerusalem, where the temple would one day be built (9-19). The non-priestly Kohathites were farther from Jerusalem (20-26), the Gershonites were mainly in the north (27-33) and the Merarites were mainly in the north and east (34-40). Once the Levites had received their cities, the allotment of Canaan was complete (41-45).

Settlement of the eastern tribes (22:1-34)

Now that the territory west of Jordan had been conquered and divided among the nine and a half tribes, the other two and a half tribes were free to return to their inheritance east of Jordan. Joshua commended them for being faithful to their word in helping their brothers conquer Canaan (22:1-4; cf. Deut 32:16-32), and warned them to remain true to

God in their new homeland (5). He then sent them back to their families with his blessing (6-9).

The eastern tribes expressed their loyalty to God and their unity with their brothers in Canaan by building an altar (10). But the western tribes misunderstood their action. They saw it as a sign not of unity, but of division. They thought the eastern tribes were rebelling against God and corrupting the religion he had given them (11-20).

In response the eastern tribes explained that they were not setting up an independent religion. On the contrary they wanted to demonstrate that they shared the same faith as their brothers across the river (21-25). They had not built the altar to offer sacrifices. They had built it solely for the purpose of reminding their descendants that they were part of Israel and worshipped the same God as their fellow Israelites (26-29).

This explanation satisfied the western tribes and peace was restored. The eastern tribes even gave the altar a special name to ensure that they never forgot its significance. They were bound to Yahweh, their covenant Lord (30-34).

23:1-24:33 JOSHUA'S FAREWELL

Nothing is recorded of events that occurred between Joshua's division of the land and his farewell addresses to the nation many years later. His life was now drawing to a close (see v. 14), and he called Israel's leaders together to pass on some encouragement and warning (23:1-2). He assured them that God would continue to fight for his people till all the remaining Canaanites were destroyed, provided his people remained true to the covenant. They were to love God, keep his commandments, and avoid the worship of all other gods (3-11). They were not to intermarry with the Canaanites who still lived among them (12-13), and were to remember that loyalty to God would bring his continued blessing, but disloyalty would bring his judgment (14-16).

Just as the people had once gone to Shechem to declare their loyalty to the covenant (see 8:30-35), so now the leaders, on behalf of the people, returned to Shechem to make a fresh declaration of loyalty (24:1). The covenant had originated with God, who brought Abraham from Mesopotamia into Canaan and promised to make from him a nation that would one day possess Canaan as its homeland (2-4). Centuries later God fulfilled that promise when he brought Israel out of Egypt (5-7), through the wilderness (8-10) and finally into Canaan (11-13). Sadly, the Israelites had demonstrated a tendency towards idolatry, whether the idolatry of Abraham's ancestors, of the Egyptians, or of the Canaanites. Therefore, they had to make a firm decision whether they were going to serve one of these gods or serve the true God, Yahweh (14-15).

The people readily declared that they would serve Yahweh alone (16-18). Joshua knew that to declare loyalty was easy, but to maintain it was not so easy. He therefore reminded the people of the terrible consequences if they broke their covenant with such a holy God (19-20). When the people swore that they knew what they were doing, Joshua challenged them to put their professed loyalty into practice immediately (21-24). He then ceremonially sealed the renewed covenant, wrote the covenant laws in a book, and set up a stone as a memorial of the people's promise to be loyal and obedient (25-28).

Joshua died in the knowledge that his strong leadership had helped the people maintain their allegiance to God. He was buried in his own piece of land in the tribal area of Ephraim (29-31). Joseph's bones, which the Israelites had brought with them from Egypt, were also buried within the area of the Joseph tribes. This was in accordance with Joseph's instructions, given centuries earlier, by which he had openly declared his faith in God's promises (32; cf. Gen 50:24-25; Exod 13:19; Heb 11:22). The high priest also was buried in Ephraim (33).

Judges

BACKGROUND

The book of Judges deals with events in Israel during the two hundred years that followed Joshua's conquest of Canaan. Israel under Joshua had won a great victory, but the people had not been fully obedient to God's command to destroy all the Canaanites. As a result those Canaanites who were left in the land became a source of trouble to Israel, both religiously and politically.

During this period Israel's history developed a pattern that is repeated many times in the book of Judges. Time and again Israel turned away from God, copied the religious practices of the Canaanites, became politically weak and finally fell under the power of neighbouring tribes or nations. But God, who used these enemies to punish his disobedient people, was long-suffering and merciful. In each case he gave them, in his time, a deliverer from among their own people who overthrew the enemy and led Israel back to himself.

These deliverers were called judges, because they carried out God's judgment in defeating the enemy and delivering his people. Other judges, less warlike, carried out God's judgment by guiding the everyday affairs of his people according to his law. From these leaders, military as well as civilian, the book takes its name.

Israel and its enemies

It appears that the various conquests by enemy nations, and the deliverances by the Israelite judges that followed, never involved the whole of Canaan. Usually the only tribes involved were those in the area of the enemy's activity. Also, some of the conquests and deliverances may have occurred in different parts of the country at the same time. For example, the story of Jephthah and the Ammonites may belong to the same period as the stories of Samson and the Philistines (Judg 10:7-8; 11:5; 13:1). There was little unity in Israel, and each tribe (or group of tribes) looked after its own area without concern for the other tribes.

The main reason for this lack of unity was the people's departure from God. If they had made him the centre of their national life, their loyalty to him would have bound them together. Their disunity

was made worse by their failure to destroy the enemy among them. Canaanite strongholds in a number of key places kept the tribes apart. In Canaan itself (the area between the Jordan River and the Mediterranean Sea) the tribes were broken into three main sections — northern, central and southern — while the eastern tribes were separated from the rest by the Jordan River.

This breaking up of Israel created not only political disunity but also religious disunity, for it meant that many of the tribes were cut off from Israel's central place of worship at Shiloh (Josh 18:1; 22:9). In short, most of the nation's troubles, material, political and spiritual, were a direct result of the people's failure to obey God and wipe out the Canaanites (Judg 1:21,27-36; cf. Deut 7:2-4; 9:5; Josh 24:14-24).

The religion of the Canaanites

Canaanite gods were known as Baalim (plural of Baal; see Judg 2:11-12; 10:10; 1 Kings 16:31), and goddesses as Ashtaroth (plural of Ashtoreth, or Astarte; see Judg 2:13; 1 Sam. 7:3-4) and Asherim (plural of Asherah; see Judg 6:25-26; 2 Kings 23:4). These were gods of nature and fertility who, among other things, were believed to have the power to increase agricultural productivity. Since Israel knew Yahweh as the Creator of nature, the people easily fell to the temptation to combine Canaanite ideas with their own and so worship Yahweh as another Baal. The word *baal* was a common Hebrew word that meant master, husband or owner, and since the Israelites knew Yahweh as their master, husband and owner, they further linked the Canaanite Baals with him (Hosea 2:5-10).

The places where the Canaanites liked to carry out their Baal rituals were the sacred hilltop sites known as high places (Num 33:51-52; 2 Kings 23:13). Among the features of these high places were the sacred wooden or stone pillars known as Asherim (named after Asherah, the goddess whom they represented; Judg 6:25-26; 1 Kings 14:23). From the beginning Israelites had worshipped Yahweh at various places in the hills (e.g. Gen 22:2; Exod 17:8-15; 19:3), and again the people readily fell to the temptation to take over the high places of Baal and use them in their worship of Yahweh. All this was in spite of God's command that the high places of Baal were to be destroyed (Num 33:52; Deut 12:2-3).

Prostitutes, male and female, were available at these high places for fertility rites. These were religious-sexual ceremonies that the people believed gave increase in crops, herds, flocks and family (1 Kings 14:23-24; Hosea 2:5,8-9; 9:1-2,10-14). In following the Baals, the Israelites were also guilty of spiritual prostitution. The covenant bond between Israel and Yahweh was likened to the marriage bond; therefore, Israel's association with Baal and other gods was spiritual adultery (Judg 2:12-13,17; Jer 2:20; 3:6-8; Hosea 2:13; 4:12).

OUTLINE

1:1-2:10   Summary of Joshua's conquest
2:11-16:31 Rule of the judges
17:1-21:25 Tribal disorder within Israel

1:1-2:10 SUMMARY OF JOSHUA'S CONQUEST

Israel's incomplete conquest (1:1-36)

The writer of the book is concerned with events 'after the death of Joshua' (see 1:1), but before describing these events he gives a background to them by outlining Israel's conquest of Canaan under Joshua. First, he summarizes the attack led by Judah and Simeon in the southern part of the central highlands (1:1-7; see notes on Josh 10:1-43).

Jerusalem was among the highland towns that Joshua captured. Later, however, it was retaken by the enemy, so that by the time Benjamin received Jerusalem in its tribal allotment, the enemy was firmly in control of the city again (8; cf. v. 21). Israel then carried the conquest south to Hebron, where Caleb won a great victory (9-10; cf. v. 20; see notes on Josh 14:6-15). Caleb's boldness encouraged Othniel, who spread the conquest even further (11-15; see notes on Josh 15:13-19).

Although the Israelite armies won control of the hill country, they were not able to maintain control of the plains, being driven back into the hills by the Canaanite chariot forces. Consequently, towns captured by Israel on the coastal plain of southern Palestine were later recovered by the Philistines (16-21). (The towns of Ashdod, Ashkelon, Gaza, Gath and Ekron were known as 'the five cities of the Philistines'; cf. 3:3; 16:23; Josh 13:3.)

Having outlined Israel's conquest in southern Canaan, the writer goes back in the story to mention part of Israel's earlier conquest in central Canaan (22-26; see notes on Josh 8:1-29). As the Israelites spread their conquest farther north they gained control of the hill country, but could not gain control in the plainland regions where the Canaanite chariot forces operated (27-30; see notes on Josh 17:7-18). In the far northern tribal areas of Naphtali and Asher, the Canaanites maintained even greater control (31-33), and the central coastal tribe of Dan was eventually forced out of its territory completely (34-36; see notes on Chapters 17 and 18 below).

Results of Israel's failure (2:1-10)

In bringing Israel into Canaan, God was faithful to his covenant promises. The Israelites, however, were not faithful to theirs. Therefore, just as Israel was once God's instrument to punish the Canaanites, so now the Canaanites would be God's instrument to punish Israel (2:1-5). After the death of Joshua and the godly leaders whom he had trained, the Israelites turned away from God. In so doing they brought Israel into an extended period of suffering and defeat, though within this period there were times of peace. These were won for them through God-sent deliverers known as judges (6-10).

2:11-16:31 RULE OF THE JUDGES

Pattern of judgment and deliverance (2:11-3:6)

When the people of Israel rejected God and began to worship Baal and other gods, God punished them. He allowed them to fall under the power of foreign tribes and nations who seized their property and ruled them cruelly (11-15). When, after many years of suffering, the people finally turned again to God, God gave them deliverers who overthrew the enemy and restored independence to Israel. But as soon as they were living in peace and contentment again, the people forgot God and returned to their idolatrous ways. This pattern was repeated generation after generation (16-19). The enemy whom the Israelites failed to destroy then became a source of trouble to them (20-23).

God used enemies in and around Palestine to test Israel's loyalty to him and to punish them when they were disobedient. He also used them to give each new generation of Israelites experience in warfare (3:1-4). Some Israelites intermarried with these people and worshipped their gods (5-6).

Othniel, Ehud and Shamgar (3:7-31)

The first invader of Israel seems to have come from Aram, which was far to the north of Palestine. The Israelite leader who finally defeated him, Othniel,

97

came from the tribe of Judah, which was in the south of Palestine (see Josh 15:13-19). It appears, therefore, that the enemy had overrun most of the land. As in other cases recorded in Judges, Israel's victory came through God's special power given to the deliverer (7-11; cf. 6:34; 11:29; 13:25; 14:6,19; 15:14).

Israel's next oppressor came from the east. The forces of Moab, assisted by Ammon and Amalek, crossed the Jordan and advanced as far as Jericho, the city of palms. From there they exercised control over the tribal area of Benjamin and possibly the border areas of Ephraim. They ruled for eighteen years (12-14). Israel's deliverer, Ehud, came from Benjamin. When the time came for him to take Israel's periodic tribute money to the Moabite king (probably at Jericho), he cunningly gained a private meeting with the king and assassinated him (15-23). Before the Moabites discovered what had happened, Ehud escaped and mobilized his soldiers (24-27). When the Moabites tried to flee back to Moab, they were cut off by the Israelites at the Jordan crossing, and mercilessly slaughtered (28-30).

Another great leader who rescued the Israelites from an enemy was Shamgar. He won his victory over the Philistines, who lived on the Mediterranean coastal plain (31).

Deliverance under Deborah (4:1-5:31)

Hazor, chief city of the north, had been conquered and burnt by Joshua (Josh 11:10-13). However, not all the people had been destroyed. Having rebuilt Hazor, they now took revenge on the northern tribes, especially Zebulun and Naphtali, and ruled them cruelly for twenty years (4:1-3). (To understand fully how God saved Israel at this time, we must read the historical outline in Chapter 4 together with the song of victory in Chapter 5.)

Israel's deliverer on this occasion was Deborah, a woman who was already established as a leading civil administrator in the nation (4-5). With her army commander Barak, she led a large Israelite force up Mt Tabor. The plan was to make the enemy commander Sisera believe there was an armed rebellion in Israel, and so draw Sisera's chariot forces out into the plain of the Kishon River, which lay below the Israelites (6-10).

The plan was successful. Soon after Sisera crossed the shallow stream, a tremendous rainstorm flooded the river. The soft ground quickly became one huge bog; the small stream became a raging river. The Canaanites were thrown into confusion as chariots became bogged, horses grew mad with fear, and soldiers drowned in the rushing waters. Certain

of victory, the Israelites rushed down upon the enemy (11-16; see also 5:20-22).

Sisera escaped and looked for safety in the tent of his friend Heber (17; cf. v. 11). But Heber was not at home, and Sisera did not know that Heber's wife Jael was on the side of Israel. Once Jael had made sure that Sisera was soundly asleep, she killed him (18-22). The Israelites' victory that day gave them the confidence and courage to fight on till they destroyed the power of the enemy to enslave them (23-24).

Deborah and Barak's song of praise recalls the dramatic activity of God, the initiative of the leaders and the willing service of the people which together produced this spectacular victory. The rainstorm that God used to fight for his people reminded them of the earthquake he sent at Mt Sinai (5:1-5; cf. Exod 19:16).

Israel had suffered enough under the cruel Canaanites, whose raiding and violence made trade, travel and farming almost impossible. They would not even allow the Israelites to make any weapons to protect themselves. Then arose Deborah! Rich and poor alike are now urged to join with Israelites everywhere in songs of praise for God's deliverance through her (6-11).

When Israel's leaders stirred themselves to overthrow the Canaanites, most of the tribes joined in enthusiastically. With Benjamin and Ephraim in the lead, and Manasseh (Machir), Zebulun, Naphtali and Issachar following, the Israelites rushed down the valley and attacked the enemy. Shame on Reuben, Gad (Gilead), Asher and Dan who were selfishly concerned with their own affairs and did not come to help the other tribes (12-18).

The Canaanites came looking for victory and reward, but instead they met defeat, because God turned the forces of nature against them (19-22). Although some in Israel selfishly refused to join in the fight against the enemy, Jael risked her life to make Israel's victory complete (23-27). The song writers pictured Sisera's mother waiting anxiously for her hero son to return, assuring herself that the reason for his delay was that he was gathering the rewards of victory. But the Israelites knew, with a feeling of vengeful delight, that Sisera would never return (28-31).

God prepares Gideon (6:1-40)

Israel's return to sinful and idolatrous ways met its punishment in the raids of the Midianites. As usual the Amalekites were pleased to join in the attack. Year by year, for seven years, the invaders rode their army of camels from the deserts of Arabia, crossed the Jordan, and raided the fields and herds of the helpless Israelites. Their attacks reached as far north as Naphtali and as far west as Gaza. So fierce were

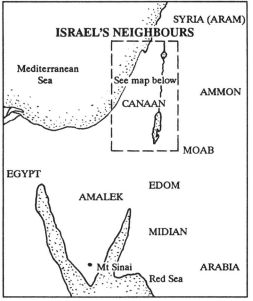

ISRAEL'S NEIGHBOURS

their attacks that the Israelites could no longer live safely in the open fields or in the towns. They were driven to a life of poverty and hardship in their mountain hiding places (6:1-6).

When the Israelites cried to God for help, God reminded them that they had been disobedient and unfaithful (7-10). Nevertheless, in his grace, he would send them a deliverer. The man he chose was Gideon (11-14). In spite of an assurance of victory, Gideon was at first unsure of God's call (15-18). Only after fire miraculously burnt up his offering was Gideon certain that God had indeed spoken to him (19-24).

Gideon began his reformation of Israel in his home town. He smashed the altar of Baal, along with its sacred wooden pillar, and built a new altar on which he offered holy sacrifices to Israel's God, Yahweh, the only true God (25-27). His father, who was apparently caretaker of the altar of Baal, was the first to see the error of his ways and turn from Baal (28-32).

The men of the town were at first angry at Gideon's action, but when he began to put together a fighting force to deal with the Midianites, they were the first to support him. People of other tribes followed their example and joined him (33-35). As the people prepared themselves to fight Midian,

Gideon's faith began to weaken, but God in his grace reassured him of victory (36-40).

Deliverance under Gideon (7:1-8:35)

God allowed Gideon only three hundred men to launch the attack against the Midianites, so that Israel might know that victory was not by military power but by God's power (7:1-8). A Midianite soldier's dream showed that an unnatural fear had come upon the Midianites. When he dreamt that a poor man's loaf of barley overthrew a rich man's tent, he thought that poverty-stricken Israel would overthrow Midian's army. The Midianites could, in fact, have wiped out the Israelites with ease (9-14). Gideon knew that victory for Israel was now certain and he prepared his men for attack (15-18).

The Midianites were thrown into confusion when they were awakened in the middle of the

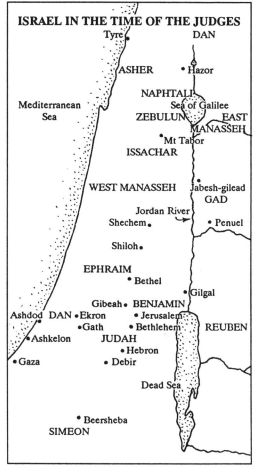

ISRAEL IN THE TIME OF THE JUDGES

night by the alarming sound of rams horns blasting, water jars breaking and Israelites yelling. When they saw lights all around the camp, they thought that Israel's army was upon them. In their panic many began swinging their swords at anything they saw move in the darkness, not realizing that they were killing their own soldiers. Others tried to escape (19-22). The larger Israelite forces then joined in the battle (23).

Gideon gave to the men of Ephraim the task of cutting off the Midianites' escape by seizing the Jordan River crossing. In doing so, the Ephraimites captured and killed two Midianite princes (24-25). However, the Ephraimites were offended because Gideon had not called them to join in the main battle. They calmed down when Gideon praised them by pointing out what a good job they had done. Whereas Gideon and his men had killed many of the ordinary Midianite soldiers, the Ephraimites had killed the two Midianite princes. The quality of Gideon's 'harvest' could not compare with that of the Ephraimites' 'gleanings' (8:1-3).

As for Gideon himself, he would not rest till he had killed the enemy kings. Not only were they the Midianite leaders, but they had also killed Gideon's brothers (4-5; cf. v. 18-19). The leaders of certain cities east of Jordan doubted that Gideon would be successful, and refused to give him needed supplies for his army. They feared that if they helped Gideon, the Midianites would later return and punish them. Gideon promised that if they would not help him, he would punish them (6-9).

Though greatly outnumbered, Gideon pursued the two kings and captured them (10-12). As he returned from battle, he punished the leaders of the Israelite cities who had refused to help (13-17). He himself then killed the kings who had killed his brothers (18-21).

By now there was a widespread feeling among the Israelites that they should be like the nations round about and have a king whose rule would pass on to his descendants after him. Gideon refused their invitation, pointing out that Yahweh was their king (22-23). Although he continued to exercise some leadership in Israel, Gideon was not the great leader in peace that he had been in war. As Aaron had once done, he made a material symbol of the unseen God, and this soon led the people into idolatry (24-28).

In spite of his refusal to be Israel's king, Gideon showed a tendency towards the sort of lifestyle that was typical of kings in neighbouring nations. Like them he built a large household of wives, concubines and children (29-32). When he died, the people easily slipped back into Baal worship. In their security and prosperity they forgot the God who had saved them (33-35).

The story of Abimelech (9:1-57)

Gideon had about seventy sons. One of these, Abimelech, was not a full-blooded Israelite, for his mother was a Shechemite. (The Shechemites were a group of Canaanites who lived peaceably among the Israelites; see Gen 12:6; 34:1-31; Josh 24:32.) With the help of some worthless Shechemites, Abimelech killed all his brothers (except one who escaped) and established himself 'king' in Shechem. His 'kingdom' probably consisted only of Shechem and a few towns round about (9:1-6).

Jotham, the brother who escaped, warned the Shechemites in a parable of the trouble they would bring upon themselves. Good men are likened to good trees: they are too concerned with giving useful and honourable service to be bothered with seeking power. By contrast Abimelech is like a bramble: he can give neither shelter nor protection. And just as a bramble can catch fire easily and burn down a forest, so would Abimelech be the means of the Shechemites' destruction (7-21).

In due course trouble arose between Abimelech and the Shechemites. Through highway robbery, the Shechemites created an atmosphere of insecurity and disorder, at the same time robbing Abimelech of his taxes (22-25). When a suitable occasion arose and Abimelech was in another town, a group of Shechemites plotted to overthrow him. The chief administrator in Shechem pretended to be on their side, but secretly he sent news to Abimelech (26-33). Abimelech came quickly and put down the rebellion (34-41).

But Abimelech did not stop at that. He decided to teach his subjects a lesson. He would destroy all the people of Shechem, both those who went out to work in the fields and those back in the town who took shelter in the city stronghold (42-49). In senseless fury Abimelech carried his attack to other towns, but his uncontrolled rage and lack of caution soon brought about his own death. The Shechemites who supported him were also destroyed, as Jotham had predicted (50-57).

Jephthah and five other judges (10:1-12:15)

Little is known of the political or military activities of the judges Tola and Jair. They both exercised power for lengthy periods, and Jair's family certainly enjoyed considerable power and prestige among the East Jordan tribes (10:1-5).

Again the Israelites turned away from Yahweh and worshipped false gods, and again they were punished. The Ammonites conquered the eastern tribes, crossed Jordan, and seized large portions of Israelite territory in Canaan as well. The Philistines attacked and conquered from the west (6-9). After eighteen years of oppression, the Israelites cried to God for help. In his mercy God saved them, though not until they got rid of their foreign gods and began to worship him again (10-16). Their deliverance from the Ammonites during the time of Jephthah is described in 10:17-12:7; their difficulties with the Philistines during the time of Samson are outlined in 13:1-16:31.

The leaders of the eastern tribes were desperate in their search for someone to lead Israel in battle against the Ammonites (17-18). The man they chose was Jephthah. The son of a prostitute, Jephthah had been cast out of his family and become the leader of a gang of bandits (11:1-6). He was tough, bitter and uncompromising, and he accepted the tribal leaders' invitation only after they agreed that he would remain their leader after the war was over (7-11).

Ammon had ruled eastern Israel for eighteen years (see 10:8). Apparently aware of feelings of restlessness and revolt in Israel, the Ammonites decided to attack. They made the excuse that Israel had taken their territory from them, so now they intended to take it back (12-13).

Jephthah replied by giving them an account of Israel's progress from Egypt to the region east of Jordan that was now in dispute. Firstly, he pointed out, Israel did not take any of this territory from peoples related to Israel, whether they were Ammonites, Edomites, or Moabites. All Israel's land east of Jordan was taken from the Amorites, who were under the judgment of God (14-22). Secondly, the land had been given to the Israelites by their God Yahweh, and his will had to be obeyed (23-24). Thirdly, the Moabite king of the time made no complaint that Israel had seized his territory. Why, then, after all these years should a dispute arise (25-26)? Jephthah appealed for understanding, but the Ammonites would not listen (27-28).

Although God gave Jephthah his special help, Jephthah was still only a slightly reformed bandit. He knew little of the character of God, and thought that by making a vow to sacrifice a person as a burnt offering to God, he could buy God's help and so ensure victory. Human sacrifice was against God's law (see Lev 18:21; Deut 12:31), but the people had forgotten that law and followed the religions of the neighbouring nations (see 10:6; cf. 2 Kings 3:26-27).

Having made his vow, Jephthah went to battle and won a great victory (29-33). On his return from battle, Jephthah found that the person whom he had to offer according to his vow was his only daughter. Nevertheless, he kept his vow and sacrificed her (34-40).

Once more the Ephraimites were offended that they, the strongest tribe in Israel, had not been invited to the battle (cf. 8:1-3). They crossed the Jordan River into the eastern territory to complain to Jephthah and to fight if necessary (12:1).

Jephthah replied that for years the eastern tribes had been asking for Ephraim's help, but had never received it. Why should they ask for it again (2-3)? The Ephraimites replied by accusing the eastern tribes of having run away from Israel; but when fighting broke out between the two groups, the Ephraimites were the ones running away. Jephthah's soldiers cut off their escape at the Jordan. The Ephraimites' attempt to disguise themselves and slip through the checkpoint was not successful, because their speech betrayed them as Ephraimites (4-6).

Having liberated his people, Jephthah then ruled over them, but after only six years he died (7). Three subsequent judges are listed, but little is known of them. From the sizes of their households it appears that they were people of wealth and influence (8-15).

A man to fight the Philistines (13:1-25)

The Philistines were by far the strongest enemy that Israel had yet met. Their forty years of rule lasted until the time of Samuel, and they continued to give trouble during the reigns of Saul and David (13:1).

Samson was the man God chose to begin the job of breaking the Philistines' rule. Before he was born, his mother was told by a messenger from God that she was to dedicate the child to God as a Nazirite for life. This meant that Samson was not to drink wine, touch anything dead, or cut his hair. These restrictions were to be a constant reminder to him and to others that he was totally dedicated to the service of God (2-7; cf. Num 6:1-21).

God's messenger repeated the instructions for the benefit of Samson's father (8-14), who then prepared to offer a sacrifice to God (15-16). When the messenger ascended towards heaven in the flames of the altar, Samson's parents realized that he was a supernatural figure, the angel of the Lord (17-23; see note on Josh 5:13-15).

In due course Samson was born. As he grew to manhood, God's special power worked in him to prepare him for the tasks ahead (24-25).

Samson's exploits (14:1-16:31)

So dominant were the Philistines in Israel, that the Israelites had decided to live with them peacefully rather than try to rise up in armed rebellion. Samson had other ideas. He thought that his marriage to a Philistine woman would give him the opportunity to do some harm to the enemy (14:1-4).

In spite of Samson's desire to help Israel, he had little respect for either his Nazirite vow or the Israelite law. He handled a dead lion, married a Philistine woman and joined in the customary wine-drinking feasts of the Philistines (5-10; cf. Deut 7:1-3). His opportunity to harm the Philistines came quickly and unexpectedly during his wedding feast. Through the deceit of his wife, he lost a bet with thirty of her Philistine friends (11-18); but he took revenge by killing thirty other Philistines, whose valuables he used to pay off his lost bet. Then, with no more desire to go on with the marriage, he returned home (19-20).

On calming down, Samson decided he would return and take the woman as his wife after all. When he found that she had been given to another, he took revenge on the Philistines by burning their harvest (15:1-5). The Philistines replied by killing Samson's wife and father-in-law, since they were the cause of the trouble. Samson, in return, killed more Philistines (6-8).

Not wishing to extend the conflict at this stage, Samson moved to a hideout near one of the towns of Judah. But the Philistines attacked the town and demanded that the Israelites hand Samson over to them. The Israelites were willing to cooperate, because Samson had brought them enough trouble (9-13). Again, however, Samson slaughtered the Philistines (14-17). The victory left him weak and thirsty, but God refreshed him, thereby providing a fitting reminder that God alone was the source of his strength (18-19).

The spectacular exploits of Samson went on for twenty years (20). Although he is called a judge, he was neither a civil administrator nor an army commander. His 'deliverances' consisted of one-man adventures against the Philistines in the areas where they had overrun Judah and Dan, the latter being Samson's tribe (see 13:2; 15:9). Samson's attacks unsettled the enemy and stirred the people of Israel from their lazy acceptance of foreign rule. He began the deliverance that eventually saw the Philistines overthrown (see 13:5b).

Samson had a moral weakness in matters concerning women, and on one occasion this almost led to his capture (16:1-3). The Philistine leaders, on learning of this weakness, worked out a plan to use the woman Delilah to trap him (4-5). Delilah's early efforts were unsuccessful, but she did not give up (6-14). Samson had paid little attention to the self-discipline demanded by his Nazirite vow, except that he allowed his hair to remain uncut. But when he removed this the last symbol of his separation unto God, he was in fact separated *from* God. The Lord who had given him his strength now left him. His abnormal power was gone, and his enemies soon captured him (15-22).

In the celebration feast that followed, the Philistines praised their god Dagon and humiliated Samson (23-25). But when Samson turned to God at last, God graciously responded. He allowed Samson a return of his former strength, so that he had a greater victory in his death than he ever had in his life. The sudden death of all the leading Philistine rulers was the turning point that gave Israel its first hope for victory (26-31).

17:1-21:25 TRIBAL DISORDER WITHIN ISRAEL

The writer of the book has now finished his account of the activity of the judges. To this he adds an appendix consisting of two stories (not necessarily placed in their correct chronological position in the book) that illustrate the disorder that existed in Israel during that period. The nation had no central government and people in the various tribes did as they pleased (see 17:6; 18:1; 19:1; 21:25). The stories record important changes that occurred in two tribes, Dan and Benjamin.

The migration of the Danites (17:1-18:31)

Micah, a man who lived in the tribal area of Ephraim, had stolen some money from his mother. When he heard the frightening curse she placed on the thief, he thought it wise to confess his guilt and return the money. To show her thanks, the mother made a silver idol to add to the other idols that were kept in the household shrine. Micah made matters worse by appointing his son, an Ephraimite, as priest (17:1-6). When a young Levite who lived in the tribal area of Judah later passed that way, Micah hired him to be priest instead of his son (7-13).

People of the tribe of Dan had never won complete control over their tribal inheritance on the Philistine coast. Squeezed between Israel's two most powerful tribes, Judah and Ephraim, and pushed back from the coast by the Philistines and the Amorites, they were left with very little area to call their own (see 1:34). They therefore sent a group of representatives to look for a better dwelling place elsewhere. The men's journey took them through Ephraim, where they stayed overnight with Micah (18:1-2). They asked Micah's guidance concerning their mission and were encouraged by his favourable reply (3-6).

Moving on, the Danite spies eventually arrived at Laish in the far north of Palestine. There they found a suitable area, fertile and well watered. It was inhabited by a quiet-living people who had made no preparations against attack, and who were so cut off from the big cities on the coast that they had no way to get help if they were suddenly attacked. Enthusiastic about what they had seen, the spies returned with their report. Soon the people of Dan were on the move, eager to conquer Laish and make it the centre of their new homeland (7-10).

On the way the Danites stopped at the house of Micah (11-13). Ignoring Micah's previous kindness to them, they raided his shrine, robbed him of his images, and bribed his priest to go with them (14-21). When Micah protested, they threatened him with swift destruction if he tried to resist them (22-26). They journeyed on to Laish, where they ruthlessly slaughtered the people and burnt the town. They then rebuilt the town according to their own plans, renamed it Dan, and used Micah's priest and images to establish their own idolatrous religion (27-31).

The war with Benjamin (19:1-21:25)

A Levite whose concubine had run away from him came to Judah looking for her. When they were reunited, her father was so pleased he did not want them to leave. They therefore stayed with him a few days, then set out to return to the Levite's home in Ephraim (19:1-9).

The route back to Ephraim took the couple through the tribal territory of Benjamin. Looking for somewhere to sleep the night, they preferred not to stay in Jerusalem, which was inhabited by foreigners, but to move on to Gibeah, where they would be among their fellow Israelites (10-14). But the people of Gibeah were not hospitable, and the Levite and his wife thought they would have to sleep in the town square. However, an old man (who was not a Benjaminite, but an Ephraimite) saw them and took them into his house (15-21).

While the Levite was enjoying the old man's hospitality, a crowd of Benjaminite men attacked the house, demanding that the old man hand over his guest for them to satisfy their sexual perversions. The old man refused, but the Levite gave them his concubine instead. They raped her throughout the night and she was found dead on the doorstep the next morning (22-26). Her husband responded to this violence by cutting the corpse into twelve pieces and sending a piece to each of Israel's twelve tribes. This was an ancient method of calling the people together to fight against a common enemy, which in this case was the wicked men of Gibeah (27-30). (For a comparable incident see 1 Samuel 1:1-11.)

Soldiers from all Israel gathered to attack Gibeah (20:1-11). Not only did the rulers of Gibeah make no attempt to punish the murderers, but the leaders of Benjamin also took their side. Benjamin decided to fight against the other eleven tribes (12-17).

At the beginning the battle went well for the Benjaminites. They knew the terrain of the country better than the Israelites, and in those hilly regions Israel's larger numbers were of no great advantage. Added to this, the Benjaminites were fighting for the lives of their people and for their homeland, whereas the Israelites shared no such personal interests. Also, the Israelites may have been over-confident with their much larger army (18-25). Only when the Israelites became desperate and turned to God in sincerity and complete dependence did God promise them victory (26-28).

In spite of the assurance of God's help, the Israelites had to plan their attack carefully and carry it out properly in order to be victorious (29-36a). The story of the battle is then repeated in greater detail to show how the Israelites operated. Their main force drew the Benjaminites out from Gibeah, after which a smaller Israelite force came out of hiding to attack the defenceless city. The soldiers of Benjamin, caught between the two Israelite forces, were massacred (36b-46). Only six hundred of the Benjaminite fighting force escaped. The Israelites meanwhile spread their attack throughout the whole tribal territory of Benjamin, burning the towns and slaughtering the people (47-48).

Soon the Israelites were sorry that they had acted in such savage haste against the Benjaminites. Almost the whole tribe had been wiped out. Now the Israelites wanted to rebuild Benjamin, but they could not see how to do it. They could not provide wives for the six hundred Benjaminite men who survived the battle, because they had earlier vowed never again to allow their daughters to marry Benjaminites (21:1-3).

The Israelites therefore looked for other ways of finding wives for the Benjaminites. To start with they made a destructive raid on the town of Jabesh-gilead and carried off the young ladies. Their excuse for this was that they were punishing Jabesh-gilead because it had not joined in the battle against Benjamin. The operation provided four hundred of the wives (4-14).

Israel's leaders then thought of how to find wives for the remaining two hundred Benjaminite men (15-17). They arranged for the men to go to a festival at Shiloh and each take a wife for himself without asking the parents' permission. Because no fight would take place, the Benjaminites could not be accused of capturing the girls; and because the parents of the girls had not actually given their daughters to the Benjaminites, they could not be accused of breaking their vow (18-22). The men did as they were told and the plan succeeded (23-24). It would have been useless for either the girls or their parents to complain about these matters, because, as the writer pointed out earlier, Israel had no central government to administer justice in inter-tribal affairs (25; cf. 17:6; 19:1).

Ruth

BACKGROUND

The story of Ruth belongs to the period of the judges, and provides a refreshing contrast with the low religious and moral condition of Israel pictured in Judges. It shows that simple trust in God and loving thought for others still existed in Israel. Here and there throughout the nation were people who tried to live their lives humbly and righteously before God. The story shows also that God was graciously caring for such people and was guiding everyday events for their good, and ultimately for the good of the nation.

OUTLINE

1:1-22   Ten years of hardship in Moab
2:1-4:22   Start of a new life in Israel

1:1-22   TEN YEARS OF HARDSHIP IN MOAB

When a severe famine struck Israel, Elimelech took his wife Naomi and their two sons across the Jordan and south to the land of Moab, in the hope of finding a living there. But Elimelech died, and within ten years his two sons, who had married Moabite wives, died also (1:1-5).

Naomi saw no future for herself in Moab, so, upon hearing that the famine in Israel had passed, she decided to return home. Her daughters-in-law loved her and decided to go with her to ease her burden (6-10).

As the daughters-in-law were thoughtful of Naomi, so she was thoughtful of them. They were both childless and would remain so if they stayed with her, as she had no other sons whom they could marry. (The custom was that if a man died childless, his brother was to have a temporary marital relation with the widow so that she might produce a son. This son would be reckoned as belonging to the dead brother, and so would carry on his name and inheritance; see Deut 25:5-10; Mark 12:19.) Naomi made it clear that they should feel no obligation to go with her. They were free to remain with their own people and begin new lives by remarrying and having families of their own (11-13).

One daughter-in-law accepted Naomi's offer and returned to her family in Moab. The other, Ruth, was determined to go on to Israel with Naomi, trusting in Naomi's God, whatever the cost (14-18). Although Naomi was welcomed home by the local townspeople, she was sad when she thought of all she had lost over the previous ten years (19-22).

2:1-4:22   START OF A NEW LIFE IN ISRAEL

Ruth works in the field of Boaz (2:1-23)

Back in Israel it soon became clear that God was in control of affairs in the lives of the two widows. According to Israelite law, when a farmer reaped his harvest he was not to send his workers through the field a second time to pick up the odd stalks of grain that the reapers dropped. These were to be left for the poor, who would follow the reapers and glean what grain they could (Lev 23:22; Deut 24:19). Ruth therefore went gleaning, to gather food for Naomi and herself. Unknown to her, the field in which she happened to glean belonged to a relative of Naomi's late husband. The man's name was Boaz (2:1-7).

Boaz had heard of Ruth's kindness to Naomi and looked for ways to reward her. He gave her food and drink, protected her from the local youths, and made sure that the reapers deliberately left extra grain for her to pick up (8-16).

Through Boaz's kindness and her own hard work, Ruth took home more grain than she had hoped for. When Naomi heard her story, she knew that God was directing events. She told Ruth that the man who had been kind to her was a close relative of Naomi's late husband (17-20). Ruth continued to glean in Boaz's field for the rest of the harvest season (21-23).

Naomi's plan (3:1-18)

By the time reaping was over, the widows had put aside enough grain to last them till the next summer. But Naomi was concerned for Ruth's future, and suggested that she marry (3:1).

One difficulty was that Naomi had no sons still living; that is, there were no brothers of Ruth's late husband whom Ruth could marry. Naomi therefore suggested Boaz, as he was apparently the closest living relative. In addition, he had shown some interest in Ruth. Naomi thought out a plan whereby Ruth could discuss the matter quietly with Boaz without the local people knowing. Accordingly, one night Ruth crept to the threshing floor where Boaz was sleeping, guarding his grain. She quietly lifted the blanket from his feet, so that as his feet grew cold he would slowly wake up. Then, while all others were asleep, she put the request to him. By asking him to 'spread his skirt over her', she was figuratively asking him to take her as his wife (2-9).

Boaz was delighted and honoured. He knew that Ruth could easily have married one of the local men much nearer her age than he. But she chose rather to be faithful to her family obligations. He therefore showed similar faithfulness by being open and honest with her. He told her there was a closer relative than he, and this man had the right to marry her. Only if this relative was not willing would Boaz take her as his wife (10-13).

Ruth remained at the threshing floor for several hours. Boaz then gave her some more grain and sent her home while it was still dark, as he did not want anyone to see her and begin to gossip (14-15). Naomi was encouraged that things were working out as she had hoped (16-18).

Boaz marries Ruth (4:1-22)

Feeling the effects of the poverty of widowhood, Naomi decided to sell her late husband's land. To prevent the land from passing out of the family, she had to ensure that it was bought (or redeemed) by the nearest relative (cf. Lev 25:23-28). In this case that person was the same one who had to produce through Ruth an heir who could carry on the names of the late Elimelech (Naomi's husband) and Mahlon (Elimelech's son and Ruth's husband). But should such an heir be born, he would also inherit the family property. That meant that the close relative who bought Naomi's land would later lose it if he produced a son through Ruth. The man was willing to buy Naomi's land if that was all he was required to do, but to marry Ruth as well would cause him financial loss (4:1-6).

By the ceremony of handing over his shoe, the man with the right to buy Naomi's property indicated that he was handing this right over to Boaz. The way was now clear for Boaz to marry Ruth. This gave Boaz the chance to keep alive the family name of Elimelech (and Mahlon), to hold on to their family property, and to marry the woman he loved (7-10). The witnesses and onlookers at the ceremony blessed Boaz and Ruth with the wish that God would make them as fruitful and prosperous as Israel's ancestors (11-12).

The child born to Boaz and Ruth meant a lot to Naomi, but what most enriched her life was the love and care of her daughter-in-law Ruth (13-15). History shows that the onlookers' good wishes for Boaz and Ruth's child were fulfilled in a greater way than they could possibly have expected. The child not merely carried on the name of Naomi's husband and son, but he became the grandfather of King David and an ancestor of Jesus the Messiah (16-22; cf. Matt 1:1,5).

1 Samuel

BACKGROUND TO 1 & 2 SAMUEL

Originally the two books of Samuel were one, and provided a continuous history of Israel from the time of the judges to the end of the reign of David. The books do not name their author, though they indicate that material in them was collected from various written records, such as those of Samuel, Nathan, Gad, David and the author(s) of the book of Jasher (1 Sam 10:25; 2 Sam 1:18; 1 Chron 27:24; 29:29).

The title 'Samuel' is taken from the man who is the leading figure in the early part of the story, and who anointed the two kings whose lives are followed through the rest of the story. The period covered by the two books is between eighty and one hundred years.

From judges to kings

The opening chapters of 1 Samuel carry on the record of Israel's history from the book of Judges. During the time of the judge Eli, Israel's political and religious life followed the pattern of the period of the judges, with the people turning away from God and falling under the power of their neighbours (1 Sam 2:12,32; 3:11-13; 4:10-11,18; cf. Judg 2:13-15). But when Samuel, probably the greatest of the judges, successfully urged the people to put away their false gods and turn again to Yahweh, God in his mercy rescued them from their enemies (1 Sam 7:3-6,13,15-17; cf. Judg 2:18; 3:9,15).

However, Samuel was not able to bring about any lasting change in the nation. His sons who succeeded him as judges were worthless, and the people demanded that the system of government be changed. Instead of government by judges, they wanted a monarchy similar to the monarchies of neighbouring nations (1 Sam 8:1-5). The outcome was the appointment of Saul as Israel's first king, but Samuel warned that this would not solve the nation's problems. Under the judges God had punished Israel for its unfaithfulness (1 Sam 12:9-11), and under the kings he would punish it just the same (1 Sam 12:13-15).

During the early days of the Israelite monarchy, the nation's leadership retained many of the features of the leadership that operated during the time of the judges. This was seen particularly in the way the leaders received the special power of God's Spirit to save Israel from its oppressors and carry out other tasks given to them (1 Sam 10:6; 11:6-11; cf. Judg 3:10; 6:34; 11:29; 14:6,19). Thus, when Saul rebelled against God and was rejected, the Spirit of God departed from him and came upon David (1 Sam 16:13-14).

But David was the last of the Spirit-gifted leaders. The people wanted, and received, a system of government where such leaders were not needed. With a firmly established monarchy, the leadership would pass automatically from father to son (1 Sam 8:19-22).

In contrast to Saul, David submitted to God and desired to carry out God's will (Ps 89:20; Acts 13:22). With David a new era began, and Israel at last found the stability it had been looking for. The remainder of 1 and 2 Samuel deals with the reign of David, whom Israelites of later ages regarded as Israel's greatest king. He established the dynasty that produced the promised Messiah (2 Sam 7:12-16; Matt 22:42; Luke 1:32-33).

OUTLINE OF 1 SAMUEL

1:1-7:17   Israel under Eli and under Samuel
8:1-12:25   Establishment of the monarchy
13:1-15:35   Saul's early victories
16:1-19:24   The rise of David
20:1-31:13   Saul's pursuit of David

1:1-7:17 ISRAEL UNDER ELI AND UNDER SAMUEL

Birth of Samuel (1:1-2:11)

Elkanah was a Levite who lived in the tribal territory of Ephraim (1:1; 1 Chron 6:33-38). Each year he took his family to the town of Shiloh to offer sacrifices to the Lord. (Since the time of Joshua, Shiloh had been the central place of worship in Israel; Josh 18:1,10; Judg 18:31.) According to the regulations for certain sacrifices, the offerer, after offering his sacrifice, received back some of the sacrificial food, which he then shared with the members of his household in a joyous fellowship meal (see Lev 7:11-16,20). For Elkanah's household the happiness of the occasion was always spoiled when one of Elkanah's wives, Peninnah, mocked the other wife, Hannah, because Hannah was unable to have children (2-8).

In deep distress, Hannah cried to God, asking him to give her a son. She promised that, if God answered her prayer, she would give her son back to God to serve him as a Nazirite for life (9-11; concerning Nazirites see notes on Num 6:1-21). The priest Eli encouraged Hannah to believe that God would answer her prayer (12-18). In due course she gave birth to a son, whom she named Samuel (19-20). When the child was two or three years old, Hannah took him to Shiloh, where she dedicated him to God for life (21-28).

Overjoyed at all that God had done for her, Hannah could now laugh at those who had mocked her (2:1). She praised God for his just action in helping the downtrodden and reversing the wrongs she had suffered. God had humbled the proud and exalted the humble (2-8). And what God had done for Hannah, he could do for others. Neither the people of Israel nor their rulers needed to fear their enemies if they trusted faithfully in the saving power of God (9-10).

Having offered her praise to God, Hannah returned home with her husband. But Samuel stayed behind at Shiloh, where he was brought up by Eli in the house of God (11). (Since the Israelites were no longer shifting the tabernacle from place to place, they had apparently carried out alterations and additions that made it a more permanent structure; see 1:9.)

Judgment on the family of Eli (2:12-3:18)

Eli the priest had become the judge, or chief administrator, in Israel. He sat at the door of the house of God where people could freely meet him to seek his advice or ask for directions in disputes (see 1:9; 4:18). His sons, it seems, carried out the routine work in connection with the sacrifices and ceremonies.

According to the Levitical law, the portion of the sacrifice that was for God had to be burnt on the altar first, after which the priest and the offerer took their portions. Eli's sons were not satisfied with this. First, they took more of the boiled meat than they should have, thus robbing the offerer of what rightly belonged to his own sacrificial meal. Second, and much worse, they took the best part of the meat before it was boiled, so that they could roast and eat it at their leisure. This showed their disrespect for God, because it meant that they took their portions

before God received his (12-17; cf. Lev 3:1-5; 7:15; 7:29-33).

While Samuel's parents experienced increasing divine blessing because of their unselfish devotion to God (18-21), Eli's sons were warned of the coming punishment because of their greed and immorality (22-25). The corruption of Eli's sons contrasted sharply with the godly development in the life of the young Samuel. God was preparing Samuel to be Eli's successor (26).

God then sent a prophet to Eli to announce a divine judgment upon the ungodly family (27-29). Eli's descendants, instead of enjoying lasting service in the priesthood, would be punished with shame, poverty and early death. Even though God might allow a descendant of Eli to continue functioning for a time as a priest, he would eventually remove the person from office. He would take the priesthood away from the family of Eli, and give it to a man more worthy of it (30-36; cf. 4:11; 14:3; 22:11-20; 1 Kings 2:26-27).

Some time later, when Samuel was probably twelve or thirteen years of age, God revealed to Samuel what previously he had made known to Eli through the prophet (3:1-14). In spite of his many weaknesses, Eli was humble enough to accept God's announced judgment as a just punishment (15-18).

Samuel – prophet, judge, priest (3:19-21)

Years passed and Samuel developed into a religious and civil leader known and respected throughout the land, from Dan in the far north to Beersheba in the far south (19-21). He was a prophet who made known God's will to the people (see 3:20-21) and a judge who ruled over the civil affairs of the people (see 7:15). In addition he was appointed by God to carry out priestly duties even though he was not a descendant of Aaron (see 7:9; 1 Chron 6:33-38).

The priesthood was by now so corrupt that it was of little spiritual help to the people. The various ceremonies and sacrifices were meaningless rituals. Consequently, God was increasingly using prophets, rather than priests, to speak to his people.

As the Spirit revealed God's message to the prophets, they passed it on to the people. Sometimes the prophets became over-excited because of the activity of the Spirit of God upon them, and their uncontrolled behaviour gave them a bad reputation (see 10:9-12; 19:20-24). In an effort to develop this religious enthusiasm for the benefit of the nation, Samuel established a school of prophets at Ramah. Others were later established in Bethel, Jericho and Gilgal (see 19:18-20; 2 Kings 2:3,5; 4:38).

Emotionalism did not feature in all prophetic preaching, nor was it essential to the prophet's ministry. The important characteristic of the prophet was that he spoke as the representative of God in announcing God's will to the people (see 22:5). The prophet's messages were therefore concerned chiefly with the people's daily affairs. Nevertheless, as the prophet urged the people to turn from their sins to God, he may also have foretold events that would follow their obedience or disobedience.

The Philistines capture the ark (4:1-22)

For many years the Philistines had oppressed Israel (Judg 13:1). Samson had begun to save Israel from them (Judg 13:5), but the Philistines now fought back and decided to extend their rule further into Israel's territory. The Israelites should have realized that their defeats were God's punishments upon them because of their sin, and turned to him in repentance. Instead they thought that they would guarantee his help by carrying the symbol of his presence (the ark of the covenant) on to the battle-field, after the manner of their heathen neighbours (4:1-4; cf. 2 Sam 5:21). God showed clearly that he had withdrawn his help from Israel by allowing the ark to be captured (5-11).

Eli must have realized that the death of his two sons in battle fulfilled God's previously announced judgment, but he seems to have been more shocked at the capture of the ark. He died that day (12-18). So too did Eli's daughter-in-law, who was also shocked at the capture of the ark. God had surely departed from Israel (19-22).

This was probably the time when Shiloh, the religious centre of the nation, was destroyed (Ps 78:60-61; Jer 7:12,14; 26:6). But the priests managed to escape to Nob, taking with them whatever they could of the house of God (see 21:1-6; 22:18-19; 1 Kings 8:4).

The ark returns (5:1-7:1)

Although God used the Philistines to judge Israel, he would not allow them to dishonour him. He showed that the capture of the ark did not mean that he was inferior to the Philistine god Dagon (5:1-5). Wherever the ark went it brought trouble to the Philistine people. A plague of mice seems to have spread a painful and deadly disease throughout the country, bringing widespread suffering and death (6-12; cf. 6:5).

The Philistines felt fairly certain that the ark was the cause of their troubles. So they decided to send it back to Israel, along with gifts to Israel's God to pay for their sin in capturing his ark (6:1-6). To test whether their theory was correct, they planned to put the ark on a new cart to be drawn by two milking cows that had never pulled a cart and had only recently calved. The cows were to be left alone to see if Israel's God directed them to take his ark back to Israel. Normally the cows would want to break loose and return to their calves (7-9).

God restored his honour by bringing his ark back without the Israelites' doing anything at all (10-12). The Israelites accepted the Philistines' gifts and offered sacrifices to God, but God killed those Israelites who looked into the ark. He wanted to impress upon the people that the ark was sacred. They were not to treat it as an object of curiosity or superstition (13-19; cf. Num 4:20). The people then took the ark and placed it in a private house in the nearby town of Kiriath-jearim (20-7:1).

Samuel's leadership (7:2-17)

During the years of Philistine oppression, Samuel's position as chief ruler in Israel became firmly established. As a religious leader he commanded the people to turn from idols and worship the Lord only, and the people responded (2-6a). As a civil leader he settled disputes among them (6b). In response to the people's repentance and Samuel's prayers for them, God gave Israel a great victory over the Philistines (7-11). The Israelites continued to fight against the Philistines till they had driven them from Israel's territory completely. From this time on, as long as Samuel remained in control of Israel, the Philistines were of no great trouble to Israel (12-14).

With the destruction of Israel's tabernacle at Shiloh, the nation's religious life centred on Samuel, who set up an altar for sacrifice in his home town of Ramah. The civil administration also centred on Samuel, as he moved in an annual circuit around four major towns where he held district courts to settle disputes (15-17).

8:1-12:25 ESTABLISHMENT OF THE MONARCHY

The people ask for a king (8:1-22)

Israel's history continued to follow the pattern set out in the book of Judges. Once the God-appointed judge (in this case, Samuel) was no longer able to exercise control over the nation (for Samuel was old and his sons who succeeded him as judges were worthless), the people turned from God and drifted into wrongdoing (8:1-3).

In search for stability within the nation, the people asked Samuel to bring the old system to an end and to give them a king as other nations had.

This was more than merely a rejection of the system of rule by judges; it was a rejection of God. The people's troubles came from their sins, not from the system of government. The remedy, therefore, was to turn to God in a new attitude of faith, love and practical holiness. Instead they turned to a new political system (4-9).

As well as rejecting God, the people of Israel were inviting social and economic hardship. Samuel reminded them of the examples they could see in the

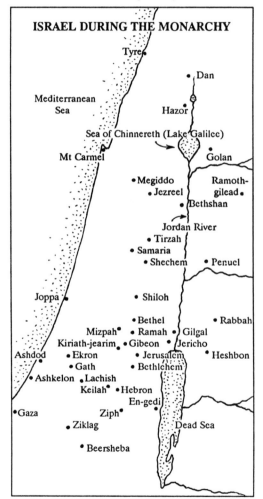

ISRAEL DURING THE MONARCHY

nations round about, where kings oppressed their people with harsh rule, forced labour and heavy taxes (10-18). But the Israelites were unmoved; they wanted a king. In particular, they wanted one who would be an impressive military leader (19-22).

Samuel's prediction about Saul (9:1-10:16)

Saul, who became Israel's first king, originally had no desire for political power and little interest in the spiritual ministry of Samuel. As the son of a wealthy landowner, he was more concerned about the loss of his father's donkeys, and the worry he might cause his father by being away so long in search of them (9:1-5). This concern led him to seek help from Samuel. He thought that Samuel, with his ability to see visions and make predictions, could tell him where the donkeys were (6-14).

God revealed to Samuel that he had chosen Saul to be Israel's king. Saul would save Israel from the Philistines, who had recently renewed their attacks (15-17). Samuel prepared Saul to receive this startling news by treating him with special honour at a sacrificial feast that was being held at that time (18-24).

The next day Samuel told Saul privately that God had chosen him to be king, after which Samuel anointed him in a brief, private ceremony (25-10:1). Samuel then predicted three things that would soon happen as proof to Saul that Samuel's predictions always came true. Most important of these three events would be the coming of God's special power upon Saul to change him from an ordinary Israelite farmer into a national leader. Saul would receive additional guidance by going to the shrine at Gilgal, where Samuel would pass on God's directions to him (2-8).

When the Spirit of God first came upon Saul, he certainly behaved differently, but those who knew him were not impressed. They were surprised that a well respected young man like Saul should associate with religious extremists and behave in such an undignified manner (9-13). But Saul did not reveal what Samuel had told him about the kingship (14-16).

Saul made king (10:17-27)

Some time later, Samuel called a meeting of the leaders of all the tribes and families in Israel to select a king (17-19). The selection was made by a system of drawing lots that finally led to one man being chosen. Two people, a confident Samuel and a nervous Saul, knew through God's previous private revelation who would be chosen (20-24).

After the selection had been made, Samuel announced publicly the rights and duties of a king (25; cf. Deut 17:14-20). Many of the people were delighted when they saw the appearance of the man who had been chosen king, but some doubted and mocked. Saul therefore made no immediate changes in the nation's administration, but returned to his farm at Gibeah (26-27). (Gibeah became the administrative centre of Israel during Saul's reign; see 11:4; 14:2; 15:34; 22:6; 26:1.)

Saul's victory over the Ammonites (11:1-15)

Within a short time Saul had the opportunity to prove to the doubters that he was the man to lead Israel. About a century earlier the Ammonites had exercised control over Israel's territory of Gilead, east of Jordan, till Jephthah overthrew them (Judg 10:7-8; 11:29-33). Now they attacked again and seemed certain of victory (11:1-3). When he heard the news, Saul called Israel's fighting men together (using a well recognized local procedure; cf. Judg 19:29) and assured the Gileadites of victory (4-9). The Israelites tricked the Ammonites into thinking they were about to surrender, but the next day Saul launched a surprise attack that smashed the Ammonite army (10-11).

Saul had led Israel to victory in his first battle, and immediately became a national hero. Samuel then arranged for a public ceremony at Gilgal, where Saul was declared king over a now unified people (12-15).

Samuel's farewell address (12:1-25)

The people's demand for a king was an insult to Samuel as well as to God. Samuel therefore called upon them to declare before God and before the king that he had been blameless in all his behaviour. He had given them no cause to be dissatisfied with his leadership (12:1-5).

In the lengthy address that followed, Samuel reminded his hearers of all that God had done in giving Israel the land of Canaan for a homeland (6-8). He reminded them also that Israel's troubles in Canaan had come from the sins of the people, not from the type of leadership. They now had the leadership they wanted, a king, but even he would not be able to save them from judgment if they sinned against God. As under the rule of the judges, so under the rule of a king, God would give his people into the hand of their enemies when they rebelled against him, and save them from their enemies when they obeyed him (9-15).

Samuel gave the people clear proof that he spoke for God in condemning them for asking for a king. In response to his word, God sent a sudden storm, even though rain did not normally fall at that time of the year (16-18). The people were terrified and realized their sin in asking for a king. But now that they had their king, there could be no turning back. Samuel could not change matters,

but he promised to keep praying for them and to keep teaching them God's way. Though no longer their political leader, he was still their priest and prophet (19-25).

13:1-15:35 SAUL'S EARLY VICTORIES

Preparing to fight the Philistines (13:1-14)

Israel's regular army consisted of two divisions, one under the command of Saul, the other under the command of Saul's son Jonathan. Other fighting men were called to join the army when needed. Such a need arose when Jonathan attacked a Philistine camp, and the Philistines replied by sending a large army to attack Israel (13:1-6a).

In a time of national emergency, Saul was apparently to go to Gilgal, where he was to wait seven days for Samuel to arrive. By that time, Israel's leaders would have gathered the army together. Samuel could then offer sacrifices to God on behalf of the nation, and pass on God's instructions to Saul (see 10:8). The current Philistine attack tested Saul's obedience. But rather than wait for Samuel, he offered the sacrifice himself. Probably his action resulted partly from impatience and partly from the desire to have complete power, religious as well as political (6b-9). Samuel saw that Saul's action was really a rebellion against the authority of God. As punishment God would one day take the kingship from him and from his family (10-14).

War against the Philistines (13:15-14:46)

After Samuel left Gilgal, Saul took his troops and joined with the other section of the Israelite army, which was under Jonathan. Together they prepared for the battle against the Philistines (15-18). The Philistines were confident of victory, partly because for many years they had so controlled metal-working activities in the area that the Israelites owned hardly any weapons. This enabled the Philistines to raid throughout Israel without fear of strong resistance (19-22). In addition they controlled the mountain pass by which the Israelites hoped to attack them (23).

Jonathan, however, without telling his father, worked out a daring plot to attack the Philistines. To begin with he took his armour-bearer, climbed up the rocky slope on the other side of the pass, and approached the Philistine camp (14:1-7). The two men tricked the Philistines by pretending they were deserting from the Israelite army. The Philistines relaxed their defences and welcomed the supposed deserters. Jonathan and his servant then attacked the unsuspecting enemy and killed twenty men

(8-14). Panic quickly spread through the Philistine camp (15).

On hearing of the Philistines' confusion, Saul hurriedly assembled a fighting force and went out to do battle. He was so eager to seize the opportunity to attack the enemy that he did not wait to receive God's directions through the priest (16-20; see v. 3). Israelites who had earlier deserted to the Philistines or hidden themselves in fear suddenly returned to Saul's side and joined in the battle (21-23).

Saul put a curse on any soldier who stopped to eat that day, as he wanted to carry the battle on unbroken till the Philistines were destroyed. It was a stupid curse, for tiredness and hunger prevented the Israelites from being fully successful (24-30).

As soon as night fell, the soldiers ate freely. By eating food that was forbidden by God's law, they showed that, although they feared to break the king's command, they did not fear to break God's. Saul was distressed when he heard what the people had done (31-35; cf. Lev 17:14). He was even more distressed when he learnt that God would not guarantee him victory in a proposed night attack on the Philistines. Assuming that one of his soldiers was responsible for this hindrance to God's help, he added to his previous rash curse an equally rash vow to punish the offender (36-39).

When it was revealed that Jonathan was the offender, Saul gave a further demonstration of his unpredictable nature. He did not carry out his vow, but heeded the voice of those who demanded Jonathan's release (40-46).

Summary of Saul's reign (14:47-52)

Despite his many weaknesses of character, Saul was a strong leader in battle and led Israel to many victories (47-48). He helped develop this strong leadership by collecting around him the best and most capable men from his own family circle and from the army (49-52).

War against the Amalekites (15:1-35)

The Amalekites came under the same curse as those Canaanite nations that were to be destroyed (15:1-3; cf. Exod 17:8-16; Deut 20:16-18; 25:17-19). Again Saul's obedience was tested, and again he failed. His kingly power gave him no right to alter God-given instructions to suit himself (4-9).

God sent Samuel to tell Saul of the consequences of his disobedience (10-16; cf. 13:13-14). Religious sacrifices and military victories were no substitute for obedience. Samuel had given Saul God's instructions, but Saul, by acting independently of those instructions, had rebelled against God. He had proved himself unfit to be king of God's people (17-23). No appeal from Saul could alter the fact that God was going to replace him as king of Israel (24-29). The most that Samuel could do for him was to accompany him in a final act of public worship (30-33). Although not removed immediately from the kingship, Saul lost for ever the services of Samuel (34-35).

16:1-19:24 THE RISE OF DAVID

David brought to the royal court (16:1-23)

When told by God to go and anoint a king to replace Saul, Samuel feared to, lest Saul kill him. God therefore told Samuel to keep the matter secret (16:1-3). Reassured by this additional word from God, Samuel went to Bethlehem, where he met the leading men of the important families in that area (4-5).

The outcome of Samuel's visit was that he anointed David, youngest son of the family of Jesse. Anointing was a way of marking out people for other important positions besides kingship, and Samuel gave no indication to the onlookers why he had anointed David. For David's sake, as well as for Samuel's, Saul was not to know that Samuel had already anointed David as Saul's successor. Many years would pass before David actually became king (6-13).

Now that the special power of God's Spirit came upon David (see v. 13), it departed from Saul. Troubled by his own jealousy and sense of insecurity, Saul became emotionally and mentally unstable. Meanwhile David matured. He became skilled in speech, writing and music, and learnt to be a brave fighter through having to defend his flocks from wild animals and Philistine raiders (14-18; cf. 17:34-36). The next step in his preparation for kingship was his introduction to Saul as one who could play music to relax the king's troubled nerves. The outcome of this was that eventually he became a permanent member of the royal court (19-23).

Goliath's challenge and defeat (17:1-58)

The Philistines again assembled their troops to fight against Israel (17:1-3). As often happened in ancient warfare, the invaders challenged the defenders by calling for a contest between the champions of the two sides (4-11). At this time David was back on his father's farm at Bethlehem, for he did not need to remain at Saul's court when Saul was away directing affairs on the battlefield (12-16).

When circumstances later brought David to the scene of the battle, he discovered that the Philistines had a champion, Goliath, whom no Israelite dared to fight (17-25). David was not even a soldier, but he volunteered to fight the Philistine (26-32). He reasoned that since Goliath had defied God he was certain of defeat, and since Israel was God's army it was certain of victory (33-40; cf. v. 26, 45). David killed Goliath without using a sword or a spear, proving that God did not need weapons to save his people (41-50). The Philistines fled in confusion, but the Israelites caught and killed many of them, then plundered the camp they left behind (51-54).

Saul did not immediately recognize David as the young man who had previously played music to calm him during his half-mad fits. It was probably after David's victory over Goliath that Saul took him into his court permanently, making him his armour-bearer and full-time court musician (55-58; see 16:21-22; 18:2).

David's success and Saul's jealousy (18:1-30)

Once David came to live at Saul's court, he and Jonathan became close friends. In fact, Jonathan promised loyalty to David as if bound to him by covenant. David continued to produce outstanding successes as a soldier, and Saul made him an officer. The promotion was popular with army officers and common people alike (18:1-5). David's popularity, however, stirred up Saul's jealousy, and Saul tried to kill him (6-11). Saul was now afraid of David, so removed him from the court by giving him a military command that kept him on the battlefield. But this only resulted in more success and more fame for David (12-16).

Determined to force David into wrongdoing, Saul offered to give his eldest daughter to David for a wife, and then deceived David by giving her to someone else. But David remained guiltless (17-19; cf. 17:25).

When Saul learnt that another of his daughters, Michal, was in love with David, he saw another opportunity to try to trap him (20-22). He asked David to kill one hundred Philistines as the bride price, thinking that David would surely be killed in the attempt. David was pleased at this sort of bride price, for he was too poor to pay money. He was successful against the Philistines, and Saul hated him even more. Through his marriage to Michal, David became part of the royal family (23-30).

By this time David had probably written some of the psalms that are now part of the biblical book of Psalms (cf. 2 Sam 23:1). The introductions and titles to these psalms indicate that a number of them were written during the time of his flight from Saul.

These, along with other psalms he wrote over a long and eventful career, give David's personal views of events that the writer of 1 and 2 Samuel describes in narrative form.

Jonathan, Michal and Samuel (19:1-24)

For a while Jonathan was successful in persuading his father to stop trying to kill David (19:1-7). However, David's further military successes made Saul jealous again. He made two more attempts on David's life, first at the palace, then at David's house. This time another of Saul's family, Michal, helped David escape (8-17; cf. Ps 59).

David found safety with Samuel at Ramah. Three times Saul sent men to arrest David, but each time they were overcome by the power of God's Spirit that worked through Samuel and his followers (18-21). In the end Saul himself went, but he too was overcome by God's Spirit. People were surprised to find Saul prophesying, but it showed how powerless he was to resist the power of God. And that same all-powerful God protected David (22-24).

20:1-31:13 SAUL'S PURSUIT OF DAVID

Jonathan helps David escape (20:1-42)

Apparently Jonathan did not know of the number of attempts that his father had made to kill David (20:1-2). When he saw that David was genuinely fearful, he agreed to co-operate with David in finding out Saul's real intentions once and for all (3-9).

Jonathan's love for David was genuine. Even though he knew that David, and not he, would be the next king, he showed no sign of jealousy. He asked only that David, on becoming king, remain loyal to him and show kindness to his descendants (10-15). The two swore loyalty to each other and so renewed their covenant (16-17).

David and Jonathan worked out a plan to let David know whether he should remain in Saul's service or flee for safety. Their sole purpose was to save David's life. They made no plot against the king, and by keeping their whole plan a tight secret, they ensured that no rumours would arise (18-23).

Even when Saul tried to make Jonathan see that David was a threat to his own future, Jonathan maintained his unselfish loyalty to David (24-31). Saul then accused Jonathan of disloyalty to his family and tried to kill him (32-34). Jonathan now had no doubts about his father's intentions. With much sadness he and David farewelled each other and David departed (35-42).

Flight from Saul (21:1-15)

The first place to which David fled was Nob, which, since the destruction of Shiloh, had become the city of priests (21:1). About this time a few personal servants joined him, according to an arrangement he had made with them earlier. David obtained food for himself and his men by deceiving Ahimelech the priest concerning the purpose of his journey. Unfortunately for him, and for Ahimelech and the other priests, he was seen by someone sympathetic to Saul (2-9).

From Nob David went to the Philistine city of Gath. He expected that the Philistines would welcome him as a deserter from the Israelite army and so give him refuge (10). But the Philistines had not yet heard of David's break with Saul. They knew only that David had killed thousands of their own Philistine people. Thinking he may have been spying in preparation for more attacks, they decided to kill him. David acted quickly, and escaped by pretending he had gone mad (11-15; see Ps 34; 56).

A fighting unit (22:1-23)

David found a hiding place in the barren regions of Adullam. Here he was joined by his family, who had fled to escape the hate and revenge of Saul (22:1; see Ps 57; 63; 142). Knowing this hard life would be too much for his aged parents, he left them in the care of the king of Moab, and returned to his home territory of Judah. By now a crowd of four hundred, mainly outlaws and discontented people, had joined David, and he soon built these into a strong fighting unit (2-5; 1 Chron 11:10,15).

Among those who joined David were many experienced soldiers who had escaped from the eastern tribes, along with a number from Benjamin and Judah. David was careful at all times to make sure that he was not welcoming spies or others whom Saul might use to destroy him (1 Chron 12:8-18). Soon the force numbered six hundred (see 23:13). Throughout the time of Saul's pursuit, David and his men remained within the tribal area of David's tribe, Judah. However, they were gradually driven either farther south into the hotter and drier regions, or farther west into the regions controlled by the Philistines.

Meanwhile Saul was accusing his soldiers and officials of being disloyal to him and of supporting David. Saul reminded them that they could expect favours and gifts from him because they were from his tribe, Benjamin. They would get nothing from David, because he would obviously favour people from his own tribe, Judah (6-8).

When Saul discovered that Ahimelech had helped David, Ahimelech pointed out that he did so because of his loyalty to Saul. He understood that David was carrying out Saul's business (9-15). Saul by now was furious beyond reason, and commanded that not only Ahimelech but all the priests of Nob be killed. Only Abiathar escaped, and he immediately went and joined David (16-23; see Ps 52).

Saul's fierce hunt (23:1-24:22)

Since Abiathar had brought with him the high priest's ephod (containing the Urim and Thummim), David was able to ask and receive God's direct guidance. God's first direction was to rescue the Israelite town of Keilah from the raiding Philistines (23:1-6). As soon as he had defeated the Philistines, David withdrew from Keilah. He knew that Saul's army was larger and better equipped than his. He knew also that he could not trust the people of Keilah to stand with him against Saul. David still recognized Saul as the legal king and did not want to fight against him. Nor did he encourage the Israelite people to fight against their king (7-13).

David hid in the hill country near Ziph, and Jonathan came to visit him. Jonathan also remained loyal to Saul as the legal king, but he reassured David that nothing had changed the relationship between the two of them (14-18).

Saul was delighted, and David distressed, when some people from Ziph told Saul where David was hiding (19-24; see Ps 54). David was saved from certain capture when Saul left hurriedly to deal with another attack by the raiding Philistines (25-29).

Having dealt with the Philistines, Saul resumed his pursuit of David (24:1-2). Saul had in his court a group of zealous followers, probably Benjaminites, who accused David of plotting against the king and urged Saul on to destroy him (see 18:22-26; 22:7; 24:9; 26:19; Ps 7). By sparing Saul when he could easily have killed him, David proved that he had no evil intentions against Saul (3-13). God knew that David had not plotted against Saul (14-15), and even Saul himself recognized that David's uprightness was the mark of a true king. He asked David to promise that when he became king he would not wipe out Saul's family. Saul, however, gave no promise to spare David. Therefore, when Saul returned home, David thought it safer to return to his hiding place (16-22).

David marries Abigail (25:1-44)

At this point we are told that Samuel died (25:1). David, at the time, was having trouble supporting his six hundred men. It seems that his men provided protection for farmers against the raiding Philistines (see v. 16, 21), and then demanded that the farmers pay them by giving them food supplies (see v. 8, 18, 27, 35). One wealthy farmer, Nabal, refused to pay and insulted David. Furious at Nabal's response, David set out with four hundred of his men to deal with him (2-13).

Only the quick thinking and wise advice of Nabal's wife, Abigail, stopped David from killing Nabal and his entire household. She sent David the required food supplies (14-22) and reminded him to keep trusting in God to defend him and destroy his enemies. Certainly, he was not to do anything he would later regret (23-31).

David was thankful for Abigail's provisions and for her advice. Events soon proved her words to be true. God removed David's enemy when Nabal suffered a stroke and died (32-38). David then married Abigail, and in so doing became part-owner of a large and prosperous farming area in Judah (39-42). He lost Michal, however, when Saul took her and gave her to someone else (43-44).

The move to Philistia (26:1-27:12)

Although he had every intention of killing Nabal, David still refused to harm Saul; but Saul remained determined to harm David (26:1-5). When another opportunity arose to kill Saul, David refused to act. He was content to leave the matter with God, who would remove Saul when he saw fit (6-12).

Once again David produced proof that he had no evil intentions towards Saul (13-17). But clearly David was becoming tired of this continual flight from the mad king. Not only was it wearying, but it was driving him from God through cutting him off from the public worship places of his people (18-20). Saul confessed his wrongdoing and promised not to harm David, but David still thought it wise to remain in the south and keep away from Saul (21-25).

Worse was to follow when David left his own territory for the safety of enemy Philistia. This time Achish, the Philistine ruler, welcomed him, because he now knew that David was Saul's enemy and not one of his army commanders. (For David's previous meeting with Achish see 21:10-15.) Also, David's army, strengthened by the addition of a number of Benjaminites skilled in long-range warfare (1 Chron 12:1-7), would be useful to the Philistines. Wisely, David obtained a separate town, Ziklag, for his people. This enabled him to avoid trouble with the Philistines and to hold his followers together. He stayed there sixteen months (27:1-7).

This was not a time of great spiritual profit for David. His previous experiences, when he was hunted by Saul in the Judean wilderness, spiritually enriched him and produced many of his psalms. By contrast, his time in Philistia was often characterized by shameful behaviour and, so far as we know, produced no psalms.

David pleased Achish and enriched his people by carrying out successful raids that Achish thought were against the Israelites or peoples friendly to the Israelites. But David lied to Achish, for the raids were against other peoples, usually those hostile to the Israelites. To his shame David directed his men to slaughter all the inhabitants of the towns he raided. In this way he made sure that no one was left to tell Achish the true story about which people David had plundered (8-12).

Another Philistine-Israelite war (28:1-29:11)

When the Philistines set out to attack Israel, Achish made David and his troops his personal bodyguard (28:1-2). Back in Israel, Saul was terrified. He asked God what he should do, but God refused to show him (3-6). So he went to a woman who consulted the spirits of the dead, hoping that through her he could get directions from Samuel (7-14).

Samuel spoke to Saul from the world of the dead, but he gave him neither comfort nor help. He merely confirmed what he had told Saul earlier concerning God's rejection of him. He made it clear that David was the man God had chosen to succeed him, and added that Saul and his sons would die in the coming battle (15-19). Saul was now more terrified than ever, but the woman gave him some food to help strengthen him for the fight ahead (20-25).

The Philistine leaders also had their problems. The four rulers who shared the military command with Achish were suspicious when they saw David with six hundred Israelites among their own forces. They well knew of David's previous victories over the Philistines, and suspected that David and his men might turn against the Philistines during the battle (29:1-5). They therefore sent David and his men back to Ziklag. David was disappointed at this, for he had possibly planned to do what the Philistine leaders suspected he would do. At the same time the Philistine leaders may have saved David from an act of folly, because if he had fought in war against his own people, they would hardly want to accept him as their king (6-11).

David's victory and Saul's defeat (30:1-31:13)

When David's men returned to Ziklag, they found it a deserted, burnt out ruin. The Amalekites had raided the cities of Philistia and Judah while all the fighting men were away at war. The shock of losing everything — wives, families and possessions — drove David to total dependence on God. It was the kind of dependence that seems to have been lacking during his sixteen months in Philistia (30:1-8).

Assisted by some capable Israelite military commanders who had deserted to him on his recent battle march (1 Chron 12:19-22), David set out after the Amalekites. He was helped also by a slave of the Amalekites who had been left to die by the roadside but who was able, after being revived, to direct David to the Amalekite camp (9-15). David's men slaughtered the Amalekites, recovered the Israelite people and goods, then plundered the possessions of the enemy (16-20).

In sharing out the plunder among his men, David guaranteed equal rewards for those who carried out the raid and those who stayed at the base camp to guard the supplies (21-25). He also shared some of the plunder among various Judean cities and local tribes, thereby giving these people good cause to support him in the future (26-31).

Meanwhile, farther north, the battle between Israel and the Philistines was raging. Overcome by the attackers, the Israelites fled. Saul's sons were killed and Saul himself was wounded. Knowing the cruel and shameful treatment that he would receive if the enemy captured him, Saul took his own life (31:1-7). The enemy therefore dishonoured his dead body instead. But the men of Jabesh-gilead, remembering that Saul had once saved them from shameful treatment by their enemies, rescued his body and gave him an honourable burial (8-13; cf. 11:1-11; 1 Chron 10:13-14).

116

2 Samuel

OUTLINE OF 2 SAMUEL

1:1-4:12 CIVIL WAR AFTER SAUL'S DEATH

Mourning for Saul and Jonathan (1:1-27)

David learnt of Saul's death from one of Saul's own men, an Amalekite who had become a citizen of Israel (1:1-4; see v. 13). The man clearly thought that by adding a few details to the story and by bringing Saul's crown to David, he could win David's favour (5-10; cf. 4:10).

As long as Saul lived, David had regarded him as the Lord's anointed king and had consistently refused to harm him (cf. 1 Sam 24:6; 26:11). He therefore reacted with anger when the Amalekite claimed to have killed Saul, and ordered his swift execution (11-16).

In spite of all Saul's hostility to him, David was generous to Saul in the song he composed in memory of him and his son Jonathan. David knew how the enemy Philistines would rejoice when they heard of Saul's death, and he wished that the news could be kept from them (17-20). He cursed the place where Saul died (21), praised the bravery of Saul and Jonathan (22-23), and recalled the prosperity that Saul brought to the people (24). Most of all, he sorrowed over the loss of his true and faithful friend Jonathan (25-27).

Two kings in Israel (2:1-3:1)

The Philistines now controlled much of Israel's territory west of Jordan (see 1 Sam 31:7). Believing that David was still friendly to them, the Philistines allowed him to become king over Judah in the south, no doubt thinking that this would help to divide and weaken Israel further. The tribes east of Jordan, however, were still free, and David quickly tried to win their support (2:1-7). But Abner (Saul's army commander and his cousin; see 1 Sam 14:50) had beaten David to it. Having escaped across Jordan, he appointed Saul's son Ishbosheth as king over all Israel (apart from Judah), though he himself was the one who had the real power (8-11).

David's army commander was his nephew Joab (1 Chron 2:13-16). Both Abner and Joab were eager to control the strategic town of Gibeon, and when the two happened to meet near the town they agreed to an armed contest between selected young men from each side (12-14). The limited contest grew into a furious battle, which Joab's army won (15-17). Joab and Abner had long been rivals (see 1 Sam 26:5-6), but for Joab the rivalry became hatred when Abner killed Joab's brother (18-25). Abner's army fared badly, and only his personal appeal to Joab brought a break in hostilities (26-32).

Over the next two years the supporters of Ishbosheth and the supporters of David were in constant conflict. Victory consistently went to those on David's side (3:1).

End of the line of Saul (3:2-4:12)

On becoming king of Judah, David followed the pattern of neighbouring kings by taking a number of wives (2-5). (For the more important people of David's family and relatives see the appendix at the end of the commentary on 2 Samuel.) Meanwhile Abner became so powerful among Ishbosheth's supporters, that Ishbosheth accused him of trying to gain the throne for himself. (According to an eastern custom, one way a person signified his claim to the throne was by claiming the king's harem; see 12:8; 16:22.) Angry and frustrated, Abner saw that Israel could not be rebuilt on the weak foundation of Ishbosheth. He therefore decided to join forces with David, and in that way help strengthen and unify Israel (6-11).

David accepted Abner's offer of support on the condition that Michal, David's first wife and Saul's daughter, be returned to him. Having Saul's daughter as wife would further strengthen David's claim to Saul's throne (12-16; cf. 1 Sam 18:20-27; 25:44). Most of Israel's leaders readily joined with Abner in transferring their allegiance to David. Only Saul's tribe, Benjamin, needed a little extra persuasion (17-21).

Joab, however, was not pleased to see Abner join David's army, for it meant he now had a rival for the post of commander-in-chief. Treacherously he killed Abner, giving the excuse that he was taking revenge on behalf of his dead brother. But David clearly considered it to be murder (22-30; cf. Num 35:19-28). David publicly showed his disapproval of Joab's deed, and regretted that one of the nation's finest leaders should die in such a manner. But David took no action against Joab (31-39; cf. 1 Kings 2:5-6,32).

With the death of Abner, Ishbosheth's kingdom collapsed, Ishbosheth himself being murdered. The royal rule of Saul's family had come to an end, as forecast by Samuel (see 1 Sam 13:13-14). All that remained of the line of succession through Jonathan was one badly crippled child (4:1-8). David, as in the previous case of murder, showed his disapproval (for Ishbosheth had done him no harm), but this time he ordered the murderers to be executed. As always, he wanted to make it clear that he would not gain Saul's throne through murder (9-12).

5:1-10:19 DAVID ESTABLISHES HIS KINGDOM

Conquest of Jerusalem (5:1-25)

All the tribes of Israel now sent a representative force of soldiers to Hebron to present themselves to David, their new king (5:1-3; 1 Chron 12:23-40). The two-year civil war had now finished, and for the next five and a half years David reigned in Hebron over a unified Israel (4-5; cf. 2:10-11).

David probably realized that so long as he remained in the territory of his own tribe in the south, the northern tribes would hesitate to give him their full and enthusiastic allegiance. He therefore set out on the bold task of making Jerusalem his capital. The conquest of Jerusalem was sure to win him nationwide support, for it had been lost to the Jebusites soon after Joshua's conquest and had remained in Jebusite hands ever since (Judg 1:8,21; 19:10-12). Also, since it belonged to no tribe and was situated centrally between the northern and southern sections of Palestine, there could be no cause for any tribal jealousy if David made his capital there.

The Jebusites thought the city's position and defences so strong that no attack against them could succeed. They mocked the Israelites by saying that even the blind and crippled along the city walls could defend the city against them. But Joab gained entrance through a water tunnel and conquered the city in a surprise attack. As a reward for his victory, he was now appointed army commander of all Israel, not just Judah (6-10; 1 Chron 11:6). David firmly established himself in his new capital by building a palace and enlarging his harem (11-16).

A new unity was appearing in Israel, and the Philistines saw this as a danger to their power. They attacked David in the area south of Jerusalem in an effort to split the country into two parts again. David lost no time in responding. He launched a surprise attack (probably from his established stronghold in Adullum; cf. 1 Chron 11:15-19), drove the enemy back, and captured and burnt their idols (17-21; 1 Chron 14:12). Later, when the Philistines launched a second attack, David drove them from Israel's territory and carried the conquest across the border into the Philistines' territory. This was a decisive victory for the Israelites, and never again did the Philistines gain power over them (22-25).

The ark brought to Jerusalem (6:1-23)

Part of the reason for Israel's weakness during Saul's reign was the king's lack of interest in the nation's religious life. David was determined to correct this state of affairs. He began by restoring the ark, symbol of God's presence, to its rightful position as the centre of Israel's religious life. (During Saul's reign the ark had remained in a country house in Kiriath-jearim, also known as Baal-judah or Baalah; 1 Sam 7:1-2; 1 Chron 13:5-6.) In bringing the ark to Jerusalem, David was aiming to make Jerusalem the religious centre of Israel as well as the royal city and administrative capital (6:1-5).

David's plans suffered an early setback when a person who touched the ark was killed. Apparently thinking that God was angry with him for moving the ark, David feared to take it any further. He left it in the nearby house of a man named Obed-edom (6-11).

God's blessing on the house of Obed-edom during the next three months made David realize that God's anger was not because of the removal of the ark. Rather it was because of the lack of respect for God that had characterized the operation. For example, the Israelites had copied the Philistines (who knew no better) by transporting the ark on a cart, instead of carrying it on the shoulders of the Levites (see v. 3; cf. Num 4:15; 7:9; 1 Sam 6:7). Therefore, when David decided to move the ark again, he was careful to do things properly (1 Chron 15:2,13-15). He was so relieved when no one was struck dead, that he stopped the procession after it had gone only six paces and offered sacrifices of thanksgiving (12-15).

At this time the tabernacle was in Gibeon (1 Chron 16:39). David made no attempt to shift it to Jerusalem, possibly because it was too old to move without causing major damage, or possibly because David was thinking of building a new and more lasting structure. When he brought the ark to Jerusalem, he placed it, to begin with, in a special tent that he had prepared for it. He and the people celebrated the great event with a sacred ritual of music, dancing, sacrifice and feasting (16-19; see 1 Chron 15:16-28). The psalm sung on this occasion praised God for giving the people of Israel their homeland, and contrasted the power of this glorious God with the weakness of heathen idols (1 Chron 16:8-36).

Michal did not share David's enthusiasm, and rebuked him for his unashamed display of joy during the procession. She thought his behaviour unfitting for a king (20-23). But David was determined to lift the spiritual life of the people. He appointed suitable men to be with the ark and guide the worship at Jerusalem, apparently under the direction of the senior priest, Abiathar. The other chief priest, Zadok, was in charge of the tabernacle at Gibeon (1 Chron 16:4-6,37-42).

God's promise and David's prayer (7:1-29)

When David expressed his desire to build God a permanent symbolic dwelling place, God reminded him through the prophet Nathan that Israel's God, Yahweh, was not limited to one land or one place. For that reason his symbolic dwelling place had been a tent, something that was movable and could be set up in any place at all (7:1-7).

Nevertheless, because the people of Israel were not spiritually in a condition where the ideal for them could work, God would allow them to build the temple (just as he had allowed them to set up the monarchy). But the building of the temple was not of immediate importance. God was more concerned that *David's* house be firmly established — referring not to his palace but to his dynasty (8-11). David would have a line of royal descendants who would rule for generation after generation in Israel. One of these would build God's temple. Even if some kings proved unworthy of his blessings, God would not alter his purposes. He had chosen the dynasty of David as the means of bringing the Messiah, the Saviour of the world (12-17; cf. Ps 2:7-9; 89:19-37; Matt 22:42; Acts 13:22-23).

God's establishment of David as king of Israel was amazing enough, but even that seemed a small thing compared with the permanent dynasty God now promised him. Deeply humbled, David hardly knew what to say. He could only praise God for all he had done, both for David personally and for the people of Israel as a whole (18-24). David prayed that God would fulfil his promise and that his people would never cease to praise him (25-29).

David's military victories (8:1-18)

To emphasize that God was strengthening the royal house of David according to his promise, the writer gives a summary of David's military victories. David conquered the Philistines and the Moabites (8:1-2; 1 Chron 18:1-2), then expanded north across the Syrian (Aramean) state of Zobah and even took control of the central Syrian province based on Damascus (3-8).

Another Syrian state, Hamath, submitted to David without a fight. Israel rapidly grew prosperous with the wealth it received from these and other conquered states (9-12). David's army, under the control of Joab, gained a notable victory over Edom, though the victory was not easily won. Abishai was the hero of the battle (13-14; 1 Chron 18:12; Ps 60).

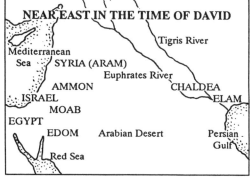

NEAR EAST IN THE TIME OF DAVID

David's rule now extended over most of the country between Egypt and the Euphrates. As his kingdom expanded, he developed and organized his administration. He also formed a personal body-guard of Cherethites and Pelethites, people who lived among the Philistines and who had joined David's fighting force during the years David lived in that area. They were tough, loyal soldiers (15-18; cf. 15:18; 20:7; 1 Kings 1:38).

Remembering former kindnesses (9:1-10:19)

Although his power was now great, David did not forget his covenant with Jonathan. Unlike other kings, David would not destroy the family of the king whom he replaced (9:1; see 1 Sam 20:12-17). David not only spared the life of Jonathan's sole surviving son, the crippled Mephibosheth, but also restored to him Saul's family property (2-8; cf. 4:4). David gave Mephibosheth the privilege of free access into the palace, and appointed one of Saul's former servants to manage his property for him (9-13).

119

Another to whom David tried to be friendly was the new king of Ammon, whose father had helped David during his flight from Saul. But the Ammonites rejected David's goodwill, suspecting that he was looking for ways of spreading his power into their country (10:1-5). They then decided to attack Israel, and even hired soldiers from various Syrian states to help them. The Israelite soldiers turned back the attackers, then, as if to show that Israel had no desire to seize Ammonite territory, returned home (6-14). (This was probably the battle referred to earlier in 8:3-8.)

The Ammonites were willing to accept defeat, but the Syrians were not. They prepared for a second attack on Israel. This time David did not stop when he had turned back the attackers, but overran their country and seized political control (15-19).

11:1-20:26 CONFLICTS IN DAVID'S FAMILY

David takes Bathsheba as wife (11:1-12:31)

While the Israelite army was out fighting another battle against Ammon, David, back in Jerusalem, committed a series of sins that brought him sorrow and trouble for the rest of his life. To begin with, he was guilty of sexual immorality with Bathsheba, wife of Uriah, one of David's top soldiers (11:1-5; cf. 23:39).

On discovering that Bathsheba was pregnant, David thought of a plan to cover up his sin. He recalled Uriah from the battle and sent him home to sleep with Bathsheba, hoping that this would make people think that Uriah was the cause of Bathsheba's pregnancy. But Uriah refused to go near his wife (6-13). David therefore sent Uriah back to the battle and arranged for him to be killed during the fighting (14-17). After waiting for confirmation from the battlefield that Uriah was dead (18-25), David took Bathsheba into his palace as a royal wife (26-27).

David was unaware that anyone in the palace knew of his sin. But Nathan knew, and he trapped David by seeking his judgment in a case where a rich sheep-owner stole and killed a poor man's pet lamb to provide food for his own meal. As expected, David condemned the guilty person (12:1-6). Nathan pointed out that David had condemned himself. In punishment for his murder of Uriah, his own family would be torn apart by murder. In punishment for his adultery with Bathsheba, his own family would be morally disgraced in the eyes of all Israel (7-12).

In genuine sorrow David confessed his sins to God (see Ps. 51) and God graciously pardoned him.

But that did not remove the distress that David would suffer as a result of his sins (13-14). (For the fulfilment of the judgments announced by Nathan see 13:10-19,28-33; 16:21-22; 18:9-15,31-33; 1 Kings 2:13-15; 2 Kings 11:1-2.)

When the child born to David and Bathsheba became sick, David prayed earnestly for it. But the child died, as Nathan had foretold (15-18). David accepted what had happened and realized it was part of God's judgment upon him (19-23). Some time later another son, Solomon, was born to David and Bathsheba (24-25).

The story now returns to the battle with the Ammonites in Rabbah that had provided David with the opportunity for his misdeeds (see 11:1,7,15). The Israelites had captured Rabbah's most strongly defended area and cut off the city's water supply. They could now easily take the whole city, and Joab called David down from Jerusalem to have the honour of leading the triumphal entry. David became king of Ammon and forced the Ammonites to work for Israel (26-31).

David's family troubles begin (13:1-14:33)

The first of the foretold disgraces that fell on David's family followed the same pattern as David's own sin: sexual immorality followed by murder, with the murderer carefully plotting how to get rid of his victim.

Amnon, David's eldest son, tried to seduce his half-sister Tamar, but when Tamar resisted him he raped her (13:1-14). Cruelly, Amnon then drove Tamar away, and the young princess cried bitterly at the loss of her virginity in such circumstances (15-19). David knew what had happened but did nothing. Tamar's brother Absalom also knew, and waited for an opportunity to take revenge on behalf of his sister (20-22).

After two years Absalom got the opportunity he was looking for and had Amnon murdered (23-29). While news of the murder was sent to David (30-33), Absalom fled to the safety of his mother's family in Geshur (34-39; cf. 3:2-3). David had now lost two sons — an adulterer who was dead and a murderer who was in exile.

Joab apparently wanted to see some stability restored to the royal household, with one man firmly recognized as heir to the throne. That man, in Joab's opinion, was Absalom. David made no attempt to bring Absalom back from exile, because this would require him to sentence him to death for murder. Joab therefore laid a plan that would enable the king to bring Absalom back safely (14:1-3). He used a woman to win from the king a judgment that in certain circumstances it was not wrong to show mercy to a murderer (4-11). The woman then used this principle to show that David should allow Absalom to return (12-17).

Although David realized that he had been tricked by Joab into making this judgment (18-20), he stuck to his decision and allowed Absalom to return. However, he did not allow Absalom to enter the royal court. In this way he showed firstly that he had not forgiven his son, and secondly that he did not consider Absalom a suitable person to succeed him as king (21-24).

Whatever David's opinion of Absalom might have been, the people in general were impressed by his handsome appearance (25-27). He was also ambitious and was becoming impatient for power. He had spent three years in exile (see 13:38) and another two years back in Jerusalem, yet he had still not been accepted by the king (28). He decided he would wait no longer. When Joab showed an unwillingness to give him further help, he persuaded Joab to take notice of him by burning Joab's fields. Without delay Joab arranged for him to meet the king, with the result that he received the king's pardon. His fierce ambition had at last brought him back into the royal court (29-33).

Absalom's rebellion (15:1-37)

By cunning and deceit over the next few years, Absalom strengthened his position and gathered himself a following, mainly among the people of Judah's country regions. He encouraged a feeling of dissatisfaction with David's administration and promised a better deal for the common people if he were in a position of authority (15:1-6).

Clearly, Absalom was plotting to seize the throne. It appears that he relied for the success of his rebellion upon the personal support he had built up among the country people. This was one reason why he chose Hebron as the place to declare himself king (7-10). The leading citizens of Jerusalem were unaware of the plot, except for the man who was possibly the mastermind behind it, David's chief adviser, Ahithophel (11-12; cf. 16:23).

The rebellion took David by surprise, because, as far as he knew, the people of Jerusalem still supported him. Now he could not be sure who was for him and who was against him. Knowing that Absalom would head for Jerusalem to claim the throne, David did not want to be trapped in the city. Nor did he want to cause the citizens unnecessary bloodshed. He therefore gathered his household and loyal troops, and fled (13-18; Ps 3). Foreigners who had defected to Israel remained loyal to David, and people from the villages near Jerusalem lamented his departure (19-23).

When the priests Abiathar and Zadok set off to escape with David, taking the ark with them, David sent them and the ark back to Jerusalem. In so doing he expressed his hope that he was not leaving Jerusalem permanently (24-29). He also intended that Abiathar and Zadok, by staying in Jerusalem with the ark, could join with David's loyal adviser Hushai to form a spy ring in the midst of Absalom's court. The priests' sons were to act as messengers to carry news to David (30-37; cf. 17:15-17).

Apparent success of the revolt (16:1-23)

As David left Jerusalem, Ziba (whom David had appointed to manage the property of Saul's grandson Mephibosheth; see 9:9-13) took the opportunity to win David's favour by bringing him food and animals to assist his escape. Ziba then told David that Mephibosheth was a traitor who was planning to seize the throne for himself. As a result David took away Mephibosheth's property and gave it to Ziba, though later events showed there was some doubt whether Mephibosheth really was a traitor (16:1-4; cf. 19:24-30).

Shimei, another of Saul's relatives, was pleased to see David humiliatingly removed from his throne, and cursed him bitterly (5-8). David showed much patience in accepting the humiliation, believing it might have been part of God's judgment upon him (9-14).

Meanwhile Absalom seized power in Jerusalem, though David's cause was helped when Hushai gained entrance into Absalom's circle of advisers (15-19). Absalom then took over his father's harem, to demonstrate to all that he was now king. By his shameful treatment of the harem women he showed his utter contempt for his father (cf. 12:11). This was all carefully planned by Ahithophel. He saw that if Absalom's revolt was to succeed, there had to be no possible chance of a reconciliation between Absalom and David (20-23).

War between Absalom and David (17:1-19:8)

Ahithophel advised Absalom that he needed to do only one thing to make his throne secure, and that was kill David. If he did this swiftly, without war or unnecessary bloodshed, the people would soon be fully behind him (17:1-4). Hushai, wishing to gain time for David to escape and organize his troops, advised against such a risky operation, for David was a very experienced soldier. He recommended that the whole Israelite army be assembled and Absalom himself lead them into battle (5-13). Being as vain as he was ambitious, Absalom liked this idea and accepted Hushai's advice (14).

At the risk of their lives, David's spies took him news of Absalom's plan (15-20), with the result that David and his men quickly escaped across Jordan (21-22). Ahithophel committed suicide. His plotting had brought Absalom to the throne, and he knew that all would be lost if Absalom followed Hushai's advice (23). David had now gained valuable time to rest his weary men, obtain provisions and plan his war strategy (24-29).

The military leaders whom David appointed over his men suggested he not go with his troops to the battle, lest he be killed. David agreed, but warned them not to kill Absalom (18:1-5). David's experienced army leaders knew better than the inexperienced Absalom how to direct the fighting in the difficult conditions of the thick forest. Absalom's forces suffered a crushing defeat (6-8). Though Joab acted against David's command in killing Absalom, he knew that this was the only way to bring the revolt to an end (9-15). Once Absalom was dead, further fighting was not necessary. Absalom had hoped for himself an honourable memorial, but he was buried in disgrace (16-18).

Not knowing how best to break the news of Absalom's death to David, Joab sent an African slave, in case the king reacted violently and killed the bearer of such bad news. But Ahimaaz, knowing that David would be overcome with grief, persuaded Joab to send him as well (19-23). Ahimaaz arrived first and tried to break the news to David softly (24-29), but when the African arrived he told David bluntly that Absalom was dead (30-33).

David's uncontrolled grief over the death of Absalom created dissatisfaction among those who had risked their lives to save him (19:1-4). Joab spoke harshly to David, telling him to stop mourning and show some appreciation of what his troops had done for him. If not, he might lose their support entirely (5-8).

David returns to Jerusalem (19:9-43)

Because the nation was still deeply divided as a result of Absalom's revolt, David did not return to Jerusalem immediately. He was waiting for the people to give an indication that they wanted him restored as king. Some people of the northern tribes had suggested they invite David back, but the people of Judah, David's own tribe, had apparently said nothing (9-10).

Knowing the rivalry that existed between Judah and the other tribes, David cunningly suggested that Judah quickly show its support for him, otherwise

it would be outdone by the other tribes. Also, in an effort to win the allegiance of those Judahites who had followed Absalom, he made Amasa, Absalom's commander, chief of his army. This was clearly unfair to Joab, who had remained loyal to David and won him the victory (11-14). (Absalom, Joab and Amasa were cousins; see 1 Chron 2:13-17.)

As he was returning to Jerusalem, David was greeted by some of the people who had met him earlier when he was fleeing (15-18a). Shimei, who had previously cursed him, now begged his favour, and David promised not to execute him (18b-23; cf. 16:5-14; but see 1 Kings 2:8-9). Mephibosheth contradicted Ziba's earlier statement to David about Mephibosheth's supposed disloyalty. It seems that David did not know whom to believe, so he divided Saul's property between the two of them (24-30; cf. 16:1-4). By taking Barzillai's son into the royal court, David rewarded Barzillai for his former kindnesses (31-38; cf. 17:27-29). The party then crossed the Jordan and headed for Jerusalem (39-40).

Judah responded so vigorously to David's call to bring him back to Jerusalem, that it outdid the other tribes (see v. 11, 40). Unfortunately, the whole affair further stirred up those inter-tribal jealousies which one day would result in the breaking up of the kingdom (41-43).

Sheba's revolt (20:1-26)

With virtually the whole nation in a state of unrest, Sheba, a Benjaminite, seized the opportunity to try to lead the northern tribes to break away from David (20:1-2). Being anxious to re-establish his kingdom in Jerusalem, David did not leave the city but sent his new commander-in-chief Amasa to assemble the army and pursue Sheba (3-4).

When Amasa was slow in assembling the army, David sent off his private army, the fighting force that had been with him since the days of his flight from Saul. David placed Abishai in charge of the operation, but Joab went also (5-7). When the troops with Abishai and Joab met the troops with Amasa, Joab murdered Amasa and again took control of the army (8-13).

Sheba's uprising apparently did not attract a large following. When he was finally trapped in the town of Abel in the far north of Israel, only a few people of his own clan were left with him (14-15). The citizens of Abel, on the advice of an old woman among them, saved their besieged town from destruction by murdering Sheba and throwing his head over the wall to Joab (16-22).

This section of the book closes with a list of the chief officials in David's administration during the latter part of his reign. The list shows certain changes and developments that had occurred over the years (23-26; cf. 8:15-18).

21:1-24:25 MISCELLANEOUS MATTERS

The writer of 2 Samuel has finished his historical record of David's reign. Since the story of David's sin with Bathsheba, the writer has mainly been concerned with showing how this one event changed the course of David's life. He now returns and records various other stories and poems to show other difficulties David faced during his reign. He shows also how God cared for him during those difficulties. (The story of David's closing years is given in the opening chapters of 1 Kings.)

Judgments and justice (21:1-22)

One of David's difficulties was a three-year famine throughout the land. God showed him that this was a judgment on Israel because Saul had slaughtered the Gibeonites. By such action Saul broke the oath that Joshua, as representative of the nation, had sworn to the Gibeonites in the name of God (21:1-2; see Josh 9:15,19-21). Saul's sin had to be cleansed and the Gibeonites' claim for justice needed to be satisfied. Therefore, seven of Saul's descendants were executed, the number seven symbolizing full satisfaction (3-9).

David was filled with sympathy when he saw how one of Saul's former concubines sorrowed for the dead men. He tried to comfort her by arranging for an honourable burial for the bones of Saul and Jonathan, possibly along with those of the seven victims. This showed also that he himself had no hatred for his former king, but had executed the seven men only in response to God's call for justice. God then lifted his judgment on Israel by ending the famine (10-14).

During one of the Philistines' many battles with Israel, a Philistine giant had apparently tried to take revenge on behalf of the dead Goliath by trying to kill David. But he himself was killed by one of David's chief men (15-17). Three other Philistine giants were killed by Israelites on different occasions (18-22; cf. 1 Chron 20:5).

Two psalms (22:1-23:7)

The first of these two psalms was written by David to celebrate his victories over his enemies. Later it was put to music for use in the temple services and appears in the book of Psalms as Psalm 18.

David began the psalm by praising God who constantly answered his prayers and saved him from death (22:1-7). God displayed his mighty power in earthquakes, wind, rain, lightning, thunder and darkness (8-16), and sometimes he used these forces to save David from his enemies (17-20). God worked on behalf of David because of David's uprightness and obedience (21-25), showing that God treats people as they deserve (26-30).

Because God is perfect in all his ways, David could always depend upon him (31-33). This God protected David and gave him ability as a soldier and a national leader (34-37), so that he repeatedly conquered his enemies (38-43). His fame spread far and wide as foreign nations submitted to his rule (44-46), but he gladly acknowledged that all his greatness came from God (47-49). Later kings of David's dynasty could likewise be assured of God's unfailing blessing (50-51).

In the second psalm David commented briefly on the blessings that a God-fearing king brought to his people. Life under such a king had a pleasantness that could be likened to that of a morning without clouds. As the sun benefited the grass after rain, so the king benefited his people (23:1-4). David's dynasty was assured of the additional blessings of stability and lasting prosperity, because of the covenant God made with David (5; cf. 7:16). But, like any wise ruler, David knew also that he had to punish the wicked, and he would not avoid this responsibility even though it was often difficult and dangerous (6-7).

David's mighty men (23:8-39)

From the hundreds of men who gathered around him during his flight from Saul, David had built a loyal and tough fighting unit. This unit remained the central strength of his army throughout his long reign (see 1 Sam 22:1-2; 30:9; 2 Sam 15:18; 18:1-2; 20:7; 1 Chron 11:10). The commander-in-chief of his army was Joab (see 8:16, 20:23).

Next in rank below Joab were three generals, or commanders, each of whom was a courageous fighter and a national hero. These men were known simply as The Three (8-12; 1 Chron 11:10-14). After The Three came The Thirty, three of whom were especially remembered for the occasion on which they risked their lives because of their devotion to David (13-17). The leader of The Thirty was Joab's brother Abishai. Another notable figure among The Thirty was Benaiah, commander of David's bodyguard (18-23; see note on 8:18).

Although the group took its name from the number thirty, there are more than thirty names in the biblical lists. This is probably because the lists include the names of those who had been killed and those who had replaced them (24-39; 1 Chron 11:20-47).

The census and its outcome (24:1-25)

Israel's increasing power and prosperity under David may have given David and his people feelings of self-praise, as if they, and not God, had been the cause of this growth. God saw that the time had come to awaken Israel to this sin. Therefore, God allowed Satan to suggest to David that he take a census of the people. David's pride in his growing nation was apparently what made the suggestion seem such a good idea, but God was going to use the event to reveal that pride and punish it (24:1-4; 1 Chron 21:1). The officials carried out the census first in the territory east of Jordan, then in the north of Canaan, and finally in the south (5-9).

Even before God acted in judgment, David's conscience told him he had sinned. Through a prophet, God offered David a choice of one of three calamities as a punishment, but David chose rather to leave the decision with God and trust in his mercy (10-14). A plague broke out in Israel, physically weakening the nation that David thought was strong. Even Jerusalem, the city that David was so proud of, would have been destroyed had not God in his mercy stopped the plague (15-17).

To show his repentance, David was told to offer sacrifices to God, but in view of the recent events he feared to go to the tabernacle at Gibeon (1 Chron 21:29-30). God therefore allowed him to remain in Jerusalem, but directed him to the hilltop farm of a man named Araunah (or Ornan). David was to buy the piece of hard ground that Araunah used as his threshing floor, and build on it an altar to offer the sacrifices (18-20). Araunah wanted to give the piece of ground to David for nothing, but David insisted that he buy it. If his offering was to be a genuine sacrifice, it had to cost him something (21-25).

Later David bought the surrounding land as well, and declared that this was the place where the temple of God would be built (1 Chron 21:25; 22:1). It was apparently the place where Abraham had offered up Isaac (2 Chron 3:1; cf. Gen. 22:2).

Summary: from Moses to David

1280 BC	Moses leads Israel out of Egypt
	Years in the wilderness
1240	Israel under Joshua enters Canaan
	Period of the judges
1050	Saul becomes Israel's first king
1010	Saul dies; David becomes king
1003	David conquers Jerusalem
970	David dies; Solomon becomes king

APPENDIX
David's family and relatives (important names only; 1 Chron 2:11-17)

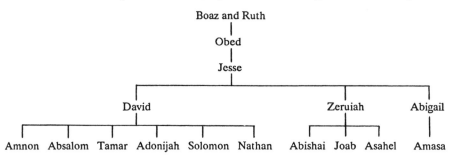

David's wives and their children (important names only; 2 Sam 5:13)

Michal	daughter of Saul	no children (1 Sam 18:27; 2 Sam 6:23)
Ahinoam	from Jezreel	mother of Amnon (1 Sam 25:43; 2 Sam 3:2; 13:1)
Abigail	formerly wife of Nabal	mother of Chileab (1 Sam 25:42; 2 Sam 3:3)
Maachah	daughter of king of Geshur	mother of Absalom and Tamar (2 Sam 3:3; 13:1,4)
Haggith		mother of Adonijah (2 Sam 3:4; 1 Kings 1:5)
Bathsheba	formerly wife of Uriah	mother of Solomon and Nathan (2 Sam 11:3; 12:24; 1 Chron 3:5; Matt 1:6; Luke 3:31)

1 Kings

BACKGROUND TO 1 & 2 KINGS

The two books of Kings (originally one book) carry on the history of Israel from the books of Samuel. They cover a period of about four centuries from the closing years of David's reign to the time the people were taken into captivity in Babylon. They describe the division of the kingdom into two, and the history, decline and fall of the separate kingdoms.

Characteristics of the books

As with the books of Joshua, Judges and Samuel, the two books of Kings have been written as prophetic history. That is, the author's main concern was not merely to record events, but to show the meaning of those events in the purposes of God. (For further discussion on the features of prophetic history see introductory notes to the book of Joshua.)

Because of this concern to see the meaning to Israel's history, the writer does not record all the events of any one era. Nor does he always place events in their chronological order. He selects and arranges his material according to its religious, rather than its political, significance. He might mention a politically important king only briefly (e.g. Omri; 1 Kings 16:21-28), but deal with politically unimportant events in some detail (e.g. the ministry of Elijah and Elisha). He deals with the affairs of surrounding kingdoms only as they are of significance in God's purposes for Israel.

The author of Kings has chosen to remain anonymous. He may have been a prophet, and he probably used the official court records, along with the records of the prophets, in preparing his book (1 Kings 11:41; 15:7,23,31; cf. 2 Chron 9:29; 33:19). Lengthy sections of the prophetical books Isaiah and Jeremiah are found also in Kings (e.g. Isa 36:1-39:8; Jer 39:1-10; 52:1-34). The whole work was probably completed after the collapse of the Israelite nation, when the people were in captivity in Babylon.

OUTLINE OF 1 KINGS

1:1-4:34 SOLOMON ESTABLISHES HIS KINGDOM

Solomon becomes king (1:1-53)

David was old and his health was failing. He needed a nurse with him continually, one of her duties being to lie with him in bed to give him warmth. Although this nurse, Abishag, was not David's concubine, many people apparently thought she was (1:1-4; see note on 2:22).

Adonijah, David's oldest surviving son, decided to establish himself as king while David was still alive, and so prevent any possible claim to the throne by Solomon later. Once he had gained the support of the senior priest Abiathar and the army commander Joab, Adonijah thought he could ignore the friends and advisers of David who favoured Solomon (5-10).

Those friends of David had more influence in the palace than Adonijah realized. Possibly the most important of them was the prophet Nathan, who apparently knew that God's will was for Solomon to be the next king (cf. 2 Sam 7:12-17; 12:24-25; 1 Chron 22:6-10). Nathan quickly thought of a plan to prompt David to declare openly that Solomon was to succeed him as king (11-14). First Bathsheba told David what Adonijah had done (15-21), then Nathan asked David if he approved of Adonijah's action (22-27). Shocked at what he heard, David declared that Solomon, not Adonijah, would be his successor (28-31).

Once roused to action, David was determined to see Solomon anointed and publicly proclaimed king (32-37). Solomon's appointment seems to have won popular support. It also had the backing of David's personal bodyguard of Cherethites and Pelethites, who were under the command of the tough Benaiah (38-40).

Adonijah's celebrations were cut short when he heard what had happened (41-48). He realized that his claim to the throne now had little chance of success. Therefore, he decided that the wisest thing to do was to acknowledge Solomon as king in return for Solomon's guarantee not to execute him (49-53).

The excitement of these events must have given David a sudden renewal of strength just before his death. He arranged a second anointing of Solomon, this time with full regal and religious ceremony, at which he presented Solomon to the people. He wanted them to see that Solomon was his divinely chosen successor (1 Chron 28:1-10; 29:20-22).

Opponents of Solomon executed (2:1-46)

As he saw his death approaching, David passed on to Solomon advice aimed at ensuring stability to his reign and good government for God's people. The first and most important point was a reminder to be faithful to God. God's promises of a prosperous kingdom and a lasting dynasty required David and his successors to be obedient to God's will. Without obedience, there was no guarantee of blessing (2:1-4; 1 Chron 22:6-16).

David's second piece of advice to Solomon was to remove those likely to rebel against him, and reward those who had remained loyal to him. David had for many years known that Joab should have been punished for the murders he had committed (see 2 Sam 3:30; 20:10). He now saw an opportunity to deal with Joab, because he knew that Solomon would not hesitate to execute one who had recently supported Adonijah (5-9).

After the death of David (10-12), Solomon soon found opportunities to get rid of his opponents. Adonijah was first to be killed. Since a new king inherited the former king's concubines, Solomon considered that Adonijah's request to marry Abishag was an attempt to claim David's throne (13-22; cf. 2 Sam 3:7; 12:8; 16:22). Adonijah was executed for treason (23-25).

Solomon then dealt with Abiathar, the high priest who, with Joab, had supported Adonijah. Abiathar was not executed, but his dismissal brought his priestly work, and the priestly work of Eli's descendants, to an end (26-27; cf. 1 Sam 2:27-36).

Next Joab was executed. He had no right to ask for mercy by clinging to the altar, as he had been guilty of wilful murder (28-35; cf. Exod 21:12-14). Joab was followed by Shimei, a relative of Saul who had always been opposed to the throne of David (see 2 Sam 16:5-14). To lessen Shimei's chances of plotting against him, Solomon would not allow him to leave Jerusalem (36-38). When Shimei went to Gath in search of runaway slaves, Solomon saw this as defiance of his authority. Shimei was promptly executed (39-46a). With all possible opponents now removed, Solomon's position was secure (46b).

Solomon's wisdom (3:1-28)

David's power had come through war and conquest; Solomon's came through clever commercial and political agreements with neighbouring countries. Solomon gave impressive public display of his loyalty to God, but he ignored God's warnings when he saw advantages to be gained through foreign alliances. His marriage to the daughter of Pharaoh guaranteed peace for Israel in a region where Egypt was the chief power, but it probably required Solomon to pay respect to Egypt's gods (3:1-3; cf. 11:1-8; Exod 34:12-16).

Although David had placed the ark of the covenant (GNB: covenant box) in a special tent in Jerusalem, the tabernacle (GNB: tent of the Lord's presence) and the remainder of its articles were still at Gibeon (1 Chron 15:1-3; 16:1,39; 21:29). Soon after being crowned king in Jerusalem, Solomon went to Gibeon for a lavish religious ceremony, as a public exhibition of his devotion to God (4; 2 Chron 1:2-6). While there, he had a dream in which God offered to give him whatever he chose. By asking for wisdom to judge between the morally right and the morally wrong, he showed his concern for the just government of God's people (5-9). God gave him all that he asked for and more (10-15).

Back in Jerusalem Solomon soon had to put this wisdom to use, when he was called upon to decide which of two prostitutes was the mother of a disputed baby (16-22). Solomon knew that both women were of low moral standard, but he did not allow such knowledge to affect his sense of justice. Many of the people of Israel might have been ungodly, but Solomon still had to understand their affairs and act with fairness when settling disputes among them (23-28).

The administration of the kingdom (4:1-34)

Details are now given of how Solomon administered Israel. First the leading religious, civil and army officials are listed (4:1-6). Solomon revised the taxation system by dividing the country into twelve zones, each of which had to provide the royal household with all its food supplies for one month of the year. These twelve zones apparently replaced the former tribal areas (7-19).

Neighbouring nations that had become part of the Israelite empire also paid taxes, and so enriched Solomon further. Israel as a nation enjoyed peace and prosperity (20-21). The monthly food supply was enormous, for it had to maintain not only the royal family and government officials, but also the army (22-28).

Because of his wisdom, Solomon was famous in countries far and near. People made collections of his proverbs and songs, and many travelled to Israel to hear his wisdom (29-34).

5:1-9:25 SOLOMON'S BUILDING PROGRAM

When David had expressed a desire to build a permanent house for God, he was told that God was more concerned with building a permanent 'house' for David, namely, a dynasty. As for a symbolic dwelling place for God, God had already shown his ideal for Israel in the tabernacle. Nevertheless, he would allow Israel to have a temple, though it would be built not by David, but by David's son Solomon (see notes on 2 Sam 7:1-17).

Despite God's emphasis on the need to build a godly family, both David and Solomon seem to have been more concerned with building a lavish temple. David may not have been allowed to build the temple himself, but he helped Solomon all he could by preparing the plan and setting aside money and materials for the building's construction. He wanted everything to be ready so that Solomon could begin construction as soon as he became king (1 Chron 22:2-16; 28:11).

But Solomon's plans were for more than a temple. His building program lasted more than twenty years, and included an expensive palace and other impressive buildings to adorn his national capital. (For details of David's preparations for the temple and its services, and his extensive instructions to Solomon, see notes on 1 Chronicles 22:2-29:30.)

Workers and materials (5:1-18)

No doubt Solomon intended the building of the temple to be a help to Israel's spiritual life, but the way he carried out the work could easily have had the opposite effect. He obtained the best of materials from Hiram, king of Tyre, but the contract with Hiram almost certainly involved religious ritual and recognition of Hiram's gods (5:1-9).

Solomon agreed to pay for all this material by sending farm produce to Hiram. But Israel's farmers may not have been happy to see their hard earned produce going to a heathen king, especially since it was only to pay for a lavish building program in the capital city (10-12). Nor would people in northern Israel be pleased to see their land handed over to Hiram to pay off Solomon's debts (see 9:11-14).

These disadvantages may not have existed had Solomon been more moderate in his plans and materials. The temple did not need to be any larger than the old tabernacle, and David seems to have left Solomon plenty of materials for its construction (1 Chron 22:2-5; 29:1-9).

Another of Solomon's policies that created feelings of dissatisfaction and rebellion was that of forced labour (see 12:4). All working men were required to give three months work to the king each year, to provide a year-round workforce of 30,000 men. One third of these were sent to Tyre to work in relays, a month at a time, cutting the timber under the supervision of Hiram's men. The timber was then floated down to the Israelite port of Joppa (see v. 6,9; 2 Chron 2:8-10,16). Besides these part-time Israelite workers, there were 150,000 full-time slaves (mainly Canaanites; 9:20-22) who did the harder work of quarrying and carrying the stone (13-18).

Overall plan of the temple (6:1-13)

The simplest way to describe Solomon's temple is as a rectangular stone building with a porch added to the front, and three storeys of storerooms added to the sides and rear. The side and rear walls of the main building were reduced in thickness by one cubit (about forty-four centimetres, or eighteen inches) for the middle storey, and by a further cubit for the top storey. This created 'steps' on which the timber beams rested to form the floors for the middle and upper storeys (6:1-6).

All stones used in the building were cut and dressed at the quarry, so that they would be as easy to handle as possible. No stoneworking tools were used at the temple site (7-10). God gave Solomon the timely reminder that the temple would be a means of blessing to him and his people only if he was obedient to God (11-13).

Details of the temple's interior (6:14-38)

Inside the temple the stonework was covered with lavishly carved wood panelling overlaid with beaten gold (14-15; see v. 22). A partition divided the main temple into two rooms. The larger front room was called the nave or Holy Place; the smaller rear room was called the inner sanctuary or Most Holy Place (16-18).

The Most Holy Place contained the ark of the covenant, symbol of God's presence (19). This room had a lower ceiling than the rest of the building (20; cf. v. 2) and, also unlike the rest of the building, was without windows (cf. 6:4; 8:12). Its entrance was closed by a curtain, a pair of doors and gold chains hung across the doorway (21-22; see v. 31; 2 Chron 3:14). Inside the room were two huge winged creatures, or cherubim, which side by side stretched across the width of the room. They were probably symbolic guardians of the ark (23-28). The doors to the Most Holy Place were of carved wood overlaid with gold, similar to the temple walls (29-32).

In the front room were the altar of incense, the table of 'presence bread' and ten lampstands, five

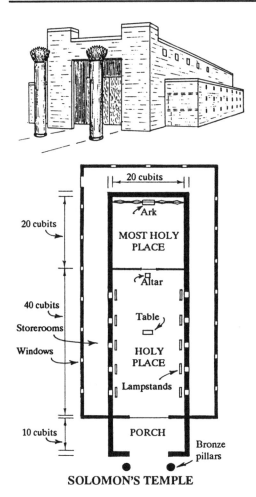

SOLOMON'S TEMPLE

on each of the two side walls (see 7:48-49). Folding doors led from the entrance porch to this room (33-35). A walled courtyard surrounded the whole building (36). The total construction time for the temple was seven years (37-38).

Construction of other buildings (7:1-12)

After finishing the temple, Solomon moved on to the next part of his building program. This was the building of a magnificent palace that took thirteen years (7:1). He also built many other expensive buildings in this national showpiece. The House of the Forest of Lebanon, so called because of its three rows of cedar pillars, was apparently a military headquarters and weapons storehouse (2-5; cf. 10:17; Isa 22:8). The Hall of Pillars was probably a meeting

hall, and the Hall of the Throne a judgment court. There was also a separate palace for his queen, the daughter of Pharaoh (6-8). All these buildings, along with the temple and Solomon's own palace, were built within the Great Court, around the perimeter of which was a stone and timber wall (9-12).

More concerning the temple (7:13-51)

Israel seems to have lost the spiritual insight and artistic skill that in the time of Moses enabled its craftsmen to design and make the decoration for God's dwelling place (cf. Exod 31:1-6). Solomon therefore hired a craftsman from Tyre to do the bronze work and other decorations for the temple, with no apparent concern for the wrong religious ideas this man may have had. By coincidence this hired craftsman was named Hiram (GNB: Huram), the same as the king (13-14; 2 Chron 2:7,13-14).

Hiram the bronzeworker made two bronze pillars that stood in front of the porch but did not support the roof. They seem to have been purely ornamental. Decorations around the bowl-shaped tops of the pillars consisted of pomegranates, large flowers and a network of interwoven chains (15-22; see v. 41-42).

A new bronze altar was made, much larger than Moses' tabernacle altar, which was now far too small for the great numbers of animals that Solomon sacrificed (see 8:64; 2 Chron 4:1). A bronze laver (GNB: tank), in the form of a huge basin supported on the backs of twelve oxen, held water for bathing and other cleansing rites (23-26). There were ten additional mobile lavers, each consisting of a bronze basin fixed on top of a trolley, or cart. The basin sat inside a square frame, on the outside of which were attached decorative panels (27-39).

The writer then lists all the articles made of bronze (40-45). The bronze casting was done at a place in the Jordan Valley where the ground was suitable (46-47). Other articles were also made, till the temple was finished in every detail and fully equipped for its services (48-51).

The ark brought to the temple (8:1-21)

People came from all over Israel to celebrate the dedication of the temple (see v. 65). The ceremony took place at the time of the mid-year festival season (8:1-2; see Lev 23:24,27,34).

In transferring the ark from David's temporary tent to the temple, Solomon, evidently remembering the mistake of his father, was careful to see that the priests and Levites carried the ark and all the holy vessels in the proper manner (3-9; cf. 2 Sam 6:1-7). The procession was accompanied by music and singing provided by the priests and Levites, all of whom were on duty for the special occasion (2 Chron 5:11-14).

Once the ark was in its rightful place, God gave the sign of his presence by filling the temple with a cloud of glory. As in the case of the tabernacle, the light of God's presence was so dazzling that human activity in the sanctuary had to cease (10-13; cf. Exod 40:34-35). Amazed at all that had happened, Solomon contrasted that day with the days of their ancestors. Ever since Israel had become a nation, God had refused to choose any city for his dwelling place; but now he chose the city of David and his son Solomon (14-21).

The dedication ceremony (8:22-9:9)

Solomon then went up on to a specially made bronze platform, knelt down and prayed to God in the presence of the assembled people (2 Chron 6:12-13). He admitted that only God's grace had allowed his father and himself to fulfil their wish of building God a symbolic dwelling place. He prayed that God's grace would rest likewise upon his royal descendants after him (22-26). Solomon knew there was no necessity for the temple, because God dwells everywhere. But he asked that God would graciously hear his prayer and the prayers of the people when they came to the temple to pray (27-30).

Because the temple was a place of prayer, Solomon thought of various circumstances when people would go there to pray. He asked that judges, such as himself, would have God's help in making legal judgments where the evidence was uncertain (31-32; cf. Exod 22:7-12). He thought of cases where God might punish his people through war, famine, disease or other disasters, and he asked that when they repented, God would forgive them (33-40).

In a public display of concern for foreigners, Solomon prayed that they too would come to know God, and that God would answer their prayers as he did those of Israelites (41-43). He asked that God would hear the Israelites when they prayed for success against their enemies in war (44-45). Finally, he asked that God would hear them when they cried for mercy from those whom he sent to punish them (46-53).

God demonstrated his acceptance of Solomon's prayer by sending fire from heaven to burn up the sacrifices (2 Chron 7:1-3). Solomon then prepared to pray for God's blessing upon the assembled people (54-55). He praised God for his faithfulness to his promises, and asked that God would help his people to obey his law (56-61). The ceremony concluded in typical fashion with large numbers of sacrifices

(62-64), and public celebrations continued for a further week (65-66).

In accepting the temple, God again reminded Solomon that the important 'house' was not the house of God (the temple), but the house of David (those whom God had appointed to govern Israel for ever). Though in relation to the people they were kings, in relation to God they were servants, and they had to be obedient to his will if they were to enjoy the fulfilment of his promises (9:1-5). Solomon had built the temple to show that God dwelt among his people. But if the king or his people rebelled against him, God would destroy the temple to show his displeasure with them (6-9).

Building development in other cities (9:10-25)

Earlier Solomon had borrowed from Hiram about four thousand kilograms of gold to help finance his ambitious building programs. In payment of these debts, Solomon gave Hiram twenty cities in northern Israel. Hiram was not satisfied with these cities and returned them (which meant that Solomon had to look for other ways to repay the loan) (10-14; see 2 Chron 8:1-2).

To strengthen Jerusalem's security, Solomon rebuilt the Millo (some sort of defence fortification) and all the damaged sections of the city wall. He also rebuilt ruined cities, established army bases at strategic points, and equipped selected cities to store the farm produce collected to maintain the government (15-19; cf. 4:7,22-28; 5:11). He made all foreigners slaves. Israelites, though not officially slaves, were treated little better (20-24; cf. 12:4).

Solomon kept the covenant requirements in relation to the annual religious festivals. His harsh treatment of his subjects, however, showed little regard for other covenant requirements, such as those concerned for people's well-being (25; cf. Exod 23:9,14-17; Lev 19:13).

9:26-11:43 OTHER FEATURES OF SOLOMON'S REIGN

Trade, fame and wealth (9:26-10:29)

Always alert in business dealings, Solomon saw the opportunity for further profits by cooperating with Hiram in trade transport. Goods from the Mediterranean were received at Hiram's port of Tyre, taken overland to the Israelite port of Ezion-geber at the northern tip of the Red Sea, then shipped east, possibly as far as India. Since the Israelites were not a seafaring people, Solomon hired seamen from Hiram to teach and guide his men. Goods that these ships brought back from the east further enriched the two kings (26-28; cf. 10:11-12,22). ('Ship of Tarshish' was a technical name for a certain kind of ocean-going merchant ship. It was not an indication of the port to which or from which a ship was sailing.)

Archaeology indicates that Solomon mined and smelted iron and copper in the region of Ezion-geber, from where he shipped the materials east (cf. Deut 8:9). The strategic and economic importance of Ezion-geber (or Elath) was a cause of frequent conflicts between Jerusalem and Edom, the original owners of the port (cf. 2 Kings 14:22; 16:6).

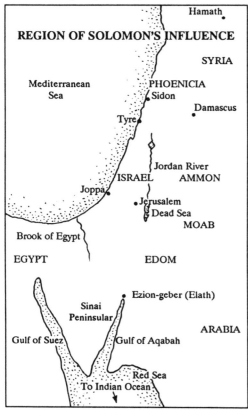

REGION OF SOLOMON'S INFLUENCE

People of other nations heard of Solomon's reputation for wisdom, and on one occasion the queen of an Arabian country visited Jerusalem to test him with hard questions. She was amazed not only at Solomon's wisdom but also at the splendour of his court (10:1-9). At the same time both she and Solomon took the opportunity to have some useful trade exchanges (10-13).

Solomon gained further wealth by taxing all goods that passed through Israel along the inter-national trade routes. He spent much of this wealth extravagantly, to give his city and palace a splendour unequalled among the nations of the region (14-22). Nations that sought his favour also brought him expensive gifts (23-25). Besides building a large horse and chariot force for himself, he became the middleman in an international horse and chariot trade that further enriched him (26-29).

The reign of Solomon saw the beginnings of a strong merchant class in Israel. Previously Israel's economy was largely agricultural and pastoral, but gradually the merchants gained control over the farmers. Over the next two centuries conditions for the farmers worsened and social injustice increased, causing prophets such as Amos, Hosea, Isaiah and Micah to condemn the corrupt society and announce its coming judgment.

Solomon's idolatry (11:1-43)

Although some of Solomon's marriages were for political purposes, most of his wives and concubines were probably given to him as gifts. These women usually brought their gods into Israel, and Solomon's weakness in worshipping these gods led finally to his downfall (11:1-8). God's judgment on Solomon and Israel was to bring the long-standing friction between northerners and southerners to a climax in the division of the kingdom. Only Solomon's tribe Judah (which had by this time absorbed Simeon in the south) along with neighbouring Benjamin would be left for Solomon's son to rule. The remaining tribes, led by Ephraim, would form the breakaway northern kingdom (9-13).

By this time the king of Egypt who had been friendly to Solomon (see 3:1) had died. The new Pharaoh, fearful of Solomon's power, encouraged any rebellion inside or outside Israel that would weaken Solomon. Hadad, crown prince of Edom, had been taken to Egypt in childhood when David conquered Edom. He grew up in Egypt, and later returned to Edom, from where he carried out guerilla attacks against Israel (14-22). Other enemies used Syria as a base from which to conduct guerilla warfare against Solomon. The leader in this case was Rezon, another who had escaped when David conquered his country (23-25; cf. 2 Sam 8:3,13).

Meanwhile the prophet Ahijah revealed that Jeroboam would be the next king. Jeroboam was one of Solomon's most capable administrators, an ambitious hard-working young man whom Solomon put in charge of the Ephraim-Manasseh workforce (26-33). Ahijah also warned Jeroboam that he had to be obedient to God. But Jeroboam's immediate concern was to gain power, and no doubt he used his position to influence his fellow northerners against Solomon and so gain a following for himself (34-39).

When Solomon tried to kill him, Jeroboam escaped to Egypt, for he knew he could be sure of Pharaoh's support. He stayed there till the death of Solomon, awaiting his opportunity to return and seize the throne of Israel (40-43).

12:1-16:28 EARLY DAYS OF THE DIVIDED KINGDOM

Revolt against Rehoboam (12:1-24)

From the time of the judges there had been tension between Judah and the northern tribes, particularly Ephraim. Rehoboam apparently knew of the possibility that the northern tribes would break away from him, and therefore he arranged for a special coronation ceremony in Shechem, one of the more important northern cities (12:1).

Jeroboam decided immediately that he would test Rehoboam's ability as a leader. He knew that Solomon's forced labour and heavy taxation policies were unpopular, and he used these to stir up the people against Rehoboam (2-5). Rehoboam realized the seriousness of the situation, but whether he relaxed or tightened his father's policies, he was doomed to failure. The northern tribes decided to break away from Rehoboam and form their own kingdom (6-17).

Rehoboam tried to force his authority on the rebels by sending his labour chief, Adoram, to deal with them. Adoram was probably the most unpopular person in Israel, and the northerners promptly murdered him. They then invited Jeroboam to be their king (18-20). Rehoboam fled to his palace in Jerusalem, from where he planned to establish his rule in the north by military force. To his credit he changed his mind when a prophet told him that this division was God's will (21-24).

With the division of the kingdom came the collapse of the empire that David and Solomon had built. One by one the subject nations regained their independence.

Two kingdoms

From this point on, the northern kingdom of ten tribes was known as Israel, the southern kingdom as Judah. Judah was the smaller of the two kingdoms in both population and area, and had the poorer country agriculturally, but politically it was more stable. It had an established dynasty, the dynasty of David, and its people, being mostly from one tribe, were fairly well unified.

By contrast there was never a strong unity in the northern kingdom. Reasons for this were the greater number of tribes in the north, the comparatively large population of Canaanites still living in the area, and the natural divisions created by mountains and rivers. Judah was more isolated, but Israel was more open to foreign interference.

The writer's plan in outlining the history of the two kingdoms is to record the reign of one king to his death, then return to the story of the other king and follow it through the same way. The length of a king's reign is at times difficult to determine, since in some cases the king shared the reign with his father during the latter's last years as king. Sometimes the length of the reign is calculated from the beginning of the joint reign, other times from the beginning of the reign as sole king. Further variations occur because the number of years of a king's reign may include the years of his ascension and death as full years, even though he reigned for only part of those years.

Writings such as 'The Books of the Chronicles of the kings of Israel and Judah', which the writer mentions frequently from here on, are not to be confused with the books called Chronicles in our Bible. Rather they were the official court records of Israel and Judah.

THE DIVIDED KINGDOM

False religion in the north (12:25-33)

Shechem, where Rehoboam had hoped to unite all Israel, now became the capital of Jeroboam's breakaway kingdom. Jeroboam established a second capital at Penuel, east of Jordan, probably with the aim of holding the allegiance of the two and a half eastern tribes (25). Later he moved his capital a short distance north to Tirzah, which remained the capital during the reigns of several kings (see 14:17; 15:21,33).

Jeroboam saw that his people might be tempted to transfer their allegiance to Rehoboam if they went to Jerusalem for sacrifices and festivals. He therefore set up his own shrines at Bethel (near his southern border) and Dan (near his northern border), complete with his own order of priests, sacrifices and festivals. This new religion included many ideas taken from the religions of Canaan and neighbouring countries. It was a rebellion against God for which the writer of Kings repeatedly condemns Jeroboam. It led Israel into increasing moral and religious corruption over the next two centuries (26-33).

Jeroboam's punishment (13:1-14:20)

God soon showed that this new form of religion was totally unacceptable to him. A prophet from Judah came to Bethel and, by bold words and dramatic actions, condemned both the people and the king (13:1-10).

However, there was another prophet, a much older man, who lived in Bethel and had apparently not spoken out against Jeroboam's wrongdoing. The old prophet seems to have been jealous of the prophet from Judah, and decided to tempt him to disobey God's command. By using lies and deceit he was successful (11-19).

As the prophet from Judah was returning home, he was killed by a lion in punishment for his disobedience (20-26). When the people of Bethel saw the lion standing quietly beside the body of the man it had killed, without either eating the body or attacking the man's donkey, they realized that this was no ordinary death. The old prophet also was shocked, and expressed his admiration for the younger man's boldness (27-32). But in spite of these warnings of judgment, Jeroboam did not change his ways (33-34).

When his son fell ill, Jeroboam sent to the prophet Ahijah for help (14:1-5). Ahijah was the person who had first told Jeroboam that he would become king. Now he told him that God would remove him and his descendants from Israel's throne, because he had led the nation into idolatry (6-11). Jeroboam received immediate assurance that this prophecy would come true when his son died, as Ahijah had foretold (12-18). Before the predicted judgment fell on Jeroboam personally, he and the people of the northern kingdom suffered much in a long battle with Judah, which by that time was under the rule of Rehoboam's son Abijah (19-20; 2 Chron 13:2-20).

Rehoboam's reign in the south (14:21-31)

The story returns to the kingdom of Judah. After the division of the kingdom, Rehoboam quickly strengthened the defences on his southern border, for he knew that Egypt was likely to support Jeroboam (cf. 11:40; see 2 Chron 11:5-12). For three years Rehoboam carried on the true worship of Yahweh. This was mainly because of the help he received from a large number of priests and Levites from the north who fled to Judah rather than participate in the corrupt religion of Jeroboam (2 Chron 11:13-17).

During this time Rehoboam ruled wisely and trained his sons as administrators. The new kingdom of Judah was strong and well organized (2 Chron 11:18-23; 12:1). Unfortunately, Rehoboam's pride increased with his power, and he tried to show himself independent of God by adopting practices of the Canaanite religions (21-24). (For details of the Canaanite religions see introductory notes to the book of Judges.)

As a judgment on Judah for this sin, God allowed the Egyptians and their allies to invade the land, capture the defence cities that Rehoboam had built, invade Jerusalem, and carry off much of the gold that Solomon had carefully stored up. Only a last minute confession of sin from Rehoboam and his governors saved Judah from destruction (25-31; 2 Chron 12:2-16).

Rehoboam's policies continued (15:1-8)

Both Rehoboam and his son Abijam (Abijah) who succeeded him were unfaithful to God, though not to the extent that Jeroboam was. False religion had official recognition in the north through the new system that Jeroboam had established, but in the south it was rather a corruption that existed alongside the orthodox worship of God (15:1-5).

Abijam thought that, because the kingdom of Judah still practised the ancient religion that God had given Israel through Moses, this would guarantee God's help in giving him victory in a war with Jeroboam. He did, in fact, defeat Jeroboam, but this was because his soldiers fought in genuine reliance on God, not because God was in any way obliged to help him (6-8; 2 Chron 13:1-22).

Asa's reformation in Judah (15:9-24)

Judah's new king, Asa, spent the first ten years of his reign getting rid of Canaanite religious practices and strengthening the nation's defences. Strong faith and a strong fighting force enabled him to defeat a huge army that invaded Judah from the south. Plunder seized at the time enriched Judah considerably (2 Chron 14:1-15).

A prophet pointed out how this victory proved that, as in the time of the judges, God blessed those who trusted in him in their distress (2 Chron 15:1-7). This encouraged Asa to move ahead more zealously with his reformation. He destroyed the remaining idols and invited all the people to sacrifice to the Lord and swear their loyalty to him. Those who joined in Asa's reforms included the faithful from the north who had migrated to Judah (2 Chron 15:8-15).

Asa then removed the queen mother, who was one of the main supporters of the false religion. He also drove out the religious prostitutes, but he did not remove all the local Baal shrines (9-15).

While Asa was busy dealing with enemies from the south, the Israelite king to the north, Baasha, took the opportunity to move into Judah's territory and build a fort at Ramah, a few kilometres north of Jerusalem (16-17). Asa took what was left of his reserve funds to bribe Syria to break its treaty with Israel and attack her. Syria was easily bribed, and gained an additional prize by seizing much of Israel's northern territory. Then, while Israel was fighting Syria in the far north, Asa attacked Ramah. He destroyed the fort and carried away the materials to build two forts for his own kingdom as protection against Israel (18-22).

This policy of trusting in foreign nations showed a weakening of Asa's trust in God, and brought him into conflict with the prophet Hanani. It was a failure of faith that repeated itself just before his death. When suffering from a disease in the feet, he looked for healing through pagan sorcerers instead of trusting in God (23-24; 2 Chron 16:7-14).

After Jeroboam (15:25-16:20)

As predicted by Ahijah, Jeroboam's dynasty soon came to an end. His son Nadab was murdered by Baasha, one of his army generals, who then declared himself king. Baasha quickly removed all possible rivals by destroying Jeroboam's entire family (25-34; cf. 14:11-14). However, Baasha was no better than Jeroboam. Because he followed Jeroboam's policies,

he would suffer Jeroboam's fate (16:1-4). Just as Baasha brought Jeroboam's dynasty to an end by murdering Jeroboam's son and wiping out the rest of his family, so Baasha's own dynasty came to an end when another army general murdered his son and wiped out his family (5-14).

The new military dictator, Zimri, misjudged the support he would receive from the army, and lasted only a week. When he saw that the army preferred the commanding officer Omri, Zimri committed suicide (15-20).

The dynasty of Omri established (16:21-28)

Confusion followed Zimri's death. Omri seized the throne but was challenged by Tibni. There was civil war for four years (see v. 15,23) before Omri was officially crowned king. Two years later he moved his capital from Tirzah to Samaria, which remained the capital till the end of the northern kingdom. It was an excellent site for a capital and enabled later kings to withstand fierce attacks and strong sieges (21-24).

During the remaining six years of his reign, Omri brought a measure of stability to Israel, though religiously he was worse than former kings (25-28). His strong rule produced a dynasty that lasted four generations. Only Jehu's dynasty, which succeeded it, lasted longer.

16:29-22:53 MINISTRY OF ELIJAH

Jezebel's Baalism in Israel (16:29-17:24)

In a new political alliance, Ahab, the new king of Israel, married Jezebel, daughter of the king-priest of Phoenicia. Ahab not only accepted his wife's Baalism, but also gave it official status in Israel by building a Baal temple in the capital (29-33). The Baalism imported by Jezebel was of a kind far more evil and far more dangerous to Israel's religion than the common Canaanite Baalism practised at the high places. Jezebel's Baalism (as we shall refer to it, to distinguish it from the common Baalism) was that of the great god Melqart, whose dwelling place was the Tyre-Sidon region of Phoenicia where Jezebel came from. Jezebel then set about making this the official religion of Israel.

The rebuilding of Jericho further demonstrated the spirit of rebellion against God that characterized Israel. The project was in direct opposition to God's clear command (34; cf. Josh 6:26).

Israel's religious life was in such danger that God intervened with an unusually large number of miracles and judgments. First he sent the prophet Elijah to announce a three-year drought throughout the land (17:1). This showed the powerlessness of Baal, who was supposed to be the God of nature and fertility. At the same time it showed the power of Yahweh, who was still God of Israel. Elijah was no doubt unpopular because of the drought, so God directed him to hide near a stream in his home territory of Gilead, east of Jordan. No one knew where he was, and he did not even need to go out to look for food, because God provided it miraculously (2-6).

When Elijah's water supply dried up (7), God sent him to Zarephath in Phoenicia. This was Baal's home territory, but the drought there was just as severe. The miraculous feeding of Elijah, the widow and her household showed that God's power was greater than Baal's even in Baal's home country; and, unlike Baal's, it could work independently of nature. The events showed also that faith, not nationality, was the basis for God's blessing (8-16; cf. Luke 4:25-26). The healing of the widow's son confirmed her faith in God, and assured Elijah of God's presence and power in the dangerous and lonely days ahead (17-24).

Elijah and the prophets of Baal (18:1-46)

After three years unbroken drought, God told Elijah that the time had come to make Ahab and Israel decide clearly whether they would follow him or Baal (18:1-2). Ahab was concerned about the effect of the drought on Israel's trade and defence (for he was in danger of losing his valuable transport animals), but he was not so concerned about the religious condition of the country. He still tried to serve both God and Baal. While his queen attacked God's prophets, his God-fearing manager of the royal household tried to protect them (3-6).

Upon returning to Israel, Elijah demanded that he meet Ahab (7-16). He declared clearly to Ahab that divided loyalty was in God's sight disloyalty. This was Ahab's sin and a chief cause of Israel's troubles (17-18).

So zealous was Jezebel in establishing her religion in Israel, that she now had hundreds of Baal prophets working for her. Elijah challenged Ahab to take the prophets of Baal to Mt Carmel (believed to be a sacred Baal site) for a public contest to reveal which was the true God (19-24). Baal was supposed to be the god of nature, but he was shown to be powerless (25-29). Yahweh showed himself to have total power over nature, by defeating Baal in a victory that involved lightning, fire and water (30-39). When the people acknowledged Yahweh's victory, Elijah took advantage of the favourable circumstances to destroy Baal's prophets (40).

Elijah gave final proof that God, not Baal, was the controller of nature by announcing that God would now end the drought. As Ahab raced his chariot home to escape the approaching storm, Elijah, in the strength of God, ran before him in triumph (41-46).

God reassures Elijah (19:1-21)

When Jezebel heard that Elijah had killed her prophets, she threatened to do the same to him. She still had great power over the people, who, despite Elijah's victory at Mt Carmel, soon returned to their idolatrous ways (19:1-2; cf. v. 10). Elijah fled south through the barren regions of Judah where, overcome with despair, he wanted only to die. But God sustained him, enabling him to keep moving south till he reached Mt Sinai, the place where God had made his covenant with Israel (3-8).

Elijah doubted whether the covenant had any more meaning for Israel. The people as a whole repeatedly rebelled against its commands, and they were spiritually unaffected by the drought and its spectacular removal (9-10). God then showed Elijah that although violent and spectacular events had some use, there would be lasting benefits only as people listened to God's voice in their hearts and responded accordingly (11-14). Through the work of an enemy king Hazael, an Israelite king Jehu and the prophet Elisha, violent and spectacular events would occur as punishments on Israel; but always there would be some who heeded God's voice and remained faithful to him (15-18).

With renewed confidence Elijah returned to Israel. Elisha showed his willingness to succeed Elijah by killing his oxen (his previous source of income) and using them to provide a farewell dinner for his family and friends (19-21).

Defeat of Ben-hadad (20:1-43)

Ahab appeared to be in serious trouble when a combined army of Syria (Aram) and neighbouring states besieged the Israelite capital Samaria and demanded heavy payments. Ahab at first submitted (20:1-4), but when their demands increased, he changed his mind and decided to fight (5-12).

A prophet assured Ahab that God would give Israel victory (13-15). Ahab's plan, based on the prophet's advice, was to send a large group of young men ahead to distract the Syrians, then follow with a surprise attack by his army. Ahab won a decisive victory, but was warned to be ready for a further battle the following spring (16-22).

The Syrians improved the combined fighting force by replacing the allied commander-kings with their own professional soldiers. They also thought they had a better chance of victory by changing the location of the battle to a region where their gods were stronger. Again Israel won, proving to the Syrians (and to Ahab) that they were mistaken in thinking God's power was limited to only certain places (23-30).

Ahab captured the enemy king Ben-hadad, but let him go after Ben-hadad agreed to give back to Israel territory that Syria had previously seized. The two kings also made a trade agreement that was very favourable to Israel. This cooperation with Syria was no doubt intended to give Israel added strength against any possible invader, but it would not have been necessary had Ahab trusted in God, as his recent victory should have taught him (31-34). A young prophet acted a parable to show Ahab that because he rejected a God-given opportunity to destroy the enemy once and for all, that enemy would return and bring increasing suffering upon Israel (35-43).

Naboth's vineyard (21:1-29)

The events so far recorded of Ahab show that his religious, military and trade policies were all contrary to God's will. The story of his seizure of Naboth's vineyard shows that he was equally ungodly in the matter of common justice. Ahab at first made an honest offer to buy Naboth's vineyard. Naboth refused, as land inherited from ancestors was an Israelite's most valued possession (21:1-4). Jezebel therefore arranged to have Naboth falsely accused and executed. People were easily bribed, officials were corrupt, and there was no one to uphold the law on behalf of the ordinary citizen (5-16).

As Ahab took possession of the vineyard, Elijah met him. The prophet announced God's judgment on Ahab, and particularly on his murderous wife Jezebel (17-24). Ahab and Jezebel had done lasting damage to Israel. Two of their sons would reign over Israel, but then the dynasty of Omri would come to an end (25-29).

Ahab and Jehoshaphat (22:1-40)

Three years after making his peace agreement with King Ben-hadad of Syria, Ahab broke it. He saw the chance to retake the border town of Ramoth-gilead, and persuaded Jehoshaphat, king of Judah, to help him (22:1-4). (Jehoshaphat had previously made an alliance with Ahab by having his son Jehoram marry Ahab's daughter Athaliah; 2 Kings 8:16-18,25-26; 2 Chron 18:1.) The professional prophets in Ahab's court were more concerned with pleasing Ahab than with telling him God's will. Jehoshaphat was not impressed with them and asked Ahab to send for another prophet, Micaiah (5-12).

Micaiah, having been warned by the messenger to agree with the court prophets, simply repeated their words. But even Ahab saw that he was not speaking what he believed (13-16). Micaiah then announced God's truth plainly: the prophets were lying and Israel would be defeated (17-23). When one of the court prophets objected to this statement, Micaiah suggested he spend time alone seeking God's will instead of merely trying to impress the king. The king responded to this rebuke by throwing Micaiah into jail (24-28).

Foolishly ignoring Micaiah's prophecy, Ahab went to war with Syria. He tried to escape death by disguising himself as an ordinary soldier, but his efforts were in vain. He was wounded early in the battle, but with much courage remained at the battle scene all day to encourage his men. He died that evening (29-36). Elijah's prophecies were starting to come true (37-40; cf. 21:19).

The good work of Jehoshaphat (22:41-53)

In spite of the reformations by Asa and Jehoshaphat, the people of Judah did not remove all the Baal shrines from the local high places. But this did not weaken Jehoshaphat's determination to reform his country. He gathered a number of selected priests, Levites and administrators, and sent them to teach God's law throughout Judah (41-43; 2 Chron 17:1-9). He also strengthened Judah's army, so that other nations thought it wise to encourage his friendship (2 Chron 17:10-19). Other notable achievements of his reign were his reform of the judicial system and his remarkable defeat of a huge enemy army through faith in God (see notes on 2 Chron 19:4-20:30).

Jehoshaphat's foolishness in going with Ahab to battle spoiled an otherwise good reign (44-46; 2 Chron 19:1-3). In accordance with his policy of cooperation with Israel, he decided to join Ahab's son Ahaziah in operating a shipping line. When the ships were wrecked, Jehoshaphat realized, as a prophet had previously pointed out, that God did not want him to continue this close association with the wicked Ahaziah (47-53; 2 Chron 20:35-37).

2 Kings

1:1-8:15 MINISTRY OF ELISHA

Elijah succeeded by Elisha (1:1-2:25)

Ahab's son Ahaziah had not reigned long when he was injured in a fall. When he sent messengers to ask foreign gods whether he would recover, Elijah met them along the way. He sent them back with a message that the king would die, because he had forsaken the true God for foreign gods (1:1-10). Ahaziah sent soldiers to arrest Elijah, apparently with the intention of killing him because of his bold words. The ungodly king lost a hundred soldiers before he realized that he could neither silence nor kill the man whom God had sent to rebuke him (11-18).

Assured of this divine protection, Elijah saw that the time had come to pass on his work to Elisha. Together they visited some of the major centres where young prophets and other faithful Israelites lived. (Schools for prophets had been established in these towns as early as the time of Samuel; see notes on 1 Samuel 3:19-21.) This was a test for Elisha, who could easily have been tempted to stay at one of the schools of the prophets instead of continuing on with Elijah (2:1-6).

Elisha stood the test. He knew that since he was Elijah's spiritual heir, he had to remain with Elijah to the end, in order to receive the spiritual power to carry on his work. The mark of the heir was that he received a double portion of the father's inheritance (7-10; cf. Deut 21:17).

When Elijah was suddenly and supernaturally taken away, Elisha knew that, in this one man, Israel had lost a defender equal to a whole army of horses and chariots. But he soon had clear proof that God's special power had now passed from Elijah to him (11-14). Back in Jericho the young prophets did not believe the report of Elijah's spectacular departure, till they had spent three fruitless days looking for him (15-18).

Elisha's first two miracles symbolized blessing and cursing, the two characteristics of his future ministry. At Jericho, where people were distressed through an unhealthy water supply, he brought healing. At Bethel, where the chief shrine of Israel's corrupt religion was situated, he brought God's curse on those who rejected his message (19-25).

The increasing importance of prophets

Ever since the time of Samuel the schools of the prophets had served a useful purpose in Israel's religious life. They were valuable training centres for young men who were enthusiastic about improving the quality of spiritual life in the nation. Although members of these schools had a reputation for unorthodox behaviour (1 Sam 10:5,9-12; 19:20-24; 2 Kings 9:11), many of them were genuine followers of God.

Elijah and Elisha did not belong to these schools, but members of the schools looked upon them as their spiritual leaders. Elisha seems to have moved from school to school, spending some time in each community (see 2:1-7,15; 4:38; 6:1). His aim was not to train the young men to be professional prophets, but to build up the godly among them and so help strengthen the faithful minority in an unfaithful nation.

The cases of Elijah and Elisha show that a person did not have to be a member of one of these schools to be a prophet. Of those prophets whose writings have been collected in the Bible, few appear to have been professional prophets. The emphasis of the true prophets was that they had been called by God, not that they had received specialist training (Jer 1:5; Ezek 2:1-5; Amos 7:14-15).

Chief characteristic of the prophets was that they were God's spokesmen in announcing his will (Judg 4:4; 1 Kings 18:18; 22:8; Jer 23:18; Ezek 2:7; Amos 2:6-16; 3:7). They brought God's message to the people of their time, and this message may have included instruction for the present and warnings or promises for the future (Isa 1:16-20; Jer 18:7-10). The prophets were mainly preachers to the general public and in some cases advisers to the nation's rulers (2 Sam 7:1-3; 2 Kings 19:1-7; Isa 7:3-4; 37:5-6; 39:5-7; Jer 7:1-7; 38:14; Zeph 2:1-3).

Elisha helps in the defeat of Moab (3:1-27)

Joram (or Jehoram) succeeded his brother Ahaziah in Israel. He was not as bad as his father Ahab, and at least showed some displeasure with Baal worship by removing a sacred pillar that his father had built (3:1-3).

After Ahab's death, Moab had revolted against Israelite rule and refused to pay tribute, but Ahaziah did nothing about it (see 1:1). Joram tried to recover this valuable source of income by a military attack in which he had the support of Judah and Edom, both of whom would benefit if Moab was weakened. The army marched around the southern end of the Dead Sea and approached Moab from the deserts of Edom (4-8).

When, after a week's march, the army had no water, Joram blamed God. Jehoshaphat knew God better and asked him through the prophet Elisha what they should do (9-12). Elisha felt no obligation to help Joram, but for the sake of Jehoshaphat he announced that God would supply enough water to meet all their needs. They were then to attack and devastate Moab. That night, probably as a result of a storm in the distant red hills of Edom, water flowed down the dry creek bed beside which the army was camped (13-20).

Next day the refreshed allies slaughtered the falsely confident Moabites and devastated their towns, farmlands and forests. They seemed certain of complete conquest of the land when suddenly, while approaching the last stronghold, they saw the Moabite king sacrifice his son. This must have so inspired the Moabites and terrified the Israelites that the allied army was forced to retreat and finally return home (21-27). Relieved of pressure from their attackers, the Moabites took the opportunity to rebuild their country. Soon they were engaging in guerilla attacks against Israel (see 13:20).

Elisha's miracles

At this point the writer of Kings departs from his chronological pattern and recounts a number of incidents to demonstrate the nature of Elisha's work. Elisha had an important part to play in God's judgment on the northern kingdom because of its unfaithfulness during the time of the dynasty of Omri. He also had to help preserve and strengthen that small body of believers in Israel who remained faithful to God (see 1 Kings 19:15-18). A collection of six stories (4:1-6:7) shows how Elisha used his supernatural powers to help preserve this small remnant when it was threatened with extinction. A second collection (6:8-8:15) deals with that part of his work which was concerned with judgment on the nation Israel.

Miracles of care for the remnant (4:1-44)

The widow of one of the prophets was in desperate trouble. She had hardly any food left and was about to lose her only means of income; for her sons were to be taken from her in payment for a debt. Elisha's miraculous provision of oil enabled her to pay the debt and so preserve a few of God's faithful in days of extreme hardship (4:1-7).

Another of Israel's faithful was the wife of a wealthy landowner. She recognized Elisha as God's representative and offered him hospitality as often as he needed it. As with the poor widow of the previous story, Elisha provided for the woman's future, in this case by promising her a son (8-17). Some years later the son died. The woman, still strong in faith, reasoned that seeing the prophet had promised her the son in the first place (even though she had not asked for a son), he had the responsibility to correct what had gone wrong. He was God's representative and she would speak with no other (18-31). She insisted that Elisha himself go to her house, and again she would accept no other. Her faith was rewarded when Elisha brought her son back to life (32-37).

Elisha moved around the schools of the young prophets to instruct and encourage the faithful. At one school, during a time of famine, food was so scarce that the men had to eat wild plants. In these circumstances they suffered a serious loss when one of their meals was ruined because somebody had mistakenly cooked a poisonous plant. God lovingly provided for them through Elisha (38-41).

On another occasion God's care for the faithful was shown when a farmer brought an offering of food that was miraculously multiplied to feed Elisha and a hundred of his followers (42-44).

More miracles of care (5:1-6:7)

Syria was Israel's most powerful neighbour during Elisha's lifetime, and was a constant source of trouble around Israel's borders. When the Syrian army commander Naaman approached the king of Israel with a request to be treated for leprosy, the king of Israel interpreted this as a trick by Syria aimed at creating war (5:1-7). Elisha, however, saw it as an opportunity to reveal God's power to the military commander whom God was preserving to lead Syria against Israel (8-14). Naaman's knowledge of the one true God was still imperfect, but at least he had a more sincere faith than many of the Israelites (15-19; cf. Luke 4:27).

Elisha had refused payment for the healing, as he was God's servant, not a wonder-worker looking for money (see v. 15-16). But most of the prophets lived in poverty, and Gehazi could not resist the temptation to seek some financial benefit from the miracle. Fittingly, he was punished by receiving Naaman's leprosy (20-27).

In one school of the prophets, their accommodation needed rebuilding, but during the work a borrowed axe head was lost. For people who could not afford an axe in the first place, this was no small loss. Again God met his people's need, showing they could always depend on him (6:1-7).

Miracles of warning to Israel (6:8-8:15)

The remaining stories of Elisha concentrate on his dealings with the rulers of Israel and Syria. God was going to use Syria to punish Israel for its sin during the period of the Omri dynasty, but first he had various lessons to teach the two nations.

On one occasion when Israel and Syria were fighting each other, Elisha repeatedly warned the Israelite king of Syrian ambushes (8-10). The Syrian king was furious when he learnt why his ambushes failed, and sent an army to capture Elisha. Instead Elisha took control of the Syrian soldiers and led them to the Israelite capital, Samaria (11-19).

Israel's king thought this a perfect opportunity to slaughter the enemy, but Elisha directed him to feed them and release them. As a result peace was temporarily restored between Israel and Syria. The whole story was a lesson to both countries that God controlled their destinies (20-23).

Some time later the Syrians returned and besieged Samaria. With people dying of starvation and no help from God in sight, the king blamed Elisha for the trouble and tried to murder him (24-33). Elisha assured the king there would be plenty of food the next day (7:1-2), but when a report reached the king that it had arrived, he was slow to believe (3-12). The report was true, and at least one person was trampled to death as people rushed to buy (13-20).

In spite of the judgment that had begun to fall on Israel, God was still caring for those who were faithful to him. The woman whose son had been raised to life (see 4:8-37) was saved from poverty by being warned of a famine soon to hit Israel. She went and lived elsewhere during the famine, but by God's control of events she received back all her property when she returned to Israel (8:1-6).

Meanwhile God was continuing to prepare Syria to be his instrument to punish Israel. The king Ben-hadad was seriously ill, but he would have recovered had not Hazael murdered him. Hazael then became king. Elisha wept when he saw the terrible suffering that Hazael would bring upon Israel (7-15; cf. 1 Kings 19:15).

8:16-12:21 REMOVAL OF JEZEBEL'S BAALISM

Jezebel's Baalism spreads to Judah (8:16-9:10)

The writer now returns to his historical account of the kings of Judah and Israel. Jehoshaphat's son Jehoram, who was married to Athaliah the daughter of Ahab and Jezebel, became king of Judah after his father's death. Through Athaliah, Jezebel's Baalism spread to Judah. Jehoram made sure that no one challenged his right to do as he pleased by killing all likely rivals. Because of this and his support for Jezebel's Baalism, he was assured of a horrible death (16-19; 2 Chron 21:4,11-15,18-20).

For David's sake God did not yet destroy Judah, though the nation certainly weakened. Edom to the south and Libnah on the Philistine border freed themselves from Judah's rule, while the Arabs and the Philistines raided and plundered with great success (20-24; 2 Chron 21:16-17).

During one of these raids most of Judah's royal family was killed. Jehoram's sole surviving son, Ahaziah, became king after his father's death (2 Chron 22:1), but in his short reign he proved to be no better than his father. He was dominated by his mother Athaliah, along with relatives of hers from the north whom she had brought into the Jerusalem palace (2 Chron 22:3-4). He joined his uncle Joram (or Jehoram) of Israel in war against Hazael of Syria. When Joram retreated to the summer palace at Jezreel to recover from wounds received in battle, Ahaziah went to visit him (25-29).

Elisha saw that the time had come for him to carry out his last major responsibility, which was to anoint Israel's army commander Jehu as king. Jehu's job was to rid Israel of the entire family of Ahab and Jezebel (9:1-10; cf. 1 Kings 19:16).

Jehu's revolution (9:11-10:14)

On hearing of Jehu's anointing as king, Jehu's senior officers swore their immediate allegiance (11-13). Without allowing time for news of the rebellion to leak out, Jehu set off for Jezreel (14-16). As he approached the city, Joram and Ahaziah, unaware of the rebellion, went out to meet him. Joram was killed on the spot, appropriately at Naboth's vineyard (17-26; cf. 1 Kings 21:17-19). Ahaziah was killed after a chase (27-29). Jehu quickly went on to Jezreel to deal with the queen mother, Jezebel. Knowing she could expect the same fate as Joram, she prepared herself to meet the executioner with royal dignity. She died a horrible death, as the prophet had foretold (30-37; cf. v. 10).

The massacre continued. After arranging for the execution of Ahab's seventy surviving male descendants in Samaria, Jehu displayed their heads as a warning to any likely rebels (10:1-8). He tried to make the people believe that the seventy had been killed directly by God, but they were probably not convinced. They well knew that the only way Jehu could make his throne safe was to kill all Ahab's descendants. God's earlier announcement of judgment on the family of Ahab gave Jehu the opportunity to carry out his plans (9-11; cf. 9:7-9). Since the late Ahaziah was a descendant of Ahab, Jehu killed Ahaziah's relatives as well (12-14).

End of Jezebel's Baalism in Israel (10:15-36)

Jehu next put into operation a plan to rid Israel of all Jezebel's Baal-worshipping followers. In this he had the cooperation of Jehonadab, a man who had led his people to give up the agricultural life (possibly because of its tendencies to Baal worship) and go back to the simple way of life followed by Abraham and the early Israelites (15-17; cf. Jer 35:6-10). Through deceit and butchery, Jehu wiped out Jezebel's Baal worshippers (18-27).

However, Jehu did not remove the idol worship established earlier by Jeroboam. This gives further indication that his anti-Baal campaign resulted from political, rather than religious, motives. Nevertheless, he destroyed the dynasty of Omri along with its particular form of Baal worship, and for this God rewarded him. His dynasty would last longer than any other in the northern kingdom (28-31).

As the story in Kings shows, Jehu went far beyond what was necessary to bring God's judgment on the dynasty of Omri. His needless butchery, still talked about a century later, would be the reason why his own dynasty would come to a bloody end (Hosea 1:4).

Jehu's massacre of all the nation's leading administrators left the nation's internal government weak and unstable (see 10:11). The slaughter of Jezebel's descendants brought the long-standing treaty with Tyre and Sidon in the north to a sudden end. The murder of Judah's king and his relatives lost Israel the support of her sister nation to the south. Jehu's withdrawal of Israel's troops from Ramoth-gilead to support his revolution weakened Israel's eastern border (see 9:4-5,11-14). Syria's king

Hazael was quick to attack, and over a time seized most of Israel's territory east of Jordan. Elisha's prophecy was coming true (32-36; cf. 8:12).

End of Jezebel's Baalism in Judah (11:1-21)

Ahaziah, king of Judah, had been assassinated the day of Jehu's revolt (see 9:27). His mother Athaliah showed herself a true daughter of Jezebel when she killed all her grandchildren (except one who escaped), seized the throne, and established her mother's Baalism in Judah. The one who escaped was the baby Joash, who was rescued by his aunt (a princess married to the high priest; 2 Chron 22:11) and hidden for six years in the temple (11:1-3).

When Joash was seven years old, the high priest Jehoiada, with the support of the palace and temple guards, claimed the throne for him. The coup was planned for a sabbath day, when the changing of the guard ensured that a much larger group of guards than usual would be at the temple (4-8). All went according to plan without bloodshed, apart from the execution of Athaliah (9-16).

Because Athaliah had interrupted the line of Davidic kings, the restoration of the Davidic king to the throne was accompanied by a renewal of the covenant. All Jerusalem celebrated the great day. The people went wild with joy, destroying Athaliah's Baal temple and all that belonged to it (17-21).

True worship restored in Judah (12:1-21)

Under the influence of Jehoiada, Joash encouraged the worship of Yahweh (12:1-3). But his project for repairing the temple (damaged by Athaliah and her followers; 2 Chron 24:7) was hindered by the priests. They lacked enthusiasm and were inefficient, and possibly dishonest, in handling the finances (4-8). Joash therefore separated the funds for the priests' personal use from the funds for the temple repairs, and placed the latter under the supervision of an official of the royal treasury. He then hired workmen who had a desire to do the work properly and honestly (9-16).

After Jehoiada's death, Joash, no longer under the strong priestly influence of his life-long adviser, turned to idolatry. When rebuked by the new high priest Zechariah, Joash had Zechariah murdered (2 Chron 24:15-22; Matt 23:35). Judgment on Joash was swift and severe. Hazael led his troops across Israel and south into Judah as far as Gath. He then turned to attack Jerusalem, and Joash saved the city only by robbing the temple treasury and sending the money to Hazael (17-18; 2 Chron 24:23-24). But he could not buy off the judgment that was to fall on him personally. Soon after the battle he was assassinated by his officers, and was not even given a royal burial (19-21; 2 Chron 24:25-27).

The prophecy of Joel

It was possibly during the early part of Joash's reign that the prophet Joel wrote his book. During that time Joash was still a boy and the government was largely in the hands of Jehoiada. If that is so, Joel was the first of the writing prophets (i.e. prophets who wrote books of the Bible).

However, the book of Joel mentions no date of writing, and it could possibly have been written many years later, perhaps after the return from captivity and even later than the time of Nehemiah. If that is the case, Joel was among the last of the writing prophets. The message of the book is straightforward and can be readily understood regardless of its date of writing.

Joel's reason for writing was a severe plague of locusts that devastated Judah. He interpreted this as a judgment on Judah for its sin, and urged the people to repent. In response to their repentance, God removed the locusts and promised to give the nation productive crops again (Joel 1:4; 2:10-14,25). Joel saw the events as symbolic of God's future judgment on all enemies and his coming blessing on all the faithful (Joel 3:16-19).

13:1-17:41 HISTORY TO THE FALL OF ISRAEL

After the anti-Baal revolution (13:1-14:22)

Jehu's son Jehoahaz followed the sins of earlier Israelite kings, and so did his people. The Syrian attacks foreseen by Elisha were so severe that, had God not mercifully intervened, the whole population would have been left homeless and the entire army destroyed (13:1-9).

The next king, Jehoash, learnt from Elisha that he would win three battles against Syria. He would have won more, had he not lacked faith in God (10-19). During Jehoash's reign Elisha died, but dramatic events at Elisha's tomb showed that the God who had worked through him was still alive and powerful (20-21). Jehoash won three battles as Elisha had foretold, and thereby regained some of Israel's lost territory (22-25).

After the murder of his father Joash, Amaziah came to the throne of Judah. Once firmly in control, he executed his father's murderers (14:1-6). He planned to attack Edom, but when a census of his army revealed that he had not enough soldiers, he hired trained men from Israel. A prophet told him to send the Israelites back, for God would

not give Judah's army victory while it contained men from the ungodly northern kingdom. Angry at missing out on the chance to raid the Edomites, the northerners raided the cities of Judah instead. Amaziah, meanwhile, attacked and defeated Edom (7; 2 Chron 25:5-13).

Foolishly, Amaziah brought back to his palace some idols of the defeated Edomites. His military victory gave him such self-assurance that he thought he could act independently of God and ignore the warnings of God's prophet (2 Chron 25:14-16). Confident in his increased military experience, he decided to attack Israel. The Israelite king warned him that Judah would be defeated, but Amaziah persisted. Judah was defeated, Amaziah was taken captive and Jerusalem was plundered (8-16; cf. 13:12). Later he was allowed to return to his throne, but apparently he was unpopular and, like his father, was assassinated (17-22).

An era of prosperity (14:23-15:7)

During the long reigns of Jeroboam II in the north and Azariah (or Uzziah) in the south, Israel and Judah experienced political stability and economic development such as they had not known since the days of David and Solomon. This was possible partly because political conditions in the region were favourable to Israel and Judah.

Syria had been used by God to punish Israel for its sins in following Baal. With the death of Hazael, Syrian power declined and Israel regained lost territory (see 13:24-25). Events further favoured Israel when Assyria, the rising power in the region, became involved with enemies to its north and for forty years did not bother Israel and Judah.

Under these conditions Jeroboam II expanded his kingdom from Hamath in the north to the Dead Sea in the south, as foretold by the prophet Jonah. This gave him control over many trade routes, which further helped Israel's economy. But religiously he was a failure, and the evils of his reign were condemned by the prophets Amos and Hosea (23-29; cf. Amos 1:1; 7:10-11; Hosea 1:1; 7:1-3).

Azariah (or Uzziah) in Judah began his reign well, mainly because of the godly instruction that he received from his teacher Zechariah (15:1-3; 2 Chron 26:1-5). He spread his rule west to the Mediterranean Sea, east over Ammonite territory, and south as far as the Red Sea and Egypt. This gave him control over important land and sea trade routes (see 14:22; 2 Chron 26:6-8). He fortified the capital city Jerusalem, improved agricultural and pastoral conditions in every region of the country, built up the armed forces and equipped his troops with the most modern weapons (2 Chron 26:9-15). His big mistake was to think that he could become religious head of the nation as well. God punished him with leprosy, and his son Jotham acted as joint ruler till Uzziah's death (4-7; 2 Chron 26:16-23).

Jonah and the Assyrians

Israel's prosperity during the era produced within many Israelites, even the prophet Jonah, a selfish, nationalistic spirit. Jonah had already successfully predicted Jeroboam II's victories over a number of enemies (see 14:25), and no doubt he would have liked to see the downfall of Assyria. The capital of Assyria, Nineveh, was already threatened by an enemy from the north. But God told Jonah to go and warn Nineveh of the coming attack, and urge the people to repent of their sins so that they might avoid destruction (Jonah 3:4-5,10).

NEIGHBOURS OF ISRAEL-JUDAH

At first Jonah refused to go, for he preferred to see Nineveh overthrown. He had to learn that God was the controller of all nations, and he would have mercy on any who turned from their sins, regardless of nationality. This was of particular importance in the case of the Assyrians, for God was preserving them to be his instrument to punish Israel.

The fiery preaching of Amos

Two hundred years earlier, in the time of Solomon, a distinct merchant class had begun to appear in Israel (see notes on 1 Kings 9:26-10:29). During the time of Jeroboam II and Uzziah (the eighth century BC), the merchants grew into a powerful group. Society was no longer built around the simple agricultural life. As commerce and trade developed, so did city life. This brought with it greed and oppression, as the upper classes exploited the poorer classes. Bribery was widespread, the courts were corrupt, and the poor were left with no way of obtaining justice.

Amos was the first of several prophets to speak out against these evils. He was a shepherd-farmer who knew how the poor suffered, because he himself had to deal with ruthless merchants and corrupt officials in selling his produce. In his fiery preaching he condemned the greed and luxury of the rich. He knew they had gained their wealth by cheating and injustice (Amos 2:6-7; 3:10,15; 6:4-6; 8:4-6). They still carried out their religious exercises, but these were worthless in God's sight as long as the worshippers persisted in wrongdoing (Amos 5:21-24; 8:10).

Most of Amos's attacks were directed against the northern kingdom (Amos 2:6; 4:1; 6:1; 7:10). The people, it seems, took little notice. Amos clearly saw what Israel's upper classes failed to see, namely, that the nation was heading for a terrible judgment from God (Amos 3:12; 6:14; 7:11).

Hosea's experiences

Despite Amos's accusations and warnings, social conditions in Israel worsened. This is seen from the writings of Hosea, who began to preach late in the reigns of Jeroboam II and Uzziah, and continued through the reigns of succeeding kings (Hosea 1:1). Like Amos, Hosea was concerned chiefly with Israel, though he referred also to Judah.

Hosea saw that Israel's society was corrupt because its religion was corrupt. The priests were as bad as the merchants and officials. Baal worship, complete with its fertility rites and prostitution, was widely practised. Israel did not know the character of Yahweh (Hosea 4:1-6,17-19; 5:4,15; 6:6-10; 7:2-4; 9:15; 13:16; cf. Amos 2:7-8).

Since Israel's covenant bond with Yahweh was likened to the marriage bond, Israel's association with other gods was really spiritual adultery. Hosea began to understand what this meant to God when his own wife left him for other lovers. But her pleasures did not last and she was sold as a slave. All this time Hosea remained faithful to his marriage covenant, and when he found his wife a slave, he bought her back. It was a picture of the covenant love of God for his unfaithful people. They too would go into captivity, but after cleansing from the filth of their adulterous association with the Canaanite gods, God would bring them back to live in their land again (Hosea 2:5-10; 3:1-5).

Chaos in Israel (15:8-26)

The long and prosperous reign of Jeroboam II brought political as well as social and religious troubles. When Jeroboam died, Israel entered a time of political chaos, as ambitious men fought to seize power. The nation lost its stability, and Assyria soon began to show interest in adding Israel to its rapidly expanding empire.

Jehu's dynasty, which began bloodily, ended bloodily when its fifth king was murdered after a reign of only six months (8-12; cf. 10:30; Hosea 1:4; Amos 7:9). The assassin, Shallum, reigned only one month before he was murdered by Menahem, who then seized the throne (13-16). Menahem survived ten years, but only by buying the protection of the Assyrian king Tiglath-pileser III (also known as Pul). This policy damaged Israel's economy, weakened its independence and opened the way for eventual conquest by Assyria (17-22).

Israel's army commander Pekah was opposed to this pro-Assyrian policy. After Menahem died and was succeeded by his son Pekahiah, Pekah murdered Pekahiah and made himself king (23-26). The plots, assassinations and repeated changes in foreign policy were condemned by God's prophets (Hosea 5:13; 7:3,7,11; 8:4; 10:3-4; 12:1).

Isaiah and Ahaz

Meanwhile Tiglath-pileser III was working towards a complete military conquest of Israel. (The prophets had already predicted such a conquest; see Hosea 10:5-8; Amos 7:17.) Realizing this, the Syrian king Rezin and the Israelite king Pekah formed a defence alliance to resist Assyria. They tried to persuade Judah's king Jotham and the succeeding king Ahaz to join them, but the kings of Judah refused. Rezin and Pekah then attacked Ahaz, with the aim of conquering Judah, putting their own king on the throne, then forcing Judah to join their anti-Assyrian alliance (see 15:37; 16:5; Isa 7:1-2,6).

As the Israel-Syrian invasion force approached, Ahaz panicked. But one man among his advisers, the prophet Isaiah, remained calm and urged the king to trust in God. Isaiah assured Ahaz that he need not fear, for Israel-Syria would not defeat Judah, but would themselves be conquered by Assyria. Ahaz had only to trust in God (Isa 7:2-9; 8:4). However, Ahaz neither trusted in God nor believed Isaiah. Instead he asked Assyria to come and help him. Isaiah warned that this was foolish, for it would put Judah under Assyria's control (Isa 8:5-8). Again Ahaz ignored the advice (see 16:7-8).

Assyria then attacked Syria and Israel. Assyria's policy was to carry off the people of a conquered country into other countries of the Assyrian Empire (to prevent rebellion breaking out in the conquered territory) and replace them with settlers from elsewhere. Therefore, when Tiglath-pileser conquered Syria, he transported the people into captivity in Assyria (732 BC). This brought the kingdom of Syria

to an end, as foretold by God's prophets (see 16:9; Isa 17:1; Amos 1:4-5). Tiglath-pileser attacked Israel also, overrunning its eastern and northern territory and taking the inhabitants into captivity (see 15:29). This was the beginning of the end for Israel.

Judah's decline under Ahaz (15:27-16:20)

The writer of Kings records the Assyrian attack mentioned above. Pekah's policy had proved fatal and he was assassinated by Hoshea, a sympathizer with Assyria. Hoshea then became king and won temporary relief for Israel by submitting to Assyria's control (27-31).

Before speaking further of Hoshea, the writer returns to the time before Pekah was assassinated. Pekah's program for the conquest of Judah had begun during the reign of Jotham, but reached its climax in the reign of Jotham's successor Ahaz. The aggression of Israel-Syria and the constant threat from Assyria prompted Jotham to build defence fortifications throughout Judah. He also made his borders secure by taking control of neighbouring Ammon (32-38; 2 Chron 27:3-6).

Because of his lack of faith in God, Ahaz had a disastrous reign. Apart from the damage he did to Judah by following other gods, he almost ruined the nation's economy by his policies in the war with Israel and Syria. Buying Assyrian aid did not save him from heavy losses in the war, and he would have suffered even more had not Israel released the war prisoners taken from Judah. His weakened country suffered further at the hands of invading Edomites from the south and Philistines from the west. He also lost the Red Sea port of Elath (Ezion-geber) (16:1-9; 2 Chron 28:5-18).

Earlier, after losing a battle with Syria, Ahaz had turned from Yahweh to worship the 'victorious' Syrian gods. He closed the temple to Yahweh in Jerusalem and built altars to foreign gods throughout Judah (2 Chron 28:22-25). But Assyria, acting on Ahaz's request, had now conquered Syria (see v. 9) and established its religion and its administration in Damascus. Ahaz now replaced the Syrians' religion with the Assyrians', and built a copy of their altar in Jerusalem (10-16). Ahaz's hiring of Assyria was so costly that he removed valuable metal from the temple to pay Tiglath-pileser (17-20). (It was after this conquest of Syria that Tiglath-pileser overran eastern and northern Israel; see 15:29.)

The importance of Isaiah

There was great variety in the kinds of people God chose to be his prophets. Whereas Amos was a poor farmer, Isaiah was a person of high social standing, an adviser to the king who was able to influence national policy. His ministry had begun long before the time of Ahaz. It began in the year of Uzziah's death and continued through the reigns of Jotham, Ahaz and Hezekiah (Isa 1:1; 6:1). The traditional belief is that he was executed during the reign of the wicked Manasseh by being sawn in two (cf. 21:1-2,16; Heb 11:37).

In the early part of the book of Isaiah, the prophet records his attempts to persuade Ahaz to trust in God, not in Assyria, to save Judah from the Israel-Syrian invasion. In the next part of the book he records his attempts to control the zeal of the good king Hezekiah, who was rather too keen to rely on help from Egypt in revolting against Assyria (see notes on 18:1-20:21). Isaiah shows that all these nations, and others as well, were under God's judgment. Judah too would be punished for its sin, and its people taken into captivity.

The final section of the book of Isaiah shows that God would not cast off his people for ever. He would preserve that minority of people who had always remained faithful to him, and through them he would rebuild the nation. God's people would return to their land and enjoy peace and prosperity once more. The Messiah-king would come, and his kingdom would spread to all nations.

Micah accuses the rich landowners

No doubt one man who cooperated with Isaiah was Micah, who prophesied during the same period of Judah's history (Isa 1:1; Micah 1:1). While Isaiah was using his influence at Jerusalem's royal court, Micah was coming to the aid of the small farmers. (He came from a farming village and was probably a farmer himself; Micah 1:1,14.) As Amos and Hosea had done before him, he condemned the injustice, greed and false religion that were widespread in Judah, especially among the upper class people of Jerusalem (Micah 3:1-3,9-11; 6:9-12; 7:3).

Micah was particularly concerned at how the rich ruthlessly gained possession of the land of the small farmers. They lent money to the farmers at high interest, then, when the farmers found it impossible to pay their debts, seized the farmers' houses and land as payment (Micah 2:1-3,9). The farmers then were required to rent their land from their new masters, which increased their burden even more. The state of affairs showed no thought for the rights of others, no understanding of true religion, and no knowledge of the character of God. It was a sure indication that Judah was heading for judgment (Micah 3:12; 6:16).

End of the northern kingdom (17:1-41)

Some time after Shalmaneser V succeeded Tiglath-pileser III as king of Assyria, the Israelite king Hoshea tried to show himself independent of Assyria by refusing to pay the annual tribute. He thought that with Egyptian support his rebellion would be successful. Shalmaneser put an end to such hopes by invading Israel and besieging Samaria. After three years Israel's defence collapsed, and Shalmaneser's successor, Sargon II, captured Samaria and carried off the survivors into captivity (722 BC). This was the end of the northern kingdom (17:1-6).

The fact that Israel's nineteen kings were spread over nine dynasties is an indication of the instability that characterized the northern kingdom throughout its history.

At this point the writer comments at length on the reason for the fall of Israel, namely, the spiritual failure of the people as a whole. Though Jeroboam I was responsible for changing the official religious policy, the real cause of the failure lay with the common people, who readily copied local religious practices. This was open disobedience to God's covenant commands given by Moses and repeated by the prophets (7-17). In the end God punished the people by making them captives in a foreign land, as they had once been in Egypt. Only Judah was left, but it too was turning from God (18-23).

In accordance with their normal policy, the Assyrians resettled people from other parts of their Empire into cities of the northern kingdom (which was now known as Samaria). These settlers tried to avoid punishment from Israel's God by combining the worship of Yahweh with their own religion. They also intermarried with the Israelites left in the land. Their descendants, known as Samaritans, being of mixed blood and mixed religion, were despised by the Jews (24-33; cf. John 4:9; 8:48). The presence of all these religions in the land God gave to Israel was in sharp contrast to God's plan, which was for Israel to worship him alone (34-41).

18:1-25:30 HISTORY TO THE FALL OF JUDAH

New policies under Hezekiah (18:1-12)

With the destruction of the kingdom of Israel in the north and the disastrous reign of Ahaz in the south, Assyrian influence in Palestine was at its peak. In spite of this, the young king Hezekiah set out on the bold task of reforming Judah's religion and freeing Judah from Assyrian power. He destroyed all the local idolatrous shrines (something that no king since David had been able to do), and because of this the writer of Kings regarded him as Judah's greatest king (18:1-6).

(For Hezekiah's extensive religious reforms see notes on 2 Chronicles 29:1-31:21. The reforms were largely external, being concerned mainly with temple services and ceremonies. There is no evidence of any lasting change in either the rulers or the people, and no direct reference to the reforms by the prophets of the time, Isaiah and Micah.)

Hezekiah realized that once he reversed his father's policy concerning Assyria, the Assyrian army would attack Jerusalem. To prepare against siege he strengthened the city's defences and improved its water supply (see 20:20; 2 Chron 32:5). Once he was assured of military support from Egypt, he revolted against Assyria by refusing to pay further tribute. Isaiah opposed this reliance on Egypt, just as during the reign of Ahaz he opposed reliance on Assyria. What Judah needed was not military help from Egypt but quiet faith in God (7-8; Isa 30:1-3,15). Assyria's recent conquest of the northern kingdom should have been a warning to Hezekiah (9-12).

Freed from Assyrian power (18:13-19:37)

When news reached Hezekiah that the Assyrian army, under the new king Sennacherib, was heading for Jerusalem, he quickly prepared the defences of the city. He also cut off any water supply outside the city that might be of help to the besieging armies. Above all, he encouraged his troops to trust in God for victory (13; 2 Chron 32:1-8). But, on seeing the strength of the siege, Hezekiah began to repent of his rebellion and offered to pay whatever money Sennacherib demanded (14-16).

After taking a large payment from Hezekiah, the Assyrian king showed that he intended to punish him anyway. He sent three senior officers to demand that Hezekiah surrender. Unknowingly, the Assyrian officers agreed with Isaiah (though for different reasons) that reliance on Egypt was useless (17-21; cf. Isa 30:1-3; 31:1-3,8). In any case, they said, God had sent the Assyrians to punish Jerusalem (22-25).

On seeing how their words troubled Jerusalem's officials, the Assyrians spoke even more boldly. They tried to persuade the common people to surrender, promising to treat them well in the lands to which they would take them (26-32). Their big mistake, however, was to insult Yahweh by claiming he was no stronger than the gods of other nations whom the Assyrians had conquered (33-37).

When Hezekiah sent to enquire about the situation from Isaiah, the reply made it clear that God would not tolerate the Assyrians' mockery

(19:1-7). The Assyrians temporarily withdrew from Jerusalem to deal with a crisis elsewhere, but sent a letter renewing their threats and challenging God to resist them (8-14). Hezekiah then presented the whole matter to God, who, being the only true and living God, was the only one who could save Jerusalem (15-19).

Isaiah brought God's reply. It condemned the Assyrians for mocking God and boasting of their achievements, especially when they were only God's instrument to carry out his judgments. God would therefore punish them and save Jerusalem (20-28). Fields not sown because of the enemy's siege would become fruitful again, and the number of genuine believers in Judah would increase (29-34).

Having announced his plans, God then acted. The Assyrian army was almost destroyed (701 BC), and although Sennacherib escaped home, he was later assassinated (35-37).

Warning concerning Babylon (20:1-21)

It seems that the events recorded in 20:1-19 occurred before those recorded in 18:13-19:37. Hezekiah was about to die, but, in answer to his prayer, God promised to extend his life. This was for the purpose of bringing Judah through the time of conflict with Assyria that has just been described (20:1-7). God gave Hezekiah a miraculous sign to prove that he would do what he had promised (8-11).

At this time Babylon was increasing in power and was looking for allies to help it overthrow Assyria. Hezekiah's illness gave the Babylonian king an excuse to send representatives to Jerusalem, in the hope that they could encourage Hezekiah to join with Babylon against Assyria. Hezekiah was proud of the prosperity he had brought to his kingdom, and was willing to cooperate (12-13; 2 Chron 32:25,31). Again Isaiah condemned this willingness to enter into foreign alliances. He saw that it would result in conquest by the allied nation (14-21).

Manasseh's evil reign (21:1-26)

Hezekiah's reformation had cleansed Judah of the outward forms of foreign religion, but the inward spiritual condition of most people had not changed. The faithful remnant was still small (see 19:30-31). Possibly under pressure from Assyria, Manasseh reversed his father's religious policy and with almost fanatical zeal reintroduced foreign religious ideas of every kind. Fifty-five years under his rule left Judah in a worse spiritual condition than that for which God had destroyed the original Canaanites (21:1-9). Therefore, God announced he would punish Judah as he had punished Israel. No later king was able to remove fully the evil that Manasseh brought upon Judah (10-16; cf. 23:26-27).

Towards the end of his life, Manasseh rebelled against Assyria. He was taken captive and brought before the Assyrian leaders at Babylon, which at that time was under the control of Assyria. Later he was allowed to return to Jerusalem. Believing that his captivity was a punishment by God for his sins, he attempted to return to the true worship of Yahweh. But it was too late to undo the damage he had done over half a century, and his reform had no lasting effect (17-18; 2 Chron 33:10-20).

Manasseh's son Amon returned to the earlier policies of his father, but after a brief reign he was murdered. Some of the leading citizens, tired of the constant cruelty and bloodshed (cf. v. 16), executed Amon's murderers and put Amon's eight year old son Josiah on the throne (about 640 BC). In this way power rested with the king's advisers, who could then follow policies that would benefit the people and restore peace and stability to Judah (19-26).

Zephaniah and Josiah

By the time he was twenty, Josiah had developed his own policy and begun reforms that lasted many years (2 Chron 34:1-5). He was possibly prompted to introduce these reforms through the preaching of the prophet Zephaniah. Zephaniah was probably not much older than Josiah and appears to have been related to him (cf. Zeph 1:1).

So far as we know, Zephaniah was the first prophet to appear in Judah for over seventy years. The Bible has no record of any prophets during the evil reigns of Manasseh and Amon. Zephaniah's work marked the beginning of a new period of prophetic activity in Judah. He lived in Jerusalem, where he denounced the same evils as Isaiah and Micah denounced a century earlier (Zeph 1:4-9; 3:3-4). His announcements of judgment no doubt prompted many of the people to change their ways and cooperate in Josiah's reforms (Zeph 2:3).

Josiah repairs the temple (22:1-20)

Included in Josiah's reformation was a project for extensive repairs to the temple, which had been damaged during the reigns of Manasseh and Amon (22:1-7). By this time Assyrian power had weakened considerably, which enabled Josiah to carry out his reformation program without interference from outside. He even extended his power into the conquered territory of the former northern kingdom (see 23:15,19; 2 Chron 34:6-7).

During the fifty-seven years when Manasseh and Amon reigned, a new generation had grown up in Judah who knew nothing of the law of God as given to Israel by Moses. When workers on the temple found some scrolls of this long-forgotten law, Josiah, on reading the scrolls, was shocked to learn how far Judah had turned away from God (8-13). He sent messengers to ask a prophet what to do, and received the reply that, despite his personal faith, Judah was doomed. But he could continue his reforming work, so that the judgment might be postponed to the reign of some future king (14-20).

Extent of Josiah's reforms (23:1-27)

Josiah was not discouraged by the prophecy of judgment on Judah. Rather he intensified his efforts to change his people. His greater reformation would now begin. To gain the cooperation of all the leading citizens, he explained to them the contents of the book on which he was basing his reforms, and invited them to join with him in renewing the covenant with God (23:1-3).

With uncompromising zeal, Josiah removed all idolatrous priests and destroyed all shrines and sacred objects associated with other gods, whether in Judah or in former Israel. After the removal of the country shrines, he centralized Judah's worship in Jerusalem where it could be properly supervised. Although most priests came to live in Jerusalem, some refused (4-14; 2 Chron 34:6-7). At Bethel he burnt the bones of the false prophets on their altar and then destroyed it, as foretold by a godly prophet of an earlier era. But he was careful not to damage the tomb where the bones of the godly prophet lay (15-20; cf. 1 Kings 13:1-3,29-32).

On the positive side, Josiah re-established the worship of Yahweh by keeping the Passover. The festival had added significance at this time, as it symbolized a fresh deliverance from bondage (21-23; for details of this Passover see 2 Chron 35:1-19). He also ordered the removal of all private household gods, and prohibited all forms of spiritism and fortune telling. Apart from Hezekiah, Josiah was the only king of Judah to receive unqualified praise from the writer of Kings (24-25; cf. 18:5).

Nevertheless, Josiah's reforms were not enough to remove the idolatrous ideas deeply rooted in the minds of the people. Few were genuinely converted, and God did not remove his earlier sentence of judgment (26-27).

Warnings from Jeremiah

Jeremiah was from a priestly family, but God called him to be a prophet. His prophetic work began about 627 BC, during the reforms of Josiah (Jer 1:1-2; cf. 2 Chron 34:3,8). But Jeremiah says little about the reforms. This was no doubt because he saw there had been no basic change in the hearts of the people, and therefore the changes in the external forms of the religion would have no lasting effect. Although Jeremiah did not discourage the zealous king from the good work he was doing, he pointed out to the people that if they did not change their behaviour and attitudes, they would not escape God's judgment (Jer 11:15; 14:12).

After the death of Josiah, Jeremiah's warnings became more urgent. He assured the people of Judah that because of their persistent rebellion against God, they would be taken captive to Babylon (Jer 21:2-7). Jeremiah became a prominent national figure during the time of Judah's later kings, and his ministry lasted till after the destruction of Jerusalem in 587 BC. He was violently opposed by leaders and common people alike, and on occasions imprisoned (Jer 20:1-6; 26:1-11; 28:1-17; 37:1-21; 38:1-28). The significance of Jeremiah and his protests will become clear as the story moves on.

Nahum and the destruction of the Assyrians

While Josiah was reigning in Judah, great changes were occurring among the more powerful countries of the region. Most important of these changes was the decline of Assyria and the rise of Babylon. This was foreseen by the prophet Nahum, whose short book is wholly concerned with the destruction of the Assyrian capital Nineveh and the end of Assyrian power (Nahum 1:1-2; 2:8). Nahum rejoiced that at last a fitting divine judgment was going to fall on such an arrogant and brutal oppressor (Nahum 2:13; 3:1,7,18-19).

Egypt and Babylon (23:28-30)

During the years of Assyria's declining power, Egypt took the opportunity to extend its influence. But Babylon had now risen to power, and in 612 BC it conquered Nineveh. Pharaoh Necho of Egypt, fearing this Babylonian expansion, went to help what was left of Assyria to withstand Babylon. He no doubt hoped that Assyria might yet form some sort of defence barrier between Egypt and Babylon.

Josiah apparently saw this Assyrian-Egyptian alliance as a threat to Judah's independence. He preferred Assyria to remain weak and tried to stop Egypt from helping it. This proved to be a fatal move. Judah was defeated and Josiah killed in battle (609 BC). By a decision of Judah's leading officials, Josiah's second son Jehoahaz (or Joahaz) was made the new king (28-30; 2 Chron 35:20-25). Meanwhile, as Babylonian power expanded, Assyria collapsed, and its national identity disappeared.

Habakkuk's problem concerning Babylon

God was preparing Babylon to be his instrument to punish Judah. The prophet Habakkuk was puzzled when he learnt of this, because he knew that the people of Babylon were even worse sinners than the people of Judah. In his book he records how he argued with God about this matter, and how God reassured him that any of the people of Judah who remained faithful to him would enjoy his favour. The Babylonians, however, because of their pride at conquering God's people, would themselves suffer God's punishment (Hab. 1:6,13; 2:4,16).

End of Judah's independence (23:31-37)

Pharaoh Necho now considered himself to be the controller of Judah, and would not accept the king chosen by the people of Judah. The unfortunate Jehoahaz was thrown into prison and later taken to Egypt, where he eventually died. Necho made Jehoahaz's older brother Jehoiakim king instead, and placed a heavy tax on Judah (31-37).

It soon became clear why the people of Judah had not chosen Jehoiakim as king. He was a proud, cruel and oppressive ruler, who murdered those who opposed him and insultingly rejected the advice of God's prophets (see 24:4; Jer 26:20-23; 36:1-32). In spite of the heavy taxes his country had to pay Egypt, he built himself luxurious royal buildings, forcing people to work on his selfish projects without payment (Jer 22:13-17).

Conquest by Babylon and captivity (24:1-17)

In 605 BC the armies of Babylon under Nebuchadnezzar conquered Egypt in the famous Battle of Carchemish (Jer 46:2). This meant that Judah now came under the control of, and paid tribute to, Babylon. When the conquerors returned to Babylon, they took with them captives from the conquered countries, including some of the most capable and well educated young men they could find among the leading families of Jerusalem. One of these was the youth Daniel (Dan 1:1-6).

After three years Jehoiakim stopped paying tribute, thinking that Nebuchadnezzar was too busy with wars elsewhere to deal with Judah. Jehoiakim depended on Egypt to support his rebellion, a policy that Jeremiah consistently opposed (Jer 2:18,36). Nebuchadnezzar did not immediately return and attack Jerusalem, but he weakened its power by allowing other countries within his Empire to raid across Judah's borders (24:1-4).

When he had put down rebellions elsewhere, Nebuchadnezzar sent his army to besiege Jerusalem. Jehoiakim the king was taken prisoner and chained ready to be sent to Babylon, but he died before the journey began. No one mourned his death, and his body was thrown on the garbage dump outside Jerusalem as if it were the carcass of an unclean animal (5-7; 2 Chron 36:6; Jer 22:18-19; 36:30).

The eighteen year old Jehoiachin (also known as Jeconiah, or Coniah) then became king. After three months he saw that further resistance was useless and surrendered (597 BC). Most of the nation's treasures, along with the king, the royal family, the palace officials and all Judah's best people, were carried off to Babylon. Among these captives was the young man Ezekiel. Only those of no use to Babylon were left in Jerusalem. Babylon then appointed Jehoiachin's uncle, Zedekiah, as king (8-17; see Ezek 1:1-3).

The destruction of Jerusalem (24:18-25:21)

All Judah's most capable administrators had been taken captive to Babylon. The few advisers who were left to Zedekiah had no true understanding of the situation, either political or religious, and persuaded the weak king to seek Egypt's help in rebelling against Babylon. This was a policy that Jeremiah clearly saw was disastrous, for it would lead only to the horrors of siege and destruction. His advice was that Judah accept its fate as God's will and submit to Babylon (18-20; 2 Chron 36:11-14; Jer 21:1-10; 27:12-15; 37:6-10).

Zedekiah, however, followed the advice of the pro-Egypt party and rebelled against Babylon. Nebuchadnezzar decided to crush the rebellious city once and for all. When Egypt came to Jerusalem's aid, the siege was temporarily lifted, but Jeremiah warned that this would only make Babylon more determined to crush Judah, and Egypt with it. The pro-Egypt party accused Jeremiah of being a traitor and had him imprisoned (Jer 37:1-38:28).

The Babylonians returned and soon Jeremiah's prophecy came true. The horrors of the siege are vividly described in the book of Lamentations (Lam. 2:10-12,19-21; 4:4-5,7-10). When, after a year and six months, the Babylonians finally made a break in the wall, Zedekiah and some of his men tried to escape, but were captured (25:1-7).

Babylonian soldiers then poured into the city, seizing anything of value that could be taken back to Babylon, and burning or smashing what remained. This was the end of Jerusalem (587 BC). The leaders of the rebellion were killed, and the most useful citizens taken captive (8-17).

In the course of arresting the chief officials of Jerusalem, the Babylonians released Jeremiah from jail and gave him full freedom to decide where he would like to live, Babylon or Judah. Jeremiah chose to stay in Judah with a small number of farmers and other poorer people who were of no use to Babylon (18-21; Jer 39:11-40:6).

In Egypt and Babylon (25:22-30)

Gedaliah was appointed governor of those who remained in Judah, and with Jeremiah's support he followed a pro-Babylon policy. He took no action against Judah's anti-Babylon military leaders who had escaped the Babylonians. Rather he encouraged them, along with others who had fled the country, to return and settle around Mizpah, north of Jerusalem (22-24; Jer 40:7-12).

Within a few months Gedaliah was murdered by the leaders of the anti-Babylon group. Fearing a revenge attack by Nebuchadnezzar, the remaining Judeans in the resettlement area fled for safety to Egypt, taking the protesting Jeremiah with them (25-26; Jer 40:13-43:7). It is believed that Jeremiah was stoned to death in Egypt by his fellow Judeans. The Babylonians, meanwhile, made their punishing raid on Judah as expected, and took captive any that they found (582 BC; Jer 52:30).

After all the centuries of God's dealings with his people, most of them were now back in Chaldea (Babylon) from where Abraham had been called, and others were back in Egypt where their ancestors had been slaves. Yet God had not cast off his people. They received a sign of hope for the future when the Babylonians released Jehoiachin from prison and promoted him to a place of honour in the Babylonian palace (in 568 BC). God was still in charge of his people's affairs, and one day a remnant would return to the homeland and rebuild the nation (27-30; cf. Jer 29:10-14).

Obadiah's accusations against Edom

When Babylon attacked and destroyed Jerusalem in 587 BC, Edom joined in, welcoming the opportunity to enrich itself and to help wipe out what remained of the Israelite nation (Ps 137:7). The prophet Obadiah, apparently one of those left behind in Judah, announced God's judgment on Edom for its hostility, particularly since Edom and Israel were brother nations (being descended from Esau and Jacob respectively) (Obad 10-14).

Ezekiel in Babylon

Among the important citizens of Jerusalem taken captive to Babylon in 597 BC (see 24:10-17) was the young priest Ezekiel. If he had hoped to return to Jerusalem to serve God in the temple, he was soon to be disappointed. Jeremiah wrote to the exiles to tell them plainly that they would probably spend the remainder of their lives in Babylon (Jer 29:1-14). Ezekiel's work for God was to be as a prophet in Babylon, not as a priest in Jerusalem. He began his prophetic ministry five years after his arrival in Babylon, and continued it for at least twenty-two years (Ezek 1:2; 29:17).

In the early days of his preaching, Ezekiel repeatedly condemned the sins of the citizens of Jerusalem. He made it clear that the suffering of the people, both those in Jerusalem and those in Babylon, was a fitting judgment from God. He warned that for those left in Jerusalem worse was yet to come. The city would be destroyed and the temple burnt when the Babylonians invaded the city for the third and final time (Ezek 6:1-7; 7:20-27; 11:9-10; 21:21-22).

At first the exiles rejected Ezekiel's message (Ezek 12:27-28). A few years later, when news reached them that Jerusalem had fallen as Ezekiel had predicted, they realized that Ezekiel was a true prophet who knew God's mind. They began to listen to his messages again, though few genuinely changed their ways (Ezek 33:21,30-33).

Nevertheless, Ezekiel was encouraged to move ahead with the next and most important part of his ministry, which was to prepare God's people for the new era that lay ahead. He looked for the day when God's people would be cleansed from their sins and worship him in spirit and in truth.

The long career of Daniel

Daniel was among the first citizens of Jerusalem to be taken captive to Babylon. (This was in 605 BC; see 24:1a; Dan 1:1-6.) He was probably only a teenager when he entered the Babylonian court to be trained as an administrator. During his long career he held some of the most important positions in Babylon's government. He outlasted the Babylonian Empire, and was still alive in the third year of the Persian king Cyrus, who had conquered Babylon in 539 BC (Dan. 10:1). He therefore lived to see the first of the Jews return to Jerusalem to rebuild the nation (2 Chron 36:22-23).

The first half of the book of Daniel records stories of Daniel and his friends that illustrate the overruling control of God in the lives of his people. The second half shows, through a series of unusual visions, how God would continue this government in the affairs of his people: first, during the confusion and conflict that would follow the period of Persian rule; second, during the events of Christ's ministry and death; and third, during the final great events connected with the return of the Messiah and the end of the world's history.

APPENDIX: The Divided Kingdom

BC	Judah (1 dynasty)	Israel (9 dynasties)	Other nations; events
930	Rehoboam Abijam (or Abijah)	Jeroboam I	
910	Asa	Nadab	
		Baasha Elah	Ben-hadad I (Syria)
		Zimri	
874		Omri Ahab	
	Jehoshaphat Jehoram	Ahaziah Joram (or Jehoram)	Ben-hadad II (Syria)
	Ahaziah		Hazael (Syria)
841	[Athaliah] Joash	Jehu	
		Jehoahaz Jehoash	Ben-hadad III (Syria)
	Amaziah		

BC	Judah (cont.)	Israel (cont.)	Other nations; events
793	Azariah (or Uzziah)	Jeroboam II	
		Zechariah	
		Shallum	
	Jotham	Menahem	Rezin (Syria)
		Pekahiah	Tiglath-pileser III (Assyria)
	Ahaz	Pekah	
732			Syria falls to Assyria
			Parts of Israel fall to Assyria (Captivity Part 1)
	Hezekiah	Hoshea	Shalmaneser V (Assyria)
722			Israel falls to Assyria (Captivity Part 2)
			Sargon II (Assyria)
	Manasseh		Sennacherib (Assyria)
			Esarhaddon (Assyria)
			Ashurbanipal (Assyria)
	Amon		
640	Josiah		
612			Assyria falls to Babylon
	Jehoahaz		
	Jehoiakim		
			Nebuchadnezzar (Babylon)
605			Babylon taxes Jerusalem (Captivity Part 1)
	Jehoiachin		
597			Babylon captures Jerusalem (Captivity Part 2)
	Zedekiah		
587			Babylon destroys Jerusalem (Captivity Part 3)
582			Babylon raids Judah again (Captivity Part 4)
558			Cyrus (Persia)
539			Babylon falls to Persia
538			Jews begin return to Jerusalem

1 Chronicles

BACKGROUND

As with Samuel and Kings, Chronicles consists of two books in our Bibles, but was only one book in the original Hebrew Bible. The writer has not recorded his name, though he has recorded the names of some books and documents from which he gathered his material (1 Chron 9:1; 27:24; 29:29; 2 Chron 9:29; 16:11; 24:27; 33:19; 35:25).

A chronicle is a record of events, and the biblical writing called Chronicles records events that took place in Israel during the period covered by the books of Samuel and Kings. But Chronicles differs from Samuel and Kings in both style and content. The Chronicler wrote for people of a specific period and with a clear purpose in mind.

Circumstances of the time

Chronicles was written many years after Israel and Judah had been taken into captivity. After the captivity of the northern kingdom (Israel) by Assyria in 732 and 722 BC, many of the people of Israel became scattered among the nations where they lived, and largely lost their national identity. Those of the former southern kingdom (Judah), who were taken captive to Babylon in a number of stages between 605 and 582 BC, largely retained their national identity. When Persia conquered Babylon in 539 BC and gave permission to the Jews to return to their homeland, those who returned were people of this latter group. Further migrations followed in succeeding generations.

Most of those who returned had never lived in Palestine and knew little of the temple that once functioned in Jerusalem. These were the people for whom the Chronicler wrote. He wanted to give them some background knowledge about their country and their religion. In particular he wanted to impress upon them that they were more than just a lot of migrants living back in the land of their forefathers. They were a continuation of that pre-captivity nation whose life had been built on the twofold foundation of the Davidic dynasty and the Levitical priesthood.

Characteristics of Chronicles

God had a purpose in restoring his people to their homeland. He was still in control of their history, and the promises he had given to David and his dynasty would yet be fulfilled. The Chronicler has therefore chosen and arranged his material carefully, so that his readers might see the importance of rebuilding their nation according to God's design. Although he traces the history of the nation from the time of its first king, Saul, he says little about Saul. He is concerned almost entirely with the Davidic line of kings and the temple in Jerusalem with which they were connected.

The northern kingdom was a breakaway from God's chosen line through David, and its religion a rebellion against the true worship of God that was centred in Jerusalem. The writer of Chronicles has no desire to interest his readers in the northern kingdom and its sinful ways. For him the Davidic line of kings is the only legitimate dynasty, Jerusalem the nation's only legitimate capital, the temple in Jerusalem its only legitimate sanctuary, and the Levitical priesthood the only legitimate religious order. In concentrating on the southern kingdom, the writer wants to show his readers how the God-given Davidic kingship and the God-given Levitical order were essential to the national life of God's people.

Because of his special interests, the writer of Chronicles gives many details that the writers of Samuel and Kings do not record. This is particularly so in relation to Israel's religious organization during the period of the monarchy. On the other hand there are many things that he does not record, such as the failures of some of the Davidic kings. His aim is not to examine the lives of individuals, but to show that the Davidic kingdom was established with the religious order as an inseparable part of Israel's national life.

The Levites are always of particular interest to the writer of Chronicles. Whereas the writers of Samuel and Kings scarcely mention them, the Chronicler mentions them repeatedly, to show the part they played in the nation's affairs. He wants to impress upon his readers that the nation functions best when the civil administration of the Davidic kings and the religious order of the Levites work in harmony as God intended.

OUTLINE OF 1 CHRONICLES

1:1-9:34 GENEALOGIES OF THE TRIBES OF ISRAEL

The long lists of names that characterize Chronicles may not make interesting reading for us today, but they were important to the original readers. First, these genealogies proved to those who returned that they were a true continuation of the former kingdom. Second, they indicated who among the people had to carry out various religious duties and who among them were of the royal family of David. The lists recorded the origin and development of each tribe in some detail, so that people would know the tribe to which they belonged.

All the tribes came from a common ancestor, Jacob, and through him from Abraham. Abraham was the true father of the nation and a key figure in God's purposes for the human race (cf. Gen 12:1-3; 13:14-17; Matt 1:2-16).

The origins of Israel (1:1-54)

As in many of the genealogies of the Bible, the genealogy here is simplified. That is, it does not list the name of every person descended from one ancestor, but selects certain people and certain generations according to the purpose of the writer. In this genealogy the writer is concerned mainly with only one line of descent from Adam.

To begin with, the writer records the line of descent from Adam to Noah (1:1-4). Although he records the descendants of Noah's three sons (5-23), he is particularly concerned with the line through Shem that produced Abraham (24-27). The nation Israel was descended from Abraham through his son Isaac and grandson Jacob, but before dealing with Israel, the writer lists people descended from Abraham's other children (28-33) and from Isaac's other son (34-54).

Descendants of Judah and Simeon (2:1-4:43)

Having listed the children of Jacob (Israel) starting with the eldest son Reuben, the writer immediately turns his attention to the tribe of Judah, the tribe that produced the dynasty of David (2:1-17). He traces the line of David first, then goes back to deal with a number of other important people in Judah and lists their descendants (18-55). On completing this, he returns to list the family of David (3:1-9), the descendants of David who reigned after him to the captivity (10-16), and further descendants who lived during the time of the captivity and later (17-24). The section concludes with a collection of miscellaneous branches from Judah's family tree (4:1-23).

The tribe of Simeon had no tribal territory of its own, but dwelt within the territory of Judah (Josh 19:1,9). It is therefore dealt with here, immediately after the listings for Judah. Some of the Simeonites' conquests, which are not mentioned elsewhere, are also recorded (24-43).

The eastern tribes (5:1-26)

At the beginning of this section, the writer gives the reason why he listed the genealogy of Judah before that of Reuben, the firstborn. Reuben had lost his rights as the firstborn (see Gen 35:22), so the ruling power in Israel was given to Judah instead. The firstborn's double portion of the inheritance went to Joseph, who received two tribes in Israel (Ephraim and Manasseh). The descendants of Reuben, along with those of Gad and half the tribe of Manasseh, dwelt on the east of Jordan, not in Canaan itself. Their territory had no natural boundaries to the north or east, and so was open to attack from the Assyrians (5:1-10).

Gad's descendants are listed next (11-17). In addition there is the account of an important victory that the two and a half eastern tribes won, thereby giving them greater security and prosperity (18-22). There is also a short list of the leading families of the eastern half of the tribe of Manasseh (23-24). The section closes by recording that the people of the two and a half eastern tribes, because of their unfaithfulness to God, were conquered by the Assyrians and taken into captivity (25-26).

The Levites (6:1-81)

Levi had three sons, Gershon, Kohath and Merari. The priesthood in Israel began with Aaron, who was descended from Levi through Kohath. From that time on, all Aaron's descendants, and no others, were priests. This means that the Levites may be divided into four groups — the priestly Kohathites, the non-priestly Kohathites, the Gershonites and the Merarites.

The Chronicler begins with the priestly line descended from Aaron through his son Eleazar, and traces the line to the time of the captivity (6:1-15). He follows this with genealogies of the Gershonites, the remaining Kohathites and the Merarites (16-30). Next he gives the genealogies of the three who were put in charge of the temple singers — Heman the Kohathite (31-38), Asaph the Gershonite (39-43) and Ethan the Merarite (44-48). (Songs from these three men, and others from a group of Levitical musicians known as the sons of Korah, have been collected in the book of Psalms; e.g. Ps 42; 44-50; 73-85; 87-89.)

Forty-eight cities had been given to the Levites after Joshua's conquest of Canaan (Josh 21:41), and these also were divided into four groups. The cities for the priestly Kohathites were all in the region around Jerusalem and therefore within easy reach of the temple (49-60). Cities for the other three Levitical groups were more distant from Jerusalem (61-65). The writer then lists the cities for these three groups: first for the non-priestly Kohathites (66-70), then for the Gershonites (71-76) and finally for the Merarites (77-81).

Genealogies of the remaining tribes (7:1-8:40)

Although the lists here are incomplete and in places difficult to follow, it seems that the tribes dealt with are Issachar (7:1-5), parts of Benjamin and Dan (6-12), Naphtali (13), the portion of Manasseh not listed earlier (14-19; cf. 5:23-24), Ephraim (20-29) and Asher (30-40).

Benjamin is given in greater detail, possibly because it included Jerusalem in its tribal territory. Also this was the only tribe that joined Judah in the southern kingdom, the kingdom that remained loyal to the Davidic dynasty (8:1-28). Benjamin also produced Israel's first king, Saul, whose family details are given (29-40).

First group to return to Jerusalem (9:1-34)

At the time of writing, the first of the exiles had just returned to Jerusalem, having been given permission by the Persian king Cyrus (2 Chron 36:22-23). The writer lists the heads of the families who returned (9:1-9). He points out that priests, Levites and temple servants also returned, to emphasize that the re-establishment of the nation Israel had to be on the basis of the religious order appointed by David before the captivity (10-16).

Just as gate-keepers were needed to guard the tabernacle and the temple in former times, so they would be needed to guard the temple in rebuilt Jerusalem (17-21). The writer records how David organized the guards' working hours and duties in the former temple (22-27). Even everyday matters, such as the care of temple equipment and the preparation of incense, spices and sacred foods, were carefully planned and supervised (28-32). People such as musicians and singers, who were to be ready for duty any time, day or night, lived in some of the temple buildings (33-34).

9:35-22:1 THE REIGN OF DAVID

End of the line of Saul (9:35-10:14)

Saul is introduced by listing his genealogy once again (35-44). However, the Chronicler passes over the reign of Saul in silence, for his concern is with the dynasty of David. Saul's death alone is recounted, since that was the means of bringing in the reign of David. It was also God's judgment on Saul for his unfaithfulness and disobedience (10:1-14; see notes on 1 Sam 31:1-13).

David made king (11:1-12:40)

It seems clear that the writer of Chronicles assumes that his readers have already read the books of Samuel and Kings. (In this commentary also it is assumed that the reader has read these books. For further details see notes and maps at the relevant places in Samuel and Kings, and the appendix at the end of Chronicles.)

In view of his readers' assumed knowledge, the Chronicler makes no attempt to record events that have little to do with his central purpose. For example, he omits all reference to the attempt by Saul's followers to continue the rule of Saul's family (2 Sam 1:1-4:12). Instead he passes straight on to the establishment of David in Jerusalem as king over all Israel (11:1-9; see notes on 2 Sam 5:1-10), and the important part that David's mighty men played in establishing and maintaining his kingdom (10-47; see notes on 2 Sam 23:8-39).

Others who gladly gave themselves to David to fight for him are also mentioned: the Benjaminites who joined him at Ziklag when he was fleeing from Saul (12:1-7; see notes on 1 Sam 27:1-7); the fearless soldiers from Gad, Benjamin and Judah who had previously joined him at his stronghold in Adullum (8-18; see notes on 1 Sam 22:1-23); and the Israelite military commanders from Manasseh who deserted to him at the time of the Philistines' last battle with Saul (19-22; see notes on 1 Sam 29:1-30:25). Finally, the writer records how all the tribes of Israel sent a representative force of troops to Hebron to present themselves to David, their new king (23-40; see notes on 2 Sam 5:1-5).

The ark comes to Jerusalem (13:1-16:7)

David knew that part of the reason for Israel's previous weakness was Saul's lack of interest in its religious life. Even the ark of the covenant, symbol of God's presence, lay forgotten in a country house. David set out to restore the ark to its rightful place at the centre of the nation's religious life. In bringing the ark to Jerusalem, his aim was to make Jerusalem the religious, as well as the political, centre of Israel. But his plans suffered an early setback because of a lack of reverence for the ark (13:1-14; see notes on 2 Sam 6:1-11).

An account of two victories over the Philistines is inserted (out of chronological order), probably to impress upon the reader how David's fame was spreading (14:1-17; see notes on 2 Sam 5:11-25).

The writer then goes back to the story of the ark and shows how, after the earlier setback, it was finally brought to Jerusalem. Nothing disastrous happened this time, because the ark was transported in the proper manner and handled with fitting reverence. It was carried on the shoulders of the Levites, who themselves were ceremonially cleansed (15:1-15; see notes on 2 Sam 6:12-15).

Music and singing, organized and directed by the Levites, accompanied the procession. The three leading singers previously named, Heman, Asaph and Ethan (see 6:31,33,39,44), were in charge of the singers, who were under the overall control of Chenaniah. Obed-edom, who had looked after the ark during its recent stay in his house (see 13:14), was appointed to be one of the guardians of the ark in Jerusalem. He was also among the official singers when not required for guard duty (16-24).

After the arrival of the ark in Jerusalem, David and the people celebrated the event with sacrifices and feasting (25-16:3; see notes on 2 Sam 6:16-23). David also appointed various officials to lead the worship. The arrangements for singing and music made on this occasion became the basis of Israel's future organized public worship (4-7).

A psalm of thanksgiving (16:8-36)

The Chronicler records a psalm that was sung in celebration of the ark's arrival in Jerusalem. It was typical of the psalms sung on such great national occasions. It began with a call to God's covenant people to worship him in praise for his faithfulness to the covenant he made with Abraham (8-13). This covenant was the work of God alone. Out of all the nations of the earth he chose Abraham, promising to make his descendants into a nation and to give them Canaan for a national homeland (14-18). In the early days, when they were few in number, Abraham's descendants could easily have been wiped out by hostile neighbours, but God miraculously preserved them (19-22).

In view of all he had done for them, God's people were urged to praise him and to proclaim his mighty acts to others. People could never really know other gods, for those gods were lifeless, but they could know the only true God, both through the created universe and through the public worship of the sanctuary (23-27). Therefore, the peoples of the world were urged to bring God worship and sacrificial offerings (28-30), and the physical creation was urged to bring him praise (31-34). His unfailing mercy was the Israelites' assurance that they could always depend on him to save them (35-36). (The above psalm is not in Samuel; the two psalms of 2 Samuel 22:1-23:7 are not in Chronicles.)

Plans for a permanent house (16:37-17:27)

On being brought to Jerusalem, the ark had been placed in a tent that David prepared for it (see v. 1). David appointed temple servants to remain with the ark to guide the worship, apparently under the direction of the senior priest, Abiathar. The other chief priest, Zadok, was in charge of the worship at the tabernacle, which was still at Gibeon (37-43).

One reason why David did not shift the tabernacle from Gibeon was that he was planning to build a permanent dwelling place for the ark in Jerusalem. He wanted to build a house for God, but God wanted rather to build a house for David. The house God wanted to build was a dynasty, a line of royal descendants, one of whom would build the temple (17:1-27; see notes on 2 Sam 7:1-29).

David's fame (18:1-22:1)

Before speaking further of the temple, the writer lists a number of David's victories in war. These records show how God was strengthening David's kingdom according to his promise, but they show also why God would not allow David to build the temple. One who had caused so much bloodshed was not a suitable person to build the nation's sacred place of worship (see 22:7-10).

The writer records victories over miscellaneous enemies (18:1-17; see notes on 2 Sam 8:1-18); victory over a combined Ammonite-Syrian attack (19:1-19; see notes on 2 Sam 10:1-19); victory over Ammon at Rabbah (20:1-3; see notes on 2 Sam 11:1; 12:26-31); and various victories over the Philistines (4-8; see notes on 2 Sam 21:18-22).

In bringing these battle stories together, the writer has omitted a number of passages from the parallel section of 2 Samuel. He is concerned with God's plan for establishing the kingdom of David, not with the fate of Saul's survivors (2 Sam 9:1-13; 21:1-17), nor with David's personal sins and family troubles (2 Sam 11:2-12:25; 13:1-20:26).

There is, however, one sin of David's that the Chronicler does record, and that is his numbering of the people. Yet even this story is recorded not to point out a personal weakness, but to show how

David bought the piece of ground on which the temple was to be built (21:1-22:1; see notes on 2 Sam 24:1-25). The writer now moves on to show how David, having bought the site, began preparations for the temple's construction.

22:2-29:30 PREPARATIONS FOR THE TEMPLE

David's encouragement to Solomon (22:2-19)

God's purpose was that Solomon, not David, should build the temple. Although David understood the reason for this and accepted it humbly, he did all he could to help Solomon in his task. He gathered construction materials in great quantities, and put all foreigners in Israel to work preparing the stones for building (2-5). Most importantly, he encouraged Solomon to seek wisdom from God and obey his commandments, so that he might govern the nation according to the law of God (6-13). David provided Solomon with further practical help by arranging for various kinds of craftsmen to be ready to start work when the time arrived. (14-16).

David's conquests gave Israel such strength and security that it was safe from attack. This allowed Solomon to concentrate on his building program without interference (17-19).

Arrangements for the Levites (23:1-26:32)

Having appointed Solomon to be his successor, David made further arrangements for the service of the temple. First, he set out a plan to distribute duties among the Levites. A census showed that there were 38,000 Levites eligible for temple service. Of these, 14,000 were official record-keepers, judges, guards, singers and musicians. The remainder were to help in the general service of the temple (23:1-6). Clearly, there were far too many Levites to work in the temple all at the same time. David therefore divided them into groups according to their families, the total number of groups coming to twenty-four (7-23).

Each Levitical group was to serve in the temple two weeks each year. (This accounted for forty-eight weeks. The remaining four weeks would be taken up with the festivals of Passover, Pentecost and Tabernacles, when all the men of Israel were to assemble at the central place of worship. On these occasions all Levites would be on duty; see Exod 23:14-17.) The work of the Levites included assisting the priests, keeping the temple clean, providing the music and singing for worship, and attending to the many practical matters connected with the sacrifices and ceremonies (24-32).

The priests also were divided into twenty-four groups, each of which served in the temple for two weeks per year as outlined above. The service alternated between the Eleazar branch and the Ithamar branch of the Aaronic family. Each priest's turn for service was decided by drawing lots (24:1-6). The names of the twenty-four priestly groups are then given (7-19), followed by a further list of some Levitical families (20-31).

Among the temple singers (a total of 4,000; see 23:5) were 288 specially skilled musicians. Included in these were twenty-four leaders (25:1-7). These 288 musicians were also divided into twenty-four groups that served in rotation. Their job was apparently to train and lead the section to which they were assigned (8-31).

There were also 4,000 gate-keepers, or temple guards (see 23:5). They too were probably divided into twenty-four groups who took turns to go on duty. The number of positions to be guarded was twenty-four (26:1-19). The wealth that David and others won for Israel through their conquests was administered by a group of treasurers, whose names are listed (20-28). The 6,000 judges (see 23:4) were most likely organized on a rotation system for their service. Some of them were concerned with the central administration, some worked only in the area west of Jordan, and some worked only among the two and a half tribes that were located east of Jordan (29-32).

Military and civilian leaders (27:1-34)

In contrast to the detail that the writer gives in the lists of the Levites, there is only a brief summary of David's military and civil leaders. Each month 24,000 men were required to do one month's military service. The twelve commanding officers (who took turns at commanding this fighting force, one month at a time) all belonged to David's group of 'mighty men' (27:1-15; see 11:10-47). Three other lists name the leaders of Israel's tribes (16-24), the officials who looked after the king's farmlands (25-31), and the king's close advisers (32-34).

Solomon presented to the people (28:1-29:30)

David had been forced to appoint Solomon as king hastily when he learnt that another son, Adonijah, was plotting to seize the throne for himself (see notes on 1 Kings 1:5-53). That very unceremonious anointing of Solomon was followed soon after by a second anointing, this time with full religious and regal ceremony (see 29:22). This second occasion is the one that the Chronicler refers to here. David presented Solomon to the people as the one who, by God's choice, would succeed him as king and build the temple (28:1-10). David gave Solomon the plans he had prepared for the temple and its service. He encouraged Solomon to persist in the work till the temple was finished and in use according to the plans he had set out (11-21).

In addition to the money and materials he had already given for the project (see 22:14), David gave a lavish offering from his own personal funds. His example prompted the people to make similarly generous offerings (29:1-9). The joyful response from the people brought from David an outburst of magnificent praise to God. He gladly acknowledged that everything that people possess comes from God; therefore, in making offerings to him, the Israelites had only given back what he had already given them. They had done this joyfully and willingly, and David prayed that they would maintain such devotion to God always (10-20).

Next day the people joined in a great festival and swore allegiance to Solomon as their new king (21-25). The writer will now continue with the story of Solomon, but before doing so he gives a brief summary of the reign of David (26-30).

2 Chronicles

OUTLINE OF 2 CHRONICLES

1:1-9:31 THE REIGN OF SOLOMON

Solomon's wisdom and wealth (1:1-17)

The writer of Chronicles is chiefly concerned with the continuation of the dynasty of David through Solomon according to God's promise, and therefore he omits stories that he considers irrelevant to his theme. He says nothing of Adonijah's attempt to gain the throne, and nothing of Solomon's alliance with Egypt (1 Kings 1:1-3:3). His initial emphasis is rather on Solomon's devotion to God from the very beginning of his reign.

To demonstrate Solomon's devotion, the writer records the impressive ceremony Solomon arranged at the tabernacle in Gibeon and his commendable request for God's wisdom in ruling Israel (1:1-13; see notes on 1 Kings 3:4-15). However, the writer omits the examples given in 1 Kings 3:16-4:34 that show Solomon's wisdom at work in the everyday affairs of the people, in his overall administration of the kingdom, and in his writings and songs.

Before describing Solomon's plans for building the temple, the writer shows that under Solomon Israel enjoyed stability and prosperity. Such a king was well able to carry out the temple building program successfully (14-17; see notes on 1 Kings 10:26-29).

Construction of the temple (2:1-7:22)

With the help of King Hiram of Tyre, Solomon prepared materials and arranged a workforce to build the planned temple (2:1-18; see notes on 1 Kings 5:1-18). Construction went on for seven years, until the temple, its furniture, its courtyard, and all other articles and decorations connected with it were completed according to plan (3:1-5:1; see notes on 1 Kings 6:1-7:51). The temple was then dedicated to God (5:2-7:22; see notes on 1 Kings 8:1-9:9).

Solomon's greatness (8:1-9:31)

Other building programs of Solomon are outlined. The Chronicler adds a note that the reason Solomon built a separate palace for his Egyptian wife was to preserve the holiness of the throne. This point is important to the Chronicler, who wants to show that the Davidic kings, on the whole, tried to remain faithful to God. He notes in addition that Solomon organized the temple services according to the plan that David had laid down (8:1-18; see notes on 1 Kings 9:10-28).

After outlining once more Solomon's wisdom, commercial ability, fame and wealth (9:1-28; see notes on 1 Kings 10:1-25), the Chronicler closes his record of Solomon's reign. He makes no mention of Solomon's idolatry and the judgment to which it was leading (1 Kings 11:1-40), for he is concerned with the continuation of the Davidic dynasty rather than with the failure of its kings (29-31; see notes on 1 Kings 11:41-43).

10:1-36:23 THE KINGS OF JUDAH

Division and its consequences (10:1-13:22)

The Chronicler records the division of the kingdom (10:1-11:4; see notes on 1 Kings 12:1-24), but omits the statement in 1 Kings 12:20 that Jeroboam was made king of the northern tribes. He does not even mention Jeroboam's reign (1 Kings 12:25-14:20). He considers that because the northerners broke away from the dynasty of David and from the true worship of God, they had no right to be called a kingdom, and certainly not the kingdom of Israel.

Unlike the writer of Kings (who calls the southern kingdom Judah and the northern kingdom Israel), the writer of Chronicles calls the southern kingdom either Judah or Israel. For him Judah is the only true kingdom, and the Davidic kings are the only legitimate kings. Nevertheless, he still accepts people from the north as Israelites, and is pleased when any return to God and the Davidic rulers (see 11:13-17; 15:9; 30:1-12). He sometimes refers to the northern kingdom as Ephraim.

Priests and Levites are often prominent in the Chronicler's account of Judah's successes. Solomon's son Rehoboam began his reign well, mainly through the influence of a large number of priests and Levites who fled to Judah from the north rather than join in Jeroboam's idolatry. As long as Rehoboam followed the ways of God as taught by the priests, Judah was strong and stable. When he introduced Canaanite religious practices, God punished him by way of a damaging invasion from Egypt (11:5-12:16; see notes on 1 Kings 14:21-31).

Abijam (or Abijah) followed the religious policy of his father in allowing the worship of Baal to exist side by side with the worship of God, but he did not completely forsake God as Jeroboam did in the north. Abijam's unexpected victory over Jeroboam in battle demonstrated that God was on the side of the king who belonged to David's dynasty and who refused to join in the false religion of the north (13:1-22; see notes on 1 Kings 15:1-8).

Reformation under Asa (14:1-16:14)

God's blessings on Asa showed his pleasure with those who removed Canaanite customs and restored the Levitical order of worship. God rewarded Asa by giving him a remarkable victory over a large and powerful army that invaded from the south. This sign of God's pleasure encouraged Asa to continue his reforms with greater boldness (14:1-15:19; see notes on 1 Kings 15:9-15).

When, however, Asa trusted in outside help instead of trusting in God, he displeased God and was rebuked by one of God's prophets. Not willing to listen to advice, he treated cruelly any of his people who opposed his policies (16:1-14; see notes on 1 Kings 15:16-24).

Towards the end of Asa's reign, Ahab came to power in the north. Under the influence of his foreign wife Jezebel, Ahab introduced a new form of Baal worship in Israel. This Baalism was far more powerful and far more evil than that practised by the common people at the local Baal shrines (1 Kings 15:25-21:29). But since these matters concerned the northern kingdom, the Chronicler, in keeping with his usual practice, does not record them.

The reign of Jehoshaphat (17:1-20:37)

Jehoshaphat carried on the reform that Asa began, by destroying all the Baal shrines that remained in Judah (17:1-6; cf. 15:17). Positively, he educated the people in the law of God by forming an official group of instructors whom he sent around Judah's towns and villages. The group consisted of civil leaders, priests and Levites (7-9). He also fortified Judah's defences and enlarged its army, so that neighbouring countries feared to attack it (10-19).

Judah's army was so strong that Ahab of Israel sought and obtained Jehoshaphat's help in a war against Syria (Aram) (18:1-34; see notes on 1 Kings 22:1-40). A prophet rebuked Jehoshaphat for this, as Ahab was a worshipper of Baal and therefore an enemy of God (19:1-3).

Jehoshaphat reformed and reorganized Judah's judicial system to eliminate injustice, guarantee fair treatment for all, and ensure that standard procedures were followed throughout the land. He set up courts and appointed judges in all the chief cities of Judah, with the main court and the chief judges in Jerusalem. The courts and the officials were divided into two kinds. Some dealt with religious matters and were under the control of the chief priest. Others dealt with civil matters and were under the control of the chief governor (4-11). This arrangement was a further indication to the Chronicler that David's dynasty governed according to the Levitical code (cf. Deut 16:18-20; 17:8-12).

Some time later, a combined army of various nations from the south and east set out to attack Judah (20:1-2). The Chronicler notes that Jehoshaphat and his people not only cried to God for help, but they did so by gathering at the temple in Jerusalem. That was the place of prayer for God's people in times of crisis (3-12; cf. 6:24-25). As a result God answered their prayer. He assured them through a prophet (who was also a Levite) that the enemy would be defeated without Judah's army having to do anything (13-17).

The priests and Levites, being very active in Judah, led the people in songs of praise even before the victory was won (18-23). After the people had plundered the defeated army, the Levitical singers led them to the temple to praise God for the victory (24-30).

Earlier, Jehoshaphat had done wrong when he formed a military partnership with Ahab (see 18:3; 19:2). Later, he did wrong again when he formed a commercial partnership with Ahab's son Ahaziah. God sent a disaster to remind Jehoshaphat that he was not to cooperate with Israel's Baal-worshipping kings (31-37; see notes on 1 Kings 22:41-50). (The Chronicler omits the other references to Ahaziah's short rule in 1 Kings 22:51-53.)

Jezebel's Baalism in Judah (21:1-23:21)

The Baalism of Ahab and Jezebel remained strong in the northern kingdom during the successive reigns of their sons Ahaziah and Joram (2 Kings 1:1-8:15). It spread to Judah in the reign of Jehoshaphat's son Jehoram, who was married to Athaliah, the daughter of Ahab and Jezebel (21:1-20; see notes on 2 Kings 8:16-24).

Judah's next king, Ahaziah, at the direction of his mother Athaliah and her northern relatives, cooperated with the idolatrous northern kingdom, and as a result met an early death (22:1-9; see notes on 2 Kings 8:25-29; 9:21-29; 10:12-14). The kings of both Judah and Israel were killed by Jehu, whose anti-Baal revolution in the northern kingdom is recorded in 2 Kings 9:1-10:36.

Upon the king of Judah's death, Athaliah seized the throne for herself. She ruled for six years, during which she did all within her power to establish the northern Baalism of her parents in Judah. But the priests and Levites remained faithful to God. The Levites were the temple guards, and the writer emphasizes the part they played (in cooperation with the palace guards) in getting rid of Athaliah and restoring the throne to the Davidic dynasty. The Chronicler also points out that although the coup took place in the temple grounds, no one except the priests and Levites entered the temple buildings. People still had to respect the temple's holiness (22:10-23:21; see notes on 2 Kings 11:1-20). The death of Athaliah marked the end of Jezebel's Baalism in Judah.

Joash and Jehoiada (24:1-27)

The reign of the new king Joash showed how a strong and godly priesthood was necessary for the proper functioning of the Davidic kings. As long as he was under the influence of the high priest Jehoiada, Joash encouraged true worship among his people. After Jehoiada died, Joash turned away from God and encouraged Canaanite worship. For this he came under God's judgment. Even his death was a punishment, notes the Chronicler, because he had murdered the priest who rebuked him (24:1-27; see notes on 2 Kings 12:1-21).

Prosperity followed by disaster (25:1-28:27)

Succeeding kings of Israel are passed over in silence (2 Kings 13:1-25). Judah was to have nothing to do with the northern kingdom, not even to the hiring of Israelite soldiers. Amaziah took the advice, and was rewarded with victory in a battle against Edom. But the victory, instead of increasing his dependence on God, gave him a feeling of independence. He turned from God and worshipped idols. The ungodly northern kingdom then became God's instrument to punish the rebellious southern kingdom (25:1-28; see notes on 2 Kings 14:1-22).

Under the rule of Jeroboam II in the north (2 Kings 14:23-29) and Uzziah (or Azariah) in the south, both kingdoms enjoyed remarkable growth and prosperity. Unfortunately, this made Uzziah proud, and he arrogantly took to himself the rights of a priest. The writer points out that although the priesthood and the kingship were both appointed by God, they were separate and independent systems. One could not take over the functions of the other (26:1-23; see notes on 2 Kings 15:1-7).

Jotham followed the good policies of his father, while being careful not to repeat his father's errors. In the Chronicler's view, Jotham's fear of God was the source of his strength and success (27:1-9; see notes on 2 Kings 15:32-38).

The great prosperity throughout both kingdoms was followed by unbelievable chaos. In the north the kingdom of Israel almost collapsed (2 Kings 15:8-31), and in the south the disastrous reign of Ahaz almost brought destruction to Judah (28:1-27; see notes on 2 Kings 16:1-20). Within a short time the northern kingdom was conquered by Assyria and its people carried away captive. This was the end of the northern kingdom (2 Kings 17:1-41).

Hezekiah's religious reforms (29:1-31:21)

Immediately he became king, Hezekiah began a thorough reformation of Judah's religion. This was prompted partly by the preaching of the prophet Micah (Jer 26:17-19; see notes on 2 Kings 18:1-12).

The Chronicler gives a detailed account of Hezekiah's work, particularly that part of it which affected the temple, the priests and the Levites. Hezekiah called a meeting of priests and Levites and told them plainly that neglect of the temple was the reason for God's anger with Judah. Their first job was to clean the rubbish out of the temple and prepare it for the recommencement of religious services (29:1-11). The temple was so filthy that a large group of Levites took more than two weeks to clean and prepare the building for use again (12-19).

Hezekiah then held a service in which sacrifices were offered for the cleansing and rededication of the king, the nation and the temple (20-24). All this was accompanied by the music and singing of the Levites as arranged by David (25-30).

When the service was finished, the people were invited to make personal offerings. They responded so promptly and generously that the priests were spiritually unprepared for, and physically unable to cope with, the renewed activity in the temple. The Levites, who showed more enthusiasm, had to be called in to help (31-36).

After the rededication of the temple, Hezekiah held a great Passover Feast. His reforms began too late for the Passover to be held in the first month of the year (the time specified in the law), so it was postponed one month (cf. Num 9:10-11). Hezekiah invited the scattered northerners who had escaped captivity, but most were not interested (30:1-12).

Those who gathered for the feast cleansed Jerusalem of all traces of false religion. Their zeal for religious purity stirred up the priests and Levites to hurry and ceremonially cleanse themselves in time for the feast. Certain visitors to Jerusalem arrived too late for the seven day purification ritual before the Passover, and joined in the feast while still unclean. On Hezekiah's request, God forgave them (13-22). The occasion was so joyous that the feast was extended one week (23-27).

Once the city of Jerusalem and its temple had been cleansed, the people went out and cleansed the country areas (31:1). Having removed false religion, Hezekiah made plans for the proper functioning of the nation's true religion. First he divided the priests and Levites into groups according to David's plan (see 1 Chron 23:1-26:32). Then he arranged for their proper support through the orderly payment of tithes and offerings by all the people (2-7).

People responded so generously that Hezekiah prepared special storage places for all the sheep, cattle and produce they offered. He also appointed officials to administer the stores, and made a register of all those eligible for support, to ensure there was no dishonesty in the administration (8-21).

Hezekiah's political administration (32:1-33)

To the writer of Chronicles, Hezekiah's religious reforms were the most important feature of his reign. Politically, he was able to remain independent of Assyria, but only because God intervened in response to his faith (32:1-23; see notes on 2 Kings 18:13-19:37). He also made Judah prosperous. But pride in his achievements led him to become friendly with Babylon, the rising power in the region. It was a policy that later brought disaster upon Judah (24-33; see notes on 2 Kings 20:1-21).

The evil of Manasseh and Amon (33:1-25)

Manasseh receives the full blame for destroying all the good work that his father had done. Over his long reign of fifty-five years he dragged the nation down to its lowest spiritual condition ever. Although he made a brief attempt at reform towards the end of his life, he could not undo the damage of the previous half a century. Nor was any king after him able to reform Judah sufficiently to save it from judgment. Like Israel, Judah would go into captivity because of its wickedness (33:1-20; see notes on 2 Kings 21:1-18). If any trace of Manasseh's reform remained after his death, Amon soon removed it (21-25; see notes on 2 Kings 21:19-26).

The final reform (34:1-35:27)

Another reform swept Judah during the reign of Josiah (34:1-33; see notes on 2 Kings 22:1-23:20). As with the reform of Hezekiah, the climax in the eyes of the Chronicler was a great Passover Feast in Jerusalem.

After returning the ark to its rightful place in the temple, the priests and Levites prepared themselves for their duties. Josiah arranged them in divisions as Hezekiah had done earlier, so that the music, singing, sacrifices and other rituals could be conducted properly. The king, his governors and the leading Levites generously provided the sacrificial animals needed by the people for the occasion. The whole festival was even more spectacular than that of Hezekiah's time (35:1-19; see notes on 2 Kings 23:21-27). Sadly, Josiah was killed in battle at only thirty-nine years of age (20-27; see notes on 2 Kings 23:28-30).

Failure, defeat and captivity (36:1-23)

The Chronicler spent much time describing the reforms of Hezekiah and Josiah, impressing upon his readers that good kings tried to be faithful to the Mosaic and Davidic covenants. They had to follow the Levitical order if they were to enjoy the promises given to the dynasty of David. With the death of Josiah, Judah quickly returned to its former ungodly ways. Successive kings followed disastrous policies, both political and religious, which resulted in God's final judgment upon the nation. He allowed Babylon to conquer Judah, destroy Jerusalem, and take the people captive to a foreign land.

It is not the Chronicler's purpose to record details of the conquest. These are given in Kings. Instead he draws attention to the reasons for Judah's destruction: the unfaithfulness of the priests and the people, and their refusal to heed the warnings of the messengers God sent to them (36:1-21; see notes on 2 Kings 23:31-25:30).

Yet God did not cast off his people for ever. About seventy years later a new age dawned, when Cyrus, the Persian king who had conquered Babylon, announced that the Jews were free to return to their homeland and rebuild their nation. As formerly, that nation was to have its life centred on the temple in Jerusalem (22-23).

APPENDIX
Index of Parallel Passages

Ezra

BACKGROUND TO EZRA AND NEHEMIAH

It seems that in Old Testament times the books of Chronicles, Ezra and Nehemiah were joined to form a continuous story. The book of Ezra begins at the point where the account in Chronicles ends.

The year was 539 BC and the Jews' period of exile in Babylon was at last over. Persia had just conquered Babylon, and the Persian king Cyrus had issued a decree giving permission to the Jews to return to their homeland (1 Chron 36:22-23; Ezra 1:1-4). The era that followed is known as the post-exilic period. Six books of the Bible deal with this period, three of them historical, the other three prophetical. The summary of events below will help towards a clearer understanding of these books.

Note: From this point on Israelites in general were commonly referred to as Jews. About two hundred years earlier, the people of the former northern kingdom of Israel had been taken captive to various nations, and in time became absorbed by those nations. But when people of the southern kingdom Judah were later taken captive to Babylon, they retained their national identity. The people of Judah were called Judeans, but this was shortened to 'Jew'. Because most of those who returned from Babylon to Palestine were from the former southern kingdom, they could be called either Israelites or Jews. There was no longer any division in Israel, and the two names, along with the name 'Hebrew', were used interchangeably (Jer 34:9; John 1:19,47; 2 Cor 11:22; Gal 2:14).

First exiles to return

After Cyrus's decree of 539 BC, many thousands of Jews returned to Jerusalem. They had their own Jewish leaders in the civil administrator Zerubbabel and the high priest Joshua (or Jeshua), but they were still within the Persian Empire and still under Persian rule. Jerusalem lay within the province known as Beyond the River (GNB: West Euphrates; NIV: Trans-Euphrates), which extended from the Euphrates River to the Mediterranean Sea (Ezra 4:10,16; 7:21,25).

Soon after arriving in Jerusalem, the Jews began to rebuild the temple. First they set up the altar, and in the second year they laid the foundation of the building (Ezra 3:1-3,8-10). However, enemies then began to oppose the builders, with the result that the work stopped (Ezra 4:1-5,24).

Haggai and Zechariah

For at least sixteen years no work was done on the construction of the temple (Ezra 4:24). Then, in 520 BC, God raised up two men from among the Jews in Jerusalem to rouse the people to get on with the job, and not to stop till it was finished. These two men were the prophets Haggai and Zechariah (Ezra 5:1-2; Hag 1:1; Zech 1:1).

As soon as the people restarted work, there was renewed opposition (Ezra 5:3). The local governor referred the matter to the Persian king Darius (Cyrus having died some years previously). Darius investigated the matter and found that Cyrus had given permission to rebuild the temple. He therefore issued a second decree, supporting the initial decree of Cyrus, to allow the work to go on (Ezra 6:6-12).

Haggai's stirring preaching brought immediate results, and soon the Jews were again at work on the reconstruction of the temple (Hag 1:2-6,12-15). Zechariah supported Haggai, and went on to give more extensive teaching designed to bring a spiritual change in the lives and outlook of the people (Zech 1:4; 6:15; 7:8-9; 13:1). Four years after the restarting of the work, the temple was finished (in 516 BC; Ezra 6:14-15; cf. 4:24).

The book of Esther

Persia's next king after Darius was Xerxes I. He was also known as Ahasuerus, and reigned from 486 to 465 BC. He is the king who features in the story recorded in the book of Esther.

Return under Ezra

Artaxerxes succeeded Xerxes I as king of Persia in 465 BC. In the seventh year of his reign (458 BC) he issued a decree giving Ezra authority and finance to go to Jerusalem and carry out reforms there (Ezra 7:1,7,13).

It will be seen, from examining the relevant dates, that the events recorded in the opening part of the book of Ezra (i.e. events relating to Zerubbabel, Joshua and the rebuilding of the temple) took

161

place before Ezra was born. The writer of the book of Ezra no doubt searched through many letters, documents and historical records to prepare much of the early part of the book. We do not reach the time of Ezra himself till half way through the book. Ezra's return was about eighty years later than Zerubbabel's. The people in Jerusalem in Ezra's time were a different generation from those who returned with Zerubbabel.

Ezra was a priest and a scribe skilled in the law of God (Ezra 7:6,12). In former days a scribe was a person who made copies of the law for those who wanted to read it, but in post-exilic days he became also a teacher of the law. He was a person whose opinions in religious matters were highly respected. In later years the scribes gained more and more power in Israel, while the prophets declined in both numbers and influence.

Nevertheless, the scribe Ezra was a man sent by God. He read the law and explained its meaning, so that it became a handbook for the people to follow in their everyday living (Ezra 7:10; Neh 8:8). Here we see the origin of the religious system known as Judaism that was developed by the scribes over the next few centuries. However, examples from the Judaism of Jesus' time show that it was spiritually unhelpful and far different in spirit from the sort of religious life that Ezra taught.

Return under Nehemiah

In the twentieth year of his reign, Artaxerxes issued a second decree allowing a government sponsored group of Jews to return to Jerusalem, this time under the leadership of Nehemiah (445 BC). The temple in Jerusalem had been finished more than seventy years earlier, but the city itself was still in a state of disrepair, and the wall around the city had not yet been rebuilt. The reconstruction of the wall and the city was the specific project for which Nehemiah received the support of Artaxerxes (Neh 2:1-8).

Ezra had gone to Jerusalem thirteen years before Nehemiah. His reforms met with only partial success, and only when Nehemiah arrived and became governor of Jerusalem did the reformation have any great effect on the population as a whole. The two men worked together in leading the people back to God (Neh 8:9). Nehemiah stayed in Jerusalem twelve years, then returned to Persia (Neh 2:1; 13:6). Some time later he came back to Jerusalem (Neh 13:6-7).

The biblical book of Nehemiah, which was written by Nehemiah himself, records the significant events of his two terms as Jerusalem's governor.

The prophet Malachi

It seems that Malachi preached in Jerusalem during the period of reform by Ezra and Nehemiah. The date of his prophecy cannot be fixed with certainty, but the sins he rebuked were similar to those that Ezra and Nehemiah had to deal with.

The people expected that, because they had come back to their land and rebuilt their temple, they were going to enjoy the unlimited blessing of God. This did not prove to be so, and as a result they began to doubt whether God really cared for them. Malachi replied that the fault was on their side, not God's. They had, by their sins, created obstacles that hindered their enjoyment of God's love (Mal 1:2,6-7; 2:17; 3:7-8,13-14).

Malachi's book brings to a close the prophetical ministry in the Old Testament history of Israel. Four hundred years would pass before the voice of a prophet would be sounded in Scripture again. It was the voice of one crying in a barren country, 'Prepare the way of the Lord, make his paths straight' (Mark 1:3).

Summary of events

BC	Persian king	Events
539	Cyrus	Cyrus captures Babylon (Dan 5:30-31)
538		Cyrus' decree; Zerubbabel returns (Ezra 1:1; 2:2) Work on temple starts (Ezra 3:1-3,8-10)
537		Work on temple stops (Ezra 4:1-5,24)
530	Cambyses	Becomes king
521	Darius I	Becomes king
520		Haggai and Zechariah prophesy (Ezra 5:1-2; Hag 1:1; Zech 1:1) Darius' decree to rebuild temple (Ezra 4:24; 6:6-12)
516		Temple finished (Ezra 6:14-15)
486	Xerxes I	Becomes king; also known as Ahasuerus (Esther 1:1)
465	Artaxerxes I	Becomes king
458		Artaxerxes' 1st decree; Ezra returns (Ezra 7:1,7,13)
445		Artaxerxes' 2nd decree; Nehemiah returns (Neh 2:1-8)
424		End of Artaxerxes' reign

OUTLINE OF EZRA

1:1-2:70 ZERUBBABEL'S RETURN

Cyrus had been ruler of Persia for some time before he conquered Babylon in 539 BC. His policy was, when he conquered a nation, to allow any people held captive by that nation to return to their homeland. Therefore, soon after he conquered Babylon (i.e. in his first year as the Jews' new ruler) he gave permission for the Jews to return to Jerusalem (1:1-4). Jeremiah's prophecy made seventy years earlier had come true: the Jews were released from Babylon's power to return to Palestine and rebuild their nation (Jer 25:1,12; 29:10).

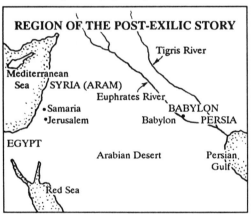

REGION OF THE POST-EXILIC STORY

Tigris River

Mediterranean Sea

SYRIA (ARAM)

Euphrates River

• Samaria

• Jerusalem

BABYLON

Babylon

PERSIA

EGYPT

Arabian Desert

Persian Gulf

Red Sea

Although all had permission to return, many chose to remain in Babylon. They were reasonably well settled and secure in Babylon, and did not want to face the risks and hardships of a new life in Jerusalem. Nevertheless, they assisted those who returned by giving them money and goods. Cyrus also gave some assistance, giving back the temple treasures and handing over a gift of money from the royal treasury to help finance the reconstruction of Jerusalem (5-11; see also 3:7; 6:4).

At first the leader of the returning exiles was Sheshbazzar (see 1:8, 5:14), but for some reason not recorded he was soon replaced by the joint leadership of Zerubbabel and Joshua (see 3:2; 5:2; Hag 1:1; 2:2). Alternatively, Sheshbazzar may have been another name for Zerubbabel.

The record of those who returned to Jerusalem begins by listing the chief men who were to assist Zerubbabel and Joshua (2:1-2). (The person named Nehemiah in this list is not the person we meet later in the book of Nehemiah.) The total number who returned was about 50,000. Some were classified according to their families (3-19), others according to the towns their families originally came from (20-35). The priests, Levites and temple servants were all listed separately (36-58). Others could not be fitted into any category (59-63). On arrival in Jerusalem, some made offerings of money towards the building of the temple. All the people were then settled in and around Jerusalem (64-70).

3:1-6:22 THE TEMPLE REBUILT

Work begins (3:1-13)

Non-Jewish people living in and around Jerusalem were not pleased at the return of the Jews to the area. The Jews were understandably afraid, and wanted to ensure God's protection by carrying out their religious duties faithfully. The mid-year festival season was approaching (see Lev 23:23-43), so the Jews quickly built an altar on which to offer their sacrifices. This marked the recommencement of regular sacrifices and festivals according to the ancient Levitical law (3:1-6).

The Jews then turned their attention to the task of rebuilding the temple. They ordered timber from Lebanon, and took stones from the ruins of the old temple and recut them for the new building (7). By the beginning of the next year they were ready to start work. Under the supervision of the Levites the work went well, and the foundation was laid amid much rejoicing. Some older people, however, had a feeling of sadness when they recalled how the splendour of the former temple had been destroyed (8-13).

Opposition stops the work (4:1-24)

As a result of Assyria's resettlement program of two centuries earlier, a race of people grew up in the area around Samaria and Jerusalem who were of mixed blood and mixed religion. They were known as Samaritans (see notes on 2 Kings 17:24-33). The Jewish leaders refused their offered help in building the temple of God, no doubt to prevent wrong ideas from corrupting Israel's religion. The Samaritan group reacted bitterly. They opposed the Jewish builders so fiercely that soon work on the temple stopped completely (4:1-5,24).

Two examples show the kind of opposition that Israel suffered. These stories do not belong to the time of Zerubbabel. They are taken from official documents of a later period, and in fact are written in a different language from the rest of the book. The writer puts them into his account at this point to give the reader an idea of how Israel was unjustly persecuted.

The first example is taken from the reign of Ahasuerus, also known as Xerxes I (6). (This king later showed favour to the Jews, as the book of Esther shows). The second belongs to the reign of Artaxerxes I. By that time the temple had long been completed and the Jews were rebuilding the walls of Jerusalem. Their Samaritan opponents wrote to Artaxerxes, accusing the Jews of fortifying Jerusalem in preparation for a rebellion against Persia (7-16). The king therefore commanded that the work cease immediately, though he reserved the right to reverse his decree at a later date if he so desired (17-23). (We learn from Nehemiah 2:1-8 that later this king did, in fact, reverse his decree and give his support to the Jews.)

The temple completed (5:1-6:22)

Having given examples of anti-Jewish activity from another era, the writer returns to the time of Zerubbabel. Because of opposition from their enemies, the Jews did no work on the temple for about sixteen years. Then the prophets Haggai and Zechariah began to stir up the people to get them working on the building once more (5:1-2).

Some local people must have objected to the renewed activity, and soon a group of officials arrived at the scene to question the legality of the building program (3-5). But the provincial governor investigated the matter fairly. He noted the Jews' claim that they had received royal permission, and sent a full report to King Darius to see whether the Jews' story was true (6-17).

A search of the official records showed that the Jews' claim was true (6:1-5). Darius therefore had no hesitation in giving permission for the work to continue. In addition he guaranteed protection for the workers, and ordered the provincial officials to provide the Jews with money and materials at the government's expense. He wanted to ensure that the building was completed according to plan, and that the Jews had enough animals and produce to re-establish the temple rituals satisfactorily (6-12).

Four years later the temple was completed and dedicated. The offerings that the people made were on behalf of all twelve tribes of Israel, for the pre-exilic division between north and south no longer existed (13-18).

A few weeks after the dedication ceremony, the people celebrated the first of the annual festivals in their new temple. This was the Feast of Passover and Unleavened Bread. Among those who gathered for the festival were local Jews who had not been part of the Babylonian exile and who had mixed with other people of the region. They were allowed to join in the festival provided they separated themselves from the mixed religion of the surrounding people (19-22).

7:1-8:36 RETURN UNDER EZRA

The temple was completed in 516 BC. Ezra's return was in 458 BC, the seventh year of the reign of Artaxerxes I (see 7:1,7). There is therefore a gap of about sixty years between Chapters 6 and 7. By the time of Ezra, former leaders such as Zerubbabel, Joshua, Haggai and Zechariah had died. Without their leadership, Israel's religious life became weak and its community life disordered. The only detailed information that the Bible gives of events during these years is found in the book of Esther.

Plans for reform (7:1-28)

Ezra was both a priest and a scribe. He had a thorough knowledge of the Jewish law and he was well respected in official circles in Persia. When he told the king of his plan to go to Jerusalem to reform the Jewish people, the king readily gave his approval (7:1-10).

In addition the king gave Ezra funds from the royal treasury to carry out his program (11-20), with the assurance of further funds from the Persian administration in Palestine should the need arise (21-24). He also gave Ezra the authority to appoint judges, set up courts and carry out punishments (25-26). The whole arrangement caused Ezra to praise God and gave him added confidence as he began his work (27-28).

Details of the journey (8:1-36)

Leaders of the family groups who returned under Ezra are listed, along with the numbers of people in the various groups (8:1-14). Surprisingly, no Levites were among them, so Ezra sent specially for some. Levites were essential, as religious service was the main purpose of Ezra's return (15-20).

The journey to Jerusalem would take Ezra and his party about four months (see 7:9). During this time they would constantly be open to attacks from robbers. Yet even though they had with them large amounts of money and treasure, Ezra refused to ask the king for an escort of armed soldiers. He considered that to do so would contradict all that he had told the king concerning the protection God would give his people. So they fasted and prayed, trusting in God alone for their safety (21-23).

Ezra kept an exact record of all the wealth that they were taking with them. When that same amount was paid into the temple treasury at the end of the journey, it proved to all that God had answered their prayers and given them safety throughout their journey (24-34). The returned exiles acknowledged God's goodness by offering sacrifices. After this, Ezra went to the local Persian officials to present the documents authorizing him to take control of the Jewish community (35-36).

9:1-10:44 THE PROBLEM OF MIXED MARRIAGES

Ezra's grief (9:1-15)

One of the first problems that Ezra dealt with was that of mixed marriages. Israelite men had married non-Israelite wives and had families by them. The practice was widespread and involved even the leaders of the community. If allowed to continue, it could destroy Israel's religion and even Israel's identity as a distinct race (9:1-2).

When told of the matter, Ezra was overcome with grief and shame. He turned to God to confess the sin on behalf of the nation (3-5). He acknowledged that God had frequently and justly punished his people for their rebellion by allowing them to fall captive to their enemies; but in his grace God always left some to carry on the nation. The present liberty and protection that Persia gave them were further evidences of God's grace (6-9). Ezra's fear was that because of this latest rebellion against his law, God would act in judgment again, but this time leave no remnant at all (10-15).

The problem solved (10:1-44)

People heard of Ezra's grief and gathered with their families to meet him. They confessed their wrong-doing and promised on oath before Ezra that they would correct it (10:1-5). But the problem could not be solved in a day, for it was widespread and its consequences were far-reaching. Ezra therefore went away to a quiet room in a friend's house where he could spend the night considering the matter before God. The result was that a meeting of all families was arranged for three days later (6-8).

The weather on the day of the meeting was unfavourable, but the people sat and shivered in the rain to hear Ezra's judgment. They were genuinely concerned to put things right. Only a few objected when Ezra announced that the offenders should get rid of their foreign wives (9-15). This was going to take time, so officials were appointed to oversee the matter. Their work took three months to complete (16-17). Mixed marriages were as widespread among the religious leaders as among the common people, but in the end all alike put away their foreign wives. They also offered sacrifices for their sin (18-44).

Nehemiah

For the background to the book of Nehemiah see the introductory notes to the book of Ezra.

OUTLINE OF NEHEMIAH

1:1-2:10 NEHEMIAH RETURNS TO JERUSALEM

Thirteen years had now passed since Artaxerxes issued his decree giving Ezra authority to go to Jerusalem and reform Israel (Ezra 7:7; Neh 2:1). Ezra's work had some early success, but when the Jews tried to strengthen Jerusalem's defences by rebuilding the city wall, their enemies accused them of planning to rebel against Persia. They reported the matter to Artaxerxes, with the result that the king issued a decree commanding that the work stop immediately (Ezra 4:7-23).

Meanwhile in Persia, Nehemiah, a Jewish official in the king's palace, had risen to the trusted rank of cupbearer (GNB: wine steward; see 1:11). When the Jews heard that one of their own people was in a position to speak to the king, they came to Persia to see him. In particular they told him of the distress that the Jews' opponents had created in Jerusalem through carrying out the king's decree (1:1-3; cf. Ezra 4:23). That decree allowed the king to reverse his decision at a later date if he desired (Ezra 4:21), and the Jewish representatives from Jerusalem no doubt hoped that Nehemiah could persuade the king to become favourable to them again.

But Nehemiah was not a mere opportunist. He was a man of God and a man of prayer. He knew that his people's troubles were largely a result of their sins, and in a spirit of humble confession he brought the matter before God and asked his help (4-11).

For four months Nehemiah prayed about the matter. He was therefore fully prepared when an opportunity arose for him to speak to the king about it. The result was that he received permission to return and carry out the reconstruction work he had planned. He was also given the necessary building materials (2:1-8). This was probably the time when he was appointed governor of Jerusalem (see 5:14).

Circumstances surrounding Nehemiah's return were different from those that had surrounded Ezra's return, and Nehemiah felt it wise to accept the king's offer of an armed escort (9; cf. Ezra 8:21-23). Officials who previously controlled the Jerusalem district were hostile when they found they had lost this area to Nehemiah. Besides being Jewish, he had authority from the Persian king that made him independent of them (10).

2:11-7:73 REBUILDING THE CITY WALL

The plan of work followed (2:11-3:32)

Rebuilding the broken-down wall was going to mean much hard work. In fact, the task was so huge that some may have said it could not be done. Therefore, before announcing his plans, Nehemiah made a secret survey himself so that he would know exactly how much work was to be done and the amount of materials that would be required (11-16). This first-hand knowledge, together with his account of how God had guided all the events leading up to his return, convinced the people that they should start rebuilding the walls. Opposition, however, seemed inevitable (17-20).

The work was properly planned. Groups of people were allotted work areas side by side around the city, so that the entire wall was built. The list of workers shows that Jews from far and near came to help. Not only builders, but priests, goldsmiths, perfumers, government officials, merchants and young women helped in the work (3:1-16). The Levites repaired the section near the high priest's house (17-21). Priests and others who were residents of Jerusalem were usually allotted those sections of the wall that were closest to the areas where they lived. People from other regions built the remaining sections (22-32).

Early opposition (4:1-23)

Since the Jews had the Persian king's approval for their building program, their opponents, being also under the government of Persia, hesitated to attack Jerusalem openly. However, they were still able to mock and ridicule, hoping that this would dishearten the people from building (4:1-5).

But the Jews were not easily discouraged and the work continued (6). The enemies therefore planned to create confusion and uncertainty among the Jews by carrying out surprise terrorist attacks on the city. On hearing of this, the Jews increased their prayer and strengthened their defences (7-9).

Jews from outlying areas informed Nehemiah of the enemies' movements (10-12), but Nehemiah still took no risks. He armed all the workers and divided them into two shifts, one working while the other stood guard. He also made arrangements for battle in case of a sudden attack (13-21). Country people who worked in the city were asked to sleep there rather than return home, in order to provide added protection at night (22-23).

The greed of the rich (5:1-19)

Another problem that Nehemiah dealt with was the tension that had developed over the years between the rich and the poor. Those in financial difficulty borrowed money from the rich to buy food and pay their land taxes to the Persian government. The rich took advantage of them by charging heavy interest. Then, when the poor could not pay, the rich took their land from them in payment, and in some cases took their children as slaves. Troubles increased when a famine hit the land, and with the rebuilding of the wall these troubles increased further, since the workers were not able to earn a normal living. The poor saw no way out of their difficulties and appealed to Nehemiah for help (5:1-5).

Nehemiah knew the greed and cunning of the rich. One of their schemes was to sell Jews to foreigners as slaves, knowing that Nehemiah's policy was for the state to buy them back (6-8). Therefore, he commanded the rich to return any people or property they had seized, and to remove all interest on loans (9-13).

Throughout the twelve years of his governorship, Nehemiah gave the people an example to follow. He did not claim benefits that were lawfully his, as he did not want to place added burdens on the people. He even fed his employees and guests out of his personal funds (14-19).

The wall completed (6:1-7:73)

With the wall nearing completion, the enemies saw that their only hope lay in getting rid of Nehemiah himself. They tried to draw him out into the country where they could murder him, but Nehemiah was aware of their tricks (6:1-4). They then spread rumours, by means of an open letter, that Nehemiah was planning a revolt against Persia, but their efforts came to nothing (5-9).

The enemies thought of yet another plan. They tried to make Nehemiah act in a way that would ruin his reputation for fearlessness before opponents and reverence for the temple. Again they failed (10-14). Even the spies and traitors whom the enemies had planted in Jerusalem were unable to stop Nehemiah from completing the wall (15-19).

Jerusalem was now surrounded with a solid wall of defence. But as usual Nehemiah took no risks. The city was only thinly populated and special precautions were necessary. In case of a surprise early morning attack, Nehemiah ordered that the city gates remain closed until all the people were awake and about their daily business. In addition he formed a city-wide guard, arranged so that each household supervised an area close to it (7:1-4).

Nehemiah then made a register of all those living in Jerusalem. It was based on lists that went back to the very first group of returned exiles, who had come to Jerusalem with Zerubbabel almost a century earlier (5-73; see notes on Ezra 2:1-70, where the same list is given).

8:1-13:31 NEHEMIAH'S REFORMS

First reading of the law (8:1-18)

The wall was finished on the twenty-fifth day of the sixth month (see 6:15). Israel's mid-year meetings and festivals were held during the seventh month (Lev 23:24,27,34), so this was a fitting occasion to assemble the people to celebrate the completion of the rebuilt wall (see 7:73b, 8:1). (The same time of the year had been chosen for the dedication of the rebuilt altar more than ninety years previously; see Ezra 3:1-6.)

At the people's request, Ezra, assisted by some Levites, read the law and explained it to the people. It must have been so long since the people had heard the law that they all listened attentively (8:1-8). When they found how far they had departed from the law, they were filled with grief. Nehemiah was concerned that the celebration, instead of being a time of joyous feasting, was turning into a time of mourning and weeping (9-12).

Next day Israel's leaders returned to hear more of God's law (13). This led in turn to a full-scale national celebration of the Feast of Tabernacles (RSV: Feast of Booths; GNB: Festival of Shelters). On this occasion the people lived in temporary shelters made of branches of trees and palm leaves, in memory of their ancestors' unsettled existence in the wilderness (14-18; see Lev 23:33-43).

Israel's confession and oath (9:1-10:39)

Two days after the end of the Feast of Tabernacles (which lasted from the fifteenth day to the twenty-second day of the month; see 8:18; Lev 23:34), the people reassembled for another reading of the law. After this came a time of confession and worship led by the Levites (9:1-5).

The prayer began by exalting God as the great Creator, and by praising him for choosing Abraham and making his covenant with him (6-8). God was faithful to his people through all their trials, whether in Egypt or in the wilderness (9-15). Even when they rebelled against him, he forgave them and brought them into the promised land (16-25). Still the people were rebellious and still God forgave them. But they continued in their disobedience. In the end, after many defeats and much oppression, they were taken captive into foreign lands, so that God might humble them and bring them to repentance (26-31). Though they were now back in their land, they were still under the rule of foreigners. They confessed that this was a just reward for their sins, for they had been disobedient to the covenant (32-37).

Having confessed their failures, the people made a fresh covenant promise to be faithful to God. They confirmed their promise with a written oath signed by their leaders on their behalf (38). Nehemiah was the first to sign (10:1), followed by the priests (2-8), Levites (9-13) and civil leaders (14-27). All the people were bound by the covenant document to be obedient to God's law (28-29).

Specific matters mentioned in the document concerned mixed marriages (30; see Exod 34:15-16), the Sabbath day and the sabbatical year (31; see Exod 20:8-10, 23:10-11; Deut 15:1-2), the temple tax (32; see Exod 30:11-16), the maintenance of the temple and its rituals (33-34), offerings of firstfruits and firstborn (35-36; see Num 18:13-18) and tithes (37-39; see Num 18:21-28).

Lists of Jerusalem residents (11:1-36)

Most of the people who returned from exile had settled in the country around Jerusalem rather than in the city itself. Therefore, because Jerusalem was thinly populated, a resettlement scheme was put into practice. Under this scheme one tenth of the residents from the country areas came to live in Jerusalem and so increase its stability. In addition to these, a large group offered willingly to come and live in the city (11:1-2).

A list is then given of the heads of the families who returned with Zerubbabel. (The descendants of these families would have been the old established residents of Jerusalem at the time the resettlement program was planned.) Apart from those belonging to the tribes of Judah and Benjamin (3-9), most seem to have been priests, Levites or other temple servants (10-21. See also notes on 1 Chron 9:1-34, where the same list is given, with a few variations and additions). Arrangements were also made for overseeing the work of the Levites, regulating the temple singers, and having a Jewish representative at the court of the Persian king (22-24). Then follows a list of reoccupied towns in the former tribal territories of Judah and Benjamin (25-36).

Lists of priests and Levites (12:1-26)

Following the lists of residents of Jerusalem are the lists of priests and Levites. The first of these records the names of those priests and Levites who returned with Zerubbabel and Joshua (12:1-9). (The Ezra mentioned in this list is not the more commonly known Ezra.) After recording the descendants of Joshua for the next six generations (10-11), the writer returns to record the heads of the other original priestly families (12-21).

Besides dealing with the families of priests, the records also deal with ordinary temple servants. Some of the records extend to an era later than the time of Nehemiah (22-26).

Dedication of the wall (12:27-13:3)

The story continues from where it left off in 10:39. After the reading of the law, the celebration of the Festival of Tabernacles and the people's oath of loyalty to the covenant, the wall was dedicated. Priests, Levites, singers, musicians and leading citizens joined in the ceremony (27-30). The people assembled at a point beside the wall on one side of the city. They then divided into two groups and set off marching in opposite directions around the wall. One group was led by Ezra (31-37), the other by Nehemiah (38-39). The two groups met on the opposite side of the city at the temple, where they joined in offering sacrifices and praising God with much rejoicing (40-43).

Officials were then appointed to oversee the collection and distribution of money and supplies that the people brought to the temple. All Israelites gave one tenth of their income to this central fund. From there it was divided among the Levites, who assisted the priests and provided music, singing and other services in the temple. The Levites in turn gave one tenth of their income to support the priests

(44-47). A further reading from the law reminded the people to keep God's temple holy. Pagans were to be refused entry (13:1-3).

Nehemiah's later reforms (13:4-31)

After serving twelve years as governor of Jerusalem, Nehemiah returned to Persia for a period (see 5:14; 13:6). During his absence the religion of the Jews deteriorated, while the Jews' old enemies, Sanballat and Tobiah, gained some influence in Jerusalem. The high priest Eliashib was especially blameworthy in this. He allowed a member of the high priestly family to marry the daughter of Sanballat (see v. 28), and gave permission to Tobiah to live in one of the temple rooms. This was directly against the law that Nehemiah tried to uphold, for Tobiah was an Ammonite (see 4:3; 13:1). On his return Nehemiah quickly corrected the disorders (4-9).

Nehemiah discovered also that the people had broken an important covenant promise made at the time of the dedication of the city wall. They had not paid tithes, with the result that the Levites had to leave the service of the temple and work for their living in the fields (10-14; cf. 10:35-39).

People were also working and trading on the Sabbath, thereby breaking another of the covenant promises (15-18; cf. 10:31). Nehemiah quickly put an end to this. By closing the city gates on the Sabbath, he prevented people from bringing their goods into the city to sell. He also stopped them from selling outside the gate or waiting there in preparation for selling as soon as the Sabbath was past (19-22).

In Ezra's day the people had taken an oath to put away their foreign wives, and in fact had done so (Ezra 10:19,44). Now the practice was widespread again, and threatened to corrupt Israel's religion. With characteristic fearlessness, Nehemiah soon corrected the situation (23-29). There is no doubt that he, more than anyone else, helped the people of his day establish their way of life on a proper religious basis according to the law of God (30-31).

Esther

BACKGROUND

The book of Esther belongs to that period of Israel's history known as the post-exilic. The story recorded in the book took place in Persia during the reign of the Persian king Xerxes I, also known as Ahasuerus, who reigned from 486 to 465 BC. (For further details of the post-exilic era see background notes to the book of Ezra.)

Persia had become ruler of the Jews more than half a century before the time of Ahasuerus, when Cyrus conquered Babylon (in 539 BC). Although Cyrus gave permission to the captive Jews to return to their homeland, many preferred to remain in Babylon (or Persia, as it now was). They felt assured of reasonable security and freedom in the land of their captivity, and did not want to face the risks and hardships of a new life in Jerusalem. They and their descendants continued to increase in prosperity, but showed little interest in re-establishing their religion as a spiritual force in their national life.

God, however, was still guarding his people. The book of Esther does not mention the name of God or the religious activities that should have been the main feature of Jewish life. But it shows that God was still ruling in their affairs, whether they acknowledged him or not. He still had a purpose for his people and he would not allow them to be destroyed.

OUTLINE

1:1-2:23   Esther becomes queen
3:1-7:10   Plan to destroy the Jews
8:1-10:3   The Jews triumphant

1:1-2:23 ESTHER BECOMES QUEEN

Officials and leading citizens from all over the Persian Empire had gathered in the winter capital for an exhibition designed to display the riches and magnificence of the royal court. The exhibition lasted six months and was brought to a fitting climax by a lavish seven-day banquet (1:1-9). The week of wine and merriment so excited the king that his sexual urges were in danger of getting out of control. Consequently, when he told his queen Vashti to display her beauty before the crowd of wine-soaked men at the banquet, Vashti refused (10-12). The queen had defied the king's authority and his pride was hurt. In anger he removed her from being queen (13-22).

For some time the king made no attempt to replace Vashti. He still had plenty of concubines, but his advisers suggested that he appoint an official queen (2:1-4). The most beautiful young women in the land were therefore brought together in the palace, where they were further beautified and trained so that the king might choose one as his queen. Among them was an orphan Jew named Esther, who had been brought up by her cousin Mordecai. But she did not reveal to anyone in the palace that she was a Jew (5-11).

After a year of beauty preparation, all the young women were taken in turn to the king. In the end he chose Esther and crowned her queen (12-18). (This happened four years after he removed Vashti; cf. 1:3; 2:16.)

Mordecai apparently worked in or around the palace (see v. 11,19). When he heard that two of the palace guards were plotting to assassinate the king, he passed on the information to the king by way of Esther. The guards were executed, and Mordecai's good deed was noted in the official records (19-23).

3:1-7:10 PLAN TO DESTROY THE JEWS

Haman plots evil (3:1-15)

Some time later, a proud and ambitious man named Haman was promoted to the position of chief minister in the Empire. He apparently demanded that people honour him almost as if he were a god. Mordecai refused, letting it be known that he was a Jew, and claiming that to give Haman such honour was against his Jewish religion. Haman was furious, and decided to get his revenge by killing all the Jews in the Empire (3:1-6). (Esther had now been queen just over four years; cf. 2:16; 3:7.)

Being superstitious, Haman cast lots to find out the best day on which to carry out his murderous plan. He gained the king's permission by pointing out how the wealth seized from the Jews would enrich the royal treasury. The king even gave his ring to Haman, which meant that Haman could put the royal seal on any order he wished to make. However, God was clearly in control of the casting of the lots, with the result that Haman would have to wait eleven months before he could carry out his plan (7-11).

Haman dared not bring forward the date of his 'lucky day'. He therefore went ahead and issued the decree, announcing that in eleven months time all Jews would be destroyed. God, meanwhile, could work in the affairs of the government and reverse the force of the decree (12-15).

Esther agrees to help the Jews (4:1-17)

Mordecai realized that the Jews' only hope now lay with Esther, who, shut up in the women's quarters of the palace, had not heard of the decree till Mordecai told her. He added that her duty now was to ask the king to cancel the decree (4:1-9).

Esther pointed out that this was not as easy as Mordecai thought, for even the queen risked her life in making a request of the king (10-11). But Mordecai believed that God would not allow the Jewish people to be destroyed, and that Esther would be his means of saving them. She therefore agreed to approach the king. First, however, she asked for three days of fasting by the Jews on her behalf (12-17).

Haman's humiliation and defeat (5:1-7:10)

After three days Esther approached the king and invited him and Haman to dinner (5:1-4). She was so pleased with their friendly response that she decided to invite them again the next day, in the hope that they would be even more favourable to her (5-8). Haman thought that the honour given him by the queen showed that she, as well as the king, was pleased with him and agreed with his anti-Jewish policy. He decided to take the opportunity of this royal favour to arrange for a decree from the king to have chief enemy Mordecai executed immediately (9-14).

Early next morning, Haman went to ask the king for Mordecai's execution. But the king had just spent the night reviewing some official records, where he was reminded that Mordecai had saved his life several years earlier. Knowing nothing of the hatred that Haman and Mordecai had for each other, the king decided that Mordecai must be rewarded (6:1-5).

The king consulted Haman about the matter, but did not tell Haman the name of the person who was to receive the proposed royal honour. Haman, thinking that the honour was for himself, suggested an extravagant public show of the king's favour (6-9). The king agreed, with the result that Haman, instead of executing Mordecai, had to carry out the king's command to honour Mordecai before the people (10-11). Haman's humiliation appeared to his family and friends as a foreshadowing of worse to come (12-13).

When the king and Haman joined Esther for dinner that night, the circumstances were entirely favourable for Esther to put her case to the king (14-7:2). The king showed no anger when he found out that Esther was Jewish, but he burst into fury when told that Haman had planned the destruction of the queen and her people. Haman threw himself down on the couch before Esther to cry for mercy, but the king, in his rage, interpreted Haman's action as an attempt at rape. He then learnt that Haman had prepared to execute the man who had saved the king's life. The king had heard enough; he condemned Haman to immediate death (3-10).

8:1-10:3 THE JEWS TRIUMPHANT

Victory and celebration (8:1-9:32)

Although Mordecai was appointed chief minister instead of Haman (8:1-2), the decree arranged by Haman was still in force. A king's decree could not be changed. However, the king gave Esther and Mordecai his authority to issue a new decree that would counteract the former one (3-8).

Esther and Mordecai acted promptly. They gave the Jews permission to take whatever action they chose in order to defend themselves against any attack on the appointed day. Because the new decree showed that the king was now sympathetic to the Jews, provincial officials would hesitate to enforce the former decree (9-14). Many non-Jewish people were so impressed by what had happened, that they became open converts to the Jewish religion (15-17).

It seems that when the day for the destruction of the Jews arrived, very few of their enemies attacked them. Rather the Jews attacked their enemies, possibly doing more than the decree gave them permission to do. To their credit, however, they refused to exercise their right to plunder the enemies' goods. The Persian officials now feared Mordecai's power, and thought it wise to give the Jews whatever help they needed (9:1-10).

At Esther's request, the Jews in the capital were given an extra day to take revenge on their enemies (11-15). This meant that although the slaughter in the provincial areas lasted only one day, in the capital it lasted two days (16-19).

Mordecai ordered that the great occasion be celebrated by feasting, exchanging gifts of food and giving to the poor (20-22). From that time on the Jews held an annual festival, known as the Feast of Purim, to celebrate their victory over Haman. The word 'purim' was the Hebrew plural of the Persian-Assyrian word *pur*, and meant 'lots'; for by casting lots, Haman decided which day was suitable for his attack. It was a day that turned into one of triumph for the Jews (23-28; cf. 3:7,13). Esther and Mordecai then issued a formal decree to confirm Mordecai's instructions concerning Purim as official law for all Jews (29-32).

Continued prosperity (10:1-3)

The book concludes by noting the greatness of Mordecai and the benefits that he brought to the Jewish people. Under his administration, non-Jewish peoples were forced to contribute more to the Empire's economy, so the burden on the Jews was eased (10:1-2). Mordecai continued in his position as chief minister in the government of Ahasuerus for many years, and under him the Jews had security and contentment (3).

Job

BACKGROUND

Among the many different types of books in the Old Testament are those known as the wisdom books. These are the books of Job, Proverbs and Ecclesiastes, though certain psalms and parts of other books might also be classified as wisdom literature.

Wisdom writings

God used various kinds of preachers and teachers to instruct and guide his people. He used priests to teach and supervise his law (Lev 10:8-11; Deut 33:10; Mal 2:7), and prophets to bring messages that would reveal his purposes and turn people from sin to obedience (Ezek 2:3-5; Amos 3:1,7-8; Micah 3:8). He also used wisdom teachers. These people, sometimes known as 'the wise', constituted a distinct category among the teachers of Israel (Jer 18:18; cf. Isa 29:14). They did not claim to receive revelations from God, but examined the everyday affairs of life and, as people of faith, instructed others in right living (Eccles 12:9-10).

The biblical literature that comes from the wisdom teachers is of two main types. One of these, represented by the book of Proverbs, deals mainly with the general principles of right and wrong as they apply to life in general; for example, the righteous will prosper but the wicked will perish (Prov 11:5-8; 12:6-7). The other, represented by Job and Ecclesiastes, looks at the exceptions to these general principles; for example, the righteous sometimes have all sorts of troubles, but the wicked enjoy peace and prosperity (Job 12:4; 21:7-13; Eccles 7:15; 8:10,14).

These features do not indicate that the wisdom teachers had conflicting interpretations of life. They show rather that wise people were able to look at various aspects of life in different ways. The same teacher could consider important issues from a variety of viewpoints. The writer of Proverbs, for example, acknowledges that an acceptable general principle may not apply equally in every case (Prov 26:4-5), while the writers of Job and Ecclesiastes recognize that, in spite of the exceptions, general principles are still the basis for wise teaching (Job 28:20-28; Eccles 7:1-13).

Wisdom teachers were godly men who looked at life with all its consistencies and inconsistencies, so that they might help God's people find meaning and purpose in the life God had given them. Though they were aware of an afterlife (Job 19:26), their main concern was to deal with the issues that people faced in the present life.

Understanding Job

Job was a wealthy, learned, God-fearing man who lived in Uz, a land somewhere in the region east of Palestine. When he was overcome by a series of disasters, his friends argued that his troubles must have been because of his secret sins. Job denied this. He knew that he was not perfect, but he also knew that the traditional views, such as those held by his learned friends, did not explain everything. The long and bitter argument that followed takes up most of the book.

The reader of the book, however, knows what neither Job nor his friends knew. Satan had made the accusation that people serve God only because of the good things they can get from him. If they get only suffering and hardship they will curse him (Job 1:9-11; 2:4-5). God allowed disasters to fall upon Job to prove the genuineness of Job's faith and enrich his experience of God (cf. James 5:11). Job's sufferings were proof not of God's judgment on him but of God's confidence in him.

In insisting that suffering must be the result of personal sin, the friends drove Job to the point where he almost lost patience with them completely; but they also drove him to God, whom Job saw as his only hope. In making his protests to God, Job may have been guilty of using rash language, but at least he took his protests to the right person.

Job was finally satisfied, not through having all his questions answered, but through meeting the God to whom he had cried. He may not have understood God's purposes, but he learnt that God's wisdom was beyond human understanding and he was worthy of a person's total trust. God was not answerable to anyone; he could do as he pleased.

In announcing his approval of Job, God showed the friends to be wrong in asserting that suffering was always the result of personal sin. He also showed

Satan to be wrong in asserting that people worship God only because of what they can get from him. Job remained true to God though he had lost everything, but in the end God blessed him with greater blessings than he had before.

Writing of the book

There is no certainty concerning the era the story of Job belongs to, nor does the book say who wrote it. However, lack of information on these matters is no hindrance to an understanding of the book. The important considerations when reading the book of Job are not those relating to its authorship and date, but those relating to its literary character. The book is a piece of Hebrew wisdom literature and, apart from its beginning and ending, is written in poetry.

We should not read the book of Job as we would those books of the Old Testament that consist mainly of prose narratives, legal commandments, or challenging sermons. This is not only because the book has the characteristics of wisdom literature already considered, but also because it is in a stylized form. This is evident throughout the book — in the narrative introduction, in the successive rounds of debate, and in the dramatic conclusion.

As in all poetry, the language and word-pictures are often striking, and the writer does not expect his readers to interpret everything literally. Nor has he designed the book to be read as a word-by-word study. Often one verse, or several verses, may be used to express one basic thought. These features are typical of Hebrew poetry, and the more we understand such features the better we will understand Job. (For more about the characteristics of Hebrew poetry see introductory notes to Psalms and Proverbs.)

OUTLINE

1:1-2:13 SATAN TESTS JOB

From prosperity to ruin (1:1-22)

A popular belief in ancient times was that prosperity and well-being were proofs of godliness, but poverty and suffering were proofs of ungodliness. They were signs that God was either rewarding or punishing a person, according to whether that person's life was good or bad. The book of Job contradicts this belief. Yet the prosperous and contented Job was indeed a godly person who was blameless in all that he did. He was concerned also for purity in the lives of all his children (1:1-5).

Meanwhile in heaven, God's court of angelic beings had assembled before him. Among them was one, Satan, whose chief concern was to move around the world looking for human failings (6-7). (In Hebrew *satan* was a common word that meant 'adversary' or 'opponent'.) Satan made the accusation to God that Job's faith was not sincere. If Job suddenly lost his family and possessions, argued Satan, his apparent devotion to God would soon disappear (8-11). God allowed Satan to test Job by removing anything that belonged to him, but he was not to harm Job's body (12).

In a series of calamities, Job lost first his working animals (13-15), then his sheep and shepherds (16), then his camels (17), and finally all his children (18-19). In spite of his overwhelming distress, Job's devotion to God did not alter (20-22).

Job's loathsome disease (2:1-13)

Not accepting defeat, Satan still claimed that Job was concerned only for himself. He would sacrifice his possessions, and even his family, provided he himself avoided suffering. He would sacrifice their skin to save his own (2:1-5). God again accepted Satan's challenge, this time allowing him to attack Job's body (6). Satan therefore afflicted Job with the most painful and loathsome disease. The faith of Job's wife failed, but Job's faith did not, even though he was treated worse than a diseased dog. He was driven from the town and forced to live at the public garbage dump (7-10).

Those who had been Job's friends in his days of prosperity deserted him. Only three, all of them (like Job) seekers of wisdom, came to comfort him. When they saw his suffering they were so overcome with grief that for several days they could say nothing, only weep (11-13).

3:1-14:22 FIRST ROUND OF ARGUMENT

Job's bitterness (3:1-26)

The long silence breaks when Job curses the day of his birth. He wishes he had never been born (3:1-7). He would like sorcerers also to curse that dark day. If they have power over the mythical sea monster Leviathan, they should have power to declare the day of his birth a day of darkness and sorrow, a day on which no person should have been born (8-10). If he had to be born, he wishes he had been stillborn. Then he would have gone straight to the place of the dead (11-16). Death releases all people from the sufferings of life, whether old or young, rich or poor, good or bad, kings or prisoners, masters or slaves (17-19).

Life only increases Job's misery. He feels that he would be better dead than alive, better in darkness than in light. It is a cruel mockery when the sole purpose of life seems to be to make him conscious of his distress, the sole purpose of light to show him how horrible are his sufferings (20-24).

Yet Job's suffering is more than physical. The inner conflict is more tormenting. According to what he has always believed, his great suffering means that he must be a great sinner, but he knows he is not. What he has always dreaded has apparently come true: he is cut off from God and he does not know why (25-26).

The debate

Although we shall see that in the end Job is proved right, this does not mean that everything he says during the debate is true (cf. 6:26; 42:1-6). Likewise, although the book will show that the arguments of the three friends are not the answer to Job's suffering, this does not mean that everything they say is wrong.

The chief fault of the three friends is that they try to explain all the facts of human suffering on the basis that suffering is always the result of personal sin. Certainly, it sometimes is, but the special knowledge we are given in Chapters 1 and 2 of God's control of events shows us that this is not always the case. No one can be certain of the underlying reason for another person's suffering.

Also, amid all the friends' words of advice there is no real sympathy for Job, and no acknowledgment of the remarkable patience and humble submission to God that he has already shown (see 1:21; 2:10). They firmly believe their traditional theories, but they have never been in Job's position where they can test those theories in practice. They are in the dangerous position of having religious beliefs without corresponding personal experience. While they talk *about* God, Job talks *to* God.

Eliphaz speaks (4:1-5:27)

The first of the three friends to speak is Eliphaz, who is probably the oldest of the three. He is also the least severe in the accusations brought against Job (4:1-2). He begins by noting that in the past Job comforted others in their troubles, but now that he

has troubles himself, his faith has failed. If Job truly honoured God and was upright in his ways, there would be no need for this despondency (3-6). The person who is innocent, argues Eliphaz, need not fear suffering or death. Such calamities are God's judgment on wrongdoing, and not even the strongest or most defiant person can withstand his judgment (7-11).

Eliphaz now tells of a hair-raising vision he saw one night (12-16). (It becomes clear, as we read Eliphaz's speeches, that this vision has become for him a standard by which he judges others.) The main point that Eliphaz learnt from his vision was that no person can be righteous before God. If angels, who live in the heavenly realm, are imperfect, how much more imperfect must human beings be who live on the earth (17-19). Their brief lives comes to an inglorious end, like a tent that collapses when its cords are cut (20-21).

According to Eliphaz, it is useless for Job to expect the angels to support his protest against God's laws (5:1). The person who rebels against God in such bitterness is a fool and will only get himself into more trouble. His house may be destroyed, his sons convicted of lawbreaking, or his fields plundered by raiders (2-5). For Eliphaz, this shows that suffering does not spring up by itself. Suffering is caused by a person's sin, just as sparks are caused by a fire (6-7).

In summary, Eliphaz's suggestion is that if he were in Job's position he would stop complaining and leave the whole matter in God's hands, for he has infinite wisdom and power (8-10). God blesses the humble and the needy, though he opposes those who think they are clever (11-16). The sufferings God uses to punish and correct people are likened to wounds. He will heal the wounds of those who submit to him (17-18). He will then bless them with protection from famine and from enemies (19-22); wild beasts will not destroy their flocks or herds (23-24); their families will multiply, and they will die contented in old age (25-26). Such is Eliphaz's advice, based on much research, and he suggests that Job accept it (27).

Job's reply to Eliphaz (6:1-7:21)

Eliphaz had rebuked Job for his impatient outburst. In reply Job acknowledges that God is the one who has sent this affliction, but he points out that if Eliphaz knew how great this suffering was he would understand why Job spoke rashly (6:1-4). An animal cries out only with good reason (for example, if it is hungry for food). Job likewise cries out only with good reason. His tormenting thoughts and Eliphaz's useless words are to him like food that makes him sick (5-7). He still refuses to curse God, and wishes that God would give him his request and kill him, even if the death is painful (8-10). He cannot endure much more suffering; he is not made of rock or bronze (11-13)!

Job expected kindness from his friends but found none. They are like useless streams that overflow with destructive ice and snow in winter, but dry up in summer (14-17). They disappoint all who go to them expecting to find something beneficial (18-21). Job has not asked his friends for money or help, but he had hoped for sympathy (22-23).

Instead Job receives from his friends nothing but rebuke for his rash words. They make no effort to understand what despair must have caused him to make such an outburst. He accuses them of being heartless, and challenges them to show him plainly where he is wrong (24-27). He is being honest with them; in return he wants some understanding. At least he wants their acknowledgment that he can tell the difference between suffering that is deserved and suffering that is not (28-30).

Life for Job has no pleasure. He looks for death as a worker looks for wages or a slave looks for rest at the end of a hard day's work. Day and night he has nothing but pain (7:1-5). Bitterly Job says that if God is going to help him, he should do it quickly, otherwise Job will soon be dead. It will then be too late for God to do anything (6-10).

This leads Job to an angry outburst addressed to God. Job asks why God must treat him with such severity, as if he were a wild monster (11-12). Tortured with pain by day and horrible dreams by night, he wants only to die (13-16). If God is so great, why doesn't he leave Job alone? Job complains that God's torment of him is so constant he does not even have time to swallow his spittle (17-19). He cannot understand why the mighty God is so concerned over the small sins of one person. Surely they are not such a burden. Surely God can forgive. If he does not hurry and forgive soon, it will be too late, because Job will be dead (20-21).

Bildad speaks (8:1-22)

After rebuking Job for his wild words against God, Bildad tells him that God is always just. Completely lacking in sympathy, Bildad reminds Job that his children have died, and cruelly concludes that it must have been because of their sin (8:1-4). Job's suffering must likewise be because of *his* sin. If, however, he is innocent, he need only pray humbly to God, and God will replace his suffering with greater blessing than he had before (5-7).

For Bildad the traditional teaching is of first importance, and this emphasis characterizes all his speeches. Job cannot, on the basis of his short experience, question what all the wisest people of previous ages have believed (8-10).

All disaster, in Bildad's view, is the consequence of personal ungodliness. As flourishing plants wither and die when the water dries up, so the rich are brought to ruin when they forget God (11-13). They are as insecure as a spider's web (14-15). They are like a fast-growing plant that is suddenly pulled up and replaced by others. Their joy is shortlived (16-19). According to Bildad, the reason for Job's terrible losses and tormenting suffering can only be Job's sin. Repentance will bring renewed strength, joy, victory and prosperity (20-22).

Job's reply to Bildad (9:1-10:22)

While agreeing with Bildad that God is just, Job argues that ordinary people are still at a disadvantage. They cannot present their side of the case satisfactorily, because God always has the wisdom and power to frustrate them. He can ask a thousand questions that they cannot answer (9:1-4). He can do what he wishes in the heavens or on the earth (5-9). He can work miracles and no one can resist him (10-12). If God overthrows those with supernatural power such as the mythical monster Rahab, what chance does a mere human like Job have (13-14)?

Job knows he has not committed great sins, but he also knows that if he tried to argue his case before God he would still lose (15-16). He would surely say something wrong and so be proved guilty. God would crush him then as he crushes him now (17-20).

Although he is blameless, Job sees no purpose in living, since God destroys the innocent and the guilty alike. There seems to be no justice (21-24). Life may be short, but it is full of pain and suffering (25-28). He can see no purpose in trying to bear suffering gladly or act uprightly, because God still condemns him as a sinner (29-31). Job feels that because God is God and he is only a man, the battle is unequal. He wants an umpire, a mediator, someone to bridge the gap by bringing the two parties together and settling the case (32-33). By himself Job cannot plead his case satisfactorily, because he is overwhelmed by the suffering God has sent him (34-35).

In bitterness Job asks God why he makes the innocent suffer, yet at the same time blesses the wicked (10:1-3). Is he like an unjust judge who punishes a person even though he knows the person is innocent (4-7)? Did God create Job simply to destroy him (8-9)? Has he kept him alive merely to torment him (10-13)? It seems to Job that it makes no difference whether he is good or bad. God's purpose seems to be to hunt him mercilessly and heap punishment upon him for even the smallest sins (14-17).

Job wishes he had never been born into a world of such injustice and suffering (18-19). He asks only for the briefest period of happiness before he dies and goes to the gloomy comfortless world of the dead (20-22).

Zophar speaks (11:1-20)

Angered at what he considers to be Job's irreverent talk, Zophar can keep silent no longer (11:1-3). He rebukes Job for claiming to be an innocent victim of injustice, and asserts that if Job really suffered according to his sin, his suffering would be much worse (4-6). God's wisdom is limitless and therefore his judgments must be true. People should neither oppose him nor expect to understand his ways (7-10). No one can deceive God, for he sees people as they really are. Only stupid people ask the sorts of questions Job has been asking (11-12).

What Job must do, says Zophar, is acknowledge his sin and turn from it (13-14). In return God will bless him with a genuinely clear conscience and a feeling of security and confidence. The miserable past will be forgotten; a bright future is assured (15-19). But if he stubbornly refuses to repent, Job can expect only increased suffering, which will lead finally to death (20).

The impression we gain from the speeches of Zophar is that he is the shallowest thinker of the three. Not surprisingly, he is also the most dogmatic and hot tempered. He has no experience such as Eliphaz's dream to support him; he does not have Bildad's knowledge of teachings handed down from the past; but he is totally confident that his view is right and all others wrong.

Job's reply to Zophar (12:1-14:22)

The reply from Job opens with a sarcastic comment on the supposed wisdom of the three friends. They have merely been repeating general truths that everybody knows (12:1-3). They do not have the troubles Job has, and they make no attempt to understand how Job feels. A good person suffers while wicked people live in peace and security (4-6).

Job does not argue with the fact that all life is in God's hands. What worries him is the interpretation of that fact (7-10). As a person tastes food before swallowing it, so Job will test the old interpretations before accepting them (11-12).

Being well taught himself, Job then quotes at length from the traditional teaching. God is perfect in wisdom and his power is irresistible (13-16). He humbles the mighty (17-22) and overthrows nations (23-25). Job knows all this as well as his friends do. What he wants to know is *why* God does these things (13:1-3). The three friends think they are speaking for God in accusing Job, but Job points out that this cannot be so, because God does not use deceit. They would be wiser to keep quiet (4-8). They themselves should fear God, because he will one day examine and judge them as they believe he has examined and judged Job (9-12).

The friends are now asked to be silent and listen as Job presents his case before God (13). He knows he is risking his life in being so bold, for an ungodly person could not survive in God's presence. Job, however, believes he is innocent. If God or anyone else can prove him guilty, he will willingly accept the death sentence (14-19). Job makes just two requests of God. First, he asks God to give him some relief from pain so that he can present his case. Second, he asks that God will not cause him to be overcome with fear as he comes into the divine presence. He wants to ask God questions, and he promises to answer any questions God asks him (20-22).

To begin with, Job asks what accusations God has against him. Why is he forced to suffer (23-25)? Is he, for example, reaping the fruits of sins done in his youth? Whatever the answer, he feels completely helpless in his present plight (26-28).

Life is short and a certain amount of trouble and wrongdoing is to be expected (14:1-5). Why then, asks Job, does God not leave people alone so that they can enjoy their short lives without unnecessary suffering (6)? Even trees are better off than people. A tree that is cut down may sprout again, but a person who is 'cut down' is dead for ever (7-10). He is (to use another picture) like a river or lake that has dried up (11-12).

Job wishes that Sheol, the place of the dead, were only a temporary dwelling place. Then, after a period when he gains relief from suffering and cleansing from sin, he could continue life in a new and more meaningful fellowship with God. If he knew this to be true, he would be able to endure his present sufferings more patiently (13-17). Instead, the only feeling that accompanies his pain is the feeling of hopelessness. He knows he will be cut off from those he loves most, never to see them or hear of them again. Like soil washed away by a river he will disappear, never to return (18-22).

15:1-21:34 SECOND ROUND OF ARGUMENT

Eliphaz speaks (15:1-35)

The three friends are offended that their collective wisdom has not humbled Job as they had hoped. They are angered that Job continues to argue with God. Therefore, in this the second round of argument they emphasize the terrors of God's judgment, hoping that this might bring Job to repentance.

Eliphaz, the least aggressive of the three, leads off again, though clearly even he is angered and offended at Job's speech. Job claims to be a wise and godly person, but his rash answers have been unprofitable and irreverent. Such speech is itself proof of his guilt (15:1-6). Does Job think that he alone has knowledge of the ways of God (7-9)? Does he think that he can ignore teaching that is the fruit of generations of experience (10)? Why does he despise the comfort of his friends and turn against them with such hostility (11-13)? If even angels are not perfect, how sinful must the rebellious, self-righteous, argumentative Job appear in God's sight (14-16. Note how Eliphaz again refers to his dream; cf. 4:18).

Job cannot ignore the lessons of experience, nor can he ignore the teaching of traditional wisdom (which, Eliphaz notes approvingly, has not been affected by foreign ideas) (17-19). Experience and traditional wisdom show clearly that pain, loss of prosperity and the feeling of hopelessness are all the results of wickedness (20-24). And the supreme wickedness, says Eliphaz, is to fight against God. When God destroys, a person should not try to rebuild (25-28).

The rebel, in punishment for his sin, suffers personal loss and an early death. He is like a healthy vine or tree that is suddenly destroyed (29-33). Such disaster is the unavoidable result of a deceitful heart (34-35).

Job's reply to Eliphaz (16:1-17:16)

Tired at this repetition of the friends' unhelpful teaching, Job says he could give similar 'comfort' if he were in their position and they in his (16:1-5). His argument with God may not have brought relief from his pain, but neither has his silence. In fact, his physical condition only becomes worse (6-8). God opposes him and people insult him. Some deliberately try to do him harm (9-11). He feels like a helpless victim that wild animals attack, like a target that archers fire at, like a weak city wall that enemy soldiers smash to pieces (12-14). He mourns and suffers, though he is innocent (15-17).

For a moment Job's faith grows strong again despite his bitter anguish. His innocent blood has been spilt on the earth, and he asks the earth to cry to heaven that justice might be done on his behalf (18). He believes he has a heavenly witness who knows he is not guilty of the wrongdoing of which people accuse him (19-21). Although he is confident that this witness hears his cries and affirms his innocence, he nevertheless fears that he is on the way to his death (22-17:2).

Job asks God himself to guarantee that in the end he will be declared righteous. He has given up expecting any understanding from those who have closed their minds to reason. He feels they have betrayed him (3-5). Job is sad that he, a godly person, must suffer such pain and insults, but his sufferings make him the more determined to do right and oppose wrong (6-9).

As he returns to consider the so-called comfort of his friends, Job becomes discouraged again. There is no wisdom in what any of them say (10). It is useless for them to try to comfort him by saying that the night of suffering will soon be past and a new day of joy will dawn. He expects only the greater darkness of death (11-16).

Bildad speaks (18:1-21)

In an angry outburst, Bildad accuses Job of not answering their arguments directly and of looking for arguments on other matters instead. Job speaks to them as if they were stupid cattle, and speaks to God as if the Creator should change the world to suit Job (18:1-4).

Then, with inexcusable heartlessness (in view of the recent calamities in Job's household), Bildad further describes the punishment that justly falls on the wicked. In his house sorrow will replace happiness and poverty will replace prosperity (5-7). This is a judgment from which he cannot escape. He is like an animal caught in a trap (8-10). He is afflicted with fear, hunger, disease and finally death (11-14). His property is destroyed and his family is wiped out (15-19). His fate becomes a lesson to all who would oppose God (20-21).

Job's reply to Bildad (19:1-29)

Again Job rebukes his friends and rejects their assertion that his sufferings prove he must be a great sinner. Even if he has sinned, he argues, that is no concern of theirs (19:1-4). As Job sees things, he has not been wicked, but God has made it look as if he has by placing him in this humiliating situation (5-6). God has used his power against Job and Job can do nothing about it. He feels helpless (7-12). Relatives, friends and servants have all turned against him (13-16). His wife has forsaken him, children laugh at him, and people in general find him repulsive (17-20). Eliphaz, Bildad and Zophar are the only ones who have chosen to stay with him. Can they not therefore take pity on him and give him some comfort (21-22)?

Job wishes that his words could be recorded permanently, so that some day someone would declare him right (23-24). At this thought Job recalls his previous wish for new life after death (see notes on 14:13-17). This time, however, his words are more than just a wish. He is now confident that there must be a new and victorious life after death, for if God is to make a declaration that Job is righteous, Job must be there to hear it. So though his body may die, he will somehow live again. In his own body, with his own eyes, he will see God (25-27).

When that day comes, justice will be done to those who at present insist that Job's suffering is the result of his secret sins. His accusers will be proved wrong and his persecutors will be punished (28-29).

Zophar speaks (20:1-29)

On hearing Job's bold forecast of punishment on his accusers (see 19:28-29), Zophar can hardly control his temper. Not only does he feel insulted, but he is burning with inward rage (20:1-3). His hasty reply is intended to hurt Job by reminding him that the wicked person's happiness and success are shortlived (4-7). The wealth he unjustly gained will not save him, and his early death will be a fitting punishment (8-11).

The wicked feed on sin, keeping it in their mouths as long as possible to enjoy its taste before swallowing it. But it will be like poison in their stomachs and will kill them (12-16). Their lives of luxury will end, and the money they gained through oppression will be lost (17-19). Because of their greed, God will punish them with poverty and misery (20-23). The sword of God's anger will pierce them and the fire of God's wrath will burn them up (24-26). Zophar triumphantly concludes that heaven and earth will unite to destroy those who fight against God (27-29).

Job's reply to Zophar (21:1-34)

There are two main reasons for Job's impatient speech. One is the frustration of arguing with a person whom he cannot see or hear. The other is the constant pain that torments him. If the friends can understand this and stop their mockery for a moment, Job will answer Zophar's statement calmly (21:1-6). The wicked are not always swiftly destroyed

as Zophar claims. Many enjoy long lives of peace, prosperity and happiness (7-13). The wicked fight against God yet prosper; Job hates wickedness yet suffers (14-16).

How often, asks Job, do the wicked suffer all the terrible judgments that the three friends have detailed (17-18)? The friends may reply that the children will reap the fruits of the parents' sins. If this is so, says Job, it still means that the wicked themselves are not punished. They do not worry about what happens to others after they die (19-21). It is wrong to try to make God's actions fit human theories, especially when those theories are contradicted by the plain realities of life (22). The fact is that all people, good and bad alike, suffer the unwelcome fate of death. This shows that sufferings and misfortunes are not an indication of a person's goodness or wickedness (23-26).

The friends say that calamity will come upon the house of the wicked (27-28), but anyone who observes events around him knows this is not always true (29-31). Some of the wicked have impressive funerals, where crowds of people attend to pay them honour (32-33). The friends are not being honest when they quote those examples that support their theories but ignore others (34).

22:1-26:14 THIRD ROUND OF ARGUMENT

Eliphaz speaks (22:1-30)

In the first two rounds Eliphaz had not been as severe on Job as the others. Now, however, he attacks Job with specific accusations. He argues that since a person can add nothing to God, God would not make Job suffer in the hope of gaining some benefit for himself. The reason for Job's suffering must lie with Job, not with God (22:1-3. Note how once again Eliphaz refers back to the main part of his dream; cf. 4:17-19). And since God would not punish Job for his reverence, he must be punishing him for his sin (4-5). Eliphaz's accusation is that Job has heartlessly oppressed others to make himself rich (6-9), and that is why God is now punishing him (10-11).

According to Eliphaz, Job practises all this evil because he thinks God is so far away that he cannot see him and will not punish him (12-14). This was the way wicked people in former ages thought and behaved. They ignored God in spite of the benefits they received from his gracious blessings (15-18). The godly rightly rejoice when they see such people consumed in fiery judgment (19-20).

In view of the certain punishment of the wicked, Eliphaz urges Job to submit humbly to God and repent (21-23). Job must learn to look for his satisfaction in God, not in wealth (24-26). Then God will answer his prayers and give him all that he desires (27-30).

Job's reply to Eliphaz (23:1-24:25)

Again Job says that he is not rebelling against God or running away from him as his friends claim. On the contrary he wants to meet God, so that he can present his case to him and listen to God's answer (23:1-5). He is confident that God will declare him innocent of the charges people have made against him (6-7).

No matter where Job has searched for God, he has not found him. He cannot see God, but God can see him. God knows he is upright, and one day, when this time of testing has proved him true, God will announce his righteousness to others (8-12). But until that day arrives, Job must bear his suffering. Nothing will change God's mind, and Job is terrified as he thinks of what God may yet require him to go through (13-17).

Job wishes there were set times when God the judge was available for the downtrodden to bring their complaints to him and obtain justice (24:1). The poor and helpless are oppressed by the rich and powerful. Driven from their homes they are forced to wander like animals in the wilderness, eating whatever food they can find and sleeping under trees and rocks (2-8). If caught they are forced to sell their children as slaves or become slaves themselves. Yet God ignores their cries for help (9-12). Meanwhile murderers, sex perverts and thieves, who rely on the cover of darkness to carry out their evil deeds, seem to escape unpunished (13-17).

The friends say that these wicked people will quickly be swept away in judgment (18-20), but from Job's observations, God allows them to go on living in comfort and security. When they die, their deaths are no different from the deaths of others (21-24). Job challenges his friends to prove him wrong in what he says (25).

Bildad speaks and Job replies (25:1-26:14)

It seems either that Job's friends have no answer to what he says or that they are tired of arguing with him and see no point in continuing the debate. Bildad has only a brief speech, to which Job replies, and Zophar does not speak at all.

In an effort to bring Job to repentance, Bildad impresses upon him the greatness of the God with whom Job argues. His kingdom is all-powerful, his armies of angelic beings more than can be counted (25:1-3). In addition, God is pure beyond human understanding, so that even the mighty universe is unclean in his sight. How then can one tiny human being claim to be sinless (4-6)?

Bildad's statement shows that he still does not understand Job's complaint. Job has never claimed to be sinless; only that he is not the terrible sinner that they, on the basis of his sufferings, accuse him of being. Tired of their words, Job, with biting sarcasm, thanks Bildad for his sympathetic understanding and congratulates him for his outstanding knowledge (26:1-4).

Job then shows that he knows as much about the power of God in the universe as Bildad does. No region is outside God's sovereignty, not even the mysterious gloomy world of the dead (5-6). The heavens also are in his power. He controls the stars, the moon and the clouds. He turns darkness into light when the sun rises above the horizon each morning (7-10). On the one hand he sends earthquakes and storms; on the other he calms the raging sea and gives fair weather (11-13). If these are but the 'whispers' of God's power, how great must be his 'thunder' (14)!

27:1-31:40 JOB'S SUMMARY

The traditional teaching (27:1-23)

According to the established pattern of the debate, Zophar should speak next, but when he does not, Job proceeds to summarize his own position. He restates that, in spite of his suffering and bitterness, he is innocent of the great wrongdoing of which they accuse him, and he assures them that he intends to remain innocent (27:1-6).

Job knows as well as his friends do that the ungodly will, in the end, be punished and no final cry for mercy will save them. Moreover, the friends' false accusations against Job put them in the class of the ungodly (7-10). They have been foolishly wasting their time in trying to teach Job the traditional doctrine concerning the punishment of the wicked. He knows all this so well that he could just as easily teach them (11-12). To prove his knowledge, Job quotes some of the traditional teaching for them to hear: the families of the wicked are wiped out (13-15), their wealth is plundered (16-17), their houses are destroyed (18-19), and their lives end in horror (20-23).

The search for true wisdom (28:1-28)

At this point there is a pause in the story while the writer inserts a poem on the pricelessness of true wisdom. The poem does not state who composed it, though it could have been spoken by Job during the period of quiet that followed the last of the friends' speeches. The theme of the poem is that, though people go to much trouble to find the riches hidden in the earth, they are not able to find the far greater riches of true wisdom.

Mining is an occupation that shows people's courage and inventiveness. While grain grows quietly above the earth, miners in dark underground tunnels dig out the minerals (28:1-6). Travellers, animals and birds move about in the world above, unaware that beneath them miners are changing the course of underground streams in search for precious metals (7-11). But people do not know how to find wisdom. They cannot dig it out of the earth, find it in the sea, or buy it with money. It is precious beyond value (12-19). Neither the living nor the dead can give wisdom (20-22).

God alone is the source of wisdom. He created everything, controls everything and knows everything (23-27). People will find wisdom only when they cease acting according to their sinful urges and act instead out of the humble desire to please God and do his will (28).

Past glory; present humiliation (29:1-30:31)

Since the three friends have nothing more to say, Job proceeds to show that in the past he had indeed tried to fear God and avoid wrongdoing. So close was his fellowship with God in those days that he could call it friendship (29:1-4). He was blessed with family happiness and prosperity (5-6). He was one of the city elders and was highly respected by the whole community (7-10).

Most rulers were corrupt, favouring the rich and oppressing the poor, but Job's impartiality and honesty were well known everywhere (11-14). He helped those who were exploited and never feared to give a judgment against the oppressors, no matter how rich or powerful they were (15-17). Job felt that in view of such uprightness he could look forward to a bright future of continued contentment and success (18-20). He would have the same freshness as in former days, when he guided people with his wise advice and cheered them with his warm understanding (21-25).

But instead of the honour and happiness he expected, Job has shame and misery. The lowest of society mock him cruelly (30:1). These worthless people had been driven into the barren wastelands in punishment for their misdeeds, but now they return to make fun of him as he sits in pain and disgrace at the garbage dump (2-8). God allows them to humiliate him without restraint, and he cannot defend himself (9-11). He feels like a city that was once glorious but is now smashed and overrun by the enemy (12-15).

In addition to suffering cruel humiliation, Job has agonizing physical pain. He gets no relief, day or night. As he rolls in agony, his clothes twist around him and become covered in the filth of burnt garbage (16-19). He cries to God, but God only sends him more pain, as if torturing him to death (20-23).

With the desperation of a person sinking into certain ruin, Job cries out for help; but no one gives him the sympathetic assistance that he once gave others (24-26). Depressed in spirit and loathsome in appearance, tortured by pain and rejected by his fellows, he can do nothing but groan (27-31).

Job reaffirms his innocence (31:1-40)

Once again Job examines his past life to see if, in fact, he has committed some great sin for which God is now punishing him. He readily acknowledges that God sees everything and that his punishment of sin is just. God knows that he has not been guilty even of unlawful sexual lust (31:1-4). He has not cheated others to enrich himself. If someone can prove that he has, he will gladly surrender all the produce of his fields (5-8). If he has committed adultery, he will gladly accept the lawful punishment due to him and will submit to the humiliation of having to surrender his wife to slavery (9-12).

Job continues: he has always been fair to his servants, knowing that they have been created by God the same as he has. He knows he is answerable to God for the way he treats them (13-15). He has looked after the poor and needy, some from childhood (16-20). He has never cooperated with corrupt judges to exploit the defenceless (21-23). He has not been greedy for money, nor has he engaged in any kind of false worship (24-28). At all times he has been forgiving to enemies and hospitable to strangers (29-32). He has never hidden the truth in fear of either popular opinion or influential people (33-34).

Having found no charge against himself, Job now challenges God to find a charge against him. If God can find such a charge, Job will be glad to have it made public so that he can answer it before God and before his fellow citizens. Then he will be able to prove himself innocent (35-37). He adds a final note that he has not gained any of his lands by dishonesty or violence (38-40).

32:1-37:24 ELIHU'S ARGUMENTS

Reasons why Elihu must speak (32:1-22)

People came for various reasons to see Job. Many were merely curious, wanting to see the former leading judge, honoured citizen and respected wise man who was now decaying at the city garbage dump. Some came to mock, others to listen to the debate. Among this latter group was an intelligent young man named Elihu.

As the debate progressed, Elihu grew restless and angry. He was angry at Job for his self-righteous assertions, and angry at the three friends for their failure to prove Job wrong. He had remained silent while the more learned men spoke, but now that he sees they are either unable or unwilling to argue with Job further, he can keep quiet no longer (32:1-5).

Elihu begins by explaining that he has kept quiet out of respect for the three older men; but, he quickly adds, God gives wisdom to young men as well (6-10). He then rebukes the three friends. He has listened carefully to their speeches and has found that none has answered Job satisfactorily. He warns them against giving up the debate by thinking that further argument with Job is useless. If they think that only God can answer Job, then Elihu is the one through whom God will speak! But Elihu will answer Job with arguments different from theirs (11-14).

The friends may have been silenced, but Elihu feels that he must speak. He is like a wine bottle ready to burst (15-20). He will speak fairly and flatter no one (21-22).

Elihu accuses Job (33:1-33)

Turning now to Job, Elihu gives the assurance that he speaks with sincerity and with respect for the God who created him (33:1-4). He also speaks as one who is on a level of equality with Job (5-7).

To begin with Elihu recalls Job's claim to be innocent and Job's accusation that God has treated him as if he were guilty (8-11). Elihu is shocked that a person could make such an accusation against God, and boldly rebukes Job (12-13). He suggests that if Job were quiet for a while, he might hear God speaking to him, possibly through a dream or vision. God will then show him his pride so that he might repent of it and be saved from destruction (14-18).

Elihu then repeats, and in some ways expands, what the other three have already said. He starts by asserting that God punishes the sinner with disease and suffering (19-21). Then, when the person is almost dead, God sends a messenger to show him his sin and lead him to repentance (22-23. Perhaps Elihu sees himself as this messenger). The person is then saved from death, his body is healed and good health returns (24-25). He rejoices in fellowship with God again, and confesses to all that though he was justly punished for his sin, God has mercifully saved him (26-28).

After giving an added warning not to ignore God's patience and mercy, Elihu challenges Job to deny the truth of his argument. If Job has nothing to say, let him listen to Elihu further (29-33).

The justice of God (34:1-35:16)

When Job does not reply to Elihu's challenge, Elihu turns to the onlookers and repeats some of Job's rash statements about the injustice of God (34:1-6). Let them judge for themselves. Surely such words prove Job's wickedness (7-9).

God is not unjust, says Elihu, and no one can tell him what to do. He is the governor of the universe (10-13). He is the source of all life and, if he wished, he could bring all life to an end (14-15). God governs perfectly and shows no special favour to the rich and powerful (16-20). Unlike earthly judges, God does not have certain set times to hear evidence, nor does he carry out investigations. He sees and knows everything, and punishes the guilty according to his perfect knowledge (21-28). No one can compel God to explain why he acts or why he keeps quiet. Whether the issues concern individuals or nations, people must simply accept God's justice (29-30).

Elihu asks Job to think about this question: if a person acknowledges his wrongdoing and promises to repent, but then demands that God reward him with favour, is that really repentance (31-33)? Not only is Job unrepentant, but he adds to his former sins by his rebellious words against God. Elihu concludes that Job deserves no relief from his sufferings (34-37).

Believing that Job has said the godly are no better off than sinners, Elihu sets out to give his reply (35:1-4). He argues that since God is infinitely higher than his human creatures, people's sin cannot harm him nor their goodness benefit him. Therefore, Job's suffering cannot be because of any unnatural action on God's part. It must be solely because of Job's wickedness (5-8).

Many cry to God for help when they are in trouble, but other times they ignore him, in spite of all he does for them. Consequently, God does not answer their prayers (9-13). How much less will he answer the prayers of Job, who rudely complains that God refuses to meet him and show his approval of him. Actually, says Elihu, God has been very patient with Job. He should have punished him even more severely because of his irreverent speech, but Job has only responded with yet more empty talk (14-16).

God's unknowable purposes (36:1-37:24)

Elihu, believing he has all the answers to Job's questions, says he will now answer Job on God's behalf (36:1-4). Certainly, God punishes the wicked, but he does not despise all who suffer. If the afflicted are truly righteous, they will soon be exalted (5-7). The reason he afflicts them is to show them their sin. If they repent, they will enjoy renewed and unbroken contentment; if not, they will suffer horrible deaths (8-12).

Only the ungodly rebel against God because of their afflictions; the righteous submit. They listen to what God teaches them through suffering and so find new life and renewed prosperity (13-16). Job's present suffering is a fitting punishment from God. No payment of money, no cry to God, no longing for death will bring him relief (17-21).

Instead of accusing God of injustice, Job should submit to his afflictions, realizing that by these God is teaching him (22-23). Elihu then reminds Job of the mighty God before whom Job should bow. This God is great beyond a person's understanding (24-26). God controls everything. He makes clouds, rain, lightning and thunder, and he uses these things to bring upon people either blessing or judgment (27-33). Thunder is like the voice of God proclaiming his majesty (37:1-5). When he sends rain, snow and ice, people have to stop work and animals look for warmth in their dens (6-10). God uses the forces of nature according to his perfect purposes (11-13).

Who is Job to argue with such a God? What does he know of God's workings (14-18)? Who can question such a God? By arguing with him, Job is running the risk of being struck dead (19-20). If even the sun is too bright for people to look at, how much more will the majesty of God blind them. People cannot fully understand God, but they know he always acts rightly. Job should not argue with God but stand in awe of him (21-24).

38:1-42:17 GOD'S ANSWER

Control of the natural world (38:1-38)

Possibly an approaching storm was what prompted Elihu's poetic praise of the God of nature (see 36:27-37:5). If so, that storm now broke, and through it the voice of God spoke to Job. Job had repeatedly challenged God to a contest. God now accepts (38:1-3).

In his reply, God asks Job questions that he cannot answer, in order to show him how little he knows of the mind and activity of the Almighty. God begins his ironical questioning of Job with a poetic description of his work in creating the world, something that he did long before Job or any other human being was born. Only angels witnessed his work (4-7). God separated the waters in the atmosphere from the waters on the earth and caused dry land to appear (8-11).

God asks Job if he is able to make the sun rise, so that those who rely on darkness to do evil are exposed. They are 'shaken' out of their hiding places as insects are shaken out of clothing (12-13). Can Job use the rays of the rising sun to create beautiful patterns and colours on the earth's surface (14-15)? Has Job been to the depths of the sea or the ends of the earth? Does he know where the sun dwells so that he can make it rise each morning and take it to its resting place each evening? He should, if he has such great knowledge as he claims (16-21).

Does Job know how God controls the weather (22-24)? Who is it that makes snow, hail, wind, rain and lightning (25-30)? Can Job control the stars (31-33)? Can he send floods or create drought as he wishes (34-38)?

Control of the animal world (38:39-39:30)

The pressure on Job increases as God continues with his unanswerable questions. From the natural world in general, God moves to the animal world. He draws Job's attention to animals that sometimes appear to have no purpose so far as human life is concerned, but are still part of God's ordering of the world.

God asks Job if he is able to order nature by providing wild animals with food (39-41), while protecting timid animals when they give birth and care for their young (39:1-4). God gives freedom to the wild ass, but at the same time controls the animal and its habitat according to his ordering of nature. Can Job do this (5-8)? Or can Job make a wild ox work like a domestic ox, when God has given the wild ox an instinct that makes it impossible to tame (9-12)?

Some things in God's creation are puzzling to humans. For example, it appears as if the ostrich neglects her eggs and has no concern for her young, because when she is frightened she runs away and leaves them. People may not understand why the ostrich behaves as it does, but God has given each animal its own particular instinct as he sees fit (13-18). God made the horse with an instinct to be trained. This is impressed upon Job with a description of the spectacular yet fearsome sight of war horses in battle (19-25).

Hawks and eagles make their nests in higher places than other birds, but they are not disadvantaged in looking for food. This is because of their remarkable eyesight, which enables them to see the tiniest objects from a great distance. Can Job compete with a Creator whose wisdom foresaw even the smallest detail (26-30)?

A direct challenge (40:1-14)

God now challenges Job to present his arguments (40:1-2). Although God's speech has not specifically dealt with the problem of Job's suffering, Job has no argument to present. God has not solved Job's intellectual problems, nor has he confirmed or denied the theories of the three friends. He has said nothing against Job, but he has shown Job that people cannot expect to understand everything about the activity of God in the complex world he has made. Job is sorry for his former rash words and has nothing more to say (3-5).

However, God is not yet finished with Job. He asks about Job's accusations of injustice in God. Does he still want to make God wrong merely to prove himself right? Does he want to be like God, to take God's place and govern the moral order of the universe, to decree what is right and what is wrong (6-9)? If so, let Job clothe himself with God's magnificent robes and sit in judgment on all who are proud and wicked. Then God will acknowledge Job's assessment of himself as correct (10-14).

Two beasts (40:15-41:34)

Before Job accepts the challenge to govern the moral order, God warns him that it is far more difficult than governing the natural and physical order. Therefore, Job must first consider what power he has over, for instance, the beasts. Two examples are sufficient to impress upon Job that he faces an impossibility. The first of these is the monster Behemoth, generally thought to be the hippopotamus. It is among the strongest creatures of God's creation (15-18), all-powerful on the land, untroubled in the water and very difficult to capture (19-24).

The second beast described to Job is Leviathan, the mythical sea monster or, possibly, the crocodile. Can Job catch one with a hook as he catches a fish?

Can he make it talk, or make it work for him, or make a pet of it? Can he sell it in the market (41:1-6)? Even if Job were able to catch one he would be sorry. He would never do it again (7-8)! If, then, no person in his right mind would dare stir up Leviathan, how unthinkable to try to stand up against God (9-11).

God then describes some fearsome features of this dragon-like beast: its armour of tough skin, its strong jaws, its terrible teeth (12-17). When it blows air and water out of its nostrils, it appears to be blowing out fire and smoke (18-21). The animal is so fearfully strong that just the sight of its movements fills even the strongest with terror (22-25). No weapon can pierce its iron-like skin (26-29). When it moves from the land into the water its movements dig up the mud like a threshing-sledge and whip up white foam on the water (30-32). This fearsome creature is the king of beasts, unconquerable by human power, yet it is part of the world God has created (33-34).

Job submits to God (42:1-6)

Although Job does not have the answer to his problems, he knows now that God does — and God will not fail. God has not given Job any reason for his sufferings, but he has given Job a fuller knowledge of the all-powerful and all-wise God, and this has changed Job's thinking.

Now Job sees that God is above all and in control of all; he is concerned about the smallest detail. Although Job may not understand the reason why God does things, he is assured that God is working according to his own purposes, and those purposes are perfect. Job has been conquered but he has also found peace, for the God who has been revealed to him is greater than Job ever imagined. Job no longer demands anything of God. He only worships (42:1-2).

Humbly Job confesses the truth of God's accusation against him that he 'darkened counsel without knowledge' (3; see 38:2). God had challenged Job to answer his questions (4; see 38:3), but Job now has nothing to say. Previously, he had a theoretical knowledge of God, but now he has personally met God. Although his questions are not answered, he himself is fully satisfied (5-6).

God exalts Job (42:7-17)

The three friends, in spite of the truths mixed in with their speeches, are now declared wrong. Job, in spite of his rash speech and irreverent protest, is now declared right. In accusing Job of great sin, the three friends had not spoken the truth, whereas Job, in claiming to be upright and not guilty of great sin, is now proved to be truthful. The friends' theory that suffering is always the result of personal sin is proved wrong, whereas Job's desire for a just God is satisfied. The friends had relied upon traditional theories, whereas Job had searched for the truth. The friends talked about God, whereas Job talked to God (7-8).

Job was not haughty in victory, nor were the friends bitter in defeat. In loving forgiveness, Job prayed for the friends, and in humble repentance the friends asked God's forgiveness by offering the sacrifices he demanded of them (9).

Apparently Job still did not know (and possibly never knew) that the main reason for his sufferings was an accusation made against him by Satan (see 1:11; 2:5). Now that Satan had been proved wrong, it was only fair that Job's former prosperity and family happiness should return. At the same time it might have shown to Job's fellow citizens, in the only way they understood, that God was pleased with Job. The turning point in Job's sufferings came when he prayed for his critics. His disease was healed, good health returned, children were born to replace those who had died, and his wealth grew to twice that of former days (10-17).

Psalms

BACKGROUND

A psalm is a hymn of praise intended to be sung to musical accompaniment. The biblical book of Psalms is a collection of 150 of these hymns. The reader of Psalms does not have to move through the book from beginning to end as with other books of the Bible, for the psalms are not successive chapters of a story, but individual songs and poems.

A collection with unity and variety

It seems that the collection of the psalms was made by a number of people over a long time. Although each psalm is a unit in itself and not necessarily connected with the psalms before or after it, certain psalms have been grouped together. They may have come from smaller collections that already existed (e.g. those of the 'sons of Korah'; see Ps 44-49) and some seem to have been arranged in a certain order (e.g. Ps 120-134).

Five major groups make up the collection and these are numbered in the Bible as Books 1 to 5 (see Outline below). At the end of the last psalm in each of the first four books a general expression of praise has been added to mark the close of the book. The very last psalm, the 150th, has been placed where it is to form a grand climax to the whole collection.

There is much variety in the types of psalms found in the book. Some express feelings of joy and confidence, others grief and uncertainty. Many of these arose out of circumstances in the lives of the individual writers (e.g. Ps 3; 75). They may have been roughly prepared in times of excitement or crisis, then later rewritten. In some cases the writers may have made adjustments and additions to make the psalms more suitable for public use (e.g Ps 54). Some psalms were written specially for use in public worship and temple festivals (e.g. Ps 38), while others were written for joyous national occasions such as coronations, victory celebrations and royal weddings (Ps 2; 18; 45).

Writers of the psalms

In many cases a psalm is introduced by a title (or heading) that gives the name of the author or the name of the person(s) from whose collection the psalm was taken. David is named as the author of seventy-three psalms, which is almost half the collection. He was a gifted musician and poet (1 Sam 16:23; 2 Sam 1:17-27; 23:1) and was the person who first arranged Israel's musicians and singers into formally recognized groups for the temple services (1 Chron 15:16-28; 16:7).

The temple musicians and singers were Levites. David arranged them into three groups, according to the three sons of Levi from whom they were descended — Gershon, Kohath and Merari. The Gershonites were under the direction of Asaph, the Kohathites under the direction of Heman (one of the 'sons of Korah') and the Merarites under the direction of Ethan (Jeduthun) (1 Chron 6:1,31-48; 15:19; 2 Chron 5:12). Asaph was a prophet (2 Chron 29:30), while Heman and Ethan, both known as Ezrahites because of their birthplace, were famed for their wisdom (1 Kings 4:31). Asaph is named as the author of twelve psalms (Ps 50; 73-83), Heman of one (Ps 88) and Ethan of one (Ps 89).

Solomon is named as the author of two psalms, which reflect respectively the splendour and wisdom for which Solomon was famous (Ps 72; 127). One psalm is noted as having come from Moses, which would make it probably the oldest in the collection (Ps 90).

Characteristics of the Psalms

In reading Psalms we should bear in mind that the book is one of poetry, specifically Hebrew poetry. The distinctive style of Hebrew poetry comes not from metre and rhyme as in traditional English poetry, but from the balanced arrangement of words and sentences. This means that when Hebrew poetry is translated into other languages, it retains some of its style and rhythm. But we should still seek to understand some of the linguistic characteristics of Hebrew poetry, as this will help us understand better what the poet is saying.

Often the poet expresses a central idea by making two parallel statements, where the second repeats the thought of the first in slightly different form (e.g. Ps 27:1; 104:28,33). Sometimes he might balance two statements, where one expresses a truth and the other either states its opposite (e.g. Ps 37:9) or gives an application (e.g. Ps 103:5,13). In other cases the poet may develop his theme through a careful arrangement of related statements (e.g. Ps 4:3-5; 91:1-2,14-16).

We can easily misinterpret the psalms if we look in too much detail at each line or sentence. We should rather treat the whole verse as a unit. At times a verse is repeated as a refrain in the psalm (e.g. Ps 42:5,11; 46:7,11; 49:12,20). A number of psalms are written in the form of an acrostic (see note on Psalms 9 and 10).

As in our hymn books today, a psalm may be introduced with practical directions for musicians and song leaders. Some Hebrew words used in these directions are of uncertain meaning, and therefore are simply transliterated into English; e.g. Shiggaion (Ps 7), Miktam (Ps 16), Maskil (Ps 55). Most likely these words indicate the kind of hymn.

Other unfamiliar Hebrew words in some of the titles may be instructions concerning the purpose of a particular psalm or the kind of occasion on which it should be sung. Additional directions may concern the type of instruments to be used (e.g. Ps 4; 5; 67) and the tune to which the psalm should be sung; e.g. 'Muth-labben' (Ps 9), 'The Hind of the Dawn' (Ps 22).

'Selah', a word that occurs in many psalms, is probably a musical direction. Its apparent purpose was to indicate a variation in the music such as a pause, a softening of the music, a build up of voices, a change in the tempo, or the repetition of a line (e.g. Ps 89:37,45,48).

Psalms and the New Testament

No matter what part of the Bible we read, we shall understand it better when we understand the events that prompted its writing. This applies to Psalms as it does to other parts of the Bible. Each psalm had a meaning to the author when he wrote. As we today understand this meaning, the Holy Spirit who inspired the writer is able to speak to us and apply the ancient Word to present circumstances. This helps us understand God better and know how we ought to live if we are to please him.

However, the New Testament writers often found truths in the Old Testament of which the original writers were not aware. The reason for this is that the New Testament writers saw Jesus Christ as the fulfilment of God's purposes for Israel. They therefore had no hesitation in taking Old Testament passages that referred originally to events in the history of Israel and applying them to Jesus (cf. Ps 68:17-18 with Eph 1:18-23; 4:8-10). Jesus was the embodiment of the ideals that God desired for his people (cf. Ps 89:3-4 with Luke 1:32-33).

Israel, as a nation and in its kings, failed to fulfil God's purposes for it. Yet the people constantly looked forward to a day of glory when evil would be destroyed and righteousness would be established under the rule of God's chosen king. Jesus, the true embodiment of Israel, so shared in his people's sufferings that in the end he bore the full force of God's wrath against sinners (cf. Ps 22:1-18 with Matt 27:39-46). But he came out victorious, bringing greater blessing than Israel had ever expected (cf. Ps 22:19-31 with Phil 2:7-11, Rev 5:9-14; cf. Ps 2:1-11 with Acts 4:25-31; 13:33-34).

Because of the union between God and his people, the sufferings of the godly in Old Testament times are an anticipation of the sufferings of Christ. (In much the same way, the sufferings of the godly in Christian times are a sharing in the sufferings of Christ; see 2 Cor 1:5; Phil 3:10.) Likewise the victories of the godly in the Old Testament are an anticipation of the victory of Christ. When the New Testament writers spoke of the fulfilment of the Old Testament in Jesus Christ, that fulfilment was not just the occurrence of events that someone had predicted. Rather it was the completion of a pattern that God had been silently directing through the varied history of his people Israel.

Messianic psalms

The word 'messiah' is a transliteration from Hebrew and means 'the anointed one'. Kings and priests (and sometimes prophets) were anointed with oil as a symbol of appointment to their position. That person whom God would send to be Israel's greatest leader — the mighty saviour-deliverer, the supreme king-priest — was popularly called the Messiah. The New Testament (Greek) equivalent of this word is 'Christ'. Because Jesus and his disciples spoke the local language of the Jews of Palestine, they would have used the local word 'Messiah'; but because the Gospels were written in Greek, the word appears in our Bible as 'Christ' (Matt 22:42; John 7:41-42).

We have seen that we may expect to see fore-shadowings of Christ in the Psalms. This does not mean, however, that because a certain verse is applicable to Christ, the whole psalm is therefore applicable. The godly psalmist wrote of the ideals that he desired for himself and others, but the only true expression of those ideals was in the perfect person, Jesus Christ. The same godly psalmist also wrote of his failures, but these could not in any way be applied to Christ.

For example, in Psalm 40, verses 1-3 and 12 are a vivid description of the experience of the sinner that could not be the experience of Jesus Christ. But verses 6-8 of the same psalm contain a principle which, though in some measure applicable to the psalmist, could find its true meaning only in Christ (Heb 10:5-9).

This application of the psalmist's language to Christ becomes more common in those psalms where the writer considers the ideals that Israel looked for in its king. As the people's representative, the king is sometimes called God's son (e.g. Ps 2:7; cf. Exod 4:22; 2 Sam 7:14), and as God's representative may even be called God (e.g. Ps 45:6; cf. Ps 82:6; John 10:34). These ideals spread out from the king to his kingdom, and are well expressed in those psalms where the writer looks for the development of this kingdom in righteousness and power.

The psalmist's idealism was fulfilled not in David or in any of the Davidic kings of the Old Testament, but in David's greatest descendant, Jesus the Messiah. Jesus became in fact what the Davidic king of the Psalms merely foreshadowed (cf. Ps 45:6-7 with Heb 1:8-9; cf. Ps 110:1 with Matt 22:44; Acts 2:34-36). The better known psalms among those commonly referred to as messianic are Psalms 2, 45, 72 and 110.

Problems in the Psalms

There are many features in the Psalms that may appear to Christians as unusual in the light of their understanding of the New Testament. The problem arises frequently throughout the collection, but this commentary will discuss each issue at length only once. For the issues and the discussions on them readers are referred to the following notes:

The state of the dead − note that follows Psalm 6.
Curses on the wicked − note that follows Psalm 7.
Longing for judgment − note that follows Psalm 10.
God's steadfast love − note that follows Psalm 13.
God's desire for praise − note that follows Psalm 30.

OUTLINE

Book 1:   Psalms 1-41
Book 2:   Psalms 42-72
Book 3:   Psalms 73-89
Book 4:   Psalms 90-106
Book 5:   Psalms 107-150

BOOK 1: PSALMS 1-41

Psalm 1   The godly and the ungodly

This psalm is really an introduction to the whole collection. It shows the life of the godly and the reward it brings, and the life of the ungodly and the judgment it will receive. God is the supreme controller of each person's destiny, and he orders everything according to his own righteousness.

In both their thought and their behaviour, the godly are different from others. They are constantly increasing their knowledge of God's Word, and as they allow that Word to change their outlook and attitudes, their character becomes more and more like God's. Their lives are marked by freshness, strength and growth (1-3). Sinners, by contrast, have no quality or stability in their lives. They have chosen the way that is worthless, and therefore their lives will bring disappointment and end in despair (4-5). God is in control of all human affairs, and he determines the reward or punishment that will result from the way each person has lived (6).

Psalm 2   God's ruler

There is no title to this psalm, though Acts 4:25 indicates that the writer was David. The psalm was probably written to celebrate some great national occasion such as the coronation of a king. It was a reminder to the king, the people and the enemy nations that the Israelite king was, in a sense, God's son, the one through whom God exercised his rule (2 Sam 7:11-16; cf. Exod 4:22). Through him God would overpower all opposition and establish his rule on the earth.

In the opening portion of the psalm the official in charge of the ceremony reminds the hearers that rebellious people, such as the leaders of enemy nations round about Israel, challenge the rule that God desires to exercise through his anointed king (1-3). The king replies that God's mighty power makes any human show of strength look so weak that it is laughable. Since the king is God's son, his adopted representative, no one can withstand his conquering power (4-7). His rule will extend to the ends of the earth (8-9).

After such an expression of confidence in God, the presiding official returns the challenge to the rebels. He calls upon them to submit to God's rule, otherwise God may turn on them in terrifying destruction (10-12).

History shows that David never experienced the triumph and glory he so confidently expressed in this psalm. The words received fuller meaning with the coming of Jesus Christ (Acts 4:25-31; 13:33-34; Heb 1:5; 5:5). They will have even more meaning in the future (1 Cor 15:24-25; Rev 12:5; 19:15).

Psalms 3-4   Morning and evening psalms

The title that introduces Psalm 3 indicates that David wrote the psalm after his son Absalom rose up in rebellion against him and seized the throne of

Israel (2 Sam 15:1-17:29). In much distress David fled Jerusalem, but he still trusted in God.

Absalom's rebellion appears to be so successful that many people think David has no chance of escape. He seems to have little hope of saving his life (3:1-2). But David's faith in God is unshakable. He lies down at night knowing that God hears his prayers and protects him; he wakes in the morning with renewed confidence (3-6). The dangers that face him only increase his trust in God; he expects nothing less than total victory (7-8).

Psalm 4 also possibly belongs to the time of David's flight from Absalom. In this psalm David begins by praying to God (4:1), and then turns to speak to his enemies and to his supporters. He accuses his enemies of disloyalty, self-seeking and too easily believing Absalom's lies in joining the rebellion. He assures them they will be defeated, for God is on the side of David (2-3). To his supporters David gives the calm advice that they must not have thoughts of hatred and revenge. Their thoughts must be centred on God and their actions must reflect their devotion to him (4-5).

Many people look to God for prosperity, in the belief that this will bring them contentment; but David, in spite of his distressing circumstances, finds greater contentment simply through trusting in God (6-7). With these thoughts he can lie down to sleep in peace and confidence (8).

Psalm 5 Joy of the godly

In another morning prayer David again recalls the attacks that certain enemies made on him. This leads him to consider the different attitudes God has towards the godly and the ungodly. David expects God to hear his prayers and save him from his enemies (1-3).

The reason for David's confidence is that his enemies belong to that group of people whose wickedness brings only opposition from God (4-6). By contrast, David worships God with a true heart and has a sincere desire to know God's ways and walk in them (7-8). The speech of the wicked reveals the evil in their hearts, and because of that evil, God will punish them. On the other hand, the joy of the righteous displays their love for God, and because of that love, God will protect them (9-12).

Psalm 6 Anxiety in a time of trouble

Through either illness or some other depressing situation, David is distressed, in both body and mind. This has caused him to search his life to see if God is using this affliction to punish him for some sin. Humbly he asks God for mercy (1-3). He fears death, and his pain and sorrow become more distressing through the personal attacks that his opponents make on him (4-7). The thought of these ungodly enemies, however, gives David confidence that God will heal him. He knows that God opposes the wicked but helps those who humbly seek him (8-10).

State of the dead

The Old Testament shows us that people do not cease to exist when they die, but it tells us little about the condition of life after death. The Hebrew word used for the unseen place and unknown state of the dead is *sheol*. Sheol was to the Israelites a place of darkness, silence and shadowy existence (Job 10:21-22; Ps 39:13; 88:3,10-12; 94:17; 115:17). Death was something unpleasant and fearful, on account of the mysterious existence that followed in sheol (Ps 6:5; 31:17; Eccles 8:8). English Bibles have translated the Hebrew *sheol* by such words as 'the grave', 'the pit' and even 'hell'.

Certainly sheol would bring nothing but terror for the wicked (Deut 33:22; Ps 16:10; 55:15; Isa 14:9-11; Ezek 32:18-32). The righteous, however, could expect that life after death would bring them joy in the presence of God (Ps 16:11; 49:15; 73:24; cf. 2 Kings 2:11). But the name 'sheol' itself signified neither a hell of torment nor a heaven of happiness. It was simply 'the world of the dead' (GNB).

Death was the great leveller. Rich and poor, good and bad, oppressor and oppressed, kings and slaves were all subject to death. All died and went to sheol, the world of the dead (Job 3:13-19; Isa 14:19-20; Ezek 32:18-32). Sheol therefore became a synonym for death, and this is usually the way the word is used in Psalms.

By the end of the Old Testament era, believers were more fully convinced that beyond death lay the resurrection (Dan 12:1-2). This confidence grew into bold assurance through Jesus Christ's death and resurrection. Christ conquered death and sheol (Matt 16:18; Rev 1:18; the Greek equivalent of *sheol* was *hades*), so that people no longer had any need to fear them (Heb 2:14-15). Through Jesus Christ, God clearly showed immortal life to be a certainty (2 Tim 1:10).

Psalm 7 Against Cush, a Benjaminite

During the reign of Saul, David won much fame for himself. Saul became jealous and attempted to murder David. When David escaped, Saul pursued him cruelly, being urged on by a group of zealous courtiers (probably from Saul's tribe of Benjamin), who accused David of plotting to overthrow the king (1 Sam 18:22-26; 22:7; 24:9; 26:19; cf. 2 Sam 16:5; 20:1).

The time was one of considerable suffering and temptation for David, but he remained guiltless throughout. He refused to do anything against Saul, whom he still acknowledged as God's anointed king. All he wanted was to save his own life (1 Sam 20:1; 24:11; 26:9). Cush, the Benjaminite against whom David wrote this psalm, was probably one of those who falsely accused David and urged Saul to destroy him.

Unjustly pursued by fierce enemies, David turns to God for protection (1-2). In a strongly worded statement he boldly declares his innocence (3-5). He appeals to the judge of heaven and earth also to declare his innocence, and in addition to condemn his enemies (6-9). David's confidence is that God always acts justly (10-11). Therefore, those who are evil should turn from their sin, otherwise they will be overtaken by God's judgment (12-13).

Since evil deeds sooner or later bring about the downfall of those who practise them, David need have no fear of his enemies. His confidence in God's overruling justice strengthens him in his present distress (14-17).

Curses on the wicked

The psalmists frequently request God to destroy the wicked without mercy (e.g. Ps 7:6; 35:8; 139:19). This appears at first to be a display of hate and revenge that should have no place in the hearts of God's people. Before considering this matter, we should, in fairness to the psalmists, note that the curses and punishments they spoke of were in keeping with the legal penalties and methods of warfare of their day. The Christian today may rightly hesitate to use such language (cf. Ps 58:6; 109:6-15; 137:9).

However, the reason the psalmists called for divine punishment was not necessarily that they wanted personal revenge. This is seen in Psalm 7:3-6, where the psalmist, before praying down divine judgment, emphasizes that he has no desire to return evil for evil personally. The psalmists' overwhelming desire was to see God's standards of righteousness established. In fact, it often seems that, in regard to righteousness, they knew God better than we do. For this reason sin appeared worse to them than it does to us. They saw sin as God sees it and hated evil as God hates it (Ps 139:21-22). They knew that wicked people had to be punished according to their wickedness (Ps 109:16-19).

Cursing in ancient times was not a burst of bad language arising out of a fit of temper or hatred. It was an announcement that people believed could release powerful forces against the evildoer. The psalmists feel something of the divine anger against sin as they call on God to punish the evildoers with the sorrows that they intended to bring upon the innocent (Ps 109:17; cf. Rom 12:9,19; Eph 4:26).

It should also be remembered that the ancient Israelites lived in the era before Jesus Christ came and revealed God's purposes more fully. They did not have the fuller understanding that Christians have of a future judgment bringing rewards and punishments. For them righteousness was to be rewarded and wickedness punished in this life; and one could not occur without the other. If God was going to establish righteousness on the earth, this would mean punishing the wicked. If he was to deliver his people, this would mean overthrowing their foes.

The psalmists may not have had as clear an understanding as Christians have of the vastness of God's grace, because the world-changing events of Christ's life, death and resurrection had not yet taken place. But they were realistic enough to see that most people would not repent. The principle behind their attacks on their enemies was this: 'God is a righteous judge . . . If people do not change their ways, God will sharpen his sword' (Ps 7:11-12; cf. 2 Thess 1:6).

Psalm 8 Divine glory and human dignity

God is so great in majesty and power that nothing in the universe can challenge his sovereign rule. The praises of children may appear to be weak and simple, but they are sufficient to silence God's enemies. God uses what appears to be powerless to overcome all the hostile forces that his enemies can gather (1-2).

This majestic power of God is seen also in the vastness of the universe that he created. How amazing, therefore, that God should give to feeble insignificant human beings a position of dignity that makes them unique among all created things; for they alone are made in the image of God (3-5; cf. Gen 1:26-30).

Human beings have a God-given authority that places them in charge of the physical world in which they live. Having been made in God's image, they rule as God's representatives (6-8). But they are not God; they are merely the image and representatives of God. Their first duty is always to bring homage, worship, praise and glory to the Lord and God whom they serve (9).

Because of sin, the human race never fulfilled God's purposes for it. Only in Christ can people be lifted out of the shame and hopelessness of sin, and enter into the glory that God intended for them (Heb 2:6-9; 1 Cor 15:21-28).

Psalms 9-10   God fights for the oppressed

In Psalms 9 and 10 we meet another kind of Hebrew verse, the acrostic. (Other acrostics are Psalms 25, 34, 37, 111, 112, 119 and 145.) In an acrostic the first word of each verse (or stanza) begins with a different letter of the 22-letter Hebrew alphabet, moving in order, so to speak, 'from A to Z'. The acrostic in this case moves unbroken through Psalms 9 and 10, indicating that originally they probably formed one psalm. The absence of a heading to Psalm 10 supports this view. The two psalms appear to belong to the days of David's kingship.

David begins with an expression of praise to God (9:1-2) because of a notable victory that God has given Israel over its enemies (3-6). This victory illustrates God's perfect justice in upholding what is right (7-8) and his unfailing love in caring for those who trust in him (9-10). David therefore calls on the whole congregation to join him in this hymn of praise (11-12).

As he recalls the enemy attacks, the grateful psalmist recalls also how he prayed desperately in the crisis and promised to offer public praise to God on his successful return to Jerusalem (13-14). Knowing that God is righteous in all his judgments, the psalmist is assured that God will punish the wicked and care for the faithful (15-18). He asks God to act decisively against those who defy him, and to show them that they are merely mortal beings (19-20).

At times it seems to the psalmist that God stands idly by while the ungodly do as they please. Self-seeking people use their power, influence and wealth to oppress the poor and trample on the rights of others (10:1-2). Because God does not act in judgment against him immediately, the unjust think that God is not concerned. They think there will be no judgment (3-6). Greed, lying, cruelty and deceit are the characteristics of such people (7-9). The more easily they crush people, the more confident they become that they have escaped God's punishment (10-11).

But God is not indifferent to the arrogance of the oppressors; nor is he indifferent to the sufferings of the oppressed. Silently, he has been taking notice of everything. God has a particular concern for those who are defenceless and easily exploited (12-14). The arrogant can never triumph over God. Those who advance themselves by oppressing others will meet with certain punishment, but those who trust in God will be delivered (15-18).

Longing for judgment

Ideas commonly associated with God's judgment are those of condemnation and punishment. Judgment is not usually something to look forward to. Yet the psalmists often long for God's judgment and rejoice in anticipation of the day when it will come (Ps 67:4; 96:12-13).

The reason for this longing for judgment is that, for the psalmists, God's judgment means the administration of justice in the everyday affairs of life. The godly were oppressed and downtrodden. Corruption, bribery and injustice meant they had no way of obtaining justice, no way of gaining a hearing, no way of getting a judgment of their case (Ps 10:1-6; 82:1-4). They knew they were in the right. That was why they longed for the day when God would act in judgment, righting the wrongs, declaring them to be right, and sentencing their oppressors to punishment (Ps 7:6-8; 9:8,12; 10:12,17-18; 35:23-24).

Psalms 11-13   Persevere . . . or give in?

There came a time when David became tired of his continual flight from Saul, not just because it was wearying, but because it was cutting him off from the public worship places of God's people (1 Sam 26:19). His spiritual life was weakened and he gave in to the temptation to leave his own country for the safety of enemy Philistia (1 Sam 27:1). This is the sort of temptation that David considers in Psalm 11, the temptation to go along with wrongdoing instead of resisting it.

If people act solely according to common sense, their suggestion in such a crisis will probably be to do what creates least hardship. After all (so the argument runs), if there is no law and order in the community, and if people in positions of power have set themselves to do evil, what can a righteous person gain by trying to resist (11:1-3)? David replies that such action really shows a lack of understanding of God's holiness and no respect for his authority. God sees and understands all. He will pour out his wrath on the wicked, but he will comfort the faithful with the security of his presence (4-7).

The theme of Psalms 10 and 11 continues in Psalm 12, and indeed right through to Psalm 17. Ungodly people hold all the positions of power and pay no attention to the opinions of those who walk in God's ways. They maintain their authority and influence only by twisting, ignoring or withholding the truth (12:1-4). But God sees and knows. He promises to protect the godly, and his promises can be trusted (5-6). His people know that their only hope is in him (7-8).

Continual persecution can be hard to bear. It tries the psalmist's patience to the limit, causing him to cry out to God, almost in despair, asking when will God deliver him from his troubles (13:1-2). If he dies, his enemies will think they have won the battle against him (3-4). However, the very act of crying out to God lightens his burden. It reminds him that the one to whom he cries has bound himself to his people with a covenant love, and he will not fail (5-6).

God's steadfast love

Frequently the psalmists rejoice in a characteristic of God that RSV translates as 'steadfast love', GNB translates as 'constant love', and other versions translate as 'loyalty', 'love', 'mercy', 'kindness' and 'loving kindness'. These are all translations of the Hebrew word *chesed*, which has the meaning of covenant loyalty or faithfulness.

A covenant was an agreement between two parties that carried with it obligations and blessings. *Chesed* was a particularly strong form of love, which bound a person to be faithful and loyal to the other party in the covenant. In the Psalms the word is used frequently to denote the loyal love and covenant faithfulness that God exercises towards his people through all their trials and joys (e.g Ps 13:5; 25:7).

Psalms 14-17 Godly people in ungodly society

Continuing the theme of Psalms 10-13 (concerning the godly person who is downtrodden), the psalmist notes what happens when people refuse to acknowledge God and live as if he does not care about their actions. The result is a corrupt society (14:1-3). Because they have rejected God they have rejected the true standard by which to judge good and evil. They live solely for themselves, with no consideration for others and no thought for God (4). But in the end victory will go to the poor and downtrodden, because God is on their side (5-7).

In Psalm 15 David considers the requirements necessary to enter the presence of God (15:1). These all have to do with character and behaviour, not with religious beliefs and observances. People must be honest in their actions, truthful in their speech, and disciplined in their avoidance of slander and gossip (2-3). They must know how to make right judgments between things that are good and things that are not. In addition they must be reliable and trustworthy, keeping their word even when it hurts. They must be generous and helpful, and never take advantage of the poor or defenceless (4-5a). Such people will dwell in the presence of God and enjoy the lasting security that only God can give (5b).

Psalm 16 is David's thanksgiving for one of the many occasions when God rescued him from what seemed to be certain death. He finds pleasure in the fellowship of God and his people, and rejects all other gods and those who worship them (16:1-4). Possessions may satisfy people and property may enrich them, but David considers that because he has God, he has all the satisfaction and wealth he desires (5-6). God is David's instructor, friend and protector, the source of his stability and security (7-8). God delivers him from death and leads him through life, giving him the constant joy of his presence (9-11).

(The feelings that David expressed in Psalm 16 may have represented ideals that he himself never fully experienced. They find their full meaning in Jesus Christ; see Acts 2:25-28; 13:35-37.)

In another prayer that probably belongs to the time of David's flight from the murderous Saul, David emphasizes his innocence in the strongest terms (17:1-5). He asks God to protect him from his enemies (6-9), after which he describes their wickedness (10-12) and pronounces their certain destruction. Their hunger for wickedness is only building up a heavier weight of judgment, which will not only fall on them but will also affect their offspring (13-14). The wicked are never satisfied, but the psalmist finds full satisfaction in his experience of God (15).

Psalm 18 David's song of victory

The outpouring of praise recorded in Psalm 18 is applicable to many of David's experiences. It was probably put into its present form after David reached the height of his power as king. He had conquered all his enemies and now controlled all the country from Egypt to the Euphrates (2 Sam 8:1-18). The psalm is also recorded in 2 Samuel 22.

David opens by declaring his love for God (1) and thanking God for hearing his prayers and saving him from death at the hands of his enemies (2-6). God revealed himself in dramatic exhibitions of his mighty power, using earthquakes and storms (7-9), wind and rain (10-11), lightning and thunder (12-15) to deliver his servant (16-19).

The reason God answered David's prayers was that David walked in God's ways and kept himself pure and humble (20-24). God's attitude to people, whether he helped them or opposed them, depended on whether they were devoted to him or rebelled against him (25-27). That is why David was always confident of God's help (28-30).

God had blessed David with good health, physical strength, natural ability, and the desire to train and practise till he was skilled in the abilities God had given him (31-34). Above all, God gave David his saving power (35-36). As a result David was able to go on to certain victory, conquering his foes (37-42), expanding his kingdom (43-45) and bringing glory to God (46-48). As he looks back on what God did for him in the past, he offers further praise for God's unfailing kindness (49-50).

Psalm 19 Knowing God

The wonders of the universe display God's glory, power and wisdom. Although these things cannot speak, day after day they tell people that there is a God and teach them something of his nature (1-4a). The sun, with its splendour and brilliance, is a particularly notable witness to God's glory (4b-6).

If, however, people are to know God personally and live according to his will, they need a more detailed knowledge than the physical creation can provide. They need God's written Word. That Word is the authoritative revelation of God's will for them. The knowledge that comes from it gives them new life, confidence, wisdom, joy, understanding and purity (7-9). It has a worth that is beyond value, and brings an enjoyment that is beyond comparison (10). It warns and instructs people, making them more sensitive to sin and giving them an increased desire to cleanse their lives and live blamelessly (11-13). As the Word does its work, they will want all their thoughts, words and actions to be pleasing to God (14).

Psalms 20-21 Before and after battle

These two psalms belong together as a pair. The former is a prayer for the king before he leads the people in battle; the latter, a thanksgiving after victory.

Addressing the king, the people call down God's power and protection upon him (20:1-2). They pray that God will remember the king's faithfulness and give him victory (3-5). The king replies that victory is certain, because he has God's help. God's power is greater than military might (6-8). In response, the people offer a further plea, brief and urgent, for God's help (9).

The people join in thanksgiving to God that he has answered their prayer of the previous psalm (see Ps 20:4). God has given the king his heart's desire, enabling him to lead his people to victory (21:1-4). Although the king receives glory because of his victory, the glory is not self-centred. It is glory given him by God, in whom he trusts (5-7). Having offered thanks to God, the people turn and address the king. They assure him that through God's power

he will continue to have victory over all his enemies (8-12). King and people then unite in praise to God (13).

Psalm 22 Suffering and salvation

At the time of the writing of this psalm, David had reached what he thought was the farthest extreme of suffering. He was almost at the point of despair. Christians know that they are required to share the sufferings of Christ (Col 1:24), but David was probably unaware that, in the experiences recorded here, he was also having a share in those sufferings. His experiences were a foretaste of the greater sufferings that the messianic king Jesus would one day endure on the cross.

Although in his suffering the psalmist trusts in God, he is puzzled that God has not answered his prayers and rescued him. After all, God rescued people of former times who trusted in him (1-5). But, thinks the psalmist, he is hardly even a man. He feels more like a worm, so painful is the cruel mockery he receives from his enemies (6-8). He feels as helpless, yet as dependent, as a baby. He therefore pleads that as God looked after him when he was a baby, so he will look after him now (9-11).

The writer's physical sufferings are beyond description. His enemies seem to him like wild animals that have surrounded their helpless victim (12-15). They are like a pack of vicious dogs that stare and gloat over him with a fierceness that tells him they are getting ready for the kill. Already they are biting at his hands and feet and tearing his clothes from him (16-18). In desperation he cries to God, for only God can save him now (19-21).

God did save him. He therefore will perform his duties according to the vow that he made when he called on God's help. He invites all the people of Israel to join him in a sacrificial feast to celebrate the fulfilment of his vow. With him they can then praise God for his great deliverance (22-26; see Lev 7:11-18 for the ceremony that marked the fulfilment of a vow). His joy overflows as he extends his call to people everywhere to bow before God and worship him because of his great salvation (27-29). From generation to generation people will praise God for all he has done (30-31).

The intensity of David's feelings caused him to use words so extravagant that their fullest meaning extended beyond his own experiences to the death of Christ and the triumphant spread of the gospel (cf. v. 1-2 with Matt 27:46; cf. v. 6-8 with Matt 27:39-43; cf. v. 14-16 with John 19:18; cf. v. 18 with John 19:23-24; cf. v. 19-21 with Heb 5:7; cf. v. 22 with Heb 2:12; cf. v. 27-31 with Matt 28:19; Phil 2:9-11).

Psalm 23   Divine shepherd and host

God's relationship with his people is like that of a shepherd to his sheep. He provides what is best for them, refreshes them continually, and guides them in the way that he knows is right. In so doing he proves himself faithful to his own nature as the covenant God of his chosen people (1-3).

Despite God's provision and guidance, there will be dangers along the way. But as a shepherd uses his club (rod) to beat off wild animals, and his crook (staff) to rescue the troubled sheep, so will God care for his people (4). Wild animals may surround them, but they can feed in safety under the protection of the heavenly shepherd. In view of God's provision of the best food for those in his care, the picture changes from the divine shepherd to the divine host. God gives special attention to his guests, just as a host in ancient times gave special honour to a guest by anointing his head with oil. The guests in God's house, however, never have to leave. They are with him for ever (5-6).

Psalm 24   The triumphal entry

Saul had taken little interest in the religious life of Israel. During his reign the ark of the covenant (or covenant box) remained in a country house in Kiriath-jearim. David set about correcting this state of affairs by restoring the ark, symbol of God's presence, to its rightful place at the centre of the nation's religious life. One of the greatest days of his life, therefore, was the day on which he brought the ark into Jerusalem (1 Sam 7:1-2; 2 Sam 6:12-19). This was probably the occasion on which Psalm 24 was first sung.

As the procession approaches the hill of the Lord (Jerusalem), a question is asked: who is able to enter the presence of the almighty Creator, Yahweh, the holy God of Israel (1-3)? The answer comes back: only those who have 'clean hands' in all their dealings with others and pure hearts in their loyalty to God (4; cf. 2 Sam 6:1-13; Ps 15:1-5). Such are God's true people, and God will defend them against their opponents (5-6).

At the gate of the city the procession stops and demands entrance in the name of the king of glory (7). The gatekeepers challenge the right of the procession to enter, by asking the identity of this king of glory. They receive the reply that he is Yahweh, the almighty God of Israel who gave the nation victory over its enemies (8-10).

Whatever meaning the song may have had to the Israelites of Old Testament times, it will have added meaning if it is sung at the king of glory's greater victory procession that is yet to come (cf. Phil 3:20-21; Rev. 19:1-8).

Psalm 25   Forgiveness and guidance

In the distressing circumstances surrounding this psalm, David is concerned that his enemies should not triumph over him. This is not only to save him from personal shame, but also to save his faith from being shaken. The rebels, not the faithful, are the ones who should be defeated (1-3). David wants to know more of God and his ways, so that in all the affairs of life he will do what is right (4-5). If past sins are the cause of his present troubles, he prays that God, in his mercy and love, will forgive them (6-7).

As he thinks of the goodness of God towards humble and repentant sinners, David is encouraged to believe that God will forgive him. More than that, God will lead him into a life of truer understanding, obedience and faithfulness (8-11). The more people revere and obey God, the more they find that God is their friend. They know more of God and are more assured in their salvation (12-14).

In his present danger David is lonely and fearful. But he keeps his eye fixed on God, trusting in him alone for help (15-17). He asks again for forgiveness of his sins and deliverance from his enemies (18-21). He asks also that God will save the nation from its troubles. If he can be the saviour of the individual, surely he can be the saviour of the nation (22).

Psalms 26-28   Living uprightly

David appeals to God to support him against those who plot evil against him. God has done a work of grace in his life, and this causes him to hate the company of worthless people and make every effort to live the sort of life that pleases God (26:1-5). He desires righteousness, delights in worship, loves to spend hours in the house of God and enjoys telling others about God (6-8). He therefore asks that he will not suffer the same end as the wicked (9-10). Though determined to do right, he knows that he will not succeed without God's help (11-12).

The psalmist is fully confident in the power of God and in God's willingness to protect him (27:1-3). His desire is to live his life as if he is in the presence of God continually. Thereby he will have protection, and his life will be one of constant strength and joy (4-6). He prays that God will hear his prayers and never turn away from him. Others might reject him, but he is confident that God's care of him will never fail (7-10). In view of the persecution he suffers, he asks that God will teach him more about the way he should live (11-12). He remains confident in God and this gives him patience. Whatever may happen, he knows that he can always depend on God's help (13-14).

In the next psalm David again is in great distress and cries out to God to save his life. He does not want to die like the wicked, for whom an early death is a fitting punishment (28:1-3). His prayer to God to punish the wicked is not because of personal bitterness or the desire for revenge. It is because they are the enemies of God and they disregard all that he has done (4-5). David knows that God will answer his prayer and thereby strengthen David's trust in him (6-7). This will also strengthen the faith of the people, who will have a better understanding of God as their defender and shepherd (8-9).

Psalm 29   God in the storm

On the occasion referred to here a furious storm displays to people something of the might and glory of God. The writer sees the storm approaching from the sea, bursting in its fury on the forest regions, then passing on into the barren areas to the south. He begins the psalm by urging heavenly beings to join with people on earth to worship God for his majesty and power (1-2).

The psalmist sees the storm gathering over the sea and approaching with the sound of loud thunder (3-4). It bursts in fury on the cedar forests of Lebanon, breaking trees like matchwood. It tosses them about with such wild power that the forest appears to be jumping around like a lively young animal (5-6). Flashes of lightning add their weird light as the wild wind moves south, shaking the forests as it goes (7-8). As the psalmist views the stripped forests and scattered wreckage left behind by the storm, he is humbled before a God of such awesome power. The whole scene speaks of the glory of the almighty God (9).

But God is more than the Lord of nature. He is the Lord of his people. He is the heavenly king, and just as he has the power to send storms and bring calm, so he is ready to bless his people with strength and peace (10-11).

Psalm 30   The danger of self-confidence

Feelings expressed in this psalm may have arisen from David's personal experience, but they also reflect Israel's experience during events leading up to the dedication of the temple (see heading to the psalm). Enemies may try to destroy, but no matter how bad the situation appears, it is never hopeless. There may be troubles, but God's deliverance will follow as surely as day follows night (1-5).

Recalling the experience, the psalmist outlines some lessons it taught him. Prosperity and security had led to self-confidence, and God's shattering intervention was necessary to remind him that his security depended solely on God's grace (6-7). Being brought near to death he cried out, asking what would God gain by killing him. If he was dead, how could he then praise God and serve him (8-10)? Now that God has rescued him, sadness is replaced by joyful celebration, and anxiety is replaced by humble thanksgiving (11-12).

God's desire for praise

Often in the Psalms there are statements where God himself is the one who is urging people to praise him. The psalmists, realizing how much God desires worship, use it as a reason to persuade him to save them from their troubles. If he allows them to die, they will no longer be able to bring him the praise he seeks (e.g. Ps 30:9).

It may seem at first that God is like a vain, self-centred person who demands that others be continually telling him how great he is. However, a closer look at the matter will show that this is not the case. In one of the psalms where God urges people to praise him (Ps 50:14,23), he also makes it clear that in no way is he in need of people's religious contributions (Ps 50:12-13). God has no selfish craving for people's attention.

Whatever people enjoy, whether it be nature, art, friend or lover, their enjoyment increases when they talk about it and praise it to others. When they are able to praise the object of enjoyment directly to itself (as in the case of a lover), their enjoyment increases further. Likewise as people praise God, their enjoyment of him is increased. Or, to put it another way, God gives more of himself to people as they worship him. Their acts of praise and worship become not only offerings to God, but also the means by which God offers himself to them. By calling upon people to praise him, God is inviting them to enjoy him to the full.

Psalm 31   Trust amid apparent hopelessness

In his distress David is dependent entirely on the merciful goodness of God (1-2). He knows God's character well enough to be assured that God will save him (3-5). God will bring victory to those who trust in him, and judgment on those who reject him for other gods (6-8).

Nevertheless, the psalmist's faith is at times shaken by the intensity of his sufferings. Physically and spiritually he feels helpless almost to the point of despair (9-10). Enemies plot against him and friends have deserted him (11-13). Yet he trusts in the steadfast love of God, believing that God will deliver him and destroy his enemies (14-18). He knows that the God in whom he trusts is unfailingly faithful to his people (19-20), and he recalls how God has saved him in the past (21-22). He urges all God's people to love and trust him with patience and courage. Then they will have the strength to bear whatever troubles they meet (23-24).

Psalm 32   The joy of the forgiven sinner

When people are honest with God and confess their sin to him, they experience the unspeakable joy of knowing that their sin is forgiven (1-2). If, however, instead of acknowledging their sin they try to push it out of the mind, they only create greater distress and tension for themselves. This can lead to a falling away in physical health (3-4). But when confession is made, forgiveness follows, the burden of the mind is removed, and people enjoy afresh the assurance of God's safe-keeping (5-7).

God now speaks, encouraging believers to listen to his teaching and walk in his ways willingly. If they stubbornly refuse, God may act against them with corrective discipline to force them back to the right path (8-9). Unconfessed sin brings punishment; confession of sin brings joy (10-11).

Psalm 33   Rejoicing in God

Israel's musicians and singers are called to unite in joyous praise to God (1-3). He is worthy of people's praise because of his faithfulness, seen in all his righteous works (4-5); because of his power, seen in creation and in his irresistible word (6-9); and because of his sovereign control, seen in the history of world events (10-12). God, being perfect in knowledge, sees the uselessness of all those achievements in which people put their trust (13-17).

Above all, God is worthy of people's praise because of the salvation he gives to those who fear him. He gives them life, protection and provision (18-19). All who humbly trust in his mercy will find that their lives develop new qualities of patience, confidence and joy (20-22).

Psalm 34   Thanks for deliverance

When he first fled from Saul to the Philistine city of Gath, David expected the Philistines would welcome him as a deserter from Israel's army, and so provide him with refuge. But the Philistines had probably not yet heard of David's break with Saul. They knew only that David had killed thousands of their own Philistine people; perhaps he was spying out their city in preparation for more slaughter. They decided to kill him, and David escaped only by pretending to be a madman. He found a new hiding place in the cave of Adullam (1 Sam 21:10-22:1).

Although the king of Gath's name was Achish, the heading to this psalm calls him Abimelech. This was a Philistine royal title (meaning 'father-king'), in the same manner as 'Pharaoh' was an Egyptian royal title (cf. Gen 20:2; 21:22; 26:26).

David trusts that God's deliverance of him will encourage others and be a cause for joint praise (1-3). His face previously showed shame and fear; now it shows radiance, for God protects and rescues the downtrodden when they cry to him (4-7). David therefore invites others to taste God's goodness for themselves. The strongest and most successful flesh-hunting beasts do not always find enough food to satisfy them, but David never suffers a shortage of supplies. He fears God, and therefore God provides for him (8-10).

To fear God requires people to speak truthfully, do good and strive for peace. This is the only way to true enjoyment in life (11-14). God punishes those who do evil but he answers the prayers of those who live uprightly, particularly when they are tempted to give up hope (15-18). Regardless of the extent of people's suffering, God is always able to preserve them through it. In the end, righteousness will lead to victory (19-22).

Psalm 35   Against false accusers

It seems that this psalm also was written during the time of David's flight from Saul. Much of his suffering during that time was because of the false accusations made against him by influential people in Saul's court. (See introductory notes to Psalm 7.)

Since David's enemies have the ferocity of men in battle, David asks God to deal with them accordingly and fight against them as a warrior (1-3). He prays that they might be turned back, scattered and brought to ruin (4-6), for they have persecuted him without cause (7-8). God alone can defend him against his attackers (9-10).

David's sorrow is the more painful when he remembers that those who now fight against him are those whom he helped, sympathized with and prayed for when they were sick or in trouble (11-14). They are hoping that David will soon be caught, so that they can pounce on him and destroy him. He knows that only God can keep him going and preserve him from their attacks (15-18). They plot evil and make false accusations against him (19-21), but he trusts that God will not allow them to gain the victory (22-25). His desire is that evil will be conquered and that righteousness will triumph (26-28).

Psalm 36 Human sin and divine love

When people habitually do what they know is wrong, the principle of lawlessness takes control of their lives. It hardens their hearts against God and blinds their eyes to their own failures, so that they cannot see the terrible judgment for which they are heading (1-2). Their wrong attitude shows itself in deceitful speech, evil actions and mischievous plottings (3-4).

God, on the other hand, is characterized by covenant love that is limitless (5), acts of righteousness that are unshakable (6), and loving provision that is inexhaustible (7-9). Blessing awaits those who trust in his faithful love; devastating ruin, those who persist in their wickedness (10-12).

Psalm 37 Opposite destinies

This psalm is an acrostic and a wisdom poem. (Concerning acrostics see notes on Psalms 9 and 10. Concerning wisdom literature see introductory notes to Job.) Other wisdom poems are found in Psalms 10, 14, 19, 49, 73 and 112.

On seeing how wicked people prosper, believers may be tempted to envy them or, worse still, to doubt God's goodness. The reminder given in this psalm is that no one should judge by outward appearances. The prosperity of worthless people will be shortlived, but the faithfulness of believers will be rewarded (1-4). Believers should therefore not be restless, impatient, or too easily angered when they see the apparent success of the wicked (5-9).

One day all the wicked will be destroyed. The meek will then be the sole possessors of the land (10-11). Lasting prosperity belongs to those who exercise patience and faith, not to those who achieve their selfish goals by wrongdoing. The evil of the wicked will eventually be the cause of their own downfall (12-15).

God will see that those who put spiritual values above material prosperity will, in due course, be materially blessed. But those who put material prosperity before everything else will find that it vanishes like smoke (16-20). Life will have its ups and downs, but through them all God will care for those believers who give generously to others (21-22). They may meet troubles, but God will never desert them. Through their difficulties God will provide for them and enrich their experience of him (23-26).

In the end justice will be done both to those who are good and to those who are bad (27-29). The good people, in God's sight, are those whose minds are so directed by God's Word that their speech and behaviour are wise and wholesome. God will not allow the wicked to gain the victory over them (30-34). As a towering cedar tree can be cut down in a few minutes, so those who tyrannize others will be suddenly destroyed (35-36). But God's goodness protects the godly and saves them in times of trouble (37-40).

Psalms 38-39 The cries of the sick

The psalmist David felt that sometimes punishment for his sins took the form of sickness (e.g. Ps 6) or opposition from those who envied or hated him (e.g. Ps 25). Both elements appear again in the prayer of Psalm 38, which, being a confession of sin, was suitable to be offered with certain sacrifices.

As the suffering David cries to God for mercy, he admits that, because of his sin, he deserves what he has got (38:1-4). He vividly describes the sickness, sores and pain that he has to endure (5-7), but his inner suffering is much greater. It leaves him crushed and repentant before God (8-10). Friends forsake him and enemies plot against him (11-12), but he bears their slanders as if he cannot hear them and cannot reply to them (13-14). He can only leave the matter in God's hands and trust that his downfall will give his enemies no cause to gloat over him or dishonour God (15-17). Although he has confessed his sins, his enemies still persecute him. He prays that God will not leave him alone in his hour of grief (18-22).

Psalm 39 views sickness in a different context from the previous psalm. As the psalmist looks back on his sickness, he asserts that he did not want to complain, in case he gave the wicked an excuse for dishonouring God. In the end, he could restrain himself no longer (39:1-3). His illness made him see how short and uncertain life is (4-6). He now sees this as all the more reason why he should trust in God and seek his forgiveness. He does not want to be mocked as one whose faith leaves him with fear and uncertainty in the face of death (7-8).

In view of all he has been through, the psalmist now asks for relief from his sufferings. The lesson God has taught him is that he should not place too high a value on the temporary things of life (9-11). He sees himself as a traveller, as a passing guest, and prays that his divine host will treat him with fitting kindness in the few days of life that remain (12-13).

Psalm 40 The life that pleases God

David here refers to some past experience in which God rescued him from what appeared to be certain death. David felt like a person who had fallen into a muddy pit and was sinking to death, but God pulled him out and put him on firm ground again. He can now continue his journey, singing as he goes and thereby encouraging others to put their trust in God (1-3). His song is one of praise to God, whose loving works on behalf of the faithful are more than can be numbered (4-5).

What God is most concerned with in the lives of believers is not the offering of animal sacrifices, but the offering of their lives; not the mere performance of religious rituals, but the willing performance of all God's will. God wants believers to open their ears to hear his instruction, then to carry it out willingly and joyfully (6-8). (This principle was carried out perfectly in the life of Jesus; see Heb 10:5-9.)

Having experienced personally the loyal love of God, David never stops telling people about it (9-10). He knows that the outflow of divine love will never cease, and with this assurance he asks God for his special protection through the persecution he is at present suffering. He does not deny that this suffering may be a punishment for past sins, but he still trusts God to save him through it (11-15). He desires that people everywhere praise God for his great salvation, and that he too might experience God's saving power once more (16-17).

Psalm 41 A friend's treachery

At the time of the writing of this psalm, David was ill and unable to help himself. One of his closest friends took the opportunity to act treacherously against him. The psalm would suit such circumstances as when his trusted adviser Ahithophel plotted his overthrow by organizing the rebellion of Absalom (see v. 9; cf. 2 Sam 15:12,31).

Those who help the needy will themselves receive help from God when they are in trouble (1-3). David knows that many are glad to see him lying helpless because of his sickness and are hoping he will die. To his face they say that they hope he will recover, but behind his back they plot against him (4-6). They encourage one another with the news that he has no hope of recovery (7-9).

David prays that he will recover so that he can deal with the plotters (10). He is confident that his uprightness before God will guarantee God's help and so bring him victory (11-13).

BOOK 2: PSALMS 42-72

Psalms 42-43 Longing for God's temple

In many ancient manuscripts Psalms 42 and 43 form one psalm. Together they express the sorrow of a devout worshipper, possibly a temple singer, who lived in the far north of Israel (see 42:6) and could no longer go to worship at the temple in Jerusalem.

This may have been because the kingdom was now divided, and the northern king would not allow his people to travel into the southern territory, where Jerusalem was situated. The king rejected the religion that was based in Jerusalem and set up his own idol-gods, one near his southern border and one in the far north where the writer of this psalm lived (1 Kings 12:28-29).

The psalmist's longing to draw near to God in his temple is likened to the intense thirst of an animal that seeks water in a dry sunburnt country (42:1-2). Ungodly friends mock him for having such strong feelings for a God who, living far away in Jerusalem, can be of no help to him (3). When he recalls how in former times he had led groups of singing worshippers to Jerusalem, his confidence in God is strengthened (4-5). As he watched the waters of those fast-flowing northern streams tumbling over the rocks, he felt that those waters were like the troubles that tumbled over him, almost drowning him in sorrow (6-7). But through all the disappointments and all the mockings of his enemies he knows that God will keep him (8-11).

Meanwhile the psalmist is still in an unsettled state of mind, because God has not yet given him his heart's desire (43:1-2). Then, as he considers the certainty of God's character, his confidence returns. He knows he will meet God at his altar on Mount Zion again (3-5).

Psalm 44 Has God forgotten his people?

Some national disaster has overtaken Israel and the people ask if God has deserted them. The tone of the psalm is not one of humility, but one of outspoken boldness in questioning God's purposes. It shows some lack of faith and submission before God (cf. Rom 8:28,31-39). But God may yet be gracious and answer such a prayer.

Through the words of the psalmist the people recall how God enabled their ancestors to conquer and inhabit Canaan (1-3). They remind God that he alone gave Israel victory, and the people praised him accordingly (4-8). Why, then, has he now deserted them? He has allowed them to be conquered, plundered, scattered and enslaved (9-12). They feel disgraced because of the insults that neighbouring nations throw at them (13-16).

What makes the insults hard to bear is that the people can see no reason why God has allowed this calamity to befall them. They do not feel as if they have forgotten God or been unfaithful to him (17-19). If they had worshipped foreign gods they could understand such severe divine punishment, but they can see nothing at all of which they have been guilty (20-22). They call upon God to wake from his sleep and do something to help them. They ask him to remember his covenant love for them and rescue them from their enemies (23-26).

Psalm 45 A royal wedding song

This song was written to be sung at the wedding of some Israelite king. The anticipation of such an occasion causes the writer's heart to overflow with joy (1).

First the writer addresses his comments to the king. Handsome in appearance, gracious in speech and strong in purpose, this one has been supremely blessed by God to fight for truth and justice (2-5). Since he is God's representative, the king will have an enduring kingdom. Since he fights for all that is right, God has given him honour and glory above all others (6-7). The writer sees this honour and glory reflected in the splendour of the wedding ceremony — the king's magnificent robes, the music being played in the ivory-decorated palace, the attendant princesses from many countries, and the presence of the queen mother (8-9).

The writer then addresses his comments to the queen. She is reminded to transfer her loyalty from her former family to the king, and is assured that he will return her love. People of subject nations will bring her gifts (10-12). The psalmist describes the majestic beauty of her bridal robes and the joyous scene as her bridesmaids and musical attendants lead her to the king (13-15). The king is then addressed again. He is given the assurance that he will have a line of royal descendants more glorious than that of his ancestors, so that his name will be honoured for ever (16-17).

As in most ceremonial songs, the words of this psalm are extravagant when applied to the Israelite king. But the same words, when applied to the King of kings, are scarcely enough to begin to describe his glory and power (cf. Heb 1:8-9; Rev 19:6-9).

Psalms 46-48 When God saved Jerusalem

Confident in tone and bold in expression, these three psalms express praise to God for delivering Jerusalem from an enemy invasion. One example of such a deliverance was on the occasion of Assyria's invasion of Judah during the reign of Hezekiah (2 Kings 18:9-19:37).

No matter what troubles he meets, whether from earthquakes, floods or wars, the person who trusts in God is not overcome by them (46:1-3). He has an inner calmness, likened to a cool refreshing stream that flows gently from God. The Almighty is still in full control, and he gives strength to his

people (4-7). God's power can smash all opposition. Therefore, opponents should stop fighting against him, and realize that he is the supreme God, the supreme ruler of the world (8-11).

The psalmist calls upon people of all nations to worship God with reverence and joy. The king who rules over all has come down from heaven, fought for his people and given them victory (47:1-4). Now he is seen returning to heaven to the sound of his people's praises (5-7). He takes his seat on his throne again, king of the world. All nations are, like Israel, under the rule of the God of Abraham (8-9).

Now that their beloved city Jerusalem has been saved, the people praise its beauty and strength. More than that, they praise the God who saved it (48:1-3). Enemies thought they could destroy Jerusalem, but God scattered them. They were broken in pieces as ships smashed in a storm (4-7). Israel's people had heard of God's marvellous acts in the past; now they have seen them with their own eyes (8). In thanks for the victory, the people flock to the temple to praise God. Throughout the towns of Judah, and even in other countries, there is rejoicing (9-11). The citizens of Jerusalem are proud of their city, but they are prouder still of their God who has preserved it (12-14).

Psalm 49 When rich and poor face death

Rich and poor alike are asked to listen as the psalmist deals with a problem of life that concerns them both (1-4). The godly have no need to be anxious when the wealthy and powerful oppose them. After all, the wealthy cannot give their money to God to stop them from dying. Money cannot buy the right to live for ever. The wealthy also must die (5-9). Whether people be wise or foolish, rich or poor, they are no better off than the beasts when it comes to escaping death (10-12).

Although all are equal in having to face death, they are not all equal in what they have to face after death. Those who foolishly rely on their wealth will find it unable to save them from ruin and decay in the world of the dead. On the other hand, the godly, who do not look to wealth to save them from the power of death, will find that God himself saves them, and leads them into a future life of joy (13-15). A person need not, therefore, fear or envy the rich, for their wealth is not lasting. It cannot save them from future ruin (16-20).

Psalm 50 True worship

In a scene that displays his awesome majesty, God commands the whole world to stand before his judgment throne (1-3). He is the righteous judge of all the peoples of the world, and his first call to judgment concerns his own people, Israel (4-6).

God's complaint against the Israelites is not that they have failed to offer sacrifices and offerings. Indeed, they have offered them continually (7-8). But God will not accept their offerings. Instead of offering their sacrifices in a spirit of humble worship, the people were offering them as if they were doing God a favour for which he should be thankful. They offered their sacrifices as if they were giving God something he needed. But God needs nothing; he already owns everything (9-11). The meat and blood of the sacrifices are of no material use to him. God is not like the mortal beings of earth who have to eat and drink to keep alive (12-13). The offerings that he accepts are those based on thanksgiving, obedience and complete trust (14-15).

Turning to judge those who are not his people, God condemns them for their disobedience, lies, adultery and slander (16-20). Because God does not act in immediate judgment against them, they think he approves of their behaviour. They are about to find out that such thinking is mistaken (21). They are warned of God's terrible judgment and invited to accept his free salvation (22-23).

Psalm 51 David's repentance

Having committed adultery with Bathsheba, David then arranged for her husband Uriah to be killed, so that he could take Bathsheba as a royal wife (2 Sam 11:1-27). The prophet Nathan found out David's sin, condemned him to his face, then pronounced God's judgment upon him (2 Sam 12:1-15). This psalm displays David's deep sorrow as he confesses his sin to God.

David makes no excuses. He acknowledges his sin and realizes that he can do nothing to receive forgiveness, except cast himself on the unfailing mercy of God (1-2). His wrongdoing has been not merely against a fellow human being but also against the holy God. It is the fruit of a human nature that from birth has been infected by sin (3-5). In the Israelite ceremony for restoring a cleansed leper, a brush made of hyssop was used to sprinkle him with sacrificial blood, and his body was washed with pure water. David refers to this ceremony as he asks God for cleansing from his sin. Once cleansed, he wants to be restored to a life of joy and gladness (6-9; cf. Lev 14:1-9).

What David fears most is to be separated from God. He therefore asks God for a new heart, one that is free of sin, so that he might enjoy God's presence and obey God's law as he ought (10-12). In gratitude for such merciful forgiveness he will never cease to praise God, and will always tell people of the salvation God offers to those who turn from their sin (13-15).

The Israelite religious system had no category of sacrifices for deliberate sins such as adultery and murder. Even if it had, David knows that God desires a humble and repentant spirit more than ritual sacrifices. The only thing David can do is come to God in his sorrow, and in a spirit of genuine repentance ask humbly for mercy (16-17).

Because David was king, his sin had dragged his country down with him. He therefore prays that his country also might be restored to God and enjoy God's blessing afresh (18-19).

Psalms 52-54 Those who act treacherously

When David fled from Saul he obtained urgently needed provisions from the priests at Nob (1 Sam 21:1-9). He was seen by Doeg, an Edomite and a servant of Saul, who reported the matter to Saul. In a typical fit of mad vengeance, Saul ordered Doeg to kill all the priests at Nob, something that Doeg was very willing to do (1 Sam 22:6-23). On hearing of Doeg's butchery, David wrote a poem against him, which has been preserved in the Bible as Psalm 52 (see heading).

David denounces Doeg for his pride, treachery and hatred of all that is good (52:1-4). Doeg will surely meet a terrible death, which good people will recognize as a just punishment from God (5-7). His impending ruin is in contrast to the fruitfulness of the believer, who lives his life in the fellowship of God and his people (8-9).

Psalm 53 is a repetition of Psalm 14 with minor adjustments. The purpose in repeating it here was probably to add further comment on the character of Doeg described in the previous psalm. For notes on the psalm see commentary on Psalm 14.

Psalm 54 also belongs to the time of David's flight from Saul. It was written against the people of the town of Ziph, who betrayed David to Saul when they found that he was hiding in the wooded hills nearby (1 Sam 23:19-24). David prays to God to save him and punish his enemies (54:1-5). Confident that God will hear him, he looks forward to the day when he can show his gratitude to God by sacrifice (6-7).

Psalm 55 Betrayed by a friend

David is worried and uncertain. He has found that so-called friends have been plotting against him (e.g. Ahithophel; 2 Sam 15:12,31; 17:1-3) and he knows not which way to turn. He remembers things he saw certain people do and realizes now that they were treacherously aimed at his downfall (1-3).

Overwhelmed by a sense of helplessness, David fears that death is upon him (4-5). He wishes that he could escape from it all. He would like to fly away like a bird, so that he could find a quiet place where he could shelter from the storm (6-8). Then he thinks again of the murderous plans that people have laid against him. Along the city walls, around the streets, in the market places, people plot against him (9-11). Most heart-breaking of all is the knowledge that the person behind this plotting is the one he thought was his closest friend (12-14). Such traitors deserve a fitting punishment (15).

In his distress David turns to God and his faith awakens. He knows that God will save those who trust in him, and overthrow those who deliberately ignore him (16-19). But he cannot forget his false friend and the treacherous way his friend has lied to him (20-21). He decides finally that the only way to be relieved of the burden on his mind is to hand it over to God. He is confident that God will look after the righteous and punish the wicked (22-23).

Psalms 56-57   David escapes from Saul

Both these psalms belong to the time when David fled from Saul, first to the city of Gath, then to the cave of Adullam. (For the historical background see introductory notes to Psalm 34.)

David is in great distress in Gath, as he learns that certain people in the city are planning to kill him (56:1-2). The increased danger he faces drives him to an increased dependence on God (3-4). Enemies watch his every move, plotting how they can best attack him (5-7). He is so tense with fear that he cannot sleep at night. He knows God takes notice of his distress, and this reassures him that God will protect him (8-11). In fact, his confidence in God is so secure that he considers his prayer as already answered. He pictures himself fulfilling his vows by offering sacrifices of thanksgiving to God for his deliverance (12-13).

Having escaped from Gath, David now takes refuge in a cave. More importantly, he takes refuge in the Most High God (57:1-3). As a lion hunts down its prey, so Saul's men hunt down David. They are like those who hunt innocent animals by laying traps for them. But they themselves are the ones who will suffer (4-6). David is so confident of God's deliverance that he pictures singers and musicians joining in praise to the God of love and faithfulness who has saved him (7-11).

Psalm 58   Corrupt judges

In Psalms 10-17 the psalmist considered the problem of the poor and innocent being trampled underfoot by people of power and wealth. (See notes on these psalms, including the special note that follows Psalm 10.) In Psalm 58 the psalmist deals more specifically with those who make such a situation possible, the corrupt judges. Evil in thoughts and actions, they are deaf to any pleas for justice (1-5). The psalmist appeals to God to break their power and destroy them, so that they disappear from human society (6-9). The righteous will rejoice when corruption and oppression receive their fitting judgment from God (10-11).

Psalm 59   Wild dogs

At the time of writing this psalm, David had not yet fled to Gath and Adullam. He was still at Saul's court, but his repeated military successes stirred up Saul's jealousy, resulting in another attempt by Saul to spear him (1 Sam 19:1-10). David escaped to the safety of his own house. Saul then laid a plot to murder him at his home, and David escaped only narrowly (1 Sam 19:11-17). This psalm concerns the attempt on David's life at his house.

The psalm opens with a plea for protection against those whose intention is to murder David (1-2). Bloodthirsty people hide in the dark, awaiting the opportunity to kill an innocent man (3-5). David likens them to a pack of wild dogs that prowl the streets at night, seeking some helpless victim that they can attack and tear to pieces (6-7). But they are powerless against God, and therefore they are powerless against those whom he defends (8-10).

David knows that God will destroy these violent people, but he does not want them killed in a way that would appear to be the result of natural causes. He wants their death to occur in such a way that people will see clearly that it is a direct judgment from the righteous God (11-13).

Meanwhile the hungry dogs still prowl. Each night they return, eagerly looking for their victim (14-15). God, however, still guards David, and each morning David praises him afresh for his faithful protection (16-17).

Psalm 60   Victory over Edom

In the war outlined in 2 Samuel 8:3-14 (and dealt with in more detail in 2 Samuel 10:1-19) David fought on many fronts. The present psalm concerns Israel's victory in a battle against Edom. Because of the widespread military activity, a number of people and places are named in the accounts in 2 Samuel and in the heading to this psalm. Also three different leaders are named as bringing victory to Israel. The first is David, who was the supreme commander in Israel. The second is Joab, who was the army

201

commander-in-chief. The third is Abishai, who was the leader of the army unit involved in the particular battle that is mentioned here (cf. heading to Ps 60 with 2 Sam 8:13; 1 Chron 18:12).

While Israel has been fighting to the north and east, Edom and its allies have attacked from the rear (i.e. the south). Israel's forces have suffered such heavy losses it appears God has deserted them. They have been thrown into confusion, as if hit by an earthquake. They stagger like a person who is drunk (1-3). Since they are God's people, will he not reverse this disaster and lead them to victory (4-5)? Surely he will, for he has given them his promise. All the enemy-occupied areas, whether west of Jordan or east, will be liberated, for they belong to Israel by God's appointment. The southern attackers – Moab, Edom and Philistia – will be overthrown and made to serve Israel (6-8).

Why then should God's people doubt him? He has not forgotten them. He will indeed lead them against the enemy strongholds and give them victory (9-12).

Psalms 61-64 Longing for God

Far from home, weary, depressed and in danger, David seeks refuge and refreshment with God. He trusts that God will bring him safely back to Jerusalem and give him the strength to carry out his promise to lead God's people in God's ways (61:1-5). The people with him add their support to his request (6-7), and David responds that he will always remain faithful to his task (8).

God alone is the strength of David's assurance (62:1-2). David's enemies think they can ruin him. They think he is as unstable as a leaning wall, as easy to push over as a broken-down fence (3-4). Actually, he is as strong and secure as a fortress, for he is built on God. All God's people should therefore take courage and realize that they can trust in God through all circumstances (5-8). The unstable ones are those who live as if God does not matter. Life is uncertain, but they put their trust in wealth, even though that wealth must soon be lost (9-10). The only ones who have true security are those who take God into account and build their lives according to his values (11-12).

At times David experiences weakness and thirst in the dry Judean wilderness, but they are nothing compared with the spiritual thirst he has to worship at Israel's sanctuary again (63:1). He praises God as he recalls the power and glory of God that he experienced at the sanctuary in former days. He looks forward to a life of continuing praise because of God's continuing love (2-4). As he lies on his bed he thinks back with much satisfaction at all God's goodness to him over the years (5-8). This gives him the confidence to believe that God will punish his enemies and bring him safely back to Jerusalem (9-11).

Again David cries to God to save him from enemies who by cunning and lying seek to kill him (64:1-4). They plot their evil carefully, thinking that God cannot see them (5-6). However, they are deceiving themselves. God will act against them suddenly and certainly, bringing shameful defeat upon them. God's decisive action will be a warning to others, and at the same time bring honour to his name (7-10).

Psalm 65 Praise for harvest, fields and flocks

As they approach God, the worshippers are aware of their failures through sin. They realize that forgiveness is necessary before they can enjoy fulness of fellowship with God in his house (1-4). They recall his great acts, both in the events of history and in the natural creation, and see these as a reason for all people, from east to west, to shout for joy (5-8).

Coming closer to home, the worshippers see God's provision in the well-watered ground, the flowing streams, the full harvest and the flourishing countryside before them (9-10). They view the scene as if God is driving through the land in his chariot to inspect its richness; and the pastures, harvest and flocks join in joyously shouting their welcome to their divine provider (11-13).

Psalm 66-67 God and the nations

It appears that in Psalm 66 the people join in singing the first part of the song, and that the king sings the latter part alone. The song opens with a call to people worldwide to sing praise to God for a notable victory he has just won for Israel (66:1-4). Centuries earlier God brought Israel out of Egypt and led the people through the Red Sea, and the same God still rules in the affairs of nations (5-9). The worshippers acknowledge that in allowing them temporarily to be defeated, God had been working for their good. His purpose was to correct their waywardness so that once again they might enjoy the freedom of life that is found only in his presence (10-12).

The king then sings his praises, promising to present sacrifices in fulfilment of the vows he made to God during the time of trouble (13-15). He urges godly people everywhere to take note of what the experience has taught him (16). Above all, it has taught him not to ignore personal wrongdoing. God answers the prayers of those who have no known sin unconfessed in their lives (17-20).

Psalm 67 shows God's loving purposes towards all the nations of the world. When the people of Israel enter into the fulness of God's blessing, they will be in a fit condition to take the message of his salvation to other nations (67:1-3). These nations will then have their way of life changed through coming under the just rule and merciful guidance of God (4-5). People everywhere will rejoice in God's good gifts and offer thanks to him (6-7).

Psalm 68   The God of Israel

This magnificent hymn of praise and triumph was no doubt written for some special occasion. It may have been the occasion on which David brought the ark to Jerusalem (see introductory notes to Psalm 24), but its language makes the psalm suitable for much wider use.

When God fights for his people, their enemies are as helpless before them as smoke before wind or wax before fire. Nothing can stop him as he rides out to do battle (1-4). God is on the side of the poor, the afflicted and the downtrodden, but he opposes those who rebel against him (5-6).

All this was demonstrated in the events of the exodus from Egypt, when God worked wonders in the skies and on the earth to release his people and punish their oppressors (7-10). It was demonstrated also in the conquest of Canaan and the events that followed. Enemy kings were conquered and driven before Israel as snowflakes are driven before the wind. The psalmist pictures the colourful scene at the Israelites' camp as the soldiers return with clothing and other goods left behind by the fleeing enemy (11-14).

Finally, Israel conquered Jerusalem, whereupon God, in the symbolic form of the covenant box, came to Mount Zion. The psalmist imagines the mighty mountains of Bashan being envious of the humble hill in Jerusalem that God chose for his dwelling place (15-16; cf. 2 Sam 5:1-10; 6:14-19).

God's conquest on behalf of his people, from the time they left Mount Sinai to the time they came to Mount Zion, is pictured in a conquest by a mighty army of chariots. The victors capture their enemies and enrich themselves by seizing the enemies' goods (17-18).

These reminders from the past encourage Israel to have confidence in God for the present and the future. He will continue to help them (19-20). From the tops of Bashan's mountains to the depths of the sea nothing can withstand God. Israel will triumph over its enemies (21-23). The psalmist then describes the triumphal procession, as singers, musicians and dancers, followed by the tribal representatives, enter the sanctuary (24-27). No longer will other nations ('beasts' and 'bulls') conquer Israel and force it to pay heavy taxes. Instead these nations will bring *their* offerings to Israel, as they submit themselves to the rule of God (28-31). All nations are urged to praise him who rules in the heavens (32-35).

Psalm 69   Undeserved suffering

As a person sinking in a muddy pit, or someone drowning in swirling floodwaters, so the psalmist fears he is being overwhelmed by his sufferings. No human help is near (1-3). His enemies cruelly injure him, forcing him to suffer for sins that he did not commit (4). He knows he is not sinless, but he also knows that he has tried to live uprightly before God. On the basis of this he cries out to God to rescue him. He does not want his enemies to triumph over him, in case other believers are discouraged (5-6).

This suffering is for God's sake. The psalmist is an outcast even among his own family (7-8). His zeal for God, his fasting, and his other acts of devotion are merely an excuse for others to mock him and insult God (9-12).

At this point the psalmist turns to consider God's steadfast love. Although his sufferings and dangers are not lessened, he believes God will rescue him from them (13-18). He has nothing but disappointment from those he thought were his friends. They have all deserted him. His enemies increase his torture by the poisoned food and bitter drink they give him (19-21). The psalmist prays that his persecutors themselves will taste something of the tortures that they have been giving him — the poisoned food, the dark hiding places, the weakness the fear, the loneliness (22-25). As they have heaped sorrow on the godly, may God heap his punishment on them (26-28).

Although in pain and despair, the psalmist still trusts in God, believing that God will hear him. He promises that his worship will be thankful and sincere, far more than the mere sacrifice of animals (29-31). His deliverance will encourage others who are harshly treated to put their whole trust in God (32-33). And if God can save the individual, he can also save the nation and make it a fitting dwelling place for the righteous (34-36).

For the wider meaning of many sections of the psalm in the experience of Jesus Christ, see Background. See also introductory and closing notes to Psalm 22. For quotations of this psalm in the New Testament cf. v. 4 with John 15:25; cf. v. 9 with John 2:17, Rom 15:3; cf. v. 21 with Matt 27:34,38; cf. v. 22-23 with Rom 11:9-10; cf. v. 24 with Rev 16:1; cf. v. 25 with Acts 1:20; cf. v. 28 with Rev 20:15.

Psalms 70-71 A lifetime of faithful service

Psalm 70 is the same as Psalm 40:13-17 (see notes). It appears in the collection as a separate psalm probably because it was short and suitable for use in temple services on certain occasions.

In Psalm 71 the believer is pictured looking back on a long life and recalling how the wicked always have opposed him. But just as God has protected him since childhood, so he will continue to do so now (71:1-6). The psalmist's life has been a constant example of the believer's trust and God's faithfulness (7-8). He prays that now, at this late stage in life, God will not withdraw his protective care. He wants no one to have cause to accuse him or God of unfaithfulness (9-13). From his youth he has proclaimed the great saving acts of God. He prays that God will not disappoint him now, and that he will continue to proclaim the message of divine salvation till life's end (14-18).

The psalmist is confident that God will give him the extra years and added strength that he needs to complete his life's work (19-21). Such assurance leads him to a final outburst of praise to this God of faithfulness and righteousness (22-24).

Psalm 72 Israel's ideal king

Solomon, the writer of this psalm, knew that God's desire was for the dynasty of David to be established permanently (2 Sam 7:8-16). He knew also that only as the king himself feared God and ruled by God's wisdom would Israel enjoy the peace and strength that God intended for it (1 Kings 3:6-9).

These points are emphasized in the present psalm, which is a prayer designed to be used by the people when praying for their king. But Solomon and the Davidic kings after him fell far short of the ideals that he sets out here. The one Davidic king who fulfils all that the prayer asks for is the Messiah, Jesus.

The king who rules in submission to God will be righteous in his character and just in his actions, defending the oppressed and crushing those who oppress them (1-4). He will be as beneficial to his people as rain is to the earth, and thereby ensure that his kingdom enjoys prosperity, righteousness, peace and long life (5-7). His kingdom will expand by taking into it other countries, and will be enriched by the tribute and resources that these countries provide (8-11). The reason for this expansion is not selfish ambition or ruthless aggression, but the moral quality of the king himself. He helps the poor and the needy, rescues the downtrodden, and considers each person's life a thing of great worth (12-14).

Riches will come to this king and people will offer prayers for him. His country will flourish agriculturally, his fame will spread and his dynasty will last for ever (15-17). The psalmist urges people everywhere to praise God who alone can do all this (18-19). An editorial note marks the conclusion of this group of psalms (20).

BOOK 3: PSALMS 73-89

Psalm 73 Why do the wicked prosper?

Asaph had a problem that almost caused him to give up the life of devotion to God. If God was a God of goodness who helped the righteous and opposed the wicked, why did worthless people prosper while Asaph suffered want (1-3)?

It seemed to Asaph that the wicked enjoyed lives of ease and plenty, then died peacefully without suffering. Yet their lives had been characterized by pride, cruelty, greed, trickery, scorn, oppression and boasting (4-9). Some of the godly were tempted to follow their example, for it seemed that God did not interfere with the wicked in their comfort (10-12). Even Asaph himself felt at times that there was no purpose in suffering for God's sake (13-14).

All this time Asaph kept his problem to himself, because he did not want his doubts to bring shame on God's people or weaken their faith (15). Only when he considered the matter from God's point of view did he see any answer to his problem (16-17). Then he saw that death will shatter the ungodly person's life of luxury, just as waking ends a pleasant dream. The wicked will wake to find that God has not been sleeping. Now he will act in terrible judgment (18-20).

Looking back, Asaph now sees how foolish he has been to doubt God. Although he has acted like an ignorant animal, the everlasting God has not left him (21-23). Asaph sees now that in God he has riches and pleasures that are permanent and beyond value. They are far greater than the temporary riches and pleasures of the ungodly (24-26). When he sees things from God's viewpoint his whole attitude is changed. He no longer envies the wicked; he finds his full satisfaction in God (27-28).

Psalm 74 Israel in captivity

This psalm belongs to the time that followed the destruction of the nation Israel. Assyria conquered the northern kingdom in 722 BC, and Babylon the southern kingdom during the years 605-587 BC. The people were taken captive into foreign lands and the temple in Jerusalem was destroyed (2 Kings 25:8-12). Now, with the centre of their religious life gone, the people feel cut off from God. Worse than that, the bitter years in captivity lead them to doubt God's faithfulness.

Has God forgotten his covenant with Israel? The people invite him to go and inspect the ruins of the city and the temple. Perhaps it will rouse him to remember his covenant and bring them back to their homeland (1-3). They describe the scene of defilement and destruction in the temple: heathen victory symbols set up in the Holy Place (4); the beautiful woodwork broken, smashed and burnt (5-8); not a messenger of God to be found anywhere in the land (9).

Surely such a sight will rouse God from his inaction and cause him to act for them (10-11). Certainly, he is not lacking in power, for he has worked for them in the past. He directed the world of nature in such a way as to save Israel (12-17). Will he not therefore silence those who dishonour him? Will he not save his helpless people according to the covenant he made with them (18-20)? By acting against the oppressors, God can defend his cause and rescue his people (21-23).

Psalms 75-76 Exalting God, not self

In a psalm designed for use in public worship, the congregation begins by thanking God for all his mighty deeds (75:1). A singer representing God replies that even when conditions in the world look hopeless, God is still in control. He will intervene when he sees fit (2-3). Therefore, the wicked should not be proud or stubborn like an ox that struggles against its master (4-5). The only exaltation that matters is that which comes from God. The opinions of people mean nothing (6-7). Punishment also comes from God, and the wicked will drink his cup of anger to the last drop (8).

The leader of the congregation then responds on the people's behalf. He gives the assurance that they will always remain loyal to their God and will cooperate with him in doing good and opposing evil (9-10).

In the next psalm God is again praised, this time for some great deliverance in saving Jerusalem from an enemy (76:1-3). His glory, majesty and power are seen in the decisive way he crushed the enemy (4-6). The one who defends Jerusalem is also Lord of the universe. Nothing can stand before him. His power is absolute in the heavens and on the earth (7-9).

Angry rebellion against God is turned into a source of praise to him, for his triumph brings glory to his name. Since God will be glorified whether

people submit or rebel, they will do well to bring glory to him willingly by offering true and humble worship (10-12).

Psalm 77 Has God's favour of old changed?

Once again Asaph has a problem that is causing him much anxiety. (For his earlier problem see Psalm 73.) He cries to God in his distress but receives no answer (1-2). The more he thinks of God's dealings with him, the more distressed he becomes. It seems that God not only refuses to comfort him, but even prevents him from sleeping (3-4). So as he lies awake on his bed, he thinks of God's kindness to him in days gone by (5-6). God was gracious to him then; has he forgotten him now? It certainly seems so. It is as if God no longer helps him (7-10).

As his thoughts go beyond his troubles his confidence in the controlling care of God returns. The whole history of Israel is proof of God's love and power (11-15). Events of particular note are Israel's crossing of the Red Sea and God's coming to his people at Mount Sinai (16-19). These events are an encouragement to Asaph. He knows that the God who guided Moses and Aaron is still the shepherd of his people (20).

Psalm 78 Lessons from history

Being a true teacher, the psalmist is concerned for the spiritual condition of his people. His present intention is to comment on events in the history of Israel so that people of future generations may take heed (1-4). God gave his law to his people to guide them. The record of his faithfulness will be an encouragement, the record of Israel's failures a warning (5-8).

The first reminder is of the stubbornness of the tribe of Ephraim in one of Israel's early battles (9-11). The psalmist does not name the particular battle). By contrast God was always faithful to Israel. For example, he freed the people from Egypt and provided for their needs miraculously (12-16; see Exod 13:21; 14:21; 17:6). But as soon as the people began to taste the hardships of desert life, they complained bitterly. They challenged God to prove his kindness and power by giving them the food they wanted (17-22). Again God graciously provided for them (23-28), but their greed became the means of their punishment (29-31; see Exod 16:1-36; 17:1-7; Num 11:1-35).

Israel's constant lack of faith was well demonstrated in the people's refusal to believe that God could give them victory over the Canaanites. In punishment they suffered disaster and death over the next forty years (32-37). Yet in his mercy God did not destroy the rebellious nation (38-41; see Num 14:1-35). By his great power he saved the Israelites from the terrible judgments he sent upon Egypt, both its land and its people (42-51; see Exod 7:1-14:31). He cared for his people as they travelled through harsh countryside, from the Red Sea to the borders of Canaan. Finally, he brought them into the land he had promised them (52-55; see Josh 24:12-13).

Soon, however, the people forgot all that God had done for them. They turned away from the true God to follow the false gods of the Canaanites (56-58; see Judg 2:11-15). This led in turn to the destruction of their place of worship at Shiloh and the loss of the ark of the covenant to the Philistines (59-64; see 1 Sam 4:1-11; Jer 7:12,14).

Again God saved his people, this time by using a man from the tribe of Judah to stir them up and lead them triumphantly (65-68). This man, David, established the sanctuary on Mount Zion and placed within it the ark of the covenant, the symbol of God's presence. In this way David showed his determination that God should be the centre of Israel's national life. Israel's history had been one of constant failure, but God in his mercy had not forsaken his people. In the symbol of the ark he dwelt among them and through the rule of his chosen king he cared for them (69-72; see 2 Sam 5:6-10; 6:1-19).

Psalms 79-80   Cries from a conquered people

Like a previous psalm of Asaph, Psalm 79 is from the time of Jerusalem's destruction and the taking of the people into captivity. (For an outline of events see introductory notes to Psalm 74.) The historical setting for Psalm 80 is not clear. Both psalms, 79 and 80, are cries to God for salvation after Israel has suffered defeat and desolation.

The scene around Jerusalem is one of horror. The temple has been destroyed, the city is in ruins, and the army is a mass of decaying corpses providing food for wild birds and animals. Shame is added to sorrow through the insults heaped on Israel by its neighbours (79:1-4).

True, the destruction of Jerusalem has been a judgment sent by God on the nation because of its sin, but, ask the people, is not that enough? Will not God now reverse his judgment and punish those who eat up his people (5-7)? They pray that God will forgive their sins and restore them to their land. In this way he will silence those nations who mock him as being powerless to save (8-10). God's captive people cry out to him to rescue them and punish those who insult him (11-13).

Again the people cry to God for some decisive action that will save them from their present plight (80:1-3). They are weighed down with grief. God has apparently forgotten them and their enemies cruelly mock them (4-7).

When they think of the nation's past glory they wonder why they must suffer such shame. Israel was like a vine transplanted from Egypt into Canaan, where it grew and spread. It covered the mountains, burst its boundaries, and reached to the Lebanon Ranges and the Euphrates River (8-11). Why then does God allow the wild beasts of the forest to plunder and destroy his vineyard? Why does he allow enemy nations to crush Israel (12-13)?

The people pray that God will rescue the suffering nation, that he will save the damaged vine and restore it to healthy growth (14-16). They pray that he will give back to Israel the strength it once had as his specially chosen nation (17-19).

Psalm 81   A festival song

In the traditions that grew up around the Jewish festivals, this song was sung annually at the Feast of Tabernacles. (For this feast see Lev 23:33-36,39-43.) The song opens with a reminder of God's command to keep this joyous festival in remembrance of his goodness in saving his people from Egypt (1-5).

God then recounts how he lifted the burden of slavery from the backs of his people and looked after them as they travelled through the barren countryside (6-7). At Mount Sinai he gave them his law, adding a promise that he would continue to provide for them if they were faithful to him (8-10). But their stubborn disobedience prevented them from receiving God's blessing (11-12). God still desires his people's repentance and wholehearted loyalty; then he can pour out more of his blessings upon them. He can give them help and provision far greater than anything their ancestors experienced in the wilderness (13-16).

Psalms 82-83   Opposition to God's just rule

Psalm 82 is written against all those who act unjustly in their position as God's representatives in administering justice. They are even called gods (v. 1,6; cf. John 10:34; Rom 13:1,4,6). However, instead of rescuing the helpless poor from the powerful rich who enslave them, they show favour to those with influence and money (82:1-4). Because they are blind to all justice, truth and mercy, there is no stability in society (5). They may have high rank, but it will not save them on the day when they themselves are judged. They will be destroyed along with other wicked people (6-8).

Another picture of opposition to God concerns an attack on Israel by enemy nations whose hatred of Israel results from their hatred of God (83:1-4). On all sides enemies gather to fight against God and his people (5-8). But just as God defeated Sisera and Jabin in the time of Deborah, and defeated the Midianites in the time of Gideon, so may he defeat the gathered armies again (9-12; see Judg 4:1-5:31, 6:1-8:28). The psalmist prays that their destruction will be complete (13-15), so that people will acknowledge God's sovereign power and praise his holy name (16-18).

Psalm 84   Joy in God's house

On account of the difficulties and dangers people faced in travelling from remote areas to Jerusalem, some Israelites could visit the temple only once or twice each year. The present psalm reflects the joy and satisfaction of one such traveller as he comes to the temple to worship (1-2). Even the birds who make their nests in the temple courtyard have meaning for this man. As they find rest in their nests, so he finds rest in God's house (3-4).

The traveller is so pleased to have arrived at the temple, that the troubles he experienced on the journey now seem nothing. Although he was faint and weary in a waterless country, God strengthened him to go on (5-7). As he offers praise to God he does not forget to pray for the king (8-9). He finds such joy in worshipping in God's house, that he would gladly put up with any difficulties, no matter how tiring the journey, just to stand at the door. He would rather go through hardships and be at the temple than remain at ease but be far away from God. The almighty God alone is the source of all true blessing (10-12).

Psalms 85-86   The steadfast love of God

Israel had again suffered God's punishment in being defeated by its enemies. The psalmist reminds God that when this happened in the past, God forgave his people and poured out his blessings on them afresh (85:1-3). Would he not, therefore, in the present crisis do the same once more (4-7)? The psalmist thinks longingly of the spiritual paradise that results when people are living in a right relation with their God. Steadfast love flows down from God and is met by covenant faithfulness from his people (8-11). And as people respond to God's unfailing goodness, the land will enter a new era of fruitfulness, bringing fresh benefits to God's people (12-13).

Psalm 86 is similar to many psalms that David wrote in his times of distress. Knowing that God is on the side of those who are treated unjustly, the psalmist calls confidently for his help. He trusts in God's steadfast love (86:1-7). God is supreme. Both creation and history show that he is the only true God (8-10). Therefore, the psalmist desires to know him better, obey him more faithfully and praise him more constantly (11-13). On the basis of God's close relation with him, he appeals to God to give him strength to escape those who are trying to kill him (14-17).

Psalm 87   Citizens of God's city

This psalm looks forward to the gathering of people of all nations into Zion, the city of God. It is a picture of God's gracious act in welcoming all who want to be his people, regardless of their nationality (cf. Matt 8:11; 28:19; Gal 3:28; 4:26; Eph 2:13-19; Rev 21:22-24).

God loves his city, the place where he dwells among his people (1-3). He brings men and women from former enemy nations and places them in his city (4). He gives them equal rights as his children along with the faithful of Israel and those of other, far off nations (5-6). All the faithful rejoice together in the refreshment and delight of God's city (7).

Psalm 88   Darkness and despair

Overcome with trials and seeing no way out of the situation, the writer prays desperately to God (1-2). He sees himself as being close to death, with no way of being rescued (3-5). He feels as if he has been left to die by both God and friends (6-8). He wants to experience God's saving power now, while he is still alive, for it will be too late when he is dead (9-12).

Looking back, the writer sees that all his life he has had nothing but suffering, yet God still seems to ignore him. In fact, it seems that God deliberately attacks him, crushing him with sorrow and taking away from him even the comfort of friends. In spite of this, he does not turn away from God, but brings his burden to him daily (13-18).

Psalm 89   Remember the covenant with David

Apparently Israel had suffered some military setback that threatened its existence. This caused some people to think that God had forsaken his anointed king. The psalmist therefore recalls the covenant promise God made to David to preserve his dynasty for ever, and on the basis of this he claims God's help (1-4; see 2 Sam 7:8-16).

Before speaking further of the covenant, the psalmist praises God for his majesty and greatness. None among the multitudes of glorious heavenly beings can compare with him (5-7). On the earth also he is all-powerful, crushing his foes, working wonders and administering justice (8-14). This one is the God of the people of Israel. He is their glory, joy and strength, the one who gave them their king (15-18).

Assured of God's perfection and sovereignty, the psalmist turns to consider the covenant that God made with Israel. He outlines how God chose David to be his anointed king (19-20), gave him victory over all his enemies (21-23), enlarged his kingdom beyond the borders of Israel (24-25) and gave him power and glory (26-27). Above all, God made a covenant with David to establish his dynasty permanently (28-29). Even if some kings proved unworthy, God promised that he would not alter his plans. He had chosen the dynasty of David as the means of bringing the Messiah (30-37).

It seems now, however, that their great and powerful God has left them. Their covenant Lord appears to have forgotten his promises (38-39). The kingdom has been ruined, the city destroyed, the land plundered (40-41). Enemies are allowed to conquer as they please. The Davidic king has lost his throne and been openly disgraced (42-45). Why, then, does God not act? Certainly, some must die, but is he going to allow these enemies to conquer and kill until the king and his people are eventually wiped out (46-48)? The psalmist prays that God will remember his covenant promise to David, save his people from their present shame, and give them freedom under the rule of their Davidic king again (49-52).

BOOK 4: PSALMS 90-106

Psalm 90   Making the most of a short life

God alone is permanent and enduring, and therefore the only true security is found in him (1-2). Human life, by contrast, is short and uncertain, and is brought to an end as God decides and when he chooses. No matter how long a person lives, even to a thousand years, the number of years is insignificant compared with the timelessness of God (3-6).

Sin has spoiled human life and brought God's judgment upon people in the form of life's troubles and finally death (7-10). The ungodly live to please themselves. They do not fear God and do not consider that they are spending their lives building up God's judgment against them. Those who love God should therefore seek God's wisdom, so that they might use their short lives in the best way possible (11-12). Since the psalmist wants to live his life wisely, he asks for God's help. Then sorrow will be replaced by joy, and his life will become one of fruitful service for God (13-17).

Psalm 91   God our protector

This psalm appears to have been used in temple worship in a time of danger. A lone singer opens with a statement of the security and protection enjoyed by those who trust in God and live their lives constantly in God's presence (1-2).

The singer then addresses his remarks directly to such believers. God will protect them from dangers, both seen and unseen, both by day and by night. Neither cruel enemies nor deadly diseases will overcome them. God will guard their lives as a mother bird guards her young and as a soldier guards his fortress (3-6). Others may fall, but those who trust in the Most High will be safe (7-8). Because they have committed themselves to God's safe-keeping in complete faith, God will direct his angels to watch over them with special care (9-12). They will triumph over the strong and fierce, the cunning and deceitful (13).

Another singer, representing God, adds his blessing. He notes that such believers have a close personal knowledge of God, love him and talk with him; consequently, God will protect, deliver, guide, comfort and honour them. He will give them the blessing of long life by which they can enjoy God's salvation to the full (14-16).

Psalms 92-93   God's rule in an evil world

According to the title, Psalm 92 was for use on the Sabbath. God is pleased when people cease their ordinary work for a day in order to engage in worshipping him and proclaiming his love (92:1-4). As they meditate upon the nature of God, their thinking will be changed. They will see from God's point of view and will understand things that are misunderstood by the ordinary person. They will see, for instance, that they need not puzzle over why the wicked prosper. God is the supreme ruler and judge, and he is always in control. In the end the wicked will be destroyed and their prosperity lost for ever (5-9).

By contrast, those who remain true to God will prosper. As a wild ox grows powerful, so the righteous will be strengthened. As privileged people are anointed with oil, so the righteous will be blessed (10-11). As magnificent trees flourish, so the righteous will be strong and fruitful. As a house built on a rocky hill is safe, so the righteous will be secure (12-15).

God is the sovereign Lord and he reigns in majesty. He existed before the universe and he rules over it (93:1-2). The opposition of the ungodly world is like a raging flood that tries to overturn his throne, but it is powerless to move him (3-4). His glory is displayed not only in his power but also in his holiness. People should therefore obey and worship him (5).

Psalm 94 God the judge of all

The psalmist, tired of the oppression caused by the proud and the wicked, calls for a fitting divine punishment on all those who oppose God and his ways (1-3). They brutally crush the poor and the helpless, thinking that God does not see them (4-7). How foolish of them. They forget that God is the one who made them. He knows what they are and what they do. He controls their destinies and will punish them for their wrongdoing (8-11).

God does not desert the godly in their troubles, and may even use their troubles to teach them lessons of patience and love. Then, when he sees the time has come to intervene, he punishes the tormentors and gives relief to their victims (12-15). But until that day comes, the suffering believer has no defence against the wicked and no source of comfort except in God alone (16-19). The wicked are in places of authority, but they oppose God whose law they should be administering. The believer's only hope is to trust in the overruling government of God (20-23).

Psalms 95-96 God the creator of the universe

Six psalms, 95 to 100, are grouped so as to form a series for use in temple worship. The first psalm opens by calling people to worship God because he is the saviour (95:1-2), the great God (3), the creator and controller of the universe (4-5), the maker of the human race (6) and, above all, the covenant Lord and shepherd of his people (7). Worship, however, must be joined to obedience. Israel's experiences in the wilderness show that people might claim to belong to God, but be so complaining, disobedient and stubborn that it is impossible for them to enjoy the inheritance God promised (8-11; cf. Exod 17:1-7; Num 11:1-23; 20:2-13; Heb 3:7-4:10).

After the worshippers have heeded the warning of the previous psalm and prepared their hearts in a right attitude of worship, they are urged to praise God with further singing. Besides praising him for his great works, they are to proclaim his wonders to others (96:1-3). Idol-gods cannot be known, because they have no life. The living and true God can be known, both through the created universe and through the worship of the sanctuary (4-6). People everywhere should therefore bring him worship, praise and sacrificial offerings (7-9). Because he is Lord of the universe, all creation joins in bringing

him praise. Because he is Lord of the world of humankind, he will establish his righteous kingdom on the earth (10-13).

Psalms 97-100 God the universal king

Psalm 97 follows on from the thought on which the previous psalm closed (namely, that God is king over the earth). It shows that holiness, righteousness and justice are the basis of God's kingdom. His judgment will be as universal as a flash of lightning and as powerful as an all-consuming fire (97:1-5). Everything will bow before his rule (6-7). His own people already recognize him as Lord and bring him fitting worship (8-9). They can experience the light and joy of his salvation in their everyday lives as they reject what is evil and choose what is good (10-12).

Continuing the theme of the previous psalm, Psalm 98 reminds the people to welcome the divine universal king. By his power, he has conquered evil and established his kingdom in righteousness and love (98:1-3). People worldwide are to praise God with music and singing because of his great victory (4-6). The physical creation is invited to join in the praise, rejoicing because of him who rules the earth with justice (7-9).

From his throne in Zion, the city of God, God rules over the earth in holiness and justice (99:1-4) and people respond with worship (5). The psalmist refers to the lives of Moses, Aaron and Samuel to show how God answered the prayers of those who submitted to his rule and obeyed his law (6-7). When people disobeyed they were punished, but when they repented God forgave them (8). The God who rules in Zion is holy, and those who worship him must also fear him (9).

Psalm 100 is the climax of this group of six psalms. People of all the world are to worship God gladly, acknowledging him as their God, their maker and their shepherd (100:1-3). They are invited to come into his temple, where they can unite in thankfully praising him for his loving faithfulness to them (4-5).

Psalm 101 Principles of government

David here sets out the principles he sought to follow in his government of Israel. In view of the high ideals outlined here, it is not surprising that people such as Joab, Ahithophel and Absalom found David a hindrance to the success of their devious plans and selfish ambitions.

The chief concerns of David are loyalty to God and justice to his people. In his personal life he is determined to be strictly honest, pure in thoughts and actions, and uncompromisingly opposed to all evil (1-4). As for those who live in his palace, his ministers and officials, he will not tolerate any who are treacherous, proud, deceitful or untruthful. He will accept only those who are trustworthy and blameless (5-7). As for the people he governs, he will be strictly just in punishing the wicked, no matter how much money and power they may have (8).

Psalm 102 The changeless God

Jerusalem is in ruins, God's people are in captivity, and a weary sufferer pours out his complaint to God (see heading to the psalm; also v. 13-17). The opening part of the prayer describes the psalmist's afflictions in a style similar to that of many psalms in the early part of the book. The writer is ill and dying, partly because he is unable to eat (1-5). He is lonely and cannot sleep (6-7). He is persecuted by his enemies and feels he has been deserted by God (8-11).

But how could God desert him? God is still Lord; he does not change (12). He is always faithful to his people. For example, he sees their love for their broken-down city, he hears their prayers, and he will rebuild their city for them. Israel will triumph over its enemies as of old (13-17). All who are oppressed and discouraged should take note of this and praise God. He will hear the cries of his captive people, release them from bondage and bring them back to their beloved Jerusalem (18-22).

There is no need to doubt God. Life is full of troubles and uncertainties (23-24), and even the natural world suffers from wear and tear (25-26), but God is changeless. His troubled people, from one generation to the next, can depend on him to rescue them and bless them (27-28).

Psalm 103 God's great love

Realizing how easily people forget God, David reminds himself of the many blessings, physical and spiritual, that God has given him. Gratefully, he praises God for them all (1-2). Sin, sickness and the prospect of a hopeless death have been replaced by forgiveness, good health and a renewed enjoyment of life (3-5).

The constant love of God for his people is seen in the history of Israel. He cares for the oppressed and shows mercy on sinners (6-8). If God acted only according to his justice, all sinners would perish. But to his justice he adds his mercy, by which sinners may be forgiven (9-12). God understands human weakness and he is kind to those who fear him (13-14).

Life is short and uncertain, but people can enjoy the everlasting blessings of God's steadfast love if they are faithfully obedient (15-18). God requires submissive obedience not only of earthly beings, but also of heavenly beings (19-21). In fact, all created things are to praise God. But in the midst of this universal praise, each individual has special cause to praise him (22).

Psalm 104 God's earth

The theme of this song of praise is the wisdom and power of God as seen in nature. The song begins by considering the splendour of the heavens. The light of the sun, the expanse of sky reaching down to meet the earth on the horizon, the movement of clouds blown by the wind, the flashes of lightning – all these things speak of the magnificence of God who dwells in and rules over the universe (1-4).

Land and sea also display the greatness of God. He determined where they should be and how far they should extend (5-7). Mountains and rivers show God's complete control over the powers of nature, so that the land is well watered and able to support life (8-13). Because of God's control, the earth supplies people and animals with food (14-15), and with all the other materials necessary for them to live in safety and security (16-18). He arranges seasons and weather, night and day, so that the natural world can meet the needs of the various forms of life (19-23).

Before going on, the psalmist pauses to praise God for the vastness of his creation and for the wisdom that designed and maintains it (24). He then returns to his consideration of the natural world by showing how the immeasurable sea speaks further of God's greatness. It is full of the most wonderful creatures. Ships sail on it for distances farther than the eye can see or the mind imagine (25-26). God is the one who provides all creatures with life and food, and who determines how long each should live (27-30). He also controls the earthquake and the volcano (31-32).

In view of the devastating power that God has within his control, the psalmist prays that he will use it to cleanse the earth of sin. Then he will have complete pleasure in his creation and in the worship that his creatures offer him (33-35).

Psalm 105 God's faithfulness to his covenant

God's covenant people Israel, the descendants of Abraham, Isaac and Jacob, are reminded to worship their God continually and to tell others of the great things he has done (1-6). In particular they are to remember God's faithfulness to the covenant he made with Abraham. This covenant was his work alone. He chose Abraham from all the people of the world, and promised to make through him a nation and to give the land of Canaan to that nation for a homeland (7-11).

In the early days, when the covenant family was small, enemies could easily have wiped it out, but God miraculously preserved it (12-15). When a famine hit the land, God preserved his people through Joseph. Although Joseph's brothers sold him as a slave, God exalted him to high office so that he could provide for his needy family (16-22).

Through Joseph, all the chosen family moved to Egypt, where they grew into a strong and unified people (23-24). Unfortunately, this brought envy and oppression from the Egyptians (25), but God worked terrible miracles to punish the Egyptians and free his people (26-36). Having freed them, God guided and preserved them according to the covenant promises given to Abraham (37-42). Finally, God led his people into the land he had promised them. This was not because of any virtue in the people, but solely because of God's grace. In thanks for his covenant faithfulness, they should be faithful in obeying his law (43-45).

Psalm 106   Israel's faithlessness to God

Like the previous psalm, this psalm recounts the history of Israel. But whereas Psalm 105 emphasized God's faithfulness, Psalm 106 emphasizes Israel's unfaithfulness and the punishments it suffered as a result.

Since God is good, people should praise and obey him. Then they will enjoy, as individuals and as a nation, the full blessings God desires for them (1-5). The psalmist admits, however, that he and those of his generation have sinned as did their ancestors (6).

The psalmist gives many examples of Israel's sin. God saved his people from Egypt by his mighty power, but they had gone only as far as the Red Sea when they rebelled against him (7; see Exod 14:1-13). God again saved them and destroyed their enemies (8-12), but in their selfishness and greed they rebelled again (13-15; see Exod 16:1-17:7; Num 11:1-35). On another occasion they rejected their divinely-given leaders (16-18; see Num 16:1-50). At Sinai they rejected God himself (19-23; see Exod 32:1-35). They gave a further demonstration of their lack of faith when they refused to believe that God could lead them victoriously into Canaan (24-27; see Num 13:1-14:35).

After forty years in the wilderness, the people again showed their stubborn disobedience when they fell into idolatry and immorality (28-31; see Num 25:1-13). Throughout those forty years their bitter complaining spirit was a constant cause for God's displeasure (32-33; see Num 20:2-13).

When at last they entered Canaan, the people forgot God and copied the idolatrous practices of their heathen neighbours (34-39; see Judg 3:6; 10:6). God used the surrounding nations to punish his people, but when they cried to him he turned in mercy and freed them from their oppressors (40-46; see Judg 2:11-23). On the basis of his unfailing mercy, the distressed people call on God to save them again (47-48).

BOOK 5: PSALMS 107-150

Psalms 107-108   Specific thanksgivings

Psalm 107 seems to be particularly appropriate to the time of the Jews' return to their homeland after their exile in Babylon. It is a song of thanksgiving to be sung by those who have been saved from some great affliction or danger (107:1-3). Four different cases are introduced by verses 4, 10, 17 and 23. Each of the cases describes the danger, notes the prayer, outlines the answer and concludes with a word of instruction and warning.

The first thanksgiving is that of homeless wanderers. Lonely, hungry and thirsty, they cried to God and were led to a place of safety and security. They should now bear in mind that complete satisfaction is found only in God (4-9). The second thanksgiving is that of people who were in prison or slavery because of their sins, but when they cried to God he set them free. They should remember that no bondage is too strong for God (10-16). The third thanksgiving is that of the sick who once suffered for their wrongdoings but have now been healed. They should respond to God's grace by telling others of what he has done for them (17-22). The fourth thanksgiving is that of people who have been saved from terrible storms at sea. They should bear in mind that God is the one who brings all peace and calm (23-32).

When people are wicked, God may turn nature against them, punishing them with thirst and hunger. But when thirsty and hungry people are in need, God sends his generous blessings of nature upon them (33-38). When rulers are wicked, God may turn them into homeless wanderers. But when the poor are oppressed, God lifts their families into places of honour (39-43).

Psalm 108 was composed for some special occasion by combining portions of two other psalms. It is a song of assurance that God will give victory on the basis of his promises. For 108:1-5 see notes on Ps 57:7-11; for 108:6-13 see notes on Ps 60:5-12.

211

Psalm 109   Those who afflict others

David complains to God about the unjust attacks of his opponents and the false accusations they bring against him (1-3). He has no desire for personal revenge; rather he has shown love for his enemies and has prayed for them (4-5).

Nevertheless, in the prayer that follows, David uses strong language as he pleads for justice to be done. With the cruelty of his enemies increasing, he hands the case over to God, the righteous judge, who will repay the wicked for their wickedness. In particular David has in mind the leader of his accusers (6-7). (See section 'Curses on the wicked' that follows notes on Psalm 7.) The evildoer will receive fitting justice if he suffers the sorrows he intended to bring upon David. The curses listed here display the character of the aggressor and the evil he intended to do to David and his family (8-15). The man ruthlessly persecuted those who could not defend themselves, and deserves a punishment that is similarly ruthless (16-20).

As for David, he is weak, sick and despised, as helpless as an insect about to be blown away. Only God can save him now (21-25). He wants God to save him and punish his persecutors in such a way that people will see the events as the direct work of God (26-29). True justice is found with God alone. David is therefore confident that God will rescue him (30-31).

Psalm 110   The ideal priest-king

Melchizedek was priest-king of the Canaanite city-state of Salem, later known as Jerusalem. He was a man so pure and upright that he was called king of peace, king of righteousness and priest of the Most High God (Heb 7:1-10). He first appears in the biblical record when he met and blessed Abraham, who was returning after a victory over some raiders. Abraham refused to take any reward from those who benefited from the victory, but instead made offerings to God's priest. In this way he acknowledged that God was sovereign ruler in human affairs (Gen 14:1-24).

When David conquered Jerusalem and set up his throne there, he became heir to Melchizedek as Jerusalem's ideal priest-king. (The Melchizedek kind of priesthood was distinct from the Aaronic kind of priesthood.) As God's representative, David also was to be king of peace, king of righteousness and priest of the Most High God. It seems that David wrote this psalm to be sung by the temple singers to celebrate the establishment of his throne in Jerusalem (2 Sam 5:6-12).

To David it seems that, with his conquest of Jerusalem, God has given him victory over all his enemies and invited him to sit in the place of supreme power (1). From Mount Zion in Jerusalem, David rules his people and conquers his foes (2). The people willingly offer themselves to the king for his service in spreading his rule throughout the land. An army of young men with the life-giving freshness of dew and the strength of youth present themselves to the king (3). Just as the authority of Melchizedek, God's representative, had no historical or national limits, so David's authority in the name of God is limitless, in time and extent (4). God will lead his king to universal conquest and rule (5-6). He will refresh him by renewing his vigour continually, till he stands victorious, master of all (7).

It becomes clear as we read the psalm that David was but a very faint picture of the universal priest-king. Jews in later times interpreted the psalm as applying to the Messiah, and Jesus agreed that this was a correct application (Matt 22:42-45; see also Matt 26:64; Acts 2:34-35; Heb 1:3,13). The Melchizedek priesthood that David inherited was a priesthood in name only, a mere title to add to the other titles held by the Israelite king. Jesus Christ's priesthood after the order of Melchizedek is complete and never-ending (Heb 5:6; 7:1-28). His final conquest and royal rule will be universal (1 Cor 15:24-25; Rev 19:11-20:6).

Psalms 111-112   God and his godly people

Equal in length and similar in form, these two psalms can be read as a pair. Both are acrostics (see note preceding Psalm 9). The former considers the greatness of God, the latter the character of his godly people.

God's wonderful works, both in creation and in history, are a cause for praise by all his worshipping people (111:1-3). In his sovereign power he took the agriculturally productive land of Canaan from its heathen inhabitants and gave it to the Israelite people according to the covenant he had made with them (4-6). His desire is that they rule themselves according to his just law (7-8). He is the mighty and holy covenant-redeemer of his people, and they should fear him, honour him, obey him and praise him (9-10).

When people respond to God in such a way, God blesses them with a respected, upright and prosperous line of descendants (112:1-3). God looks after those who are fair in their treatment of others and generous with their money (4-6). Their lives will be enriched with a sense of security and confidence, so that they fear nothing (7-8). The satisfaction that comes from such lives is in sharp contrast to the envy and hopelessness of the wicked (9-10).

Psalms 113-114 When hope seems gone

Psalms 113 to 118 form a collection called the Hallel. Israelites sang the Hallel at various annual festivals, the most important of which was the Passover. They sang Psalms 113 and 114 before eating the meal, and Psalms 115 to 118 after (cf. Matt 26:30).

From east to west, now and for ever, God is worthy to be worshipped by those who serve him (113:1-4). Although he is enthroned in the highest place, he is concerned about his creatures on earth (5-6). He helps those who are downtrodden and gives new life and purpose to those who have given up all hope (7-9).

The merciful salvation of God was seen in the events of the exodus. God released his people from the humiliating slavery of Egypt and gave them new life by dwelling among them (114:1-2). In the course of doing this, he divided the Red Sea, stopped the flow of the Jordan River and sent an earthquake on Mount Sinai (3-4). All was the work of God alone. Not only did he rescue them from their hopeless situation in Egypt, but he also looked after them throughout their journey to Canaan (5-8).

Psalms 115-117 Saved from death

God was always faithful to Israel, though the Israelites were often unfaithful to him. Their sins brought God's punishment upon them, causing their pagan neighbours to mock them with the accusation that their God was unable to help them and had deserted them (115:1-2). The Israelites reply that their God is alive and in full control. The pagan gods, by contrast, are useless, and the reason they are useless is that they are lifeless. Those who trust in them will achieve nothing (3-8).

Israel's people will therefore trust in God for help and protection (9-11). They know that he will bless them and their descendants after them, for he is the almighty Creator (12-15). He has given the earth to humankind as a dwelling place, but has limited the number of years that each person may live on it. Therefore, God's people should make sure that they fill their few short years with praise to him (16-18).

In Psalm 116 an individual worshipper brings a sacrifice to God to pay his vows and offer thanks (see v. 17-18). Before offering his sacrifice, he pauses to think quietly on the great mercy and love of God. As he does so, he finds that his own love towards God increases, particularly when he recalls how God has answered his prayers and saved his life (116:1-4).

He has personally experienced God's compassion and goodness (5-7). When he was unable to help himself and when so-called friends proved useless, he still trusted God. He prayed, and God gave him new life (8-11). He will now publicly thank God by offering prayers and sacrifices in fulfilment of his vow (12-14). He sees how highly God values the life of the believer. God does not allow him to die, as if death is a thing of no importance in God's sight. God preserves him alive, and for this he offers overflowing thanks (15-19).

God's loyal love to Israel should cause his people to spread the good news of his love to other nations. This, in turn, will cause the people of those nations to bring their praise to him (117:1-2).

Psalm 118 A procession of thanksgiving

Originally this hymn was apparently sung by a combination of the temple singers, the congregation and the king, to mark some great national occasion such as a victory in battle. The scene is set in the temple, where the royal procession enters the gates and moves to the altar (see v. 19,20,27).

The singers call Israel to worship, and the congregation responds with praise to God for his steadfast love (1-4). The king then recounts how, in answer to prayer, God saved him from his enemies (5-7). The people respond that God is worthy of people's trust (8-9). The king describes the hopeless position he had been in, with enemies attacking him on every side, but with God's help he overthrew them (10-14). The people respond that God is all-powerful (15-16).

After expressing his confidence in God and his gratitude for God's chastening, the king commands that the temple gates be opened to him (17-19). The gatekeepers open the gates, but add the reminder that only the righteous can enter God's temple (20). The king responds by thanking God for his righteous salvation, for this alone enables him to enter God's presence (21).

The people then sing their rejoicings. When the king had been on the edge of shameful defeat, he seemed like a useless builder's brick that the builders had thrown away in disgust. Now, with his triumph, the same brick seems to have been brought back and made the chief cornerstone, giving perfection and character to the building (22-25).

From the altar in the temple courtyard, the priests sing their welcome as the worshippers, in procession and waving branches of palm trees, draw near. The palm branches give the appearance of binding the worshippers together as they surround the altar in preparation for the sacrifice (26-27). Before the sacrificial ceremony commences, the king, followed by the congregation, offers a final thanksgiving (28-29).

Psalm 119 Love for God's word

This psalm is a lengthy meditation addressed to God on the excellencies of his law. The law here refers not to legal requirements such as in the law of Moses, but to the whole of God's instruction for humankind in general. Therefore, God's law is also called his word, commandments, sayings, judgments, statutes, ordinances, instructions, precepts, injunctions, testimonies, promise, way and path. At least one of these words occurs in almost every verse of the psalm.

An acrostic in form, the psalm is divided into twenty-two sections, corresponding to the twenty-two letters of the Hebrew alphabet. Each section has eight verses, and all eight verses in any one section begin with the same letter. (For example, one might imagine an acrostic poem in English with the first eight lines all beginning with A, the second eight lines all beginning with B, and so on down to Z.)

Verses 1-16: In a confident opening statement the psalmist expresses the happiness enjoyed by those who live according to God's word (1-3). The psalmist then addresses God, praying that he himself will understand God's word and be obedient in following it (4-8). A good knowledge of God's word is a safeguard against sin (9-11). This knowledge is obtained by asking God's help in understanding his teaching, thinking it over and declaring it to others. Above all, the person must find pleasure in God's word and have a desire to know it and practise it (12-16).

Verses 17-32: The psalmist knows that if he has this desire to be guided by God's word, his life will be full of purpose and meaning. Though he may be unsure of his future (17-20), mocked by friends (21-22), or persecuted by rulers (23), he will always be loyal to God's word (24). This gives him the confidence to trust in God when he is in distress. God's word strengthens him (25-28). He therefore prays for increased understanding and greater inner strength to refuse what is evil and choose what is good (29-32).

Verses 33-48: For the psalmist, life is built around devotion to God's word. He does not want to be sidetracked by trying to gain wealth or prestige (33-37). What he dreads most is to displease God. What he longs for is a life directed by God through his word (38-40). The word gives him assurance of salvation, which in turn gives him courage to answer those who mock him (41-43), confidence to live in the freedom God has given him (44-45), and boldness to speak about God to the nation's rulers (46-48).

Verses 49-64: God's word brings comfort to the suffering believer (49-52), but it also stirs up feelings of righteous anger against those who deliberately ignore God's standards (53). However, the psalmist does not allow discouragement to overwhelm him. He gains renewed vigour from fresh meditation on God's word (54-56). Love for the word leads to enjoyment of God himself (57-58). It produces a life of obedience and prayer. It brings hatred from the wicked, but the believer finds new friendship among those who share his love for God (59-64).

Verses 65-80: In a world of sin, an understanding of God's word is essential to guide the godly in the way that is right (65-66). When they stray from God's path, God may send afflictions to bring them back. The afflictions in the case of the psalmist are the lies with which the wicked slander him (67-72). But the God who made him is developing his character through these afflictions. By coming through his trial with a firmer faith in God, he has been an encouragement to others (73-76). He prays that if his enemies attack him again, they, not he, will be defeated. As a result the godly will be further encouraged (77-80).

Verses 81-96: During periods of suffering, the psalmist has at times wondered why God is slow to act in saving him as he promised. He feels as useless and lifeless as a dried-up wineskin (81-83). Yet he does not lose hope. He still trusts in the steadfast love of God to deliver him from the treachery of his persecutors (84-88). God and his word are lasting and unchangeable. His promises are sure (89-91). This encourages him to believe that God will save him through his trials (92-96).

Verses 97-112: When the psalmist is taught by God through studying and meditating on his word, he learns true wisdom. He is wiser than all the worldly-wise, in spite of their years of experience (97-100). The wisdom that comes from God's word produces moral uprightness and sound judgment (101-104). It shows the psalmist how he should behave when he is afflicted (105-107), when he is praying or worshipping (108) and when he is in danger (109-110). It gives him constant and deep-seated joy (111-112).

Verses 113-128: Another result of loving God's word is a hatred of all that is evil and all that hinders the pursuit of good (113-117). God will punish those who deliberately rebel against his word. This is all the more reason why people should fear God and obey him (118-120). In view of his own obedience and God's promise, the psalmist asks God to save him from those who persecute him and break God's law (121-124). His enemies despise God's law, but he delights in it (125-128).

Verses 129-144: So wonderful is the instruction of God's word that God's loyal servant has a hunger to know more of it. He knows that by following God's word he has victory over sin and temptation (129-134). He weeps to think that people would trample underfoot such noble teaching (135-136). Their irreverence causes him further sorrow, for they are cutting themselves off from the knowledge of God. Only through God's word can people develop a true understanding of God's justice, righteousness and faithfulness (137-140). As for the psalmist, he finds God's word reliable and true, and a constant source of comfort, joy and instruction (141-144).

Verses 145-160: Obedience to God's word brings confidence in prayer, but that does not lessen the need for self-discipline, whether in studying the word or in praying (145-148). Whatever the danger, God is always near those who are loyal to him (149-152). As the psalmist's troubles increase, his pleas become more urgent. He reminds God that he has been loyal to the divinely given word, and asks God to save him (153-156). On the basis of God's love, truth and justice, he pleads for God's help (157-160).

Verses 161-176: Because he rejoices in God's instruction, the psalmist is steadfast amid persecution and consistent in his daily prayers (161-164). His life is one of inner peace and stability. In quiet confidence he waits for God to save him (165-168). The psalmist concludes his long meditation with a summary of his main requests: an understanding of God's word (169), deliverance from affliction (170), boldness to proclaim the excellencies of God's word (171-172), constant help from God because of his constant obedience to the word (173-175), and God's correcting hand upon him when he strays from God's path (176).

Psalms 120-124 To Jerusalem for worship

Each of the fifteen psalms 120 to 134 is entitled 'A Song of Ascents' (RSV; NIV). These psalms were apparently sung by worshippers from the country areas as they made the journey up to Jerusalem for the various annual festivals.

Whether or not the psalms were written for this purpose, they have been arranged in a sequence that reflects the feelings of the travellers. They provide expressions of worship for the travellers as they set out from distant regions, travel through the country, come to Jerusalem, and finally join in the temple ceremonies.

The collection opens with a cry from one who lives in a distant region and is bitterly persecuted by his neighbours (120:1-2). Their insults pierce him like sharp arrows and burn him like red-hot coals. He prays that God's punishment of them will be just as painful (3-4). He is tired of being victimized. He feels as if he lives in a far-off land where he is surrounded by attackers from hostile tribes. He will set out for Jerusalem and seek some peace and refreshment of spirit in God's house (5-7).

As he journeys through the hill country, the man knows that God who made the hills cares for him (121:1-2). Even when he sleeps by the roadside at night, God, who never sleeps, watches over him (3-4). God protects him from dangers by day and by night (5-6). Surely, God will take him to Jerusalem and bring him safely home again (7-8).

In the excitement of anticipation, the traveller pictures his dream as fulfilled. He recalls a psalm of David and pictures himself at last standing in Jerusalem as David once did (122:1-2). He sees it as a beautiful, well-built city, where the tribes of Israel are united in their worship of God, and where God rules his people through the throne of David (3-5). He prays that God will always preserve the city and prosper its people (6-8). He himself will do all he can for the city's good (9).

Ungodly people mock the poor traveller, and others who have now joined him, for putting up with such hardships just to attend a religious festival in Jerusalem. The worshippers ask God to give them some relief by silencing those who mock them (123:1-4).

The persecuted travellers once more recall the experience of David and sing one of his psalms that reflects their own experience. As David was persecuted, so are they. Only through God's grace and power have they been kept from much worse treatment (124:1-3). Their enemies are as violent and destructive as a raging flood (4-5), as cruel as wild animals (6) and as cunning as bird-trappers (7), but the travellers have the great Creator on their side (8).

Psalms 125-128 Lessons from Jerusalem

As the worshippers journey towards Jerusalem, they recall some of the varied experiences that the city has passed through. They see these as typical of the experiences of God's people as a whole. Believers are like Jerusalem in that they are completely secure and fully protected (125:1-2). Although Jerusalem sometimes came under the rule of its enemies, God never allowed these enemies to control it for long, in case God's people lost their devotion to him (3). In the same way God cares for the righteous and punishes their enemies (4-5).

On another occasion God saved Jerusalem from some who plundered the land and threatened to destroy the capital. Israel rejoiced in God's loving deliverance (126:1-3). But their problems were not over. Hard work lay ahead of them if they were to restore the land. They relied on God to provide water in the dry Negeb region, but they realized that they would have to work hard and long before they could enjoy the fruits of the land again. The lesson for the travellers is that they must persevere if they are to enjoy God's blessing (4-6).

Whether in governing Jerusalem or in building a family, people must acknowledge the sovereign rule of God. If they become nervous wrecks because of worry-filled days and sleepless nights, their faith in God is shown to be weak (127:1-2). The travellers receive a further encouragement to trust in God by the reminder that a large and healthy family is a blessing from God. It also gives a person stability, strength and honour in society (3-5)

If people's lives are characterized by trust, obedience and perseverance, they will enjoy the blessings of personal security and a happy home (128:1-4). Wherever God dwells, whether in the sense of dwelling in the family or in the sense of dwelling in Jerusalem, his people there will enjoy his fullest blessing (5-6).

Psalms 129-131 Preparing for worship

Thinking back on the sorrows of Israel's history, the travellers recall that ever since the days of the nation's 'youth' in Egypt, Israel has had suffering. The backs of the people had been whipped when they were slaves, but God cut the cords that bound them in slavery and set them free (129:1-4). Now again they are troubled by those who hate them. They pray that God will turn back their enemies and make them as useless as stalks of grass that wither and die in the sun (5-7). Left without friends, their enemies will have no one to help them (8).

A sense of their own sinfulness overcomes the travellers as they approach the temple. They know that they need forgiveness, for no person in a sinful condition can stand before the holy God in his temple (130:1-4). They wait for the assurance of God's forgiveness with the same longing as watchmen on night duty wait for the light of dawn (5-6). But all the time they have a quiet confidence that God, in his love, will forgive them (7-8).

Realizing that they are forgiven, the grateful worshippers are now ready to enter God's temple in holy worship. The importance of the occasion fills them with such a sense of awe that they are genuinely humbled before God. They confess that they cannot understand all about God and his ways, though at the same time they rest in the knowledge of his nearness and comfort (131:1-3).

Psalms 132-134 A house of prayer for Israel

A visit to the temple is a fitting occasion to recall the origins of the temple. David, with much difficulty, brought the ark (or covenant box) to Jerusalem with the aim of building God a house (132:1-5; cf. 2 Sam 6:3-13; 7:1-3; see also introductory notes to Psalm 24). Previously the ark had been at Kiriath-jearim, also known as Baale-judah and here called 'the fields of Jaar'. David therefore went from Bethlehem (Ephrathah) to Kiriath-jearim to collect the ark and bring it to Jerusalem (6-9; see 2 Sam 6:2,14-19; 1 Chron 13:5).

Although David wanted to build God a house in Jerusalem, God wanted to do something far greater for David. God wanted to build David a house in Jerusalem; not a house of stone, but a line of royal descendants to rule from Zion where the living God dwelt (10-14; cf. 2 Sam 7:4-16). God would give his people all they needed for healthy lives, physically and spiritually (15-16). He would give the Davidic king power, prosperity, victory and glory (17-18).

The psalmist rejoices to see Israelites from all parts of the country worshipping together in unity in Jerusalem. He considers it a precious sight, having a pleasantness that he likens to the perfume of the sweet-smelling oils used to anoint Israel's high priest. It has a freshness like the dew that falls on Mount Hermon (133:1-3).

At the end of the day's festival activities, the worshippers wish the priests and Levites good-night on a note of praise to God (134:1-2). The priests and Levites respond by wishing the worshippers God's blessing (3). This concludes the fifteen Songs of Ascents.

Psalms 135-136 God's choice of Israel

Two hymns for use in Israel's public worship appear here side by side. The first is a hymn of praise, the second a hymn of thanksgiving. The two hymns are similar in that they both recall God's loving acts in nature and on behalf of his people Israel. These acts display God's incomparable greatness on the one hand and show up the uselessness of the gods of the heathen on the other.

A call goes out to the worshippers gathered in the temple to praise God because he has chosen the nation Israel to be his people (135:1-4). God's choice of Israel is particularly significant, because anything God does is deliberate. It is as sure and certain as his acts in the creation and control of nature (5-7). He demonstrated his special care for the people of Israel by rescuing them from Egypt, conquering their foes and giving them Canaan for their homeland (8-14). By contrast the so-called gods of other nations are merely useless pieces of metal (15-18). All Israelites should therefore offer thankful worship to their covenant God (19-21).

In the Jewish tradition, Psalm 136 was sung after the Hallel at the Passover Feast (see note introducing Psalm 113). In each verse the leader sings of the greatness of God, and the congregation replies that this is seen in his loyal love to his people, a love that will never end. Israel's God is good, and he is the only true God (136:1-3). He has perfect wisdom and he made all things (4-9). He saved his people from Egypt (10-15), gave them victory over their enemies (16-20) and led them into Canaan (21-22). All this was not because his people deserved his blessings, but because he exercised his steadfast love towards them (23-26).

Psalm 137   Against the Babylonians

The Israelites who first sang this song were captives in Babylon, working in a slave camp beside one of Babylon's rivers. The Babylonian slave-masters tried to create some amusement for themselves (and some torment for their victims) by asking the downcast slaves to sing some of the merry songs of glorious Jerusalem (1-3). The cruel insults of the slave-masters pierce the hearts of the Israelites, because their beloved Jerusalem is in ruins. How can they forget all that Jerusalem means to them by singing songs that would now be a mockery? And all this just to amuse the slave-masters! They would rather be struck dumb than do such a thing (4-6).

At the time of Jerusalem's destruction, the Edomites had encouraged the Babylonians (7), but the Babylonians were the ones who were mainly responsible for the merciless slaughter of the people of Jerusalem. The psalmist announces a curse on the Babylonians, so that they might be punished by suffering the sort of butchery that they inflicted on others (8-9).

Psalm 138   A God for everyone

David imagines himself showing all lifeless gods how useless they are and how great is the only true God. This God loves his people, answers their prayers and gives them the strength to face life's difficulties with boldness (138:1-3).

The rulers of other nations ought also to know this God, for in God's sight their high position does not make them any better than the poor and lowly (4-6). This encourages the psalmist, because those in positions of power are often the ones most strongly opposed to him. Some even try to kill him. He knows that God will be true to his promise and save him (7-8).

Psalm 139   The all-knowing, ever-present God

God knows all about the psalmist — what he does, what he thinks, where he goes and what he says (139:1-4). Because of the realization that God is all around him, the psalmist sometimes feels helpless (5-6). A person may be tempted to look for some escape from such an overpowering presence, but no escape is possible. This may bring fear to rebels but it brings comfort to believers (7-8). Wherever they travel, God is with them (9-10). In darkness or in light, God sees them constantly (11-12).

Being the Creator, God has perfect knowledge of those he created. He knows their innermost thoughts as well as their physical characteristics, and has a detailed knowledge of their lives that are yet to be (13-16). As the psalmist meditates on the mysterious purposes and wonderful works of God, he finds they are too vast to understand and too numerous to count. When he awakes after his meditation he knows that God is still with him (17-18).

Through his meditation the psalmist has grown so close to God that he sees the wicked as God sees them and hates evil as God hates it. He therefore prays that God will act in righteous judgment (19-22). Nevertheless, he knows also that he himself is not perfect. He prays that God will show him his sin, cleanse him, and lead him into a life of holiness (23-24).

Psalms 140-143   Troubles for the godly

These four psalms are similar, and from the title of Psalm 142 it appears that all four belong to the time when David was fleeing from Saul. (See introductory notes to Psalm 34.)

Treachery and slander are the chief weapons that David's enemies use to attack him. These men have the poison of snakes and the cunning of hunters (140:1-5). But Yahweh is David's God, his defender in whom he trusts for victory (6-8). David's enemies will receive a fitting punishment if they suffer the torments that they intended to inflict upon David (9-11). The righteous will praise God when they see his justice in punishing the wicked and delivering the innocent (12-13).

When a person is the victim of slanderous talk, such as David was at the time, he is tempted to use strong words and unwise speech in return. David prays that he may be kept from such sins. He does not want to follow the evil ways of the wicked (141:1-4). If a godly person ever has cause to rebuke him, David prays that he may receive it as a blessing, as if he has been anointed with oil. But he will always remain opposed to evil (5). People will be forced to take notice when God acts, for his punishments will leave the wicked completely shattered (6-7). Meanwhile, the wicked still live, and David prays that he will be saved from the traps they have set for him (8-10).

Still pursued by his enemies, David escaped from Gath and fled to the cave of Adullam, though at the time of this psalm others have not yet joined him (1 Sam 22:1). He is overcome by a feeling of terrible loneliness. Feeling that no one cares for him, he cries out to God (142:1-4). He prays that God will deal with his enemies and so enable him to live a normal life in freedom and security again (5-7).

The frightening thought occurs to David that God might be using the enemy to punish him for his sins. He knows that he, like others, is a sinner, and there is no way of escaping punishment if God decides to act. He therefore casts himself entirely on the mercy of God for forgiveness and deliverance (143:1-2). David tells God about his troubles, how he has been pursued and is forced to live in darkness in the cave (3-4). He thinks of God's mighty acts in the past and prays that God will save him again (5-6). He fears the hopelessness of those who die without God. He longs for a greater experience of God (7-8). He prays that God, having rescued him, will instruct and guide him in the future (9-12).

Psalm 144 A king's praise

Most of the verses in this psalm are found in some form in other parts of the book. This composition was probably made for use by the king on a special occasion of national celebration.

Israel's king praises the almighty God for his strong protection, which has repeatedly brought victory for his people over their enemies (1-2). As his thoughts broaden, the king praises God for his concern for the human race in general, particularly since men and women are unworthy of all God's kindness (3-4). God has saved his people from enemies in the past, and they can depend on him to save them in present and future crises (5-8). The result of God's victories will be that the king will

bring him praise and express his continued trust in God as his deliverer (9-11).

Looking to the future, the king prays that the nation will enter a new age, where security and prosperity are enjoyed by all. He prays that families will grow and flourish, that fields and flocks will be fruitful, and that people will enjoy peace and contentment. But he reminds the people that they can expect such blessings only if they maintain their loyalty to God (12-15).

Psalms 145-146 God is gracious and merciful

The book of Psalms closes with six hymns of general praise. The first of these is David's 'Song of Praise' and in the Hebrew is an acrostic. The other five have no titles, but each begins and ends with the words 'Praise the Lord'.

God is great and worthy to be the object of people's praise, day and night, for ever and ever (145:1-3). Those who know God's greatness should meditate upon it and proclaim it to others (4-7). Not only is God great, but he is full of goodness, showing covenant faithfulness to his people and gracious love to people everywhere (8-9). Those who have tasted his love should show their gratitude by praising him and telling others of his mighty works. In this way they will help spread his rule to the lives of others (10-13a).

The generous help and free gifts of God are always available to all his creatures (13b-16). He is on the side of those who call upon him, honour him and love him, but he is against those who in their sin reject the offer of his mercy (17-20). All creation, and in particular his people, should bring him unending praise (21).

No matter how stable people may appear to be, they can never be fully relied upon. They do not have unlimited power and their lives may be cut short at any time (146:1-4). God, on the other hand, can be relied upon, for he is the all-powerful Creator and his life never ends (5-6). Also, he has special care for those suffering from poverty, injustice, physical handicaps and social insecurity (7-10).

Psalms 147-150 Praise the Lord

God's people should praise him constantly for his merciful and loving care: his care over them in particular (147:1-2), his care over those who sorrow (3), his care over all his creation (4), and his special care for the downtrodden (5-6). God delights to provide for the physical needs of his creatures (7-9). But of all his creatures, those he delights in most are those who humbly trust in his steadfast love (10-11). That is why he delights in Israel above other nations. He protects his people and gives them food to enjoy (12-14). By sending bitterly cold weather he toughens them to endure hardship; by sending pleasant weather he reminds them that he is still caring for them (15-18). Above all, he has given them his word. Through this word they can know him better and as a result bring him further joy (19-20).

All creation displays the wonders of God and so brings praise to him. From the angelic beings to the beasts of the earth, praise goes up to him. From the farthest regions of outer space to the depths of the sea, his name is praised (148:1-10). Human beings in particular should praise him. Without distinction of age or rank, the people of the world should exalt God. They should praise him not only because he is the sovereign Lord of the universe, but also because through Israel he has made himself known to them (11-14).

As the people of Israel gather to worship, they have special cause to praise God. Besides being the one who created them, he is the one who rules over them. He is their king (149:1-3). In addition, they are God's representatives in promoting his rule through-out the world. Therefore, salvation from attackers and victory over enemies are a cause for praise to God and national celebration (4-5). But if God's rule is to be established in the world, the rebels must first be punished (6-9).

The final psalm forms a climax to the whole book. Worshippers at the temple join with angels in the heavens to praise God for the greatness of his person and his deeds (150:1-2). In every way possible people everywhere should praise God (3-6).

Proverbs

BACKGROUND

In the ancient world, as in the world today, the wisdom of experience was often summarized in short easily-remembered sayings known as proverbs. The biblical book of proverbs is largely a collection of Hebrew proverbs, mostly from Solomon (Prov 1:1; 10:1; 25:1). It also contains lectures on the benefits of wisdom (Chapters 1-9) along with material from non-Hebrew sources (Prov 30:1; 31:1). (Concerning wisdom literature in general see introductory notes to the book of Job.)

Wisdom for living

The teachers of ancient Israel realized that people needed wisdom if they were to handle the everyday affairs of life satisfactorily. The wisdom that is taught in Proverbs therefore covers a wide range of subjects. Some of it deals with apparently minor matters such as talking too much, bad table manners and laziness. Other parts are concerned with wider issues such as sexual morality, family responsibilities, business ethics, local community affairs and national government.

Although the proverbs and other teachings collected in the book are largely Israelite in origin, they contain similarities to the wisdom teaching of neighbouring countries. The Bible acknowledges that non-Israelite peoples also had wisdom (1 Kings 4:30; Jer 49:7; 50:35; Acts 7:22), and the Israelites and their neighbours found helpful instruction in each other's proverbs. At times wise people from various countries visited each other to test each other's knowledge and increase their own (1 Kings 4:31-34; 10:1).

However, the Israelites were careful not to take from their neighbours any teaching that reflected ideas of idolatry, immorality or self-seeking. The basis of Israelite wisdom was the fear of God (Prov 1:7). Israelite proverbs differed from other proverbs in that they were created or selected by people who knew God's law and wished to apply it to everyday life. Therefore, although the wisdom taught in the book of Proverbs is practical, it is not worldly. It is a wisdom that comes from God. Worldly wisdom may easily encourage selfish ambition regardless of the interests of others. Godly wisdom encourages practical righteousness that puts God's values first. It is based on an understanding of God's righteousness (cf. James 3:13-18).

Writers and editors

Despite the variety of material collected in Proverbs, the book is not disjointed. Its date of composition is uncertain, but Solomon was the main author and much of the collection may have been made during his reign.

The first section of the book consists mainly of a lengthy talk from a teacher to a pupil (or from a father to a son) on the importance of choosing wisdom and avoiding folly. This basic instruction prepares the reader for Solomon's collection of 375 miscellaneous proverbs (his own and others) that follows (Prov 10:1). Solomon wrote and collected a total of three thousand proverbs (1 Kings 4:32), and no doubt his proverbs in this book were selected from that collection.

After this there are two collections of miscellaneous teachings of other Israelite wise men (Prov 22:17). A further collection of 128 of Solomon's proverbs was added about two hundred years later, probably at the time of Hezekiah's reformation (Prov 25:1; cf. 2 Chron 29:1-31:21). The book closes with three shorter sections. The first records the wisdom of Agur, who was probably a non-Israelite (Prov 30:1). The second comes from the wisdom of King Lemuel, another non-Israelite (Prov 31:1). The third is an anonymous poem in praise of the perfect wife (Prov 31:10).

In some sections of the book, the original editors have brought together proverbs that concern the same subject. In general, however, teaching on any one subject is scattered throughout the book. Among the topics that most frequently occur are wisdom, folly, laziness, speech, friendship, family, life and death.

Style of the book

Most of the book of Proverbs is written in poetry. (Concerning Hebrew poetry see background notes to Psalms.) The poetry in Proverbs consists largely of two-line units, where the two lines present an obvious parallelism. They may express the same idea in different words (Prov 16:16), support one central idea with an application (Prov 16:21), develop a basic statement by showing its outcome (Prov 3:6), or emphasize opposite truths by placing two statements in contrast (Prov 11:5).

We should not read Proverbs as if it were prose, nor should we read it as if it were a novel. This means we should probably not read the book straight through all at once. The units of instruction are short and straightforward, designed to make readers stop and think. The wisdom teachers, by presenting their teaching in a poetic form, encourage their readers to memorize it, so they can put it into practice in the various circumstances they meet.

OUTLINE

1:1-9:18 THE VALUE OF WISDOM

Purpose of the book (1:1-7)

The instruction given in the book of Proverbs aims at producing wisdom. This wisdom involves not only growth in knowledge, but also the ability to use that knowledge in discerning what is right and true, then acting accordingly. It calls for training and discipline. The result will be purity in personal behaviour and justice in dealings with others (1:1-3).

Although this wisdom is available to the young and immature, even the wise and experienced have need of it. Proverbs help develop the mind as people think out their meanings. These meanings are sometimes expressed in figures of speech, other times plainly; sometimes with humour, other times with irony. But the guiding principle in searching for true wisdom is a respectful relationship with the holy God (4-7).

Heed instruction; avoid bad company (1:8-19)

Having introduced his subject, the writer now gives the first of a series of lessons on the value of wisdom. Throughout these lessons he speaks as a father to a son, drawing from his own experience to give advice and warning (8-9).

The first warning concerns bad companions, especially those who lead others astray with the tempting offer of instant wealth through robbery and violence (10-14). The writer hopes that the inexperienced youth, being forewarned, will not be caught by such temptations, just as a bird will not fall into a trap that its sees being set for it (15-17). Those who

look for wealth through violence will, in the end, find that their evil plans bring about their own destruction (18-19).

Wisdom addresses the people (1:20-33)

To help people see what he is saying about wisdom, the writer tries to give illustrations that anyone can understand. He does not discuss wisdom as an abstract principle, but pictures it as being in the form of a person (i.e. personified). He speaks of wisdom as if it were a dignified and well respected woman who stands in the streets and market places of the town and speaks openly and plainly to those who pass by (20-21).

The woman addresses her words largely to three classes of people – the simple, the scoffers and the fools. The simple are those who are irresponsible and easily influenced. The scoffers (or mockers) are those who are arrogantly confident in their own ability and scornful of the opinions of others. The fools are those who have no interest in right thinking or right behaviour. They are not people whose mental ability is below average, but normal intelligent people who are lazy or careless in their attitude to what is worthwhile and what is not (22).

Those who refuse to listen to the voice of wisdom and go their own way will finally meet disaster. As they recall the wisdom that they ignored, that wisdom seems now to mock them (23-27). Wisdom's words are proved to be true, but they are now of no use. It is too late for wisdom to help, and now they will suffer the consequences (28-31). To ignore God's wisdom brings ruin; to seek it brings security (32-33).

The rewards of seeking wisdom (2:1-22)

People must spare no effort in diligently searching for wisdom. At the same time they must remember that the true goal of their search is not academic achievement but spiritual growth through knowing God better (2:1-5). However, when they obtain this wisdom, they cannot claim to have achieved it by their own abilities; it is the gift of God. He rewards those who seek genuinely (6).

Not only does God give wisdom to those who earnestly seek it, but he also watches over them (7-8). He gives them inner satisfaction through their greater understanding of what is right (9-10). This enlightened understanding helps protect them from those who have scheming minds and find pleasure in wrongdoing (11-15). Also it will save them from falling to the temptations of immoral women. These women, in making prostitutes of themselves, have left their husbands, despised God and bought lasting damage to themselves and their lovers (16-19). By contrast, those who obtain wisdom have useful lives that bring lasting benefits to all (20-22).

The whole life for God (3:1-35)

Obedience and loyalty to God, in addition to guaranteeing his favour, produce the kind of life that most people acknowledge as honourable (3:1-4). If, instead of trusting in their own wisdom and ability, people live in an attitude of reverential trust in God, they can be assured that God will direct them in all their affairs. God will remove obstacles and lead them to their desired goals (5-8).

Personal income is one part of everyday life where people must honour God. They should give God the first share, not the leftovers. God, in turn, will honour the givers (9-10). But God's blessings do not always mean prosperity. Sometimes he may show his love by allowing people to meet difficulties, with the purpose of correcting faults and improving character (11-12).

Riches cannot buy wisdom, but those who gain wisdom are rich in all that people most desire (13-18). By wisdom God created and maintains the world (19-20). People likewise should live and work by wisdom, thereby ensuring for themselves contentment and security (21-24). Wisdom will enable them to be confident at all times and prompt in helping others (25-28). They will not create trouble or co-operate in plans that hurt others (29-31). God is on the side of the humble, not the selfish or the scornful (32-35).

Wisdom the inner guide (4:1-27)

The writer further instructs his 'sons' by passing on teaching that his own 'father' once gave him. The main point of that teaching was that, more than anything else, he was to get wisdom and insight (4:1-5). The first step in getting wisdom is the desire for it. Once obtained, wisdom will bring into the life of the possessor a new measure of security, honour and beauty (6-9).

By living according to God's wisdom, people will have true freedom, and at the same time will be morally upright (10-13). They will not join in the evil deeds of those whose thoughts and actions are governed by the desire to do wrong (14-17). The more people do right, the better they understand life; the more they do wrong, the more confused their understanding becomes. Consequently, their mistakes become more frequent and more disastrous (18-19).

In addition to reminding themselves constantly of the instruction they have received, the disciples must keep their heart and mind, their whole inner person, in a state of moral and spiritual good health (20-23). Since the tongue and eyes can easily lead to wrongdoing, a person must control them through developing and maintaining right thinking and right attitudes (24-27).

Temptations to sexual immorality (5:1-23)

Strong warning is given to beware of the prostitute and the temptations she offers. (The frequency of this warning in Proverbs indicates that prostitution must have been a widespread social evil at the time.) The pleasure that the prostitute brings is shortlived, but the bitterness that follows is lasting. It leads eventually to death (5:1-6).

A man must flee the temptations offered by such immoral company, otherwise he may finish a physical and moral ruin. Moreover, he could find that he loses his possessions to those who have mercilessly deceived him (7-10). In addition to being disgraced by his own conduct, he will be overcome by despair as he thinks back on his stupidity in refusing to heed advice (11-14).

The married man should be faithful to his wife and seek his sexual pleasures in her alone. He should seek no pleasures from the immoral women who move around the streets and market places trying to seduce people (15-20). Married or single, a man must bear in mind that God sees everything. He must remember also that if he lacks self-discipline he will fall to temptation and eventually bring suffering upon himself (21-23).

Rashness, laziness and troublemaking (6:1-19)

A person can easily get into serious difficulties by agreeing to be a financial guarantor for a friend (or a stranger), as the friend may get so far into debt that the guarantor is ruined. If the guarantor realizes that he made a rash promise, he should act quickly. He should not rest till he has gone back to his friend, told him of his true position, and withdrawn his guarantee. Only in this way will he save himself from possible disaster (6:1-5).

Though believers should not be anxious about the future, neither should they be thoughtless or lazy. They should learn a lesson from the ant. It works diligently to provide for its future security (6-8). People have only themselves to blame if they are too lazy to get up and work and as a result fall into poverty (9-11).

Another kind of person heading for disaster is the troublemaker. People of this kind are skilled at making subtle suggestions by their movements and words, and soon create conflict (12-15). All forms of deceit and plotting are as hateful to God as the more obvious sins of haughtiness and violence. Eyes, tongue, mind, hands and feet can all lead a person into sin (16-19).

More about sexual misbehaviour (6:20-7:27)

Sometimes teaching can be so well known that people no longer take any notice of it. Therefore, they must remind themselves to be obedient to familiar truths (20-22). One matter concerning which the writer repeats his earlier warnings is sexual immorality. Offenders are merely destroying themselves (23-29). People may not despise a desperately hungry person who steals food; nevertheless, the person must be dealt with and made to repay (with interest) what was stolen. But people will certainly despise a man who takes another's wife; and there is no repayment he can make that will calm the anger of the offended husband (30-35).

Chapter 7 gives a colourful picture of how an immoral woman can trap a weak, easily led young man. The section opens with a renewed emphasis on the importance of a young man's getting wisdom and holding on to it firmly. Then he will know best how to resist the temptations he meets (7:1-5).

The writer imagines himself looking out the window and seeing a silly young man wandering around the streets at night (6-9). The young man is met by a prostitute who sees him as a likely customer (10-12). She assures him that there is nothing wrong with going to bed with her. After all, she is a very religious person who has just been to the temple, and she had the feeling that she would meet this particular man (13-17). Furthermore, her husband is away for a few weeks on business. Clearly, all the circumstances indicate that the young man is meant to go with her (18-20).

After some indecision the man gives in, and in exchange for a night's pleasure his whole life is spoiled (21-23). All young men should take note and resist the temptations offered by such women (24-27).

Eternal wisdom available to all (8:1-36)

Once again wisdom is personified as a woman standing in a public place and speaking to the people who pass by (8:1-3; cf. 1:20-21). Even the immature and foolish can learn wisdom (4-5). One characteristic of wisdom is speech that is wholesome, true and straightforward (6-9). The instruction given by wisdom is beyond value, for it produces all those qualities most necessary for a truly worthwhile life. Yet it will not lead to pride, for people can only have this wisdom if they humbly fear God (10-13).

Wisdom in a country's ruler will produce justice in the land (14-16). All who seek wisdom will find that they are genuinely enriched, both materially and spiritually (17-21).

The eternal God is the source of wisdom. It existed before the universe and, in fact, God created the universe by wisdom (22-29). Because of this, the completed creation, particularly the human creation, was a source of joy to God (30-31). People must seek wisdom daily if they are to find real life. If they are neglectful they will be the losers. To hate wisdom is fatal (32-36).

Invitations from 'Wisdom' and 'Folly' (9:1-18)

Wisdom is again personified in a gracious lady. This time she invites the silly and the ignorant to a great feast that she has prepared in her magnificent house. She wants them to come and enjoy the life-giving gifts of wisdom and discernment that she freely offers (9:1-6).

Whether people desire wisdom depends largely upon the character they have developed in themselves over the years. When people grow conceited in their opinions and blind to their failures, they usually react with bitterness when criticized. Those who are wise welcome criticism and so increase their wisdom (7-9). People are responsible individually for their own gain or loss of wisdom. Everything depends on whether they are willing to learn from God (10-12).

In contrast to the invitation of the gracious lady Wisdom is the invitation of the shameless prostitute Folly. She also invites the silly and the ignorant, but the only thing she can offer is stolen food to be eaten in secret — unlawful pleasures that ruin a person's life (13-18).

10:1-22:16 PROVERBS OF SOLOMON

The proverbs in this section are usually written in a simple two-line form, each proverb usually being equal to one verse in our Bible. Although the editor of the book has in parts brought together proverbs dealing with a similar subject or principle, each proverb must be considered by itself.

Clearly there is not enough space in a commentary of this size to explain each separate proverb. Readers will gain most benefit from Proverbs by reading it over a period (for example, a chapter at a time, with an interval between chapters), pausing to consider each proverb and how it applies to daily life. These proverbs are practical examples of how the wisdom and folly dealt with in Chapters 1-9 may be applied to everyday human experience.

Wisdom in practice (10:1-32)

The selection begins with proverbs that comment on some themes of the previous section — wisdom and folly, righteousness and wickedness, laziness and diligence. The proverbs point out the good and bad effects these things have on those who practise them and those associated with them (10:1-5). Behaviour indicates character, and a person's reputation lives on after death (6-7). Wisdom comes by learning, not by boasting; security comes by uprightness, not by dishonest dealings (8-9).

Some people, by cunning actions and words, create trouble. Others, by speaking openly in love, make peace (10-12). The wise keep their knowledge for use on the right occasions; fools speak when they should not and so bring themselves trouble (13-14).

Money may, for a while, increase personal security, but people must earn it honestly and use it wisely if it is to improve the quality of their lives (15-17). If people have hatred in their hearts, their words will be either hypocritical or slanderous. If they are honest and sincere, their words will be well chosen and helpful to the hearers (18-21).

Because the foolish and the wicked build their lives on things that are material and temporary, they fear sudden disaster. But disaster will indeed befall them. The righteous build their lives on things of more lasting value. They therefore maintain their security and contentment, in spite of the troubles they meet (22-25). Lazy people are an annoyance to their employers (26).

God promises long life, gladness and divine protection to the righteous. He assures the wicked that when he acts against them their lives will finish in disappointment and despair (27-30). The speech of the righteous is wise and gracious, but that of the wicked is deceitful and hurtful (31-32).

Prosperity; uprightness; generosity (11:1-31)

People are foolish to try to get rich by dishonest methods, because dishonesty brings judgment from which riches cannot save (11:1-4). By their blameless conduct, people ensure their ultimate victory; by crookedness they ensure their downfall (5-8). When good people have influence in a city, the citizens live in peace and happiness. But each city also has its troublemakers, who are a nuisance to their neighbours and create unrest in the community (9-11). Because of the trouble these people cause through their harmful speech, the city's leaders must provide firm but wise direction (12-14).

A further warning is given against making rash guarantees (15; see notes on 6:1-5). Violence may bring prosperity, but the prosperity is deceptive, for it is shortlived. By contrast, kindness brings honour and a lasting reward (16-18). God is in control of the lives of all people, and he makes sure that the righteous life is the only worthwhile life (19-20). There are irregularities, both real and apparent, in the relationship between the inner lives and outer circumstances of some people, but in the end justice will be done (21-23).

Generosity will not result in poverty, for God will reward the generous person. But people curse those who hold back food in a time of scarcity in the hope of forcing the price up (24-26). No matter what people look for, good or evil, they will get it, but if they look for security through wealth they will be disappointed (27-29). The righteous, by their good lives, bring blessing to others. If even they at times suffer from God's just punishment, how much more will the wicked suffer (30-31).

Honest speech and honest work (12:1-28)

There are further proverbs on attitudes towards criticism (12:1-2; see notes on 9:7-9), the stability of the righteous (3) and the value of a good wife (4). The righteous, besides having good principles, have the courage to speak up at risk to themselves in order to save others (5-7).

If people live humbly and in keeping with their financial capacity, they may not achieve high social status, but at least they will remain free of debt. They are wiser than those who spend money lavishly in an effort to impress others but become poor and hungry in the process (8-9). Likewise if people ensure their security by working hard, they are wiser than those who waste time and money on things that are useless. Honest work, like honest speech, is considerate of others and brings satisfaction to those who practise it (10-14).

Those who have genuine wisdom will listen to advice and ignore insults (15-16). They will always speak the truth, but in such a way that their words heal, not injure (17-19). By speaking in this way they will bring pleasure to God and joy to themselves (20-22). Good people will keep silent rather than display their knowledge, but they will always have a fitting word of encouragement or guidance for those who need it (23-26). By contrast, the lazy will never get what they want, and may fall into the power of others (27-28).

Satisfaction amid life's hardships (13:1-25)

Parental advice is one of the benefits of life. Those who habitually ignore it will develop an attitude of scorning all opinions except their own (13:1). Good words bring a reward, but treacherous words can result in violence. Discipline in speech is necessary, because rash words lead to disaster (2-3). Discipline is necessary also in work and behaviour, otherwise a person's life may end in ruin. Security is found in honesty (4-6).

The poor might at times pretend they are rich (since there are some advantages in wealth), but the rich, out of meanness, might pretend they are poor (7-8). If people acquire wealth quickly, they often spend it rashly. If they work hard for it, they usually make it last longer (9-11).

When people see their hopes fulfilled they have joy; when they take notice of the teachings of the wise they have refreshment (12-14). Sound common sense will win them the respect of others and bring them personal satisfaction. They will achieve their goals. Fools, on the other hand, have not enough sense either to hide their folly or to turn from paths that are leading them to ruin (15-19). The sorts of experiences people meet in life, for better or for worse, depend to some extent on the company they keep (20-21).

There is a recognition of justice when the wicked rich lose the wealth that they have gained through exploiting the poor. Although injustice will always be reversed in the end, parents must act as justly as possible now in training their children and preparing for their children's future (22-25).

Hidden feelings and motives (14:1-35)

Wisdom builds, but folly destroys. People's actions reveal their attitude to God (14:1-2). The wisdom of their speech and their commitment to hard work are among the things that determine whether they progress or come to ruin (3-5). Those who think they know everything can never become truly wise and therefore can never have right discernment in the moral issues of life (6-8).

Good people may prosper and evil people may suffer loss, but outward appearances do not tell the full story. Hidden within the heart there may be a joy or a sadness that no one can share (9-14). Those who believe anything, who throw away caution, or who act in quick temper are only increasing their folly (15-18). The wicked may have a secret respect for those who are genuinely good, but they despise the poor, because they know they can get nothing from them (19-21).

The next five proverbs urge pure motives, hard work, wisdom, truthful speech and reverence for God (22-27). No one can live without depending on others; even a king cannot exist without his people (28). Bad temper affects people's health as well

as their personality, but oppressing the poor affects their relation with God (29-31). Righteousness and wisdom bring benefits in whatever sphere they are practised, whether in private life or in the political affairs of the nation (32-35).

Bringing joy to others (15:1-33)

Words can easily cheer others or enrage them, help them or hinder them. Therefore, people should think carefully about what they say (15:1-5). In addition to being wise in their speech, they must be honest in the way they earn their income (6-7). In fact, they must be upright in all aspects of their daily lives. Only then will God, from whom nothing can be hidden, accept their sacrifices and prayers (8-11). Another matter concerning habits of speech is that those who readily criticize others are usually offended when others criticize them (12).

Inner joy enables believers to be outwardly cheerful, even amid afflictions. Because they fear God and love others, they are truly contented even though not wealthy (13-17). A series of warnings shows that wrongdoing creates its own hardships: bad temper causes arguments (18); laziness means harder work in the long run (19); folly creates family tensions (20); ignorance results in plans going wrong (21-22).

Those who bring joy to others can be assured of God's goodness to them (23-24), but God opposes those who plot evil and use their positions of power to exploit the poor and the defenceless (25-29). A cheerful face, like good news, brings refreshment to others (30). Again the book records that to gain wisdom, people must be willing to learn, reverent towards God and humble in spirit (31-33).

Laying plans and making decisions (16:1-33)

A person may make plans, but God is the one who determines their outcome. He knows the person's unseen motives and controls events according to his purposes. It is important, therefore, always to bring God into one's planning (16:1-4). God punishes the arrogant but has mercy on those who fear him (5-6). He protects them from harm and guides them on the right pathway (7-9).

When a king's wisdom comes from God, his decisions will be right. He will show no partiality but will punish evil, commend good, and insist that all trading practices be fair and honest (10-15). The person who is truly rich is not the one who has money, but the one who is wise, upright, humble, obedient and faithful (16-20).

Pleasant speech is not hypocritical if it springs from a pure heart. It benefits the speakers for it gives their words persuasiveness, and it benefits the hearers for it improves their minds (21-24). People can readily deceive themselves, but they cannot escape the plain fact that if they do not work they will go hungry (25-26). In contrast to the pleasant speech just mentioned, abusive speech, whispering and sly scheming create only trouble (27-30). Living uprightly guarantees honour in old age; controlling one's passions guarantees strength; referring matters to God guarantees right decisions (31-33).

Friends and fools (17:1-28)

A peaceful family life, no matter how simple, is a great blessing, but a son may miss out on his family inheritance through his own folly (17:1-2). God's dealings with his people are always for a good purpose, to make them better than they were before (3). To listen to evil talk is as bad as to speak evil oneself; to take pleasure in another's troubles is as bad as to cause those troubles (4-5).

Other proverbs concern the appreciation that the old and the young should have for each other (6), the need for fitting speech (7), the prosperity so easily yet wrongfully gained through bribery (8), and the different attitudes of the peacemaker and the troublemaker (9).

Fools are dangerous because they are stubborn, rebellious, and not open to reason (10-13). Through them a minor disagreement can become a major conflict. They think that by paying fees to teachers they will get wisdom, but they do not have a mind to learn (14-16).

When in trouble a person can depend on a true friend for help, but help need not go so far that it brings the friend to ruin (17-18). When people through wrongdoing advance themselves in order to boast of their higher status, they invite disaster (19-20). Folly leads to grief, and that in turn leads to ill health. Cheerfulness, by contrast, helps keep a person healthy (21-22). Innocent people suffer unjustly because of corrupt officials, and a fool's parents suffer because of their son's folly. Fools wander aimlessly, but intelligent people consider all their actions wisely (23-26). A mark of wisdom is to think before speaking (27-28).

(The frequent references to bribery and false witnesses indicate that corruption of the courts was widespread in the days of the writer; see 14:5,25; 17:8,15,23,26; 18:5; 19:5,9,28.)

Real strength (18:1-24)

When people become too confident in their own opinions, they are liable to break away from former friends. They become unreasonable in discussion and blind to the viewpoints of others. Those who despise others will themselves be disgraced (18:1-3). The words of the wise bring refreshment, but those of a fool or a gossip bring destruction (4-8).

Those who leave work undone are almost as bad as those who wreck what already has been done (9). Those who trust in God know they are safe, but those who trust in their wealth only think they are safe. One day they will find that pride leads to disaster. God exalts those who willingly take the lowest place (10-12).

Strength of mind and spirit is more important in the battle of life than strength of body. The wise listen to opinions from all available sources before giving their judgment (13-15). People may try to win a judge's favour by giving him gifts or telling him only those parts of a story that support their viewpoint. In some cases the only way a judge may be able to settle a dispute is by the drawing of lots (16-18).

People may become strong friends or strong enemies, depending on how they are treated. Words will bring a person good or ill, depending on what they mean and how they are spoken (19-21). True friendship is not easily broken, nor does it make a distinction between the richer partner and the poorer partner. But a good wife is the best friend of all (22-24).

Lessons heeded and ignored (19:1-29)

Moral uprightness is more important than wealth, and wise action is more important than hasty action. People are foolish when they blame God for the trouble they bring upon themselves through their own mistakes (19:1-3).

Often the reason the rich have many friends is that these 'friends' hope to gain personally from their wealth or influence (4-6). The poor lose their friends, though in a sense they are rich if they maintain their understanding (7-8). People should behave in a way that befits their social status, though to misrepresent the truth is always wrong (9-10). If they are mature, they will not allow themselves to be easily offended and will know how to control their temper (11-12).

Stupidity, quarrelling, laziness and a lack of parental discipline will destroy family happiness. Wise, sympathetic, yet firm, dealings by the parents will build it (13-18). Bad tempered people never seem to learn, and as a result bring trouble upon themselves repeatedly (19-20).

God directs affairs in people's lives, and desires from them reverent loyalty. He blesses the obedient, but not the lazy (21-24). Physical punishment is often the only method of correction that fools understand, but sensible people listen to rebukes and learn from them (25-29).

Honesty (20:1-30)

Wise people will not become drunkards, will not needlessly anger those in authority, will avoid quarrelling and will work to support themselves (20:1-4). They will also have the ability to draw out the deepest feelings and intentions of those with whom they deal (5). Many people boast of their loyalty but few practise it. To live honestly is the best way to guarantee a good future for one's children (6-7). A king learns by experience to discern between right and wrong in cases brought before him for a decision; yet he knows that he, like anyone else, has a sinful heart (8-9).

God hates cheating. If ordinary people can, to some extent, know the state of other people's hearts by what they see them do, how much more can God who made them (10-12). Conscientious workers are satisfied in the knowledge that they make a living honestly. Shrewd buyers may boast that they have obtained a good article cheaply by complaining about it, but they may find that their boasting is shortlived (13-17). Wise people will listen to advice, beware of gossip and give to their parents the honour due to them (18-20).

Impatience can lead to wrongdoing, whether in obtaining a coveted inheritance, in wanting to see an offender punished, or in offering a gift in a rash vow. Patience will enable a person to wait for God; he will direct in the way that is right (21-25). A king's punishments may be severe but they must be just (26). A sensitive conscience should show people their faults so that they can correct them. But if the conscience becomes dulled, more painful action may be needed to correct faults (27-30).

God at work in people's lives (21:1-31)

As God directs the course along which a stream flows, so he guides the decisions of national rulers according to his plan (21:1). God knows people's motives and he will not accept their sacrifices if their thoughts and actions are wrong (2-4). Prosperity that comes through diligence is a fitting reward, but prosperity that comes through greed, lying and violence is a deadly trap (5-8). Some people make life unpleasant for those who live in the same house, and others deliberately do evil wherever they can. They will come to ruin, but the righteous will enjoy blessing (9-12).

Some people live solely for themselves, ignoring the needy and bribing the influential so that they can get whatever they want and live in complete comfort. One day they will justly suffer for their selfishness and dishonesty (13-17). By suffering the evil they planned against the innocent, the wicked become the ransom for the innocent (18). Wise people save for the future. At the same time they realize that the only way to build lasting treasure is to practise righteousness and kindness (19-21).

Wisdom is more important than military might, and control of the tongue is a good defence against trouble (22-23). Religious acts done with wrong intentions are hateful to God, along with pride, laziness and selfish desires (24-27). Whether in general speech or in sworn testimony before a court, a person must give a genuine testimony of the truth, not merely put on a bold face to impress others (28-29). It is useless to fight against God, and just as useless to fight without him (30-31).

Children and adults (22:1-16)

People vary in reputation and status, but they should respect one another as being equally God's creatures (22:1-2). Wise people will act with caution and humility. They will bring up their children in a way that prepares them for the experiences they will face in the life ahead (3-6). Those who borrow will fall into the power of the lenders, and this can lead to unjust treatment of the poor by the rich. Such oppression will be punished, but generosity will be rewarded (7-9).

When people are trying to work together as a group, harmony and understanding are essential. It is better to get rid of, than to tolerate, the person who makes trouble. A sincere person is an asset (10-11). God wants people to act according to truth and knowledge. He has no pleasure in the lazy who make excuses or the immoral who seduce others (12-14). Wise parental discipline can correct childish foolishness. Adult greed can lead to persecution of the poor and bribery of the rich, but in due course it will be punished (15-16).

22:17-24:34 SAYINGS OF THE WISE

The correct use of proverbs (22:17-29)

In this section the sayings are longer and often cover several verses, whereas in the previous section each verse was usually a separate proverb. The section begins with an appeal to the disciples to listen carefully to the instruction, to memorize it and to put it to practical use. It will strengthen their trust in God and give them the ability to answer correctly anyone who questions them concerning what is right and true (17-21).

The opening proverbs repeat warnings already met in the book — warnings against exploiting the poor (22-23), getting into bad company (24-25) and giving rash pledges (26-27). One proverb condemns the practice of stealing land by shifting boundary markers (28), and another commends diligence in work (29).

Social-climbers and others (23:1-35)

Those who seek status like to mix with the upper classes and try to copy their habits. But because of their ignorance of how to eat fine foods, they make fools of themselves and so spoil their chances of progressing up the social ladder. The food they desire becomes the means of their downfall (23:1-3). The desire for wealth can lead to disappointment (4-5), and the efforts to win the favour of others may win only their disfavour. This may particularly be the case when the wealthy are miserly; for they may be thinking all the time of how much it is costing them to entertain those who seek their favour (6-8).

Trying to teach wisdom to fools is a waste of time (9). Exploitation of the poor is dangerous, for God is their protector (10-11). If people are keen to learn wisdom, and just as keen to train their children likewise, they will have deep satisfaction (12-16).

When the wicked prosper, the righteous should not envy them, but realize that God in his time will punish evil and reward good (17-18). Those who cannot control their eating and drinking habits only create trouble for themselves (19-21). Children should respect their parents. If from an early age they are taught the value of goodness and wisdom, they will bring joy to their parents in later life (22-25). Prostitution leads not only to personal ruin but also to social decay (26-28).

Among the fruits of drunkenness are sorrow, trouble, physical injury and bad health (29-30). Drinking may be enjoyable, but when drunkenness results, the person's stomach, eyesight, mind, speech and ability to walk are all badly affected (31-34). Yet the drunkard declares that he suffers no ill effects from drink, and boasts that he is looking forward to more (35).

Godly and ungodly citizens (24:1-34)

In contrast to the destructive schemes of the wicked are the constructive acts of the wise. A life built by wisdom is likened to a strongly built and richly furnished house (24:1-4). Wisdom gives people real strength and success, but folly gives them nothing worthwhile, not even sensible words that can benefit their fellow citizens (5-7). (In ancient times the place where citizens liked to gather was the open area just inside the city gate; v. 7. There they discussed community affairs and dealt with matters of business and justice.)

Those who constantly plan evil or scorn others are a menace to society (8-9). So are the moral cowards who give in when hardship arises or who refuse to help the afflicted and the oppressed, claiming they did not know of their troubles (10-12). By contrast, those who allow wisdom to teach them find that its fruits are sweet and lasting (13-14).

Righteous people need not plot the overthrow of the wicked, for the destruction of the wicked will come of itself. The righteous will overcome repeated hardships but the wicked will not (15-16). The wicked are certain to be overthrown, but when this happens the righteous should not gloat over them (17-20). Rather the righteous should maintain an attitude of reverence towards God and honour towards the civil authorities (21-22).

People respect a judge who is impartial; they despise one who shows favouritism (23-26). It is wise to be assured of a reliable source of income before taking on the heavy financial burden of building a house (27). Revenge is a terrible thing, especially when people combine it with false accusation in order to get their own way (28-29). If people sleep when they should be working, they demonstrate their stupidity as well as their their laziness. They will surely end in poverty and disgrace (30-34).

25:1-29:27 MORE PROVERBS OF SOLOMON

Relations with others (25:1-28)

God has no obligation to explain to anyone the reasons for his actions. A king, however, has a duty to his people to investigate the causes of events that affect them, though he need not reveal to them his deepest thoughts (25:1-3). Some advisers to the king may be ungodly or treacherous, and should be removed if the king is to rule righteously (4-5). It is better to wait to be invited to a higher rank than to be boastfully ambitious and then lose face when demoted (6-7).

A warning is given against being too hasty in making an accusation against someone. A private talk with the accused person may reveal that the accuser did not have all the facts. It may also save the accuser the shame of being disproved in court and thereby receiving the unwelcome reputation of being a talebearer who cannot be trusted (8-10). Words fittingly spoken, even in reproof, benefit the hearers, as cool water refreshes farmers working in the hot sun. Idle boasting, on the other hand, helps no one (11-14). Quiet words are often more effective than brute force (15).

Without self-control in eating, people can harm their health. Without self-control in visiting their neighbours, they can make themselves unpopular (16-17). Among the neighbourhood nuisances are those who make false accusations, those who let down friends in times of need, and those who are flippant when among mourners (18-20). People who suffer unjustly, instead of reacting in bitterness, should treat the wrongdoers as friends. This may make the wrongdoers so ashamed that they will change their ways (21-22).

Those who are bitter, argumentative, critical, or otherwise negative in their words can cause much damage, but when people bring good news they bring refreshment (23-25). When people give in to what they know is wrong, use flattery, seek praise, or lack self-control, they demonstrate their weakness of character (26-28).

Fools and troublemakers (26:1-28)

Only a fool honours a fool, and only a fool curses another without cause. Such a curse cannot come true (26:1-2). People with wisdom know on which occasions to ignore a fool and on which occasions to answer him (3-5). Fools cannot be trusted. For them, proverbs are as useless as paralysed legs, and honour is as useless as a stone tied to the sling that is supposed to throw it out (6-8). Fools with a little knowledge can be dangerous. As employees, they can create trouble for their fellow workers. But a conceited person is worse than a fool (9-12).

Always making excuses, too lazy to get out of bed or help themselves, lazy people nevertheless think they know everything (13-16). All communities have their troublemakers: busybodies (17); double-talkers who, when they see the damage they have done, say they were only joking (18-19); gossips, without whom many quarrels would have ended long ago (20-22); and smooth talkers whose pleasant words hide their evil intentions (23-26). Having ruined others, the troublemakers finally ruin themselves (27-28).

The valuable things of life (27:1-27)

Over-confidence, self-praise, stupidity and jealousy must all be avoided (27:1-4). True friends will show the inner love they have for each other by being open and honest with each other. Over-pleasantness may be a sign of a deceitful heart (5-6). Those with many possessions do not find contentment; the poor are more than satisfied if they can get what the rich throw away (7). Among the most priceless of possessions are a happy home and faithful friends (8-10).

Common sense will save people a lot of trouble and bring happiness to their parents (11-12), but those who give rash guarantees must be prepared to suffer the consequences (13). A loudmouthed but insincere friend is a curse, and a nagging wife can make life miserable (14-16). Where there is true understanding, differences of personality and viewpoint are of benefit to all concerned. Faithfulness to one another brings its reward (17-18).

The mind of a person reflects the true self. Therefore, a person's worth must be judged by reputation and character, not by possessions or wealth. Material things cannot fully satisfy (19-21). The character of the fool is easily judged, for no amount of corrective discipline will bring any lasting change (22). Instead of thinking only of building up wealth, a person should combine conscientiousness in daily work with trust in God's provision (23-27).

Selfish ambition (28:1-28)

A bad conscience makes a person a coward, but a clear conscience gives a person courage (28:1). Some characteristics of a corrupt society are instability in the government, exploitation of fellow citizens (even among the poorer classes), lawlessness, reversal of moral standards, injustice and greed. In spite of this, some will always remain true to God (2-7).

Even those who are religious may be guilty of exploiting the poor and misleading the upright, but their religious exercises will not help them escape God's judgment. Those who are poor yet godly see this truth and believe that one day they will prosper, whereas their oppressors will suffer (8-12). Hidden sins and a hardened conscience alike bring God's judgment (13-14).

Although an individual may suffer a lifetime for causing the death of another, a whole nation may suffer because of the fury and ignorance of a despotic ruler (15-17). Those who live and work honestly need not fear the future (18-19), but those who are greedy will in the end be driven into poverty. Some are so greedy they can be bribed even by a piece of bread (20-22)!

No one should neglect these warnings, for a sincere rebuke is better than flattery (23). In their greed for riches, people at times cheat their parents, stir up trouble, become self-centred, neglect the poor and ignore injustice. But those who live only for themselves will one day suffer as they have made others suffer (24-28).

Authority with justice (29:1-27)

Many themes that we have already met in Proverbs are repeated in this section: stubbornness, good and bad government, family values, prostitution, justice, flattery, cunning and concern for the poor (29:1-7). Scoffers are more than just fools; they are trouble-makers. They are not open to reason and cannot control their temper (8-11).

Unjust rulers oppress innocent citizens, and the rich persecute the poor, but good and bad alike receive the blessings that God gives to people in general (12-13). The ruler of a country and the head of a family should work for the contentment and well-being of those for whom they are responsible, but they can expect success only if they themselves are good and just. The pursuit of righteousness leads to stability (14-17).

One reason for a nation's spiritual or moral decay is its neglect of the revealed word of God (18). A stubborn servant is a problem for his master, but a shrewd servant, if he receives too many favours, could one day take over his master's property (19-21). Those who are bad tempered or arrogant bring trouble, not just to others but also to themselves (22-23).

When a person who was partner in a crime refuses to give evidence to the judge, his guilt increases (24). There can be no justice when the basis of people's decision-making is fear of those who are influential or partiality towards those who are their friends (25-27).

30:1-31:31 OTHER COLLECTIONS OF WISE SAYINGS

The personal testimony of Agur (30:1-9)

Agur, some of whose sayings are collected here, was apparently a well known wisdom teacher in the Palestine region. He begins his instruction with a confession that though he longs to know God he cannot, because he is merely a man. No human being can do the great works God has done. Agur challenges his hearers to tell him the name of any person (or the name of that person's son, if they prefer) who has been to heaven and returned to tell people what God is like (30:1-4). God's words, and his only, are true, and they are always reliable. Agur has such a respect for the truth of God's word that he does not want to teach anything that is contrary to it (5-6).

As for the comforts of life, Agur aims at moderation. He desires neither riches nor poverty, lest he be tempted to live as though independent of God (if he were rich) or tempted to steal (if he were poor). His moral values and his lifestyle were inseparable (7-9).

The wise sayings of Agur (30:10-33)

It is wise not to be hasty in reporting a person for a supposed wrongdoing. Such action could rebound with harm to the talebearer if the person is innocent (10). The arrogant despise those whom they should respect, while considering that they themselves are not only blameless, but superior to their fellows. They are merciless in their treatment of those whom they should rather help (11-14).

The expression 'three things . . . and four' in the proverbs that follow is a figure of speech indicating that the writer is giving only three or four examples. The complete list would be much longer. A leech's constant appetite for blood is used as an illustration of unlimited or unfulfilled longing. Four examples are given: the place of the dead is always looking for more occupants; a woman unable to have children can never have her deepest desires fulfilled; the earth always cries out for more water; a fire will keep burning as long as it is fed (15-16). A proud person's arrogance likewise knows no limits, till death brings it to a fitting end (17).

Skill and grace in mastering difficulties are to be admired (18-19); but the cunning that delights in seducing innocent victims is hateful, especially when the guilty person feels no shame (20). Among the most unbearable of people are those who suddenly gain power or status when previously they were nothing (21-23).

Even tiny creatures are wise. They provide for their future, secure themselves against danger, cooperate with one another through order and discipline, and reach the places of highest power in the land (24-28). Other things are commended for their impressive appearance of dignity and assurance (29-31), but a commendable appearance must be accompanied by humility, purity of heart and peace-loving behaviour (32-33).

A mother's advice to a king (31:1-9)

King Lemuel was probably a non-Israelite from a neighbouring nation, but his mother appears to have been a God-fearing woman who vowed her son to God (31:1-2). The main desire of some kings was to get themselves as much pleasure as possible, chiefly through women and wine. Lemuel is warned that such interests distract a king from his proper duties and result in lawlessness and injustice (3-5). Strong drink deadens pain and dulls the mind. Therefore, among the people who seek after it are those whose distress is so great that life seems to have no more hope for them. The king should not seek after it, for he must have a clear mind at all times, so that he can judge with justice and defend the downtrodden (6-9).

The ideal wife (31:10-31)

In the original language this section is an acrostic poem. That is, each of the poem's twenty-two verses begins with a different letter of the Hebrew alphabet in order.

A good wife makes the perfect partner. Her husband, knowing this, trusts in her and depends upon her (10-12). She is kind, clever at buying and selling, diligent, conscientious, and a good manager of the household (13-16). She is energetic and tireless, both in helping the family income and in carrying out household tasks (17-19). Though a good business-woman, she is not hard-hearted. Though careful in handling money, she is not miserly. She gives generous help to the poor and needy (20).

In like manner this ideal wife is generous towards her family. When making clothes she uses good cloth, so that all in her household look well dressed and, through her foresight, enjoy good protection when bad weather comes. The respect that people have for her husband is due in large measure to her (21-25). Through her wise words, kindness, consideration, diligence and reverence for God, the family is uplifted. Her children and her husband delight in her and the community at large honours her (26-31).

Ecclesiastes

BACKGROUND

The title of the book, Ecclesiastes, comes from the Septuagint, the first Greek translation of the Old Testament. The translators took the title from the Hebrew word *qohelet*, the name that the writer of the book uses for himself. It has been translated by such English words as preacher (RSV), teacher (NIV) and philosopher (GNB) (Eccles 1:1,12).

Although the writer does not tell us his name, he was probably a well known wisdom teacher in Jerusalem. A number of of his illustrations reflect the viewpoint of those with status and wealth, which suggests that his students were mainly from upper class families (cf. Eccles 5:11-14; 6:1-2; 8:2-3; 10:4). But he also taught the common people at large (Eccles 12:9).

Teaching style

A common practice in those times was for an author to write as if he were some well known person in the past whose life would form a background for his own teaching. This is what the writer of Ecclesiastes appears to do in the opening chapters of his book. He quotes what was probably a saying of King Solomon, 'Vanity of vanities, all is vanity', and, placing himself in the position of Solomon, develops his message. He shows that all the wealth, pleasure, wisdom and power that people may gain will, in the end, be of no benefit to them if they have wrong attitudes to life and to God.

Ecclesiastes is not a story or argument that moves through the book in an unbroken development from the first verse to the last. Rather it is a collection of some of the writer's teachings, and was probably put into its present form late in the writer's life. Nevertheless, each section is related to the book's central message. That message is presented at length in the opening two chapters, then is restated and discussed, in part or in whole, in the following sections. Although each section forms a unit by itself, the book is not disjointed. The writer has to some extent grouped sections where the subject matter is similar.

Like other Hebrew wisdom teachers, the writer is concerned with the apparent contradictions of life. (For a background to the wisdom writings in general see introductory notes to the book of Job.) He is not content to accept comfortable orthodox theories, but examines the frustrations and injustices that at times make life appear to be useless and without meaning. But he is not a pessimist. He has a strong faith in God, and this faith gives him his interpretation of life.

Meaning of the book

We must not read Ecclesiastes as if the writer is a priest or a prophet. He is not trying to explain the meaning of atonement, nor is he calling people to repentance. He is a wisdom teacher who wants to encourage God's people to find the meaning in life that God intended. His interpretation of life, built around the basic truths that God is sovereign and God is the Creator, may be summarized as follows.

No matter what benefits people gain for themselves in life, they are cancelled by the certainty of death. Life seems useless (Eccles 2:14,18; 6:1-6). Yet through it all God is in control, directing events according to his purposes (Eccles 3:11a,14; 8:15b). The writer is frustrated that he cannot know God's purposes, but he never doubts that such purposes exist (Eccles 3:11; 8:16-17; 9:1a). People should not therefore waste their time and energy searching after what God has kept to himself, but concentrate on enjoying what God has given to them, namely, life (Eccles 3:12-13; 5:18-19).

God is the sovereign Lord who controls all that happens in people's lives. At the same time he is the Creator who has given his world to the people he created. Therefore, people should accept whatever God determines for them, but at the same time they should find enjoyment in God's world and in all their activities in that world (Eccles 2:24; 9:7-10). But this enjoyment must not be selfish or without restraint, for they will only enjoy life properly as they act with wisdom rather than folly, and as they do good rather than evil (Eccles 7:5,7-9,19).

OUTLINE

1:1-4:16 ACCEPT THE LIFE GOD GIVES AND ENJOY IT

Is there a purpose to life? (1:1-11)

At times life does not appear to have much meaning. People have to work to keep themselves alive, but in the end they lose everything they have worked for. Generation after generation passes, but the same things still happen (1:1-4). The sun rises and sets, then the next day the cycle is repeated. The wind blows and circles around, coming back to begin its course all over again. Rivers flow unceasingly into the sea, but the sea is never full and the rivers never dry up (5-7). Life is wearisome; nothing satisfies; history will go on repeating itself; past generations die and are forgotten, and the same will happen to future generations (8-11).

Lessons from experience (1:12-2:26)

Writing as Solomon, the author now looks back and describes the experiences of a truly wise and wealthy man who searched for a meaning to life. First he tried the study of wisdom, but it led only to misery and frustration. Some things could not be made to fit any sort of consistent pattern; others, which in theory may have solved some problems, in practice did not exist (12-15). His learning and experience enabled him to tell the difference between wisdom and folly, but they were unable to help him find a meaning to life. His greater wisdom only increased his frustration and bitterness (16-18).

Continuing his search, the great king turned to pleasures of various kinds, but they did not provide the answer (2:1-3). He used his knowledge and resources in extravagant building programs and agricultural projects, and his household had everything he needed for a life of luxury and pleasure (4-8). All his achievements brought him a certain amount of satisfaction. But as he looks back he confesses that they brought him no nearer to solving the mystery of life's purpose (9-11).

Kings can build for themselves huge fortunes and accomplish impressive works, but even the wealthiest and most ambitious of kings found that all this did not bring satisfaction. What chance, then, does anyone else have? The frustrated searcher turned therefore to consider the subject of wisdom again (12). He reminded himself of the obvious truth that wisdom is better than folly (13), but he recalled also that the wise person dies the same as the fool, and both alike are soon forgotten (14-17).

Not only has wisdom no advantage over folly; diligence has no advantage over idleness. A person uses all his knowledge and skill in his work, spending long days labouring and sleepless nights worrying, but when he dies all that he has built up is left to someone else. Not only that, but the person who inherits all this did not work for it and may even foolishly waste it (18-23).

The writer now reaches one positive conclusion concerning the purpose of life. God intends people to enjoy the good things of life and to find enjoyment in their work. This is God's gift. Those who accept this gift please God. To them God gives the wisdom and ability to enjoy his gift. Those who do not accept this gracious gift from God, but who spend their energies trying to achieve happiness by their own wisdom and efforts, find that all they build up for themselves will be lost. In despair they cry out again that life is useless (24-26).

Events controlled by God's fixed order (3:1-15)

In 1:1-11 the author considered the ceaseless toil and repetition in the natural world and decided that life was useless. Now (ignoring for the moment the conclusions he has just outlined in 2:24-26) he considers the fixed order of events in the world. It appears to him that everything happens at the time God has decided it will happen. In view of this, all human effort to improve life is useless. People can change nothing (3:1-9).

Human beings may have a desire to know God and the realities of the unseen eternal world, but they still cannot understand God's ways. The writer is confident that God does everything perfectly according to his plan, but he is also frustrated because he does not know what that plan is. People can only accept whatever God sends them and find pleasure in it (10-13). They can change nothing; events will go on repeating themselves according to God's fixed purposes. Their realization of this keeps them in a state of fear before God (14-15).

Injustice in the world (3:16-4:3)

Having acknowledged God's order in human events, the writer now observes that the 'order' is, at times, not very orderly. For example, injustice abounds (16). Maybe, thinks the writer, God will put everything right in a judgment day in the afterlife (17). On the other hand, thinks he, there may not be an afterlife. He observes that people die the same as animals, as if God is trying to show that they are no different from the beasts. Also, he asks, can it be proved that people have life after death? The best they can do, concludes the writer, is to enjoy life while they can (18-22).

Although the enjoyment of life is a desirable goal, the world has so much cruelty and oppression that many people have no way of finding any sort of enjoyment. It would be better for these sufferers if they were dead; better still if they had never been born (4:1-3).

The uselessness of achievement (4:4-16)

Several examples illustrate how useless much human activity is. Some people drive themselves in their work but can never relax and enjoy it, because they are always worrying about being ahead of everyone else. Others do not work at all and so ruin themselves. Both extremes should be avoided. People should work for a living and enjoy it, but they should not be so ambitious that they create trouble for themselves (4-6).

Other unhappy people are those who spend all their time making money which they neither use themselves nor give to others (7-8). Those who cut themselves off from others, such as these rich misers, really harm themselves, for cooperation with others increases personal security (9-12).

Probably no one experiences the worthlessness of success and fame more than the great man who falls from power. He may have risen from poverty to fame, from prison to the throne, but if he refuses to listen to advice, any intelligent youth could rule better than he (13-14). In fact, among the thousands of people over whom a king rules there may just happen to be such an intelligent youth, who will overthrow the king and seize the throne for himself. But he, like the former king, will soon be forgotten (15-16).

5:1-10:20 MAKE THE MOST OF LIFE'S FRUSTRATIONS

Advice about religion (5:1-7)

Among the many affairs of everyday life that the writer deals with is the matter of religious practices. First he warns that the offering of sacrifices is useless if the worshippers have no desire to listen to God's word or obey it (5:1). Those thinking of making vows must consider their vows carefully before telling them to God. Too many words may lead to foolish vows, just as too much work can produce bad dreams (2-3).

People are not forced to make vows, but having made them they must do as they have promised. If they break their vows, it is useless to make excuses to the temple officials. That will not help the offenders escape the chastisement of God (4-6). Therefore, the writer reminds his readers again to avoid silly thoughts and foolish speech, and above all to fear God (7).

Advice about money (5:8-6:12)

Greed for money is a common social evil and the cause of much suffering. Because of such greed, government officials exploit poor farmers. Each official makes sure he takes as much money as he can, so that after he has passed some of it on to those above him who protect him, he has enough left for himself. As for the farmers, besides losing their profits to corrupt officials, they must also give some of their harvest as a tax to the king (8-9).

Prosperity does not satisfy, because the more people have, the more they want. The rich may lie awake at night worrying about their money, while labourers sleep soundly (10-12). Another frustration for the rich is that they may lose all their money in an unsuccessful business deal. In the end they have nothing to pass on to their children in spite of a lifetime of hard work (13-17). Life is short, and people should use the possessions and the work God has given them to bring themselves enjoyment, not trouble. This is God's will (18-20).

Two further examples illustrate the deceitfulness of riches. People may have wealth but not be able to enjoy it. Then, when they die, the benefits of their wealth are enjoyed by others, who may not even be relatives (6:1-3). Others may have everything that enables them to enjoy their wealth but they refuse to. They might live to a great age, but die in misery and are forgotten. A baby born dead, never having seen the world's light, is better off than such people (4-6).

No matter how much people have, they are never satisfied. Why, then, do they waste time and effort trying to improve themselves? They would do better to find enjoyment in what they have than always to want something else (7-9). After all, they cannot change what God has determined. Neither can they argue with God. They do not know what is best for them in this short life, nor do they know what will happen after they die (10-12).

Proverbs about life and death (7:1-14)

The writer now faces up to the fact that people have to make their way through life in spite of its various misfortunes. Through a collection of proverbs he points out that whatever circumstances they find themselves in, they should use them to the best advantage.

To begin with, people should desire a good reputation. If they live worthwhile lives, the day of their death will be more important than the day of their birth. It will be the climax that confirms their good reputation for ever (7:1). In view of this, they should always bear in mind the certainty of death, and not waste their lives on empty pleasures (2-4).

People who understand life will prefer the sincere rebuke of a wise person to the empty praise of a fool (5-6). They will avoid the temptation to get rich through oppression and bribery, knowing that these ruin a person's character (7). They will not be impatient or hot-tempered, and will not try to escape present troubles by wishing to be back in the past (8-10). They will recognize that wisdom and money, when used together, can improve the quality of life, but they will also accept the various circumstances they meet as being God's will for them. They cannot change what God has determined, but they can enjoy whatever good they meet (11-14).

Avoid extremes (7:15-29)

One of the puzzles of life is that bad people often have long and prosperous lives, but good people suffer and sometimes die before they have had a chance to enjoy life. The writer suggests that people follow a middle course through life, where they do not ruin their lives through being either over-zealous for goodness and wisdom or over-tolerant towards sin and foolishness. Those who fear God will be successful in avoiding both extremes (15-18).

Certainly, wisdom is better than folly and right is better than wrong, but the reality is that everyone sins sometimes. Before condemning others, people should realize that they may have been guilty of similar things themselves (19-22).

Again the writer points out how his search for absolute wisdom failed. He found that the meaning of existence was beyond his understanding. So he turned to consider practical wisdom in relation to human conduct, and discovered the disaster that results from wickedness and stupidity (23-25). His own experience taught him the ruin that an immoral woman can bring to the man who falls victim to her temptations. He also came to the conclusion that, though he might find one man in a thousand whom he could respect, he could not find one such woman. For this he blames not God but the human race in general. People have become too smart for their own good (26-29).

Compromise, despair and joy (8:1-17)

Wisdom helps people see the underlying meaning of things and teaches them that to act with pleasantness is better than to act with harshness (8:1). If, for example, people work in the king's palace, they will do what the king says, partly because they have sworn before God to be obedient and partly because they will be punished if they disobey. But if they find the king's command unreasonable, wisdom will show them a way out. They will wait for a suitable opportunity to act, then act in such a way that, though they do not disobey the king, neither do they sin against their conscience (2-5).

Despite the compromise he recommends, the writer knows that people remain uneasy about the outcome and about the future in general. They know they have no control over life or death. Just as there is no escape from a battle, so there is no guaranteed success to wrongdoers (6-8).

Often there appears to be no principle of justice at work in the world. The wicked go unpunished and, even when they are dead and buried, people still praise them for their achievements in life (9-10). It seems that this lack of punishment encourages people to sin (11-12a). The writer knows what the traditional teachers say: that those who fear God will be rewarded and those who are wicked will be punished (12b-13). But he also knows that often the opposite is true (14). People should not despair over these problems, but rather enjoy whatever God has given them in life (15). They should not spend weary days and sleepless nights puzzling over problems to which only God knows the answer (16-17).

Life's opportunities (9:1-12)

A person may believe that life is under the control of God, but still not know whether the experiences one meets in life are a sign of God's pleasure or a sign of his anger. The same fate, death, comes to all (9:1-3). Good people have no advantage over the bad. The only advantage is that of the living over the dead. The living can still do things, but the dead are useless and forgotten (4-6).

Therefore, people should enjoy life to the full while they have the opportunity, as there will be no further opportunity when they are dead. Festive occasions, marital relations and daily work are all part of the order that God has instituted for human society, and he wants people to enjoy them (7-10). Much in life seems to depend on chance. Those who deserve success may miss out because of some misfortune; those who do not deserve defeat may be overtaken by calamity (11-12).

Thoughts on wisdom and folly (9:13-10:20)

A simple story illustrates how a person may be wise and humble, but the good he does is not appreciated by those who benefit from it. Riches, status and a show of power are the things people admire. If a person lacks these, he is ignored or despised, even though his quiet words of wisdom may save a city from destruction (13-18).

One foolish act can spoil a lot of good. Stupidity leads to wrongdoing and marks a person out as a fool in the eyes of everyone (10:1-3). But when a ruler acts like a fool, the wise person will be patient and not panic. Unfortunately, fools often get into places of authority, but more capable people are not given a chance (4-7). In most activities there is some danger, so people should be careful and plan ahead; otherwise, instead of enjoying success they may meet disaster (8-11).

Fools talk without thinking of the consequences of their words and so get themselves into trouble. They waste their time with much talk about the future, even though no one can know the future. They waste their energy in useless work. They have no idea where they are going (12-15).

Immature rulers, who think only of their own comforts and ignore the needs of the people, bring hardship and discontent to the country they rule (16-17). Laziness leads to decay. If people want to enjoy the good things of life, they must work so that they can earn the money to buy them (18-19). The wise will learn how to control their thoughts and, consequently, their words and actions. In this way they will keep out of trouble (20).

11:1-12:14 HAVE A POSITIVE ATTITUDE TO LIFE

Boldness in spite of uncertainty (11:1-8)

It is typical of the writer that he encourages a positive attitude to life. True, life may be uncertain, but that is no reason to refuse to act positively. Regardless of what people decide to do, they must work at it boldly in spite of the risks, expecting results in due time. However, they should not put all their goods or money into one project. Then, if they meet misfortune in one place, the rest of the investment will be safe (11:1-2).

The world of nature shows that there are many things in life that people can neither control nor alter. There is much they do not know. If they always wait till they are certain before putting their plans into action, they will never do anything (3-5). Rather their attitude should be positive and optimistic (6). Life is compared to the light of day, death to the darkness of night. People should therefore enjoy life to the full while the light of day lasts (7-8).

Advice to young people (11:9-12:8)

God's will is that people enjoy life. In fact, they have a responsibility to do so. The writer urges young people especially to take note of this and not to misuse their mental or physical powers through developing wrong attitudes to life. However, their enjoyment of life must be according to a proper understanding of God and his character. They, like all others, are answerable to him for their behaviour (9-10).

Young people should remember that God is the Creator, the giver of life and all that goes with it. They should accept life from his hand and enjoy it as he intended. The opportunity will have passed by the time old age comes (12:1).

The writer pictures old age as a run-down house in a cold dark winter. The old person, now at the end of his life, is shaky, bent, half blind, half deaf, unable to sleep well, fearful of heights and afraid to walk along the street. He has lost all desire for life's pleasures (2-5). Finally, death overtakes him. He is (to use another picture) like a broken bowl or a smashed water jar. God who first gave him life now takes it back. Life has run its course and has led, in the end, to nothing (6-8).

Final comments (12:9-14)

Those whom the writer taught were not only the sons of the rich who attended the wisdom schools, but also ordinary people around the city. His method of study was to consider all the wise teachings relevant to his subject, select the most suitable, then arrange them in a way that was interesting and helpful to his audience. However, he never twisted the truth to suit his own purposes (9-10). True wisdom teaching, such as that which the writer speaks of here, comes from God. It helps people on and sticks in their minds (11).

A final warning is necessary. Too much study can be harmful, especially if it goes beyond what is taught by the wisdom teachers (12). All people have a basic responsibility to fear God and obey his commandments. They are answerable to God for everything they do (13-14).

Song of Songs

BACKGROUND

The intellectual and literary abilities of Solomon earned him recognition as one of Israel's greatest wisdom teachers and song writers (1 Kings 4:29-34). His accumulation of wives and concubines made him perhaps its most famous lover (1 Kings 11:1-4). Not surprisingly, he was traditionally regarded as the author of the collection of love poems known as the Song of Songs, or the Song of Solomon. The book names Solomon as its author and makes reference to the splendour of Solomon and his court (Song of Songs 1:1,5; 3:7-11; 8:11-12).

This does not mean, however, that Solomon is the chief character of the book, or that the poems are concerned with him personally. A poet can write about others besides himself. Readers of the Song of Songs in fact often have difficulty working out who the poems are about, as separate poems can be understood in different ways. In some poems all the words may be from one speaker, but in others they form a dialogue. They may even include the words of additional speakers. Some poems describe actual feelings and events, but others recount dreams. The poems may recall the past, speak of the present or look forward to the future.

Interpretation of the book

Since readers have to work out for themselves who the various speakers are, many interpretations of the book have been suggested. These are reflected in the sub-headings that translators of different versions of the Bible have introduced.

Some interpretations of the book see it as a drama concerning Solomon himself. Among these there are two main viewpoints. The first sees only two main characters, Solomon and a Shulammite girl, who fall in love and marry. (The meaning of 'Shulammite' is not clear. The word may have come from the name of the village where the girl lived.) The other view is that there are not two main characters but three — a young shepherd, a Shulammite girl and King Solomon. The shepherd and the girl are deeply in love, but Solomon has taken the girl from her shepherd-lover, put her into his harem and now unsuccessfully tries to win her love.

Other interpretations take the view that the book is not a drama at all and that it is not about Solomon. Rather it is a collection of love poems recounting the exchanges of love between a young man and a young woman. This is the view taken in the commentary below. Only two main characters are involved, an unnamed shepherd-farmer and an unnamed country girl whose love for each other is expressed in a series of poems.

There is a basic unity to the book. Certain features recur throughout, and there is a general development that reflects the maturing relationship between the two lovers. There is a progression from the longing for a distant lover in the opening poem to what appears to be the home-coming of a married couple in the final poem. But the poems are not necessarily in chronological order, and in places it is uncertain whether they have been written before or after marriage.

The following notes will simply deal with the two people as lovers, whether engaged or married. In biblical times people considered engagement to be as binding as marriage, and this meant that love poems may have contained erotic expressions. But this did not give the lovers permission for sexual relations before marriage.

Love between the sexes

In the order that God has laid down for human society, sexual love between a man and a woman has its rightful place. One reason for the inclusion of the Song of Songs in the Scriptures may have been to show God's approval of sexual love. Always, however, the love is in the context of a relationship where a man and a woman commit themselves to each other in marriage, to the exclusion of all others (Song of Songs 2:16; 6:3; 7:10; 8:6).

The detailed and unashamed descriptions of love between a man and a woman, though they may embarrass some present-day readers, reflect the purity and pleasure of a love relation between the sexes. Figures of speech that the lovers use may seem strange to people of a different language and culture, but in their original setting they were no doubt regarded as compliments of the highest order. The language of lovers is always extravagant, and in the Song of Songs the beauty and power of the language displays the intensity of human love in a way not found elsewhere in the Bible.

OUTLINE

1:1-2:7 OPENING EXCHANGES OF PRAISE

The girl longs for her lover (1:1-7)

After an introductory note (1:1), the collection opens with a poem spoken by the girl in praise of her absent lover. At times she imagines she is speaking to him, at times she thinks about him, but always she longs for his love and attention. She thinks that all girls must love such a handsome young man. To her he is king, and she imagines the coming wedding day when he takes her into his room, praises her beauty and makes love to her (2-4).

Aware that men have a liking for lighter skinned girls such as those of Jerusalem, the girl makes excuses for her dark skin. She is a farm girl who has worked in the sun, and she compares the colour of her skin to that of black goat-hair tents. Yet she knows that her lover makes a better comparison when he likens her to the beautiful curtains of Solomon's palace. The reason for her dark skin is that her hard-hearted brothers have made her look after the family vineyards, with the result that she has not had time to look after the 'vineyard' of her own appearance (5-6).

The girl wishes she knew where her lover was feeding his sheep. Then she could go straight to him without having to wander from flock to flock looking for him (7).

The lovers talk together (1:8-2:7)

In reply to the girl's longing, the man invites her to come and join him in the fields (8). He praises her beauty and promises to give her the finest jewellery (9-11). The girl responds that her greatest joy is just to be in his presence and let her love flow out to him (12-14). After the man further praises the girl's beauty (15), she expresses her desire to be with him in the fields again, where they can lie down together in the shade of the trees (16-17).

The girl regards herself as nothing special – just a country maiden, just a small wildflower in a large field (2:1). Yes, replies her lover, but she is the only flower in the field. Compared with her, all the other girls are brambles (2). And her lover, replies she, is like a tree that surpasses all the other trees of the forest. He protects, strengthens and refreshes her. His company is to her a feast of joy and love (3-6).

In view of the girl's strong desire for her lover, a warning is given (in the form of an appeal to the easily excited young women of Jerusalem). The warning shows the danger of trying to stir up love when a person is not ready for it (7).

2:8-6:3 MEMORIES AND DREAMS

Springtime and night-time (2:8-3:5)

A fresh poem begins with the girl's recalling the coming of her shepherd-lover across the hills to visit her at her house (8-9). She remembers his words as he invited her to go with him to visit the fields and vineyards, where the dreariness of winter had passed and the new life of spring was bursting out (10-15). But now she is alone again and he is in the fields looking after his sheep. She longs for the day when he will return to her (16-17).

Because she thought constantly about her lover by day, the girl often dreamt about him at night. On one occasion she dreamt that she was walking around the streets of her home town looking for him. When, to her delight, she found him, she immediately took him back to her family home (3:1-4). She adds her reminder that, when two people have such love for each other, it does no good to stir up their feelings further (5).

A wedding procession (3:6-5:1)

As the wedding day approaches, the girl pictures the coming of the bridegroom for her as a royal wedding procession — King Solomon in all his glory coming to this humble country town to claim his bride. She pictures the scene as the procession approaches amid clouds of perfumed incense. The centre of attraction is the king himself, carried on his gold and silver carriage and surrounded by fully armed royal guards in brilliant uniforms (6-11).

The bridegroom meets his bride and praises her in the most extravagant language (4:1-5). He looks forward to the first night with this one who, to him, is flawless, the one who fulfils all his ideals (6-7). In making his bride his own, he feels like a conqueror who has taken a person from a well defended stronghold. Yet he feels also like one who has himself been conquered, for his bride has stolen his heart (8-11). Everything about her is pure and lovely. She is like a fragrant garden where he can find delight and refreshment for ever (12-15).

In response the bride wishes that the wind would blow upon her 'garden', so that her lover might smell its fragrance and come into it (16). The bridegroom accepts the invitation, comes to his 'garden' (his bride) and takes the girl as his own. Friends then announce their blessing on the bridal couple (5:1).

A dream of frustration (5:2-6:3)

Another dream reflects the girl's unfulfilled longing as she waits impatiently for her wedding day. She dreams that while she is asleep, her lover has travelled through the night to come to her and now he knocks on her door (2).

Only half awake, the girl is slow to get out of bed and answer the door. She finds it a nuisance, as she has just bathed and got herself dressed for bed (3). Suddenly she realizes what has happened: her lover has come for her! Excitedly she hurries to the door and opens it to welcome him. But she has delayed too long and now he has gone (4-6). She rushes into the streets looking for him, but receives no sympathy from the nightwatchmen. To them a girl in her bedclothes who rushes around the streets at night must be a prostitute, and they treat her harshly (7).

Desperately the frustrated dreamer appeals to the women of Jerusalem to help her find her lover, but the women's reply is uncooperative. Why is her lover more special than anyone else's that they should help her find him (8-9)? The girl replies that in appearance, build and personality he surpasses all others (10-16). If he is so wonderful, reply the women, they would like to go with her to meet him (6:1). At this the girl remembers that she has not really lost him, for she has only had a dream. She knows where he is. He is at home on the farm, faithful to her as ever (2-3).

6:4-8:14 THE STRENGTH OF TRUE LOVE

Desires for each other (6:4-7:13)

Using language that he has used before, the man again praises the girl's loveliness (4-7; cf. 4:1-3). The nation's most beautiful women may have been chosen for the palace harem, but they must look with envy upon the beauty of the lovely farm girl who is his beloved (8-10). In a brief parenthesis that follows, the two lovers are reminded of an occasion when they met on the farm. The girl was carried away by her lover's charms as if taken away by a prince on his chariot (11-12). The theme quickly returns to the praise of the girl, with the harem women asking her to display her beauty for them.

But neither she nor her lover want people to gaze upon her as if she were a common dance girl (13).

The girl's unclothed loveliness is for her lover's appreciation and no one else's. He then describes her beauty from her feet to her head (7:1-5), and adds a short erotic song expressing his great desire for her (6-9a). The girl replies that she belongs solely to him. She wants to go for a walk with him through the fields and vineyards, where together they can enjoy each other's love (9b-13).

Restrained behaviour (8:1-4)

A brief poem addressed by the girl to her lover displays the frustration that the two felt in not being able to show their love to each other openly. The girl comments that if they were brother and sister they would at least be able to kiss in public (8:1-3). But fitting expressions of love between the two will come in their own good time. They do not need anyone to arouse them (4).

At home with family and friends (8:5-14)

The final poem sees the lovers walking along the road on their way home (5a). As they approach the house, the girl is reminded that the place where they fell in love was the garden of the home where her lover was born (5b). She then praises the power of love that binds her to him. True love demands total possession of each by the other. It is indestructible and beyond value (6-7).

The girl recalls the words of her older brothers when she was only in her early teens. Her brothers had helped her develop that strength of character that enabled her to retain her purity when unworthy men approached her. If, like a wall, she resisted such men, her brothers would honour her. If, like a door, she tended to yield to them, her brothers would protect her (8-9). Now, as one who has resisted and who has retained her purity to the maturity of adulthood, she enjoys contentment with her one and only true love (10).

Solomon spent extravagantly maintaining his harem, an action likened here to the costly business of maintaining a vineyard by using hired workers. So far as the lover and his beloved are concerned, Solomon may keep his wealth and the hired workers may keep their wages. As for the small 'vineyard' (the girl), she is not for hire. She belongs solely to her lover (11-12). The man asks his beloved to speak, so that he and his friends may hear her voice (13). She does, by echoing her words of former years when she desired that he come quickly and take her to be his own (14; cf. 2:8-9).

Old Testament Prophecy

INTRODUCTION

In modern usage, the words 'prophecy' and 'prophet' are usually concerned with foretelling events. A prophet is a person who predicts (for example, a weather prophet). This was not the chief usage of the words in Old Testament times. Prophecy basically meant making known the will of God. A prophet was a spokesperson for God.

This definition of a prophet was well illustrated in the case of Aaron, who was Moses' prophet. He was Moses' spokesman. Moses was leader of the nation, but Aaron was the one who announced Moses' directions to Israel (Exod 4:10-16; 7:1-2). In the same way a prophet of God announced God's will to the people (1 Kings 22:7-8; Jer 1:7,9; Ezek 3:4,27; Amos 3:7).

The true prophet could be appointed only by God (Jer 1:5,9; Ezek 2:3-7; Amos 7:15), and was therefore known as a man of God (1 Sam 2:27; 9:6; 1 Kings 13:1-2), a messenger of God (Hag 1:13), or a servant of God (2 Kings 17:23; Jer 7:25). Sometimes he was called a seer (meaning 'one who sees'), because he may have seen God's message in a vision (1 Sam 9:9,18-19; Zech 1:7-8).

The prophetical books

A clear indication of the Israelites' view of prophecy is seen in the way they arranged the books of the Old Testament. They divided their Bible into three portions, which they called the Law, the Prophets and the Writings. The Law consisted of the five books of Moses. The Prophets consisted of the Former Prophets (Joshua, Judges, Samuel and Kings) and the Latter Prophets (Isaiah, Jeremiah, Ezekiel and the twelve so-called Minor Prophets). The Writings consisted of the miscellaneous other books.

From the composition of the Former Prophets group we see that the books that we call historical the Israelites called prophetical. The reason for this is that these books were written from the prophetic viewpoint (most of Israel's historians were prophets; cf. 1 Chron 29:29; 2 Chron 9:29; 12:15), showing how God was working out his purposes in the lives of his people. In summary it might be said that in the Former Prophets God revealed himself in the history of the nation Israel, while in the Latter Prophets he revealed himself through the words of his spokesmen.

Because the Israelites had this understanding of prophecy, they excluded Chronicles from the Former Prophets and Daniel from the Latter Prophets. Chronicles was written from the priestly viewpoint rather than the prophetic. Daniel was written in the apocalyptic style rather than the prophetic. (In the type of literature known as apocalyptic, the revelations were based on dreams and visions, where weird animals, mysterious numbers and unnatural events were used symbolically to warn or encourage God's people.)

Professional prophets

The prophets whose writings have been collected in the Bible (commonly referred to as the writing prophets) date from the eighth century BC, but prophets had been active in Israel long before the time of these men. As preachers and spiritual guides, they brought God's message to his people (Judg 4:4; 1 Sam 3:20; 2 Sam 7:2).

In the time of Samuel there were many enthusiastic young prophets, but they were often guilty of uncontrolled behaviour that gave prophets a poor reputation (1 Sam 10:5,9-12; 19:20-24; cf. 2 Kings 9:11; cf. Amos 7:14). In an effort to redirect this religious enthusiasm for Israel's spiritual benefit, Samuel established a school of prophets at Ramah. This was followed by additional schools in other towns (1 Sam 19:18-20; 2 Kings 2:3,5; 4:38).

When Israel's religion was under threat because of the Baal worship introduced by Jezebel, the prophets Elijah and Elisha found many genuine followers of God in these schools. These young men (the 'sons of the prophets') maintained the worship of God in a nation that had largely sold itself to Baal (2 Kings 2:1-7,15; 4:38; 6:1).

By the time of the writing prophets about two hundred years later, many of those who passed through the schools of the prophets were more concerned with being religious professionals than with spiritually feeding God's people. Few of the writing prophets appear to have been professionals. Their emphasis was that the true prophet had been called by God, not that he had received professional training (Jer 1:4-8; Amos 7:14-15).

True and false prophets

Religion was an important part of Israelite life, and people often consulted prophets about their affairs. Consequently, prophets often lived and functioned near Israel's public places of worship (1 Sam 9:11-12; 10:5; 1 Kings 13:1-2; 18:30; Jer 35:4; Amos 7:12-13). Some of them were advisers to kings and officials, for through them God could give directions when leaders had to make important decisions (2 Sam 7:1-3; 24:11-12; 1 Kings 22:6-8; 2 Kings 19:1-7; Jer 38:14-17).

Because the prophets received their income from the people to whom they ministered, many of them gave in to the temptation to prophesy the sorts of things that they knew their hearers wanted to hear. This guaranteed good rewards and stability in their jobs, but it brought condemnation from genuine believers. Because of this dishonesty and greed, they were known as false prophets (1 Kings 22:13-18; Jer 6:13-14; 23:16-17; Micah 2:11; 3:5-7,11; Zeph 3:4).

Although they were called prophets, these men were not God's spokesmen. They were appointed by themselves, not by God. They spoke according to their own selfish desires, not according to the mind of God (Jer 14:14; 23:21-22; Ezek 13:1-3,17). Instead of rebuking the people for their sin, they maintained their popularity by assuring the people that God was pleased with them. Actually, the nation was heading for judgment, and the corruption of the prophets was one reason for that judgment (Jer 23:11-17; Ezek 13:8-16,22).

The test of a prophet, whether he was true or false, was not whether his predictions came true (for even the predictions of a false prophet might come true). The test was whether he led people in the ways of God (Deut 13:1-5; Jer 23:21-22,29-32; Hosea 9:7-8). Clearly, if a prophet made a bold assertion that his prediction would come true and it did not, he was a false prophet (Deut 18:22).

True prophets were concerned chiefly not with foretelling events, but with leading the people to repentance and faith (Micah 3:8; 7:18; Zeph 2:1-3). They often opposed formal religious practices, not because the practices themselves were wrong, but because the people carried them out in the wrong spirit. Religious exercises were of value only if the people were godly in their attitudes and behaviour. They were no substitute for morality. People had to be humble before God and righteous in their dealings with their fellows if God was to accept their outward expressions of worship (Isa 1:12-17; Amos 5:21-24; Micah 6:6-8).

Current events and future hopes

Since the prophet's main purpose was to bring God's message to the people of his time, prediction was not an essential part of the message. However, it often played a part, because the God who is concerned about the present is the God who controls the future.

Therefore, as the prophets urged people to turn from their sins and obey God, they often spoke of events that would follow the people's obedience or disobedience. The prediction was not just to satisfy curiosity about the future, but had an important moral purpose. It taught people how they should act now (Isa 1:18-20; Hosea 11:1-11; 14:1-7).

In relation to this it should be noted that predictions were usually conditional, even when the prophet did not mention the conditions in his prophecy. For example, a prediction of good may not have been fulfilled if the people were disobedient. A prediction of disaster may not have been fulfilled if the people repented (Jer 18:7-10; 26:17-19; Jonah 3:4,10).

Like all the godly in Israel, the prophets looked forward to that great day when God would punish evil, destroy all enemies, cleanse the earth and establish his righteousness in the world (Isa 24:17-23; 32:1-4). The one who would rule in this golden age was known as the Messiah, meaning 'the anointed one' (cf. Ps 2:1-7). (In Old Testament times kings, priests, and sometimes prophets were appointed to their positions by the ceremony of anointing. Holy oil was poured over the head of the person as a sign that he now had the right, and the responsibility, to perform the duties required by his position; cf. Exod 28:41; 1 Sam 10:1; 1 Kings 1:39; 19:16.)

The preachers of the Old Testament pictured the Messiah as a king, a conqueror and a saviour. They lived in the expectation that a king of the dynasty of David would reign in a worldwide kingdom of peace and righteousness (Isa 9:6-7; 11:1-5; 32:1; Jer 23:5; Zech 6:12-13). But they spoke also of a prophetic figure whom they pictured as a servant, a sufferer and a victim (Deut 18:15,18; Isa 52:13-14; 53:4-7; Zech 12:10). What they did not see was that both pictures applied to the same person. The Messiah who finally came was both a king and a servant, both a conqueror and a sufferer, both a saviour and a victim (cf. 1 Peter 1:10-12).

Another point that the prophets did not see was that this person would fulfil God's purposes for humankind not all at once, but through two separate

241

entrances into the world. The New Testament makes it clear that the promised Messiah was Jesus Christ (Matt 11:2-6; 22:41-45; Luke 1:32-33; 24:19,25-26; Rev 5:5). The Messiah's first coming began with Jesus' birth and ended with his death, resurrection and ascension. At his second coming he will judge the world and lead his people into the era of the new heavens and the new earth (Heb 1:5-9; 9:27-28; Rev 19:11-16; 21:1-4).

Problems concerning time

This apparent inconsistency in relation to time is typical of all prophetic prediction. Within the one prediction there may be some parts fulfilled within the prophet's lifetime, other parts fulfilled within a hundred years or so, and other parts still not yet fulfilled (e.g. Joel 2:24-32; Hag 2:20-23).

The reason for this is that the prophet sees things from God's point of view, and God does not live in the sort of time system that operates in the world of our experience (Jer 23:22; Ezek 8:1-3; 11:24). The prophet sees and knows in a way that is different from that of the ordinary person. It is as if he steps out of the world of time into the world of eternity, where time as we know it does not exist (2 Peter 3:8; Rev 1:8).

Consequently, the prophet may speak of events in language of the future, the present, or the past tense (e.g. Isa 9:6-7; 53:1-9; Jer 51:52-57). In the course of history as ordinary people see it, events may be separated from one another by hundreds or even thousands of years, but in the message of the prophet they may not be separated at all. They may be mentioned together as if they happened almost at the same time (e.g. Isa 53:1-12; 61:1-9; Ezek 34:20-24; Mal 2:17-3:4).

The language of prophecy

Early prophets such as Deborah, Samuel, Nathan, Elijah and Elisha have left little or no record of their prophecies. But the biblical accounts of their ministries show that they sometimes passed on their messages by means of stories and actions (2 Sam 12:1-7; 1 Kings 11:29-31). In later times prophets frequently wrote down their messages as well as, or instead of, speaking them (Isa 30:8; Jer 29:1,25; 30:2; 36:1-4). Some also acted them (Isa 20:1-6; Jer 19:1-3; Ezek 5:1-12).

Of the prophecies that have been written down, most are in the form of poetry. The reason for this is probably that poetry is better able to express a person's deeper thoughts and feelings. It is also easier to memorize than prose, and this would help people in remembering and passing on the message (Isa 55:6-9; Joel 1:2-4; Amos 3:1-8).

Hebrew poetry has no rhyme or metre as in English poetry. Its style and rhythm come largely from its arrangement of words and sentences. The most common form is that in which the first line of a verse contains the main thought, and the following line (or lines) then adds weight to this thought either by repeating it in a slightly different form (Isa 30:3; 32:3), by stating its opposite (Nahum 1:6-7; Hab 2:4), or by adding some further explanation or contrast (Isa 55:2-3; Jer 9:4-6; Hosea 8:7).

When reading the poetry of the prophets, we should be concerned not so much with the meaning of each separate phrase or line, as with the meaning of the verse (or verses) as a unit. We should also remember that poets create vivid word pictures and use exaggerated language to express their thoughts. They do not expect us always to interpret their words literally (Isa 40:12; Amos 9:13; Micah 4:4).

Isaiah

BACKGROUND

Isaiah lived during that period of Old Testament history when the Israelite nation was divided into two kingdoms. The division occurred about 930 BC, soon after the reign of Solomon (1 Kings 11:9-13; 12:16-20), and resulted in a northern kingdom of ten tribes and a southern kingdom of two tribes.

The northern kingdom continued to call itself Israel, though in fact it was the breakaway part of the nation. It dissociated itself from both the dynasty of David and the religion that centred on the temple in Jerusalem (1 Kings 12:25-33). The early centres of administration were Shechem and then Tirzah, but within fifty years a new and well fortified capital was established at Samaria, and this was still the capital in the time of Isaiah.

The southern kingdom called itself Judah, after the tribe that formed its major part. Jerusalem, which had been the capital of the entire nation in the time of David and Solomon, was now the capital only of Judah. The dynasty of David continued to rule in Jerusalem, but now it ruled only over the southern kingdom. The Jerusalem temple remained the centre of Judah's religious life in spite of the false religion that repeatedly troubled the nation.

A prophet and a statesman

God's servant Isaiah lived in Jerusalem, where he was an adviser to several kings of Judah. He was a person of importance, and over many years he used his position to try to influence Judah's policies in both local and international affairs. His work began in the year of King Uzziah's death (740 BC), and continued through the reigns of Jotham, Ahaz and Hezekiah (Isa 1:1; 6:1,8-9). According to traditional Jewish belief, he was executed during the reign of the wicked king Manasseh by being sawn in two (cf. Heb 11:37).

Much of the early part of Isaiah's book is concerned with his attempts to persuade the ungodly Ahaz to trust in God instead of seeking military help from Assyria. The next portion of the book records his attempts to control the zeal of the good king Hezekiah, who was so keen to free Judah from Assyrian power that he too sought foreign military aid, in this case from Egypt.

Isaiah saw that Assyria and Egypt, along with many other nations among Judah's neighbours, were opposed to Israel's God, who was the one and only true God. The prophet therefore announced God's judgments upon each of them in turn. But he saw also that Judah was rebellious against God. The nation was heading for a terrible judgment that

DIVIDED KINGDOM OF ISRAEL-JUDAH

would see the people taken into captivity in a foreign land. Through all these events, however, God would preserve the remnant, that minority of the people who remained faithful to him.

The final section of the book, which was probably written much later than the earlier parts, shows God's purposes in preserving the remnant. From this faithful group would come the beginning of new life for God's people. When the people

243

acknowledged the justice of God's punishment and received cleansing from past sins, they would return to their land and enjoy peace and prosperity once more. This future glory of Israel is described at length, with particular emphasis on the qualities of the messianic king who would rule and the world-wide blessing that his kingdom would bring.

Conditions of Isaiah's time

With the long and prosperous reigns of Uzziah (or Azariah) in Judah and Jeroboam II in Israel, both kingdoms enjoyed expansion and progress (2 Kings 14:23-25,28; 15:1-7; 2 Chron 26:1-15). However, the prosperity brought with it severe religious, social, moral and political evils. The prophets of this time, Amos and Hosea, tirelessly denounced the moral and religious corruption of the people, and tried to defend the poor against the exploitation of the rich (Amos 2:6-7; 3:10,15; 6:4-6; 8:4-6; Hosea 4:1-6; 6:6-10; 7:2-4; 12:7-9).

The work of these two prophets was soon strengthened by that of Isaiah, and a few years later by that of Micah. Although the four prophets carried out their work in different parts of Israel and Judah, and although each had his own emphasis, they all saw the same evils and announced the same judgment (cf. Isa 1:12-23; 3:14-17; 5:11-13; 5:20-23; Micah 2:1-5,8-9; 3:1-3,9-12; 7:3).

Isaiah, being in a better position than the other three to influence the king, tried also to develop a greater concern for God's standards in the government of the nation. He saw what was happening in Jerusalem, and knew that Judah was heading for inevitable judgment. Yet the troubles of Judah were inseparably linked with those of Israel, and much in Isaiah's book relates also to the northern kingdom.

Political instability in Israel

When Jeroboam II died (753 BC), the northern kingdom Israel entered a time of political chaos as ambitious men fought to seize power. The new king reigned only six months before being murdered, but his assassin reigned only one month before suffering a similar fate at the hands of Menahem, who then became king (2 Kings 15:8-16).

Israel quickly lost its stability, and Assyria soon began to show interest in adding Israel to its rapidly expanding empire. Menahem survived only through buying the protection of the Assyrian king Tiglath-pileser III (also known as Pul). The Israelite army commander Pekah was opposed to this pro-Assyrian policy. When Menahem died and was succeeded by his son, Pekah murdered the new king and seized the throne for himself (2 Kings 15:17-26).

Israel and Syria attack Judah

Tiglath-pileser III now planned a complete military takeover of Israel. (God's prophets had already predicted such a conquest; Hosea 10:5-8; Amos 7:17.) To strengthen the defence against Assyria, the Syrian (Aramean) king Rezin and the Israelite king Pekah entered into a joint defence agreement. They tried to persuade the Judean king Jotham and the succeeding king Ahaz to join them, but the Judean kings refused. Rezin and Pekah then attacked Ahaz, apparently with the aim of conquering Judah, putting their own king on the Judean throne, then forcing Judah to join their anti-Assyrian alliance. This attack took place in 735 BC (2 Kings 15:37; 16:5; Isa 7:1-2,6).

On learning that the Israelite-Syrian army was nearing Jerusalem, Ahaz panicked. Isaiah remained calm and urged the king to trust in God, assuring him that he had nothing to fear. Israel and Syria would not defeat Judah, but would themselves be

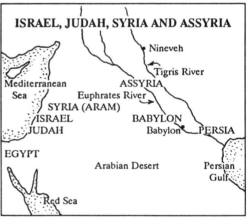

ISRAEL, JUDAH, SYRIA AND ASSYRIA

conquered by Assyria. Ahaz had only to believe God (2 Kings 16:5; Isa 7:2-9; 8:4). But Ahaz neither trusted God nor believed Isaiah. Instead he decided to ask Assyria to come and help him. Isaiah warned that this was a foolish move, because it would place Judah under Assyria's control. Again Ahaz ignored the advice (2 Kings 16:7-8; Isa 8:5-8).

In response to Ahaz's request, Assyria attacked Syria and Israel. When Assyria conquered a country, its policy was to take the people captive into other parts of the Assyrian Empire and replace them with settlers from elsewhere. This helped to prevent rebellion breaking out in the conquered territory. Therefore, when Tiglath-pileser III conquered Syria, he carried off the people into captivity in Assyria (2 Kings 16:9). This happened in 732 BC and marked the end of the kingdom of Syria, as foretold by the prophets (Isa 17:1; Amos 1:4-5).

Tiglath-pileser continued his attack across the border of Syria and into Israel. He seized much of Israel's eastern and northern territory, and carried off the inhabitants into captivity (2 Kings 15:29). This was the beginning of the end for Israel. The nation was finally conquered by Assyria and its people taken captive into foreign lands in 722 BC (2 Kings 17:1-6).

Judah's new policies under Hezekiah

The Assyrians were now dominant in Palestine. In the north they had replaced former Israelite inhabitants with settlers from elsewhere (2 Kings 17:24), and in the south they had imposed a heavy tribute on the Judean king Ahaz (2 Kings 16:7-8). But when the young Hezekiah succeeded Ahaz in Judah, he set out on the bold task of freeing Judah from all Assyrian influence, whether military, political or religious.

Hezekiah's first action was to reform Judah's corrupt religion. He destroyed all idolatrous shrines, cleansed and rededicated the temple, reinstituted various festivals and ceremonies, and organized the priests and Levites according to the arrangements originally set out by David (2 Kings 18:1-6; 2 Chron 29:1-31:21).

It is doubtful, however, that Hezekiah's reforms brought any lasting change in the lives of the people in general. Hezekiah is commended for the good work he did (2 Kings 18:5), but the prophets of the time, Isaiah and Micah, do not mention his reforms. They saw that, in spite of the renewed religious activity, people had not changed inwardly. They gave little evidence of genuine faith and repentance (Isa 1:11-20; Micah 6:6-8).

In relation to Assyria's military and political dominance of Judah, Hezekiah was equally zealous for reform. But before he declared his new policy on foreign affairs, he fortified Jerusalem's defences, strengthened the city wall and improved the city's water supply as a precaution against possible siege (2 Kings 20:20; 2 Chron 32:5-6). Then, assured of military backing from Egypt, he revolted against Assyria by refusing to pay further tribute (2 Kings 18:7-8).

Isaiah opposed this dependence upon Egypt, just as during the reign of Ahaz he had opposed dependence upon Assyria. Judah's need was not for military help from Egypt but for quiet faith in God (Isa 30:1-3,15; 31:1,3). In response to Hezekiah's rebellion, Assyria attacked Jerusalem (701 BC; Isa 36:1-6). The book of Isaiah gives a lengthy account of events surrounding the attack and Jerusalem's miraculous deliverance.

Captivity and return

After the account of Jerusalem's deliverance from the Assyrian siege, there is a gap in the record of approximately 150 years. This gap occurs between Chapters 39 and 40, and forms a natural division in the book. In fact, Chapters 40-66 are so different in content and style from Chapters 1-39, that some biblical scholars suggest they were not written by Isaiah, but come from some person or persons of a later generation.

In brief, what happened during this intervening period was that Assyria was conquered by Babylon (612 BC), who then conquered Judah, carried the people captive to Babylon and destroyed Jerusalem (605-587 BC). The messages recorded in the latter section of Isaiah were intended originally for the Judean captives in Babylon.

During this time of the Judeans' captivity, events foreseen by the prophet began to happen. In neighbouring Persia a man named Cyrus had risen to power, and one by one conquered most of the surrounding nations. Then, in 539 BC, he conquered Babylon, and immediately gave permission to the captive Jews to return to their land (Ezra 1:1-4). Many returned and immediately began to rebuild the temple, but because of delays through opposition it was not finished till 516 BC (Ezra 6:14-15).

THE USE OF NAMES

The name Yahweh

In the Hebrew Bible a number of words are used for God, the most common of which are translated in English Bibles as 'God' (Hebrew: el or elohim) and 'the LORD'. The latter of these two words, which is always printed in capitals, has a distinctive significance in the Old Testament. Where God is called 'Lord' (and the whole word is not in capitals), the Hebrew word is usually adon or adonai, a word that indicates God's sovereignty as lord and master. But where he is called 'LORD' (in capitals) the Hebrew word is yahweh, the name of the Hebrews' God.

There is some mystery concerning the origin and usage of this name. Israel's ancestors knew God as Yahweh (Gen 12:1; 26:2; 28:21; 49:18), but the people as a whole seem to have first understood the significance of the name only at the time of their escape from Egypt under Moses. God revealed himself to Moses as 'I am who I am' (Exod 3:14; sometimes translated 'I will be who I will be'), and Moses was to pass this revelation on to the people.

In revealing himself in this way, God was providing an explanation of what the name Yahweh should have meant to his people. In the Hebrew language the word translated 'I am' is related to the name of God, Yahweh.

Originally the Hebrew language was written using consonants only. The absence of vowels was no problem, because readers knew how to put in the vowels as they read. The name of Israel's God was written as YHWH (without vowels) but pronounced apparently as Yahweh. There can be no absolute certainty about this pronunciation, because there are no Hebrew records old enough to record it.

By the time the Hebrews had developed the practice of adding vowels to the written language, they no longer spoke the name YHWH. This, they claimed, showed their reverence for the holy name of God, but for many it was more a superstition. Whatever the reason for it, the practice developed that when the Hebrews read the Scriptures, instead of speaking the word YHWH, they used the word *adonai* (meaning 'lord' or 'master').

When, about 300 BC, a version of the Hebrew Bible added vowels to the consonants, it put the vowels of *adonai* to the consonants YHWH. This produced a new word, Jehovah, though the Hebrews still preferred to substitute *adonai* for YHWH when speaking. English translations of the Bible have usually avoided the pronunciation problem by using 'the LORD' (in capitals) instead of YHWH.

Names of nations

A common practice among the Old Testament prophets was to refer to countries by some representative feature, such as a king (Isa 14:4; Ezek 28:2), a god (Isa 46:1; Jer 48:46), a river (Isa 8:7; Jer 2:18), a mountain (Isa 1:27; Ezek 35:2), a tribe (Isa 7:2; Jer 49:8), or a city (Isa 9:8-9; Jer 49:3). The reader of the prophets will therefore find that the northern kingdom Israel is often called either by the name of its leading tribe, Ephraim, or by the name of its capital, Samaria. In the same way the southern kingdom Judah is sometimes called by the name of its capital, Jerusalem. Among foreign nations, those most commonly referred to by their capital cities are Assyria (called Nineveh) and Syria (called Damascus).

Names of Israelites

During the years of the captivity in Babylon and the subsequent reconstruction of Israel, it became increasingly common to refer to Israelites as Jews. The background to this change of usage goes back to the time of the divided kingdom.

When the people of the former northern kingdom (Israel) were taken captive to various countries by Assyria, they became absorbed into the nations where they lived and largely lost their national identity. But when the people of the former southern kingdom (Judah) were taken into captivity in Babylon, they retained their national identity. The people of Judah were called Judeans, which was later shortened to 'Jew'.

After Persia's conquest of Babylon, captives from Babylon returned to the ancient Israelite homeland. This meant that most of those involved in the rebuilding of Israel were Judeans, or Jews. But they were also Israelites, according to the meaning of the name that went back to the nation's origins. There was no longer any division in Israel between north and south, and the names 'Israelite' and 'Jew', along with the ancient name 'Hebrew', were used interchangeably (Jer 34:9; John 1:19,47; 2 Cor 11:22; Gal. 2:14).

OUTLINE

1:1-6:13 JUDAH AN UNCLEAN PEOPLE

God judges Judah (1:1-9)

The opening chapter introduces most of the main issues that the prophet is to deal with, and therefore is a summary of the overall message of the book. The scene is one of judgment. God is the judge, his people the accused, heaven and earth the witnesses. The charge is that Judah has rebelled against God. Even animals are grateful for what their masters do for them, but the people of Judah show no gratitude to their heavenly Father (1:1-3).

Isaiah declares that the sinful people are more than ungrateful to God; they despise him (4). God has punished them repeatedly by sending enemy armies to attack them, with the aim that they see their sin and return to him. His punishment has been so consistent that Judah is likened to a person who has been beaten and flogged till he is bruised and cut from head to toe. But Judah is still stubbornly unrepentant (5-8). It would have been destroyed long ago, had not God shown mercy on account of the few faithful believers scattered throughout the nation (9).

Religious and moral corruption (1:10-31)

No doubt the people thought they were pleasing God by offering sacrifices, attending public worship services, and keeping the special Israelite feasts; but because their everyday lives were full of sin, their religious exercises were hateful to God. No matter how correct the form of worship, God will not accept it unless the people show a corresponding zeal for right behaviour (10-15).

The people must turn from their selfishness and treachery, and begin to show love and honesty in their everyday dealings if they want to be pleasing to God (16-17). He is ready and able to cleanse them, but whether he will depends on them. They must be willing to stop pleasing themselves and obey him instead. God wants them to enjoy prosperity in their land, but if they refuse to change their ways they will meet only disaster (18-20).

Jerusalem is so morally filthy that it is likened to a prostitute. The city that was once pure is now unclean. It is like silver that has become covered with dirt, like wine that has been watered down. The rulers and judges are corrupt, favouring the rich in return for bribes, but ignoring the poor and denying them justice (21-23).

God loves Jerusalem (Zion), and therefore he will not tolerate this wrongdoing. He will act in judgment against the rebels, like a refining fire that burns away the rubbish and leaves the metal pure. Corrupt rulers and judges will be replaced by those who are just. Jerusalem, instead of being like a prostitute, will be like a faithful wife (24-26). In the end the righteous will triumph, while the wicked will be overthrown (27-28).

People engage in heathen worship in the hope of increasing their prosperity, but in the end they will find that it does them no good (29). They are proud of the power they have gained through their evil ways, but they will find that, unless they turn from their corruption and idolatry, this power will be the means of their destruction. It will be like a spark that sets a forest on fire (30-31).

Baal worship

From the early days of their settlement in Canaan, the Israelites had been led astray by the worship of local gods, collectively known as Baalim (the Hebrew plural of Baal). Joshua warned the original settlers of the dangers of idolatry (Josh 24:14-15),

but by the time of the judges it was a major national problem. It continued to be a problem throughout the history of the Israelite kingdom, and was in fact one of the chief reasons for the captivity of both Israel and Judah. Because Isaiah, like most of the prophets, refers to Baal worship often, present-day readers need to have some understanding of how Baal worship functioned if they are to understand the book of Isaiah. For further details see introductory notes to Judges, sub-heading 'The religion of the Canaanites'.

Jerusalem as it should be and as it is (2:1-22)

God's people always looked for the day when Jerusalem would be the religious centre of the world, where people of all nations would go to be taught the ways of God. In that day there would be no more war, but contentment and prosperity (2:1-4). (A note on the new Jerusalem is included in the introduction to Chapters 40-66, where the subject of Jerusalem's future glory is considered more fully.) Such hope for the future is all the more reason why Judah should walk in the ways of God now (5).

But the people of Judah, instead of leading other nations to know God and enjoy his peace, follow the idolatry and superstitious practices of those nations. Instead of trusting in God, they spend much energy building up their wealth and increasing their fighting force (6-8). Because they proudly trust in their own achievements, God will bring them low. God alone is to be exalted (9-11).

Israel and Judah had always hoped for the time when God would give them victory over all their enemies. Isaiah warns them that before God acts against their enemies, he must act against them (12). All the things they proudly trust in for security, whether natural resources, defence fortifications or prosperous trade, will be destroyed (13-16). Neither arrogant self-confidence nor devotion to idols will save them (17-18).

People will see the worthlessness of the things in which they have trusted, and will flee in a last desperate effort for safety when the day of God's judgment comes (19-21). They will at last see the uselessness of putting confidence in anything of human origin (22).

Ungodly society (3:1-4:1)

Isaiah now gives a picture of the end of a society characterized by human self-sufficiency and self-centredness. The government collapses, resulting in a shortage of basic necessities such as food and water. Judah had previously depended for leadership on a variety of people, good and bad — statesmen, soldiers, judges, prophets, magicians — but now no one can be found to lead the country (3:1-3). Power falls into the hands of immature youths, and lawlessness results. People show no respect for former social values, but seize every opportunity to advance themselves and exploit their fellows (4-5).

In a time when food and clothing are so scarce, anyone who appears a little better off than others will be invited to take over the leadership in an effort to restore order in the chaotic city. But he will quickly make excuses and refuse the invitation, for no one will want to be leader in such a troubled time (6-7).

The people arrogantly declare themselves to be independent of God. They boast of their new-found moral freedom and are proud of their immoral acts (8-9). All the wrongdoers will suffer a fitting punishment, but the righteous will escape (10-11). The nation is almost without leadership, because the former leaders have either fled or been overthrown. Their corruption is the reason for the present crisis. They used their positions entirely for their own benefit, and now the nation has come to ruin (12-15).

These leaders oppressed and robbed the poor so that their wives could dress themselves lavishly. But women who once enjoyed the luxury of the upper classes now suffer humiliation (16-17). Their extravagance is replaced by poverty, their vanity by shame (18-24). They once tried to tempt men with their artificial beauty, but now they will find themselves begging men to marry them, so that they will not be left childless. So many men will be killed in battle that there will not be enough husbands for all the women (25-4:1).

New life (4:2-6)

Having judged his people and removed sin, God blesses the righteous that remain. This new blessing is symbolized by a tree that bursts into new life and by a field that brings fresh growth. A new Israel is born where the people of God are those whom he has saved and made holy (2-4). In the new Jerusalem God dwells among and protects his people in a relationship far more wonderful than in previous times (5-6).

God's love and Judah's response (5:1-30)

Judah and Israel together are likened to God's vineyard. God did everything possible to make it healthy, beautiful and fruitful, and he expected a good harvest of grapes, but the people brought God none of the fruit he expected (5:1-4). He therefore will cease to care for them, so that they might be left to suffer whatever ruin their sin brings upon them. Israel has already been destroyed and Judah will now follow (5-7).

Examples of the sins that brought this judgment are now given. The first people to be condemned are the rich landowners, who lend money to the poor at high rates of interest, then seize their lands when they are unable to pay their debts. But the houses and lands that the rich have dishonestly gained will bring them no profit (8-10).

Next to be condemned are the leading citizens of Jerusalem, who live only for pleasure and have fallen under the power of strong drink. Their greed will be replaced by tormenting thirst when they are carried captive into a foreign country. Many will die. The 'greedy one' in that day will be the world of the dead (Hebrew: *sheol*), who will eagerly 'swallow up' the multitudes killed by the enemy (11-14). God's justice will be carried out upon Jerusalem and the wicked city will be left in ruins. Its only inhabitants will be sheep and goats, for all the people will have been taken into captivity (15-17).

The prophet pictures the people of Jerusalem as having so much sin that they pull it along by the cartload. Some actually boast of the amount of sin they commit and challenge God to stop them (18-19). Others try to reverse God's standards by calling evil good and good evil. They claim that they know everything and have no need of God (20-21). Judges and officials love the social life of the upper classes. They are not interested in administering justice, but only in increasing their own luxury through collecting bribes (22-23).

When a nation claims to be God's people but defiantly ignores his standards, it only invites his judgment. It is like a field of dry grass about to be burnt (24-25). God responds by sending against it an enemy nation whose army is so highly disciplined, well equipped and fiercely aggressive that Judah cannot possible escape (26-30).

God's call of Isaiah (6:1-13)

Isaiah has gone to some length to describe Judah's spiritual and moral corruption before he mentions God's call to him to be a prophet. His reason for doing this seems to be that he wants his readers to see why God called him. Their understanding of conditions in Judah will help them understand the sort of task that lay before him.

King Uzziah's death marked the end of an era of prosperity unequalled in Judah's history. Yet this era brought with it the corruption that Isaiah has just described, and left the people with no respect for God and no knowledge of what his holiness demanded of them. Isaiah sees that God is glorious and majestic, the supreme ruler over Judah and all other nations. Even God's sinless heavenly servants dare not look on his glory, but busy themselves serving and praising him (6:1-4).

The vision of God's holiness makes Isaiah realize that not only are the people among whom he lives sinful, but so too is he. Therefore, before he can be God's messenger to others, his own sin must be cleansed. God graciously does this for him by removing his sin and transferring to him the benefits of God's holiness, symbolized in the coals from the altar (5-7).

When God asks who will take his message to such a corrupt people, Isaiah volunteers; but God quickly tells him that his task is going to be difficult. The more he preaches, the more his hearers will reject his message. As a result they will sink deeper into sin, and so make it increasingly difficult for them ever to turn to God and be forgiven (8-10).

Isaiah asks God how long such hardness will last, and receives the reply that there is no hope for any rapid improvement. On the contrary the condition of the nation will worsen, till eventually judgment must fall. Judah's cities will be destroyed and its people taken into captivity (11-12). But God will preserve the few who remain faithful to him, and from these will grow up a new people for God. To illustrate this destruction, apparent death and new life, God gives Isaiah the picture of a huge tree that is chopped down, so that only the stump remains; but from this stump springs new life (13).

7:1-12:6 JUDAH IN THE REIGN OF AHAZ

Chapters 7-12 belong to the reign of Ahaz, when Pekah the king of Israel and Rezin the king of Syria (Aram) joined forces to attack Ahaz, with the aim of forcing Judah into their anti-Assyrian alliance. Before reading these chapters, readers should be familiar with the historical background given in the introduction under the heading 'Israel and Syria attack Judah'.

Isaiah's message for Ahaz (7:1-25)

When the Judean king Ahaz hears of the approach of the Israelite-Syrian army, he and all his people are terrified (7:1-2). While Ahaz is inspecting Jerusalem's water supply in preparation for the siege, Isaiah meets him and points out that he need not fear Israel or Syria, nor need he ask Assyria for help. God is on the side of Judah. Pekah and Rezin plan

to conquer Judah and put their own king on Judah's throne, but they will not succeed. They think they can overthrow Judah in a fiery conquest, but they are no more dangerous than the smoke from two smouldering sticks (3-6). Israel and Syria, along with their kings, are nearing the end of their existence. If Ahaz believes God he has nothing to fear; but if he does not, nothing will save him (7-9).

(Only three years after this prophecy, Syria fell to Assyria, and ten years later so did Israel. Within 65 years of Isaiah's prophecy, people of the former northern kingdom had become so scattered that they no longer had any national identity; see v. 8b.)

God then invites Ahaz to ask for a sign as an assurance of God's help. Ahaz responds with an attempt to appear religious, by saying that he will not put God to the test (10-12).

Whether Ahaz asks for a sign or not, God promises to give one. Ahaz will have reassurance that God is with Judah when he hears of the birth of a child whose mother has named him Immanuel (meaning 'God with us'). By the time this child is two or three years old, Israel and Syria will be powerless to trouble Judah further. But at the same time Judah will be troubled by a different enemy, the nation Assyria. There will be extensive damage, particularly to the farmlands. Crops will be ruined and the people will have to rely on animals and insects for their food (13-17; see also notes on 9:1-7 below).

Armies from Egypt and Assyria will invade Judah, covering the the land like insects and leaving it bare and fruitless (18-20). With all the crops destroyed, cultivated land will become wild again. The scattered inhabitants who remain will wander from place to place with their few animals, living off the products of these animals and any other wild food they can find (21-25).

Isaiah's son a sign for the people (8:1-10)

God then gives a second sign to guarantee the defeat of Israel and Syria. The sign of Immanuel had been given to the royal household, but this sign is given to the people. Another child is to be born, this one to Isaiah and his wife. The name of the child, Maher-shalal-hash-baz (meaning 'the spoil hastens, the plunder comes quickly'; cf. GNB: Quick Loot, Fast Plunder), is announced publicly in advance so that the birth of the child will give added assurance to the people that God's promises come true. The significance of the sign is that within a year or so of the child's birth, Judah's enemies (Israel and Syria) will be defeated and their goods seized by the conqueror (8:1-4).

The people of Judah, however, are unmoved; they still refuse to believe. They reject the help of God (likened to the waters of the gently flowing canal of Shiloah in Jerusalem), and prefer instead the help of Assyria (likened to the waters of the mighty river Euphrates). This river will not only destroy Israel and Syria, but will overflow into Judah, the land of Immanuel, almost drowning the people (5-8).

Then, turning to address Israel and Syria, Isaiah tells them that their plans for the conquest of Judah will not succeed. They have no chance of victory, because Judah is the land of Immanuel – 'God with us' (9-10).

Judah rejects Isaiah's preaching (8:11-22)

Once again God reminds Isaiah to trust in him alone. Isaiah is not to follow Ahaz and the people, whether in fearing the Israelite-Syrian alliance or in trusting in Judah's alliance with Assyria (11-12). God should be the means of Judah's safety; but if the people do not trust in him they will find that he is the means of their destruction (13-15).

When neither the king nor the people heed the messages he brings them from God, Isaiah ceases his public preaching for a time. He concentrates instead on building up the faith of the few who believe God and who will be preserved through the coming judgment. They will guard and preserve the teaching that God has delivered to his people through Isaiah (16-17; cf. 6:13).

This reminds Isaiah of the truth of the signs that God gave to Judah through him and his sons. The elder son, Shearjashub (meaning 'a remnant shall return'), speaks of judgment on Judah from which only the faithful few will be saved. The younger son, Maher-shalal-hash-baz (meaning 'the spoil hastens, the plunder comes quickly'), suggests that Assyria will invade and plunder not only Israel and Syria, but also Judah (18; cf. 7:3; 8:1-4). Nothing but terrifying judgment awaits a people who have turned from God and his teaching to practise witchcraft and spiritism (19-22).

Messiah, Prince of Peace (9:1-7)

The southern kingdom under Ahaz was about to enter a time of increasing distress and darkness (see 8:21-22). The northern kingdom was about to be attacked by Assyria, and the tribes of Zebulun and Naphtali in the far north Galilean region were about to be taken into captivity (2 Kings 15:29). Yet out of this darkness and from this conquered northern area will come the great deliverer, the Messiah, to lead his people to victory and to introduce an era of light,

joy and peace. Oppressors will be overthrown and war will be banished (9:1-5).

This Messiah is the true Immanuel, 'God with us', and he was pictured in the child born in Ahaz's day. The sign of Immanuel was given not merely to Ahaz personally, but to Ahaz as representative of the dynasty of David. Now the eternal God comes to dwell among humankind in the person of Jesus Christ, the mighty Messiah-King, the great descendant of David, who brings everlasting peace and rules with justice for ever (6-7; cf. 7:13-14; Matt 1:21-23; 2:2).

The fall of Israel (9:8-10:4)

Isaiah now describes the situation in the northern kingdom Israel, which becomes weakened by enemy attacks and finally is conquered by Assyria. The northerners refuse to acknowledge that God is the one who has brought this catastrophe upon them. They make a show of self-assurance by saying they will rebuild, bigger and better, whatever their enemies have destroyed (8-12).

Because the people refuse to repent, God will punish them further. His purpose is to remove the whole nation from the land (13-14). Sin dominates in every level of Israel's society, from civil and religious leaders to the common people. Therefore, all must fall under God's judgment (15-17).

As a fire destroys a forest, so the people's wickedness has destroyed their nation. This catastrophe has been sent by God, as a punishment on the people for their sins (18-19). They are greedy and jealous, and attack each other like a lot of wild animals (20-21). Special blame is placed on the judges and civil leaders who, through injustice and corruption, have oppressed the people while making themselves rich. But their wealth will not save them when God sends a foreign army to destroy the nation and take its survivors captive (10:1-4).

Assyria's pride and punishment (10:5-34)

God is angry with the rebellious people of Israel and has used Assyria to punish them (5-6). Assyria, however, has no concern for God's purposes and thinks it has won its victories by its own might. It therefore decides to attack Jerusalem, confident that it will conquer Judah as it has conquered other nations (7-9). It thinks that because the gods of other nations have not been able to save them from Assyria's might, the God of Judah will not be able to save Jerusalem (10-11). This boastful self-confidence and lack of respect for Yahweh is Assyria's big mistake. God will not allow it to go unpunished (12-14).

Assyria is merely a tool that God uses to do his work, but when that tool tries to make itself greater than the one who uses it, it must be destroyed. Assyria will come to a humiliating end. It will be like a mighty forest that is burnt down, like a strong soldier who grows sick and dies (15-19).

Israel may be destroyed and Judah attacked, but God will always preserve the remnant of faithful believers who trust in him and not in military alliances. Those who trust in Assyria will come under Assyria's power, and in the end will cause their nation to be taken into captivity. But a remnant will return and rebuild the nation (20-23).

On the basis of these certainties, Isaiah appeals to Judah once again not to fear Assyria nor to ask help from it. Assyria will be defeated, just as enemies in Israel's past history have been (24-27). Isaiah then paints a vivid picture of an Assyrian attack on Jerusalem — the setting up of the base camp, the rapid approach over the mountains and through the valleys, the conquest of towns along the way, the flight of the citizens (28-32). But the Assyrian army is suddenly smashed by God, like a giant tree that is chopped down and comes crashing to the ground (33-34).

The Messiah's kingdom (11:1-12:6)

A leading theme of this part of the book is that God preserves a remnant out of the destruction of Israel and Judah. Earlier this remnant was likened to the stump of a tree from which springs new life (see 6:13). The remnant is now identified with the royal line of David (son of Jesse) from which comes the Messiah (11:1). The Messiah reverences God and, having the Spirit of God in unlimited measure, knows how to apply God's wisdom in ruling God's people. He is the Prince of Peace who governs with perfect love and perfect justice. He is not deceived by outward appearances, and has a particular concern for those who are the victims of injustice and oppression (2-5).

In the Messiah's kingdom there is no hate, fear, cruelty or danger, but perfect peace and harmony. People truly know God, and therefore they no longer do evil to each other (6-9).

The blessings of the Messiah's kingdom were foreshadowed in the return of the Jews from their captivity in Babylon. The prophet pictures God's people coming from many nations to dwell together under the Messiah's rule (10-12). The tension that once existed between Israel and Judah is now gone, for the two kingdoms are united again. They work together in overpowering any nation that threatens the peace of the messianic kingdom (13-14). In a

migration of people likened to the exodus from Egypt, those held in foreign captivity return to their homeland (15-16).

Just as Moses and his people sang a song of praise to God for his deliverance from Egypt, so the returned exiles sing their praise to God for his deliverance from Babylon. Now that he has forgiven them, they have no need to fear. God's salvation brings with it confidence, strength, refreshment and joy (12:1-3). Those who have received this salvation not only want to praise God, but they also want to tell others of him and all that he has done (4-6).

13:1-23:18 MESSAGES FOR VARIOUS NATIONS

All the nations are under the rule of God, who controls their rise to power and their final destruction according to his purposes. This is the truth that the prophet teaches in the collection of prophecies against various nations in Chapters 13 to 23. The first message is for Babylon, which in Isaiah's day had not yet risen to a position of international power. The fall of Babylon that is pictured in these chapters would not take place for more than one hundred and fifty years.

The pride and fall of Babylon (13:1-14:23)

Although a combined army of Medes and Persians overthrew Babylon, God was the one who moved them to do it. The prophet pictures the scene as the Medo-Persian army gets ready for battle, with soldiers shouting, signalling, organizing themselves and preparing their weapons (13:1-5). The people of Babylon shake with fear as they see that defeat is upon them (6-8). It is, for them, the day of the Lord, the day of God's great intervention in judgment (9-10). The chief cause of Babylon's punishment is its pride, for it boasted of its achievements, mocked God and dealt with people ruthlessly. When God decides that he will no longer tolerate the arrogance of the haughty, he pours out his wrath (11-13).

Enemy armies who invade the proud city show no mercy on its inhabitants, whether they be native Babylonians or foreigners (14-16). The Babylonians try to bribe the Medes into turning back, but the Medes will not listen. They carry on with the slaughter and destruction, till the people are wiped out (17-18). The city that was once beautiful is left a ruin, inhabited only by wild animals (19-22).

A further reason for the overthrow of Babylon is now revealed. God wants to break the power of Babylon, so that the captive Jews can be released and return to their homeland. Peoples who once oppressed the Jews will now help them rebuild their ruined nation (14:1-2). (The permission for the Jews' return was given by the conquering Persian king, Cyrus.)

Then comes a song that the Jews sang to the disgrace of their former master, the king of Babylon. The king is seen as the embodiment of all Babylon's pride and evil (3-6). Now that he is dead and the captive Jews are free from his rule, the whole world rejoices. Nations feel a sense of relief after years of Babylonian oppression (7-8).

Those in the world of the dead welcome the fallen king, reminding him that though he was all-powerful in life, he is no better than they in death (9-11). Arrogant and ambitious, seeking after the highest place, the greatest honour and supreme power, he is brought down to the lowest place, the greatest shame and complete weakness (12-15). Those who see him can scarcely recognize him as the one who destroyed kingdoms and enslaved entire nations. They find it hard to believe that one who terrified the world can come to such a humiliating end (16-17).

Most kings are buried with honour, but this king is treated with disgrace. He is left unburied, his corpse thrown out to rot in the sun. His sons also are to be killed, to make sure they have no opportunity to copy their father (18-21). The power of Babylon must be destroyed, so that the nation can never rise again (22-23).

Concerning Assyria and Philistia (14:24-32)

In Isaiah's day the immediate threat came not from Babylon but from Assyria. But Assyria will suffer the same fate as Babylon. It may invade the land of Judah, but in that same land it will be defeated and its power over Judah broken (24-25). The almighty God has determined this, and therefore no one will be able to prevent it (26-27).

Ahaz had always tried to follow a pro-Assyrian policy, in spite of objections from Isaiah. Ahaz's son and successor, Hezekiah, was firmly opposed to Assyria. The rulers of neighbouring Philistia apparently knew this, for soon after the death of Ahaz they sent representatives to try to persuade Hezekiah to join them in rebelling against Assyria. It seemed a suitable opportunity, as Assyria had just suffered some sort of military setback. Isaiah warns against being foolishly optimistic. Assyria will soon recover and meet any rebellion with a ferocity greater than before, leaving the land desolate (28-31). The answer to give the Philistine messengers is that Judah will not cooperate in the plan but will trust entirely in God (32).

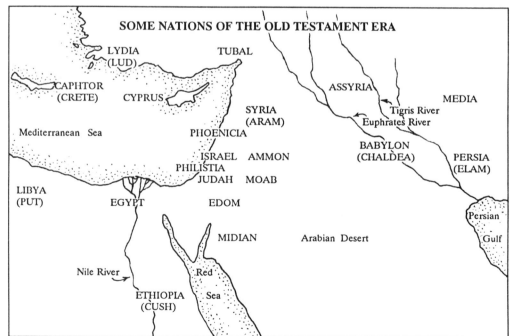

SOME NATIONS OF THE OLD TESTAMENT ERA

Devastation in Moab (15:1-16:14)

The place names mentioned in these two chapters indicate that the attack on Moab comes from the north, most likely from Assyria. The attack is swift and ruthless, and towns fall in a night. Wherever a person looks, there is mourning (15:1-4). Even Isaiah weeps as he sees the people fleeing pitifully, rushing along the streets, across the streams and over the fields that have been damaged by the invading armies. They take with them whatever precious possessions they can carry (5-7). There has already been plenty of bloodshed, but Isaiah sees that more is to come (8-9).

In desperation Moab's leaders send an urgent request to Jerusalem, asking the Judean leaders to allow Moab's fleeing and scattered refugees to enter Judah. With their request they send a gift of lambs as an expression of appreciation for the help they hope to receive (16:1-4a). The messengers from Moab try to win the Judeans' favour by declaring their confidence in Judah's future. They express the hope that Judah will conquer all enemies, and that the dynasty of David will continue to prosper till it achieves fully its ideals of faithfulness, love, righteousness and justice (4b-5).

However, the Judean rulers, remembering the Moabites' insults in the past, do not trust them. They refuse to help, no matter how much the Moabites weep and wail (6-7). Nevertheless, Isaiah feels pity for them as he sees their country ruined and their vineyards destroyed in the devastation of war (8-11). Moab's hour of judgment has come, and all the Moabites' prayers to their gods will not save them (12-14).

Syria and Israel condemned (17:1-14)

This message belongs to the time of Ahaz, when Israel and Syria joined forces to attack Judah. The two attackers will themselves be destroyed (17:1-3). Israel in particular will suffer, because the nation has turned away from God. Throughout the nation, however, the scattered few remain faithful to God and these will be spared. They are likened to the odd pieces of fruit that remain on the trees after the harvest has been gathered (4-6).

The judgments will be so severe that some of the people will turn from their idolatry and cry to God for help. But for Israel as a whole there will be no help. The nation has followed Canaanite religious practices, and its destruction will be a fitting divine punishment (7-9). People plant sacred gardens and dedicate them to foreign gods, in the hope that this will bring rapid growth in their crops. But if they succeed in getting quick crops, those crops will be trampled and destroyed by the invading army (10-11).

By contrast the nation that remains faithful to God will be protected. Enemies may come against it like a flood, but (to change the illustration) they will be turned back like chaff blown by the wind (12-14).

Alliance with Ethiopia refused (18:1-7)

Along the upper reaches of the Nile River was the country known as Ethiopia (RSV), Sudan (GNB) or Cush (NIV). It was a land of tall smooth-skinned people, but also a land plagued by swarms of buzzing insects. From this country a group of government representatives came to visit Judah, travelling down the Nile and across to Jerusalem. They apparently hoped to gain Hezekiah's cooperation in an attack against Assyria. Isaiah sends them back as he had done the Philistine representatives earlier (18:1-2; cf. 14:28-32).

Judah's need is to trust in God, not in foreign alliances. Even if the Assyrian army reaches the mountains of Judah and signals for the final attack on Jerusalem, the Judeans must keep trusting in God. God has been quietly watching the Assyrians' advance and at the right time he will cut them down, as a farmer cuts down the ripened grain. Birds will feed on the corpses of the dead soldiers (3-6). A group of Ethiopian representatives will then come to Jerusalem again, this time to thank God for his defeat of the Assyrians (7).

Egypt's punishment and conversion (19:1-25)

At various times Judah was tempted to rely on Egypt for help against aggressors. Isaiah shows in this message how useless such reliance is. He pictures the day when God acts against Egypt, and sees that all Egypt's magic and all her gods cannot save her. Civil war breaks out, followed by the harsh rule of a dictator (19:1-4).

Drought causes the Nile, Egypt's only water supply, to dry up. This ruins the nation's farming, fishing and cotton industries, and creates nationwide unemployment (5-10). Try as they may, the nation's rulers and advisers cannot solve its problems, for those problems have been sent upon them by God (11-13). As a result the nation is reduced to helplessness. No one knows what to do (14-15).

Having been humbled, Egypt fears Judah. It also fears Judah's almighty God, Yahweh (16-17). Judeans then migrate to Egypt and establish the worship of Yahweh in places where people had once worshipped heathen gods. God now treats the people of Egypt as previously he treated those of

Israel and Judah. He delivers them from their oppressors, punishes them for their sins, and forgives them when they repent (18-22). People from Egypt, along with people from other former enemies of Israel-Judah, will have an equal part with the people of Israel-Judah in God's universal kingdom (23-25).

Further warning against alliances (20:1-6)

Previous messages have shown Hezekiah the uselessness of forming alliances with Philistia, Ethiopia or Egypt for the purpose of fighting against Assyria (see 14:28-32; 18:1-6; 19:1-15). To emphasize the point afresh, Isaiah acts a message for everybody to see. He dresses himself as a prisoner of war, to show the people of Judah what will happen to them if they enter foreign alliances instead of trusting God for victory over Assyria. After three years the people have proof of the wisdom of Isaiah's advice. The Assyrians capture the Philistine city of Ashdod, after which they invade Egypt and Ethiopia and carry away many captives (20:1-4).

Philistia's hope of military help from Egypt and Ethiopia is sadly disappointed. This causes Judah to realize how disastrous it would have been to trust in any of those countries for its security (5-6).

Vision of the fall of Babylon (21:1-10)

The next message of judgment concerns 'the wilderness of the sea' (RSV), which we soon learn is another name for mighty Babylon. The prophet has a vision of its destruction, which occurred in 539 BC when the combined forces of Persia (Elam) and Media conquered the city (21:1-2). (Daniel 5:1-31 records the story of Babylon's capture while the king was feasting with his mighty men.)

Although the prophet always longed for the destruction of Judah's oppressors, now that the time has come he turns away in horror. The sight of the slaughter is terrifying (3-4). Babylon's leaders, who should be preparing the nation's defences, are all feasting merrily when the enemy attacks. They are suddenly stirred to action, but it is too late (5).

In his vision the prophet sends a man to Babylon to report what he sees (6-7). The man reports that he sees the invading army approaching, and he knows that this is the end for Babylon (8-9). This is good news for God's people, as it means that the nation that so long oppressed them has finally been overthrown (10).

Edomites and Arabs (21:11-17)

The prophet has a short message for the people of Edom, who cry out from their stronghold in Mt Seir, asking how much longer they must be oppressed.

The answer is not encouraging. They will get a brief relief from their sufferings, but then they will be oppressed again (11-12).

Wandering Arabs also will suffer from the cruel attacks of the invaders. Thirsty and hungry, they will flee from place to place looking for safety and shelter (13-15). But whatever refuge they find will be only temporary, and within a year even the bravest of the Arab tribal peoples will virtually be wiped out (16-17).

Jerusalem besieged (22:1-25)

In Judah, the land where the prophet had his visions of judgment on other nations, he recalls one of God's judgments on Judah, namely, the Assyrians' siege of Jerusalem. On that occasion the city was saved only through the faith of Hezekiah and Isaiah (2 Kings 18:13-19:37).

Ignoring the gracious intervention of God that had miraculously saved them, the people celebrate as if they had won the victory themselves. Isaiah is disgusted at the light-hearted attitude of the people, particularly when he recalls their cowardly behaviour during the siege. The city's leading officials fled the doomed city, only to be killed or captured by the enemy (22:1-4).

The prophet describes the scene during the siege. Outside Jerusalem enemy forces spread across the countryside, while battering rams try to smash the city walls. Soldiers hired from various countries are eager to start fighting (5-8a). Inside Jerusalem soldiers rush to the army headquarters for weapons, and there is much activity to save the city's water supply. Where the city wall is crumbling under the enemy attacks, the Jerusalemites desperately build it up, even demolishing their houses to obtain bricks for the work. But they do not turn to God for help (8b-11).

Other citizens, however, feel sure that Jerusalem will fall. They do nothing to help, but enjoy themselves as much as they can while they can. They show no repentance for the sins that have brought this disaster upon them (12-14).

Shebna, Hezekiah's chief official, is condemned for using his position for the benefit of himself instead of for the benefit of the people. He loved the honour of a procession of chariots preceding him wherever he went, but now he will be shamefully removed from office. Instead of having a magnificent funeral, he will be buried in disgrace (15-19). His position, which was the top decision-making position in the land after the king, will be taken by Eliakim (20-23). But Eliakim will be used by his relatives and friends for their own advantage, and this will eventually be the cause of his downfall (24-25). (By the time of the siege, Eliakim had already been promoted and Shebna demoted; see 2 Kings 18:18.)

Judgment on Phoenicia (23:1-18)

Commerce was the source of Phoenicia's power. Its merchant navy was well known throughout the ancient world, and Phoenician traders sailed to ports far and near. Phoenicia's own ports, Tyre and Sidon, were among the most prosperous cities of the time, but because of their commercial greed and corruption they too will be destroyed.

The prophet pictures the scene in various places when Tyre falls. Phoenician traders who have sailed to Cyprus are shocked when they hear the news. The sea without Phoenician ships is like a mother without children. Egypt panics on hearing the news, because her valuable grain trade is now ruined (23:1-5).

In former times the Phoenicians made colonies of other countries, but now they are forced to flee to other countries in search of refuge (6-7). The proud people are humiliated, and this humiliation has been brought upon them by God himself (8-9). In the far off port of Tarshish (in Spain) there is confusion and despair, because the city has depended much on Phoenician trade for its well-being. God has now destroyed Phoenicia, and there will be no escape for its greedy merchants (10-12). The nation that God uses to carry out his judgment on Phoenicia is Babylon (Chaldea) (13-14).

After an interval Phoenicia will revive, and will show the same interest as formerly in commercial activities. The prophet likens these activities to those of a prostitute, since they are guided by immoral greed and selfish desires, and give no thought for God's standards (15-17). Nevertheless, God will receive glory even from Phoenicia. In due course God's people will benefit from the wealth and merchandise of Phoenicia, and they will dedicate some of this to God (18; cf. Matt 15:21-28; Acts 21:2-6).

24:1-27:13 FINAL JUDGMENT AND SALVATION

The judgment of various contemporary nations leads the prophet to consider God's final great judgment on the world. Naturally, his illustrations are taken from the world that he knew, and the nations he mentions are those of his time, but the principles of judgment and salvation that he presents are those of the unchangeable God. They will find their fullest expression in God's mighty triumph at the end of the world's history.

Some will mourn, others rejoice (24:1-25:12)

When God judges sinners, he will make no distinctions on the basis of status or class. All who have rebelled against God and ignored his law will be punished (24:1-5). There will be few survivors (6). In a world where people previously lived mainly to enjoy themselves, the most noticeable feature will be an absence of joy and merriment (7-11). The only ones spared in the widespread judgment will be the few who have remained faithful to God. These are compared to the odd grapes left here and there after harvest (12-13).

This remnant then praises God for his salvation. The prophet finds it difficult to share their joyous feelings, for he thinks of the sinful people around him and foresees their terrible punishment (14-16). There will be no way of escape when that day of judgment comes. The world will stagger and fall under the weight of its sins (17-20).

High rank will not save those who have rebelled against God. The rulers of nations will be thrown together like prisoners locked in a crowded dungeon as they await their final punishment (21-22). After all the sinners are removed, God will reign in glory so dazzling that even the sun and moon will appear dark by comparison (23).

At this reminder of the final triumph and glory of God, the prophet breaks forth in a song of praise to him whose victory has been planned from the beginning. When people see God destroy the things they have proudly built, they will turn and praise him (25:1-3). He will give relief to those who are oppressed and will silence the boastful oppressors (4-5).

God will celebrate his victory with a great feast, and introduce an era of joy where all signs of mourning are removed and the possibility of death is gone for ever (6-8). God's people rejoice in his salvation (9), but his enemies suffer humiliating destruction. Their boasting cannot save them, and all their clever achievements finish in ruin (10-12).

Final victory for the godly (26:1-27:1)

Having destroyed the city built by human hands (that is, humankind's whole ungodly way of life; 25:2), God now builds his city. It is a city for the righteous, an eternal dwelling place for those who have experienced the perfect peace that comes through complete trust in God (26:1-3). Those who trust in him have stability and security, but those who trust in themselves are overthrown. God's city stands for ever; the world's city is smashed to the ground and trampled in the dust (4-6).

Godly people long to know God and his ways better, so that they can live righteously according to his directions. They desire this knowledge for others also, because only when people know God can they truly know what righteousness is (7-9). The ungodly do not know God and so cannot live uprightly (10-11). The righteous know that God cares for them, and they respond with loyalty to him, even when they are oppressed by their enemies (12-13). In due course, however, the enemies are destroyed, but the righteous have peace. Their numbers increase, and God's blessing spreads throughout the land (14-15).

The righteous then recall how they have cried to God in their distress, but have received no apparent answer. All their efforts and all their expectations have come to nothing. They feel the disappointment and frustration of a woman who suffers birth pains but produces no child. Many of the godly have died without seeing any victory (16-18). Their victory must therefore lie in the future, when their bodies will be triumphantly raised from death (19).

God's people need not fear his wrath, for he will protect them when he carries out his work of judgment on a sinful world (20-21). By contrast his enemies, symbolized here by fierce monsters, will suffer his deadly punishment (27:1).

Shameful exile and glorious return (27:2-13)

From its beginning, Israel was God's chosen people. God compares the nation to a beautiful vineyard, which he has cared for and guarded continually (2-3). Israel's enemies are likened to thorns and briars, and unless they repent of their wrongdoing and seek God's forgiveness, they will suffer a fiery destruction (4-5). Israel, by contrast, will flourish like a giant tree and bring blessing to the whole world (6).

Before that can happen, however, God must deal with Israel because of its sins. The nation, in both its northern and southern kingdoms, must be punished because it has turned away from the true God to serve the false gods of its neighbours. God does not punish his people as severely as he punishes his enemies. Those nations he destroys, but his own people he only sends into captivity, so that when their sins are removed they can return to their own land (7-9).

The desolation of their homeland is a just punishment that God sends upon his rebellious people (10-11). But when their punishment is ended, they will be gathered from many places back into their land, as grain is gathered together after it has been threshed (12-13).

28:1-33:24 HEZEKIAH AND THE ASSYRIANS

Before reading Chapters 28-33, readers should be familiar with the historical background found in the introduction under the heading 'Judah's new policies under Hezekiah'. Hezekiah reversed the policies of his father Ahaz. Whereas Ahaz sought help from Assyria to oppose Israel and Syria, Hezekiah sought help from Egypt to oppose Assyria. Isaiah opposed both policies alike. Faith in God, not reliance on foreign powers, is Judah's only hope for survival. The messages collected in these chapters were probably delivered by Isaiah during the three or four years from Hezekiah's revolt against Assyria to the miraculous rescue of Jerusalem in 701 BC.

Bad leadership and its results (28:1-29)

Although his rebukes are directed mainly against Judah, Isaiah opens the section with a short message he once preached against Israel. (The reason for this, as Isaiah will soon point out, is that the message is now equally relevant to Judah.)

The nation's rulers are a lot of drunkards, who live only to enjoy themselves and do not care about the welfare of the people. Because they are heavy wine-drinkers, they are likened to a flourishing vineyard. A severe hailstorm (symbol of the Assyrian invasion) will now destroy the vineyard, and enemy soldiers will trample the grapes underfoot (28:1-4). Nevertheless, the few who remain faithful to God will not be forsaken. God will give them his wisdom and strength, enabling them to come through the crisis successfully (5-6).

At this point Isaiah makes it plain that his prophecy against Israel applies also to Judah. Its leaders also are drunkards, even the religious leaders (7-8). They are annoyed at Isaiah for his persistent teaching, and indignantly ask him if he thinks he is teaching children. They are tired of hearing his same simple message over and over, telling them to turn from their evil ways and trust in God (9-10). Through Isaiah God has promised them true peace and perfect rest. If they refuse to listen to these clear and simple words, God will speak to them in a different language, one that they will not understand. That is, they will hear the foreign language of the Assyrian armies whom God sends against them to punish them (11-13).

Judah has made an agreement with Egypt to rebel against Assyria, but God sees it as a rebellion against him. It is like an agreement with the world of the dead instead of with the living God. It is based on falsehood instead of on God's truth (14-15). God is the only reliable foundation on whom Judah can build its hopes. If the Judeans trusted in him, they would not need to go running to Egypt for help (16). God will act in righteous judgment against his faithless people. Their alliance with Egypt will be as powerless against Assyria as a temporary shelter is against raging floodwaters (17-18).

Day and night the ferocious Assyrian attack will go on. The people of Judah will find that all their preparation has not been enough to give them the comfort they hoped for (19-20). In the place where David punished his enemies, David's people will be punished by their enemies. And the more they ignore Isaiah's warnings, the more difficult it will be for them to escape the punishment (21-22; cf. 1 Chron 14:11,16).

A farmer knows from experience that he must use different methods of planting and threshing for different crops. God likewise uses different methods in his dealings with people, and his actions are always based on his perfect knowledge (23-29).

God saves Jerusalem (29:1-24)

Isaiah then presents a frightening picture of the Assyrian siege of Jerusalem (called 'Ariel' in RSV and NIV, and 'God's altar' in GNB). The people think that their city is safe and that the cycle of annual festivals will go on indefinitely. Suddenly, they find their lives threatened by a terrible siege. Throughout the city people are distressed and humiliated, as the doomed city cries out to God, as it were, from the grave (29:1-4).

The enemy armies think their conquest of Jerusalem is certain, when unexpectedly God intervenes and miraculously saves the city. The enemy's disappointment is like that of a distressed person who has a pleasant dream, then awakes only to find it is not true (5-8; 2 Kings 19:35).

As usual the people of Judah do not respond to Isaiah's prophecy. They are morally dull and spiritually blind, and seem to have no ability at all to understand God's message. It is to them like a book that remains closed (9-12). They carry out the religious traditions, but they know nothing of God and are not even interested in him. They are fit only for God's judgment (13-14).

In planning alliances without thought for God, the people of Judah are deliberately ignoring the God who created them (15-16). God can do more

for them than they can ask or think. He has planned a great future for Judah, where those who humbly trust in him will find complete satisfaction and contentment (17-19). However, those who are cruel, dishonest, selfish and unbelieving will have no share in this future, because God will first remove them in judgment (20-21).

When sin is removed there will be no more cause for shame. God's people will truly belong to him, and will have a genuine desire to understand his character and to walk in his ways (22-24).

The folly of relying on Egypt (30:1-33)

All Isaiah's warnings against an alliance with Egypt are in vain. As he learns that a group of Judean representatives is on its way to Egypt, he points out again how disastrous this alliance will prove to be. Judah's reliance on Egypt is against God's will and in the end will bring only disgrace upon Judah (30:1-5).

Isaiah pictures the dangerous journey, as a caravan of donkeys and camels carry Judah's payment through the dry southern region of Judah towards Egypt. He knows that the journey is a waste of time, money and effort (6). Judah thinks of Egypt as a great dragon (Rahab) that will help it overthrow enemy Assyria, but Isaiah knows that Egypt will be powerless to help — like a dragon that sits still and does nothing (7).

The prophet writes this discouraging message down as a permanent record that the people have been warned (8). But the sinful people do not want to hear messages that come from God. They want to hear only those things that please them (9-11). They trust for their national defence in a treaty with Egypt, which, to them, is like a high wall that protects them from enemy Assyria. But this wall will collapse on top of them (12-14).

Instead of trusting quietly in God the people trust in military strength. This is only inviting defeat, because the military strength of Assyria is greater than that of Egypt (15-17). God wants to help his people, but first he wants them to learn to trust in him (18).

Despite Judah's rebellion, God in his mercy does not cast them off for ever (19). He is the great teacher who punishes his people when they turn from him, so that they might see their wrongdoing, give up their sinful ways and return to walk in the ways of God (20-22). Then God will pour out upon them the blessings of nature to an extent they have never before experienced (23-26). Upon their enemies, God will pour out his holy wrath (27-28). The people of God will celebrate their victory with much gladness and singing (29), but the Assyrians will be destroyed without mercy, as if burnt in a huge bonfire (30-33).

Egypt cannot save Judah (31:1-9)

Isaiah again condemns the Judeans for relying on Egypt instead of on God. The Judeans think they are wise, but actually they are foolish. Real wisdom rests with God, and he knows best how to overthrow Assyria. As for Egypt, it will be defeated, and when it falls, Judah also will fall (31:1-3).

Judah should learn to trust in God. A lion is not terrified by the shouts of shepherds, and God is not terrified by the threats of the Assyrians. He will protect Jerusalem as a mother bird protects her young (4-5). God desires that this whole experience will lead the people of Judah to repent of their sins and throw away their idols (6-7). They will see that victory over the Assyrians comes neither from Egypt nor from idols, but from the living God. He will act against the Assyrians and they will be miraculously defeated (8-9).

A kingdom of righteousness (32:1-20)

Looking beyond the victory over the Assyrians, Isaiah sees the day when the people of God are under the rule of an ideal government. At the head of this government is a king whose chief officials share his characteristics of integrity, justice and mercy. Together they give their people protection and contentment (32:1-2).

In such a kingdom the people as a whole reflect in their lives the qualities of their rulers. They have a desire to know more of God and his ways and to live lives of greater usefulness to others (3-4). If people speak foolishly, act selfishly, or plot cunningly how to exploit the disadvantaged, they will find that in such a society they are shown up to be what they really are (5-7). In the same way the upright will be recognized for what they are, and honoured accordingly (8).

Returning to the Jerusalem of his own time, Isaiah announces that the upper class women who live luxuriously will suddenly find themselves poor. The vineyards that provide them with a constant supply of wine will be destroyed, and the city where they find their pleasure will be smashed to ruins (9-14).

Only after the removal of all these evils does the ideal age begin. This age is characterized by justice and righteousness, because the people have God's Spirit poured out upon them (15-16). The result is peace, safety, joy, freedom and prosperity such as people have never known before (17-20).

Assyria defeated; Jerusalem blessed (33:1-24)

In speaking again about the current situation, Isaiah announces God's judgment on the Assyrians. They have plundered greedily and acted treacherously (33:1). Isaiah cries to God to save Jerusalem, so that the enemy armies will flee and the Jerusalemites can seize the goods left behind (2-4). Assured that God will act, the prophet praises him before the actual victory. God gives his people security and wisdom, and they respond with reverence and trust (5-6).

Isaiah then hears of the treachery of Assyria towards the Judean representatives who came to negotiate a peace settlement. Assyria accepted from Judah the heavy fine it demanded as the price of peace, then betrayed Judah by saying it would attack Jerusalem just the same. Judah's administration in the country areas had broken down as a result of the Assyrian invasion, so the Assyrians decided to finish the job properly by capturing the capital, Jerusalem (7-9; see 2 Kings 18:13-37).

But God will now act. He will fight against the Assyrians, turning their expected victory into a shattering defeat. His action will be so devastating that people everywhere will be amazed (10-13). God will act against the Jerusalemites also, sparing only those who live uprightly and who refuse to join in the misdeeds of the ungodly (14-16).

With the besieging armies gone, the people will look out on the open fields again. They will cheer their king as he appears before them in his royal robes (17). No longer will they hear the foreign language of the Assyrian generals who took the Judeans' money and then betrayed them (18-19). People will flock to Jerusalem for the feasts and festivals as in former days (20). Jerusalem will be safe, like a city on the edge of a broad river where no enemy warships approach and therefore no one needs to prepare any ships for battle. The city, by God's forgiving mercy, will be a place of good health and ample provision (21-24).

34:1-35:10 MORE ABOUT JUDGMENT AND SALVATION

Jerusalem's final triumph over Assyria is followed by further pictures of God's final judgment on the world and the blessings that will follow. (See notes on the introduction to 24:1-27:13.) God's enemies in this section are represented by one of Israel's most ancient enemies, Edom.

Punishment of the wicked (34:1-17)

God calls sinners together to hear his judgment and receive his punishment. This judgment affects people worldwide, and involves the entire physical creation. Nothing in the heavens or on the earth can exist independently of God and nothing can withstand his power (34:1-4). One picture of this judgment is that of a great slaughter of animals, as if for sacrifice. The rebellious will fall by the sword of God's judgment (5-7). They will suffer a fitting punishment for their persecution and slaughter of God's people (8).

The scene then shifts to the earthly homeland of these people. Their country will be turned into a place of terrible torment, fear and confusion, a place that no human being would ever want to inhabit (9-11). The glory of its kingdom will be gone, and the ruins of its military defences will be inhabited by all sorts of fearsome animals and dreaded demons (12-15). This judgment has been determined by God, who has recorded the details in a book so that people everywhere might be assured that it is his doing (16-17).

A paradise for God's people (35:1-10)

In contrast to the terrifying end that awaits the wicked, the final state that God has prepared for the righteous is one of peace, joy and beauty. As judgment was pictured in the devastation of the land of Edom, so salvation is pictured in the restoration of the land of Israel. The picture is that of a desert that turns into a beautiful garden or a mighty forest. The Lord God dwells there and strengthens his people (35:1-4).

All the effects of sin are now banished, as God brings physical healing both to people's bodies and to the world of nature. There is perfect contentment and total satisfaction (5-7). God forgives his people's sins and prepares the way for them to come from all nations to dwell with him in his city. Nothing that is sinful or in any way harmful or dangerous will be allowed to enter. God's people will come to his city with joy, like captives returning from a foreign country, or like people flocking to Jerusalem for a festival (8-10).

36:1-39:8 HISTORICAL APPENDIX

The historical record in this appendix is almost identical to that found in 2 Kings 18:13-20:19. There seem to be two main reasons for this appendix. First, it provides the background to Isaiah's messages concerning Hezekiah and the Assyrians that have just been considered (Chapters 28-33). Second, it shows how Babylon began to become involved in Judean affairs, and so provides a fitting introduction to the second part of the book.

The Assyrian attack (36:1-22)

Once Hezekiah was satisfied that he had military backing from Egypt, he took the bold step of rebelling against the overlord, Assyria. He declared his independence of Assyria by refusing to pay further tribute (cf. 30:1-2; 2 Kings 18:7b).

After dealing with rebellions elsewhere, the Assyrian army, under the new king Sennacherib, set out to attack Jerusalem. When Hezekiah heard that the enemy had conquered the Judean countryside and was approaching Jerusalem, he quickly prepared the city's defences and cut off any water supply outside the city that might have been of use to the besieging armies (36:1; 2 Chron. 32:2-5).

Upon seeing the size of the Assyrian army, Hezekiah was sorry he had rebelled and offered to pay Sennacherib whatever amount he demanded (2 Kings 18:14-16). Sennacherib took a large sum of money, but then treacherously declared that he intended to punish Jerusalem anyway. He sent some of his chief officers to try to persuade Hezekiah to surrender, pointing out the uselessness of reliance on Egypt for help. In this the Assyrian officials agreed with the prophet Isaiah, though for different reasons (2-6).

The Assyrians went on to say that to depend on Yahweh was equally useless, as Yahweh was the one who had sent them to destroy Jerusalem. Their statements showed they had an inaccurate understanding of Judah's religion, but they felt confident that neither Judah's God nor Judah's army could withstand them (7-10).

When they found that Jerusalem's leaders were not willing to cooperate, the Assyrian officials turned to address the common people (11-12). They tried to win the people's approval by promising good treatment for them if they deserted Hezekiah and surrendered unconditionally (13-17). They brought about their own undoing, however, by insulting Israel's God. They claimed that Yahweh was no better than the gods of other nations that Assyria had conquered, and they challenged him to rescue Jerusalem from their crushing siege (18-20). In spite of the Assyrians' promises and threats, the common people remained loyal to Hezekiah (21-22).

Assyria defeated (37:1-38)

Hezekiah now realized his mistake in ignoring Isaiah and relying on Egypt. In a humble but open acknowledgment that Judah's plight was desperate, he sent to ask Isaiah to appeal to God for help (37:1-4). Isaiah reassured Hezekiah that God would not tolerate Assyria's mockery of him (5-7).

When the Assyrians temporarily withdrew from Jerusalem to deal with an enemy attack to the south-west, they sent a letter renewing their threats. They reminded the Jerusalemites that none of the gods of the nations had been able to save those nations from Assyria (8-13).

Hezekiah then presented the whole matter to God in complete trust (14). Although he wanted deliverance from the Assyrians, he was concerned also for the honour of God's name. He did not deny that the Assyrians had conquered many nations, but he objected to their insults against Yahweh. He wanted to be saved from the Assyrians in such a way that people everywhere would see that Yahweh was the only true God (15-20).

Isaiah, being God's spokesman, brought God's reply to Hezekiah. God knew what had happened, and he condemned Assyria for insulting him and despising his people (21-23). Assyria boasted of its achievements, when in fact it had been no more than God's instrument to carry out his judgments (24-27). Because of Assyria's blasphemy, God would now punish Assyria and save Jerusalem (28-29). The area around Jerusalem, where fields had not been farmed because of the besieging armies, would be sown afresh and become productive again. But more important than agricultural increase would be the increase in the number of truly faithful believers in Judah (30-32).

God showed that he could save Jerusalem from the Assyrians without the people of Jerusalem needing to carry out any military activity at all (33-35). Having announced his plans, God acted. He inflicted the Assyrian army with a deadly plague, so that it suffered heavy losses and was forced to flee. Some time later, back in Assyria, Sennacherib was assassinated (36-38).

Hezekiah's illness and recovery (38:1-22)

The events recorded in Chapters 38 and 39 probably happened before those of the previous chapters. Hezekiah was about to die (38:1), but in answer to his prayer God gave him an extension of life. It seems that the reason for preserving Hezekiah's life was to enable him to bring Judah through the time of conflict with Assyria (2-6). God gave Hezekiah a miraculous sign to confirm that this extension of life was according to the divine will (7-8).

Hezekiah then sang a psalm of praise to God for his recovery. He had expected to die, and his lack of knowledge of the future life gave him no cause for joy at all. Life seemed to him so short. Death, it seemed, would cut him off from all living things,

even God (9-13). He was depressed, knowing he could do nothing to help himself, for life and death were in God's hands (14-15).

This realization, however, now gave Hezekiah cause for hope. If his life was in God's hands, God could save him. He realized that his sickness had been sent by God for his own benefit, so that his faith might be strengthened (16-17). He could not praise God if he were dead, but he could if he remained alive. He therefore determined that he would keep on praising God, both privately before his children and publicly in the temple (18-20).

Isaiah, who had announced God's promise of healing to the king (see v. 4-6), adds a note to explain how the healing may have come about (21-22).

Warning concerning Babylon (39:1-8)

At this time Babylon was increasing in power and was looking for allies to help it resist Assyria. Hezekiah's illness gave the Babylonian king an excuse to send representatives to Jerusalem with the aim of encouraging Hezekiah to join with Babylon against Assyria. Hezekiah's faith, which had been strengthened through his miraculous recovery from death, soon weakened. He could not resist the temptation of yet another anti-Assyrian alliance. He was proud of the prosperity he had brought to his kingdom (see 2 Chron 32:25,31), and he was pleased at the opportunity to impress Babylon. He therefore gladly showed his willingness to cooperate in the anti-Assyrian plot (39:1-2).

Isaiah seems to have suspected that Hezekiah was preparing the way for another alliance against Assyria (3-4). Once again the prophet condemned this willingness to enter foreign alliances. He saw that it would only result in conquest by the allied power. Judah would be conquered and its people carried captive to Babylon (5-8).

40:1-48:22 RETURN FROM BABYLON

Between Chapters 39 and 40 there is a gap of about one hundred and fifty years. The scene suddenly changes from Jerusalem in the time of Hezekiah (701 BC) to the distant kingdom of Babylon where the Judeans are held captive. (For the background to the Babylonian captivity see introductory notes, 'Captivity and return'.) From now on no distinction is made between the northern kingdom Israel and the southern kingdom Judah. The emphasis rather is on encouraging all those living in exile to be ready to return to their ancient homeland and, beginning in Jerusalem, to build a new Israel.

New Jerusalem

Much of Chapters 40-66 is concerned with the glorious future that the captive Israelites could look forward to in the rebuilt Jerusalem. The era that began with their return from exile is known as the post-exilic era. However, many of the blessings pictured in these chapters are far greater than those of restored Israel.

As in former days, so in the post-exilic era, the nation turned away from God. The account in the four Gospels shows clearly that the Israel of Jesus' time was as far from God as the Israel of Isaiah's time (cf. Isa 29:13; Mark 7:6-8; 15:12-13). But, as in Isaiah's time, there were always those who believed, even though their number was small (cf. Isa 8:11-18; John 1:11-12; 6:66-69). This faithful remnant of the old Israel became the nucleus of the new people of God, the Christian church (Acts 1:13-15). The new Israel consists of Abraham's spiritual offspring. The new Jerusalem is a spiritual community of those of all nations who are born 'from above' (Gal 3:14; 3:26-29; 4:26-28).

Even this new community does not at present experience the full blessings pictured in Isaiah. The Messiah's kingdom has yet to be displayed in its full glory (Matt 25:31-34). But Isaiah's message seems to point to more than the coming of the Messiah in glory. The complete fulfilment of the prophet's message awaits the final state of all things, when God dwells for ever with all his redeemed people in a new order of life never before experienced (Rev 21:1-22:5).

God reassures his people (40:1-11)

According to Israelite custom, when the members of a family received an inheritance from their father, the eldest son received twice the amount that the others received. The nation Israel, being God's 'firstborn son' (Exod 4:22), likewise receive double from God, in punishment as well as blessing. The people's punishment in being taken captive to Babylon is proof that they are still God's 'firstborn son' and that he still has a special love for them. Now that he has dealt with their sins, he is ready to bless them afresh (40:1-2).

Just as people prepare a smooth highway for a king when he travels across the country, so God has prepared the way for his people to return to their land. Loyal subjects may watch a royal procession, but the whole world will watch when Israel returns to its homeland (3-5).

The prophet, representing the new Jerusalem, announces this good news to the captives. What people do is unreliable and temporary, but what God does is reliable and permanent. The restoration of ruined Jerusalem and the regathering of scattered Israel is certain, because God will do it (6-9). By his mighty power God will conquer the enemy. His reward will be to enjoy fellowship with his people again, caring for them as a shepherd cares for his sheep (10-11).

Israel's incomparable God (40:12-31)

Should any doubt God's ability to re-establish Israel in its homeland, the psalm of praise that follows drives away those doubts. God is the great Creator; the universe appears insignificant compared with him. He does whatever he wants, without any help or advice from his creatures (12-14). Israel has no need to fear Babylon or any other ruling power, for nations also are insignificant and powerless before him (15-17). How absurd, therefore, for people to make lifeless idols and trust in them instead of in the living, almighty God. Yahweh's people need have no fear of Babylon's gods (18-20).

Since Yahweh created all and rules over all, the leaders of the nations are as powerless before him as ants or grasshoppers. They are as easily destroyed as dry grass (21-24). On the earth or in the heavens, God controls all (25-26).

In view of all this, the Jewish exiles need not become discouraged through thinking that God is either unwilling or unable to help them. He has not forgotten them, nor has he lost his power. Through him the weak can be made strong (27-29). Those who trust in their own strength will fail, no matter how capable they may appear to be. But those who trust in God will be constantly strengthened by his power, which will lead them on victoriously (30-31).

The living God and idols (41:1-29)

At that time Cyrus of Persia had been expanding his empire. He had conquered all the countries to the north and east, and was now threatening Babylon. The prophet imagines God calling the nations to assemble before him and asking them a question: who is it that has stirred up Cyrus to carry out this conquest? The answer: Yahweh (41:1-4).

As the armies of Cyrus approach these nations the people panic, and in their distress call upon their gods for protection. Isaiah pictures the goldsmiths and other craftsmen helping and encouraging each other as they work overtime to meet the heavy demand for idols (5-7).

The people of Israel, by contrast, are the people of the living God. He chose them long ago and he has not forgotten them. He is always present to strengthen and protect them (8-10). They need not fear their enemies, for God will fight for them – and no enemy can stand against him (11-13).

By God's power Israel will be victorious. As a farmer threshes and winnows wheat, so Israel will crush and scatter its enemies (14-16). God will answer the prayers of his people, and provide them with all they need for a healthy and prosperous life. His gracious gifts will be a demonstration of his character that all can see (17-20).

God then challenges the gods of the nations to prove their power by predicting coming events. Not only are they unable to predict the future, they cannot even relate the past. He challenges them to prove their existence by doing anything at all, good or bad, but again they are unable. They are lifeless (21-24). God points out that he predicts correctly and acts decisively. None of the gods of the nations predicted Cyrus's conquest, but the God of Israel did (25-27). These gods can neither predict events nor answer questions. Being lifeless, they can only deceive those who worship them (28-29).

The Servant of Yahweh

In 42:1-4 we meet the first of the four so-called Servant Songs. (The others are in 49:1-6, 50:4-9 and 52:13-53:12.) The songs do not always give a clear indication who this servant is. In some cases the whole nation Israel is the servant, in other cases it is the faithful within Israel, while in some cases it is the Messiah, Jesus Christ.

The probable reason for this threefold meaning is that Israel as a whole failed, and the spiritual blessings God desired for Israel were experienced only by the faithful few who truly believed God. Yet even this faithful remnant did not experience the full blessings God intended for his people. God's purposes for Israel were fulfilled only in Jesus the Messiah. The nation Israel was Abraham's natural offspring (John 8:37); the few faithful believers within Israel, often referred to as the remnant, were his spiritual offspring (Rom 9:6-7; Gal 3:29); but the Messiah himself was the one and only perfect offspring, in whom all God's purposes for Israel were fulfilled and through whom people of all nations are blessed (Gal 3:16; cf. Gen 12:1-3,7).

Although the people of Israel repeatedly failed and suffered God's punishment, they nevertheless looked forward to a golden age of glory and power. The expectancy of a golden age naturally became greater as the exiles in Babylon learnt that they were about to return to their land. But, having returned and rebuilt their nation, they again failed. Jesus

Christ, the embodiment of ideal Israel, not only suffered God's punishment because of his people's sins, but brought the glory and power that Israel hoped for but never achieved (cf. Isa 42:1-4 with Matt 12:17-21; cf. Isa 53:4 with Matt 8:17).

Success and failure of God's servant (42:1-25)

In the previous chapter the servant of Yahweh was identified with Israel (see 41:8). Israel is probably again the servant who is identified here, but the ideals outlined in this song never became a reality in the nation. They did, to some extent, characterize the faithful remnant, but they found their perfect expression only in the one who embodied the ideals God desired, Jesus Christ. The prophet foresees that this servant of Yahweh, though empowered by God's Spirit and concerned with establishing God's justice in the world, will never make a show to attract attention to himself, never hurt those who sorrow, and never turn away from those of even the weakest faith (42:1-4).

The result of the servant's work will be the salvation of people from many nations. Through his servant, the Creator will send the message of his salvation to the people of his creation, to turn them from darkness to light, from bondage to freedom (5-7). Yahweh, the eternal God and all-powerful redeemer, needs no help from idols in this. He will bring his purposes to fulfilment through his servant. The Jews' salvation out of bondage in Babylon will be a sign and a guarantee of a much wider salvation that is yet to come (8-9).

This statement of God's purposes brings forth an outburst of praise. From various parts of creation and from various nations of the world, people join in singing praises to the merciful God (10-12). This same God, however, will destroy those who fight against him (13).

God himself then speaks. He had appeared to be inactive and silent during the time of the Jews' captivity in Babylon, but now he will act decisively. He will lead his people out of the blindness and darkness of captivity back to the land of their ancestors (14-16). At this demonstration of God's power, all those who trusted in idols will feel foolish and ashamed (17).

Having set out his ideal purposes for Israel (see v. 1-4), God now displays the condition of Israel that brought about its captivity in Babylon. Spiritually the people were blind and deaf, and stubbornly refused to see God's truth or listen to his voice (18-20). God had given them his law so that they might bring other nations to know him and praise him. Instead they disobeyed his law and were plundered by those nations (21-22). The calamities that befell Israel were not accidental; they were sent by God. But because the people did not know God, they did not know the meaning of the events that brought about their defeat and captivity (23-25).

Redemption through God's grace (43:1-28)

Despite Israel's failure and subsequent punishment, God has not cast off his people for ever. God used the power of foreign nations to enslave them and bring sufferings and hardships upon them, but he will now destroy the power of those nations. He will make them pay the ransom price for the redemption of captive Israel. They will fall so that Israel can go free (43:1-4). Wherever the captives are, they are still God's people, and he will bring them back to their land (5-7).

God challenges the nations to meet him in court to see who controls the history of the world, Yahweh or the gods of the nations. If they can prove that their gods have knowledge of past events or can predict future events, they are invited to bring these gods with them to court, along with any other witnesses they can find to support their claims (8-9). As for Yahweh, his sole witness will be Israel. The history of Israel proves that God's predictions always come true and that he is the only God. People can therefore be assured that when he predicts Israel's release and return to its land, this prediction also will come true (10-13).

For Israel's sake, God will overthrow Babylon. He is still Israel's covenant God, and once again he will redeem his people from bondage (14-15). Just as he miraculously led Israel through the Red Sea and across the desert in the time of Moses, so he will lead his people to the promised land again (16-19). As on the former occasion, he will protect them from danger and provide for their needs along the way (20-21).

This restoration of Israel to its land will be entirely by God's grace. The people certainly do not deserve it. While they have been in captivity, God has not demanded that they maintain the sacrificial ritual. He has placed no added burden upon them. But they have not shown their gratitude to him through prayer or other expressions of worship. They ignore God and continue in their sinful and selfish ways (22-24).

God is still willing to forgive his people, if only they will honestly examine themselves and admit their wrongdoing (25-26). The history of Israel shows, however, that the people do not repent readily. From the time of Jacob to the time of their captivity, they and their rulers have consistently rebelled against God and brought divine judgment upon them (27-28).

Israel's God and man-made gods (44:1-28)

Not only is God willing to forgive his people, but he wants to pour out the power of his Spirit upon them so that new spiritual life will spring up within them. This will enable them to evangelize the Gentiles, who will then join the descendants of Jacob in worshipping the God of Israel (44:1-5). Israel's redeemer is the only God. He knows the end from the beginning and his people can depend on him always (6-8).

In contrast to the one true and living God are the many lifeless gods that workmen make. But how can a *man* make a *god*? What he makes must be inferior to himself, not greater. By making idols a person lowers his own status and brings shame upon himself (9-11).

When a craftsman makes an idol of metal, he gets hot and tired from his work, and the idol can do nothing to help him (12). When a craftsman makes an idol of wood, he has to use a tree that the living God has made to grow. After the man has chopped the tree down, he uses part of it to make a fire to cook his meals, and uses another part of it to make an idol that he then worships (13-17). To worship man-made things is clearly absurd, but those who worship them cannot see this, because they are spiritually blind (18-20).

The prophet then returns to consider the one true God and what he has done for his people. He has chosen them to belong to him, forgiven them their sins and saved them from their enemies (21-23). He is their redeemer as well as their creator, and he is now about to prove wrong those who forecast the destruction of Israel (24-25). As the prophet has already announced, God is going to act on behalf of his people. At his direction Cyrus will conquer Babylon and permit the Jews to return and rebuild Jerusalem (26-28).

God uses Cyrus (45:1-19)

Cyrus's many victories, and the power and wealth he gained through them, were all planned by God. God was preparing the way so that Cyrus could conquer Babylon and release the Jews. Throughout these events, Cyrus did not know God and was unaware that God was using him to carry out his purposes for Israel (45:1-4).

To Cyrus, his release of the captive Jews was a relatively minor event in his long and glorious career, but in the eyes of God it was the purpose for which he had risen to international power. When people recognize this as God's doing, they will praise him as the only true God (5-7). Israel, meanwhile, will enter a new era of divine blessing (8).

Some Israelites may have questioned God's wisdom in using a heathen king to bring about their restoration. God replies that they have no right to argue with him or question the way he deals with his children (9-11). God is the creator and controller of the universe. He has used Cyrus to give the Jews their freedom and the chance to rebuild Jerusalem, and the Jews have not needed to do anything. For this they should be thankful to God (12-13).

In addition, people of other foreign nations will give their assistance to Israel. They will forsake their idol-gods for the God who cannot be seen, the God of Israel (14-17). God always works to a plan, whether in creation or in the history of Israel. The chaos that resulted from Babylon's destruction of Jerusalem is no cause for Jews to turn away from God in disappointment. They must not think that he has lost control of events or that he has some new mysterious plan for them. He will be true to his word and do for his people what he has purposed for them (18-19).

Babylon's helpless gods (45:20-46:13)

Cyrus's conquest of Babylon will prove to those Babylonians who survive that to trust in idols for victory is useless. Wooden gods could not foresee Cyrus's conquest, but Yahweh, the only true God, predicted it long ago (20-21). People of surrounding nations may previously have fought against Yahweh by trusting in idols, but now they should forsake those idols and submit to the living God. Then they will find victory, righteousness and strength, and will join with all God's true people in bringing him praise (22-25).

The prophet pictures the Babylonian refugees as they flee from the armies of Cyrus, taking with them whatever personal possessions they can carry. The Babylonian gods (two of the most important of which were Bel and Nebo), instead of saving the people, have to be saved by them. So far from helping the people, they only become a hindrance and a burden, causing the donkeys and oxen to groan under the extra weight they have to carry (46:1-2). The people of Yahweh, by contrast, are carried by him. The God who made them cares for them, and will continue to care for them to the very end (3-4). Gods of silver and gold cost their worshippers much in money, time and effort, but they cannot do anything to save their worshippers from trouble (5-7).

Many of the Jews had once been tempted to follow the idolatrous ways of the Babylonians. They are reminded that Yahweh alone is God (8-9). The future is under his control, and at the right moment he will call Cyrus to come and destroy Babylon and release the Jews (10-11). Those Jews who stubbornly refuse to trust in God must therefore change their ways, if they want to share in the blessings of the new Israel (12-13).

Judgment on Babylon (47:1-15)

The great nation Babylon is likened to a beautiful and vain young lady who is now disgraced. She once lived in luxury, but now is made to sit in the dirt, forced to work like a slave girl, stripped of her beautiful clothing and made to walk around naked (47:1-3). God's judgment on Babylon brings freedom to Israel (4).

Pride is the reason for Babylon's downfall. God's desire was to use Babylon to punish Israel, but Babylon has gone beyond the limits God set and has acted with unnecessary cruelty (5-7). Proud of the place of honour she has gained among the nations, she acts as if she is God. Therefore, God will punish her. She thinks she is unconquerable, but God will suddenly destroy her (8-9).

In her arrogance Babylon thinks that she can do as she likes and no one can stop her (10-11). She thinks that her rise to power is a result of guidance received through her knowledge of magic and astrology. The prophet challenges her to keep trusting in magic and astrology, and see if that will save her from God's judgment (12-13). What she will find is that the magicians and astrologers themselves will fall under God's judgment. They will be destroyed, as straw is burnt in a fire. No one will be able to save Babylon from the coming judgment (14-15).

The past and the future (48:1-22)

Before returning to their homeland, the people are reminded of the sins that led the nation into captivity. They must not repeat former errors. The people's chief failing was that they honoured God with their words but not with their conduct (48:1-2). Knowing their tendency towards idolatry, God gave his people advance revelations of his will, to prevent them from turning to idols for guidance. But they still stubbornly rejected his teaching (3-5).

Nevertheless, God once again tells them his plans in advance, namely, that he is going to lead them back to their land. But he makes the announcement at the last minute, as it were, for their previous history has shown that they cannot be trusted. God is not going to give them the chance to claim that idols have brought them this deliverance (6-8).

God has been very patient with his people. He likens his work with them to that of a refiner, who puts silver in the fire to burn up the rubbish and leave the metal pure. In the same way God has 'refined' the people of Israel, but they have proved worthless. However, for the sake of his own honour, God does not destroy them (9-11).

The God who called Israel to be his people still looks after them. The God who made the world still controls its history. He brings Cyrus to Babylon to conquer Israel's oppressor and free the captive people (12-15). God has always spoken openly with his people, and now he does so again, by sending his messenger the prophet to make his plans known to them (16).

Because God wanted only the best for his people, he was saddened to see the suffering they had brought on themselves through their stubborn disobedience. If they had paid attention to his instruction, they would have enjoyed unbroken peace and prosperity (17-19). God is now delighted that they are about to leave Babylon and return to their land. He will protect and provide for them, but if they want to enjoy peace in their land they must live uprightly (20-22).

49:1-55:13 THE SALVATION OF GOD'S PEOPLE

The servant's task (49:1-7)

Leaving behind the subject of Cyrus's conquest, the prophecy now develops the theme of the servant of Yahweh. The second Servant Song begins by recording how Israel was chosen by God to be his servant, and prepared by God to do his work. As Israel did the work faithfully, it would bring praise to God (49:1-3).

Israel as a whole failed, but from generation to generation a minority within Israel, the remnant, remained loyal to Yahweh as his servant. They were unable to save their people from captivity, but they still trusted in God that he would bring some good from their work (4). They now see God's purpose in preserving and strengthening the faithful remnant through the captivity. He wants to use them to lead his people back to their land, from where they will send the light of his salvation to the darkened heathen nations (5-6). God's servant will then no longer suffer the shame that Israel experienced in the captivity. On the contrary, those who once despised God's servant will now give him honour,

proving to all that God is faithful to his people and faithful to his word (7).

Again the nation as a whole failed in its task, though, as always, a small minority remained faithful (cf. Luke 1:16-17; John 20:21; Acts 13:46-47). Jesus the Messiah, the perfection of Israel, was the one who truly brought his people back to God, sent the light of God's salvation to the Gentiles, and receives homage from people of all nations (Matt 1:21; Luke 2:30-32; Acts 26:23; Rom 15:8-12; Rev 3:7).

Israel rebuilt (49:8-50:3)

Once more God promises the return of the captive Jews to their homeland. God will protect them along the journey and help them as they rebuild their ruined country (8-10). Whether exiled in Babylon or scattered in other places, the people will return home amid much rejoicing (11-13).

Some of the Jews thought God had forgotten them. God now shows that for him this is impossible (14-16). Israel will return and rebuild its homeland. Opponents who try to ruin Israel's work will not be successful and will leave in shame and defeat (17-18). People born in exile will flock to the rebuilt Jerusalem. The land previously uninhabited and in ruins will become well populated and prosperous again (19-21). Scattered Jews in other countries will also return, helped by generous aid from the nations among whom they have lived (22-23).

Among the exiles were some who apparently doubted the prophet's promise of restoration, for Babylon seemed unconquerable. How can a captive people possibly be freed when they are in the grip of such a powerful tyrant (24)? God replies that he can do it. He reminds the doubting exiles that he is the all-powerful God and Israel's covenant redeemer. He will crush the Babylonians in a judgment suited to the cruel oppression that they inflicted on their helpless victims (25-26).

Other Jews blamed God for their troubles, as if he had cast them off like a husband who divorces his wife or a father who sells his children to pay off his debts. God replies that they have no evidence to support such an accusation, for he has neither 'divorced' them nor 'sold' them. Rather their sins are the cause of their troubles (50:1). They ignored God when he spoke to them through his servants the prophets. But he still loves them and has the power to save them. Nothing in all creation can withstand his power (2-3).

The servant's patient endurance (50:4-11)

In this, the third Servant Song, the words again may have an application to the experiences of Israel among the nations. In particular they reflect the experiences of the few faithful Jews who tried to teach, warn and comfort their ungodly fellow exiles in Babylon. The song becomes even more meaningful when applied to the experiences of the Messiah himself.

The servant is taught by God day by day, so that he can give teaching and encouragement to those who need it. Although people respond with opposition and physical violence, the servant does not give up. He learns the meaning of obedience by the things he suffers (4-6). He perseveres because he knows that he has acted blamelessly and that God is with him. And if God is on his side, no one can triumph over him. Those who make accusations against him will not prove him guilty, but will themselves be put to shame (7-9).

In a world of darkness faithful believers walk confidently and do not fall, because they trust in God. Others, who do not trust in God but who make their own 'fire' to give them light, will find in the end that the fire burns them. In other words, when people depend on human scheming instead of depending on God, they will find in the end that their scheming is the cause of their downfall (10-11).

God of the impossible (51:1-23)

To the captive Jews it must have seemed almost impossible to escape from the powerful grip of the tyrant Babylon, make the long journey over harsh territory and then rebuild their ruined country. God encourages them with reminders of the apparently impossible things he has done for them in the past. The very origin of Israel was something of a miracle. God built a nation out of one couple, even though the man and his wife were past the age when they might normally expect to have children. The same God is still active; he can perform a miracle again and restore Jerusalem (51:1-3).

From this rebuilt Jerusalem, God's salvation will spread throughout the world. This salvation will not be temporary and political, but eternal and spiritual. People of all nations will receive new life and hope when they come to know God (4-6). The Israelites should be encouraged as they see what God is about to do through them. They should have no fear of their present oppressors (7-8).

A cry from the captive Israelites urges God to act on their behalf. As he overthrew Egypt (here symbolized by Rahab, the mythical dragon of the Nile) and led his people through the Red Sea and into Canaan, so may he overthrow Babylon and lead his people back to Jerusalem. They look expectantly

to a new age when sorrow is banished and they live in Zion in unbroken contentment (9-11).

God reassures Israel with the reply that he is the Creator, the eternal one. Israel's enemies, by contrast, are merely creatures, who one day must die. Israel has no need, therefore, to fear Babylon's might and fury (12-13). Yahweh, Israel's covenant God, is the Almighty. He is in control of all affairs and he will release his captive people. More than that, he will give them his teaching so that they can know him and serve him (14-16).

Jerusalem fell, but it is now about to rise again. The Babylonian attack on Jerusalem was a punishment sent by God to bring about the collapse of the city and the destruction of Judah. The judgment is likened to a strong drink given to a person to make him drunk, so that he staggers and falls (17-20). This strong drink is now to be taken from Judah and given to Babylon, so that it will stagger and fall. God is going to destroy Babylon as he destroyed Judah (21-23).

Joy in Jerusalem (52:1-12)

In view of these promises, the prophet urges the captive Jews to prepare for the return to Jerusalem. The city that heathen armies defiled and destroyed will be rebuilt, to become strong, holy and beautiful again (52:1-2).

God will redeem his people from slavery, but he will not pay the slave-owner (Babylon) any ransom (3). In earlier days the Israelites were made slaves in Egypt, even though they went there in peace. They then established themselves in Canaan, but again they fell into bondage. Some were taken captive to Assyria, and now the rest are slaves in Babylon. The oppressor nations paid nothing for their slaves, and God will pay nothing to release the slaves. Rather, he will punish the slave-owners, particularly since they have mocked him (4-5). Then the doubting Israelites will see clearly that their God is the controller of history (6).

Overjoyed at this reminder of the triumph of God, the prophet pictures a messenger going from Babylon to Jerusalem to announce the good news that God reigns supreme. The people of Israel will return and Jerusalem will be rebuilt (7). He pictures the watchmen in Jerusalem rejoicing as they see the first lot of exiles returning to the city. Onlookers from other nations will see God's power displayed (8-10).

As he pictures the first exiles leaving Babylon, the prophet reminds those carrying the temple vessels to keep themselves ceremonially clean (11; cf. Ezra 1:7-11). He cannot help but contrast the quiet and orderly departure on this occasion with the hurried exodus from Egypt when Israel set out for its land the first time (12).

Israel and the Messiah

The fourth Servant Song (52:13-53:12) emphasizes the contrast between Israel's sufferings at the hands of the Babylonians and the coming glory in the restored nation. The song, however, does more than merely contrast suffering and glory. It reveals that the two are inseparably connected, that suffering is necessary before glory. It shows for the first time that the servant must die. He must bear punishment of sin before he can enjoy the glory that God has promised.

Previous statements in the book have made it clear that Israel is the servant who has sinned, who is punished, and who looks for future glory (see 41:8; 42:19-25; 49:5-7). But this song makes it clear that the removal of sin and the blessings of glory are possible only as another takes the punishment on behalf of the sinful servant. Yet the one who bears Israel's sin is also called God's servant. The servant dies for the servant; the suffering servant dies for the sinful servant.

It may be, then, that the Israel of the exile suffered for the sins of Israel of former generations; or that the faithful remnant in exile suffered because of the sins of the people as a whole in exile. The suffering, however, is not only *because* of Israel's sins, but to *take away* Israel's sins. Certain sins of Israel, such as idolatry, were removed through the exile, but the removal of sin in its fullest sense could come about only through Jesus the Messiah. Jesus was the ideal Israel, the perfect servant, who takes away his people's sin through bearing the punishment for them (Matt 1:21; Heb 2:14-17).

Jesus does even more than that. He dies for the sin not only of Israel, but also of the world. Only in him do people have complete forgiveness of sin, and only in him will they experience future glory (John 1:29; Heb 2:9-10).

The fourth Servant Song speaks of Israel's sufferings at the hands of the Babylonians and its glory in the rebuilt Jerusalem. But those events do not fully satisfy the language of the song. They are but dim pictures of the sufferings of Christ and the glory that follows (1 Peter 1:11).

The servant's suffering and glory (52:13-53:12)

Just as people were startled at the sight of the servant's great sufferings, so will they be startled at the sight of his great glory. They will be struck dumb, as it were, as they witness a sight more glorious than they or anyone else could ever have imagined (13-15).

Many people find it hard to believe that God will give his servant such power and magnificence, because when they look at the servant they see just an ordinary person of insignificant beginnings. They liken him to a small plant growing in dry and infertile ground — so different from the magnificent trees that stand majestically in the tall forests. They see nothing in his appearance that is impressive or attractive. On the contrary, when they see the extent of his sufferings they turn away from him in disgust, like people repelled by the sight of a diseased person (53:1-3).

At first those who see the servant's intense suffering think that he is being punished by God for some wrong he has done. However, as they think further they realize that he is suffering not for his own sins, but for the sins of others; in fact, *their* sins. They are the ones who have turned away from God and they are the ones for whom the servant dies. It is for them that he bears God's punishment (4-6).

The servant is treated cruelly, but he bears it silently. Those who judge him show neither mercy nor justice; they just send him off to be killed. His fellow citizens are just as heartless, and show no concern that he suffers death unjustly. Yet he bears all this for the sake of those who are sinners (7-8). Those who hate him leave him to die in disgrace like a criminal, but those who love him give him an honourable burial. They know he has done no wrong (9).

Despite the inhumanity of people, the servant's death is according to God's will. It is a sacrifice for the removal of sin. But beyond the sorrow of death is the joy of the resurrection. The servant is satisfied when he sees the fruits of his suffering, namely, a multitude of spiritual children who are forgiven their sins and accounted righteous before God because of his death (10-11). The sufferer becomes the conqueror and receives a conqueror's reward. Because he willingly took the place of sinners and prayed for their forgiveness, he is now exalted to the highest place (12).

Yahweh and Israel reunited (54:1-17)

Israel is likened to the wife of Yahweh. Her exile in Babylon was like a period of divorce when God separated her from him because of her sins. During this time she did not increase or prosper as a nation. She is now to return to God and to her homeland, where she will produce greater increase than in the days before the captivity. As an Arab has to enlarge his tent to accommodate more children, so Israel will have to enlarge its borders to accommodate this increase (54:1-3).

When Israel returns to her husband, she will no longer bear the shame of her separation. In love God will forgive her and take her back to himself (4-6). His discipline of Israel was only temporary, and now he looks forward to a glad reunion and a lasting relationship (7-8). He promises that he will not send the nation into such a shameful exile again (9-10).

The new Israel, built by God himself, will have the beauty of a city built of precious stones (11-12). God will teach his ways to those who dwell in the city, so that justice and righteousness become the most noticeable features of their way of life (13-14). God is the creator of the world and the controller of all human activity in the world. He will make sure that no one who fights against his people will be victorious (15-17).

God's free provision (55:1-13)

Many of the Jews had made life reasonably tolerable for themselves in Babylon. The prophet knew that they were so settled that they might not want to uproot themselves and face the hardships of life back in their desolated homeland. Many were more concerned with making life easier for themselves than with knowing God and looking to him for their provision. God warns against this self-centred attitude and invites them to trust fully in him. The blessings he gives are free. They cannot be bought with money, but they bring more satisfaction than all the temporary benefits that people might manage to gain (55:1-2).

If the people respond to God's purposes for them, the divine blessings will extend far beyond the borders of the restored nation. When God's people take his message to other nations, people who previously had no knowledge of God will become followers of the God of Israel. God's people will see his covenant promises to David fulfilled beyond their expectations (3-5).

First, however, God requires repentance. When people turn from their sin to God, he forgives them freely according to his mercy (6-7). This mercy is so great that it is beyond human understanding. What God has prepared for his people is greater than they have ever imagined (8-9).

As surely as rain soaks into the ground and makes plants grow (it does not float back up to the clouds), so will God's promise of Israel's restoration come true (it will not return to God fruitless). God will lead his people out of Babylon and back to their homeland. The world of nature will rejoice

along with God's people, and their land will become fruitful again (10-13).

56:1-66:24 PRESENT SHAME AND FUTURE GLORY

Having looked beyond the Babylonian captivity to the Jews' imminent return to their homeland, the prophet now sees the people resettled in and around Jerusalem. What he sees causes him to realize that this is not the golden age after all. Social and religious sins once again become a characteristic of the national life of Israel. The prophet contrasts this corrupt state of affairs with conditions in the ideal Jerusalem of the future.

In this section, as in the previous sections (Chapters 40-48 and 49-55), we must remember that we are reading poetry, where the pictures are vivid and the language exaggerated. We do not need to interpret the prophecies literally (e.g. mountains do not literally have voices and trees do not literally have hands; cf. 55:12). The important consideration for the reader is not merely what the prophecies say, but what they mean.

Of particular importance is the spiritual significance of the prophecies, and this is the aspect that the New Testament emphasizes. The prophecies of Isaiah take on new meaning once Jesus Christ has come.

Thus, the glorious kingdom that God promised Israel is, above all, a spiritual kingdom centred in Jesus the Messiah (32:1-8; cf. Luke 17:21). The faithful remnant of Israel is in fact the true Israel (10:20-23; cf. Rom 9:6-7,27-33). The spiritual, not the natural, descendants of Abraham are the real people of God (41:8; cf. Gal 3:29). The salvation of God is proclaimed worldwide and people of all nations join in one body to be his people (54:1-3; cf. Gal 4:26-28). The new Jerusalem for which believers hope is not material and earthly like the old, but is spiritual and from heaven (60:1-22; cf. Rev 21:1-4; 21:22-27).

True worshippers (56:1-8)

God reminds his people that life in the rebuilt nation must be based on his law. This applies to laws that concern social justice as well as those that concern religious practices (56:1-2).

When the Jews returned to Jerusalem, some Gentile converts returned with them. Among these were several eunuchs, possibly people who were previously connected with the palaces in Babylon and Persia. The law of Moses made it plain that eunuchs were to be excluded from the tabernacle worship, probably to discourage the Israelites from making their own people eunuchs (Deut 23:1). But in the new Jerusalem all foreigners, eunuchs or otherwise, who honour God and keep his law should be allowed to worship in the temple along with godly Israelites (3-5).

Love and obedience towards God, not physical or national characteristics, are the important things in God's sight. The temple is for the use of all people, not just Jews, because God's mercy is for all people (6-8).

Corruption and idolatry (56:9-57:21)

The Assyrian captivity of the northerners and the Babylonian captivity of the southerners did not include the whole populations. Those who were of no use to the conquerors were left behind, along with scattered country people who escaped the enemy. These and their descendants soon followed the old religious practices of the Canaanite people. They worshipped idols, offered human sacrifices to the god Molech, and practised fertility rites with religious prostitutes, all in the hope of becoming prosperous (2 Kings 17:24-41). Those who engaged in these practices tried to join in the worship of Yahweh when the Jews returned from captivity.

Israel's spiritual leaders should have been like alert watchmen, who warned the people of these dangers and instructed them in the ways of God. Instead, says the prophet, they are like lazy, overfed watchdogs who can only sleep. They are interested only in personal gain and do not care for the people. The civil leaders (likened to bad shepherds) are equally greedy and corrupt (9-12).

In such conditions the righteous are the ones who suffer. They find relief only when they rest in death (57:1-2). The wicked, meanwhile, carry on with their witchcraft, immorality, idolatry and child sacrifice. They do not realize that by their behaviour they are challenging God and inviting his judgment (3-6). Although their idolatrous practices involve costly sacrifices, shameful behaviour and tiresome journeys, they persist in them, hoping vainly for a better life (7-10).

Although the people have turned from God to worthless idols, God has been patient with them. But his patience has not led them to repentance. They will now find that their gods will not save them from God's punishment (11-13).

By contrast, God will help those faithful to him, no matter what obstacles are in their way. Although he is exalted above the heavens, he also dwells with those who humbly acknowledge their sin and turn from it (14-15). He may punish them when they do

wrong, but he does not remain angry with them. When they humbly acknowledge their wrong and show their desire to please him again, he gives them new life and strength (16-18). The repentant enjoy peace and fellowship with God, but the wicked live in a turmoil of uncleanness. They will be excluded from God's peace for ever (19-21).

True religion (58:1-14)

The Jews thought they were a righteous people because they carried out the daily rituals required by the law. The prophet is about to show them that in spite of all this they are still sinners. In fact, their attitude towards these rituals is their chief sin (58:1-2).

For example, many practise fasting not because they are truly humble before God, but because they hope God will be impressed with their actions. But at the same time as they fast, they oppress their workers and fight with one another. They act and dress in a way that shows they are fasting, but such fasting is worthless in God's sight (3-5). God would rather that they cease oppressing others and begin to help the poor and needy (6-7). Only then will he be pleased with them; only then will he accept their worship and answer their prayers (8-9a).

When the people stop treating others with contempt, God will show kindness to them. When they sacrifice their comfort for the sake of those who are ill-treated and hungry, God will bless them. He will give them fresh spiritual life and restore their country to the strength of former days (9b-12). Religious observances are important, but people must carry them out from right motives. Whether practising fasting or keeping the sabbath traditions, the important thing is to honour God, not to seek personal benefit (13-14).

Society incapable of reform (59:1-21)

Ungodly society is heading for destruction. The reason for this is not that God is powerless to save people, but that people's sins have cut them off from God, the only one who can save them. They have filled the land with violence, lies and treachery (59:1-3).

Because of the corruption of the courts, there is no justice in society (4). Wickedness multiplies as evil people spread their poison and trap the innocent in their plots. They try to cover their sin with a show of respectability, but they are not successful (5-6). Because their thoughts are evil, their actions also are evil. Always devious, they are a constant source of trouble to others. They know nothing of such basic virtues as kindness, honesty and justice (7-8).

The prophet then joins with the people in confessing their sin. They would like to see an end to oppression and injustice, but they hope in vain. They live in a society of moral darkness that they themselves have created (9-11). They have turned away from following God and have developed a way of life where honesty and truth are ignored (12-13). Injustice and corruption are everywhere, from the highest law courts down to the market places of the common people. The person who tries to be honest suffers persecution from those who find it more convenient to cooperate with the corrupt system. God sees all this and it displeases him (14-15).

God sees that the human race cannot reform itself. What is needed is the intervention of God. In purity and justice he acts against the sinners, with the result that people worldwide acknowledge his lordship (16-19). Those who repent of their sins enter a new relationship with him. They become his true people and enjoy the spiritual blessings of his covenant with them (20-21).

A glorious kingdom (60:1-22)

In Chapters 60-62 the scene returns to Babylon, where the captive Israelites look forward to the return to their homeland and the reconstruction of their national life. Here, more than in the previous chapters, the blessings seem to go far beyond those experienced by post-exilic Israel. (See sub-section 'New Jerusalem' at the introduction to Chapters 40-66.)

When sin is removed and enemies are punished, Israel will receive the glory it has always hoped for. Not only will scattered Jews return to their land, but people of all nations will come to Jerusalem to worship the God of Israel (60:1-5). Some countries send camels loaded with treasure. Others send animals that guarantee a constant supply for the sacrifices in the rebuilt temple (6-7). Ships bring people and goods from countries across the sea to enrich Israel (8-9).

Foreigners help rebuild Jerusalem, and demonstrate their submission to Israel by the constant supply of gifts they bring to the city (10-12). Some of the nations provide valuable building materials for the new temple (13). Nations that in the past attacked Israel now become its subjects. Those who previously plundered and disgraced Israel now bring it riches and honour (14-16).

Jerusalem is established with beauty, security and strength. Violence and cruelty are replaced by peace and righteousness (17-18). Lights are not necessary, because God's glory fills every place.

There is no sadness and no sin. Since the sovereign God is in control there is perfect security and universal prosperity (19-22).

Good news for the exiles (61:1-62:12)

God's Spirit gives the prophet some good news to pass on to the Jews held captive in Babylon. They will be released to return to their land, but their captors will be punished (61:1-2). When they arrive in Jerusalem, they may be overcome with grief because of the ruin and devastation they see around them. But God will encourage and strengthen them so that they can rebuild their beloved city (3-4).

Foreigners will carry out the everyday duties for the Jews and contribute liberally to the national income. This will enable the Jews to concentrate on the more important matters of worshipping and serving God (5-6). God will give blessings to his people that are far beyond anything they have ever expected. In justice he will compensate them for the plundering they have suffered at the hands of their enemies (7-9).

In thanks the prophet praises God in advance for saving Israel and giving it glory, a glory that he likens to the beauty of wedding garments. As surely as seeds sprout and grow, so just as surely will God save Israel and bring praise to himself from people of all nations (10-11).

But at the time of writing, the prophet is still in Babylon and Israel has not yet been saved. The prophet will therefore not cease praying for Israel till it has been restored to its land in glory (62:1-3). The nation will then no longer be like an unfaithful wife living alone and in disgrace. Her husband still loves her and will take her back. As the deserted woman becomes happily married again, so the desolate nation will again rejoice in fellowship with Yahweh (4-5).

In Jerusalem watchmen wait expectantly for the first returning exiles. The prophet urges these watchmen to join him in unceasing prayer that God will soon fulfil his promise and bring his people back, never to be plundered again (6-9). He then commands people to go out and prepare the way for Israel's release from Babylon and return to Jerusalem. Israel will again be known as the people whom God has redeemed (10-12).

God's holy anger (63:1-6)

When Babylon made its last attack on Jerusalem (587 BC), Edom joined in, taking wicked delight in helping to destroy the Israelite nation. God's messengers announced his judgment on Edom for this (Ps 137:7; Obad 1,10-14; cf. Mal 1:4-5), though in the denunciation in the present chapter, Edom may be a symbol for all God's enemies. (Compare the picture that follows with Revelation 14:18-20; 19:13-16.)

On seeing a person clothed in red approaching him from Edom, the prophet asks who it is. The person replies that he is the Lord, who punishes his enemies but saves his people (63:1). The prophet asks why his clothes are red (2), and receives the reply that they are red with the blood of slaughtered enemies. When God acts in his righteous anger, the blood of sinners runs freely over the earth, in much the same way as juice runs out of grapes when workers tread them in a winepress. Since God alone is all-holy and all-powerful, he alone can carry out this judgment (3-6).

A prayer for Israel (63:7-64:12)

The prophet's prayer for God's suffering people begins by recalling God's great acts of love in the past (7). Because Israel was his people, God saved them from slavery in Egypt, though when they rebelled against him, they were punished (8-10). Nevertheless, God forgave them. Therefore, asks the prophet, could not this God of mercy and love, who has done such great things for Israel in the past, also save his people from captivity in Babylon now (11-14)?

It seems as if God has withdrawn into his heavenly dwelling place, for there is no evidence of his mercy upon his people. The prophet realizes that if Abraham and Jacob, Israel's earthly fathers, saw their descendants in captivity, they would be ashamed of them and want to have nothing to do with them. But he prays that God, their true Father, will not cast them off (15-16). It seems, however, as if he has. He has allowed the Babylonians to destroy their temple and take them to a foreign land, where there is no evidence that Yahweh is their God or that they are his people (17-19).

God has revealed himself and saved his people with supernatural acts in the past, and the prophet longs that he might do so again. The enemies of God would then be overthrown (64:1-3). By contrast, those whose chief pleasure is to please God know that God helps them in the most unexpected ways (4-5a). They also know that, despite their desire to please God, they are still self-willed sinners. Even their best deeds are polluted by sin. They often forget God and have only themselves to blame for the troubles that result (5b-7).

Although they have failed miserably, the people know that God is still their Father. He may punish them, but he still loves them (8-9). Therefore, asks

the prophet, is not the destruction he has sent upon Judah sufficient punishment? Can God not see the desolation of Jerusalem and take pity on the ruined city? Will he not now forgive his people and bring them back to their land (10-12)?

God's people: servants or rebels? (65:1-16)

It was God's desire that Israel seek him and enjoy his blessings, but instead the nation rebelled against him and stubbornly went its own way. Only a minority within Israel, along with those of Gentile nations who turned to Israel's God, were really God's people (65:1-2). As for the people of Israel as a whole, they had throughout their long history repeatedly made God angry. They sacrificed to other gods, consulted the spirits of the dead and ate forbidden food, yet all the time they claimed that they were holy but other nations were unclean (3-5). Consequently, God had punished Israel and sent the people into captivity (6-7).

Amid all the religious corruption of Israel there is still a faithful remnant. They are like a few good grapes in a bad bunch. For their sake God will restore Israel to its land, where faithful believers will worship and serve him in peace and content-ment (8-10). But those who ignore his warnings and continue to worship foreign gods will be destroyed (11-12).

The minority of faithful believers, those who worship and obey God, are God's truly chosen ones, God's true servants. They will be blessed with God's favour. The rest of the nation, those who ignore God, will be disgraced with God's punishment (13-14). Although the ungodly will be destroyed, their name will continue to be used by the faithful as a symbol of the curse of God upon disobedience. The faithful, by contrast, will be given a new name, to indicate God's favour upon them. They will live in loyal dependence on the faithful God (15-16).

A new creation (65:17-25)

Israel's condition in the time of the prophet is then contrasted with conditions in the new Jerusalem, the kingdom of the Messiah. That kingdom is not an improved version of the old Israelite kingdom, but is something entirely new. It is a new creation, where the quality of life will be different from that of the present world. Sorrow will be replaced by rejoicing. Life will not be cut short except where God acts in judgment (17-20).

In the new creation people will have complete satisfaction. They will not experience the sufferings and frustrations that result from sin, but will enjoy life as God intended them to enjoy it (21-23). The absence of sin will mean that, above all, they will live in perfect fellowship with God. The world of nature also will benefit in this new era of genuine peace and harmony (24-25).

Attitudes towards ritual (66:1-6)

This chapter continues the contrast between the majority of Israel who were the people of God in name only, and the godly minority who were his true people. The returning exiles were glad to hear that the temple was to be rebuilt, but the prophet reminds them that they are mistaken if they think that God's sole dwelling place is a temple. God dwells everywhere. They are also mistaken if they think that God's chief requirement for people is that they carry out religious ceremonies. What God most desires is their humble acknowledgment of sin and their genuine repentance (66:1-2).

Without this humble attitude of heart, killing an innocent animal in sacrifice is as bad as killing a person; presenting holy offerings is as bad as presenting unclean things; so-called worship of God is as bad as worship of idols. Correct religious ritual, without obedience in the common things of everyday life, will not help a person escape the judgment of God (3-4).

Genuine believers, who emphasize that to fear God is more important than to be ritually correct, are excluded from the religious ceremonies by the ritualists. They are mocked with the challenge to show openly that God is on their side (5). God's judgment on these sinners will begin at the very place where they mock him, the temple (6).

New people and a new age (66:7-24)

Usually there is a long period of development before a group of people becomes a nation, but the new nation Israel will appear suddenly and unexpectedly, like a baby born before the due date (7-9). As with the birth of a baby, there is much rejoicing over the birth of the new nation (10-11). The 'baby' grows strong and active because God is the one who nourishes it. Under the controlling hand of God, Israel prospers (12-14).

While Israel enjoys God's blessings, enemy nations suffer. God's people have new life, but the rebels are punished with death (15-16). In particular, God's judgment falls upon those who reject his law and engage in idolatrous rituals (17).

The day of God's great intervention in history displays his glory to the people of the world, bringing destruction to some and salvation to others. Gentiles from far-off nations, together with Jews scattered in those nations, flock to Jerusalem to worship God. No distinction is made between Jew and Gentile; all have access to the house of God, and all have equal right to worship and serve him (18-21). In the new age all the redeemed join in the unending worship of God. Those who rebel against him and reject his love suffer unending punishment (22-24).

Jeremiah

INTRODUCTION

An obvious feature of the book of Jeremiah is the unusually large amount it reveals of the author's personality. Jeremiah, like other prophets, knew that if he faithfully announced God's message he would be unpopular, but his writings reveal the deeper tensions that developed within him. He was sad at the ungodly state of his people, and he unceasingly denounced the false religious practices, wrong social behaviour and foolish government actions that characterized the nation. The bitter persecution he received was distressing enough, but much more distressing was the feeling that God had been unfair to him.

If we are to understand the difficulties and conflicts that Jeremiah faced, we must first understand the condition of the people to whom he preached. A century earlier the former northern kingdom (Israel) had been destroyed and its people scattered among the nations of the Assyrian Empire. Now the southern kingdom (Judah) was heading for a similar judgment, and Jeremiah's task was to warn the unrepentant people that the day of reckoning was almost upon them.

RELIGIOUS BACKGROUND

Josiah's reformation

The reign of Josiah (640-609 BC) brought with it a reformation of Judah's religion and a revival of genuine prophetic activity in the nation. The person who initiated the reforms was Josiah himself, and the most important person in the renewed prophetic activity was Jeremiah.

When Josiah came to the throne of Judah, he inherited a country that was religiously and morally corrupt. The two kings before him, Manasseh and Amon, had reigned for a total of fifty-seven years, during which they had dragged Judah down to a religious and moral condition worse than that for which God had destroyed the original Canaanites. Manasseh introduced foreign religious practices of every kind, and developed a national policy (which Amon followed) of promoting these practices in place of the true worship of Yahweh (2 Kings 21:1-9; 21:16,19-22). Josiah, on becoming firmly established

as king, set out to reform Judah. His aim was to rid Judah of all these evils and re-establish the worship of Yahweh as taught in the law of Moses.

The generation that had grown up during the time of Manasseh and Amon knew almost nothing of the law that God had given to Israel at Mt Sinai. When workmen were repairing the temple and found some scrolls of this long-forgotten law, Josiah was able to read it for himself. He was shocked to find how far Judah had turned away from God, but this only increased his zeal for reform. He removed all idolatrous priests and destroyed all shrines and other sacred objects associated with false gods. He re-introduced the Passover, centralized the worship in Jerusalem where it could be properly supervised, and prohibited all forms of spiritism and fortune-telling (2 Kings 22:1-23:25).

However, Josiah's reforms were not enough to remove the idolatrous ideas that were deeply rooted in the minds of the people. Although religious disorders were removed and proper practices introduced, few people were changed inwardly. The nation was still rebellious against God and was heading for certain judgment (2 Kings 23:26-27).

Jeremiah's view of Judah's religion

In 627 BC, during the reign of Josiah, Jeremiah began his prophetic work (Jer 1:1-2). But he makes little reference to Josiah's reformation. Being a prophet, he saw there had been no real change in the hearts of the people, and therefore the changes in the external forms of the religion would have no lasting effect (Jer 9:25-26; 11:15). In fact, idolatrous practices soon returned (Jer 7:16-20; 19:3-9).

While not discouraging the zealous king from carrying on with his good work, Jeremiah tried to strike deeper into the hearts and consciences of the people. He was not opposed to Josiah's revival of the sacrificial system, for people still had to be obedient to the law (Jer 17:21-22,26); but he pointed out that unless people had a moral and spiritual reformation, they would certainly fall under God's judgment (Jer 14:12).

The most important period of Jeremiah's work began after Josiah's death. His warnings became more intense as he assured the people that, because of their persistence in wrong attitudes and wrong behaviour, they would be taken captive to Babylon (Jer 10:17-18; 21:2-7; 26:1-6).

God's messenger rejected

People did not like to hear Jeremiah's repeated announcements that the Babylonians would conquer Jerusalem, destroy the temple and take the people captive. As a result he suffered constant persecution. He was violently opposed by his own family (Jer 12:6), by the people of his home town (Jer 11:19-21), by the citizens of Jerusalem in general (Jer 15:10,20; 18:18; 20:7), by the religious leaders (Jer 20:1-2; 28:10-11; 29:24-28), by the civil authorities (Jer 37:11-15; 38:1-6,24-27) and by the kings of Judah (Jer 36:26; 37:18). He was flogged (Jer 20:2; 37:15), on occasions imprisoned (Jer 20:1-2; 37:15,21; 38:13) and often threatened with death (Jer 11:21; 26:7-9; 36:19,26; 38:4,15).

Jeremiah never married (Jer 16:2) and for much of his life he had few friends. Society at large would have nothing to do with him (Jer 15:10,17), and after a while he was not even allowed to enter the temple (Jer 36:5). His loneliness increased when he was forbidden to join in ordinary community activities such as feasts and funerals (Jer 16:5,8). Nevertheless, some people in places of influence at times gained protection for him against his persecutors (Jer 26:24; 38:7-13; 40:5-6).

HISTORICAL BACKGROUND

Readers of Jeremiah may at times find the book confusing because the prophecies and narratives are not arranged in chronological order. To help towards a clearer understanding of the book, the following summary gives the sequence of local and international events that form the background to Jeremiah's messages.

Collapse of Assyrian power

One factor that favoured Josiah in his reform was the decline of Assyria, who had, till then, been the chief power in the region. Assyria had destroyed Judah's sister kingdom to the north a century earlier (2 Kings 17:5-6) and had made life difficult for the Judean kings of the time (see introductory notes to Isaiah). By the time of Josiah Assyrian power had weakened sufficiently for Josiah to carry out reforms in his country without interference from hostile neighbours.

As the power of Assyria declined, Babylon and Egypt expanded their influence in the region. When Babylon conquered the Assyrian capital Nineveh in 612 BC, Pharaoh Necho of Egypt set out to resist any further Babylonian expansion. He apparently hoped that he could strengthen the remains of Assyria's western territory, so that it might form a defence barrier between Egypt and Babylon.

Since Judah lay between Egypt and Assyria, the Judean king Josiah saw this alliance between the two nations as a threat to Judah's independence. He preferred Assyria to remain weak, and attempted to stop Pharaoh's army as it passed through Palestine on its way to Assyria. This proved to be a disastrous decision. Judah was defeated and Josiah was killed in battle (609 BC; 2 Kings 23:28-30). Assyria could withstand the superior forces of Babylon no longer, and soon collapsed. It became absorbed into the Babylonian Empire and lost for ever its separate national identity.

End of Judah's independence

Following Josiah's death, the people of Judah made Josiah's second son, Jehoahaz, the nation's new king (2 Kings 23:30). But Pharaoh Necho now considered himself the controller of Judah and he would not accept the king whom the Judeans had chosen. He removed Jehoahaz and took him captive to Egypt, then put Jehoahaz's older brother, Jehoiakim, on the throne instead. He also placed a heavy tax on Judah (2 Kings 23:31-34).

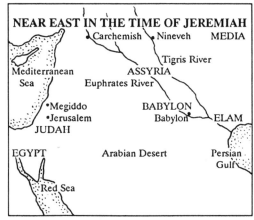

NEAR EAST IN THE TIME OF JEREMIAH

Once Jehoiakim began to rule, it soon became clear why the people had not chosen him as king. He was a proud, cruel and oppressive ruler, who did not hesitate to murder any who opposed him or even displeased him (2 Kings 24:4; Jer 26:20-23; 36:21-26). Despite the heavy taxes his country had to pay Egypt, he built himself luxurious royal buildings. To make matters worse, he forced the builders to work on his selfish projects without payment (Jer 22:13-18).

Beginning of Babylon's conquest

The long struggle between Egypt and Babylon came to a climax when the armies of Babylon conquered Egypt in a famous battle at Carchemish, on the Euphrates River, in 605 BC (Jer 46:2). This meant that Judah now came under the control of Babylon and had to pay its taxes to Babylon instead of to Egypt.

When the victorious Babylonians returned to their homeland, they took captive with them a number of capable and well educated young men from the leading families of Jerusalem. These young men, among whom were Daniel and his three friends, were to be trained as administrators in the Babylonian government (Dan 1:1-6).

After three years Jehoiakim rebelled against Babylon by refusing to pay further taxes. This was a dangerous decision, but Jehoiakim apparently hoped that Nebuchadnezzar would be too busy with wars elsewhere to deal with the rebellion of a small country such as Judah. Although Nebuchadnezzar did not attack Jerusalem immediately, neither did he ignore it. His anti-Judean tactic was to encourage neighbouring countries under his control to carry out guerilla attacks against Judah, and so undermine whatever economic, political or military stability might have remained (2 Kings 24:1-2).

In due course, after he had established his authority in other troublesome regions, Nebuchadnezzar sent his armies to besiege Jerusalem. It seems that by this time the people of Jerusalem could tolerate the worthless Jehoiakim no longer, and handed him over to the Babylonians in an attempt to win concessions for themselves. Although the city had not fallen, Jehoiakim found himself a captive in the enemy's hands. He was chained ready to be sent to Babylon, but he died before the journey began. No one mourned his death, and his body was thrown on the garbage dump outside Jerusalem, as if it were the carcass of an unclean animal (2 Chron 36:6; Jer 22:18-19; 36:30).

The eighteen year old Jehoiachin (also known as Jeconiah, or Coniah) became king, but after three months he saw the uselessness of resisting the Babylonians further. He therefore surrendered, in the hope that he could lessen Jerusalem's suffering and gain reasonable treatment from the conquerors (597 BC; 2 Kings 24:10-12).

Having captured Jerusalem, the Babylonians lessened the likelihood of further revolt by carrying off most of Judah's wealth and all its best people to their own country. They left behind only those they had no use for, and appointed Jehoiachin's uncle, Zedekiah (another son of Josiah), as king over them (2 Kings 24:12-17).

The destruction of Jerusalem

Zedekiah was a weak king, easily persuaded by influential people. With all Judah's most capable administrators taken to Babylon, Zedekiah's government was dominated by self-seeking officials who had poor political judgment and no religious insight. They were constantly urging Zedekiah to seek Egypt's help and rebel against Babylon. Jeremiah opposed any policy of rebellion against Babylon, knowing that it would lead only to the horrors of siege and destruction. He advised Judah to accept its fate as God's will and submit to Babylon (2 Kings 24:18-20; Jer 21:1-10; 27:12-22).

Foolishly, Zedekiah followed the advice of the pro-Egyptian party and rebelled against Babylon. Nebuchadnezzar lost patience and, determined to put an end to Jerusalem's rebellion, sent his armies to crush the city in one final great siege. When Egypt came to Jerusalem's aid, the siege was temporarily lifted, but Jeremiah assured the Jerusalemites that Babylon would return to crush both Egypt and Judah. The pro-Egyptian party accused Jeremiah of being a traitor and had him beaten and thrown into prison (Jer 37:1-21).

Soon the Babylonians returned and Jeremiah's prophecy came true. (The book of Lamentations gives a vivid picture of the dreadful conditions in and around Jerusalem during the siege; see Lam 2:10-12,19-21; 4:4-5,7-9.) When, after a siege lasting a year and a half, the Babylonians finally made a break in the wall, Zedekiah and some of his men tried to escape, but were captured by the enemy (2 Kings 25:1-7).

The victorious Babylonian soldiers then overran Jerusalem, seizing anything of value that could be taken back to Babylon and burning or smashing what remained. The temple was destroyed and the city left in ruins. The Babylonians executed the leaders of the rebellion and took all the most useful citizens captive. They released Jeremiah from prison and gave him full freedom to decide where he would like to live, Babylon or Judah. Jeremiah decided to stay in Judah, along with a small number of farmers and other poorer people who were of no use to Babylon (2 Kings 25:8-21; Jer 39:13-14; 40:4-6). This was the end of Jerusalem (587 BC).

Jeremiah taken to Egypt

Gedaliah, one of the few leaders in Jerusalem who had not supported Zedekiah's pro-Egyptian policy, was appointed by the Babylonians as governor over those who remained in Judah. With Jeremiah's support he followed a pro-Babylon policy. He took no action against those anti-Babylonian military leaders of Judah who had managed to escape the Babylonian army. Instead he encouraged them, along with other refugees who had fled the country, to return and settle around his administrative headquarters at Mizpah, a town north-west of Jerusalem (2 Kings 25:22-24; Jer 40:7-12).

The anti-Babylon group, however, had still not learnt the lessons Jeremiah had been trying to teach them. Refusing to accept Babylon's domination, they plotted against the governor Babylon had appointed, and when a suitable occasion arose they murdered him. Fearing a revenge attack by Nebuchadnezzar, the remaining Judeans of the resettlement area fled for their lives to Egypt, taking a protesting Jeremiah with them (2 Kings 25:25-26; Jer 40:13-43:7).

Even in Egypt, the country whose help he had always rejected, Jeremiah's continued to announce God's message. But God's people refused to heed it (Jer 43:8-44:30). According to tradition they became so hostile that eventually they stoned him to death.

The use of names

During the time of the divided kingdom, the custom was to refer to the northern kingdom as Israel (or Samaria, after its capital), and the southern kingdom as Judah (or Jerusalem, after its capital). (For further details about the use of names see introductory notes to Isaiah.) By the time of Jeremiah only Judah remained, so there was no further need to distinguish between the former northern and southern kingdoms. Jeremiah sometimes uses the name Israel when referring to Judah, for he uses the word according to its ancient and more general usage, not according to its specific usage during the time of the divided kingdom.

To avoid confusion, these notes will refer to the southern kingdom only by its name Judah. The name Israel will be used only to apply to the northern part of the divided kingdom, except in those places where the context makes it clear that the reference is to ancient Israel (e.g. Israel in the time of Moses).

OUTLINE

1:1-6:30 JEREMIAH'S EARLY MINISTRY

The call of Jeremiah (1:1-10)

Jeremiah belonged to a priestly family that lived not far from Jerusalem. However, he may never have practised as a priest, for God's will was that he be a prophet. His prophetic ministry lasted at least forty years. It began in 627 BC (the thirteenth year of Josiah's reign) and continued into the era that followed the destruction of Jerusalem in 587 BC (1:1-3).

God had chosen Jeremiah to be a prophet before he was born. He was to be God's messenger to Judah and the surrounding nations (4-5). At the time God called him to be a prophet, Jeremiah was probably no more than twenty years of age. When he objected that he was too young and inexperienced for such a task, God replied that he would be with him and give him the message to speak. Jeremiah had no cause to be afraid (6-8).

Much of Jeremiah's message would not be popular and at times would appear to be pessimistic because of its repeated announcements of God's judgment. Nevertheless, judgment was necessary, because proud self-confidence must be broken down and the corruption of sin removed before new spiritual life can grow up (9-10).

Two visions (1:11-19)

To encourage Jeremiah in the work that lay ahead of him, God gave him two visions. The almond, first tree to bloom in spring, symbolized God's watchfulness and constant readiness to keep his promises (11-12. The Hebrew word for 'almond' sounds like the Hebrew word for 'watching'). The giant boiling pot, tilted from the north so as to pour its contents over Judah, symbolized a foreign army entering Judah from the north and overrunning the country. This was a judgment brought about by God because of Judah's idolatry (13-16).

God told Jeremiah he was not to be afraid in announcing Judah's doom, for God cannot use a coward. He warned that Jeremiah had a lifetime of opposition ahead of him, but at the same time he promised to specially strengthen his servant. All the attacks on Jeremiah, whether from political leaders, religious leaders or the people at large, would not overcome him, because God would strengthen and defend him (17-19).

A nation's unfaithfulness (2:1-19)

While Josiah was reconstructing the outward form of Judah's religion, Jeremiah was searching into the deeply rooted attitudes of the people and trying to bring about a truly spiritual change. He contrasts the nation's present sad condition with its devotion to God in former days. Israel once loved God, as a bride loves her husband. She was like the firstfruits of the harvest that belonged to God, and those who plundered her were punished (2:1-3).

God now challenges the nation to produce proof that her turning away from God has resulted from any failure on God's part. He brought his people out of Egypt, cared for them on their long journey through harsh dry country, and gave them a pleasant fertile land to live in. But they polluted the land by their wickedness. Under the leadership of ungodly priests, ignorant teachers, corrupt rulers and worthless prophets, they turned away from God and followed the religious practices of their heathen neighbours (4-8).

Therefore, God lays a charge of unfaithfulness against his people, and calls upon the sun, moon and stars that shine upon them to be his witnesses. Heathen nations remain true to their gods, even though those gods may be lifeless and useless. Israel and Judah, by contrast, exchanged the true and living God for useless idols (9-12). They acted like people who turned away from the natural spring that gave them a permanent supply of pure water, and trusted for their water supply in a cracked cistern they had made themselves (13).

Israel and Judah boasted that they were God's children, but now they are becoming slaves of other nations. A century earlier Assyria had invaded the northern kingdom, destroyed its cities and taken its people into captivity (14-15). Other nations now threatened the southern kingdom. God warns that it is useless and foolish for Judah to ask either Egypt or Assyria to help defend it against enemy invasions. It is useless because such attacks are a judgment on Judah for its disobedience. It is foolish because, in seeking aid from a more powerful nation, Judah is placing itself under that nation's religious influence and political power (16-19).

Idolatry and immorality (2:20-37)

In associating with Baal and other gods, Judah has broken the covenant bond with Yahweh. Judah's unfaithfulness is likened to adultery (20). (Throughout the following chapters, Jeremiah makes repeated reference to the beliefs and practices of Baalism, and to the significance they had in leading God's people into spiritual adultery and prostitution. For information that will help to understand Jeremiah's teaching, see introductory notes to Judges, subheading 'The religion of the Canaanites'.)

Two brief illustrations picture Judah's uselessness for God. In one illustration the nation is likened to a well cultivated vine that has grown wild. In the other it is likened to a filthy object that no amount of washing can cleanse (21-22). But the main illustration in this section is that of a woman who has left her husband for other men. Judah, however, claims that she cannot be held responsible for her idolatry. She is like an innocent person who has been led astray. God replies that, far from being innocent, she has actually lusted after other gods — as an animal in heat lusts for a mate. She has gone looking for foreign gods with the eagerness of a thirsty traveller who walks the desert searching for water till the sandals drop off his feet (23-25).

God's people will bring disgrace upon themselves because of their rebellion against him. They worship idols of wood and stone, but when these idols prove powerless to help them in a time of need, they turn back to God and expect him to save them. God will surely send shameful calamity upon such a worthless nation. Then the people will find out that their idols cannot save them (26-28).

As a father punishes his children to correct them, so God has punished his people, but it has not resulted in any change within them (29-30). He has not treated them harshly. They should feel no need to want to be 'free' from him. Yet they have done what would seem impossible: they have forgotten the one who gave them glory (31-32).

The wickedness of the people of Judah has become so great that they can even teach prostitutes how to be immoral. A person might happen to shed blood in defending himself against a robber, but the people of Judah attack the poor and helpless simply because they love violence. Their consciences have become so dull that they cannot see their wrongdoing (33-35). They have turned from God to trust in Egypt and Assyria, but these nations will prove to be treacherous friends. They will bring injury and shame upon Judah (36-37).

Judah unfaithful and unashamed (3:1-5)

By her spiritual adultery Judah has broken the marriage bond with Yahweh and defiled the land. In her immorality and idolatry she has acted like a prostitute who lures lovers in the city streets. She is like a desert outlaw who looks for innocent victims along the country's highways (3:1-2).

God sent drought to bring Judah to repentance, but the nation has remained unmoved. She is so shameless she even looks like a prostitute (3). Yet she is bold enough to ask God to act like an overkind father and give her whatever she wants. But

God will act in righteousness against her because of her sin (4-5).

Need for true repentance (3:6-18)

King Josiah had tried to reform Judah, but because people had not changed inwardly, the reformation affected only the external forms of religion. Looking from God's viewpoint, Jeremiah calls the people's so-called repentance a pretence (see v. 10). Judah had seen her sister nation Israel divorced from God and sent into captivity because of her spiritual adultery, but Israel's experience taught her nothing. She is now doing what Israel did. In accepting Josiah's reforms she pretends to be returning to God, but she is not sincere (6-10).

Judah's spiritual adultery is more blameworthy than Israel's, because she ignored the warning God gave her through the divine judgment poured out on Israel (11). Jeremiah promises the northerners that if they acknowledge their unfaithfulness and turn from it, God will bring them from captivity back to their own land (12-14). He will give them new leaders, who will lead the people in his ways (15). There will be no need for the ark of the covenant as symbol of God's presence, because God himself will dwell among them. He will rule over a united and obedient people (16-18).

Repentance means genuine change (3:19-4:4)

God wanted the relationship between him and his people to be like that between a father and a son, or between a husband and a wife. But his people have been rebellious and unfaithful (19-20). In hope, the prophet pictures the people turning from their false worship at Baal's high places and crying out to God for forgiveness. In response God promises that if they truly repent, he will forgive them and heal them (21-22a).

The people then turn to God and confess their sins. They admit that the worship of Baal has been a deception; instead of bringing them prosperity it has brought them disaster. They are ashamed of themselves, and return to Yahweh in acknowledgment that he alone is God (22b-25).

God reminds the people that if they repent, their repentance must be genuine. They must remove every trace of idolatry from their lives and renew their oath of absolute loyalty to him. Only then will they be able to serve him by taking his message to the nations (4:1-2).

People must break up their hardened hearts and remove wrongdoing from their lives, just as farmers break up the hard ground and remove weeds before they plant new seed. Inward change,

not outward ceremony, is what is needed. Without such repentance, the nation will be destroyed in divine judgment (3-4).

The coming invasion (4:5-31)

Jeremiah now pictures the terrible judgment that will fall on Judah if it does not repent. With the enemy army sweeping down upon Judah from the north, a trumpeter sounds the alarm and the people of Judah flee to their walled cities for safety (5-6). Like an enraged lion the enemy prepares to pounce upon its victim. God is about to pour out his anger on the unfaithful people (7-8).

Judah's leaders, both civil and religious, are shocked at the sudden catastrophe that overtakes them. They now realize that by believing the false prophets, they have deceived themselves. They mistakenly thought that God would never allow a heathen nation to destroy them (9-10).

God's judgment burns up his people like a scorching desert wind (11-12). As Jeremiah pictures the enemy's horses and chariots sweeping across the northern frontier, he makes a last desperate plea to the Jerusalemites to repent (13-14). He sees the invasion forces moving down from Dan, crossing Ephraim's mountains, spreading over the country and besieging cities as they head for their main prize, Jerusalem. The people of Judah have brought this disaster upon themselves because of the way they have lived. They are about to reap the fruits of their ungodliness and idolatry (15-18).

Jeremiah can scarcely bear to look at the scene of destruction, and cries out in his distress (19-21). God assures him that the judgment is just. In their stupidity the people have rejected God and devoted themselves to wrongdoing. Now they are suffering the consequences (22).

To the prophet it seems that, with the fall of Judah, the earth has become barren, waste, dark and silent (23-26). God's judgment is so devastating that, were it not for his mercy, the people would be wiped out (27-28). In country towns people flee before the enemy and look for hiding places in forests and caves (29). Jerusalem tries to win favour with the enemy, as a prostitute tries to win the favour of lovers, but the enemy is not fooled. Jerusalem's end is as horrible as that of a brutally murdered prostitute; her screams are as piercing as those of a woman in agonizing childbirth (30-31).

Sins of Jerusalem and Judah (5:1-19)

A search of Jerusalem reveals that the city is wholly corrupt. Injustice and selfishness abound. People claim they belong to God and they swear oaths by his name, but they remain untouched by the lessons he is trying to teach them (5:1-3). There may be some excuse for the poor and uneducated if they know nothing of God's law, but the upper classes are just as ignorant. This indicates that the problem lies not with people's social background or material well-being, but with their hardened hearts. All alike reject the authority of God's law and refuse to be bound by his standards (4-5).

Jerusalem is ripe for judgment. The invading armies are likened to wild beasts ready to pounce and kill (6). In addition to being idolatrous, the people are so morally degraded they are little better than animals. There can be no forgiveness, only punishment, for a nation such as this (7-9).

As a vineyard is stripped, so Judah will be destroyed, though the destruction will not be total (10-11). The people have deceived themselves. They have refused to believe the words of God's prophets, and keep telling themselves that God will not destroy his own people. God will therefore act against them decisively, according to the judgments he announces by his prophet Jeremiah (12-14).

Through Jeremiah, God tells the people of Judah that a foreign nation will invade their country, and neither Judah's armed forces nor its defence fortifications will prevent widespread slaughter and ruin (15-17). But the nation will not be completely wiped out. Those who survive the attack will be taken captive to a foreign land, which will be a fitting punishment for their disloyalty in serving foreign gods in their own land (18-19).

A corrupt society (5:20-31)

The people of Judah do not fear God for his mighty power (20-21), nor do they give him thanks for the benefits he gives them through nature (22-24). They think they can go their own way regardless of God, but in so doing they miss out on his blessings (25).

By cruelty, cunning and bribery, the wealthy increase their power, but the poor cannot obtain justice in even the smallest affairs. Administrators and judges alike are corrupt (26-28). God sees all this, and will not allow it to go unpunished (29). He sees also that priests and prophets cooperate in the wrongdoing, while the people in general, instead of rebuking them, encourage them. Judah is a nation of corrupt and greedy people who are concerned only for their immediate prosperity. They cannot see that they are heading for a dreadful end (30-31).

Destruction of Jerusalem and Judah (6:1-30)

Jeremiah warns that the enemy forces will invade from the north. The citizens of Jerusalem should

therefore flee from the city to the hilly regions south of Jerusalem, where they may be able to find refuge from the invaders (6:1-2). As shepherds lead their sheep to feed in new pastures, so will the enemy commanders lead their forces to 'devour' Jerusalem. They will attack by day and by night (3-5). In building their siegeworks around the city, the enemy soldiers will ruin the nearby fields and forests. The reason for Jerusalem's destruction is that the city is morally corrupt and spiritually sick (6-8).

The enemy will be as thorough in destruction as a grape-picker is in picking every grape he can find on the vine. Jeremiah hopes that some might be spared, but he can find none who will listen to his message. Therefore, he can announce only judgment (9-11a). In this judgment, no age group will be spared. All property will be seized by the plundering invaders (11b-12). Common people and religious leaders alike are shamelessly corrupt, but all they have gained through injustice will be lost. Priests and prophets assure the people that all is well, when in fact the nation is doomed (13-15).

God has urged the people to follow the ways of godly people of the past who kept his law. He has warned them of punishment if they ignore him. But it has all been without result (16-17). God therefore announces to the nations of the world that his people will now reap the fruit of their disobedience (18-19). The people offer incense and sacrifices, but God is not pleased with such offerings when the offerers do not listen to his teaching. Religious exercises will not save a disobedient people from God's judgment (20-21).

Judah will be powerless against the invading armies of this cruel, well equipped enemy (22-24). Even innocent civilians, when fleeing to safety in the country, should be careful to keep well clear of the enemy forces (25-26).

As God's servant, Jeremiah is like a refiner of silver who tries to remove the dross (wickedness) from the precious metal (God's people). But the people refuse to be refined. They do not want to be separated from their evil. They are therefore rejected as worthless (27-30).

7:1-20:18 THE SPIRITUAL CONDITION OF JUDAH

Jeremiah at the temple (7:1-15)

This message seems to belong to the period of religious decline that followed the death of Josiah. Though Josiah had done well to restore the temple, the people developed a wrong, even superstitious, attitude towards it. They felt that it was sacred, that it belonged to God, and that therefore he would not allow any enemy to destroy it. They thought that the presence of the temple in Jerusalem guaranteed the city against capture by the enemy. God now tells Jeremiah to stand outside the temple and announce to the people that in thinking this way they are deceiving themselves. Only by changing their ways and replacing injustice with godliness will they save their temple, their city and their nation from certain destruction (7:1-7).

Jeremiah points out the stupidity of the people in thinking they can do as they wish and still expect God to save them. They are immoral, dishonest, violent and idolatrous, yet they think they are safe because they offer sacrifices in his temple (8-11). Shiloh was once the religious centre of the nation, the place where the tabernacle was set up; but God allowed Shiloh and the tabernacle to be invaded and smashed because of the people's wickedness. For the

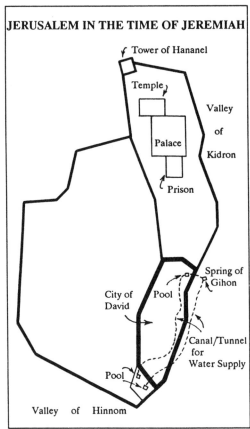

JERUSALEM IN THE TIME OF JEREMIAH

- Tower of Hananel
- Temple
- Valley
- of
- Palace
- Kidron
- Prison
- Spring of Gihon
- City of David
- Pool
- Canal/Tunnel for Water Supply
- Pool
- Valley of Hinnom

same reason he will now allow Jerusalem and its temple to be destroyed (12-15; cf. Josh 18:1; 1 Sam 1:3; Ps 78:60).

No hope for an idolatrous people (7:16-8:3)

God now tells Jeremiah that it is useless for him to persist in praying for the safety of the Judeans. They have so given themselves to idolatrous practices that nothing can save them from God's judgment. Throughout the cities and towns of Judah people worship foreign gods, but in the process they harm themselves (16-19). The harm will be much greater when God's judgment falls on them (20).

While openly worshipping heathen gods, the people also offer sacrifices to Yahweh. The offering of sacrifices was part of the religious system God gave to Israel through Moses, but the first thing God demanded of his people was always obedience (21-23). Israel's history shows that sacrifices will never save a stubborn and disobedient people from punishment (24-26).

Most of the people will ignore the prophet's warnings, but he must persist in announcing God's message (27-28). Jeremiah tells the people to shave off their hair as a sign of mourning for the death that is soon to overtake their nation (29). They have brought idolatrous practices into God's temple, and just outside Jerusalem they have established a site for the heathen practice of sacrificing children to the god Molech (30-31). But the place where they have slaughtered their children will become a dump for their own corpses. There they will rot in the sun and be eaten by foul birds (32-34; cf. 2 Kings 21:6; 23:10).

Not satisfied with butchering the helpless people, the invaders will do all they can to heap disgrace upon Judah. They will even drag out the bones of the nation's honoured dead from their tombs and scatter them like garbage on the ground. But such disgrace is preferable to the horror that will be experienced by people who live through those days (8:1-3).

Tophet and the Valley of Hinnom

The place where the Judeans offered their children as burnt sacrifices was the Valley of Ben Hinnom, on the southern side of the city. The valley got its name from the son of Hinnom (the Hebrew *ben* meaning 'son') who at one time probably owned the land that stretched along the valley. The name Tophet seems to have meant 'place of burning' and was used originally in relation to the place in the Valley of Hinnom where people burnt their children as sacrifices. This was also the place where people from

Jerusalem dumped broken pottery (see 19:1-2). In time it became a public garbage dump and fires burnt there continually.

When transliterated from Hebrew to Greek, 'Valley of Hinnom' (Hebrew: *ge-hinnom*) becomes *gehenna*. This was the word that Jesus used for the place of final punishment of the wicked, and is commonly translated 'hell' (Matt 10:28; 18:9; 23:33). The Valley of Hinnom was associated with judgment and burning (see 7:31-32; 19:4-7), and therefore *gehenna* became a fitting word to denote the place or state of eternal punishment (Mark 9:43-48; cf Matt 18:8-9; Rev 20:10,15).

Sin and its punishment (8:4-17)

It is natural for a person who falls to pick himself up again, but the people of Jerusalem who have fallen spiritually make no attempt to return to God (4-6). It is natural for a bird to obey the laws of instinct and know the time to migrate, but the people of Jerusalem do not know the laws of God or when to return to him (7).

The teachers of the law, the wisdom teachers, the priests and the prophets have all led the people astray. Instead of denouncing wrongdoing, they have told the people there is nothing to fear. They work solely for the benefits they hope to receive for themselves, but their gains will all be lost (8-11). Their behaviour is shameful, though they themselves feel no shame. They are supposed to be servants of God, but they are as useless as fruit trees that bear no fruit (12-13).

When the enemy invades, the people will realize that this is God's judgment on them because of their sin, but it will then be too late. There will be no safety for them, not even inside the walled cities. They have deceived themselves and now they must bear the consequences (14-15). The prophet sees them shaking with fear as the enemy armies descend on them from the north (16-17).

Mourning for Judah (8:18-9:22)

The prophet is overcome with grief as he foresees the tragic end of the nation. The people wonder why God their King does not save them. God replies that it is because of their idolatry. They now realize that they can no longer expect his salvation (18-20). Nothing can heal Judah's spiritual sickness now; the end has come. And nothing can heal the wounds of grief in Jeremiah's heart as he sees his people suffer (21-22).

Jeremiah is unable to express the extent of his grief. He feels he could weep for ever (9:1). On the other hand, he knows that the judgment is fitting. As he returns to consider the sinful city in which he lives, he wishes he could leave it and go to some quiet resting-place in the country (2).

Since Judah's society is characterized by lies and deceit (3-6), God warns that it is heading for a fiery judgment (7-9). The prophet foresees the desolation in Judah, with its cities ruined, its pasture lands destroyed, and its people either killed or taken captive to a foreign land (10-11).

If anyone asks why the land has been desolated (12), the answer is that the people have turned away from Yahweh and followed heathen gods. They have turned away from the law of God and followed their own stubborn hearts (13-16). In their distress and sorrow the people invite the professional mourners to come and wail over the dead city (17-19). This time, however, the mourning is real. Rich and poor, young and old die alike. Their corpses lie unburied in the streets and fields (20-22).

Knowledge of the only true God (9:23-10:16)

People may have knowledge, power and wealth, but these are no substitute for a true understanding and knowledge of God (23-24). The Judeans may have been circumcised as a sign that they are the covenant people of God, but in their hearts they have not been true to God or the covenant. They might as well be uncircumcised like their heathen neighbours. Israel's rite of circumcision is no more beneficial to disobedient people than the heathen rite of cutting the hair into certain shapes (25-26).

Jeremiah warns God's people against copying the practices of other nations and worshipping the sun, moon and stars. He warns them also against worshipping idols, which he describes as merely decorated pieces of wood (10:1-5). Judah's God, Yahweh, is not just one among many national gods. He is the only God, incomparable and all-powerful (6-7). People may be very artistic in carving or moulding their idols, and may go to much expense to clothe and decorate them, but the idols are still senseless and worthless. Yahweh alone is the true and living God (8-10).

Idols cannot make anything or do anything (11), but God created the universe and keeps it going. Idols are lifeless, and those who make them have no sense; but God is a living being, and all his works are the products of his wisdom (12-15). This God is the almighty Yahweh, the one who created all things and who chose Israel to be his people (16).

Prepare for captivity (10:17-25)

Picturing Jerusalem under siege, Jeremiah sadly tells the people that the end has almost come. They should collect their few remaining belongings and prepare for the long journey to captivity in Babylon (17-18). The people mourn for their nation, which has fallen like a collapsed tent. Chiefly to blame for this catastrophe are the nation's worthless leaders (19-21). Jeremiah then imagines the enemy armies roaring down from the north and desolating the towns of Judah (22).

As he pleads to God on behalf of his fellow countrymen, Jeremiah reminds God that people are naturally weak and are easily led astray (23). He asks, therefore, that God will not punish Judah too severely and that Judah will accept his correction. He prays that God's wrath will be poured out not upon Judah, but upon those ungodly nations who attack Judah with needless cruelty (24-25).

The broken covenant (11:1-17)

God had made a covenant with Israel after the people came out of Egypt, assuring them of blessing if they obeyed his law and punishment if they disobeyed. God now tells Jeremiah to remind the people of these conditions of the covenant (11:1-5). Past lessons should be a warning to them that unless they change their ways, they are heading for disaster (6-8). However, the people prefer to ignore the warnings. Like their forefathers they rebel against God and follow false gods (9-10). The towns of Judah are full of false gods, but the people will now find that these gods are powerless to save them from God's judgment (11-13).

It is too late to pray for Judah's deliverance. All her rituals and ceremonies will not save her from the punishment due to her (14-15). God intended Judah to be like a beautiful green olive tree, but when the storm of his judgment breaks, that olive tree will, as it were, be struck by lightning and burnt up. By worshipping Baal, Judah has brought about its own destruction (16-17).

A plot against Jeremiah (11:18-23)

The people of Anathoth, Jeremiah's home town, had become angry with Jeremiah. They did not like his uncompromising opposition to their false religious practices and his constant predictions of certain judgment. When God warned Jeremiah that they were plotting to kill him, Jeremiah cried to God for help (18-21). God now replies with a promise that he will protect Jeremiah and punish his would-be murderers (22-23).

Jeremiah's complaint; God's answer (12:1-17)

As he thinks back on the treachery of the people of Anathoth, Jeremiah is prompted to complain to God. Innocent people suffer, whereas wicked people live at ease. Why is it, he asks, that God allows the wicked to prosper? God gives them life and food, and they grow fat and prosperous, though their hearts are far from God (12:1-2). Jeremiah, by contrast, remains true to God, yet he suffers. Indeed, the whole land suffers because of the sins of people who are arrogant and evil. Jeremiah wishes they could all be destroyed (3-4).

In reply God rebukes his servant with some challenging questions. If he is discouraged by the comparatively small opposition of the people of his home town, how will he overcome the far greater opposition that he will face from the nation at large? If he is running from the opposition of a few friends and relatives, how will he survive when he faces a jungle of wild animals (5-6)?

God then assures Jeremiah that there *is* justice, and in God's time the wicked will be punished. Judah may be compared to God's household and God's beloved, but she has fought against God like a wild beast or a killer bird. God will therefore use other 'wild beasts' and 'wild birds' (enemy nations) to devour her (7-9). In another picture, Judah is likened to God's vineyard. But the leaders of the nation have trampled down his vineyard, and the enemy will now come in and destroy it completely. Judah will reap the fruits of her sin (10-13).

Not only Judah will be conquered, but also the neighbouring nations. They took advantage of Judah's weakened position to carry out raids against it (cf. 2 Kings 24:1-2), but they themselves will now be raided. Like Judah, they will go into captivity in Babylon (14). However, if any of these conquered nations renounces Baal and swears allegiance to Yahweh, then, like Judah, it will be brought back to its homeland (15-17).

A nation useless and disgraced (13:1-27)

In an effort to emphasize God's warnings to Judah more forcefully, Jeremiah gave them an illustration that they could all see. He took a piece of clean new cloth, put it around his waist, then walked to a distant river where he buried the cloth in the river bank. Some time later he returned to the river and brought back the cloth for all to see. It was now rotten and useless (13:1-7). The meaning is that Judah, the nation that was supposed to be morally pure and tied closely to God, has now become rotten and useless. Because it has rebelled against Yahweh and served other gods, it too will be taken to a distant land (8-11).

God then instructed Jeremiah to give a second illustration of warning to the people of Judah. To them there was nothing unusual in the sight of wine jars filled with wine, for they liked to enjoy their wrongly gained prosperity to the full. Jeremiah explains that wine, instead of symbolizing pleasure, now symbolizes wrath, God's wrath. The nation will drink that wrath till it becomes drunk and unable to save itself from disaster (12-14).

Jeremiah has a sincere love for his country and will be deeply grieved to see such a catastrophe occur. He urges the proud nation to humble itself and turn to God, otherwise judgment will overtake it, as darkness overtakes a frightened traveller in dangerous hill country (15-17). The king and others of the royal family will suffer the humiliation of being stripped of their royalty and taken to Babylon as common prisoners, along with citizens from the farthest areas of the kingdom (18-19).

Judah had once been friends with Babylon (2 Kings 20:12-19). How great, then, will be Judah's surprise when it sees Babylon's armies descending upon it from the north. They will attack Judah with the ruthlessness of wolves attacking sheep or a rapist attacking a woman (20-22). Judah's sin is so deeply embedded that reform is now impossible. The nation will be driven off into captivity, just as chaff is driven away by the desert wind (23-25). It has acted like a prostitute, and will be punished with public disgrace like a prostitute (26-27).

Drought, disease and war (14:1-15:9)

A severe drought had hit Judah. People in all walks of life, from nobles to farmers, were affected by it, and they covered their heads as a sign of their distress. They had difficulty in getting enough water to keep themselves alive, and their animals were beginning to suffer from disease. Some had already died because of the lack of food (14:1-6).

Pleading on behalf of the people, Jeremiah confesses the nation's sins. He asks God to cease acting as if he were an uninterested traveller passing through a strange land, and instead act to help them. After all, the land is his and so are the people (7-9). In reply God points out that he cannot overlook their sin. Jeremiah should stop pleading for them, because nothing can now save them from God's judgment, a judgment that will come through war, famine and disease (10-12).

Jeremiah tells God that prophets have been assuring the people that these calamities will not overtake them (13). God replies that such prophets are false prophets. They will perish in shame and so will all those who believe them. The people have welcomed these prophecies of peace, because by such assurances they feel free to increase their wrongdoing without fear of punishment (14-16). Jeremiah weeps publicly to impress upon people the sorrow he feels as he foresees their terrible suffering (17-18).

Though his past pleas have not been answered, Jeremiah pleads with God yet once more. On behalf of the people he confesses their wrongdoing and asks that God will be merciful to them and give them rain. He prays that God will not forsake his people but will remember his covenant with them. There is no other God they can call upon to help them (19-22).

God replies that though Moses and Samuel had in the past pleaded successfully on behalf of the people (e.g. Exod 32:11-14; Num 14:13-25; 1 Sam. 7:5-9; 12:19-25), the nation has now passed the point where God can extend his mercy further. The false religion promoted by Manasseh still controls the attitudes of the people, and the nation will come to a cruel and humiliating end (15:1-4).

Time and again God has punished his people, with the purpose that they might acknowledge their sin and return to him; but always it has been without result. They do not deserve any further pity (5-6). The final slaughter is too horrible to imagine, but when people refuse to change their ways, such a judgment becomes inevitable (7-9).

Jeremiah's anguish; God's comfort (15:10-21)

The prophet again complains to God because of the unjust treatment he suffers. He has done no harm to the people, and in fact has pleaded on their behalf for God's mercy upon them, yet they hate him. They are angered at his attacks on their sin and his forecasts of judgment. Their hearts are as hard as iron (10-12). God's word is that the Judeans will be invaded, plundered and taken captive (13-14).

Knowing that God is understanding, Jeremiah asks that he will protect him from death and deal with his persecutors (15). He was glad to be God's representative, to receive God's message and pass it on to the people; but when they heard that message and knew that the prophet was angry with them because of their sin, they cut themselves off from him. Lonely and discouraged, Jeremiah feels that even God has failed him. He feels like a thirsty person who has come to a stream, only to find that the stream has dried up (16-18).

In response God tells Jeremiah that he must stop speaking idle words of self-pity, and speak useful words as a true servant of God should. He must not copy the people and their worthless attitudes; they must copy him. If they continue to oppose him, God will protect him (19-21).

Symbolic actions (16:1-21)

Again God instructs his prophet concerning certain courses of action designed to attract the people's attention. Jeremiah is to be a living reminder to the Judeans of what will happen to them if they do not repent. Firstly, he is not to marry or have children, as a grim warning to people that those with families will have greater distress when the final slaughter comes (16:1-4). Secondly, he is not to attend any funeral, as a warning that when Judah falls there will be no funerals, since the dead will lie unburied (5-7). Thirdly, he is not to join in any feast, as a sign that soon all merriment will be gone from Judah for ever (8-9).

When people question Jeremiah about his strange behaviour and the doom to which it points, he must give a forthright explanation. He must tell them plainly that this judgment is because of their rebellion against God in following false gods (10-13). Beyond the judgment there will be restoration. Just as God delivered Israel from slavery in Egypt, so in due course will he bring his people from captivity in Babylon back into their own land (14-15). First, however, they must go into captivity. As fish caught in a net or beasts hunted down by hunters, so the Judeans will be captured and dragged off to a foreign land (16-18).

As the prophet looks beyond the captivity to the restoration, he offers a prayer that expresses his confidence in God. He sees a day when God's people will return to their land and people of other nations will join with them to worship Yahweh as the only God (19-21).

Wrong attitudes and their outcome (17:1-13)

Baal worship has become so much a part of the people's everyday lives that God sees it as engraved on their hearts. It is so widely practised in Judah that it cannot be removed from the land unless the people themselves are removed (17:1-4). Those who ignore God and trust in themselves are likened to a useless stunted bush that tries to grow in barren ground. Those who trust in God are likened to a healthy green tree that flourishes in well-watered fertile soil (5-8).

Because of the deceitfulness of the human heart, people may not understand their own actions and motives. Only God knows the hidden attitudes of their hearts, and he treats people accordingly (9-10). Those who gain riches by dishonest methods are also deceiving themselves. They will one day lose their riches, just as a bird that hatches eggs stolen from another bird's nest will lose the young birds

when they grow and fly away (11). The only security in life is with the eternal God, whose presence is symbolized in the temple. But even the temple will not save those who turn away from him. The nation's hope is in a person, not a building (12-13).

Forthright messages (17:14-27)

Jeremiah is still distressed and once more appeals to God for help. His complaint is that the people mock him when they do not see his prophecies come true (14-15). He reminds God that he has done no more than announce the message God has given him. He personally does not wish doom upon the nation. Therefore, he asks God to be his protector against his persecutors (16-18).

One of God's commands to Jeremiah was that he go around the various city gates and warn the people of Jerusalem not to work on the Sabbath day (19-21). They are not to repeat the sins of their ancestors, but are to keep the Sabbath day holy, according to the covenant (22-23). If the people are obedient to the requirements of the covenant, they will enjoy the blessings promised in the covenant. God will give them prosperity and contentment under the rule of Davidic kings indefinitely (24-26). But if they persist in their disobedience, the nation will be overthrown (27).

Lessons from the potter (18:1-23)

A potter can make a lump of clay into whatever shape he wants. He can also change the kind of vessel he is making, if he thinks that conditions require it (18:1-4). As a potter determines the kind of vessel he makes, so God determines the destinies of nations, and this is the lesson that the people of Judah must learn (5-6). He may announce judgments on a nation, but he may withdraw those judgments if the nation repents. On the other hand, he may promise blessings to a nation, but he may withdraw those blessings if the nation rebels (7-10). Jeremiah assures Judah that it can be saved from the coming destruction if it returns to God (11). Judah, however, refuses to change its ways (12).

In turning from God to idols, Judah has done something that is almost unbelievable. Such action is as unnatural as that of a virgin who suddenly turns prostitute, or of a snow-fed mountain stream that suddenly dries up (13-15). Onlookers shake their heads in amazement at Judah's folly. It can lead only to calamity (16-17).

Some of the Judeans plotted mischief against Jeremiah because of his outspoken criticisms. They refused to acknowledge him as God's spokesman. They comforted themselves in the assurance that they were loyal followers of the official priests, wisdom teachers and prophets, who, of course, approved of their sinful ways (18). Jeremiah reminds God that he has prayed for these people, and now they are returning evil for good (19-20). As he asks God to fight for him, he prays that God will destroy the plotters and their followers, according to the curse that the law of Moses pronounced upon the rebellious (21-23; cf. Deut 28:15-68).

The broken pot (19:1-20:6)

In another acted parable Jeremiah, carrying an earthenware pot in his hand, took the leaders of Jerusalem to a place outside the city walls where old pottery was dumped. This was in the valley where the Judeans once sacrificed their children to Molech and carried out other pagan rites (19:1-2; see 7:30-34 and section, 'Tophet and the Valley of Hinnom').

Through their leaders, the people of Judah are told that in this valley, where they have killed their children, they themselves will be killed. The place had been named the Valley of Hinnom, but the prophet announces that in the future it will be called the Valley of Slaughter (3-6). When the Babylonians finally destroy Jerusalem, many Judeans will be slaughtered in this valley, while those who remain in the besieged city will be so near to starvation that they will eat their own children (7-9).

Jeremiah then smashed the pot, to symbolize God's coming judgment on Jerusalem. The city will be smashed, destroyed. Tophet, which is already unclean through its association with idolatry, will become a dump for corpses. The defilement of Tophet will be the measure of Jerusalem's defilement (10-13).

Having made his announcement at the site of the coming slaughter, Jeremiah returned to the temple, where he repeated the announcement of judgment (14-15). Pashhur, the chief officer of the temple, furious at Jeremiah's words, arrested him, flogged him and imprisoned him for the night (20:1-2). But Jeremiah would not be silenced. He boldly announced that Pashhur himself would see the people slaughtered and the city plundered and destroyed. After that, Pashhur would be taken off to humiliating captivity in Babylon, where he would die (3-6).

Jeremiah complains again (20:7-18)

The prophet feels that God has not been fair to him. God has called him to be a prophet against his personal wishes, then, when he faithfully announces God's message, the people mock and curse him (7-8). If he decides to keep quiet he finds he cannot, for God's word burns within him and he must proclaim it. Even his friends have turned against him and now treacherously plot his downfall (9-10). When he remembers that God is on his side, he is assured that his enemies will not overcome him (11-13); but when he thinks about his own bitter experience of life, he wishes he had never been born (14-18).

Jeremiah's inner conflicts

An examination of the preceding chapters shows that Jeremiah was a true patriot who loved his people and his country dearly (8:18-9:1; 14:19-22). No one could honestly doubt his loyalty. He was filled with unspeakable sorrow when he had to announce his country's overthrow and urge his fellow Judeans to submit to the enemy (4:19-22; 10:17-21; 14:17-18; 17:16-17). He was deeply hurt when accused of being a traitor (37:13; 38:1-6); he preferred rather that people heed his warnings and repent, and so avoid the threatened calamity (7:5-7; 13:15-17; 26:16-19; 36:1-3).

The false prophets, by contrast, assured the people of safety, victory and peace. They knew that as long as they spoke words that pleased the people, they would receive suitable financial rewards (6:13; 8:11). Jeremiah wished for peace too, but he knew that there could be no peace as long as the people continued in their stubborn rebellion against God. He became increasingly distressed as he saw that the people's optimism, encouraged by the false prophets, would result in disappointment (7:1-15; 14:13-18; 23:9).

Much as it hurt him to announce these divine judgments to his people, Jeremiah did it faithfully as God's messenger (20:8-10). How great, then, was his agony of spirit as the people turned against him (11:19; 18:18). In bitterness he turned to God, arguing with God because of the cruel reward he received in return for his devoted loyalty (12:1-4; 15:10-12,17-18; 20:14-18). God rebuked his servant for this self-pity, though at the same time he gave him added strength for the greater conflicts that lay ahead (12:5-6; 15:19-21).

These experiences of Jeremiah emphasized the reality and importance of an individual's personal relationship with God. Those with no personal fellowship with God did not truly know God, even though they may have called themselves prophets (23:18,21-22). But those who sought God with the whole heart found him (29:13).

Jeremiah foresaw the day when this close relationship with God would be experienced by all

God's people. God would make a new covenant, one characterized not by a community's conformity to a religious system, but by an individual's personal relationship with himself (31:31-34).

21:1-25:38 WARNINGS TO KINGS AND FALSE PROPHETS

A message for Zedekiah (21:1-10)

This message was given late in the reign of Judah's last king, Zedekiah. Jerusalem was under its last great siege, which resulted in its fall and destruction in 587 BC. The king sent to Jeremiah and asked that he would pray to God to save Jerusalem from the Babylonians (21:1-2). Jeremiah replies that God will not save Jerusalem but will fight for the Babylonians (Chaldeans) against Jerusalem. Many of the people within the city will die, and those who survive will be taken captive to Babylon (3-7). Since this is God's judgment, the people of Jerusalem have no chance of success against the invaders. Jeremiah tells them they would do better to surrender and so save their lives (8-10).

A king's responsibility (21:11-22:9)

As he has no doubt done many times, Jeremiah tells the leaders of Judah that they must correct the widespread social injustice that has corrupted their nation. If they do not, God will destroy the nation in judgment (11-12). They are deceiving themselves if they think that God will not allow anyone to attack Jerusalem. They are going to be disappointed if they think that the city's fortified position guarantees its safety (13-14).

The king has a duty to provide justice for all, no matter what their status in life. By ruling uprightly the king will ensure the continuance of the Davidic dynasty, but by ungodliness he is only helping to bring that dynasty to an end (22:1-5). As a mighty forest is cut down and burnt, so Judah will be destroyed if it forsakes God. When the king and his people abandon the covenant and worship other gods, they have no further assurance of God's saving power (6-9).

Concerning Shallum (22:10-12)

Jehoahaz, also known as Shallum, was made king by the people of Judah after his father Josiah was killed in battle. But after reigning three months, he was deposed and taken prisoner to Egypt (2 Kings 23:29-34). Jeremiah says that the people should mourn more for Shallum than for Josiah. At least Josiah died a hero on the battlefield, but Shallum will die a captive in a foreign land (10-12).

Concerning Jehoiakim (22:13-23)

Jehoiakim, another son of Josiah, was made king by Egypt in place of the unfortunate Jehoahaz. Jehoiakim was a cruel and oppressive ruler. In a time of extreme hardship, when the people were already burdened with heavy taxes to pay the overlord Egypt, Jehoiakim built luxurious palaces for himself. He demonstrated his contempt for his people by treating them almost as slaves and forcing them to work on his grand building projects without payment. He was the complete opposite of his father, who had shown a particular concern for the poor and needy (13-17; cf. 2 Kings 23:34-37).

God's response to Jehoiakim's evil is to assure him of a humiliating death. No one will mourn for him and he will receive no funeral. His dead body will be thrown on to the garbage dump outside Jerusalem as if it were the remains of an unclean animal (18-19; see also 36:30). The mountainous regions from which Jehoiakim obtained the luxuries for his extravagant living will be destroyed. His allies will be crushed, and the Jerusalem leaders who cooperated with him in his corrupt government will be driven into captivity as if blown by a strong wind (20-23).

Concerning Jehoiachin (22:24-30)

On Jehoiakim's death, his eighteen year old son Jehoiachin (also known Jeconiah, or Coniah) was made king. He was doomed to a short reign of only three months followed by a long captivity in Babylon. Other members of the royal family would also go into captivity, along with many of the leading citizens of Jerusalem (24-27; cf. 2 Kings 24:8-15). Jehoiachin died in a foreign country, and no son of his became king after him (28-30; but see also 2 Kings 25:27-30).

Return from captivity (23:1-8)

Judah's political leaders are likened to shepherds over a flock, but instead of caring for the sheep they have exploited them. They are the ones chiefly responsible for driving God's flock into captivity, and therefore God will punish them (23:1-2). Even in a foreign country, however, the flock still belongs to God. He does not forget his people, but will bring them back to their homeland and give them good leaders (3-4).

As a new branch shoots from the stump of a fallen tree, so will new leadership shoot from the fallen dynasty of David. The rule of the Davidic dynasty will be restored, so that it can reach its goal in a king who will be the embodiment of God's righteousness, the true Messiah (5-6). The nation's return from exile will be a sign of God's covenant faithfulness, just as his deliverance from Egypt was in the days of Moses (7-8).

Lying prophets (23:9-32)

From denouncing the political leaders, Jeremiah turns to denounce the spiritual leaders. He is filled with sorrow and anguish as he thinks of the evil of these people and the terrible judgment God will send them (9). They have encouraged idolatrous worship and immoral behaviour in every place, even in the temple of God. For this reason the land has already experienced God's judgment and worse is to come (10-12).

Baal worship in the northern kingdom and its capital Samaria was bad enough, but the situation is even worse in the southern capital, Jerusalem. The place is as immoral as Sodom or Gomorrah and is worthy of divine punishment (13-15).

The false prophets speak not God's words but their own. They encourage the people to do as they please, assuring them that God will not punish them (16-17). The reason the false prophets do not understand God's wrath is that they do not understand God. Their minds have never been taught by him (18-20). In spite of this they preach as if their words are the words of God (21). If the false prophets had heard God's words as Jeremiah had, they would announce God's judgment on wrongdoers, not his approval of them. They would be turning people from sin, not encouraging them in it (22).

When false prophets say what they like as if God cannot hear or see them, they are demonstrating their folly. Nothing can be hidden from God (23-24). God sees what they are doing and he is displeased. Their 'prophecies' originate in their own dreams and ideas (25-27).

The messages of the false prophets are like straw, whereas the messages of the true prophets are like wheat. They nourish what is good. At the same time they are like fire or a hammer, because they destroy what is worthless (28-29). False prophets only lie and deceive. They even take the words of the true prophets and misapply them in order to support their own ideas. In this way they lead people astray (30-32).

God's burden (23:33-40)

Prophets often spoke of their message as a 'burden' from God. It was a responsibility they had to discharge by announcing it to the people. Sometimes people went to prophets, particularly those whom Jeremiah calls false prophets, to ask them for a message, or burden, that would give them direction

or guidance. God tells Jeremiah that if they ask him for a burden, he is to tell them that *they* are the burden. They are a burden so heavy that God cannot carry them any longer. He will therefore get rid of them by throwing them into captivity (33).

The false prophets misused the word 'burden', so that no matter what announcement they made, they claimed it to be a burden from God. For this reason God commands the true prophets, such as Jeremiah, not to use the word any more (34-37). When false prophets persist in using the word, they show their defiance of God and their intention to deceive his people. God's punishment will be to treat them as a burden and throw them away. As those whom God has cast off, they will be taken captives to a distant land (38-40).

Good and bad figs (24:1-10)

On the occasion of Babylon's attack on Jerusalem in 597 BC, the king Jehoiachin (Jeconiah) was taken captive to Babylon, along with the best of Judah's people. The people that Babylon did not want were left in Judah and placed under the control of Zedekiah, the new king appointed by Babylon (2 Kings 24:10-17). Jeremiah's vision of two baskets of figs was concerned with these events (24:1-3).

The people left behind in Jerusalem thought that they had God's approval, because they were still in their homeland, whereas the others had been punished with shameful exile. Jeremiah points out that this is not so. Those taken captive are the 'good figs'. The shock of the captivity will awaken many of them to see their sin, repent of it and return to the Lord. God will then bring them back into their land, where they will enjoy a new and living relationship with him (4-7).

Those who remain in Jerusalem are the 'bad figs'. They continue in their evil ways and think that by relying on Egypt they will escape the power of the Babylonians. Jeremiah tells them that, far from escaping, they will come to the most humiliating and horrible end (8-10).

Seventy years captivity (25:1-14)

Babylon conquered Egypt in 605 BC (the fourth year of Jehoiakim's reign according to Judean reckoning, the third year of his reign according to Babylonian reckoning; cf. Dan 1:1-6). Judah therefore came for the first time under the direct control of Babylon. Jeremiah now clearly sees his prophecies being fulfilled before his eyes. He reminds the people that for over twenty years he has been bringing God's message to them but they have not listened (25:1-3). He has urged them to turn from their sin and idolatry, promising that if they did, God would allow them to remain in their land. But they have ignored his words and as a result brought harm upon themselves (4-7).

God is now going to punish Judah, and will use Babylon as his instrument of punishment. Joy and gladness will cease from Judah, the land will be left in ruins, and the people will be taken captive to Babylon. They will remain under Babylon's rule for seventy years (8-11).

However, Babylon has no right to do as it pleases. When it acts as if it is greater than God, it too will be destroyed. The outcome of this will be the release of God's people, so that after their seventy years of captivity, they will be able to return to their homeland (12-14).

Judgment on various nations (25:15-38)

God is righteous and holy, and in justice pours out his wrath on those who arrogantly defy his authority. His judgment upon wicked nations is likened to a cup of wine given to a person to make him drunk so that he staggers and falls (15-16). Through the spreading conquests of the Babylonian armies, God has punished Judah (17-18), along with a variety of other nations far and near (19-25). But in the end Babylon, the agent God has used to carry out his judgment, will itself be the object of God's wrath (26. Sheshach is another name for Babylon). No nation can escape once God has determined to punish it (27-28), and Judah, God's chosen nation, will be the first to suffer (29).

A further picture of the terrible judgment to fall on the wicked is that of a lion's attack on a flock of sheep. When the judge of all the earth acts in his holy judgment, the wicked will find no place of refuge (30-31). The bodies of the dead will lie rotting and stinking in the sun, like manure (32-33). The leaders of the people (shepherds of the flock) will look for a way of escape when the day of disaster comes, but they too will perish (34-35). As shepherds cry out when they see violence at work within their peaceful pastures, so Judah's leaders will wail when they see the Babylonian armies desolating their land (36-38).

26:1-34:22 PROPHECIES OF EXILE AND RETURN

The dangerous life of a prophet (26:1-24)

Again Jeremiah went to the temple, where he could preach to people who came from all over Judah to worship. He stood in the open court and urged the worshippers to give up their sinful ways and return to God (26:1-3). If they refused, the temple would be demolished, as the tabernacle had been at Shiloh several centuries earlier (4-6; see notes on 7:1-15; cf. also 19:14-20:6).

Religious officials and ordinary citizens alike were so angered at Jeremiah's words that a riot threatened to develop and Jeremiah was in serious physical danger (7-9). When the city officials rushed to the temple to intervene in the crisis, the leaders among the crowd demanded that Jeremiah be executed (10-11).

Jeremiah defended himself by pointing out that he had only been speaking the message God gave him. His real desire was that the people repent, for only by such action would they save themselves and their temple from destruction (12-15). The city officials accepted his defence (16). Other respected leaders supported them, adding that instead of trying to kill the prophet, people should take notice of his warnings. If they changed their ways, they would save themselves from disaster. In this they would be following the good example of a former Judean king, Hezekiah, who heeded the prophet of his day (17-19; cf. Micah 3:12).

Although Jeremiah on this occasion escaped death, another prophet who spoke a similar message did not. This man, Uriah, had heard of a threat to his life and fled to Egypt, but the wicked Jehoiakim had him brought back to Jerusalem and executed (20-23). Jeremiah received some protection at this dangerous time through the loyalty of an influential friend, Ahikam (24). (Ahikam seems to have been an important palace official. He had been a key man in the launching of Josiah's reforms; see 2 Kings 22:11-14.)

Submit to Babylon (27:1-22)

Early in the reign of Zedekiah, representatives from various neighbouring countries came to Jerusalem, in the hope of forming an alliance with Zedekiah against Babylon. Jeremiah delivered God's message to them, illustrating the message by putting an ox's yoke on his neck. The meaning was that the people were to submit to the yoke, or rule, of Babylon. This was God's will, and there was no use rebelling against it. Babylon would not be overthrown till God's time for it had come (27:1-7).

This message applied to all nations. All had to acknowledge Babylon's overlordship, regardless of the pronouncements of self-appointed prophets in Judah or fortune-tellers in other nations. Those who resisted Babylon were only inviting disaster and ruin (8-11). Jeremiah repeated the message for the benefit of the Judean king in particular, since he had mistakenly placed his hope in the assurances given by the false prophets (12-15).

The priests of Jerusalem were also building up false confidence in people. They announced that Babylon would soon be overthrown, and the temple vessels that Nebuchadnezzar had taken to Babylon would be returned. Such prophecies were lies (16-17; cf. Dan 1:2; 2 Kings 24:13). The priests and prophets should rather have been urging the people to repent and so prevent any further plundering of the temple by the Babylonians (18).

But Jeremiah knew that the people would not repent. As a result the few remaining treasures in the temple would also be taken to Babylon. Only in the distant future, when Babylon's power was gone, would these temple treasures return to Jerusalem (19-22).

Hananiah's false prophecy (28:1-17)

One of the temple prophets, Hananiah, publicly contradicted Jeremiah. He asserted that he had received a revelation from God that showed that within two years Babylon would be overthrown. The captive people and the temple treasures would then return to Jerusalem (28:1-4). Jeremiah replied that he wished such would be the case (5-6), but wishing for a thing does not make it come true. Some prophesy doom, others prophesy peace, but when the events take place then people will know who was right (7-9).

Hananiah, angry at Jeremiah's words, took the yoke from him and broke it. In this way he expressed his belief that God would break the yoke of Babylon. Jeremiah did nothing, but awaited a word from God (10-11). When that word came, it announced that the nations under Babylon's yoke would suffer even greater distress than they had so far experienced. The wooden yoke would be replaced by an iron yoke (12-14). As for the false prophet, within a few months he would die (15-16). Jeremiah's prophecy came true, but Hananiah's did not (17).

Letters to the captives in Babylon (29:1-32)

In 597 BC several thousand of Jerusalem's most capable people were taken captive to Babylon. Among them were some false prophets who began to predict, as Hananiah had done, that Babylon was about to fall and that the Judean captives were about to return to Jerusalem. Jeremiah, on hearing of this, wrote a letter to the community of captives (29:1-3).

The advice Jeremiah gives to the exiles is that they settle down to a more or less permanent way of life, as they will not be returning to Judah in the near future. They should try also to increase their numbers, for this would help them build towards a strong future (4-6). They should work for the good of the nation under whose government they live, and should not believe the predictions of the false prophets (7-9). The people will be in captivity for seventy years, but these will be years of discipline, during which God will prepare them for a better future (10-11). After this time of discipline, they will be in a better condition to enjoy true fellowship with God in their homeland again (12-14).

Turning from the exiles who were deceived by false prophets, Jeremiah has a few words concerning those still in Jerusalem who were similarly deceived, (15-16). The Jerusalemites had made no attempt to reform in spite of God's warnings, and therefore they too will be punished. Some will die at the hand of the enemy, and others will be taken to join their fellow Judeans in captivity (17-19). The two false prophets, who by their deceptive announcements and immoral behaviour have been leading the exiles astray, will be publicly executed by the Babylonian rulers (20-23).

On hearing Jeremiah's letter read in Babylon, another of the false prophets among the exiles, Shemaiah, was furious. He wrote a letter to the priests in Jerusalem, accusing Jeremiah of being a madman and demanding that he be arrested and imprisoned (24-28).

Jeremiah then sent a letter back to the exiles, accusing Shemaiah of being a self-appointed prophet and a deceiver. As punishment, neither he nor any of his offspring would live to see the fulfilment of God's promise in the people's return to their homeland (29-32).

Disease, suffering and healing (30:1-24)

Although he has been prophesying the captivity of Judah, Jeremiah knows also that after seventy years the people will return to their homeland. A theme of hope and encouragement runs through the next few chapters (30:1-3).

The suffering of God's people will almost be more than they can bear, but God assures them that it will not last indefinitely (4-7). He will release them from bondage and give them independence and peace under the rule of the Davidic dynasty again (8-9). Nations who have oppressed Judah will be destroyed, but God will not destroy Judah. He will discipline Judah because of its sins, but when the people repent he will re-establish them as a nation (10-11).

Nothing can save Judah from either the present distress or the greater distress to follow. The nation is like a person who has an incurable disease (12-13). As an immoral woman tries to win the favour of lovers, so Judah has tried to gain the help of other nations. But those she thought were allies will prove useless to her (14-15). The covenant God, Yahweh, is the only one who can restore his people. By his own power he will destroy Judah's oppressors and heal her incurable disease (16-17).

Jerusalem will be rebuilt and its former power and prosperity will be restored. The population will increase to compensate for those slaughtered in the Babylonian destruction, and the streets of the city will be full of rejoicing again (18-20). The people will have their own kings to rule over them and they will worship God sincerely, as befitting those who belong to God (21-22). But before these glorious days come, God must punish the nation Judah for its wickedness (23-24).

The people return home (31:1-22)

God has not forgotten any of his people who have been driven into a harsh existence in distant countries. Those of both the northern kingdom Israel and the southern kingdom Judah will share in the restoration to the land of their ancestors (31:1-3). They will be reunited in a land of renewed contentment and prosperity. They will join again in the national religious festivals at Jerusalem (4-6).

The prophet pictures the joyous journey back to Palestine. Even the blind and the lame join in the long trek back, because God strengthens them and supplies their needs along the way. He cares for them as a father cares for his firstborn son (7-9). The God who scattered his people in many lands now gathers them. He releases them from the power of those who have held them captive (10-11). God will protect and care for his people, giving them agricultural prosperity, social contentment and religious satisfaction (12-14).

When the people go into captivity there is weeping and mourning (15), but God wants this to be replaced with rejoicing and hope (16-17). First, however, the people must acknowledge that they have sinned and that God has acted justly in punishing them. They pray to God in an attitude of humble repentance (18-19), and God, as their loving and merciful Father, forgives them (20).

In view of their expected return, the prophet suggests that when the people go into captivity, they leave markers along the way. This will enable them to know the pathway back to their homeland. Although the nation goes into captivity as an unfaithful daughter, she will be cleansed and will return as a pure bride. God is going to reverse the normal course of events; he is going to create something new (21-22).

A new city and a new age (31:23-40)

Jeremiah has a vision of Jerusalem as a city of righteousness and Judah as a land of contentment. It is a vision that gives him the satisfaction of a pleasant dream (23-26). God had been responsible for the devastation of their land in the past, but he will also be responsible for its productivity in the future (27-28). The people by then will have learnt the lessons of their captivity. They will no longer blame their forefathers for their misfortunes, but will realize that people are punished for their own sins (29-30).

The people of Israel had been unfaithful to the covenant that God made with them at Sinai, and therefore they never enjoyed the close relation with God that he intended for them. God now promises to make a new covenant (31-32).

God's new covenant will not be spoiled by people's imperfections, because it will not depend upon their obedience to a set of laws. God will change people by working within them, by giving them a better knowledge of his will and the inner strength to carry it out. Instead of priests alone being able to approach God, all will know God. People will not need priests as mediators between them and God, because God himself will deal with their sins. He will remove all barriers and bring them into direct fellowship with himself (33-34).

(This new covenant came into being through the death of Jesus Christ. All who have faith in him receive its blessings. For the New Testament development of Jeremiah's prophecy see Heb 8:6-13; 9:15; 10:12-18; Gal 3:14,28-29.)

As surely as God will continue to control the universe, so just as surely will he restore Israel and Judah to their land (35-37). Jerusalem will be rebuilt and possibly extended beyond its former boundaries. Places around the city that were formerly defiled will be purified, so that Jerusalem becomes a city entirely dedicated to God (38-40).

Jeremiah buys a field (32:1-15)

At the time of Babylon's final siege of Jerusalem, just before the city fell, Jeremiah was imprisoned (32:1-2). The king, Zedekiah, considered Jeremiah a traitor because he forecast the defeat of the city and the captivity of the king (3-5).

However, Jeremiah also forecast that the land of Judah would not be lost for ever, and that one day the people would repossess it. An opportunity now arose for Jeremiah to give practical demonstration of his faith in this future restoration. A relative of Jeremiah owned a piece of land that was occupied by the enemy armies. In these circumstances he saw no benefit in retaining ownership of the land, so gave Jeremiah the offer to buy it from him (6-8; cf. v. 24-25).

Jeremiah, having confidence in God's promises concerning Judah's future, bought the land (9). In carrying out the transaction he made sure that everything was done according to the legal requirements and that there were public witnesses (10-12). He then put the title deeds in an earthenware pot for safe-keeping. He had faith to believe that some relative of a later generation would receive the right to inherit the land when the people returned from captivity (13-15).

God reassures Jeremiah (32:16-44)

After buying the field, Jeremiah began to have doubts. It seemed to him almost too much to expect that God could allow such a worthless people ever to return to their land. He therefore prayed to God (16), seeking to reassure himself that nothing is too hard for a God who is so loving and powerful (17-19). He reminds God of his steadfast faithfulness and miraculous power, which had saved his people in the past (20-22). But the people have been disobedient and have now brought this justly deserved punishment upon themselves (23). With the enemy siege machines battering the city walls, Jeremiah fears that Jerusalem's end has come. He wonders whether, in buying the field, he has correctly understood God's will (24-25).

God replies that nothing is too hard for him. Certainly he will destroy Jerusalem (26-29), for this is a judgment on the nation because of its idolatry (30-31). Kings, administrators, priests, prophets and common people alike have turned from God and followed pagan religions (32-35). However, after God has disciplined his people in foreign lands, he will bring them back to their land (36-37). He will do a work within them so that they will know him in a more spiritual relationship than they have previously experienced. They will have a renewed devotion to God and a fresh experience of God's blessing (38-41).

Jeremiah need have no doubts about the wisdom of buying the piece of land from his relative. The day will certainly come when this piece of land will be returned to Jeremiah's family. In fact, throughout the country people will buy and sell land as they did before (42-44).

The nation restored (33:1-26)

After this reassurance, God encourages Jeremiah to ask for further revelations of his plans for his people (3:1-3). Because of his imprisonment, Jeremiah may not know what is happening in and around the city. God shows him that the people of Jerusalem are desperate. They are demolishing houses and palaces in order to obtain materials to strengthen the city walls against the enemy's battering rams. But they are wasting their time, as the city is going to be destroyed (4-5).

Nevertheless, God will not forsake his people. After he has cleansed them from their sin, he will bring them back and they will rebuild the city to God's glory (6-9). In the cities of Judah there will be joy, in the pastures there will be peace, and in the temple there will be the sound of praise to God (10-13).

Once more a king of the dynasty of David will rule over Israel, and Jerusalem will be the city of God's salvation. Both the king and the city will be true expressions of God's righteousness (14-16; cf. 23:5-6). The Davidic dynasty and the Levitical priesthood will work together in perfect harmony, and worship will ascend to God perpetually (17-18). As certainly as night follows day and day follows night, God will fulfil his covenant promises to the dynasty of David and the tribe of Levi. Civil and religious power will work together for the good of his people as God intended (19-22).

When God punishes Israel and Judah, some people claim that he has rejected them. God tells Jeremiah that he has not. Despite their sin, they are still the descendants of Abraham, Isaac and Jacob, and they are still his people (23-26).

Note: After the time of exile, Zerubbabel, a descendant of David in the kingly line, became governor of Jerusalem (Hag 2:20-23; Matt 1:12,17), and Joshua, a descendant of Aaron, became high priest (Hag 1:1). There was peaceful cooperation between them and together they helped to re-establish Israel (Zech 6:13). But Israel did not maintain its loyalty to God. The nation never experienced fully all the blessings that Jeremiah pictures in this chapter. These blessings come in their fulness only through Jesus Christ, the messianic Son of David, the Great High Priest (Matt 22:42-44; Acts 13:33-34; Heb 4:14; 10:11-18).

Treacherous slave-owners (34:1-22)

Again Jeremiah tells King Zedekiah that Jerusalem will fall to the Babylonians. Zedekiah himself will be taken to Babylon but will not be executed. When he eventually dies he will be given a fitting royal funeral (34:1-7).

Earlier, when the Babylonians laid siege to Jerusalem, Zedekiah issued a command that slave-owners were to release all their Hebrew slaves. He no doubt hoped that his action would win God's favour, and he probably thought it had succeeded when an army from Egypt came to Jerusalem's aid and the Babylonians temporarily withdrew (v. 21; see also 37:5). Having gained the relief from siege they were looking for, the slave-owners then recaptured their slaves (8-11).

Through Jeremiah God now announces his judgment on the actions of the slave-owners. He approves of their releasing the slaves, for this is in keeping with the law he gave to Israel in the time of Moses (12-15; cf. Exod 21:2; Deut 15:12-14). But by recapturing the slaves, they have shown their contempt for God and his law (16).

Besides disregarding the law of God, the slave-owners have broken their promise (their covenant). God will therefore punish them according to the oath that people swear when making a covenant. (The ancient practice was that the two parties to a covenant walked between the pieces of a slaughtered animal and called down the animal's fate upon themselves if they broke the covenant.) In the case of the treacherous slave-owners of Jerusalem, this means that they will now be slaughtered (17-20). God will recall the Babylonian armies to complete their conquest of Jerusalem (21-22).

35:1-45:5 EVENTS IN JUDAH AND EGYPT

A lesson from the Rechabites (35:1-19)

Events recorded in the book of Jeremiah are not in chronological order, and Jeremiah now takes the readers back to the reign of Jehoiakim. He recounts a story concerning the Rechabites, a community of local tribal people who lived peaceably among the Israelites (1 Chron 2:55). The Rechabites were forbidden by their long-standing customs to drink wine. They were true worshippers of Yahweh and were fiercely anti-Baal (cf. 2 Kings 10:15-16,23-27). God told Jeremiah to test their loyalty to their ideals by offering them wine to drink (35:1-2). Jeremiah carried out the test in the temple, where officials could witness the event (3-5).

The Rechabites refused to touch the wine. They pointed out that their ancestors had forbidden them to drink wine or to carry on agricultural occupations of any sort (apparently because of the temptations to

Baal worship that such occupations provided). They had always lived a simple nomadic life, living in tents rather than building houses (6-9). This nomadic life also enabled them to avoid the corrupting influences of city life; though when the Babylonian armies invaded Judah, they had been forced to flee to Jerusalem for temporary refuge (10-11).

Jeremiah now uses this as a lesson to the people of Judah. The Rechabites remain faithful to the laws of their ancestors, but the Judeans are not faithful to the law of God (12-16). God therefore will preserve the Rechabites through the bloodshed that will come upon Jerusalem (17-19).

Jehoiakim burn's Jeremiah's scroll (36:1-32)

God commanded Jeremiah to write down all the prophecies he had given during the previous twenty years and announce them again to Judah. Perhaps even yet the nation would repent and so escape God's judgment (36:1-3).

Over the next year Jeremiah wrote down the messages, using Baruch as his scribe. Since Jeremiah was forbidden to enter the temple (see 20:1-2; 26:7-9), he arranged for Baruch to go on his behalf and read the scroll to the people (4-7). (Baruch was the brother of a leading palace official; see 32:12; 51:59.) The day Jeremiah chose for the reading of the scroll was a national day of fasting, when large crowds were at the temple. Baruch read the scroll from a prominent position where most in the temple could see him (8-10).

Among the crowd who listened to Baruch was the son of one of the city's leaders. When the young man told his father and the other city officials of the events at the temple, they invited Baruch to come and read the scroll to them (11-15). They were shocked at the serious accusations and predictions in the scroll, and decided to tell the king. They suggested, however, that Baruch and Jeremiah hide themselves for the sake of safety (16-19).

The suggestion of the city leaders proved to be life-saving advice for the two servants of God. When the king heard the scroll read, instead of taking heed, he defiantly burnt the scroll and sent to have Jeremiah and Baruch arrested. But they could not be found (20-26).

God told Jeremiah to rewrite the prophecies of the scroll that Jehoiakim had destroyed (27-28). In addition to the former prophecies was a special prophecy concerning Jehoiakim, who was assured of a horrible and disgraceful death (29-31; cf. 22:18-19). Baruch then wrote the scroll anew, adding further messages of God's judgment (32).

Jeremiah imprisoned (37:1-21)

Having dealt with events in the reign of Jehoiakim in the previous two chapters, the story now returns to the reign of Zedekiah. As in the case of Jehoiakim, Zedekiah ignored the warnings of God's prophets (37:1-2).

During Babylon's final great siege of Jerusalem, Egypt sent an army to help the Jerusalemites. When the Egyptians approached, the Babylonians lifted the siege and went to deal with the new threat elsewhere. Zedekiah sent a message to Jeremiah, asking him to pray that the Babylonians' withdrawal would be permanent. Jerusalem would then be able to live in peace (3-5).

Jeremiah replied that the Egyptians would retreat and the Babylonians would return. After laying siege to Jerusalem again, they would then conquer and burn it (6-8). Jerusalem's defeat was certain. Even if the Babylonians suffered heavy losses and were left with only wounded men lying in tents, they would still take Jerusalem (9-10).

The temporary lift of the siege gave Jeremiah the opportunity to go into the country to attend to some business concerning his family's property. But a guard at the city gate, suspecting that Jeremiah was going to see the Babylonians, arrested him and charged him with being a traitor (11-13). Jeremiah denied the charge, but it made no difference. He was flogged, then thrown into a temporary prison that had been set up in the house of a government official (14-15).

When the Babylonian army returned (contrary to the predictions of the false prophets) the king sent again to ask Jeremiah what hope there was for Jerusalem. The prophet's reply was the same as before: the city would be conquered (16-19). Though disappointed at Jeremiah's reply, Zedekiah at least respected the prophet's honesty. In response to Jeremiah's request, Zedekiah gave him better prison accommodation and a better provision of food (20-21).

Jeremiah's escape from death (38:1-28)

The chief officials in Jerusalem were a powerful group. They hated Jeremiah for his unchanging message of 'submit to Babylon or perish', and they managed to force the king to hand over Jeremiah to them for execution (38:1-5). They dropped him into a filthy disused well and left him there to die (6).

There was, however, in Zedekiah's court an African who had risen to a position of responsibility and who was favourable to Jeremiah. In an action that showed considerable courage, the man pleaded with the king on Jeremiah's behalf (7-9). The result was that he was able to change the weak king's mind, rescue the prophet from the well and return him to his temporary prison accommodation in the palace barracks (10-13; cf. 37:21).

The king sent for Jeremiah to question him again about the city's future. Jeremiah agreed to talk only after gaining the king's assurance that he would not be unjustly treated again (14-16).

Jeremiah's message, however, was no more encouraging than it had been previously. Zedekiah's only hope was to surrender to Babylon (17-18; cf. 37:17). Zedekiah feared that if he surrendered, he might receive disgraceful treatment from his people (19). Jeremiah replied that if he did not repent he would still receive disgraceful treatment from his people, and from the Babylonians as well. The helpless Judean women, raped by enemy soldiers and officials, would in bitterness blame Zedekiah for their plight, because he had been so easily deceived by his advisers (20-23).

Zedekiah and Jeremiah agreed not to reveal the content of their conversation to the king's officials, who were still plotting to kill Jeremiah. In this way Jeremiah escaped death, though he was still kept under military guard at the palace barracks (24-28).

The fall of Jerusalem (39:1-18)

After eighteen months of siege, the Babylonian armies finally broke through the walls of Jerusalem (39:1-2). Zedekiah tried to escape by night, but was quickly captured and brought face to face with the king of Babylon, as Jeremiah foretold. Although he was not executed, Zedekiah suffered cruel treatment before being taken captive to Babylon (3-7; cf. 34:2-3). The Babylonians then burnt Jerusalem, destroyed the city walls and took the citizens into captivity. They left behind only the poorest of the people, who were of no use to them (8-10).

God protected his servant Jeremiah through the enemy invasion, as he had promised (cf. 1:8). The Babylonians released him from imprisonment and placed him in the care of Gedaliah, the son of Jeremiah's friend Ahikam (11-14; cf. 26:24). God also protected the African who saved Jeremiah's life. Through Jeremiah, God assured the man that he would be safe from both the Judean rulers and the enemy soldiers (15-18; cf. 38:8-9).

Jeremiah and Gedaliah (40:1-12)

After being released from prison, Jeremiah was apparently recaptured when the Babylonian soldiers were assembling the people to be taken captive to Babylon. When the Babylonian leaders discovered what had happened, they realized a mistake had been made and released him again (40:1). They gave him freedom either to go to Babylon or to remain in Judah (2-4). Jeremiah chose to remain in his homeland. There he maintained his close association with Gedaliah, whom the Babylonians had appointed governor over the people left behind in Judah. He set up his headquarters at the town of Mizpah, north-west of Jerusalem (5-6).

The new governor then began the task of restoring order, peace and productivity in Judah. He saw that it would be useless for those who remained of Judah's army to attempt any sort of military action against the Babylonian occupation forces. He advised instead that all the people, farmers and soldiers alike, settle down and help make Judah's damaged farmland productive again. This would ensure for themselves a fairly comfortable existence under their new rulers (7-10).

Gedaliah also welcomed home those Judeans who had fled to neighbouring countries to escape the Babylonian army. Under Gedaliah's leadership, the Judean people soon saw their country becoming productive again (11-12).

Ishmael's plot against Gedaliah (40:13-41:18)

One of the former army commanders, Ishmael, was opposed to Gedaliah's policy of submission to Babylon. With Ammonite support he plotted to kill Gedaliah. So sincere and trusting was Gedaliah, that when told of the plot, he refused to believe it (13-16). Gedaliah apparently took no precautions against the reported treachery, and when a suitable time arrived Ishmael carried out his brutal plot. He murdered Gedaliah, along with all the Judean officials and Babylonian supervisors at Gedaliah's headquarters (41:1-3).

Ishmael wanted no news of the assassination to be made public till he had carried out the next stage of his plan. But he was surprised by the arrival of a group of men travelling to Jerusalem to mourn the destruction of the temple (4-5). To prevent news of the assassination leaking out, Ishmael killed the travellers, though some saved their lives by telling Ishmael where he could find needed food supplies (6-9). Ishmael, it seems, panicked. Not knowing exactly what to do, he decided to take the whole population of Mizpah captive to Ammon (10).

Johanan, who had first warned Gedaliah of the plot against him (see 40:13-16), decided to pursue Ishmael. He rescued the captive people of Mizpah, but Ishmael escaped into Ammon (11-15). Fearing revenge from the Babylonians because of Ishmael's rebellion, the people of Mizpah decided it would be safer to look for refuge in Egypt than to return to Mizpah (16-18).

Jeremiah opposes going to Egypt (42:1-22)

As Jeremiah had been living at Mizpah, he was probably among the people who had been captured by Ishmael and who were now thinking of fleeing to Egypt. These people therefore asked him to seek God's guidance for them (42:1-3). Jeremiah agreed to their request, and they promised to do whatever God said, whether it pleased them or not (4-6).

After ten days Jeremiah received God's answer, and quickly passed it on to the people (7-9). God's directions were clear. The people were to stay in the land and were not to fear Babylon. God would give them protection and provision (10-12).

If the people disobeyed, thinking that by going to Egypt they would escape war and hardship, they would be disappointed. God would punish them by bringing upon them in Egypt the war and hardship they had tried to escape (13-17). As the people in Jerusalem had been punished for disobeying God, so would these people, if they rejected God's word through Jeremiah (18).

Jeremiah knew that the people had already decided to go to Egypt before they asked him for God's guidance. He therefore warned them of the terrible consequences of their stubbornness (19-22).

The move to Egypt (43:1-13)

In flatly rejecting Jeremiah's advice, the people gave proof that they had already made up their minds to go to Egypt. In spite of all his previous prophecies' being proved true, they accused him of being a liar (43:1-2). They also turned against Baruch, who had apparently given similar advice against going to Egypt. They accused him of being a Babylonian agent and of influencing Jeremiah against them (3). They then left for Egypt, forcibly taking Jeremiah and Baruch with them (4-7).

On arriving in Egypt, Jeremiah warned the Judeans that they would still not escape Babylon. He illustrated this by burying two stones in the pavement outside one of Pharaoh's palaces. On these stones, Jeremiah foretold, Babylon would build its throne; that is, Babylonian power would spread to Egypt (8-10). Babylon would overpower Egypt with the ease that a shepherd picks insects off his coat. Egypt's temples would be burnt and its people taken captive (11-13).

Message to the Judeans in Egypt (44:1-30)

Once they had settled down in Egypt, the Judeans soon copied Egyptian religious practices. Jeremiah begins his warnings to them with the reminder of what happened to Jerusalem. The city was destroyed and the people of Judah sent into Babylonian exile because of their false religion and idolatry (44:1-6). Yet the Judeans who escaped to Egypt have not heeded the lesson. God had promised to preserve a minority of the people taken captive to Babylon, but he will preserve none of those who have escaped to Egypt. They show no sign of repentance, but worship the gods of Egypt as they once worshipped other false gods in Jerusalem (7-10).

God announces that his judgment will follow the Judeans to Egypt till they are destroyed. Some will die through war, others through famine. The only survivors will be a few fugitives who escape back to Judah (11-14).

The people's arrogant response to the message from God shows their rebellious spirit and their determination to continue in their idolatry. They argue that during the reign of Manasseh, when the worship of foreign gods was at its peak (cf. 2 Kings 21:3-5), there was neither war nor famine. But when Josiah removed idolatry and established the worship of Yahweh (cf. 2 Kings 23:4-5), Judah suffered from both war and famine (15-18). Moreover, the idolatry had the full approval of the heads of households all over Judah (19).

In reply Jeremiah points out that the worship of foreign gods was the reason for Judah's calamities and ultimate downfall. The idolatrous practices of Manasseh's time were so deeply rooted that Josiah's reform could not remove them (20-23; cf. 2 Kings 23:26-27).

The prophet challenges the people to continue their worship of false gods and see whether or not they will be punished (24-25). But he knows the outcome: they will be destroyed, never to dishonour the holy name of God again (26-27). Only a few who escape will live to see Jeremiah's prophecy come true (28). The Judeans in Egypt will have a sure sign of their coming doom when they see Pharaoh, in whom they have trusted, overthrown (29-30).

A message for Baruch (45:1-5)

Jeremiah gave this word of encouragement to his assistant Baruch on the occasion when Baruch had to read the scroll of God's judgments to the people (45:1; see 36:1-32). Baruch was distressed, but, says Jeremiah, think how much more distressed is God, who is about to destroy the very nation that he has built up (2-4). Baruch was thinking how his unpopular announcements might affect his own security or advancement; but, says Jeremiah, when divine judgment falls on Judah, Baruch will be thankful enough just to come out alive (5).

46:1-51:64 MESSAGES FOR FOREIGN NATIONS

Although Jeremiah's main ministry was to Judah, he had also been called to proclaim God's message to the surrounding nations (see 1:5,10). This section of Jeremiah's book brings together a number of the messages that the prophet announced to foreign nations during the many years of his ministry (cf. 25:13). By these messages, the prophet shows that as God deals justly with Judah, so he deals justly with Judah's neighbours.

The order in which the messages have been arranged does not follow the order of the events they announce. The arrangement is more according to the geographic location of the countries, starting with Egypt in the south and moving north and east towards Mesopotamia. The climax of the series deals with the nation that dominated the affairs of most countries in the region, Babylon. (For the nations dealt with here, see map located at Isaiah 13-23, where another group of messages to various nations is recorded.)

A message concerning Egypt (46:1-12)

Egypt's first defeat by Babylon was in 605 BC at Carchemish. That battle marked the beginning of the end for Egyptian overlordship in the region, and brought Judea for the first time under the control of Babylon (46:1-2). Jeremiah pictures the activity and excitement as the Egyptian soldiers prepare for battle (3-4). They go out confidently but are surprised by the ferocity of the Babylonian attack. The Egyptians turn and flee but are cut off at the Euphrates River (5-6).

In another picture of the same battle, the prophet sees Egypt's army surging forward like the Nile in flood. Strengthened with skilled soldiers hired from a number of neighbouring countries, the Egyptian forces feel they are so strong they could conquer the whole earth (7-9). But the day is not one of victory for Egypt. It is a day of God's judgment, and the Egyptians suffer great slaughter (10). All Egypt's skills in using medicine cannot heal her wounds. News of Egypt's defeat spreads far and wide (11-12).

A second message concerning Egypt (46:13-28)

Jeremiah now foresees another defeat of Egypt by Babylon, this one not on foreign soil but in the land of Egypt itself (13). Egyptian cities fall as the Babylonian armies advance. Egypt's gods are not able to hold back the enemy. Hired soldiers flee from the battle-front and look for safety in their own countries (14-16). Pharaoh is accused of being a loud-mouthed boaster who does nothing when the hour for action comes (17).

Babylon towers over Egypt as Mount Tabor towers over its neighbouring territory and as Mount Carmel towers over the sea beside it. The Egyptians cannot overthrow Babylon, and should prepare for captivity (18-19). As cattle flee from the biting gadfly, so the Egyptians flee from the Babylonian attackers (20-21). The Egyptians are (to use another picture) like a snake that wriggles away into its hole in search of safety. In yet another picture, the Babylonians in their attack on Egypt are likened to woodmen cutting down a forest (22-24).

Egypt and its gods will be punished, but the nation will not be completely destroyed. One day it will revive (25-26). As for the Judeans, they will be exiled in foreign countries, but one day they will return to their land. There they will enjoy peace and security again (27-28).

A message concerning Philistia (47:1-7)

The prophet sees that Babylon will conquer Philistia also, overrunning the land as a river overflows its banks and floods the fields (47:1-2). When Babylon's horses and chariots sweep down, the Philistines flee in panic, each selfishly concerned only with saving himself. No one cares about the plight of others. Any possible help from Tyre and Sidon is cut off, and the cities of Philistia mourn their destruction (3-5).

Jeremiah imagines the Philistines crying out to God, asking him to stop the Babylonian slaughter. The prophet then answers on God's behalf, pointing out that God's judgment must continue till it is complete (6-7).

A message concerning Moab (48:1-47)

Moab was one nation that tried to form an alliance with Judah against Babylon (see 27:1-3). Moab will now suffer Babylon's anger. Jeremiah pictures the scene: the land devastated, fortresses smashed, cities destroyed, people crying out in distress, refugees fleeing from the invading armies (48:1-6).

Chemosh, Moab's national god, cannot save the nation. Rather, it will be taken into captivity along with Moab's civil and religious leaders. The towns of Moab will be left desolate (7-9). In destroying Moab, the Babylonians are executing God's work of judgment. Therefore, they must carry that work out to its completion (10).

Because its people had not previously been taken into exile, Moab is likened to wine that is allowed to sit in a jar undisturbed. But now, because its people are to be taken captive to Babylon, it is likened to wine that is to be emptied out of its jar (11-12). The Moabites will lose trust in their god who has proved powerless to save them (13). The best of Moab's soldiers will be killed in the dreadful slaughter, and there will be widespread mourning over the shattered nation (14-17).

People throughout Moab will be shocked to hear how the nation's defences have been ruined. The proud nation will be disgraced (18-20), the mighty nation broken, as God's judgment spreads from one Moabite city to the next (21-25).

The people of Moab once despised and mocked Israel and Judah, but now they will be despised and mocked themselves. They will drink God's wrath till they are drunk and vomit (26-27). Once proud and arrogant, the Moabites will now be forced to flee in shame to look for refuge in the caves and dens of the mountains (28-30). Jeremiah even feels pity for them, as he sees their widespread power broken, their crops destroyed, their country ruined (31-36). The people shave their heads, cut their flesh and put on sackcloth as signs of their mourning, but it is too late. Moab is finished. It is like a broken pot that is thrown on the rubbish heap (37-39).

In a final declaration of Moab's destruction, the prophet pictures Babylon swooping down on Moab as an eagle swoops down on its prey (40-43). No matter which way they turn, there will be no escape for those on whom God's judgment falls (44). Moab's chief cities will be burnt and its people taken captive (45-46; cf. Num 21:28-29). Yet God, in his mercy, will again preserve a remnant (47).

A message concerning Ammon (49:1-6)

Like its brother nation Moab, Ammon was a distant relative of the nation Judah. (Ammon and Moab were descended from Lot; Judah was descended from Lot's uncle, Abraham; cf. Gen 12:5; 19:36-38). Ammon and Moab occupied part of the tableland region east of the Jordan River, which meant they were the immediate neighbours of Israel and Judah to the east.

About a century before the time of Jeremiah, Assyria had conquered the northern kingdom Israel and carried the people into captivity (2 Kings 15:29; 17:6). Ammon apparently then took the opportunity to seize the territory of Gad, one of Israel's border tribes. But Ammon forgot that Israel was still God's people. Jeremiah tells Ammon that it will be conquered and its capital, Rabbah, destroyed. Israel will then repossess its own territory (49:1-2). (Molech, or Milcom, was Ammon's national god.)

Ammon was proud of the wealth it had built up and thought it was secure against attack. Jeremiah tells the Ammonites that economic prosperity will not save them when the enemy invades. They will be taken into captivity (3-5), though later a remnant will return to the homeland (6).

A message concerning Edom (49:7-22)

The Edomites, the descendants of Esau, prided themselves that they were cleverer than peoples of surrounding nations. They were confident that their country was safe against attack because its rugged mountains provided it with a good defence system. The prophet tells them that neither their wisdom nor their defences will save them from the destruction that God has determined for them (7-8).

A vineyard worker picks the grapes that are ripe but leaves the rest; a house burglar steals only what he wants and leaves the remaining goods in the house; but the enemy's attack on Edom will aim at total destruction. Even those who hide in caves in the mountains will not escape (9-10). However, God will take care of all those who become orphans or widows as a result of the battle (11).

If people less deserving of God's wrath must suffer his punishment, how much heavier will be the punishment of the wicked Edomites. God assures them that the prosperous towns in which they pride themselves will be left in ruins and become places of horror (12-13).

The Edomites think that the fortifications they have set up throughout their rocky hill country have made them secure against attack. They think they are unconquerable, but they deceive themselves. Jeremiah warns them that no matter how high up the mountains they go, or how strong they make their defences, nothing will save them from the coming judgment (14-16).

Edom's overthrow will be complete. Like the cities of Sodom and Gomorrah it will be left a desolation (17-18). As a lion comes from the jungle and destroys a flock of sheep, so will the enemy come and destroy Edom. No one will be able to withstand the army that God chooses to carry out his judgment (19-20). The Edomite soldiers will be powerless against their attackers. Their wailing will be heard to the borders of their land and beyond (21-22).

A message concerning Damascus (49:23-27)

Damascus was the capital of the country that in ancient times was known as Aram and later became known as Syria. The city had been conquered by Assyria in 732 BC (2 Kings 16:9), but when Jeremiah began his ministry it was still occupied, having become a provincial centre within the Assyrian Empire. Jeremiah now foresees that it is about to

suffer the horrors of war and defeat again, because Babylon is about to conquer Assyria.

This prophecy must have been given early in Jeremiah's career, for his ministry began in 627 BC, and Babylon's conquest of Assyria occurred only fifteen years later, in 612 BC. Jeremiah sees the Syrians filled with fear and a sense of helplessness as they hear that Babylon's armies are approaching (23-24). Again Damascus is to become the scene of slaughter and destruction, as the Babylonian army ruthlessly takes over the city (25-27).

A message concerning Kedar (49:28-33)

Even the wandering tribes of the desert will suffer from the Babylonian invasions. The particular tribe that Jeremiah mentions is Kedar, which occupied a region known as Hazor. The people of Kedar lived in tents, kept flocks of sheep, and were shrewd traders (Ps 120:5; Isa 60:7; Ezek 27:21). Jeremiah announces that their settlements will be wrecked, their animals will be taken, and they themselves will flee in terror (28-30).

At the same time the calamity is a judgment of God upon these desert tribes. Their practice was to raid towns that the Babylonians attacked, and then return to their desert settlements where they themselves were out of the path of the Babylonian forces. Now their safety will come to an end, and their plunder will be lost (31-33)

A message concerning Elam (49:34-39)

The message concerning the ancient kingdom of Elam came at the beginning of Zedekiah's reign. At that time Zedekiah was trying to form an alliance with other nations west of Babylon, with the aim of resisting the spread of Babylon's power (34; cf. 27:1-3,12).

Jeremiah's message here shows that Zedekiah was wasting his time. Babylon's power will spread so widely that even countries to its *east*, such as Elam, will be overthrown (35-38). But Elam's overthrow will not be permanent (39). History records that Elam later became part of Persia, which in turn conquered Babylon (Ezra 1:2).

A message concerning Babylon (50:1-46)

Finally, Jeremiah sees that the nation that God used to punish Judah will itself be punished. Bel, or Merodach (Marduk), the chief god of Babylon, will be powerless to save Babylon when the attack comes (50:1-3).

Since the Judeans will by this time have humbly repented before God, the downfall of Babylon will give them the opportunity to return to the land where their ancestors once lived (4-5). (When Cyrus of Persia conquered Babylon in 539 BC, he promptly gave permission to the Jews to return; see 2 Chron 36:22-23.)

Judah's leaders have been guilty, for they have led the nation astray (6), but the Babylonians have also been guilty (in spite of their denials), for they have done to Judah as they wished (7). Therefore, while the Jews will return from Babylon (in fact, they will be the first of the captive nations to find freedom), Babylon itself will be punished (8-10).

Arrogant self-confident Babylon boasted that it had conquered and plundered Judah, the people of Yahweh (11). Now Babylon will be disgraced, as the wrath of God is poured out upon it (12-13). The attackers will be as ferocious against Babylon as Babylon has been against others. Once it has been defeated, the nations it has held captive will escape to their own lands (14-16).

The northern kingdom Israel had been conquered by Assyria, then Assyria by Babylon, so that the exiled people of Israel as well as those of Judah eventually came under Babylon's power. But now Babylon will fall. Israel and Judah will return to their land, a united and forgiven people (17-20).

Continuing with his pictures of the downfall of Babylon, the prophet sees the attackers being urged to go up and attack its various cities (21-22). Like a hammer Babylon had smashed others, but now Babylon itself will be smashed. Its stores of food will be destroyed and its soldiers killed (23-27). The captive Judeans will return home, where they will praise God for justly punishing their oppressor (28), but the arrogant Babylonians will be left with no one to help them (29-32). God redeems those who are oppressed but punishes those who oppress them (33-34).

No matter how wise Babylon's rulers, how clever its sorcerers or how strong its soldiers, all alike will be killed. The nation's chariot forces will be destroyed and its treasures plundered (35-37). Through drought and war the land will be ruined and left unsuitable for human habitation (38-40).

The prophet pictures the fear of Babylon's king as he hears the news of the onrushing conquest by Persia and its allies (41-43). When God acts against Babylon there is no hope of escape. Babylon is likened to a flock of sheep attacked by a lion. In terror it cries out as it comes to a cruel and bitter end (44-46).

The overthrow of Babylon (51:1-33)

When a farmer, after reaping his harvest, winnows the wheat, he throws it into the air so that as the wind blows away the chaff, he can gather the grain for himself. Similarly, when God 'winnows' Babylon he will make a separation between the Babylonians and his own people. He will 'blow away' the former in judgment, but will preserve the latter for himself (51:1-5).

God had used Babylon to punish other nations, but now Babylon itself will suffer God's wrath. It will be like a drunken man who falls and cannot rise, like a wounded man who cannot be healed. Meanwhile the nations that Babylon afflicted will be freed from their bondage and able to return to their homelands (6-9). God makes sure that in the end justice is done (10).

Jeremiah then pictures the army of Medes and Persians preparing for the final attack on Babylon. He warns the people of Babylon that their end is drawing near and soon enemy soldiers will swarm into their city (11-14). All Babylon's gods will be powerless to save. Such gods are lifeless, worthless and useless. There is only one true God, and that God is he who made and controls the universe (15-18). This same God has chosen the Israelite nation, the descendants of Jacob, to be his people (19). He is the God who controls history, and therefore he may use any nation to punish another, according to his purposes (20-23).

Babylon will be punished because of the way it has treated Judah (24). It appears to be as strong and unconquerable as a mountain, but God will smash it to pieces and leave it a barren waste (25-26). Again the prophet pictures the scene as nations join forces to fight against Babylon (27-29). Confusion is widespread as the attackers overrun Babylon's strongholds, and messengers carry news to the king that his army is suffering heavy losses. It is being crushed like grain trampled on the threshing floor (30-33).

Response to Babylon's overthrow (51:34-58)

Jeremiah recalls the desperate prayers of the people of Judah who often complained to God about Babylon's unrestrained greed and cruelty. They cried to God that he would hold Babylon responsible for the violence they suffered, and now God is about to answer their prayers (34-35).

God will defend the cause of his people and punish Babylon by destroying it. The nation will be conquered and the city will be left a heap of ruins (36-37). The Babylonians, who like lions had attacked and killed the sheep, will now themselves be slaughtered like sheep (38-40). The proud and mighty city (also known as Sheshach), along with its god Bel, will be defeated and disgraced. Enemy soldiers will pour into the city like an overflowing sea, and Babylon's power over captive nations will at last be broken (41-44).

The prophet gives a warning to the captive Jews in Babylon not to be hesitant or doubting because of the conflicting rumours they hear. They must be ready to flee at the first opportunity (45-46). Babylon is to fall because of its many sins, and in particular its sins against God's people. The arrogant ruler will be disgraced, and nations everywhere will rejoice (47-49).

In view of what is about to happen, the Judean exiles must cease their monotonous complaint that they have been shamed and God's temple dishonoured by Babylon's armies. The time has come for them to start thinking seriously about returning to Jerusalem, for Babylon's end is fast approaching (50-53).

Yahweh, the God of Israel, is the one who has determined Babylon's destruction. He is the Lord Almighty, the only divine King. His work of judgment will bring destruction to the city and death to all the nation's mighty men (54-57). Babylon's huge walls will not withstand the attackers that God sends against his enemy (58).

Jeremiah's message sent to Babylon (51:59-64)

When Jeremiah finished writing down his announcement of Babylon's downfall, he sent it with Seraiah to be read to the exiles in Babylon. (Seraiah was the brother of Baruch and probably a court official; cf. v. 59 with 32:12.) On this occasion, Seraiah went with Zedekiah on a visit the king made to Babylon in the fourth year of his reign (59-62).

After reading the scroll to the exiles, Seraiah was to tie a stone to it and throw it into the Euphrates, the river on which Babylon was built. This was to symbolize that Babylon would sink, never to rise again (63-64).

52:1-34 HISTORICAL APPENDIX

This appendix is similar to 2 Kings 24:18-25:30. The probable reason for its inclusion is to show how Jeremiah's prophecies concerning Jerusalem's last days were fulfilled.

Judah's king during its last tragic years was Zedekiah. He was a weak king, whose reign was characterized throughout by religious failure and political indecision. Finally, after years of uncertain plotting, he decided to rebel openly against his overlord Babylon (52:1-3). Nebuchadnezzar could be

patient with Zedekiah no longer and decided to crush Jerusalem once and for all. Soon his armies besieged the rebellious city (4-5).

Zedekiah had plotted his rebellion in co-operation with Egypt, and when Egypt eventually came to Jerusalem's aid, Babylon temporarily lifted the siege. However, as Jeremiah had warned, the Babylonians soon forced the Egyptians to retreat. They then resumed their siege, with a determination to maintain it till the city fell (see 37:1-21).

The longer the siege lasted, the more desperate the situation in Jerusalem became. Throughout the city people were dying of disease and starvation (6; see Lam 2:10-12,19-21; 4:4-5,7-9). After eighteen months of siege, the Babylonians broke through the city walls. With Jerusalem now doomed, Zedekiah and some of his men tried to escape, but were captured by enemy soldiers. Zedekiah was blinded, chained and taken off to prison in Babylon (7-11; see 39:1-7).

Babylonian soldiers then overran Jerusalem. They destroyed most of the city, including the temple, the palace and much of the city walls (12-14). They took most of the people into captivity, leaving behind only those that were of no use to them (15-16). They also stripped the temple of its valuable metals, taking its furnishings, decorations, vessels and utensils to Babylon. Things too large to carry whole were broken up so that they could be carried more easily (17-23). The leaders of the rebellion — the chief priests, top army officers and leading palace officials – were executed (24-27).

The writer concludes by recording the numbers of people taken into captivity at the times of the separate invasions. The smallness of his numbers, compared with those given in the book of 2 Kings, indicates that Jeremiah may have counted only the heads of the families. Some were taken captive in 597 BC, after Jehoiachin's surrender (28; see 2 Kings 24:14-16); others in 587 BC, the year of the events recorded in this chapter (29); others later again, in 582 BC, after Ishmael's assassination of Gedaliah (30; see Chapters 40-42).

In 561 BC, however, the new Babylonian king released the former Judean king Jehoiachin from prison and promoted him to a place of honour in the Babylonian palace. To the captive Jews this was a sign that God had not forgotten them and that he was still in control of their affairs. It gave them hope that they would yet be released and return to their homeland (31-34; cf. 2 Kings 24:8-15; 25:27-30).

APPENDIX
Contents of Jeremiah according to chronology

Not all Jeremiah's prophecies can be assigned with certainty to a particular king's reign. This applies especially to the first twenty chapters, where many of the messages would fit the reigns of either Josiah or Jehoiakim. Nevertheless, if the reader wants to trace the prophecies and events of Jeremiah's time in some sort of chronological sequence (omitting the prophecies concerning foreign nations in Chapters 46-51), the following order of chapters is suggested:

Reign of Josiah (640-609 BC)   Chapters 1-6
Reign of Jehoahaz (609 BC)   Chapter 22 (verses10-12 only)
Reign of Jehoiakim (609-597 BC)   Chapters 7-20, 26, 22 (verses 1-9,13-23), 23, 25, 35, 36, 45
Reign of Jehoiachin (597 BC)   Chapter 22 (verses 24-30)
Reign of Zedekiah (597-587 BC)   Chapters 24, 27-33, 21, 34, 37-39, 52 (verses 1-30)
After the fall of Jerusalem   Chapters 40-44, 52 (verses 31-34)

Judah's last days

Jer 52	BC	Babylonian action	Judeans taken captive
-	605	Jerusalem taxed	Leading youths (Dan 1:1-4; 2 Kings 24:1a)
v. 28	597	Jerusalem captured	All the best people (2 Kings 24:10-17)
v. 29	587	Jerusalem destroyed	Most of remainder (2 Kings 25:1-17)
v. 30	582	Judah raided again	Leftovers in country (after Jer 41:17-18)
v. 31ff	561	Jehoiachin released	(Hope for future return) (2 Kings 25:27-30)

Lamentations

BACKGROUND

The word 'lamentations', though not used as much today as in former times, is an ordinary English word that denotes expressions of sorrow, grief or distress. The biblical book of Lamentations is a collection of five poems that express the writer's sorrow over the fall of Jerusalem to the armies of Babylon in 587 BC. (For details of the events of that time see the section 'Historical Background' in the introductory notes to the book of Jeremiah.)

A poet and his poems

There is no statement in the book of Lamentations to inform us who wrote it, though the popular view is that the author was Jeremiah. Whoever the author was, he must have lived in Jerusalem during the final siege and ultimate collapse of the city. He witnessed the horror of those days and had first-hand knowledge of the hardships that the survivors in Judah experienced.

Clearly the author of the book was a person of considerable literary skill and spiritual insight. His poems arouse feelings of pity and sympathy in the reader, but they also show the firmness of his faith. In the depressing circumstances about which he writes, he still took his troubles to God.

Each of the five poems represents one chapter in the English Bible. By his arrangement of the poems, the author has provided a sharp contrast between despair and hope. The central poem, which has 66 verses, deals with certain basic issues of people's relationship with God, such as faith and doubt, punishment and salvation, justice and mercy, repentance and forgiveness. The other four poems, which have 22 verses each, deal with the sufferings of those who lived in Jerusalem and the surrounding countryside, and are arranged equally either side of the central poem.

A further feature of the poems has specifically to do with the original language and therefore is not evident in English. In the Hebrew of the poems of Chapters 1, 2 and 4, each verse begins with a different letter of the 22-letter Hebrew alphabet, the order of letters being from the first letter of the alphabet to the last. In the 66-verse poem of Chapter 3, there are 22 sets of three verses each. All three verses in each set begin with the same letter, and the initial letters of each set again follow the order of the Hebrew alphabet. The poem of Chapter 5, though having 22 verses, does not maintain the alphabetical arrangement.

THE FIVE POEMS

Desolation in Jerusalem (1:1-22)

Jerusalem, once a busy commercial city, is now empty. She is like a woman who has lost her husband, like a princess who has become a slave. The nations (her 'lovers') who she thought would help her have proved useless, some even treacherous (1:1-3).

When Jerusalem's hour of crisis came, all her leaders fled, leaving the people to be attacked, plundered and taken captive. Now that all the usual activities of daily life have ceased, there remain only the memories of the pleasant way of life she once enjoyed – and the memory of how her enemies laughed at her downfall (4-7).

The reason for Jerusalem's desolation is her sin. In her idolatry and wickedness she had acted like an immoral woman; now she has been treated like one (8-9). Babylonian soldiers not only entered the temple (something that was forbidden to foreigners) but also plundered its precious metals and took its sacred treasures. The starving people in the crushed city try to trade their personal possessions with the enemy soldiers in a desperate effort to obtain bread (10-11).

In anguish the personified city asks those who pass by if they feel any pity for her because of the suffering God has sent her. She has been attacked, burnt, and left in a condition of hopeless ruin (12-13). Her sins have weighed her down as a heavy yoke weighs down on the neck of a working animal. Consequently, when God sent the enemy armies against her, she was so weak and helpless that she was unable to withstand them (14-16).

Although she does not receive the sympathy for which she cries out, she is not bitter against God. She knows God has justly punished her for her sins. She warns others to learn from her experience (17-18). When she called for help, none came. Some of the people starved to death in the siege, others were killed or taken captive when the city finally fell (19-20).

Jerusalem's grief is made worse by the mockery of her neighbours. They rejoice over the fall of Jerusalem, yet they themselves are wicked. She prays that God will carry out justice against them as he has carried it out against Judah (21-22).

Sufferings sent by God (2:1-22)

In this poem the main theme is that the calamity that has befallen Judah has been the work of God. He has humbled the exalted nation; he has turned her glory into darkness (2:1). City and field, temple and fortress have been destroyed by him. They expected God to be the defender of his people, but he has been the attacker. Far from showing pity towards them, he has been angry with them (2-5).

God has destroyed the temple and left it looking like an old broken-down hut in a neglected garden. Religious festivals and ceremonies have ceased. In the sacred house of God, heathen soldiers have shouted wildly as they plundered and smashed (6-7). As builders are thorough in measuring and building a wall, so God has been thorough in destroying Jerusalem's wall. He has allowed the enemy to invade the city, and now all Jerusalem's leaders are gone (8-9).

The writer weeps as he describes the scene in Jerusalem at the height of the siege. Starvation is widespread, and the city's leaders can do nothing to help. Children search the streets for scraps of food till eventually they collapse and die (10-13).

Now that the city has fallen, people can see how the false prophets misled them in giving assurances of deliverance. They should have spoken like the genuine prophets, who condemned the people's sins and warned of God's judgment if they did not repent (14; cf. Jer 14:13-16; 23:14-17). Now the genuine prophets' predictions of judgment have come true. Jerusalem's enemies mock the fallen city (15-17; cf. Jer 24:8-10; 27:12-15).

Again the writer pictures the heartbreaking scene in besieged Jerusalem, with starving people crying out to God for mercy. Some even kill their own children for food (18-20). As pilgrims flock to Jerusalem at the time of an annual festival, so enemy soldiers now pour into the city, but only to slaughter its citizens (21-22).

Grief, repentance and hope (3:1-66)

This poem is different in style from the previous two. The poet speaks as if he is the representative of all Judah, describing Judah's sufferings as if they were his own. And those sufferings are God's righteous judgment (3:1-3). He is like a starving man ready to die. Indeed, he feels as if he already dwells in the world of the dead (4-6). He is like a man chained and locked inside a stone prison from which there is no way out (7-9).

To the writer God seems like a wild animal that tears its prey to pieces, or like a hunter who has shot his prey with an arrow (10-12). Mocked and afflicted, the writer feels like one who has been punished by being forced to eat and drink things that are harmful to him (13-15). He is like a person whose face has been rubbed in the ground and whose joy for life has gone (16-18). He feels hurt and depressed, yet in all the darkness of his suffering he now sees a ray of hope (19-21).

God may punish, but the writer still trusts in him. He knows that God's steadfast love does not change. It is constant and reliable (22-24). God disciplines and trains, but those who are patient will enjoy the fulness of his salvation (25-27). Humility and submission are important, even submission to the enemy that God sends as his agent of judgment (28-30).

The people of God can be assured that he does not reject them for ever and that he has no pleasure in punishing them. Nevertheless, punishment is necessary (31-33). But God does not approve of punishment that is unnecessarily cruel, ignores a person's rights or perverts justice (34-36).

When people know that God is in control of all things, and confess that God's judgment is just, they will bear his punishment patiently (37-39). The writer therefore urges the people of his shattered country to examine themselves, to recognize their sin, to acknowledge that the punishment they have received is just, and to turn to God and seek his forgiveness (40-42).

Speaking as if he is the whole nation of Judah, the writer acknowledges his sin. He confesses that it has been a barrier or cloud between him and God, preventing God from hearing his prayers for mercy. As a result he has been ruined and disgraced (43-45). He is filled with grief because of the cruelty and mockery he has suffered at the hands of his enemies (46-48). He weeps when he looks at the terrible suffering that has fallen upon the people of Jerusalem (49-51).

The writer feels like a bird that has been hunted or a person who has been thrown down a well to drown (52-54). But now that he is repentant, God hears his cries for help and assures him that he need not be afraid (55-57). He knows at last that God has saved him. At the same time he reminds God of the cruelty of those who have persecuted him (58-60), for they have heartlessly mocked and jeered the afflicted (61-63). He leaves the judgment of such people in God's hands (64-66).

Corrupt leaders disgraced (4:1-22)

Jerusalem's former glory is contrasted with her present ruin. The once glorious temple, now defiled and shattered, is symbolic of the once glorious people now shamed and broken. Jerusalem's dead lie in the streets like pieces of broken pottery (4:1-2). The writer recalls again the scene of horror during the siege. Wild beasts provide food for their young, but in Jerusalem mothers are unable to provide food for their children. Rich nobles die on the streets like beggars (3-5).

Sodom's punishment was great, but Jerusalem's is greater; for Sodom was destroyed in a day, but Jerusalem is destroyed amid long and bitter agony (6). Even those of the upper classes, who spent much time and money making themselves look beautiful, are now ugly through disease and starvation (7-8). It would be better to be killed in battle than to starve to death or be forced to eat one's children (9-10). The Jerusalemites thought that because Yahweh was their God, no enemy could conquer their city, but now Yahweh himself has destroyed it (11-12).

Chiefly to blame for Jerusalem's downfall are its corrupt leaders, especially the prophets and priests. They, more than anyone else, have been responsible for the injustices that have brought God's judgment on the city (13). Realizing this, the people now treat their former leaders like lepers and drive them out of the city. When the fugitives try to settle in other places, the local people refuse to receive them (14-16).

The writer recalls how Jerusalem expected to be rescued by Egypt, but no deliverance came. Instead the Babylonians came, making the Jerusalemites prisoners in their own city (17-18; cf. Jer 37:6-10). Those who tried to flee to the mountains were caught, including the king Zedekiah, in whom the people had falsely placed their trust (19-20; cf. Jer 39:3-5).

Edom rejoiced to see its ancient enemy Judah overthrown; but Edom too will be overthrown and, unlike Judah, will not rise again. The destruction of Jerusalem is temporary, but Edom's destruction will be permanent (21-22; cf. Jer 49:7-13; Ps 137:7; Obad 10-14).

A prayer for mercy (5:1-22)

This poem was apparently written in Judah some time after the fall of Jerusalem. Only the people of no use to Babylon were left in the land, and this poem reflects the hardships they faced (cf. Jer 52:16).

In a plea to God for mercy, the people remind him of their present shame (5:1). Death has broken up their families, and the invaders have taken over their houses and lands (2-3). They live and work like slaves in their own country, and have to buy water from their foreign overlords (4-5). Their ancestors tried to keep the nation alive by seeking help from Egypt and Assyria, but they actually brought the nation to ruin. Now the people have to submit to Babylonian guards who are little more than slaves (6-8).

Conditions in Judah are terrible. The people have to search the barren country regions for food, and in doing so they risk death from desert bandits (9-10). Judean women are raped, former leaders are tortured, and children are forced to work like slaves (11-13). The old way of life has gone, and with it has gone all celebration and rejoicing (14-15). People everywhere are unhappy, discouraged and ashamed. They acknowledge that their sin has brought all this upon them (16-18).

In a final desperate plea, the people cry to the sovereign ruler of the world not to reject them but to bring them back to himself. They ask that he will restore their nation and give them the happiness they once enjoyed. God is eternal and unchangeable, and they are his people; surely he will not forget them (19-22).

Ezekiel

BACKGROUND

The era through which Ezekiel lived was one of great change in the Palestine region. It was an era that saw Babylon's rise to power, the destruction of Jerusalem and the captivity of God's people in a foreign land. All these events had an effect on Ezekiel's personal life and on the work God called him to do. Readers should therefore be familiar with the history of the period in order to understand the man Ezekiel and the message he has preserved in his book.

Judah conquered by Babylon

More than a century before the time of Ezekiel, Assyria had destroyed the northern kingdom Israel and scattered the people in foreign lands. The days of Ezekiel's childhood coincided with the last days of Assyria's power. In 612 BC Assyria was conquered by Babylon, who went on to defeat Egypt at the Battle of Carchemish in 605 BC. With this victory, Babylon became the master of all the nations in the region, including Judah (2 Kings 24:1a,7; Jer 46:2). (For a map showing the locations of these nations, see introductory notes to Jeremiah. For an explanation of the names used of various nations see introductory notes to Isaiah.)

The Babylonian conquerors allowed the Judean king Jehoiakim to continue reigning in Jerusalem, but they placed a heavy tax on Judah. They also took captive to Babylon a small number of intelligent young men whom they chose from the leading families of Jerusalem. One of these was Daniel (Dan 1:1-6).

After submitting to Babylon for several years, Judah rebelled (2 Kings 24:1b). Babylon refrained from taking direct action against Judah till the time was suitable. Then, in 597 BC, its armies returned and attacked Jerusalem. At the time of this attack Judah's worthless king Jehoiakim died and the eighteen year old Jehoiachin came to the throne. When, after reigning only three months, he saw that Jerusalem could not withstand the Babylonians indefinitely, he surrendered. All the nation's best people were carried off to Babylon, among them the young man Ezekiel. Only those whom Babylon did not want were left in Jerusalem, and over these

the Babylonians appointed Zedekiah, Jehoiachin's uncle, as king (2 Kings 24:8-17).

With all Judah's most capable administrators now captive in Babylon, Zedekiah was left with an inexperienced government. Few of his advisers were politically or spiritually mature, and they persuaded the weak king to seek Egypt's help in rebelling against Babylon. The prophet Jeremiah opposed this policy untiringly, for he saw that it would lead only to the horrors of siege and destruction. He advised Judah to accept its fate as God's will and submit to Babylon (2 Kings 24:18-20; Jer 21:1-10; 27:12-22; 37:6-10).

Ignoring Jeremiah's advice, Zedekiah rebelled against Babylon. Nebuchadnezzar's armies returned, and through a cruel siege that lasted a year and six months they crushed the rebellious city. This was the end of Jerusalem (587 BC). The city and its temple were destroyed and many of the people taken captive. Only the poorest of the people were left in the land, along with scattered villagers in country areas (2 Kings 25:1-12).

Ezekiel in Babylon

Many of the people taken captive to Babylon in 597 BC expected that soon they would return to Jerusalem. Ezekiel, who was one of these captives, no doubt shared their hopes. He was a young priest (Ezek 1:3) and he was probably looking forward to the day when he would serve in the temple in Jerusalem. Any such hopes were destroyed when he heard from Jeremiah's letter to the exiles that they would spend the rest of their lives in Babylon (Jer 29:1-10). God told Ezekiel that his work was to be as a prophet in Babylon, not as a priest in Jerusalem. Ezekiel began his prophetic work five years after arriving in Babylon and it lasted at least twenty-two years (Ezek 1:2; 29:17).

In the early days of his preaching, Ezekiel denounced the sins of Jerusalem and announced the city's coming destruction. He made it clear that the people's present suffering, whether in Jerusalem or in Babylon, was a fitting judgment from God. He warned that for those left in Jerusalem worse was to come, for the city would be destroyed and the temple burnt down when the Babylonians invaded the city for the third and final time (Ezek 4:1-2; 5:12; 6:1-7; 7:5-9).

Ezekiel's hearers at first rejected his message, claiming that his announcements of the destruction of Jerusalem applied to a future generation, not to them (Ezek 12:27-28). A few years later, when news reached the exiles that Jerusalem had fallen as Ezekiel had prophesied, the people were forced to acknowledge that Ezekiel was a true prophet who knew God's mind. They started to listen to his teaching, though few genuinely changed their ways (Ezek 33:21,30-33).

Nevertheless, Ezekiel was encouraged to move ahead to his main task, which was the spiritual preparation of God's people for the new age God had promised them. He looked forward to the day when God's people, cleansed inwardly from their sin, would worship him truly from the heart and serve him in loving obedience.

Life of the exiles

When taken captive to Babylon, the Jews were not locked up as if in prison. They were placed in various settlements around the country and put to work as unpaid labourers for the Babylonian government (Ezek 3:15). Though they were often treated harshly by their Babylonian overseers (Ps 137:1-6), they were allowed a measure of freedom to live their family and communal lives in these settlements as they pleased (Jer 29:4-7).

Characteristics of Ezekiel's prophecies

Although he lived in a foreign country and had no chance of serving in God's temple, Ezekiel retained his interest in the proper functioning of Israel's religious system. He had been trained for the priesthood, and his book shows the priest's concern for detail in matters relating to the temple and its services. The exactitude of the priest is further seen in Ezekiel's practice of carefully dating his messages. He usually dated these according to the year of the exile of King Jehoiachin, which was also the year of his own exile.

Probably the best known characteristic of the book of Ezekiel is its symbolism, something that was naturally of interest to a priest. The interpretation of this symbolism is complicated by the fact that Ezekiel was such an unusual person. He seems to have possessed abnormal mental powers and was able to have unnatural visions. He had a vivid imagination and was emotionally sensitive. He often acted in the strangest manner. All this makes it difficult to understand his book, and encourages caution in interpreting his visions and actions.

OUTLINE

1:1-3:27 THE CALL OF EZEKIEL

A vision of God's glory (1:1-28)

Ezekiel lived in a Jewish settlement that bordered the Chebar River. He had been in Babylon five years and was now thirty years of age, the age at which he normally would have begun his priestly service in the temple in Jerusalem (cf. Num 4:2-3). But he had no chance now of returning to Jerusalem. Instead God called him to be a prophet, who would take his message to his people in Babylon (1:1-3).

The call came as Ezekiel was watching a storm approach across the desert. He was looking with particular interest at the startling changes of colour produced across the sky by the reflection of the lightning in the dark thunderclouds. Just then he saw something that appeared to come out of the clouds (4).

Ezekiel would soon discover that the object was a fiery chariot, but his first observation was that it was in the shape of a hollow square, with a living creature standing upright at each corner. These living creatures were of an order of heavenly beings known as cherubim (see 10:20). Each had a human body but four faces, and their outstretched wings met to form the sides of the square. Other wings formed their clothing. The whole thing seemed to be alive and could move in any direction (5-12). Lightning flashed from something that looked like burning coals or a blazing torch that was contained in the middle of the square (13-14).

At each corner of the square was a wheel, which actually looked more like two wheels, one at right angles to the other. By now he could see clearly that the fiery object was a chariot, and the wheels enabled the chariot to move freely in any direction. Even the wheels were alive, for they shared the life of the living creatures (15-21).

When the chariot moved, the sound of the movement of the creatures' outstretched wings was like a waterfall or thunder. When the chariot stopped, the creatures lowered their wings. Above the heads of the creatures was a shining platform that supported the throne of God (22-25). Seated above this throne and surrounded by a rainbow was a fiery figure, human in outline but so dazzling that Ezekiel could not describe it. Overcome by this awesome vision, he could only fall down and listen to the voice speaking to him (26-28).

Sent to a stubborn people (2:1-3:15)

In contrast to the glorious and almighty God, Ezekiel is addressed merely as 'son of man'. This was a Hebrew phrase which here simply means 'man' (GNB: mortal man) and which is used consistently throughout the book when Ezekiel is addressed (2:1-2). God was going to send Ezekiel with his message to his rebellious people (3). Ezekiel was warned that he might suffer cruel treatment at the hands of his countrymen, but he had to persevere. Whether they heeded his words or not, they would at least know that he was God's prophet, because the power of God would be at work in him (4-7).

Ezekiel was not to share the stubborn attitude of the people. He had to declare all that God told him to declare, even when the message was one of 'lamentation, mourning and woe'. He had to eat the scroll containing God's message, thereby signifying that he made God's message his own before giving it to others (8-10). When, in obedience to God, Ezekiel ate the scroll, he unexpectedly found it a sweetly satisfying experience (3:1-3).

God reminded Ezekiel, however, that the exiles would not listen to him. Foreign nations might heed God's word, but not Israel (4-7). God gave Ezekiel a special toughness, so that he would not give in when he came against the hardened opposition of Israel (8-11).

The vision now ended. Ezekiel felt God's power upon him and heard the sound of God's chariot-throne as it departed. God's word within him was changing his attitude as he began to see Israel's sin from God's viewpoint. His heart became heavy as he returned to the camp (12-14). He waited seven days for God's word to have its full effect on him before he began to pass it on to the exiles (15).

A faithful watchman (3:16-27)

As a watchman warns people in the city of a coming attack, so Ezekiel was to warn the exiles, so that they might turn away from sin and be saved from further calamity (16-17). If Ezekiel gave a warning and people ignored it, those people would bear the responsibility for their own death. But if Ezekiel failed to give the warning, Ezekiel would be held responsible for their death, and would himself suffer the death penalty (18-21).

Before Ezekiel began his ministry, God had one further instruction for him (22-23). Ezekiel was shown that he must speak God's message only when God directed him. To emphasize this, God required Ezekiel not to speak or leave his house until God allowed him. In a dramatic demonstration of this restriction, God may have caused Ezekiel to suffer some sort of illness. Alternatively, Ezekiel may have voluntarily acted dumb and allowed someone to bind him with ropes. When God's time came for Ezekiel to be released, he was to go and announce God's message to the rebellious people (24-27).

4:1-7:27 JUDGMENT AGAINST JERUSALEM

Siege and exile (4:1-17)

Prophets often acted their messages instead of, or in addition to, speaking them. Ezekiel drew a rough picture of Jerusalem on a brick, placed the brick on the ground, then with sticks, stones, clay and markings in the sand, he modelled a siege of the city. The message to the exiles was that they had no chance of an early return to Jerusalem. On the contrary, Jerusalem could expect further attack. God would not defend the city; rather he would cut himself off from it. The prophet symbolized the barrier between God and sinful Jerusalem by taking an iron cooking plate and holding it between himself (representing God) and the model of the besieged city (4:1-3).

The prophet's next acted parable lasted more than a year. Each day he spent a period lying on his side facing his model of besieged Jerusalem. He was bound with cords so that he could not move, to symbolize that God's people could not escape the judgment of their sins. However, his arm was left bare, to demonstrate God's determination to fight against Jerusalem. The number of days he lay on his left side was for the number of years from the northern kingdom's breakaway from Jerusalem to the end of the captivity. The number of days he lay on his right side was for the number of years from the fall of Jerusalem to the end of the captivity (4-8).

In the third acted parable, Ezekiel ate a starvation diet each day, to symbolize the scarcity of food and water in Jerusalem during the last great siege (9-11; see v. 16-17). He was told to cook the food on a fire of human dung. In this way he would picture the uncleanness of the food that the people would be forced to eat, both during the siege and later in the foreign countries to which they would be scattered (12-13). When Ezekiel complained that it was unfair to ask him to use human dung to make the fire, God allowed him to use cow's dung instead. This was a fuel commonly used by people in that part of the world (14-17).

Jerusalem destroyed (5:1-17)

The last of this group of four acted parables was again concerned with the siege of Jerusalem. It dealt more specifically with the dreadful fate that awaited the citizens.

Ezekiel shaved his hair, weighed it, then divided it into three equal parts. One part he burnt on his model city (the brick), symbolizing the death of one third of the city's people through famine and disease. The second part he scattered around the model city, then chopped up the hair with a sword, symbolizing the slaughter of many in fighting around the city. The third portion he scattered to the wind, symbolizing those who would be taken captive to Babylon or otherwise scattered among the nations. Many of those who attempted to flee the city would be ruthlessly killed by the enemy (5:1-2; see v. 12).

In a symbolic expression of hope, Ezekiel then picked up a few of the scattered hairs and put them in his clothing, indicating that a remnant would be saved. But even some of these would perish (3-4).

Jerusalem was the centre of God's chosen nation, but its people had behaved worse than the people of heathen nations round about (5-6). God would therefore punish Jerusalem with a terrible judgment (7-9). Starvation during the siege would make the people so desperate for food that some would kill their children and eat them. They would experience the horrors of famine, disease, slaughter and captivity that Ezekiel had pictured (10-12). God would act as he saw fit. His judgment would be a punishment on Jerusalem and a warning to other nations (13-17).

The idolatry of Israel (6:1-14)

From the time of the judges (the period that followed Israel's settlement of Canaan) the people of Israel had copied Canaanite religious practices. Canaanite gods, collectively known as Baalim (plural of Baal) were gods of nature, and Israelites used the Canaanite shrines throughout the countryside as places to offer worship to Yahweh. These shrines were called 'high places' because they were usually built on the tops of hills and mountains. Israel's false worship at these high places was largely the reason for the nation's unfaithfulness to God and its consequent punishment. Ezekiel, in keeping with the preaching of earlier prophets, announced God's judgment on the idolatrous shrines (6:1-4). The

idol-worshipping Israelites would be slaughtered in the coming judgment, and their corpses would lie scattered over these pagan hilltop sites along with the remains of the demolished altars and broken idols (5-7).

Of those taken captive to foreign countries, some would realize that God had been just in punishing them for their idolatry. In shame at their former waywardness they would turn again to God (8-10). God's triumph over all the wicked would be celebrated by the clapping of hands and the stamping of feet. Throughout Israel, from south to north, the rebels would be punished and God's honour restored. Then all would know that Yahweh was the one true God (11-14).

The end is near (7:1-27)

Many Jews thought that Jerusalem would never be conquered. Ezekiel announced with certainty that the city would fall. God had been longsuffering and merciful, and had saved the city many times, but the people stubbornly refused to repent. Now the time for God's judgment had come (7:1-4). One disaster would follow another, till the wicked city was destroyed (5-9).

As a tree blossoms, so Jerusalem's sin was full-grown. The city was about to fall; rich and poor were about to lose everything. Therefore, a buyer was not to rejoice in a good deal he had made, nor a seller mourn because he had lost his property. Neither was the seller to hope that one day he would regain his property (10-13).

The citizens of Jerusalem might prepare for battle, but all such preparation would be useless. Jerusalem was doomed (14). People trapped in the besieged city would die of starvation. Those in the fields and villages outside would be killed by enemy soldiers. Any who managed to escape would only face a miserable existence in their mountain hiding places (15-16). Everywhere there would be a feeling of hopelessness. The money that the Jerusalemites had unjustly gained would be of no use to them when there was no food to buy. In despair they would throw their money away (17-19). Their idols, richly ornamented and expensive, would be stolen by the invaders, and God's 'precious place', the Jerusalem temple, would be profaned as irreverent Babylonian soldiers invaded, plundered and in the end destroyed it (20-22).

Terrified by the violence of the attack, people would look on helplessly as the invaders seized their houses (23-25). Neither religious nor civil leaders would be able to save Jerusalem from being overrun by the hated foreigners. The calamity would be a fitting judgment on the city for its religious rebellion and moral waywardness (26-27).

8:1-24:27 THE SINS OF JERUSALEM

Idolatry in the temple (8:1-18)

A year and two months had now passed since God called Ezekiel to be a prophet. By this time people recognized him as a prophet, and leaders among the exiles came to discuss their affairs with him (8:1; cf. 1:1-2). While the leaders were sitting talking with him, Ezekiel was suddenly caught up by the Spirit of God and taken, as it were, to Jerusalem (2-3).

Ezekiel knew immediately that these visions were from God, because the first thing he saw was a vision of the glory of God similar to that which he had seen earlier (4; cf. 1:1-28). In this vision Ezekiel was taken to the temple where, as he was about to enter the inner court, he saw an idol that stirred God to jealousy (5-6).

From there Ezekiel went by a secret door into a hidden room (7-9). There he saw a gathering of Jerusalem's leaders, who were secretly worshipping pictures of animals painted on the walls. Foolishly, they thought God could not see them (10-13). In another part of the temple Ezekiel saw women carrying out ritual mourning as part of their worship of the foreign god, Tammuz (14-15). Finally, Ezekiel came into the inner court of the temple, where he saw a group of priests who had turned their backs on the temple and were worshipping the sun. 'Putting the branch to the nose' was part of the ritual and a particularly offensive insult to God (16-18).

Execution of the sinners (9:1-11)

God's punishment of Jerusalem was illustrated by a vision in which God sent his executioners to carry out his work of judgment on the sinful people. First, however, he sent a special servant to put a mark on those who opposed the city's wickedness, so that they might be preserved through the coming bloodshed (9:1-4). The first place where the judgment fell was the temple, where the nation's leaders had led the people astray with their wickedness and idolatry. The temple was soon defiled with the corpses scattered around its courts (5-7).

The northern kingdom had been destroyed long ago, and now many from the southern kingdom were killed or taken captive. Ezekiel feared that with the slaughter in Jerusalem the last remains of the ancient nation would be wiped out (8). God assured the prophet that his judgment was just. The people acted as if God did not matter; now they were to

suffer the consequences. But safety was guaranteed for those believers who stood firm for God amid the nationwide ungodliness (9-11).

God's glory departs from the temple (10:1-22)

In the present series of visions the fiery chariot-throne of God was in the court of the temple (see 8:3-4). The glory of God (that is, the symbolic form of God over the throne) had risen from the throne and come to rest on the threshold of the temple. From there God had directed his agents in the execution of the citizens of Jerusalem (see 9:3). From this same position on the temple threshold, God now gave further commands to the man who had previously sealed the faithful for preservation. God told him to go and take some coals from the vacant chariot-throne and scatter them over the city of Jerusalem, to symbolize that the coming fiery destruction of Jerusalem was directed by God himself (10:1-5).

The man then went to the chariot-throne to carry out God's commands. As Ezekiel describes how one of the cherubim helped the man collect the coals, he adds a note to explain that the cherubim had hands (6-8).

Ezekiel must have been so interested in the details of the chariot-throne that he repeated much of the description given in the opening chapter. He apparently wanted to impress upon his readers that the chariot-throne he saw at the temple was the same as that which he had seen earlier (9-17). He then saw God return to his chariot-throne and begin to leave the temple. But, as if unwilling to leave, he moved only as far as the temple gate, then stopped (18-19).

An additional note explains that the 'living creatures' Ezekiel described earlier were cherubim. Cherubim were the winged creatures who guarded the covenant box in the Most Holy Place (cf. Exod 25:20-22). In other words, the God whom Ezekiel saw enthroned above the cherubim was the same God who was enthroned above the mercy seat (the lid of the covenant box) in the Most Holy Place. This God, Israel's covenant God Yahweh, was the one now about to leave his temple, slaughter his people and destroy his city (20-22).

Judgment on Jerusalem's leaders (11:1-13)

At the east gate of the temple, where God's chariot-throne had temporarily stopped (see 10:19), Ezekiel saw in vision a group of twenty-five of the city's political leaders. The wrong advice of these men was one reason why Jerusalem was heading for certain ruin (11:1-2). (At the time of this vision, the last great siege of Jerusalem, foretold in earlier chapters, had not yet happened.)

Jeremiah had been telling the people that to fight against Babylon was fatal, for God had sent the Babylonians to punish Jerusalem. The city should therefore surrender (Jer 21:8-10). These leaders, on the other hand, were stirring up the people to resist Babylon. They recommended that building programs in the city be stopped so that more men would be available to fight. They were confident that they were safe in Jerusalem. The city walls would protect the inhabitants from the Babylonians, just as a cooking pot protects the flesh inside it from the fire (3-4).

God's word to Jerusalem's leaders is that he knows what they are thinking, but the city will fall in spite of their confidence (5-6). The innocent people, whom these corrupt leaders have killed, are now the fortunate ones, for they will be spared the bloodshed that is to come upon Jerusalem. They are the only pieces of flesh to be safe from the fire. As for the leaders, they will be taken out of the cooking pot, dragged out of their imagined security in Jerusalem, and executed at the border of Israel as the victorious Babylonian armies return home (7-12). (For the fulfilment of this prophecy see 2 Kings 25:18-21.)

Ezekiel saw one of Jerusalem's leaders drop dead as he was speaking. The prophet was again filled with fear as he saw the determination of God to punish his rebellious people (13).

Hope for the future (11:14-25)

Those left in Jerusalem thought they were God's favoured people. They thought their security was guaranteed because they lived in the city where his temple was situated. They looked upon the exiles as having been cast off by God, forsaken and unclean in a foreign land (14-15). To the contrary, Ezekiel points out that the exiles are God's favoured people, the remnant whom he has preserved. When they repent of their idolatry and rebellion, he will bring them back to their land (16-18). He will restore them to a new covenant relationship with himself, and put within them a new spirit that will make them more responsive to his will. The rebellious, however, will be punished (19-21).

As a final demonstration that God would no longer dwell among or protect the people living in Jerusalem, the chariot-throne bearing the glory of God departed from the temple, went out of the city and came to rest on a nearby mountain. God had left Jerusalem, but he was still within reach if the people decided to repent (22-23).

Now that the series of visions was finished, Ezekiel returned to normal. In spirit he was no longer in Jerusalem, but back in Babylon, where he recounted his experiences to the exiles (24-25; cf. 8:1-4).

Pictures of exile (12:1-16)

It appears that many of the exiles were rebellious against God because of his message of doom, and were still hoping for an early return to Jerusalem (12:1-2). God therefore commanded Ezekiel to act another message for them. He was to show that the exiles had no chance of returning to Jerusalem. On the contrary, the Jerusalemites would come to join the exiles in Babylon. Ezekiel's daytime act was to gather a few belongings that an exile could carry with him and set off into the country. His nighttime act was a little different. He dug through the wall of his home, then tried to escape with his bundle of belongings into the night (3-7).

Next morning Ezekiel explained his actions to the people. His daytime act pictured the people of Jerusalem going into exile (8-11). His nighttime act pictured King Zedekiah's attempt, at the time of Babylon's last great siege of Jerusalem, to escape from the city by night. But he was captured, blinded and taken into exile (12-13; see 2 Kings 25:2-7). His leading officials were killed and the common people taken into captivity (14-15).

Out of this catastrophe, however, God would preserve the repentant minority. These would assure the people among whom they lived that Jerusalem's destruction was not because Babylon's gods were more powerful than Jerusalem's God, Yahweh. It was because Yahweh himself commanded it. God would destroy Jerusalem as a punishment upon his people for their sins (16).

Messages to be heeded (12:17-28)

Ezekiel's starvation diet symbolized the shortage of food in Jerusalem during the last great siege (see 4:9-17). He was now told that, when he ate, he was to act as if he were stricken with terror, to emphasize the horror of the events about to overtake Jerusalem (17-20).

Many of the exiles doubted the truth of the messages that Ezekiel announced. They argued that days, months, and even years passed, but they did not see his prophecies fulfilled (21-22). God's reply was that the prophecies were now about to be fulfilled, and false prophecies of an early return to Jerusalem would cease (23-25). Others did not doubt the truth of Ezekiel's message, but claimed that the events he foresaw would all happen in the distant future. Again God said that the prophesied events were about to happen (26-28).

Condemnation of false prophets (13:1-23)

False prophets were a constant danger, both those in Jerusalem and those among the exiles in Babylon. They were bad guides, spiritually and morally, because they proclaimed only what they themselves wanted. They had no knowledge of the mind of God (13:1-3). Judah was falling into ruins, but the false prophets, instead of helping to repair and strengthen the nation, cunningly exploited the situation for their own benefit. They were like foxes digging holes around the city wall and so helping its ruin. They should have been like builders trying to strengthen the wall so that it would not crumble (4-7).

Ezekiel announced God's certain punishment on the false prophets. They would lose, to begin with, their place of honour in society, then their citizenship, and finally their right to live in God's land (8-9).

If these preachers had been true prophets, they would have destroyed the people's mistaken hopes of peace and security. Instead they encouraged them. In Ezekiel's illustration they white-washed an insecure wall to cover the cracks, whereas they should have demolished it. God announced that he would send a storm of rain, hail and wind, and the wall would collapse, burying the false prophets beneath it. They would perish along with the nation (10-16).

Among the false prophets were a number of women, who helped the decay of the nation by practising witchcraft. They used magic wristbands and veils in their weird rituals, casting deadly spells over their innocent victims, while protecting the evil people who consulted them (17-19). By their strange powers these witches disheartened the righteous and encouraged the wicked. God declared that he would now destroy their powers and release those whom they kept in bondage (20-23).

Idolatry in the heart (14:1-11)

Once again the leaders of the exiles came to see if Ezekiel had any helpful advice for them. He did, but not of the kind they were seeking. Although these men were outwardly loyal to Yahweh, inwardly they were attracted to the Babylonian gods. God told Ezekiel that he would not speak to such people through his prophet, but would speak directly. He would speak in a decisive act of judgment that would remove this tendency towards idolatry from the hearts of his people. Then they would become truly loyal to him (14:1-5).

God wanted his people to be cleansed from idolatry, in thought as well as in actions. He had his own way of dealing with the person who, idolatrous in heart, secretly consulted a false prophet (6-8). Should the prophet give a comforting message to such an enquirer, his action would indicate that he was more concerned with pleasing people than with pleasing God. It would prove that he was a false prophet. God would allow the man to speak his deceiving words, and on the basis of this clear evidence would then destroy him, along with his idolatrous enquirer (9-11).

Justice in punishing Jerusalem (14:12-23)

Some were no doubt saying that God would not destroy Jerusalem as Ezekiel had been prophesying. God would surely spare the city out of consideration for the godly people within it, even though such godly people may have been few in number. Ezekiel replied that even if some of the godliest people who ever lived were in the city, God would still destroy it; though he would deliver the godly (12-14). God's punishment could take various forms, but the same basic principle would apply (15-18). The righteousness of a few would not save the wicked from their just punishment (19-20).

Later some citizens of Jerusalem would escape the slaughter and come to join the exiles in Babylon. Then the exiles would see how corrupt the people of Jerusalem really were. The exiles would at last realize that God's judgment on the city was indeed just (21-23).

The useless vine (15:1-8)

Judah was one nation among many, like a vine among the trees of the forest. The question is asked: Is the timber of the vine better than the timber of other trees? The answer: No; as timber it is useless, not even fit to make a peg from which to hang a cooking pot. It is still more useless if it has been half burnt in a fire (15:1-5).

The nation Judah was useless and was already half destroyed through Babylon's attacks. Like the half-burnt vine thrown back on the fire, Jerusalem will be destroyed in the coming judgment (6-8).

The unfaithfulness of Jerusalem (16:1-43)

In this chapter Ezekiel describes Judah's relationship with Yahweh by means of a long and colourful illustration. The ancient nation Israel began life in Canaan as a hated people of mixed blood and mixed culture. It was like an unwanted baby girl thrown out at birth and left to die (16:1-5). Then a passing traveller (Yahweh) picked the baby up and gave it a chance to live. The girl survived and grew, though without training or upbringing (6-7).

Many years later, by which time the girl had reached an age when she might marry, the same traveller happened to see her again. She had not been washed or clothed since birth. The man then lovingly bathed her, clothed her, married her, and made her so beautiful that her fame spread to other nations. So likewise, after the Israelites had spent centuries away from God in Egypt, he saved them from shame and made them his own people by covenant at Mt Sinai (8-14).

But the woman was not faithful to the marriage covenant. Israel was unfaithful to the one who had done so much for her. Leaving him to serve other gods, she became a spiritual prostitute. She built shrines and altars to other gods, and offered to those gods the things that Yahweh had freely given her (15-19). To make matters worse, she participated in the pagan practice of offering her children as human sacrifices (20-22).

As a prostitute uses brothels to attract her customers, so Israel built idol shrines throughout her towns and villages (23-25). She further demonstrated her spiritual prostitution by forsaking God and making political alliances with other countries. Even those nations, Israel's lovers, were ashamed of her immoral behaviour, but Israel kept lusting for more (26-29). In fact, her lust was so great that it was abnormal. Usually the customer pays the prostitute, but in the case of the prostitute Israel she paid the customer, so that she could multiply her immoral acts (30-34).

According to Israelite practice, the punishment for an adulteress was to be stripped naked, paraded in public and then stoned to death. Judah would therefore be punished, with its countryside stripped bare and the nation destroyed by enemy invaders. The nations who would inflict this disaster upon her would be the very nations whose favour she had tried to win by her prostitution (35-41). All this would be at the direction of God himself, whose love for Israel was the reason for his anger with her (42-43).

Worthless sisters (16:44-63)

Ezekiel refers back to Israel's mixed parentage in Canaan to introduce two sisters of the prostitute (who, in Ezekiel's time was identified with Judah's capital Jerusalem). The two sisters were the cities Samaria (capital of the former northern kingdom) and Sodom. Both cities were destroyed by God's judgment, but Jerusalem's sin was worse than both (44-48). Sodom was well known for its greed and

immorality, Samaria for its idolatry, but both cities now appeared righteous compared with Jerusalem. Surely, the destruction of Jerusalem was inescapable (49-52).

Samaria and Sodom may each have had some satisfaction in seeing Jerusalem suffer the same fate as they had suffered. Yet all three had hope for the future. After the overthrow of Babylon, the three regions of Palestine represented by these three cities would be restored and inhabited again (53-55). In the meantime Jerusalem had to bear the shame of its immoral behaviour. In times past, Jerusalem was ashamed to mention the sin of Sodom, but now her reputation was just as bad (56-58).

Looking beyond the coming judgment, Ezekiel saw the day when a humbled and forgiven Jerusalem would exercise authority over all her neighbours. The granting of this authority would not be because of any right that Jerusalem had under the old covenant. Rather it would be a free act of God's forgiving grace (59-62). As Jerusalem remembered her shameful behaviour in the past, she would be kept from any feelings of pride (63).

Zedekiah's treachery (17:1-21)

Another detailed illustration showed the exiles the significance of political developments in Jerusalem. Much had happened since they were taken from the city in 597 BC.

In Ezekiel's illustration a giant eagle broke off the top branches of a young cedar tree and carried them into a land of trade (17:1-4). (In 597 BC Babylon captured Jehoiachin, the Judean king, along with all the best of the people of Jerusalem, and carried them into Babylon; see 2 Kings 24:10-16.) Back in the land of the cedar tree, the eagle planted a native seed that grew into a vine, but it was low-spreading and was obedient to the eagle (5-6). (Back in Jerusalem, Babylon appointed another member of the Judean royal family, Zedekiah, king instead of Jehoiachin. Zedekiah was allowed only a limited independence, and had to remain submissive to Babylon; see 2 Kings 24:17.)

Then another giant eagle, equally as impressive as the first, appeared on the scene, whereupon the vine transferred its allegiance from its former master to this new eagle (7-8). (Zedekiah rebelled against Babylon by entering into an anti-Babylon military treaty with Egypt; see 2 Kings 24:20b; Jer 37:2-10.) The first eagle will therefore pull up the vine and cut off its branches, leaving it to wither and die (9-10). (Babylon will destroy Jerusalem and take Zedekiah into humiliating exile in Babylon, where he will die; see 2 Kings 25:1-12; Jer 37:8-10.)

Ezekiel's interpretation of the illustration gives special emphasis to Zedekiah's treachery in breaking his treaty with Babylon. Zedekiah had sworn an oath of allegiance to Nebuchadnezzar in the name of Yahweh (11-14), but he broke that oath in seeking Egypt's aid. In punishment he was taken captive to Babylon (15-18). Because he swore the oath in God's name, God dealt with Zedekiah's treachery as if it were against himself (19-21).

God's promise (17:22-24)

Returning to the former illustration, Ezekiel shows that God, not an eagle, will now take a branch from the top of the cedar tree. He will plant it on the top of a mountain, where it will grow into a huge and magnificent tree, bringing benefits to birds and animals of all kinds (22-23). (From the Davidic line of kings God will take one, the Messiah, and through him establish a kingdom that will bring blessing to the whole world.) High trees will be made low and green trees will dry up, but God's tree will flourish (24). (Nations such as Babylon and Egypt will perish, but God's kingdom will be exalted.)

Each person is responsible (18:1-32)

Many of the exiles complained that it was unjust that they should suffer because of the sins of the previous generation. True, the present captivity had resulted from the continuing decay of the nation over several generations, but the exiles could not deny that they too had sinned. There could be no excuses. They are individually responsible for their wrongdoings and they are punished accordingly (18:1-4).

Examples of sins are then given. These include joining in idol feasts at the high places, immorality, exploitation of the weakness of others, and lack of concern for those in need. The person who avoids these sins and does what is right will enjoy the blessing of God (5-9).

If this good person has a son who does evil, the son will be punished for his sin (10-13). If this wicked son produces, in turn, a son who does good, the good man will be rewarded for his goodness, though his wicked father will be punished (14-18). Each is either rewarded or punished according to whether he has done good or evil, regardless of how his father may have acted (19-20).

God wants sinners to repent, so that they can receive forgiveness and enjoy God's blessings in life. But if they deliberately choose the way of sin, nothing is left for them but judgment (21-24). The exiles had accused God of being unjust, but they, because of their wickedness, are the ones who are unjust (25-29). God in his justice will punish those

who sin, though it gives him no pleasure. He prefers that they repent of their sin and be forgiven; and to each person who repents, God will give eternal life (30-32).

Mourning for Judah's kings (19:1-14)

Although the prophet realized that God's judgment on the sinful people of Judah was fitting, he felt sorry for those Judean kings who fell victim to the foreign invaders (19:1). Judah was like a mother lion whose young lions became kings to rule over nations. However, when Egypt in 609 BC gained control of the region, Judah's king Jehoahaz was captured, bound and taken to Egypt, where he later died (2-4; see 2 Kings 23:31-34).

The next 'lion' had all the fierce and aggressive characteristics of Judah's next king, Jehoiakim (5-8; see 2 Kings 23:36-37; 24:1; Jer 22:13-19). Unlike the kings before and after him, Jehoiakim died not in a foreign country but in Jerusalem (Jer 22:19). His son and successor, Jehoiachin, was captured and taken prisoner to Babylon. Although Jehoiachin reigned only three months, he showed he had the same evil characteristics as his father (9; see 2 Kings 24:8-15).

Judah is pictured also as a strong healthy vine, and her kings as fruitful branches of that vine. But the 'vine' withered and was taken, along with its last rightful king, Jehoiachin, into the dry and thirsty land of Babylon (10-13). Back in Jerusalem the king appointed by Babylon proved to be a 'fire' who destroyed the little that remained of the vine. Through Zedekiah both the nation and the Davidic line of kings came to an end (14; see 2 Kings 24:20-25:21).

Idolatry in the past (20:1-26)

Ezekiel records another occasion when the leaders of the exiles came to him with certain questions. God told him not to waste time dealing with their questions (20:1-3). Rather Ezekiel was to deal with the more important issue of the people's false understanding of God. Since wrong attitudes had been passed on from generation to generation, Ezekiel began to recount Israel's history from the time the people were in Egypt (4-6). Even in Egypt they had been attracted to idols and had displayed the rebellion that was to characterize their long history. God could rightly have destroyed the people then, but he refrained. He did not want the Egyptians to misunderstand his actions and accuse him of evil (7-9).

In his grace God saved the people from Egypt and gave them his rules for right living. He also gave them the Sabbath rest day as a sign that they were his people by covenant (10-12). Again they rebelled and again God withheld his judgment when he may have justly destroyed them (13-17). Time and time again they rebelled, but God still withheld his judgment (18-22). He warned them that if they persisted in their disobedience and idolatry he would scatter them among foreign nations. He would leave them to harm themselves by following heathen customs such as child sacrifice (23-26).

Past mistakes must not be repeated (20:27-44)

Having clearly illustrated that Israel had always shown a tendency to idolatry, Ezekiel now began to apply the lessons of history to his fellow exiles in Babylon. He reminded them that as soon as the people of Israel settled in Canaan they copied the religious practices of the Canaanites (27-29). Those of Ezekiel's day were just as idolatrous in heart and were thinking of copying the idolatrous ways of Babylon. God warns that he will not allow this to happen (30-32).

As he saved his people from Egypt, so God will save them from Babylon. He will bring them back to their homeland (33-34). Again they will pass through the wilderness, but this time God will take firm control of them. He will sort them as a shepherd sorts sheep, removing those who still want to worship idols. This time only those loyal to him will inherit the promised land (35-38).

With all their idolatrous tendencies left behind in Babylon, God's people will worship him in holiness in Jerusalem. They will offer sacrifices that are acceptable to him (39-40). When surrounding nations see Yahweh and his people living in true holiness, they will appreciate the character of Israel's God (41-42). The people of Israel will then have a proper understanding of God and will be ashamed of their former unfaithfulness (43-44).

Babylon's terrifying attack (20:45-21:17)

The usual way to travel from Babylon to Jerusalem was by a semi-circular route that avoided the Arabian desert by following the Euphrates River to the north-west then turning south towards Judah. (See map 'Near East in the time of Jeremiah.) Ezekiel put himself in the position of the Babylonian army as it moved south into Judah, overrunning and destroying the country as an uncontrollable bushfire. None would escape its terror (45-48). But the people did not understand Ezekiel's message (49).

Ezekiel therefore changed his symbol of God's judgment from fire to a sword. This sword would bring slaughter, not just to Jerusalem but to the whole land of Judah (21:1-5). Ezekiel's display of

bitter grief showed his hearers how frightening this coming judgment would be (6-7).

To emphasize his message and illustrate its urgency, Ezekiel gave a dramatic demonstration of a swordsman cutting down his enemy. The Judeans had not heeded when God used a stick to discipline them. He would therefore use the sharpened sword of Babylon to slay them (8-13). While acting the part of a swordsman, Ezekiel also acted the part of the onlookers, by occasionally clapping his hands at the swordsman's display. In this way he indicated God's approval of Judah's destruction (14-17).

No possibility of escape (21:18-32)

In another acted message, the prophet drew a map on the ground, showing a road out of Babylon that branched in two directions. One led to Jerusalem, the other to Rabbah, capital of Ammon. By means of markings on the map, Ezekiel indicated that the king of Babylon had arrived at the road junction and was trying to decide whether to go and attack Rabbah or go and besiege Jerusalem. The king used three superstitious methods to determine which way to go: drawing lots (using arrows for lots), consulting idols, and looking into the liver of a sacrificed animal (18-21).

The decision of the Babylonian king was to besiege Jerusalem (22). The Jerusalemites, however, were not worried by this news. They took no notice of what they considered to be Babylonian superstitions. They trusted instead in their treaty with Egypt. But it would make no difference to the outcome; Jerusalem would be captured (23).

Jerusalem was doomed because of its sin; so was Zedekiah, and for the same reason. The proud king would suffer the greatest humiliation. There would not be another king over Israel till the Messiah came, to whom the throne rightly belonged (24-27).

Meanwhile the Ammonites, having escaped the Babylonian attack, took the opportunity to join in crushing Jerusalem. They were encouraged in this by lying prophets who assured them they were doing God's work. The true prophet Ezekiel told them they were only making certain their own punishment (28-29). The Ammonites were not God's instrument for punishing Jerusalem. When they returned to their own country, God would punish them (by means of a Babylonian attack) for their unprovoked attack on his people (30-32).

National decay (22:1-31)

With Jerusalem's end approaching, God again told Ezekiel to show the city its sins and the humiliating judgment that these sins would bring upon it (22:1-5). Powerful people exploited others, without any respect for the laws of God or the dignity of their fellow human beings (6-8). The corrupt city was characterized by lies, violence, idolatry, bribery, oppression and sexual sins of the worse kind (9-12). God warned that in punishment for its wickedness, he would destroy the city and scatter its people among the nations (13-16).

As a refiner puts metals into a furnace to refine them, so God would gather the people in Jerusalem for a fiery judgment. But instead of the refining process producing pure metal, it would show that there was nothing but worthless metal. As the fire of the furnace melts the metal, so God in his anger would punish Jerusalem (17-22).

Jerusalem's wickedness extended to people in all sections of the community. Leaders made themselves rich through oppression and violence, while priests encouraged corruption by ignoring God's law (23-27). Prophets approved of wrongdoing for the sake of their own gain, and the people as a whole took advantage of any who were less fortunate than themselves (28-29). Not one person among all the country's official leaders was prepared to work for God in trying to stop the nation from crumbling to ruin (30-31).

Two prostitute sisters (23:1-35)

God's chosen nation was saved from Egypt and settled in Canaan, but it soon divided into two, the northern kingdom Israel (capital: Samaria) and the southern kingdom Judah (capital: Jerusalem). The prophet likens these two kingdoms to two sisters who became prostitutes (23:1-4).

The prostitution of Israel and Judah was their unfaithfulness to God in forming military alliances with foreign nations instead of trusting in him. Israel, the northern kingdom, was impressed with the might of Assyria, but in forming an alliance with the superior power she accepted also that country's gods (5-8). Assyria, having used Israel for its own satisfaction, then savagely attacked and killed her (9-10).

Judah failed to learn from Israel's experience. She too made alliances, first with Assyria and later with Babylon (Chaldea) (11-16). Then, with the feeling of disgust that often follows immorality, Judah turned away from Babylon. Soon she went lusting again, this time seeking the favours of Egypt, hoping for Egyptian aid to fight against Babylon (17-21).

Therefore, Judah's former lover, Babylon, with the assistance of other peoples from the Babylonian

region, will return and attack her (22-24). It will be a time of terrible suffering as the people are cruelly humiliated, butchered and plundered (25-27), yet the whole terrifying experience will be a fitting punishment because of Judah's disgusting prostitution (28-30). She will suffer the same fate as her sister kingdom to the north. She too will drink the cup of God's wrath (31-35).

Judgment on the two sisters (23:36-49)

The prophet links the two kingdoms for his summary of God's judgment on them. Both kingdoms had copied the religious practices of their treaty partners, even to the extent of offering their children as blood sacrifices to foreign gods. They deliberately broke God's law and defiled his temple (36-39).

Both kingdoms acted like prostitutes, enticing foreign nations so that they could join with them in unions that were immoral and ungodly (40-41). These foreign nations are likened to pleasure-seeking men from the desert who bring jewellery and ornaments to pay the prostitutes for their services (42-44). As righteous judges sentence prostitutes to a fitting punishment, so God will now judge Judah (45). As an adulteress is stoned to death and her property burnt, so will Jerusalem and her people be destroyed (46-49).

The cooking pot (24:1-14)

On the day Babylon began its siege of Jerusalem, Ezekiel spoke another message (24:1-2; see 2 Kings 25:1). Previously the Jerusalemites had boasted that the walls of the city would protect them from the Babylonian armies as a cooking pot protects the meat within from the fire (see 11:3). Ezekiel now uses the illustration of the cooking pot in an entirely opposite sense. The people of Jerusalem (the meat in the pot) are going to be 'cooked alive' by the 'fire' of the besieging armies of Babylon (3-5).

The cooking pot illustration is then used again. The pot, covered in rust and filth, cannot be cleansed, and the meat within it must be thrown out. Jerusalem is morally filthy beyond cleansing, and the people will be taken out of it into captivity (6).

One reason for Jerusalem's punishment is the innocent blood that has been shed in the city. That blood, which has cried out for vengeance and which till now has not been answered, will now receive a decisive response from God (7-8). Once the contents of the pot have been thrown out, the pot itself will melt in the intense heat of the fire. Only in this way can the filth of the pot be removed; and only by the destruction of Jerusalem can *its* filth be removed (9-14).

314

Death of Ezekiel's wife (24:15-27)

It came as a shock to Ezekiel to learn from God that his wife was about to die. He was told not to show any of the usual signs of mourning, but to go about his business as usual. Before his wife died, Ezekiel told the people what would happen (15-18).

As expected, the people asked Ezekiel why he was not observing the usual mourning customs (19). Ezekiel explained that he was demonstrating how the exiles would react when they heard news of the destruction of their temple and the slaughter of their relatives. Being exiles in the land of the conqueror, they could hardly show public signs of mourning, though they would groan privately to one another in their unspeakable grief (20-24).

When news of the fall of Jerusalem reached the exiles, the restrictions God had placed on Ezekiel's speech and movements would be lifted. The people would at last realize the truth of his message and be prepared to listen to him (25-27; cf. 3:22-27; 33:21-22).

25:1-32:32 JUDGMENTS AGAINST FOREIGN NATIONS

Once the exiles had been awakened, Ezekiel's next task was to instruct them further about God's future purposes for them. But before doing so, he shows how God will deal with Israel's former oppressors. God is the controller not only of Israel's destiny but also of the destinies of other nations. He will not allow sin to go unpunished, and he will especially deal with the four neighbouring nations who supported Babylon at the fall of Jerusalem. (For the nations dealt with in this section, see map located at Isaiah 13-23, where another group of messages to various nations is recorded.)

Ammon, Moab, Edom and Philistia (25:1-17)

The Ammonites had taken wicked delight in seeing Jerusalem and its temple destroyed. Now God is going to deal with them (25:1-3). They will be overrun by desert tribesmen from the east who will turn Ammon's cities into pasture lands for their animals (4-7).

Moab will suffer the same fate as Ammon. Its sin was to despise Judah's God, Yahweh, by claiming that he was no different from the gods of other nations. They thought that he was powerless to protect his temple from devastation. He will now show his power by devastating Moab (8-11).

Edom had acted with unnecessary violence and treachery against Judah, and helped Babylon in the final destruction of Jerusalem. The Jews themselves will be God's instrument in punishing Edom (12-14; see also Ps 137:7; Obad 10-14).

The Philistines, ancient enemies of Israel, had also acted in bitter revenge against Jerusalem when they saw the city about to fall. Therefore, they too will cease to be a nation (15-17)

Overthrow of Tyre (26:1-21)

Tyre, on the Mediterranean coast of Phoenicia, just north of Palestine, was a leading commercial centre in the ancient world. The city was in two parts, one built on the mainland coast, the other on an island a short distance offshore. Tyre rejoiced at the fall of Jerusalem, for the way was now open for it to take over the important trade routes that passed through Jerusalem (26:1-2). The prophet announces that in the years ahead, armies from various nations will overrun both Tyre's island and mainland portions, leaving it devastated and bare (3-6).

Babylon will be the first nation that God sends against Tyre. The mainland city will be besieged and will suffer extensive damage at the hands of Nebuchadnezzar's well equipped attackers (7-11). When the city is later destroyed, the enemy will empty the rubble into the sea, forming a road across to the island city, which, in turn, will be overthrown (12-14).

Coastal cities around the Mediterranean will mourn the loss of this trading giant, on whom they have depended for trade and economic prosperity (15-18). In pictorial language the prophet describes Tyre as sinking beneath the sea, never to be seen again (19-21).

Mourning for Tyre (27:1-36)

This chapter continues the theme of Tyre's overthrow. It is in the form of a funeral song that Tyre's trading partners sing as they mourn the city's death (27:1-2).

The song begins by recalling the glory of Tyre's past. The prosperous commercial city is likened to a magnificent merchant ship, beautifully made from best quality materials taken from all parts of the trading world. Her planks, masts, oars and decking were made of the best timbers, her sails from the finest linen, her colours of the most expensive dyes (3-7). The oarsmen, sailors and craftsmen who made up her crew were highly skilled men drawn from many countries (8-9).

Tyre's prosperity appeared to be secure, for the city was well defended by an army of hired soldiers chosen from many countries (10-11). The city's commercial strength was unequalled. Countries from the west to the east, from the north to the south, traded with Tyre. The trade covered an enormous range of merchandise, from minerals to animals, from spices to slaves (12-24).

However, Tyre's great commercial enterprise brought with it great danger. The ship became overloaded and, when caught in a storm at sea, sank. All its merchandise was lost and all its crew drowned (25-27). All Tyre's trading partners now mourn its loss (28-31), though their mourning is as much out of pity for themselves as out of pity for Tyre. The chief reason for their sorrow is that, with the loss of Tyre, they have lost the trading partner who, more than any other, has been the source of their wealth (32-36).

Judgment on the king of Tyre (28:1-19)

The king of Tyre, as representative of the whole nation, is now condemned on account of the pride for which Tyre was famous. Because of the wealth and strength that the country gained through clever trading, Tyre saw itself as all-powerful, answerable to no one. It considered itself to be a god among the nations of the commercial world (28:1-5).

Yahweh, the only true God, will tolerate Tyre's arrogance no longer. The day of Tyre's judgment has come (6-7). The city in both its island and mainland sections will become rubble and will be thrown into the sea. The king who thought he was a god will be killed by the foreigners whom he despised, and his body thrown into the sea (8-10).

Tyre, still represented in its king, thought of itself as one who lived in paradise — wealthy, wise, happy, in need of nothing (11-13). Not satisfied with the security it enjoyed and the dominion it exercised over God's earth, Tyre fell into the sin of wanting to be like God. Just as those who lived in the original paradise were driven out for their arrogance and rebellion, so proud Tyre will be shamefully removed from its place of honour and power (14-17). By the selfish greed and arrogant ambition of its trading activity, Tyre has corrupted itself. It will therefore come to a humiliating end by being smashed and burnt before the gaze of the nations through whom it has made itself rich (18-19).

Judgment on Sidon (28:20-26)

Sidon, to the north of Tyre, was another neighbouring state that had oppressed Israel. It too will experience a bloody judgment (20-23). As a result God's people will have relief from suffering and a more enlightened understanding of him (24). When God has destroyed their enemies, he will bring them back to live contentedly in their land again. His righteous dealings with them will be a striking demonstration to the surrounding nations that the God of Israel is holy (25-26).

Judgment on Egypt (29:1-16)

At the time Ezekiel delivered this prophecy against Egypt, Jerusalem was besieged by the Babylonian armies (29:1; see 2 Kings 25:1-2). The Judean king Zedekiah depended upon Egyptian aid in rebelling against Babylon, but Ezekiel knows that to depend on Egypt is to invite defeat. By his condemnation of Egypt in this message, he shows how unacceptable any Judean-Egyptian alliance is in God's sight (2; cf. 17:15-18; Jer 37:6-10).

In this very pictorial prophecy, Egypt is likened to the mythical monster who thought he owned the Nile. God says he will catch this monster, drag it out of the river and leave it to lie in the fields, where it will become food for foul birds and animals. Egypt will fall to foreign powers (3-5).

Ezekiel then gives another illustration. Judah at times had depended on Egypt for help, as a cripple depends on a walking stick. Egypt, however, proved to be not a walking stick but a reed, which broke and brought injury to the person who depended on it. For its treachery to Judah, Egypt will be punished (6-9a; cf. Isa 36:6). For its pride also it will be punished, and its land will be left desolate (9b-12). Although God will later restore Egypt, it will never regain its former power (13-16).

Babylon's victory over Egypt (29:17-21)

A much later prophecy is put into the collection at this point, to show how God's judgment on Egypt was carried out. The year was 571 BC (17).

Babylon took thirteen years of hard work to conquer Tyre, and this left the Babylonian soldiers worn out. To make matters worse, they did not gain the profit they expected from the conquered city, because the people of Tyre had apparently shipped out much of their wealth during the thirteen years of siege (18). Therefore, the Babylonian forces will turn south and conquer Egypt, assured by God that the rewards of victory in Egypt will compensate for what they missed at Tyre. In both cases they were 'hired' by God to carry out his judgment, and he would make sure they received fitting 'wages' (19-20). The fulfilment of this prophecy will be proof to Israel of God's power (21).

Desolation of Egypt (30:1-26)

God's coming judgment on Egypt will be a day of terror for other nations besides Egypt (30:1-3), because when Egypt falls many of its neighbouring allies will suffer also (4-5). These allies will be terrified as news reaches them of the calamities in Egypt. The invading army will overrun Egypt from north to south, killing the people and burning their cities (6-8). The people in neighbouring Ethiopia (NIV: Cush; GNB: Sudan) will be terror-stricken, knowing that they will be the next victims of this ruthless attacker (9).

The nation that God will use to smash Egypt is mighty Babylon. In addition to sending armies, God will send a drought to dry up the Nile, so that the whole land of Egypt will be left desolate (10-12). Cities throughout the country will be destroyed, strongholds burnt, idols smashed, leaders killed, and people taken captive (13-19).

Already God's judgment on Egypt had begun. Egypt had suffered one defeat by Babylon, and was not able to repair the damage or regain former strength. Babylon had, so to speak, broken one of Pharaoh's arms (20-21). Babylon is now about to break Pharaoh's other arm. It is about to gain another major victory, and Egypt's power will be smashed completely (22-26).

The mighty cedar tree (31:1-18)

Pharaoh, and through him Egypt, is likened to a giant cedar tree, well watered and tall, which provides shelter for birds and animals alike. It is a picture of the strong and proud kingdom of Egypt, upon whom neighbouring countries relied for protection (31:1-6). (Some versions suggest that this poem was written concerning Assyria. If that is the case, the writer quotes it here so that Egypt might learn the lesson.)

Other countries were impressed by Egypt and envied its stability and strength (7-9). But no matter how impressive the tree is, foreigners will cut it down. Egypt will be conquered (10-13). The ruin of Egypt will be a warning to others not to be dominated by pride and selfish ambition (14).

As the trees of the forest mourn the death of this mighty cedar tree, so will nations tremble when they hear of the fall of Egypt. Other nations who had 'died' previously will feel some comfort to learn that mighty Egypt has now suffered the same fate (15-17). The once glorious nation now lies in humiliation among the dishonoured dead (18).

The end of Egypt (32:1-32)

Again Pharaoh (or Egypt) is likened to the mytho-logical monster of the Nile who will be caught, dragged out of the river and left to rot in the sun. His blood will flow over the land and his carcass will be meat for birds and wild animals (32:1-6; cf. 29:3-5). A terrifying darkness throughout the country

will impress upon people that this judgment is the work of the sovereign God (7-8).

Neighbouring nations will tremble when they see multitudes of Egyptian people killed by the invaders or taken into foreign captivity (9-12). With people and animals wiped out, the land will be left desolate. The waters of Egypt will be clear and its rivers will flow smoothly, unpolluted and undis-turbed by any form of life (13-16).

Ezekiel returns to his picture of Egypt's sinking into Sheol, the dark silent world of the dead. With mocking words, the dead welcome the formerly proud nation to join them in the place of shame and uncleanness (17-21; cf. 31:15-18).

Already in the world of the dead are certain cruel nations of the past, such as Assyria, Elam, Meshech and Tubal. These nations formerly terrified others, but now they lie useless and dishonoured (22-27). Egypt will now join them (28). Other nations that Ezekiel has already denounced, such as Edom and Sidon, will finish in the same place (29-30). The only comfort for Egypt will be to learn that it is not the only nation to suffer such a humiliating end (31-32).

33:1-39:29 RETURN TO THE LAND

A new phase in Ezekiel's work (33:1-20)

Up till now Ezekiel's messages have been concerned mainly with God's judgment – first his judgment on Jerusalem, then his judgment on other nations. Now that Jerusalem has fallen (see v. 21), the prophet concentrates more on the task of building up the exiles. He wants them to be a new people who will be ready to repossess the land when God's time comes. This, however, is going to involve some stern warnings. Ezekiel is therefore reminded again that he is like a watchman on the city wall who must warn the people when he sees danger approaching (33:1-6). Whether the people heed him or ignore him, he must carry out his duty faithfully (7-9; cf. 3:16-21).

For the first time, the exiles show sorrow for their past sin. Some are even tempted to despair. Ezekiel assures them that God does not delight in punishment. He would rather they repent. Then he will forgive the past and they can make a new beginning (10-11).

The prophet reminds the people that each individual has a personal responsibility to do what is right in order to enjoy the blessings of God. Good deeds of the past will not save a person from judgment if that person deliberately turns back to sin. Bad deeds of the past will not be held against a person if that person turns from them (12-16; cf. 18:5-24). If people suffer God's punishment, it is because they have done wrong, not because God is unjust (17-20; cf. 18:25-32).

News from Jerusalem (33:21-33)

As soon as news reached the exiles that Jerusalem had fallen as Ezekiel had foretold, Ezekiel knew that the new phase of his work was to begin. The former restrictions on his speech and movements were lifted (21-22; cf. 24:25-27).

Ezekiel received news also of certain selfish and dishonest practices among the Jews who were left in the country areas of Judah. Some of these people had seized the land of those taken into exile. They argued that if Abraham (only one person) had been given the right to inherit Canaan, surely they (a much greater number) had the right to accumulate property there (23-24).

God's reply through Ezekiel is clear. The Jews scattered in Judah have no right to possess any of the land, since they commit the same sins as the Jerusalemites — sins for which Jerusalem was destroyed and its people taken into captivity (25-26). Those who happened to escape the Babylonians are not the people who will repossess the promised land. On the contrary, they will be punished as the Jerusalemites were punished (27-29).

Meanwhile the exiles in Babylon had developed a more favourable attitude towards Ezekiel. Now that his prediction of the fall of Jerusalem had come true, they were convinced that he was a true prophet. As a result they came to listen to what else he had to say (30). But they were concerned only with any advantages that they might gain to make life easier for themselves in Babylon. They listened to Ezekiel as they might listen to an entertainer. They took no notice of his moral instruction (31-32). Only after they had been restored to the promised land would people understand fully that this was the goal for which Ezekiel had been trying to prepare them (33).

Rulers past and future (34:1-31)

The leaders of Israel, whether of the northern kingdom or the southern, were supposed to be shepherds, but instead of caring for the people they exploited them. Their sole concern was for themselves (34:1-4). Because of their neglect of the flock, the sheep were attacked and scattered. Because of the corruption of its leaders, Israel was destroyed by hostile nations and its people taken captive into foreign countries (5-6).

God will therefore punish the shepherds, but he will rescue the scattered sheep and bring them back to their home (7-10). God himself will be their new shepherd. He will feed them and care for them (11-15). While being sympathetic to those who are afflicted, he will act with strict justice against those who are oppressive (16).

Having taken the flock under his control and care, the true shepherd will remove from it those who, in their greed and selfishness, spoiled the pastures and dirtied the water for others. God will punish those who made themselves rich and powerful by trampling on the rights of their fellow citizens (17-19). When God has removed those who oppressed others for their own advantage, he will set up his Messiah to rule over his people in love and righteousness. The ideal that David wished for but never experienced will then be a reality (20-24).

Ezekiel speaks of the new relationship between God and his people as a covenant of peace. A bond of harmony exists between the good shepherd and his sheep. As the shepherd protects his flock from wild animals and gives his sheep good pastures, so God will protect his people from their enemies and give them agricultural prosperity (25-29). His people will respond with true loyalty. They will be his people, and he will be their God (30-31).

Edom punished (35:1-15)

Since the Jews were to inherit their land again, any foreign nation that attempted to occupy that land for itself had to be overcome. One such nation was Edom, symbolized here by its distinctive landmark, Mt Seir (35:1-4). Edom had a long record of bitter hatred of Israel, and with wicked vindictiveness had gladly helped Babylon crush Jerusalem in 587 BC. Therefore, Edom itself will be crushed. It will suffer the slaughter it made Jerusalem suffer. Its people will be wiped out and its land left uninhabited (5-9; see notes on 25:12-14).

Edom was determined to take over the territory of Judah for itself, but God saw Edom's action as an attack upon him. Since Judah was God's people and their land was his territory, Edom's curses against Judah were really blasphemies against God (10-13). Far from taking over Judah's land, Edom will be destroyed and its land left a desolation (14-15).

Restoration assured (36:1-15)

With the removal of the people of Israel from their ancient homeland (both northern and southern kingdoms) certain neighbouring nations took the opportunity to seize Israel's former territory for themselves (36:1-2). God comforts his people with the reminder that the land rightly belongs to him, and he will not tolerate the contempt of these enemies (3-5). He will now deal justly with those who despised his people (6-7).

Having dealt with his enemies, God will bring the people of Israel back to their former territory. The deserted land will be repopulated, cities will be rebuilt, farm and pasture lands will again become productive, and flocks and herds will increase (8-12). In the past the land may at times have appeared to be hostile to its inhabitants, but now it will be favourable to them (13-15).

For the sake of God's holy name (36:16-38)

God had driven the people of Israel out of their land because their sins had made them unclean in his sight (16-19). Onlooking nations, however, did not see it that way. They mocked God, saying that the removal of Israel from its land showed that he was weak. He could not save his people from the superior gods of the nations (20-21).

Therefore, God will correct this misunderstanding and restore his honour by bringing Israel back to its land (22-24). He will cleanse his people from their idolatry and put a new spirit within them. Then, instead of being stubborn as in former days, they will have a readiness to do God's will (25-27). The land will give them the best of agricultural blessings (28-30). They will be ashamed when they remember their bad conduct in the past, whereas God will be honoured by the nations that once mocked him (31-32).

These nations will be amazed when they see the fertility of the formerly desolated land and the prosperity of the formerly conquered people. They will realize that God is not weak as they supposed, but is working in Israel's history according to his plan (33-36). As flocks of sacrificial animals once filled Jerusalem at festival times, so will multitudes of Jews fill Israel's cities again (37-38).

The nation revived and reunited (37:1-28)

With Jerusalem destroyed and the people in exile, Israel's national life had come to an end. To Ezekiel it appeared as if a great army had been slaughtered in battle and the bodies of the dead left to rot in the sun. All that was left was a lot of dry bones. Israel's condition appeared to be beyond hope (37:1-3).

God now promises Ezekiel that he will do the impossible. He will bring Israel back to life as if he brings the scattered bones together, puts flesh on them and breathes life into them. Dead Israel will become a living nation again, but only through the direct creative action of God (4-10).

The interpretation of the vision is combined with another picture illustrating Israel's revival. This is the picture of buried bodies coming back to life. Again the renewal of life is only by the direct activity of God (11-14).

When the nation is re-established in its own land, there will not be the division that previously existed between the southern kingdom (Judah) and the northern kingdom (Ephraim). To demonstrate the unity of this new kingdom, Ezekiel took two sticks, symbolizing the two former kingdoms, and held them together so that they appeared as one (15-19). In explaining the meaning of his actions to the people, Ezekiel stressed that there will be no idolatry in the restored nation (20-23).

The king who will rule over this unified nation will be none other than the promised Messiah of the dynasty of David. The people will live in the land promised to their ancestors and they will walk in God's ways (24-25). God will give his people the covenant blessings. He will establish his everlasting presence among them, and all people will know that Israel is his people (26-28).

Strange prophecies

Chapters 38 and 39 give a pictorial description of an attack by evil powers on the people of God. The setting for this attack is the land of the restored people of Israel, who are enjoying an existence of peace and contentment.

Restored Israel did, in fact, suffer an onslaught by evil powers when, in 171-165 BC, Antiochus Epiphanes butchered their people and almost wiped out their religion. But it is clear from a reading of the two chapters that the language cannot be interpreted literally of the period of Antiochus or any other period of Israel's recorded history.

As with some of Ezekiel's other visions, the meaning extends beyond the period of post-exilic Israel. It speaks of the final victory that God has prepared for his people in a hostile world. The vision is concerned only with that limited area of the world with which the exiles were familiar, but its meaning is relevant to God's people in any age, no matter where they live (cf. Rev 20:7-10). The purpose of the vision is not to teach the exiles history, but to show people in general, and God's people in particular, that God is holy and that his sovereign purposes will be fulfilled (see 38:23; 39:21-22).

Invasion by the armies of Gog (38:1-23)

To the Jews of Ezekiel's day, the nations referred to here would represent the most distant regions of the world — 'the four corners of the earth'. They are

319

led by a man called Gog, who lives to the north in the land of Magog and who is ruler of the joint kingdom of Meshech-Tubal (38:1-3). He will lead an attack on Israel and will be helped by other countries from the east (Persia), from the south (Cush and Put, meaning probably Ethiopia and Libya), and from the north (Gomer and Beth-togarmah). But because God is working in history, the attackers, not the people of God, are the ones who are doomed (4-6).

This combined army will launch its attack some time after the people of God are contentedly settled back in their land. God urges the enemies on in their preparations for battle, as he is going to use the occasion of the joint attack to destroy them all in one final great act of judgment (7-9; cf. v. 3-4).

Gog plans to take advantage of the peaceful circumstances in Palestine, where the nation Israel is no longer concerned with war. He will attack its defenceless cities and seize so much spoil that the greed of other nations will be aroused. They will then come and join with Gog, hoping to share the spoil (10-13).

After carefully laying his plans, Gog acts, but he does not realize that God is in control of events (14-16). God has been waiting for him, and now he deals with him (17-18). Through earthquakes, floods, fire, disease and bloodshed, God wipes out the forces of Gog (19-23).

Destruction of the armies of Gog (39:1-29)

Ezekiel repeats that God was the one who drew out the forces of Gog, his purpose being to destroy them (39:1-3). Their dead soldiers lie unburied in the fields, and their cities are in ashes (4-6). The terrible massacre helps people to see how frightening is the power of God when he acts in holy anger against evil (7-8).

So great were the armies of Gog in size, that their weapons provide firewood for the people of Israel for the next seven years (9-10). Collecting and burying the corpses takes seven months (11-13). When this task is finished, people search the land thoroughly to make sure that not even a bone of one of Gog's men remains in Israel. All trace of the forces of evil must be removed, so that the land is completely cleansed (14-16).

Returning to the picture of the unburied corpses, Ezekiel invites wild beasts and foul birds to come and feast on them. It will be a feast such as they have never had before (17-20). The destruction of Gog, like the captivity of Israel, shows to people everywhere that God is holy and just in dealing with sin (21-24). But whereas Gog is the power of

evil, Israel is the people of God. Gog is destroyed, but Israel is restored. The people come back to their land, to live in close fellowship with Yahweh, their redeemer and saviour (25-29).

40:1-48:35 THE NEW AGE

In this the final section of his book, Ezekiel adds to the picture he has already given of Israel's restoration to the land and the golden age that will follow. He has already dealt at length with the return to the land; now he deals with matters relating to the people's way of life within the land. In particular he deals with the temple and the city.

Although the blessings outlined by Ezekiel were intended for restored Israel, the nation missed out on the blessings when it turned away from God as in former days. But some remained true to God, and the faithful remnant of old Israel became the nucleus of the new people of God, the Christian church. The new Jerusalem is a spiritual community of those of all nations who are 'born from above' (Gal 3:26-29; 4:26-28).

This new community can learn from Ezekiel's visions, even though the visions were given for the benefit of people of Ezekiel's time. But even this new community may not at present experience the full blessings pictured by Ezekiel. The visions seem to point beyond, to the time when the kingdom of Jesus Christ will be established in its fullest glory. The great expectation of God's people is the new age yet to come, when God will dwell for ever with all his redeemed people in an order of existence never before experienced.

Pictures and language

In revealing certain characteristics of life in his eternal kingdom, God used words and illustrations that people of Ezekiel's day could understand. Since the immediate hope for those people was to return to their land and rebuild the temple and city, God used this immediate hope as his means of instructing them concerning his ultimate purposes. The restoration was a shadow or picture of greater things to come.

Just as the details of Ezekiel's previous visions are not to be understood in a literal or physical sense, so neither are the details of his visions of the new temple and the new Jerusalem. Ezekiel was a priest, and he best understood the ideal life of God's people in terms of an ideal religious system. He saw a temple where God dwelt among his people and was worshipped by them in a religious order that was perfect in every detail (e.g. 43:10-12). He saw a

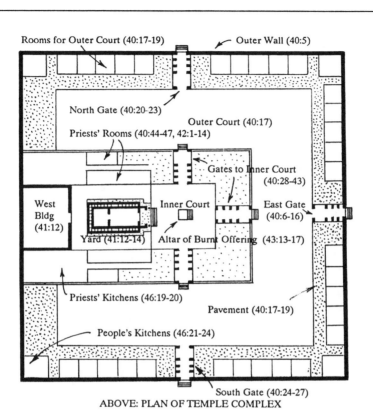

Rooms for Outer Court (40:17-19)

Outer Wall (40:5)

North Gate (40:20-23)

Outer Court (40:17)

Priests' Rooms (40:44-47, 42:1-14)

Gates to Inner Court (40:28-43)

West Bldg (41:12)

Inner Court

East Gate (40:6-16)

Yard (41:12-14)

Altar of Burnt Offering (43:13-17)

Priests' Kitchens (46:19-20)

Pavement (40:17-19)

People's Kitchens (46:21-24)

South Gate (40:24-27)

ABOVE: PLAN OF TEMPLE COMPLEX

BELOW: ENLARGEMENT OF TEMPLE PROPER

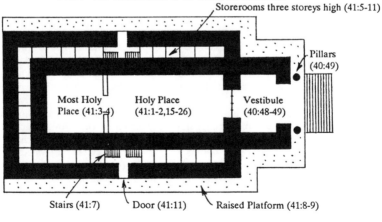

Storerooms three storeys high (41:5-11)

Pillars (40:49)

Most Holy Place (41:3-4)

Holy Place (41:1-2,15-26)

Vestibule (40:48-49)

Stairs (41:7)

Door (41:11)

Raised Platform (41:8-9)

EZEKIEL'S TEMPLE

321

nation whose ideal existence was possible only because everything was perfectly arranged around the central presence of God (e.g. 48:8,20,35).

Ezekiel, like all seers, was concerned with spiritual realities more than with physical details. Nevertheless, he had to use examples from the physical world to illustrate the spiritual, because the physical world was the only world that he and his readers knew. In this he may be compared with another seer, John, the writer of the book of Revelation. As Ezekiel used the illustration of a temple, John used the illustration of a city. Both were concerned with informing their readers of that quality of life that can find its fullest expression only in the age to come.

The temple: outer and inner courts (40:1-47)

It was now twenty-five years since Ezekiel had been taken to Babylon, and fourteen years since the fall of Jerusalem. One day he had a vision in which he imagined himself back in Israel where, from a high hill, he saw a huge temple. To help him understand its size and details he had a heavenly guide, who carried a linen tape for measuring long distance, and a reed (just over three metres long) for measuring shorter distances. The exactness of the measurements no doubt indicated that God does everything to perfection (40:1-4).

The first thing Ezekiel saw was the wall that surrounded the temple complex (5). This complex was square in plan and was entered through a huge tunnel-like gate in the eastern wall. To pass through this gate a person had to go up a flight of steps, cross a threshold (6), walk along a passage (on each side of which were three small rooms, or alcoves, for the temple guards), cross another threshold, then pass through a larger room (called the vestibule, or portico) into the outer court of the temple (7-9). The measurements of the various rooms within the gateway are given (10-15). They all had light and ventilation openings, and were decorated with carvings of palm trees (16).

Built around the inside of the outer wall were thirty rooms (probably for the use of worshippers) which opened on to the outer court (17-19). There were gates in the north and south sides of the main outer wall. These gates were similar to the main gate in the eastern wall that has just been described (20-27).

Inside the outer court was a smaller, inner court. This inner court was on a higher level than the outer court (cf. v. 18) and was entered on either the south, east, or north sides by ascending a flight of steps and passing through a gate similar to those

in the outer walls (28-37). The vestibule (or portico) of each gate to the inner court had eight tables for slaughtering the sacrificial animals (38-41), and four tables on which the various utensils used in the sacrifices were kept (42-43).

On the inside of the walls enclosing the inner court were rooms for the priests. Rooms on the north were for those priests responsible for the daily routines of the temple. Rooms on the south were for those priests responsible for the sacrifices. The altar of burnt offering was positioned in the centre of the inner court (44-47).

The temple proper (40:48-41:26)

From the inner court the way into the temple proper was up a flight of steps on the western side of the court, between two pillars at the top of the steps, and through a vestibule or entrance room (48-49). From the vestibule an entrance led into the nave or Holy Place (the outer sanctuary). From the nave a narrower entrance led into the Most Holy Place (the inner sanctuary) (41:1-4).

Attached externally to the sides and rear of the temple proper were three storeys of storerooms, probably used for storing the tithes and offerings brought by the people. The side and rear walls of the main building were reduced in thickness for the middle storey, and reduced further for the top storey. This created 'steps', or ledges, in the outer face of the main walls. The timber beams that formed the floors of the middle and top storeys rested on these steps (5-7). Access to the storerooms was through two doors in the bottom storey. These doors, one on the north side and one on the south, opened on to the raised platform, or terrace, on which the temple stood (8-11).

To the sides and rear of this paved platform was an open area called the temple yard (or courtyard). At the rear of this yard, backing on to the western outer wall, was another building. Referred to simply as the west building, it was possibly an additional storehouse (12). The measurements of the temple and its immediate surroundings demonstrated the perfection of the whole. Everything was carefully planned; nothing was left to chance (13-15a).

Windows were positioned high in the side walls of the temple so as to open above the lean-to roof of the attached storerooms. The inner walls of the temple, extending from the floor up over the doors to the underside of these high windows, were panelled with richly carved wood (15b-20).

The doors of the Holy Place and the Most Holy Place were in two halves, each of which could be folded. In front of the doors that led into the

Most Holy Place was a piece of furniture that looked partly like an altar and partly like a table (21-26).

The priests' rooms (42:1-20)

Ezekiel now gives further details concerning the rooms for the priests located in the inner court (see 40:44-47). There were two priests' buildings, one on the north side of the temple proper, the other on the south.

First the building on the north side is described. It was three storeys high and divided lengthways by a passage. On the temple yard side of this passage were three storeys consisting of one long narrow room on each storey. On the outer court side were three storeys of storerooms. The second storey on each side had a gallery, or verandah, attached to the rooms. On the third storey the rooms were narrower but the gallery wider. Since the rooms of each storey were narrower than those of the storey below, the buildings had a stepped appearance (42:1-6). The block on the outer court side of the passage took up only half the area of the block on the temple yard side. The other half of the area on the outer court side was separated from the passage by a wall but was open at the end, thereby forming a sheltered entrance to the bottom storey (7-9).

The priests' building on the south side of the temple proper was the same as that on the north (10-12). The various blocks of rooms within these two buildings were used by the priests when they changed their clothes or when they ate the food of the people's offerings (13-14).

Ezekiel's heavenly guide then left the inner court, went through the outer court, through the gate, and out of the temple compound. He measured the whole temple complex and found it to be square. The high wall enclosing this complex was to protect the holy things of God from the uncleanness of everyday life outside (15-20).

God returns to the temple (43:1-12)

Nineteen years earlier, Ezekiel had seen visions in which God left the temple, went out of Jerusalem to a nearby mountain, then destroyed the city and its inhabitants (see 8:1; 9:1-11; 10:19; 11:22-24). Now, with the new temple established, he sees God returning by the same route, coming to his temple and filling it with glory (43:1-5).

God then told Ezekiel that this temple was to be his earthly dwelling place. It was holy, and his people were not to defile it as their ancestors had defiled the previous temple, through worshipping idols and burying their kings there (6-9). Ezekiel was to describe the new temple to the exiles and explain to them how it was to function. His purpose was to help them understand more of God's holiness, so that they might live obediently and avoid wrongdoing (10-12).

Altar of sacrifice (43:13-27)

Positioned centrally in the inner court was the altar of burnt offering. In appearance it looked like three large square boxes placed one on top of the other, with the largest on the bottom and the smallest on the top, giving a stepped appearance. The whole structure was set on a large base built into the pavement. It was so huge that it needed steps so that the priest could climb up to reach the top level, on which the sacrifices were offered (13-17).

The altar was to be dedicated to the holy service of God in a ceremony involving sin offerings (indicating cleansing) and burnt offerings (indicating consecration). Only those priests descended from Zadok were allowed to carry out the actual sacrifice on the altar (18-24). The dedication ceremony was to last one week. After this the altar could be used for normal sacrificial offerings (25-27).

Service in the temple (44:1-31)

Because the glory of God had entered the temple through the east gate of the outer court, no human being was considered worthy to enter by this gate. It therefore had always to be kept shut (44:1-2). The king, however, could eat his sacrificial meal in the vestibule that was on the inside of the east gate. He had to enter the temple compound by either the north or the south gate, then enter the vestibule from the courtyard side (3).

The presence of God's glory in the temple meant that there were restrictions concerning those allowed to enter it. God did not want his temple to be defiled through the introduction of heathen practices (4-5). Therefore, only God's covenant people could enter the temple. Foreigners were not allowed even to be employed as temple servants (6-9; cf. Josh 9:23,27; 2 Kings 11:4-8).

Day to day duties in the temple, such as guarding its gates and helping with arrangements for the sacrifices, were to be carried out by the Levites along with those priests who were not of the family of Zadok. These non-Zadokite priests were excluded from higher responsibilities because of their idolatry in former days (10-14).

Zadokite priests, who were given full priestly responsibility, were to keep strictly all the laws concerning priests. They were not to allow anything connected with the sanctuary, not even the clothes they wore in the sanctuary, to be polluted through

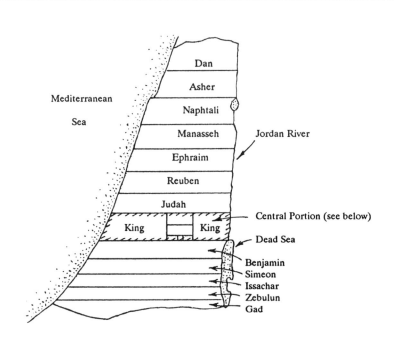

ABOVE: THE 12 TRIBAL DIVISIONS (47:14; 48:1-8,23-29)

BELOW: THE CENTRAL PORTION (45:1-8; 48:8-22)

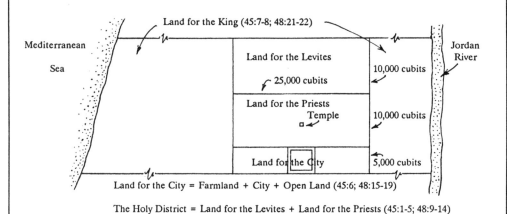

Land for the City = Farmland + City + Open Land (45:6; 48:15-19)

The Holy District = Land for the Levites + Land for the Priests (45:1-5; 48:9-14)

DIVISION OF THE LAND

contact with people or things from the unclean world outside (15-19; cf. 42:14). In their appearance, habits, family life, purity and uprightness they were to be an example to the people of the true meaning of holiness (20-24). If for any reason they became ceremonially unclean, they had to go through the full purification rituals (25-27).

As in former days, priests were not to own any land. Their income and food supplies were to come from the various offerings of the people. However, the kind of food they ate was subject to the same restrictions as applied to the food of people in general (28-31).

Land for priests, Levites and king (45:1-12)

Clearly the division of the land described here was symbolic and stylized. Straight lines can easily be drawn on a flat sheet of paper, but a land of hills, valleys and streams, such as Palestine, could not be divided in this way. Ezekiel's division emphasized the important issues to be considered in the ideal division of the land.

Following the principle that operated in the offering of tithes and firstfruits to God, a section of the land was first set apart as God's portion. This was an acknowledgment that all the land was really his. Within this portion was the temple, surrounded by an open space to emphasize the separation of the holy things of God from the unclean things of everyday life outside. Priests and Levites were given first consideration in the resettlement arrangements, so that they could be near the temple. The portion of land in which the temple was situated was given to the priests, and a portion of the same size adjoining it given to the Levites (45:1-5). On the other side of the priests' land was land for the city (6).

Extending out to the Mediterranean Sea in the west and to the Jordan River in the east was land for the king. The king was to be satisfied with this generous allotment and was not to seize land that belonged to common people in other parts of the country (7-8).

While on the subject of taking advantage of others, Ezekiel adds further warnings. Rulers were not to use their positions of power for their own benefit, and merchants were not to cheat their customers. All weights and measures had to be exact (9-12).

Offerings and festivals (45:13-46:15)

All the people had a part in providing the offerings for national religious festivals. The offerings were collected by the king, who then offered them in sacrifice on behalf of his people (13-17). At the beginning and end of the first week of the new year, sacrifices were offered for the cleansing of the temple (18-20). The two main annual festivals to be celebrated at the temple were the Feast of Passover and Unleavened Bread at the beginning of the year (21-24; cf. Lev 23:4-8), and the Feast of Tabernacles (GNB: Festival of Shelters) half way through the year (25; cf. Lev 23:34-36).

The east gate leading from the outer court to the inner court was closed every day except the weekly Sabbath and the monthly day of the new moon, when the king presented sacrifices on behalf of the nation. On these days the king, and he alone, could enter the vestibule of the gate and watch the priests carry out the sacrificial rituals inside, but he could not pass through the gate (46:1-2; see also v. 8. Only priests and Levites were allowed into the inner court). The people were to gather in the outer court in front of the gate (3). The weekly and monthly sacrifices were to be according to the laws laid down (4-8).

Certain rules aimed at maintaining order when people crowded the outer court during the annual festivals. Upon entering the gate, people were to keep moving in one direction and exit through the gate on the opposite side (9-10). If the king offered a voluntary offering, he could watch the ritual connected with it by standing in the east gate as mentioned previously (11-12). In addition to the nation's weekly, monthly and annual sacrifices, there was a daily sacrifice (13-15).

More about the land and the temple (46:16-24)

If the king marked off a piece of his land and gave it to one of his sons, it remained the permanent property of the son. But if he made a similar gift to one of his servants, the land returned to the king at the year of jubilee. (Concerning the year of jubilee see Lev 25:8-34.) This ensured that the royal family retained possession of its land, and that the king was not tempted to seize other people's land to compensate for what he gave away (16-18).

Returning to the details of the temple, Ezekiel adds that there were kitchens inside the enclosure of the inner court. These were provided so that the priests who offered the sacrifices (i.e. the Zadokite priests; see 44:15-16) could cook their portions of food from the holy offerings, without having to go outside the holy enclosure (19-20). There were also kitchens in the four corners of the outer court, where other temple officials (i.e. the Levites and non-Zadokite priests; see 44:10-14) cooked those portions of the sacrificial food that belonged to the common people (21-24).

The river of life (47:1-12)

Upon completing his description of the temple and its rituals, Ezekiel moves on to the remarkable climax to his visions. He saw a trickle of water coming from under the door of the temple, then flowing across the court and under the main outer wall (just south of the east gate) (47:1-2). The stream headed east, rapidly growing wider and deeper until, within a very short distance, it became a large river (3-6a).

The first thing that Ezekiel noticed about this remarkable river was the number of trees growing along its banks (6b-7). He then learnt that the river was flowing towards the Dead Sea, and all along its course it brought life into previously stagnant waters (though it left some areas of salt that would be useful to the people of the land). The trees that grew on its banks, besides providing a constant supply of nourishing food, brought healing to the sick. The river pictured the healing, nourishing, life-giving blessings that flow from the presence of God to his people (8-12; cf. Rev 22:1-2).

Boundaries of the land (47:13-23)

In restored Israel the land was to be divided equally among the nation's twelve tribes. Levi had no tribal allotment, but Joseph, who received the firstborn's blessing, had two, Ephraim and Manasseh (13-14; cf. Gen 48:5; 1 Chron 5:1).

The overall boundaries of the land are given. The northern boundary went from a point near Tyre on the coast to the Jordan headwaters. The eastern boundary followed the Jordan to the southern end of the Dead Sea. The southern boundary went from there to the Wadi (or Brook) of Egypt, which it then followed to the coast. The western boundary was the Mediterranean coast (15-20).

In the matter of land allocation, foreigners who lived among the Israelites had equal rights with them. They were to be given land in the territory of the tribe in which they lived (21-23).

Divisions of the land (48:1-29)

Land to the north of the specially allocated central portion (see 45:1-8) was divided into seven equal portions by drawing parallel lines from the Mediterranean Sea to the eastern boundary. Although the terrain of the country would make such a division impossible in practice, the division had meaning. It indicated a measure of equality among the tribes (for their portions were equal in area; see 47:14), though there was a difference in responsibility (for the more important tribes were closer to Jerusalem and the temple) (48:1-7).

In the centre of the land was the special portion for temple, priests, Levites, city and king (8; see notes on 45:1-8). The central section of this portion contained the site for the temple and was given to the priests (9-12). The section bordering it to the north was for the Levites (13-14).

The section bordering the priests' portion to the south was for the nation's capital and its citizens. The city proper was a square, surrounded by a strip of open land, and was inhabited by people taken from all twelve tribes. To the west and east of the city were farming areas, where food was grown to support the people of the city (15-19). The entire portion of land for priests, Levites and national capital was square in plan (20). Either side of this central square portion was land for the king (21-22; see 45:7-8).

To the south of the central portion were the remaining five tribes in their parallel strips of land. Again the more privileged tribes were closer to Jerusalem and the temple (23-29).

The gates of Jerusalem (48:30-35)

As he brings the account of his visions to a close, Ezekiel speaks again of the city. He points out that it had twelve gates, three in each of its four sides, representing the entire people of God (30-34; cf. Rev 21:12-14). Having restored his people to their land and re-established their national and religious life according to his perfect plan, God now dwells with them for ever (35; cf. Rev 21:23).

Daniel

BACKGROUND

The book of Daniel is set in the time of the Jews' exile in Babylon. This was the period that introduced the final stage of Israel's Old Testament history, which led in turn to the new era that dawned with the coming of Jesus Christ.

From the New Testament it is clear that the book of Daniel had an influence in later generations. The name that Jesus commonly used for himself, the Son of man, came from Daniel's vision of the God-sent universal king (Dan 7:13-14; Mark 2:28; 14:62). Jesus referred to Daniel's visions in warning the Jews of troubled times ahead (Matt 24:15), and John, in the book of Revelation, recorded visions where many features come from the book of Daniel (cf. Dan Chap. 2, 7 and 8 with Rev Chap. 11, 12, 13 and 17). The writer to the Hebrews referred to the man Daniel as an example of the person who has genuine faith (Heb 11:33).

The long career of Daniel

Daniel was one of the first citizens of Jerusalem to be carried off captive when Judah fell under the control of Babylon in 605 BC. This was the fourth year of the reign of the Judean king Jehoiakim (third year according to Babylonian reckoning), when Judah was rapidly approaching its end (2 Kings 24:1a; Jer 25:1; Dan 1:1-6). (For the history of this era see introductory notes to Ezekiel.)

At the time of his removal to Babylon, Daniel was only a teenager. He was one of a select group of intelligent young men whom the Babylonians chose from the upper class families of Jerusalem, with the aim of training them to be administrators in the royal court at Babylon (Dan 1:4).

During his long career in Babylon, Daniel held some of the top positions in the government. He outlasted the Babylonian Empire and was still alive in the third year of Cyrus, the Persian king who conquered Babylon in 539 BC (Dan 10:1). He therefore lived to see the first Jewish exiles return to Jerusalem to rebuild their nation (Ezra 1:1-4).

A book for the times

Jewish affairs were greatly affected by the changes and crises that occurred throughout the period covered by the book of Daniel. But God's people were not to lose their trust in him. A prominent theme in Daniel is the sovereignty of God. The book shows that God is in control of human affairs, whether everyday matters in the lives of his people or events relating to the rise and fall of nations.

The first half of the book records stories of Daniel and his friends that illustrate the care of God for those who were faithful to him. The second half shows, through a series of unusual visions, how God would continue his government in the affairs of his people during great events that were yet to take place.

These revelations were concerned mainly with the long period of confusion and conflict that followed the period of Persian rule and reached its climax in the events of the New Testament era. The New Testament writers, in turn, take details of these revelations and apply them to the great events connected with the return of Jesus Christ and the end of the age.

Features of the book

Because of his gift to understand and make known God's will, Daniel has been referred to since New Testament times as a prophet (Matt 24:15). But the Jews who arranged the books within the Hebrew Bible (equivalent to our Old Testament) did not so regard him. They did not include his book among the prophets, but put it with the miscellaneous writings. This was probably because they looked upon Daniel more as a statesman in the Babylonian palace than as a preacher who brought God's word to his people.

Nevertheless, Daniel was one through whom God revealed his purposes, and God usually did this by means of dreams and visions. As a result the book of Daniel has many characteristics of that kind of literature known as apocalyptic (from the Greek *apokalupto*, meaning 'to reveal or uncover').

In apocalyptic writings the visions are always strange or unnatural, with weird symbolism that frequently features fearsome beasts and mysterious numbers. The visions are given by God, interpreted by angels, and usually concern great conflicts out of which God and his people triumph. Although the overall meaning of a vision may be fairly clear, the details are often difficult. In seeking to understand these visions, the present-day reader must always bear in mind that any suggested interpretation must contain an element of uncertainty.

OUTLINE

1:1-6:28 STORIES ABOUT DANIEL AND HIS FRIENDS

Training for Nebuchadnezzar's court (1:1-21)

Babylon's first attack on Jerusalem came in 605 BC, during the reign of the Judean king Jehoiakim. In keeping with the usual practice among conquerors in ancient times, the Babylonian king Nebuchadnezzar plundered the temple of the conquered people, carried off its sacred objects and placed them in his own temple. In this way Nebuchadnezzar demonstrated his belief that Babylon's gods were superior to the God of the Jews (1:1-2).

Nebuchadnezzar also took back to Babylon a number of Jewish young men chosen from the upper class families of Jerusalem, his purpose being to prepare them for high positions in his royal court (see 'Background' above). He chose men whose good looks would add to the grace of his palace and whose intelligence would enable them to learn Babylonian ways quickly. He wanted them to be skilled in Babylonian law and wisdom, particularly Chaldean wisdom (3-4). (The Chaldeans were the dominant race among the Babylonian people, and the one to which Nebuchadnezzar belonged. Their wise men were famous for their skill in astrology, magic and ancient languages.)

The Babylonians put strong pressure on the young Jewish captives to break with their old religion and culture. To begin with they gave them Babylonian names (containing names of Babylonian gods) to replace their Hebrew names (which contained the name of the Hebrews' God). Also they gave them a share of the same food served to the Babylonian king (5-7).

Four of the Jewish youths, led by Daniel, asked to be excused from eating the king's food. They considered it unclean, either because it was of a kind forbidden by Jewish law, or because it represented fellowship with a heathen king and his idols (8). The official in charge of the court trainees refused their request. He feared that the simpler food the youths requested would have a bad effect on their appearance, and that he would be blamed for it (9-10). But Daniel and his friends made a secret arrangement with their personal dining attendant, so that they were served only the simpler food that they desired (11-16).

God rewarded the young men's faithfulness to him and their diligence in study. He gave them the attractive appearance that the king wanted and an understanding that in all spheres of learning was better than that of their fellows. He gave them also the ability to recognize the difference between the true and the false in Babylonian wisdom, and to Daniel he gave the extraordinary ability to understand visions and dreams (17-20). History shows that Daniel so enjoyed God's favour that he was still a person of importance even after the Babylonian Empire had fallen (21; cf. 10:1).

Nebuchadnezzar's dream (2:1-23)

Soon after completing their early training, Daniel and his friends were faced with a severe test. Nebuchadnezzar had a dream and wanted his wise men to tell him its meaning. However, he would not, or could not, tell them the dream. He insisted that they first describe the dream to him accurately, and then he could be sure that their interpretation also was accurate (2:1-6). The wise men replied that the king's demand was unreasonable. No person anywhere had such knowledge (7-11). Furious at their reply, the king ordered that all Babylon's wise men be executed (12).

Perhaps Daniel and his friends had kept themselves separate from the Babylonian magicians and sorcerers, for they did not appear with them before the king. When the king's guards came to arrest them to be executed, Daniel bravely went to the king and successfully asked for extra time to consider the matter (13-16). He immediately returned home and gathered his three friends with him to pray to their God (17-18).

That night God revealed the dream and its interpretation to Daniel in a vision. Without waiting to check with the king whether his vision of the dream was the same as the king's, Daniel confidently thanked God for answering his prayer (19). He praised God as the all-wise and all-powerful ruler of the world, who controls history, determines the destinies of kings, gives wisdom to the faithful and reveals mysteries to his servants (20-23).

The meaning of the dream (2:24-49).

Daniel had no thought of taking the opportunity to exalt himself above his unfortunate fellow officials. Rather he first of all ensured that they would not be

1. BABYLONIAN EMPIRE

3. GREEK EMPIRE

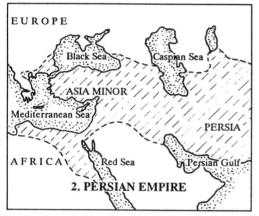

2. PERSIAN EMPIRE

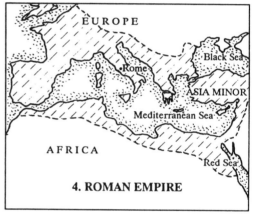

4. ROMAN EMPIRE

executed (24) and even supported their statement that no person could be expected to meet the king's demand (25-27). Certainly, Daniel would tell the king the dream and its meaning, but the revelation was due entirely to God, not to any special skill that Daniel possessed (28-30).

What Nebuchadnezzar saw was a huge statue. It was made of a variety of substances, which, from head to feet, decreased in value while increasing in strength — except that the feet, which supported the statue, were brittle. A huge stone, supernaturally formed, struck the statue in the feet so that the whole structure crumbled to dust and was blown away. The stone, however, grew into a mountain that covered the whole earth (31-35).

The dream concerned the future of Nebuchadnezzar's kingdom and the climax to which coming events would lead (see v. 29). Its chief purpose so far as Nebuchadnezzar was concerned was to show him that God is the sovereign ruler of the world, and

he sets up kingdoms and destroys them according to his own will.

In the light of later history, the meaning of the dream appears to be as follows. The mighty Babylonian Empire headed by Nebuchadnezzar (the head of gold) would soon be replaced by the Medo-Persian Empire (the chest and arms of silver) as the ruling power in the world as Nebuchadnezzar knew it. The Medo-Persian Empire would in turn be replaced by the Greek Empire (belly and thighs of bronze), and this in turn by the Roman Empire (legs of iron) (36-40). The Roman Empire would take in more scattered states than any of the previous empires, but would not be able to hold its empire together in a stable union (feet partly of iron, partly of clay) (41-43).

During the time of this Roman Empire, God would intervene. The mighty empires of human achievement, which started with Babylon and lasted till Rome, would crumble before the coming of a

329

supernatural king, Jesus Christ (the supernatural stone that smashed the image). The kingdom of God introduced by Jesus Christ would spread worldwide and would last for ever (the stone became a great mountain and filled the whole earth) (44-45).

Though Nebuchadnezzar was forced to acknowledge the superiority of Daniel's God, he did not yet acknowledge that he was the only true God (46-47). The king promoted Daniel to chief administrator in the kingdom and head over his council of advisers. But Daniel, in his hour of greatness, did not forget his friends. He had them appointed administrators with responsibilities over various country regions, but he himself remained at the palace in the city of Babylon (48-49).

Saved from the fiery furnace (3:1-30)

Within Nebuchadnezzar's kingdom were people of many races, languages and religions. In a plan to create greater unity among these people, Nebuchadnezzar made a huge image as a national religious symbol, and demanded that all citizens, great and small, bow before it. He set up the image in open plain country where it could be seen from afar, then called all the leading officials from the country areas to a dedication ceremony (3:1-3). He gave instructions concerning the ritual to be followed in worshipping the image, and laid down the penalty for any who disobeyed (4-7).

Some Babylonian officials were jealous of the three Jews who had been recently appointed as provincial administrators. When they saw that the Jews refused to bow to the image, they were pleased to have an opportunity to bring accusations against them before Nebuchadnezzar (8-12). The king found it difficult to believe that people he had recently honoured would be so ungrateful and rebellious. Although he was furious with them, he gave them another chance, warning them that no God could save them once they were thrown into a fiery furnace (13-15).

The three men again refused to obey. They had no doubt that if the sentence against them was carried out, God could save them if he so chose. Whether he *would* save them, they were not sure. Either way, they were determined not to worship the king's image and were prepared to accept the consequences (16-18).

Nebuchadnezzar, now in a rage, had the men bound and thrown into a fiery furnace (19-23). His rage quickly turned to fear when he saw that God sent his heavenly messenger to save them (24-25). The whole experience humbled Nebuchadnezzar. He praised the Jews' God, and issued a decree that gave the Jews religious freedom and protected them from further persecution. He also gave the three men higher positions in his government (26-30).

Nebuchadnezzar's madness (4:1-37)

In this chapter Nebuchadnezzar recounts, for the benefit of his subjects, an experience that humbled his pride and brought him to acknowledge Yahweh as the one and only true God (4:1-3). It all began when Nebuchadnezzar had a puzzling dream. After getting no help from his Babylonian wise men, he told it to Daniel in the hope of discovering its meaning (4-9).

The first thing that Nebuchadnezzar saw in his dream was a giant tree. It towered over the world and provided food and shelter for all creatures everywhere (10-12). A heavenly messenger then announced that this tree would be cut down, though its stump would be preserved (13-15a). The tree was also a person, who then lived for a time as an animal in the fields (15b-16). Angels announced that the purpose of the dream was to show that God rules over all the world's kingdoms and gives them to anyone he chooses (17-18).

Daniel, after hesitating at first, revealed that the dream applied to the great and powerful Nebuchadnezzar himself (19-22). The king would suffer a period of mental illness when, imagining he was an animal, he would go and live like an animal in the field. Although he would not be able to rule during this time, God would preserve his kingdom for him. Eventually he would come to realize that God, not he, was the all-powerful one who decided the destinies of nations. Then God would give him back his throne (23-26).

After revealing the dream's meaning, Daniel gave the king some advice. He urged the king to cease the oppression and injustice that characterized his rule, and begin instead to administer justice for the welfare of his people. Perhaps he would then avoid the threatened disaster (27).

God gave Nebuchadnezzar a year to repent as Daniel had urged, but the king would not change. Instead of repenting, he only grew more defiant and proud. The result was that God acted, and Daniel's dreadful forecasts concerning Nebuchadnezzar came true (28-33).

Only after Nebuchadnezzar lost his sense of self-importance and humbly submitted to God did his sanity return. Previously he had acknowledged that Daniel's God was one among many gods, maybe even the best god (see 2:47; 3:29), but now he openly acknowledged that Daniel's God was the one and only true God, to whom he must bow. This God is the one who determines the destinies of individuals and nations according to his will (34-37).

Belshazzar's feast (5:1-31)

The events of this chapter took place in 539 BC. If Daniel was about fifteen years of age when taken captive to Babylon in 605 BC, he would now be over eighty. Nebuchadnezzar had long been dead. The present king, Nabonidus, was absent in distant territories for much of his reign, and the rule of the country was largely in the hands of his son Belshazzar. The queen who appears in the story (v. 10) was probably the queen mother, wife of Nabonidus. Nebuchadnezzar is referred to in the story as Belshazzar's father (v. 2,11), not in the sense of being father by blood, but in the sense of being predecessor as king.

While the armies of Persia were preparing for their final attack on Babylon, Belshazzar and most of Babylon's leaders were enjoying themselves at an extravagant banquet. Belshazzar knew of the expanding power of the Medo-Persians, but he was so self-confident that he thought nothing could shake his mighty kingdom. He also knew of the God of the Jews who had humbled Nebuchadnezzar, but he showed his contempt for this God by taking the Jews' sacred vessels to use in his banquet of drunkenness and idolatry (5:1-4).

At the height of the feast, Belshazzar was overcome with a sickening terror when a hand suddenly appeared and wrote mysterious words on the wall (5-6). Panic-stricken, he asked his wise men to explain what it all meant. He promised that the one who explained the mystery would be given the next highest place in the kingdom after him. No one was successful (7-9).

When news of the confusion reached the queen mother, she came to the banquet hall to tell the king how Daniel had interpreted mysteries for Nebuchadnezzar many years previously (10-12. At this time Daniel no longer occupied a position of power in Babylon, either because of his age or because of the change in kings). Though able to interpret the writing, Daniel refused the king's reward (13-17). Also, he reminded Belshazzar of how God had humbled the mighty Nebuchadnezzar (18-21), yet although Belshazzar knew all this he deliberately treated God with contempt (22-23). Therefore, God sent him this terrifying message (24).

Daniel recognized three well known Aramaic words in the mysterious writing: *mene*, meaning 'numbered'; *tekel*, meaning 'weighed'; and *parsin* (plural of *peres*), meaning 'divided'. He then offered his interpretation of the words. God had numbered the days of Belshazzar's kingdom and fixed the day when it would collapse; he had judged (weighed) Belshazzar and found him to be a failure; he would divide Belshazzar's kingdom and give it to the Medes and Persians (25-28).

That night, before Belshazzar's banquet was over, Babylon fell to the armies of Medo-Persia under the leadership of the Persian king Cyrus. The Darius mentioned in the story could have been Cyrus under an alternative name, or it could have been a Median general whom Cyrus appointed over Babylon. He is not the Darius mentioned elsewhere in the Old Testament (29-31).

Daniel in the lion's den (6:1-28)

There had been no opportunity for Daniel to enjoy his return to high office, because Babylon fell the night he was reinstated (see 5:29-30). But the new rulers would have known of his record under Nebuchadnezzar, so they made him one of the three presidents appointed to administer the nation (6:1-2).

Daniel had such obvious ability that the other two presidents soon became jealous of him. They wanted to get rid of him, but were unable to find any accusation of mismanagement to bring against him. They saw that their only chance lay in bringing in a new religious law that Daniel's conscience would not allow him to obey (3-5).

In putting their suggestion to the king, the two men used words that made the king think Daniel agreed with them. Their suggestion was that for the next month all prayers to all gods had to pass through the king. It was a common Medo-Persian practice for the king to act as representative of the gods, so Darius agreed to the suggestion and made it law (6-9).

By the time Daniel heard about the new law, it had already been approved and sealed by the king, so he could do nothing to have it changed. He made no effort to obey it, and proceeded to pray to God as he had before (10). His enemies worked out a plan to catch him in the act of breaking their evil law, so that they could accuse him to the king (11-13). They had him condemned and thrown into a den of lions, even though this was against the king's wishes (14-18).

God's miraculous deliverance of Daniel showed that the kind of worship that he accepted was not the state-controlled worship, but Daniel's kind of worship. Daniel had refused to sin against his conscience, had done nothing against the king, had not retaliated against his enemies, and above all had trusted in God (19-22; cf. Heb 11:33). After punishing the plotters (23-24), the king issued a decree commanding that all his subjects respect the God of Daniel (25-27). As for Daniel himself, he continued to prosper in the high positions he held in the Persian administration (28).

7:1-12:13 DANIEL'S VISIONS

Although the visions collected in this section of the book are in approximate chronological order, there is no obvious connection leading one on to the next. Each vision has a separate and distinct message.

A vision of four beasts (7:1-14)

In the first vision (whose chronological position would be between Chapters 4 and 5), Daniel saw a severe storm stirring up the sea, then, coming up out of the raging waters, four strange beasts. The meaning (partly explained later in the chapter) seems to be that God was working in the affairs of the region, stirring up events that produced in turn four kingdoms (7:1-3; see also v. 17).

The four kingdoms represented here are the same four kingdoms illustrated in Chapter 2, but there is a difference in emphasis. Whereas the vision given to the heathen king Nebuchadnezzar dealt in general with the historical significance of the events symbolized, the vision given to God's servant Daniel dealt more with how these events would affect the people of God. The emphasis in Chapter 2 was that God controls the rise and fall of empires. The emphasis in Chapter 7 is that God preserves his people through the opposition that these empires bring.

Babylon, the kingdom symbolized by the first beast, was proud, ruthless and unconquerable at the beginning, but later its cruel power softened and it became more humane (4). The second beast, already eating one victim and getting ready to pounce on another, symbolized the Medo-Persian Empire in its greedy conquest (5). The third beast pictured the swift conquest by Alexander the Great and the spread of the Greek Empire (6).

The fourth beast, so horrible and terrible that it was beyond description, symbolized brutal all-conquering Rome. From the many kingdoms ('ten horns') brought together in the Roman Empire, one leader (a 'little horn') emerged as more ruthless than all others. He murdered those who opposed him and established himself as a cruel unchallengeable dictator (7-8).

Daniel then had a vision of the fiery chariot-throne of God, upon which sat the Lord of the universe. He would judge his creatures with absolute purity and fearful justice (9-10). The 'little horn' dictator made such claims to power that God could tolerate him no longer. His day of judgment had come. The three previous kingdoms were merely overthrown — taken over rather than wiped out. This fourth kingdom, however, under the absolute rule of its arrogant dictator, was completely and mercilessly destroyed (11-12).

In place of this anti-God kingdom a new kingdom was set up, one that was different from all that had gone before. It was set up not by a beast-like figure but by a man-like figure. This was the universal kingdom of God (13-14).

Interpretation of the vision (7:15-28)

One of God's heavenly servants explained to Daniel the meaning of the vision. The kingdoms of the world may arrogantly oppose God in their ruthless drive for supremacy, but the kingdom that triumphs in the end is the kingdom of God, the people of God (15-18).

A reason is then given for God's devastating judgment on the 'little horn' dictator of the fourth beast: he had used his power to make war against God's people (19-22). He blasphemously challenged the Almighty and cruelly persecuted his people, even making special laws so that the whole power of the state could be turned against them. But God allowed him to rule only for a time, then suddenly intervened and destroyed him (23-26). Once again God's kingdom triumphed; his people were victorious (27). Daniel was disturbed as he considered what the vision foretold (28).

History shows that the Roman Empire used its power with arrogance and cruelty. It blasphemed God and persecuted his people without restraint. But God's people triumphed and the kingdom of God remained unconquerable, whereas the Roman Empire crumbled and even the most brutal of its emperors was destroyed. So will it be with all the 'beasts' and all the 'little horns', till the Son of man returns in power and glory, and his people in the fullest sense inherit his everlasting kingdom (v. 13-14,27; cf. Matt 24:30-31; 25:31-33; Mark 13:26; 14:61-62).

Vision of the ram and the goat (8:1-14)

This vision is easier to understand than that of the previous chapter (which was given to Daniel two years earlier; cf. 7:1; 8:1). This is partly because of the interpretation given to Daniel, and partly because of ancient records that show a remarkable correspondence between details of the vision and events as they actually happened.

It was now almost 550 BC, and though Babylon was still the dominant power in the region, Persia had now begun to challenge it. The significant event of 550 BC was Persia's conquest of the formerly great kingdom of Media. Then, in 539 BC, the combined armies of Persia and Media conquered Babylon. This combined Medo-Persian power was pictured in the vision as a ram, one of whose horns (Persia) was higher than the other (Media) (8:1-4; see also v. 20).

Persia ruled till about 333 BC, when Alexander the Great came from the west and with unbelievable speed overran the Persian Empire. His Greek Empire was symbolized in Daniel's vision as a goat, with Alexander as the large horn between the goat's eyes. But at the height of his power, when only thirty-two years of age, Alexander suddenly died. His empire soon split into four sectors ('four new horns') (5-8; see also. v. 21-22).

One of these sectors was centred on Syria. From this sector there arose, many years later, a king ('a little horn') who attacked God's people and even God himself ('the stars of heaven and the Prince of those stars'). This king, Antiochus Epiphanes, stopped the regular sacrifices that the Jews offered each morning and evening, set up Greek idols and a heathen altar in their holy temple, and forced the Jews to carry out practices that he knew their law prohibited (9-12; see also v. 23-25).

This attack on the Jewish religion lasted more than three years (1150 days, or 2300 morning and evening sacrifices). It came to an end in 165 BC, when the Jews regained control of their temple. They then cleansed and rededicated it to the holy worship of God (13-14).

Gabriel explains the vision (8:15-27)

An interpreting angel named Gabriel then set out to explain to the frightened Daniel the meaning of the vision of the ram and the goat (15-18). It was chiefly concerned with the climax of the Jews' troubles, when God would intervene in mighty judgment against Antiochus (19). But first the Medo-Persian and Greek Empires had to be established (20-22). Cruel, cunning, arrogant and powerful, Antiochus would slaughter the Jews, defile the temple and blaspheme God. But God, in his time, would destroy him (23-25).

Gabriel revealed to Daniel that the terrifying events would not take place for some time. This, however, was small comfort, and for several days Daniel lay sick and depressed at the thought of what lay ahead for his people (26-27).

Daniel's prayer (9:1-23)

Persia conquered Babylon in 539 BC and Darius was placed in charge of the newly conquered territory (see 5:31). The Jews' seventy years captivity in Babylon, which Jeremiah had predicted, was now almost complete, and Daniel looked for their return to their homeland (9:1-2; see Jer 29:10). But he knew that repentance was necessary if they were to enjoy God's blessing, and therefore he came to God in prayer on behalf of his people (3).

Casting himself and his people entirely upon the unfailing love of God, Daniel confessed that they had rebelled against his word and disobeyed his messengers (4-6). He acknowledged God's justice in punishing them and scattering them among the nations, but reminded himself that God was also merciful and forgiving (7-10). Through the law of Moses, God warned his people of the consequences of disobedience, but they ignored his warnings. As a result Jerusalem was destroyed and the people taken captive to a foreign land. Yet they had still not asked God's forgiveness (11-14).

Daniel humbly confessed that the calamity that fell upon the nation was a just punishment for a sinful people. He now asked that God, on the basis of his mercy, would forgive. He prayed that God, for the sake of his great name, would act without delay and bring his people out of Babylon and back to their land, as once he had brought them out of Egypt (15-19).

While Daniel was still praying, the heavenly messenger Gabriel brought him God's answer. God had heard his prayer and would bring the Jews back to their land. However, God would give additional revelations, and Daniel would need to think about them carefully if he wanted to understand them (20-23).

The seventy weeks (9:24-27)

Possibly no other portion of the Bible has produced as many interpretations as Daniel's 'seventy weeks'. This is for two main reasons. First, it is not clear who or what many of the symbols or statements refer to. Second, if a 'week' equals seven years, the timetable of 490 years does not correspond exactly with the historical record of events, no matter what meaning we give to the symbols or what method of chronological reckoning we use.

The following interpretation, which is only one among many possible explanations, does not attempt to draw up a timetable based on seventy lots of seven years. Rather it understands the seventy weeks as symbolic of the era about to dawn in answer to

Daniel's prayer. The three divisions within the seventy weeks are therefore seen as symbolic of three phases within that era.

With the Jews' return to their homeland, the old era of seventy years captivity in Babylon would end (see v. 2), and a new era of seventy 'weeks' in Jerusalem would begin. During this period God would bring his age-long purposes to fulfilment. He would deal with sin finally and completely, and in its place would establish everlasting righteousness. Through the arrival of the promised Messiah, God would set his seal of absolute authority upon the visions of the prophets, for their predictions had now come true. As for the Messiah himself, he would be exalted to his rightful place in the holy presence of God (24).

At the time of Gabriel's revelation to Daniel, Persia had just taken control of the Jewish exiles in Babylon (see v. 1) and the Persian king was about to issue a decree allowing the Jews to return to Jerusalem to rebuild their city and temple (Ezra 1:1-4). Gabriel's message was that the first period (seven weeks) would see the city and the temple largely rebuilt, but the next several hundred years (sixty-two weeks) would be a time of constant trouble for Israel (25).

Following this time of trouble God's anointed one, the Messiah, would come (seventieth week), but his people would reject him and kill him. After this an enemy army would pour into Jerusalem like a flood, destroying both city and temple (26). (This predicted calamity occurred when the Roman armies under Titus destroyed Jerusalem in AD 70.)

The Messiah would bring in a new covenant. In the middle of the seventieth week he would be killed and the Jewish sacrifices would cease for ever. But in killing their Messiah, the Jews were preparing their own punishment. They were going to bring upon themselves the 'awful horror' and 'desolating abomination' of ruthless Roman attack. They, as well as their city and temple, would be destroyed. The Romans would be so savage in their attack that they too would be punished (27; cf. Matt 23:37-38; 24:15-22).

A vision beside the Tigris (10:1-11:1)

Daniel's final vision was also his longest, and his account of it lasts till the end of the book. At this time Cyrus was in the third year of his rule over the Jews (10:1). The Jews who had returned to their land had already met so much opposition that they had stopped rebuilding their temple (Ezra 4:1-5,24).

Perhaps this opposition was part of the cause of Daniel's sadness (2-3). Whatever the cause, his mourning and fasting provided the circumstances in which he came face to face with a man-like figure more glorious than any he had met previously (4-6). The presence of this glorious figure was so overpowering that the people with Daniel fled and hid themselves, even though they had not seen him. Daniel remained, but was overcome with weakness (7-9).

First of all the superhuman messenger gave Daniel fresh strength. He then told Daniel that God was pleased with his humble attitude and sincere desire to know more of God and his ways. God had heard Daniel's prayer when he started praying three weeks previously, and had sent this messenger to him (10-12; cf. v. 2-3), but the messenger had been delayed by forces opposed to God. One reason for the Jews' present troubles was that an evil spiritual power was behind the rulers of Persia. This evil spirit tried to prevent the messenger from reaching Daniel, but Michael, a good spirit who worked on behalf of God's people, came and won control over the evil spirit, thereby releasing the messenger to come to Daniel (13-14).

On hearing about the spiritual conflicts going on in the unseen world, Daniel was again overcome with weakness and needed to be strengthened by God's heavenly messenger (15-19). Just as two years earlier this messenger had helped Michael (probably in securing the Jews' release from Persia), so now Michael would help the messenger. The two would fight on behalf of the Jews against the evil power behind Persia. Then, later, when Greece overthrew Persia, they would fight against other evil powers behind Greece (20-11:1).

Kings from the north and the south (11:2-20)

The messenger went on to describe to Daniel the conflicts involving Persia and Greece as they would affect the Jews. This account runs on unbroken through Chapters 11 and 12. The comments on these chapters below are designed to outline the history of the period and to show how events followed the pattern of the predictions given to Daniel.

After the death of Cyrus, the states in the region of Greece steadily grew in power. (Although there was no 'official' Greek nation at that time, these notes will use the name Greece to refer to the region in general. The most important of the Greek states was Macedonia in the north, which later became the centre of the Greek Empire.)

Earlier Persian kings had some outstanding successes against these Greek states, but the Greeks eventually re-established their independence and began to expand their power. Probably the most notable victory came in 333 BC, when the armies of Alexander the Great took control of the eastern Mediterranean region. The Greek conquest then spread rapidly through western Asia and northern Africa. Then, within only a few years of establishing his power, Alexander unexpectedly died, and his vast empire was divided among four of his generals (2-4; cf. 7:6; 8:8).

In the eastern areas of this divided empire there were two main sectors, Egyptian to the south and Syrian to the north. When the Syrian sector became dominant (under the leadership of a man who had previously served under the Egyptian leader), the struggle between the two sectors increased. Israel, caught between the two power centres, suffered much because of these conflicts (5).

Later an alliance was established between the south and the north when the Egyptian king gave his daughter in marriage to the Syrian king. But the marriage broke up and eventually the Syrian king was murdered (6). The woman's brother then invaded and plundered Syria. This was about 246 BC (7-8). During the next fifty years Syria and Egypt invaded each other on several occasions, both sides tasting victory and defeat (9-13).

A decisive battle as far as the people of Israel were concerned was fought in 198 BC. Some of the Jews joined with the Syrians against Egypt, thinking they were fulfilling a prophetic vision that would bring benefits to themselves. In the end they only brought themselves greater trouble, because Syria not only conquered Egypt but also took firm control of Palestine (14-16).

The Syrian king tried to gain full control of the Egyptian throne by giving his daughter in marriage to the king of Egypt, but the scheme did not bring him the success he hoped for (17). He then attacked Greece, but was defeated and forced to flee back to Syria, where he died (18-19). The new king, in order to obtain money to pay the victorious enemy, was attempting to plunder the Jewish temple treasures when he was suddenly murdered (20).

The rise of Antiochus Epiphanes (11:21-28)

Antiochus Epiphanes then became king over the region controlled by Syria. He was not the legal heir, but by bribery and flattery he managed to gain the throne. He was a 'contemptible person' (RSV), treacherous, cruel, greedy and ambitious for power. He devised the most evil schemes to deceive his allies, crush his enemies and plunder the defenceless (21-24).

Within a short time, Antiochus had conquered Egypt, helped by certain traitors in the Egyptian administration who betrayed their king (25-26). He tried to form a partnership with the new king that he had appointed in Egypt, but this king was as deceitful as Antiochus, and the partnership soon failed. Antiochus returned to Syria, planning to carry out the chief aim of his program, the destruction of the Jews and their religion (27-28).

Antiochus attacks the Jews (11:29-45)

Before he had a chance to launch his anti-Jewish campaign, Antiochus heard there was unrest in Egypt, so he returned south to put down the rebellion. But Egypt called in the help of a foreign navy and Antiochus was forced to flee back to Palestine. On his arrival in Jerusalem, he found that fighting had broken out between rival Jewish groups. One of these groups consisted of people who were loyal to their ancient religion, the other of people who were prepared to change their beliefs and practices to gain political benefits from their foreign overlords. Already angry because of his defeat in Egypt, Antiochus eagerly took the opportunity to attack the Jews (29-30).

The enraged Antiochus slaughtered Jews in thousands, made others slaves, and prohibited all from keeping their religious laws. Worse than this, he set up a Greek idol and a Greek altar in the Jewish temple, then sacrificed animals that the Jews considered unclean. To loyal Jews this was 'the abomination that makes desolate' (RSV), 'the awful horror' (GNB). Though some Jews joined Antiochus in order to save their lives, others stood firm no matter what it cost them (31-33).

Jewish resistance to Antiochus was led by a courageous priest and his five sons, known as the Maccabees. They persuaded many to join them in their fight for religious freedom. Amid all the persecution some Jews failed, but others stood firm and were martyred for their faith. The effect of the persecution among the people at large was one of spiritual cleansing. Purified faith enabled the faithful to stand firm, with the result that in 165 BC, after more than three years of fighting, they regained their religious independence and rededicated their temple (34-35).

In addition to blaspheming the God of the Jews, Antiochus dishonoured the Syrian and Greek gods. Considering himself to be above every god, he replaced the existing gods with others brought from elsewhere. He rewarded those who flattered him, by giving them gifts of land and promoting them to positions of power (36-39).

Towards the end of his reign Antiochus was attacked by Egypt. He began his successful counter-attack by overrunning Palestine and once again slaughtering the unfortunate Jews, though he did not invade neighbouring states that were hostile to the Jews. He then moved down to take over Egypt along with those African states that were under Egypt's control (40-43).

When he was later attacked from the north-east by the Parthians, Antiochus left his temporary head-quarters on the plains of Palestine and went out with his usual fury and confidence to meet the attack. But when returning from the battle he suddenly and unexpectedly died (44-45).

End of an era (12:1-13)

Having concluded his lengthy revelation concerning the arrogance, ambition and brutality of Antiochus Epiphanes, the interpreting angel gave encourage-ment to Daniel. He pointed out that the great angel Michael would fight on behalf of the Jews during the period of Antiochus's persecution. Those who were truly God's people would be saved through their time of suffering. Though good and bad alike would be killed in the widespread massacre, the righteous had no need to fear. They received the assurance that one day God would raise them to enjoy eternal life, whereas the wicked would be raised to suffer eternal disgrace. A special reward awaited those who could turn others from selfish wrongdoing to the ways of God (12:1-3).

Daniel was not yet to announce publicly the revelation that God had given him. He was to make sure that it was kept safe till the climax of Jewish suffering arrived with the appearance of Antiochus. Through Daniel's prophecy true believers would then receive enlightenment from God concerning his purposes. The unfaithful, by contrast, would never discover God's purposes, no matter how hard they tried (4).

Two other angels appeared to Daniel, to assure him that God had set a limit to the period that he would allow his people to suffer under Antiochus (5-7). They informed him also of the outcome of the dreadful persecution. Many Jews would renounce their religion to preserve their lives, but in so doing would lose the only life worth having. Others would stand firm, and as a result their lives would be strengthened and purified (8-10).

History records that the period of Antiochus's apparent triumph, which began when he stopped the Jewish sacrifices and ended when the Jews rededicated the temple, was about three and a half years. This period is described as 'a time, two times and half a time', or 1290 days. Many did not live to see the end of the persecution, having been martyred for their unfailing commitment to God. Those who survived, though they had a longer time of suffering, received a blessing that made their suffering seem worthwhile. After three and a half years of persecution, they had the joy of seeing their temple rededicated and the temple services in full operation again. Their religion had survived the onslaught (11-12).

Daniel went to his 'rest' in the grave before these events happened. However, he was assured that he would still have a place in the final triumph of God's people (13).

The pattern repeated

Although Daniel's understanding had been helped by the interpreting angel, the visions and revelations that God gave him had more significance than he may have realized. Their symbolic meaning extended beyond the period of conflict that followed the Jews' return from Babylon. The terrible suffering under Antiochus, though it was the last great persecution of the Jews before the coming of the Messiah, was by no means the end of their troubles.

When the Messiah came, the Jewish people as a whole rejected him and brought upon themselves, at the hands of Rome, greater suffering than they had ever experienced before (cf. 7:23-25). Jesus more than once connected the Jews' rejection of him with the 'desolating abomination' and 'awful horror' of the Romans' destruction of Jerusalem (Matt 21:37-41; 23:37-38; 24:15-22,32-33; Luke 21:20-24; 23:28-31).

Many years after the destruction of Jerusalem, John wrote of the persecution of God's people, using symbolism that again was taken from the book of Daniel (Rev 11:1-3; 12:6-7,14; 13:1-12; 17:8-14). An anti-God spirit had motivated the persecutors of the Jews in Old Testament times, and now the same anti-God spirit was motivating the persecutors of Christians in New Testament times. The anti-God spirit was now specifically anti-Christ. This spirit is always hostile to God and his people (1 John 2:18), and will have its fullest expression in the antichrist who will appear at the end of the age and who will be destroyed by Christ at his coming (2 Thess 2:3-12; Rev 19:20).

Whatever the era and whoever the antichrist, the message for God's people is always one of encouragement: 'he who endures to the end shall be saved' (Dan 12:12; Matt 24:13; 2 Tim 2:11-12; Rev 12:11; 13:10; 20:4). In the end all the powers of this world must give way to the rule of God, whose people inherit his eternal kingdom (Dan 7:27; Matt 25:34; Rev 11:15; 19:1-8).

APPENDIX
Summary of important events

605 BC	First Jewish exiles taken to Babylon
597	More Jewish exiles taken to Babylon
587	Jerusalem destroyed; final deportation to Babylon
558	Cyrus becomes king of Persia
550	Persia conquers Media
539	Persia conquers Babylon
538	First Jews return to Jerusalem
	Work starts on rebuilding the temple (under leadership of Zerubbabel)
516	Temple finished
458	More Jews return to Jerusalem (with Ezra)
445	Nehemiah goes to Jerusalem as governor
333	Alexander the Great overpowers Persia
323	Alexander's empire splits into various sectors
	301-198 Palestine ruled by Egyptian sector
	198-143 Palestine ruled by Syrian sector
171	Antiochus Epiphanes becomes king of Syrian sector
168	Antiochus Epiphanes desecrates the Jewish temple
165	Jews under the Maccabees retake the temple
143	Palestine becomes independent again
63	Rome takes over Palestine
6	Birth of Jesus Christ
AD 31	Death and resurrection of Jesus Christ
70	Destruction of Jerusalem by the Romans

Hosea

BACKGROUND

Hosea belongs to the period of Israelite history when the ancient nation was divided into two kingdoms, Israel in the north and Judah in the south. His ministry began during the reigns of Jeroboam II in Israel and Uzziah in Judah, and continued through the reigns of succeeding kings (Hosea 1:1).

A time of prosperity

Jeroboam II and Uzziah (or Azariah) came to power about the same time, in the early part of the eighth century BC. Both had long and prosperous reigns. During their time Israel and Judah experienced stability such as they had not known since the days of David, and economic prosperity unparalleled in their history. This was possible partly because the political situation in the region favoured Israel and Judah. Syria, the former major power, had declined, and Assyria, the rising power, was involved in a struggle with nations to its north and for forty years did not bother Israel and Judah.

Under these conditions Jeroboam II expanded his kingdom from Hamath in the north to the Dead Sea in the south, as foretold by the prophet Jonah. This gave him control over many of the region's trade routes, which helped considerably to increase Israel's strength. Religiously, however, he was a failure (2 Kings 14:23-29).

Uzziah, meanwhile, was extending his kingdom. He spread his rule west over Philistine territory, east over Ammonite territory, and south as far as the Red Sea and Egypt. He fortified Jerusalem, improved farming and pastoral conditions throughout the country, built up the armed forces, and equipped his army with the most modern weapons. His great mistake was to think that he could be religious head of the nation as well, and for this misguided zeal he was severely punished (2 Kings 15:1-7; 2 Chron 26:6-23).

Social conditions

The economic development of the eighth century brought with it greed and corruption far greater than anything Israel or Judah had experienced previously. Those who benefited from the prosperity were not the ordinary people (such as the farmers, who made up the majority of the population) but the officials and merchants. These were the people of power and influence. They exploited the poor as they pleased, knowing that because of the corruption of the courts, the poor had no way to defend themselves.

Godly people began to see that such practices would lead eventually to God's judgment in the destruction of the nation. The first prophet of this period whose writings are recorded was Amos, who directed his attacks mainly against the upper class people of the northern kingdom. (For fuller details of the social corruption of the time see background notes to Amos.)

Hosea's experiences

In spite of Amos's accusations and warnings, social conditions in Israel worsened. This is seen from the writings of Hosea. Like Amos, Hosea was concerned chiefly with the northern kingdom, though at times he referred to the southern kingdom.

Not only the merchants and officials but also the priests oppressed the poor. The religion was now completely corrupt, and this was what Hosea particularly opposed. He saw this as the cause of all Israel's evil. Baal worship, complete with its fertility rites and prostitution (see 'Baal worship' below), was more widely practised than in Amos's day. Israel knew nothing of the character of Yahweh (Hosea 4:1-6,17-19; 5:4; 6:6-10; 7:14-16; 8:5-6; 13:6; cf. Amos 2:7-8).

Since the covenant bond between Israel and Yahweh was likened to the marriage bond, Israel's association with other gods was really spiritual adultery. Hosea had this impressed upon him when his own wife, Gomer, committed adultery. She left him for other lovers. But her pleasures did not last and she was sold as a slave. All this time Hosea remained faithful to his marriage covenant and still loved his erring wife. When he found her a slave he therefore bought her back.

Hosea's love for his wife was a picture of the covenant love of God for his unfaithful people. They too would go into captivity, but when they had been cleansed of the filth of their adulterous association with the Canaanite gods, they would be brought back to live in their land again.

Baal worship

Canaanite gods were known as Baalim (plural of Baal, a word meaning 'master, owner, or husband'). Goddesses were known either as Ashtaroth (plural of Ashtoreth) or Asherim (plural of Asherah). These were gods of nature that people believed had the power to increase fertility in human beings, animals and soil alike.

From the early days of their settlement in Canaan, the Israelites had been easily led astray by the local Canaanite religions. They saw similarities between the worship of Yahweh and the worship of the local gods, and soon they combined the two. After all, they thought, Yahweh was the God of nature, and he was Israel's husband and master (Hebrew: *baal*). Also, the Canaanites worshipped at altars on the tops of hills (the 'high places'), just as Israel's leaders did in the past. Among the features of the Baalist places of worship were sacred gardens and pillars, the latter being known as Asherim (plural of Asherah, the goddess after whom they were named).

At these high places there were prostitutes, both male and female, with whom worshippers could conduct fertility rites. These were religious-sexual ceremonies that the worshippers believed could influence the gods to give increase in family, herds, flocks and crops. In forsaking Yahweh for Baal, Israelites were guilty of prostitution, both spiritual and literal (Hosea 2:5,8; 4:10-13; 7:14-16; 9:1-2).

Political decline in Israel and Judah

The social and religious evils that developed during the reigns of Jeroboam II and Uzziah continued in the reigns of the kings who followed. There were also serious political troubles.

In Israel Jeroboam had been in such firm control for so long, that when he died there was no one capable of governing the country as he had. The result was political chaos, as ambitious men fought to seize power. A series of plots and assassinations resulted in frequent changes of government and the nation quickly lost its stability (2 Kings 15:8-26).

Within a short time Assyria began to show interest in adding Israel to its rapidly expanding empire. As successive Israelite kings changed between pro-Assyrian and anti-Assyrian policies, Assyria became increasingly involved in Israel's affairs (2 Kings 15:19,29; 17:3-4). Finally, in 722 BC, Assyria conquered Israel and carried its people into captivity (2 Kings 17:5-6).

Political conditions in Judah were, for a while, more stable than in Israel. This was mainly because Jotham, the son of Uzziah, continued his father's policies (2 Kings 15:32-36). But the next king, Ahaz, had a disastrous reign. Politically weak, he led Judah into an alliance with Assyria that almost destroyed Judah's independence. Religiously he was a failure (2 Kings 16:1-20). The next king, Hezekiah, made a courageous effort to restore Judah's independence and reform its religion (2 Kings 18:1-19:37). (For fuller details of the reigns of Jotham, Ahaz and Hezekiah, see background notes to Micah, subheading 'Political events'.)

OUTLINE

1:1-3:5	Hosea's family life and its lessons
4:1-8:14	Israel's moral corruption
9:1-13:16	Israel's punishment
14:1-9	God's forgiving love

1:1-3:5 HOSEA'S FAMILY LIFE AND ITS LESSONS

Hosea, Gomer and their children (1:1-2:1)

The prophet begins his book by outlining his experiences with his unfaithful wife, Gomer. Gomer was probably not a prostitute when Hosea was told to marry her. In recording the story, Hosea is looking back over the events that happened, recalling that the woman whom he married and who bore him children became a prostitute. Gomer's unfaithfulness in leaving him for other men pictured Israel's unfaithfulness in leaving Yahweh for the gods of neighbouring peoples (1:1-3).

Hosea had three children, all of whom were given names with symbolic meaning. The first foretold judgment on the dynasty of Jehu, to which Jeroboam II belonged. God's appointment of Jehu as king was for the purpose of destroying the wicked family of Ahab and Jezebel, but Jehu used it as an opportunity to satisfy his ambition for absolute power. He treacherously destroyed all opponents in a series of brutal massacres, but now the dynasty he established will come to an end (4-5; cf. 2 Kings 9:6-10; 10:1-27).

The name of the second child foretold that God will no longer have pity on the northern kingdom, but will allow it to suffer the full penalty of its sins. However, he will not yet withdraw his mercy from Judah, but will protect it by his miraculous power (6-7; cf. 2 Kings 19:21-37). By the time the third child was born, God no longer recognized Israel as his people. The nation (and, later, Judah as well) will be cut off from him and taken into captivity (8-9).

Despite these judgments, God will have pity on Israel and Judah; they will once more become his people. In Jezreel, where God's judgment fell, they will rejoice again. Israel and Judah will be brought back to their homeland and reunited as one people (10-2:1).

Unfaithful Israel (2:2-23)

In Chapter 2 Hosea's sons are apparently now grown up and Hosea asks them to plead with their mother to return to him. In the same way the minority of faithful believers in Israel plead with the faithless nation to return to God (2).

Israel's adultery was to follow Baal instead of Yahweh. The people believed that Baal was the god of nature and he would give them happiness. Just as a husband could strip his unfaithful wife and send her away naked, so God will, by drought and conquest, strip Israel's land, leaving it bare and fruitless (3-5).

God creates other hindrances designed to stop Israel from going after Baal and to help her return to him, but she persists in pursuing Baal. Only when she cannot get what she wants from Baal does she selfishly turn back to Yahweh, hoping he can do better for her (6-7).

In his grace God receives unfaithful Israel back, but by ruining the productivity of the land he will show her that he, not Baal, is the controller of nature (8-9). As an adulterous wife is shamed by being stripped naked, so the nation that is committing spiritual adultery with Baal will be shamed as her land is stripped bare (10-13).

After she acknowledges her wrong, God will win Israel back to himself. When Israel first entered her land, the Valley of Achor (GNB: Trouble Valley) brought warnings of judgment (see Josh 7:22-26), but when she returns it will bring hope (14-15). No longer will she try to follow both Yahweh and Baal. Yahweh will be her only husband. In fact, she will be so determined to avoid any identification of Yahweh with Baal, that she will refuse to use the word *baal* when speaking of Yahweh as her husband or master. She will use the alternative word *ish* (16-17). Yahweh will protect her from all dangers, whether from the world of nature or from the world of people. He is God of nature and God of history (18).

The 're-marriage' will be based on God's standards and maintained by his loving faithfulness to the marriage covenant. Israel will know Yahweh and be inseparably united with him (19-20). He, the only God of nature, will then give to Israel the blessings of nature that she desired. The curses signified by the names of Hosea's three children will then be turned into blessings (21-23).

Steadfast love (3:1-5)

The story now returns to relate how Hosea, having found that his prostitute wife had become a slave, bought her back. In the same way God will buy back his adulterous people from slavery (3:1-2).

But Gomer had first to undergo a period of discipline and live with Hosea as a slave, not as a wife. Israel likewise must have a period of discipline. She must live in captivity in a foreign land, where she will be without her own civil government and will be separated from all objects connected with former religious practices, good and bad. Only when she willingly responds to God's love and seeks him will she be truly his (3-5).

The love that God showed to Israel (and Hosea to Gomer) is a special kind of love that in Hebrew is called *chesed*. It is translated in the RSV as 'steadfast love', in the GNB as 'constant love' and in other versions as 'mercy', 'kindness' and 'loving kindness'.

Chesed love is covenant loyalty and faithfulness. A covenant is an agreement between two parties that carries with it obligations and blessings. In the case of Hosea and Gomer, that covenant is the marriage covenant, and *chesed* is that particularly strong form of love by which the two persons in that covenant are bound to be loyal to each other. This idea forms a basic theme of the book of Hosea. God exercised loyal love and covenant faithfulness towards his people, but they were not loving and faithful to him in return. Their *chesed* 'vanished like the morning mist' (see 6:4-6).

4:1-8:14 ISRAEL'S MORAL CORRUPTION

Hosea now turns from his personal experiences to the conditions in Israel that they illustrated. There appears to be little chronological order or logical development in this section. It consists of collections of numerous short messages that Hosea apparently delivered on various occasions over a number of years.

Corrupt religion; corrupt people (4:1-5:7)

The people have no knowledge of God or his law, and therefore they are unfaithful to him and deceitful in their dealings with one another. Their wickedness is the reason for the present drought they are suffering (4:1-3).

Chiefly to blame for this nationwide corruption are the priests. They have not taught God's law to the people (4-6). Instead they have encouraged the people to offer more sacrifices so that they (the priests) can profit. Since they receive the meat of the sin offering, the priests welcome the people's sins. The more the people sin, the more sin offerings the priests receive (7-8). The priests are as bad as people in general and are guilty of the same sins. They look for increase in their families, flocks and herds through the Baal practice of carrying out sexual rites with religious prostitutes. God will make sure that their hopes are disappointed (9-10).

Throughout the land people follow religious practices of the worst kind. They become drunk at their religious feasts. They look for guidance by superstitious ceremonies using sacred sticks. They offer sacrifices under sacred trees at the Baal high places. Their young women become religious prostitutes, though the chief blame lies with the men, who, by their immoral desires, made the women into prostitutes (11-14).

Judah is warned not to follow Israel in trying to mix the worship of the living God with the false religion that operates at places such as Gilgal. God cannot bless those who stubbornly go their own way (15-16). The idolatry, greed and immorality of Israel will be the cause of its destruction (17-19).

Priests, common people and the royal family are all corrupt. They are condemned as spiritual prostitutes and slaves to the false religion that is practised throughout the nation. The prophet names some of the more popular Baal centres (5:1-3). The people are firmly held by the power of idolatry and unable to return to God. They still offer their animal sacrifices, but God does not accept them. They are not his children, but the children of prostitution. Within a short time God will send another judgment upon them in the form of further devastation of their crops (4-7).

Foreign policies (5:8-15)

During the reigns of the Judean kings Jotham and Ahaz, Israel and Syria tried to persuade Judah to join them in an alliance aimed at resisting the spreading power of Assyria. When Judah refused to cooperate, Israel and Syria attacked Jerusalem, whereupon Ahaz, contrary to Isaiah's advice, asked Assyria for help. Assyria replied by conquering Syria and much of Israel. But Judah's independence also suffered, because in asking Assyria for help, it placed itself under Assyria's power (2 Kings 16:5-9; Isa 7:1-9; 8:4).

Hosea sees Israel going to battle and knows that the nation is about to bring a fitting calamity upon itself. He also condemns Judah, who took the opportunity to seize some of Israel's territory. He sees the inner decay of both kingdoms as a judgment of God upon them (8-12).

When Israel's foreign policy proved fatal, the king Pekah was assassinated by Hoshea, a sympathizer with Assyria who then became king (2 Kings 15:30; 17:3). But Assyria could not solve Israel's problems any more than it could Judah's. Both Israel

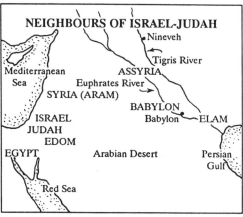

NEIGHBOURS OF ISRAEL-JUDAH

and Judah were morally sick. They turned to foreign nations to help them instead of turning from their sins to God. Now they will find that God will use foreign nations to punish them. As a lion destroys a lamb, so God will destroy Israel and Judah (13-14). He will give no help to his people till they repent of their sins and seek him afresh (15).

Insincere repentance (6:1-6)

In view of God's warning in the previous chapter (see 5:15), the people decide to make a confession of repentance. But their confession is not sincere. They offer it to God in the hope that it will satisfy him and bring from him a speedy response. If God helps them, their future blessings are guaranteed (6:1-3).

God sees that the people's promise to return to him is nothing but words; their hearts have not changed. They have no covenant loyalty towards God, no love for him and no desire to know him. As long as they are without these qualities, all their sacrifices and offerings are useless. Religious exercises will not save a rebellious people from judgment (4-6).

Treachery, robbery and murder (6:7-7:7)

Priests and common citizens alike are guilty of treachery, robbery and murder. Hosea again names the places where they have practised these evils. He announces that the people, along with all their religious ceremonies and sacrifices, are repulsive to God (7-10). God wants to give blessings to his people, but they prevent such blessings because they refuse to repent. They prefer to continue with their cheating, stealing and violence (11-7:2).

The death of Jeroboam II was followed by a series of plots, conspiracies and assassinations (see 2 Kings 15:8-26). The successful assassin, who then became king, was pleased with the treacherous deeds of his fellow plotters, but he himself was not safe from the plotting of others. Just as a baker keeps the fire low until the dough is ready for an increase in heat, so these men plot their evil secretly until the time is ripe to murder the king (3-4). Pretending to be friends, they feast with him so that they can get him drunk, then murder him (5-7).

Alliances with other nations (7:8-16)

Israel is useless, like a cake that is burnt on one side but uncooked on the other. It has ruined itself by relying too much on other nations and too little on God. As a result Israel has, without realizing it, come under the power of these nations. God has allowed this to happen as a punishment on his people, but because of their arrogance they refuse to acknowledge the fact and will not return to God (8-10). Foolishly they make alliances, first with one nation then with another, but God sees all such alliances as rebellion against him. Far from saving the people, these alliances will be the cause of their destruction (11-13).

Like Baal worshippers, the Israelites wail and dance and cut themselves with knives, hoping that Baal will respond by giving them good harvests from their fields and vineyards. God is the one who has trained and strengthened them, but they have treacherously turned against him. They are as useless to God as a crooked bow is to an archer. Their defiant attitude towards him will lead to certain punishment (14-16).

A rebellious kingdom (8:1-14)

The people of Israel claim to know God, but they have broken their covenant with him and sinned against his law. God will use the Assyrian army (here symbolized by an eagle) to bring his punishment upon them (8:1-3). Their kings are not people appointed by God but traitors who murder to gain power. The centre of their religion is not God but the golden calves set up as idols in their cities (4-6; see 1 Kings 12:29-30).

Israel's foreign policy, besides being rebellious towards God, is politically foolish. The nation will now reap the fruits of its folly in disappointment and destruction. It will come under enemy control (already some of the people have been taken into captivity; 2 Kings 15:29), and finally the nation will come to an end (7-8). Israel has acted stubbornly like a wild ass and therefore will be treated like a wild ass. It will be left to wander alone — leaderless, oppressed and without friends (9-10).

Religious ceremonies, intended originally to be a help, have become a cause of sin. The people enjoy offering sacrifices because of the feast that follows; but God rejects their sacrifices because they are not interested in knowing or following the moral teachings of his law (11-13). Their prosperity is only hastening their day of judgment (14).

9:1-13:16 ISRAEL'S PUNISHMENT
Punishments to fit the sins (9:1-17)

Baal worship and its accompanying immoral rituals were aimed at increasing the produce from farms and vineyards. As a punishment God will destroy the farms and vineyards and send the people into captivity. There they will be forced to eat food that to them is unclean (9:1-3). They will not be able to

DIVIDED KINGDOM OF ISRAEL-JUDAH

offer the usual food and wine offerings; in fact, they will barely have enough to keep themselves alive. Meanwhile the land in which they once lived will become wild again through neglect (4-6).

The people do not like Hosea's denunciations and warnings. He is God's messenger to them, the nation's watchman, but they call him a fool and a madman. They even plot to kill him (7-8). Their sin is as great as that of Gibeah in the time of the judges (9; see Judg 19:1-20:48).

When God brought the people of Israel out of Egypt and led them through the wilderness, his desire was that they enter a new era of fruitfulness. But even before they reached the promised land, they had turned to Baalism and its immorality (10; see Num. 25:1-5). Such unfaithfulness has characterized the people ever since. They practise sexual rites, hoping that their families will increase. God's punishment, fittingly, will cause their families to decrease (11-14). Because of their Baal practices (as, for example, at Gilgal), they will be fruitless instead of fruitful. They will go into shameful captivity in a foreign land (15-17).

Reaping what they have sown (10:1-15)

The more prosperous the people of Israel become, the more they increase their worship of Baal. The more certain, therefore, is their coming judgment (10:1-2). No one can be trusted. Injustice, like a poisonous plant, is having a deadly effect. It is killing the nation. The people do not fear God, and as a result will fall under his judgment. They, along with their king and the golden calf that they worship, will be carried off to Assyria (3-6). The land will be ruined and the Baal altars will become overgrown with weeds (7-8). Again, Israel's sin is compared to that of the Benjaminites in Gibeah, and their punishment is just as certain (9-10).

God compares Israel to a young ox whose original work (threshing) was not hard. But Israel has been so rebellious that if she is to avoid God's judgment she will have to do much harder work (ploughing). She must break up the hard, barren, long-neglected soil so that it can produce spiritual fruit for God (11-12). The people reap what they sow. They have sown evil and are now reaping a harvest of social injustice. They have trusted in the military strength of foreign nations, and so will be destroyed by the military strength of foreign nations (13-15).

The Father's love (11:1-11)

As a father loves a son, so God loved Israel and saved his people from slavery in Egypt. They turned from God to serve idols, but God still loved them and cared for them (11:1-4). However, they have refused to return to God, and now they are about to go into slavery again, this time in Assyria (5-7).

It hurts God to have to punish those whom he loves. He must punish them for their wickedness, because he cannot ignore sin. But within his justice there is mercy. His love is stronger and more faithful than anything that is found in human relationships. He will remove his people from their land, but he will not destroy them for ever as he did Sodom, Gomorrah and other cities (8-9; see Deut 29:23). God will overpower the enemies of Israel, release his people from captivity and bring them back to their homeland (10-11).

Deceit and wilfulness (11:12-12:14)

Israel's political agreements with foreign nations, whether concerning trade or defence, are unlawful in God's eyes. They are based on lies and dishonesty (11:12-12:1).

Such deceit has been a characteristic of Israel from the time of the nation's forefather, Jacob (the original Israel). From birth Jacob showed a desire to get his own way. As an adult he struggled even with God. Only when he was forced finally to give in did he win the blessing he so eagerly desired (2-5; see Gen 25:22-26; 32:24-30). In the same way the people who are descended from him and who bear his name must give in by turning from their sinful ways to God. Only in this way will they receive God's blessing (6).

Merchants have become wealthy by cheating and oppressing the poor, but now they are to receive fitting justice. They have used their wealth to bribe judges and administrators, but they cannot use it to bribe God. Their prosperous cities and luxurious houses will be destroyed and the people of Israel will be forced to live in tents, as they did on their journey from Egypt to Canaan. This was an experience that Israelites recalled each year when they lived in small temporary shelters during the Feast of Tabernacles (7-9; cf. Lev 23:40-43).

God had used prophets to speak to his people in many ways, but the people repeatedly ignored the messages and are now to suffer the consequences. Their heathen altars will be destroyed and left like heaps of stones in a field (10-11).

Jacob was a shepherd who looked after sheep, but Moses was a shepherd who looked after people. He was a prophet who led God's people Israel, but just as the people of Israel rebelled against Moses so they have rebelled against all the prophets after him. Their rebellion against God's messengers is really a rebellion against God himself. They have made God angry with them and thereby have made their own punishment certain (12-14).

The destruction of Israel (13:1-16)

Ephraim prided itself that it was the leading tribe in Israel and that the other tribes did as Ephraim told them. Ephraim must therefore bear the responsibility for the development of Baal worship in Israel. As the morning dew quickly vanishes with the rising of the sun, so Ephraim, and all the other tribes with it, will soon disappear (13:1-3).

God saved the Israelites from slavery, looked after them in the wilderness and gave them a land, but in their prosperity they forgot him (4-6). God will now destroy them. There will be no escape (7-8). Israel's original desire for a king was a rejection of God. The people will now find that the king will not give them the security they hoped for. The monarchy, as well as the nation, is doomed (9-11; cf. 1 Sam 10:19; 12:13-15).

Israel has been piling up sin for years, and the punishment for that sin is now to fall upon it in the form of national destruction. There is hope of salvation and new life if the nation responds to God, but it stubbornly refuses to. It is like an unborn child which, when the time for birth has come, refuses to come out of its mother's womb, and so dies (12-13). There can be no more mercy. Death is

certain (14). As a hot wind from the desert can destroy the countryside, so the Assyrian army will destroy Israel. It will show no mercy (15-16).

14:1-9 GOD'S FORGIVING LOVE

God loves Israel in spite of its sin and rebellion, and he still desires the people's repentance rather than their destruction. He even gives them the words of confession to use in asking his forgiveness. In this prayer they acknowledge their sin, and promise that they will no longer look to foreign nations for help. They will not worship man-made gods, but will trust entirely in God and his mercy (14:1-3).

If they repent, God in his love will give them a spirit of faithfulness to replace their present unfaithfulness. He will bless them with refreshment, beauty and strength, and help them develop fruitful lives for him (4-7). God assures his people that he will give them blessings far greater than those they looked for, but never received, from their worship of Baal and their pursuit of prosperity (8).

The prophet closes his book with a wisdom saying to remind his readers that if they heed his message they will find blessing, but if they ignore it, they will meet disaster (9). We know from history that the people did not respond to God's appeal. The nation Israel (the northern kingdom) was conquered by Assyria in 722 BC, its cities destroyed, and its people taken into foreign captivity (2 Kings 17:1-6).

Joel

BACKGROUND

Among the prophets of the Old Testament, Joel differs from most of the others in that he does not state the period during which he preached. One suggestion is that he prophesied in Judah around the period 835-830 BC, during the reign of the boy-king Joash. This would explain why the book does not mention Syria, Assyria or Babylon, the chief enemies during the time of the divided kingdom, as these nations had not yet begun to interfere in Judah's affairs. It would also explain why the prophet does not mention a reigning king, for at that time the government of the country was largely in the hands of the priest Jehoiada (2 Kings 11:1-21; 12:1-2). The prominence of Jehoiada may also account for Joel's interest in the temple and its services (Joel 1:9,13; 2:12,15-17).

An alternative suggestion is that the book was written after the Jews' return from captivity. The most likely period is either 520-510 BC (after the ministry of Haggai and Zechariah and the rebuilding of the temple) or around 400 BC (a generation or so after the reforms of Ezra and Nehemiah). According to these suggestions, Joel is among either the first or the last of the writing prophets.

Purpose of the book

In spite of the absence of a specific date, the present-day reader should have no great difficulty in understanding the book of Joel. This is because the single event that forms the book's basis is not concerned with details of Judah's local politics or international affairs. The event is a severe locust plague, and the setting appears to be Jerusalem and the surrounding countryside.

The locust plague brought extensive agricultural damage and created widespread suffering to the people. What made the plague even more devastating was its occurrence at the height of a crippling drought. Joel interpreted these events as God's judgment on Judah for its sin. He promised the people that if they repented, God would renew his blessing by giving them productive crops and a more enlightened knowledge of himself. Joel saw these events as symbolic of God's future judgment on all enemies and his blessing on his people.

OUTLINE

1:1-2:11 THE GREAT LOCUST PLAGUE

Effects of the plague (1:1-20)

So devastating is the current locust plague, that even the oldest people cannot remember anything like it. The whole countryside has been stripped bare. Joel tells the people to pass the story of the plague on to their children and grandchildren, so that it will not be forgotten (1:1-4). Those who have greedily lived for their own pleasure are punished. They will no longer get drunk with wine, because the locusts have destroyed the vineyards (5-7).

The people mourn as a young bride mourns when she has lost her bridegroom. She had looked forward to happiness, but instead she has misery (8). The priests mourn, because with the destruction of the fields and vineyards the people cannot bring their cereal and wine offerings (9). The ground mourns, because it cannot fulfil its natural purpose of producing grain, wine and oil (10). And the farmers mourn, because their crops have been ruined (11-12).

Joel now reveals that the locust plague is not an accident; it is a direct judgment from God. The priests therefore must lead the nation in repentance. First they must show their own repentance, then they must gather the leaders and people together to cry to the Lord for mercy (13-14).

The people must acknowledge that this disaster is from God. It is a foretaste of the great day of the Lord when he intervenes in judgment in the affairs of the human race. They have the evidence before their eyes in the form of hungry people, ruined crops and starving animals. Surely, they must see that this is God's judgment upon them (15-18). Therefore, God is the one to whom the prophet cries; he alone can save the nation from total ruin (19-20).

An army of locusts (2:1-11)

Joel now pictures the approaching swarms of locusts as a person in Jerusalem sees them. He compares them to an enemy army and commands the watchman on the city wall to blow the trumpet to warn the city's inhabitants of the attack. The swarms are so thick that they look like black clouds as they sweep down over the mountains (2:1-2). They spread over the countryside like an uncontrollable bushfire, turning healthy farmlands into barren wastes (3). People are terrified. They are helpless before the onslaught of this destructive army (4-6).

Finally, the locusts attack Jerusalem. City walls cannot keep this enemy out, as locusts swarm into the city and through the houses (7-9). The clouds of insects are so thick they blot out the sun. The darkness demonstrates to all that this is God's judgment and the day of the Lord is upon them (10-11).

2:12-32 GOD'S MERCY ON THE REPENTANT

Repentance and restoration (2:12-27)

Although God is the one who has sent this judgment, it is not too late for the people to ask for his mercy. However, this must be accompanied by genuine inward repentance, not just by the outward show of torn clothing, sackcloth and ashes. God may then restore their fields and vineyards, and they will be able to worship him with their cereal and wine offerings again (12-14).

Once more a trumpet is blown, but this time to call the people to the temple to seek God's mercy. No one is to be excluded, not even the children. All are to fast and mourn, even people who would normally be rejoicing and celebrating, such as those who have just been married (15-16). The priests gather in the temple court between the porch and the altar, and lead the people in prayer (17).

God accepts the people's repentance and promises to remove the locusts. He will drive them out to perish in the desert regions to the south, in the Dead Sea to the east, and in the Mediterranean Sea to the west. There may be some unpleasantness at first because of the smell from the millions of decaying locust carcasses, some lying in heaps on the ground, others washed up on to the shores. But after this, the land will become productive again (18-22). God will give good rains and good harvests to compensate for the losses suffered during the locust plague (23-25). This whole experience of judgment, repentance, forgiveness, blessing and thanksgiving will cause them to know God better (26-27).

Promise of the Spirit (2:28-32)

People may readily turn to God in days of hardship, but many of them just as readily forget God and become self-satisfied as soon as prosperity returns. They will be more obedient to God when they have a better understanding of his will. They will be more genuine in their devotion to him when they realize that his blessings consist of more than grain, wine and oil. Joel looks forward to the day when God will give all his people this better understanding by putting his Spirit within each one, regardless of age, sex or social status. It will not be like former times, when God gave his Spirit only to certain people for special tasks on special occasions (28-29).

All this must happen before the final great day of the Lord dawns. The darkness and terror of the locust plague is only a faint picture of the horror of that last great judgment. On that day believers will be saved but sinners will perish (30-32).

In New Testament times Peter saw a fulfilment of Joel's prophecy in the remarkable events of the Day of Pentecost. With the death, resurrection and ascension of Christ, a new age had dawned. The Spirit was now given to all God's people. Those who called on God's name had the assurance of salvation, but those who persisted in their sin had the assurance of judgment and condemnation (Acts 2:14-21; cf. John 16:7-15).

3:1-21 FINAL PUNISHMENT AND BLESSING

Up till now Joel has been emphasizing aspects of the day of the Lord that were not so well known, for example, judgment on *all* sinners, including Israel-Judah, and blessing on *all* the faithful, regardless of age, sex or status. Now he deals with aspects that were better known, namely, the salvation of God's people and the judgment of their enemies. However, he wants his readers to understand these matters in the light of what he has already told them about God's worldwide salvation and universal judgment. The people of God can be confident of their own salvation and their enemies' condemnation only if they have first repented of their sin (see 2:32; cf. Acts 2:37-39; 17:30-31).

Enemy nations judged (3:1-15)

Joel pictures enemy nations gathering for a last attack on Jerusalem. But these nations do not realize that God is the one who has brought them together. He is now going to execute his judgment upon them for their crimes against Judah. Chief among these crimes are their seizure of Judah's territory and their treatment of Judah's people, whether in driving them into other countries or in selling them as slaves (3:1-3). Tyre, Sidon and Philistia are examples of those nations that fought with Judah, plundered the Jerusalem temple and sold the people into slavery. In punishment God will now treat them as they treated Judah (4-8; cf. 2 Chron 21:16-17).

Returning to the picture of nations gathering for war in the valley outside Jerusalem, the prophet ironically urges the enemy armies to make full preparation for the battle. He then calls upon God to send down his angelic armies (his 'warriors'; v. 11b) to be ready to carry out his sentence of judgment upon the enemy (9-12).

God's moment of decision comes and he announces his verdict on the nations. They are guilty, their wickedness is great, and therefore they must die. They are cut down like grapes from a vine; their blood flows like grapejuice overflowing a winepress. The valley of God's judgment is filled with the bodies of dead soldiers (13-15).

Blessings for God's people (3:16-21)

The time of God's judgment on his enemies is also the time of his deliverance of Jerusalem. He protects his people from punishment, purifies them from uncleanness, and gives them peace and prosperity (16-18). Having punished all enemies (symbolized here by Egypt and Edom), God now dwells among his people for ever. The persecutors receive their just punishment, but the righteous enter into eternal life (19-21).

The day of the Lord

In his book Joel has shown how the events surrounding the locust plague were a picture and a foretaste of greater events that were yet to take place. He has shown how the day of the Lord brings both judgment and salvation. For the parallel between the judgment of the day of the Lord in Joel's day (the locust plague) and the judgment of the final great day of the Lord, compare 2:3 with 2:30; 2:10a with 3:16a; 2:10b with 3:15; 2:11a with 3:11b. For a parallel between the blessings on God's people after the locust plague and after God's final great intervention in human affairs, compare 2:23-24 with 3:18; 2:26-27 with 3:16b-17.

Amos

BACKGROUND

Amos was the first of four prophets who prophesied during the eighth century BC, the others being Hosea, Isaiah and Micah. This was the time of the divided Israelite kingdom, and each of the writers carefully dated his writings according to the kings of Israel and Judah in whose reigns he prophesied. This helps the present-day reader to build up a picture of the circumstances surrounding each prophet's ministry.

The background notes to Hosea provide a summary of social, religious and political conditions in Israel and Judah during the time of the earlier eighth century prophets. A reading of those notes will provide a useful introduction to the notes on Amos below. Maps showing the divided kingdom and the neighbours of Israel-Judah are also located in the notes on Hosea.

Increased prosperity brings social evils

At the time Amos began his preaching, Jeroboam II reigned in the northern kingdom Israel, and Uzziah (also known as Azariah) reigned in the southern kingdom Judah. Under these kings, both nations enjoyed prosperity, but with the prosperity came changes that religiously, socially and morally were for the worse.

The rise of the merchant class, which began two hundred years earlier during the reign of Solomon, reached its peak during the time of Jeroboam II and Uzziah. No longer was society built around the simple agricultural life. With the rapid growth of commerce and trade, city life developed, and this brought social evils on a scale that neither Israel nor Judah had known before. Rapid prosperity for some meant increased poverty for others. As the upper classes grew in wealth and power they exploited the lower classes. Bribery and corruption flourished, even in the law courts, leaving the poor with no means of obtaining justice.

The fiery preaching of Amos

Amos, with bold attacks on the rich merchants and unjust rulers of Israel, was the first of the prophets to come to the defence of the poor. He was a shepherd-farmer who lived in a lonely village in the north of Judah, but most of his attacks are directed at Israel. This is probably because when he took his fruit and wool across the border to sell in the markets of Bethel and other towns, he saw the corruption of Israel's city life. He had first-hand knowledge of the situation, because he himself had to deal with the ruthless merchants and corrupt officials.

In his fiery sermons Amos condemned the disgusting greed and extravagant luxury of the rich, for he knew that they had gained their wealth by cheating, oppression and injustice (Amos 2:6-7; 3:10,15; 5:10-12; 6:4-6; 8:4-6). They kept the religious festivals with much enthusiasm, paid their tithes and offered elaborate sacrifices, but all these things were worthless in God's sight so long as the worshippers persisted in their social injustice (Amos 5:21-24; 8:3,10). Amos clearly saw what Israel's upper classes did not see, namely, that the nation was heading for a terrible divine judgment (Amos 7:11).

OUTLINE

1:1-2:16 JUDGMENTS ON VARIOUS NATIONS

It seems that Amos announced most, if not all, of his message in Bethel, an important religious and commercial centre near Israel's southern border (see 7:10). He gained the attention of his audience by first announcing God's judgment on Israel's neighbours. This news no doubt pleased his hearers, but for Amos it was part of his build-up to the climax, which announced God's judgment on Israel.

The first three nations that Amos condemned were foreign nations unrelated to Israel. The next three were relatives of Israel, thus bringing the judgment nearer. (Edom was descended from Esau; Ammon and Moab were descended from Lot.) Judgment became uncomfortably close when Israel's sister nation Judah was condemned. Finally, Israel was condemned. The announcement of judgment was longer for Israel than for any other nation. Yet it was only an introduction to the series of messages concerning Israel that fills up the rest of the book.

Judgment on Israel's neighbours (1:1-2:5)

Amos dates his prophecy according to a local earthquake that was well known to his original readers but is not mentioned in the biblical record. He is a shepherd but his announcement of judgment is like the roar of a lion. He is the mouthpiece for God, who declares from his dwelling place in Jerusalem that this judgment will affect all Israel. Lowland pastures and fertile hill country alike will dry up under the force of God's action (1:1-2).

The words that God uses to introduce each announcement of judgment — 'for three sins and for four I will not turn away from punishment' — show that the nation has sinned again and again, and can no longer escape punishment. God has been patient, to give sinners the opportunity to repent, but when they refuse to repent, judgment becomes inevitable. Sin has overflowed; judgment must fall.

Syria (capital: Damascus) is condemned to destruction and captivity because of its unrestrained cruelty. Under the kings Hazael and Ben-hadad, Syria tortured and butchered its victims by the most brutal methods (3-5; cf. 2 Kings 8:12-13; 10:32-33; 13:3,7,22). Philistia captured cities and sold entire populations as slaves — men, women and children. In punishment Philistia's own chief cities (Gaza, Ashdod, Ashkelon and Ekron) will be destroyed (6-8). The Phoenician city of Tyre, the leading commercial centre of the region, will also be conquered and burnt to the ground. It deceived its treaty partners, and bought and sold slaves as it would any other merchandise (9-10).

Edom is condemned for savagely attacking Israel without any thought for the blood relation between the two nations (11-12). Ammon (capital: Rabbah) also will suffer a devastating judgment, because it mercilessly killed whole populations, including defenceless women and children, merely to expand its territory (13-15). Moab, which bordered Ammon to the south, will be invaded by foreign armies. In an overwhelming judgment from God its cities will be burnt and its leaders killed, because it acted with uncontrolled hatred towards an enemy (2:1-3).

The six nations previously mentioned did not have God's law so they are not condemned by that law. They are condemned for ignoring the knowledge of right and wrong that God has put in the hearts of all people. Their inhumanity and cruelty are inexcusable (cf. Rom 2:12-15). But Judah did have God's law. It is condemned for disobeying that law and going its own way (4-5).

Judgment on Israel (2:6-16)

Israel is corrupt, socially, morally and religiously. Judges and officials favour those who bribe them, with the result that the poor and the innocent receive unjust treatment. The rich lend to the poor, then take them as slaves when they cannot repay their debts, even though the debt may be as little as the price of a pair of sandals (6-7a).

The wealthy seize the clothes of the poor as guarantees for the repayment of debts (even though the law of Moses prohibited the seizure of clothes and other essential items as guarantees; see Deut 24:6,10-13). But since the wealthy have no desire to wear the clothes of the poor, they find an alternative use of them. They spread them out beside the Baal altars to make beds, where they engage in sexual rites with religious prostitutes. Their religious feasts become drinking parties, but again the wine comes from people who have been exploited. Corrupt officials place unjust fines on poor people such as farmers, then, when the farmers are unable to pay their fines, the officials seize their wine as payment (7b-8).

God had richly blessed the people of Israel, bringing them out of slavery, destroying the former inhabitants of Canaan, and giving them a prosperous land to dwell in (9-10). He gave them prophets and Nazirites for their spiritual upbuilding, but they rejected both (11-12; for Nazirites see Num 6:1-21). God will therefore crush his people, as an ox-cart loaded with grain crushes whatever is beneath it. Nothing will save them from his judgment. They will be destroyed (13-16).

3:1-6:14 REASONS FOR ISRAEL'S PUNISHMENT

The prophet's responsibility (3:1-8)

Many Israelites thought that because they were God's people, they could do as they liked without fear of punishment. On the contrary, says Amos, God's choice of them to be his people is all the more reason why he will punish them if they are disobedient (3:1-2).

To prevent the people from thinking that he is making idle threats, Amos points out that he has good reason for speaking with such boldness. He gives a list of illustrations to show that there is a reason for everything. For example, if people go on a journey together, the reason is they have arranged it. If a lion roars, the reason is it has caught its prey.

If a bird-trap shuts, the reason is a bird has been caught in it. If troops assemble for battle, the reason is the city fears an attack (3-6). Likewise if a prophet speaks boldly, the reason is God has given him a warning to pass on to the people. They should therefore take notice (7-8).

The corruption of Samaria (3:9-4:3)

Amos tries to shame the people of Israel (capital: Samaria) by inviting their enemies to come and see how bad the nation is, with all its oppression, lawlessness, violence and greed (9-10). Israel will surely be conquered and plundered. The only things that will remain as a reminder of former luxury will be a few scraps of furniture. The remains of the nation will be like the remains of a sheep that has been attacked and eaten by wild animals (11-12). The altars of the Baal worshippers and the luxurious houses of the corrupt upper classes will be smashed to pieces (13-15).

The wealthy women, who have urged their husbands on to exploit the poor simply to increase their own extravagance, are likened to a lot of fat cows. When the enemy conquers Samaria, these women will be taken captive and led out, like cows, through the gaps in the broken city wall (4:1-3).

Religion without God (4:4-13)

In words of cutting irony, Amos calls the people to the places of worship, encouraging them to continue their zealous but unspiritual religious exercises. The more they do so, the more they will increase their sin. They are corrupt, immoral, ungodly, greedy, lawless and violent, yet they love to make a show of their religious zeal. Amos mocks them by urging them to offer their sacrifices daily (normally, private citizens did this yearly), to offer their tithes every three days (instead of every three years), to present their sacrifices with leaven (which was forbidden), and to advertise their free-will offerings (instead of offering them privately) (4-5).

God sent famine and drought, with the aim that the people would see these things as a punishment from him and so turn from their sins; but they did not (6-8). Mildew and locusts destroyed much of their crops; disease, war and an earthquake killed many of their people; but there was still no sign of repentance (9-11). God will therefore act in a more terrible judgment. It will be too late to repent and Israel will be forced to meet its God (12-13).

God requires repentance (5:1-15)

The prophet again recalls past warnings that the people had consistently ignored. He sees vividly that the result of the people's stubbornness will be the destruction of Israel. Samaria will be conquered and most of Israel's army wiped out (5:1-3).

What God wants is not an increase in religious ceremonies but a turning in heart and life to him. He does not want processions to religious holy places (which, in any case, will be destroyed) but the administration of civil justice that is fair to all (4-7). The all-powerful God will punish those who build up their power through oppressing others (8-9).

When corrupt people are accused by the poor of being dishonest, they respond with increased hatred and cruelty. They use their power to force the poor into greater hardship, then with the money they have dishonestly gained they build bigger and more luxurious houses and gardens. They are able to do all this without fear of opposition, because they bribe government officials and no one dares to speak out against them (10-13. The 'gate' in an ancient eastern city was the business and community centre, the place where people gathered to talk and where the city elders gave judgments in disputes). The people of Israel will escape God's punishment only if they change their ways individually and restore justice in their society (14-15).

The day of the Lord (5:16-27)

God's terrible judgment will result in grief and mourning throughout the nation, in city and country areas alike (16-17). This intervention of God in judgment is commonly called the day of the Lord. Israelites thought that this day would be one of victory and rejoicing for them because their enemies would be destroyed. Amos tells them that when God acts in judgment, he will act against *all* the wicked, and Israel will be the first to suffer. There will be no way of escape, no place of safety, when God's judgment falls (18-20).

Amos repeats that the remedy for the people's troubles is not to increase their religious rituals and ceremonies, but to change their conduct. Feasts and sacrifices are of value only when the offerers are doing God's will in their daily lives. They must behave with justice and uprightness towards their fellows if their religious exercises are to be acceptable to God (21-24).

The people's sacrifices, besides being offered without any thought of moral holiness or obedience, were corrupted through false religion. This was not the way Israelites offered sacrifices in the time of Moses. God will now punish Israel. Their sacrifices will cease, and they, with their foreign gods, will be taken into captivity (25-27).

Pride and its punishment (6:1-14)

Israel's leaders deceive themselves that the nation is secure. They live prosperously and see no possibility of any immediate crisis. Amos reminds them that other nations were stronger than Israel and other cities more prosperous than Samaria, but they still fell to enemy armies (6:1-3). These upper class people live in luxury, without any concern for the injustice that is ruining the nation. When Israel is conquered, they will be in the first group taken into captivity (4-7).

Amos pictures the scene when the enemy lays siege to Samaria. The people die in thousands because of famine and plague. When a person comes to a house to take away the corpse of a relative to burn it, the lone survivor in the house warns him not to speak, and certainly not to mention the name of Yahweh. They do not want to attract God's attention, in case he punishes them even more. They realize that God himself is the one who has sent this catastrophe (8-11).

A horse cannot run up a rocky cliff and a farmer cannot plough the sea, yet the people of Israel have done what seems equally impossible. They have turned justice into injustice, and right into wrong (12). They have also foolishly boasted of their military strength because they have overrun two small towns. God tells them that he will send an army to overrun their whole country, from north to south (13-14).

7:1-9:10 VISIONS OF JUDGMENT

God's patience before judgment (7:1-9)

Farmers paid their taxes by giving the king the first reaping of their harvest. After this a second crop grew up, which provided the main harvest for the people. It was this second crop that Amos, in his vision, saw threatened with destruction from a plague of locusts. If God judged Israel in this way, it might never recover. When Amos pleaded on Israel's behalf for God's mercy, God answered his prayer (7:1-3). God later answered a similar prayer after he had threatened to burn up the land with drought (4-6).

However, when Amos saw the people as a whole persist in their sin, he knew that judgment could no longer be avoided. As a builder tests a wall with a plumb-line to see if it is straight, so God tests Israel according to his perfect standard to see if it is morally upright. He finds that it is crooked beyond repair and must be demolished. Corrupt religion and corrupt administration have been the cause of the

country's failure, and these are things upon which the judgment falls most heavily (7-9).

Amos and Amaziah (7:10-17)

Amaziah the priest heard Amos's preaching at Bethel, and was furious that he so boldly denounced Israel's religious practices. He planned to get rid of the unwelcome prophet by accusing him of treason because of his announcements of judgment on the royal house (10-11; see also v. 9).

The king apparently took no interest in the priest's accusations. Amaziah therefore tried to persuade Amos to return to Judah, where people would welcome his prophecies against Israel and so pay him generously (12-13). Amos replies that he is not a professional prophet and never has been. He is a common farmer whom God called to announce his message to Israel (14-15). In addition he has a message for Amaziah. When Israel is eventually conquered, Amaziah's wife will become a prostitute for the enemy soldiers, his children will be killed, and his land will be divided up by the conquerors (16-17).

Israel nears its end (8:1-14)

Just as the harvest comes to an end and the fruit is gathered into baskets, so Israel has come to its end and will be punished. Celebration will be turned to mourning, and hope will be replaced by despair. When the enemy attacks, the slaughter will be so extensive that bodies will lie unburied in the streets and fields for days (8:1-3).

Amos returns to conditions in Israel to indicate that one reason for the nation's downfall is the upper classes' exploitation of the lower classes (4). Greedy merchants, annoyed that they must stop work whenever there is a religious holy day, can hardly wait for the holy day to pass, so that they can get back to the job of making money. They have no principles of honesty. When selling grain they use undersized measures, and when weighing the buyer's money they use extra heavy weights. They also sell leftover grain, which normally would be given to the poor or fed to cattle (5-6).

The coming judgment will smash the sinful people like an earthquake and overthrow them like a flood (7-8). Not merely physical darkness but spiritual darkness will cover the nation, without even the small amount of light at present supplied by the prophets. In their mourning and distress people will suddenly become hungry for God's word, but they will not find it, no matter how hard they search (9-12). Neither the vigour of the nation's youth nor the imagined power of its false gods will be able to save Israel when God's judgment finally falls (13-14).

No possibility of escape (9:1-10)

In the final vision God causes a shrine to collapse on the heads of the worshippers. The picture is that of God's judgment on the people of Israel because of their false religion (9:1). None will escape his judgment. No place is beyond his reach (2-4). He is the God of nature, the controller of the universe. He has the power to carry out his plans (5-6).

Some Israelites might object that this could not happen to them, because they are God's chosen people. He brought them out of Egypt and he would not send them into a foreign country again. Amos points out that past blessings are not a guarantee of present safety. God directed the movements of other nations, not just Israel, but when people are sinful he will punish them, regardless of their nationality. In this matter Israelites have no advantage over people of other nationalities, such as Ethiopians, Philistines or Syrians. God will destroy Israel, but he will preserve the minority within Israel who remain faithful to him. Through these he will fulfil his purposes (7-8).

Amos gives a final picture of the certain judgment that is to fall on the sinful Israelites. As no pebble or other worthless matter falls through a sieve, so no sinner will escape God's judgment. If people think that because they are Israelites they will not experience God's judgment, they are only deceiving themselves (9-10).

9:11-15 HOPE FOR THE FUTURE

Beyond judgment Amos sees God's forgiveness. Captivity in a foreign land will bring to an end the old division between the northern state of Israel and the southern state of Judah. God will bring the reunited people back into their land, where they will live in security and prosperity under the rule of the restored Davidic dynasty. Israel's rule will extend over other nations, here represented by Edom (11-12). The land will become so productive that grain will grow faster than farmers can harvest it. The reaper will not be able to finish his work before the next planting is due. Cities will be rebuilt and the people will live in happiness and safety (13-15).

The blessings that the prophet pictures here are far greater than those experienced by post-exilic Israel. In the New Testament Amos's picture of the rule of the Davidic king over the nations is applied to the expansion of Christ's kingdom among the Gentiles (Acts 15:13-18; cf. Eph 3:6). No doubt there will be an greater application in the future (cf. Rom 8:19-23; 1 Cor 15:24-28; Rev 22:1-5).

Obadiah

BACKGROUND

The book of Obadiah belongs to the period that followed Jerusalem's final collapse and ultimate destruction by the Babylonians in 587 BC. Nothing is known of Obadiah's ministry apart from what is contained in the short book that bears his name, though he must have been one of the few genuine prophets left in Judah at the time of its overthrow and captivity. His book is concerned with God's judgment on the nation Edom.

Edom and the fall of Jerusalem

When the armies of Babylon finally broke through the walls of Jerusalem and destroyed the city, the Edomites joined in, taking wicked delight in helping to wipe out the last traces of the ancient Israelite nation (Ps 137:7; Ezek 35:1-5,12,15). The prophet Obadiah, writing some time later, announced God's judgment on Edom for acting with such hostility against its brother nation, whom it should rather have helped.

(The nation Israel was descended from Jacob, the nation Edom from Jacob's brother Esau; see Gen 25:23-26; 32:28; 36:1,8-9. For examples of the hatred that existed, first between the two brothers and later between the two nations descended from them, see Gen 27:36,39-45; Num 20:14-21; 2 Sam 8:13-14; 1 Kings 11:15-16; 2 Kings 8:20-22; 14:7; 16:6; 2 Chron 25:11-12; 28:17.)

Edom was situated south of Judah, between the Dead Sea and the Gulf of Aqabah, the north-eastern arm of the Red Sea. (See maps located in the commentaries on Numbers and Hosea.) It was a land of rugged mountains that provided it with strong defences against enemy attacks. Chief among its mountains was Mt Seir, after which the nation was sometimes called (Gen 32:3; 36:8-9; Deut 2:1-5; Ezek 35:2,15).

The chief towns of Edom were Sela (Petra), Bozrah and Teman in the inland regions, and Ezion-geber on the Gulf of Aqabah. The Edomites, particularly those from the district of Teman, were famous for their wisdom and cunning (Job 2:11; Jer 49:7), but no amount of cleverness would deliver them from the impending judgment from God. As

Obadiah predicted, the nation Edom was subsequently destroyed and its land devastated by enemy invasions (Mal 1:2-4).

OBADIAH'S MESSAGE

Edom's sin (1-14)

The Edomites thought their land was unconquerable because of the defence system that they had built throughout their rocky mountains. Obadiah warns them that no matter how high up the mountains they go or how strong they make their defences, nothing will save them from the coming destruction. Already the enemy armies are preparing to attack Edom (1-4).

A house burglar steals only what he wants, and leaves the remainder of the goods in the house; a vineyard worker picks the grapes that are ripe and leaves the rest; but when the enemy soldiers plunder Edom they will take everything. They will seize even the treasures that the Edomites have hidden in caves in the mountains (5-6).

Edom prided itself in its political skill and military strategy. Its leaders thought they were cleverer than the leaders of neighbouring nations, and often used their cunning to cheat their allies. Their shame in defeat will therefore be the greater when they discover that some of these neighbouring nations, who they thought were trusted allies, have betrayed them and helped bring about their downfall (7-9).

Obadiah now gives the reason why God will punish Edom so severely. When th Babylonian armies attacked and plundered Jerusalem, Edom did nothing to help its brother nation. Rather the opposite; it gladly helped the attackers (10-11). The Edomites were glad to see Jerusalem plundered, and even joined in the plundering. Worse than that, they helped the Babylonians capture the Jerusalemites by cutting off the escape route of those who tried to flee (12-14).

The day of the Lord (15-21)

In the day of the Lord, God will intervene in human affairs and punish sinners according to their sins. The Edomites celebrated their plunder of Jerusalem by holding wild drinking parties among the ruins of the temple on Mt Zion. They, as well as Jerusalem's other enemies, will now be drunk in a different way. They will drink the cup of God's wrath until, unable to stand any longer, they will stagger and fall (15-16).

Having punished Jerusalem's enemies, God will release his people from captivity and bring them back to their homeland. He will restore holiness to Mt Zion, but send a fitting judgment upon Edom. He will destroy Edom as a fire burns up a field of dry grass (17-18).

From Jerusalem the re-established Israelite nation will expand south into Edomite territory, west over Philistine territory, north over its own territory that the Philistines had seized, and east across Jordan to retake former territory there (19; cf. Amos 9:12). Captives will be taken from various camps in foreign countries and resettled permanently in their own land, from Phoenicia in the north to the Negeb in the south (20). Israel will then rule over former enemies, showing clearly to everyone that God controls all history. Sovereign rule belongs to him (21).

Jonah

BACKGROUND

In contrast to other prophetical books, the book of Jonah does not record the name of its author. The book takes its name from the chief person in the story, a prophet who at one time correctly predicted the growth of the northern kingdom Israel under Jeroboam II (see 2 Kings 14:23,25 and associated map). A further contrast to other prophetical books is that Jonah contains little of the prophet's actual preaching. The book is mostly narrative and, again in contrast to most of the prophetical writings, is mostly in prose.

Purpose of the book

During the reign of Jeroboam II (793-753 BC), the nation Israel enjoyed such prosperity that people easily developed selfish nationalistic attitudes. (For conditions of the time see background to Hosea.) Even God's prophet Jonah was affected by this narrow-minded spirit.

No doubt Jonah was satisfied to see the fulfilment of his forecasts of Jeroboam's victories. He would have been far more satisfied to see the downfall of Assyria, whose rising power was about the only threat that Israel saw to its own independence. Already Assyria's capital Nineveh was threatened by an enemy from the north. Jonah was therefore surprised and angry when God told him to go and warn Nineveh of the coming attack. He was to urge the people to repent of their wickedness so that they might avoid a terrifying destruction (Jonah 3:4-5,10).

Jonah's first reaction was to refuse to go, for he would rather see Nineveh destroyed than spared such a fitting judgment. Jonah needed to learn that God was the controller of all nations, and he would have mercy on any people or nation as he wished, even on the wicked Ninevites.

As for God's people, since they had often experienced the love and mercy of God, they should show similar love and mercy to others. God took no pleasure in destroying people, and neither should they. Rather they should, like God, desire their repentance and forgiveness (Jonah 4:11; cf. Acts 11:18; Rom 3:29; 9:15).

OUTLINE

1:1-17 JONAH'S DISOBEDIENCE AND ITS RESULTS

When God commanded Jonah to go and warn the sinful people of Nineveh of coming judgment, Jonah not only refused but fled in the opposite direction. He boarded a ship and headed for the distant Mediterranean port of Tarshish, somewhere in the region of Spain (1:1-3). But God determined to bring Jonah back. His first action was to send a fierce storm that threatened to sink the ship. The seamen, who were not Hebrews, prayed to their gods to save them, and tried to persuade Jonah to pray to his (4-6).

On seeing that their prayers brought no results, the seamen concluded that the storm must have been a supernatural punishment upon someone in the ship. When they drew lots to identify the guilty person, the lot indicated Jonah (7). Jonah confessed his sin, acknowledging that this was God's judgment upon him. He suggested that the only way the seamen would save their lives would be to throw him overboard (8-12).

Although they were pagans, the seamen pitied Jonah and respected Jonah's God (which was in sharp contrast to Jonah's lack of pity for the pagan Ninevites and lack of respect for God). Only when they were convinced that nothing else would save them did they throw Jonah overboard (13-16). Jonah apparently lost consciousness and was drowning, when God saved his life by sending a great fish to swallow him (17).

2:1-10 A PSALM OF THANKSGIVING

Jonah regained consciousness inside the great fish. This almost unbelievable experience caused him to believe that it was God's way of saving his life. From inside the fish he then thanked God for saving him from drowning. He seems to have remembered phrases from various psalms and prayers used in

355

temple worship, and he brought these together to form his own prayer of thanksgiving.

In the opening words of the psalm Jonah recalled his prayer of desperation as he found himself overcome by the rough seas. He was sinking into what he feared was the world of the dead (2:1-3). As he sank deeper, the pressure of water increased and he could feel himself losing consciousness. He felt that his end had come and that he would be cut off from God for ever (4-6). The next thing he knew was that he was alive, inside the great fish. God had answered his prayer and saved him (7-8).

Jonah had no idea how he would return to the world of his fellow human beings, but he knew that if God had done this much for him, the same God would finish his work and save him fully. In confidence he offered thanks for his salvation, even though it was still not complete. God rewarded his faith and gratitude by delivering him from the fish (9-10).

Various attempts have been made to prove and disprove that a person could be swallowed by a great fish or whale and still live. Regardless of these arguments, the events described in Jonah were still the miraculous work of God. It was highly unlikely that such an animal should have been at the spot where Jonah was thrown overboard, that it should have swallowed him, and that the place it vomited him up should have been near the mainland shore. The entire course of events to this point, as well as what was to follow, was a demonstration of God's sovereignty. He had complete power over the natural world, he was in control of events, and he showed mercy on sinners.

3:1-4:11 THE NINEVITES' REPENTANCE

Jonah's preaching in Nineveh (3:1-10)

God repeated his command to Jonah to go and preach in Nineveh, and this time Jonah obeyed (3:1-3). God's message was that within forty days Nineveh would, because of its wickedness, be overthrown. The Ninevites, leaders and common people alike, heeded the warning and turned in repentance to God (4-5). The king even issued a decree commanding a moral reformation in the city (6-9). As a result of the Ninevites' repentance, God withdrew his threat of destruction (10).

A lesson about mercy (4:1-11)

It now became clear why Jonah did not want to preach in Nineveh. He wanted the Ninevites to be destroyed, not spared; he wanted them to be punished, not forgiven. He knew that God was merciful to sinners, but he wanted this divine blessing reserved solely for the people of Israel. He would rather die than see Gentiles forgiven the same as Israelites (4:1-3).

God wanted to make Jonah see that he had no right to be angry, but Jonah refused to listen. Apparently still hoping that God would change his mind and destroy Nineveh, he went outside the city, built himself a temporary shelter, and waited to see what would happen at the end of the forty days (4-5).

Since Jonah had not responded to God's earlier rebuke, God now gave him an object lesson in sympathy. When Jonah's shelter proved inadequate to protect him from the heat of the sun, God made a big leafy plant grow up to provide Jonah with shade. As a result Jonah felt thankful. Then God made the plant die, and exposed Jonah to the blazing sun and a burning wind. As a result Jonah became angry (6-8).

Jonah did not want the plant to die, and neither did God want the people of Nineveh to die. Jonah felt sorry for a plant that he had not made and that lasted only one day. How much more should God feel sorry for the people of Nineveh whom he had made and who, in their ignorance, had faced total destruction (9-11).

Micah

BACKGROUND

The eighth century BC brought some remarkable developments in the political and social life of Palestine, both in the northern kingdom Israel and in the southern kingdom Judah. Agriculture and commerce thrived, but with the rapid growth of wealth came the temptations of greed, corruption, injustice and immorality. This in turn resulted in rebukes and warnings from God's messengers, the prophets. Micah was the last of four prophets of this period whose writings have been preserved in the Bible.

Amos and Hosea, the first of this group, brought God's message mainly to the northern kingdom. The other two, Isaiah and Micah, were concerned more with the southern kingdom, and prophesied during the same period (Isa 1:1; Micah 1:1). Both were particularly concerned with the sins of the capital city, Jerusalem. There are many similarities between their books, and it has even been suggested that Micah might have been one of Isaiah's disciples (cf. Isa 8:16).

Social conditions

Judah's prosperity was not evenly spread throughout the population. Those who gained most from the flourishing economic activity were the merchants, officials and upper class city people in general. They became wealthy largely by exploiting poorer people such as farmers, and with their wealth came social and political power. Corruption in the law courts made it easy for them to do as they wished, with the result that as they increased their wealth, the poor were driven into greater poverty. (See also background notes to Amos and Hosea.)

This cruel injustice was hateful to God, and through his prophets he warned of the judgment that would fall on the nation if the people did not change their ways. Isaiah was a person of influence in Jerusalem, an adviser to the king who used his position to try to develop a greater concern for God's standards in the government of the nation. Micah, by contrast, was from a small farming village, and was particularly concerned about the plight of the poor farmers. He condemned the greed of the rich people in the cities, and defended those who were the victims of their oppression.

One of the farmers' main problems came from the economic pressure put on them by people in positions of power and influence. Because of the corruption of the officials and merchants, farmers were forced to borrow from the wealthy to keep themselves in business. The wealthy lent money at interest so high that the farmers found it impossible to repay their debts. The creditors then seized the farmers' possessions as payment — firstly clothing and household items (Micah 2:8), then, when these were not enough, the farmers' houses and land (Micah 2:1-3,9). In the end the farmers became tenants who were forced to rent their land from their new masters, which increased their burden even more.

This whole sorry state of affairs showed no thought for the rights of others, no understanding of the nature of true religion, and no knowledge of the character of God. Micah told the people that as long as their lives were characterized by such behaviour, they could never be pleasing to God, no matter how much they appeared to worship him by religious ceremonies (Micah 6:6-8). Unless the people turned from their sinful practices, Judah was heading for certain judgment (Micah 3:12; 6:16).

Political events

Micah prophesied during the reigns of the Judean kings Jotham, Ahaz and Hezekiah. (The overall extent of these three reigns was approximately from 740 to 687 BC.) Political conditions were reasonably stable during the reign of Jotham, but during the reign of Ahaz they became very unsettled. Ahaz weakened Judah's independence and almost ruined its economy through buying Assyrian protection against other enemies. This was a policy that Isaiah strongly opposed (2 Kings 16:1-9; Isa 7:1-9; 8:5-8). (For relevant maps of the period see commentary on Hosea.)

The next king, Hezekiah, reformed Judah's religion and set out to rid Judah of all Assyrian influence. There is no doubt that Hezekiah was influenced in his reforms by the preaching of Micah (Jer 26:18-19). He was also influenced by Isaiah. But when, instead of trusting in God for victory against Assyria, he trusted in military alliances with Egypt and other nations, Isaiah opposed him (2 Kings 18:1-7; Isa 30:1-3,15). On one occasion Jerusalem was saved from what could have been a crushing siege by Assyria only through the miraculous intervention of God (2 Kings 18:13-19:37).

During the time of Micah's activity the northern kingdom Israel was conquered by Assyria and the people taken into captivity (in 722 BC; see 2 Kings 18:9-12). From that time on, the southern kingdom Judah was all that remained of the once united kingdom over which David had ruled. In contrast to the usual practice of referring to the northern and southern kingdoms as Israel and Judah respectively, Micah often makes no distinction. He uses the names Israel and Jacob to apply to the people in general. The comments below will follow Micah's more general usage of the name Israel, though it should be remembered that Micah is mainly concerned with the southern kingdom.

OUTLINE

1:1-3:12   Samaria and Jerusalem doomed
4:1-5:15   The ideal kingdom
6:1-7:20   God accuses and the people reply

1:1-3:12 SAMARIA AND JERUSALEM DOOMED

A picture of coming destruction (1:1-16)

The prophet Micah was from a country village in the Judean foothills between the central mountain range and the coastal plain. He was probably a farmer, and he directed his attacks at the upper class city dwellers who drove the farmers into poverty. They lived in luxury by exploiting the poor. As a Judean he was concerned mainly with conditions in his country's capital, Jerusalem, but he also attacked the northern capital, Samaria (1:1).

Micah pictures the two cities crushed by the enemy, as if destroyed by the combined force of a volcano and an earthquake. This is God's judgment on the two kingdoms because of the sins of the people in Samaria and Jerusalem (2-5). Instead of being faithful to God, they went after idols. They were like a prostitute who goes after lovers. These idols and all the sacred objects associated with them (likened to the rewards a prostitute gains from her lovers) will be smashed to pieces, and Samaria will be left a heap of ruins (6-7). All these evils cause Micah unspeakable grief. They had their origins in the northern kingdom, but they have now spread to the southern kingdom. Consequently, it too will be punished (8-9).

In a short poem, announced no doubt with much feeling, the prophet pictures the advance of an enemy army as it moves along the coastal plain then turns east over the hills to attack Jerusalem. He sees the distress it brings in the various towns along the way as people are slaughtered and captured (10-11). Some flee with their goods loaded on horses and chariots; others look for safety by buying protection from better fortified towns; but their efforts are useless. Nothing will save them from defeat and captivity (12-16).

Those who oppress the poor (2:1-13)

To an Israelite, a person's land was his most prized possession. It was not only his means of income, but also part of the family heritage handed down from generation to generation. But the greedy money-lenders cared nothing for that. Micah pictures them lying awake at night working out schemes to seize the farmer's land and, if possible, take the farmer and his family as slaves. They have money and power, and therefore they can do as they wish without thought for the rights of others (2:1-2; cf. 1 Kings 21:1-16).

God announces that he will punish them by treating them as they treat others. *They* will be oppressed, *their* land will be seized and divided up (by the invading armies), and *they* will be taken away as captives (3-5).

Some of the hearers object that Micah should not preach like this (6). Micah and the people alike should know that a God of patience will not hastily punish his people and will, in fact, reward those who do good to others (7). The trouble is, says Micah, that the people are not doing good to others. They take the property of those who have done them no wrong, and drive honest women and children from their homes (8-9). They, in turn, will be driven out of *their* homes. God gave them the land of Canaan as a place of rest, but they have made it unclean. Therefore, they must be removed from it (10).

The people do not want to hear moral teaching from God's prophet. They would rather hear from the false prophets who, being greedy and dishonest like themselves, talk only of the pleasures of life (11).

Although the nation will go into captivity, there will always be a minority in the nation who remain faithful to God. God will bring them back to their land. In Babylon they will be like a flock of sheep locked up in a foreign fold, but their shepherd, God, will break the wall of the fold and lead them out. He will take them into a new fold in their own land (12-13).

Corrupt leaders (3:1-12)

The nation's civil leaders are the first to be condemned, because they have reversed the standards of justice. Greedy officials cooperate with corrupt judges to exploit the people for their own benefit. Because of the cruel oppression that they have practised, God will not save them from the fury of the enemy, no matter how much they cry for his help (3:1-4).

Religious leaders are also condemned. Prophets preach words of comfort and approval to those who give them food and money, but announce judgment on those who refuse. Such men will cease to be prophets, because God will not speak through them (5-7). God will speak only through those (such as Micah) who refuse to alter his message to please the hearers (8).

Priests are just as corrupt as the civil leaders and prophets, and do religious service only for those who pay them well. Yet all these leaders think that God will protect them simply because his temple is situated in their city (9-11).

God can tolerate the corruption of these leaders no longer. He will smash their city, and their temple with it (12). (As a result of this prophecy, the king Hezekiah determined to take stronger action in reforming Judah. The success of his reformation won for Judah a postponement of the threatened judgment; see Jer 26:18-19.)

4:1-5:15 THE IDEAL KINGDOM

Shame replaced by glory (4:1-5:1)

Previously Micah recorded God's promise that the people of Israel would come from captivity back to their land (see 2:12-13). He now looks beyond that to the greater day when God's ideal king reigns and Jerusalem is the religious centre of the world. People of all nations desire to worship God and learn his law, with the result that there is universal peace and contentment (4:1-4). This future hope encourages Micah and his few fellow believers to be more faithful to God now (5).

Micah sees the people in captivity as a flock of sheep that have been attacked, injured and scattered. The remains of this flock will be gathered again, healed, and brought back to their own land to become a strong nation once more (6-8). The prophet then pictures the siege of Jerusalem and the suffering of its inhabitants. They will be taken captive to Babylon, but after a period God will bring them back (9-10).

Another illustration of the triumph of God's people is given in the form of a vision where the prophet sees the overthrow of a great army that besieges Jerusalem. The army is composed of soldiers of many nations, who await their chance to break down the walls and plunder the city. They scoff at the people and dishonour the king, not realizing that God has brought them together so that he might destroy them the more easily — all in one place at one time. They will be punished by God's almighty power, crushed as the grain on the threshing floor is crushed under the hoofs of the oxen (11-5:1).

(There was in the time of Micah a siege of Jerusalem similar to the one described here. On that occasion Assyria was the nation that besieged Jerusalem and mocked God, but God miraculously saved the city, preserved his people and destroyed the attackers; see 2 Kings 18:13-19:37.)

God's chosen king (5:2-15)

Ruling over Israel in this golden age will be a king specially chosen by God. He will have only a humble beginning, being born in the small Judean town of Bethlehem. But his ancestry will go back to ancient times, to the great king David, who himself came from Bethlehem and whose dynasty was guaranteed by God to last for ever. This king will have full right to David's throne, and through him God's promises to David will be fulfilled (2; cf. 1 Sam 17:12; 2 Sam 7:16; Matt 2:6; John 7:42).

Until this person is born, however, Israel will continue to be troubled by enemies; but when he comes, Israel's scattered believers will be united under his rule. He will rule in the strength that comes from God to nourish and protect God's people (3-4).

Israel will have plenty of good leaders and will be safe from all enemies. Any who try to invade Israel, whether they be Assyrians or other enemies, will find themselves driven back and conquered by Israel (5-6). The people of God will take his truth to all nations. Like dew they will be the means of refreshment and new life to those who seek God. But like a lion they will be the means of destruction to those who oppose him (7-9).

People of the new Israel will now enjoy God fully, because God will remove all that previously kept them from trusting in him. At various times Israel and Judah had been tempted to trust in military strength, fortified cities, occult practices,

Baal worship and heathen armies, but now all such things will be destroyed (10-15).

6:1-7:20 GOD ACCUSES AND THE PEOPLE REPLY

What God desires (6:1-16)

Returning to conditions in his own time, Micah pictures a courtroom where, with the heavens and earth as witnesses, God accuses his people of unfaithfulness (6:1-2). God recalls the great things he has done for them, as if asking why they treat him so badly in return (3-5).

The people's reply shows their misunderstanding. They ask what sort of worship God wants. Does he want sacrifices that are exact according to the letter of the law? Or an increase in the number of sacrifices? Or more lavish sacrifices? Or even heathen sacrifices? If God tells them what he wants, they will try to please him (6-7).

God replies that he has already shown them (particularly through Amos, Hosea and Isaiah) what he wants, namely, justice and love towards their fellow human beings, and faithfulness and humility towards God. Correct sacrifices and enthusiastic religious exercises are of no value if the people do not have right attitudes and right conduct (8).

Micah warns that God sees the rich merchants throughout Judah's cities and he takes note of their crooked business methods. When selling grain they use undersized measures, and when weighing the buyer's money they use extra heavy weights. They become rich through violence, lies and trickery (9-12). God will make sure that these cheats do not enjoy the good things they have built up for themselves. Through drought, famine and enemy attacks he will destroy their dishonestly gained wealth, and finally destroy them (13-16).

Sin, repentance and forgiveness (7:1-20)

Speaking as one of the genuine believers in the nation, Micah confesses that God's accusations are true. The prophet can find nothing to satisfy him in the life of the people as a whole. Judah as a nation is fruitless and of no use to God (7:1).

All around him Micah sees a society that is in a state of moral decay. Gang warfare is widespread, and law-breakers buy protection from judges. Rich businessmen and other influential persons bribe government officials to cooperate with them in their evil plans (2-3). Even the best of them cannot be trusted. Treachery and deceit are so widely practised that people cannot trust even their friends and relatives (4-6).

Those who remain faithful to God know that they are part of a nation that is doomed for judgment. But they know also that somehow God will save the faithful (7). Micah acknowledges the justice of God's punishment in allowing the people to be taken into captivity. Enemies may rejoice because of their conquest of Israel and Judah, but they themselves will in turn be conquered. Those among God's people who have remained faithful to him will then return to their homeland (8-10). Jerusalem will be rebuilt, and people from other nations will return with the believing Jews to settle in the new Jerusalem. Other nations will then find that it is their turn to suffer devastation because of their sins (11-13).

In a concluding prayer Micah appeals to God, the great shepherd, to rescue, protect and feed his people. He asks that God will work miracles for them as he did in the time of Moses (14-15). People of other nations will no longer fight against Israel, but will humbly acknowledge God's almighty power and submit to his rule (16-17).

These thoughts prompt a final expression of praise from Micah. No words can describe the excellencies of Israel's God. He is a God of mercy, faithfulness and constant love, and only because of these characteristics does he forgive the sins of his people. His punishment of them is temporary, but his forgiveness is eternal (18-20).

Nahum

BACKGROUND

Most of the short book of Nahum is concerned with the coming judgment of Assyria, and particularly with the destruction of its capital, Nineveh. The Assyrians had been cruel enemies of Israel and Judah, but Nahum saw that the day of judgment for them was now approaching.

The Assyrian oppression

Assyria had risen to power more than a century before the time of Nahum. From its base in Mesopotamia, it established an empire that soon began to spread over nations of the Palestine region. It conquered Syria in 732 BC, and Israel (the northern part of the divided Israelite kingdom) in 722 BC, taking the peoples of both nations into captivity (2 Kings 15:29; 16:9; 17:3-6).

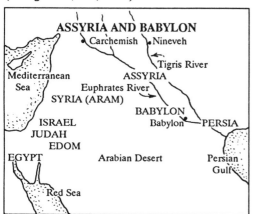

With the fall of Israel, the southern kingdom of Judah became open to Assyrian aggression, and for the next one hundred years had a constant struggle to keep itself independent. At times Judah was under the power of Assyria and had to pay it heavy taxes; at other times it managed to reassert its independence; but always it was in a state of tension, if not conflict, with Assyria (2 Kings 16:7-20; 18:7-37; 19:37; 2 Chron 28:16,20-21; 30:6; 33:11).

By the time of Josiah, who began to reign in Judah in 640 BC, Assyria's power had weakened considerably. This enabled Josiah to carry out much needed religious and social reforms without the threat of interference from Assyria. During Josiah's reign there was a revival of prophetic activity in Judah, with the ministry of the prophets Zephaniah, Jeremiah, Nahum and Habakkuk. (For the relation of Josiah's reforms to this prophetic activity see background notes to Zephaniah.)

With Assyria weakening and Babylon growing stronger, Nahum foresaw what the people of Judah had desperately wanted for more than a century, the end of Assyrian power. His description of Nineveh's overthrow is dramatic, colourful and full of feeling. He rejoiced that at last a fitting divine judgment was to fall upon the nation whose cruelty made it one of the most barbarous oppressors in history. In 612 BC Nineveh was conquered as Nahum foretold, falling to the armies of Babylon.

OUTLINE

1:1-15   The power of God
2:1-3:19   The destruction of Nineveh

1:1-15 THE POWER OF GOD

God is the great judge, the all-powerful ruler of the universe. On the one hand he is patient with the rebellious, but on the other he is zealous for righteousness. His punishment of the guilty is severe, but it is also just (1:1-3a). Through storms, winds, droughts and earthquakes he sends judgments that bring total destruction. When his wrath is poured out on sinners, no one can escape (3b-6).

Being so mighty, God can protect those who trust in him, and destroy those who fight against him (7-8). Nahum warns all enemies that it is useless to plot against God, for he can destroy them with one blow. He will not need to strike twice (9-11).

Turning to address the people of God, Nahum promises that God will not punish them further. He will free them from the enemy's power (12-13). Nahum tells the Assyrians that their gods will be destroyed (14), but tells the Judeans that their God will be victorious. Soon a messenger will bring them news of the overthrow of Assyria, whereupon they should worship God with thanks, sincerity and joy (15).

2:1-3:19 THE DESTRUCTION OF NINEVEH

Destroyed because of cruelty (2:1-13)

Chapters 2 and 3 consist of two separate poems on the same subject, the destruction of Nineveh and the reasons for it. Nahum begins his graphic description of the attack on Nineveh by calling upon the watchman on the city wall to alert the city that the enemy is approaching. God is now going to destroy those who destroyed Israel and oppressed Judah (2:1-2).

The prophet pictures the brightly uniformed soldiers, the gleaming chariots and the prancing horses as the enemy army approaches the city walls. The officers who lead the attack are so keen for battle that they stumble in their haste (3-5). Enemy soldiers break open the water gates, flooding the city and throwing it into confusion. Some of the soldiers capture the queen and the palace harem, while others plunder the city (6-9).

So ruthless and cruel were the Assyrians in their treatment of the nations they attacked, that the prophet likens them to wild animals. They are like ferocious lions that savagely attacked smaller helpless animals and then dragged them back to their den. But now the lions are dead and the den is empty. The few surviving Ninevites look with horror on their devastated city (10-13).

Destroyed because of greed (3:1-19)

Not only was Assyria cruel, but it was also greedy. Often it conquered nations solely to plunder them. Nahum likens it to a prostitute, for it thought only of money and pleasure and gave no thought for morality. The prophet gives another vivid picture of the battle scene in Nineveh as God acts in judgment against the guilty people (3:1-4).

Like a prostitute Nineveh dressed herself with lavish adornments and lived in luxury by tempting and deceiving others. Her splendour will be replaced by shame. She will be like a prostitute who is stripped and made to walk naked in the streets. Those whom she deceived and robbed will now laugh at her (5-7).

Nahum reminds Nineveh of what happened to the city of Thebes in Egypt. It was well defended and had strong allies, but it was conquered and its people taken into captivity (8-10). The same will happen to Nineveh. Its outlying fortresses will be demolished as easily as ripe figs are shaken from a tree. When troops in the city hear of this they will lose courage and the city will be overthrown (11-13). They may store water in case of a siege, and strengthen the city walls to withstand the battering rams, but all their precautions and preparations will prove to be useless. The city will be burnt to the ground and left as bare as a field that has been stripped by locusts (14-15a).

The merchants, officials and others involved in Nineveh's commerce are likened to a swarm of locusts. But just as locusts fly away when the sun gets hot, so these will flee when Nineveh is attacked (15b-17). Assyria's leaders will be killed, leaving the people leaderless and an easy prey for the attackers. Assyria will fall, never to rise again. Those who suffered from its cruelty will then rejoice (18-19).

Habakkuk

BACKGROUND

Although Habakkuk does not mention the Judean kings of his time, the contents of his book indicate the era in which he prophesied. He announced his message during the closing years of the kingdom of Judah, when Babylon had risen to power and Judah was threatened with conquest.

The prophet and the Babylonians

With its conquest of Assyria in 612 BC, Babylon became the leading power in the region of Mesopotamia and Palestine. Then in 605 BC it defeated Egypt at Carchemish on the Euphrates River (see map located in the commentary on Nahum). Since Egypt had earlier defeated Judah, this meant that Babylon replaced Egypt as Judah's overlord (2 Kings 23:33-35; 24:7; Dan 1:1-4).

When Judah rebelled against Babylon, the Babylonian armies captured Jerusalem, took all the best people into captivity, and appointed a new king over those who remained in the city (597 BC; 2 Kings 24:10-17). When, after some years, the new king also rebelled, Babylon finally lost patience. It destroyed Jerusalem and took most of the remaining people into captivity. This was the end of the kingdom of Judah (587 BC; 2 Kings 25:1-12).

The prophet Habakkuk lived during the early days of this build-up of Babylonian control over Judah. His book records how he argued with God when he learnt that God was preparing Babylon to be his instrument to punish Judah. Habakkuk was confused, perhaps angry, because he knew that the Babylonians were worse sinners than the Judeans. God assured Habakkuk that any of the Judeans who remained faithful to him had no cause for fear. Although the nation as a whole would be destroyed, the faithful would enjoy his favour.

God had a message for the Babylonians as well. They had no cause for self-satisfaction. They had shown an intolerable arrogance in conquering God's people, and therefore they too would suffer a divine judgment.

Habakkuk's faith was strengthened through his dialogue with God. He may not have received the detailed explanations from God that he was looking for, but he received a revelation of God's power and wisdom that gave him a better knowledge of God and a determination to remain faithful to him.

OUTLINE

1:1-2:5   Habakkuk complains and God answers
2:6-20   Babylon's sins
3:1-19   Habakkuk trusts in God's judgment

1:1-2:5 HABAKKUK COMPLAINS AND GOD ANSWERS

First complaint and answer (1:1-11)

Despite Habakkuk's zealous preaching and fervent prayer, Judah shows no sign of improvement. All around him the prophet sees violence, lawlessness, injustice and all sorts of other social evils. Knowing God is holy and just, he asks God how long will he allow this wickedness to go unpunished (1:1-4).

God replies that he is preparing the Babylonians (Chaldeans) to punish Judah. God has not told the Judeans about this, because he knows they would not believe him. They would not believe that he would use such a wicked nation to punish his own people (5-6). Then follows a description of the Babylonians that demonstrates the ruthlessness of their sweeping conquests. Arrogant and powerful, they do as they wish regardless of laws, justice, kings or armies (7-11).

Second complaint and answer (1:12-2:5)

Habakkuk replies to God by asking a further question. If Judah is God's people for ever, and if God is holy, how can he use Babylon to punish Judah when the Babylonians are more wicked than the Judeans (12-13)? It seems to Habakkuk that God has the same standards as the Babylonians. They treat the people of nations as if they were no better than fish in the sea — there to be caught for the fisherman's enjoyment (14-15). The Babylonians' power is their god. Their appetite for conquest will never be satisfied. They will go on killing and plundering (16-17).

Having made his complaint, the prophet awaits God's answer (2:1). The answer is that the greed, pride and violence of the Babylonians will be the means of their downfall. Some time may pass before the judgment falls, but it certainly will fall. Wickedness always brings defeat in the end, just as moral uprightness always leads to victory. There is a message in this for the Judeans also: the greedy are never satisfied, but the righteous find genuine contentment in their loyalty to God (2-5).

2:6-20 BABYLON'S SINS

The prophet now announces judgment on evildoers, listing five sins that God must punish. He introduces each condemnation with the words, 'Woe to him who . . .' (GNB: 'You are doomed!'). The evildoer here is probably Babylon, but the condemnation has an application also to the Judeans. In fact, it applies to people of any age and race.

The lust for power and wealth (2:6-11)

To illustrate Babylon's lust for power, the prophet refers to the practice of money-lending, which was the cause of much injustice and hardship in society. Babylon is like a merciless money-lender who, by charging high interest that the debtor cannot repay, gets as many people into his power as possible. But these enslaved people will suddenly arise and overthrow their wicked master. They will do to him what he previously did to them (6-8).

Babylon has made itself wealthy and secure by treating other nations shamefully. It is like a bird that builds its nest high in a tree away from trouble, where it can live in ease and comfort. But Babylon's luxury will be a witness against it in the day of judgment, and so ensure for it a fitting punishment (9-11).

Destruction, cruelty and idolatry (2:12-20)

In its ruthless conquests Babylon destroyed cities and nations, often with the sole aim of enriching itself. It seized the wealth and manpower of these nations and used them to make its own national capital magnificent. It does not realize that God alone is ruler of the world, and the great city that Babylon has built will one day be burnt to the ground (12-14).

God used Babylon to punish other nations, a judgment that the prophet likens to a cup of strong drink that is given to a person to make him drunk. But the Babylonians went beyond the limits that God set. They cruelly butchered people and took delight in mocking their victims. God will therefore punish the Babylonians and they will be the ones to drink God's cup of punishment. They will be drunk and others will mock them. They will become the victims of violence, and their land, flocks, cities and people will be destroyed (15-17).

Finally, the idolatry of the Babylonians is condemned. They thought their idols gave them victory, but such lifeless creations are powerless. They can do nothing but deceive those who trust in them. The living God will show that he alone is the controller of the world (18-20).

3:1-19 HABAKKUK TRUSTS IN GOD'S JUDGMENT

The psalm of Chapter 3 has no direct connection with Judah and the Babylonians. Nevertheless, it is relevant to what Habakkuk has just written, for it describes the appearance of God in his work of judging the nations and saving his people. The psalm is introduced by what appears to be the name of the tune to which it was sung (3:1).

Habakkuk recalls the mighty works that God has done for his people in the past, and he prays that God will act on their behalf again. However, he knows that when God's anger is stirred against sinners, Israel's enemies may not be the only ones to suffer. God's people also are sinners, and therefore the prophet prays for God's mercy when he deals with them (2).

God's judgment is pictured in a number of illustrations, some of which appear to be taken from the story of Israel's escape from Egypt and journey to Canaan under Moses. The judgment is like a thunderstorm that is seen approaching over the tops of the southern mountains (3-4); like a plague from which no one escapes (5); like an earthquake that terrorizes the nations and shakes the mountains (6); like a desert wind that blows down the Arab's tents (7); like the overthrow of enemies in battle, whether by armies or by the spectacular intervention of the forces of nature (8-9); like a flood that sweeps everything away (10); like an eclipse of the sun that leaves the earth in darkness (11); like the triumph of a warrior who kills his enemies and saves his people (12-15).

The prophet trembles as he thinks of such a judgment. His only hope is to trust in the controlling justice and mercy of God (16). Fields and flocks may be destroyed, but he will remain faithful to God. He will rest contented in the knowledge that a God of infinite wisdom and power knows what he is doing, and his will is perfect. Such deep trust is the answer to the questions, doubts and complaints that he had earlier expressed (17-19).

Zephaniah

BACKGROUND

From the information given in the biblical records, it seems that Zephaniah was the first prophet to appear in Judah since the conclusion of Isaiah and Micah's ministry seventy years earlier. His preaching marked the beginning of a new era of prophetic activity in Judah, but it was an era that also saw the destruction of Jerusalem and the end of the kingdom of Judah.

A prophet in Jerusalem

For much of the seventy years before Zephaniah, the king over Judah was the wicked Manasseh. After his fifty-five years on the throne, Judah was in a worse spiritual condition than the original Canaanites, whom God had destroyed. His reign was marked by cruelty, bloodshed, immorality and foreign religious practices of every kind. The damage he did to Judah could not be fully corrected by any king who came after him, and it resulted in the destruction of Judah (2 Kings 21:1-9,16; 23:26-27).

Manasseh's son Amon followed his father's policies, but after a reign of only two years he was murdered. The leaders of Judah were by now tired of political and social violence, so they executed Amon's murderers and put Amon's eight year old son Josiah on the throne (640 BC). In this way they could act as advisers to the king and so develop a national policy that would restore justice and stability to the nation (2 Kings 21:19-22:2).

By the time he was twenty years of age, Josiah had developed his own national policy and had begun religious reforms that lasted many years (2 Chron 34:3-4). (For details see 2 Kings 22:3-23:25; 2 Chron 34:1-35:27.) The ministry of the prophet Zephaniah may have had some part in prompting the king to introduce his reforms. Zephaniah was a young man probably not much older than Josiah and appears to have been related to him (both being descended from Hezekiah; see Zeph 1:1; cf. 2 Kings 20:21; 21:18,24).

Zephaniah lived in Jerusalem, where he saw and denounced the same evils as Isaiah and Micah denounced almost a century earlier. His preaching no doubt prompted many of the people to change their ways and cooperate in Josiah's reforms. It may

also have helped produce the renewed prophetic ministry in Judah. Other prophets of Zephaniah's time were Jeremiah, Nahum and Habakkuk, and these were followed after the destruction of Jerusalem by Obadiah and Ezekiel.

OUTLINE

1:1-3:8   Punishment of sinners
3:9-20   Salvation for the repentant

1:1-3:8 PUNISHMENT OF SINNERS

Sins of Jerusalem (1:1-18)

The prophet opens with a general statement about judgment that probably comes as no surprise to the people of Jerusalem. He announces that God will destroy sin from the earth (1:1-3). What surprises the hearers is Zephaniah's assertion that God will destroy *them*, for they too are sinners (4a). Anti-God practices established by Manasseh still exist, such as the worship of Baal, the worship of the stars and the worship of Milcom (Molech). These practices will be dramatically removed, together with those who engage in them (4b-6; cf. 2 Kings 21:3-6).

As an offerer kills his sacrificial animal and invites his guests to eat it, so God will slaughter the people of Judah and allow them to be swallowed up by the Babylonian armies (7). During the reigns of Manasseh and Amon, foreign religious customs, violence and cheating were widespread. Particularly blameworthy were members of the royal family, along with government officials and others who through corruption had won favour with the royal household. All will be punished (8-9).

When God searches through Jerusalem he will catch and punish the dishonest merchants. Cries will be heard from various parts of the city — the Fish Gate, the Second Quarter (the newer part of the city), the hills, and the Mortar (the market area in the lower part of the city). God will deal with the merchants who have made themselves rich by ignoring him and cheating others (10-13).

It will seem that the day of the world's final great judgment has come. People in places of power will suddenly find themselves powerless against God's judgments. Walled cities and other defence installations will give no protection (14-16). The former leaders and other influential persons will find that they are as helpless and defenceless as the blind and the poor whom they have exploited (17-18).

The certainty of judgment (2:1-15)

In spite of the certainty of judgment, there is still hope for those who will turn to God in humility and faith. The only ones to escape the divine wrath will be those who renounce their former wrongdoing and determine to live in obedience to God (2:1-3).

To impress upon the Jerusalemites that no sinners will escape God's wrath, Zechariah gives them examples of coming judgment on neighbouring nations. The first judgment concerns regions to the west of Judah. The greedy Jerusalem merchants are told that the rich commercial cities of Philistia will be destroyed and their inhabitants killed. The ruined cities will become sheep pastures, and the new inhabitants will be those Jerusalemites who have responded to the prophet's appeal of verse 3 and repented (4-7).

Moab and Ammon, to the east of Judah, will suffer a worse fate than the Philistines. Their lands will be so devastated that they will not be useful even for feeding sheep. The reason for this severe judgment is that in their pride they mocked God's people and therefore mocked God (8-11).

To the south the nation of Ethiopia (GNB: Sudan; NIV: Cush) will fall under God's judgment (12), and to the north mighty Assyria will be destroyed. Assyria had confidently boasted that it ruled the world, but now it will be left a wilderness. It will be fit only to be a dwelling place for birds and wild beasts (13-15).

More sins of Jerusalem (3:1-8)

Zephaniah now returns to consider further the sins of Jerusalem. Injustice and oppression are widespread, and people who are guilty of such evils take no notice of the prophet's rebukes (3:1-2). Officials and judges are corrupt. More savage than lions and greedier than wolves, they favour only those who pay them well. Religious leaders are just as bad, and use their position to gain benefits for themselves (3-4).

Daily, God has showed the people what is right, but they are too absorbed in their own selfish pursuits to take any notice of him (5). He has punished other nations to show them the results of sin, but again it has made no difference. They merely increase their corruption (6-7). By reminding them of the certainty of final judgment, Zephaniah urges the people to repent before it is too late (8).

3:9-20 SALVATION FOR THE REPENTANT

When all the sinners have been destroyed, the humble who have previously turned from their sin (see 2:1-3) will then enjoy a new life of peace and blessing. In the midst of judgment there is mercy for the repentant. Cleansed sinners from all nations will worship and serve God with pure hearts (9-10). No longer will Jerusalem be characterized by the pride, rebellion, dishonesty and deceit of Zephaniah's day. Wrongdoing will be removed from the community of God's people (11-13).

Although God's people may previously have had sorrow because of his punishments upon them, now they will have joy. They will dwell together with God, their king, without fear of further judgment (14-15). In view of this promising future, they are not to be lazy or discouraged, but alert and full of confidence. Defeat will be replaced by victory. God will take away their shame and in his love give them new life (16-18). Exiles will be gathered from the lands of their oppression and be established again in their own land. Under God's rule they will share with him in receiving praise from the whole earth (19-20).

Haggai

BACKGROUND

Haggai and Zechariah worked together in Jerusalem during the period that followed the Jews' return from captivity in Babylon. Two hundred years earlier the former northern kingdom Israel had been conquered by Assyria and the people taken captive into foreign countries (722 BC; 2 Kings 17:1-6). Some time later people of the former southern kingdom Judah suffered a similar fate when they were conquered by the Babylonians and taken captive to Babylon (605-587 BC; 2 Kings 24:1-25:12). People of the former northern kingdom were largely absorbed by the nations among whom they lived, but not so the people of the former southern kingdom. They retained their national identity, and these were the ones who returned to reconstruct the ancient Israelite nation.

Though there was no longer a division between northerners and southerners, most of those who returned were from the former southern kingdom, Judah. These were once known as Judeans, but this was shortened to 'Jews', which now became a common name for Israelites in general.

The event that made the Jews' return possible was Persia's conquest of Babylon in 539 BC. When the Persian king Cyrus gave permission for captive peoples to return to their homelands, a large group of Jews migrated to Jerusalem. Though under the overall control of Persia, they were allowed to establish their own leadership in Jerusalem. Their early leaders were the governor Zerubbabel and the high priest Joshua (or Jeshua). These were still the leaders when Haggai and Zechariah began their ministry (Ezra 2:1-2; 5:1-2).

The preaching of Haggai and Zechariah

Soon after arriving in Jerusalem, the Jews showed their desire to rebuild the temple on Mt Zion. They set up an altar of sacrifice, and in the second year they started to lay the foundation of the temple (Ezra 3:1-3,8-10). However, local people began to oppose the builders, with the result that the work stopped (Ezra 4:1-5,24).

For about sixteen years no work was done on the rebuilding of the temple. Because of this, God raised up the prophets Haggai and Zechariah to work among his people. They began preaching in 520 BC, their job being to stir up the people to get on with the job and not stop till it was finished (Ezra 5:1-2; Hag 1:1; Zech 1:1).

People blamed opposition from local enemies and hardship from famine as the reasons for not building. The prophets saw that these were not the real reasons. The problem lay with the people themselves. They were not willing to work for God, though they were quite energetic when working for themselves. The problem was spiritual, not political or material (Hag 1:2-4,9-10).

This opinion of the prophets was soon proved to be correct, for when the people restarted the work and opposition broke out afresh, the Persian king encouraged the Jews. He even issued a second decree to confirm the decree of the former king Cyrus. In addition he gave financial assistance to make sure the work was finished satisfactorily (Ezra 5:3; 6:6-12).

The early preaching of Haggai and Zechariah was designed to get the Jews started and encourage them through their early difficulties. This ministry lasted almost six months and, according to the record preserved in the Bible, consisted of four messages from Haggai and two from Zechariah. Two years later Zechariah delivered his third message. Zechariah's remaining two messages seem to come from a period much later in his life.

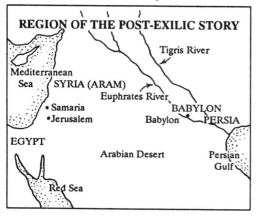

REGION OF THE POST-EXILIC STORY

Tigris River

Mediterranean Sea

SYRIA (ARAM)

Euphrates River

• Samaria

• Jerusalem

BABYLON

Babylon

PERSIA

EGYPT

Arabian Desert

Persian Gulf

Red Sea

Characteristics of the two books

While Haggai's preaching was straightforward and easy to understand, Zechariah's consisted largely of vivid accounts of unusual visions and dramatic messages given to him by God. As a result, his preaching required more thought on the part of his hearers. This type of preaching (or writing) was known as apocalyptic. (Concerning characteristics of apocalyptic writings see background to Daniel.)

Haggai was mainly concerned with rousing the people from their spiritual laziness to get them working on the rebuilding of the temple. Zechariah supported Haggai in this urgent ministry, but went on to give further teaching. He wanted to see a lasting spiritual change in the lives and outlook of the people, so that they would be better equipped to serve God in the future.

Through Zechariah, God was further preparing his people for the purpose for which he had chosen them. That purpose would find its fulfilment in the coming of the Messiah, the establishment of his kingdom, and the salvation of people worldwide. The latter half of Zechariah's book (consisting of two messages delivered probably later in his life) shows that the Jews' task would not be easy. There would be bitter conflicts with the forces of evil, but in the end God's kingdom would triumph.

Summary of contents

The table below shows the sequence of the messages and events recorded in Haggai and Zechariah.

BC	Mth	Day	Message/Event	Reference
521			Darius as king	
520	6	1	Hag 1st message	Hag 1:1-11
	6	24	Temple started	Hag 1:12-15
	7	21	Hag 2nd message	Hag 2:1-9
	8		Zech 1st message	Zech 1:1-6
	9	24	Hag 3rd message	Hag 2:10-19
	9	24	Hag 4th message	Hag 2:20-23
	11	24	Zech 2nd message	Zech 1:7-6:15
518	9	4	Zech 3rd message	Zech 7:1-8:23
516	12	3	Temple finished	Ezra 6:14-15
years later			Zech 1st oracle	Zech 9:1-11:17
late in life			Zech 2nd oracle	Zech 12:1-14:21

THE PROPHECY OF HAGGAI

Haggai's rebuke and its results (1:1-15)

The Jews were making excuses for not building the temple, saying that they were suffering a time of personal hardship and enemy opposition. They claimed it was not yet time to begin the work (1:1-2). Yet they could build houses for themselves. In fact, they had taken much of the available timber and used it extravagantly in their own homes, even though timber was in short supply and was needed for the temple (3-4). Because of their selfishness God had punished them with poverty and famine (5-6).

People complained that they could not build the temple because they were poor. Rather, replied the prophet, they were poor because they would not build the temple. They were selfish, thinking only of what they wanted, not what God wanted. Therefore, they had to go back to the forests and cut timber for the temple (7-11).

Haggai's forthright preaching brought quick results. The people, realizing the truth of his accusations, responded to his appeal, and in little more than three weeks had restarted work on the temple. When they began to obey God and fear him, he promised to be with them (12-15).

A message of encouragement (2:1-9)

Although the foundation of the temple had been laid sixteen years earlier, it had no doubt been damaged during the years of neglect. More work was necessary before construction could begin on the building itself. After the people had been at work for about a month, they could see enough of the rebuilt foundation to form an idea of the size of the proposed temple. Some of the very old people, remembering Solomon's magnificent temple, may have commented that this new temple was not very impressive by comparison. Haggai saw that this would discourage the builders, so he brought them a message of encouragement (2:1-3). As God's spokesman, Haggai passed on God's assurance that he was with them, just as he had been with their ancestors when he brought them out of Egypt (4-5).

Just as God shook the earth with the giving of the law at Mt Sinai, so through this temple he would 'shake' heaven and earth in a far greater way. Through the temple, he was reconstructing the religious centre of the Jewish nation, for this was the nation from which the Messiah was to come. Israel's temple would receive greater splendour than the discouraged workmen imagined. God, who was the real owner of the world's wealth, would direct rulers of other nations to bring their silver and gold to beautify it (6-8; cf. Ezra 6:8-12).

However, far greater glory would come through the multitudes from many nations who would join with Israel in the true temple. The Messiah's real dwelling place would be among all the redeemed in a living temple that he would establish in the world in glory. The temporary hardships of the Jewish builders would appear as nothing compared with the splendour of that day (9).

Promises of blessing (2:10-19)

At the end of three months all the foundation work was finished (cf. 1:14-15; 2:18). Zechariah had successfully urged the people to repent (Zech 1:1-6), and now Haggai emphasized again that spiritual cleansing was the only way by which they could enjoy God's blessing (10).

Haggai reminded the people that their wrong attitudes in the past had been the cause of all their troubles. He gave an illustration to show that contact with unclean things made a person unclean, but contact with holy things did not make a person holy. As long as they had neglected the temple and let it lie as a ruined 'dead' thing in their midst, they had been unclean and therefore unacceptable to God. All their religious activity had not made them holy, no matter how much it brought them in contact with holy things (11-14).

The people's selfishness and disobedience had brought God's judgment upon them in damage to their crops and a shortage of food. Now that they had turned from their selfish ways and obeyed God, things would change (15-17). God would reverse the unfavourable agricultural conditions and give them fruitful crops again. His promise would begin to come true from that very day; for on that day, by completing the foundations of the temple, they had given visible proof that their obedience was genuine (18-19).

A personal message for Zerubbabel (2:20-23)

Later the same day Haggai delivered another encouraging message, this time to Zerubbabel the governor (20). Zerubbabel was a descendant of David in the line of kings who reigned in Jerusalem, and he was entitled to the throne of Israel (Matt 1:6-12). But because Israel was still under Persian rule he was allowed to be only governor.

Despite these restrictions, Haggai encouraged Zerubbabel with the assurance that he was still God's specially chosen representative. Through him God would not only re-establish the nation Israel, but would overthrow all nations and establish God's worldwide kingdom. Zerubbabel did not live to see the fulfilment of Haggai's words, but the promise passed on to one of his descendants, Jesus the Messiah, in whom the prophecy will find its fullest meaning (21-23; cf. Matt 1:12-16).

Zechariah

BACKGROUND

Zechariah was a fellow worker with Haggai in bringing God's message to the Jews in Jerusalem at the beginning of the post-exilic period. Their chief concern during the early days of their ministry was to arouse the Jews from their selfish laziness and urge them to rebuild the temple. Zechariah went on to give teaching over a wide range of issues, as part of his task to prepare people for the era of the Messiah that lay ahead.

The introductory notes to Haggai give background details for both Haggai and Zechariah, and the reader should be familiar with that material before continuing with the present study. The notes that introduce Haggai also discuss characteristics of Zechariah that mark it out as a different kind of book from Haggai.

OUTLINE

1:1-6:15 ZECHARIAH'S VISIONS

Call to repentance (1:1-6)

At the time Zechariah delivered his first message, Haggai had already been preaching for about two months (1:1; cf. Hag 1:1). In his two recorded messages of that time, Haggai had shown that all Israel's current difficulties were because of the people's selfishness and disobedience in failing to rebuild the temple. As a result of Haggai's preaching the people stirred themselves and started building again (Hag 1:1-2:9).

Zechariah now joins Haggai in the preaching, recalling that disobedience to the prophets of former times had led to hardship and finally captivity (2-3). The people should therefore learn from their forefathers' experiences and take notice of the words of the prophets. This means not simply that they must rebuild the temple, but more importantly that they must acknowledge their sin, accept God's discipline, turn from their disobedience and begin a new life of devotion to God (4-6).

Eight visions

The section 1:7-6:8 consists of a series of eight visions. These are arranged with the two most important visions in the centre, and the remaining visions in two equal groups, one on either side.

At the time that Zechariah received these visions, work on rebuilding the temple had been going on for five months, three months of which were taken up with preparing the foundations (cf. v. 7 with Hag 1:14-15; 2:18). The people would clearly benefit from some encouragement and direction. The first three visions are largely messages of encouragement to the builders, the middle two are of special encouragement to the leaders Joshua and Zerubbabel, and the final three give assurance of ultimate victory for God and his people.

Encouragement to the builders (1:7-2:13)

In the first vision some mounted patrol officers have just returned from a tour of duty and report to a rider on a red horse who is standing among some trees (7-10). The patrol officers report that throughout the empire all is calm and peaceful (11).

This report may be good news for the Persians but it is not for the Jews, who have now been in bondage to foreign overlords for more than seventy years. They long for freedom and pray for God's mercy (12-13). God tells them that although he used foreign nations to punish them, those nations went beyond the limits he had set. He loves his people and he knows what their enemies have done to them (14-15). Therefore, he will now turn and help Israel again. The temple will be finished, and the city rebuilt and made prosperous once more (16-17).

The second vision assures the Jews that they need have no fear of foreign overlords. Nations may attack them from all sides, using their power to oppress Israel as wild beasts use their horns to terrify their victims, but their success will not last. As each wild beast is overcome by a workman who smashes it with a hammer, so each nation that attacks Israel will be overthrown (18-21).

In the third vision Zechariah sees a young man going out to measure Jerusalem in preparation for the rebuilding of its walls (2:1-2). But a messenger stops him, for the rebuilt city will extend beyond the walls of the former city. In fact, it will not need walls, because God will be its protector (3-5).

Those Jews still in Babylon may have made living conditions reasonably comfortable for themselves, but they should beware of becoming too settled. They should return to Jerusalem as quickly as possible, both to enjoy its blessings and to avoid the punishment about to fall on their captors (6-9). God gives further encouragement to those working on the temple by assuring them that it will be the means by which he dwells among his people again. Citizens of other nations will renounce their gods and come to join with Israel as the people of God (10-13).

Encouragement to Joshua (3:1-10)

Zechariah then has a vision in which he sees Satan accuse the high priest Joshua (and therefore the people he represents) of being unclean. Because of their long exile in idolatrous Babylon, they are no longer fit to enter God's presence. In other words, Satan is hinting that the people are wasting their time building the temple. Since they are unclean, no sacrifices that they offer there will be acceptable to God (3:1; see also v. 3).

God replies that he has not cast off his chosen people. Their time of exile in Babylon has been his punishment on them because of their sin, but now he has saved them. He has snatched them from the hand of their enemies, brought them back to their land and cleansed their sin. Now he is going to set up the temple and its priesthood for them once again (2-5).

Joshua and his fellow priests are warned to be faithful to God in carrying out their duties in the new temple that God will put in their care. Joshua will then be able to enter the presence of God without fear of Satan's accusations (6-7). The re-establishment of the Israelite priesthood is a further sign to assure the people that their Messiah will come (8. For the significance of the messianic title 'the Branch' see commentary on 6:12-13). A specially engraved stone is to be set in the temple as a reminder of what the Messiah will do. He will cleanse the land of sin and bring in a new era of contentment and prosperity (9-10).

Encouragement to Zerubbabel (4:1-14)

The next vision is of a seven-headed lampstand standing between two olive trees. The olive trees pour their oil into a central bowl on top of the lampstand. The oil from this central bowl then feeds the seven lamps that provide the light. This means that the lamps do not need anyone to look after them. Light is provided supernaturally through the constant supply of oil from the trees (4:1-5; see also v. 12).

This vision was of particular encouragement to Zerubbabel who, in his task of reconstructing the temple, faced mountainous obstacles. His authority was limited by Persia; he had a shortage of labour and materials; his workers were discouraged by certain Jews who despised the new building as being small in comparison with Solomon's magnificent temple; and he was surrounded by hostile foreigners who tried to hinder the work. God now gives him a message of encouragement and reassurance. Just as the lamps receive a continuous supply of oil supernaturally, so the temple will be finished through the power of God's Spirit. God's power, not human power, is to be the source of Zerubbabel's strength (6-10a).

Zechariah then records an additional meaning given to the two olive trees. Through the Davidic prince Zerubbabel and the high priest Joshua, God will supply spiritual power to Israel. This will enable Israel to send forth the light of God throughout the whole earth (10b-14).

Assurance of final victory (5:1-6:8)

Previously God gave a promise that the Messiah will remove sin from the land (see 3:9b). This will come either through forgiveness (in the case of those who repent) or destruction (in the case of those who continue in their sin). This latter judgment is now pictured in the vision of a huge flying scroll that announces God's judgment on all those who choose to ignore God's law. No one has any excuse, because the scroll is large enough for all to read and it flies over the whole land so that all can see it (5:1-3). Whether wrong actions are directed against God or against others, the wrongdoers will not escape judgment (4).

In the past Israel often fell into idolatry, with its accompanying sin of sexual immorality. Therefore, idolatry and everything associated with it must be removed from Israel's land. In Zechariah's vision, idolatry is symbolized by a large container, inside which is a woman, probably a prostitute (5-8). The container and its contents are then carried away to the distant land of Babylon. There the woman will be at home among the ungodly idol worshippers awaiting final punishment; but the land of Israel will at last be free of her defiling influence (9-11).

Having cleared the land of sin, God establishes the kingdom of the Messiah with its worldwide authority. This seems to be the meaning of the final vision, which begins with the appearance of four chariots coming out from the stronghold where God dwells (6:1-4). The chariots speed to the four corners of the earth to spread God's rule throughout the world (5-7). God is particularly pleased to see the nations to the north conquered, for that was the direction from which most of the enemy conquests of Israel came (8).

Israel's captivity and re-establishment in its land was a foreshadowing of the events pictured in these three visions — the punishment of sinners, the removal of idolatry and the setting up of the Messiah's kingdom. Restored Israel had turned from its sins, put away idolatry, and was now in the process of establishing a God-centred national life once again through the rebuilding of the temple.

The crowning of Joshua (6:9-15)

Just as the setting up of the Messiah's kingdom will be marked by the crowning of the Messiah as universal king, so the re-establishment of the nation Israel was marked by the crowning of Joshua. The crown was made from gold and silver brought from Babylon by some exiles who had recently arrived in Jerusalem (9-11).

A coronation of the high priest was unusual, but because the restored nation of Israel was still under Persian rule, a coronation of the Davidic prince Zerubbabel may have appeared to be an act of rebellion. But the Persians were not likely to object to a religious ceremony marking the restoration of Israel's national life and the reconstruction of their temple.

Zechariah's words, spoken on behalf of God, further indicate that the crown rightly belonged to Zerubbabel; for though the words were addressed to Joshua they applied to Zerubbabel. It was Zerubbabel, not Joshua, who was the 'branch' in David's family tree, the royal descendant entitled to the throne of Israel. Joshua's rightful place was as the high priest who assisted the civil ruler. The two men, because of the peaceful understanding between them, led the nation in the ways of God. Their joint rule fittingly foreshadowed the rule of the true 'Branch', the king-priest Messiah (12-13; cf. 3:8; see also notes on Hag 2:20-23).

The three recently returned exiles who supplied the gold and silver for the crown were apparently witnesses at the ceremony. The crowning took place in the house of their friend Josiah, and the crown was later placed in the completed temple in Jerusalem. There it was displayed as a memorial to those who gave it and as a symbolic guarantee of greater things to come (14-15).

7:1-8:23 A QUESTION ABOUT CERTAIN FASTS

Mourning over the past (7:1-14)

In captivity the Jews had instituted four fasts to mourn the destruction of Jerusalem. One fast was in the tenth month, which was the month the Babylonians laid siege to the city. One was in the fourth month, to mark the day eighteen months later when the Babylonians broke through the walls and invaded the city. Another was in the fifth month, to mark the destruction of the temple. The other was in the seventh month, to mark the murder of Gedaliah, the last Jewish ruler in Jerusalem (see 8:18-19; cf. 2 Kings 25:1-4,8-9,25).

Now that the temple was beginning to take shape (for it had been under construction more than two years) a question arose in the minds of certain Jews. With the temple rebuilt, should they still keep the fasts that had been instituted in Babylon as memorials of destruction (7:1-3)?

Zechariah replies that those fasts had no value in God's sight anyway. Self-pity, not repentance towards God, was what prompted the people to keep them. Furthermore, the destruction they commemorated came about only because they had been disobedient to God's prophets. Through their own stubbornness, the people were driven out of what used to be a prosperous land (4-7).

The Jews of Zechariah's day should not repeat the sins of their ancestors. Rather they should show their obedience to God in lives of active justice, love and mercy towards their fellows. They must avoid the temptation to exploit those who, for one reason or another, are disadvantaged (8-10). The heartless attitude of their ancestors towards the needy was a reflection of a more deep-seated problem, their hardness of heart towards God (11-12). Because they ignored God's instruction to them through the prophets, God ignored their prayers to him when the enemy attacked. As a result they were taken into foreign captivity (13-14).

Confidence for the future (8:1-23)

Zechariah goes on to outline the blessings that will come to Jerusalem when God dwells there. God's love for Jerusalem was the reason why he punished it so severely. With corresponding zeal he will restore it to a favoured place according to his covenant promises (8:1-3).

In the new community of God's people, there will be no place for fear or violence. Old and young alike will enjoy lives of freedom and contentment greater than they imagined possible (4-6). Above all, they will enjoy true fellowship with God. After their years of captivity they will now begin to experience the blessings God always intended for them (7-8).

Since the people had restarted work on the temple, conditions in Jerusalem had changed. God removed the afflictions of drought and enemy action that he had used to punish them in the past (9-11). In their place he now gives blessings of agricultural prosperity and peace (12-13). These blessings will continue and will increase, but the people on their part must continue to behave rightly towards God and towards one another (14-17).

In view of all that God will do, the people should not waste time mourning over calamities of the past. Instead they should look confidently to the future and turn their fasts of mourning into feasts of joy (18-19). In contrast to the relatively few Jews who were at that time rebuilding the temple and city, multitudes of Gentiles from far and wide will come to Jerusalem to seek the God of Israel (20-23).

9:1-14:21 THE TRIUMPH OF THE MESSIAH

Israel always looked forward to a messianic day of glory and power. The people longed for the day when all enemies would be destroyed, and righteousness would be established in the land under the rule of the Messiah. The nation's re-establishment under Zerubbabel and Joshua was a foretaste of that great day. Israel could expect to see its former enemies conquered and full independence restored in its land.

This in fact happened. The years 334-326 BC saw the Greek conqueror Alexander the Great spread his rule over all those countries that had previously controlled Israel. Although Alexander's conquests included Israel, the time came when Israel finally won full independence under the Maccabees (143 BC). In due course the Messiah came in the person of Jesus Christ, but by this time the Jews, through their own sin, had lost their independence. Worse still, they rejected their Messiah.

The prophecies of Zechariah have to some extent been fulfilled, but they still await a greater fulfilment. This will take place when Jesus Christ returns to conquer all enemies and establish his universal rule of peace and joy. In Zechariah the time factor therefore has little meaning. Events that cover many years, or perhaps are separated by centuries, may be condensed into one verse. Much shorter periods may be dealt with at length.

Zechariah's prophecies are not descriptions of historical events that he happens to have written in advance. They are a revelation of God's purposes given to instruct, warn, encourage, guide and inform his people. Their fulfilment may take different forms in different eras. In some cases the fulfilment may be closely related to events belonging to the time from Alexander to the Maccabees; in others it may be more concerned with the greater events of Christ's life and work; and in yet others it may relate more fully to the future events of the return of Christ and the age to come.

Enemies punished; freedom restored (9:1-17)

The prophet outlines how Israel will move from its present position (in its own land but still under Persian rule) to full independence, and then into the era of the Messiah's rule. He sees an invading army moving down from the north. First it conquers the Syrian cities of Hadrach, Damascus and Hamath, then the Phoenician cities of Tyre and Sidon (9:1-4). From there it moves down the coastal plain to conquer the Philistine cities of Ashkelon, Gaza, Ekron and Ashdod. The Philistine practice of eating unclean food will cease, and the Philistines will become part of Israel, as the Jebusites had in the time of David (5-7; cf. 2 Sam 5:6-10). Jerusalem, however, will be preserved. Although it will come into the enemy's sphere of control, it will not be destroyed (8).

(History records that an invasion such as the above took place when Alexander's armies swept through the region, conquering many of Israel's former enemies, including its current master, Persia. Although Alexander took control of Jerusalem, he did not destroy it.)

Greek rule may spread over Palestine, but eventually it will be overthrown. God's king will then reign in Jerusalem, though not as a warlike conqueror. He will enter the city in quiet yet royal dignity, and establish a worldwide reign of peace (9-10).

Now that he has pointed to the climax of Israel's glory through the reign of the Messiah, the prophet returns to the time of Alexander. He shows that God will set his people free according to the covenant he made with them at Sinai (11-12). Israel will become a weapon in God's hand to slaughter its enemies and thereby carry out God's judgment upon the nations (13-15). On gaining its freedom, the nation will settle down to a life of security, joy and prosperity (16-17).

Problems of leadership (10:1-11:3)

At the time this prophecy was given, the temple had long been finished and life in Jerusalem was not as it had been previously. Zerubbabel and Joshua had apparently died, and without strong leadership the Jews drifted into the ungodly ways of neighbouring nations. Some were using idolatrous objects as magic charms, in the belief that these would bring good rains and good crops. Zechariah tells them to stop such practices and trust in God alone (10:1-2).

God is angry with Israel's leaders, who have no concern for the people they rule. God will replace them with strong, stable, dependable leaders, who in God's strength will overthrow the ruling power (3-5). Jews who are still scattered throughout other lands will return to their homeland, where they will live in confidence and joy under God's protection (6-7). The movement of people to the promised land will be like the migration from Egypt to Canaan in the time of Moses (8-11). In response to God's grace his people will worship and obey him (12).

As for bad leaders, their judgment is certain, no matter how great and mighty they think themselves to be. They increase their power and wealth by oppressing the people without mercy, and therefore God will punish them without mercy. His judgment will be like a raging fire sweeping through the proud forests, where not even the strongest and fiercest animals will escape (11:1-3).

Two short plays about leadership (11:4-17)

After announcing God's judgment on Israel's bad leaders (see 11:1-3), Zechariah demonstrates that judgment in two short plays. In these plays he acts the part of a shepherd, representing the leaders of God's people.

In the first play God told Zechariah to act the part of a good shepherd. Zechariah was to look after a people oppressed and exploited by bad shepherds, whose sole aim was to enrich themselves. They cared nothing for the flock. God showed Zechariah, however, that his efforts were doomed to failure. Leaders and common people alike were heading for a fitting punishment (4-6).

Nevertheless, Zechariah acted his short drama. With a shepherd's stick called 'grace' (or 'favour') he tried to give the sheep the gracious and beneficial leadership that God desired for them. With another stick, called 'union', he tried to bind them closer to one another in national peace and harmony. He even destroyed the three bad shepherds. In return the people were angry with him. They were so far removed from the ways of God that they preferred the bad shepherds to the good shepherd (7-8).

Zechariah therefore broke his two sticks, to show the people that he would no longer be their shepherd (9-11; see also v. 14). When he suggested

that they might pay him his wages, they gave him such a small amount that it was an insult. This was especially so since the wages really belonged to God, whom he served (12-13). He knew that the people preferred the sort of society where the greedy could get what they wanted by exploiting others. In the end such a society would destroy itself (14).

In the second play Zechariah played the part of a bad shepherd, which was the sort of shepherd Israel wanted. This cruel and selfish leadership was what the people deserved, and would be God's means of punishing them (15-17).

There may have been events in Zechariah's day or soon after that corresponded to the two plays he acted. Certainly, there was a striking correspondence with conditions among the Jews of Jesus' day. The people rejected him, preferring the bad leadership of the Pharisees, Sadducees, scribes, priests and elders (cf. John 10:7-13,26-31). They crucified the one whom God graciously gave to save them. They fought among themselves and with the Roman authorities who governed them, and finally brought upon themselves slaughter and destruction at the hands of Rome in AD 70.

Victory, but with mourning (12:1-13:1)

On occasions God used Gentile nations to punish his people Israel, but if his desire was to fight for Israel, no enemy attack could be successful. On the occasion that Zechariah speaks of in Chapter 12, God strengthens his people to overthrow the armies that besiege Jerusalem (12:1-3). The charging horses of the enemy are thrown into confusion as God comes to the help of his people. The Jewish leaders acknowledge that, above all, God is the cause of Jerusalem's victory (4-5).

The Jewish fighters who lead the attack against the enemy are not from Jerusalem, but from the country areas round about. This prevents the people of Jerusalem from boasting that they have been responsible for the destruction of the enemy. Fitting honour is given to their brave brothers from the country (6-7). All, however, realize that God is really the one who has saved Jerusalem (8-9).

God's people may have won a great victory, but the victory has been costly. As they mourn their dead, the people are humbled to a new attitude of sorrow for their wrongdoing, and they cry to God for mercy. The chief cause of their mourning is their realization that a man whom they had recently murdered was the one whom God had sent to save them. They may have objected to his announcements or directions concerning the battle, but now they realize that they should have honoured him (10). There is mourning throughout the land, but it is particularly intense among those connected with the civil and religious leadership in Jerusalem (11-14). Yet God's forgiveness is available to all who are genuinely sorry for their disobedience and treachery (13:1).

False prophets and true shepherd (13:2-9)

Having introduced the subject of forgiveness and cleansing, Zechariah goes on to deal with those evils that had to be removed from the land. One of Israel's chief sins was idolatry, and this had been encouraged by the false prophets. Therefore, all false prophets must be killed (2-3).

If a false prophet escapes, he might try to preserve his life by throwing away his prophet's cloak and disguising himself as a farmer. But he will not be able to remove the scars on his back. (Such scars were a characteristic of sorcerers and false prophets. They were made by cutting 'magic' marks in the skin; see Lev 19:28; 1 Kings 18:28.) If someone notices the scars, the false prophet will lie to protect himself, saying that he received the scars through a fight or an accident in a friend's house (4-6).

Zechariah returns to the subject of leadership, using again the illustration of the shepherd. (The leader referred to here may be the person of 12:10 who was killed by his own countrymen.) The leader of God's choice is one who is close to God and who truly cares for God's people. But the people kill him and persecute his followers. As a result of this shepherd's death, the majority of his people fall under divine judgment. The minority who are left go through a time of suffering, but through this they become better people and come into closer fellowship with the God in whom they have trusted. These are God's true people (7-9).

No doubt this true shepherd was Jesus the Messiah (Matt 26:31; John 19:37). His own people killed him, and with his death the majority of Israel fell under God's judgment. Some, however, were saved. These became God's true people, though they

suffered persecution at the hands of the rebellious (Rom 9:6-8; 11:5-7; Gal 4:28-29).

The Messiah's kingdom (14:1-21)

In the final section of his book, Zechariah outlines briefly the worldwide triumph of the Messiah. Since those for whom he writes are familiar only with the region around Palestine, he limits the geographical details to that area. Other pictures are likewise taken from the way of life familiar to the Jews.

The scene opens with the enemies of God mistakenly thinking that at last they have conquered his people (Jerusalem). Confident that they have achieved victory, they sit down in the middle of the city to divide the plunder, while the Jews are either led away captive or imprisoned in the city (14:1-2). Suddenly God acts in supernatural judgment. As he once divided the Red Sea to give his people a way of escape from the Egyptians, so he divides the mountains east of Jerusalem to give his people a way of escape from the enemy-occupied city (3-5).

God gives his people satisfaction and provision by altering the course of nature for their benefit. They lack nothing (6-8). God now establishes his throne in a restored and repopulated Jerusalem, from where he rules over all the earth. Mountains around the city are flattened so that Jerusalem is lifted up in the eyes of all nations and Israel's God is worshipped worldwide (9-11).

Enemies are destroyed in a terrifying judgment, and Israel is compensated for all that it previously lost to plundering armies (12-15). Survivors among the nations are required to come to Jerusalem to worship God. This ingathering of nations is likened to Israel's ingathering of harvest fruits at the Feast of Tabernacles (Festival of Shelters) at the end of each agricultural year (16-19).

No longer is there a difference between sacred and non-sacred articles. Everything is holy and fit for the service of God, even household pots and pans and bells on the necks of horses. Since all things are holy, traders are no longer needed in the temple to exchange non-sacred for sacred goods. True holiness will at last be established in the world (20-21).

Malachi

BACKGROUND

The meaning of the Hebrew word *malachi* is 'my messenger'. Since a prophet was God's messenger, some have thought that 'Malachi' in the opening verse is not a person's name but a statement that the writer is a genuine messenger from God. (The same word is used of another messenger of God in Malachi 3:1.) The usual understanding is that the writer, in calling himself Malachi, is introducing himself by his own name, as do the other writing prophets.

Conditions in Israel

After Persia's conquest of Babylon in 539 BC, the first lot of Jewish exiles returned to Jerusalem and set about rebuilding their city and temple. They were under the leadership of the governor Zerubbabel and the high priest Joshua, and these were helped by the prophets Haggai and Zechariah (Ezra 5:1-2). It was largely a result of the stirring preaching of the prophets that the temple was finished (in 516 BC; Ezra 6:14-15). (For further details of this period see background to Haggai.)

Little is known of affairs in Israel during the next sixty years. A new generation grew up, and without the strong leadership provided by Zerubbabel, Joshua, Haggai and Zechariah, the people drifted from God. When news of this reached Persia, a godly Jewish priest named Ezra obtained authority and finance from the Persian king, Artaxerxes, to go to Jerusalem and carry out reforms there. This was in 458 BC (Ezra 7:7,11-26).

Ezra's reforms met with only limited success. But when Nehemiah arrived in Jerusalem thirteen years later (445 BC) more extensive changes began to take place. Nehemiah also was a Jew who had previously lived in Babylon, and he also came to Jerusalem with authority from Artaxerxes. He was the king's appointed governor over Jerusalem (Neh 2:1-8; 5:14-15). Ezra and Nehemiah then worked together to lead the people back to God (Neh 8:9; 12:26).

It seems that Malachi carried out his ministry some time during this period of post-exilic reform by Ezra and Nehemiah. The date of his book cannot be fixed with certainty, but the sins he rebuked were similar to those that Ezra and Nehemiah had to deal with.

The people apparently expected that because they had come back to their land and rebuilt their temple, they were going to enjoy the unlimited blessing of God. This did not prove to be so, and as a result people began to doubt whether God really cared for them. Malachi replied that the fault was on their side, not God's. They had, by their sins, created barriers that hindered the flow and enjoyment of God's love.

OUTLINE

1:1-5 God's love for Israel
1:6-3:18 Sins of the people
4:1-6 God's care in the day of judgment

1:1-5 GOD'S LOVE FOR ISRAEL

People may pride themselves that they are God's people, yet displease him through living to please themselves. Malachi learns through experience that when such people are rebuked, they usually take offence. Their reaction is to point out, in a hurt tone of voice, that they are innocent and have been treated unfairly. Malachi's method of dealing with them is to quote their complaints (note the number of times he says, 'You say . . .' or something similar; e.g. 1:2,6-7; 2:17; 3:7,13-15), then to show that they have no right to make such complaints. They should not blame God, but blame themselves.

The people's main complaint is that God does not love them. If he does, they argue, let him prove it to them by giving them comfort and prosperity instead of hardship and poverty. Malachi will soon show them the reasons for their difficulties, but first he wants to make them see that they have clear proof of God's love. This is seen in God's choice of Jacob and not Esau, though there was nothing in Jacob that made him more lovable than his brother (1:1-2).

Jacob's descendants, Israel, have been punished but they are now back in their God-given homeland. But Esau's descendants, Edom, have suffered a judgment from which their nation will never recover. The destruction throughout Edom's land will be a reminder to people of future generations of Edom's incurable wickedness (3-5).

1:6-3:18 SINS OF THE PEOPLE

Disgraceful sacrifices (1:6-14)

Israel, as God's people, should honour him as their father and reverence him as their master. Instead they insult him. They offer to God animals that are lame, sick and blind. They would never think of offering such animals to the governor, yet they offer them to God and expect him to be pleased with them (6-9). They would do better to close the temple doors and have no sacrifices at all than to offer worship like that. Even Gentiles offer more sincere worship (10-12).

To the Jews the whole worship ritual is boring. Not only do they insult God by the standard of their offerings, but they also cheat him. When in trouble they promise to sacrifice something of value if he saves them, but once they are saved they give him something worthless (13-14).

Unworthy priests (2:1-9)

The priests are chiefly to blame for the poor spiritual condition of Israel. If they do not quickly reform their ways, God will punish them. He will reduce their income from the people's tithes and offerings, and bring public disgrace upon them. He may even remove them from their position as priests, in order to stop the priesthood from becoming so corrupt that it has to be abolished. God prefers to maintain the priesthood, according to the promise he gave to the tribe of Levi (2:1-4).

Priests are not merely officials who look after temple rituals. They are supposed to be the spiritual and moral guides of the people. The early priests taught the people, by their personal example as well as by their instruction, how to know God and live righteously (5-6; cf. Num 25:11-13). Priests are servants of God who have the responsibility to teach people God's law and give them practical instruction concerning everyday affairs (7; cf. Deut 33:10). But the priests of Malachi's day have failed to uphold God's standards, either by teaching or by practice, and so have led Israel astray. They favour the rich and powerful, and as a result are despised by the common people (8-9).

Divorces and mixed marriages (2:10-16)

Marriage disorders were a further cause of Israel's troubles. Many Jewish men had married idolatrous heathen women, and introduced idolatrous practices into the holy worship of God (cf. Ezra 9:1-2; Neh 13:23-27). Not only did these Jewish men marry idol

worshippers, but they divorced their Jewish wives to do so. They despised both the marriage covenant and the covenant God made with Israel at Sinai. God designed the covenant to promote family and national unity, but these men break up families and intermarry with pagans (10-11). Malachi warns that God will act in decisive judgment against those guilty of such selfishness and disloyalty (12).

The wrongdoers are upset that God no longer accepts their ritual sacrifices and offerings, but they show no concern at their own unfaithfulness in breaking a marriage covenant that God himself had witnessed (13-14). By marrying idolatrous wives they show that they have no real desire to bring their children up to know and follow God. They also show that they are unconcerned that their former wives are left to face lives of hardship (15-16).

Cheating God (2:17-3:18)

When the Jews saw surrounding nations prosper while they suffered hardship, they complained that God was not just. Other nations made no effort to keep God's law, whereas Israel was his people (17). Malachi replies that if justice is what the Jews want, then justice is what they will have; but they must realize that such justice will apply to them as well as to their heathen neighbours. They have asked for the God of justice; now he will come and do his work of justice among them (3:1).

God will intervene in human affairs and bless his people as they wish, but first he will have to cleanse them of all uncleanness, rebellion and social injustice — and this will be a very painful process. Those who resist his cleansing and continue in their sin will be punished with swift destruction (2-5). (The intervention of God spoken of here was the coming of Jesus Christ. The messenger who came before him was John the Baptist; see Matt 3:10-12; 11:10; John 3:27-28.)

If the people want to escape hardship, they should be asking for mercy, not justice; for their hardship, though a punishment, is a merciful punishment. As always, God has been extremely patient with them. If God always acted according to strict justice (as they are claiming he should) they would all have been destroyed long ago (6-7).

Because of drought, locust plagues and plant diseases, they have had poor crops, but all these disasters have been sent by God. They are his punishment upon them because they have kept for themselves what rightly belongs to him. In their selfishness they have failed to give him their tithes and offerings (8-9). They must change their ways and be honest with God. Then he will bless them with good rains and good crops. The result of their generosity will be that they become more contented and their land becomes a better place in which to live (10-12).

Many of the people continue to murmur against God. They complain that it is useless to try to live to please him, as they still suffer hardships. By contrast, those who openly defy him seem to prosper (13-15). Others, however, will not allow themselves to be influenced by such talk. They encourage one another to remain faithful to God, believing that he will never forsake them. The difference between these two classes — those who truly serve God and those who do not — will be clearly seen in the day of judgment (16-18).

4:1-6 GOD'S CARE IN THE DAY OF JUDGMENT

God's action in destroying the wicked in the day of judgment is pictured in the illustration of a farmer burning off his field after he has harvested his grain. The righteous are likened to the farmer's calves, which were previously tied up in the dark stalls but are now set free. They burst forth to go leaping and skipping over the recently burnt-off fields. As the sun shines down upon them it brings healing and vigour into their lives of newfound joy and freedom (4:1-3).

In view of their coming salvation, the righteous should remain faithful to God's law. In addition they should look expectantly for the appearing of the Messiah's forerunner, symbolized here under the name 'Elijah'. If the people respond to the preaching of this Elijah, they will be united in one spirit with their believing forefathers, Abraham, Isaac and Jacob. But if they refuse to repent, they will meet divine judgment (4-6).

The symbolic Elijah was John the Baptist (Matt 11:10-15; 17:10-13; Luke 1:13-17). After Malachi, John was the next prophet whose voice was heard in Scripture. The time of the Messiah's appearing had arrived, and John's voice announced, 'Prepare the way of the Lord, make his paths straight' (Mark 1:3; John 1:19-28; 3:26-30).

The New Testament World

JEWS AND THEIR RELIGION

In the time of Jesus the social, religious and political conditions of Israel were vastly different from those of Old Testament times. Many of the changes came about during the period between the close of the Old Testament era and the beginning of the New. The origins of the changes, however, go back into the national life of Israel during the time of the Old Testament monarchy. A brief survey of events and developments in Israel will help towards a better understanding of the life and ministry of Jesus.

Hebrews, Israelites or Jews

About a thousand years before the time of Christ, David established in Jerusalem a dynasty through which God promised to bring the universal king, the Messiah (2 Sam 7:12-16; Ps 2:6-9; Isa 9:6-7; 11:1-9). David was followed by Solomon, but after Solomon the kingdom divided into two. The northern section broke away from the dynasty of David, but it still called itself Israel. The city that eventually became its capital was Samaria. The southern kingdom became known as Judah, after its leading tribe. It remained loyal to the dynasty of David, whose kings continued to reign in Jerusalem, but now over only the southern kingdom.

When the people of the northern kingdom were conquered by Assyria and taken into foreign captivity (722 BC), they became absorbed into the countries of their exile and largely lost their national identity. But when the people of the southern kingdom were conquered and taken captive to Babylon (605-587 BC), they largely remained in one region and retained their national identity. The people of Judah were called Judeans, and this was later shortened to 'Jew' (Jer 34:9).

After Persia's conquest of Babylon (539 BC), captives from Babylon returned to their Israelite homeland. This meant that those who rebuilt Israel were largely Judeans, or Jews. But they were also Israelites according to the name's original meaning (for they were descended from the man whose name was Israel, Jacob). There was no longer a division in the nation between north and south, and the names 'Israelite' and 'Jew', along with the ancient name 'Hebrew', were used interchangeably (John 1:19,47; 2 Cor 11:22; Gal 2:14).

Jews and Samaritans

The Samaritans were a race of people that emerged after the Assyrians' conquest of the northern kingdom in 722 BC. The Assyrians' policy was to move conquered peoples into other countries. Therefore, after they had taken the Israelites into foreign captivity, they resettled people from other parts of their empire into the cities of the former northern kingdom, mainly in the region around Samaria (2 Kings 17:6,24).

These settlers tried to avoid punishment from Israel's God, Yahweh, by combining the worship of Yahweh with their own religious practices (2 Kings 17:25-33). They also intermarried with the Israelite people left in the land, resulting in the emergence of a new racial group, the Samaritans. By the time the Jews had returned to Jerusalem (after Persia's conquest of Babylon in 539 BC), the Samaritans were well established in the land.

When the Jews began to rebuild Jerusalem and its temple, the Samaritans offered to help, but the Jewish leaders rejected them. They saw the Samaritans as a people of mixed blood and mixed religion, and feared they would introduce corrupt ideas into Israel's religion. The Samaritans reacted bitterly and opposed the Jews throughout their building program (Ezra 4:1-5; Neh 4:1-9). Although

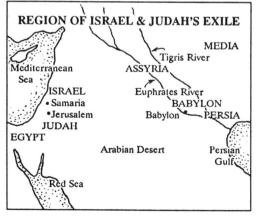

REGION OF ISRAEL & JUDAH'S EXILE

MEDIA
Tigris River
ASSYRIA
Mediterranean Sea
ISRAEL
Euphrates River
• Samaria
BABYLON
• Jerusalem
Babylon
PERSIA
JUDAH
EGYPT
Arabian Desert
Persian Gulf
Red Sea

the Jews eventually completed the building program, some of the leading Samaritans, through cunning and deceit, gained influence in Jerusalem. They introduced corrupt religious and social practices, but within a few years were driven from the city in disgrace (Neh 13:1-9,23-28).

Sacred places and sacred writings

As a result of the Jews' constant rejection of them, the Samaritans turned their attention to organizing their own religion, to make it more distinct from the religion of the Jews. One development was the building of a temple of their own on Mt Gerizim, a place of religious significance located not far from Samaria (cf. Deut 11:29; 27:12; Josh 8:33). This only increased the hatred between Jews and Samaritans, and this hatred continued into New Testament times (Luke 9:52-54; John 4:9).

In defending their actions, the Samaritans used selected parts of the Pentateuch (the five books of Moses), but they became so extreme that they almost treated the remaining Old Testament books as being of no importance. Their chief beliefs were that there was only one God, Moses was his only prophet, the law of Moses was the only authoritative teaching, and Mt Gerizim was the only true place of worship (cf. Deut 27:12; John 4:20).

The Jews, by contrast, had so many sacred writings that they were forced, by the arguments of the Samaritans, to consider which were the Word of God and which were not. This led, in time, to the acceptance of the thirty-nine books that form our Old Testament. This might be called the Jewish Bible, though the arrangement of books differs from that of the Old Testament in the Christian Bible.

The Jewish synagogue

With the rebuilding of Jerusalem and the temple, sacrificial rituals again became part of the Jewish religion. These had not been possible when the people were in exile in Babylon, with the result that greater emphasis was placed on teaching and obeying the moral teachings of the law. Although sacrificial rituals were now restored, the emphasis on teaching the law was maintained. This is clearly seen in the work of Ezra and Nehemiah, who gathered the people together in Jerusalem to read them the law and explain its meaning (Neh 8:1-4,7-8; 9:1-3). In the years that followed, such teaching activity was partly the reason for erecting local meeting places known as synagogues (from a Greek word meaning 'to gather or bring together').

Wherever the Jews settled they built themselves synagogues (Mark 1:21; Luke 4:16; John 6:59; Acts 13:5,14). These were centres for prayer, worship, teaching, fellowship and administration of local Jewish affairs. The synagogue leaders became the acknowledged leaders of the Jewish community and were called elders (Matt 21:23; Luke 7:3-5). The chief elder was known as the ruler (Mark 5:22; Acts 22:19). Elders had power to punish wrongdoers, even to the extent of flogging them or expelling them from the synagogue community (Matt 10:17; 23:34; John 9:22).

A synagogue was a simple building, consisting of a main meeting room entered through a porch, with an open court outside. It had no altar and no sacrifices were offered there. Women and men sat on opposite sides of the room, and the leaders sat in the chief seats, facing the audience (Matt 23:6).

Synagogue services were conducted at least every Sabbath and were under the control of leaders (Mark 1:21; Acts 13:14-15). The service opened with prayers, followed by readings from Old Testament scrolls that were kept in a special box and handed to the reader by an attendant (Luke 4:16-17,20; Acts 15:21). Either a local leader or an invited person then delivered an address based on one of the readings (Luke 4:16-22; Acts 13:15; 17:10-11), after which the service was closed with prayers.

In the everyday functions of the Jewish religion, synagogues became more important than the temple in Jerusalem. But later teachers were far removed in spirit from Ezra and Nehemiah, and by the time of Jesus the synagogues were more a hindrance than a help to God's purposes. The Jewish religion had changed so much that it is commonly referred to as Judaism, to distinguish it from the religion set out in the law of Moses.

Teachers of the law (scribes)

Chiefly to blame for the development of Judaism were the scribes, or teachers of the law. In the days before mechanical printing, scribes were those who made written copies of the sacred writings. Theirs was a specialized job, and because of their skill in copying details of the law exactly, people regarded them as experts on matters of the law (Ezra 7:6,10).

Although the priests were supposed to be the teachers in Israel (Deut 33:10; Mal. 2:7), people now went rather to the scribes to have problems of the law explained. During the four to five hundred years between the time of Ezra and the time of Jesus, the scribes grew in power and prestige. They became known as teachers of the law, lawyers and rabbis (Matt 22:35; 23:2-7).

There was a great difference between the explanations of the law given by Ezra and those given by the scribes of Jesus' time. Over the years the scribes had developed their own system, which consisted of countless laws to surround the central law of Moses. Some of these new laws grew out of legal cases that the scribes had judged; others grew out of traditions that had been handed down. The scribes forced their laws upon the Jewish people, till the whole lawkeeping system became a heavy burden (Matt 15:1-9; 23:2-4).

Being leaders and teachers in the synagogues, the scribes enjoyed prestige and power in the Jewish community (Matt 23:6-7). They taught in the temple in Jerusalem, and established schools where they trained disciples (Luke 2:46; Acts 22:3). They then sent these disciples to spread their teaching far and wide (Matt 23:15). Most of the scribes belonged to the party of the Pharisees, one of the two major groups that developed within Judaism (Matt 5:20; 23:2; Acts 5:34).

The Jewish Council (Sanhedrin)

As early as the time of Ezra, groups of elders and judges had been appointed to administer the law in Jewish affairs (Ezra 7:25-26; 10:14). This practice was followed in the local synagogue committees, but as these committees grew in power a more rigid system of Jewish rule developed. Although any local Jewish council could be called a Sanhedrin, the word was most commonly used for the supreme Jewish Council in Jerusalem.

The Jerusalem Sanhedrin consisted of a maximum of seventy members, not counting the high priest, who occupied the position of president. Its composition changed from time to time, but in New Testament times it consisted of scribes, elders, priests and other respected citizens. It included people from both main Jewish parties, the Pharisees and the Sadducees (Matt 26:3,57-59; Acts 5:17,34; 23:1,6).

Rome gave the Sanhedrin authority to arrest, judge and punish Jewish people in relation to certain religious and civil matters (Acts 5:17-21,40; 9:2). The Sanhedrin could condemn a person to death, though according to its own law it could not pass such a sentence at night (Luke 22:66), and according to Roman law it could not carry out the sentence (John 18:31). The Jewish authorities had to convince the Roman authorities that the person deserved death, after which the Romans themselves carried out the execution (Luke 23:1-4,24). However, the Romans knew the difficulties of governing the Jews, and they sometimes feared to deny the Jews their wishes or even to intervene when there was mob violence (Matt 27:24-26; cf. Acts 7:57-58).

JEWS UNDER FOREIGN RULE

Although the Jews were ruled by Rome in the time of Jesus, many features of the Jewish way of life were the result of political events in the pre-Roman period. The Persians, who had conquered Babylon in 539 BC and helped the Jews to rebuild their ancient homeland, remained the Jews' overlord for the next two hundred years. But rapid changes occurred with the dramatic conquests of Alexander the Great and the establishment of the Greek Empire.

Greek rule and influence

Alexander was from Macedonia, the northern part of present-day Greece. In little more than a year he overran Asia Minor and took control of much of the eastern Mediterranean region (333 BC). His conquests spread rapidly through parts of northern

THE GREEK EMPIRE

Africa and western Asia, then continued over what remained of the Persian Empire till they reached India.

Wherever they went the Greeks planted Greek culture. The Greek language became commonly spoken throughout the region, and remained so into the New Testament era in spite of the rise of Roman power. People in local regions continued to speak their own languages (the Jews of Palestine spoke Aramaic, a language related to Hebrew), but they usually spoke Greek as well (cf. Mark 5:41; 15:34; John 19:20; Acts 14:11; 22:2). The New Testament was written in Greek.

Greek architecture spread through the building of magnificent new cities, and Greek philosophy changed the thinking of people everywhere (1 Cor. 1:20-22). The Greeks brought some help to the people they governed, by providing a standard of education, sport, entertainment and social welfare that most people had never known before. Those who absorbed this Greek culture were regarded as civilized; all others were regarded as barbarians (Rom 1:14).

Alexander died while at the height of his power (323 BC) and his vast empire was divided among his generals. In the early days after the break-up there were four dominant leaders, but power struggles among them (and others) continued for many years. By 301 BC there were three main sectors in the divided empire: one in the west centred on Macedonia, and two in the east centred respectively on Egypt to the south and Syria to the north.

At first Palestine was within the Egyptian sector, where each of the Greek rulers took the name Ptolemy. Under the Ptolemies the Jews had a reasonably peaceful existence. During this time, in the recently built city of Alexandria in Egypt, a group of about seventy Jewish scholars translated the Hebrew Bible into Greek. This translation is known as the Septuagint (meaning 'seventy' and usually abbreviated as LXX). In New Testament times both Jews and Christians used the Septuagint as well as the Hebrew Old Testament. When the New Testament writers quoted the Old Testament, they usually used the Septuagint rather than make their own translation from the Hebrew.

Changes in Israel

Some of the later Ptolemies became hostile to the Jews, but conditions worsened when the Syrian sector conquered the Egyptian sector and so brought Palestine under its control (198 BC). The Greek kings who ruled Syria were known as the Seleucids, after the king who founded the dynasty. Most of the kings gave themselves the name Antiochus, after Antioch, the capital of the Seleucid kingdom that the founder of the dynasty built in 300 BC (cf. Acts 11:20; 13:1,4).

Israel had now been under Greek rule for more than a hundred years, and Greek customs and ideas were having an influence on the Jews' religion and way of life. Divisions began to appear among the Jewish people. Some Jews not only tolerated this Greek influence but actively encouraged it. In doing so they won favours from the Greek rulers and had themselves appointed to important positions in the Jewish system. Others firmly opposed all Greek influence, particularly the influence of Greek rulers in Jewish religious affairs.

When fighting broke out in Jerusalem between rival Jewish factions, the Seleucid king of the time, Antiochus IV Epiphanes, mistakenly thought that the people were rebelling against him. He invaded Jerusalem, killed Jews in thousands, made others slaves, burnt the Jewish Scriptures, forced Jews to eat forbidden food and compelled them to work on the Sabbath day. He set up a Greek altar in the Jewish temple, then, using animals that the Jews considered unclean, offered sacrifices to the Greek gods. To the Jews this was 'the awful horror' (GNB), 'the abomination that makes desolate' (RSV) (Dan 11:31). But Antiochus failed to realize that the Jews were zealous for their religion and would not stand idly by and allow him to destroy it.

Jewish resistance led by the Maccabees

The Jews' fight for religious freedom began through a priest named Mattathias. He and his five sons (known as the Maccabees, after Judas Maccabeus, his son and the leader of the group) escaped from Jerusalem, put together a small army and began to carry out surprise attacks against the forces of Antiochus. The attacks were so successful that after about three years the Maccabees had overthrown the pro-Greek party of Jewish priests in Jerusalem and cleansed and rededicated the temple (165 BC). From that time on, the Jewish people celebrated the great event in the annual Feast of Dedication (John 10:22).

Encouraged by their remarkable victory, the Maccabees (also known as the Hasmoneans, after their old family name) decided to keep fighting till they had won political freedom as well. But the religiously strict Jews, who had previously opposed Greek political interference in their religion, also opposed the Maccabees' drive for political power. They believed that the Maccabees had done their job by restoring the temple and regaining religious freedom for the Jews. They should not have any part in politics.

These opposing viewpoints eventually produced the two main parties that divided the Jewish people, the Sadducees and the Pharisees. The Sadducees wanted political power, whereas the Pharisees were content to have religious freedom. The Maccabees carried on the war in spite of the Jewish opposition, and after twenty years won political independence (143 BC).

Sadducees and Pharisees

After four and a half centuries under Babylon, Persia, and then Greece, the Jews were free again. However, they were now clearly divided, under the domination of two major parties. On the one side were the pro-political priests and leaders (the later Sadducees) who were wealthy, powerful and favoured by the Hasmonean rulers. On the other side were the anti-political traditionalists (the later Pharisees), who were poor, powerless and favoured by the common people. The differences between the two parties increased as each developed its own beliefs and practices.

The Pharisees' chief aim was to keep the law in all its details; not so much the law of Moses as the countless laws developed and taught by the teachers of the law, the scribes. They were particularly strict in keeping rules relating to religious observances such as fasting (Luke 18:11-12), tithing (Matt 23:23), Sabbath-keeping (Matt 12:1-2), the taking of oaths (Matt 23:16-22) and ritual cleanliness (Mark 7:1-9). The name 'Pharisees' meant 'the separated ones', and many were so convinced they were God's only true people that they kept themselves apart from others (Acts 26:5; Gal 2:12).

If the Pharisees were the party of the scribes, the Sadducees were the party of the priests (Acts 5:17). (Their name possibly comes from Zadok, a priest of Solomon's time whose descendants were regarded as the only legitimate priests; 1 Kings 1:38-39; Ezek 44:15-16). The Sadducees' strategy was to use the religious and political structures of Jewish society to gain power for themselves. Since they controlled the priesthood, one of the main channels of power, it suited them to emphasize the temple rituals. However, they had little interest in the traditions of the scribes. The only Jewish law they acknowledged was the written law of Moses (Luke 20:27-28).

Sadducees and Pharisees had several other well known differences, chiefly in matters of their beliefs. The Sadducees did not believe in the continued existence of the soul after death, the resurrection of the body, the directing will of God in life's events, or the existence of angelic beings, all of which were important beliefs to the Pharisees (Matt 22:23; Acts 4:1-2; 23:7-8).

End of Jewish independence

The Hasmoneans ruled for almost one hundred years. Under them political, religious and military power joined together, so that the Hasmonean ruler was at the same time governor, high priest and commander-in-chief of the army.

During the period of Hasmonean rule the Pharisees were often the ones who suffered. They welcomed the chance to reverse the situation when a later queen showed herself favourable to them. But when she died, fighting broke out between her two sons, one of whom favoured the Pharisees, the other the Sadducees. At that time Rome's power was spreading towards Palestine, and as General Pompey had his army nearby in Syria, both sides asked for his help. Pompey settled the dispute by leading his army into Jerusalem and taking control himself. Thus, in 63 BC, Jewish independence came to an end.

Herod the Great

One of the two brothers who sought Rome's support was appointed by the Roman administration as political head and high priest of Judea. He proved to be a weak leader. He was very much under the influence of an Idumean friend Antipater, who was cunningly planning to gain control himself. (Idumea was a region in the south of Judea that was inhabited by a mixture of Jews, Arabs and the remains of the nation once known as Edom.) In the end Antipater was appointed governor of Judea, with his two sons in the top two positions under him.

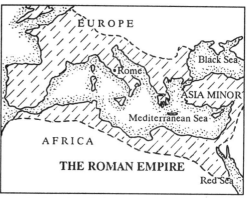

THE ROMAN EMPIRE

At that time Judea, and in fact the whole of the eastern Mediterranean region, was troubled by a succession of power struggles, divisions and wars. Antipater was eventually murdered and his sons overthrown. But one of the sons, who had developed even greater cunning than his father, escaped to Rome, from where he had himself appointed the new governor of Judea and given the title of king. This person we know as Herod the Great.

Through treachery and murder, Herod removed all possible rivals. Then, having made his position safe, he began to develop and expand his kingdom. He ruled Judea for thirty-three years (37-4 BC). He carried out impressive building programs, two of his most notable achievements being the rebuilding of Samaria and the construction of Caesarea as a Mediterranean port. In Jerusalem he built a military fortress, government buildings, a palace for himself and a magnificent temple for the Jews (Matt 27:27; Mark 13:1; John 2:20; Acts 23:10,35).

In spite of the benefits Herod brought them, the Jews hated him. This was partly because of his mixed blood (though he was Jewish by religion) and partly because of his ruthlessness in murdering any he thought a threat to his position. His butchery was well demonstrated in his massacre of the Bethlehem babies at the time of Jesus' birth (Matt 2:13,16).

Family of Herod

Before he died, Herod divided his kingdom between three of his sons, though they, like their father, could rule only within the authority Rome gave them. The southern and central parts of Palestine (Judea and Samaria) went to Archelaus, a man as cruel as his father but without his father's ability (Matt 2:22). The northern part of Palestine (Galilee) and the

area east of Jordan (Decapolis and Perea) went to Herod Antipas, the man who later killed John the Baptist and who agreed to the killing of Jesus (Mark 6:14-29; Luke 3:1; 23:6-12). The areas north-east of the Sea of Galilee (Iturea and Trachonitis) went to Herod Philip, a man of milder nature than the rest of his family (Luke 3:1).

Direct Roman rule

Archelaus was so cruel and unjust that in AD 6 the people of Judea and Samaria asked Rome to remove him and govern them directly. From that time on, Judea and Samaria were ruled by Roman governors, or procurators, with headquarters at Caesarea. The procurators of Judea and Samaria mentioned in the Bible are Pilate, Felix and Festus (Matt 27:2; Acts 23:24,33; 25:1).

The only exception to this rule by procurators was the brief 'reign' of Herod Agrippa I, a grandson of Herod the Great (Acts 12:1-4,20-23). Through winning favour with Rome, he gained the former territories of Herod Philip (in AD 37) and Herod Antipas (in AD 39). In AD 41 he gained Judea and Samaria, and for three years he ruled almost the entire 'kingdom' of Herod the Great. Upon his death in AD 44, Judea and Samaria returned to the rule of Roman governors.

Earlier, when a governor from Rome replaced Archelaus (AD 6), the Jews for the first time had to pay taxes to the Romans direct instead of through the Herodian ruler. When Rome conducted a census to assess this tax, a group of Jews led by a man called Judas the Galilean rebelled, claiming that it was wrong for the people of God to pay tax to a pagan emperor (Acts 5:37). Because of their zeal in trying to free Israel from pagan influence, they became known as Zealots, or Patriots, and formed a minor political-religious party in Israel (Luke 6:15; Acts 1:13).

The zealots were so opposed to Roman rule that they were prepared to fight against it. Rome's mismanagement of Jewish affairs increased their determination, and in AD 66 they revolted openly by taking control of Jerusalem. There was much turmoil and bloodshed during the next four years, but the Romans gradually reasserted their control, first in Galilee then throughout Judea. Finally, in a series of brutal and devastating attacks, they conquered Jerusalem, massacred the people, burnt the temple and left the city in ruins (AD 70). So far as Rome was concerned, the Jewish nation was finished.

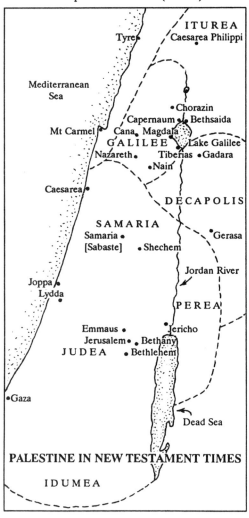

PALESTINE IN NEW TESTAMENT TIMES

ISRAEL UNDER PERSIA, GREECE AND ROME

539 BC	Persia conquers Babylon; releases Jews from captivity
	Jewish nation rebuilt in Palestine, but under Persian rule
333	Alexander the Great overpowers Persia; conquers entire Empire within two years
323	Alexander dies; Greek Empire divided into several sectors
	301-198 BC Palestine ruled by Egyptian sector
	198-143 BC Palestine ruled by Syrian sector
143	Jews win complete independence, but divided through political and religious conflicts
63	Jews lose independence; Rome takes over Palestine
37	Herod the Great becomes Rome-appointed ruler of Palestine
4	Herod the Great dies; his 'kingdom' divided between his sons
	Archelaus ruler of Judea and Samaria
	Herod Antipas ruler of Galilee, Decapolis and Perea
	Herod Philip ruler of regions north-east of Jordan
AD 6	Archelaus replaced; Judea and Samaria ruled by Roman governors
	Pontius Pilate fifth Roman governor of Judea and Samaria (AD 26-36)
37	Herod Agrippa I gains territories of Herod Philip (AD 37) and Herod Antipas (AD 39),
	followed by Judea and Samaria (AD 41); rules whole of Palestine for three years
44	Herod Agrippa I dies; most of Palestine returns to rule by Roman governors
	Herod Agrippa II rules far northern regions of Palestine (AD 48-70)
	Felix (AD 52-60), Festus (AD 60-62) Roman governors of Judea and Samaria
70	Fall of Jerusalem

PART OF HEROD THE GREAT'S FAMILY

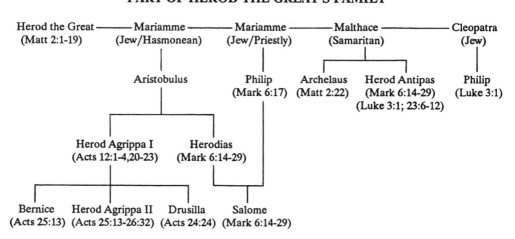

385

Introduction to the Four Gospels

THE WRITING OF THE GOSPELS

According to long-established practice, the first four books of the New Testament are known as Gospels. This is probably because they record the gospel, or good news, of the coming of Jesus Christ, the world's Saviour.

Each of the four Gospel writers had a special purpose in writing his book, and he selected and used his material accordingly. Each gave his own emphasis to teachings and events taken from the life of Jesus, according to the plan and purpose of his book. The writers wrote for different people, who lived in various countries and came from different racial and religious backgrounds. Yet there is no disagreement in the picture of Jesus Christ that the four writers present: he is divine and human, Lord of all and the Saviour of people everywhere (Matt 11:27-30; Mark 2:10,28; Luke 2:11,29-32; John 5:20-25).

The Gospels are not biographies of Jesus, and make no attempt to give a detailed or chronological account of Jesus' life. Nevertheless, they give all the facts that people need to know in order to believe in Jesus as the Son of God and so have life through him (John 20:31).

Record of Jesus' life

Taken together the four Gospels present a picture of three main periods in Jesus' life. These three periods are his early childhood, his public ministry (i.e. his teachings, healings, miracles, etc.) and his death, burial and resurrection.

The stories of events leading to, including, and immediately following Jesus' birth are given at some length. Nothing more is written about his childhood until he was twelve years old, and even then only one incident is recorded. But that incident is enough to show that even at such an early age Jesus knew he had a special relation with God, for he was God's Son (Luke 2:49; cf. 1:35).

Nothing more is recorded in the Bible of the next eighteen years (approximately) of Jesus' life. Then, when about thirty years old, he began his public ministry (Luke 3:23), and this lasted about three and a half years. Much of his work was done in Galilee, the northern part of Palestine, though he met his fiercest opposition in Judea in the south, particularly in Jerusalem, the centre of Jewish religious power. The religious leaders considered that Jesus was guilty of blasphemy in claiming to be the Son of God, and they were constantly looking for an opportunity to kill him. Jesus, however, continued to carry out his ministry openly, knowing that he would be arrested and killed only when he had finished his ministry and the time appointed by his Father had come (Luke 13:31-33; John 8:20; 13:1; 17:1,4).

Jesus' last week in Jerusalem was full of tension and activity, and is recorded in greater detail than any other part of his life. He entered Jerusalem as Israel's Messiah-king, cleansed the temple, debated with hostile Jewish opponents, gave teaching to his disciples on many subjects, then allowed himself to be arrested, cruelly treated, falsely condemned and crucified. Then follows an account of his burial, resurrection, and activity after his resurrection. Finally, he returned to his Father with the promise that one day he would come again (Luke 24:50-51; Acts 1:9-11).

Extent of Jesus' ministry

If we had only the Gospels of Matthew, Mark and Luke, we might think that the public ministry of Jesus lasted barely a year and that he spent almost the whole of that time in the north. John's Gospel records more of his work in the south, particularly in and around Jerusalem. It also provides information that shows clearly that the ministry of Jesus lasted several years.

John mentions three specific Passover Feasts (John 2:13; 6:1,4; 13:1) and possibly a fourth (John 5:1. It is widely assumed that the unnamed feast mentioned here was the Passover). Because the Passover Feast was held only once a year, the record of four Passovers would indicate that the public ministry of Jesus must have covered at least three years.

The broad divisions of Jesus' ministry are set out in the following table. We should bear in mind, however, that we cannot with certainty assign every portion of the Gospel accounts to a particular time or place in Jesus' life.

Jesus baptized in Jordan; tempted by Satan; begins his public ministry; visits Cana and Capernaum in Galilee	3 months (approx.)
1st Passover – Jesus goes to Jerusalem (John 2:13)	
From Jerusalem Jesus goes through Samaria to Galilee; remainder of year spent in Galilee	1 year
2nd Passover – Jesus goes to Jerusalem (John 5:1)	
Jesus returns to Galilee; further work around Lake of Galilee and in other northern areas	1 year
3rd Passover – Jesus in Galilee prior to feast (John 6:1,4)	
Further work in Galilee and other northern areas; through Samaria to Jerusalem for Jewish festivals; work around Jordan valley	1 year
4th Passover – Jesus goes to Jerusalem; crucifixion (John 13:1)	
Jesus with his disciples in various places in Judea and Galilee; ascension	6 weeks (approx.)

Re-telling the story of Jesus

Soon after Jesus' ascension, his disciples began the task of spreading the good news of the salvation he had brought. They started in Jerusalem and several thousand were converted (Acts 1:8; 2:41,47; 4:5; 5:14; 6:7). From Jerusalem the gospel spread to neighbouring provinces, then to countries beyond, till Christianity was firmly established in western Asia and eastern Europe (Acts 8:5,40, 11:19-20; 13:4,14; 16:11-12; 18:1; 28:13-15). This growth took place over a period of about thirty years (the AD 30s to the 60s).

Those who became Christians were taught the stories that recounted the activity and teaching of Jesus. This emphasis on the life of Jesus was one reason why apostles had to be personal associates who had been with Jesus from his baptism to his ascension. They could give first-hand accounts of what he said and did, and in particular could give eye-witness testimony to his resurrection (Acts 1:21-22; 3:15; 5:32; 10:36-41). The apostles carefully instructed new believers, who memorized the stories and sayings of Jesus and went out to spread the good news to others. New converts were taught similarly, and they too went out to teach and make disciples of others (Matt 28:18-20; Acts 2:42; 8:4; 2 Tim 2:2).

As the years passed and the church grew, those who had seen and heard Jesus became fewer in number and more widely scattered. In order to preserve what these witnesses taught about Jesus, people began to prepare written accounts of things Jesus said and did (Luke 1:1). In this sort of activity we can see the origins of the four Gospels, the first of which was probably written about AD 60, and the last about AD 90. Although we do not know all the details concerning how or when each book was written, we can find enough evidence in the books themselves and in other first century writings to make the following explanation a possibility.

Two related accounts

It seems that Mark's Gospel was the first to be written. Mark had assisted the apostle Peter in missionary work that took them through the north of Asia Minor and brought them eventually to Rome (cf. 1 Peter 1:1; 5:13). When Peter left to go on further journeys, Mark remained for a while in Rome. The Roman Christians asked Mark to write down the story of Jesus as they had heard it from Peter, with the result that he wrote the book that we know as Mark's Gospel.

Mark was was still in Rome when Paul arrived as a prisoner, accompanied by Luke and Aristarchus (Acts 27:2; 28:16). In letters Paul wrote from Rome at this time, he mentions that Mark, Luke and Aristarchus were all with him, and they surely would have got to know each other well (Col. 4:10,14; Philem 24).

Over the years Luke also had been preparing an account of the life of Jesus. No doubt he did much research during the two years he had recently spent with Paul in Palestine (Acts 24:27). Others had already written accounts of Jesus' life and ministry (Luke 1:1), and Luke gathered material from these as well as from people still living in Palestine who had seen and heard Jesus. When he arrived in Rome and met Mark, he took some of Mark's material to add to his own and so bring his book to completion.

Whereas Mark wrote for a group of Christians, Luke wrote for someone who was probably not a Christian. This person, Theophilus, appears to have been a government official of some importance, and Luke's purpose was to give him a trustworthy account of the origins of Christianity (Luke 1:1-4). Luke's account was so long that it was divided into two books. The first, which covers events from the birth of Jesus to his ascension, we know as Luke's Gospel. The second, which covers events from Jesus' ascension to Paul's arrival in Rome, we know as the Acts of the Apostles (cf. Acts 1:1-2).

A third related account

The Gospel of Matthew appears to have been written about ten years after the Gospels of Mark and Luke. Matthew's concern was to produce an account of Jesus' ministry that was especially suited to the needs of Christians of Jewish background. His book shows a particular interest in the fulfilment of God's purposes concerning Israel's Messiah, and the responsibility of the Messiah's people to spread his message to the Gentiles. According to early records, the Jewish Christians for whom Matthew wrote were those of Syria and Palestine.

By this time Mark's Gospel had become more widely known, and because it represented Peter's account of Jesus' ministry, it was well respected. Matthew therefore saved himself a lot of work by using much of Mark's material in his own book. (About 90% of Mark is found in Matthew.) There is also a lot of material common to Matthew and Luke that is not found in Mark. This material, commonly referred to as Q, probably came from one or more of the many writings in use at the time (cf. Luke 1:1). This common material Q consists mainly of sayings and teachings of Jesus, in contrast to stories about him.

Because of the parallels between Matthew, Mark and Luke, the three books are often referred to as the Synoptic Gospels (meaning Gospels that 'see from the same viewpoint', in contrast to the Gospel of John). Each of the Synoptic Gospels, however, has material of its own that has no parallel in the other Gospels. In Mark this amount is less than 5%, in Matthew about 28%, and in Luke about 45%.

A different kind of book

John's Gospel is different in form and style from the other three Gospels. The book was written probably within the last decade or so of the first century, by which time the other three Gospels were widely known. Although John follows the same general development of the story from Jesus' baptism to his resurrection, his purpose was not to produce another narrative account of Jesus' ministry. He selected only a few stories of Jesus, but recorded at length the teaching that arose out of them. He wanted to instruct people in basic Christian truth concerning who Jesus was and what this meant for the people of the world.

The reason John wrote his Gospel was that in the region where he lived (probably Ephesus, in western Asia Minor), people were confused because of the activity of false teachers. Some of these denied that Jesus was fully divine, others that he was fully human. John opposed these teachers (cf. 1 John 2:18-23,26; 4:1-3), but his chief reason for writing was not negative. He had a positive purpose, and that was to lead people to see Jesus as the Son of God and so to find true life through him (John 20:30-31).

Much of John's Gospel therefore consists of teaching, but most of this teaching comes from the recorded words of Jesus himself. In comparison with the Synoptic Gospels, action stories are few. More than 90% of the material in John's Gospel is not found in the other Gospels.

INTRODUCTION TO MATTHEW

The writer and his readers

Matthew's Gospel does not record the name of its author or the purpose for which he wrote the book. The title 'Matthew', given to it in the second century, reflects the early church's belief that the author was the apostle Matthew. There was, however, some uncertainty concerning the stages of development that the book went through before the final version appeared. Whether or not Matthew himself actually produced the finished product, it seems clear that his writings (referred to in second century documents) must have at least provided a major source of material for the book.

Like the rest of the New Testament, the Gospel of Matthew was written in Greek. It seems to have been written for Greek-speaking Jewish Christians of Syria and Palestine, to reassure them that Jesus was the Messiah promised in the Old Testament, and he fulfilled the purposes for which God chose Israel. The Jewish Christians, as the people of the Messiah, were not to fail in evangelizing the Gentiles as Israel of Old Testament times had failed, but were to be energetic in spreading the gospel to all nations (Matt 28:19-20; cf. 8:11-12; 11:20-24; 24:14).

A likely place for the writing of such a book is Antioch in Syria, which was closely connected with the Jewish churches of the region and the mission to the Gentile nations (Acts 11:19-22,27-29; 13:1-4; 15:1-3,22). (For further details on the writing of Matthew's Gospel see previous section, 'The Writing of the Gospels'.)

Matthew the tax collector

Evidence within the Gospel supports the view that the writer was Matthew the tax collector, who later became one of the twelve apostles. When Mark and Luke list the twelve apostles, they name Matthew but do not record his occupation (Mark 3:18; Luke 6:15). When they mention the tax collector who became a follower of Jesus, they call him not Matthew but Levi, which was his other name (Mark 2:14-17; Luke 5:27-32). They seem, out of kindness to Matthew, to avoid mentioning that he was once a tax collector, for the Jews despised those of their own people who collected taxes on behalf of the oppressor Rome.

Matthew, far from hiding the fact that he was once a tax collector, states it clearly. He uses the name Matthew, not Levi, in speaking of his response to Jesus' call (Matt 9:9-13), and when listing the twelve apostles he states his previous occupation (Matt 10:3). The book reflects the gratitude that a tax collector would feel in being chosen by Jesus to be an apostle. Stories about the dangers of money reflect the lessons learnt by one whose life was once dominated by greed (Matt 18:23-35; 20:1-16; 27:3-10; 28:12-13).

The place where Matthew worked as a tax collector was Capernaum, on the shore of Lake Galilee (Mark 2:1,13-14). He had a good income and owned a house large enough to entertain a large number of people (Luke 5:29). He seems to have enjoyed a secure and stable lifestyle, but he left all this for the risky business of following Jesus and spreading the good news of his kingdom (Matt 10:5-23). He was involved in the establishment of the early church (Acts 1:13), but the Bible gives no details of his later ministry.

Arrangement of Matthew's material

Matthew's Gospel may contain much that is in Mark and Luke, but the treatment of the material is different. Luke, for example, has usually grouped together stories that are exclusive to him, and kept them separate from stories that he has taken from Mark. But Matthew has adjusted and rearranged all his material, regardless of its source. He has made each part fit into the plan of his book in a way that makes it inseparable from the rest. He records more teaching and less action in comparison with Mark and Luke, and his material is not always in chronological order.

In Matthew the material is arranged according to subject matter rather than chronology. It is built around five main teaching sections where Jesus instructs his followers in what he requires of those who enter his kingdom. Each of the five sections concludes with a statement such as 'When Jesus had finished these sayings . . .' (Matt 7:28; 11:1; 13:53; 19:1; 26:1). The five sections concern the personal behaviour of those in Christ's kingdom (Chapters 5-7), proclamation of the message of the kingdom (Chapter 10), parables of the kingdom (Chapter 13), attitudes to others within the kingdom (Chapters 18) and the climax of the kingdom at the return of Christ (Chapters 24-25).

A teaching purpose

The characteristic flavour of the Gospel of Matthew comes mainly from the material that is found only in Matthew. Included in this are many quotations from the Old Testament. Matthew often introduces these quotations by a statement showing how the Old Testament was fulfilled in Jesus (Matt 1:22; 4:14; 8:17; 13:35; 21:4; 27:9).

In particular Matthew shows that Jesus was the promised Messiah, the son of David, the fulfilment of God's purposes for Israel (Matt 1:1,17; 2:6; 9:27; 11:2-6; 16:16; 21:9; 26:63-64). The kingdom of God was the rule of God, and in Jesus that kingdom had entered the world (Matt 4:17,23; 5:3; 12:28; 18:1-4; 24:14). Jesus was the king, though he was not the sort of king that most people had expected (Matt 4:8-10; 21:5,9-11; 25:31,34; 26:52-53; 27:11). (For further discussion on the kingdom of God and the Messiah see the section 'Jesus and the Kingdom' that follows.)

Jewish Christians were often persecuted by unbelieving Jews for forsaking the religion of their ancestors. Matthew reassured these Christians by pointing out that they were not the ones who had wandered away from the Old Testament religion. Rather they had found the true fulfilment of it. Jesus did not contradict the law, but brought out its full meaning (Matt 5:17).

Matthew not only taught the Jewish Christians the high standards of behaviour required of them, but urged them to be energetic in spreading the good news of the kingdom to others (Matt 5:13-16; 10:5-8; 24:14; 28:19-20). The unbelieving Jews, who zealously kept the traditions, were consistently condemned (Matt 15:1-9; 23:1-36). They missed out on the promised kingdom, with the result that the gospel was sent to the Gentiles, and many believed (Matt 3:7-9; 8:11-12; 12:21,38-42; 21:43). Jesus had laid the foundation of his church, and no opposition, whether from the Jews or the Romans, could overpower it (Matt 16:18).

INTRODUCTION TO MARK

Authorship

Like the other three Gospels, Mark is anonymous. However, from the first century the commonly held view has been that the author is John Mark of Jerusalem, and that his Gospel reflects Peter's account of Jesus' ministry.

Mark came from a prominent family in the early Jerusalem church. His parents were wealthy enough to own a large house and employ servants (Acts 12:12-13) and at least one of his close relatives, Barnabas, was a reasonably prosperous landowner (Acts 4:36-37; Col. 4:10). The traditional belief is that Mark's family home was the place where Jesus held the last supper and where the disciples met in the early days of the church (Luke 22:11-13; Acts 1:13).

Mark's service in the gospel

Perhaps the first reference to Mark is in the story of the young man who followed Jesus and his friends to the Garden of Gethsemane but fled when opponents tried to seize him. This story appears only in Mark's Gospel (Mark 14:51-52). According to a common practice, an author might include a reference to himself but not use his own name directly (cf. John 13:23; 2 Cor 12:2).

Because the early church leaders met in Mark's family home, Mark would have known Peter and other early Christian leaders (Acts 12:12-14). Paul and Barnabas were impressed with him sufficiently to take him with them from Jerusalem to Antioch in Syria, and then to Cyprus and Asia Minor on a missionary journey (Acts 12:25; 13:1-5).

After only a short time, Mark left Paul and Barnabas and returned to Jerusalem (Acts 13:13). Paul thought this showed a weakness in Mark and refused to take him on his next missionary journey. When Paul and Barnabas quarrelled about the matter and separated, Barnabas took Mark on a return mission to Cyprus (Acts 15:36-41).

The Bible records nothing of Mark's activities during the next ten years or so. Other early records, however, provide evidence that he spent some time with Peter evangelizing the northern regions of Asia Minor. He became so closely associated with Peter that Peter referred to him as his son (1 Peter 5:13). Later the two visited Rome, where Peter helped the church by his teaching on the life and ministry of Jesus. When Peter left Rome, Mark stayed behind, and in response to the needs of the local Christians he wrote down the story of Jesus as they had heard it from Peter. The result was Mark's Gospel. (For further reference to Mark's ministry in Rome see earlier section 'The Writing of the Gospels'.)

Paul visited Rome while Mark was there, and recommended him as one who could be of help to young Christians (Col. 4:10). A few years later, when Paul was awaiting execution, he called for Mark to be with him in his final days (2 Tim 4:11).

Features of Mark's Gospel

In Mark's Gospel there are many features that reflect the interests and character of Peter. Apart from events surrounding Jesus' death and resurrection, most of Jesus' ministry recorded in Mark was centred in Galilee, where Peter's home town of Capernaum seems to have been Jesus' base. In fact, his real base may have been Peter's own house (Mark 1:21,29; 2:1; 9:33).

The account in Mark shows the characteristic haste of Peter, as it rushes on from one story to the next. The language is usually more clearcut than in the parallels of the other Gospels, reported statements are more direct and details are more vivid. This is particularly so in describing Jesus' actions and emotions (Mark 1:41; 3:5; 4:38; 6:6; 10:14,16,21,32). The genuineness of Peter is seen in that his mistakes are more openly reported than in the other Gospels (Mark 9:5-6; 14:66-72), whereas incidents that might bring him praise are omitted (cf. Matt 14:29; 16:17).

As the story of Jesus was set in Palestine, the Gentiles in Rome needed certain details explained. Consequently, Mark translated Hebrew or Aramaic expressions (Mark 3:17; 5:41; 7:11,34; 15:22,34) and explained Jewish beliefs and practices (Mark 7:3-4; 12:18,42; 14:12; 15:42).

Persecution of Christians

During the decade of the sixties, the government intensified its persecution of Christians, particularly after Nero blamed Christians for the great fire of Rome in AD 64. Just before this, Peter had written a letter from Rome (which he code-named Babylon; 1 Peter 5:13) to Christians in northern Asia Minor to warn them that, although they were already being persecuted, worse was to come. He gave them encouragement to face their trials positively and to look forward to a victorious future (1 Peter 1:6; 2:20-23; 3:14-17; 4:12-16). Not long after this he himself was executed by Rome (2 Peter 1:14; cf. John 21:18-19).

Mark's Gospel, like 1 Peter, was written at the beginning of this time of increasing persecution. It reminded the Roman Christians (from Peter's own experience of the life and teaching of Jesus) that they would need strength and patience to endure misunderstandings, false accusations, persecution and possibly betrayal (Mark 3:21,30; 4:17; 8:34-38; 10:30; 13:9,13; 14:41,71-72; 15:15,19,32).

Mark's view of Jesus

The Gospel of Mark records more action than the other Gospels, but less of Jesus' teaching. Its basic teaching purpose, as the opening verse indicates, is to show that Jesus is the Son of God (Mark 1:1). According to Mark, the entire ministry of Jesus showed that he was a divine person in human form, the Messiah who came from God.

At the baptism of Jesus, the starting point of his public ministry, God's declaration concerning Jesus showed what this unique ministry would involve. That declaration combined Old Testament quotations relating to the Davidic Messiah and the Servant of the Lord, showing that Jesus' way to kingly glory was to be that of the suffering servant (Mark 1:11; cf. Ps 2:7; Isa 42:1). Jesus was the heavenly Son of man to whom God promised a worldwide and everlasting kingdom, but he would receive that kingdom only by way of crucifixion (Mark 8:29-31,38; 10:45; 14:62; cf. Dan 7:13-14). (For the meaning of 'Son of man' and 'Son of God' see 'Jesus and the Kingdom' below.)

As might be expected, the death of Jesus is the climax of Mark's Gospel, but Mark draws attention to the confession of Jesus that brought about that death. Mark alone records that when the Sanhedrin asked Jesus if he was the Messiah, the Son of God, Jesus replied openly, 'I am'. Jesus then expanded his answer to show that he was both messianic Son of God and heavenly Son of man, and he was on the way to his kingly and heavenly glory (Mark 14:61-64).

Throughout his Gospel, Mark reinforces this essential truth that Jesus was the Son of God. Demons knew that Jesus was the Son of God (Mark 3:11; 5:7), Jesus' disciples recognized it (Mark 8:29), and the Father confirmed it at his transfiguration (Mark 9:7). Jesus declared it plainly to his disciples and to his enemies (Mark 13:32; 14:61-62), and even a Roman centurion at the cross was forced to admit it (Mark 15:39).

INTRODUCTION TO LUKE

Luke and Theophilus

The opening words of the Gospel of Luke and the book of Acts indicate that the two books were written by the same person. Together they form a continuous record of the origins of Christianity, from the birth of its founder to the arrival of its greatest missionary in Rome.

Both books were written for a man named Theophilus, who, from the title by which he is addressed, appears to have been a person of some importance, possibly a high-ranking official in the Roman government (Luke 1:1-4; Acts 1:1-2). The books do not record the name of the writer, but the common belief from the time of the early church is that it was Luke.

A Gentile historian

It seems certain that Luke was a Gentile, and therefore the only New Testament writer who was not a Jew. Early records suggest that he was born in Antioch in Syria, though at the time of Paul's missionary travels he seems to have lived in Philippi, in the north of present-day Greece.

By profession Luke was a doctor (Col 4:14), but he became also a skilled historian. He carefully dated the beginning of his story according to well known events (Luke 2:1-2; 3:1-2), and the findings of archaeology have confirmed the exactness of the technical words he used for places and officials (Acts 13:7; 16:12,35; 18:12,16; 19:31,35)

Luke first appears in the biblical record when he joined Paul in north-western Asia Minor and accompanied him on Christianity's first missionary thrust into Europe. Luke's movements can, to some extent, be traced by his use of the word 'we' when he was with the missionary party and the word 'they' when he was not. Paul's first centre of evangelism in Europe was Philippi (Acts 16:10-12), and Luke remained there when Paul moved on to other parts of Greece (Acts 17:1). He rejoined Paul several years later when, on a subsequent journey, Paul passed through Philippi on his way to Jerusalem (Acts 20:5-6).

It seems that from this time on, Luke remained with Paul as one of his most valued fellow workers. When Paul was arrested in Jerusalem and then imprisoned in Caesarea, Luke remained close by. He no doubt used the time to gather information from eye witnesses of the life of Jesus to include in his Gospel (Luke 1:2-3). When, at the end of a two-year imprisonment, Paul was sent to Rome, Luke accompanied him (Acts 27:1; 28:16). He was with Paul during a further two-year imprisonment in Rome, and during this time he finished the writing of his Gospel and Acts (Acts 28:30; Col 4:14; Philem 24). (For further details of events in Rome that helped Luke in his writings, see earlier section 'The Writing of the Gospels'.)

Luke concluded his two-part record at the point he had chosen. Christianity's greatest ambassador was proclaiming the gospel openly and unhindered in the very heart of the Empire (Acts 28:31). But the end of Luke's book did not mean the end of Paul's life. As had happened many times before, Paul was released from his imprisonment and went on further travels. After visiting churches in various countries he was again arrested, then taken to Rome where this time he faced execution. Luke was still with him, and in fact was the only one with him as Paul awaited the executioner (2 Tim 4:6,11).

Stories with a purpose

Of the four Gospels, Luke is the longest and most orderly. It covers more of the life of Jesus than the other Gospels, though like them it does not attempt to give a biography of Jesus. The writer has gathered and arranged his material with a definite purpose in mind, and with much skill has produced a book that contains more of the well known stories of Jesus than any other.

In writing his account, Luke was concerned with more than providing Theophilus with a record of historical details. He selected and presented his material in a way that defended and promoted Christianity. He wanted to show that God in his love had a plan of salvation for a sinful humanity, and that in accordance with that plan Jesus Christ came to be the Saviour. Those who believed in Jesus received the promised salvation, then spread the message of that salvation worldwide (Luke 1:17; 1:68-73; 2:11; 3:4-6; 4:18,21; 19:10; 24:44-48; cf. Acts 1:8). (Most of the statements and stories represented by the references above, and by those that follow, are found only in Luke.)

A Saviour for all

Luke shows that although Jesus belonged to the Jewish race and grew up in the Jewish religion, the salvation he brought was not in any way tied to the Jews. People did not have to adopt the Jewish religion or the Jewish way of life to be saved. Certainly, the religion of Israel had prepared the way for Jesus, but now that he had come it had fulfilled its purpose. The salvation he brought was for people everywhere, regardless of race. The Jews enjoyed no favoured treatment, and the Gentiles suffered no prejudice against them (Luke 2:32; 3:6-8; cf. Acts 15:6-11). In fact, Jesus was often more appreciated by Gentiles than by Jews, with the result that Gentiles received his salvation, but Jews missed out (Luke 4:25-27; 7:9; 11:31-32; 17:11-18).

Just as there was no distinction on the basis of race or religion, so there was no distinction on the basis of social class. Salvation was available equally to all. Luke illustrates this (and in so doing gives a warning to Theophilus) by showing that often the socially respectable missed out on salvation, but the socially despised received it (Luke 7:29-30; 10:30-37; 16:19-31; 18:9-14; 19:1-9).

In developing this theme, Luke draws attention to the various kinds of socially disadvantaged people who received God's blessings. Among these were slaves (Luke 7:2-7; 12:37), aliens (Luke 10:30-37; 17:16), the poor (Luke 1:53; 2:7; 6:20; 7:22) and women (Luke 1:28; 2:36-38; 7:37-48; 8:2; 13:11-13), in particular, widows (Luke 4:25; 7:12-15; 18:1-7; 21:1-4).

INTRODUCTION TO JOHN

An associate of Jesus

Early tradition and biblical evidence indicate that 'the disciple whom Jesus loved' was John the son of Zebedee, and that this John was the author of John's Gospel (John 21:20,24). Although the other Gospel writers mention John by name often, his name does not appear in John's Gospel. This is no doubt because the writer follows the common practice of using the descriptive name by which he was known rather than his real name (John 13:23; 19:26; 21:7). His use of the name may also have indicated his gratitude for all that Jesus had done for him.

The family of John lived in a town on the shores of Lake Galilee. He and his brother James worked with their father Zebedee as fishermen, along with Peter and Andrew, brothers from another local family (Matt 4:18-21; Luke 5:10). John's mother, Salome, appears to have been the sister of Mary the mother of Jesus (Matt 27:56; Mark 15:40; John 19:25).

Both pairs of brothers seem to have responded to the preaching of John the Baptist and looked expectantly for the promised Saviour. When Jesus arrived, they were among the first to join him (Matt 4:22; John 1:35-40). All four were later included in Jesus' group of twelve apostles (Matt 10:2), and Peter, James and John developed into an inner circle that was especially close to Jesus (Mark 5:37; 9:2; 14:33).

Jesus called James and John 'sons of thunder', probably because they were sometimes impatient and over-zealous (Mark 3:17; Luke 9:49-56). As Peter became increasingly more prominent among the twelve, James and John tried to outdo him by seeking from Jesus the top two positions in his kingdom. The only guarantee Jesus gave them was of coming persecution (Matt 20:20-28). By the time of Jesus' ascension, Peter and John were clearly the two leading apostles (Luke 22:8; John 19:26-27; 20:2-9; 21:20).

A church leader

In the early days of the church, Peter and John provided the main leadership and bore the main persecution (Acts 1:13; 3:1-11; 4:13-20; 5:40). They were among the first to show that the church must accept non-Jews equally with Jews (Acts 8:14-17,25) and they encouraged the evangelization of the Gentiles (Gal 2:9).

The Bible contains little additional information about John's ministry. Non-biblical writings indicate that he lived to a very old age (cf. John 21:20-23) and spent most of his later years in and around Ephesus, from where he wrote his Gospel and Letters. He was known as 'the elder' (2 John 1; 3 John 1) and has been traditionally regarded as the writer of Revelation. If that is so, he probably spent his final years as a prisoner on the island of Patmos, off the coast from Ephesus (Rev 1:9).

Battle with false teachers

Churches of the Ephesus region had long been troubled by false teaching (cf. Acts 20:17,29-30; Rev 2:2). The teaching was an early form of Gnosticism, a heresy that became very destructive during the second century. The Gnostics tried to explain some of the mysteries of the universe — such as the relation between good and evil, spirit and matter, God and people — by combining Christian belief with pagan philosophy. Because they denied there could be a perfect union between things that appeared to be opposites, some denied that Jesus

was fully a human being, others that he was fully God.

John firmly opposed both these errors. But his writings were more than merely a defence against false teaching. He had a positive purpose, and that was to lead people to faith in Christ, so that they might experience the full and eternal life that Christ made possible (John 20:31; cf. 1:4; 3:15; 4:14; 5:24; 6:27; 8:12; 10:10; 11:25; 14:6; 17:3; see also 1 John 1:1-3; 5:13). (For the relation of John to the other Gospels see earlier section, 'The Writing of the Gospels'.)

The uniqueness of Jesus

From the outset of his Gospel, John asserted that Jesus was divine (John 1:1) and human (John 1:14). He was eternal (John 1:2), he created all things (John 1:3) and he came from the heavenly world to reveal God to the human race (John 1:18; 3:13; 5:18-19; 6:62; 8:23,26; 14:9,11). He was also fully human. He had a material body with normal physical characteristics (John 4:6-7; 9:6; 12:3; 19:34), and he experienced normal human emotions (John 11:35; 12:27; 19:26-27).

If the heretical Gnostics of the AD 90s had trouble accepting Jesus' uniqueness, so did the orthodox Jews of the AD 30s. John's method of teaching the confused people of Ephesus was to recount the stories and teachings of Jesus. He had many stories of Jesus available to him (John 21:25), but he chose to use only a few. He did not just recount incidents from Jesus' life, but showed the significance of the incidents. For this reason he called them 'signs' (John 20:30; cf. 2:11; 4:54; 6:14; 7:31; 12:18,37).

Jesus' signs showed not only that he was the Messiah, but also that he was the Son of God (John 20:31). The Jews considered it blasphemy that a person who had grown up among them should claim to be God (John 6:42; 8:53-59; 10:33; 19:7). As a result, the signs that Jesus performed were usually followed by long debates with the Jews (e.g. the miracle in John 5:1-15 followed by the debate in 5:16-47; the miracle in John 9:1-12 followed by the debate 9:13-10:38). These and other debates that Jesus had with the Jews provided John with much of his teaching material. He used the actual words of Jesus to teach Christian truth (e.g. John 7:1-39; 8:12-58).

When John and one of the other Gospel writers recorded the same miracle, they treated the material differently. The other writers did little more than tell the story, whereas John followed the story with lengthy teaching that arose out of it (cf. Matt

14:13-21 with John 6:1-14 and the teaching that follows in John 6:26-65).

Since John was concerned with the meaning and significance of events, he recorded some of Jesus' conversations with people at length (e.g. with Nicodemus in John 3:1-15 and with the Samaritan woman in John 4:1-26). In a similar way he used the account of the Last Supper, which the other writers recorded only briefly, to provide four chapters of teaching on important Christian doctrines. Again the teaching came direct from the lips of Jesus (John 13:1-16:33).

At the centre of all the doctrinal discussions was the fact that Jesus was God in human form. The Jews had always considered Jesus' claim to divinity as a reason to get rid of him (John 7:28-30; 10:33,39) and in the end they had their wish (John 11:25,53; cf. Mark 14:61-64).

Jerusalem was the centre of this opposition to Jesus and consequently was the place where many of his debates with the Jews occurred. Because of John's usage of these debates for his teaching material, much of John's Gospel is set in Jerusalem (John 2:13; 5:1; 7:14,25; 8:20; 10:22-23; 11:1). This is in sharp contrast to the other Gospels, which are concerned more with Galilee and make little mention of Jerusalem, apart from the few days leading up to Jesus' crucifixion.

Jesus and the Kingdom

KINGDOM OF GOD

A major theme of the Bible is the kingdom of God. It runs through the Old Testament, but is more fully developed in the Gospels. Jesus showed that through him the kingdom found its fullest meaning.

Rule of God

In its broadest sense, the kingdom of God is the rule of God. It is not a territory over which God reigns but the rule that he exercises. It is not defined by physical boundaries, time or nationality, but by the sovereign rule and authority of God (Exod 15:18; Ps 103:19; 145:10-13).

Jesus spoke of God's kingdom in this sense. Those who seek God's kingdom seek his rule in their lives (Matt 6:33), and those who receive God's kingdom receive his rule in their lives (Mark 10:15). When they enter the kingdom, they enter the realm where they accept God's rule (Matt 21:31), and they pray that others also will accept it (Matt 6:10).

The world is under the power of Satan and in a state of rebellion against God (2 Cor 4:4; 1 John 5:19). Therefore, when Jesus brought the kingdom into the world, he demonstrated God's rule in the defeat of Satan. As Jesus announced the good news of the kingdom, he gave evidence of his power by healing those whom Satan had afflicted by disease and evil spirits (Matt 4:23-24). As he delivered people from Satan's bondage he gave evidence that God's kingdom (his authority, power and rule) had come among humankind (Matt 12:28; Mark 1:27; Luke 10:9,17-18).

Note: The Bible uses the expressions 'kingdom of God' and 'kingdom of heaven' interchangeably. They are different names for the same thing (Matt 19:23-24). Jews had a traditional fear of misusing the name of God, and therefore they often used words such as 'heaven' instead (Dan 4:25-26; Luke 15:18; John 3:27). Matthew, who wrote his Gospel for Jews, usually (but not always) speaks of the kingdom of heaven, whereas the other writers call it the kingdom of God (Matt 19:14; Mark 10:14; Luke 18:16).

Present and future

Jesus' teaching on God's kingdom was in contrast to the popular Jewish belief of the time. The Jews believed that the kingdom was a future national and political kingdom centred on Israel. Jesus pointed out that God's kingdom was already among them. It was present in him (Luke 10:9; 17:20-21). Those who submitted to Christ's rule entered Christ's kingdom, and thereby received forgiveness of sins and eternal life (Matt 21:31; Mark 10:14-15; John 3:3). The same is true of people of any era. Those who believe in Christ enter his kingdom and receive its blessings (Rom 14:17; Col 1:13).

Yet Jesus spoke also of the kingdom as something belonging to the future (Mark 14:25). It would be established only after his death and resurrection (Luke 22:15-16,28-30; 24:26; cf. Rev 5:6-12; 11:15). Moreover, Jesus said that those who were already believers would enter his kingdom at his return (Matt 7:21-23; 13:41-43; 25:31-34; cf. 1 Cor 15:50; 2 Pet 1:11).

Therefore, although the kingdom of God is already present, it also awaits the future. Since the kingdom is the rule of God, believers enter it when they believe, but they will experience its full blessings only when Christ returns to banish evil and reign in righteousness (1 Cor 15:24-26). In being both present and future, the kingdom has the same characteristics as salvation and eternal life. To 'enter the kingdom of God' is to 'have eternal life' or to 'be saved'. The Bible uses the expressions interchangeably (Matt 19:16,23-25).

Just as believers experience the kingdom of God now and will do so more fully in the future, so they have eternal life now but will experience it more fully in the future (John 5:24,29). Likewise they have salvation now, but they will have it in its fulness at the return of Christ (Eph 2:8; Heb 9:28). Eternal life is the life of the kingdom of God, the life of the age to come. But because the kingdom of God has come among humankind now, believers have eternal life now (Matt 25:34,46; Luke 23:42-43; John 3:3,5,36; 5:24).

JESUS THE MESSIAH

The title 'Messiah' is a Hebrew word that means 'the anointed one'. In Old Testament times, the people of Israel appointed kings and priests (and sometimes prophets) to their official positions by the ceremony of anointing. A special anointing oil was poured over the head of the person as a sign that he now had the right, and the responsibility, to perform the duties required by his position (Exod 28:41; 1 Kings 1:39; 19:16).

By far the most common usage of 'anointed' in a title was in relation to the Israelite king. He was known as 'the Lord's anointed' (1 Sam 24:10; Ps 18:50; 20:6). That person whom Israelites looked for as their great deliverer-king was popularly called the Messiah. The New Testament (Greek) equivalent of this word is 'Christ'. Jesus and his disciples spoke the local language of Palestine, and therefore the word they would have used was 'Messiah'; but the Gospels were written in Greek, and therefore the word appears in the Bible as 'Christ' (Matt 22:42; John 1:41; 7:41-42).

Old Testament expectations

In the days of Israel's beginnings, God indicated that the leadership of the nation would belong to the tribe of Judah. From this tribe would come a leader who would rule all nations in a reign of peace and prosperity (Gen 49:9-12). In developing this plan, God promised King David (who was from the tribe of Judah) an everlasting dynasty (2 Sam 7:16). From that time on, Israelites looked expectantly for the ideal king, a descendant of David who would destroy all enemies and reign in a worldwide kingdom of righteousness and peace. They called this coming saviour-king the Messiah (Ps 89:3-4; Isa 11:1-10; 32:1; Jer 23:5; Ezek 34:23-24; Micah 5:2; cf. Luke 1:32-33; Rev 5:5).

Because God promised to treat David's son and successor as his own son, Israelites regarded every king in the royal line of David as, in a sense, God's son. He was the one through whom God exercised his rule. Above all, the Messiah was God's son (2 Sam 7:14; Ps 2:6-7; cf. Mark 10:47; 12:35; 14:61). Israelites saw victories over their enemies as fore-shadowings of the victory of the Messiah, and praised their kings in language that vividly expressed the ideals they looked for in the messianic kingdom (e.g. Psalms 2; 45; 72; 110).

Besides being a king, the promised Messiah had priestly characteristics as well. He would not be a priest in the Levitical system, but he would exercise the joint rule of king-priest after the manner of Melchizedek (Ps 110:1-7; cf. Matt 22:41-45; Heb 5:6). He would also have prophetic characteristics, in that he would be God's messenger to announce God's will to his people (Deut 18:15; cf. Luke 24:19; John 6:14; 7:40; Acts 3:22-23).

Jesus and the Jews

By the time of Jesus, Jewish expectation of the Messiah had little to do with the Messiah's spiritual ministry. Most Jews were not concerned with being delivered from the power of sin or submitting to the righteous rule of God. They were more concerned with being delivered from the power of Rome and establishing an independent Israelite kingdom of prosperity and peace. For this reason Jesus did not immediately announce his messiahship openly. He did not want to attract the wrong sort of following. When people followed him because they expected political and material benefits, he resisted them (John 6:15,26; cf. Matt 4:8-10).

When others, for better reasons, recognized Jesus as the Messiah, he told them not to broadcast the fact (Matt 9:27-30; 16:13-20). The title by which Jesus usually referred to himself was not 'Messiah', but 'Son of man' (Matt 17:22; 20:18,28; for further discussion see below).

Towards the end of his ministry, when Jesus knew that his work was nearing completion and his crucifixion was approaching, he allowed people to speak openly of him as the Messiah (Matt 21:14-16; 22:41-45). He entered Jerusalem as Israel's Messiah-king (Matt 21:1-11) and declared his messiahship before the Sanhedrin, adding that as Son of God he was on equality with God, and as Son of man he had gained an eternal kingdom (Mark 14:60-62; Luke 22:70-71). To Pilate he indicated that he was a king, though neither his kingship nor his kingdom were of the kind that most people expected or wanted (Matt 27:11; John 18:33-37; cf. Acts 17:7).

The Messiah's suffering and victory

Many believers of Jesus' time still thought of the Messiah in relation to a visible worldwide kingdom centred on Israel, and they were puzzled when Jesus did not set up such a kingdom (Matt 11:2-3; Luke 19:11; 24:21; Acts 1:6). Jesus pointed out that God's kingdom had come through him; the messianic age had begun. He was the Messiah, and his ministry was proof of this (Isa. 35:5-6; 61:1; Matt 4:23; 11:4-5; 12:28; Luke 4:18; 17:20-21; 18:35-43).

What the disciples could not understand was that the Messiah had to die. They knew that the Old Testament spoke of God's suffering servant (Isa. 49:7; 50:6; 52:13-53:12) just as they knew that it spoke of the Messiah, but they did not connect the two. Jesus showed that he was both the suffering servant and the victorious Messiah. The Messiah had to die before he could enter his glory (Matt 16:13-23; 20:25-28; Luke 24:25-27; Acts 4:27).

If the disciples of Jesus understood little of his statements about his coming death, they understood even less of his statements about his resurrection (Mark 8:29-32; 9:31-32). But after he died and rose to new life, everything became clear. They saw the resurrection as God's great and final confirmation that Jesus was the Messiah. His death was the way to victory for him and deliverance for his people (Acts 2:31-32,36; 10:38-43; Col 1:13-14,20).

The early Christians so identified the victorious Messiah with the risen Jesus that the Greek word for Messiah (Christ) became a personal name for Jesus. Over the years the two names were often joined as Jesus Christ or Christ Jesus, and the name Christ was often used without any direct reference to messiahship (Phil 1:15-16,18,21). In general the Gospels and the early part of Acts use 'Christ' mainly as a title (meaning 'the Messiah'), and other parts of the New Testament use it mainly as a name (John 1:20; 10:24; 1 Peter 4:14; 5:10,14).

SON OF MAN

Of all the names, pictures and titles of Jesus in the Gospels, 'Son of man' is the one that Jesus used most and others used least. It hardly occurs outside the Gospels, and inside the Gospels is used almost solely by Jesus. In ordinary speech it could be just a poetic word for 'person' (Num 23:19; Ezek 2:1-3), but people realized that Jesus used it with special significance. It was an unusual way for a person to refer to himself, but Jesus wanted people to think about who he was and what his mission involved (John 12:34).

A heavenly figure

The title 'Son of man' comes from a vision recorded in Daniel, where a person 'like a son of man' came into the heavenly presence of God and received from him a universal and everlasting kingdom (Dan 7:13-14). The 'Son of man' was connected with the coming of the kingdom of God. Jesus made it clear that, through him, the kingdom of God had come into the world (Matt 4:23-24; 12:28; see 'Kingdom of God' above). That kingdom will find its fullest expression when the Son of man returns at the end of the age to remove all evil and establish righteousness eternally (Dan 7:13-14; Matt 13:41-43; 24:30-31; Mark 8:38).

An additional feature of the vision in Daniel is the connection between the Son of man and the people of God. Though the Son of man receives the kingdom, he shares it with his people (Dan 7:14,27). Jesus, the heavenly Son of man, therefore promised his followers that they would share with him in the kingdom's final triumph (Matt 19:28; 25:31-34).

An earthly figure

Since 'son of man' could be used in everyday speech to refer to an ordinary human being (Ps 8:4; Ezek 2:8), the expression had an added significance when used of Jesus. Although it pointed to his deity (for he was the heavenly Son of God; John 3:13; 6:62), it pointed also to his humanity (for he was a man, a member of the human race; Matt 8:20). The Son of man was a unique person who, being divine and human, brought the authority of God into the world of humankind (Mark 2:10,28; John 5:27).

In relation to the kingdom of God, the heavenly Son of man was in fact an earthly figure, who was born in the royal line of David and had claim to the messianic throne. Because of the Jews' misguided nationalistic ambitions, Jesus rarely spoke of himself specifically as the Messiah. By using 'Son of man' instead, he was claiming to be the Messiah without using the word 'Messiah'. He knew people found the name 'Son of man' puzzling, but he wanted them to consider the evidence of his life and ministry and discover for themselves his true identity (Matt 16:13-16; John 9:35-36; 12:34).

When the Jewish leaders finally understood what Jesus meant by calling himself the Son of man, they accused him of blasphemy and had him killed. They saw that he claimed to be not only a messianic figure in the line of David, but also a heavenly figure on equality with God (Mark 14:61-64).

Jesus' death did not take him by surprise, as he knew that the heavenly Son of man had to become the suffering servant. He had to suffer and die before he could receive his kingdom (Mark 8:31; 9:12; 10:45; John 3:13-14; 8:28). Also, he had to rise from the dead (Mark 9:31). God therefore raised him up and gave him glory, a glory that will be fully revealed when the Son of man returns in the triumph of his kingdom (Mark 8:38; 13:26; 14:62).

SON OF GOD

When the Bible speaks of Jesus as God's Son, the meaning is unique. Elsewhere in the Bible Israel is called God's son (Exod 4:22), the Davidic king is called God's son (2 Sam 7:14) and in particular the Messiah is called God's son (Ps 2:7; Luke 1:32-33). But Jesus was more than God's Son in any of these senses. He was God's Son in the sense that he was God. He did not become God's Son through being the Messiah; rather, he became the Messiah because he already was God's pre-existent Son (Matt 22:42-45; John 1:34,49; 20:31).

Eternally the Son

God is a trinity of Father, Son and Holy Spirit, all of whom are equally and eternally God. Jesus' sonship does not mean that he was created by the Father or is inferior to the Father. He has the same Godhead and character as the Father (Matt 11:27; John 1:1,14,18; 8:19; 10:30,38; 14:9), the same powers, authority and responsibilities as the Father (John 3:35; 5:21-22,43; 13:3) and the same thought and purpose as the Father (John 5:17-20,30; 8:16,28-29; 14:10,24).

The relation between Jesus (the Son of God) and his Father is unique, and should not be confused with the relation between believers (sons of God) and their heavenly Father. Jesus' sonship is eternal. The Father and the Son have always existed in a relation in which both are equally and unchangeably God. Believers, by contrast, become sons of God only through faith in Jesus Christ. God *makes* them his sons, but he never made Jesus his Son. Jesus always has been the Son (John 1:18; 5:37; 8:18-19; 17:1-5; cf. Gal 4:5-7).

When Jesus talked with believers about God the Father, he was therefore careful to make a distinction between 'my Father' and 'your Father' (Matt 5:16; Luke 2:49; 12:30; John 5:17-18; 20:17). Nevertheless, through Christ believers come into such a close personal relation with the Father that they can address him as 'Abba', as Jesus did (Mark 14:36; Rom 8:15).

The Son's mission

Although the Son existed with his Father from all eternity, he willingly became a human being in order to fulfil his Father's purposes for the salvation of human beings and the conquest of evil (Rom 8:3; Gal 4:4-5; Heb 2:14-15). When Jesus was born in Bethlehem, the Son added humanity to the deity that he always had. His entrance into human life came about through God's supernatural work in the body of Mary, so that the baby born was both fully human and uniquely divine (Luke 1:30-31,35; 2:42,49). Jesus grew up in a relation with his Father that was shared by no other (Luke 2:49; John 5:19; 8:28-29), and this relation was confirmed at certain events during his public ministry (Matt 3:17; 17:5; John 12:27-30).

Jesus' followers usually spoke of Jesus' sonship in relation to his divine person and total unity with the Father (Matt 16:16; John 20:31; 1 John 2:23; 4:15), but Jesus himself usually spoke of it in relation to his earthly ministry and total submission to the Father (Mark 13:32; John 4:34; 5:19; 7:16; 8:28,42). The Father sent the Son to be the Saviour of the world, and the Son's obedience to this mission meant that he had to suffer and die (John 3:14-16; 12:27; 1 John 4:9-10,14). The Son finished the work, being obedient even to death (John 17:4; Phil 2:8), and the Father declared his complete satisfaction with his Son through the victory of the resurrection (Rom 1:4; Phil 2:9-11).

However, the Son's mission involved more than the salvation of believers. The Father had entrusted him with the task of overcoming all rebellion and restoring all things to a state of perfect submission to the sovereign God (John 5:20-29; Eph 1:10; 1 John 3:8). That mission extends to the whole universe, and will reach its climax when the last enemy, death, is banished for ever (Heb 2:14; 1 Cor 15:25,26). The Son conquered sin at the cross, and the power of that conquest will eventually remove the last traces of sin. The Son will restore all things to the Father, and the triumph of God will be complete. God will be everything to everyone (1 Cor 15:24,28).

JESUS AS LORD

Many people addressed Jesus as Lord (Matt 20:33; Mark 7:28; Luke 7:6), but when his disciples used the title of him, or when he used the title of himself, 'Lord' had much more meaning (Luke 19:34; 24:34; John 11:27; 13:6,13-14; 20:28; 21:7). The early church developed the more meaningful usage of the word till it became one of the most distinctive expressions of the Christian community.

Hebrew and Greek backgrounds

The Greek word that is translated 'Lord' in the New Testament is *kurios*, the word used in the Greek translation of the Old Testament for the Hebrew word *yahweh* (i.e. Jehovah) (cf. Ps 32:2 with Rom 4:8; cf. Isa 40:13 with Rom 11:34). Yahweh, the name of God, was a mysterious name that Jews of later times considered so sacred that they refused to speak it. Linguistically, the name was connected with the expression 'I am' and referred to the eternal, unchangeable, self-sufficient and ever-present God (Exod 3:13-16).

Jesus identified himself with Yahweh by calling himself 'I am' (John 8:58; see also John 4:26; 6:35; 8:12; 10:7,11; 11:25; 14:6; 18:5; Mark 14:62). The New Testament writers also identified Jesus with the God of the Old Testament, and repeatedly quoted Old Testament references to Yahweh as applying to Jesus (cf. Ps 16:8 with Acts 2:24-25; cf. Isa 40:3 with

Mark 1:1-3; cf. Jer 9:23-24 with 1 Cor 1:30-31; cf. Isa 8:13 with 1 Peter 3:15; cf. Ps 110:1 with Matt 22:41-45).

Both the words of Jesus and the quotations of the New Testament writers reflect the Hebrew background of the New Testament. According to that background, to call Jesus 'Lord' was to call him God. But most of the early Christians did not come from a Hebrew background. They were Gentiles, not Jews, and they had no history of the usage of the name Yahweh to influence their thinking. Yet to them also, to call Jesus 'Lord' (*kurios*) was to call him God. Their understanding of *kurios* came from its usage in the Greek-speaking Gentile world in which they lived.

In common speech, *kurios* may sometimes have meant no more than 'sir' or 'master' (Matt 21:30; Luke 12:36,45; John 12:21; Acts 25:26), but it was also used in relation to deity, such as when people referred to the Greek and Roman gods (1 Cor 8:5). The Greek-speaking Christians' use of this word for Jesus showed that they considered him to be God — not just one of many gods, but the one true God. This one was the creator and ruler of the universe, and the controller of life and death (Acts 1:24; 13:10-12; 17:24; Rom 14:9,11; 1 Tim 6:15-16; Rev 17:14).

Glorified and triumphant

Through the glorious resurrection and exaltation of Jesus Christ, God declared dramatically the absolute lordship of Christ (Acts 2:36; Rom 1:4; Phil 2:9-11). Believers in Christ are also Christ's servants and disciples. They gladly acknowledge him as Lord and willingly submit to him as to one who has complete authority over their lives. At the same time they love him as one who has saved them and given them new joy, peace and hope (John 20:28; Acts 10:36; Rom 10:9; 1 Cor 1:2-3; Eph 1:22-23; 2 Thess 3:16; Rev 22:20).

When God's chosen time comes, the lordship of Jesus Christ, at present unrecognized by the world, will be openly displayed (1 Cor 2:6-8; 15:24-26; cf. Heb 2:9; 9:28). He will return in power and glory, to enjoy the final fruits of the victory he won through his life, death and resurrection. In that great day there will be universal acknowledgment that he is indeed Lord (Phil 2:11; 1 Thess 4:15-17; 2 Thess 1:7; Rev 19:16).

Index to the Four Gospels

	Subject	Matt	Mark	Luke	John
39.	A right attitude to the law	5:17-20			
40.	Legal obedience is not enough	5:21-48		6:27-36	
				12:57-59	
41.	Giving, praying and fasting	6:1-18		11:1-4	
42.	Concern about material things	6:19-34		12:22-34	
43.	Judging others	7:1-6		6:37-42	
44.	Prayers of request	7:7-12		11:5-13	
45.	The two ways	7:13-29		6:43-49	

In Jerusalem again

	Subject	Matt	Mark	Luke	John
46.	Healing at Bethesda and its outcome				5:1-29
47.	Witnesses to Jesus				5:30-47

Back in Galilee

	Subject	Matt	Mark	Luke	John
48.	Centurion's servant; widow's son	8:5-13		7:1-17	
49.	Messengers from John the Baptist	11:1-19		7:18-35	
50.	The judgment and mercy of God	11:20-30			
51.	In the house of Simon the Pharisee			7:36-50	
52.	Blasphemy of the Holy Spirit	12:22-45	3:22-30	11:14-36	
53.	Jesus and his family	12:46-50	3:20-21	8:19-21	
			3:31-35		

Parables

	Subject	Matt	Mark	Luke	John
54.	The sower	13:1-23	4:1-29	8:1-18	
55.	Wheat and weeds; mustard seed; yeast	13:24-43	4:30-34	13:18-21	
56.	Hidden treasure; pearl; fishing net	13:44-52			

Around the Lake of Galilee

	Subject	Matt	Mark	Luke	John
57.	Jesus calms the storm	8:23-27	4:35-41	8:22-25	
58.	Demon power overcome at Gadara	8:28-34	5:1-20	8:26-39	
59.	Jairus' daughter and a woman healed	9:18-26	5:21-43	8:40-56	
60.	Jesus heals the blind and the dumb	9:27-34	8:22-26		
61.	Jesus rejected at Nazareth	13:53-58	6:1-6		
62.	The twelve sent out	10:5-42	6:7-13	9:1-6	
63.	Concern about safety and security			12:4-21	
64.	Death of John the Baptist	14:1-12	6:14-29	9:7-9	
65.	Feeding the five thousand	14:13-21	6:30-44	9:10-17	6:1-14
66.	Jesus walks on the sea	14:22-36	6:45-56		6:15-21
67.	The bread of life				6:22-59
68.	Words of eternal life				6:60-71
69.	Teaching about cleansing	15:1-20	7:1-23		

Further work in the north

	Subject	Matt	Mark	Luke	John
70.	In Tyre and Sidon	15:21-28	7:24-30		
71.	Ministry in the Decapolis	15:29-39	7:31-8:10		
72.	Beware of Pharisees and Sadducees	16:1-12	8:11-21	12:1-3	
				12:54-56	
73.	Peter's confession of the Messiah	16:13-23	8:27-33	9:18-22	
74.	Test of true discipleship	16:24-28	8:34-9:1	9:23-27	
75.	The transfiguration	17:1-13	9:2-13	9:28-36	
76.	Healing of an uncontrollable boy	17:14-21	9:14-29	9:37-43	
77.	Payment of the temple tax	17:24-27			
78.	Lessons in humility	17:22-23	9:30-50	9:44-50	
		18:1-14			

Subject	Matt	Mark	Luke	John
122. Authority of Jesus questioned	21:23-32	11:27-33	20:1-8	
123. The wicked vineyard keepers	21:33-46	12:1-12	20:9-18	
124. The royal wedding feast	22:1-14			
125. A question about paying taxes	22:15-22	12:13-17	20:19-26	
126. Marriage and the resurrection	22:23-33	12:18-27	20:27-40	
127. The greatest commandment	22:34-40	12:28-34		
128. Who is the Messiah?	22:41-46	12:35-37	20:41-44	
129. More about scribes and Pharisees	23:1-39	12:38-40	20:45-47	
130. The widow's offering		12:41-44	21:1-4	
131. The coming crisis	24:1-31	13:1-27	21:5-28	
132. A warning to be alert always	24:32-51	13:28-37	21:29-38	
133. The ten girls	25:1-13			
134. The three employees	25:14-30			
135. Sheep and goats	25:31-46			

Betrayal, trial and crucifixion

Subject	Matt	Mark	Luke	John
136. The seed must die				12:20-26
137. Final message to the Jews				12:27-50
138. The plot to capture Jesus	26:1-16	14:1-11	22:1-6	
139. Jesus prepares the Passover	26:17-19	14:12-16	22:7-13	
140. Washing the disciples' feet				13:1-20
141. A traitor among them	26:20-25	14:17-21	22:21-23	13:21-35
142. The Lord's Supper instituted	26:26-30	14:22-26	22:14-20	
143. The way to the Father				14:1-14
144. Promise of the Holy Spirit				14:15-31
145. Union with Jesus				15:1-27
146. Work of the Holy Spirit				16:1-15
147. Difficulties ahead for the disciples				16:16-33
148. Jesus' prayer				17:1-26
149. Disciples' failure foretold	26:31-35	14:27-31	22:24-38	13:36-38
150. Jesus prays in Gethsemane	26:36-46	14:32-42	22:39-46	18:1
151. The arrest of Jesus	26:47-56	14:43-52	22:47-53	18:2-11
152. At the high priest's house	26:57-75	14:53-72	22:54-65	18:12-27
153. The Sanhedrin's judgment	27:1-2	15:1	22:66-71	
154. Death of Judas	27:3-10			
155. Before Pilate and Herod	27:11-14	15:2-5	23:1-12	18:28-38
156. Jesus before the people	27:15-31	15:6-20	23:13-25	18:39-40
				19:1-16
157. Journey to Golgotha	27:32	15:21	23:26-31	19:17
158. The crucifixion	27:33-44	15:22-32	23:32-43	19:18-24
159. The death	27:45-56	15:33-41	23:44-49	19:25-37
160. The burial	27:57-66	15:42-47	23:50-56	19:38-42

Resurrection and ascension

Subject	Matt	Mark	Luke	John
161. Morning of the resurrection	28:1-15	16:1-11	24:1-12	20:1-18
162. On the road to Emmaus		16:12-13	24:13-35	
163. Sunday night in Jerusalem		16:14	24:36-49	20:19-23
164. One week later				20:24-31
165. At the Sea of Tiberias				21:1-25
166. On a mountain in Galilee	28:16-20	16:15-18		
167. The ascension		16:19-20	24:50-53	

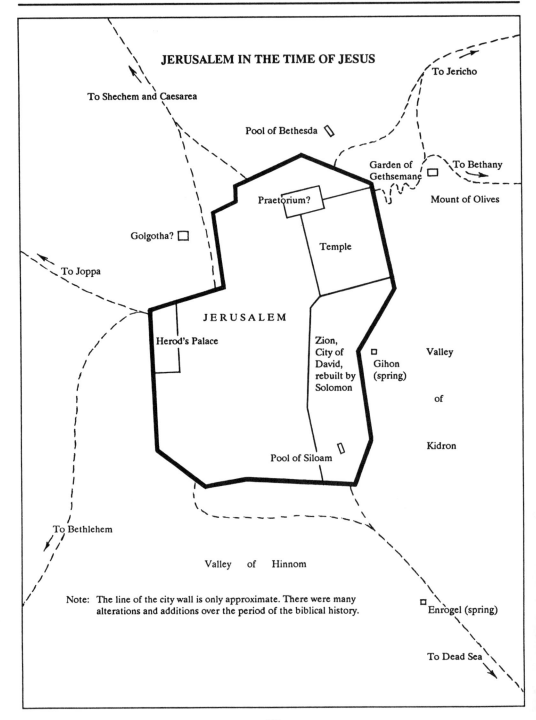

JERUSALEM IN THE TIME OF JESUS

To Jericho

To Shechem and Caesarea

Pool of Bethesda

Garden of Gethsemane — To Bethany

Praetorium?

Mount of Olives

Golgotha?

Temple

To Joppa

JERUSALEM

Herod's Palace

Zion, City of David, rebuilt by Solomon

Gihon (spring)

Valley

of

Kidron

Pool of Siloam

To Bethlehem

Valley   of   Hinnom

Note: The line of the city wall is only approximate. There were many alterations and additions over the period of the biblical history.

Enrogel (spring)

To Dead Sea

404

The Four Gospels

THE EARLY LIFE OF JESUS

1. Luke's introduction (Luke 1:1-4)

Of the four Gospel writers, Luke is the only one who introduces his book by setting out briefly the circumstances of his writing. He wanted to prepare an account of the life and ministry of Jesus, but unlike others who prepared similar books, he was not an eye witness of the things about which he wrote. He therefore could prepare his book only after careful research (Luke 1:1-3). He wrote for a person of rank named Theophilus, to give him a reliable account of who Jesus was and what he had done (Luke 1:4). (Concerning Theophilus see also 'The Writing of the Gospels'.)

2. Birth of John the Baptist foretold (Luke 1:5-25)

Zechariah, the father of John the Baptist, was a priest. Because all male descendants of Aaron were priests, there were, even in Old Testament times, too many priests for the amount of work to be done. David therefore divided them into twenty-four divisions, and each division served for two weeks each year. Zechariah belonged to the division of Abijah (Luke 1:5; cf. 1 Chron 24:1-19). (All priests would be required for duty during the Feasts of Passover, Pentecost and Tabernacles, which together would account for the remaining four weeks of the year; cf. Exod 23:14-17.)

Each morning and each evening one priest was chosen by lot to go into the temple and burn incense while the people outside prayed. Priests valued this duty as something they would probably do only once in a lifetime; but for Zechariah the joy of the occasion was mixed with personal disappointment, as his own prayers had not been answered. He and his wife Elizabeth had prayed for many years that God would give them a child, but they were still childless (Luke 1:6-10).

While Zechariah was carrying out his priestly duties, God showed him that his prayers would now be answered. Elizabeth would have a child, to be named John, who would become a special messenger from God to his people. He would be equipped by God's Spirit for his ministry, and he would live under the restrictions of a person set apart for God (Luke 1:11-15; cf. Num 6:1-8). John's task was to call the people of Israel to repentance. If they responded to his preaching, they would be united in spirit with their ancestors Abraham, Isaac and Jacob, and would be ready to welcome the Messiah (Luke 1:16-17; cf. Mal 4:5-6).

Although Zechariah had the faith to pray, he did not have the faith to believe the answer to his prayer. As a chastisement for his lack of faith, he became dumb for a period (Luke 1:18-22). God did not, however, withdraw his promise. When Zechariah's time of service at the temple was over, he returned to his home, and soon Elizabeth became pregnant (Luke 1:23-25).

3. An angel prepares Mary (Luke 1:26-38)

Six months after Gabriel appeared to Zechariah in the temple in Jerusalem, the same angel appeared to Mary in the town of Nazareth in Galilee. Mary was engaged to be married to a man named Joseph (Luke 1:26-28). She was startled and puzzled when the angel told her that, though still a virgin, she would give birth to a son, and this son would be the promised Messiah. He would be in a unique sense God's Son and his kingdom would be eternal (Luke 1:29-34). Mary's pregnancy would come about not through any sexual relations with Joseph, but through the direct creative power of the Spirit of God. The son born to her would be of Adam's race but free of any trace of Adam's sin. He would not be one whom God merely adopted as his son, but one who was actually God's Son. He would be the head of a new creation (Luke 1:35).

Mary knew that in the eyes of the public her pregnancy would spoil her honourable reputation, but she humbly submitted herself to the will of God. If she had any doubts about what God could do, Elizabeth's recent experience might have been an encouragement to her. The two women were close relatives (Luke 1:36-38).

4. Mary visits Elizabeth (Luke 1:39-56)

With the time drawing near when Elizabeth would give birth, Mary travelled south to visit her. The honour that Elizabeth gave to Mary at their meeting was symbolic of the honour that John would give to Jesus (Luke 1:39-45).

Mary's song of praise reflects her total submission and deep gratitude to God for what he was doing through her. The song (sometimes called the 'Magnificat', from the opening words in the Latin version) has many similarities to the song of Hannah, whose son Samuel was also a gift from God in unusual circumstances (cf. 1 Sam 2:1-10). Mary begins by recalling God's love in choosing her, an ordinary human being, to be the means of bringing his blessing to humankind (Luke 1:46-49). God did not use the rich, the mighty or the proud, but the poor and lowly who feared him (Luke 1:50-53). In showing grace to Mary and mercy to Israel, God was being faithful to the promises he gave to Israel's ancestors (Luke 1:54-56; cf. Gen 12:1-3).

5. Birth of John the Baptist (Luke 1:57-80)

Elizabeth's son was born amid much rejoicing, and eight days later was circumcised in accordance with the law of Israel. Circumcision was a minor surgical operation carried out on all Israelite baby boys, and was the covenant sign that Israel was God's people. At this ceremony the child was usually given his name (Luke 1:57-60; cf. 2:21; Gen 17:9-14; Lev 12:3). When relatives tried to interfere in the naming of the child, Zechariah proved his obedience to God by insisting that the child be named John. In response God removed Zechariah's dumbness (Luke 1:61-66; cf. v. 13, 20).

Zechariah then broke forth in a hymn of praise to God. His first words of praise were not for his son, but for the Saviour whom his son would announce. This Saviour was the Davidic Messiah and the redeemer of his people. In accordance with the covenant God made with Abraham, the Messiah would deliver God's people from bondage so that they might serve him in reverence, holiness and righteousness (Luke 1:67-75).

As he turned his attention to his own son, Zechariah was reminded that John's task was to lead people from darkness to light through repentance of their sins. In this way he would correct the false ideas people had of the Messiah and prepare the way for them to welcome him. A new age would dawn (Luke 1:76-79). But before John could prepare others to receive the Messiah, he himself had to be prepared (Luke 1:80).

6. Genealogies of Jesus (Matt 1:1-17; Luke 3:23-38)

The genealogies recorded by Matthew and Luke show how the birth of Jesus fulfilled the promises made to Abraham (Gen 12:2-3; 22:18). Matthew, writing for the Jews, begins his genealogy with Abraham, father of the Jewish race (Matt 1:1-2a). Luke, writing for non-Jews, traces Jesus' genealogy back past Abraham to Adam, to emphasize Jesus' union with the whole human race (Luke 3:34b-38).

Between Abraham and David the two genealogies are the same (Matt 1:2b-6a; Luke 3:32-34a), but between David and Jesus they are different, as they follow two lines of descent that started with David and came together in Jesus (Matt 1:6b-16; Luke 3:23-31).

Matthew's genealogy shows that Jesus had legal right to the throne of David, for he was in the royal line of descent that came through Solomon and other kings of Judah down to Joseph. Jesus therefore fulfilled the promise that the Messiah would be one of David's royal descendants (2 Sam 7:12-16; Jer 23:5). But both writers point out that though Joseph was Jesus' legal father he was not his natural father (Matt 1:16; Luke 3:23).

The genealogies do not necessarily list every person in the line of descent. As is often the case, they may be selective and stylized, to make them fit a simple scheme. Matthew, for example, omits some names to produce an arrangement of three sets of fourteen (Matt 1:17).

Luke's genealogy gives further proof that Jesus was descended from David, by tracing his ancestry through the line of another of David's sons, Nathan. This may represent another line of descent from David to Joseph, or it may represent the line of descent from David to Mary (but Mary's name is not shown, since the genealogies record only the names of the males). If the latter is the case, Joseph was the 'son' of Heli only because of his marriage to Mary (i.e. Mary was the daughter of Heli, Joseph the son-in-law). It is possible that Mary's mother was from the tribe of Levi and descended from Aaron (cf. Luke 1:5,36) and her father from the tribe of Judah and descended from David (cf. Luke 1:32,69).

7. Birth of Jesus (Matt 1:18-25)

Joseph and Mary were not yet married, when Joseph was shocked to learn that Mary was pregnant. Since Mary had been promised to him in marriage, Joseph had the right, according to Jewish custom, to report the matter to the authorities and have Mary dealt with for marital unfaithfulness. Joseph was a morally upright man but he was also compassionate. Instead of acting spitefully towards Mary, he tried to protect her from public shame by breaking the engagement secretly. God then intervened to show Joseph that

Mary's pregnancy was miraculous, pure and of the Holy Spirit. The son to be born to her would be Israel's long-awaited Messiah, whose mission was not to save his people from foreign domination but to save them from sin (Matt 1:18-21).

Being a person of faith, Joseph believed God. He took Mary as his wife, though he had no sexual relations with her before the birth of Jesus (Matt 1:22-25).

8. Shepherds visit the stable (Luke 2:1-20)

Joseph and Mary lived in Nazareth in the north of Palestine (see Luke 1:26-27), but the town to which they belonged according to their ancestry was Bethlehem, the birthplace of their forefather David. When the government issued an order that all people were to return to their ancestral town for a census (probably for taxation purposes), Joseph and Mary made the journey to Bethlehem. The town was so overcrowded with travellers returning for the census that they could find nowhere to stay except in a stable with animals. There Mary gave birth to Jesus (Luke 2:1-7).

The first people to be told the news that Israel's Messiah had been born were a group of shepherds in the fields near Bethlehem. God's gift of such a Saviour was evidence of his good pleasure towards humankind and his desire that people everywhere be brought into a relationship of peace with him (Luke 2:8-14). The shepherds hurried to visit the new-born child, then spread the news of their wonderful discovery (Luke 2:15-20).

9. Temple ceremonies in Jerusalem (Luke 2:21-24)

After Jesus was born, his parents were required to carry out three ceremonies according to the law of Moses. The first of these was circumcision (Luke 2:21; see note on Luke 1:59).

For the second ceremony Mary and Joseph made the ten kilometre journey to Jerusalem, where they went to the temple to present their firstborn to God. Ever since God saved Israel's firstborn at the time of the original Passover, the firstborn of all Israel's people and cattle belonged to him. At the age of one month the firstborn was taken to the temple, presented to God, then bought back by a payment of five shekels (see Exod 13:2; Num 18:15-16).

The third ceremony was the ritual purification of the mother after childbirth. In the case of a male child this took place forty days after the birth, when the mother presented a lamb for a burnt offering and a bird for a sin offering. If she was too poor to afford a lamb she could offer another bird instead (see Lev 12:1-8).

Jesus' parents carried out these two ceremonies on the same visit to Jerusalem. Their poverty is indicated by their choice of the sacrifice available for those too poor to afford the normal sacrifice (Luke 2:22-24).

10. Simeon and Anna (Luke 2:25-38)

In separate incidents, two people at the temple recognized Jesus as the promised Messiah. The first was a man named Simeon. Unlike most Jews, Simeon had the spiritual insight to understand the sort of person the Messiah would be. He acknowledged that Jesus was the promised Messiah, and that he would bring glory to Israel and salvation to the Gentiles (Luke 2:25-32).

Having praised God for the coming of Jesus, Simeon turned to address Mary. He saw that one day Jesus would create a division among the Jewish people. Many would reject him and so fall under God's punishment, but others would receive him and so rise to salvation. People's opposition to Jesus would show up the sinfulness of their hearts, and at the same time bring pain and sorrow to the heart of his mother (Luke 2:33-35).

The other faithful Jew who saw Jesus and his parents in the temple was an elderly woman named Anna. In some ways her life had been lonely, but she had never grown bitter. She sacrificed time and personal comforts so that she could devote herself to worship and prayer. Throughout her long life she never stopped believing that salvation would come through the promised Messiah. On seeing Jesus she knew that this was the one for whom she had waited (Luke 2:36-38).

11. Herod and the Magi (Matt 2:1-18)

It seems that after the ceremonies in Jerusalem, Joseph and Mary returned with Jesus to Bethlehem. Because most of the travellers had now gone, they were able to move into the house (see Matt 2:11). Meanwhile, in a country to the east, men known as Magi (people who study the stars) had worked out that a new king was born in Judea and they came to Jerusalem looking for him (Matt 2:1-2).

Herod the Great was ruler of Judea at the time, and he had no desire to see a rival Jewish king set up. From the Magi he learnt the time of the new king's birth, and from the Jewish scholars he learnt the place of his birth. He urged the Magi to locate the child then report back to him so that he could go and pay homage (Matt 2:3-8). The Magi found Jesus and worshipped him, but when they learnt that

Herod planned to kill him, they returned home without first reporting to Herod (Matt 2:9-12). Mary and Joseph also learnt of Herod's planned treachery, and escaped with the child to the safety of Egypt (Matt 2:13-15).

When, after some time, the Magi did not return, Herod saw that the only way to be certain of destroying the new king was to kill all male children under two years of age in the Bethlehem area. He fixed the age of the doomed children according to details given him by the Magi, which suggests that Jesus by this time was between one and two years old (Matt 2:16-18). (For Herod and his family see earlier section, 'The New Testament World'.)

12. Return to Nazareth (Matt 2:19-23; Luke 2:39-40)

Upon hearing of Herod's death, Joseph and Mary returned with the infant Jesus to Palestine (Matt 2:19-21). Since the new king Archelaus was as unjust and cruel as his father Herod, they considered it unsafe to stay in Judea, so went north to their home town of Nazareth. As the years of Jesus' childhood passed, he developed in body, mind and spirit (Matt 2:22-23; Luke 2:39-40).

13. Jesus twelve years old (Luke 2:41-52)

Joseph and Mary, being sincere and faithful Jews, went to Jerusalem for the Passover each year. Jesus, who accompanied them on the occasion recorded here, was twelve years old at the time. At this age Jewish boys were being prepared for entrance into the adult affairs of the synagogue (Luke 2:41-42).

In the Jewish form of instruction, teacher and student often took turns at asking and answering questions, many of which were concerned with details of the law. The teachers in Jerusalem noted that Jesus was different from other students, both in the questions he asked and the answers he gave. His concern was not with trivial details of the traditional teaching, but with a real understanding of the mind and ways of God (Luke 2:43-47). He reminded his parents of his unique relationship with his heavenly Father and of the need for him to know and do his Father's will. They did not fully understand what he meant, but Mary kept thinking about it. Jesus, on his part, realized that he still had to be obedient to his earthly parents (Luke 2:48-52).

JESUS BEGINS HIS MINISTRY

14. The eternal Word (John 1:1-18)

To Israelites of Old Testament times, God's word was more than something merely written down or spoken out. It was something active, so that when God expressed his will, that will was carried out. God spoke, and it was done (Gen 1:3; Ps 33:9; Isa 55:10-11). By his active word, God created the universe (Gen 1:6,9,14; Ps 33:6). God's word had such life and power that people thought of it almost as if it were a person — God's living agent or messenger (Ps 107:20; 147:15,18).

In John's Gospel Jesus is called the Word (Greek: *logos*). Greek philosophers used *logos* in speaking of what they believed to be the principle of reason in the universe. John may have kept this in mind when he was writing, but he uses *logos* mainly in the Old Testament sense. The Word of God is the living and active agent of God, which existed before creation and was the means by which God created. It is not just like a person, but *is* a person – not 'it' but 'he'. He is not just with God; he is God. Though distinct from the Father, he is inseparably one with him (John 1:1-3). He is the source not only of physical life but also of the full and spiritual life that God desires people to have. He brings the light of God into the world, and not even the darkness caused by sin can put it out (John 1:4-5).

John the Baptist announced the coming of Jesus as the light of the world. John called people to faith and repentance so that they would be prepared to receive Jesus, but John himself could not give them the light and life of God. Only Jesus could do that (John 1:6-9).

Jesus' coming into the world was like the coming of a person to his home town. But the people who lived in the 'town', especially his own people Israel, refused to receive him. Any, however, who did receive him, whether Israelites or others, became his true people. Such people are God's true children. They come into this privileged relationship not through birth into a particular family or nation, nor through the actions of others on their behalf, but only through their personal reception of Jesus Christ (John 1:10-13).

When a person writes or speaks, the words he uses are really part of himself. They may have been in his mind for years, but they remain unknown unless he writes or speaks them. As long as the eternal Word remained with God in the unseen heavenly world, it was to a large extent hidden and unknown, but when God became a human being in the person of Jesus, the Word could be seen and heard by all (John 1:14; see also v. 18).

Although John preceded Jesus, in both his birth and his ministry, Jesus preceded John in that he was the eternal Word. The one who had always existed as God now took upon himself human form and made God known to humankind. He showed people what God was like not by commanding them to keep the law given to Israel, but by supplying grace and truth in unlimited supply to meet all their needs (John 1:15-18).

15. Preaching of John the Baptist (Mt 3:1-12; Mark 1:1-8; Luke 3:1-17; John 1:19-28)

The preaching of John soon attracted opposition from the Jewish religious leaders. They sent representatives to question him and then report back on what he taught and who he claimed to be. John denied that he was promoting himself as some new leader in Israel. He did not consider himself to be either the prophet of Deuteronomy 18:15,18 or the 'Elijah' promised in Malachi 4:5. He was only a voice calling people to turn from their sin and be baptized, and so prepare themselves to receive the Messiah. He was like a messenger sent ahead of the king to tell people to clear the way for the royal arrival (Matt 3:1-6; Luke 3:1-6; John 1:19-23).

John commanded all people to repent, no matter who they were. Those who were descendants of Abraham were no more privileged in the eyes of God than the stones on the ground. All people, regardless of nationality, religion or social status, were to leave their selfish and sinful ways, and produce results in their daily lives that would prove their repentance to be genuine (Matt 3:7-10; Luke 3:7-14).

Although John baptized people to show they had repented and been forgiven their past sins, his baptism gave them no power to live a pure life. It was merely a preparation for one who was far greater than John. Jesus Christ would give the Holy Spirit, which, like fire, would burn up the useless chaff of the heart, leaving the pure wheat to feed and strengthen the life (Matt 3:11-12; Luke 3:15-17; John 1:24-28).

16. Baptism of Jesus (Matt 3:13-17; Mark 1:9-11; Luke 3:21-22; John 1:29-34)

In due course John publicly introduced Jesus as the Messiah, the Son of God, for whom he had prepared the way. John's introduction contained none of the popular Jewish ideas of a political or military leader who would bring in a golden age for Israel. Instead it suggested that the Messiah would die, like a lamb offered in sacrifice for the cleansing of sin (John 1:29-30). John then pointed out that he himself was not at first certain that Jesus was the Messiah, but when he saw the Holy Spirit descend on Jesus at his baptism, he was left in no doubt. John's explanation indicates that Jesus' baptism took place before his public introduction (John 1:31-34).

When Jesus approached John to be baptized, John hesitated, because he knew Jesus was superior to him in character, status and authority. But Jesus insisted. He wanted to begin his ministry with a public declaration of his devotion to God. Baptism was an act of obedience carried out by those who declared themselves on the side of God and his righteousness. Jesus was baptized to show that, like all the faithful, he was obedient to God and he intended to carry out all God's purposes. His baptism displayed his identification, or solidarity, not only with the faithful minority of Israel but also with the human race in general. It was an identification that would lead to a far greater baptism at Golgotha, when as the representative of his fellow human beings he would bear the full penalty of sin (Matt 3:13-15).

Having shown his intentions openly, Jesus received openly the assurance that his Father was pleased with him. The Father's announcement, by combining a quote concerning the Davidic Messiah with one concerning the Servant of the Lord (see Ps 2:7; Isa 42:1), gave an indication that Jesus' way to kingly glory was to be that of the suffering servant. In appointing Jesus to his public ministry, the Father poured out upon him the Holy Spirit, through whose power he would carry out his messianic work (Matt 3:16-17; cf. Isa 11:1-2; 61:1; Acts 10:37-38).

17. Temptation of Jesus (Matt 4:1-11; Mark 1:12-13; Luke 4:1-13)

Immediately after being appointed to his messianic ministry, Jesus was tempted by Satan to use his messianic powers in the wrong way. (For the identification of the devil with Satan see Revelation 20:2.) Satan's aim was to make Jesus act according to his own will instead of in obedience to his Father.

Jesus had gone many weeks without eating and was obviously very hungry. Satan therefore used Jesus' natural desire for food to suggest that he should use his supernatural powers to create food and eat it. Jesus knew that food was necessary for a person's physical needs, but he also knew that obedience to God was more important. God alone would decide when and how his fast would end (Matt 4:1-4).

Living in a world of unbelievers, Jesus could be very frustrated at their refusal to accept him. He was therefore tempted to perform some spectacular feat that would prove once and for all that he was the

Son of God. For instance, he could jump from the top of the temple in front of the people, asking God to keep him from being hurt. But to call upon God to save him from an act of suicide would be sin. It would be putting God to the test by demanding that he act in a certain way merely to satisfy an individual's selfish desire (Matt 4:5-7).

Then came the temptation to gain worldwide rule through compromising with Satan and using his methods to gain power. As the Messiah, Jesus had been promised a worldwide kingdom, but the way to that kingdom was through laying down his life in sacrifice. God wants people to enter his kingdom because they have a willing desire to serve him, not because they are the helpless subjects of force or cunning (Matt 4:8-10).

In each case Jesus answered the temptations by quoting principles taken directly from the Scriptures. All the references were to the experiences of Israel in the wilderness (Deut 6:13,16; 8:3), suggesting again the identification that the Messiah felt with his people in their varied experiences.

These were not Satan's only temptations (Luke 4:13). Jesus continued to be tempted with suggestions to put his physical needs before his Father's will (see John 4:31-34), to prove his messiahship to unbelievers by performing miracles (see Matt 16:1-4) and to gain a kingdom through any way but the cross (see Matt 16:21-23; John 6:15).

18. The first disciples (John 1:35-51)

John the Baptist no doubt felt he had successfully completed part of his work when two of his disciples left him to follow Jesus. One of these was Andrew, the other probably John (who does not mention his own name in his Gospel). Andrew then brought his brother Simon to Jesus. Jesus saw some characteristic in Simon that caused him to give him the name 'Rock'. (The Aramaic word that Jesus used is transliterated as Cephas. The equivalent Greek word is transliterated as Peter.) These men believed Jesus to be the Messiah of whom John spoke, but they had little understanding of the nature of Jesus' messiahship (John 1:35-42).

The party travelled north to Galilee, where they were joined by two more, Philip and Nathanael. (It seems that Nathanael was also called Bartholemew.) Nathanael was surprised to hear that the Messiah came from such an insignificant town as Nazareth in Galilee (John 1:43-46). But when he discovered that Jesus knew all about him even though they had not met, he was convinced that Jesus was the messianic king and the Son of God. Jesus was like a ladder

connecting earth to heaven, bringing God to the world and making it possible for the world to come to God (John 1:47-51).

19. Marriage feast in Cana (John 2:1-12)

At a marriage feast in Cana attended by Jesus and some relatives and friends, the host was embarrassed when he learnt that the supply of wine had run out. Mary told Jesus, apparently thinking he could work a miracle to provide extra wine. In this way he could display his messianic power and so convince people who he was. Jesus reminded her that he could not perform miracles just to please relatives and friends. This was not a time for a public demonstration of his messiahship (John 2:1-5).

Nevertheless, Jesus helped the host out of the difficulty. He performed the miracle privately, but the host immediately noticed the superior quality of the wine he produced. By this miracle Jesus showed his disciples, for the first time, something of the glorious power of the Messiah (John 2:6-11). He then moved back to Capernaum on the shore of Lake Galilee (John 2:12).

EARLY WORK IN JUDEA AND SAMARIA

20. Cleansing the temple (John 2:13-25)

From Capernaum Jesus went to Jerusalem for the Passover (John 2:13). When he visited the temple he found that its outer court (the Court of the Gentiles) was crowded with Jewish merchants and money changers. The merchants were selling animals for sacrifice, and the money changers were exchanging foreign money for money acceptable to the temple authorities. The place looked more like a market than a place of prayer. Jesus was so angry at what he saw that he took bold action to cleanse the temple of all commercial activity (John 2:14-16).

The Jews objected to Jesus' interfering with the temple and challenged him to perform some miracle as evidence that he had authority from God to act in such a way. Jesus referred to the sign of his resurrection as his authority, but no one understood its meaning at the time. Jesus knew that because of his zeal for the purity of God's house the Jews would eventually kill him, but he would rise from the dead and bring in a new era of life for the world (John 2:17-22).

At that time few had a genuine belief in Jesus as Saviour. Many said they believed in him but their faith was not soundly based. They were impressed with Jesus' miracles, but had little idea of what was involved in being disciples of the Messiah. Jesus

410

could not trust people to be loyal followers if their 'belief' in him was little more than enthusiasm for his spectacular deeds (John 2:23-25).

21. Jesus and Nicodemus (3:1-21)

Nicodemus, a member of the Jewish Council, or Sanhedrin, was impressed with Jesus' miracles, but faith based on miracles alone is not enough. There must be inner cleansing, a complete change of heart brought about by the creative power of the Spirit of God. Only then can a person enter the kingdom of God (John 3:1-5; cf. Ezek 36:25-27).

Jews prided themselves that they were born Jews, and thought this guaranteed their entrance into the kingdom of God. Jesus was not concerned with physical birth or an earthly kingdom. He was talking about the work of God's Spirit that gives repentant sinners new life and so enables them to enter God's kingdom. Like the wind, the work of the Spirit is mysterious. It cannot be seen, though its results certainly can (John 3:6-8). Those who have personally experienced God know this new life. Those who think only in terms of earthly things will never know it (John 3:9-12).

True, no person has ever gone up into heaven to learn all about God and his ways, but Jesus Christ has come down from heaven and shown people what God is like. He is God's gift to the world. His death on the cross is God's way of salvation, and if people under condemnation turn to him and believe, they will have eternal life (John 3:13-15).

God's purpose in sending his Son into the world was positive. He wanted people to believe in him and so have eternal life. But if people prefer the darkness of their own sin to the light of salvation through Jesus, they bring judgment upon themselves by their own choice (John 3:16-18). Now that Jesus has come into the world, the difference between light and darkness, good and evil, is clearly seen. People either come into the light of Jesus for cleansing or remain in the darkness of their sin. Once they have come into God's light, they see that every action of their new life is only the result of God's work within them (John 3:19-21).

22. John the Baptist's work complete (John 3:22-36)

While Jesus and his disciples were preaching and baptizing in Judea, John the Baptist was spending the closing days of his ministry preaching and baptizing further north, in the region of the Jordan Valley (John 3:22-24). Some of John's disciples were becoming jealous of Jesus' popularity, and John had to rebuke them. He reminded them that his work was only to prepare the way for Jesus. That work was now finished. John was like the friend of a bridegroom who made the necessary preparations for a wedding, but withdrew once the bridegroom arrived (John 3:25-30).

John was just an ordinary person, born into the world like any other, but Jesus came from heaven, speaking God's words. Most people rejected this divine messenger, though some believed (John 3:31-33; cf. 1:11-12). God revealed himself to the world through Jesus, and Jesus carried out his mission perfectly through the power of God's Spirit working through him. Those who accepted Jesus' teaching showed they believed God, but those who refused it placed themselves under God's judgment (John 3:34-36).

23. Jesus in Samaria (John 4:1-42)

When the Pharisees saw the crowds following Jesus they took an increasing interest in him. No doubt they were becoming jealous and soon might become violent. Jesus therefore decided to leave Judea for Galilee (John 4:1-3).

As Jesus approached one of the villages of Samaria, he began a conversation with a Samaritan woman whom he met at a well (John 4:4-9). The woman had a similar problem to Nicodemus in that she interpreted Jesus' words literally instead of figuratively. She did not understand that when Jesus offered her living water, he was not speaking of ordinary water but of eternal life. If she accepted what he offered, her deepest needs would be satisfied for ever (John 4:10-15).

Realizing that the woman would have to see her personal sin before she could see her spiritual need, Jesus began to speak of her marital affairs. At first she tried to hide her sins, but Jesus' searching remarks soon made her realize that she was in the presence of one with divine knowledge (John 4:16-19). She therefore turned the conversation to religion by referring to the dispute between Jews and Samaritans about the location of the temple. (Concerning relations between Jews and Samaritans see earlier section, 'The New Testament World'.) Jesus told her that the important matters were not those of race or locality, but those that concerned a right attitude of spirit and a right relation with God (John 4:20-24).

The woman saw that the conversation was leading to things she knew nothing about. She therefore tried to finish it quickly by saying that she would wait for the Messiah to come and explain it all to her. Jesus replied that the Messiah was already talking to her (John 4:25-26). In wonder and excitement the woman hurried back to tell the villagers of her discovery and urge them to come and see this remarkable person (John 4:27-30).

Next it was the disciples who interpreted Jesus' words literally instead of figuratively. This time the subject was food. Jesus told them that his strength came from obedience to the will of God. That was his real food, and he intended to keep feeding on it till he finished the work he came to do (John 4:31-34).

After a farmer sows the seed, he may have to wait many months before he reaps the harvest. But in the case of the Samaritan woman, the seed sown in her heart was already bearing fruit, for the Samaritan villagers were already hurrying across the fields to learn about Jesus. Jesus had sown; the disciples would reap. It was a foretaste of the harvest they would reap from seed sown by messengers of God who had gone before them, from the prophets of Old Testament times to John the Baptist (John 4:35-38).

Though the woman had introduced the villagers to Jesus, they needed to exercise personal faith if they were to receive the eternal life he offered. Many responded in genuine faith, realizing that Jesus was a Saviour whose blessings were not limited to selected races or nations (John 4:39-42).

EARLY WORK IN GALILEE

24. Changing situations (Matt 4:12-17; Mark 1:14-15; Lk 3:18-20; 4:14-15; Jn 4:43-45)

Somewhere about this time John the Baptist was imprisoned. (Concerning his imprisonment see notes on Matt 14:1-12; Mark 6:14-29; Luke 9:7-9.) Jesus meanwhile continued north into Galilee, where the people's enthusiastic welcome was in sharp contrast to the suspicion of the people in Judea (Matt 4:12-16; John 4:43-45). He pointed out, however, that the kingdom he announced was not for those seeking political or material benefits. It was only for those who humbly and wholeheartedly turned from their sins (Matt 4:17).

25. Son of an official healed (John 4:46-54)

Jesus was in the town of Cana when a government official arrived from Capernaum with an urgent request for Jesus to heal his son. Again Jesus was careful not to perform miracles to satisfy those who thought of him as merely a wonder-worker. But when he saw the man's distress, he accepted what little faith the man had and announced that the son would live (John 4:46-50). The man accepted Jesus' word and set out for home. When he learnt of the

time and circumstances of his son's healing, he came to complete faith, along with his household (John 4:51-54).

26. The synagogue at Nazareth (Luke 4:16-30)

Soon after returning to Galilee, Jesus visited his home town of Nazareth. Being a genuine God-fearing Israelite, he went on the Sabbath to join with other Jews in worshipping God at the synagogue. In keeping with the synagogue custom of standing to read and sitting to preach, Jesus stood and read Isaiah 61:1-2, then sat down and explained how the passage applied to him. He was the Messiah who brought God's salvation to a world oppressed by sin (Luke 4:16-21).

The people were surprised that the one they previously knew only as the carpenter's son could preach so well. But before they would accept him as the Messiah, they wanted him to do miracles in Nazareth as he had done in other places. Jesus refused. He knew they did not believe in him but were interested only in seeing some spectacular performance (Luke 4:22-23).

Jesus quoted a proverb to show that God's messengers are often not appreciated by those among whom they live, but are welcomed by people elsewhere. He gave two illustrations from the Old Testament. Elijah was unpopular in Israel but welcomed by a woman in Phoenicia. Elisha was rejected by Israelites, but was sought by a soldier from Syria. When Israelites rejected God's servants, God sent his blessings to people of other countries (Luke 4:24-27; cf. 1 Kings 17:9-16; 2 Kings 5:1-14). The lesson for the people of Jesus' home town was that if they did not want God's blessing, it would be sent to others, even to the despised Gentiles, and they would receive it.

The people of Nazareth understood what Jesus was saying and burst into anger. Their actions showed that Jesus had read the condition of their hearts correctly, for instead of believing they tried to murder him. But Jesus escaped unharmed (Luke 4:28-30).

27. Call of Peter, Andrew, James and John (Matt 4:18-22; Mark 1:16-20; Luke 5:1-11)

From the hills of Nazareth the story moves to the fishing villages of Capernaum and Bethsaida on the northern shore of Lake Galilee. The fishermen brothers Peter and Andrew had already met Jesus and accepted him as the Messiah. So too, it seems, had another pair of fishermen brothers, James and John (see notes on John 1:35-42). Jesus now asked the four men to take the further step of leaving their occupations so that they could become his followers in the task of bringing people into the kingdom God (Mark 1:16-20).

Peter learnt more of what lay ahead when, after a day on which they had caught no fish, Jesus told him to let down the nets again. Peter obeyed, with the result that he caught so many fish the nets almost broke (Luke 5:1-7). The incident impressed upon Peter that Jesus was indeed Lord, and in humble submission he fell at the feet of Jesus and confessed his sinfulness (Luke 5:8-11).

Note: The Sea (or Lake) of Galilee, the Sea (or Lake) of Gennesaret, and the Sea (or Lake) of Tiberias were three names for the same place.

28. Man with an evil spirit healed (Mark 1:21-28; Luke 4:31-37)

While in Capernaum Jesus preached in the local synagogue. People noticed that his teaching was very much different from that of the Jewish religious teachers. Instead of arguing about small points of the law he taught the truth of God plainly. All who heard had no doubt that this was God's message taught with his authority (Mark 1:21-22).

On this occasion, however, Jesus' teaching was violently opposed by evil satanic powers that had taken control of a man in the audience. Such demons opposed Jesus throughout his ministry, but they were never victorious over him. News of Jesus' authority over evil spirits spread quickly throughout northern Palestine (Mark 1:23-28).

29. Many sick people healed (Matt 4:23-25; 8:14-17; Mark 1:29-39; Luke 4:38-44)

Further examples of the ministry of Jesus show the presence and power of the kingdom of God in healing those afflicted by Satan (Matt 4:23-25; Mark 1:29-34). (For the significance of the kingdom of God see earlier section, 'Jesus and the Kingdom'.) On one occasion when Jesus was staying in Capernaum, he went outside the town to find a quiet place to pray to his Father. Peter thought he was losing valuable opportunities, as the town was full of people looking for him. Jesus replied that no matter how many needy people were in Capernaum, he could not stay there all the time. He had to work and preach in other towns as well (Mark 1:35-39).

30. Jesus cleanses a leper (Matt 8:1-4; Mark 1:40-45; Luke 5:12-16)

People with leprosy and other skin diseases were considered unclean and a danger to public health. They were outcasts from society (Lev 13:45-46). If they were healed they had to offer sacrifices to symbolize their cleansing and express their thanks (Lev 14:1-20).

On the first recorded occasion when Jesus healed a leper, he did what anyone else would normally avoid doing; he touched the man. He then told the man to present himself to the priest (whose duty was to examine him and confirm that he had been healed; Lev 14:3) and to offer the sacrifices required by the law. He also told the man, clearly and firmly, not to broadcast what had happened, as he did not want to attract people who were curious to see a miracle-worker but had no sense of spiritual need (Mark 1:40-44).

The man disobeyed and as a result Jesus' work was hindered. So many people came to see him that he was unable to teach in the towns as he wished. He continued to help the needy, but the pressures upon him caused him all the more to seek his Father's will through prayer (Mark 1:45; Luke 5:16).

31. Jesus heals a paralyzed man (Matt 9:1-8; Mark 2:1-12; Luke 5:17-26)

This story shows the first signs of organized Jewish opposition to Jesus. A group of religious leaders from Jerusalem, Judea and Galilee came, with evil motives, to find out for themselves what Jesus was doing and saying (Luke 5:17).

Some friends of a paralyzed man were so sure Jesus could heal him that they allowed no obstacle to stop them from bringing the man to him. In his response Jesus did more than heal the man. He went to the root of all suffering in a fallen world, sin, and on the basis of the faith that had been displayed, he announced forgiveness of the man's sins. The Jewish leaders saw that Jesus was claiming to be God, for only God can forgive sins. Either Jesus was God or he was a blasphemer (Luke 5:18-21).

Jesus left his critics in no doubt of the meaning of his words and actions. A person can just as easily say 'You are forgiven' as say 'You are healed', but whereas the first statement cannot be proved by external evidence, the second statement can. If, therefore, Jesus' claim to heal the man's disease could be proved true, his claim to forgive the man's sins must also be accepted as true. When the man, in response to Jesus' words, stood up and walked, the onlookers had clear proof that Jesus was all that he claimed to be (Luke 5:22-26).

32. Call of Matthew (Matt 9:9-13; Mark 2:13-17; Luke 5:27-32)

The next person to join Jesus' group of chosen disciples was the tax collector Matthew, also known

413

as Levi (Matt 9:9; Mark 2:13-14). Matthew took Jesus home for a meal and invited his fellow tax collectors and other friends to come and meet his new master. Jews despised tax collectors as being unpatriotic, dishonest and irreligious. The Pharisees despised Jesus when they saw him eating with them (Matt 9:10-11; Luke 5:27-30).

Jesus replied that if tax collectors were as bad as the Pharisees claimed, then tax collectors were just the sort of people who needed his help. God was pleased with Jesus' action in showing mercy to outcasts. He was not pleased with the sacrifices of those who thought they were superior to others (Matt 9:12-13; Luke 5:31-32).

33. Why Jesus' disciples did not fast (Matt 9:14-17; Mark 2:18-22; Luke 5:33-39)

Both John the Baptist's disciples and the Pharisees were slow to realize that Jesus' coming had brought in a new era. Their traditional ceremonies and fastings were now of no use. The coming of Jesus may be compared to the coming of a bridegroom to his wedding feast. In a time of such joy no one thinks of fasting, and therefore Jesus' disciples did not fast while he was with them. But Jesus would be taken away from them and killed, and then they would fast because of their great sorrow. Their sorrow, however, would be turned into joy, because Jesus would rise from death victoriously (Mark 2:18-20; Luke 5:33-35).

Jesus reminded his hearers that, now that he had come, they should not expect to continue the old traditions of the Jewish religion. He had not come to repair, improve or update Judaism. Judaism was useless, worn out, finished. Jesus brought something that was entirely new. Judaism was like an old worn out coat that could not be mended; it was like a brittle old wineskin that could not stand the pressure of new wine (Mark 2:21-22; Luke 5:36-38). Yet the Pharisees preferred their old worn out religion (Luke 5:39).

34. Picking corn on the Sabbath (Matt 12:1-8; Mark 2:23-28; Luke 6:1-5)

When the Pharisees criticized Jesus' disciples for picking a few pieces of corn to eat on the Sabbath, Jesus defended his disciples by referring to two examples from the Old Testament. First, when David and his men were very hungry and urgently needed food, they were rightly allowed to eat the holy bread of the tabernacle, which normally only priests were allowed to eat (Matt 12:1-4; cf. 1 Sam 21:1-6). Second, even the Levitical priests worked on

the Sabbath, for they had to prepare and offer the sacrifices (Matt 12:5; cf. Num 28:9-10).

These two examples show that in a case of necessity the legal requirement of the law may be overruled. Life is more important than ritual. To exercise mercy is more important than to offer sacrifices. Jesus is more important than the temple. People are more important than the Sabbath. The Sabbath was given for people's benefit, not for their discomfort; and since Jesus is the messianic Son of man, he has authority to decide how the Sabbath can best be used (Matt 12:6-8; Mark 2:27-28).

35. Man with a withered hand (Matt 12:9-21; Mark 3:1-6; Luke 6:6-11)

If an animal fell into a pit on the Sabbath day, the Jews would not hesitate to rescue it the same day. Yet they criticized Jesus for healing a man on the Sabbath. Although no list of rules sets out all that a person should or should not do to keep the Sabbath holy, it is always right to do good on the Sabbath. To save life is better than to kill, and in this case Jesus was helping to save life. The Pharisees, by contrast, were looking for ways to kill him (Matt 12:9-14; Mark 3:1-6).

Jesus left his critics and went on to his work elsewhere. Matthew saw this as a further stage in the fulfilment of the prophecy that God's chosen servant, who had now appeared in the person of Jesus, would take the gospel to all people. This servant never tried to make a show of greatness, never hurt those who sorrowed, and never turned away from those of even the weakest faith (Matt 12:15-21; cf. Isa 42:1-4).

36. Jesus chooses the twelve apostles (Matt 9:35-10:4; Mark 3:7-19; Luke 6:12-19)

The more Jesus' work grew, the more people came seeking him; and the more deeply saddened he became as he saw the confused and helpless spiritual condition of the Jewish people. There were plenty of opportunities for worthwhile work but there were few workers, and Jesus asked his followers to pray that God would supply the right workers to meet the need (Matt 9:35-38; Mark 3:7-12).

So urgent was the need that Jesus decided to appoint twelve helpers immediately. He therefore spent the night in prayer and in the morning announced his choice. The twelve were to be known as apostles (from the Greek word *apostello*, meaning 'to send'), as Jesus was to send them out in the service of the kingdom. To begin with he would keep them with him for their spiritual training, then he would send them out equipped with his messianic authority to heal those afflicted by Satan and urge people to enter the kingdom of God. The era of the Messiah had arrived. As twelve tribes had formed the basis of the old people of God, so twelve apostles would be the basis of the new (Matt 10:1; Mark 3:13-15; Luke 6:12-13). The following list includes alternative names by which some of the apostles were known.

Simon Peter, or Cephas	Matt 10:2;	John 1:42
Andrew, brother of Peter	Matt 10:2;	John 1:40
James, son of Zebedee	Mark 3:17;	Luke 8:51
John, brother of James	Mark 3:17;	John 21:20
Philip	Matt 10:3;	John 6:5
Bartholemew, or Nathanael	Matt 10:3;	John 21:2
Thomas, the Twin (Didymus)	Matt 10:3;	John 21:2
Matthew, or Levi	Matt 10:3;	Luke 5:27
James, son of Alphaeus	Matt 10:3;	Acts 1:13
Thaddaeus, or Lebbaeus, or Judas the son of James	Matt 10:3;	Luke 6:16
Simon the Zealot, the Patriot, or the Cananaean	Matt 10:4;	Luke 6:15
Judas Iscariot	Matt 10:4;	Luke 22:48

THE SERMON ON THE MOUNT

When people enter Jesus' kingdom they enter a new life. They come under the rule of Jesus and, as his disciples, listen to his teaching and put it into practice. Their behaviour is not governed by a set of rules such as the law of Moses, but by the character of Jesus, who wants to reproduce that character in them. The collection of Jesus' teachings commonly known as the Sermon on the Mount deals with the attitudes, behaviour and responsibilities of those who have come under the lordship of Jesus Christ.

37. Citizens of the kingdom (Matt 5:1-12; Luke 6:20-26)

The section opens with a series of short two-line statements commonly known as Beatitudes (from the Latin word for 'blessed'). In present-day English 'blessed' is probably not as good a translation as 'happy' (GNB). Jesus is not making a formal declaration of divine favour, but announcing the true happiness of those who live according to the life of the kingdom. For example, those who humbly acknowledge that they need God's help in everything will enjoy God's kingdom, for it was made for such people. In that kingdom there is no room for those who are proudly self-sufficient (Matt 5:1-3).

Those who sorrow because of the power of sin in the world will have their sorrow turned to joy when they see sin finally destroyed. God will remove the arrogant from the earth and give it as a dwelling place to the truly humble. The people who in the end will be fully satisfied are not those who selfishly pursue their own ambitions, but those who long to do what God wants and to see his will done in the world around them (Matt 5:4-6).

When people realize the greatness of God's mercy to them, they will be more merciful to others. In return they will receive yet more mercy from God. If, with a pure heart, they try to please God and not themselves, they will be fittingly rewarded with a vision of God himself (Matt 5:7-8). God's children reflect the true character of their Father when they help those who have quarrelled to become friends again. They prove themselves to be worthy citizens of God's kingdom when they stand for him against wrongdoing, even though they may suffer as a result (Matt 5:9-10). When persecuted for Christ's sake they rejoice, knowing that they are thereby united with God's true people of former days (Matt 5:11-12).

In contrast to those who put God's interests first, some people direct all their efforts towards making life better for themselves. They may have much success at accumulating wealth, building a comfortable life and gaining popularity, but that is all the success they will ever have. The future will bring them disappointment, sorrow and eternal loss (Luke 6:20-26).

38. Christ's people in the world (Matt 5:13-16)

Salt can be used to preserve food from decay and to give food flavour. Christ's people should have a similar effect upon the world, as they resist the corrupting effects of sin and help make the world a better place to live. But if they do not discipline themselves to develop and maintain this salt-like quality, they will be of no use for God (Matt 5:13-14).

The followers of Jesus are lights for God in a dark world. Like a city on a hill they will be noticed by all; like a candle on a stand they will give light to others. Just as a candle is not hidden but is put in a place where it gives light, so Christians will not hide themselves but will live and work in places where they can bring people to know and worship God (Matt 5:15-16).

39. A right attitude to the law (Matt 5:17-20)

In a lengthy section that runs through to the end of the chapter, Jesus points out that it is not good enough merely to follow the teachings of the scribes and Pharisees. Realizing that people may think he is in some way opposed to the law of Moses, Jesus explains at the outset that this is not so. He does not abolish the Old Testament or overthrow its authority. On the contrary he gives it fuller meaning. He is its goal, and it finds its fulfilment in him (Matt 5:17-18).

Jesus does not teach anyone to ignore the instruction of the Old Testament, but he makes it clear that even if they keep all the commandments (as the Pharisees claimed to do), they still will not gain entrance into the kingdom of God. Salvation is not by works. The righteousness that God desires cannot be achieved by keeping rules and regulations. It can result only from an inward change that starts with faith and repentance and is developed through genuine love and submission to Jesus (Matt 5:19-20).

40. Legal obedience is not enough (Matt 5:21-48; Luke 6:27-36; 12:57-59)

After his explanation concerning right and wrong attitudes to the law, Jesus gives a number of examples. He introduces these examples with statements such as 'You have heard that it was said in the past'. This is not the same as 'It is written'. Jesus is not quoting from the Old Testament but from the teachings of the scribes and Pharisees. He is not contradicting the law but the interpretations of the law that the scribes taught. In so doing he explains the real meaning of the law and the necessity for more than mere legal obedience. He is not writing a new law, but showing his people that they must have a new attitude. The Jewish religious leaders used the law to govern outward actions, but Jesus wants to control the heart.

In his first example Jesus shows that to refrain from murder is not enough. The spirit of anger and revenge that leads to murder must be removed from the heart (Matt 5:21-22). Besides controlling their anger, disciples of Jesus should try to make peace with those who are angry with them. Even in worldly affairs an offender would be wise to reach agreement with his opponent quickly. Otherwise he may find himself in worse circumstances by receiving an unfavourable judgment in court (Matt 5:23-26).

Like murder, adultery is the final fruit of wrong thoughts and uncontrolled feelings. The eye sees, the mind desires and the body acts. Therefore, the eye, as well as the rest of the body, must be brought under control, whatever the cost. Temptation must be cut at the source (Matt 5:27-30).

Another common sin that resulted from a misunderstanding of the law was divorce. In a time of widespread social disorder, Moses had introduced a law to prevent easy divorce and protect innocent partners (Deut 24:1-4). Certain teachers then twisted the meaning of Moses' law to allow easy divorce. Jesus rejected such use of the law and referred them back to God's original standard (Matt 5:31-32).

Many Jews considered that if, in swearing an oath, they did not use God's name, they were not bound by that oath. If they swore 'by heaven', 'by earth', 'by Jerusalem' or 'by the head' and then broke their oath, they felt no guilt, because such oaths did not use the name of God. Jesus says they should not need to swear oaths at all. *Everything* they say should be true, honest and straightforward (Matt 5:33-37).

When Moses laid down a law code for civil governments, he established the principle that the punishment had to fit the crime. 'An eye for an eye, a tooth for a tooth, a scratch for a scratch' meant that there had to be a heavy punishment for a major offence, and a light punishment for a minor offence (Exod 21:23-25). But once again people took a legal regulation of civil government and twisted it to suit their purposes. They now felt free to take personal revenge on anyone who did them wrong. Jesus shows that his followers must not demand their rights every time they are wronged, but show loving forgiveness (attitudes that also were taught in the law of Moses; Exod 23:4-5; Lev 19:17-18). The spirit that rules in their hearts must not be the same as that which rules in the code of legal justice (Matt 5:38-42).

The saying that encouraged Jews to hate their enemies did not come from the law of Moses, as the above Old Testament references clearly show. It came from the traditions of the scribes. God's people must love their enemies. They are doing nothing exceptional if they love only those who are friends, for even the ungodly do that. The Christians' example is found in God, who gives rain and food to those who love him and those who hate him. He makes no distinctions, and as Christians follow his example, their character will become increasingly like his (Matt 5:43-48).

41. Giving, praying and fasting (Matt 6:1-18; Luke 11:1-4)

If the followers of Jesus give help to the needy with the aim of winning people's praise, their giving is of no value in God's sight. They will have their reward in the praise they seek, but will miss out on any reward from God. They should keep matters of giving secret from even their closest friends (Matt 6:1-4).

Prayer also is a private matter. Believers do not need to make a show of prayerful zeal, as if their heavenly Father needs long and impressive prayers to rouse him to action. He is not like the lifeless idols of the heathen, but is a loving Father who understands his children's needs (Matt 6:5-8).

In encouraging believers to pray confidently, Jesus provides a model for them to follow. Although they can speak to God with the freedom of children speaking to a father, they should do so reverently, remembering that he is holy. An expression of worship ensures that his glory comes before their needs (Matt 6:9). Believers should pray for God's rule in their lives and in the lives of others, whether as individuals or among people in general. Their prayers may concern great things such as the completion of God's eternal plan, or small things such as the provision of daily needs (Matt 6:10-11). They should confess their sins, remembering that God will forgive them only if they forgive others. They should also ask for God's control in the affairs of life, so that difficulties they meet will not cause them to fall into sin (Matt 6:12-15).

If at any time believers accompany their prayers with fasting, they should not try to impress others by making themselves look sad. Their fasting will be of no value in God's sight if they use it to win people's praise. When they fast they should act and dress normally (Matt 6:16-18).

42. Concern about material things (Matt 6:19-34; Luke 12:22-34)

People who come into the kingdom of God should not view the material things of earthly life as others view them. They should put God's interests first and be generous in giving to others. Those who set their hearts on material things are being disloyal to God, and guarantee bitter disappointment for themselves in the end (Matt 6:19-21).

To illustrate the results of right and wrong attitudes to material things, Jesus referred to a local belief about the results of good and bad eyesight. People believed that eyes were like windows that allowed light to enter the body and keep it in good health. Healthy eyes meant a healthy body (light); diseased eyes meant a diseased body (darkness). A healthy view of material things will result in a healthy spiritual life; but an unhealthy view will mean that the natural spiritual darkness already in the heart will become even darker (Matt 6:22-23). A person can be a slave of only one master at a time. If people devote their attention to increasing their prosperity and comfort, they can no longer claim to be loyal to God (Matt 6:24).

Others, however, get into bondage to material things not because they are greedy, but because they worry too much about having enough money to look after themselves. They should realize that if God gives life, he can also give what is necessary to maintain life (Matt 6:25-27). If he cares for lesser things such as birds, flowers and grass, he can certainly care for his people. Believers should not be anxious concerning their material needs. Those who do not know God might be anxious, but believers should trust in God and put the interests of his kingdom first. They are under his rule and they should trust that as day to day difficulties arise, he will provide the answer (Matt 6:28-34).

43. Judging others (Matt 7:1-6; Luke 6:37-42)

People who continually find fault with others only invite judgment upon themselves, both from their fellows and from God. In pointing to the faults in others, they attract attention to themselves. They too have faults, and though they themselves may be unaware of them, other people see them very clearly (Matt 7:1-5).

Nevertheless, there is a kind of judgment that is necessary. Those who present the gospel must be able to judge the difference between people who genuinely want to know about God and people who only want to mock and abuse. A person does not give good meat to filthy dogs, nor does he give pearls to pigs (Matt 7:6).

The followers of Jesus must learn to make proper judgments if they are to help others. As teachers they are examples, and God will reward them according to the example they give, whether for good or for bad. They must remember that they cannot lead the blind if they themselves are blind. In particular, they must not lead others astray by faultfinding (Luke 6:37-42).

44. Prayers of request (Matt 7:7-12; Luke 11:5-13)

Jesus gave two illustrations to show his followers that they can put their requests to God confidently. Even a tired and uncooperative neighbour can be persuaded by a person's persistence into giving him what he needs. How much more will God, who is a loving Father, supply all the needs of his children (Luke 11:5-10). Christians do not have to beg from a

God who is unwilling to give. They go to God as children go to their father, confident that he will not disappoint them or give them less than they ask (Matt 7:7-12; Luke 11:11-13).

45. The two ways (Matt 7:13-29; Luke 6:43-49)

There are two ways of life. One is the easy way of pleasing self, which most choose and which leads to destruction. The other is the narrow way of denying self for Jesus' sake, which leads to life (Matt 7:13-14).

One reason why many do not follow the narrow way is that they are deceived by those who teach their own views on how people can find meaning in life. Their teaching at first sounds reasonable, but in the end it proves to be destructive. The teachers appear to be as harmless as sheep, but actually they are as dangerous as wolves. A bad tree produces bad fruit, and wrong teaching produces wrong behaviour (Matt 7:15-20).

Another reason why people do not follow the narrow way is that they deceive themselves. They think that because they attach themselves to Jesus' followers they will enter Jesus' kingdom. They may even preach in Jesus' name, but if they have never had a personal experience of God through faith and repentance, they too will go to the place of destruction (Matt 7:21-23). If people hear Jesus' teaching but do not act upon it, they are deceiving themselves and heading for disaster. They are like a person who builds a house that looks solid but has no foundation, and so is destroyed when the storm of testing comes (Matt 7:24-27).

The difference between Jesus' teaching and the teaching of the scribes was obvious to all. The scribes referred to respected teachers of the past for their authority, but Jesus spoke on his own authority. The scribes could only repeat the regulations of Judaism, but Jesus interpreted the law with an authority that came from God (Matt 7:28-29).

IN JERUSALEM AGAIN

46. Healing at Bethesda and its outcome (John 5:1-29)

Jesus came from Galilee to Jerusalem for a Jewish religious festival. While there he visited a pool where many blind and crippled people hoped to find healing (John 5:1-5). One of the men asked Jesus for help, not to heal him (for he did not know who Jesus was) but to assist him into the pool. Jesus responded by healing him instantly (John 5:6-9). As the healing took place on the Sabbath, the Jewish leaders were anxious to find out who

was responsible. Jesus must have known that the healed man's wrongdoing was partly the cause of his troubles, and urged him to repent. But the man's response was to report Jesus to those who were looking for him (John 5:10-15).

When the Jewish leaders accused Jesus of breaking the Sabbath laws, he replied that his Father also works on the Sabbath. Day by day he maintains the world and cares for his creatures. When he makes the sun to rise, the rain to fall and the grass to grow on the Sabbath, he does not break the law. Jesus is united with his Father, and he does not sin when he carries out acts of mercy on the Sabbath (John 5:16-17).

The Jews objected even more strongly when they heard Jesus call God his Father. Jesus replied that in all their work the Father and the Son are united. They are separate persons, but one God. In healing on the Sabbath, Jesus was not acting against the Father's commands, but doing what the Father wanted (John 5:18-20a).

Because Jesus is God, he will do even greater works than this; he will raise the dead to life and bring in final judgment. Those who reject the Son dishonour God, but those who receive the Son pass immediately from spiritual death to spiritual life (John 5:20b-24). When the dead are raised for final judgment, that judgment will be carried out by the Son. But there will be no condemnation for those who have received the life that he offers (John 5:25-29).

47. Witness to Jesus (John 5:30-47)

Jesus acted with God's authority, but he would not give evidence on his own behalf to try to convince the Jews. God was his witness, and Jesus accepted his witness even if the Jews did not (John 5:30-32). With God as his witness, Jesus needed no other, but if the Jews wanted earthly witnesses, they were available. Jesus gave them three, which would satisfy those who wanted to judge him according to the requirements for witnesses under Jewish law (cf. Deut 19:15). The first was John the Baptist. His announcement of the coming of the Messiah was like the introduction of a lamp in a dark place. People at first welcomed him, but when they saw that he was calling them to turn from their sinful ways they lost interest (John 5:33-35).

The second witness was the work of Jesus. His miracles were visible proof of the presence and power of the invisible God. But again the Jews did not believe (John 5:36-38). Third, there were the Old Testament Scriptures, which the Jews studied diligently, thinking that by keeping the law they would gain eternal life. Yet their studies did not lead them to accept the Saviour to whom the Scriptures pointed, and therefore they did not receive eternal life (John 5:39-40).

Unlike the Jews, Jesus did not look for human praise. The Jews welcomed those who appointed themselves teachers, but rejected the one whom God appointed (John 5:41-44). If they understood the real meaning of Moses' law instead of arguing about rules and regulations, they would welcome Jesus. They would see that he was the one to whom Moses' teaching pointed. In rejecting him they rejected Moses, and so were condemned by the very things that Moses wrote (John 5:45-47).

BACK IN GALILEE

48. Centurion's servant; widow's son
(Matt 8:5-13; Luke 7:1-17)

Back in Capernaum, a Roman centurion asked Jesus to heal one of his servants who was dying. However, he did not expect Jesus to come to his house. Being an army officer, he operated in a system of authority where he needed only to give a command and it was carried out. He believed that Jesus carried the authority of God, and he needed only to say the word and the servant would be healed (Matt 8:5-9; Luke 7:1-8).

Jesus saw that this Roman had more faith than the Jews. He used the incident to warn the Jews that many of them would be left out of God's kingdom, but Gentiles from countries far and near would, because of their faith, be included (Matt 8:10-13; Luke 7:9-10).

In another northern town, Nain, Jesus raised a widow's son to life. It seems that in this case he acted not because of any request, but solely because of the pity he felt for the woman. With her husband and her only son dead, she was faced with hardship and poverty for the rest of her life. Jesus therefore stopped the funeral procession and gave her son back to her (Luke 7:11-17).

49. Messengers from John the Baptist
(Matt 11:1-19; Luke 7:18-35)

Shut up in prison, John the Baptist received only irregular and possibly inaccurate reports of Jesus' ministry. These reports must have caused him to wonder whether Jesus really was the Messiah he foretold. Jesus sent back the message that he was carrying out a ministry of relief to the oppressed, which was the sort of ministry foretold of the Messiah in the Old Testament (Matt 11:1-5; cf. Isa 35:5-6; 61:1). Many were disappointed that Jesus did not bring the political victories they expected of the Messiah, but Jesus promised a special blessing to those who understood his ministry and did not lose heart (Matt 11:6).

To prevent anyone from speaking ill of John because of his questioning, Jesus pointed out what a great man he was. John was not weak in character, uncertain of himself or easily swayed by the opinions of others. Nor did he seek comfort or prestige. He was a prophet, and like many of the prophets he endured a life of hardship (Matt 11:7-10).

John was the last and greatest figure of the era before the Messiah, but because he belonged to that era he was less blessed than the humblest believer who enters the Messiah's kingdom. Although some opposed the kingdom violently, others spared no effort to enter it (Matt 11:11-12). In preparing the way for the kingdom and introducing the Messiah, John was the 'Elijah' of whom the prophet Malachi spoke (Matt 11:13-15; cf. Mal 4:5).

Those who believed and obeyed the preaching of John were pleased to hear Jesus' commendation of him. But the religious leaders, who hated John, were angry (Luke 7:29-30).

Jesus likened the people of his day to a lot of quarrelling children playing in the streets. They could not agree to play a lively wedding game, nor could they agree to play a slower funeral game. Nothing satisfied them. The Jews acted like those children. They criticized John because he followed strict rules about food and drink and lived like a hermit in the desert; they criticized Jesus because he had no such rules about food and drink and mixed with the most disreputable people in society. But God had a purpose in sending John and Jesus with their separate missions, and his wisdom was proved in the changed lives of those who accepted their messages (Matt 11:16-19).

50. The judgment and mercy of God
(Matt 11:20-30)

The Galilean towns of Bethsaida, Chorazin and Capernaum, where Jesus did much of his work, were not as immoral as certain Gentile cities of the Old Testament era such as Tyre, Sidon and Sodom. However, because the Galilean towns had witnessed the ministry of Jesus then deliberately rejected him, they would suffer a more severe judgment than the Gentile towns that had never heard of him. Their greater privilege placed upon them a greater responsibility, and this meant that their failure would bring a greater judgment (Matt 11:20-24).

Very few of the privileged and learned classes turned to Jesus, as they felt comfortably secure and satisfied with their achievements in life. But many who felt helpless turned to Jesus to satisfy their deepest needs, and through him came into a new relationship with God. They found true refreshment in learning from Jesus and obeying his teachings. In submitting to his lordship they found true life (Matt 11:25-30).

51. In the house of Simon the Pharisee (Luke 7:36-50)

Like most Pharisees, Simon no doubt kept the laws of holiness and thought that God was more pleased with him than with socially despised people such as tax collectors and prostitutes. He was therefore surprised that Jesus allowed a prostitute to wash his feet. In Simon's view this showed that Jesus did not have divine knowledge, otherwise he would know the sort of person the woman was and would not allow her to touch him (Luke 7:36-39).

Jesus knew Simon's thoughts, so told a story to contrast Simon's attitude with the woman's (Luke 7:40-43). Simon had never come to Jesus in search of forgiveness, because he had never felt the need. Consequently, he had no reason to feel any love or gratitude towards Jesus. The woman, however, had apparently heard Jesus' message of forgiveness and, being sorry for her sins, trusted in his forgiving love. She then showed her love and gratitude in the most meaningful way she new (Luke 7:44-50).

52. Blasphemy of the Holy Spirit (Matt 12:22-45; Mark 3:22-30; Luke 11:14-36)

On one occasion when Jesus cast out demons, the Pharisees accused him of doing it by the power of Satan, the prince of demons (Matt 12:22-24; Luke 11:14-16). Jesus replied that if the prince of demons used his own power to cast out demons, he would be creating civil war in his own kingdom. He would be destroying himself. The only way a strong man can be defeated is if a stronger man overpowers him. In casting out demons Jesus showed that he was stronger than Satan. His reign, which would result in the destruction of Satan, had begun (Matt 12:25-29; Luke 11:17-22).

God could forgive the doubts and misunderstandings people had about Jesus, but he would not forgive their defiant rejection of the clear evidence that all Jesus' works were good and that they originated in God. Those who called God's Spirit Satan, who called good evil, had put themselves in a position where they had no way of acknowledging God's goodness. Therefore, they had no way of receiving his forgiveness (Matt 12:30-32).

The good works that Jesus did were evidence of his goodness, just as good fruit is evidence of a good tree. Likewise the evil works of the Pharisees were evidence of their evil hearts, and this evidence will be used against them in the day of judgment (Matt 12:33-37).

Again the Pharisees asked Jesus to perform a miracle as a sign that he was the Messiah, and again Jesus refused. The only sign would be his resurrection from the dead, which would be the Father's unmistakable confirmation that Jesus was his Son. By their rejection of Jesus, they were guaranteeing that in the judgment day they would be in a far worse position than the heathen. The queen of the Gentile kingdom of Sheba recognized Solomon's wisdom, and the people of the heathen city of Nineveh repented at Jonah's preaching, but the Jews of Jesus' time stubbornly refused to accept him as the Messiah (Matt 12:38-42; Luke 11:29-32).

Jesus gave an illustration to show that people could not remain neutral. If they were not wholeheartedly committed to him, in the end they would be against him. They would be like a person who benefits temporarily by being cleansed of demons, but because he does nothing positive to fill his life with better things, he becomes possessed by even worse demons. The people of Jesus' time benefited temporarily from his gracious ministry, but if they did not positively turn from their sin and accept him as the God-sent Saviour, they would in the end be under a more severe condemnation than they were originally (Matt 12:43-45; Luke 11:23-28).

If people allowed God's light to shine into their hearts, it would drive out the darkness and enable them to take this light to others. But if they rejected the light, the darkness within them would become even darker (Luke 11:33-36).

53. Jesus and his family (Matt 12:46-50; Mark 3:20-21,31-35; Luke 8:19-21)

The children of Mary and Joseph born after Jesus were James, Joseph, Simon, Judas and at least two daughters (cf. Matt 13:55-56; Mark 6:3). At first they did not accept Jesus as the Messiah, but thought he was suffering from some sort of religious madness (Mark 3:20-21; cf. John 7:3-5). Jesus must have been saddened to see such an attitude in his brothers and sisters, but he knew that more important than natural relationships were spiritual relationships. All who obey God are related to him and to one another in the vast family of God (Mark 3:31-35).

PARABLES

54. The sower (Matt 13:1-23; Mark 4:1-29; Luke 8:1-18)

To visit all the towns of Galilee was a huge task. Jesus and his disciples were helped in this work by a group of women who went with them to look after their daily needs (Luke 8:1-3). Crowds of people came to see Jesus wherever he went, and were often a hindrance to the progress of the gospel. It seems that one reason Jesus began to teach extensively in parables was to separate those who were genuinely interested from those who were merely curious (Matt 13:1-3a; Mark 4:1-2).

The parable of the sower draws its lessons from the four different kinds of soil rather than from the work of the sower. The preacher puts the message of the kingdom into people's hearts as a farmer puts seed into the ground. But people's hearts vary just as the soil in different places varies. Some people hear the message but do not understand it because they are not interested. Others show early interest but soon give up because they have no deep spiritual concern. Others are too worried about the affairs of everyday life. Only a few respond to the message in faith, but when they do their lives are changed and a spiritual harvest results (Matt 13:3b-9,18-23; Mark 4:3-9,13-20).

Parables may provide a pictorial way to teach truth, but they are more than just illustrations. Their purpose is to make the hearers think about the teaching. Those who gladly receive Jesus' teaching will find the parables full of meaning. As a result their ability to understand God's truth will increase. But those who have no genuine interest in Jesus' teaching will see no meaning in the parables at all. Worse still, their spiritual blindness will become darker, and their stubborn hearts more hardened. Because their wills are opposed to Jesus, their minds cannot appreciate his teaching, and consequently their sins remain unforgiven (Matt 13:10-17; Mark 4:10-12).

Although the teaching of parables may cause the idly curious to lose interest in Jesus, the basic purpose of a parable is to enlighten, not to darken. A parable is like a lamp, which is put on a stand to give light, not hidden under a bowl or under a bed. The more thought people give to their master's teaching, the more enlightenment and blessing they will receive in return. But if they are lazy and give no thought to the teaching, their ability to appreciate spiritual truth will decrease, until eventually it is completely gone (Mark 4:21-25).

Returning to the picture of the sower, Jesus shows that good seed will always produce healthy plants and good fruit if given the opportunity. The farmer sows the seed, but he must wait for the soil to react with the seed and make it grow. Likewise the messenger of the gospel must have patient faith in God as the message does its work in people's hearts (Mark 4:26-29).

55. Wheat and weeds; mustard seed; yeast (Mt 13:24-43; Mk 4:30-34; Lk 13:18-21)

In another parable, two types of seed produce two types of plants in the same field. The plants, wheat and weeds, are not separated while they are growing, but are left till harvest time. Then the wheat is put into the farmer's barn but the weeds are destroyed (Matt 13:24-30).

As with the parable of the sower, Jesus gave his disciples an interpretation (Matt 13:34-36; cf. v. 10,16-18). In the present world those who are in the kingdom of God live alongside those who are not. This was contrary to popular Jewish thinking, which expected the kingdom to come in one mighty act that would destroy all enemies and set up God's universal rule of righteousness and peace. Jesus points out that his kingdom is in the world already, but it will have its climax at the end of world history. When that time comes the wicked will be destroyed but the righteous will share in the kingdom's triumph (Matt 13:37-43).

The parable of the mustard seed foretells the expansion of the kingdom, as seen in the remarkable growth of the church. From small beginnings it grows to a vast community that covers the entire earth (Matt 13:31-32). A similar truth is illustrated by the parable of the yeast (or leaven). As a small amount of yeast spreads through a lump of dough, so will the apparently small kingdom of Jesus spread through the world (Matt 13:33).

56. Hidden treasure; pearl; fishing net (Matt 13:44-52)

Two parables show that when people are convinced of the priceless and lasting value of the kingdom of God, they will make any sacrifice to enter it (Matt 13:44-46). Yet those in the kingdom still live in a world where the righteous and the wicked exist together. Even among those who claim to be in the kingdom are the true and the false. These will be separated at the last judgment (Matt 13:47-50).

Jesus' teachings are likened to valuable goods that are put in a storeroom where they are added to the things that the owner already has, namely, the Old Testament Scriptures. The disciples of Jesus have a wealth of teaching available for their benefit (Matt 13:51-52).

AROUND THE LAKE OF GALILEE

57. Jesus calms the storm (Matt 8:23-27; Mark 4:35-41; Luke 8:22-25)

A well known feature of Lake Galilee was that fierce storms blew up quickly. Jesus had suggested that the group sail across the lake, but the disciples expressed disappointment with him when a storm arose and he did nothing to help. Instead he was sleeping in the back of the boat, perhaps an indication of his tiredness from constant work (Mark 4:35-38).

The disciples still did not understand fully the divine power of Jesus, and he rebuked them for their lack of faith. When a word from him was sufficient to calm the wild forces of nature, they were struck with a mixture of wonder and fear. The sovereign Lord of creation was among them (Mark 4:39-41; cf. Ps. 89:9).

58. Demon power overcome at Gadara (Matt 8:28-34; Mark 5:1-20; Luke 8:26-39)

Another place that Jesus visited was the district to the east and south of the Lake of Galilee known as Gadara. The people were mainly Gentiles and were known as Gadarenes (sometimes as Gerasenes, after the chief town of the district, or even Gergesenes, after another local town) (Matt 8:28; Mark 5:1). Jesus was met there by a man whose body had been cruelly taken over by demons. To release the man from his torment, Jesus commanded the demons to come out of him. The demons knew that Jesus was the Son of God and that one day he would judge them, but they were angry that he came to interfere with them before the appointed time (Matt 8:29; Mark 5:2-8).

Jesus commanded the man to tell him his name, so that the man might see how great a power of evil had possessed him. The demons saw that judgment was upon them, and begged Jesus not to send them immediately to the place where evil spirits are punished (Mark 5:9-10; Luke 8:30-31).

The demons preferred to remain in the bodies of living things than go to the place of punishment. Therefore, if they were not allowed to remain in the man's body, they would rather enter the bodies of animals, even pigs. Jesus gave them their request, but they met their judgment nevertheless, for the pigs went mad and drowned in the sea. By sending the demons into the pigs, Jesus gave dramatic visible proof of his power over demons, and at the same time he showed to all what a vast number of demons had possessed the man (Mark 5:11-13).

To Jesus the life of one person was more important than the lives of two thousand pigs. The local villagers were more concerned about their farms and, fearful of what might happen if Jesus remained in the district any longer, begged him to leave (Mark 5:14-17). Jesus left, leaving the man to spread the good news of the Saviour throughout the area. Since these people were Gentiles, there was no need for the man to keep quiet about the miracle. Gentiles were not likely to use Jesus' messiahship for political purposes (Mark 5:18-20; cf. Matt 8:4, 9:30, 12:16; John 6:14-15).

59. Jairus' daughter and a woman healed (Mt 9:18-26; Mk 5:21-43; Lk 8:40-56)

Back in the Jewish regions, a synagogue elder named Jairus asked Jesus to come and heal his seriously ill daughter. Seeing that the man had faith, Jesus set off for his house (Mark 5:21-24). On the way they were interrupted by a sick woman who believed that if she could only touch Jesus' clothing she would be healed (Mark 5:25-29). Jesus knew that someone was seeking his help in this way, and did not want the person to be left with any superstitious ideas. He therefore searched for the woman so that she might show her faith openly and be healed completely (Mark 5:30-34).

Jairus' faith was tested when he heard that while Jesus was healing the woman, his daughter had died. Jesus responded by working a greater miracle than Jairus expected, for he brought the girl back to life. He allowed only five people to see the miracle, and he told them not to tell others what they had seen. He did not want people flocking to him for the wrong reasons (Mark 5:35-43).

60. Jesus heals the blind and the dumb (Matt 9:27-34; Mark 8:22-26)

Two blind men, in begging Jesus to heal them, used his messianic title Son of David, but Jesus did not heal them till he was certain that they had genuine faith. No doubt there were many in Israel who had no feeling of spiritual need but who were willing to call Jesus by messianic titles simply for the purpose of receiving benefits from him. Again, to avoid attracting the wrong sort of following, Jesus warned the men not to tell anyone what had happened (Matt 9:27-31). Although some people misinterpreted Jesus' miracles because they were impressed with his power, others misinterpreted them because they hated him (Matt 9:32-34).

Another blind man who came to Jesus for healing apparently had some lack in his faith. Jesus saw this, and so after an initial act of healing asked the man whether he could see properly. Lack of complete faith had hindered the healing. Nevertheless, Jesus did not leave the man with his sight only partly restored. He completed the healing, thereby giving the man normal eyesight and at the same time strengthening his faith (Mark 8:22-26).

61. Jesus rejected at Nazareth (Matt 13:53-58; Mark 6:1-6)

It is not clear whether this visit of Jesus to Nazareth is the same as that referred to in Luke 4:16-30 or another visit. If it was a second visit, it would have taken place a year later, but the result was the same as on the previous occasion. The people were surprised that a person they had known only as a carpenter could preach so well, but they refused to accept the evidence and admit that this one was indeed God (Matt 13:53-57; Mark 6:1-4). They refused to believe in him and, as usual, Jesus would not use his miracles to force people to believe. But out of compassion he privately healed a few sick people (Matt 13:58; Mark 6:5-6).

62. The twelve sent out (Matt 10:5-42; Mark 6:7-13; Luke 9:1-6)

Jesus sent out the twelve apostles to preach the good news that the kingdom of the Messiah had come. The miraculous powers of the Messiah were given to them also, so that the knowledge of his love and mercy might spread more quickly throughout the land (Luke 9:1-2).

There would be no time during Jesus' lifetime to spread the gospel worldwide, so the apostles had to concentrate on Israel. After Jesus' death and resurrection they could then take the gospel to the countries beyond (Matt 10:5-8; cf. 28:19-20). They were to take with them only the bare necessities for daily needs, so as not to be hindered in their travels. Also they were not to waste time preaching to people who refused to listen, when others in nearby areas had not even heard (Matt 10:9-15; Luke 9:3-6).

Although they preached good news and did good works, the apostles could expect persecution. If brought to trial, whether before Jewish leaders or government officials, they would have the help of God's Spirit in giving them the right words to say (Matt 10:16-20). They would meet opposition from friends and relatives, but they were to press on urgently in their mission. They would not even cover the whole of Palestine within the time of Jesus' earthly ministry (Matt 10:21-23).

As servants of Jesus, the apostles could expect the same sort of opposition as their master received (Matt 10:24-25), but they were not to fear to teach publicly the things Jesus had taught them privately (Matt 10:26-27). They were to maintain a reverent obedience to God, knowing that as their heavenly Father he would watch over them. He never forsakes those who are faithful to him (Matt 10:28-33).

The followers of Jesus must not expect ease and comfort. They must put loyalty to Jesus before all other loyalties, and this may result in conflict and division, even within their own families. They must be prepared for hardship, persecution and possibly death, but in the end they will not be the losers. In sacrificing the life of self-pleasing in order to please their Lord, they will find life in its truest sense (Matt 10:34-39). All who welcome Jesus' messengers into their homes are really welcoming Jesus who sent them, and God the Father who sent him. Help given to Jesus' messengers will be rewarded as if given to Jesus himself (Matt 10:40-42).

63. Concern about safety and security (Luke 12:4-21)

Some teaching that Jesus gave to the twelve apostles is repeated in other parts of the Gospels. This may have been given to the followers of Jesus in general, particularly those instructions and warnings that concerned putting loyalty to Jesus before the desire for personal safety (Luke 12:4-12; see notes on Matt 10:28-33 above).

On one occasion when a crowd was listening to such teaching from Jesus, there was one person who showed no understanding of what Jesus was saying. Contrary to Jesus' teaching, personal safety and security were his main concern. He wanted Jesus to force his brother to give him a bigger share of an inheritance they had received. Jesus was not a rabbi who settled disputes about the law; he was a teacher from God and he was concerned about people's greed (Luke 12:13-15). He therefore told the story of a rich but foolish farmer who thought only of his prosperity, security and comfort. Suddenly the farmer died. Not only was his wealth of no further use, but it had prevented him from obtaining true heavenly riches (Luke 12:16-21).

64. Death of John the Baptist (Matt 14:1-12; Mark 6:14-29; Luke 9:7-9)

By this time John the Baptist had been executed. When Herod heard the news of Jesus' miracles, he feared that Jesus was really John come back to life and that supernatural powers were working in him (Matt 14:1-2; Mark 6:14-16). (The Herod referred to here was Herod Antipas, a son of Herod the Great; see earlier section, 'The New Testament World'.)

Having mentioned John's death, the writers go back to record the events that led up to it. Herod had imprisoned John because John had accused him of adultery in marrying Herodias, wife of Herod's brother, Philip (Mark 6:17-18; cf. Matt 4:12; 11:2). Herod both respected and feared John, as he knew that John was a godly man and that his accusations were true. But no amount of discussion with John could persuade Herod to conquer his passions and give up Herodias (Mark 6:19-20).

John's place of imprisonment was apparently the dungeon of Herod's palace. Although this gave Herod the opportunity to speak to him often, it also made it easier for Herodias when an opportunity arose for her to get rid of him. She hated John for his interference, and was quick to act when she saw the chance to have him executed (Mark 6:21-29).

65. Feeding the five thousand (Matt 14:13-21; Mark 6:30-44; Luke 9:10-17; John 6:1-14)

When the apostles returned from their first tour around the country areas, they met Jesus in Galilee and tried to have a quiet time alone with him (Mark 6:30-32; John 6:1). Jesus also was in need of a rest, but he was filled with pity when he saw the crowds of people flocking to him in their need. They appeared to him as a flock of spiritually starved sheep that had no food because there was no shepherd to feed them (Mark 6:33-34; John 6:2-4).

The apostles were soon reminded that Jesus alone could satisfy the spiritual needs of the people. Without him the apostles were not able to satisfy even the people's physical needs. With five small loaves and two fish, Jesus miraculously fed a huge crowd, reminding the apostles that the miracles they had done on their missionary tour had resulted solely from Jesus' power working in them (Mark 6:35-44; John 6:5-13). But to many of the people, the miracle was a sign that Jesus was the promised great prophet. Like Moses, he had miraculously fed God's people in the wilderness (John 6:14; see Exod 16:1-36; Deut 18:15; 1 Cor 10:1-5).

66. Jesus walks on the sea (Matt 14:22-36; Mark 6:45-56; John 6:15-21)

On seeing Jesus' miracle with the bread and fish, many wanted to make him king immediately. This no doubt would have pleased many of Jesus' followers, but for him it presented a possible temptation. He therefore sent his disciples to Bethsaida, while he escaped into the hills where he could be alone and pray (Matt 14:22-23; Mark 6:45-46; John 6:15).

Bethsaida was not far from the place where Jesus had fed the five thousand (see Luke 9:10-11). Both places were on the shore of the lake, but separated by a small bay. To escape the crowd the disciples decided to row across the lake, making it appear that they were heading for Bethsaida, which was near Capernaum (John 6:16-17).

Again a storm suddenly arose, blowing the boat off course and making rowing almost impossible. Jesus came to his disciples walking on the water, but instead of responding with faith they were fearful. Peter made a bolder response, but his confidence was shortlived (Matt 14:24-30; Mark 6:47-50). Jesus was disappointed that again their faith failed in a crisis. Although they had seen his power in feeding the five thousand, they did not understand that the same power was still available to help them (Matt 14:31-33; Mark 6:51-52). So much had they been blown off course before Jesus came to them, that they landed at Gennesaret, a long way west of their goal (Mark 6:53-56).

67. The bread of life (John 6:22-59)

Many Jews were determined to find Jesus and make him king. Although he had escaped from them after the feeding of the multitude, they were out the next day looking for him (John 6:22-24).

Jesus knew that these people wanted him to be king not because they felt any spiritual need, but because they thought he had magical powers that could supply all their daily needs. He urged them not to think just of physical and temporal blessings, but to seek the spiritual and eternal life that he offered (John 6:25-27). People cannot earn this life through doing good works; they can only accept it by faith (John 6:28-29). Jesus does not need to make food fall from heaven as in Moses' day in order to prove his power. He himself is the true bread from heaven (John 6:30-33).

This bread from heaven is not some common everyday thing that people can have simply to satisfy their appetite. It is a spiritual provision available to those who, being drawn by the Father to the Son, give themselves to him in faith (John 6:34-37). As Jesus does the work that his Father sent him to do, he brings believers into the life of God's kingdom, eternal life. They have this eternal life now, and they will enjoy it in its fulness following the victorious resurrection at the end of the age (John 6:38-40).

Jesus' hearers objected that he had no right to speak such words, for he was not God. He had not come from heaven but from a Galilean family, as people well knew. Jesus repeated what he had said previously, to impress upon them that the salvation he brought came from heaven and was the work of the invisible God (John 6:41-47). However, the only way this salvation can become possible is through Jesus' giving himself as a sacrifice for sin. People can have eternal life only through Jesus' death (John 6:48-51).

The true bread that Jesus came to give was his flesh and blood offered in sacrifice. Unless people eat and drink this 'food' they cannot be saved. That is, unless they accept Jesus' sacrifice for themselves in faith, they cannot have eternal life, either now or in the future (John 5:52-59).

68. Words of eternal life (John 6:60-71)

Many of the people who followed Jesus found his teaching about the bread of life hard to understand. Jesus told them that if they had difficulty believing this, they would be positively amazed when they saw him going bodily back to heaven. Their difficulties arose because they were thinking only of physical flesh and blood, and failed to see the spiritual truths they illustrated. They still did not understand how eternal life could result from Jesus' death (John 6:60-65).

Those who were more interested in earthly benefits than spiritual life were disappointed in Jesus' teaching and turned back from following him. Not so the apostles. All, except for Judas Iscariot, maintained their deep trust in their Lord. They knew that the words he spoke were true and life-giving (John 6:66-71).

69. Teaching about cleansing (Matt 15:1-20; Mark 7:1-23)

A common practice of the Jews in Jesus' time was the ceremonial washing of hands. They believed that those who came in contact with 'unclean' people or things had to pour water over their hands to cleanse themselves. This was not a command of the law of Moses but a tradition of the Pharisees (Mark 7:1-5). Jesus argued that such traditions not only caused people to misunderstand the law, but stopped them from doing the more important things that the law required (Mark 7:6-8).

In support of this assertion, Jesus gave an example. The law of Moses taught people to respect and care for their aged parents, but the Jews had added a tradition that enabled them to ignore their parents. They could make a vow that when they died, their money and goods would be given to the temple. Having promised such things to God, they said they were not free to give them to anyone else, such as needy parents. Yet they themselves continued to enjoy their possessions as long as they lived. Their tradition contradicted the plain teaching of the law (Mark 7:9-13).

The Jews would not eat certain foods, believing that such foods made them unclean. Jesus said that just as eating with unwashed hands did not make a person unclean, neither did eating prohibited foods (Mark 7:14-16). The people really unacceptable with God were those who taught such traditions (Matt 15:12-14).

What makes a person unclean is the evil that comes out of the mouth, not the food that goes into it. The source of all evil is a wicked heart, and this is what must be cleansed if a person is to be acceptable with God. The Pharisees' traditions of cleansing prevented them from seeing this, even though it was the goal towards which Moses' laws of cleansing pointed (Mark 7:17-23).

FURTHER WORK IN THE NORTH

70. In Tyre and Sidon (Matt 15:21-28; Mark 7:24-30)

To get some peace and quiet away from the crowds, Jesus and his disciples went out of Palestine to the Gentile towns of Tyre and Sidon on the Phoenician coast (Matt 15:21; Mark 7:24). When a woman of that area asked Jesus to drive a demon out of her daughter, he tested the genuineness of her faith before helping her. At first he did not answer; but the woman persisted (Matt 15:22-23).

Jesus then told the woman that his work was with Israel, not with the surrounding nations. But her pleas for help continued (Matt 15:24-25). Jesus added that the people of Israel were the favoured 'children' to benefit from his ministry, and it was not right to neglect them to feed the Gentile 'dogs'. Still not giving up, the woman replied that although she was an unworthy Gentile 'dog', not fit to eat with the 'children' at Israel's table, she would be satisfied to eat the crumbs that fell to the floor. Jesus was impressed with the genuineness of the woman's faith and granted her request immediately (Matt 15:26-28).

71. Ministry in the Decapolis (Matt 15:29-39; Mark 7:31-8:10)

From the Mediterranean towns of Phoenicia, Jesus returned to the region around the Sea of Galilee, then continued on into the Decapolis, where the population was largely Gentile. It seems that for a period his ministry was mainly among Gentiles, and many became believers in the God of Israel (Matt 15:29-31; Mark 7:31). One of the people he healed was a deaf and dumb man. Because of the man's deafness, Jesus used actions rather than words to ensure that the man's faith was active and that he understood Jesus' actions (Mark 7:32-37).

Again Jesus had compassion when he saw a multitude of hungry people around him and he decided to feed them. On the previous occasion the crowd consisted largely of Jews (see John 6:14-15), but on this occasion it probably consisted largely of Gentiles. That may have been why the disciples doubted whether Jesus would use his power to feed them (Matt 15:32-33; Mark 8:1-4). But he fed them as miraculously as he had the Jews (Matt 15:34-39; Mark 8:5-10).

72. Beware of Pharisees and Sadducees (Matt 16:1-12; Mark 8:11-21; Luke 12:1-3,54-56)

In spite of all that Jesus had done, the Pharisees and Sadducees still demanded he produce a special sign to satisfy them. Jesus refused. They could look at the sky and work out what the weather would be like, but when they looked at Jesus' miracles they refused to believe what the miracles told them, namely, that Jesus was the Son of God. The only sign Jesus would give them would be his resurrection. Jonah came back to life after three days of apparent death, but Jesus would come back to life after three days of actual death. By this unmistakable sign the Father would prove to all that Jesus is his Son (Matt 16:1-4; Luke 12:54-56).

Sin is compared to yeast, or leaven, in that it affects everything it touches. The Pharisees, the Sadducees and Herod were evil influences that spread through Israel as yeast spreads through a lump of dough. Jesus warned his disciples to beware of the yeast-like effect of these people. His probable meaning was that they were not to be influenced by the wrong teaching and hypocrisy of the Pharisees and Sadducees or the ungodly ways of people like Herod (Matt 16:5-6; Mark 8:14-15; Luke 12:1).

The apostles missed the meaning of Jesus' illustration. They thought he wanted some bread (but not bread baked with certain types of yeast) and were worried that they did not have any. This showed that although they had twice seen him miraculously feed a large crowd, they still lacked the faith to believe he could provide for them. In addition they lacked spiritual understanding, and saw the meaning of Jesus' illustration only after he explained it to them (Matt 16:7-12; Mark 8:16-21; Luke 12:2-3).

73. Peter's confession of the Messiah (Matt 16:13-23; Mark 8:27-33; Luke 9:18-22)

Jesus and the apostles travelled up to Caesarea Philippi, in the far north of Palestine. While there, Jesus asked the apostles who they believed him to be. Peter, probably speaking for the group, replied that he was the promised Messiah, the Son of God (Matt 16:13-16).

Delighted at this insight, Jesus told the group (through words addressed to their spokesman Peter) that they would be the foundation on which he would build his church, and no power would be able to conquer it (Matt 16:17-18; cf. Eph 2:20). By preaching the gospel they would open the kingdom to all who wished to enter. They would carry Jesus' authority with them, so that the things they did on earth in his name would be confirmed in heaven (Matt 16:19; cf. Acts 2:32; 3:6,16,19). But that was still in the future. For the present they were to support him in his ministry, but they were not to proclaim his messiahship openly till the appointed time had come (Matt 16:20).

Jesus then made it clear that in order to fulfil his messianic ministry, he had to suffer, die and rise again. Peter's objection to this showed that the apostles still did not understand the true nature of the Messiah's work. The suggestion that Jesus should turn back from the cross was yet another temptation by Satan. It was an attempt to persuade him to gain his kingdom by some way other than death, and so cause him to fail in the very thing he came to do (Matt 16:21-23; cf. 4:8-10).

74. Test of true discipleship (Matt 16:24-28; Mark 8:34-9:1; Luke 9:23-27)

Immediately after telling his disciples of his coming suffering and death, Jesus told them they had to be prepared for similar treatment. The disciples of Jesus are those who have given their lives to Jesus, and they will be obedient to their master even if it leads to hardship, persecution and death. They will no longer rule their own lives, but will deny themselves personal desires in order to please Jesus. In sacrificing the life that puts self first, they will find the only true life. On the other hand those who live for themselves may gain what they want in the present world, but they will lose the only life of lasting value, eternal life (Matt 16:24-27).

Jesus promised his disciples that those who accompanied him in his ministry would, in their present lifetime, see something of the triumph of the Son of man's glorious kingdom. This was possibly a reference to the victorious expansion of the church after Jesus' resurrection and ascension (Matt 16:28; Mark 9:1). (For the significance of the name 'Son of man', see earlier section, 'Jesus and the Kingdom'.)

75. The transfiguration (Matt 17:1-13; Mark 9:2-13; Luke 9:28-36)

Jesus' transfiguration took place on a high mountain, possibly Mount Hermon, which was not far from Caesarea Philippi. The event was a revelation of Christ's glory and was witnessed by only three chosen apostles. In coming into the world as a human being, Jesus had laid his divine glory aside, but now it reappeared briefly through a human body. It gave an indication of the glory he would receive after he had finished the work he came to do (Matt 17:1-2; Luke 9:28-29).

Moses and Elijah appeared with Jesus during his transfiguration, possibly to symbolize that the law and the prophets found their fulfilment in him. He was the one to whom the entire Old Testament pointed. They talked with Jesus about his coming death, confirming what Jesus had recently told the apostles. The Messiah had to die before he could enter his glory (Matt 17:3; Luke 9:30-31).

The apostles were confused about what was happening, but the Father's voice from heaven told them that it was an expression of his satisfaction with the entire ministry of Jesus. By combining words from one of David's psalms with words from one of Isaiah's servant songs, God declared that the kingly Messiah would lay down his life as the suffering servant. This Messiah was also God's prophet, and people were to listen to his message (Matt 17:4-5; Luke 9:32-35; cf. Ps 2:7; Isa 42:1; Deut 18:15,18; Acts 3:22).

When the transfiguration was over and Jesus' appearance returned to normal, he again told the apostles that they were not yet to reveal what they had learnt (Matt 17:6-9; Luke 9:36). The vision of Elijah prompted the apostles to ask if Elijah would come before the Messiah. If Jesus was the Messiah, why had Elijah not come? Jesus replied that John the Baptist was the promised Elijah, but just as people rejected the Messiah's forerunner so would they reject the Messiah (Matt 17:10-13).

76. Healing of an uncontrollable boy (Matt 17:14-21; Mark 9:14-29; Luke 9:37-43)

While the faith of the three apostles on the mountain was being strengthened, the faith of the other nine on the plain below was failing. They were unable to cure a boy who suffered from sudden fits that made him uncontrollable (Mark 9:14-18). After the heavenly experiences on the mountain, Jesus felt the frustration of work in a world that was full of human failure (Mark 9:19). Nevertheless, he did not despise the uncertain faith that the boy's father expressed, and he quickly healed the boy (Mark 9:20-27).

The reason for the disciples' failure was their lack of faith. What they needed was not a large amount of faith but the right kind of faith. They needed a faith that relied completely upon the unlimited capacity of the all-powerful God and that expressed itself through sincere prayer (Matt 17:20-21; Mark 9:28-29).

77. Payment of the temple tax (Matt 17:24-27)

Jesus was staying at Peter's house in Capernaum when Jewish officials came to collect the annual temple tax of a half-shekel per person (Matt 17:24; cf. Exod 30:11-16). Jesus told Peter that he and his disciples no longer needed to pay the temple tax. Now that the Messiah had come, the Jerusalem temple had lost its importance. God now dwelt in a new 'temple', the disciples of the Messiah. They were God's people, and just as a king does not collect taxes from his family, neither does God. However, the Jewish officials would not understand this, so rather than create misunderstanding, Jesus agreed to pay the tax (Matt 17:25-27).

78. Lessons in humility (Matt 17:22-23; 18:1-14; Mark 9:30-50; Luke 9:44-50)

Despite Jesus' statement to his disciples that he was heading towards humiliating suffering and death (Matt 17:22-23; Mark 9:30-32; Luke 9:44-45), they were arguing among themselves about who would have the important places in his kingdom. Jesus rebuked them, explaining that the way to spiritual greatness is through choosing the lowest place and serving others. To enter the kingdom of God, people must humbly accept that they have no more status than a child. Receiving Christ is not concerned with prestige as in the case of those who receive an earthly king. It is as humble an act as receiving a small child (Matt 18:1-5; Mark 9:33-37; Luke 9:46-48).

If people want to be disciples of Jesus, they should not despise those who appear weak and insignificant. Indeed, they should take severe action against themselves to remove from their lives anything that might cause them to follow their own desires instead of submitting to Jesus. Wrong desires prevent people from receiving Jesus and lead only to hell (Matt 18:6-9; Mark 9:42-48). God will test and cleanse the disciples, but if they want to be useful for him in leading people to Jesus, they must cease their quarrelling and make sure that they themselves are pure in heart (Mark 9:49-50).

Jesus' disciples should have a loving concern for the weak, the helpless and the lost. They should not want any to miss out on his salvation (Matt 18:10-14). They must love others, and not act like those who tried to stop a man from casting out demons in Jesus' name because he did not belong to Jesus' apostolic group. The man feared God, and God used him to deliver people from the power of evil. He was not an enemy of Jesus, and the apostles were not to despise him or hinder him in his work. If people do acts of kindness to others, and do them with the right motives, God will reward them no matter how insignificant those acts may appear to be (Mark 9:38-41; Luke 9:49-50).

79. Lessons in forgiveness (Matt 18:15-35)

Disciples of Jesus should be willing to forgive fellow believers who sin against them, but they should also be concerned that offenders realize their sin and turn from it. In each case the believer should go to the offender privately and point out the wrongdoing, so that the person might be spiritually helped. If this fails, two or three others should be called in, firstly to make sure that the offender is in fact guilty and secondly to appeal for reconciliation. If this also fails, the entire community of believers should appeal to the offender. Should there still be no change, believers should treat the offender as if no longer part of their fellowship; though they should also desire the person's repentance and restoration (Matt 18:15-18).

God has given his people the responsibility to deal with such cases, and they must find out God's will and do it. If they are to be confident that their actions carry God's authority, they will not act in haste or out of personal prejudice. They have Jesus' assurance that as they talk and pray about the matter, he will be with them, silently giving his guidance and help (Matt 18:19-20).

Peter asked how many times Jesus' followers should forgive before taking the severe action that Jesus had just outlined. Jesus' reply shows that the severe action was not intended to be an alternative to forgiveness. Believers do not take action against offenders out of spite, but out of a concern for the offenders' spiritual good. Regardless of how many times offenders do them wrong, believers must still forgive them (Matt 18:21-22).

To illustrate the point, Jesus told a story. A king forgave a servant a huge debt, but the servant then refused to forgive a fellow servant a small debt (Matt 18:23-30). When the king heard of his servant's behaviour, he withdrew his forgiveness (Matt 18:31-34). The lesson is that God will not forgive people if they do not forgive others (Matt 18:35; cf. 6:12).

THROUGH SAMARIA TO JUDEA

80. Rejected in Samaria (Luke 9:51-56)

Jesus left Galilee and headed for Jerusalem. He knew that Jerusalem was the place where his work would finish, but first he had much to do in Samaria, Judea and certain areas east of Jordan.

The Samaritans had for centuries been enemies of the Jews, and hated the Jews' passing through their territory on the way to Jerusalem. Jesus wanted to be friendly with them but they did not want his friendship (Luke 9:51-53). In return James and John wanted God to destroy the Samaritans. Their request showed that they still knew little of the immeasurable love that Jesus had for rebellious sinners (Luke 9:54-56).

81. The cost of being a disciple (Matt 8:18-22; Luke 9:57-62)

Three men came to Jesus saying they wanted to be disciples, but they did not realize the sacrifices they would have to make in following Jesus. The first man was told to think seriously about his professed intentions, because following Jesus would bring with it physical hardship and discomfort (Luke 9:57-58). The second was warned that responsibilities towards Jesus must come before ordinary worldly responsibilities. The spiritually dead, whose interests are only in this life, can look after the everyday matters of life; the disciples of Jesus have to attend to the more important business of the kingdom of God (Luke 9:59-60). The third man was warned that Jesus' disciples must give themselves to him completely. There is no place for those whose real interests are elsewhere (Luke 9:61-62).

82. The mission of the seventy (Luke 10:1-24)

Earlier Jesus had sent twelve apostles into the northern areas because the work was more than he could do by himself in the short time available. Now, for a similar reason, he sent a much larger number into the southern regions through which he was travelling (Luke 10:1-2). The instructions Jesus gave to the seventy were similar to those he had given to the twelve (Luke 10:3-12; see also notes on Matt

10:5-42). Being reminded of the earlier mission in the north, Luke records Jesus' announcement of judgment on certain northern citizens who would not believe (Luke 10:13-16; see notes on Matt 11:20-24).

Luke goes on immediately to record the success of the seventy, though many months probably passed before they returned. Jesus saw this success as a triumph over Satan and a guarantee of his ultimate destruction. But the servants of God should always remember that their greatest cause for praise is not what they have done for God, but what God has done for them (Luke 10:17-20).

Because Jesus is the Son of God, his power in the lives of his humblest disciples gives them a knowledge of things of which the wise in this world know nothing. Through Jesus, believers have a knowledge of God the Father (Luke 10:21-22). Godly people of former ages wanted to know things that have now been revealed to Jesus' disciples, but they were unable to, because in those days the Messiah had not yet come (Luke 10:23-24).

83. Who is my neighbour? (Luke 10:25-37)

A Jewish teacher of the law came to Jesus to test him with a question about eternal life. His question showed that he thought of eternal life as something to be obtained by some special act. Jesus' reply showed that obtaining eternal life is inseparably linked with the way people live their daily lives. If they do not put God before all things and their neighbour before themselves, they can have no assurance of eternal life (Luke 10:25-28).

The teacher was disappointed with this answer and, in an attempt to excuse his own failings, asked how anyone could know who was or was not his neighbour (Luke 10:29). In reply Jesus told a story in which a traveller was beaten, robbed, and left to die. Two Jews, one a priest and the other a Levite, deliberately passed him by, but a Samaritan stopped and helped him (Luke 10:30-35). Jesus then forced the questioner to answer his own question. The example that he had to follow was not that of the religious purists, but that of the despised foreigner. If a person loves his neighbour as himself, he will act kindly towards anyone that he happens to meet, even enemies (Luke 10:36-37).

84. Jesus in the house of Mary and Martha (Luke 10:38-42)

There must have been much tension in Jesus' heart as he steadily moved closer to the climax of his work. But with his disciples in need of his teaching and people everywhere in need of his help, he had little time for relaxation. Therefore, to get away from the crowd, he stopped for some quiet fellowship at the house of Mary and Martha (Luke 10:38). (Mary and Martha, along with their brother Lazarus, lived in the village of Bethany, just outside Jerusalem; John 11:1,18.)

Martha busied herself preparing a large meal, determined to provide the best possible hospitality for their distinguished guest. Jesus did not want a lavish meal, especially when it was prepared in such a complaining spirit as Martha showed. A simple meal was sufficient, as he was looking only for some quiet fellowship with his friends. Mary understood this, and as a result she benefited from the Lord's instructive conversation (Luke 10:39-42).

IN JERUSALEM FOR JEWISH FESTIVALS

85. Family opposition (John 7:1-13)

At one stage of his ministry Jesus spent time in Jerusalem attending some annual Jewish festivals. The first of these was the Feast of Tabernacles (GNB: Festival of Shelters), when Jews lived in temporary shelters in memory of the time their ancestors dwelt in the wilderness. It also marked the end of the agricultural year, when all the produce of the land had been gathered in and the people rejoiced in thanksgiving to God (Lev 23:33-43; Deut 16:13-15). People usually flocked to Jerusalem for the festival. Jesus' brothers therefore suggested that if he was the Messiah (which they doubted), this was a good opportunity to prove it openly by performing spectacular miracles (John 7:1-5).

Self-seeking people might welcome the chance to prove their claims, but Jesus refused. He would continue to preach God's message faithfully, even if people hated him for it. He would not use the Feast of Tabernacles to show himself as the Messiah, but would await the time appointed by his Father (John 7:6-9). Later, when he did attend the feast, he avoided publicity. He was now well known throughout the country, and attracted interest and comment wherever he went (John 7:10-13).

86. Jesus teaches in the temple (John 7:14-44)

The Feast of Tabernacles lasted a week. After the excitement of the first two or three days had died down, Jesus began to teach in the temple. People were impressed with his teaching, though he taught not to gain honour for himself but to bring glory to God who had sent him. If people loved God and wanted to do his will, they would see that what Jesus taught was the truth of God (John 7:14-18). The

Jews accused Jesus of breaking the law, because on a previous occasion he had healed a man on the Sabbath (see John 5:1-16). But, replied Jesus, they themselves did not hesitate to circumcise a child on the Sabbath (John 7:19-24).

People were amazed at Jesus' boldness in so speaking, and even more amazed that he was not arrested and killed. Maybe, some thought, the religious leaders were convinced that he was the Messiah. They soon changed their minds, however, when they remembered that Jesus was from Galilee. They had always believed that no one would know where the Messiah would come from. Jesus pointed out to them that his real place of origin was not Galilee, but heaven. He was sent by God (John 7:25-29).

The words of Jesus caused division among the Jews, with some bitterly opposed to him and others convinced that he was the Messiah. The leaders of the Sanhedrin became concerned that many were believing in Jesus, and they sent temple guards to arrest him. But the temple guards were powerless to do anything. No one could arrest or kill him until the time appointed by his Father. When that time arrived he would die, rise to life, and return to his Father in heaven. His opponents would not be able to find him, because he would be in a place that they could never reach. Their unbelief excluded them from heaven eternally (John 7:30-34).

Again the Jews misunderstood Jesus' words. They thought that when he said he was going away, he was planning to go preaching among the Gentiles (John 7:35-36).

Jesus brought the feast to a fitting climax by offering to satisfy all who, in their spiritual need, came to him for help. He would work a life-giving change within them. After returning to his Father, he would send the Holy Spirit to dwell within all who believed in him (John 7:37-39). The people's reaction to this teaching was mixed. Some believed, some were confused and some were opposed, but still no one arrested him (John 7:40-44).

87. Argument in the Sanhedrin (John 7:45-53)

The leaders of the Sanhedrin were furious when the temple guards returned without Jesus. The guards said that they could not arrest one who gave such powerful teaching. Angrily the rulers replied that perhaps some of the uneducated masses believed in Jesus, but certainly none of the teachers, leaders, or other well instructed Jews (John 7:45-49).

When Nicodemus, who was a member of the Sanhedrin (cf. John 3:1), suggested that they should at least give Jesus a fair hearing, he was quickly silenced. The Sanhedrin was not interested in finding out the truth, but only in getting rid of Jesus (John 7:50-53).

88. Woman caught in adultery (John 8:1-11)

When Jesus returned to the temple the next day, the scribes and Pharisees brought to him a woman whom they had caught in adultery, and asked him to give a judgment. This was not because they wanted to find out God's will, but because they wanted to trap Jesus and so have an accusation to bring against him. If he did not condemn the woman to death, they could accuse him to the Sanhedrin of defying the law. If he did condemn her to death, they could accuse him to the government of usurping Rome's authority (John 8:1-6a).

Jesus saw their cunning and refused to give a legal judgment. Instead he challenged the woman's accusers to exercise some moral judgment on themselves, with the result that none had the courage to pursue the matter further (John 8:6b-9). It was not Jesus' duty to condemn the woman, for he was neither a witness nor a judge. He was the Saviour of sinners, and having given the woman a practical lesson in truth and purity, he urged her to make a total break with her sinful past (John 8:10-11).

89. The light of the world (John 8:12-20)

In response to Jesus' statement that he was the light of the world, the Pharisees argued that he had no right to testify on his own behalf. In their view he had no supporting witnesses (John 8:12-13). Jesus replied that he did have the right to bear witness to himself, because he came from God and was united with God. God was his supporting witness, and that should have been sufficient (John 8:14).

The Jews were wrong in their judgments against Jesus, because they judged in a totally human way. The time for Jesus to act as the world's judge had not yet come, but even if he carried out such work immediately, his judgment would be true, again because of the unity between the Father and the Son (John 8:15-16). If the Jews insisted on having two witnesses as the law required, they had them in the Father and the Son. The two were in agreement, and therefore the Jews had to accept their testimony (John 8:17-18). The reason that Jesus' opponents failed to grasp what he was saying was that they did not know God (John 8:19-20).

90. Belief and unbelief (John 8:21-30)

Because the Jews could never get their minds above earthly things, they could never accept Jesus' claim that he came from God. By rejecting him they lost all chance of having their sins forgiven. They would die in their sins and thereby be excluded from heaven, the place to which Jesus would return after his death and resurrection (John 8:21-26).

Most of the people still did not understand how Jesus could be the Son of God, but one day in the near future they would have clear proof. They would see Jesus die on the cross, but then, by the power of God, rise from the dead. This would be an unmistakable demonstration of the unity between the Father and the Son (John 8:27-29). Some who heard Jesus speak did not wait for the events he spoke of, but put their faith in him immediately (John 8:30).

91. True freedom; true sonship (John 8:31-59)

Jesus used an illustration from slavery to show the people how he could help them in their need. They all knew that slaves could not free themselves. The only person who could free them was the owner of the house in which the slave worked, or the owner's son, acting on his father's authority. The Jews were slaves, in bondage to sin and unable to free themselves. The only one who could free them was God, acting through his Son Jesus. They would find their true freedom through faith in Jesus and continual obedience to his teaching. Again the Jews did not understand the spiritual truth Jesus was illustrating. Thinking only of ordinary earthly life, they argued that they had never been slaves of any nation. They had the freedom of sons, Abraham's sons (John 8:31-36).

To explain further, Jesus told his Jewish hearers that spiritually they were not sons of Abraham at all, but sons of the devil. They were trying to kill Jesus, and murder was a characteristic inherited from their spiritual father the devil, not from their earthly father Abraham (John 8:37-40).

Beginning at last to see that Jesus was applying the illustration to their relationship with God, the Jews argued with him accordingly, but again they missed his meaning. They thought, perhaps, that he was accusing them of being like the Samaritans, who were of mixed blood and mixed religion. They assured him that they were pure sons of Abraham nationally and pure sons of God spiritually (John 8:41). Jesus responded that if God was their Father they would welcome his Son as their Messiah, not try to kill him. They would believe his teaching, not dispute it. Truly, their father was not God, but the devil (John 8:42-47).

The Jews gave further proof that God was not their Father when they insulted his Son and so guaranteed God's judgment upon them. The Son is not concerned with gaining honour for himself. His chief concerns are to give honour to the Father on the one hand, and life to believers on the other (John 8:48-51). The Jews objected that Jesus was boasting to be greater than Abraham. Jesus replied that he was not boasting but merely telling the truth: he was united with God (John 8:52-55).

As for Abraham, he himself acknowledged Jesus to be greater by rejoicing when he foresaw the coming of the Messiah. The Jews objected that Jesus could not know Abraham's thoughts, because Abraham had died hundreds of years before Jesus was born. They were angered more when Jesus said that he existed even before Abraham. Jesus is the eternal God. The Jews considered such a claim to be blasphemy and immediately but unsuccessfully tried to kill him (John 8:56-59).

92. Dispute concerning a blind man (John 9:1-41)

Some Jews believed that diseases and physical disabilities were the result of either a person's own sins or the sins of the person's parents. When Jesus met a blind man, his disciples asked him which was the most likely cause of the man's blindness (John 9:1-2).

Jesus was not interested in discussing theoretical questions just to satisfy people's curiosity. He was more concerned with healing the man, and in this way he would bring glory to God. His time in the world was limited, and that meant he should use every opportunity to do the work that his Father sent him to do (John 9:3-5). He therefore healed the man, and immediately there was much interest among the local people. They could scarcely believe what had happened (John 9:6-12).

The healing had taken place on the Sabbath day. In the eyes of the Pharisees, Jesus had broken the Sabbath laws and therefore he was a sinner. In the eyes of others, including the man himself, Jesus had healed a person born blind, and therefore he must have come from God (John 9:13-17). Rather than accept the fact that a miracle had occurred, the Pharisees tried to argue that the man had not been blind in the first place. The man's parents confirmed that he had been born blind, but they would not talk about the healing because of their fear of the Jewish leaders (John 9:18-23).

Despite the pressure that the Pharisees put on the man, he refused to change his story or condemn Jesus. He mocked the Pharisees for their persistent questioning, asking if they too wanted to become Jesus' disciples (John 9:24-27). The more the man argued with them, the angrier the Pharisees became. They had no answer to his simple step by step reasoning, so attacked him with abusive language and then threw him out of the synagogue (John 9:28-34).

Jesus found the man and made known to him that the one who healed him was indeed the Saviour sent by God. The man's faith was strengthened and in humble gratitude he worshipped (John 9:35-38).

The way people responded to Jesus showed their true spiritual condition. Some called themselves teachers and thought they possessed religious insight, but in fact they were spiritually blind. Others knew they were blind and in the darkness of sin, but when they turned to Jesus they saw the light of God. There could be some excuse for those who were blind through ignorance, but there could be only condemnation for those who claimed to have knowledge but deliberately rejected the plain evidence before them (John 9:39-41).

93. The good shepherd (John 10:1-21)

In the story of the good shepherd, Jesus was continuing the teaching he had begun after healing the blind man. Among his hearers were the Pharisees (see John 9:40), but they could not see that he was contrasting their treatment of the blind man with his. They acted like thieves and robbers, but Jesus acted like a good shepherd. As a result the man rejected the leadership of the Pharisees, but he clearly recognized Jesus as the shepherd-saviour and gladly followed him (John 10:1-6).

To explain further, Jesus likened himself to a door, by which people could come to God and so find life, freedom, protection and provision. But the Jewish leaders, instead of leading people to God, exploited and oppressed them (John 10:7-10).

Jesus was the true shepherd and spiritual leader of the people, but the scribes and Pharisees fought against him, setting themselves up as leaders. By teaching human traditions instead of God's commandments, they enslaved the Jewish people and strengthened their own power. Like thieves they robbed the flock, like wolves they destroyed it, and like hired labourers they worked for their own profit without any real concern for the flock. By contrast, Jesus sacrificed everything for his flock, even being prepared to die for it so that his sheep might be saved (John 10:11-13).

The flock of Jesus consists not merely of those in the sheepfold of Israel, but includes people of all nations and languages. They are drawn together as one flock under the shepherd Jesus. The understanding between the shepherd and the sheep is the same as the understanding between the Father and the Son (John 10:14-16). The basis of the relationship between Jesus and his flock is his death and resurrection. He has complete authority over life and death, and his enemies are powerless to take his life from him. Yet he willingly lays down that life so that he might save his people (John 10:17-18; cf. Acts 20:28).

Those who heard Jesus responded in strikingly different ways. Some said he was mad, but others accepted his words as being consistent with his work in healing the blind man. The opposite reactions that people had to Jesus determined their opposite destinies (John 10:19-21; cf. 9:39).

94. At the Feast of Dedication (John 10:22-42)

The Feast of Dedication commemorated the re-dedication of the temple in 165 BC after the defeat of Antiochus Epiphanes (see 'The New Testament World'). It was held about two months after the Feast of Tabernacles (cf. John 7:2) and was the Jews' only winter festival (cf. John 10:22).

Many Jews felt it was time Jesus made a clear public statement that he was the Messiah. Jesus replied that his works were a clear enough statement, but most of the Jews refused to recognize them (John 10:22-26). Some, however, accepted him and followed him, and these were his true people. They had eternal life, and their eternal security was guaranteed by both Jesus and his heavenly Father, with whom he was inseparably united (John 10:27-30).

The Jews again burst into anger, claiming that Jesus was calling himself God. Jesus replied that in one Old Testament passage even Israel's rulers were called 'gods', because of the God-given authority they exercised. How much more should the one who was united with the heavenly Father call himself God (John 10:31-36). But Jesus did not want the Jews to excuse their unbelief by arguing about words. The works that Jesus did were sufficient proof of his divine origin (John 10:37-38).

Once more the Jews tried to seize Jesus, but he escaped and left Jerusalem. This time he went across Jordan into Perea, where the people's ready belief was in sharp contrast to the hardness of the people in Jerusalem (John 10:39-42).

AROUND THE JORDAN VALLEY

95. Jesus accuses Pharisees and scribes (Luke 11:37-54)

The Pharisees thought that religion consisted of keeping ceremonial laws. Yet their hearts were full of wicked plans to advance themselves while at the same time they oppressed others. They took great care in washing their hands and cleaning cups and plates, but made no effort to clean the evil out of their hearts (Luke 11:37-41).

In calculating the amount of their offerings to God, the Pharisees were very strict in measuring exactly one tenth of their garden produce, even counting the seeds and stalks. But this was of no value if they did not practise love, mercy and justice towards their fellows (Luke 11:42). They were proud and vain, always looking for people's praise, but in God's sight they were as unclean as graves full of decaying bodies. And just as graves spread their uncleanness to people who touched them, so the Pharisees spread their uncleanness to all who came in contact with them (Luke 11:43-44).

The scribes felt insulted when they heard Jesus speak against the Pharisees like this, because they were the professional teachers who laid down the laws that the Pharisees followed. Jesus saw this as all the more reason to condemn them, because they burdened others with laws that they were unable to keep themselves (Luke 11:45-46). They honoured dead prophets with lavish tombs, but persecuted living prophets who brought them God's message. Some they killed, as their ancestors had done in Old Testament times. They shared in the violence of their ancestors, and would suffer accordingly (Luke 11:47-51).

Because the scribes' detailed interpretations of Scripture were difficult to understand, they had, in effect, shut people off from God's Word. They were skilful in twisting the meaning of words, and used this ability constantly to try to trick Jesus into saying something whereby they could find fault with him (Luke 11:52-54).

96. Be prepared at all times (Luke 12:35-53)

The followers of Jesus must always be ready for whatever circumstances they meet. They are likened to household servants waiting for their master to return home after a feast. Whether the master arrives home earlier or later than expected, he will be pleased if the servants are ready and waiting for him. Though they have merely done their duty, he may give them an unexpected reward by serving them a meal (Luke 12:35-38).

Another illustration of readiness concerns a householder who secures his house against burglary. Since he does not know when a burglar is likely to break in, he keeps the house secure constantly (Luke 12:39). Jesus used both illustrations to remind his followers to be ready always for 'the coming of

the Son of man', whether in the coming crisis in Jerusalem or in the final crisis at the end of the age (Luke 12:40).

When Peter asked if the parable applied only to the apostles or to people in general, Jesus gave no direct answer but told another parable (Luke 12:41). The master of a household appointed one of his servants to the position of manager over all the other servants while he went away on a trip. He gave the manager-servant instructions concerning the running of the household, but when the master was away longer than expected, the man thought he could do as he liked. Suddenly the master returned and, on discovering what had happened, dealt severely with the manager-servant (Luke 12:42-46). All the servants guilty of wrongdoing were punished, but the one who had more detailed knowledge of his master's will was punished more severely. Everyone is accountable to God, but God expects more of those who know more (Luke 12:47-48).

Jesus gave one more warning about the need to be prepared for the crisis ahead. He felt a mounting tension as he saw that the cross would mean fiery judgment for some, a baptism of suffering for himself, and conflict for those who are opposed by hostile relatives because of their loyalty to him (Luke 12:49-53).

97. Warning to the Jewish nation (Luke 13:1-9)

Two recent tragedies were fresh in the minds of the Jewish people. One was caused by Pilate, the Roman governor of Judea, when he killed a number of Galilean Jews while they were offering sacrifices at the temple in Jerusalem. The other was caused by the collapse of a tower that killed a number of Jerusalem citizens. Some Jews thought that because the victims of these tragedies met such terrible deaths, they must have been worse sinners than others. Jesus pointed out that this was not so. In fact, the rest of the Jews would suffer a far worse fate if they did not repent and accept the Messiah (Luke 13:1-5).

Israel had been unfaithful and worthless to God, like a fig tree that never produced fruit. God had been patient, but now he was giving the nation one last chance to repent and accept the Messiah. If the people persisted in their stubbornness, judgment would fall upon them (Luke 13:6-9).

98. A woman healed in the synagogue (Luke 13:10-17)

While Jesus was preaching in a Sabbath day service in the synagogue, he saw a woman in the audience who was obviously distressed because of a crippling disease. In his mercy he healed her (Luke 13:10-13). The ruler of the synagogue was angry because Jesus healed on the Sabbath, and told the people not to come for healing on the Sabbath in future. Jesus showed up the hypocrisy of the man, and those who supported him, by reminding them that they fed their cattle on the Sabbath. Surely, then, he could heal a crippled woman (Luke 13:14-17).

99. The first shall be last (Luke 13:22-35)

As Jesus moved through the towns of the Jordan Valley, he stressed that people should believe in him without delay, because they would not have the opportunity to hear from him again. Many were concerned with theoretical questions about who would or would not be saved. Jesus explained that people individually should first be sure of their own salvation, because on the judgment day many who thought they were in God's kingdom would find themselves left outside (Luke 13:22-24).

Some Jews boasted that they would enter the kingdom of God because they were descendants of Abraham; others, because they had eaten with Jesus or heard him preach in their towns. All alike would find themselves condemned to hell if they did not turn from their sins. Their places in the kingdom would be taken by the Gentiles, whom they despised (Luke 13:25-30).

Certain Pharisees tried to frighten Jesus with a threat from Herod, through whose territory Jesus was travelling. Jesus knew that Herod wanted him out of the way, but he replied that he would continue his work until he finished it in Jerusalem (Luke 13:31-33). The city that Jesus loved, in finally rejecting him, would guarantee its own punishment. The nation was spiritually desolate, and once the Romans had finished with it (in AD 70), it would be physically desolate. There would be no blessing for the Jews until they repented and acknowledged Jesus as their Messiah (Luke 13:34-35).

100. In the house of a Pharisee (Luke 14:1-24)

When Jesus visited the house of a prominent Pharisee on the Sabbath day, his critics were waiting to see if he would heal a sick man who was there. When Jesus asked them if healing on the Sabbath was lawful, they refused to answer. Jesus again pointed out the hypocrisy of those who would care for animals on the Sabbath but not for people (Luke 14:1-6).

As mealtime approached, Jesus noticed some guests choosing the places of honour at the table. He warned that those who seek status or prestige are in danger of being humiliated. God exalts only those who willingly take the lowest place (Luke 14:7-11). Jesus had a similar warning for the host. His reason for doing good should not be to win favour with people who can be of use to him. Rather he should do good out of genuine love, not expecting anything in return (Luke 14:12-14).

One of the guests, hearing Jesus' illustrations about feasting, tried to impress him with a comment concerning the coming great feast in the kingdom of God (Luke 14:15). In reply Jesus told a parable designed to make the man, and the other guests, realize that many who thought themselves assured of a place in the kingdom were going to miss out.

Jesus likened the kingdom to a feast to which many were invited, but for various reasons they all refused. This was how most of the Jews treated Jesus' invitation. They felt they were good enough already and did not need to repent (Luke 14:16-20). Consequently, the religiously respectable people were left out of the kingdom, but outcasts such as beggars, tax collectors and prostitutes were included. Even Gentiles from far off places accepted the invitation that the Jews refused (Luke 14:21-24).

101. More about discipleship (Luke 14:25-35)

The crowds that followed Jesus thought he was on the way to a throne. Jesus told them he was on the way to a cross. If they wanted to follow him they had to understand what his kingdom was like and what his followers could expect. They had to love him above everything else, and had to be prepared for self-sacrifice and even death (Luke 14:25-27).

Like a farmer building a tower or a king going to war, the person wanting to be a disciple of Jesus had first to consider what it would cost and what it would involve (Luke 14:28-32). If people were not prepared to give everything for the sake of Jesus, their lives could be of no use to him. They would be as useless as salt that had no saltiness (Luke 14:33-35).

102. Lost sheep; lost coin; lost son (Luke 15:1-32)

Jesus told these three short stories to answer the scribes and Pharisees, who had complained that he mixed with tax collectors and other low class people. The more respectable Jews considered such people unworthy of God's blessings. They were angry that Jesus showed interest in them and that many of them responded to his message (Luke 15:1-2).

The stories of the lost sheep and the lost coin show that God does more than welcome sinners; he actually goes looking for them. And when they repent, he rejoices. The Pharisees, however, did not consider themselves sinners. Therefore, they could not repent and so they brought no pleasure to God (Luke 15:3-10).

In the story of the lost son there is again a contrast between those who considered they had done everything right and needed no repentance (the elder brother) and those who were obviously sinners but who knew it (the younger brother) (Luke 15:11-19). There is also a contrast between the pardoning love of God (the father who welcomes the rebel home) and the cold and merciless attitude of the Pharisees (the older brother who was angry because of the welcome the rebel received) (Luke 15:20-30).

Because the Pharisees knew God's law, they had an advantage over the tax collectors, but because they were self-righteous they never saw themselves as 'dead' or 'lost'. They therefore never came to God in repentance. As a result they were left out of the kingdom, but sinners entered it (Luke 15:31-32).

103. The shrewd manager (Luke 16:1-17)

This story was told not to the Pharisees but to the disciples of Jesus. It concerned a shrewd business-man whom the owner of a business appointed as manager. In this business, dealings were made by exchange of goods rather than payment of money, a practice that enabled the manager to cheat the owner. When the owner found out, he decided to dismiss him (Luke 16:1-2).

The manager then thought of a plan to ensure help from his business friends after his dismissal, as he did not want to become a beggar or a labourer. He therefore reduced the amounts that his business friends owed, so that they could pay their debts quickly. More importantly, they would feel obliged to return some favour to the manager after he had lost his job. The owner, being something of a scoundrel himself, appreciated such cunning (Luke 16:3-8).

Such, said Jesus, is the way of the world. If Christians had the diligence and foresight in spiritual matters that others have in worldly matters, they would be better people and enjoy a more lasting reward. If they used their material possessions to help others, they would gain true friends now and lasting prosperity in the life to come (Luke 16:9).

God's people should realize that they are answerable to him for the way they use their goods and money. In God's sight they are not owners of these things but managers. If they are generous in using what God has entrusted to them, God will reward them with permanent riches. If they are selfish, there will be no reward (Luke 16:10-12). They have become slaves to money and therefore they are disloyal to God (Luke 16:13).

The Pharisees considered wealth to be a reward for keeping the law, and they sneered at Jesus' teaching. Jesus replied that God was not impressed with their show of righteousness, for he saw their pride-filled hearts. They did not realize that the old era of the law had passed and the kingdom announced by John had arrived. The only ones who understand the real meaning of the law are those in the kingdom. The godly are therefore zealous to enter it (Luke 16:14-17).

104. The rich man and Lazarus (Luke 16:19-31)

To illustrate the truth he had just been teaching, Jesus told the story of an unnamed rich man and a beggar named Lazarus. The rich man pictured those who lived to please themselves and felt no need of God; the beggar pictured those who were helpless and depended entirely upon God's mercy. In their existence after death, the beggar sat beside Abraham in the heavenly feast, resting his body, as it were, against Abraham, but the rich man was in great pain in hades, awaiting final punishment (Luke 16:19-24).

The rich man had been so concerned with building his wealth and enjoying it that he had forgotten God and no longer noticed the needs of others. After death he saw where his selfishness had led him, but by then it was too late to change. His determination to live for himself was his own decision, and that decision excluded him from heaven (Luke 16:25-26).

Being concerned about his brothers who were still alive, the rich man wanted Lazarus to go and warn them. But even the miracle of someone rising from death would not cause such people to give up their selfish ways. They had the message of salvation in the Scriptures, but if they rejected that, nothing else could save them (Luke 16:27-31).

105. Duty, faith and gratitude (Luke 17:1-19)

Whether in relation to money (as illustrated in the previous stories) or any other matter likely to cause temptation, Jesus' followers must not cause young believers to sin (Luke 17:1-2). They must try to correct those who do wrong to them, but at the same time forgive them, no matter how many times the offence is repeated (Luke 17:3-4). Concerning faith, they should remember that God is not concerned with how much they have, but with whether they have truly placed it in him (Luke 17:5-6).

Those who serve Jesus should not feel proud of themselves, as if their master has an obligation to give them a special reward. Their good works are their duty, and no matter how hard they work, they still owe God more (Luke 17:7-10).

Many become so used to receiving God's blessings that they forget to thank him in return. Others, who have not previously known God, may display true gratitude the first time they become aware of God's goodness to them. This was demonstrated on an occasion when Jesus healed ten lepers. He then sent them to the priest as the Jewish law required, but none of the Jews in the group returned to give him thanks. The only one who thanked him was a foreigner (Luke 17:11-19).

106. Coming of the kingdom (Luke 17:20-37)

The Pharisees were looking for visible signs so that they could work out when the Messiah's kingdom would begin. Jesus told them that since he was the Messiah and was living among them, the Messiah's kingdom had already begun (Luke 17:20-21; cf. Matt 16:1-4).

Turning to his disciples, Jesus added that one day he would be taken from them. In their longing for him to return they were not to be led astray by rumours and false prophecies. His coming would be visible and unmistakable (Luke 17:22-25).

As in the days of Noah and of Lot, people will be carrying out their everyday duties when the divine judgment will suddenly fall (Luke 17:26-30). It will then be too late for people to do anything to save themselves. There will be an irreversible separation between those who have lived for themselves and those who have put God's interests first (Luke 17:31-36). God's great intervention in human affairs will affect people worldwide. Wherever there is sin, there the divine judgment will fall (Luke 17:37).

107. Two parables about prayer (Luke 18:1-14)

Because there may be an apparent delay before his return, Jesus told a parable to encourage his disciples. They may suffer injustice from opponents of the gospel, but they must persevere in prayer, confident that God will hear them (Luke 18:1). If an ungodly judge will give a just judgment to a helpless widow solely to be rid of her ceaseless pleading, how much more will the holy God answer the cries of his persecuted people. The world may be unbelieving, but the disciples of Jesus must maintain their faith to the end (Luke 18:2-8).

In the second story Jesus rebuked those law-abiding people who thought their behaviour made them and their prayers acceptable with God. The Pharisee recounted his good deeds, and expected God to be pleased with him. He despised the tax collector, and was sure that God did too (Luke 18:9-12). But the tax collector made no attempt to impress God. He simply confessed himself a sinner and asked God for mercy. God accepted the man who humbly repented, but rejected the one who boasted of his virtue (Luke 18:13-14).

108. Questions about divorce (Matt 19:1-12; Mark 10:1-12; Luke 16:18)

Again the Pharisees tried to trap Jesus into saying something that would give them grounds to accuse him of error. This time they chose the subject of divorce, where different viewpoints among Jewish teachers often caused arguments. Jesus referred them back to God's original standard, which was that a man and a woman live together, independent of parents, in a permanent union (Matt 19:1-6). Moses set out laws to limit divorce and introduce some order into a very disorderly community. He permitted divorce not because he approved of it, but because people had created problems through their disobedience. Under normal circumstances divorce should not be allowed at all, though there may be an exception in the case of adultery (Matt 19:7-9; cf. 5:31-32).

The disciples thought that if a man had to be bound to his wife in such a way, maybe it would be safer not to marry. Jesus replied that marriage was the normal pattern for adult life, though not necessarily the pattern for everyone. Some may choose not to marry, possibly because of physical defects or possibly because they want to serve God without the hindrances that may be created by family responsibilities (Matt 19:10-12).

109. Jesus blesses the children (Mt 19:13-15; Mark 10:13-16; Luke 18:15-17)

Many people thought that they could gain entrance into the kingdom of God through their own efforts. Jesus referred to the children gathered around him to illustrate that this was not so (Mark 10:13-14). People must realize that in relation to entering his kingdom they are as helpless and dependent as children. There is no room in his kingdom for those who hold high opinions of themselves, or who think they will gain eternal life through their wisdom or good works (Mark 10:15-16).

110. The rich young man (Matt 19:16-30; Mark 10:17-31; Luke 18:18-30)

A wealthy young man came to Jesus and asked what special deeds he should do to gain eternal life. Jesus responded that there was no need to ask him, because God had already told him in the Ten Commandments what he should do (Matt 19:16-19). The man boasted that he had kept most of the commandments, but Jesus saw that at least he had failed in the last, which said 'Do not covet'. While people around him were suffering from hunger and poverty, he was building up wealth. His desire for comfort and prosperity prevented him from giving himself to God, and so prevented him from receiving eternal life. If he wanted eternal life, he would have to get rid of the things that stood in its way (Matt 19:20-22).

Wealth makes people independent of others, and for this reason the rich often find it difficult to acknowledge that they are not independent of God. Their wealth makes them no better in God's sight than anyone else. As a result few of the rich enter the kingdom of God. Actually, no one at all could enter that kingdom apart from the work of God. By his grace he accepts those who humble themselves before him (Matt 19:23-26).

Nevertheless, those who make sacrifices for the sake of Jesus will find that what they receive in eternity is incomparably greater than anything they may have lost in the present world. They may have to sacrifice wealth, status, family or friends, but in the age to come they will reign with Christ (Matt 19:27-30).

111. Workers in the vineyard (Matt 20:1-16)

Jesus' purpose in telling this story was to illustrate what he had just said concerning God's unexpected gift to those who at present appear to be disadvantaged (see Matt 19:30). He was not setting out rules for wages and employment, but giving an illustration of God's grace. The sovereign God takes pity on a needy world, and generously gives his salvation to all who accept his offer.

At the beginning of the day, a landowner hired people to work in his vineyard for an agreed wage (Matt 20:1-2). At several stages through the day he hired additional workers, then at the end of the day paid them their wages (Matt 20:3-8).

When those who had worked all day found that the landowner paid the same amount to the late-comers as he paid to them, they complained. The landowner reminded them that he had paid them the amount they had agreed to, and if he paid others the same amount, that was his concern. The discontent arose not because of any injustice in the landowner, but because of jealousy in the all-day workers (Matt 20:9-15).

The blessings of the kingdom are the same for all who enter, whether Jews who had worshipped God for centuries, or Gentiles who had just been saved from heathenism; whether scribes who had studied God's law for many years, or tax collectors who had just repented; whether those who had served God for a lifetime, or those converted in old age. But whereas the most unlikely people entered the kingdom, those for whom it had been prepared were excluded (Matt 20:16).

112. The request of James and John (Matt 20:17-28; Mark 10:32-45; Luke 18:31-34)

As Jesus journeyed towards Jerusalem, he again spoke of his coming death and resurrection, but again his disciples misunderstood. They were still thinking mainly of an earthly kingdom of political power (Matt 20:17-19; Mark 10:32-34).

James and John therefore came to Jesus with a request that they might have the top positions in the kingdom (Matt 20:20-21; Mark 10:35-37). Jesus, by using the words 'cup' and 'baptism' as symbols of his suffering and death, showed them that he had to suffer and die before he could enjoy the triumph and glory of his kingdom. They still did not understand, and boldly stated that they were prepared to suffer with him. Jesus replied that they would indeed suffer for his sake (cf. Acts 12:2; Rev 1:9), but their position in the kingdom was dependent on the Father alone. And he showed no favouritism (Matt 20:22-23; Mark 10:38-40).

In wanting to be ahead of the other apostles, James and John probably had Peter particularly in mind, but all the other apostles were angry when they discovered what had happened. Jesus then repeated and expanded teaching he had given earlier about the difference between worldly and spiritual greatness (cf. Mark 9:33-35). In the kingdoms of the world people compete with each other to achieve power, but in the kingdom of God true greatness comes from humble and willing service. The perfect example is Jesus himself, who at that time was about to lay down his life so that people in bondage to sin might be set free (Matt 20:24-28; Mark 10:41-45).

113. Blind men near Jericho (Matt 20:29-34; Mark 10:46-52; Luke 18:35-43)

It seems that Jesus healed several blind beggars as he passed through Jericho (Matt 20:29-30; Mark 10:46; Luke 18:35). The men were determined to attract the attention of Jesus and called out loudly, addressing him by his messianic title, son of David. Jesus called the men to him, and although he clearly saw their need, he asked them what they wanted. He wanted them to declare their faith boldly, and thereby strengthen it. In response to their expression of faith, Jesus healed them (Matt 20:31-34; Mark 10:47-52).

114. Jesus and Zacchaeus (Luke 19:1-10)

Zacchaeus was the chief tax collector of Jericho and was wealthy. He wanted to see Jesus, and Jesus wanted to talk to him. So Jesus went to his house, much to the disapproval of the local citizens (Luke 19:1-7).

The outcome of Jesus' visit was that Zacchaeus repented and believed in Jesus. To show that his repentance was genuine, Zacchaeus repaid (with generous interest) those he had cheated and gave freely even to those he had not cheated (Luke 19:8). Being a tax collector, he was despised by his fellow Jews as one not worthy to be called a 'son of Abraham'. But that was no reason for him to be cut off from salvation. On the contrary, sinners such as this were the people that Jesus came to save. And once Zacchaeus was saved, he was a true 'son of Abraham', a genuine believer (Luke 19:9-10).

115. Parable of the pounds (Luke 19:11-27)

As Jesus drew nearer to Jerusalem, those with him became excited, thinking he was about to establish a world-conquering kingdom. Jesus corrected their misunderstanding by telling them a parable (Luke 19:11). He was like a man who was entitled to a kingdom, but who had first to go to the seat of power in a distant country to have his kingdom confirmed, after which he would return to claim it. Before he left for the distant country, he gave an equal amount of money to each of ten trusted servants, who were to use it to promote their master's interests during his absence. The meaning was that Jesus would soon leave the world, but he gave to each of his servants the task of living for him in such a way that his kingdom would continue to grow (Luke 19:12-13).

The citizens in the parable did not want the new king, and in like manner the Jews did not want Jesus (Luke 19:14). But the loyal servants (the followers of Jesus) continued to work for their master. When he returned he examined their work and rewarded each according to his diligence. If the servant used his master's money profitably he was rewarded; if he was lazy he suffered loss. The master did not expect all the servants to be equally successful, but he accepted no excuses for laziness (Luke 19:15-25).

For the followers of Jesus the lesson is that those who work diligently find that their ability increases, and so they are given more responsibility. Those who are lazy find that they lose whatever ability they have, and cannot be trusted with any further responsibility (Luke 19:26). For those who reject Jesus the lesson is that they will suffer a terrible judgment (Luke 19:27).

BACK TO JUDEA

116. Resurrection of Lazarus (John 11:1-44)

While Jesus was still in the region between the Jordan and Jerusalem, he heard that his friend Lazarus, who lived in Bethany, was seriously ill. Jesus did not hurry to Bethany, because he knew that Lazarus was already dead. By raising him to life, Jesus would give unmistakable evidence of his unity with the Father (John 11:1-6).

After waiting two days, Jesus decided to set out for Bethany. The disciples tried to stop him, fearing that the Jews of that area would try to kill him. Jesus assured them that the time for his death had not yet come. He would travel safely as a person walking in broad daylight. Because he walked in God's light, he would be unharmed by the evil powers of darkness (John 11:7-10). His raising of Lazarus would show his power over death and so strengthen the disciples' faith. Such words of assurance gave the disciples courage to go with him in spite of the dangers (John 11:11-16).

A distressed Martha met Jesus along the way. She believed that although, humanly speaking, it was too late to do anything for her dead brother, Jesus may yet be able to call upon his Father's power and bring Lazarus back to life (John 11:17-22).

It was small comfort to Martha to know that Lazarus would be raised to life at the resurrection of the just. Jesus enlightened her by saying that *he* is the resurrection and the life. Here and now, in this life, those who are spiritually dead because of sin may have eternal life through him. They will go on living and enjoying this life even though their physical bodies may die (John 11:23-26). Martha fully believed all that Jesus was saying, and added her confident confession that he was the Messiah, the Son of God and the Saviour of the world (John 11:27). She then hurried home and brought Mary to meet him (John 11:28-32).

Jesus' statement about eternal life (v. 26) did not mean that physical death was of no concern to him. He saw it as an enemy that had to be destroyed, for it was a weapon of Satan, who had the power of death (cf. 1 Cor 15:26; Heb 2:14-15). When he saw how Satan used this weapon to fill his beloved friends with grief, he was filled with sorrow and anger (John 11:33-37).

Determined to win a victory over Satan, Jesus went to the tomb. Before raising Lazarus to life, he thanked God publicly (so that those standing by could hear) for always hearing his prayers. The Father and the Son were united in power and purpose (John 11:38-42). Jesus then called out in a loud voice (again for the benefit of those standing by) and Lazarus miraculously was raised to life (John 11:43-44).

117. Jews plot to kill Jesus (John 11:45-57)

As a result of his miraculous works, Jesus was becoming more famous every day. The Sanhedrin feared that the nation might accept him as the leader of a messianic uprising against Rome, which would lead to Rome's intervention. The outcome could be the loss of the Jews' religious privileges and even the destruction of their temple (John 11:45-48).

Caiaphas, who was high priest and president of the Sanhedrin, suggested they get rid of Jesus and so remove the possibility of Rome's intervention. Jesus should die so that the nation might be saved. These words had a meaning that Caiaphas never intended, as if they were a prophecy of the outcome of Jesus' death; for his death saves not only the Jewish people, but people of every nation who believe in him (John 11:49-52).

While the Jewish leaders plotted his death, Jesus took his disciples to a quiet place away from the crowd (John 11:53-54). Back in Jerusalem people from the country began to arrive in preparation for the coming Passover Festival. Many were uneasy as they thought about what might happen if Jesus came to the city for the festival (John 11:55-57).

118. Jesus returns to Bethany (John 12:1-11)

Before going on to Jerusalem, Jesus returned to Bethany, where Mary, Martha and Lazarus lived. Mary, believing this was probably the last time Jesus would be with them, showed her devotion by washing his feet with expensive perfume (John 12:1-4). Judas objected that the use of expensive perfume in this way was a waste of money. In answer Jesus told his disciples that he would be with them only a little longer, then would be crucified. He saw Mary's act as a symbolic anointing of his body in preparation for burial (John 12:5-8).

Once it became known that Jesus was in the house, a crowd gathered. Some were just curious sightseers, but many became genuine believers. The Jewish leaders were right in thinking that the raising of Lazarus would attract a following for Jesus. They

therefore became more determined to kill him and decided to kill Lazarus as well (John 12:9-11).

FINAL TEACHING IN JERUSALEM

119. The triumphal entry (Mt 21:1-11; Mk 11:1-11; Lk 19:28-44; Jn 12:12-19)

The time had now come for Jesus to challenge his opponents openly by a clear public demonstration that he was Israel's Messiah. The Jewish leaders wanted to arrest him, but when told of his whereabouts they feared to take action. They were unsure of the extent of Jesus' popular support (cf. John 11:57; 12:9-11).

To make sure that nothing stopped him from making a bold public entry into Jerusalem, Jesus had made a secret arrangement with some unnamed villagers who would provide the donkey that he would ride. By using a pre-arranged password, two of his disciples collected the donkey and brought it to him (Matt 21:1-3; Luke 19:28-34).

As the messianic king, the son of David, Jesus then entered his royal city of Zion. He came not riding a horse as a conquering warlord, but sitting on a donkey as a king of peace, as the Scriptures foretold (see Zech 9:9). People who were in Jerusalem for the Passover, along with local residents, welcomed him as the Messiah. They may not have understood the nature of his messiahship, but they were enthusiastic in their acceptance of him (Matt 21:4-11; Luke 19:35-38; John 12:12-16. (The word 'Hosanna', meaning 'Save us, O Lord', came from two Hebrew words found in Psalm 118, where Israel's victorious king was welcomed with the words, 'Blessed is he who comes in the name of the Lord'; Ps 118:25-26. By New Testament times the two expressions, used together, had become a declaration of praise to God for the promised Messiah.)

The Pharisees were annoyed at the welcome Jesus received and unsuccessfully tried to persuade him to silence the people (Luke 19:39-40). As the news of Jesus' raising of Lazarus spread, more and more people flocked to see him. The thing the Pharisees most feared was happening before their eyes (John 12:17-19).

Jesus, however, was not deceived by this enthusiastic welcome. He knew that when people properly understood the nature of his messiahship, they would turn against him. The nation as a whole would reject him, and in the judgment to follow, Jerusalem would be destroyed (Luke 19:41-44). The significance of Jesus' entry into Jerusalem was not political but spiritual, and therefore he went not to the palace but to the temple. He took note of what was happening there, then returned with his disciples to Bethany, where they spent the night (Mark 11:11).

120. Jesus cleanses the temple (Matt 21:12-17; Mark 11:15-19; Luke 19:45-48)

At the beginning of his public ministry Jesus had cleansed the temple (see John 2:13-25), but old practices had returned. Now that he had come to his messianic city he cleansed it again. By his action he showed God's judgment on those who had forgotten the real purpose of religious exercises and used them chiefly to make money (Matt 21:12-13).

God was more pleased with Jesus' action in healing the blind and the crippled than with all the religious activity of the Jews. Even the children saw the worth of Jesus' action and shouted their praises accordingly. The temple authorities were angered at such behaviour by the children in the temple, but Jesus responded that the children clearly saw what the religious leaders could not, namely, that Jesus was the Messiah (Matt 21:14-16). Again, at the end of the day Jesus returned to Bethany (Matt 21:17).

121. Jesus curses the fig tree (Matt 21:18-22; Mark 11:12-14,20-26)

In the morning, as Jesus and his disciples walked from Bethany back to Jerusalem, they passed a fig tree that Jesus saw as symbolic of the Jewish nation. He went to the fig tree looking for fruit but found none. Similarly he came to the Jewish nation looking for spiritual fruit, but in spite of all its outward signs of religion, spiritually it produced no fruit for God. By causing the fig tree to dry up, Jesus illustrated the judgment that would fall on the nation after it finally rejected its Messiah (Matt 21:18-20; Mark 11:12-14,20-21).

The incident was also a lesson on the effectiveness of prayer. When people make requests to God, they must have undoubting faith in the one to whom they pray and a forgiving attitude towards others (Matt 21:21-22; Mark 11:22-26).

122. Authority of Jesus questioned (Matt 21:23-32; Mark 11:27-33; Luke 20:1-8)

When Jesus returned to the temple, the Jewish religious leaders came to trap him with a question. They hoped to find something in his answer that would enable them to bring a charge, civil or religious, against him. They asked him by what authority he acted the way he did, particularly in

overthrowing the established practices of the Jewish temple (Matt 21:23).

Instead of answering directly, Jesus adjusted the question and turned it back on the religious leaders, so that they were the ones who found difficulty in answering. In doing this, Jesus was not trying to avoid telling the truth, but trying to make them see the truth. If they gave him a correct answer to his question, they would have the answer to their own question. Jesus' question concerned the authority of John the Baptist. If they acknowledged that John was sent by God, they were acknowledging that Jesus also was sent by God, because John's message was to announce the arrival of Jesus as God's chosen Messiah. If they denied that John was sent by God, they could expect trouble from the crowds, because many people still held John in high esteem (Matt 21:24-27).

When the leaders would not answer, Jesus told a story to rebuke them once more for their refusal to repent. He likened sinners such as tax collectors and prostitutes to a son who at first disobeyed his father but later changed his mind. The sinners repented of their wrongdoing and so entered God's kingdom. He likened the Pharisees to another son, who pretended to be obedient but, in fact, did not obey. The Pharisees claimed to be obedient to God, but they refused to obey John's call to repentance (Matt 21:28-32).

123. The wicked vineyard keepers (Matt 21:33-46; Mark 12:1-12; Luke 20:9-18)

This parable pictures Israel as a vineyard, God as the owner of the vineyard, and the Jewish religious leaders as the tenants who looked after it. Just as the tenants beat and killed the servants whom the owner sent to them, so Israel's leaders persecuted and killed God's messengers, from Old Testament prophets to John the Baptist. Now they were about to reject God's Son himself (Matt 21:33-39). By rejecting him the Jews were bringing punishment on themselves. God would take away the privileges from Israel and give them to the Gentiles (Matt 21:40-41).

Another picture illustrated this truth. Jesus was likened to the cornerstone of a building, which in ancient buildings was the stone upon which the structure depended. In rejecting Jesus, the Jews were like builders who threw away the cornerstone. God now took this rejected stone and used it in the construction of a new building, the Christian church. This new community would be mainly Gentile, and all of it built around and built into Jesus

Christ (Matt 21:42-43). People's attitude to Jesus determined their destiny, and those who rejected him guaranteed their own destruction. The leaders of the Jews knew he was talking about them and wanted to arrest him, but they were not sure how the crowd would react (Matt 21:44-46).

124. The royal wedding feast (Matt 22:1-14)

Throughout the Old Testament period and into the New, God sent his messengers to Israel, but the people ignored his message. God was like a king who invited people to a wedding feast for his son, but when the time for the feast arrived, they refused to come (Matt 22:1-5). This was a picture of the refusal of the Jews to accept Jesus' message and enter the kingdom of God. Their rejection of Jesus would bring God's judgment upon them and result in the destruction of Jerusalem (Matt 22:6-7). Meanwhile, the invitation that the Jews refused went to the Gentiles instead, and there was a great response (Matt 22:8-10).

However, not all the people who responded to the invitation were genuine. Some were like the man who thought he would like to go to the feast, but was either too lazy or too busy with his own affairs to prepare himself properly. The king had issued an invitation to all, but he denied entrance to those who wanted to gain the benefits of his feast without changing their self-centred ways. Jesus invited all to enter his kingdom, but there was no place for those who said they believed but showed no change in their attitudes and behaviour (Matt 22:11-14; cf. 7:21-23; 11:29; 13:20-21; 16:24).

125. A question about paying taxes (Matt 22:15-22; Mark 12:13-17; Luke 20:19-26)

The Herodians were a group of Jews who, unlike most Jews, were favourable to the rule of the Herods and therefore (indirectly) to the rule of Rome. Normally, they had little in common with the Pharisees, but the two groups were willing to co-operate in an attempt to trap Jesus. They asked him was it lawful for Jews to pay taxes to Rome (Matt 22:15-17; Luke 20:19-22).

If Jesus replied 'Yes', the Pharisees would accuse him before the Jewish people of being a traitor. If he answered 'No', the Herodians would accuse him before the Roman authorities of treason. Jesus replied that duty to God and duty to civil authorities are not in opposition. People owe to each a debt for the services and benefits they receive. They should give to civil authorities that which is due to them, and give to God all that they owe him (Matt 22:18-22; Luke 20:23-26).

126. Marriage and the resurrection (Matt 22:23-33; Mark 12:18-27; Luke 20:27-40)

Next a group of Sadducees came to Jesus with a question. According to the law of Moses, if a man died childless, his brother was to have a temporary marital relationship with the widow for the purpose of producing an heir (Deut 25:5-6). The question put by the Sadducees concerned an unlikely situation where a widow would meet seven husbands, all brothers, in the resurrection. Since Sadducees did not believe in any form of life after death, their question was intended to make fun of Jesus and the doctrine of the resurrection (Luke 20:27-33). (For other beliefs of the Sadducees see earlier section, 'The New Testament World'.)

Jesus told the Sadducees that their question was without meaning, because Israel's laws applied only to life in the present physical world. Life in the age to come is not a continuation of present earthly life, but is a different kind of life altogether (Luke 20:34-36; cf. 1 Cor 15:35-44).

To show that life after death was a fact they could not deny, Jesus quoted from the book of Exodus (which, being part of the Pentateuch, was one of the few parts of the Scriptures that the Sadducees read). Long after Abraham, Isaac and Jacob had died, the Scriptures spoke of God as having a living personal relationship with them. They must therefore still be living, even though their bodies are dead and buried (Luke 20:37-38; cf. Exod 3:6). Some of the scribes (probably Pharisees) were impressed with Jesus' answer and were pleased to see the Sadducees silenced (Luke 20:39-40).

127. The greatest commandment (Matt 22:34-40; Mark 12:28-34)

When a teacher of the law asked Jesus which was the greatest commandment, Jesus gave an answer that went beyond what the questioner expected. All the commandments of the law could be summarized under the word 'love'. A person's first responsibility is to love God; the second is to love one's fellow human beings. The fact that people are *commanded* to love shows that love is primarily a matter of doing, not feeling. It is an attitude of loyal obedience that governs a person's mind, will and emotions (Mark 12:28-31; cf. Deut 6:4-5; Lev 19:18).

The questioner immediately saw that such a requirement as this was greater than all the requirements of the sacrificial system. He realized that God required change within people's hearts more than formal obedience to ceremonial laws. He began to see what many of the Jews failed to see, and in so doing made definite progress towards the kingdom of God (Mark 12:32-34).

128. Who is the Messiah? (Matt 22:41-46; Mark 12:35-37; Luke 20:41-44)

Some of the questions that Jesus' opponents put to him were unimportant, even senseless. He now put to them the really important question: what was their view of the Messiah? Jews understood the Messiah to be the son (descendant) of David, but thought of him almost solely as a political figure who would rule Israel in a golden age. Jesus wanted to show that this view was inadequate. The Messiah was far more than the son of David (Matt 22:41-42).

Jesus referred his hearers to Psalm 110, a psalm that Jews of his time regarded as messianic. The psalm had been written a thousand years earlier, to be sung by the temple singers in praise of King David after he conquered Jerusalem and established his throne there. But the person who wrote the words was David himself; and, as Jesus pointed out, they were written under the inspiration of the Spirit in praise of the Messiah. This means that the opening words of the psalm, where the temple singers expressed homage to David by calling him 'my Lord', were the same words by which David expressed homage to the Messiah. The Messiah, who everyone knew was David's descendant, was also David's Lord. The Messiah was not only an earthly figure but also a divine figure (Matt 22:43-45; cf. Acts 2:34-36).

The people understood, at least to some extent, the meaning of Jesus' words and dared not try to trick him with any more questions. He was telling them, yet again, that his work was not to revive and expand the old earthly kingdom of Israel, but to establish an entirely different kind of kingdom, the kingdom of God (Matt 22:46).

129. More about scribes and Pharisees (Matt 23:1-39; Mark 12:38-40; Luke 20:45-47)

Instead of teaching only the law of Moses, the scribes and Pharisees added countless laws of their own. Instead of making the people's load lighter, they made it heavier. People could profit from listening to the scribes' teaching of Moses' law, but they were not to copy the scribes' behaviour (Matt 23:1-4).

Jesus gave two specific reasons for his condemnation of the scribes. First, they wanted to make a display of their religious devotion so that they might win praise from others. Second, they paid strict attention to small details of law-keeping but they ignored the law's real meaning. Jesus gave a list of examples.

Phylacteries were small leather boxes containing finely written portions of the law that people strapped on their foreheads and arms. Tassels were decorations sewn on the fringes of their clothes to remind them to keep God's law. The scribes made their phylacteries and tassels extra large to impress people with their devotion to the law (Matt 23:5; cf. Num 15:38-39; Deut 11:18).

In public meetings the scribes tried to get the most important seats, and they loved the feeling of status when their students greeted them respectfully in public. Jesus rebuked them with the reminder that the only true teacher, father and master was God, and he would humble those who tried to make themselves great (Matt 23:6-12). They made themselves appear religious with their long prayers, yet they heartlessly took advantage of the poor (Mark 12:40).

Besides not believing in Jesus themselves, the scribes stopped others from believing. If they succeeded in converting a Gentile to Judaism, they usually turned the person into such an extremist that he was more worthy of God's punishment than they were (Matt 23:13-15).

Jews were careful in swearing oaths, so that they could have an excuse if they broke their oath. If they swore by certain things they felt obliged to keep their oath, but if they swore by others they felt no guilt if they ignored their oath. Jesus repeated teaching given earlier that all oaths were binding, no matter what people swore by, and God the supreme judge would hold them responsible (Matt 23:16-22; see notes on Matt 5:33-37).

Jesus also repeated some of the accusations he had made elsewhere against the Pharisees and scribes. They concentrated on minor details of their own law but ignored the important teachings of God's law. Their efforts to appear religious were an attempt to hide their inner corruption (Matt 23:23-28; see notes on Luke 11:37-44). Like their ancestors, they would not be satisfied until they had killed all God's messengers. They would even kill the Messiah himself. Therefore, all God's judgment against his murderous people, including that which he had withheld from former generations, would fall on them. They would live to see their city destroyed and their national life brought to an end (Matt 23:29-36; see notes on Luke 11:47-51).

In rejecting the Messiah who had come among them, the Jews were rejecting their only hope. They would not experience God's blessing till they turned and welcomed Jesus as their Messiah and Saviour (Matt 23:37-39; see notes on Luke 13:31-35).

130. The widow's offering (Mark 12:41-44; Luke 21:1-4)

In one of the courts of the temple were large containers into which people dropped their gifts of money. The containers were in an open place, and onlookers could easily see how much people put in. Also, those who gave a lot could easily attract attention to themselves. Jesus noticed that some of the rich gave generously, but a poor widow gave an amount so small that it was almost of no value in the local market place (Mark 12:41-42).

Jesus, however, was more concerned with how people gave than the amount they gave. He considered that the widow gave more than anyone else, because he measured the gift not by its commercial value but by the degree of sacrifice of the giver. A heart of true devotion, not money, was the valuable thing in his kingdom (Mark 12:43-44).

131. The coming crisis (Matt 24:1-31; Mark 13:1-27; Luke 21:5-28)

Through his parables and other teachings, Jesus had spoken a number of times of his going away and his return in glory, which would bring in the climax of the age, the triumph of his kingdom and final judgment. His disciples apparently connected these events with the predicted destruction of Jerusalem. Therefore, when Jesus spoke of the destruction of the temple, his disciples immediately connected this with the return of the Messiah and the end of the age. They asked him what significant events would occur before these final great events (Matt 24:1-3; Luke 21:5-7).

In reply Jesus told them that the destruction of Jerusalem and its temple was not necessarily connected with the return of the Messiah or the end of the age. They were not to believe rumours they might hear from time to time that the Messiah had returned, for there would always be false prophets who tried to attract a following for themselves. Nor were they to think that all wars, famines, earthquakes or plagues were sure signs that the end was near (Matt 24:4-8; Luke 21:8-11).

The end would not come till the gospel had spread throughout the world, and this goal would be reached only after much opposition. God's servants would be persecuted by enemies and betrayed by friends; many would be killed. Only by love and unfailing faith in God would the survivors be able to endure their trials. Even if their sufferings resulted in death, God would preserve them for his heavenly kingdom (Matt 24:9-14; Luke 21:12-19).

Although the people of Jesus' day would not see the final events of the world's history, many of them would certainly see a foreshadowing of those events; for they would live to witness the horror of the Romans' destruction of Jerusalem.

On seeing the awful sight of Rome's armies approaching the city, people would flee to the hills, without even waiting to collect their belongings. They would find escape particularly difficult if the attack came in winter (when weather conditions would slow them down), or on the Sabbath (when religious regulations would restrict them). Women and children especially would suffer. The enemy's savage attack would be more terrible and destructive than anything they had known. In fact, if God did not stop the butchery, no one would be left alive. The people would be massacred, the temple burnt and the city destroyed. The event would be a repeat of the atrocities of Antiochus Epiphanes, only many times worse – an 'awful horror' (GNB), a 'desolating sacrilege' (RSV), an 'abomination that causes desolation' (NIV) (Matt 24:15-22; Luke 21:20-24; cf. Dan 9:27; 11:31; see 'The New Testament World').

During the time these troubles were building up, false prophets would try to draw Jesus' disciples into their group. With clever tricks and comforting words they would assure them that the Messiah had returned and was hiding in some safe place, waiting to lead his people to victory. The disciples of Jesus were not to believe such rumours. Jesus' return would be as sudden, as open, and as startling as a flash of lightning. When God's great intervention eventually occurred, it would be plain for all to see (Matt 24:23-28).

Jesus did not return at the fall of Jerusalem, nor immediately after. It seems, then, that his prophecy still awaits its greater fulfilment. If that is so, there could be a repeat of conditions such as those during the destruction of Jerusalem in AD 70, but on a wider scale and with greater intensity. The powers of nature on earth and in space will be thrown into confusion, nations will be in turmoil, and people everywhere will be filled with fear. The present age will come to an end as Jesus returns in power and glory to save his own and judge his enemies (Matt 24:29-31; Luke 21:25-28).

132. A warning to be alert always (Matt 24:32-51; Mark 13:28-37; Luke 21:29-38)

Just as the first leaves on a fig tree indicate that summer is coming, so when the disciples see the false messiahs, the persecution and the approach of the Roman armies, they will know that the destruction of Jerusalem and the Jewish nation is upon them. People of Jesus' day would see the fulfilment of these things in their own lifetime (Matt 24:32-35; Luke 21:29-33).

As for the day when the Son of man will return in the glory of his kingdom, no one knows when that will be except the Father (Matt 24:36; cf. Dan 7:13-14). People will be carrying on their daily business, ignoring God's warnings just as people did in the days of Noah. But just as the flood was God's means of judgment on those people, so Jesus' return will bring judgment on sinners and salvation to his people (Matt 24:37-41; see notes on Luke 17:22-37).

Jesus' coming will be as unexpected as that of a thief who breaks into a house while the owner is asleep (Matt 24:42-44; see notes on Luke 12:39-40). The disciples of Jesus must therefore be prepared for his return at all times. They must not settle down to a life of self-pleasing but live faithfully for him (Matt 24:45-51; see notes on Luke 12:42-46).

133. The ten girls (Matt 25:1-13)

Matthew 25 records three stories or pictures from Jesus, all of which illustrate the teaching he had just given. He would leave the world for an unknown length of time, then return. Those who prepared themselves for his return would enter his kingdom with joy; those who did not would suffer loss. The three passages show three reasons for people's failure – thoughtlessness, laziness and indifference.

A Jewish marriage followed a period of engagement that was almost as binding as marriage. At the marriage the bridegroom, with his friends, went and brought the bride from her father's house to his own house, where the feast was held. This was the procession that the ten girls in the story went out to meet (Matt 25:1).

Some of the girls, however, were foolish, for they did not consider the possibility that the bridegroom might not come at the time they expected. When his arrival was delayed, they were unprepared (Matt 25:2-9). In due course the bridegroom came, but there was then no time to make preparations. The foolish girls were locked outside the house and had no further chance of going in to the wedding feast (Matt 25:10-12).

In the same way, because of carelessness, many will not be prepared when the Son of man comes. Consequently, they will miss out on the blessings they had hoped for in his kingdom (Matt 25:13).

134. The three employees (Matt 25:14-30)

In the second story, a businessman who went away on a journey left his business in the care of three trusted employees. He gave money to the three men, the amounts they received varying according to their business abilities. Two of the men worked well and made good profits, but the third was lazy and did nothing (Matt 25:14-18).

When the owner returned, he was pleased to see that the first two men had worked well, and he rewarded them by giving them added responsibility (Matt 25:19-23). The lazy employee tried to excuse himself by saying that he feared he might trade at a loss and so anger his employer. He received the reply that if he thought his employer was so hungry for money that he looked only for profits and had no interest in honest work, he should have put the money in the bank. Then he would have at least gained some profits through the interest that the bank paid (Matt 25:24-27).

The meaning of the story is that God gives people different capacities and abilities, and they are to use these in the business of expanding his kingdom. Those who use their gifts will be rewarded with increased capacity and ability, but those who neglect their gifts will become useless. The day of reckoning will bring joy for some but disappointment for others (Matt 25:28-30).

135. Sheep and goats (Matt 25:31-46)

Jesus' third example opens with a description of his return in power and glory to judge the world. His judgment reveals that, no matter what nation a person may come from, there are only two types of people in the world, compared in the story to sheep and goats (Matt 25:31-33).

The 'sheep' are God's people, who give proof of this by the practical love they show to others, often at the expense of their own convenience and comfort. Because they are unselfish, they may not be aware of all the good they do or the appreciation that others have of their kindness. But Jesus notices. He has so identified himself with the needy that he sees any kindness done to them as kindness done to himself (Matt 25:34-40).

The 'goats', by contrast, are those who think only of themselves. Their lack of interest in the misery and suffering of others shows their lack of love for Jesus. They know nothing of his character and have never learnt to deny themselves for his sake. There is no place for them in Jesus' kingdom; their punishment is certain (Matt 25:41-46). As in the stories of the ten girls and the three employees, people are condemned for their failure to do good rather than any deliberate wrongdoing.

BETRAYAL, TRIAL AND CRUCIFIXION

136. The seed must die (John 12:20-26)

Among the crowds that went to Jerusalem for the Passover Festival were some Greeks. They had joined themselves to the synagogue communities where they lived, and now they wanted to see Jesus (John 12:20-22).

When the Lord heard of the Greeks' request, his response was to announce that the climax of his mission had arrived and he was now about to lay down his life. He apparently saw these Greeks as the firstfruits of a great Gentile harvest that would result from his death. Grains of wheat must die and be buried before they can grow up and produce a harvest. Likewise Jesus had to die so that multitudes from all nations might find eternal life. The principle of 'death before life' applies also to those who follow Jesus. For his sake they must sacrifice their lives of self-pleasing before they can be fruitful for him. People will despise them as they despised Jesus, but God will honour them (John 12:23-26).

137. Final message to the Jews (John 12:27-50)

Jesus trembled as he thought of the suffering that awaited him, but he was determined to finish the work he had come to do. He prayed that through his death he would glorify his Father, and his Father responded in a voice from heaven that the prayer would be answered (John 12:27-29). As the startled onlookers were wondering what they had heard, Jesus told them that the time for Satan's defeat was approaching. Through Jesus' crucifixion, people of all nations would be delivered from Satan's power and brought into the liberty of the kingdom of God (John 12:30-33).

The people were puzzled at Jesus' statement. He spoke of himself as 'the Son of man', but if he used this expression to mean 'the Messiah', how could the Messiah die on the cross? They thought the Messiah would live for ever. Jesus had no more time to reason with them, but urged them to believe in him immediately and so walk in the light while he was still on earth. Otherwise the darkness would come upon them and they would be lost eternally (John 12:34-36).

Most of the Jewish people were stubborn in their unbelief, as Isaiah had prophesied. Any who believed in him were afraid to say so openly, for fear of being put out of the synagogue (John 12:37-43).

In his final words to the crowd, Jesus explained that to believe in him was to believe in God; to reject him was to reject God (John 12:44-46). Jesus came to save people, not to condemn them, and the words he spoke were the words of God. But in the day of judgment those same words would be a witness for the condemnation of those who rejected them (John 12:47-50).

138. The plot to capture Jesus (Matt 26:1-16; Mark 14:1-11; Luke 22:1-6)

The Passover was only two days away, and Jesus knew its significance in relation to his coming death. Israelites kept the Feast of Passover and Unleavened Bread as an annual week-long festival in commemoration of ancient Israel's deliverance from Egypt. God 'passed over' those houses where a lamb had been sacrificed in the place of those under judgment (Exod 12:1-13). The people then escaped from bondage. For the next week they ate bread made without leaven, because they had to cook it in haste as they travelled (Exod 12:14-20,39). The time for a greater deliverance had now arrived. Jesus would die as the true Passover lamb, to bear the penalty of sin and release sinners from its bondage (Matt 26:1-2; cf. 1 Cor 5:7).

People in Jerusalem were excited as the festival approached. The chief priests therefore planned to wait until it was finished before arresting Jesus, as they did not want to be responsible for a riot (Matt 26:3-5). But when Judas came to them and offered to betray Jesus to them, their task was made easier. Judas could advise them of Jesus' movements, so that they could arrest him quietly without the people knowing (Matt 26:14-16).

Between the account of the Jews' plotting and Judas' treachery, Matthew and Mark have inserted the account of an anointing of Jesus at Bethany. This may have been the anointing recorded earlier by John, and could have been put into the story at this point to contrast the loving devotion of a true believer with the violence and treachery of others. If the three accounts refer to the same occasion, Simon the leper must have been the owner of the house where Mary, Martha and Lazarus lived. Possibly he was their father (Matt 26:6-13; see notes on John 12:1-8).

139. Jesus prepares the Passover (Matt 26:17-19; Mark 14:12-16; Luke 22:7-13)

Normally the Jews killed the sacrificial lamb on the afternoon of Passover day, and ate it together in a meal that night (cf. Exod 12:6,8). Jesus knew he was to die as the sacrificial lamb on Passover day, and therefore he prepared the meal a day earlier. He would eat the meal with his disciples the evening before Passover, but probably without a lamb, since he himself was to be the lamb.

Knowing that the Jews were looking for him to arrest him, Jesus secretly made careful arrangements for the feast. No one knew where it would be held except two unnamed disciples, who were apparently unknown even to the twelve apostles. This arrangement prevented Judas from giving any advance information to the Jewish leaders (Mark 14:12-15). Two of the apostles met the two unnamed disciples, and between them they prepared the place for the Passover (the 'upper room') and the food and drink for the meal (Mark 14:16).

140. Washing the disciples' feet (John 13:1-20)

When they gathered for the meal that night, Jesus took the place of a servant and washed the disciples' feet. By this action he symbolized firstly, the need for humility, and secondly, that he, the perfect servant, would cleanse people from sin through his death (John 13:1-5). Peter, not understanding this symbolic action, objected. Jesus responded that if he refused to let Jesus cleanse him, he could not be Jesus' disciple. By this cleansing, Jesus was referring to cleansing from sin, something that Peter would understand more fully after Jesus had died, risen and been glorified (John 13:6-8; cf. Acts 5:30-31; 1 Peter 1:18-21; 2:24).

Peter thought that if washing the feet symbolized cleansing, he should be washed all over, to ensure complete cleansing. Again he did not realize that this was what Jesus had just symbolized. The disciples (with the exception of Judas) were already cleansed all over, and needed no further symbolic cleansing. The only washing necessary was the washing of the feet, and that was not for cleansing but for humility (John 13:9-11).

Jesus had given the apostles an example. If he, their Lord and teacher, humbled himself by washing their feet, how much more should they, his servants, humble themselves in serving one another (John 13:12-17). Jesus knew that Judas was a traitor, but the rest were his servants and messengers. Those who received them received him and his Father (John 13:18-20).

141. A traitor among them (Mt 26:20-25; Mk 14:17-21; Lk 22:21-23; Jn 13:21-35)

The apostles were surprised when Jesus announced that one of them would betray him, for they did not suspect treachery among them. Perhaps they thought that one of them might unintentionally betray him through speaking carelessly. But Judas knew what Jesus meant (Matt 26:20-22; John 13:21-25). When Jesus took a piece of bread, dipped it in the dish and gave it to Judas, he was giving Judas a special honour. It was as if Jesus was making a last appeal to him. But Judas' heart was set on doing evil. Jesus knew Judas' intentions, but the apostles still did not suspect him of being a traitor (Matt 26:23-25; John 13:26-30).

Judas' departure from the room made the death of Jesus certain, though for Jesus that death would be not a misfortune but a glorious triumph. His death would bring glory to God by displaying his immeasurable love for sinful men and women. It would also bring grief to his disciples as they saw their master taken from them. But they were to show no bitterness in their grief; rather, a forgiving love, by which others would see that they were indeed disciples of Jesus (John 13:31-35).

142. The Lord's Supper instituted (Matt 26:26-30; Mark 14:22-26; Luke 22:14-20)

By the time of Jesus, the Jewish Passover had developed into a set form with a number of added procedures. Among the additions was a cup of wine, for which the head of the household offered a prayer of thanks (or blessing; cf. 1 Cor 10:16). He filled this cup and passed it among the participants, both before and after the eating of unleavened bread. The participants also sang a collection of psalms known as the Hallel (Psalms 113-118). They sang two of the psalms before eating the lamb, the other psalms after. Some of these features are evident in the Gospels' account of the Passover meal that Jesus had with his disciples the night before his crucifixion. It is sometimes called the Last Supper, and was the occasion on which Jesus instituted the communion meal later known as the Lord's Supper (cf. 1 Cor 11:23-26).

Jesus took some of the bread and wine on the table, gave thanks, and distributed it among his disciples as symbols of his body and blood to be offered in sacrifice. His blood sealed God's covenant, that unconditional promise of forgiveness and eternal life to all who receive Jesus Christ as Lord and Saviour. Israelites kept the Passover in remembrance of God's gracious work in saving them through the Passover lamb; the disciples of the Lord Jesus keep the Lord's Supper in remembrance of the one through whose death they are saved from sin and given eternal life (Matt 26:26-27; Luke 22:17-20; cf. Jer 31:31-34).

When Jesus returns, they will no longer need to remember him with bread and wine. Jesus and his people will be together in his triumphant kingdom, sharing the joy of the great messianic feast (Matt 26:28-29; Luke 22:14-16).

During the meal in the upper room, Jesus had much to say to his disciples. This is represented by the teaching recorded in John Chapters 14-16, to which is added a prayer of Jesus in Chapter 17. At the end of the meal they left the room for the Mount of Olives (Matt 26:30).

143. The way to the Father (John 14:1-14)

The disciples by now surely knew that Jesus was soon to die. He therefore comforted them by saying he was going to his Father to prepare a permanent dwelling place for them, and one day he would return to take them to be with him for ever. He had told them often enough that if they followed him as loyal followers, they would share in his final victory (John 14:1-4).

Thomas misunderstood, thinking that Jesus was speaking of a physical location and a physical journey. He wanted Jesus to show them the way so that they would have no difficulty in following him later. Jesus explained that the 'way' to the Father was through the Son. Jesus had brought the truth of God and eternal life to the human race, and to know him was to know God. To know the Son was to know the Father (John 14:5-7).

Philip also misunderstood. He wanted a special revelation of the Father, though he should have known after more than three years with Jesus that Jesus and the Father were inseparably united. Jesus' words and actions were the Father's words and actions (John 14:8-11). Jesus may have been about to die, but God's work in the world was not about to end. When Jesus returned to the Father he would send the Holy Spirit, and through the power of the Spirit and prayer the disciples would do even greater works than Jesus had done. Jesus' ministry had been limited to a few years in Palestine, but his disciples would travel to other countries and reach the whole world for God. Jesus' return to the Father would bring in a new era (John 14:12-14).

144. Promise of the Holy Spirit (John 14:15-31)

In assuring the disciples of the blessings that would follow his return to the Father (see John 14:12), Jesus had not specifically mentioned the Holy Spirit. Now he explained. When he returned to the Father, he would send the Holy Spirit as the Counsellor, or Helper, to guide, instruct and strengthen them.

Those who did not believe in Jesus would not be able to understand how this Helper worked, because their understanding was limited to the things of the world in which they lived (John 14:15-17). Soon Jesus would leave the world, but he would not desert his disciples. Although people in general would see him no longer, his disciples would, in a sense, continue to see him. They would see and know him spiritually, because he would live within them. He would love them, and in return they would love him (John 14:18-21).

Judas Thaddaeus (not Judas the betrayer), still thinking of Jesus' physical body, could not understand how the disciples would see him but others would not. Jesus replied that not only the Son, but the Father also, would live with them, provided they gave proof of their love for him by following his teachings. The Holy Spirit would help them recall those teachings (John 14:22-26).

Jesus saw that his disciples were confused and unsettled, and promised them his peace. By this he did not mean a life free from trouble, but an inward calm such as he had. Though outwardly afflicted, inwardly he had peace. The disciples should not have been troubled about Jesus' coming death, but glad that by that death he was bringing to completion the work his Father had given him to do (John 14:27-29). Though sinless and in no way under Satan's power, Jesus would allow Satan's servants to betray and kill him, so that through his death he might fulfil his Father's will and save sinners (John 14:30-31).

145. Union with Jesus (John 15:1-27)

In themselves believers have no life, strength or spiritual power. All that they have comes from Jesus Christ. If he is likened to a vine, they are likened to the branches, which means that they can bear spiritual fruit only as they are united in him. As they allow the Father to remove the hindrances of sin from their lives, they will bear even more fruit (John 15:1-5).

Those who bear no fruit are like the dead branches of a vine. Though attached to it, they receive no life from it. They say they are disciples of Jesus, but they have no spiritual union with him and in the end they will be destroyed. Such a person was Judas Iscariot (John 15:6).

If people are true disciples, they will prove it by the fruits that their spiritual union with Jesus produces. Among those fruits are obedience, love, joy and effective prayer (John 15:7-11). Jesus wants his disciples to serve him willingly, lovingly and with understanding. For this reason he chose the twelve apostles and trained them to know God's ways. If their service is based on a true knowledge of God and the true exercise of self-sacrificing love, they can expect it to result in lasting fruit (John 15:12-17).

Union with Jesus, however, will bring some suffering, because disciples, like their master, will be hated by the world. Loyalty to Jesus will bring persecution (John 15:18-20). Jesus' teaching and work showed clearly that he came from God. Those who heard and saw him had no excuse for not believing him. In fact, their clearer knowledge increased their guilt. They may have claimed to be worshippers of God, but if they hated Jesus they hated God (John 15:21-25).

The apostles also had heard Jesus' words and seen his works, but they had believed. Therefore, they could be assured of the Spirit's help as they witnessed to Jesus during the difficult time that lay ahead (John 15:26-27; cf. Acts 4:8-12; 5:32).

146. Work of the Holy Spirit (John 16:1-15)

As long as Jesus had been with his disciples, the full force of people's opposition had been directed at him, not at them. Now that he was about to leave them, he warned them that this hatred would be turned on them (John 16:1-4). However, because of their grief concerning his coming departure, they scarcely understood his warning. Nor could they see the joy that lay before him in being reunited with his Father (John 16:5-6).

When Jesus departed, the Holy Spirit would come to take Jesus' place with his disciples, to defend them and accuse their opponents. He would show the world to be wrong in three things in particular — sin, righteousness and judgment (John 16:7-8). He would show that sin is the cause of unbelief in Jesus; that Jesus' death is the way to God, a fact that is proved by his resurrection and ascension; and that judgment on sinners is certain because Satan has been conquered by Jesus' death (John 16:9-11).

Jesus could tell his disciples no more at that time, as they were too grief-stricken to take it in. After he left them, the Holy Spirit would instruct them further and help them to understand. The teaching of the Spirit would not be something new, but a development of the teaching they had already heard from Jesus. It would concern both the present and the future (John 16:12-15).

147. Difficulties ahead for the disciples (John 16:16-33)

Within the next twenty-four hours Jesus would be taken from his disciples, but three days later, after his resurrection, they would see him again. Their sorrow would be replaced by joy, just as a woman's pains before giving birth are replaced by joy after the child is born (John 16:16-22). Jesus' victory through death and resurrection would give them a confidence in God that they never had before. They would see Jesus Christ as the mediator through whom they could confidently pray to the Father and thankfully receive the Father's blessings (John 16:23-24).

After his resurrection Jesus would no longer need to speak to the disciples in figurative language, because the resurrection would give them a clearer view of the purpose of his mission. Also, no longer would they depend on Jesus to do their praying for them. They would learn to approach the Father personally and with confidence. Yet even this would be possible only because of who Jesus was and what he had done (John 16:25-28).

The disciples' faith was strengthened by Jesus' words, but they did not realize that a few hours later their faith would be put to the test. Frightened and confused they would forsake their Lord in his final hours. But the lapse would only be temporary; through his victory, they also would triumph (John 16:29-33).

148. Jesus' prayer (John 17:1-26)

Having announced his victory over the world (see John 16:33), Jesus now offers a prayer that reflects the triumph of his completed work. He begins by speaking of his relationship with the Father. Jesus' work was to reveal God to the world so that people might receive eternal life through him. He prays that by dying on the cross and successfully finishing his work, he will bring glory to his Father. At the same time, his death will bring glory to himself, for it will enable him to return to his Father and enjoy the glory that was his before he came into the world (John 17:1-5).

Although most people did not believe in Jesus, some did, such as the apostles. They believed the evidence they saw and heard that Jesus was God and that he had come from the Father to make God known (John 17:6-8).

This thought leads Jesus to the second part of his prayer, which is for his disciples. He prays that they will live in such a way as to show his glory to the world (John 17:9-10). Their unity will display the unity that exists between the Father and the Son. Jesus asks that they will remain faithful to him and not be defeated by the evil that is in the world . He wants them to share with him the triumphant joy that comes through successfully completing the work the Father had committed to him (John 17:11-13).

When Jesus leaves the world, his disciples will carry on his work. He prays therefore that they will be neither discouraged by the world's hatred nor corrupted by its sin (John 17:14-17). Just as Jesus gave himself to God to carry out his work, so he desires his disciples to give themselves to God for the task of spreading his message throughout the world (John 17:18-19).

In the final part of his prayer, Jesus prays for those who will believe through the preaching of that initial group of disciples and so become God's new people, the Christian church. He prays that the same unity as exists between the Father and the Son will bind the believers together, so that through them others too will believe (John 17:20-23). Jesus desires that in the age to come, when he enjoys the glory that was his before the world began, all who have trusted in him will be there with him. Meanwhile, in the present world of unbelief, they will learn more of him as they share in the love that the Father has for the Son. The world will begin to know God when it sees the love of Jesus in his people (John 17:24-26).

149. Disciples' failure foretold (Mt 26:31-35; Mk 14:27-31; Lk 22:24-38; Jn 13:36-38)

Despite all that Jesus had shown and taught his disciples about humility, and in spite of the death he was about to die for them, they were still arguing about who was the greatest among them. Jesus reminded them again of the different standards in the earthly and heavenly kingdoms. He had given them an example in the way he lived among them, showing that true greatness lay in serving others (Luke 22:24-27). They had stood by him in all his trials, and he wanted them to maintain their loyalty through the time of his suffering and death. Their reward would be to share his rule in the triumphant kingdom (Luke 22:28-30).

Jesus knew, however, that they would all run away and leave him in his final hour. They would be like sheep who scatter in panic when the shepherd is killed. Peter boldly assured Jesus that though others might leave him, he would not. But Jesus knew Peter better than Peter knew himself. Peter would deny him, but the experience would teach him lessons that would remove his self-assurance and give him a new strength in God. After Jesus rose from death and returned to the father, Peter would be the one through whom the group of disciples would learn to be confident and courageous (Matt

26:31-35; Luke 22:31-34; John 13:36-38; cf. Acts 4:13-31; 5:17-32).

In figurative language Jesus then told them to prepare for the new life ahead. It would be much tougher than anything they had previously known or experienced; they would have difficulty just in preserving their lives (Luke 22:35-37). The disciples misunderstood Jesus' words, but Jesus felt he had said enough on the matter for the time being, and he left them to think about it (Luke 22:38).

150. Jesus prays in Gethsemane (Mt 26:36-46; Mk 14:32-42; Lk 22:39-46; Jn 18:1)

It must have been getting towards midnight by the time Jesus and his disciples reached the Garden of Gethsemane. Then, taking Peter, James and John with him, Jesus moved to a spot where they could be alone. He was filled with anguish and horror as he saw clearly what his death would mean. The three friends could do little to lessen his anguish except stay awake in sympathy with him. He had to battle against the temptation to avoid the suffering that lay ahead, but the battle was one he had to fight and win alone (Mark 14:32-34; Luke 22:39-40).

The 'cup' of suffering that caused Jesus such distress was not just physical suffering, great though that was. Above all it was the inner agony as the sinless one, God's Son, took upon himself the sin of his human creatures and bore God's wrath on their behalf (cf. 2 Cor 5:21; Heb 2:9; 1 Peter 2:24). It was an experience no one else could know, for no one else had Jesus' sinlessness or shared his relationship with the Father. Jesus had a real human will, and when he considered the ordeal that lay ahead, a conflict arose within him. As he fought against the temptation to avoid the cross, his agony of mind was so intense that he perspired what appeared to be blood. But he won the battle, and determined that he would willingly submit to whatever his Father would have him go through (Mark 14:35-36; Luke 22:41-44).

Perhaps the reason why the disciples were unable to stay awake was not simply that they were over-tired, but that they were unable to withstand the satanic forces at work in the garden. Jesus saw their weakness and urged them to be alert and pray for strength, because they too were going to be put to the test. They would face the temptation to deny Jesus in order to save themselves (Mark 14:37-40; Luke 22:45-46).

Jesus, by contrast, would give himself without reservation, in order to save others. The decisive victory he won in the garden enabled him to meet his betrayal, trial and death with renewed courage and assurance (Mark 14:41-42).

151. The arrest of Jesus (Matt 26:47-56; Mark 14:43-52; Luke 22:47-53; John 18:2-11)

In the strength of the victory won at Gethsemane, Jesus went to meet his enemies. Judas knew the garden, for Jesus had often met there with his apostles. In the middle of the night, Judas took a group of temple guards and Roman soldiers to seize Jesus. By working under the cover of darkness, he kept the operation hidden from any who were likely to be sympathizers with Jesus. But Jesus needed no supporters to defend him, and Judas needed no force to arrest him. The armed men who came with Judas fell to the ground when they met Jesus, but he surrendered himself to them. He requested only that they not harm his friends (Matt 26:47-50; Luke 22:47-48; John 18:2-9).

The apostles, however, wanted to fight. Jesus told them that if they practised violence they would suffer violence. Moreover, if Jesus wanted defenders he could draw upon supernatural forces (Matt 26:51-56a; Luke 22:49-53; John 18:10-11). A scuffle apparently broke out and the apostles all fled. The soldiers managed to grab a young man who had followed Jesus to the garden, but he escaped (Matt 26:56b; Mark 14:51-52).

From early Christian times the common belief has been that the young man of this story was Mark, the author of the Gospel of Mark. It appears that his family home was the house of the upper room (where Jesus had just come from) and that it became a common meeting place for the apostles in the early days of the church (see Mark 14:14-15; Acts 1:12-14; 2:1; 12:12).

152. At the high priest's house (Mt 26:57-75; Mk 14:53-72; Lk 22:54-65; Jn 18:12-27)

Annas and his son-in-law Caiaphas apparently lived in the same house. Annas had been the previous high priest and, though replaced by Caiaphas, was still well respected and influential. Jesus' captors took him to Annas first, while Peter and John, who had followed at a distance, waited in the courtyard. By now it was well past midnight and into the early hours of the morning (John 18:12-18; Luke 22:54).

When Annas asked Jesus questions about his teaching, Jesus replied that it was known to all. He had no need to testify on his own behalf (contrary to Jewish law) when many other witnesses could be called in. After being ill-treated for giving an honest and unanswerable reply, he was sent to Caiaphas (John 18:19-24).

Caiaphas had called the Sanhedrin together, determined to condemn Jesus without delay, even though it was illegal for the Sanhedrin to meet at night to judge an offence that carried the death sentence. The Jewish leaders' whole purpose was to get some statement from Jesus that they could use to charge him with blasphemy and so condemn him to death (Matt 26:57-63; Mark 14:53-61). They were soon satisfied when Jesus said he was the Messiah, the Son of God and the Son of man, and he was on the way to receiving the glorious kingdom given him by God (Matt 26:64; Mark 14:62; see earlier section, 'Jesus and the Kingdom'). With an outburst of violent abuse the Jewish leaders condemned him as worthy of death (Matt 26:65-68; Mark 14:63-65).

While Jesus was before Caiaphas and the other Jewish leaders inside the building, Peter sat in the courtyard, waiting anxiously. When a servant girl recognized him as a follower of Jesus, he denied any association with him (Matt 26:69-70; Luke 22:55-57). A little later another person recognized him and told the people standing by, but again he disowned Jesus, this time with an oath (Matt 26:71-72; Luke 22:58).

About an hour later some of the bystanders approached Peter again, convinced he was a follower of Jesus, but Peter's denial was even stronger than before. The crowing of a cock indicated to all that daylight was approaching. It also reminded Peter of his folly in boasting that he could never fail. Just then Jesus happened to see Peter in the courtyard, and as their eyes met Peter was overcome with grief and went away weeping bitterly (Matt 26:73-75; cf. v. 31-35; Luke 22:59-62; cf. v. 31-34).

153. The Sanhedrin's judgment (Matt 27:1-2; Mark 15:1; Luke 22:66-71)

It had been a long night for Jesus — the Passover meal, the institution of the Lord's Supper, the washing of the disciples' feet, the lengthy teaching in the upper room, the walk to Gethsemane, the agonizing time in the garden, the arrest, the walk back to the city, and the questioning and rough handling at the high priest's house. It was now daybreak, which meant that a legal sentence could be passed. Jesus therefore was made to stand before the Sanhedrin for a brief repetition of the investigation just concluded (Matt 27:1; Luke 22:66-71). The Jewish leaders could then make a formal charge against him to present to the Roman authorities. In doing so, they had to convince the Roman governor that the accused person deserved execution (Matt 27:2).

154. Death of Judas (Matt 27:3-10)

Judas knew he had done wrong in betraying Jesus. He showed no repentance or desire to correct this wrong, but before he committed suicide he made an effort to ease his guilty conscience by returning the money. The priests had not hesitated to use temple money in paying Judas to bring about Jesus' death, but now they tried to appear righteous by refusing to put the money into the temple treasury (Matt 27:3-6).

In the meantime Judas went out into a field, tied a rope around his neck and hanged himself. It seems that in doing so he injured himself internally and his stomach burst. When the body was found in the field, the priests used Judas' returned money to buy the field in his name. Originally it was known as Potter's Field, but later it was called Field of Blood and was used as a cemetery for Gentiles (Matt 27:7-10; cf. Acts 1:18-19).

155. Before Pilate and Herod (Mt 27:11-14; Mk 15:2-5; Lk 23:1-12; Jn 18:28-38)

Pilate, the governor of the area, usually lived in the provincial capital Caesarea, but he came to Jerusalem during Jewish festivals to help maintain order. His official residence and administration centre in Jerusalem was called the praetorium. The Jewish leaders, wanting to have Jesus dealt with and out of the way before the festival started, took him to Pilate early in the morning (Luke 23:1; John 18:28-29).

The Jews had charged Jesus with blasphemy for calling himself the Son of God, but when they took him to Pilate they twisted the charge. They emphasized not that he claimed to be God but that he claimed to be above Caesar. They suggested he was a political rebel trying to lead a messianic uprising that would overthrow Roman rule and set up an independent Jewish state (Luke 23:2). Pilate tried to dismiss the case, but the Jews would not drop their charges (John 18:30-32).

Jesus then gave Pilate the true picture. He explained that his kingdom was not concerned with political power, and had nothing to do with national uprisings. It was a spiritual kingdom and it was based on truth. Pilate did not grasp the full meaning of Jesus' explanation, but he understood enough to be convinced that Jesus was not a political rebel. He suspected that the Jews had handed him over for judgment because they were jealous of his religious

following (Matt 27:11-14,18; Luke 23:3-5; John 18:33-38).

When Pilate learnt that Jesus was from Galilee, which was not under his control, he tried to avoid the issue by sending Jesus to the Galilean governor Herod, who also was in Jerusalem for the festival (Luke 23:6-7). But Jesus refused to speak to Herod, and made no attempt to defend himself against the false accusations the Jewish leaders made against him. After mocking him cruelly, Herod sent him back to Pilate (Luke 23:8-12).

156. Jesus before the people (Mt 27:15-31; Mk 15:6-20; Lk 23:13-25; Jn 18:39-19:16)

Although assured that Jesus was innocent, Pilate felt it wise to give the Jews some satisfaction; for by this time a crowd had gathered and he did not want a riot to break out. He therefore offered to punish Jesus by flogging, and consider the matter finished (Luke 23:13-16).

But the people yelled for Jesus to be crucified. Pilate did not want the situation to get out of control, so made another offer. He agreed to accept the Jews' accusation of Jesus' guilt, but he offered to give Jesus the special pardon reserved for one criminal each Passover season (Matt 27:15-18).

By this time the priests scattered throughout the crowd had the people under their power. They quickly spread the word that the prisoner they wanted released was not Jesus, but Barabbas, a rebel who had once taken a leading part in a local anti-Rome uprising (see Mark 15:7; Luke 23:19). Pilate, unaware of the influence of the priests in the crowd and thinking that Jesus had widespread support, agreed to allow the crowd to choose between the two, no doubt thinking they would choose Jesus. As he waited for them to make their choice, his wife sent him a warning not to condemn Jesus (Matt 27:19-20).

If supporters of Jesus were in the crowd, they were a minority. People in general were more likely to support a nationalist like Barabbas. Finally, they succeeded in having Barabbas released and Jesus condemned to be crucified. They accepted responsibility for this decision and called down God's judgment upon them and their children if they were wrong (a judgment that possibly fell on them with the destruction of Jerusalem in AD 70). Jesus was then taken and flogged as the first step towards crucifixion (Matt 27:21-26; Luke 23:18-25; John 18:39-40; 19:1).

While some soldiers were preparing for the execution, those in Pilate's palace cruelly made fun of Jesus. They mocked him as 'king' by putting some old soldiers clothes on him for a royal robe and thorns on his head for a crown. They hit him over the head with a stick that was supposed to be his sceptre, and spat in his face and punched him as mock signs of homage (Matt 27:27-31; John 19:2-3).

Pilate showed this pitiful figure to the crowd, apparently hoping it might make them feel ashamed and change their minds; but it only increased their hatred (John 19:4-6). Pilate became more uneasy when he heard that Jesus claimed to be the Son of God. Maybe, thought Pilate, this man was one of the gods. He became even more anxious to set Jesus free when Jesus told him that God would hold him responsible for the way he used his authority. Pilate was guilty for condemning a man he knew was innocent, but Caiaphas and the other Jews who handed Jesus over to him were more guilty (John 19:7-11).

Again Pilate tried to release Jesus, but the Jews reminded him that he himself could be in danger if he released a person guilty of treason. This disturbed Pilate further, and after a final offer that the Jews rejected, he handed Jesus over to be crucified. The Jews' declaration of loyalty to Caesar demonstrated their hypocrisy and confirmed their rejection of God (John 19:12-16).

157. Journey to Golgotha (Matt 27:32; Mark 15:21; Luke 23:26-31; John 19:17)

As the prisoners set out for the place of execution, Jesus was made to carry his cross (John 19:17). He must have been weak from the brutal flogging, and when it appeared he was about to collapse, a passer-by was forced to carry it for him. This man, Simon, was from northern Africa and had apparently come to Jerusalem for the Passover (Luke 23:26).

Among the crowd that followed Jesus were some women who wept and wailed at the dreadful sight. Jesus told them not to weep because of what they saw happening to him. One day they also would suffer. When the Romans later attacked Jerusalem, women now sad because they had no children would be better off than others, for they would not have to witness their children being slaughtered. If Rome crucified an innocent man such as Jesus, how brutal would they be in dealing with people guilty of open rebellion (Luke 23:27-31).

158. The crucifixion (Matt 27:33-44; Mark 15:22-32; Luke 23:32-43; John 19:18-24)

Golgotha, the place of Jesus' crucifixion, was a hill beside a main road just outside Jerusalem. The

procession arrived there about 9 a.m. (Matt 27:33; Mark 15:25). (It is difficult to calculate the exact times of all the incidents that took place on the day of Jesus' crucifixion. People in those days did not carry clocks, and the times given in the Gospels are only approximate. In some cases the writers may have estimated their times at different stages of the same event. Also, they may have used different methods of reckoning. Matthew, Mark and Luke usually count the hours from 6 a.m. and 6 p.m., but John seems to reckon differently.)

Great though Jesus' suffering was, his agony of spirit was greater. He was bearing the burden of human sin, and thereby was conquering Satan and releasing people from the power of sin and death. He was determined to face death at its worst, fully conscious of what he was going through. Therefore, he refused the offer of drugged wine intended to deaden the pain and dull the mind (Matt 27:34).

Meanwhile, the four soldiers who carried out the crucifixion threw dice to decide how they would divide Jesus' personal possessions. Above his head they attached a sign announcing the charge for which he was condemned, so that those who passed by could read it. As he hung there, Jesus had insults thrown at him by the common people, by members of the Sanhedrin (who came to see their sentence carried out), and by the two criminals crucified with him. All mocked with the same theme — he claimed to save others but he could not save himself. This was true, though not in the sense the mockers intended; for only by willingly sacrificing himself could he save guilty sinners (Matt 27:35-44; Luke 23:32-39; John 19:18-24). One of the criminals, realizing this, repented and experienced the saving power of Jesus that very day (Luke 23:40-43).

159. The death (Matt 27:45-56; Mark 15:33-41; Luke 23:44-49; John 19:25-37)

Jesus' mother, Mary, had followed him to the cross and stayed by him during his ordeal. Among those who comforted her were John and three women: Mary's sister Salome, who was the wife of Zebedee and the mother of the apostles James and John; another Mary, who was the wife of Clopas and the mother of James and Joses; and another Mary, who came from the town of Magdala in Galilee and was known as Mary Magdalene. These women had at first stood away from the cross, but later came and stood nearby (Matt 27:55-56; Mark 15:40-41; Luke 23:49; John 19:25-27).

From the time the soldiers began the crucifixion to the time Jesus died was about six hours (cf Mark

15:25,33). During the last three hours (from noon to 3 p.m.) a strange darkness covered the land, as the wrath of God against sin fell upon Jesus. For this reason he was separated, for the only time, from the Father with whom he had enjoyed unbroken fellowship from all eternity. Sin separates from God, and in bearing the penalty of sin, Jesus experienced that desolation (Matt 27:45-49; Luke 23:44-45).

Nevertheless, at the very time he suffered such desolation, Jesus was in harmony with his Father's will. He wanted his final words to his Father to be loud enough for all to hear, and therefore he asked for something to moisten his dry mouth. The words he spoke made known to all that he was placing his spirit in his Father's hands. His final cry of triumph, 'It is finished', confirmed that even in his death he was still in control. No one took his life from him; he gave it up in a voluntary, unique act. He had completed the work that his Father sent him to do (Matt 27:50; Luke 23:46; John 19:28-30).

At the moment of Jesus' death (about 3 p.m.) there was an earthquake in the Jerusalem area. In the temple the curtain that blocked entrance into the symbolic presence of God was torn in two. It was a striking demonstration that Jesus had brought the Jewish religious system to an end and opened the way for all into God's presence. The earthquake also caused graves to break open, and certain believers of the old era were raised to life, indicating dramatically that Jesus' death was the way to final triumph over death itself (Matt 27:51-53; cf. 1 Cor 15:20-26; Heb 2:14-15).

Another truth illustrated by the remarkable events connected with Jesus' death was that he was the true Passover lamb. He died on the afternoon of Passover day, at the same time as the Jews back in Jerusalem were killing their lambs in preparation for the meal that night. And because he was the true Passover lamb, not a bone in his body was broken. Normally, the soldiers broke the victims' legs to hasten their death, but they had no need to do this to Jesus, because he was already dead. Instead, one of the soldiers plunged his spear deep into Jesus' body (John 19:31-37).

In contrast to the lack of feeling shown by most of the soldiers, the centurion in charge of the execution was filled with wonder at what he saw. He was convinced that Jesus was all he claimed to be (Matt 27:54; Luke 23:47).

Others also changed their attitudes to Jesus because of the events at Golgotha. Many who had come from Jerusalem as spectators returned in sorrow and fear, wondering what it all meant (Luke 23:48).

160. The burial (Mt 27:57-66; Mk 15:42-47; Lk 23:50-56; Jn 19:38-42)

Two members of the Sanhedrin did not agree with the decision to crucify Jesus. They were Nicodemus (cf. John 3:1-12; 7:45-52) and Joseph, the latter being a man from the Judean town of Arimathea. Joseph, like many rich people, had built a fine tomb to be used one day for himself, but he sacrificed it so that Jesus could have an honourable burial. The two men took the body down from the cross late on the Friday afternoon (cf. Deut 21:22-23), and prepared it for burial by wrapping it in cloth with spices. They then laid it in Joseph's tomb. The women who went to the tomb with Joseph and Nicodemus hurried home to prepare more spices and ointments before the Sabbath day of rest (Mark 15:42-47; Luke 23:50-56; John 19:38-42).

At the request of the Jewish leaders, Pilate set a guard of Roman soldiers at the tomb to ensure that no one could remove Jesus' body. In view of Jesus' predictions of resurrection, the Jews wanted to make sure that the tomb was closed securely and sealed against any interference (Matt 27:62-66).

RESURRECTION AND ASCENSION

161. Morning of the resurrection (Mt 28:1-15; Mk 16:1-11; Lk 24:1-12; Jn 20:1-18)

It is not surprising that there are differences in the accounts of what people saw on the Sunday morning when Jesus rose from the dead. The sight of the empty tomb and the heavenly messengers produced a mixture of reactions — excitement, joy, anxiety, fear, wonder. There was confusion as people rushed here and there to tell others. One writer records what he heard from some, another what he heard from others. But there is no variation in the basic facts: the tomb was empty and Jesus had risen. The following summary suggests the possible order of events.

1. At the first sign of dawn two groups of women set out from separate places to take spices to anoint the body of Jesus. One group consisted of three women (Mary Magdalene, Mary the mother of James and Joses, and Salome the mother of the apostles James and John). The other group consisted of Joanna and some friends (Matt 28:1; Mark 16:1-3; Luke 24:1,10).

2. The group of three women arrived at the tomb first and found the stone rolled away. Mary Magdalene panicked and, without seeing the

angel or hearing the voice, ran to tell Peter and John that the body had been stolen (John 20:1-2). But the other Mary and Salome remained. They met one angel sitting on the stone outside the tomb, and another sitting inside the tomb. Upon hearing that Jesus had risen and desired to be reunited with his disciples in Galilee, they rushed off to the place where the apostles were gathered, eager to pass on the exciting news (Matt 28:2-7; Mark 16:4-8).

3. Meanwhile the Roman guards fled the tomb and hurried across the city to tell the chief priests what had happened. These priests were the ones who had set the guard in the first place, and their purpose was to prevent Jesus' followers from stealing the body. Now the same priests bribed the guards to spread the story that Jesus' followers stole the body while the guards slept. The priests had earlier been worried that Jesus' disciples might deceive people, but now they themselves were the deceivers (Matt 28:11-13; cf. 27:62-66). If Pilate heard the story of the guards sleeping on duty, the Jewish leaders promised to protect them by bribing Pilate (Matt 28:14-15).

4. Back at the tomb, a few minutes after the first group of women had departed, Joanna and her friends arrived. They went inside, met two angels, heard the news of Jesus' resurrection, and hurried off to tell the apostles (Luke 24:2-8).

5. Soon after the women left the tomb, Peter and John arrived, went inside and saw the linen cloth lying neatly folded. They believed the evidence they saw that Jesus must have risen from the dead, but they left the tomb confused, not understanding the significance of the event (John 20:3-10; Luke 24:12).

6. Mary Magdalene, who followed Peter and John back to the tomb, arrived after they had left. She remained there alone, weeping. Then she saw the two angels inside the tomb and, on turning round, saw a man whom she did not immediately recognize (Mark 16:9; John 20:11-15). When she discovered that the man was Jesus, she took hold of him as if not wanting to let him go. Jesus told her she had no need to cling to him in this way, as he was not ascending to heaven immediately (though he would within a few weeks). She should not become dependent on his physical presence, otherwise she would be disappointed again. She was to go and tell the apostles what he had told her (John 20:16-17).

7. Shortly after appearing to Mary Magdalene, Jesus appeared to the other women of her group (the other Mary and Salome) as they were on their way to tell the apostles of their discovery (Matt 28:8-10).

8. The two groups of women reached the house of the apostles about the same time, followed soon after by Mary Magdalene. They told the apostles of what they had seen at the tomb and of their separate meetings with the risen Jesus, but the apostles believed neither Mary nor the other women (Mark 16:10-11; Luke 24:9-11; John 20:18). (All the events summarized in sections 1 to 8 above probably happened within the space of an hour or so.)

162. On the road to Emmaus (Mark 16:12-13; Luke 24:13-35)

That afternoon Jesus joined two sorrowful disciples who were walking from Jerusalem to the village of Emmaus, but they did not recognize him (Mark 16:12; Luke 24:13-16). When they started to explain their sadness, they expressed surprise that their unknown companion had not heard about the crucifixion of Jesus. Their understanding of Jesus' mission was not very clear, for they had hoped he would bring national liberation to Israel; but they believed in him nevertheless, and they condemned the leaders of the Jews for crucifying him (Luke 24:17-21). Furthermore, they had heard first-hand reports from those who saw the empty tomb and heard the angels' announcements of his resurrection (Luke 24:22-24).

Jesus then gave the two disciples a proper understanding of the Messiah and his mission, by referring them to the Scriptures. He showed that the Old Testament consistently pointed to a Saviour-Messiah who had to suffer before he could enter his glory. The death and resurrection of Jesus brought to completion the pattern that God had been working through the history of his people (Luke 24:25-27).

When almost at Emmaus, Jesus and the two disciples stopped for their evening meal. As Jesus gave thanks and broke the bread to begin the meal, the disciples suddenly recognized who he was. He immediately disappeared from their sight, such was the mysterious nature of his resurrection body (Luke 24:28-31). The two disciples were deeply stirred by his teaching and, without waiting to rest their weary bodies, hurried back the twelve kilometres to Jerusalem to tell the apostles and other disciples of their discovery. In the meantime Peter also had met the risen Jesus (Mark 16:13; Luke 24:32-35; cf. 1 Cor 15:5).

163. Sunday night in Jerusalem (Mark 16:14; Luke 24:36-49; John 20:19-23)

While the disciples were together discussing these miraculous appearances, Jesus suddenly appeared among them in the room, even though the doors were locked. This made them think they were seeing a ghost who could pass through walls, but Jesus calmed their fears by showing them his body of flesh and bones, complete with the scars of crucifixion. He also ate some fish, showing that his body had normal physical functions (Luke 24:36-43; John 20:19-20).

Jesus gave the group of disciples the teaching he had given the two on the road to Emmaus (Luke 24:44-46). They were witnesses of his ministry, death and resurrection, and he entrusted to them the task of taking his message to all nations. Equipped by his Spirit, they would be his representatives in the world. This was a great responsibility, because as they preached the gospel, people would either believe it and be forgiven, or reject it and suffer judgment (Luke 24:47-49; John 20:21-23).

164. One week later (John 20:24-31)

Thomas had been absent when Jesus appeared among the disciples in the locked room, and refused to accept the word of the others that he was alive (John 20:24-25). His doubts vanished when Jesus appeared among the disciples (this time including Thomas) in the same locked room the next Sunday night. But faith that depended on seeing Jesus' actual body was not good enough, because soon he would return to his Father and people would no longer see him (John 20:26-29). However, they could still hear the preaching of his disciples or read their written records. Through believing in Jesus as the Messiah, the Son of God, they could have eternal life (John 20:30-31).

Note: In Bible times people had various ways of counting the number of days in a specified period. Often they included both the day on which the period began and the day on which it concluded. In discussing events on two consecutive Sundays, most people today would refer to the second as being 'a week later' (John 20:26 GNB, NIV), but many in Bible times would refer to it as being 'eight days later' (John 20:26 RSV), because they counted both Sundays. By the same reckoning, Jesus was in the tomb three days (Friday, Saturday, Sunday), though the actual time was probably about thirty-six hours (from about 6 p.m. Friday to 6 a.m. Sunday).

165. At the Sea of Tiberias (John 21:1-25)

The disciples then returned to Galilee to wait for Jesus as they had been instructed (see Matt 26:32;

28:10). Seven of them had spent an unsuccessful night fishing on Lake Galilee (the Sea of Tiberias) when Jesus appeared at the shore. He called out some directions to them, and although they did not recognize him they did as he said. As a result they caught a large number of fish (John 21:1-6).

No doubt some of the disciples recalled a similar incident years earlier, and this may have led John to recognize the person on the shore as Jesus (cf. Luke 5:1-11). The disciples were reminded again of the authority of Jesus and their dependence on him (John 21:7-9). They were reminded also of his care for them, as he prepared and served them breakfast (John 21:10-14).

Peter had once boasted that he loved Jesus more than the other disciples did, and that although they might fail him, he would not (see Mark 14:29). Yet three times he publicly disowned Jesus. Three times, therefore, he was asked publicly if he loved Jesus, as a reminder to him of the danger of over-confidence. Jesus' public conversation with Peter also showed the others that he had forgiven him. More than that he gave Peter the responsibility to care for his people through the difficult days of the church's beginning (cf. Luke 22:31-32). As a leader in that early group, receiving the full force of Jewish persecution, Peter would need more love for Jesus than the others (John 21:15-17).

If Peter was to follow Jesus, he would no longer be free to live the independent life of an energetic young fisherman. His life would be one of constant sacrifice and hard work in caring for Jesus' people. In the end he would be captured and killed on account of his loyalty to Jesus (John 21:18-19; cf. 13:36).

As for John, Jesus refused to give any indication of how his life would end. Some misinterpreted this to mean that John would never die, so John added a note at the end of his book to correct the misunderstanding (John 21:20-23). He also pointed out that he had made no attempt to give a detailed account of the life of Jesus; but what he had given was the testimony of an eye witness, and it was to be believed (John 21:24-25).

166. On a mountain in Galilee (Matt 28:16-20; Mark 16:15-18)

The apostles had an indication why Jesus had told them to go to Galilee when he took them up one of the mountains. From there they could look out to the next stage of the kingdom's mission, the Gentile nations beyond. The three and a half years public ministry of Jesus had been limited to Israel (cf. Matt 10:5-6; 15:24; Rom 15:8), but the ministry that the risen Jesus now passed on to his disciples extended to all nations without distinction. His power would be in his disciples, preserving them through dangers and enabling them to perform remarkable works (Matt 28:16-17; Mark 16:15-18).

Jesus' purpose in this activity was to establish his church (cf. Matt 16:18), as his followers preached the gospel, baptized those who believed, and taught the converts to understand and follow his teachings. As the converts, in turn, passed the message on to others, the church would continue its worldwide expansion, assured always that the victorious Jesus was working with his people (Matt 28:18-20).

167. The ascension (Mark 16:19-20; Luke 24:50-53)

From Jesus' resurrection to his ascension was about six weeks, and during that time he gave his disciples further teaching on the kingdom of God (Acts 1:3). The overall content of that teaching is probably represented by the summary attached to the story of his first Sunday night appearance to the disciples. He showed them how his ministry on earth was the climax of God's Old Testament purposes and the starting point for worldwide expansion through his followers. A clear understanding of God's purposes, together with their own eye witness accounts of Jesus' death and resurrection, would give them confidence in taking the gospel to others (see Luke 24:44-49; Acts 1:8).

When the time arrived for Jesus to leave his disciples and return to his Father, the disciples were no longer confused but confident. Again Jesus was to be taken from them, but this time instead of fleeing in fear and distress, they accompanied him to the place chosen for his departure. From near Bethany, the village on the slopes of Mount Olivet just outside Jerusalem, Jesus left his disciples, with the promise that one day he would return (Mark 16:19; Luke 24:50-51; cf. Acts 1:9-12).

The disciples returned to Jerusalem praising God, and a few days later received the Holy Spirit as Jesus had promised. They began their task of preaching the good news about Jesus and multitudes believed. Their risen Lord was working with them (Mark 16:20; Luke 24:52-53; cf. Acts 2:1-4,41-47; 4:10-12).

Acts

INTRODUCTION

Acts is an important book for our understanding of the origins and growth of the early church. Its longer title, The Acts of the Apostles, reflects the prominence of the apostles Peter and John in the early days of the church, and the prominence of the apostle Paul in the subsequent expansion of the church into the Gentile world. The book is important also for our understanding of the writings of the New Testament as a whole. Paul's earlier letters all belong to the period of Acts, and present-day readers will understand even the remaining letters of the New Testament better when they are familiar with Acts.

The writer of Acts

Early Christian records, including the record within the Bible itself, indicate that Luke wrote the book of Acts. The book was the second of two volumes that Luke wrote, the first being Luke's Gospel. Luke wrote for a person of some importance named Theophilus, to give him a trustworthy account of Christianity from the birth of its founder to the arrival of its greatest apostle in Rome (Luke 1:1-4; Acts 1:1-2).

Luke was a doctor by profession (Col 4:14), but he became also a skilled historian. Secular historians acknowledge him as a reliable writer, whose record is a valuable source of information on a period that changed the course of world history. He carefully dated the beginning of his story according to well known events in secular history (Luke 1:5; 2:1-2; 3:1-2), and the findings of archaeology confirm the exactness of the technical words he used in relation to places and officials (Acts 13:7; 16:12,35; 18:12,16; 19:31,35).

Parts of Acts are Luke's eye-witness accounts, indicated by his use of 'we' and 'us' in some of the narratives. On two of Paul's missionary journeys he spent some time travelling with Paul (Acts 16:10-12; 20:5-6,13; 21:1,7,17), and he accompanied Paul on the journey to Rome that concludes the book (Acts 27:1-3; 28:16; cf. Philem 23-24).

From the title of honour that Luke uses in addressing Theophilus, it seems that Theophilus might have been a high ranking official in the Roman government (Luke 1:3; cf. Acts 23:26; 26:25). Whether he was or not, there is no doubt that at the time Luke wrote (in the early AD 60s) the Roman government was paying increasing attention to Christianity. Luke was therefore concerned to point out that Christianity was in no way rebellious to Roman rule and was not a threat to law and order. To understand why such a defence of Christianity was necessary, we should first consider the circumstances of the Roman Empire in which the Christians lived.

Emperor worship

During the last century of the pre-Christian era, Rome had spread its power far and wide, but this did not immediately produce the Roman Empire as we know it in the New Testament. After the assassination of Julius Caesar in 44 BC, Rome went through a disastrous time of civil war, political confusion and social upheaval. Thousands of people were poor and without work, and lawlessness was widespread. Corruption flourished among government officials, and ambitious army generals were constantly plotting for more power.

Then, in 27 BC, arose one man who was able firstly to control, then to correct, the disorders. He became the first ruler of what became known as the Roman Empire, and he took the name of Caesar Augustus (Luke 2:1). He was so honoured by the people that the rulers of the Roman Empire after him took his name, Caesar, as the title of the Emperor (Luke 3:1; 20:22; Acts 25:11,25).

The people were so thankful for the peace and order that Augustus brought that they praised him in language usually used only for the gods. From this arose Emperor worship, which became the official religion of the Empire. The government allowed other religions, but those religions had first to be officially registered. Nevertheless, all people had to offer worship to the Emperor's image, even if they belonged to one of the other (registered) religions. The only exception concerned the Jews. The Roman authorities did not force Jews to join in Emperor worship, because they knew that Jews would never bow to any idol. As long as the Roman authorities thought that Christianity was part of the Jewish religion, they took no action against the Christians. But once they saw that it was a new religion, different from Judaism and therefore outside the law, they persecuted the Christians cruelly.

Roman citizenship

Originally, a Roman citizen was an inhabitant of Rome, whose citizens were given special privileges by the Emperor. Later, the government extended Roman citizenship to people of other cities and provinces, as well as to people who had given outstanding service to the Empire. Some people were able to buy Roman citizenship. People could have Roman citizenship even if they were not of Roman blood, and this citizenship passed on to their children (Acts 22:28).

Roman citizens could not lawfully be bound or beaten by local judges or officials, nor could they be executed without a verdict from a general meeting of the people. If they were not satisfied with the justice they received, they could appeal direct to the Emperor (Acts 16:37; 22:25-29; 25:11).

Communications

There was much trade and travel between the provinces of the Roman Empire. Government officials, businessmen and soldiers went to all parts of the Empire to promote trade and maintain peace. They usually settled in towns that the Romans called colonies. These were towns established as centres of Roman life in a non-Roman world, and their citizens enjoyed the right of self-government and the privileges of Roman citizenship. Among these Roman colonies were Pisidian Antioch, Lystra, Troas, Corinth and Philippi (Acts 16:12).

These and other important towns were linked to each other and to Rome by a system of roads that the Romans built throughout their Empire. The early Christian missionaries chose important towns along these roads as centres for the extension of the gospel. Once strong churches were established in these centres, the gospel would quickly spread to other places along the roads and in the regions round about.

The Greek language, which had become widely used during the time of the Greek Empire, was now the most commonly spoken language of the Roman Empire. This helped considerably towards the rapid spread of Christianity to the peoples of many nations. Local people of different regions continued to speak their own languages (the Jews of Palestine, for example, spoke Aramaic, a language related to Hebrew), but they usually spoke Greek as well (cf. Mark 5:41; 15:34; John 19:20; Acts 14:11; 22:2).

Greek was also the language most widely used for reading and writing. The New Testament was written in Greek — not the classical Greek of the scholars, but the common Greek of the ordinary people. Yet it was still a rich and powerful language, well suited to be the means by which God made known his purposes to the world.

Jews in the Roman Empire

Over the centuries Jews had become scattered throughout the lands of the Roman Empire. Some of these had migrated in search of better commercial opportunities, and others had fled as refugees in times of oppression. Then there were those who had been taken captive to foreign lands by conquerors such as Babylon, and those who had moved elsewhere when given permission by overlords such as Persia. They were known as 'the Jews of the Dispersion' or 'the scattered Jews' (John 7:35; James 1:1; 1 Peter 1:1; cf. 2 Kings 15:29; 17:6; 24:14-15; 25:11; Ezra 1:1-4).

Because they and their ancestors had lived in other countries so long, most of these Jews spoke only Greek. They had no knowledge of Palestinian languages such as Hebrew and Aramaic. However, they maintained their Jewish identity and unity through following the religion of their ancestors. Wherever they lived they built synagogues as centres for worship, teaching and supervision of Jewish affairs in general (Luke 4:16-17,31-33; 12:11; Acts 13:14; 17:1; 18:7-8). They kept the traditions of the law of Moses and went to Jerusalem for various ceremonies and festivals (John 5:1; 7:1-3).

Many Gentiles were attracted by the high moral standards of the Jewish religion and often joined in the synagogue services. Some were even circumcised and baptized as Jews, and so became known as proselytes, or converts to Judaism (Acts 2:10-11; 6:5). Most, however, did not become full proselytes, preferring simply to attend the synagogue, listen to the teaching, and keep certain sabbath and food laws. These were called God-fearers, or worshippers of God (Acts 10:1-2; 16:14). Many of these Gentiles, having already a knowledge of God and a desire to worship him, readily became Christians when they first heard the gospel of Jesus Christ (Acts 13:43; 14:1; 17:4).

God's true people

Throughout his book Luke made it clear to Theophilus that Christians, not the followers of Judaism, were the true people of God. Christianity was not an illegal religion, but the legitimate continuation of the religion established by Abraham and developed through Moses, David and the Israelite nation (Acts 2:31-33; 13:26-33; 15:15-18; 26:22-23; 28:23).

This progression from the old era to the new, from the Jewish age to the Christian, came about through Jesus Christ. He was God's Saviour for the world, the Messiah of whom the Jewish religion spoke and for whom it prepared the way (Acts 2:36; 3:18; 9:22; 17:3; 18:5,28). Though he had physically left the world and returned to his heavenly Father, he was in a sense still in the world. Through the Holy Spirit he lived within his followers, the Christians, and through them he continued to work (Acts 1:4-5; 2:33; 3:6,16; 4:30-31; 5:31-32). The growth of the church was the ongoing work of the living Christ, acting by his Spirit through his followers (Acts 8:39; 9:17,31; 10:19,45; 13:2,4; 15:28; 16:7-7).

Christians were people who cared for others. They brought help and healing to those who were sick, distressed, lonely, and poor (Acts 3:2-6; 5:15-16; 9:32-41; 11:28-29; 14:8-10; 28:7-9). They may have been involved at times in civil disturbances, but Luke pointed out by one example after another that they were never the trouble-makers. Consistently the Roman authorities declared the Christians to be innocent (Acts 16:37-39; 18:12-16; 19:31,37; 23:29; 25:18; 26:31-32; 28:30-31). In almost every case where there was trouble involving the Christians, the Jews were to blame (Acts 9:23,29; 13:50; 14:2,5,19; 17:5,13; 18:12-17; 21:27).

Luke's entire story emphasized the triumph of the Christian gospel and the life-giving blessings it brought for all people, regardless of race. The first part of the story had concluded with the triumphant return of the risen Christ to his heavenly Father (Luke 24:50-53). The second part begins at the same point (Acts 1:1-11) and shows how, in only thirty years, Christianity grew from a handful of believers in Jerusalem to a vast community that brought new life and hope to Asia Minor, eastern Europe, and even to Rome itself (Acts 28:31).

OUTLINE

1:1-2:47 BIRTH OF THE CHURCH

The task ahead (1:1-11)

Theophilus, to whom the book is addressed, was apparently a person of influence to whom Luke wished to give a reliable account of the origins and development of Christianity. In his Gospel, Luke had told Theophilus of what Jesus began to do through his life, death and resurrection (1:1-2; cf. Luke 1:1-4). Luke now goes on to tell Theophilus what Jesus continued to do through his followers.

On the occasions when Jesus appeared to his apostles after his resurrection, he taught them the significance of his death and resurrection in relation to the kingdom of God that they were now to proclaim. They would be able to begin this work within a few days, after Jesus returned to his heavenly Father and sent them the gift of his Spirit as he had promised (3-4; cf. John 14:26; 15:26; 16:7; Mark 1:8).

The apostles, thinking more about possible political independence for Israel than about their responsibility to preach the gospel, misunderstood Jesus' words. Jesus told them not to spend time thinking about things that God did not intend them to know, but to go and tell people everywhere that he was alive and triumphant. Jesus would no longer be with them physically, but through the Spirit he would come and live in them to enable them to carry on the work that he had started (5-8; cf. John 14:12,16-18). He would make no more appearances to the apostles for the time being, but some time in the future he would return to be physically with his people again (9-11).

Jesus' plan for the expansion of the gospel was that it spread out in ever widening circles — from Jerusalem into the surrounding province, then into neighbouring regions, and eventually into every part of the world (v. 8). The book of Acts shows how the work started in Jerusalem (Chapters 1-7), expanded through Judea, Samaria and Syria (Chapters 8-12), and kept on moving out till it reached the heart of the Empire (Chapters 13-28).

A replacement for Judas (1:12-26)

After Jesus' departure, the apostles returned to Jerusalem, where they met and prayed with various people, among them Jesus' mother and brothers. During the time of Jesus' ministry, his brothers had not believed in him as the Son of God, but the resurrection must have turned them to true faith (12-14; cf. John 7:5; 1 Cor 15:7).

Soon after, the apostles met with just over a hundred other Christians in Jerusalem to choose an apostle to replace Judas. Luke adds a note outlining how Judas had died. When Judas returned the betrayal money to the priests, the priests felt they could not put the money into the temple treasury, so used it to buy a field in Judas' name. This field was the place where Judas killed himself, and later it became a cemetery for Gentiles (15-20; see Matt 27:3-10).

The replacement apostle had to be an eye witness of the events of Jesus' public ministry, and particularly of his resurrection. Two were found, equally qualified and apparently equally suitable. The apostles therefore laid the matter before God in complete faith, believing that if they drew lots to decide between the two, the result would indicate God's choice (21-26).

Apostles and their duties

The word 'apostle' meant 'a sent one'. Jesus gave the name to his chosen twelve because he sent them out, equipped with his messianic powers, to spread the message of the kingdom (Matt 10:1-7; Luke 6:13). They were to spread the message throughout Israel first (Matt 10:5-7), as preparation for the worldwide mission to follow (Matt 28:19-20). The significance of the number twelve was that just as twelve tribes had been the basis of the old people of God, so twelve apostles would be the basis of the new people of God, the Christian church (Matt 16:18; Eph 2:20; Rev 21:12,14).

By choosing a replacement for Judas, the apostles showed that at first they considered it necessary to maintain the unit of twelve. Some years later when James was executed (Acts 12:1-2), they did not feel the same need to find a replacement, probably because by that time the original twelve-member group had largely fulfilled its purpose. It had provided the first-hand witness to Jesus' life, death and resurrection that Jesus wanted (Luke 24:46-48; John 15:27; Acts 1:21-22), it had established the church on the basis of Jesus' teaching (John 14:26; Acts 2:42; 6:4) and it had overseen the expansion of Christianity from Jerusalem into the wider world beyond (Matt 28:19-20; Acts 1:8; 8:14; 10:44-48). It no longer functioned as a group and the unit of twelve no longer needed to be maintained.

However, the office of apostle continued to be recognized, and as the church grew, an increasing number of people were recognized as apostles (Acts 14:14; Rom 16:7). It even became necessary to warn against false apostles (2 Cor 11:13; Rev 2:2). From this it is clear that the title of apostle applied to a wider group of people than the twelve (1 Cor 9:1; 15:8-11; Gal 1:19).

Apostles in this broader sense continued to preserve, teach and develop the truths of the Christian gospel, and people accepted their teaching as having the authority of God's Word (1 Cor 1:1; 12:28; 14:37; 1 Thess 2:13; 2 Thess 2:15; 2 Peter 3:15-16; cf. John 16:13-14). This apostolic authority extended to all aspects of the church's life (Acts 5:1-11; 2 Cor 12:12; 13:1-3; 2 Thess 3:4,14), though apostles rarely forced their authority upon people. They usually preferred that Christians develop maturity by making their own decisions and using their spiritual gifts (Acts 15:6; 2 Cor 1:24; 13:10; Eph 4:11-13).

It seems that apostles did not pass on their office to the next generation. They had been God's provision to link the ministry of Christ with the birth of the church, and to ensure that the church was built upon a proper foundation (Eph 2:20). As the Christian teaching became firmly established in written form (2 Thess 2:15) and as the churches became firmly established through local elders (Acts 14:23; 20:28), the necessity for apostles decreased. The apostolic office had fulfilled its purpose and after the first century it died out.

The church is born (2:1-13)

Pentecost was a Jewish harvest festival held on the Sunday fifty days after Passover, when Israelites presented the first portion of their harvest to God (Lev 23:15-21). It was therefore a fitting day to mark the birth of the Christian church. Christ, the true Passover had been sacrificed (1 Cor 5:7), and now fifty days later God poured out his Spirit on that small group of disciples who were to become the first members of the church of Jesus Christ.

In Old Testament times a person who received a special gift of God's Spirit may have announced a message from God as evidence of the Spirit's presence (e.g. Num 11:26). So also on the Day of Pentecost, when the followers of Jesus received the promised gift of his Spirit, they spoke words from God, and they did so in 'other tongues'. This means that their speech was in words that did not belong to their own language and that they did not understand, unless someone interpreted them (2:1-4; cf. 1 Cor 14:13-19).

When the disciples moved from the house into the street outside (possibly on the way to the temple), people were attracted by the noisy activity. Some Jews of the Dispersion who were in Jerusalem for the festival recognized their local languages in the speech of the disciples and praised God. Others recognized no languages at all and accused the disciples of being drunk (5-13).

Peter's preaching (2:14-42)

Seeing the people's interest, Peter addressed them, this time speaking in his normal language. His address shows some features of the early apostolic preaching. First he quoted from the Old Testament, to show that the Pentecost events fulfilled what the prophets foretold. To Peter the important point of the prophecy was that God poured out his Spirit on everyone — not everyone whether believers or not, but everyone within the community of God's people, whether male or female, young or old, slave or free (14-21; see v. 39).

Peter followed this with a short summary of Jesus' work, death and resurrection, showing that in spite of human injustice, God was working out his purposes (22-24). Next he quoted Old Testament Scriptures that Jews in general believed referred to the Messiah. Although David was the author of the passages quoted, the words could not refer to him, as he was dead, whereas the person referred to here was alive. This person, though not David, was a descendant of David; in fact, the Messiah. And this Messiah was Jesus, who had risen from the dead, returned to his Father in heaven, and sent the Holy Spirit upon his disciples (25-36). ('Messiah' was a Hebrew word meaning 'the anointed one'. It was used to refer to the descendant of David who would be God's chosen king and saviour, not just for Israel, but for the world. The Greek equivalent of 'Messiah' was 'Christ'.)

Finally, Peter called on the people to turn from their sins and believe in Jesus Christ. Because these people were part of the 'wicked generation' of Jews who killed the Messiah Jesus (cf. v. 23,40), they were to show their change of heart by being baptized in the name of the Messiah Jesus. They had to show publicly that they believed Jesus to be the Christ, the one whose divine authority was shown by the mighty works that God did through him (cf. v. 22). In this way they, and in fact people of any generation, would receive the same gift of the Holy Spirit as the apostles and others had just received (37-40).

With the addition of three thousand people, the church now consisted largely of new believers, but these believers soon grew into a strong body. They were built up through learning the teachings of Jesus passed on to them by the apostles, and through joining in fellowship where they worshipped and shared in the Lord's Supper (41-42).

Baptism with the Spirit

Both John the Baptist and Jesus had foretold the outpouring of the Holy Spirit described by Luke,

referring to it as a baptism (Matt 3:11; Acts 1:4-5). The baptism with the Holy Spirit may be defined as that event on the Day of Pentecost by which the risen Christ gave the Holy Spirit to his disciples as he had promised and, in so doing, united them into one body, the church (Acts 2:33; 11:15-16; 1 Cor 12:13).

On the Day of Pentecost two separate groups received the baptism, or gift, of the Spirit. The first was the group of apostles and others mentioned in Acts 1:15 and 2:1-4, the second the group of three thousand mentioned in Acts 2:37-42. But there were several important differences between the two groups.

The first group consisted of people who were already believers and who had to wait till after Jesus' ascension to receive the Spirit. The second group consisted of people who became believers only after hearing Peter preach on the Day of Pentecost and who received the Holy Spirit immediately. The experience of those of the first group (i.e. their speaking in tongues) should not be considered the normal experience of the Christian, because of the special circumstances in their case. They had lived with Jesus and could receive the Holy Spirit only after Jesus had completed his work and returned to the Father (John 7:39; 16:7). The experience of those of the second group, who received the Holy Spirit when they believed, without any unusual happenings, was the normal experience of Christians, then as well as now.

Of all the people in the New Testament who received the Holy Spirit (meaning, in other words, all Christians; see Rom 8:9-11), in only two other places, both special cases, does it state that the people spoke in tongues (see notes on Acts 10:44-48; 19:1-6).

Christians of all eras have a part in what occurred on the Day of Pentecost. Through that baptism of the Spirit they are, the moment they believe, made part of Christ's body, the church, and made sharers in his Spirit (1 Cor 12:13). Jesus' promised gift of the Holy Spirit, given initially at Pentecost, extends through the ages to all who repent and believe the gospel (Acts 2:38-39).

Life in the new community (2:43-47)

The early Christians had such a strong sense of unity that they brought their money and possessions together to form a central pool, from which all could receive help as they had need (43-45). Perhaps they were too hasty in sharing out their collective wealth, because soon none was left. As a result other churches (who did not copy the idea of a central pool) had to send money to help them through their difficulties (cf. Rom 15:26; Gal 2:10).

In addition to having fellowship in each others homes, the Christians went to the temple for public prayer and witness day by day. Their numbers increased continually, as others who were attracted by this new life of joy and love joined them. They enjoyed the goodwill of the citizens of Jerusalem in general (46-47).

3:1-5:42 RAPID GROWTH AND GREAT POPULARITY

Preaching in the temple (3:1-26)

On one of their visits to the temple, Peter and John healed a crippled beggar. The man had been lying at the gate that led from the outer public court to the inner courts where only Jews were allowed, but as soon as he was healed he followed the apostles into the temple, jumping and praising God (3:1-10).

After prayer the three men returned to the public court, where they found that a crowd of curious onlookers had gathered. Peter took the opportunity to tell the people that this healing was further proof that the Jesus whom they crucified was the Messiah. Jesus had healed cripples, and his messianic power was continuing to work through his disciples (see v. 6; cf. Matt 11:2-6). But that power was available only through faith in him as the Messiah who, having died, was now victoriously alive (11-16).

If the Jews repented of their sin in crucifying Jesus, God would forgive them. They would then experience all those blessings of the messianic age that they longed for and that the prophets of Old Testament times had spoken of. The climax of those blessings would be the return of Jesus Christ himself (17-21). The Jews of the New Testament era were the ones who, above all others, could experience the fulfilment of the covenant promises God gave to their ancestors; but first they had to turn from their sins and believe in Jesus as their Messiah. To reject him would bring destruction (22-26).

Growth brings opposition (4:1-31)

During the centuries leading up to the Christian era (see 'The New Testament World'), several parties had arisen within the Jewish religion. The most important of these were the Pharisees and the Sadducees.

The Pharisees came mainly from the common people, and tried to preserve the Jewish way of life from the corruption of foreign ideas and political ambition. They were concerned with the outward show of religion, but not so concerned with correct attitudes of heart (Matt 12:1-2; 15:1-2; 23:5,23-28). The Sadducees came mainly from the wealthy classes and were more concerned with exercising power in Jewish society than with following tradition. They were the high priestly party and had controlling power in the Sanhedrin, the supreme Jewish council that sat in Jerusalem (Matt 16:11-12; 26:57,59; Acts 5:17). A major difference of faith between the two parties was that the Pharisees believed in a physical resurrection of the dead, but the Sadducees did not (Matt 22:23; Acts 23:8).

When the number of Christians in Jerusalem increased rapidly as a result of Peter's preaching (the men alone numbered about five thousand), the Sadducees became angry. In particular, they were angry because all these people were responding to a message that was based on a belief in Jesus' resurrection. The Sadducees therefore had no hesitation in using their priestly power to arrest Peter and John and bring them before the Sanhedrin (4:1-4).

Once again Peter accused the Jews, especially their leaders, of rejecting and crucifying the Messiah (cf. v. 10-11 with 2:23; 3:13-15). God, by contrast, raised him from death and gave him the place of highest honour. Jesus fulfilled the Old Testament messianic promises, and if the Jews rejected him, no other way of salvation was available to them (5-12).

Although the apostles had not been taught in the Jewish law schools, they had been taught by Jesus. The members of the Sanhedrin recognized this and found it as difficult to argue with the apostles as it had been to argue with Jesus. To make matters more difficult for them, the healed man was proof that Jesus was still alive and working miracles (13-14). Since the apostles had broken no laws, and since the healing had increased the Christians' popularity, the Jewish leaders dared not punish the apostles. They could do no more than command them to stop preaching in the name of Jesus. But the apostles refused to obey (15-22).

The apostles considered this opposition to be a continuation of the opposition that Jesus himself experienced at the hands of the ruling authorities. The Christians had learnt from the Old Testament to expect such opposition, but they prayed that through the power of God's Spirit they would have boldness to continue Jesus' messianic ministry of preaching and healing (23-31).

Sin, cleansing and further growth (4:32-5:16)

Believers continued to sell their property and bring money from the sales to the apostles for distribution among the poor (32-35). One example of generosity came from a Jew from Cyprus who so consistently helped and encouraged others that people gave him a name to suit his character, Barnabas (meaning 'son of encouragement') (36-37).

There was no rule that forced people to sell their property. When Ananias and Sapphira sold some property, their sin was not that they kept part of the money for themselves, but that they lied through saying they had handed over all the money. After the unbroken triumphs of the weeks since Pentecost, this entrance of deliberate sin into the church must have shocked the apostles. As often happened when there was deliberate sin at the start of a new stage in God's unfolding plan for his people, God emphasized the seriousness of sin in a dramatic judgment (5:1-10). (Comparable judgments on deliberate sin occurred in the Garden of Eden, at the establishment of the Levitical priesthood and upon Israel's entrance into Canaan; Gen 3:1-24; Lev 10:1-7; Josh 7:1-26.)

Such severe judgments emphasized the holiness God demanded. They also reminded his people that all were sinners, and only his grace kept them alive and allowed them to serve him (11).

Far from slowing down the growth of the church, the judgment removed the sin that could have hindered growth. Although people saw that insincerity had no place in the church, vast numbers continued to join the church. Meanwhile, the healing ministry of Jesus continued to operate through the apostles (12-16; cf. Matt 14:35-36).

Opposition from Jewish leaders (5:17-42)

A sizable portion of the population of Jerusalem was now Christian (cf. 2:41,47; 4:4,16,17; 5:14,16,28). And the more the church grew, the more jealous and angry the Sadducees became. Again they brought the apostles before the Sanhedrin, though God showed he could rescue them at any time, should he so desire (17-21a). The apostles knew that, because of their widespread popular support, they could have successfully resisted arrest, but they chose not to. Instead they trusted in the overruling power of the sovereign God whom they served (21b-26).

The Sadducees in particular were angry; for they, being the high priestly party, were the ones whom the apostles blamed for the death of Jesus (27-28; cf. 4:6,10; 5:17). Also this new movement was based on a belief in Jesus' physical resurrection, something that the Sadducees believed could not happen but that the apostles repeatedly claimed they had witnessed. The apostles refused to alter their message, but assured the Sanhedrin that forgiveness was available to the repentant (29-32).

Though the Sadducee majority in the Sanhedrin would gladly have killed the apostles, a respected Pharisee teacher named Gamaliel persuaded the Sanhedrin not to. The Pharisees were pleased to see so many believing in the resurrection, for it gave support to their belief against the Sadducees'. They regarded the Christians as sincerely religious Jews who, though unusually enthusiastic, were orthodox enough to attend the temple daily to preach and pray (see 2:46; 3:1; 5:12,25,42). Gamaliel advised against opposing the new movement, in case it was from God. If it was not, it would collapse anyway (33-39).

Acting on Gamaliel's advice, the Sanhedrin released the apostles. But the Sadducees gained some satisfaction by having the apostles beaten for disobeying a previous Sanhedrin command (40; cf. 4:17; 5:28). This was the first time that Christians suffered physical punishment for their faith in Jesus, but they rejoiced through it all (41-42).

6:1-8:3 CHANGES IN JERUSALEM

Organizing church affairs (6:1-6)

In the Jerusalem church there were two types of Jews, those brought up in Palestine who spoke Aramaic and those brought up in other places (such as Jews of the Dispersion) who spoke only Greek. The Greek-speaking Jews were known as Hellenists. Throughout Palestine there was tension between the two groups, and this tension carried over into the church. The Hellenists complained that, when widows were given their daily share from the common pool, the Hellenist widows were being neglected (6:1).

To ensure that the daily distribution of food was handled fairly and in the right spirit, the apostles invited the church to choose seven suitable men, whom the apostles then appointed to look after the work. It appears from their Greek names that those chosen were Hellenists (2-6). With the appointment of these men, the apostles took the first steps towards the organization of the the church.

Deacons (church helpers)

When Christianity later spread to nearby regions, other churches followed Jerusalem's example of appointing people to look after specific affairs. As a result an order of deacons, or church helpers, became a regular feature of life in the early church (Phil 1:1; 1 Tim 3:8). The word 'deacon' was related to the words used to denote the Jerusalem seven and their work. It was the common Greek word for servant or minister (Rom 12:7; Eph 6:21; Col 4:17).

The New Testament nowhere defines the work of deacons. In the case of the Jerusalem seven, their main purpose was to accept responsibility for certain everyday tasks and so give the apostles more time for prayer and teaching (Acts 6:4). In churches that later grew up elsewhere, pastoral care and church leadership were the responsibilities of the elders. Deacons were a separate group who had other responsibilities (Phil 1:1; 1 Tim 3:1,8; cf. Acts 20:28; Rom 12:6-8; 1 Peter 5:1-5). The variety of needs within the church meant that opportunities existed for both men deacons and women deacons (Rom 16:1-2; 1 Tim 3:11; cf. Luke 8:1-3; 1 Tim 5:10).

Deacons were to be spiritual people, for right attitudes were necessary even in carrying out routine activities (Acts 6:3; 1 Tim 3:9). But the work of deacons was not limited to such activities. Two of the Jerusalem seven, for example, were gifted preachers (Acts 6:5,8-10; 8:5).

The Bible records no instructions concerning how deacons were appointed, though the action of the Jerusalem church may suggest some guidelines. The church leaders apparently invited the church members to select suitable people, taking into account their character, behaviour, ability, family life and Christian commitment (Acts 6:3a; 1 Tim 3:8-13). After due prayer and consideration, the elders made the appointment (Acts 6:3b; 1 Tim 3:10), in the understanding that only Spirit-gifted and Spirit-controlled people could properly do the work of deacons (1 Cor 12:4-7,11; 1 Peter 4:11).

Preaching of Stephen (6:7-15)

With the conversion of a large number of priests (not high priestly Sadducees, but ordinary temple officials), the Christians' ties with the temple might have become even stronger (7). But the preaching of Stephen quickly saw those ties broken decisively, at least in the case of the Hellenists. Stephen was one of the seven men who administered the church's welfare work, but he was also a prominent preacher and miracle-worker (8).

Stephen saw that Christianity and Judaism could not go hand in hand. With Jesus' death and resurrection, Judaism was finished. The Jewish religious system, along with its laws, ceremonies, priests and temple, had fulfilled its purpose and was now replaced by something new. When the Jews heard Stephen preaching these things in one of the Hellenists' synagogues in Jerusalem, they reported him to the Sanhedrin for preaching against Judaism (9-15). The Sadducees were pleased at last to have an accusation against the Christians that was certain to win popular support. They knew that the people would not tolerate this threat to their national religion (see v. 12).

Stephen before the Sanhedrin (7:1-60)

The defence that Stephen made before the Sanhedrin was not designed to win its approval. He outlined Israel's history to demonstrate two main points. First, God had never shown himself to be limited to one dwelling place, or even one locality (therefore the Jews were mistaken in attaching such importance to the temple in Jerusalem). Second, the people of Israel had always rejected the messengers of God (therefore their rejection of the Messiah Jesus was not surprising).

Although Canaan was the land that God gave to Abraham and his descendants, God was present with Abraham even in the distant land of Mesopotamia (7:1-8). The people of Israel showed their rejection of God's servants from the beginning, when their ancestors, out of jealousy, rejected Joseph and sold him as a slave into Egypt. Yet God was with Joseph in Egypt (9-16).

Some years later, the people of Israel rejected Moses, not understanding that God had sent him to be their deliverer (17-29). For forty years Moses lived as an exile in the wilderness, but even there God appeared to him (30-34). The man whom the people rejected became the people's saviour, with the promise that a greater messenger of God was yet to come (35-37). But the people rebelled against Moses and disobeyed God (38-43).

Originally, God's symbolic dwelling place was a movable tent, something that could be set up anywhere at all, demonstrating that God was not limited to one place. When Solomon later built a permanent temple in Jerusalem, people developed the mistaken idea that this temple was the only place where God dwelt (44-50). The Jews of Stephen's time, like their ancestors, misunderstood God, resisted his Spirit, disobeyed his law and rejected his messengers. Finally, they killed the Messiah himself (51-53).

On hearing these words, the members of the Sanhedrin could keep silent no longer. But Stephen, remaining calm, supported Jesus' claim that he, the Messiah, shared equality with God. To the Jews, Stephen was repeating the blasphemy for which they had killed Jesus. In a burst of uncontrolled anger they rushed upon him, dragged him out of the city and stoned him to death. But before he died, Stephen, again following the example of Jesus, committed his life to God and asked forgiveness for his murderers (54-60; cf. Mark 14:62-64; Luke 23:34,46).

464

Christians driven out of Jerusalem (8:1-3)

With the killing of Stephen, fierce persecution broke out against the Christians in Jerusalem. No longer did the Pharisees favour the Christians; in fact, it was a Pharisee, Saul, who led the persecution. The Christians were attacked, imprisoned, or driven violently from the city, but they did not deny their faith. Although they previously went to the temple daily, they now saw the truth of what Stephen had taught, and they were prepared to suffer for it (8:1-3).

It seems that only the Hellenist Christians were driven from the city. (Stephen was a Hellenist; see 6:8-9.) Apparently the Aramaic-speaking Christians were allowed to stay (cf. 9:26; 11:2). This Jerusalem church, without the Hellenists, later became very narrow in its outlook and was a source of trouble to other churches. The Hellenists, on the other hand, became a means of blessing to the whole world.

8:4-9:31 THROUGHOUT PALESTINE AND BEYOND

Christianity enters Samaria (8:4-25)

In the time of the Roman Empire, the region of Samaria was the central part of Palestine and along with the neighbouring region of Judea was governed from Caesarea. The origins of the Samaritans go back to Old Testament times, when Samaria was the name of the chief city of the region.

After Assyria had conquered the central and northern parts of Israel and taken the people into captivity (722 BC), it moved people from other parts of its empire into Samaria and surrounding towns. These settlers intermarried with Israelites still left in the land and combined the Israelite form of worship with their own. This resulted in a race of mixed blood and mixed religion known as the Samaritans (2 Kings 17:5-6,24-33; Ezra 4:9-10). When the Jews returned from captivity and settled in and around Jerusalem (538 BC), tension arose between Jews and Samaritans (Ezra 4:1-4), and this tension lasted into New Testament times (Luke 9:52-53; John 4:9).

Philip, a Hellenist, appears to have been the first person to take the gospel into Samaria. As a result of his preaching and miraculous works, many Samaritans believed and were baptized (4-8). A well known local magician, Simon, was so impressed by these miracles that he too was baptized, hoping no doubt that he could learn the secret of Philip's power (9-13).

When the apostles in Jerusalem heard of the conversion of so many Samaritans, they sent Peter and John to Samaria to pray that the Samaritans would receive the Holy Spirit. The reason why the Samaritans did not receive the Spirit immediately they believed was probably that God first wanted the apostles to be convinced that Samaritan believers shared the same privileges as Jewish believers. The long-standing hostility between Jews and Samaritans (an attitude that even the apostles were recently guilty of; Luke 9:52-56) was not to be carried over into the church. By using the apostles to be his means of giving the Holy Spirit to the Samaritans, God demonstrated publicly that Samaritans were accepted into the church on an equal standing with the Jews and with the full support of the apostles (14-17).

As a sign that they had received the Holy Spirit, the Samaritans apparently spoke in tongues. This impressed Simon even more, and he would gladly have paid money to have the sort of power over people that he thought the apostles had. Instead he received an assurance of God's judgment (18-24). As for the apostles, they not only welcomed the Samaritans but they also preached the gospel in many of the Samaritan villages (25).

Christianity enters Philistia (8:26-40)

From Samaria Philip headed south towards the region of Philistia on the Mediterranean coast (26). On the way he met another non-Jewish person who responded to his preaching. This man, a government official from Ethiopia in north Africa, was already one of the God-fearers and was reading the Old Testament when Philip met him (27-29). However, he did not understand what he was reading. When Philip explained the Scriptures to him, the man learnt the meaning of Jesus' death, became a believer and was baptized (30-38). The man was overjoyed as he continued his journey homeward, and no doubt readily spread the good news of Jesus Christ among his fellow Africans. Philip, meanwhile, preached around the towns of Philistia, then moved north along the coast till he came to the provincial capital, Caesarea (39-40).

Conversion of Saul (9:1-19a)

The name by which Christianity was known was 'the Way' (see 9:2; 19:9,23; 22:4; 24:14,22). Possibly the name originated with the Christians themselves, who believed their movement was the way of the Lord, the way of salvation and the way of life. But to the Christians' opponents the name represented a movement that had to be destroyed.

By this time the gospel had spread north at least as far as the Syrian city of Damascus, which had a large Jewish population. The Sanhedrin therefore sent fiery young Saul to arrest any Christians who still attended the synagogue and bring them to Jerusalem for trial (9:1-2). But before Saul reached Damascus he had an encounter with the risen Jesus that convinced him that Jesus was Lord and Christ, as the Christians claimed. The persecutor became a disciple of Jesus (3-9; cf. 2:36; 1 Cor 9:1; 15:8).

REGION OF PAUL'S FIRST MISSIONARY JOURNEY (ACTS 13-14)

REGION OF EARLY EXPANSION OUT FROM JERUSALEM (ACTS 1-12)

Through one of the local Damascus Christians, God revealed that he had chosen Saul to go to distant countries, taking the gospel to rulers and common citizens alike, to Gentiles and Jews without distinction (10-15). This would be a difficult task (16), but God prepared him for it by filling him with the Holy Spirit. Saul demonstrated openly his break with the old life and his start of the new by being baptized (17-19a).

Saul's entire background and training had been used by God to help prepare him for the work ahead (Gal 1:15-16). He was a full-blooded Jew born in Tarsus, a town in Cilicia in south-west Asia Minor (Acts 22:3; Phil 3:5). He inherited Roman citizenship from birth (Acts 16:37; 22:26-28), had a Roman name, Paul (Acts 13:9), and grew up to speak both Greek and Hebrew (Acts 21:37,40). As a religiously zealous youth, Saul moved to Jerusalem where he studied Jewish law according to the strict Pharisee traditions, his teacher being the well known Rabbi Gamaliel (Acts 22:3; 23:6; 26:5). Like all Jewish young men he learnt a trade, which in his case was tent-making (Acts 18:3).

All the influences in Saul's upbringing and education, whether Greek, Hebrew or Roman, had an effect on his life and ministry. The Greek influence taught him how to think clearly and analyse issues (Eph 3:1-6), the Hebrew influence helped him develop a character of moral uprightness (Phil 3:6), and the Roman influence gave him an international outlook that led to his great plan for the spread of Christianity (Rom 15:19-24).

In Damascus, Arabia, Jerusalem and Tarsus (9:19b-31)

People throughout Damascus soon knew of Saul's conversion. He openly joined with the Christians and argued convincingly against the Jews (19b-22). Part of the next three years he spent in Arabia, after which he returned to Damascus (Gal 1:17-18). His activities there stirred up such violent opposition that he fled to save his life (23-25; 2 Cor 11:32-33).

When Saul arrived in Jerusalem, the Christians did not welcome him. They feared that he was only pretending to be a Christian, so that when he found out who the true Christians were he could imprison them. Barnabas apparently knew him better and introduced him to the two leading apostles who were in Jerusalem at the time, Peter and James the Lord's brother (26-27; Gal 1:18-19).

Saul made good use of his two weeks in Jerusalem by preaching the good news of Jesus Christ. Not surprisingly, this made the Jews angry, as they were the ones who three years previously had sent him to crush Christianity. When they made plans to kill him, Saul escaped to his home town of Tarsus in Cilicia (28-30; Gal 1:21).

At that time the rest of the churches in Judea did not know Saul personally, but they certainly knew of his conversion, because without his fiery leadership the persecution had died down and the churches were left in peace (31; Gal 1:22-24).

9:32-12:25 JERUSALEM AND THE GENTILES

Peter in Lydda and Joppa (9:32-43)

While God was preparing Paul for the Gentile mission ahead, he was also broadening the vision of Peter and other church leaders. Peter moved out from Jerusalem and visited some of the Christian groups that had sprung up in the semi-Gentile coastal plain area where Philip had preached earlier (cf. 8:40). At Lydda he healed a paralyzed man (32-35) and at nearby Joppa he raised a woman to life. In both places news of the miracles spread and many people believed (36-42). By staying with a person whose trade the Jews considered unclean, Peter demonstrated a more relaxed attitude towards former Jewish restrictions (43).

European converts (10:1-48)

In the Roman regiment based in Caesarea was a centurion named Cornelius, a man who was such a sincere God-fearer that all his household followed his faith. In response to his expressions of faith and acts of kindness, God promised to send Peter to tell him the good news of Jesus Christ by which he could be saved (10:1-8; cf. 11:14).

First, however, God wanted to teach Peter certain lessons. God gave him a vision to show him that the old Jewish food laws were of no further use. There was no longer a distinction between clean foods and unclean foods, and therefore Peter was free to eat all foods (9-16). While Peter was thinking about the meaning of the vision, God told him to go to Caesarea to meet the Roman, Cornelius (17-23a). By the time Peter left for Caesarea the next day, he had learnt the meaning of the vision. If certain kinds of food were not unclean, neither were certain kinds of people. Peter was not to be afraid of mixing with the Gentiles (23b-29).

After Cornelius welcomed him (30-33), Peter began his address. He emphasized at the outset that, although Israel was God's means of sending the Saviour Jesus, in the matter of personal salvation God did not favour one nation above another (34-36). Peter then summarized the events of Jesus' life, death and resurrection (37-42), and concluded by repeating that forgiveness was available to people of any nationality (43).

Cornelius and his household, being already prepared for the gospel, readily believed when they heard it. Immediately, they received the gift of the Holy Spirit direct from God, without an apostle doing anything at all. It was like a repeat of the Pentecost events, but this time with Gentiles, not Jews (44-46; cf. 11:15-17). Peter saw clearly that God had accepted these Gentiles and he had no hesitation in baptizing them (47-48).

Reaction of the Jerusalem church (11:1-18)

Many in the Jerusalem church criticized Peter for what had happened in the house of Cornelius. Their minds were so moulded by Jewish thinking that they could think of Christianity only as an improved form of Judaism. They were pleased when Gentile proselytes or God-fearers accepted Jewish ways, but they were not pleased when people of any nationality entered the community of God's people without any thought for the Jewish laws concerning foods, cleansing and circumcision (11:1-3).

Peter therefore explained to his critics how God had corrected his prejudice against the Gentiles (4-14) and how the Gentiles had received all God's blessings on the same basis as the Jews (15-17). Although they accepted Peter's explanation and praised God (18), they were not fully convinced, and soon trouble broke out again (see 15:1,5).

A new work in Antioch (11:19-26)

While the apostles and others were spreading the gospel in various places, an interesting work grew up in Antioch in Syria. Some Christians who had been scattered from Jerusalem at the time of Stephen's death preached among the Greek population of Antioch and many believed (19-21). When the leaders of the Jerusalem church heard this, they sent Barnabas to Antioch. This was a wise choice, for Barnabas was from nearby Cyprus and had a much broader outlook than those Jews who had never been outside Judea. He had the ability to understand and help the new converts, and under his wise guidance the church grew rapidly (22-24).

Within a short time there was more work than Barnabas himself could manage. He wanted a helper, but the person had to be of the right sort. Therefore, he did not go back to Jerusalem to look for help, but went to Tarsus to get Saul. The last mention of Saul in the story was ten years earlier (see note following 11:30), and now he returned with Barnabas to help the Antioch church. For the next year they preached and taught, among Christians and non-Christians, with the result that the church grew even more (25-26).

The language spoken in Antioch was Greek. Consequently, when the disciples spoke about Jesus, instead of using the Hebrew word 'Messiah' they used the equivalent Greek word 'Christ'. The local citizens heard the disciples use this word continually and, although it had no significance for them, it gave them an easy name by which to identify this group of religious people — 'Christ's people' or 'Christians'. Elsewhere in Acts, Christians are called believers, disciples, followers, brothers and saints (or God's holy people) (see 5:14; 9:1,32; 11:1). To the Jews they were known as Nazarenes (see 24:5).

Fellowship between churches (11:27-30)

Towards the end of Barnabas and Saul's year in Antioch, some prophets from Jerusalem visited the Antioch church. One of them warned of a coming famine that would bring much suffering to the believers in Jerusalem. The Antioch believers (who were Gentiles) demonstrated the meaning of true fellowship by sacrificing their own money and goods to help their troubled Jewish brothers (27-29). The offering was taken to Jerusalem by Barnabas, Saul and Titus (30; Gal 2:1).

This was only Saul's second visit to Jerusalem since he had become a Christian fourteen years earlier. His first visit was three years after his conversion (Gal 1:18; Acts 9:26-30). The only certain knowledge we have of the other eleven years concerns the last year, which he spent with Barnabas in Antioch (v. 26). Now, with Barnabas, he went from Antioch to Jerusalem (v. 30; see Gal 2:1). While in Jerusalem they met the leading apostles, Peter, John and James the Lord's brother, who reassured them that their work among the Gentiles had the full support of the Jerusalem leaders (Gal 2:9-10). Barnabas and Saul then returned to Antioch (Acts 12:25).

Prophets

In biblical language, prophets were spokesmen for God, preachers who brought God's message to the people of their time (Ezek 3:4,27; Hag 1:13). They were not primarily predictors (which is the usual meaning in everyday speech today), though in urging people to turn from sin they may have foretold the blessings or judgments that would follow their obedience or disobedience (Isa 1:18-20; Jer 17:7-10). In Old Testament times the prophets were Israel's great preachers, and John the Baptist continued the line of prophet-preachers into the New Testament era (Matt 11:13-14; Luke 3:3-7,16-18).

When Jesus established the new community of God's people, the Christian church, he appointed that prophets have a part to play in the church's life. Like apostles, they were one of his gifts to help the growth of the church (1 Cor 12:28; Eph 4:11). Also, like apostles, they became less necessary as the authoritative Christian teaching became increasingly available in written form. It seems that they were not needed after the first century. They were Christ's special provision to ensure that the early church was built on a proper foundation and in accordance with God's plan (Eph 2:20; 3:4-6).

Prophets sometimes gave special directions in particular situations (Acts 11:27-30; 13:1; 21:9-11), though their main ministry was the steady teaching of God's message to build up the believers (Acts 15:32; 1 Cor 14:3-5,31). They may have received messages direct from God (1 Cor 14:6; Rev 1:1-3) and may have preached without preparation (1 Cor 14:29-31). But they were still responsible for what they said and for the control they exercised over themselves (1 Cor 14:32). Likewise the hearers were responsible to examine what was said and not to accept anything without testing it first (1 Cor 14:29; 1 Thess 5:20-21; 1 John 4:1; 2 John 10).

In exceptional circumstances, people who were not recognized prophets in the church may have prophesied (Acts 19:6). Because this increased the possibility of false prophets, God gave to certain Christians the ability to discern more readily the difference between the true and the false (Matt 7:15; 24:24; 1 Cor 12:10; Rev 2:20).

Events in Jerusalem (12:1-25)

Back in Jerusalem the church was experiencing much difficulty. The Jews in general were becoming restless concerning the free mixing between Jewish and Gentile Christians, and were angry at the apostles for encouraging it. The governor at that time, Herod Agrippa I (a grandson of Herod the Great), knew it was not wise to let the Jews become too excited. Therefore, in an effort to please them he took action against the apostles by having one of them, James, executed (12:1-2).

The execution of James pleased the Jews more than Herod expected, so next time he planned to kill the leading apostle, Peter (3-5). However, in answer to the prayers of the Jerusalem church, Peter miraculously escaped (6-11). After a brief visit to assure the Christians he was free again, Peter fled to a safer place (12-19).

Herod, by contrast, suffered a horrible death. The people of Tyre and Sidon, anxious to ensure a constant food supply from Herod's territory, had tried to win his favour with a show of extravagant flattery. Herod accepted the praise as if he was God, and was punished for it (20-23). The persecutor died but the church continued to grow (24-25).

James the Lord's brother

With the apostles' becoming more involved with matters outside Jerusalem, James the brother of

Jesus was now the most prominent leader in the Jerusalem church (Acts 12:17; 15:13; Gal 1:18-19; 2:9,12). He apparently became a believer only after Jesus' resurrection (1 Cor 15:7; cf. Mark 6:3; John 7:5), and was a foundation member of the Jerusalem church (Acts 1:14).

Although most of the Jews in the Jerusalem church still held to former beliefs and customs, James was not a slave to the law. Continually he tried to encourage his fellow Jews to be more tolerant of others (Acts 15:13,19). The common people respected him for his sincere faith and called him James the Just.

The character of James' life and teaching can be seen in the letter in the New Testament that bears his name (James 1:1). It gives teaching on how to face trials and temptations, on the character of true faith, and on many practical matters such as the control of the tongue, the use of wealth and the exercise of patience (James 1:3,12; 2:14-17; 3:2,13; 4:1-2; 5:8).

13:1-14:28 INTO ASIA MINOR (FIRST MISSIONARY JOURNEY)

Zeal of the church in Antioch (13:1-3)

The church at Antioch, which was the first Gentile church, was also the first church to see its responsibility to send off missionaries to distant places. It became the 'jumping off point' for the establishment of other churches. For this purpose it decided to send off its two most gifted and experienced leaders, Barnabas and Saul (now to be called by his Roman name, Paul). The church showed its identification with the missionaries as its representatives in the simple ceremony of the church leaders' placing their hands on them and committing them to God (13:1-3).

Preaching in Cyprus (13:4-12)

Barnabas and Paul took with them as their young assistant John Mark, a relative of Barnabas who had come back with them from Jerusalem (see 12:12,25; Col 4:10). (John Mark was probably the young man mentioned in Mark 14:51-52. Later he wrote the book known as Mark's Gospel.) The three sailed for Cyprus, the home of Barnabas, and immediately began preaching in the synagogues (4-5). They headed west for the provincial capital of Paphos, preaching the gospel from one end of the island to the other. One result of their preaching was that the governor of the island believed, in spite of the efforts of a local Jewish magician (who also claimed to be a prophet) to persuade him otherwise (6-12).

To Antioch in Pisidia (13:13-52)

When the trio arrived at Perga on the mainland of Asia Minor, John Mark, for some unknown reason, left the other two and returned to Jerusalem. Paul considered this a serious failure on Mark's part (13; see 15:38).

From Perga, Paul and Barnabas moved north into the province of Galatia and came to the town of Antioch, often referred to as Pisidian Antioch to distinguish it from Antioch in Syria. There they preached in the synagogue just as they had done in the towns of Cyprus (14-16). (Before the time of the Roman Empire, Asia Minor consisted of a collection of small independent states. When the Romans took control, they redivided the area to form a lesser number of Roman provinces. The large central province that they named Galatia included within it the region of Pisidia and parts of the former kingdoms of Phrygia and Lycaonia.)

Paul's address to the synagogue audience was similar to the addresses of Peter and Stephen (see notes on 2:14-42; 7:1-53). He began by outlining the history of Israel, showing that the promised Saviour had come in the person of Jesus Christ (17-25). Although the Jews in Jerusalem rejected and killed Jesus (26-29), God raised him from death to show openly that he was the promised Son of David, the great Messiah (30-37). All who repented of their sins and believed in him would find forgiveness and salvation (38-41).

The audience, which consisted of Jews along with Gentile proselytes and God-fearers, responded well to the message. These people did not usually hear such an exposition of the Scriptures, and they looked forward to hearing more (42-43).

Next week almost the entire population of Antioch came to the synagogue to hear the missionaries preach. This made the Jews jealous and angry. They feared that the missionaries were stealing their Gentile converts by offering an easier religion, one that promised salvation through faith without regard for the Jewish law (44-45). Paul and Barnabas replied that God's plan was for Israel to carry his message of salvation to the Gentiles, and for this reason the missionaries preached the gospel to the Jews first. But if the Jews would not accept salvation, how could they preach it to the Gentiles? Therefore, Paul and Barnabas turned from the Jews and offered it to the Gentiles direct (46-47).

The missionaries' straightforward words and the Gentiles' ready response angered the Jews even more, and they drove the two men from the city. Yet the converts, being true disciples, not only stood firm for God after the missionaries departed, but spread the gospel throughout the region (48-52).

Other churches in Galatia (14:1-28)

Paul and Barnabas moved on to the town of Iconium, where events followed the same pattern as in Antioch. They preached in the synagogue and both Jews and Gentiles believed. But as the number of converts increased, the people of the city became clearly divided between supporters of the apostles and supporters of the Jewish leaders. Because of the threat of murder, the apostles fled the city and went to Lystra (14:1-7).

When the apostles healed a crippled man in Lystra, the people thought they must have been two of the Greek gods, so prepared offerings for them (8-13). At first the apostles did not know what was happening, as they did not understand the local language (v. 11), but as soon as they found out they corrected the misunderstanding. In the synagogues they had based their preaching on the revelation of God in the Old Testament, but on this occasion their preaching had a different basis. Idol worshippers knew nothing of the Old Testament, so the apostles explained something of the character of God from his activity in the world of nature (14-18).

Again the Jews stirred up opposition and Paul was almost killed (19). Possibly the wounds he later referred to in his Letter to the Galatians were the result of injuries he received on this occasion (Gal 6:17).

The apostles then moved on to Derbe, where they founded another church (20). Not lacking in courage, they returned through the cities where they had only recently been persecuted, for they knew how important it was to strengthen the young churches and appoint elders. The apostles had given these new converts a solid foundation of teaching, and they trusted God to uphold and guide them (21-23).

After a short time in Perga, which they had missed on the outward journey, the two apostles returned to the church that had sent them out. With thanks to God they told of the work that he had done among the Gentiles through them (24-28).

Elders (church leaders)

The appointment of elders was part of God's plan to give spiritual leadership to the churches. In Old Testament Israel the leaders of the community were known as elders (Exod 24:1; Deut 21:1-6; Ruth 4:2-11) and in the Israel of New Testament times people called elders administered Jewish affairs through the synagogues (Mark 15:1; Luke 7:3). In similar fashion there were elders to provide leadership to the new community of God's people, the church.

In the early days of Acts when the Jerusalem church was the only church, the leaders were the apostles (Acts 4:37; 6:2-4). As the apostles' work outside Jerusalem increased, there arose within the Jerusalem church a group of elders that was distinct from the apostles (Acts 11:30; 15:6). Other churches followed this practice, though the New Testament writers did not always give the elders an official title. The emphasis was more on the work they did than the office they held (Acts 13:1; 14:23; 1 Cor 16:16; 1 Thess 5:12-13; Heb 13:7,17; 1 Peter 5:1-2).

This truth is evident in the variety of words that the Bible uses for elders — shepherds, overseers, guardians, leaders and bishops. Most of these words come from only two words in the Greek of the original New Testament, *presbuteroi* and *episkopoi*. Both Greek words seem to apply to the same person and office. For example (in the words of the RSV), in Acts 20:17 Paul sent for the elders (*presbuteroi*) of the Ephesian church, but when they came (v. 28) he called them guardians (*episkopoi*). Likewise in Titus 1:5 he told Titus to appoint elders (*presbuteroi*), then in the same sentence (v. 7) he called them bishops (*episkopoi*). In reference to any specific local church Paul always used the plural 'elders' rather than the singular 'elder' (Acts 14:23; 20:17; Phil 1:1; 1 Thess 5:12).

Elders were shepherds who led, ruled, guided and cared for the flock (Acts 20:28; 1 Tim 3:5; 5:17; Heb 13:17; 1 Peter 5:1-3). They had to have some ability at teaching (1 Tim 3:2) so that they could feed the church with instruction that was helpful and protect it from what was harmful (Acts 20:28-30; 1 Tim 6:3-5; Titus 1:9; 2 John 7-11). The church on its part was to support financially those who sacrificed their time and income to minister to it (Gal 6:6; 1 Tim 5:17-18).

Besides having the right abilities, elders were to be blameless in their character and behaviour (1 Tim 3:1-7; Titus 1:5-9). They were to be examples to the church, and were never to use their authority to advance their own interests or force their personal wishes upon others (Heb 13:7; 1 Peter 5:2-3).

The Bible contains no specific instructions concerning the procedure for choosing and appointing elders. In the case of a new church, it seems that the first elders were appointed by the founders of the church (Acts 14:23). Normally, an appointment was not made too soon after a person's conversion, as time was necessary for spiritual character and gift to develop (1 Tim 3:6; 5:22). Although those making the appointment needed to realize that only the Holy Spirit could really make a person an elder (Acts 20:28; 1 Cor 12:11,28), they needed to realize also that elders could function properly only if they had the church's respect and confidence (1 Thess 5:12-13; Heb 13:17). For this reason they probably shared in prayer and consultation with the church before making the appointment (cf. Acts 6:3).

As a church grew, other people developed the sorts of spiritual gifts that directed them towards eldership (1 Tim 3:1). In addition, existing leaders had a responsibility to train those who possessed the right leadership abilities (2 Tim 2:2; cf. Acts 16:2-3). No doubt the existing elders were the ones who made the new appointments (1 Tim 4:14; cf. Acts 1:21-26), but again only in fellowship with the church as a whole (cf. Acts 15:22).

THE CHURCH AND ITS FUNCTION

At this point it may be helpful to look back over what we have learnt of the church so far and add a few more notes concerning how the early churches operated.

God's plan in operation

After the repeated failures that marked the early days of human history, God declared his purpose to choose for himself a people through whom he would provide a salvation for all the world. He began by choosing one man, Abraham, and promising to make from him a nation that would be in a special sense God's people and his channel of blessing to the whole world. The people of this nation, Israel, were therefore both Abraham's physical descendants and God's chosen people (Gen 12:1-3; Exod 6:7; 19:5-6; John 8:37).

This did not mean, however, that all those born into the Israelite race were, on account of their nationality, automatically forgiven their sins and blessed with God's eternal favour. On the contrary the history of Israel shows that from the beginning most of the people were ungodly and unrepentant. Those who, like Abraham, truly trusted God and desired to obey him were always only a minority within the nation (Isa 1:4,11-20; Rom 11:2-7; Heb 3:16). These were God's true people, the true Israel, the true descendants of Abraham (Rom 2:28-29; 4:9-12; 9:6-8).

From this faithful minority came one person, Jesus the Messiah, who was the divinely chosen descendant of Abraham to whom God's promises to Abraham pointed. All God's ideals for Israel and all

his promised blessings for the human race were fulfilled in Jesus (Gal 3:16). Jesus then took the few remaining faithful Israelites of his day and made them the nucleus of God's new people, the Christian church (Matt 16:18). The church, then, was both old and new. It was old in that it was a continuation of that body of believers who in every age remained faithful to God. It was new in that it did not formally come into being till after the death, resurrection and ascension of Jesus (Matt 16:18,21; Titus 2:14; 1 Peter 2:9).

The word used by Jesus and translated 'church' meant originally a collection of people – a meeting, gathering or community. It was used for the Old Testament community of Israel, and was particularly suitable for the new community, the Christian church, that came into existence on the Day of Pentecost (Exod 12:6; 35:1; Deut 9:10; 23:3; Acts 2:1-4; 5:11; 7:38; 8:1).

The body of Christ

As the church grew, Christians understood its meaning more fully. They saw that Christ and the church are inseparably united and make up one complete whole, just as the head and the body make up one complete person. Through his resurrection and ascension, Christ became Head of the church. He has supreme authority over it and is the source of its life, growth and strength (Eph 1:20-23; 4:15-16; Col 1:18; 2:19). Another picture of the relationship between Christ and the church is that of marriage. This emphasizes Christ's love for the church and shows how, in order to gain the church as his bride, he laid down his life in sacrifice (Eph 5:23,25).

Both the picture of the body and the picture of marriage illustrate Christ's headship of the church (Eph 1:22-23; 5:23). Both pictures also make it clear that God accepts the church as holy and faultless only because it shares the life and righteousness of Christ (Eph 5:26-27; Col 1:22).

This view of the church in all its perfection as the body of Christ is one that God alone sees. The view that people in general see is of the church in a world of sin where it is troubled by imperfection and failure (cf. 1 Cor 1:2 with 1 Cor 3:1-3; cf. Eph 1:1-4 with Eph 4:25-32). God sees the church as the full number of believers of all nations and all eras, a vast international community commonly referred to as the church universal. People see the church only in the form of those believers living in a particular place at a particular time.

Within what society sees as the visible church are those who are genuine believers and those who are not. People often find it difficult to tell the difference between the two, but God knows all things and he will make the decisive separation on the day of final judgment (Matt 13:47-50; 1 Cor 10:1-11; 2 Cor 13:5).

The local church

This leads to the most common usage of the word 'church', and that is to denote the meeting together of a group of Christians in a particular locality. This community is the church in that locality. It is the local expression, a sort of miniature, of the timeless universal church (Acts 13:1; 1 Cor 1:2).

The story of the early church in Acts shows that when people repented and believed the gospel, they were baptized (Acts 2:38,41; 10:48). By their faith they became members of Christ's body, the church, and they showed the truth of this union by joining with other Christians in their locality. That is, having become part of the timeless universal church, they now became part of the local church (Acts 2:41,47).

Churches in New Testament times met in private homes or any other ready-made places they could find (Acts 12:12; 19:9, 20:7-8; Rom 16:5,14-15). Their meetings were to be orderly and, above all, spiritually helpful (1 Cor 14:26,40). The believers were built up through being taught the Scriptures and through having fellowship with each other by praying, worshipping, singing praises and observing the Lord's Supper together (Acts 2:42; 20:7,27; 1 Cor 11:23-33; 14:15).

From the church, believers went out to make known the gospel to others. They baptized those who believed, brought them into the fellowship of the church and taught them the Christian teaching, so that they too might become true disciples of Jesus Christ (Matt 28:19-20; Acts 1:7-8; 8:4; Col 1:27-29). They recognized that their responsibilities applied to distant regions as well as to their own localities (Matt 28:19; Acts 13:2-4; Rom 15:19-20); and besides preaching the gospel they helped the victims of disease, hunger and injustice (Acts 3:2-6; 11:28-29; 16:16-18; Rom 12:8,13; James 1:27; 2:14-16; cf. Matt 25:34-40).

Each local church, though having fellowship with other local churches (Acts 11:29; 18:27; 1 Cor 16:1-4), was responsible directly to the Head, Jesus Christ, in all things. There was no central organization or head church to control all others, and no set of laws either to hold the churches together in one body or to hold all the believers in one church together. Unity came through a oneness of faith in the Spirit, with Christ as the Head (Eph 4:4-6).

Christians thought of the church not as an organization or institution, but as a family. Christ was the Head, and all the believers were brothers and sisters (Gal 6:10; Eph 2:19). The strength of the church came not from any organizational system, but from the spiritual life that each believer possessed and that all believers shared in common (Phil 1:7; 2:1-2; 1 John 1:3).

Leadership in the churches

The Bible gives few details concerning how the early churches arranged their meetings and carried out their functions. No set form was laid down. That does not mean that the churches lacked leadership or that they carried out their work without thought and planning. Churches had elders to be responsible for spiritual care, growth and direction, and deacons to look after some of the church's more routine affairs (Phil. 1:1; see earlier notes). People in those leadership positions may have been gifted in various ways, since God gave a range of gifts to build up his people within the life of the body. Among these gifts were apostles, prophets, evangelists, pastors and teachers (Eph 4:11-13).

Apostles and prophets seem to have been especially suited to the time of the church's infancy (Eph 2:20; see earlier notes). Evangelists were, according to the meaning of the word, those who preached, announced or proclaimed the gospel, or good news. Their chief concern was to make known the gospel to those who had not heard it, and plant churches in places where previously there were none (Acts 8:5,40; 14:21, 16:10; Rom 10:14-15; 15:19-20; 2 Cor 10:16; 2 Tim 4:5).

Pastors were those whose special ministry was spiritual care. In the language of the original New Testament writings there was a close connection between the words 'pastor', 'shepherd' and 'flock', indicating that many of the qualities of the pastor were similar to those we have already considered in relation to elders (John 21:15-17; 1 Peter 5:1-4). Pastors were not a separate group from teachers, for the way they fed the flock was through teaching the Word (Acts 20:27-28; cf. 6:2-4). In fact, where pastors and teachers are mentioned together in Ephesians 4:11, the grammatical connection between the two words indicates that both words refer to the same people, pastor-teachers.

Teachers, being also pastors, had more than the ability to understand and teach the Word clearly. They taught in such a way that the members of the church were strengthened in their faith and equipped to serve God (Rom 12:7; 1 Cor 12:28; Eph 4:11-12). They helped Christians develop the ability to discern between teaching that was wholesome and teaching that was not, and so grow towards spiritual maturity (Eph 4:13-14; Col 1:28; 2:4; 1 Thess 5:20-21; 1 Tim 1:3-5; 4:6-8; Heb 5:12-14).

From the above data we can see that there was some overlap between the gifts mentioned in the New Testament. People were not divided too sharply into separate categories, and some combined within them several of the gifts; e.g. Paul (Rom 15:20; 1 Tim 1:1; 2:7), James (Gal 1:19; 2:9-10), Timothy (1 Tim 4:13-16; 2 Tim 4:5), Barnabas (Acts 11:22-26; 14:14), Silas (Acts 15:32; 17:10-14) and others.

Responsibilities of church members

God's purpose was not for these specially gifted people to do all the spiritual work in the church, or to be so dominant that the church members became completely dependent on them. On the contrary, they were to use their gifts to teach, train and build up other Christians and so prepare them for fuller Christian service. In this way individual Christians grew to spiritual maturity and the church as a body was built up (Eph 4:11-16; 2 Tim 2:1-2; cf. 1 Cor 14:3-4,12,26).

Paul pointed out to the early Christians that in a local church each member had a gift for the service of God, given by the Holy Spirit according to his will (1 Cor 12:11,18). He likened the church to the human body: a living organism made up of many parts, all with different functions to perform. Yet with the variety there was equality. The church, unlike ancient Israel, had no exclusive class of religious officials who had spiritual privileges that ordinary people did not have (Rom 12:4-8; 1 Cor 12:12,27; Eph 2:18-20). Many gifts operated in the early churches, but Christians were to use them in dependence upon the Spirit's power and in keeping with the Spirit's teaching (1 Cor 12:4-11).

If a local church was to operate properly, all the people in that church needed to find out what gifts the Holy Spirit had either given them or withheld from them, then develop the gifts they had (Rom 12:6-8; 1 Tim 4:14-16). This would leave no room for pride on the one hand or jealousy on the other, but through the care of the members one for the other the church would be built up (1 Cor 12:14-30).

15:1-35 FIRST MAJOR CHURCH PROBLEM

Judaisers trouble the churches (15:1)

The writer of Acts has already shown that many of the Jewish Christians in Jerusalem were not happy that Gentiles should be received into the church as equal with Jews, but without having to follow the Jewish laws (see 11:1-3). Peter may have silenced them once (see 11:18), but many still retained their old Jewish attitudes and ideas.

A group of these Jews now came from Jerusalem to Antioch in Syria, teaching that Gentile converts had to be circumcised and keep the law of Moses (15:1; see also v. 5). These men claimed they had authority from James, but James later denied this (Gal 2:12; cf. Acts 15:24). They argued so persuasively that even mature Christians such as Peter and Barnabas stopped eating with the Gentile Christians in case they broke Jewish food laws. Paul, who before his conversion was as zealous a Jew as any, saw that the teaching of the Judaisers was contrary to the Christian gospel. A forthright public rebuke from Paul resulted in Peter and Barnabas realizing their error and resuming fellowship with the Gentiles (Gal 2:11-16; cf. Acts 15:6-12).

Paul writes to the Galatians

Soon after correcting the trouble in Antioch, Paul heard that the Judaisers had spread their teachings to the newly planted churches of Galatia (Antioch, Iconium, Lystra, and Derbe) and some of the new Christians were being led astray. Angered at this, Paul immediately sent off a sharply worded letter, known to us as the Letter to the Galatians (Gal 1:6; 3:1).

In this letter Paul pointed out that there was only one gospel, the one he preached, and that the law of Moses has no authority over Christians. They are justified by faith in Christ and live by the same faith. Though free from the law of Moses, they are not lawless, but under the direction of the indwelling Spirit of Christ (Gal 3:3; 5:1,13,16,18).

To Jerusalem to discuss the problem (15:2-21)

The trouble created by the Judaisers had now spread to the farthermost parts of the church, so the matter needed to be settled quickly and decisively. Because the teaching came from Jerusalem, that was the place to discuss the matter. The church at Antioch therefore appointed Paul, Barnabas and other leaders to go to Jerusalem as its representatives. Along the way and after their arrival in Jerusalem, they reported on the widespread turning to God among the Gentiles, but as soon as the meeting began the Judaisers spoke against them (2-5). (This Jerusalem meeting is sometimes referred to as the Council of Jerusalem.)

After lengthy debate, Peter vigorously opposed the Judaisers and defended the Gentiles, asserting that Gentiles should not have to keep the Jewish law. The way of salvation and entrance into the full Christian fellowship was by faith alone, and was the same for Jews and Gentiles. This principle was basic to the gospel and could not be changed (6-11). The recent experiences of Paul and Barnabas reinforced this principle (12).

James agreed with Peter, Paul and Barnabas, adding that the events they were witnessing — the coming of the Messiah, the establishment of his kingdom and the expansion of that kingdom among the Gentiles — had been foretold by the prophets of Old Testament times (13-18).

In summing up the discussion, James repeated that no attempt should be made to put the Gentiles under the Jewish law (19). However, one problem remained. Jewish attitudes to social issues had been moulded by centuries of submission to the law of Moses, whereas Gentiles had no such law and as a result their moral standards were lower. The Jews considered many Gentile practices improper, such as the eating of any sort of food at all, regardless of how it had been killed or whether it had been offered to idols. James therefore suggested that the Gentile Christians would help improve relations between the two groups if they were careful not to engage in practices that the Jews considered offensive (20-21).

Letter from Jerusalem (15:22-35)

Acknowledging the wisdom of James' suggestion, the Antioch representatives were pleased to take back with them two leading men from the Jerusalem church, Judas and Silas, to help create a better understanding between the Jewish and Gentile groups (22).

The party also carried a letter from the Jerusalem meeting that expressed regret concerning the Judaisers' trouble-making and encouraged the Gentiles to be considerate of their Jewish brothers. The letter was not one of command, because all churches were independent of each other and none had the right to dictate to another. Yet there was a unity between them because of the common life they shared in Christ. If Christians were to enjoy that unity, they had to exercise love towards those who held different opinions on matters of lesser importance (23-29).

When the group arrived in Antioch, the local Christians were greatly encouraged to hear the outcome of the Jerusalem meeting, and gladly accepted the letter that the leaders passed on to them (30-31). They also profited from the preaching of Judas and Silas. But because they had been unsettled by the recent difficulties, Paul and Barnabas stayed on for a while to strengthen and reassure them (32-35).

15:36-18:22 INTO EUROPE (SECOND MISSIONARY JOURNEY)

Choosing a partner (15:36-41)

Paul and Barnabas thought that, in view of the recent troubles with the Judaisers, they should revisit the newly established churches in Galatia (36). Unfortunately, they could not agree on whether to take Mark with them. Barnabas wanted to but Paul refused, as he considered Mark to be unreliable. In the end they separated, Barnabas going to his native Cyprus with Mark, and Paul going to his native Cilicia with Silas (37-41).

Silas had, by his actions at the Jerusalem meeting and by his Christian service at Antioch, shown himself to be a person of ability and wisdom. Also, as Paul was to visit the churches where the Judaisers had just been, he no doubt saw some value in having with him a member of the Jerusalem church. Added to this, Silas was, like Paul, a Roman citizen (see 16:37), which would be an advantage in the Gentile areas.

Across Asia Minor to Troas (16:1-10)

Upon arriving in Lystra, Paul and Silas were joined by Timothy, a young man whom the elders of the Galatian churches considered suited to the task ahead (1 Tim 1:18; 4:14). Timothy was half-Jewish, and Paul thought it wise that he be circumcised, apparently hoping that this would gain acceptance for Timothy with the Jewish population wherever the missionaries went. The circumcision of Timothy was for practical, not religious, purposes, in keeping with Paul's principle that while working with the Jews he would live like the Jews so that he might win them for Christ (16:1-3; cf. 1 Cor 9:20).

As they passed through the Galatian towns, the missionaries delivered copies of the Jerusalem letter to the churches. This letter added further weight to what Paul had said to them in his own recent letter (4-5).

Leaving Galatia they entered the province of Asia, but God did not allow them to preach there. They headed north towards the province of Bithynia, but again God prevented them from carrying out their plans. So they headed west across the region of Mysia to the town of Troas, from where they prepared to sail to Europe. Their destination was to be the province of Macedonia, the northern part of present-day Greece. These unexpected changes in Paul's missionary movements showed that although he knew the importance of planning his work, he knew also the importance of obeying whenever God directed him otherwise (6-10).

Philippi – first church in Europe (16:11-40)

The missionaries left Troas with another addition to the party, Luke, the author of the book (note the word 'we' in verse 11). Luke's home appears to have been in Philippi, the city to which the group was now heading (11-12). It seems that Philippi had few Jews and no synagogue, but a group of God-fearers met for prayer at the river bank. The missionaries joined with them and made known to them the gospel of Jesus Christ. As a result a cloth merchant named Lydia became a Christian and, through her, her household also believed (13-15).

Not all the interest that the preachers created in Philippi was favourable. Trouble began when they healed a slave girl who, because of an evil spirit that possessed her, earned much money for her owners by telling fortunes (16-18). When her owners found she could no longer be used to earn them money, they attacked the missionaries and created a riot. Paul and Silas were arrested, flogged and thrown into prison without trial or questioning (19-24).

Yet even in prison Paul and Silas found the opportunity to talk about Jesus Christ. The outcome was the conversion of the jailer along with his household (25-34). Next morning Paul and Silas were allowed to go free, but they refused to go until they received an apology from the local officials. Paul claimed that the officials had no right to flog Roman citizens, especially without trial (35-40).

Through Macedonia to Athens (17:1-15)

In recording the groups' departure from Philippi and subsequent movements, the writer uses 'they' rather than 'we', indicating that Luke stayed behind in Philippi. The others moved on to Thessalonica, where over the next three Sabbaths their preaching in the synagogue brought good results (17:1-4). (If this visit to Thessalonica was the one referred to in Philippians 4:16, they probably stayed longer than three weeks, since the Philippians twice sent gifts to him there.)

As usual the missionaries' successes stirred up the jealousy of the Jews. With the help of some hooligans, the Jews caused an uproar and attacked the house of Jason where Paul had been staying. When they discovered that Paul was not at home,

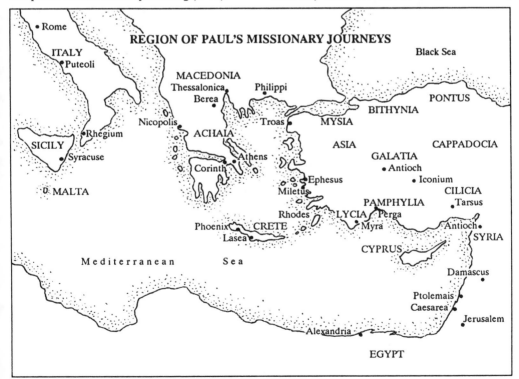

475

they seized Jason instead and took him to the city officials. They accused Jason of helping a group of Jewish rebels who were planning to set up their own king, Jesus, in rebellion against Caesar. When no one could find Paul and his party, the officials held Jason responsible to see that there was no further trouble. The payment of money that they took from Jason may have involved a guarantee that Paul would leave the city and not return (5-9; cf. 1 Thess 2:18). (Although Paul did not visit Thessalonica again on this journey, he may have visited it on his next journey; see 20:1-2.)

At Berea the story of Jewish opposition was much the same (10-13). Paul was forced to depart, leaving Silas and Timothy behind while he went on to Athens. From Athens he sent a message telling them to rejoin him at once (14-15). After they met him in Athens, Paul sent them back to Macedonia, Timothy going to Thessalonica and Silas probably to Philippi (see 1 Thess 3:1-2; cf. Acts 18:5).

Paul in Athens (17:16-34)

Athens was in the province of Achaia, the southern part of present-day Greece. It was the chief centre of learning in the Roman Empire, a place where philosophy, religion and politics were taught and discussed freely. When some local philosophers heard Paul preaching in the public places of the city, they invited him to give an account of his religion to the council of philosophers known as the Areopagus. This was an ancient council that exercised control over those who lectured publicly in Athens. When Paul preached, he so often linked the name 'Jesus' with the word 'resurrection' (Greek: *anastasis*) that the philosophers thought he was introducing them to two gods, Jesus and Anastasis (16-21).

The Areopagus was divided largely between two schools of Greek philosophers, the Epicureans and the Stoics (v. 18). The Epicureans believed that because nothing in the world is lasting or stable, people should not become too involved in the affairs of life. They should seek contentment through living calmly, and should try to avoid all pain, desire, unpleasant feelings and superstitious fears. This was how the gods lived, and for this reason they took little interest in human affairs. The Stoics believed that everything is determined by a universal Mind or Reason. Therefore, people should accept whatever they meet in life without fear or complaint, and adjust their lives to fit what nature has determined for them. Self-discipline was essential; reason was always to have control over feelings.

Paul confidently announced to the members of the Areopagus that he would explain to them the nature of the God whom they did not know (22-23). This God was the Creator and Controller of the universe and the Lord of all humankind. Yet he was a God whom human beings could know, for they were made in his image (24-28). In former ages God had been patient with the ignorance of a sinful human race, but now that Jesus had come he held people responsible for their acceptance or rejection of him. Forgiveness was available to those who repented of their sin, but punishment faced those who refused to repent. By raising Jesus from death, God showed that Jesus was the one through whom he would deal with people, whether in forgiveness or in punishment (29-31).

The Epicureans would have agreed with Paul that God needs nothing from human beings (v. 25). The Stoics would have agreed that there is a supreme God who is the source of all life and who determines when and where the peoples of the earth should live (v. 24-26,28). But both alike found that Paul's teaching about the resurrection was not worthy of serious consideration. Not all Athenians, however, rejected Paul's message (32-34).

Across to Corinth (18:1-4)

Corinth was a strategic commercial centre situated on a well used Roman road. It was also an important port, and like many ports it was full of all sorts of vice. Its reputation was so bad that people referred to a person of loose morals as one who 'behaved like a Corinthian'. Yet Paul planted a church there and, not surprisingly, it became one of the most colourful and unorthodox churches of all.

As he often did on his travels, Paul earned his living in Corinth by working for a time at his trade of tentmaking (cf. 1 Thess 2:9; 2 Thess 3:8). In so doing he met a Jewish married couple, Aquila and Priscilla, who were also tentmakers and who were to become his lifelong friends. They, along with other Jews, had recently been forced to leave Rome by command of the Emperor (18:1-3). No doubt they went with Paul to the synagogue, where he preached the gospel (4).

Paul writes to the Thessalonians

At that time Silas and Timothy returned from Macedonia, bringing with them gifts of money for Paul from the Macedonian churches. This provision released Paul from his tentmaking and enabled him to spend all his time preaching (see 18:5; cf. 2 Cor 11:8-9; Phil 4:15). Paul was so pleased with the good news that Timothy brought from Thessalonica that he wrote and sent off a letter which we know as First Thessalonians (1 Thess 3:6).

Paul was particularly pleased to hear that his hasty departure from Thessalonica had not hindered the progress of God's work there. Despite constant persecution, the church continued to grow, and within a short time had spread the gospel throughout the surrounding districts (1 Thess 1:6-8; 2:13-14). Sadly, some criticized Paul for leaving the new converts in Thessalonica to face the anti-Christian trouble that initially had been stirred up through him. Paul defended himself against these accusations and at the same time encouraged the Christians to stand firm amid the opposition (1 Thess 2:1-8,17-18; 3:3-5). He also gave instruction concerning certain aspects of Christian behaviour and cleared up some misunderstandings concerning the return of Jesus Christ (1 Thess 4:1,9,13; 5:1-2).

Within a short time, perhaps only a few weeks, Paul heard that some of the Thessalonians had misunderstood parts of his letter, particularly those parts dealing with Christ's return. He therefore sent off a second letter, which is known to us as Second Thessalonians.

Some mistakenly thought that when Paul said Jesus Christ would return 'suddenly' he meant 'immediately'. There were even those who thought that if Christ was about to return, there was no purpose in working any longer. As a result they became idle and a burden to others. Paul corrected the misunderstandings (2 Thess 2:1-3), rebuked the idle (2 Thess 3:6-12), gave further encouragement to the persecuted (2 Thess 1:4-5) and urged all to stand firm in the truth (2 Thess 2:15).

Eighteen months in Corinth (18:5-17)

Meanwhile in Corinth, Paul was having the usual trouble with the Jews. They forced him out of the synagogue, so he went and preached in the house of Titius Justus, a Gentile God-fearer who lived next door (5-7). Crispus, the ruler of the synagogue, himself believed (8; cf. 1 Cor 1:14), and possibly the new ruler of the synagogue, Sosthenes, later believed also (see v. 17; cf. 1 Cor 1:1).

In spite of the constant opposition, Paul kept preaching, and during the year and a half that he stayed in Corinth the church grew (9-11). On one occasion when the Jews tried to lay a charge against Paul, the governor refused to hear them. He looked upon Paul's party as a group within Judaism, and saw the dispute as a religious matter that the Jews would have to settle themselves (12-16). The local people, seeing that the governor was unsympathetic to the Jews, took the opportunity to express their anti-Jewish feelings by beating up one of the Jewish leaders (17).

Return to Antioch (18:18-22)

Paul then prepared to return home. At Cenchreae, from where the ship sailed, he fulfilled a vow (probably a Nazirite vow; see Num 6:1-21) which for some reason he had taken upon himself (18). He sailed across to Ephesus where he stayed a short while. His preaching created much interest and probably resulted in the start of a church in that city. Then, leaving Aquila and Priscilla in Ephesus, he sailed for his home church in Antioch, though he hoped to return to Ephesus soon (19-22).

18:23-21:16 BACK TO ASIA MINOR AND EUROPE (THIRD MISSIONARY JOURNEY)

Through Galatia to Ephesus (18:23-19:7)

On his third great journey to the west, Paul set out by visiting the churches of Galatia once again. This was the fourth time he had visited these churches and he had also written them a letter (23; cf. 13:14,51; 14:21; 16:2-6).

In the meantime a learned Jew named Apollos had come to Ephesus from Alexandria in Egypt. Like many of the Jewish teachers in Alexandria, he had a detailed knowledge of Old Testament references to the Messiah and was able to teach impressively. However, he lacked knowledge of certain Christian teachings until Aquila and Priscilla explained them to him (24-26). Later, when he moved across to Corinth, he was of great help to the church there and added considerably to the good work Paul had done previously (27-28; 1 Cor 3:6). Unfortunately, the Corinthian church divided into factions, because people made favourites of various teachers. This was a problem that Paul soon had to deal with (1 Cor 1:12; 3:4).

On arriving in Ephesus, Paul met a group of twelve people who had repented and been baptized as taught by John the Baptist. But they did not know that since the death and resurrection of Jesus, the form of baptism that John proclaimed was no longer in use. The one whom John announced had come, and the baptism with the Spirit that John promised had been given (on the Day of Pentecost; cf. Matt 3:11; Acts 1:4-5; 2:16-17,33). When they understood this they were baptized in water as disciples of Jesus Christ, and received the Holy Spirit as the original disciples had at Pentecost (19:1-7).

Ephesus and the surrounding region (19:8-22)

After Paul had preached for three months in the synagogue, the Jews forced him out, so he went and taught in the lecture hall of Tyrannus. He carried on his teaching work there for the next two years, during which the disciples took the message into the surrounding countryside (8-10). This activity seems to have resulted in churches being founded, without Paul's help, in the towns of Colossae, Hierapolis and Laodicea (Col 2:1; 4:13), and possibly also Smyrna, Pergamum, Thyatira, Sardis and Philadelphia (Rev 2:8,12,18; 3:1,7).

The healing ministry of the Messiah that had worked through Peter and John continued to work through Paul (11-12; cf. 3:1-16; 5:12-16; 9:33-35). Some itinerant Jewish wonder-workers, impressed with Paul's ability to drive out demons in the name of Jesus, tried to copy him, but were themselves violently attacked by the demons (13-16). Sorcery, magic and superstition were widespread in Ephesus, but God's power was at work in the city and large numbers of people turned to him (17-20).

As the churches in the province of Asia grew stronger, Paul began planning his future movements. His ultimate aim was to go to Rome, so that he could help establish Christianity more firmly in the heart of the Empire (cf. Rom 1:11-15). But first he wanted to go to Jerusalem. During the past year or so he had been organizing a collection of money to take to the poor Christians in Jerusalem, a plan that he hoped would bind the Jewish and Gentile churches together (1 Cor 16:1-4; 2 Cor 8:1-24; 9:1-5; Rom 15:23-27). His purpose in sending two fellow workers to Macedonia was probably to help promote and organize this project (21-22).

A riot in Ephesus (19:23-41)

Paul preached and taught in Ephesus for almost three years (see 20:31), and many people became Christians. Ephesus was considered to be the home of the goddess Artemis (or Diana), and the citizens of Ephesus were the honoured guardians of the magnificent temple of Artemis in their city. With so many people turning from the worship of Artemis, the temple was losing its popularity. Furthermore, local silversmiths who made small images and household shrines of the goddess were going out of business (23-27).

Angry at their loss of income, the silversmiths stirred up the people against Paul and his fellow missionaries, and a riot broke out. Since any who did not worship Artemis were in danger, the Jews tried to protect themselves by pointing out that they were not associated with the Christians. But the mob refused to listen (28-34).

In calming the riotous crowd, the city's chief official defended Paul and his party. At the same time he warned the people not to take the law into their own hands again, because Rome would not tolerate such disorder (35-41). Although on this occasion Paul did not suffer physical violence, on other occasions during his stay in Ephesus he certainly did (1 Cor 15:32; 2 Cor 1:8-9).

Travels and writings of this time

During this three year period, most of which Paul spent in Ephesus, much happened that is not recorded in Acts. However, as we read Paul's letters we can understand more of his activity during this time. The following is a suggested summary of events:

1. While in Ephesus, Paul wrote to the church in Corinth on various practical and moral issues. The letter has not been preserved (1 Cor 5:9).
2. Paul sent Timothy and Erastus to Macedonia (Acts 19:22) and from there to Corinth, in an effort to deal with problems in the Corinthian church (1 Cor 4:17; 16:10). Certain people in the church had developed strong feelings against Paul and even questioned his standing as an apostle (1 Cor 4:8-13,18-21).
3. Meanwhile some Corinthian believers (people from Chloe's household) arrived in Ephesus with bad news about the state of affairs in Corinth. Quarrels and factions had developed in the church because people made favourites of their teachers (1 Cor 1:11-12). Further problems arose because of immorality in the church and lawsuits between Christians (1 Cor 5:1; 6:1). In addition, representatives from the church came to Paul in Ephesus with questions on a variety of other matters (1 Cor 7:1; 8:1; 12:1; 16:17).
4. These concerns prompted Paul to write the church another letter, known to us as 1 Corinthians. It was probably taken to Corinth direct by boat so that it reached the church before Timothy (1 Cor 16:8-10). The letter dealt with the problems Paul had heard about, and answered questions concerning marriage, food offered to idols, spiritual gifts, order in the church, the coming resurrection and the collection for the Jerusalem Christians.
5. Earlier Paul had planned to visit Macedonia and then Corinth (Acts 19:21; 1 Cor 16:5-7). But when Timothy returned from Corinth with the news that neither his visit nor Paul's latest letter had been able to improve the situation, Paul changed his plans. He made a hurried trip across to Corinth (as he had warned; 1 Cor 4:19-21) in an effort to deal with the trouble-makers. This was Paul's second visit to Corinth, and later he looked back on it as one that gave both him and the Corinthians much distress (2 Cor 2:1; 13:2).

6. Paul could not stay long in Corinth, but he planned to revisit the church as soon as his work in Ephesus was finished (2 Cor 1:15-16).
7. Back in Ephesus, Paul soon heard that his recent trip to Corinth, instead of helping to improve matters, made his opponents more rebellious. He was furious, but thought it wise not to rush back and perhaps act in a way he might later regret (2 Cor 1:23). Instead he wrote a letter, a very severe letter, in which he urged the church to take firm action against those who opposed his Christ-given authority. Although Paul refers to the letter in his writings, it has not been preserved. It was taken to Corinth by Titus (2 Cor 2:3-4; 7:8; 12:18).
8. Upon completing his work in Ephesus, Paul went north to Troas, where Titus was to meet him after delivering the letter to the Corinthians. But Titus had not yet arrived. Paul was so anxious to get news from Corinth that, rather than wait for Titus in Troas, he went across to Macedonia to meet him sooner (2 Cor 2:12-13; cf. Acts 20:1).
9. Titus met Paul in Macedonia (probably Philippi) and told him that the severe letter had produced favourable results. The Corinthians were no longer rebellious (2 Cor 7:5-6). Without delay Paul wrote yet another letter to the Corinthians, the letter we know as 2 Corinthians, and sent it with Titus and two others (2 Cor 8:16-18,22-23). In this letter Paul expressed his joy at the Corinthians' change of heart, explained his recent actions, described the transforming power of the gospel, gave further details of the collection for the poor Christians in Jerusalem, and defended his apostolic ministry.

Through Macedonia and Achaia (20:1-2)

As seen in paragraph 8 of the above summary, at the end of Paul's three years in Ephesus he travelled north to Troas and then across to Macedonia (20:1). After meeting Titus and writing 2 Corinthians, Paul moved around other parts of the region and then headed south towards Achaia (2). Possibly one place he visited was Illyricum, a region that in New Testament times included the Roman province of Dalmatia and in modern times includes the country of Albania (Rom 15:19; cf. 2 Tim 4:10).

Paul writes to the Romans

In due course Paul arrived in the south of Greece and stayed there three months (see 20:3). No doubt he spent much of this time with the church in Corinth (2 Cor 13:1), for he wanted to be assured that it was stable and strong before he expanded his work to the west (2 Cor 10:15-16). From Corinth the next base in his planned move westward was Rome (Acts 19:21).

A church already existed in Rome. Paul had not planted it, as he had not yet been to Rome (Rom 1:13; 15:22). Most likely those who planted it were Christians from other parts of the Empire who travelled to Rome or went there to live (cf. Acts 2:10; Rom 16:3-16). Paul saw Rome as a key centre from which to spread the gospel farther to the west, perhaps even as far as Spain (Rom 15:23-24,28-29). More than that he saw that if Christianity had a strong base in the heart of the Empire, it would readily spread throughout the Empire. He therefore wrote to the church in Rome to make sure that the Roman Christians themselves had a clear understanding of the gospel and that they shared his vision for worldwide evangelism (Rom 1:10-15; 10:12-17; 15:14-16).

At the time of writing, Paul was staying in Corinth with Gaius, one of the earliest Corinthian converts and probably a respected leader in the church (Rom 16:23; cf. 1 Cor 1:14). Another local Christian, Phoebe, was going to Rome and took the letter on Paul's behalf. She was a deacon in the church at Cenchreae, one of the port areas of Corinth (Rom 16:1-2).

Return to Macedonia and Troas (20:3-12)

Although Paul was planning to visit Rome, his immediate concern was to go to Jerusalem with the money he had been collecting from the Gentile churches (Rom 15:24-26; Acts 19:21). But just as he was about to set sail, he heard of a Jewish plot to kill him. So he changed his plans and returned through Macedonia (3). In Macedonia, probably at Philippi, Luke rejoined the party (indicated by the renewed use of 'we' and 'us' in the narrative). They then sailed across to Troas, where they joined the representatives of the Gentile churches who were to go with Paul to Jerusalem (4-6; cf. 1 Cor 16:3).

It seems that, by this time, Sunday had become a special day for Christians, when they met for fellowship and worship (7; cf. 1 Cor 16:2; Rev 1:10). During Paul's final meeting with the Christians in Troas, the all-night discussion was interrupted when a young man fell out of a window to his death; but Paul restored him to life (8-12).

To Jerusalem with the offering (20:13-21:16)

From Troas Paul went by land to Assos, where he rejoined the rest of the party and sailed to Miletus (13-16). Since Miletus was only about fifty kilometres from Ephesus, Paul took the opportunity to call the elders of the Ephesian church to come and meet him. He wanted to give them some final encouragement and pass on helpful warnings (17).

Paul's opponents in Asia had probably been trying to turn the Christians against him. Therefore, he reminded the Ephesian elders of his tireless work in Ephesus and of the constant danger he faced from the Jews (18-24).

The Christians at Ephesus also were about to be shaken by serious troubles. Paul knew that, in spite of his preaching in Ephesus, people both from within the church and from outside would try to destroy the work of God in that city. The elders would need to be watchful, understanding, hardworking and strong if the church was to withstand Satan's attacks (25-31). Paul reassured the elders that by God's grace and through his Word they would be built up. He also reminded them that, like him, they were to sacrifice their rights and comforts for the sake of others, and never use their position of leadership for personal profit (32-38).

From Miletus Paul and his party sailed to Patara, where they changed ships and sailed across the Mediterranean to Phoenicia (21:1-3). They had fellowship with the Christians at Tyre, Ptolemais and Caesarea, where churches had been founded by those scattered after the killing of Stephen. One of those early evangelists, Philip, was still in Caesarea and Paul's party stayed with him several days (4-9; cf. 8:4-5,40; 11:19). In Caesarea, as in Tyre, prophets warned Paul of the trouble that he would meet in Jerusalem, but he was determined to go on (10-14; see also v. 4).

Finally, Paul reached his destination, Jerusalem. There he stayed with Mnason, who was a Jewish Christian from Cyprus and an early member of the Jerusalem church. He was probably one of the few in Jerusalem who were fully in agreement with Paul's work among the Gentiles (15-16).

21:17-23:35 JERUSALEM FINALLY REJECTS THE GOSPEL

Danger in Jerusalem (21:17-26)

Over the previous ten years the church in Jerusalem had become narrower in its outlook. As leaders of broader outlook such as Peter, John and Barnabas moved out to other areas, the Jewish Christians left in Jerusalem slipped back into legalism. At the Jerusalem meeting of Chapter 15, James and his like-minded fellow elders had successfully defended the Gentiles, but they now had little influence over the members at large. Those who wished to put

all Christians under the Jewish law, though silenced at the Jerusalem meeting, had not changed their former views, and now their number had grown to many thousands (see v. 20).

The elders of the Jerusalem church were glad to receive the offering from the Gentile churches (17-19), but this had little effect on the thinking of most of the church members. The legalistic Jews were not concerned greatly about what Paul taught the Gentiles, but they were angered to hear reports that he taught the Jews not to keep the law of Moses or the traditions of their ancestors (20-21). James and his friends suggested that Paul prove to the Jerusalemites that he was as religious a Jew as any, by joining with four other Jews in a purification ceremony in the temple (22-25).

Being willing to do almost anything to win his fellow Jews, Paul joined in the ceremony (26; cf. 1 Cor 9:20-23). Whether he was right or wrong in doing so is not clear. Certainly the plan was not a success, for it got Paul into serious trouble that left him a prisoner of Rome for most of the next five years.

The crowd attacks Paul (21:27-36)

Paul, James and the elders were so busy trying to please the Jerusalem Jews that they may have forgotten Paul's constant enemies, the Asian Jews (cf. 20:18-19; 2 Cor 1:8). These were the ones who brought about his downfall. Because they saw him in the streets with a Gentile friend from Ephesus, they accused him (wrongly) of taking the Gentile into a part of the temple where Gentiles were forbidden (27-29). When a riot broke out, the mob seized Paul and tried to kill him (30-31).

The Roman troops in Jerusalem were well trained to control Jewish riots, and on this occasion only their swift action prevented Paul from being murdered (32). Lysias, the military commander, had no idea who Paul was or what he had done to make the Jews angry, but he was determined to see him dealt with properly according to Roman law, not by mob violence (33-36).

Paul's reply to the crowd (21:37-22:29)

By his command of the situation, Paul showed much physical courage and mental alertness. One minute he was snatched from a violent death, the next he was able to address a mob of wildly excited Jews who were screaming for his blood. He spoke with such power that a rioting crowd of would-be murderers listened to him in silence (37-40).

Paul wanted to show that he was a zealous Jew, called by God to serve him. He told of his Jewish upbringing and education, and of his religious zeal in persecuting those he thought to be law-breakers (22:1-5). But then the risen Jesus intervened and he became a believer (6-11). Through the announcement of a respected and law-abiding Jew named Ananias, he learnt of God's purpose for him to take the gospel to people everywhere (12-16). Above all he wanted his own people, the Jews, to hear the gospel, and only when they rejected it did God send him to preach it among the Gentiles (17-21).

As soon as Paul mentioned his mission to the Gentiles, uproar broke out afresh. All Paul's speech and all the crowd's shouting were in Aramaic, which the Roman commander probably could not understand. So he decided there was only one way to find out the truth, and that was by flogging (22-24). When Paul told the soldiers that he was a Roman citizen, they quickly untied him. They knew how close they themselves had come to being law-breakers (25-29).

Before the Sanhedrin (22:30-23:11)

Still wanting to find out the story behind this remarkable man, Lysias called the Jewish Sanhedrin to examine him (30). Paul soon saw, however, that the Sanhedrin was already set against him and he was not likely to get justice there (23:1-5).

Paul therefore changed his tactics. The one who had spoken to the Roman commander in Greek, addressed the mob in Aramaic, announced himself as God's apostle to the Gentiles and claimed to be a Roman citizen, now called himself a Jewish Pharisee! He was being condemned because of his orthodox Pharisaic belief in the resurrection (6).

The immediate result of Paul's declaration was that the Sanhedrin split in two, Pharisees against Sadducees. Some Pharisees thought Paul was not such a bad person after all (much the same as another Pharisee had said of Peter and John in a similar Sanhedrin dispute more than twenty years earlier; see 5:33-39). In the uproar that followed, the Roman soldiers again saved Paul from possible death (7-10). The Lord was still with Paul and eventually would bring him to Rome (11).

Sent to Caesarea (23:12-35)

The Jews were not finished yet. They decided to ask Lysias to send Paul to the Sanhedrin for a fresh trial the next day, so they could attack and kill him on the way (12-15). Unfortunately for the Jews, the plan was discovered and reported to Lysias (16-22).

Knowing that the Jews would carry out their plan if at all possible, Lysias thought it better to remove Paul from Jerusalem altogether. He decided to send Paul to the provincial capital, Caesarea, where he would come under the direct control of the provincial governor (23-24). In sending a letter to the governor, Lysias carefully rearranged the story to make sure that no blame could be placed on him (25-30). As Paul left Jerusalem for the last time, he had still not seen the fulfilment of his lifelong wish of unity between Jerusalem and the Gentile churches. But he did not give up his fight against Jewish misunderstandings (31-35).

24:1-28:31 PAUL FAREWELLS THE EAST; GOES TO ROME

Imprisoned in Caesarea two years (24:1-27)

In the trial before Felix, the Jews used a professional lawyer to present their case (24:1-4). They made three accusations against Paul. Firstly, he created uprisings among the Jews, the suggestion being that he was stirring up rebellion against Rome. Secondly, he was a leader of the Nazarenes, a religious group that operated without government permission and therefore was probably rebellious against Rome. Thirdly, he had defiled the temple in Jerusalem (5-9).

Paul began his defence by denying that he had stirred up the people in Jerusalem. No one could prove such a claim (10-13). Secondly, he admitted that he was a follower of 'the Way', but this was the true continuation and completion of the ancient Israelite religion. It was not a new sect, neither was it false. Paul believed in the resurrection of the dead, as did most Jews, and he worshipped the same God as they did (14-16). Finally, he had not defiled the temple; in fact, he had carried out a ceremony of purification. In addition he had brought gifts to help his fellow Jews in their need. The Sanhedrin's only accusation against him concerned his belief in the resurrection, and even that was supported by only one section of it (17-21).

Felix knew the Jews well and plainly saw that Paul was not guilty, but out of fear of the Jews he would not release him. So Paul spent the next two years in prison, though he was allowed to receive visits from friends (22-23; see v. 27). Felix wanted to find out more about Paul's Christian beliefs, but he became uncomfortable when Paul spoke of the need for right behaviour and the certainty of coming judgment. Paul could have been released had he been willing to pay the bribe Felix was seeking, but he refused. Felix therefore left him in prison till the arrival of the next governor, who could handle the case as he wished (24-27).

No hope of justice in Judea (25:1-12)

When the new governor, Festus, arrived in Palestine, the Jews were quick to accuse Paul afresh. They no doubt thought that the new governor's lack of experience in handling Jewish affairs would help them win a judgment against Paul (25:1-5).

The trial before Festus was much the same as the one before Felix, but the confused Festus was not sure how to handle the case. He saw no reason why Paul should be in prison, yet he thought it wise to gain the goodwill of the Jews from the outset of his governorship. He therefore suggested that Paul go to Jerusalem and have the case dealt with there, perhaps before the Sanhedrin with Festus himself as the judge (6-9).

Paul could tolerate this injustice no longer. Neither Felix nor Festus had found him guilty of any wrongdoing, yet he had been kept a prisoner of Rome for two years; and all this merely to satisfy the Jews. Paul saw clearly that he would receive no justice from either Festus or the Sanhedrin, so he turned to the final court of appeal open to every Roman citizen, that of Caesar himself (10-12).

Paul again declared innocent (25:13-26:32)

Among those who came to Caesarea to pay their respects to the new governor was Herod Agrippa II. This man was the son of Herod Agrippa I (the governor mentioned in 12:1-4,20-23) and the brother of Bernice and Drusilla (13; cf. 24:24; see 'The New Testament World'). He was Rome's appointed ruler over certain areas in the far north of Palestine, but he had no power in the region governed by Festus. He was, however, an expert on Jewish affairs (see 26:3,27,31), and Festus was quick to seek his advice on Paul's case (14-22).

Festus' problem was that he had to send Paul to Caesar for trial, but he had no idea what to say to Caesar about the case. He did not know what accusations the Jews brought against Paul or why they wanted him executed (23-27).

Paul was pleased at last to have the opportunity to put his case before a ruler who had a good knowledge of the Jewish religion (26:1-3). His account of events was similar to that which he gave to the Jewish mob in Jerusalem two years earlier, but with an occasional change of emphasis to suit the present audience. Like most loyal Jews, Paul believed in the resurrection of the dead, but when he preached that Jesus' resurrection brought the Jews' age-long hopes to fulfilment, they persecuted him (4-8).

To some extent Paul could understand the Jews' feelings, because he himself had once persecuted the followers of Jesus (9-11). But the risen Lord Jesus appeared to him and sent him to preach the forgiveness of sins to all people, Jews and Gentiles alike (12-18). Paul willingly obeyed, because he now saw that the salvation brought by Jesus the Messiah was the fulfilment of all that the law and the prophets foretold (19-23).

Festus could not follow the argument at all and thought that Paul was mad (24). Agrippa, however, was familiar with the Old Testament Scriptures and understood what Paul was saying. Paul therefore appealed to him for support (25-27). Agrippa replied, either light-heartedly or sarcastically, that Paul was being over-enthusiastic if he thought he could convert him to Christianity in such a short time (28-29). Nevertheless, he was honest enough to admit that Paul had done nothing that deserved imprisonment (30-32).

By one example after another Luke was making it clear to Theophilus that the Christians were not unlawful or rebellious. In addition to those already mentioned who found no guilt in Paul (namely, the Jerusalem army commander, the Jewish Sanhedrin and two Roman governors), an independent expert on Jewish affairs also declared him to be innocent.

From Caesarea to Rome (27:1-28:15)

Festus arranged for a centurion and a unit of Roman soldiers to take Paul, along with a number of other prisoners, to Rome. Two Christians also went with Paul, his loyal friend Luke and a church leader from Thessalonica named Aristarchus (27:1-2; cf. 19:29; 20:4). They began the journey on a ship that took them as far as Myra in Asia Minor. There they changed to one of the huge grain ships that sailed between Alexandria and Italy. After several days they came to the island of Crete (3-8).

At the port of Fair Havens (Safe Harbours), Paul advised the ship's officers not to sail any further till the dangerous winter season had passed. But they rejected Paul's advice and decided to move on to the next Cretan port, Phoenix, which they considered to be a better place to spend the winter (9-12).

Soon all were sorry that they had not listened to Paul. A fierce storm struck, and it seemed certain that the ship would sink and all on board would drown (13-20). Paul believed otherwise. God had assured him that, although the ship would be lost, all on board would be saved, and Paul himself would eventually reach Rome (21-26).

Paul's natural qualities of leadership soon saw him take control of the situation, in spite of his being a prisoner. When the ship was about to run aground and some sailors tried to escape, the Roman guard acted on Paul's advice and stopped them (27-32). When Paul warned that people were endangering their lives by going so long without eating, the ship's officers likewise heeded his words (33-38). Only the centurion's respect for Paul stopped the soldiers from killing the prisoners when the ship broke up. In the end all those on board the ship escaped safely to land (39-44).

The island on which they landed was Malta. The local people were kind and helpful to them all, but again Paul was the one who created the most interest (28:1-6). Although he was legally a prisoner, he and his party spent three days with the island's chief official as his special guests. In return for the hospitality received from the islanders, Paul and Luke attended to many of their medical needs (7-10).

Three months after landing on Malta, when winter was over and sailing was again safe, Paul's party boarded another Alexandrian grain ship and sailed for Puteoli in Italy. From there they went by road to Rome, being met by Christians from Rome at a number of places along the way (11-15).

Paul in Rome (28:16-31)

In Rome Paul enjoyed a limited freedom. He was allowed to live in his own house and people could visit him freely, though a Roman soldier guarded him constantly (16; cf. v. 30).

Soon after arriving he invited the Jewish leaders in Rome to come and see him. He outlined the events that had brought him to Rome and pointed out that he had done nothing contrary to Jewish law. He made it clear that he brought no accusation against the Jewish people; his appeal to Caesar was solely to prove his innocence (17-20).

The Jewish leaders gave the surprising reply that they had heard no reports about Paul, though they knew that people everywhere were turning against the Christians (21-22). It seems likely that, once Paul had left Palestine, the Jerusalem Jews felt they had achieved their main goal. They may not even have sent an accusation to Rome; for if they had failed to win the support of Felix and Festus in their own country, they had little hope of winning the support of Caesar in anti-Jewish Rome. Also, if Festus sent any official papers, they probably went down with the ship.

As usual Paul preached his message to the Jews first, showing from the Old Testament that the gospel he preached was the true fulfilment of the religion of Israel. But, as in other places, most of the Jews rejected his message. This also, said Paul, had been foretold by the Old Testament Scriptures. Therefore, he would once again turn and proclaim the message to the Gentiles and they would believe (23-29).

Paul's two-year house imprisonment probably included a fixed period of eighteen months during which his accusers could present their case. If, as seems likely, the Jerusalem Jews presented no case, the authorities in Rome could take no action. Any further relevant correspondence between Rome and the authorities in Palestine would account for the remaining six months.

The point Luke emphasizes concerning Paul's two years in Rome is a positive one, namely, that Christianity's leading representative was allowed to preach the gospel freely in Rome, and Roman officials had first-hand knowledge of his activity. Clearly, the Roman authorities did not consider Christianity an unlawful or politically dangerous religion. Paul proclaimed the kingdom of God in the heart of the Empire just as he had proclaimed it elsewhere. And on that triumphant note, Luke concludes his story (30-31).

The Post-Acts Period

PAUL IN ROME

During Paul's two-year imprisonment in Rome a number of people from distant places came to visit him. The news Paul received from these visitors prompted him to send off a number of letters, some of which have been collected in the New Testament.

Letter to the church in Colossae

One person to visit Paul in Rome was Epaphras, a Christian from Colossae in Asia Minor. The church in Colossae was probably formed during Paul's long stay in Ephesus, when the converts he trained took the gospel into the surrounding countryside (Acts 19:9-10). Epaphras, in fact, seems to have been the person mainly responsible for founding the church in Colossae (Col 1:6-7; 4:12). Now a problem had arisen that Epaphras was unable to deal with, so he went to Rome to seek Paul's help.

A strange form of teaching had found its way into the Colossian church. It was an early form of Gnosticism, a religious philosophy that combined Christian belief with pagan mythology. It also contained features taken from Judaism, mainly in connection with ceremonial laws and sacred rituals (Col 2:16,20-21).

The false teachers were concerned with trying to harmonize things that they considered to be in conflict with each other, such as good and evil, spirit and matter, God and man. Because they believed matter to be evil, they argued that a God who is holy could not come in contact with human beings who are sinful. They taught that there were countless intermediate beings, part-spirit and part-matter, who helped bridge the gap between God and the human race, and Jesus Christ was one of them. People were required to worship these beings if they were to gain victory over evil and eventually reach God (Col 2:8-10,18).

Paul opposed this teaching, pointing out that Jesus Christ is the only mediator between God and the human race, and the only person able to save sinful human beings. He is the supreme God who is over and above every being, spirit or material, yet he is the perfect human being who by his death conquered evil and brings repentant sinners into union with God (Col 1:15-22; 2:9,15). This union

means that on the one hand believers can have victory over evil, and on the other that Christ's life can be reproduced in them (Col 3:3-5,10).

Letter to Philemon

While Epaphras was with Paul, another person from Colossae arrived at Paul's place of imprisonment in Rome. This person, Onesimus, was a slave who worked for Philemon, the Christian in whose house the Colossian church met (Philem 1-2,10).

Onesimus had escaped from his master and fled to Rome in search of a new life of freedom. But upon meeting Paul he was converted. He knew that since he was now a Christian, he should correct past wrongdoings and return to his master, but he was understandably fearful. Paul knew Philemon well, so wrote him a letter asking him to forgive Onesimus and receive him back as a brother in Christ. Not only was Philemon to welcome Onesimus back to his household, but the church was to welcome him as a new and useful addition to its fellowship (Philem 10-20; cf. Col 4:9).

Letter to the church in Ephesus

Paul apparently learnt from Epaphras that the false teaching was not confined to Colossae. He therefore wrote another letter to send back to the region, as a means of passing on teaching to the churches as a whole. This letter, known to us as Ephesians, was more general than Paul's other letters. It made no specific references to individuals or incidents in a particular church, but dealt with broader issues of Christian faith and practice. It gave further teaching on matters discussed in Colossians, such as the uniqueness of Christ, his victory over evil spiritual forces, his union with his people, and the results that this union should produce in the lives of Christians (Eph 1:20-23; 2:2-6; 4:1,17; 6:12).

Ephesians seems to have been one of several similar letters that Paul sent to the churches of the region. Perhaps the name of the receiving church was written into the introduction of each letter as it was delivered. If so, that would explain why some ancient manuscripts include the word 'Ephesus' in the introduction, but others omit it (Eph 1:1). Paul's letter to the church in Laodicea may have been another copy of this letter (Col 4:16). The person who delivered these letters, Tychicus, also passed on news of Paul's circumstances in Rome (Eph 6:21-22; Col 4:7-9).

Though held prisoner in Rome, Paul was not alone. Luke and Aristarchus, who had travelled with him from Caesarea, were still there (Col 4:10,14; Philem 24). So were Mark and Timothy, who had travelled with him on his missionary journeys (Col 1:1; 4:10; Philem 1,24). There was also a Jew, Jesus Justus (Col 4:11), and another friend, Demas (Col 4:14; Philem 24). No doubt his Christian friends in Rome visited him often (Rom 16:1-15).

Letter to the church in Philippi

Possibly it was during this two-year period in Rome that Paul wrote his letter to the Philippians. The letter records that Paul was a prisoner at the time of writing (Phil 1:13), but it does not record where he was imprisoned. The account of his life shows that he was imprisoned in many places and on many occasions (Acts 16:23; 22:23-30; 24:23-27; 28:16,30; 2 Cor 11:23), but the present imprisonment in Rome seems the most likely setting for the writing of Philippians.

The church in Philippi showed its concern for Paul by sending one of its members, Epaphroditus, to Rome to help him and give him a gift from the church. Paul wrote to thank the Philippians for their gift (Phil 1:5; 4:18) and to correct wrong attitudes that had arisen in the church (Phil 2:1-4,14; 4:2-3). The Philippians were not to be discouraged because of his imprisonment, for he had many opportunities to teach and preach (Phil 1:12-14). Christians in Rome were able to help him, including some who were in the government service (Phil 4:21-22).

PAUL REVISITS THE CHURCHES

Free again

Although the result of his trial was in doubt for so long, Paul remained hopeful that he would be released. He told the Philippians that he expected to visit them soon (Phil 1:25,27; 2:24), and earlier he had told Philemon of his plans to visit Colossae (Philem 22). Almost certainly he was released at the end of his two years imprisonment. What happened after his release is not certain, but from details in the letters he wrote to Timothy and Titus, we can work out at least some of his movements.

Helping Timothy and Titus

One place that Paul visited after leaving Rome was the island of Crete. It seems that among those who accompanied him on this trip were two co-workers

from former years, Timothy and Titus. Paul found that the churches of Crete were in confusion, mainly because of false teachers. He stayed for a while to help correct the difficulties, but when he had to move on to other places he left Titus behind to carry on the work and establish proper leadership in the churches (Titus 1:5,10-11).

When Paul came to Ephesus he found further problems of false teaching. He had once warned the Ephesian elders that false teachers would create confusion in the church (Acts 20:29-30), and now that had happened. Self-appointed 'experts' were ruining the church with unprofitable teaching based on ancient myths, legends, laws and genealogies (1 Tim 1:4-7; 4:1-3; 6:3-5). Some of the teaching was so harmful that Paul believed the only way to deal with the unrepentant offenders was to put them out of the church (1 Tim 1:19-20).

After some time Paul departed from Ephesus to go to Macedonia, but he left Timothy behind to give further help to the church (1 Tim 1:3). In Macedonia Paul no doubt fulfilled his wish of revisiting the Philippian church (cf. Phil 2:24; 4:1). But he was concerned for the two men he had left behind in Crete and Ephesus, and decided to write them each a letter. The two letters, Titus and 1 Timothy, are similar in many ways, though 1 Timothy is much longer and more personal.

In both letters Paul encourages his two fellow workers to be confident in carrying out the task entrusted to them (1 Tim 1:3,18; 4:6,11-12; Titus 1:5; 2:15), to establish some order and leadership in the churches (1 Tim 2:1,8; 3:1-13; 5:17; Titus 1:6-9; 2:2-8), to instruct people in Christian truth (1 Tim 3:14-15; 4:13-14; 6:20; Titus 2:1; 3:8) and not to waste time arguing about senseless issues (1 Tim 4:7; 6:20; Titus 3:9).

Imprisoned again

Some time after writing to Timothy and Titus, Paul left Macedonia. His exact route is unknown, but among the places he visited were Corinth in the south of Greece and Miletus on the west coast of Asia Minor (2 Tim 4:20). He also visited Troas to the north. The fact that he left behind some of his valued possessions at Troas suggests he may have been arrested there and forced to leave in a hurry (2 Tim 4:13). Wherever he was arrested, he was taken to Rome once more, and from prison wrote his final letter, 2 Timothy (2 Tim 1:8; 2:9).

When the authorities in Rome laid charges against Paul, some of his friends deserted him. But the God who always stood by him rescued him from violence and enabled him to proclaim the gospel to the Roman officials (2 Tim 4:16-17). Nevertheless, he did not have the optimism of his first imprisonment. Instead of looking forward to release, he expected only execution (2 Tim 4:6-8).

Knowing that time was running out, Paul wrote to Timothy to give him further encouragement and make a number of urgent requests. The church in Ephesus was still troubled by false teachers, and Paul wanted Timothy to stand firm in teaching the Christian truth (2 Tim 1:6-8,14; 2:3,15; 3:14-17; 4:2,5). At the same time he was to avoid time-wasting arguments with people whose chief aim was to make trouble (2 Tim 2:14,16,23; 3:5).

Two people who would no doubt be of help to Timothy in his difficult task were Aquila and Priscilla, who were now back in Ephesus after their second period of residence in Rome (2 Tim 4:19; cf. Acts 18:2,18-19,24-26; Rom 16:3). The family of Onesiphorus, who had given Paul valuable help in Rome, were also now back in Ephesus and likewise would be a help to Timothy (2 Tim 1:16-18; 4:19).

Martyrdom in Rome

Several urgent requests that Paul sent to Timothy indicate the distress of his final imprisonment. As he sat in his unhealthy cell, he was beginning to feel cold and he missed his books (2 Tim 4:13,21). He was also lonely. Demas, who had been with him faithfully during his first imprisonment, had now left him (2 Tim 4:10; cf. Col 4:14). Others had gone to various places in the service of God (2 Tim 4:10,12). Some of the local Roman Christians visited him (2 Tim 4:21), but only Luke could stay with him for any length of time (2 Tim 4:11).

The two people Paul most wanted with him in his closing days were Timothy and Mark, the two who, as young men, had set out with him on his early missionary journeys. Mark was most likely working in Colossae, not far from Ephesus, so Timothy would have had no difficulty going to fetch him (2 Tim 4:9,11; cf. Col 4:10). Whether they reached Rome in time is not certain. The apostle to the Gentiles, who throughout his life had never been far from death at the hands of the Jews, was finally beheaded by imperial Rome (about AD 62).

THE MINISTRY OF PETER

Encouraging the persecuted

By this time persecution was breaking out against the Christians throughout the Empire. As long as Christianity was thought to be a branch of Judaism, it was protected by law, because Judaism was a legal religion. But people in general were becoming more aware of the differences between Christianity and Judaism. When the Jews in Jerusalem killed James the Lord's brother (about the same time as Paul was martyred in Rome), everybody could see clearly that Christianity was not a movement within Judaism. It was plainly an unlawful religion.

In addition to this, people hated Christians because they could not mix freely in a society whose practices they saw as idolatrous and immoral. The Emperor Nero, who began a sensible reign ten years previously, was by now senselessly brutal and bitterly anti-Christian. He blamed Christians for the great fire of Rome (AD 64), with the result that fierce persecution broke out. About this time Peter wrote the letter that we know as 1 Peter. Its purpose was to encourage Christians to bear persecution patiently, even if it meant death (1 Peter 2:20-23; 3:14-15; 4:12-19), and to assure them of their living hope and glorious future (1 Peter 1:3-9).

But where has Peter been all these years? We last read of him in relation to the meeting with Paul and other leaders at Jerusalem thirteen or fourteen years earlier (Acts 15:6-7,12-13). We shall therefore go back to the time immediately after that meeting to see if we can fill in some of the gaps in our knowledge concerning Peter.

Peter and Mark

When Barnabas left Paul before the start of Paul's second missionary journey, he went to Cyprus with Mark, while Paul and Silas went through Asia Minor to Europe (Acts 15:36-41). Early records indicate that after Barnabas and Mark finished their work in Cyprus, Mark joined Peter. These two then worked together for many years, preaching and teaching throughout the northern regions of Asia Minor that Paul had been forbidden to enter (Acts 16:7-8; 1 Peter 1:1).

There is good evidence to indicate that, after this, Peter and Mark went to Rome for a period and taught the Christians there. When Peter left, Mark stayed behind, and the Romans Christians asked Mark to write down the story of Jesus as they had heard it from Peter. Mark did as they requested and the result was Mark's Gospel.

Peter's influence in Mark's Gospel is seen in the rapid movement of the story, the straightforward reporting, the direct language and the vivid detail (Mark 1:30,41; 3:5; 4:38; 6:39; 10:14,21,32). This is particularly so when the story concerns Peter's mistakes (Mark 9:5-6; 14:66-72). Peter and Mark helped the Gentiles in Rome to understand the story of Jesus better by giving translations of Aramaic expressions (Mark 3:17; 5:41; 7:11,34; 15:22,34) and explanations of Jewish beliefs and practices (Mark 7:3-4; 12:18; 14:12; 15:42).

Mark and Luke

About this time, Paul arrived in Rome as a prisoner for the first time, having with him Aristarchus and Luke (Acts 28:16,30; cf. 27:2). Both Mark and Luke were therefore in Rome when Paul wrote the letters of his first imprisonment, and no doubt they got to know each other well (Col 4:10,14; Philem 24). Over the years Luke had been collecting and preparing materials for the book he himself was planning to write, and on arrival in Rome was pleased to find Mark's completed record. He was able to take some of Mark's material and include it in his own book, which eventually appeared in two volumes, Luke's Gospel and Acts.

In his Gospel, as in Acts, Luke wanted to show that Jesus Christ was God's Saviour for people everywhere, regardless of race (Luke 2:32; 3:6-8; 4:25-27; 7:9), and that his followers had a responsibility to spread the message of that salvation everywhere (Luke 4:18; 19:10; 24:47). The concern that Jesus' followers showed for the poor, the sick, the despised and other socially disadvantaged people was something they had learnt from him (Luke 6:20; 7:12,22; 13:11; 17:16).

Peter and Silas

After Paul's release from imprisonment, Mark also left Rome. Later, Paul was imprisoned in Rome again and, believing he was near death, sent for Mark and Timothy to come to him (2 Tim 4:9,11). Whether or not they reached Rome before Paul was executed, Mark seems to have stayed on in Rome, and was still there when Peter visited the city again (1 Peter 5:13. The early Christians referred to Rome symbolically as Babylon, the centre of organized opposition to God). Peter's co-worker at this time was Silas, the person who had gone with Paul on his second missionary journey. Using Silas as his secretary, Peter then wrote the letter referred to above (1 Peter) and sent it to the churches of northern Asia Minor that he had helped to evangelize (1 Peter 1:1; 5:12).

Peter and Jude

A year or so later, when Peter was in Rome again, he heard of the activities of false teachers around the churches to whom he had previously written. He therefore wrote and sent off a second letter (2 Peter 3:1). In it he opposed the false teachers, who claimed that faith was not related to behaviour, and therefore immoral practices were not wrong for those with higher spiritual knowledge (2 Peter 1:5-7;

2:1-3). Peter also opposed those who mocked the Christians' belief in Christ's return. He urged them to repent before it was too late, because Christ's return would bring in the final judgment (2 Peter 3:3-4,9-10).

At the time of writing this letter, Peter was probably awaiting execution (2 Peter 1:14; cf. John 21:18-19). According to tradition he was crucified in Rome during the latter half of the AD 60s.

The sort of false teaching dealt with in 2 Peter was causing growing concern among the churches. Another New Testament letter written to oppose it was the letter of Jude (Jude 4,19). The writer was probably a younger brother of Jesus and, like his older brother James, may have become a believer after the resurrection (Mark 6:3; John 7:3-5; Acts 1:14). The similarities between 2 Peter and Jude suggest that the two writers may have used a commonly accepted form of argument in opposing the false teaching. This destructive mixture of philosophy and religion was yet another early form of Gnosticism.

CLOSE OF AN ERA

Discouragement among Hebrew Christians

With the increasing persecution of Christians during the reign of Nero, some of the Jewish Christians began to wonder if they had done right in turning from Judaism to Christianity. They had believed that Israel's Old Testament religion fulfilled its purpose in Christ and that the temple in Jerusalem was to be destroyed. Yet thirty years after Jesus' death, the temple was still standing and the Jewish religious system was still functioning.

To some Jewish Christians it seemed that Judaism was as firm as ever, whereas Christianity was heading for disaster. Many became discouraged and stopped joining in the meetings of the church, while some even gave up their Christian faith and went back to Judaism. The Letter to the Hebrews was written in an effort to correct this backsliding (Heb 6:4-6,9-12; 10:23-25,35-39).

The writer of this letter does not record his name, though he must have been a well known Christian teacher of the time. He was probably a Jew (Heb 1:1), and both he and his readers had received the gospel through the apostles or others who had heard Jesus (Heb 2:3). The letter does not say where these disheartened Jewish Christians lived, but the writer hoped to visit them soon (Heb 13:19).

By one example after another, the writer contrasted the imperfections of the Jewish religious system with the perfection of Christ. Everything of the old era that was temporary, incomplete or insufficient found its fulfilment in him. He was far above prophets, angels, leaders and priests, and his one sacrifice did what all the Jewish sacrifices could never do (Heb 9:11-14; 10:11-18). If the Jewish Christians suffered because of their faith, they were only experiencing what all God's faithful people experienced. But the faithful endured (Heb 11:36-40; 12:1-2; 13:23). Even Jesus Christ suffered, but he also endured, and in God's time he was gloriously triumphant (Heb 12:2-4).

Final break with Judaism

During the AD 60s there was a growing feeling of unrest throughout the Jewish population of Judea, not so much because of the Christians as because of the Romans. Most Jews had always hated Rome, but their hatred increased as the Roman governors of Judea increasingly mismanaged Jewish affairs. The anti-Roman extremists among the Jews were now prepared for open rebellion against Rome.

When war broke out the Jews were encouraged by some early successes, but they could not withstand Rome indefinitely. In due course the Roman armies, after conquering Galilee, Perea and Judea, laid siege to Jerusalem. At first they met strong opposition from the Jews, but by AD 70 they had conquered the city and reduced much of it, including the temple, to rubble. Although this devastated Judaism, it had a good effect on Christianity, because all the old visible ties with Judaism were now completely broken.

Preserving the Gospel records

About forty years had now passed since the death of Jesus Christ. Many of those who had been witnesses of Jesus' ministry were now scattered far and wide, and others had died. Because Christians wanted to preserve the teachings that these men handed down, many collections of the sayings and works of Jesus began to appear (Luke 1:1-2).

We have seen how Mark prepared an account of the ministry of Jesus for the Roman Christians, and as time passed this account became widely used among the churches. Luke also had prepared a written record, which, though designed for someone who was probably a government official, was also becoming widely known. Now another person, Matthew, prepared his Gospel. He used some of the material that Mark and others had already prepared, but the characteristic flavour of his Gospel comes from the extra material he added and the way he arranged it. Early records suggest that he wrote for Greek-speaking Jewish Christians in Syria.

Matthew was concerned to show that Jesus was the promised Messiah (Matt 9:27; 11:2-6), the one to whom the Old Testament pointed (Matt 2:5-6; 12:17-21), the fulfilment of God's purposes for Israel (Matt 1:17; 5:17), and the king through whom God's kingdom came into the world (Matt 4:17; 12:28; 27:11). Those who repented and believed the gospel were the people of Christ's kingdom, no matter what their nationality, whereas those who clung to the traditional Jewish religion were not (Matt 3:7-10; 8:11-12; 21:43; 23:23-28).

Jewish Christians were therefore not to fall into the errors of the unbelieving Jews. They were to develop a standard of behaviour that consisted of more than merely keeping laws (Matt 5:22,28,42; 20:26), and they were to spread the good news of the kingdom to all people, regardless of race (Matt 5:13-16; 12:21; 24:14; 28:19-20).

The fourth Gospel

Towards the end of the century another account of Christ's ministry appeared, this time in Ephesus. The writer was the last living member of the original apostolic group, John, 'the disciple whom Jesus loved' (John 21:20,24). By that time the other three Gospels were widely known. John therefore did not write another narrative account of Jesus' ministry, but selected a number of incidents and showed what they signified. Most of these incidents involved miracles (or 'signs') which showed that Jesus was the Messianic Son of God (John 20:30-31). Usually they were followed by long debates between Jesus and the Jews (e.g. John 5:1-15 followed by 5:16-47; John 9:1-12 followed by 9:13-10:39).

Gnostic-type teachings were by now a bigger problem than ever, especially in the region around Ephesus. Some teachers denied that Jesus was fully divine, others that he was fully human. John firmly opposed both errors (John 1:1,14,18; 3:13; 19:28,34). But he was concerned with more than just opposing false teaching. He wanted to lead people to faith in Christ, so that they might experience the full and eternal life that Christ made possible (John 1:4; 3:15; 6:27; 10:10; 14:6; 20:31).

John's letters

Soon after writing his Gospel, John wrote a letter that was sent around the churches of the Ephesus region. Because of the Gnostic-type teachings, many Christians were confused. John denounced the false teachers as enemies of Christ. Their denial of either his deity or his humanity was an attack on the very foundation of Christian belief (1 John 2:18-19,22,26; 4:1-3). John wanted the believers to be assured of their salvation in Christ (1 John 5:13), and resistant to those who encouraged sin by teaching that the behaviour of the body did not affect the purity of the soul (1 John 2:4; 3:6,8). Christians were to be self-disciplined and loving (1 John 2:6; 3:3,17; 5:3).

The false teaching was being spread around the churches by travelling preachers. John wrote the short letter known as 2 John to warn one particular church not to allow the false teachers into their gatherings (2 John 10-11).

On the other hand some travelling preachers were genuine preachers of the true gospel. But in one church a dictatorial person named Diotrephes refused to accept them. He claimed that they were followers of John, whom he opposed. John therefore wrote a short personal note (3 John) to one of the better leaders in the church, his friend Gaius, to help and encourage him (3 John 1,5,9-10).

Victory, not defeat

Ever since the outbreak of the persecution under Nero, the church had suffered official persecution. Although this persecution eased on occasions, it intensified during the reign of Domitian (AD 81-96). Thousands of Christians were killed, tortured or sent to work as slaves in various parts of the Empire. Oppression increased, evil men prospered, people in general became anti-Christian, and the government enforced Emperor worship as a settled policy. In addition, churches were troubled within by false teachers who encouraged Christians to join in practices that were pagan and immoral. These were the circumstances in which John received from God the messages recorded in the book of Revelation (Rev 1:1; 2:10,13-14; 6:9-11; 22:6).

John knew of the suffering that Christians were experiencing, for he himself had been arrested on account of his faith. He was being held prisoner on Patmos, an island off the coast from Ephesus. He sent his book to seven well known churches of the province of Asia, from where the message would spread to the smaller churches round about. The person who delivered the book probably took it to Ephesus first, then moved in a circuit around the other churches and back to Ephesus, from where he returned to Patmos (Rev 1:9-11).

Because of the difficulties that the churches faced, some Christians renounced their faith and others became discouraged. Many were confused, for it seemed that Jesus Christ, the glorious king they expected to return in power, was either unable or unwilling to save them from the power of Rome.

Through John, Jesus reassured his people that he was still in control, though he did not give them false hopes by promising quick relief. On the contrary he prepared them for greater endurance by revealing both the troubles that lay ahead and the ultimate victory that awaited those who stood firm for him. He was still the ruler of the world and he was still in control. In God's time he would return to punish his enemies, save his people, and bring in a new age of eternal peace and joy (Rev 1:5; 12:10-11; 19:15-16; 21:1-4).

CHRONOLOGY OF THE NEW TESTAMENT ERA

Roman Emperors	New Testament Events (dates approximate)	
Caesar Augustus (27 BC - AD 14) (Lk 2:1)	BC 6	Birth of Jesus
Tiberius (AD 14-37) (Lk 3:1)	AD 28	Baptism of Jesus
	31	Crucifixion of Jesus
	32	Conversion of Paul
Caligula (37-41)	35	Paul's first visit to Jerusalem (Acts 9:26)
Claudius (41-54) (Acts 18:2)	46	Paul's second visit to Jerusalem (Acts 11:30)
	46	Paul begins First Missionary Journey
	49	Jerusalem Council
	49	Paul begins Second Missionary Journey
	53	Paul begins Third Missionary Journey
Nero (54-68)	57	Paul to Jerusalem with the collection (Acts 21:17)
	60	Paul arrives in Rome (Acts 28:16)
Galba (68-69)	62-68	Deaths of James the Just, Paul and Peter
Otho; Vitellius (69)		
Vespasian (69-79)	70	Fall of Jerusalem
Titus (79-81)		
Domitian (81-96)	98	Death of the apostle John

Romans

BACKGROUND

Paul's letter to the Romans provides the New Testament's most carefully developed exposition of the Christian gospel. It sets out in a progressive and orderly arrangement the theological basis of the message of salvation that Paul preached. But at the same time it is a letter. Although Paul intended his presentation of the gospel to be a means of teaching Christian truth in general, he also had a definite missionary purpose in sending it to the church in Rome.

Paul's purpose for the Romans

The church in Rome was already well established when Paul wrote this letter to it. Paul did not found the church in Rome, and at the time of writing he had not even visited the city (Rom 1:13; 15:22). The church may have been founded by Roman Jews and proselytes who responded to Peter's preaching in Jerusalem on the Day of Pentecost and then took their new-found faith back to Rome (Acts 2:10). Christians from other parts of the Empire who went to live or work in Rome would also have helped to establish the church there (cf. Rom 16:3-15).

At the time of writing, Paul was nearing the end of his third missionary journey. He was in Corinth (Acts 20:2-3; Rom 16:23; cf. 1 Cor 1:14), making final preparations to go to Jerusalem with a gift of money that a number of the Gentile churches had donated to the Jewish Christians in Jerusalem (Rom 15:25-27; cf. Acts 19:21). Upon completing his work in Jerusalem, Paul intended going to Rome (Rom 15:28).

Rome was the centre of the Empire, and Paul saw that if the Roman church was firmly established in the gospel and keenly aware of its missionary responsibilities, Christianity would spread throughout the Empire. He therefore wrote to help the church understand its mission and to prepare it for the additional teaching he would give when he arrived (Rom 1:10-15; 10:12-17; 15:14-16,29). After spending some time in Rome, Paul wanted to move into the unevangelized regions to the west, till eventually he reached Spain (Rom 15:20,23-24,28).

Another issue that concerned Paul was the tension between Gentile and Jewish Christians in the Roman church. Some years earlier the anti-Jewish feeling in Rome was so strong that the Emperor expelled all Jews from the city (Acts 18:2), but they had now returned. In writing to the church, Paul sometimes spoke specifically to the Jews (Rom 2:17-19; 3:9; 4:1), other times specifically to the Gentiles (Rom 1:13-16; 11:13; 15:14-16). He warned against anti-Jewish feelings in the church (Rom 11:17-24; 15:27), and encouraged Jews and Gentiles to be tolerant of each other (Rom 14:1-23). The gospel is for all people equally, because all are sinners. Whether Jews or Gentiles, they can be saved only by God's grace (Rom 2:9-11; 3:9,23; 10:12; 11:32; 15:8-9).

Paul sent the letter to Rome with Phoebe, a Christian from a nearby church who was going to Rome at the time. Phoebe was a deacon in the church at Cenchreae, one of the port areas of Corinth (Rom 16:1-2).

OUTLINE

1:1-17   Paul introduces himself and his subject
1:18-3:20   Humankind's sinful condition
3:21-5:21   The way of salvation
6:1-8:39   The way of holiness
9:1-11:36   A problem concerning Israel
12:1-15:13   Christian faith in practice
15:14-16:27 Plans, greetings and farewell

1:1-17 PAUL INTRODUCES HIMSELF AND HIS SUBJECT

In keeping with the practice of the time, Paul introduces himself at the beginning of his letter. He is a servant and apostle of God, called to preach the gospel. This gospel, or good news, was promised in the Old Testament writings and became a reality through Jesus Christ. As to his humanity, Jesus was a descendant of David, but as to his deity, he is the Son of God, a fact shown clearly and powerfully by his resurrection (1:1-4). This Jesus is the one who gave to Paul the task of taking the gospel to people of all nations, which is one reason why he now writes to the people in Rome (5-7).

Churches everywhere know about the faith of the Roman Christians (8). Not only does Paul pray for them but he wants to visit them, so that both he and they might be strengthened as they profit from each other's spiritual gifts (9-12). Until now he has not been able to visit them, even though he has often wanted to. His duty is to preach the gospel to people of all nations and cultures, and that makes him all the more eager to visit Rome (13-15).

Paul then gives a summary of the subject that he will expound in the following chapters. He wants his readers to have the same confidence in the gospel as he has, for the gospel is humankind's only hope. People, because of their sin, are weak and unable to save themselves, but God in his power can save them from sin and accept them as righteous in his sight. Through the gospel God can put people right with himself and still be righteous in doing so. But though this salvation is available to all, it is effective only in the lives of those who believe. Only by faith, and never by works, can sinners receive the status of righteousness that God in his grace gives (16-17).

1:18-3:20 HUMANKIND'S SINFUL CONDITION

The Gentile world (1:18-32)

Because God is holy, just and true, he has an attitude of wrath, or righteous anger, against all that is wrong. He is opposed to sin in all its forms, and therefore guilty sinners are under his judgment. The Gentiles may not have received the teaching about God that the Jews have received, but they cannot excuse themselves by saying they know nothing about God. The created universe should tell them that there is a supreme being, a powerful Creator, whom they should worship (18-20).

Instead of giving glory to God, however, people have insulted him. Instead of worshipping him as the Creator, they have made created things their idols. They claim to be wise, but actually are fools (21-23).

Idols have no life, and as a result those who worship them feel free to practise all kinds of sin, without fear of punishment. But God does not ignore their sin, and one way he punishes them is to leave them to follow their own sinful desires. As a result they go deeper and deeper into sin, both men and women, and in due course they reap the fruit of their sinful behaviour (24-27).

Sin is not limited to degrading sexual behaviour. Its effects are seen in every part of the human character, as it corrupts people's inner feelings and spoils their personal relationships (28-31). Even when people know their behaviour is wrong, they persist in it, and reassure themselves by approving of the wrongdoing of others (32).

The Jewish world (2:1-29)

Not only are pagan Gentiles under God's condemnation, Jews are also. Jews find fault with their Gentile neighbours, yet they do the same things themselves (2:1). They know that God is just and that he punishes sin. Therefore, when they suffer no immediate punishment for their behaviour, they think that God approves of them and will not punish them. They do not realize that in his kindness and patience he is giving them time to repent (2-4).

Those who increase their sin also increase their punishment, because God judges people according to what they do. They deceive themselves if they think they can live as they please and still claim eternal life. By contrast those who have eternal life, the life of the age to come, will show it by the way they live now (5-8). This applies to all people, Jews and Gentiles alike. God will show no favouritism on the day of judgment (9-11).

The Jews' knowledge of the law of Moses is of no benefit to them if they do not obey it. In fact, if people know the law and disobey it, they will be punished more severely than those who have never heard of it. God will judge the Jews according to the law of Moses, but not the Gentiles, for he did not give the law of Moses to the Gentiles (12-13). Nevertheless, Gentiles have a conscience, which, though not as clearcut a standard as the law, gives them at least some knowledge of right and wrong. The conscience is like a law within their own hearts, and God judges them according to their obedience or disobedience to that 'law' (14-16).

Jews were proud of the blessings they enjoyed as God's people. They boasted that they knew God's law, and thought that they could teach it to others (17-20). But they themselves did not practise what they taught, and so brought shame on the name of God (21-24).

Paul reminds the Jews that religious rites such as circumcision are of no value unless the person's life is in keeping with the meaning of the rite. Circumcision was a sign God gave to Israel that spoke of cleansing and holiness; but an uncircumcised person with a pure life is more acceptable to God than a circumcised person with an impure life (25-27). The true Jews, the true people of God, are not those who have the mark of circumcision, but those who have pure hearts (28-29). (Circumcision was a minor surgical operation performed on Jewish boys when they were eight days old. It was a rite that God gave to the father of the race, Abraham, and it passed on to all male descendants as a physical sign that Israel was God's covenant people; see Gen. 17:9-14.)

Some Jewish objections (3:1-8)

Many Jews might argue with Paul by putting to him a fairly obvious question. If what he said was true, why did God choose Israel as his special people (3:1)? Paul replies that God chose them so that through them he could make himself known to the people of the world. The Old Testament Scriptures, for example, were given to the human race by way of the Jews (2). The sad truth is that many of these favoured Jewish people have proved unfaithful to God, but he is still willing to save them. In fact, their unfaithfulness only shows how faithful God is (3-4).

There are some, however, who dispute the truth of Paul's teaching. They argue, irreverently, that if their unbelief has shown God's righteousness more clearly, it has been of service to God, and God is therefore unjust in punishing them (5). Certainly not, replies Paul. If that were the case there could never be any standards of judgment. Consequently, God could never judge the world (6). If the Jews are going to argue like that, says Paul, why do they accuse him of being a sinner because of the things he teaches? By their argument, Paul's 'sin' would help display God's righteousness just the same (7). In the end this reasoning would lead people to the dangerous belief that they may do evil in order to get a favourable result (8).

All humankind is sinful (3:9-20)

From his discussion on the state of the Gentile and Jewish worlds, Paul concludes that the whole human race is under the power of sin (9). He quotes from the Old Testament Scriptures to show how sin affects every part of human life. Sin causes people to be rebellious against God, both in their thoughts and in their actions (10-12). It causes their speech to be harmful and destructive (13-14) and their plans to be violently selfish (15-17). They have no respect for God, but live to please themselves (18).

Those Scriptures were written originally not in relation to Gentiles, but in relation to Jews, to whom God had given his law. But if Jewish people are judged guilty because they could not keep God's law, the Gentiles, who show the same characteristics, must also be under God's condemnation. The whole human race is guilty, and the law can do nothing but show up that guilt. There is no possibility that a person can be put right in God's sight by keeping its commandments (19-20).

3:21-5:21 THE WAY OF SALVATION (JUSTIFICATION)

Now that he has established that all humankind is sinful and under God's condemnation, Paul moves on to explain the salvation that God has made available through Jesus Christ. The following outline introduces a number of ideas and words that Paul uses in this section.

God's love

It is true that God loves sinners and wants to forgive them (2 Peter 3:9; 1 John 4:16), but genuine love also acts justly. It does not ignore wrongdoing. Suppose, for example, that a judge has before him a criminal who has rightly been found guilty. The judge places a fine on him and assures him that if he does not pay he will be sent to jail. The man has no money but pleads not to be sent to jail, so the judge, feeling sorry for him, forgives him and lets him go free. What the judge has displayed is not love, but an irrational emotion that is easily influenced regardless of what is right and just.

Suppose, on the other hand, that the judge acts out of genuine love. He places the same fine on the man and insists that it be paid. Being aware of the man's personal circumstances, he feels sorry for him, but he knows that genuine love does what is right, even if it is costly. He therefore goes to the man privately and, out of his own pocket, gives the man the money to pay the fine. The same judge who laid down the penalty has paid the fine on the man's behalf.

This is what God has done for repentant sinners. He is a loving and forgiving God, but he does not ignore sin. He is just and holy, and he cannot treat sin as if it does not matter. He will do only what is pure and honourable, even though it may be costly to himself.

In order to save his guilty human creatures, God entered the stream of human life in the person of Jesus Christ (John 1:14; Phil 2:6-7). Though he lived in the world of human existence and experienced life's hardships and frustrations, Jesus lived a perfect life. He never broke God's law, in thought, attitude, intention or action (1 Peter 2:22; 1 John 3:5), and so was not under God's judgment. Yet he willingly paid sin's penalty on behalf of the guilty. That penalty was death (Rom 6:23), and Jesus died in the place of, or as the substitute for, guilty sinners (Rom 5:6; 1 Peter 2:24).

We can see now what divine love has done. God the righteous judge laid down the punishment for sin, but through Jesus' death on the cross, he himself has taken that punishment. His justice is satisfied in paying sin's penalty, while his love flows out in forgiving the sinner (2 Cor 5:21).

Justification

Paul uses the words 'justify' and 'justification' in what might be called a legal sense. The picture is that of a courtroom, where justification is that act of the judge by which he declares a person to be righteous, or in the right. It is the opposite of condemn, which means to declare a person guilty, or in the wrong (cf. Deut 25:1; Job 32:2; Matt 12:37). (The words 'justify' and 'righteous' are different parts of the same word in the original languages of the Bible.)

Concerning the relationship between sinners and God, justification means that God declares repentant sinners righteous before him. He makes them right with himself. Sinners are not made righteous in the sense that they are made into perfect people who cannot sin any more. Certainly, their lives will be changed so that righteousness, not sin, becomes their chief characteristic (as Paul will explain later in the letter; cf. Rom 6:1-2,15-19; 8:10,12-13). But the truth that is emphasized in justification is that repentant sinners are *declared* righteous. They are given a righteousness that is not their own. God gives them a new status through Christ, a new standing that makes them fit for the presence of a holy God (Rom 4:6-8; 2 Cor 5:21). God now sees them as being 'in Christ', and accepts them not because of anything they have done, but because of what Christ has done through his death and resurrection (Rom 3:27-28; 4:24-25; Phil 3:9).

Only through the work of Jesus Christ is God able to be righteous in justifying those who have faith in him. Jesus bore their sins in his body on the cross, so that God can give his righteousness to them (Rom 3:24-26; 1 Peter 2:24). And once God has declared them righteous, no one can condemn them as sinners or even lay a charge against them (Rom 8:33-34). God does all this freely by his grace, his good favour which they do not deserve (Rom 3:24; Titus 2:11; 3:4-7).

Justification is more than forgiveness

When people do wrong against us we may forgive them, but that does not declare them righteous. When God forgives he also justifies. He does more than remove sin and hostility; he brings sinners into a right relationship with himself (Rom 3:25-26; 5:6-11; 8:1-2). Forgiveness is negative; justification is positive. Forgiveness removes condemnation; justification gives righteousness. Forgiveness is something

that believers are always in need of because they are always likely to sin (Matt 6:12); justification is a declaration once and for all that God accepts them in his Son (Rom 5:1-2).

The forgiveness that believers need constantly concerns not their justification before God but their fellowship with God. Paul will explain later in his letter how believers have a constant battle with the evil effects of sin in the world. When they fail they may disappoint themselves and spoil their fellowship with God, but they can be assured that if they confess their sin God will forgive (1 John 1:9). Their justification, however, is never in question. Christ's death deals with sin's penalty for believers of all generations, past, present and future. Likewise it deals with the penalty for all the sins of individual believers, whether those sins be past, present or future (Rom 5:9,16).

Propitiation and reconciliation

Human sin has separated people from God and left them in a condition of spiritual helplessness where they are unable to bring themselves back to God (Isa 59:2; Rom 8:7-8; Eph 2:3). God always has an attitude of wrath against sin, and nothing sinners can do is able to propitiate God (i.e. pacify him, quiet his anger, remove his hostility or win his favour).

Pagans would sometimes try to calm the wrath of their gods by offering sacrifices; they would try to propitiate their gods. But guilty sinners cannot act towards God like that. Nothing they do can turn away God's wrath or win his favour. The only way God is propitiated is by the sacrificial death of Jesus Christ, who has been 'set forth as a propitiation' (Rom 3:25; Heb 2:17; 1 John 2:2; 4:10. RSV says 'expiation'; NIV says 'sacrifice of atonement'; GNB says 'the means by which people's sins are forgiven').

Propitiation means, then, that God's holy wrath against sin has been satisfied by the sacrificial death of Christ, and therefore God can show mercy on believing sinners. Once the cause of hostility (sin) has been removed, sinners can be reconciled, or brought back, to God. This is entirely the work of God. He replaces hostility with peace, and changes enemies into friends (Rom 5:10-11; 2 Cor 5:18-19; Col 1:20-22).

Faith

All that has been said so far is not true of the whole human race. It is true only of those who believe. Salvation is available to all, but it is effective only in those who have faith. In other words, faith is the means by which a person receives salvation (Rom 1:16; 3:22,25). (In the Greek of the New Testament, 'faith' and 'believe' are different parts of the same word.)

When the Bible speaks about faith in relation to salvation, it is not speaking about some inner strength that enables people to triumph over difficulties. Faith is more concerned with helplessness than with strength. Faith is reliance. It is an attitude whereby people give up all their own efforts to win salvation, no matter how good they be, and trust completely in Christ, and him alone, for their salvation (Gal 2:16; Eph 2:8-9). It is not merely an intellectual acknowledgment of certain facts (though clearly believers must know what they are trusting in), but a belief wherein people turn to Christ and cling to him with the whole heart. It is not accepting certain things as true, but trusting in a person, Jesus Christ, and all that he has done through his life, death and resurrection (Rom 4:22-25; cf. John 3:14-15; 20:30-31).

A traveller waiting to board an aircraft may believe that it will fly, and may even understand how it flies, but that belief will not take him to his destination. He must exercise his faith in the aircraft by walking on to it. He commits himself to it, trusts in it, relies upon it. That is what the Bible means by faith. People not merely know about Jesus Christ, but trust in him. They rely upon what Christ has done for them, not on anything they do themselves. Faith in Christ means commitment to him. It takes people out of themselves and puts them into Christ (Rom 3:22; Gal 2:20-21; 3:26; 2 Tim 1:12; 1 John 5:12-13).

Yet faith in itself does not save. It is simply the means by which sinners accept the salvation that Christ offers. Salvation is not a reward for faith; it is a gift that no one deserves, but it can be received by faith (Rom 3:25, 5:15).

Faith is not something a person can boast about. All the merit lies in the object of faith, which is Jesus Christ (John 3:16). When the traveller walks on to the aircraft, he has not done anything to boast about. The power to get him to his destination lies in the aircraft, not in him, and he can do no more than put his trust in it. Faith is not trying, but ceasing from one's own efforts. It is not doing, but relying on what Christ has done. It is not feeling, but accepting God's promises as true and trusting in them (Rom 4:16; 10:4-5; Titus 3:4-5).

Since faith in Christ means committal to him, it involves turning from one's self-centredness. It involves a complete change of mind, attitude and behaviour, a turn-around that the Scriptures call repentance. In explaining the doctrinal basis of the gospel for the benefit of the Roman church, Paul emphasizes the importance of faith (Rom 1:16), but when he preached to non-Christians in general he consistently emphasized that true faith is inseparably linked with repentance (Acts 20:21; cf. 3:19; 11:21; Mark 1:15).

Redemption

Another word that the New Testament uses to picture salvation is redemption. In Bible times a slave could be set free from the bondage of slavery by the payment of a price, often called the ransom price. The slave was 'bought back', or redeemed, and the whole affair was known as the redemption of the slave (Lev 25:47-48). (The words 'redeem' and 'ransom' are related to the same root in the original languages.) God's deliverance of Israel from the power of its enemies was also called redemption, the most notable example being his redemption of Israel from bondage in Egypt (Exod 6:6).

Sinners are in bondage to sin and under sentence of death (John 8:34; Rom 6:17,23), but Jesus gave his life as a ransom to pay the price of sin and release sinners from its power (Matt 20:28; Rom 3:24; Eph 1:7). Again redemption is entirely the work of God. He buys sinners back, and the redemption price is the blood of Christ – his life laid down in sacrifice (Heb 9:12; 1 Peter 1:18-19). Christ has freed believers from the power of sin, and they must show this to be true by the way they live (Rom 6:16-18; 1 Cor 7:23; Heb 2:14-15).

Saved by grace, through faith (3:21-31)

The law cannot make people right with God (see v. 20), but God himself can. Because of Christ's death, God can now declare sinners righteous and still himself be righteous in doing so. He gives sinners a righteousness that makes them acceptable to him. It is not their own righteousness, but comes from God through Christ and is received by faith (21-22). Since all have sinned, all can be justified, but only because of the grace of God and because of what Christ has done (23-24).

When Christ died on the cross, he took the punishment of sin that God's holy wrath demanded. Now that God's righteous demands have been satisfied, his grace can flow out in giving a righteous status in Christ to any who will receive it by faith. Even the sins of those who lived before the time of Christ were forgiven on the basis of Christ's death. God accepted those who had faith in him. Their sacrifices could never remove sin (cf. Heb 10:4), but they could be an expression of faith by which they acknowledged their sin as being worthy of God's punishment and called on God's mercy to forgive them. God therefore accepted believing sinners, 'passing over' their sins, as it were, until Christ came and bore the full punishment (cf. Heb 9:15). Christ's death is the basis on which God justifies all who have faith in him, whether they lived before or after the time of Christ (25-26).

This plan of salvation leaves no room for human boasting, because it depends not on anything that people might do, but entirely on what God does. All that sinners can do is trust in what someone else has done, and there is no cause for boasting in that. This is true for both Jews and Gentiles (27-30). The righteous requirement of the law is therefore upheld. The law demanded death for those who broke it; Christ died to meet its full requirements on behalf of guilty sinners (31).

Some examples (4:1-25)

To illustrate what he has just been teaching, Paul refers to the example of Abraham. Abraham was justified because of his faith, not because of any good deeds that he did (4:1-3). (To understand the illustrations concerning Abraham that follow, read Genesis 12:1-3; 15:1-6; 16:1-16; 17:15-22; 18:1-15; 21:1-21.)

Righteousness is a gift received by faith, not payment for work that a person does (4-5). David, as well as Abraham, knew that righteousness comes only through God's grace, not through one's good works (6-8). It has nothing to do with circumcision either, because Abraham was justified before he was circumcised. He received circumcision later, as an outward sign of the inward faith that he already had. He might be called the spiritual father of all who are justified by faith, whether Jews or Gentiles (9-12).

Neither has this righteousness anything to do with the law, because Abraham simply accepted God's promise by faith. He did not have to work for it by trying to keep rules. The law does not make people righteous. It only shows up their disobedience and so brings God's wrath upon them (13-15).

The principle underlying God's dealings with humankind, Jews and Gentiles alike, is that he gives his promises by grace, and people receive them by faith (16). God promised childless Abraham that he would be the father of a multitude of people. Although Abraham and Sarah were well past the age when they might normally expect to have children, Abraham still trusted God's promise and believed God could do the impossible (17-21). God accepted Abraham as righteous because Abraham trusted him to do what he had promised. In like manner God

will accept as righteous those who trust for their salvation in what Christ has done for them through his death and resurrection (22-25).

The believer's assurance (5:1-11)

When God justifies people (declares them to be righteous, or puts them right with him), he brings them into a relationship of peace with himself. In his grace he accepts them into his holy presence, and assures them of one day sharing his glory (5:1-2). Believers' anticipation of future glory is what the Bible calls hope. Hope in this sense is not a mere wish for something, but the expectation of something that is certain. It is an assured belief that enables believers to persevere through difficulties, and in the process develop Christian character. They have purpose and confidence in this perseverance because the love of God fills their hearts through the Holy Spirit (3-5).

This same love caused Jesus Christ to give his life for sinners. We may at times hear of someone who would give his life for a good person, but Christ died for those who are bad. He died for sinners (6-8). In his death Jesus bore the full wrath of God so that sinners might escape it and be reconciled to God. But Jesus triumphed over death, so that those whom he reconciles are guaranteed a victorious salvation, both in the present life and in the life to come (9-11).

Adam and Christ (5:12-21)

The Bible views the human race as existing originally in Adam. Therefore, when Adam sinned, humankind in general was involved in his sin. This doctrine is known as original sin; that is, humankind sinned originally in Adam (12).

It is true that sin is disobedience to a law, whether that law is in the form of the commandment God gave to Adam or in the form of the law-code he gave to Moses. Yet sin is present even where there is no law. This is clearly seen in the biblical record of the period from Adam to Moses. During that period no specific law-code (such as the law of Moses) was in force, yet death was the common experience of people everywhere. Since human death was the consequence of sin, this shows that sin affected the whole human race, not just Adam (13-14).

Adam's sin has brought disastrous consequences for the entire human race, but God's grace is more than able to cancel those consequences. His gift is not just the opposite of Adam's sin; it is far more. Adam's one act of sin brought condemnation and death, but God's gift of salvation through Jesus Christ brings justification and life, even though people have repeated Adam's sin countless times (15-16). As humankind's representative head, Adam brought death. As humankind's new representative head, Christ brings life (17). In contrast to Adam's one act of sin is Christ's one act of righteousness, his death on the cross. Adam was disobedient once, and through him all became sinners. Christ was obedient always, throughout his entire life and even to death, and through him all can be put right with God (18-19).

Although God gave the law to Israel for the people's good (cf. Lev 18:5; Deut 10:13), in practice it showed up their sin. When the law shows people how much they fall short of God's standard, sin appears to increase. But no matter how much it increases, God's grace through Christ can always triumph over it (20-21).

6:1-8:39 THE WAY OF HOLINESS (SANCTIFICATION)

Having spoken about justification by faith (how believers can be put right with God), Paul goes on to speak about sanctification by faith (how believers can live lives of practical holiness). In some of the other New Testament writings, 'sanctify' means 'declare holy', in much the same way as 'justify' means 'declare righteous'. ('Sanctify' and 'holy' are different parts of the same word in the original languages.) Sanctification, like justification, denotes what God does for believers on the basis of Christ's death (Heb 10:14; 1 Peter 1:2). The main emphasis in Romans, however, is on the practical expression of sanctification. Since God has declared believers righteous and holy, they must *be* righteous and holy in practice (Rom 6:19,22). The following outline will introduce some of the ideas and words that Paul uses in developing this subject.

Sinful human nature

When Adam sinned, he corrupted human nature. This means that all human beings, because of their union with Adam, are born with a sinful nature. Paul commonly calls this sinful human nature the flesh (Ps 51:5; Rom 5:12; 7:18; Gal 5:16-17).

People do not need anyone to teach them to do wrong. They do it naturally, from birth. Sinful behaviour is only the outward sign of a much deeper problem, and that is a sinful heart, mind and will (Jer 17:9; Mark 7:20-23; Eph 2:3). Every part of human life is affected by this disease of sin, including all that people are (their nature) and all that they do (their deeds) (Gen 6:5; Matt 7:18; Rom 7:18). This doctrine, known as total depravity, does not mean

that all people are equally sinful, but that every part of human nature is affected by sin. The corruption is total.

Because of such forces as conscience, will-power, civil laws and social customs, not all people show this sinful condition equally. But in spite of the good that they do, human nature is still directed by sin. The flesh is hostile to God's law and will not submit to it (Isa 64:6; Rom 8:7-8). This creates constant conflict in people's lives, because when they want to do right they repeatedly do wrong. Sin is like a cruel master that they cannot escape, no matter how much they may want to (John 8:34; Rom 7:21-23). Yet all people are still responsible for their own actions, and have the ability to say 'yes' or 'no' when tempted to sin (1 Cor 10:13; James 1:14).

Victory through Christ

Jesus was born with a human nature, but his human nature was not affected by sin (1 John 3:5). He lived in complete obedience to God's law, died to pay its penalty on behalf of sinners, then rose victoriously to new life. In dealing with sin he broke its power so that people might no longer be enslaved by it (Rom 8:3; Heb 2:14-15). The old life that believers once lived, all that each person once was as a sinful descendant of Adam — the 'old self', the 'old being' — was crucified with Christ. Believers now have a new nature. They share in the life of Christ and are indwelt by the Holy Spirit (Rom 6:6; 8:9; Col 3:9-10; 2 Peter 1:4).

Nevertheless, believers still live in a world where everything suffers from the effects of sin. Their old nature, the flesh, though condemned by Christ at the cross, is not yet destroyed. It will be with them till the end of his present earthly life, but because of Christ they need not remain in its power (Rom 6:14,18; 8:1-2).

There is therefore a continual conflict in the lives of believers, the old nature fighting against the new, the flesh fighting against the Spirit (Rom 8:5; Gal 5:17). The flesh always wants to do evil, and if believers give way to it, it will bring them under its power again, ruling them like an evil master and making them useless for God. They can resist the power of the old nature by making sure that their behaviour is directed and controlled by the Spirit (Rom 6:12-18; 8:4; Gal 5:16).

Christians have no obligation to the flesh. They must not trust it or give it any opportunity to satisfy its evil desires (Rom 8:12-13; 13:14; Phil 3:3). Paul wants to show that Christ has already won the victory over the flesh, and through the power of

Christ's indwelling Spirit believers can claim this victory as theirs daily (Rom 6:6-7; 8:1-3).

Freedom from sin (6:1-23)

In 5:20-21 Paul concluded that, no matter how much sin increases, God's grace increases all the more to meet it. He now warns against using that truth as an excuse for carelessness about sin. Christians ought not to sin. Their union with Christ means that with Christ they died to sin, with Christ they were buried, and with Christ they rose to new life. They pictured this in their baptism and they must now show it to be true in their daily lives (6:1-4).

For believers in Christ, the old life has gone, the new has come. When people die, no one can make any more demands on them. So also when believers died to sin through Christ, the full penalty that sin demanded was met for them. They are free from sin. It has no power over them (5-7). But having died for sin, Jesus rose again, and now sin and death can touch him no more. Because believers are 'in Christ', this death to sin and victorious entry into new life becomes theirs as well. They must believe it to be true and live accordingly (8-11). If, however, they allow sin to have the opportunity, it will conquer and rule them again. Therefore, they must give every part of themselves to God, so that God, not sin, might work through them (12-13). The law cannot enable people to overcome the power of sin, but God's grace can (14).

The freedom that grace gives is freedom from sin, not freedom from God. It does not allow people to sin with ease, as some think, for that would lead them back to slavery to their former master, sin. No matter what people do regularly, whether sin or righteousness, it will soon have power over them (15-16). Instead of allowing careless habits to drag them back into the bondage of sin, believers should concentrate on obeying the teachings of righteousness and so become true servants of God (17-18). This will enable them to produce lives of practical holiness (19).

Sinners feel no obligation to righteousness, but neither do they get any satisfaction from sin. They get only disappointment, bondage and death (20-21). Being a slave of God brings satisfaction and holiness in the present world, and the fulness of eternal life in the age to come (22-23).

The law cannot help (7:1-25)

Through Christ, believers have not only died to sin, they have died to the law also, which means that their lives are now different. Paul gives an example. If a husband dies, the wife is no longer bound to him

and is free to marry again. Likewise believers have died to the law so that the bond between them and the law is broken. However, they have been raised to new life and are now united to another, the living Christ (7:1-4). Formerly, they found that the more the law forbids something, the more the human heart wants to do it. But the fruit of that broken law is death (5). Now that they are dead to the law, they can serve God with a willing heart. They no longer live in fear, because they are no longer under the law's dreadful power (6).

This does not mean that the law is sinful. Quite the opposite; the law is holy, and this holiness shows people how sinful they are. Paul describes his own former experience to show that when there is no law, people do not seem to notice sin. Sin lies motionless, so to speak, as if it were dead. But as soon as people learn about a specific commandment, sin springs to life and stirs up evil desires. It makes people want to do what they are told not to do. Thus the commandment 'Do not covet' taught Paul how to covet (7-9). Instead of bringing life, the law stirred up sin which brought death (10-11). The fault lies not with the law, which is holy and good, but with the sinful nature, which is so hopelessly bad that it reacts against what is good (12-13).

Paul refers to his own experience again, to show that the more believers try to live holy lives by keeping the law, the more they fail. Again, the sin lies not in the law but in human beings. They cannot do the things they know they should do; they do the things they know they should not do (14-17). This constant defeat shows the power of indwelling sin and the inability of believers to conquer it in their own strength (18-20). They know that the law is good and they want to obey it, but the law cannot give them power over their sinful nature (21-23). How then can they get the victory? Not through themselves at all, but through Jesus Christ (24-25a).

Before moving on to explain how Jesus Christ gives this victory, Paul summarizes the previous section. The conflict he has described is between the sincere desire to keep God's law and the pull of the old nature towards sin (25b).

Victory through the Spirit (8:1-17)

The reason believers can have victory through Christ is that the power of the indwelling Spirit of Christ is greater than the power of the old sinful nature. The downward pull of the sinful nature may be likened to the downward pull of the earth's gravity. A stone thrown into the air will fall to the ground, because it has no life or power to overcome the force of gravity. A bird thrown into the air will fly away, because it has a living power that enables it to overcome the downward pull of the earth. It has a new 'law', life, which is greater than the 'law' of gravity. Likewise in Christ believers have a new upward force of the Spirit that is greater than the downward pull of the old sinful nature (8:1-2).

Efforts to keep the law cannot produce righteousness, because the sinful nature is so bad it cannot be cured, or even improved. It can only be condemned to destruction, and Christ did this by his death on the cross. When, however, believers live according to the power of the Spirit, they can develop in their lives the righteousness that the law aimed at but could not produce (3-4). The mind cannot be controlled at the same time by both the old sinful nature and the Spirit. One results in hostility to God, the other in peace. One leads to death, the other to life (5-8).

The Spirit within believers is the Spirit of Christ. Through the Spirit, Christ dwells within them, giving them spiritual life, victory over the sinful nature, and in the end freedom from even the last physical effects of sin, death (9-11).

Since the flesh is no longer their master, Christians should not obey it. Rather they should kill off its sinful actions (12-13). They are now children of God, free from the fear of bondage and led by the Spirit. Their union with Christ means that one day they will share in the Father's inheritance, but it also means that in the present life they must share in Christ's suffering (14-17).

Christian confidence (8:18-39)

Whatever sufferings believers may experience, they are of little significance when compared with the glory to be revealed on the day of final victory (18). On that day the physical creation, which from the time of Adam has suffered because of human sin (cf. Gen 1:28-30; 3:17-18), will enter its full glory along with redeemed human life (19-22). All the effects of sin will be removed, and believers will be raised from the dead in imperishable spiritual bodies suited to life in the coming age (23; cf. 1 Cor 15:42-57). Christians, being saved by faith, do not yet experience all that God has promised, but they look to the future with patience and confidence (24-25).

The same Spirit who gives hope for the future gives help in the present. When believers' prayers are unable to express their deepest thoughts and feelings, the indwelling Spirit pleads to God on their behalf. And God knows the mind of the Spirit (26-27). This concern that God has for his people involves everything. He is at work in all their affairs,

right from his eternal choice of them to be his sons to his act of final glorification when they will share the likeness of Jesus Christ (28-30).

Christians need have no doubts about any aspect of their salvation. If God has given the greatest of all gifts, the gift of his Son, nothing is beyond him (31-32). They need not fear any accusations against them, because the one who has declared them righteous is God himself, and he has done so on the basis of the perfect work of Jesus Christ (33-34). Nor should they fear persecution or even martyrdom, because through Christ they are assured of final victory (35-37). No matter what happens to them, nothing can separate them from the unchanging love of God (38-39).

9:1-11:36 A PROBLEM CONCERNING ISRAEL

The problem stated (9:1-5)

As Paul thinks about the greatness of the salvation God has provided, he is filled with sorrow, because his own people, the Jews, have rejected it. He would do anything to see them repent and believe (9:1-3). God chose Israel to be his own special people and prepared them in many ways to receive the gospel. He gave them, among other things, the privileges of sonship, the security of the covenant, a form of worship, a law-code to live by and many outstanding leaders, but when the gospel finally came to them in the person of Christ, they rejected it (4-5). Paul now considers whether God's plan has failed and whether there is any hope for Israel.

God chooses according to his will (9:6-29)

Paul's first assertion is that the promise of God has not failed. He reminds his readers of what he said earlier, namely, that people who are Israelites physically are not necessarily Israelites spiritually. In other words, not all who are physically descended from Jacob (Israel) are the true people of God in the spiritual sense (6; cf. 2:28-29; 4:11-12).

To illustrate that not all descendants of a chosen person are truly God's people, Paul refers to the fathers of the nation. Abraham, for example, had several sons and many descendants, but the only descendants who were God's covenant people were those who came through Isaac. People belonged to God because of his promise, not because of their physical descent (7-9). Isaac, in turn, had two sons, Esau and Jacob, but God chose Jacob to be the father of his people and rejected Esau (10-13).

God's choice of one and rejection of the other does not mean that God is unjust. All people are sinners and none deserves his favour, but because he is God he may choose to have mercy on some (14-16). He may also choose to harden some, such as people like Pharaoh who persistently rebel against him. But always he does what is right, according to his perfect will (17-18).

The opponents of God may argue that God is unjust to save some and harden others. Paul replies sharply by asking who do people imagine themselves to be if they think they can argue with God? God is not answerable to the human beings he created. A potter does not have to tell a lump of clay why he decides to make it into either a beautiful bowl or a common pot (19-21). So it is with God. He is always patient and longsuffering towards sinners, but when he chooses to show his judgment and power in some and his mercy and glory in others, no one can question his right to exercise his power (22-23). In choosing his people, therefore, God may decide to call Gentiles as well as Jews (24).

Even the Old Testament records the principle that God may call those who were previously not his people and make them his people. This is what he has now done in building his new people, the church, largely from Gentiles (25-26). He has included in this people only a minority from Israel, since most of the Israelites, as in Old Testament times, have been stubbornly rebellious (27-29).

Israel responsible for its own loss (9:30-10:21)

Whatever God's purposes may be, the Jews are still responsible for their own loss. They cannot say God has rejected them. They have rejected God. Gentiles, who have no law, are justified by faith, and Jews can be too, if they will believe instead of trying to win God's favour through keeping the law. They will not accept that the way of salvation for them is the same as for the Gentiles – through faith in Christ (30-33). Paul wants the Jews to be saved, but they cannot be saved while trying to create their own righteousness through law-keeping. They must admit they are helpless sinners and accept the righteousness of God through Christ (10:1-4).

The language of law says, 'Do all this and you will live'. The problem is that none is able to keep the law perfectly. All are condemned to death (5). The language of faith says, 'Do nothing. Do not try to climb the heavens or search the depths, for Christ has already come down from heaven to earth, has been crucified, buried and raised from the dead. He can be yours through faith right where you are (6-8). Believe in him as your risen Saviour, declare him to be your Lord, and you will receive from God the righteousness that saves (9-10). This applies to all

who cast themselves upon God in faith, Jews and Gentiles alike' (11-13).

Before people can believe this message, they must hear it. Therefore, Christians must be sent to proclaim it (14-15). Not all will accept the message, but Christians must proclaim it nevertheless. And the message they proclaim is the good news concerning Jesus Christ (16-17). The Jews have indeed heard this message, so they have no excuse (18). Their problem is not that they have not heard or understood it, but that they have refused to believe it (see v. 16). They become angry and envious when they see their supposedly ignorant Gentile neighbours accepting the gospel, but they themselves will not listen to it (19-21).

Salvation sent to the Gentiles (11:1-24)

All the above does not mean that God has totally rejected his people Israel. The fact that Paul has received salvation is proof that he has not (11:1). Just as in Elijah's time there was a minority in Israel who did not turn away from God, so too in Paul's time there is a minority whom God owns as his (2-5). These are God's people not because of their good works, but because of God's grace (6). They are few in number, but they have obtained the righteousness and salvation that Israel always wanted. As for the rebellious people as a whole, God has acted in judgment upon them by making them blind and deaf to the truth (7-10; cf. 9:17-18).

God's judgment on the people of Israel does not mean that they are now without hope. Their rejection of Christ has resulted in the enrichment of the world, through the preaching of the gospel to the Gentiles and the growth of God's people into a vast international community. How much greater, then, will be the blessing when the Jews accept the gospel (11-12). Paul reminds his Gentile readers of one result he hopes for as he preaches to the Gentiles. His desires that his fruit among them might stir the Jews to jealousy and cause some to believe (13-14). He likens such Jewish believers to the first loaf of a batch or the root of a tree. They give hope of more to come (15-16).

The great family of God is compared to an olive tree. Until now this tree had been Jewish in its roots, trunk and branches. When the Jews rejected Christ, many of these Jewish branches were broken off, and branches from a wild olive tree (Gentiles) were grafted, or joined, into it instead (17). The Gentiles should not despise the Jews or feel proud of themselves because they have now come into the family of God. They should remember that the Jews were the ones who prepared the way for the gospel that the Gentiles have now believed. Without this Jewish preparation, the Gentiles' salvation would not be possible (18).

God broke off cultivated Jewish branches because of their unbelief, and in his kindness grafted in wild Gentile branches instead. But if the Gentiles become arrogant, God can break them off also (19-22). If God can do what is contrary to nature and graft wild branches into the tree, he will have no difficulty in grafting cultivated Jewish branches into the parent tree again. The only reason why God holds back is the Jews' refusal to give up their unbelief (23-24).

Completion of God's great plan (11:25-36)

The Gentiles should not feel self-satisfied, but rather understand the purposes of God that Paul has now revealed to them. God has used the hardening of Israel to give the Gentiles the opportunity to receive the gospel, but neither the hardening of Israel nor the opportunity for the Gentiles will last for ever. God is using the conversion of the Gentiles to bring about the salvation of Israel. When Paul uses the words 'full number' and 'all' in speaking of the salvation of the Gentiles and of Israel, he is not saying that every Gentile and every Israelite will be saved. He has clearly shown earlier that faith, not nationality, is the basis of salvation. What he reveals here is how God is bringing about the completion of his great plan to build for himself a universal and everlasting people (25-27).

In turning from Israel to the Gentiles, God has not forgotten the promises he made to Israel's ancestors. He still has a special love for Israel, and that is why he wants the conversion of Gentiles to lead to the conversion of Jews (28-29). Gentiles and Jews have both in turn been disobedient; but just as the Jews were the means of God's mercy going to the Gentiles, so the Gentiles are now the means of his mercy going to the Jews. Because all are proved sinners, God can have mercy on all (30-32).

God's sovereign choice, far from being unjust, has been the means of his mercy being extended to people of all nations. This displays his unsearchable wisdom and causes his thankful people to give him praise and glory (33-36).

12:1-15:13 CHRISTIAN FAITH IN PRACTICE

Responsibilities and relationships (12:1-21)

For eleven chapters Paul has been explaining what God in his mercy has done, and will yet do, for repentant sinners. Now he reminds those who have experienced this mercy that the most fitting act of worship by which they can show their thanks is to offer themselves as living sacrifices to God. No longer are they to think and act like non-Christians. Their minds must be changed so that they see issues from a different point of view, God's point of view. As they learn to think in a more Christian way, they will know God's will better and their actions will be more pleasing to him (12:1-2).

This does not mean that they will become proud or hold high opinions of themselves. Rather they will learn to be more honest in acknowledging whatever abilities and limitations they have. They will recognize that as members of Christ's body, the church, all have been given different abilities (3-5). All should be diligent in carrying out the task for which God has fitted them, whether in the leadership roles in the church or in the various ministries to the needy (6-8).

Christians must be sincere and straightforward in everything they do. They must in particular have a loving care for those who are fellow members of Christ's body (9-10). Besides being spiritually enthusiastic, they must work hard at developing qualities of perseverance and prayerfulness. They must also be generous in giving practical help to their fellow believers (11-13).

These positive attitudes must be shown also towards those who are outside the church, even to persecutors (14-16). Christians should not look for revenge against those who do them wrong, but should try to live peacefully with everyone (17-18). The punishment of persecutors is a matter for God to decide. The responsibility of Christians is to treat them as if they were friends. This may in the end make the persecutors feel so ashamed that they will repent of their wrongdoing (19-21).

Duties to rulers and to others (13:1-14)

Since God is the source of all authority, governments exercise power by his permission. Christians should therefore obey the ruling authorities (13:1-2). If they keep the laws of the country, Christians have nothing to fear. They should have no difficulty in cooperating with the government, because the basic functions of government are the promotion of the well-being of society and the restraint of wrongdoing, and these functions are in keeping with Christian ideals (3-4). Christians should obey the law and pay their taxes, not just because they fear the penalties, but because they see these duties as further ways of acknowledging God's rule in the world (5-7).

Christians should also have good relations with their fellow citizens, again not just because the law tells them to, but because Christian love has changed them within (8-10). With the day of final salvation drawing nearer day by day, the time available for the development of truly Christian character grows shorter and shorter. Paul therefore urges Christians to wake up before it is too late. They must not behave as non-Christians do, and must not give the sinful nature any chance to do its evil work. They must live in the victory of Christ, with behaviour that reflects his character (11-14).

The use of Christian liberty (14:1-15:13)

Although Christians are free from religious rules and regulations such as those found in Moses' law, some have difficulty living with such freedom. Because their faith is not strong, they have their own laws which they feel bound to keep. Other Christians should accept such people warmly into their fellowship and not argue with them about personal opinions (14:1).

Some of the Jewish Christians in the church in Rome had grown little in their faith and still kept old Jewish food laws, but stronger Christians ate any food at all. Paul warns the stronger Christians not to look down on their weaker fellows, and warns the weaker ones not to criticize those who feel free to eat anything. Christians are servants of the Lord, and he is able to uphold them even when their fellow Christians might think they will fall (2-4).

In addition to keeping food laws, some Jewish Christians observed special holy days. The principle of the individual's responsibility to Christ again applies. Both strong and weak Christians recognize Christ's lordship in such matters, and all should make up their minds about what they believe is right for them in the circumstances (5-6). Christians live not to please themselves but to please Christ, who bought them for himself through his death and resurrection. They are answerable to him for all their actions (7-9). Christ the Lord is the one who will judge his servants. Those servants have no need to judge each other (10-12).

It is better that all Christians, instead of judging each other, make sure they do not damage others by causing them to do wrong. Things that are harmless to some people are sinful to others (13-14). Weaker believers may feel that a certain action is wrong, but if they see stronger believers doing it and they follow their example, they sin against their conscience. The liberty of the stronger believers therefore becomes a cause of sin. It leads weaker believers to do what they feel is wrong, and this in turn could bring ruin to their Christian lives (15-16). The important things in the Christian life are not food and drink, but the things that bring about peace and upbuilding (17-19).

Happy indeed are Christians of strong faith whose consciences are not in bondage to laws and rules concerning matters of lesser importance. But in certain circumstances they should refuse to exercise the freedom that their consciences allow, so that their actions do not spoil the work of God in the lives of others (20-23).

The strong must have a sympathetic understanding of the weak, and not act to please only themselves. Christ is the perfect example of one who always acted out of consideration for others, no matter what it cost him (15:1-3). Through the Scriptures, as well as through the example of Christ, God encourages Christians to live in unity with one another (4-6).

Christ received all and served all, whether strong or weak, Jew or Gentile, and Christians must do the same (7-9). Jewish Christians should be thankful for Christ's faithfulness in fulfilling the promises given to Israel. Gentile Christians should be thankful for his mercy in extending salvation to them (10-12). Both should rejoice together in the hope, joy and peace that God gives through the Holy Spirit (13; cf. 14:17).

15:14-16:27 PLANS, GREETINGS AND FAREWELL

Mission to Gentiles and Jews (15:14-33)

Paul has not written to the Roman believers because he doubts their ability to understand or teach the truth. He has written because he wants to give them added assurance in the principles of the gospel that they have already received. This is because, as apostle to the Gentiles, he wishes that the work among the Gentiles everywhere, including Rome, be acceptable to God (14-16). Paul has good reason to be pleased as he thinks of his mission among the Gentiles, though his emphasis is not on what he has done but on what God has done through him (17-19a). He has preached the gospel among the Gentiles from Jerusalem to Illyricum (a region north-west of Greece), mainly in places where it has not been preached previously (19b-21).

This concern to make the gospel known in the unevangelized regions is the reason why Paul has not yet visited Rome (22). Now that he has finished his work in Greece, he feels free at last to go to Italy. From Rome he wants to move farther west and preach the gospel in other unevangelized areas, even as far as Spain (23-24). First, however, he is going to deliver a gift of money from the Gentile churches to the poor Christians in Jerusalem. He believes it is fitting that the Gentiles make this offering to their Jewish brothers, since they owe their salvation to the Jews in the first place (25-27). He will then come to Rome and go on to Spain (28-29).

Paul requests the prayers of the Christians in Rome on two specific matters. He asks them to pray firstly that the unbelieving Jews will not attack him, and secondly that the Jerusalem church will accept him gladly (30-33).

Personal greetings (16:1-27)

The person who took this letter to Rome was Phoebe, a woman well respected for her work in the church in Cenchreae, one of the seaports of Corinth. She had been a tireless helper of Paul and many others, and Paul asks the Roman Christians to welcome her (16:1-2).

Paul then sends greetings to a number of people whom he had met during his missionary travels and who now lived in Rome. First among these were Paul's loyal friends, Aquila and Priscilla. They were now back in Rome after a time in Ephesus, and a local church met in their home (3-5; cf. Acts 18:1-3,18-19,24-26). Little is known of most of the others whom Paul mentions. There were both Jews and Gentiles, and some, such as Junias and Andronicus, were prominent Christian workers (6-11). Paul mentions a number of women who were well known for their Christian service, and one in particular who had been a great personal help to him (12-13). He sends greetings to two additional households where groups of Christians met (14-16).

A warning is given to beware of those who, by their smooth talk, mislead people and create divisions within the fellowship (17-18). Wise leaders, however, will not be deceived by flattering speech. They will recognize Satan at work among them, and will triumph over him (19-20).

Various people who were with Paul in Corinth join him in sending greetings. These include his secretary Tertius and his host Gaius (21-24; cf. 1 Cor 1:14). Paul finishes his letter with a further note of praise to God, who through the old order prepared the way for the new life that the Christian gospel has now made possible. It is a life that people of all nations can have through faith and obedience (25-27).

1 Corinthians

BACKGROUND

Corinth was a prosperous manufacturing centre and seaport in Achaia, the southern part of Greece. A main road connected it with important towns to the north, and sea routes connected it with other ports to the east, west and south. The city was so well known for its immorality and vice that people commonly referred to a person of loose morals as one who 'behaved like a Corinthian'. Yet Paul planted a church there, and it soon became one of the most colourful and troublesome churches of them all.

Origins of the church

Paul established the church in Corinth during his second missionary journey. He began his work there by preaching in the synagogue each Sabbath and working during the week at his trade of tentmaking (Acts 18:1-4). When the Jews forced him out of the synagogue, he went and preached in the house next door. An early convert was Crispus, the ruler of the synagogue. Another convert, Sosthenes, seems to have been the ruler of the synagogue who succeeded Crispus (Acts 18:6-8,17; 1 Cor 1:1,14). Many of the converts, however, came not from the synagogue, where there was a strong moral influence, but from the ungodly community at large, where immorality, vice and idolatry were widespread (1 Cor 1:26-27; 6:9-11,15; 10:25-28).

During the eighteen months that Paul stayed in Corinth he suffered constant opposition, but by the time he left he had firmly established the Corinthian church (Acts 18:9-12,18). Among the churches that grew up in the region round about was one at Cenchreae, Corinth's port area to the east (Acts 18:18; Rom 16:1).

Letters to Corinth

Some time after returning to his home church in Syria, Paul set out on his third missionary journey (Acts 18:22-23). He moved quickly to Ephesus on the west coast of Asia Minor, and stayed there for most of the next three years (Acts 19:1; 20:31). While in Ephesus, Paul heard that some of the Corinthians had moral difficulties, so he wrote them a letter to pass on helpful advice. The letter has not been preserved (1 Cor 5:9). Paul heard also that some Corinthians had developed strong feelings against him personally, and even doubted whether he was really an apostle. He therefore sent Timothy and Erastus to Corinth (by way of Macedonia) to deal with problems in the church (Acts 19:22; 1 Cor 4:8-13,18-21).

In the meantime some believers from Corinth arrived in Ephesus. They gave Paul the disturbing news that factions had developed in the Corinthian church because people foolishly made favourites of various teachers (1 Cor 1:10-13). Paul heard also of a serious case of sexual immorality in the church (1 Cor 5:1) and of disputes between Christians in

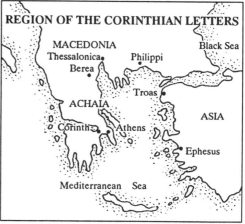

REGION OF THE CORINTHIAN LETTERS

MACEDONIA
Thessalonica
Berea
Philippi
Black Sea
Troas
ACHAIA
ASIA
Corinth
Athens
Ephesus
Mediterranean Sea

the public law courts (1 Cor 6:1). Soon after this, a group of representatives from Corinth arrived with a letter setting out questions on a variety of issues that needed attention (1 Cor 7:1; 16:17). Among these issues were such things as marriage, food offered to idols, the use of spiritual gifts in the church, the coming resurrection and the collection for the poor Christians in Jerusalem (1 Cor 7:1; 8:1; 12:1; 15:1; 16:1).

With all these matters before him, Paul wrote the lengthy letter that we know as 1 Corinthians. It seems that he sent the letter to Corinth direct by boat, as he expected it to arrive there before Timothy (1 Cor 16:8-10).

OUTLINE

1:1-9 INTRODUCTION

The Corinthian Christians may be in a sad spiritual condition, but Paul addresses them as God's holy people. They are sanctified in Christ Jesus, having a holy standing before God because of what Christ has done for them. Paul now wants to instruct them so that they might live as God's holy people should (1:1-3).

Through the grace of God, the Corinthian Christians have been specially enriched in such gifts as knowledge and speech, enabling them to understand and explain the truth (4-5). In fact, they are not lacking in any spiritual gift. They have plenty of ability, but they must allow God to control it, if they want to be blameless when they stand before Christ (6-9).

1:10-4:21 DIVISIONS IN THE CHURCH

No blame upon Paul (1:10-17)

Paul urges the Corinthian Christians to stop their quarrelling and be united (10). He has heard from people from Chloe's household that the Christians have divided themselves into factions. Some called themselves Paul's party. Others, who were impressed with the preaching of Apollos (cf. Acts 18:24-28), formed the Apollos party. Perhaps it was the Jewish group who claimed to be followers of Peter; while a fourth group claimed even higher leadership than that of Paul, Apollos or Peter, by calling themselves Christ's special party (11-12).

With a few ironical questions, Paul rebukes all the parties. He is thankful that he baptized only a few people in Corinth, namely, Crispus, Gaius and the household of Stephanus (cf. Acts 18:8; Rom 16:23; 1 Cor 16:15,17). No one can now accuse him of baptizing people with the aim of gaining a personal following. Nor did he make any attempt to attract followers by displaying much wisdom or ability in his preaching. His sole aim was to preach the gospel of Christ crucified, so that people might be saved (13-17).

Contrasts in wisdom and power (1:18-31)

The whole idea of salvation from sin through the death of Christ on the cross appears foolish to the average person, but to believers it shows God's power (18). God's way has always been different from that of people in general. Whether they be Greek philosophers, Jewish scholars, or just ordinary citizens, people always think their schemes and ideas are full of wisdom; but God shows them up to be foolish (19-20).

God, in his wisdom, saves people by way of the cross and no other. People think this way to be foolish, but no matter how much they try to know God through their own wisdom, they will never succeed (21).

The Jews want miraculous signs to prove that Jesus is the mighty Messiah, but instead they see him crucified. To them this shows not power, but weakness. A crucified Messiah is in their view a stumbling block, something that they will not believe and that consequently prevents them from receiving God's salvation. As for the Greeks, they consider the whole idea to be mere foolishness. But to believers, Jews or Greeks, it gives proof of God's power and wisdom. The cross alone can conquer sin and bring salvation (22-24). That which the Greeks think to be foolish proves to be wiser than anything people can imagine. That which the Jews think to be weak proves to be stronger than anything people can accomplish (25).

As further proof that this salvation has nothing to do with human wisdom, Paul reminds the Corinthians of the types of people who make up their church. Few of them hold important positions in the academic, political or social world. Yet God has taken them and made them his people, to prove that he does not accept anyone on the basis of natural ability or worldly status. No one can therefore boast before him (26-29). Wisdom is found not in personal achievement but in what God has done in Christ. Through Christ, God has put believers right with himself, declared them to be holy and set them free from the power of sin. Everything centres in Christ. Believers boast in him alone (30-31).

Worldly and spiritual wisdom (2:1-16)

Paul reminds the Corinthians that when he was among them he did not try to impress them with any great show of learning. He preached the plain gospel without trying to make it attractive to any one class of people (2:1-2). During his time in Corinth, Paul had been physically weak and lacked his usual boldness. As a result his preaching was not at all impressive. Yet this was no great disappointment to him, because he wanted his converts to stand in the power of God, not to become attached to the preacher because they were impressed with his style (3-5).

Although the gospel does not depend on human wisdom, that is no reason to look down on it as though it were something inferior. Christianity has a superiority and dignity of its own. It is based on the wisdom of God, which makes all human wisdom appear weak and insignificant (6-7). Lack of this wisdom was what caused people to crucify Christ. On the other hand, those who have this wisdom enter into blessings that the ordinary people of the world cannot understand. The only ones who can understand these things are those who have the Spirit of God (8-10).

Just as a person's own spirit, and no one else's, knows what is going on inside that person, so the Spirit of God, and no one else, knows what is going on within God. Therefore, only those who have the Spirit of God can know the mind of God (11-12). They receive instructions from God through the Spirit and pass on these instructions to others, not by means of worldly wisdom, but by the same Spirit. Those who receive the instruction will likewise have understanding through the work of that Spirit within them (13).

Ordinary people of the world reject the things of God as foolish, because they do not have his Spirit and therefore do not have the means of understanding them (14). Those who have the Spirit of God are able to form judgments on all things, because now that Christ has changed their thinking, they see things from Christ's point of view. But those without God's Spirit are unable to form judgments on things of the Spirit, and therefore are unable to judge spiritual issues in the lives of believers (15-16).

Lack of spiritual growth (3:1-9)

When Paul was in Corinth a year or two previously, he could not speak to the believers as spiritual people (such as those just described in 2:6-16), because they were then little different from ordinary, natural people of the world. They were babes in Christ and Paul treated them so. He did not find fault with them then, because one expects new converts to be like that; but he does find fault with them now, because they are *still* like that (3:1-2). They are like people 'of the flesh', people whose lives are characterized by the old sinful nature. They are like the people of the world that Paul has just been describing in Chapter 2. Their behaviour is

not according to the wisdom of God, but according to the wisdom of the world. Their quarrels and divisions are proof of this (3-4).

Some of the Corinthians were exalting Paul, others exalting Apollos. But Paul and Apollos are not in opposition; they are working together. The work of God in Corinth is likened to a field in which Paul did the planting, and Apollos the watering. Though the two have different functions, both are necessary, but neither of them can make the plants grow. Only God can do that (5-6). Those who plant will not see as much fruit as those who water or those who reap. For that reason the reward does not depend on the fruit people see but on the work they faithfully carry out (7-9).

Christian activity tested (3:10-23)

The Corinthians are likened also to a building. Paul laid the foundation, and now other Christians, in particular the teachers, have the responsibility to build on that foundation (10). There is only one foundation, Jesus Christ, but the structure may be built in all sorts of ways. People may build something of lasting worth through using valuable materials (gold, silver and precious stones), or they may build something of no lasting worth through using cheap materials (wood, grass and straw) (11-12).

When each building is tested by fire on the day of judgment, quality alone will count. The valuable materials will survive, but the cheap materials will be burnt up. Christians who have made the effort to grow spiritually have built something that is permanent and worthy of reward. Christians who have lived like ordinary people of the world have built nothing permanent and in the end will lose everything. They will be like those who run from a burning house but lose all their possessions. They themselves are saved, but they have nothing to show after a lifetime of activity (13-15).

Since the church (that is, the group of believers as a whole) is the temple of God, it must be holy. God will act in judgment on those who destroy his temple through division or makes it unclean through sinful behaviour (16-17).

Paul returns to the subject of wisdom, because the divisions in Corinth were caused by those who considered themselves wise in following favourite teachers. The humblest believer can understand the things of God, whereas those who are wise by the world's standards cannot. Heavenly wisdom is foolishness to the ordinary people of the world; but the wisdom of the world is foolishness to God (18-20). By attaching themselves to one particular teacher, the Corinthians are not increasing God's blessing, but limiting it. All teachers are theirs, not just one. Since they belong to Christ, their blessings are unlimited (21-23).

Attitudes towards God's servants (4:1-21)

What the Corinthians think about the servants of God is not important. God is the one who gives his servants their work and they are responsible to him, not to anyone else (4:1-2). Paul is not concerned about the Corinthians' assessment of him. Even Paul himself cannot properly assess how true his service has been. He may not know of any failure in his service, but that does not mean he is faultless. The only judgment that matters is the one that will take place at Christ's return, when he examines motives and reveals hidden attitudes (3-5).

The Corinthians should stop boasting of their attachment to certain teachers, as if it shows that they are superior to others. All these teachers are but God's gift to them; and no one has cause for personal boasting about something that, after all, was freely given by another (6-7).

Paul shows his disappointment concerning the unchristian attitudes at Corinth by the irony he uses in comparing the pride of the Corinthians with the humiliation of the apostles. The Corinthians thought they were superior Christians. Paul says that he wishes they were, so that he and other apostles might be built up in the faith through them! It appears that the apostles, instead of being the leaders of the Christian community, are the most backward. They are openly humiliated, as people about to be killed in the public arena. They are fools, weak and despised, so different from the mighty Corinthians (8-10)! On account of his service for Jesus Christ, Paul suffers constant hardship and unceasing persecution. He is cursed, beaten and treated as the lowest of the low, yet he always returns good for evil (11-13).

In writing to the Corinthians like this, Paul is warning them as a father might warn his children (14-15). He wants them to remember the things he taught them, by word and example, when he was among them. The teaching he gave them is no different from what he gives in other churches, and to remind them of it he is sending Timothy to them. Perhaps Timothy can help the church back to the right path (16-17).

This sending of Timothy does not mean that Paul himself is afraid to go, as his opponents claim. He will not hesitate to go if he believes it is God's will; and he will soon find out whether these opponents are as good as they say they are. He urges them to change their ways quickly, otherwise his visit will be marked by unpleasant discipline instead of enjoyable fellowship (18-21).

5:1-6:20 MORAL FAULTS IN THE CHURCH

Adulterous living (5:1-13)

Paul now turns to the second difficulty that had been reported. In this case the sin was one that would hardly be found even among the pagan Greeks. A man was living in adultery with his father's wife, probably a minor wife or the wife of a remarriage. Yet the Christians did nothing about the shameful situation. They thought they were so advanced in their Christian experience that there was no need to restrict the freedom of the church members. Actually, says Paul, they should have put the guilty man out of the church (5:1-2).

Though absent from Corinth, Paul quickly takes action. He urges the church to meet and deal with the matter immediately. The man must be put out of the community of God's people; that is, out of the sphere where God rules, into the sphere where Satan rules. The purpose of this is 'that the flesh might be destroyed', an expression that may refer to physical disease or even death. Such severe physical punishment in this world may be necessary so that the man's spirit may be saved in the next (3-5; cf. Mark 9:43-47; Acts 5:1-11; 1 Cor 11:30).

The Corinthians are foolish to think themselves so free from rules and laws that they can allow such things to go on. By keeping such sin among them they are really helping to destroy their own church. Sin spreads throughout a group of people in the same way as yeast spreads throughout a lump of dough (6). The Christian life is likened to a festival such as Israel's Feast of Passover and Unleavened Bread. Just as Israelites cleaned all leaven out of their houses at the time of the Passover, so the Corinthians should clean the leaven of sin out of their church, because Christ the true Passover Lamb has already been sacrificed (7-8).

Paul had given instructions on these matters in his previous letter, but the Corinthians misunderstood them. He did not mean that Christians should have nothing to do with the sinful people they meet in the world, because that would require them to leave the world altogether (9-10). Rather he meant that Christians are to have no close fellowship with those who say they are believers but deny it by their shameful behaviour (11).

Christians are not required to judge non-Christians for their sins, but they are required to take action against sin in the church. In the case in question, this will mean the removal of the guilty person from the church fellowship (12-13).

Lawsuits before heathen judges (6:1-11)

If a dispute arises between believers, it should be settled within the church, not in a public court of law (6:1). If Christians are to share in the future judgment of the world, surely they can judge everyday affairs of the present life (2-3). The Corinthians boast of their wisdom, yet not one among them is wise enough to decide the matter. Instead they shame themselves by taking Christian problems to non-Christian people for a decision (4-6).

Christians should not have lawsuits at all. They should be willing to suffer ill-treatment, as Jesus taught, but at Corinth they attack and cheat each other (7-8). They behave like the sorts of people they were before they became Christians. God has declared them righteous and holy through Jesus Christ, and therefore they should be righteous and holy in their conduct (9-11).

Unlawful sexual freedom (6:12-20)

The Corinthians had claimed that since they were not in bondage to laws they could do as they wished. Paul replies that this is not so. Not all things are helpful, and some may lead a person into a new kind of bondage (12).

Certain people at Corinth even claimed that just as the stomach needs a constant supply of food to satisfy it, so the body needs unrestrained sexual pleasure for its satisfaction. Paul denies this. The body's main purpose is not concerned with sex but with God. It is the means by which people serve God and by which God functions in people (13). It is a body which, in the case of believers, will one day be raised in glory and which is already united spiritually with Christ. Such a body should not, therefore, be united physically with a prostitute (14-17).

Immorality is a sin against the dignity of one's own body. For the believer it is a sin also against the temple of God, for the believer's body is the Holy Spirit's dwelling place. Whatever is not fitting in God's temple is not fitting in the body of the believer (18-19). God has bought believers out of the slavery of sin at the price of Christ's life. They belong to him, not to themselves, and therefore they must use their bodies for his glory (20).

7:1-40 CHRISTIAN MARRIAGE

Responsibilities of marriage (7:1-9)

Paul now deals with those matters concerning which the Corinthians had written. One problem concerned marriage. Some thought it more honourable

and a sign of moral purity not to marry. Paul replies that marriage is honourable. It is the normal course God has set out for humankind, though there are exceptions. In some cases it may be better not to marry (he will explain this in a moment), but because Corinth is an immoral city and full of temptation, it is better to marry (7:1-2).

In marriage both husband and wife have their rights, but they also have obligations to each other (3-4). In some circumstances husband and wife may feel such a need for increased prayer that they agree not to have sexual relations for a time. But this is exceptional. They should resume normal marital relations as soon as possible, so that Satan does not rouse their natural passions wrongly (5).

There are no rules that Paul can lay down to demand that people marry or not marry, though his personal preference is that they be like him and remain single. In this way they can serve God without the added responsibilities of marriage. He realizes, however, that everything depends on how God has prepared each person (6-7).

Concerning the unmarried and widows, Paul recommends that they remain single. But if in their single state they are only going to burn with sexual desire, they would do better to marry (8-9).

Problems of separation and divorce (7:10-16)

Paul claims the authority of Christ in reminding the Corinthians that a Christian husband and wife should not separate (cf. Matt 19:6). If they do, every effort should be made to bring them together again. If this fails, they must remain single (10-11).

In the examples that follow, Paul knows of no command of Christ to quote, though he believes his advice carries the authority of the Spirit of God (see v. 40). He considers situations other than those of normal Christian marriage, such as when one partner of a pagan marriage subsequently becomes a Christian. (He does not consider the possibility of believers marrying unbelievers. They will marry only 'in the Lord'; see v. 39.) If the unbelieving partner is willing to continue the marriage, the believer should also be willing (12-13).

Such a union between a believer and an unbeliever is not considered unclean, neither is any child born of that union. God considers it a holy and lawful union on account of the believing partner (14). If, however, the unbeliever is unwilling to continue the marriage and departs, the believer must let it be so and consider the marriage at an end. There is no point in forcing the unbeliever to continue the marriage in the hope of making the person a Christian if such action is only going to cause quarrels. Marriage, after all, is intended to bring peace and contentment. Nevertheless, there will be cases where the unbelieving partner comes to believe in Christ (15-16).

The life of God's choosing (7:17-24)

God wants Christians to be patient and to accept that their current state of affairs is God's will for them for the present (17). Believers may have differences in marital, national or social status, but this should make no difference to their spiritual well-being. The important issue is obedience to God's commandments. Even those who are slaves should feel no inferiority, but if they can be free, so much the better (18-21).

More important than status in the world is status before God. Believers who are slaves in the world have the liberty of God's children, while believers who are free citizens in the world are God's slaves. God has freed all believers from the bondage of sin. They should not allow themselves to be enslaved again through following the ways of an ungodly society (22-24).

The unmarried and widows (7:25-40)

Corinth was at that time troubled by some unusually distressing circumstances. In view of this, Paul felt it best for people, whether married or single, to stay as they were for the time being. The responsibilities that go with marriage and a family would only add to the current difficulties (25-28). This was not the time for people to create further problems for themselves by making changes or becoming more involved in worldly affairs. It was a time to remain steady and remember the importance of eternal things (29-31). The married, being anxious for their families, must spend time looking after them. The unmarried, being free from such worry, can give themselves fully to the service of God (32-35).

In spite of his advice against marriage during the current crisis, Paul realized that Corinth's low moral standards provided many temptations for single men and women. If such people were anxious to marry, they should not be prevented, in case the temptations proved too much for them (36). But for those without such strong passions, it would be better in the present circumstances not to marry (37). Both courses of action are right, but the latter is preferable (38).

Finally, Paul has some advice for widows. Christian marriage is a lifelong union, broken only by death. When the husband dies, the widow is free to remarry, provided she marries another believer. Here again Paul's advice is that, because of the current crisis, she would be wiser to remain single (39-40). (See 1 Timothy 5:14 for Paul's advice to widows in different circumstances.)

8:1-11:1 FOOD OFFERED TO IDOLS

In Corinth, as in other places, temples were not just religious centres but also popular eating places. This created problems for the Christians, because the food was usually first offered to idols and Christians were not sure whether they should eat it. A related problem concerned food they bought in the market, for it also may have been first offered to idols. These are the issues Paul now deals with, though they lead him to the more important issue of the exercise of Christian rights and freedom.

Different attitudes to idols (8:1-13)

The Corinthians boast that they have knowledge on the subject of idols. They know what is false and what is not. But, Paul answers, knowledge is not enough. It is never perfect and can lead to pride. Christians must be guided in their behaviour by love, not merely by knowledge. Only in this way can they grow to full maturity (8:1-3).

Some Christians, claiming to have strong faith, have no hesitation in eating food offered to idols. To them an idol is only a piece of wood or stone. Paul agrees that an idol is a lifeless object (though he will explain the meaning of making offerings to these lifeless objects in 10:19-20). He knows also that, although there are countless gods and deities, there is only one God and only one Lord (4-6).

Not all Christians, however, feel that an idol is only a piece of wood or stone. Some have for many years worshipped idols as if they were real. Their consciences are easily affected by anything connected with idolatry, and they feel it would be wrong to eat what has been offered to idols (7).

Though the kind of food people eat may not be important (8), that is no reason for those of 'strong' faith to eat in the temple feasts. If people of 'weak' faith follow their example and eat also, they sin, through doing what their consciences tell them is wrong (9-10). God then holds the 'strong' Christians responsible for doing lasting damage to the lives of the 'weak'. They sin against their fellow believers and against Christ (11-12). Paul's own attitude in such matters is that he would rather not eat at all than eat and harm another (13).

Paul's example (9:1-23)

The principle Paul has been teaching in the previous chapter is that no matter what rights Christians may have, they should be willing to sacrifice those rights for the sake of others. He now demonstrates that principle with a number of personal examples.

Paul has the same rights as others, and in fact more, since he is an apostle. But he does not always exercise his rights. Some people have misunderstood this and think that he is not an apostle at all. Paul points out that the existence of the Corinthian church is living proof of his faithfulness in his apostolic ministry (9:1-2). Paul and Barnabas (and their dependants) have as much right as the other apostles to travel and live at the expense of the church. But they deny themselves this privilege and work to earn their living, so as not to be a financial burden to the church (3-6).

Any workers, whether they be soldiers, farmers, shepherds or servants of the church, have the right to receive their living from their occupation (7). This principle is found also in the law of Moses. An animal that treads out the grain is allowed to eat the grain as it works (8-9; Deut 25:4). Just as the farmer expects to get something to eat from the results of his work, so does Paul. He has worked hard in spiritual service in Corinth and he is entitled to a material reward (10-11).

Others have received gifts from the Corinthians, but Paul has not. He has not exercised his right, because he does not want financial matters to be a hindrance to the work in Corinth (12). Both the law of Moses and the teachings of Jesus show that Paul has the right to claim financial support from the Corinthians (13-14; Deut 18:1; Luke 10:7-8).

In writing like this, Paul is not trying to shame the Corinthians into giving him financial assistance. He prefers things as they are. He preaches the gospel, not because he wants to boast about his work or income, but because he is compelled to preach (15-16). Whether he preaches willingly or not, he must preach. His reward is the knowledge that he preaches freely without claiming his rights to financial support (17-18). He sacrifices his own freedom in order to serve others, his aim being to get people to listen to his message and accept it (19). This applies to all whom he helps, whether Jews, Gentiles, or 'weak' Christians such as those who will not eat food offered to idols (20-23).

Necessity for self-discipline (9:24-27)

Christianity is a life of effort. As runners in a race strain to the full to win the prize, so Christians should put all their effort into whatever they do (24). As athletes undergo strict training in their pursuit of victory, so Christians should deny themselves lawful pleasures and foods in order to be more useful for God (25). Paul has purpose and effort in all that he

does. He is like a runner who heads for the finishing line or a boxer who aims to land his punches. He spares no effort in his program of vigorous self-discipline to keep himself fit. He realizes that it is dangerously easy to warn and instruct others, then fall into sin himself and be disqualified (26-27).

Warnings from history (10:1-13)

Paul now illustrates from the history of Israel that some might join in the fellowship of God's people, but miss out on the final blessing. All the people of Israel were united with Moses in their escape from Egypt and all enjoyed God's provision through none other than Christ himself. But only two, Joshua and Caleb, entered into the blessing of the promised land. The rest disobeyed and were punished (10:1-5). (For relevant stories see Exod 13:17-22; 14:21-29; 16:1-17:7; Num 13:1-14:35.)

These events should be a warning to Christians. Idolatry can give a feeling of self-satisfaction that results in moral laziness. This leads to the relaxing of control over sinful desires and finally to sexual immorality. This was what happened to Israel (6-8; see Exod 32:1-6; Num 25:1-9). Christians should not put God to the test by seeing how far they can go without his acting in judgment. The Israelites did and were destroyed (9; see Num 21:5-9). They complained bitterly against him and were punished (10; see Num 16:1-50).

All these things are a warning to the Christians in Corinth not to be too confident in thinking they can join in idol feasts and not be affected by them. Tests and temptations will indeed come, but there will always be a way out. There can be no excuses. They must be loyal to God (11-13).

Avoid idol feasts (10:14-22)

In view of the dangers of idolatry, there is only one wise course to take in relation to idolatrous feasts, and that is to have nothing to do with them (14-15). Those who receive bread and wine in the Lord's Supper are united with Christ in one body and spiritually share in him (16-17). Likewise in the Israelite sacrificial system those who eat the food of the sacrifices are united with the altar on which the sacrifices are offered (18). Christians cannot say, therefore, that eating food in idolatrous feasts has nothing to do with idolatry. Maybe the idol is only a piece of wood or stone, but the people who make offerings to it do not see it as such. They are, in fact, sacrificing to evil spirits (19-20).

Just as eating food at the Lord's Supper means having fellowship with the Lord, so eating food at idolatrous feasts means having fellowship with the idol, or worse, with the evil spirits behind the idol. Now that the Corinthians know the true meaning of eating food offered to idols, they must cease the practice at once, otherwise God might act against them in judgment (21-22).

Consideration of fellow believers (10:23-11:1)

Some things that are allowable are not helpful. If Christians think of others before they think of themselves, they will refrain from certain things in case others copy them and are weakened spiritually as a result (23-24).

The Corinthians should understand that the reason why they must not join in idol feasts is that eating involves fellowship with the idol and its demons. It is not that the physical properties of the food are in any way changed. Therefore, when Christians buy food at the market or eat in the house of pagan friends, they must not create unnecessary problems by asking whether the food has been offered to idols. If they do not know, it does not matter. They should eat the food and be thankful to God who gave it (25-27).

If, however, someone tells them the food has been offered to idols, they should not eat it. They do not want others to think they agree with idol worship. Christians do wrong when they use their personal liberty in a way that causes others to sin. If by eating food they harm others, their thanksgiving for the food becomes meaningless (28-30).

To summarize, Christians should be guided in their behaviour not by their knowledge of the rights they have, but by their consideration for the glory of God and the well-being of their fellows (31-32). This is the way Paul lives, and he wants the Corinthians to follow his example, just as he follows Christ's (33-11:1).

11:2-34 ORDER IN PUBLIC WORSHIP

When women pray or prophesy (11:2-16)

Paul had heard from the visitors from Corinth of disorder in the public worship of the church. To start with, some of the Corinthian women were speaking in the church services without the veil over their heads. This was shameful by current social standards in that part of the world. Paul argues that Christians do not have to show their new-found freedom by rejecting the local customs of politeness and etiquette. In fact, these customs may reflect a basic God-given principle.

Although he praises the Corinthians for their steadfastness in following his teachings (2), Paul realizes that certain matters still need attention. He reminds them that the woman is under the authority of the man, just as the man is under the authority of Christ (3). The head covering may be seen as a sign of that relationship. Therefore, a man should not wear a head covering when he prays or prophesies, because he is not under any creature's authority; but a woman should, because she is under the authority of the man. To have her head uncovered is as shameful as to have it shaved bare (4-6). Woman was made from man and for man, and though she has a special status as the glory of man, she is nonetheless under his authority (7-9). The angels observe this order in the church (10).

This does not mean that the woman is inferior or that the man is superior. Neither man nor woman can exist without the other (11-12). The Corinthians can see for themselves that it is shameful for a woman to pray with her head uncovered. It is as shameful as for a man to have long hair like a woman, or a woman to have short hair like a man. The environment in which they live should tell them what is natural and what is not, and this order should be reflected in the church (13-15). Paul does not want to argue the matter further, but he reminds them that what he has just outlined is the common practice among the churches (16).

The Lord's Supper (11:17-34)

God's purpose was that the Lord's Supper should demonstrate and strengthen the unity of his people in one body (see 10:16-17), but the way the church in Corinth practised it, it produced the opposite effect. It caused Christians to break into opposing groups. The only advantage in this, Paul ironically points out, is that it enables a person to see how many good Christians there really are (17-19).

The practice in those days was that when Christians met for the Lord's Supper, all who could afford to brought along food and drink to share with the poor in a common meal. At the end they ate the Lord's Supper. The common meal was called a love feast, but at Corinth it showed little sign of love. The ceremonial meal was called the Lord's Supper, but at Corinth it was very much their own supper. The rich greedily ate their own food without sharing it with others and without even waiting for everyone to arrive. So the poor went hungry, while the rich feasted and became drunk. Paul says that those who shame themselves and the church in this way would do better to eat at home (20-22).

Paul then gives them the true meaning of the Lord's Supper, as the Lord had revealed it to him. The eating of bread and drinking of wine together is a communion with Christ, a spiritual sharing together in his body and blood (cf. 10:16). It is a fresh enjoyment of and proclamation of the benefits of his death. It is also a reminder that through his death the old era has passed and the full blessings of the new covenant have become the possession of all Christ's people (23-26).

Nobody should join in this act of communion thoughtlessly. All should examine themselves to make sure their conduct and attitude are in keeping with the Supper's meaning (27-28). If they join in it thoughtlessly, as if it were just an ordinary meal, they bring God's judgment upon themselves. Indeed, some in the church have, because of their wrong behaviour, suffered such judgment in sickness and death (29-30). Christians should examine themselves honestly to see what they are really like. If not, God may send them difficulties to bring them back from the wrong way and save them from the judgment that awaits sinners (31-32).

Therefore, Paul concludes, the Corinthians should cease their shameful rush and greed at the Lord's Supper and remember what it is for. It is not just a feast (33-34).

12:1-14:40 SPIRITUAL GIFTS IN THE CHURCH

The variety of gifts (12:1-11)

Some unusual spiritual gifts operated in the early church. One of these caused people to speak with strange sounds (commonly referred to as 'tongues') that neither they nor the hearers understood unless someone interpreted them. Some at Corinth, still influenced by attitudes from former idolatrous days, were impressed by such things and considered those who so spoke to be spiritually superior. However, the situation got out of control and people said things that were wrong, such as 'Jesus be cursed!' This shows, says Paul, that speaking in tongues is not necessarily speaking by the Holy Spirit (12:1-3).

Different gifts and different types of service do not indicate different levels of spirituality. Nor should they produce competition or jealousy, for the same triune God works through a variety of people for the spiritual development of all (4-7).

Whatever the gifts, they are all given by the Spirit of God. Some people have gifts of wisdom and knowledge (8). Others have unusual abilities, such as faith to do the apparently impossible and power to heal sickness and disease (9). Further gifts enable various people to work miracles, to speak words from God, to tell the difference between those gifts that come from the Spirit and those that do not, to speak in tongues, and to interpret tongues so that they become understandable to the hearers (10). The one God gives all these gifts, and he gives them according to his will (11).

Unity in spite of many gifts (12:12-31)

The human body is made up of many parts, all with different functions, yet there is a basic unity throughout the body. So it is in the church which is Christ's body. All believers, without distinction, are introduced into and united in that body through the baptism of the Spirit. The same Spirit dwells within each one (12-13).

Many parts make up the body, and all are necessary for its proper functioning. Those without more obvious gifts should not think there is no place for them in the church. In the body of Christ, as in the human body, each part has its own special task (14-20).

God has so designed the body that no matter how important one part may be, it cannot function properly without dependence upon all the other parts (21). People with more obvious gifts should not look down on others. Certain parts of the body may appear at first to be less important, but the body cannot do without them (22). Other parts of the body are less presentable, but they are the parts we clothe more attractively. Just as there is harmony between the various parts of the body, so there should be in the church (23-25). In addition, there should be unity. When one part of the body suffers, the whole body suffers; when one part is honoured, the whole is honoured. There is no competition (26).

It is clear, then, that all Christians are part of the body but their gifts vary widely, from the more important gifts to the less important (27-28). All gifts are necessary, but not everybody can do everything (29-30). Christians should desire the higher gifts, but there is something greater than even the highest gift that all, whether great or small, can have, and that is love. Paul will explain what he means in the next chapter (31).

Love is greater than the gifts (13:1-13)

The Corinthians were impressed with people who exercised the more spectacular gifts. Paul reminds them that no matter what gifts they have — tongues, prophecy, wisdom, knowledge, faith — if they lack love they are not merely unimportant, they are nothing (13:1-2). People may be so generous with their goods and money that in the end they themselves become poor. They may be so faithful to their duty that they sacrifice their lives. But without love they have gained nothing (3).

Paul then describes some of the qualities of love. Chief of these is that it thinks of others, not of self. Love is patient, kind, humble, forgiving, self-controlled and always thoughtful of the feelings of others. It is not boastful, bad mannered, resentful or irritable (4-5). At the same time it upholds God's standards of righteousness, always rejoicing in what is true and never in what is wrong. It is trusting and persevering, and always looks positively to the ultimate fulfilment of God's purposes (6-7).

The various gifts are temporary and imperfect, for they are limited to life in the present world. But love is permanent, and endures into the age to come (8-10). The gifts Christians exercise are likened to the changing abilities and capacities in the life of a growing child, but love is likened to the maturity of adulthood (11). In the present world Christians have only a limited understanding of eternal things. Their view of the age to come is unclear. When face to face with Christ they will know these things clearly, just as God knows them clearly (12). The important issue for Christians is not the display of their spiritual gifts, but the exercise of faith, hope, and above all, love (13).

The gift of tongues (14:1-25)

In the light of his teaching on the variety of spiritual gifts and the importance of love, Paul now considers the problem that had arisen in the Corinthian church concerning tongues. The gift is allowable, but prophecy is preferable. This is because those who speak in tongues speak to God, not to their fellow worshippers, and therefore are of spiritual help only to themselves (unless someone interprets for them). Prophets, however, speak to all and so build up the whole church (14:1-5). (GNB calls prophets 'those who proclaim God's message', since they passed on to the people the revelation that God gave specifically to them.)

It would be pointless if Paul came to the Christians in Corinth and spoke in tongues that no one understood. It would be much better to give them some revelation or teaching in their own language, so that they could learn from it and be built up spiritually (6).

Paul follows with two illustrations to emphasize the importance of speaking in a way that means something to the hearers. The purpose of playing a musical instrument is to get a tune out of it, not to make a meaningless noise. The purpose of blowing a bugle on the battlefield is to alert the soldiers to prepare for battle (7-8). Likewise with speech the purpose is to be understood. Tongues that no one understands are as useless to the hearers as a foreign language that they have never heard before (9-11). Christians should desire those gifts that are going to be of help to others in teaching them and building them up in the faith (12).

If people have the gift of tongues, they should pray also for the gift to interpret them. Their mind as well as their spirit will then benefit, because they pray and sing with understanding (13-15). They should think also of others in the church. If the hearers do not understand what the speaker is saying, they can neither benefit from it nor express their support for it (16-17). Paul is thankful to have the gift of tongues, but in the church he would rather speak in ordinary language that will instruct and strengthen the hearers (18-19).

The Corinthians' love for the spectacular shows that they are childish in their thinking. It is good to have the innocence of childhood concerning evil, but in their minds they must be mature adults (20). In one famous Old Testament event, the strange speech of the Assyrian invaders was a sign to God's unfaithful people of coming judgment. In a similar way tongues may be a warning of God's judgment to those who stubbornly refuse to trust in him (21-22a; cf. Deut 28:49; Isa 28:11-12). Prophecy, by contrast, strengthens the hearts of believers with a message from God (22b).

If those who know nothing about Christianity come into a Christian meeting where various people are speaking in different tongues, they may think that the speakers are mad. But if the speakers are prophesying, God's word may speak to the hearers and bring them to know God (23-25).

Order and upbuilding (14:26-40)

At the meetings of the Corinthian church, the Christians came prepared to take part in the service in a variety of ways. The guiding rule was that everything was to be spiritually helpful (26). But confusion arose because several spoke in different tongues at the same time, often with no interpreter. Paul says that if no interpreter is present, they must keep quiet. Even if an interpreter is present, they must speak in turn, and then no more than two or three (27-28).

Similar instructions are given to prophets. They must restrict their participation to two or three, and the hearers must examine what is said and not accept it blindly (29). The prophets must keep control of themselves and make sure that everything is orderly and of value to the hearers (30-33). The women must be orderly too. It is not their job to instruct the church or question the preacher. They can discuss their questions with their husbands at home (34-35). The Corinthians must not get the idea that there are special rules of conduct just for them (36).

Some of the Corinthians thought they had the special gift of being able to tell what was of God and what was not. Paul suggests that if this is the case, they should show it by acknowledging that what he is saying comes from God (37-38). Although they should not disallow tongues, they should positively encourage prophecy. Above all, everything must be orderly and helpful to the spiritual upbuilding of the church (39-40).

15:1-58 THE DOCTRINE OF THE RESURRECTION

The fact of Christ's resurrection (15:1-11)

Among the Corinthians were some who denied that there will be a physical resurrection of the dead. Paul points out in this chapter that the truth of the resurrection is part of the gospel which they believed and by which they are saved (15:1-2).

The gospel Paul preaches has been given him by God. It has as its basis the death, burial and resurrection of Jesus Christ (3-4). Paul then gives a list of eye witnesses to Christ's resurrection, including Peter, James the Lord's brother and many others, most of whom were still living should anyone want to question them. These eye witnesses could confirm that the resurrection of Christ was an undeniable fact (5-7).

Last of all the risen Lord appeared to Paul himself, who at the time was on the road to Damascus to arrest and imprison Christians (see Acts 9:3-6). God's choice of the fierce persecutor to be his special apostle was unnatural and unexpected. Yet through God's grace, Paul did a greater work than all the other apostles. He is careful to point out, however, that he and his fellow apostles all preached the same gospel (8-11).

A guarantee of final victory (15:12-28)

To those who claim there will be no bodily resurrection of the dead, Paul replies that if this is true it means that Christ has not been raised. In that case the gospel he preaches is not true and the believer's faith is without foundation (12-14). Furthermore, it means that the preachers of the gospel have misled their hearers. For if Christ has not been raised from the dead, he is certainly not the victorious Saviour. He has not conquered sin; sin has conquered him (15-17). Those who died believing in Christ have likewise been for ever conquered by sin and death. As for those believers still living, they are to be

pitied for putting up with hardship in the hope of a better life to come if, as the doubters argue, there is no such future life (18-19).

Christ's return guarantees the resurrection of all believers. They will not merely be brought back to life, but they will enter into a new kind of life, one where death will no longer have any part. Death is the result of sin, and all who are descended from Adam will die; but all who have faith in Christ will triumph over death. This victorious resurrection of believers will take place at Christ's return (20-23).

With the final banishment of death itself, Christ will see the victory he won at the cross effectual to the last outpost of rebellion. Having established full and complete authority over everything and everyone, he will deliver up this authority to his Father (24-26). The work for which the Son willingly became subject to the Father will then be complete. Everything will be subject to him who is Lord of all (27-28).

A source of encouragement (15:29-34)

It seems that another strange practice the church in Corinth had introduced was that of baptizing people on behalf of those who had died unbaptized. Paul does not stop to discuss whether this was a desirable practice; he simply asks what meaning can it have if there is no future resurrection? If people do not believe in the resurrection but practise baptism for the dead, they are demonstrating something they do not believe in (29).

There are no doubts about the resurrection in Paul's mind. On the contrary his assurance of the resurrection and the victory it will bring encourages him amid daily trials. In Ephesus (the place from which he writes) he is daily in danger of being killed because of his faithfulness in preaching the gospel. If, however, there is no hope of a future and better life, he suffers for nothing. He would do better to forget about preaching the gospel and have a good time while he still has the opportunity (30-32).

Paul warns the Corinthians not to deceive themselves. If they mix with people who deny the resurrection, they will soon have wrong ideas about God, and this in turn will lead to wrong behaviour (33-34).

The resurrection body (15:35-58)

Some people mocked the idea of the resurrection by asking how could bodies that have decayed in the earth be raised to life again. Paul answers with an illustration. A seed dies when it is put in the ground, but this is part of the process of bringing forth new life in the form of a plant that grows up out of the ground. What grows up is different from what was buried, but in a sense it is the same thing. It is dry and dead looking when put in the ground, but fresh and beautiful when it appears as a living plant (35-37). The doubters should remember also that plant life takes many different forms. So does animal life (38-39). God gives a different life, beauty and form to different things, depending on his purposes for them (40-41).

In similar manner the resurrection body is different from the body that is buried in the ground. The body that is buried is perishable, unattractive, and powerless; the body that is raised is imperishable, beautiful, and strong. Just as the present body is suited to the needs of present earthly life, so the resurrection body is suited to the needs of the spiritual life of the age to come (42-44).

Adam was the first of a race of physical, earthly people; Christ is the first of a race of spiritual, heavenly people. Adam's body was the pattern for the bodies of people in the present life; Christ's body is the pattern for the bodies of believers in the life to come (45-49). Believers will have their physical bodies of the present life changed into spiritual bodies suited for life in the heavenly kingdom (50).

The change from the physical to the spiritual will take place when Christ returns and the dead are raised. All Christians, both those who have died and those still alive, will have their physical perishable bodies changed instantly into spiritual imperishable bodies (51-53). Death will have no more power over believers. Sin, which makes death fearful and which uses the law to hold people in this state of fear, will be finally destroyed (54-57).

Believers have no reason to be hesitant or doubtful concerning the coming resurrection. Rather they will find that they have greater confidence and purpose in their Christian life and service as they understand the full meaning that the resurrection has for them (58).

16:1-24 FINAL INSTRUCTIONS

Plans for the collection (16:1-4)

For many years Paul had been concerned for the poor Christians in Jerusalem, and he was always doing his best to help them (Acts 11:27-30; Gal 2:10). During his third missionary journey he had been organizing a collection of money and goods among the Gentile churches to take to Jerusalem. He hoped that as the Jerusalem Christians saw the loving concern that the Gentile churches had for

them, they would feel a greater sense of unity and fellowship with their Gentile brothers in other countries (cf. Acts 24:17; Rom 15:25-27). (Paul talks about this collection more fully in 2 Cor 8:1-9:15.)

The Corinthians were participating in this collection and had written to Paul about it. In response Paul advises them to put their offerings into the fund each Sunday, so that the money will be ready when he visits Corinth. The amount people give will depend on the amount they earn (16:1-2). The church should also choose representatives to take the money to Jerusalem, and when Paul comes to Corinth he will write letters to introduce these men to the Jerusalem church. In fact, he might even go with them (3-4).

Personal notes and farewell (16:5-24)

Paul's plan is to visit Macedonia and then move south to Corinth. He realizes that the church in Corinth needs further help, so when he comes he wants to spend some time there (5-7). He is not sure when he will make this visit, as he currently has much urgent work to do in Ephesus (8-9).

When Timothy arrives in Corinth (cf. Acts 19:22), the Christians are not to treat him with any less respect than they would Paul, for Timothy and he are doing the same work. Paul is anxious for Timothy to return to Ephesus as soon as possible, so that he might find out whether the situation in Corinth has improved (10-11). Paul tells them he has suggested that Apollos pay them another visit, but Apollos feels the time is not yet suitable (12).

Paul urges the Corinthians not to act like children any longer, but to act like responsible mature adults (13-14). Not all of them have acted immaturely. There are faithful hard-working people like those of the household of Stephanus, and the church should follow their leadership (15-16). The other two men who have come with Stephanus to seek Paul's advice are likewise ones whom the church should follow (17-18).

A number of people and churches of the province of Asia join Paul in sending greetings to the Corinthians. Among these are Aquila and Priscilla, and the church in Ephesus that meets in their house (19-20; cf. Acts 18:18-19,24-26).

Finally, Paul takes the pen from his secretary to sign the letter himself (21; cf. 2 Thess 3:17). In his own handwriting he adds a warning to those who are disloyal to Christ, expresses his longing for Christ to return, and sends his love to all the believers in Corinth (22-24).

2 Corinthians

BACKGROUND

In his previous letter Paul had spoken of his plans to move from Ephesus north to Macedonia and then down to Corinth (1 Cor 16:5-7; cf. Acts 19:21). However, when Timothy returned from Corinth to Ephesus (cf. 1 Cor 16:10-11), the news that he brought was so disturbing that Paul changed his plans. The New Testament does not record Paul's travels of this period in any detail, but occasional references to them give us at least some understanding of events.

A painful visit and a severe letter

When Paul learnt that neither his lengthy letter nor Timothy's recent visit had brought any improvement in the Corinthian church, he made a trip to Corinth direct by boat. He had already warned that he would come and deal with the trouble-makers if they did not change their ways (1 Cor 4:19-21), and now he did as he had said. This was only Paul's second visit to Corinth. It gave him such distress that when he looked back on it later he referred to it as a painful visit (2 Cor 2:1; 13:2).

Though painful, the visit was only brief, but Paul hoped to visit the church again soon (2 Cor 1:15-16). Within a short while news reached him in Ephesus that nothing had improved in Corinth. In fact, his recent visit only made his opponents more rebellious. Paul's immediate thought was to rush back to Corinth and deal with the rebels, but upon consideration he thought it better not to. He did not want to act hastily or do anything that he might later regret (2 Cor 1:23).

Instead Paul wrote a letter. It was a very severe letter, which challenged the church to deal with those who opposed his apostolic authority. The letter was taken to the Corinthian church by Titus, but it seems not to have been preserved (2 Cor 2:3-4; 7:8; 12:18).

Titus took the letter to Corinth direct, but he was to return via Macedonia and meet Paul in Troas. Paul meanwhile finished his work in Ephesus and moved north to Troas, but he was so anxious to get news of the Corinthians' response to his letter, that he could not bear waiting for Titus. So he left Troas and went looking for him in Macedonia (2 Cor 2:12-13; cf. Acts 20:1). Paul met Titus in Macedonia and was overjoyed at the good news Titus brought. As a result of the severe letter, the trouble-makers in Corinth had realized their error and stopped opposing Paul (2 Cor 7:5-6).

With much relief, Paul wrote yet another letter (known to us as 2 Corinthians) and sent it to Corinth with Titus and two others (2 Cor 8:16-18,22-23). In view of the recent troubles, Paul wrote at length concerning various aspects of Christian service. The final section of the letter, Chapters 10-13, is such a strong defence of Paul's apostolic authority, that some Bible scholars believe it is the severe letter that he wrote previously.

OUTLINE

1:1-11 INTRODUCTION AND ENCOURAGEMENT

Paul greets the Corinthian church, along with other Christians in Achaia, in the name of the God of all comfort (1:1-3). One reason why Christians suffer all kinds of troubles is that they may know how to sympathize with and help others who are similarly troubled. Just as they share in Christ's sufferings, so they can share in his comfort (4-5). When the Corinthians see the divine comfort Paul experiences in his sufferings, they should be encouraged to bear their own sufferings (6-7).

The troubles that Paul suffered in the province of Asia were so severe that they almost led to his death. But they also caused him to see clearly that he himself was completely helpless, and therefore he needed to trust entirely in God (8-9). This gives him the assurance that in the future God will likewise deliver him. If the believers in Corinth pray for God's protection over him in his work, they will also have good reason to give thanks when God answers their prayers (10-11).

1:12-2:17 PAUL EXPLAINS HIS RECENT ACTIONS

Reasons for changing his plans (1:12-2:4)

Certain people in Corinth had accused Paul of insincerity. According to them, Paul tried to give the impression through his conduct and his letters that he felt in a certain way, when he did not feel that way at all. Paul denies this. In all his behaviour, whether in dealing with people in general or in dealing with the Corinthians in particular, he has been sincere and straightforward. The same is true of his letter-writing. He hopes the Corinthians will believe this, so that in the coming judgment neither they nor he will feel shame on account of wrong attitudes (12-14).

In the recent past, Paul had twice been forced to change his plans for a visit to Corinth. His first plan was to go to Macedonia, down to Corinth and then to Jerusalem (Acts 19:21; 1 Cor 16:5-7). His second plan was to go to Corinth first, up to Macedonia, back to Corinth and then to Jerusalem. The advantage of this second plan was that the Corinthians would benefit from his ministry twice. When he was forced to change this plan also, the Corinthians accused him of not keeping his word, of being like an ordinary person of the world who says 'Yes' one day and 'No' the next (15-17).

Again Paul denies the accusation. To act in such a way would be contrary to the character of Christ that Paul had preached to them. There was nothing uncertain about Christ. The fulfilment of all God's promises in him shows that he always said 'Yes' to his Father's will. And Christians add their 'Yes' by saying 'Amen', by which they mean 'Yes, indeed, this person is the Truth of God' (18-20). The Christian life is one of assurance and stability, because it is from God, it is in Christ, and it is guaranteed by the Holy Spirit (21-22).

Paul's decision against going to Corinth was not because he lacked certainty or courage. Rather it was because he wished to spare the Corinthians the unpleasantness of his stern treatment (23). He does not want them to think he is a dictator; but they must realize the importance of discipline if they are to have true happiness (24).

Neither Paul nor the Corinthians would have wanted him to pay them another painful visit. Paul's desire was to enjoy fellowship with them, but this would not have been possible had they been full of sorrow. So instead of visiting them personally, he wrote to them. The purpose of the severe letter was not to hurt them, but to urge them to repent. He wrote out of love, so that his next visit to them would be an occasion for joy (2:1-4).

Forgiveness for the offender (2:5-11)

In this section Paul speaks about an offender and his offence, and although we do not know to whom or what he was referring, the Corinthians did. The offence seems to have concerned Paul personally (perhaps a denial of his apostolic authority), and was one reason for Paul's severe letter. The issue caused sorrow for the church and for Paul (5). The church finally dealt with the offender, probably by excluding him from the fellowship for a period (6).

Paul now has to warn the Corinthians not to be hard and unforgiving. The man had shown sorrow and repentance for his sin, and the church should now lovingly welcome him back. If they continue to treat him harshly, their action could have bad results instead of good, through driving the man away from God in bitterness and sorrow (7-8).

The Corinthians had demonstrated their unity with Paul in dealing with the offender. He wants them to demonstrate that unity again, by forgiving the man and receiving him back (9-10). If they fail to forgive, Satan may use the opportunity to do further damage, both to the man and to the church (11).

Paul's sincerity in his ministry (2:12-17)

Once again Paul states that all his movements were guided by an interest for the Corinthians, not for himself. He was so keen to meet Titus and hear news of the Corinthians that he could not concentrate on his work in Troas. So rather than wait for Titus in Troas he went across to Macedonia, in the hope of meeting him there (12-13).

The good news that Titus brought from Corinth leads Paul to an outburst of praise to God. He pictures the preachers of the gospel joining Christ in his victory procession. The gospel is triumphant. In another illustration he likens the gospel to a sweet smell that spreads everywhere (14). But some reject the gospel, and to them it is an offensive stench that kills. The preachers whom God calls to carry such a message of life and death have a great responsibility. They are not hawkers trying to sell goods for their own gain, but announcers of God's message. They have no mixed motives, but are concerned only for the spiritual well-being of others (15-17).

3:1-6:13 TRUE CHRISTIAN SERVICE

The servant and the message (3:1-18)

Some of the teachers who came to Corinth brought with them letters of recommendation from their home churches, and claimed that these letters gave them authority to teach. Paul carried no such letters, with the result that his opponents suggested he had no right to teach. Paul replies that pieces of paper do not guarantee the truth of people's ministry. A better means of judging is by the fruit of their work. The Corinthian church, which is the fruit of Paul's work in Corinth, is all the recommendation he needs. This is the work of the Spirit of God, and is far greater recommendation than a mere letter. The gospel produces fruit that no set of laws can produce (3:1-3).

Paul has confidence in his ministry, but it is a confidence that rests in God, not in himself. What changes people is the gospel, not any personal ability that Paul might have (4-5). He is a servant of the new covenant, by which the Spirit of God gives believers new life within. The old covenant (the law of Moses) set out written laws, but in the end it brought death, because the people were unable to keep it (6).

The contrast between the old covenant and the new is now illustrated by reference to the story in Exodus 34:29-35. When Moses, after receiving the law from God, came down from the mountain, his face shone with a brightness that reflected the glory of God. His face was so bright that he had to cover it with a cloth, as the people were afraid to approach him. Paul's point is this: if the covenant that brought condemnation and death came with glory, how much more glory must the new covenant have which brings righteousness and life (7-9). If the covenant that was temporary came with glory, how much more glory must the new covenant have which is permanent (10-11).

After Moses had been away from the presence of God for a while, the brightness of his face faded, but the veil over his face prevented Israelites from seeing this fading brightness. To Paul, this fading brightness symbolized the fading away and eventual end of the old covenant. The permanence of the new covenant, by contrast, gives Paul confidence in all that he says and does (12-13).

In a sense there is still a veil that belongs to the old covenant. It is the veil that covers the minds of the Jews, for they read the Old Testament but refuse to see Christ as its fulfilment. Consequently, they cannot properly understand it (14-15). When Moses went in before the Lord he removed the veil. Similarly, when Jews turn to Jesus Christ, the veil is removed. Through the work of the Spirit, Christ sets them free from the bondage of sin and the law (16-17). Christians also must make sure that there is no veil between them and their Lord. The better

they know Christ personally, the more they will be changed so that they become increasingly like him (18).

The life and work of a servant (4:1-18)

God's true servants do not avoid their responsibilities or use dishonest methods. They do not change the plain meaning of God's Word to suit themselves, but teach that Word faithfully and directly (4:1-2). Not all will believe, because Satan blinds their minds, but true preachers remember always that the message they preach is Christ's, not theirs. Then, when the hearers allow the light of that message to shine into their hearts, they see Christ as their Lord and God (3-6).

It seems strange that the priceless treasure of knowing Christ should be given to ordinary human beings, people beset by troubles and imperfections. It is like putting costly jewellery into an earthenware pot (7). Paul's life is not one of glory and honour; it is one of continual suffering and trouble. Yet his faith is never shaken. After all, if Christ suffered such things, his disciples should not be surprised when they too suffer. But this same life of Christ in him turns these sufferings into victories (8-11). Such a life is worthwhile when it is the means of bringing spiritual life to others (12).

As with the psalmist, so with Paul, his faith in God causes him to express his confidence amid all his afflictions (13; cf. Ps 116:9-11). Even if his sufferings lead to death, that will not mean defeat, because death itself will be conquered by Jesus Christ (14). Meanwhile the unfailing servant of God makes every effort to build up more and more people in the knowledge of God, and so bring glory to him (15).

In view of all this, Paul does not become discouraged. Though physically troubled and weary, he is inwardly strengthened. He sees his sufferings as small and temporary when compared with the unseen and eternal glories that one day will be his (16-18).

Confidence and courage (5:1-10)

Christians receive further encouragement amid daily trials through the knowledge that the present body is only temporary. It is like a tent in which a person lives for a short time, whereas what God has prepared for the future life is a permanent home (5:1). Another illustration likens the present body to clothes that cover a person. Again this is only temporary. One day all that is earthly and temporary will be replaced by that which is spiritual and eternal (2-4). The indwelling Holy Spirit is the guarantee that one day believers will enjoy the fulness of life for which God is at present preparing them (5).

At present believers are physically separated from Christ, but the desire to be with him is a continual source of encouragement. They do not at present see Christ, but live by faith in him (6-8). They are further reminded of the need to live faithfully when they realize that being with Christ will bring not only glory, but also judgment. Their life will be examined and they will receive what Christ considers is due to them, whether for better or for worse (9-10).

The power of love (5:11-6:13)

Because Paul knows that he is accountable to Christ, he knows what it means to fear the Lord, and this makes him more diligent in his service. God knows that his motives are pure and he trusts that the Corinthians know also (11).

In making these statements, Paul is not trying to write a recommendation for himself. He is trying to give his supporters reason to be bold in defending him against those who criticize him (12). They may have seen him display his feelings in different ways at various times, but they know he never acted out of self-interest (13). His constant awareness of Christ's love was the inner spiritual power that guided his actions. Christ died the death that sinners should have died, firstly to bear the penalty of their sins, and secondly to put an end to living for self. From now on they should live for him (14-15).

Before he became a Christian, Paul had judged Jesus by the standards of the ordinary person of the world, and in so doing had judged him wrongly. Now he no longer judges Jesus, or anyone else, from a merely human standpoint, because in Christ he sees everything in a new light. Old attitudes go and new attitudes replace them (16-17).

This changing from the old to the new is done by God through Jesus Christ. It is part of the total work that God does as he reconciles people to himself, and turns sinners into his friends. Having reconciled them, God then sends them out to preach the message of reconciliation to others, so that other sinners might be brought to God (18-20). The basis of this message is the death of Christ. Through the judgment of sin in Christ, God is able to forgive repentant sinners and give them a righteous standing before him (21).

Some at Corinth had heard this message but not responded to it. They were still spiritually dead. Paul therefore offers salvation to them once again, and they must decide whether to accept it or reject it (6:1-2). They are not to make excuses by trying to find fault with Paul, for he has never given anyone grounds for rejecting the gospel (3). He has had all kinds of difficult experiences (4-5), but through them all he has proved his genuineness by the spiritual quality of his life and the truth and power of his message (6-7). Some people have honoured him, others insulted him, but in all circumstances he has shown by his consistent behaviour that he is a true servant of God (8-10).

The Corinthians have not returned to Paul the open-hearted love that he has shown them. He has room in his heart for them, but they have no room in their hearts for him (11-12). He appeals to them to return his love (13).

6:14-7:16 CONCERNING PREVIOUS CORRESPONDENCE

The Christian in ungodly society (6:14-7:1)

Apparently the Corinthians still misunderstood what Paul was trying to teach them about relationships with unbelievers (cf. 1 Cor 5:9-11). Previously they thought it meant cutting themselves off from unbelievers completely. Now they go to the other extreme and think their relationships can be as close as they like, even to marriage. Not so, says Paul. There must be no permanent and binding relations with unbelievers. The new life of Christians is as different from the life of non-Christians as light is from darkness or as Christ is from Satan (14-15).

The church is the temple of God, and so is the individual Christian (cf. 1 Cor 3:16; 6:19). God dwells within his people, and his dwelling place must be holy. Being united with idol worshippers is the same as bringing a heathen idol into God's temple (16). Christians can have no part in the ungodliness of the sinful society in which they live. They are now members of the family of God, and their relationship with their heavenly Father is more important than all their physical and earthly relationships (17-18). In view of this, they must make sure they are cleansed from the impurities of the ungodly world, so that they might be holy before God (7:1).

Joy at the Corinthians' repentance (7:2-16)

Again Paul appeals to the Corinthians to open their hearts to him, and not to feel hesitant because of the accusations his enemies have made. Nothing in life or death can separate him from them. He assures them that he is overjoyed at the news he has just heard concerning them (2-4).

Paul recalls the restlessness he felt in Macedonia as he awaited Titus' return with news from Corinth. He recalls also the joy he experienced when

Titus recounted how he had been comforted when he saw the Corinthians' changed attitude towards Paul. That severe letter had been worthwhile. Titus' visit had been fruitful (5-7).

At first Paul had felt sorry for writing as he did, but now he is glad to see that the sorrow which the letter brought them was the means of bringing them to repentance (8-9). This is because their sorrow was not just shame at wrongdoing, but real sorrow and repentance before God. They acknowledged their sin to God and asked him to forgive them. Because they saw themselves from God's point of view, they spared no effort in clearing up the wrongdoing that was among them (10-11). Paul is satisfied that the letter has achieved its purpose. That purpose was not to hurt people, but to help them view matters under the searching eye of God (12).

Before Paul sent Titus with that severe letter, he boasted to Titus of his confidence that the Corinthians would see their wrongdoing and repent. He therefore has added joy to know that not only did Titus find them repentant, but he was also filled with love for them (13-16).

8:1-9:15 COLLECTION FOR THE POOR IN JERUSALEM

About a year earlier Paul had given instructions to the Corinthians about the collection of money he was organizing for the poor Christians in Jerusalem (1 Cor 16:1-4). The Corinthians had made a start (see 9:2), but in the meantime they became so concerned with their own difficulties that they neglected their responsibilities in the matter. Now that they have cleared up their local troubles, Paul reminds them of the importance of this exercise in Christian giving.

Paul urges the Corinthians to give (8:1-15)

The giving of the Christians in Macedonia is an example of true Christian giving. They might have suffered from persecution and poverty, but they gave generously – not only as much as they were able but far more, and without any urging from Paul (8:1-3). In fact, they begged Paul to allow them the privilege of taking part in the offering. Such an attitude was possible only because they first gave themselves to the Lord, for him to use them as he desired (4-5). Paul will now send Titus to Corinth to encourage the believers to complete what they had started. The enthusiasm they show in other spiritual exercises should be shown in their giving also (6-7).

There are no rules to force Christians to give. They should give out of love. Through love, Christ gave everything, leaving the glory of heaven for a sinful world, so that he might save sinners and give them a share in his riches (8-9). The Corinthians should likewise show sacrificial love, by completing the work that they began the previous year. There is no law to determine the amount they should give. It will depend on how much they have (10-12).

Although the Corinthians may be financially better off than Christians in some other churches, Paul does not want to burden them unfairly. Nevertheless, they should realize that while they are able to help poorer churches, they should. They must bear in mind also that they do not know the future. One day they themselves may be poor and the Jerusalem church able to send help to them (13-14). The principle is not that all must receive an equal amount, but that all must have enough according to their needs, with no greed and no starving (15).

Arrangements for the collection (8:16-9:5)

Titus is just as keen as Paul to see this collection completed successfully (16-17). He is travelling to Corinth with two other well known Christians. One of them has been chosen by several churches as their representative to join Paul and the other representatives who will later take the money to Jerusalem. The other is a proven friend of Paul's who has the interests of the Corinthians at heart. The reason for sending three people is to ensure that no one, whether inside or outside the church, has any cause to doubt Paul's uprightness or sincerity. Everything must be done openly and honestly (18-22). By participating whole-heartedly in this offering, the Corinthians will display the generous love of which Paul has often boasted (23-24).

Paul feels he must speak further on the matter. He reminds the Corinthians of their enthusiasm the previous year, and of the fact that his boasting of their enthusiasm had stirred the Macedonians to join in the offering (9:1-2). He is sending these three men ahead to ensure the collection is completed before he arrives. If he comes and finds them not ready, he will be ashamed because of his over-confidence, and the Corinthians will be ashamed because of their laziness. Also it will mean that when he arrives he will have to stir them to make a hurried collection. This would not be an honourable way to do things. It would be more like paying a tax than willingly making an offering to God (3-5).

The blessing of Christian giving (9:6-15)

God takes notice of the way Christians give, and if they give generously he rewards them generously. People should decide thoughtfully the amount they should give, then give it joyfully (6-7). They need not fear poverty if they give much, because God is able to increase his supply to ensure that generous givers still have more than they need (8-10; cf. Prov 11:24). The threefold result of true giving is that the poor are helped, the givers are blessed, and God is glorified in thanksgiving (11-12). The giving of the Corinthians will prove the genuineness of their faith. It will also join givers and receivers together in fellowship in Christ, who is the greatest gift of all, the gift given by God himself (13-15).

The Corinthians responded to Paul's appeal. Later, when he was in Corinth, he wrote to the Romans saying, 'At present I am going to Jerusalem with aid for the saints, for Macedonia and Achaia have been pleased to make some contribution for the poor among the saints in Jerusalem. They were pleased to do it . . .' (Rom 15:25-27).

10:1-13:14 APOSTOLIC AUTHORITY

In spite of all Paul has said, there were still trouble-makers at Corinth. Certain travelling preachers had gained some standing in the church and continued to make accusations against Paul. Paul refers to them ironically as 'super apostles', and more directly as 'false apostles' (see 11:5,13).

Spiritual power; worthless boasting (10:1-18)

These so-called apostles repeatedly questioned the authority of Paul and succeeded in winning some of the Corinthians over to their side. They accused Paul of trying to make himself appear tough and bold when writing letters to them, but of being weak and cowardly when face to face with them. He was no apostle, they claimed, just an ordinary person with ordinary worldly attitudes. Paul replies that what they mistakenly thought was weakness was really tolerance. He had made every effort to control his feelings, in order to show kindness and patience towards the Corinthians. Only when everything else fails will he use with severity the apostolic authority that is his by right (10:1-2).

Worldly people force others into submission by exercising their power and authority. Christians submit to Jesus Christ and depend upon his power and authority. This is a far greater force with which to fight evil. It destroys pride and makes even the mind obedient to Christ (3-5). But if the false apostles refuse to join with the rest of the church in submitting to Paul's instructions, he is ready to use his apostolic authority to deal with them (6).

The false apostles claim that they have Christ's authority; so does Paul (7). The difference is that

Paul has proof of his authority. He has built up converts and churches, whereas the false apostles have brought only harm and ruin (8). In writing like this, Paul is not trying to frighten his readers into submission, as his opponents claim. When he comes they will find out for themselves that what he says, he does (9-11). Nor is he trying to compete with the false apostles in seeing how highly he can praise himself (12).

In coming to Corinth, the false apostles are trespassing on Paul's ground, since he was the first to take the gospel there. Unlike them Paul keeps to the limits God has given him. God's call for him was to be a pioneer missionary to the Gentiles (cf. Acts 9:15; Rom 1:5; 15:16,20; Gal 2:9). He will not, therefore, interfere with the fruit of another person's work (13-14). Corinth marks the western extent of Paul's ministry so far, and before he moves into unreached regions farther west, he wants to make sure that the Corinthian church is strong and healthy (15-16). He is not saying all this to praise himself. The one whom he praises is God (17-18).

Paul is not inferior to others (11:1-15)

Although he knows that boasting is foolish, Paul feels he must say a few things to prevent the Corinthians from believing the propaganda of these men who set themselves up as super apostles. He feels for the Corinthians with the kind of jealousy that a father feels for his daughter. He has brought them from the darkness of heathenism into the light of God's world, so that he might present them as a bride to Christ (11:1-2). Paul is afraid that these false apostles will deceive the Corinthians just as Satan deceived Eve. He knows that the Corinthians have a tendency to accept wrong teaching very easily (3-4).

Even if Paul does not have the skilled speech and persuasive style of the false apostles, he is not inferior to them. At least he teaches the truth, and that is what is important (5-6).

Paul had a right to be financially supported by those to whom he ministered, but when he was at Corinth he had earned his living by making tents. He did this so that the Corinthians could be built up in their knowledge of the Christian teaching without having to worry about supporting him. He even accepted gifts from other churches so as to remain financially independent of the Corinthians. But he received no thanks for his efforts. The false apostles (who came later and who did accept money from the Corinthians) used it as 'proof' to the church that Paul was merely a labourer and not an apostle at all (7-9).

One reason why Paul supports himself is his love for the Corinthians. He has no intention of changing his practice of self-support, because he wants the Corinthians to see the difference between the true apostle and the false apostles (10-12). These men seek only their own gain. They make themselves look like servants of God, but really they are servants of Satan. Their ultimate punishment is certain (13-15).

Paul's experiences as an apostle (11:16-33)

All boasting is foolish, but since the Corinthians have heard much boasting from others, Paul decides they shall hear some from him (16). This is not the way Christ spoke, but Paul hopes it may do something to bring them to their senses. After all, he says cuttingly, they tolerate other fools, why not tolerate him (17-19)? The false apostles had enslaved the Corinthians and then cruelly taken their money. In comparison with such slave-masters, Paul is weak indeed (20-21)!

The false apostles claimed to be learned Jews, pure Hebrews. So is Paul (22). Concerning the more important matter of service, however, Paul is far superior. He has worked harder and suffered more in the spread of the gospel, even to the point of death time and again. He quotes specific examples of his experiences, most of which are either not recorded or not detailed in Acts (23-27). More than all these trials was the inner trial of the constant anxiety from which he was never free, his concern for the churches. Paul felt every weakness and every problem among his converts as if it were his own (28-29).

Remarkably, Paul's boasting is almost entirely concerned with things that the normally boastful person is ashamed to speak about, namely, personal humiliations. Yet God knows that in recounting these experiences Paul has not been exaggerating or twisting the truth (30-31). One final story comes to mind. It concerns the time he escaped from Damascus, when Jewish opponents had persuaded the governor to send soldiers to arrest him (32-33; see Acts 9:23-25).

A genuine case for boasting (12:1-10)

Before leaving the subject of boasting, Paul wants to give one more example (12:1). Fourteen years previously he had seen a vision, but because he does not want to exalt himself, he speaks about his experience in the third person, referring to himself simply as 'a man'. By some unknown means he was taken up into Paradise, where he heard and saw things that God does not normally allow people to know (2-4). He is not telling this story so that the Corinthians will have a higher opinion of him. He wants people to judge him only from their personal experience of him, from what they themselves have seen him do and heard him say (5-6).

It would be easy for Paul to have feelings of self-importance because of his visions, but God intervened to make sure this would not happen. He sent Paul some particular trial (or trials) that constantly hindered him in his work (7). (Notice that Paul now departs from his original intention of speaking in the third person and reverts to speaking directly in the first person — not 'a man' but 'me'.) God did not answer Paul's prayer to remove this trial, but that was to Paul's advantage, because it made him constantly dependent on God's grace and power. The greater Paul's sense of weakness, the more he realized the need to cast himself upon God. Therein lies his strength (8-10).

Plan to visit Corinth again (12:11-21)

The Corinthians have forced Paul to this foolish boasting through their believing the accusations that the false apostles made against him. He reminds them also of the miracles and wonders he performed among them, in spite of great difficulties. All these examples should make them see clearly that he is not a second-class apostle (11-12). His refusal to live at the Corinthians' expense was for the purpose of helping them. But instead of being thankful to him, they have been offended. They regard his action as an insult to their church. With great irony Paul asks their forgiveness for what he has done (13).

What Paul wants is the Corinthians themselves, not their money. He is coming to visit them again and he still will not take financial support from them. He will spend not only his money but also his time and energy for them, as a parent would for his children (14-15).

Some of the Corinthians made the hurtful accusation that Paul was deceitful. They said that although he did not take money from them openly, he managed to get it from them by other, more cunning, methods (16). Paul points out that this is nonsense. The Corinthians well know that he and those whom he sent had been open and straight-forward in everything (17-18).

Paul has not been saying all this because he feels answerable to the Corinthians. He is answerable to God, not to them. Nevertheless, he trusts that they may have been helped by what he has said (19). Many of them are still childish in their thinking and behaviour, and they need to change urgently. Otherwise when Paul visits them, he will feel shame instead of pride, sorrow instead of joy. He does not want to have to act severely once again (20-21).

Final appeal for order (13:1-14)

As he writes, Paul is already on his way to Corinth. He therefore repeats his former warning that if the Corinthians do not discipline the trouble-makers among them, he will be forced to discipline them himself when he arrives. He will determine the truth of matters not according to gossip but according to evidence that can be tested (13:1-2). They have wanted proof of Paul's Christ-given authority, but when they see it in action among them, they will be sorry. People once thought Christ was weak, just as the Corinthians think Paul is weak; but the resurrection power and authority seen in Christ will be seen also in Paul (3-4).

The Corinthians have been examining Paul, demanding that he show proof of his apostolic authority. Now he calls upon them to examine themselves and show proof of their Christian faith (5). If they fail the test, Paul will have to prove his apostolic authority by using it; that is, he will pass the test. If they pass the test, Paul will be content not to use his authority, even though some may say it is because he has no authority; that is, they will consider he has failed the test (6-7).

Paul is not greatly concerned whether he passes the test in their eyes. He is more concerned with upholding the truth of the Christian gospel (8). He wants to build up other people in the faith more than build a reputation for himself. He wants to see them spiritually strong, even though this will leave him no opportunity to demonstrate his divinely given power among them. That is why he is writing now. He wants to give them the opportunity to change their ways, so that he might spare them the unpleasant experience of tasting his apostolic authority in judgment (9-10).

In conclusion, Paul urges the Corinthians to take notice of his advice and correct the troubles in the church, so that there might be unity, peace, love and joy among them (11-13). They are more likely to experience these specific blessings as they experience the more basic blessings of the gospel. Through that gospel the Father has exercised his love towards them, Christ in his grace has saved them, and the Spirit has given them true fellowship with God through coming to dwell within them (14).

Galatians

BACKGROUND

During his first missionary journey into Asia Minor, Paul evangelized the southern part of the Roman province of Galatia, and established churches in the towns of Antioch, Iconium, Lystra and Derbe (Acts 13:13-14:23). These are the churches he addresses in his letter to the Galatians. (See maps located in the commentary on Acts.)

Jewish difficulties

The early chapters of Acts record that the Christian church was born in Jerusalem, and in the beginning consisted almost entirely of Jews. As the disciples moved out to other areas, large numbers of Gentiles believed and so became part of the expanding church. With Jews and Gentiles in the same church, difficulties soon arose.

Many of the Christian Jews in Jerusalem were still very Jewish in their outlook, and looked upon Christianity as a sort of improved Judaism. As Jews they had been pleased to see a few Gentiles become converts to Judaism from time to time, but they were not pleased at what they now saw happening in the church. They did not think it right that people of any nationality could enter the community of God's people without any thought for Jewish laws relating to food, cleansing and circumcision.

On one occasion Jewish traditionalists in the Jerusalem church rebuked Peter for eating with Gentiles, but when Peter explained how God had shown him that he blesses Jews and Gentiles alike, they said no more (Acts 11:1-18). However, many were not fully convinced, and when Paul returned to Syrian Antioch after his first missionary journey, trouble broke out again.

Trouble in Syrian Antioch

While Paul was in Antioch, a group of Jews came from Jerusalem and taught the Gentile Christians that they were required to be circumcised and keep the law of Moses (Acts 14:26-28; 15:1,5). These men claimed to have authority from James (the brother of Jesus and the most prominent leader in the Jerusalem church), but James later denied this (Gal 2:12; Acts 15:24). They argued so cleverly that even mature Christians such as Peter and Barnabas

stopped eating with the Gentiles in case they broke Jewish food laws (Gal 2:12-13).

Paul, who had been as zealous a Jew as any before his conversion, saw that the teaching of the Judaisers was contrary to the Christian gospel. His forthright public rebuke caused Peter and Barnabas to see their error and resume their fellowship with the Gentiles (Gal 2:11,14; cf. Acts 15:6-12).

Trouble in Galatia

Soon after Paul corrected the trouble at Antioch, he heard that the Judaisers had spread their teaching to the recently established churches in Galatia. He was angry at the Judaisers for upsetting the young Christians, and shocked that the Christians had believed them (Gal 1:6; 3:1). In response he sent off the sharply worded letter known to us as Galatians.

In this letter Paul asserts that Christians are saved by faith and live by faith. They are not saved by the law of Moses, nor are they governed by it; yet at the same time they are not lawless. They are under the direction of the indwelling Spirit of God (Gal 3:3; 5:1,13,16,18).

The problem caused by the Judaisers had now spread to the most distant parts of the church. It therefore needed to be dealt with quickly and decisively. Because the teaching had come from Jerusalem, that was the place to discuss the matter. Therefore, after he sent off his letter to the churches of Galatia, Paul went to Jerusalem with Barnabas and others from Antioch to settle the matter once and for all (Acts 15:2-35).

OUTLINE

1:1-2:21 PAUL'S GOSPEL IS THE ONLY GOSPEL

Rebuke to the Galatians (1:1-10)

At the outset Paul reminds the Galatians that his call to be an apostle did not come from any human source or through any human agency. It came direct from God. The gospel that God called him to preach is the good news that by the grace of God and through the death of Christ, people can be saved from their sins (1:1-5).

Paul is amazed and angered to hear that many of the Galatians are turning away from this, the only true gospel. Instead they are believing the Judaistic teaching that they must keep the law to be saved (6-7). He twice pronounces the curse of God on all who preach contrary to the one true gospel (8-9). The Judaisers had accused Paul of not preaching circumcision, to make it easy for Gentiles to join the church. He preached to please people, they claimed. Can they still say so, after hearing him use such severe language as this? This is not the language of a person trying to win someone's favour! No; Paul's aim is to please Christ, not his hearers (10).

Paul's gospel came direct from God (1:11-24)

Again Paul emphasizes that the gospel he preaches was not of human invention and came from no human source. He received it through the direct work of God in him (11-12). He supports this claim by pointing out that his preaching of this gospel has nothing to do with his religious background. He had been brought up a strict Jew, opposed to Christianity, educated in the law and obedient to the traditions (13-14).

Nor did any of the apostles, leading Christians, or existing churches have any part in helping Paul form his gospel. To demonstrate this, he gives a brief account of his movements during his first few years as a Christian. He begins by pointing out that after his conversion he did not go to see the church leaders in Jerusalem, but went away to the loneliness of Arabia, and then returned to Damascus (15-17; see Acts 9:1-25).

The first visit Paul made to Jerusalem as a Christian was fully three years after his conversion. Even then he stayed only fifteen days. During that time he met only one of the original apostles (Peter), along with James the brother of Jesus (18-20). Some at Jerusalem got to know him a little (see Acts 9:26-29), but elsewhere in Judea no one knew him personally. But they all knew of his conversion, because without his fiery leadership the persecution had died down. After this short time in Jerusalem he went to the provinces of Syria and Cilicia (21-24; see Acts 9:30-31). (For a summary of references in Acts and Galatians to Paul's early years as a Christian see Appendix.)

Jerusalem supports Paul's gospel (2:1-10)

Fourteen years after his conversion (i.e. eleven years after the visit mentioned in 1:18), Paul went to Jerusalem again, this time with Barnabas and Titus (2:1; see Acts 11:27-30). He did not go to seek the apostles' approval, for he had no doubts about the truth and authority of the gospel he preached. Rather he met the apostles as one of equal standing with them, and explained to them his work among the Gentiles. He wanted complete understanding with them concerning the nature of the true gospel. There was not one gospel for the Jews and another for the Gentiles (2).

Judaisers had tried to force Paul to circumcise Titus, one of his Gentile converts. Paul refused and the apostles in Jerusalem supported him. They agreed that the gospel as Paul preached it was complete; additional rites from the Jewish law were not necessary (3-6). More than that, they were in full agreement with Paul and Barnabas in their work among the Gentiles. They realized that God had called them to this work, just as he had called James, Peter and John to work among the Jews (7-9).

The only request the Jerusalem leaders made was that Paul and Barnabas remember the needs of the poor Christians in Jerusalem. This was something Paul was always ready to do. In fact, he had just brought an offering to Jerusalem from the church in Syrian Antioch (10; see Acts 11:30).

Saved by faith alone (2:11-21)

Being assured of the fellowship of the Jerusalem leaders, Paul and Barnabas returned to Antioch (see Acts 12:25). From there they set out on their first missionary journey (see Acts 13:1-3). On returning to Antioch at the end of the journey, they came into conflict with a group of Judaisers who had come from Jerusalem. These men claimed to have the authority of James, and taught that Christians should keep the Jewish laws concerning food, circumcision and other matters. Their teaching was so persuasive that Peter, Barnabas and most of the Jews stopped eating with the Gentiles (11-13). Paul rebuked Peter publicly for his inconsistency (14).

Jews such as Paul and Peter were saved by faith in Christ, not by obedience to the law. How useless, then, to go back to something that could not save them in the first place (15-16). To put the argument another way: if Gentile Christians are wrong for not keeping the law, Jewish Christians must also be wrong for being justified apart from the law. And since Christ is the one who justifies them, he too must be wrong. Clearly, such a possibility is absurd (17). Rather, the real sin is to go back to keeping the law after being justified apart from the law (18).

The law cannot bring life; it can only condemn to death all who have broken it. Christ took this punishment for sinners by his death on the cross. When sinners turn to Jesus Christ in faith they are removed from the law's power (for the law can have no power over those who are now 'dead'), and given new life, the life of Christ. Having been saved by faith without the law, they now live by faith without the law (19-20). The conclusion is that if sinners can be justified by law, Christ need not have died (21).

Justification by faith

Paul often speaks of sinners being justified (GNB: put right with God). He uses the word in a legal sense, where he likens God's act of justification to that of a judge who declares a person to be righteous, or in the right. To justify is the opposite of to condemn, which means to declare a person guilty, or in the wrong (cf. Deut 25:1; Matt 12:37). ('Justify' and 'righteous' are different parts of the same word in the original languages of the Bible.)

Justification does not mean that God *makes* repentant sinners righteous in the sense that they now have some inner power that enables them to work to achieve perfection. It means that God *declares* them righteous. He gives them a righteousness that is not their own — a new status, a new standing, that makes them fit for the presence of a holy God (Rom 4:6-8; 2 Cor 5:21). God now sees believers as being 'in Christ', and accepts them not because of anything they have done, but because of what Christ has done through his death and resurrection (Rom 3:27-28; 4:24-25; Phil 3:9).

Through the work of Jesus Christ, God is able to be righteous in justifying those who have faith in him. Because Jesus bore their sin, God can now declare them righteous (Rom 3:24-26; 1 Peter 2:24). God does this freely by his grace, and repentant sinners accept it by faith (Rom 3:24; Titus 2:11; 3:4-7).

Faith is chiefly concerned not with knowledge but with trust. It is not simply an acceptance of certain facts, but a reliance upon Jesus Christ for all that salvation means (Rom 3:22; Gal 2:20-21; 3:26). Faith in itself does not save. It is simply the means by which sinners accept the salvation that Christ offers. The merit lies not in faith itself, but in the object of faith. Salvation is not a reward for faith, but a gift that God offers to undeserving sinners (Rom 3:25; 5:15). When people by faith accept what Christ has done for them, God declares them righteous on account of Christ and assures them that they need never again fear the condemnation of sin (Rom 8:33-34; 1 John 5:12-13).

3:1-4:31 LAW-KEEPING HAS NO PLACE IN THE GOSPEL

Experience of the Galatians (3:1-5)

When the Galatians first heard the gospel from Paul, they understood clearly that salvation was based solely on Christ's death, and they gladly received it by faith. Now, because they have fallen under the power of the Judaisers, they have turned from this gospel and are trying to live according to the law (3:1-2). If the almighty power of God's Spirit was necessary to save them from the penalty of sin, how do they expect to triumph over sin in their lives by their own efforts to keep the law (3)? Surely they must know that the miracles they experienced among them came as a result of faith, not because of law-keeping. If they forsake Christ for the law, all those experiences have done them no good at all (4-5; cf. Acts 14:3).

Example of Abraham (3:6-14)

Abraham's life demonstrates that God justifies on the basis of faith, not law-keeping. (To understand the illustrations that follow, read Genesis 12:1-3; 13:14-18; 15:1-6; 22:15-18.) Abraham was justified not because he kept the law, but because he believed God. The law, with its rules about circumcision, had not yet been given. The real children of Abraham are not those who have been circumcised according to the law, but those who have been saved by faith (6-7). The Old Testament long ago declared that Gentiles would be saved the same way as Abraham — by faith (8-9).

Those who try to win God's favour by keeping the law are condemned to death by that law when they break it. Since all break it, all are condemned (10). Another reason why people cannot be justified through the law is that justification is by faith; but the law requires obedience, not faith (11-12). Christ's death on the cross was the clear sign to all that he bore the curse of God. He suffered the death penalty on behalf of the law-breakers, so that all who believe in him might escape the law's curse. Like Abraham, they are justified by faith (13-14).

God's law and God's promise (3:15-22)

Paul then adds an illustration to show that God's basis for justification (which, from the beginning, was faith) was not changed by the law. When people sign an important document, no one can alter its contents; when God makes a covenant, he does not change it (15). God made a promise that through the offspring (singular) of Abraham all peoples would be blessed. This was fulfilled in Christ, who gives salvation to all who have faith in him (16). The law, which came hundreds of years after Abraham, could not alter this promise or add conditions to it. People are justified by faith as Abraham was, according to God's promise (17-18).

If the law did not bring salvation, why was it given? Certainly, it was intended to be beneficial to those who received it (Lev 18:5; Deut 10:13), but it also showed people how far they fell short of God's standards. In so doing, it encouraged them to acknowledge their sin and seek God's forgiveness. Like a light switched on in a dark and dirty room, the law showed up the filth but could not remove it. It was a temporary provision that impressed upon people their inability to keep God's commands, and so prepared them to welcome the Saviour. It was given specifically to Israel, the nation God chose to be his covenant people, and, as in all covenant arrangements, it required the people to keep their part of the contract. In establishing the covenant, Moses acted as mediator between God and Israel, and angels were God's messengers who delivered the law to Moses (19).

By contrast, when God made his unconditional promise to Abraham, he was the sole contracting party. There was therefore no need for a mediator. God was issuing a promise, not laying down laws. He was showing that salvation depends solely on his grace; it is not a reward for law-keeping (20).

The law God gave to Moses neither replaced nor conflicted with the promise he gave to Abraham. The purpose of the law and the purpose of the promise were different. God never intended the law to be a means of salvation. It showed people God's standards, but showed them also how helpless they were to meet those standards. It impressed upon them that they could receive life and righteousness only by the promised gift of God, and they had to receive that gift by faith (21-22).

The law's purpose illustrated (3:23-4:7)

Jews under the law were like children under the control of a guardian, but this was only in anticipation of the coming of Christ. When he came, those who trusted in him were forgiven the sins they had committed against the law and were put right with God. Instead of being like children under a guardian, they now enjoyed the freedom of full-grown mature sons of God (23-26). Since the coming of Christ, all believers are united in him and are God's children, regardless of race, social status, sex or the law. Being part of Christ, they are part of Abraham's promised offspring. Those justified by faith are Abraham's true descendants (27-29).

Paul gives another example, similar to the first, to illustrate the law's function. A child who inherits his father's property cannot do as he likes with it until he has reached the age of an adult. Though legally the owner, in reality he is little different from a slave, being under the control of guardians who manage his affairs for him (4:1-2). This illustrates the position of those previously under the law. They were like children receiving instruction. But Christ came and fulfilled the law's requirements, so that those under its control could be released to enjoy their inheritance as adult sons of God (3-7).

Paul's concern for the Galatians (4:8-20)

Before they believed in Christ, most of the Galatians were pagans, in bondage to idols of wood and stone. Now that they have come to know the true God, they are foolish to get into bondage again by trying to keep the Jewish law. By doing so they are not going forward in their Christian lives; they are going backwards (8-11).

The Galatians should live as those free from the law, just as Paul does. He feels sorry for them, not angry with them. He does not consider their error to be an attack on him personally, and he still has the most pleasant memories of their kindness to him when he was ill while visiting them (12-14). They would have done anything for him then, and he hopes they will not turn against him now because of his attempts to correct their error (15-16).

Part of the Judaisers' tactics in trying to gain control over the Galatians was to turn them against Paul personally. Paul is certainly not jealous when others show interest in his converts after he has gone, provided they have pure motives (17-18). He is concerned only for the Galatians' good and he is prepared to put up with any suffering to help their Christian lives grow and develop. If it were possible he would visit them rather than write, for he is worried about them (19-20).

Example of Hagar and Sarah (4:21-31)

Paul now attacks the Judaisers by using a form of argument that they themselves liked to use. He returns to the story of Abraham to show that law-keeping is slavery and it cannot be mixed with grace. (For the background to the illustration that follows read Genesis 15:1-6; 16:1-16; 17:15-22; 18:1-15; 21:1-21.) Abraham had two sons, Ishmael, who was born as a result of human arrangements that lacked any exercise of faith, and Isaac, who was born in fulfilment of God's promise. The mother of Ishmael was the slave woman Hagar; the mother of Isaac was Abraham's true wife Sarah (21-23).

Hagar is likened to the covenant of law given by God to Israel at Mt Sinai; Sarah is likened to the covenant of grace given freely to all people from heaven. The spiritual descendants of the slave woman are the Jerusalem Judaisers of Paul's day; the spiritual descendants of the free woman are those saved by God's grace through faith (24-26). The Jews, children of Abraham by natural descent, have largely failed to be God's people; the Gentiles, who previously had neither life nor hope but who now largely make up the church, become Abraham's spiritual children. Thus, in Paul's illustration, the slave woman finishes with few offspring, but the free woman, who was formerly childless, now has a multitude of descendants (27).

Ishmael is likened to the Jews who are slaves under the bondage of the law; Isaac is likened to those saved by God's grace and freed from the law. Just as Ishmael persecuted Isaac, so the Jews under the law now persecute those who are God's people through his grace. Children of the law and children of grace cannot live together; the former must be thrown out. There is no place for law-keeping in God's family (28-31).

5:1-6:18 THE FRUITS OF CHRISTIAN LIBERTY

No place for law-keeping (5:1-12)

Through the death of Christ, believers have been freed from the bondage of the law. They should therefore live as free people (5:1).

If circumcision is necessary for salvation, Christ is of no use. Also, those who want to keep the law about circumcision must keep the whole law. They cannot choose one command and ignore others to suit themselves. If they try to find salvation through law-keeping, they cut themselves off from the salvation that comes from Christ through God's grace (2-4). That salvation has nothing to do with circumcision. It is received by faith, is guaranteed by the Holy Spirit and produces a response of love in the lives of believers (5-6).

The Galatians were progressing spiritually until the Judaisers arrived. The new teaching these people have brought with them is not from God and will eventually corrupt the whole church if it is not stopped immediately. Certain punishment lies ahead for these false teachers (7-10).

Apparently the Judaisers had twisted some of Paul's words to try to convince the Galatians that even their apostle taught that circumcision was necessary. If this was so, replies Paul, he would have no more trouble from the Jews. The reason the Jews opposed him was that he preached that the cross, not circumcision, was the way to salvation. He wishes that these Judaisers would not stop at circumcision but go the whole way and emasculate themselves, so that they might no longer trouble the Christians (11-12).

True freedom; true Christianity (5:13-26)

Christian freedom does not mean that believers may do as they like. On the contrary, they must think of others and act to please them. This is what the law commands, but those who want to put themselves under the law cannot do it. Instead they are unkind and cruel to each other. The goal that the law aims at is not reached by trying to keep the law, but by acting with true Christian liberty (13-15).

Sooner or later Christians find that they do not always do the good that their consciences tell them to do, because the sinful human nature fights against God's Spirit within them. The way they triumph over these wrong desires is not by putting themselves under the law, but by allowing God's Spirit to direct their lives (16-18). Even if people put themselves under the law, rebellious human nature produces only those evils that the law forbids and that exclude people from God's kingdom (19-21).

If, on the other hand, Christians allow God's Spirit to control them, their lives become full of the most pleasing virtues — the opposite of those things that the law forbids (22-23). Their lives should demonstrate the truth that their sinful nature has been crucified with Christ and has no further power over them. They are now controlled by God's Spirit (24-26).

Some Christian responsibilities (6:1-10)

When they live by the Spirit's power, believers will want to be of spiritual help to others. They will not be harshly critical when they see other believers caught in wrongdoing, but will feel the sorrow of others as if it were their own. They will remember how easily anyone can be overcome by temptation (6:1-2). People are foolish when they compare themselves with others in order to feel satisfied about their own spirituality. Each person is answerable to God for his or her own behaviour, regardless of what other people may have done (3-5).

Christians must help support financially those who teach them (6). They should not deceive themselves in this matter. Christians, like farmers, reap what they sow. If they live to please themselves according to their natural desires, in the end they will reap the fruit of all natural desires, which is disappointment and death. On the other hand, if they put God's affairs before their own, their lives will produce qualities of eternal value (7-8). This is the season for sowing, not reaping. By untiringly helping others, whether financially or otherwise, believers guarantee for themselves future reward of lasting worth (9-10).

Summary and farewell (6:11-18)

Up till now Paul's secretary has been writing down his words as he speaks. Now Paul takes the pen and with large bold letters writes a conclusion to the letter (11). One reason why the Judaisers insist on circumcision is to escape the persecution they will receive if they preach Christ's death as the way of salvation. Although they preach the necessity of circumcision, they are not interested in keeping the law. They want only to boast of success in getting many converts (12-13).

Paul does not boast about what he has done, nor about the virtues of carrying out or not carrying out a particular religious ceremony. He boasts only about what Christ has done for him on the cross. Christ has given him a new life, so that sinful things may no longer attract him and his sinful nature may no longer desire them (14-15). Those who live according to this principle are the true people of God, the true descendants of Abraham (16).

Slaves had scars made in their bodies to show which master they belonged to. The important mark in Paul's body is not circumcision, which marks a person as a slave of the law, but scars he received in his service as a willing slave for Jesus Christ (17). (Paul may be referring to scars he received when he was stoned by opponents in Galatia; see Acts 14:19.) He closes his letter by encouraging the Galatians once more to stand firm in the grace of God (18).

APPENDIX
Summary of Paul's movements

AD	Event	Acts	Gal
32	Paul converted on way to Damascus	9:1-22	1:13-17
	Chosen to go to the Gentiles	9:15	1:16
	From Damascus goes to Arabia	-	1:17
	Returns to Damascus	9:23-25	1:17
35	Goes to Jerusalem for first time (3 years after his conversion)	9:26	1:18
	Meets apostles Peter and James	9:27	1:18-19
	Stays only a short time (15 days)	9:28-29	1:18
	Goes through Syria to Tarsus in Cilicia	9:30	1:21
	Without Paul, persecution dies down	9:31	1:22-24
	No recorded movements for 10 years		
45	Goes from Tarsus to Antioch	11:25-26	-
	Stays in Antioch one year	11:26	-
46	Goes to Jerusalem with Barnabas and Titus (14 yrs after his conversion)	11:30	2:1-10
	Meets apostles James, Peter and John	-	2:7-9
	Returns from Jerusalem to Antioch	12:25	-
	Goes on first missionary journey, then returns to Antioch	13:1-14:28	-
49	Judaisers go to Antioch	15:1,24	2:12-13
	Paul rebukes Peter and Barnabas	-	2:11-14
	Judaisers go to Galatia	-	1:6-9
	Paul writes his letter to the Galatians		
	Meeting in Jerusalem	15:2-29	-

Ephesians

BACKGROUND

The letter of Paul that we know as Ephesians is more general than his other letters. Much of it is concerned with the union that exists between Christ and the church, and the results that this union should produce in the lives of Christians. Paul says nothing specific about his relations with the church in Ephesus or with individuals in the church, even though he spent more time with the Ephesian church than with any other.

At the time Paul wrote this letter, a particular kind of false teaching had caused trouble among the churches in and around Ephesus. Paul's special messenger apparently took a number of copies of the same letter and distributed them around these churches. Someone may have written the name of the receiving church into the introduction as copies were distributed. If this was the case, it would explain why some ancient manuscripts include the word 'Ephesus' in the opening greeting, but others omit it (Eph 1:1; see translators' note). Paul's letter to the church in the nearby town of Laodicea may have been another copy of this letter (Col 4:16).

The Ephesus region

Christianity probably came to Ephesus when Paul visited the city towards the end of his second missionary journey. He could not stay long, but left his friends Aquila and Priscilla there, and as soon as possible returned (Acts 18:18-23; 19:1). Ephesus was the chief city of the Roman province of Asia (in western Asia Minor; see map in the commentary on Acts), and Paul saw that if Christianity was established in Ephesus it would spread throughout the province.

Paul's ministry in Ephesus lasted three years and was the major work of his third missionary journey (Acts 20:31). In strengthening the church he trained many disciples, and these, it seems, were the people who took the gospel to the scattered towns and villages of the province (Acts 19:8-10). This outreach was probably the cause of churches being founded in Colossae, Hierapolis and Laodicea (Col 1:7; 2:1; 4:13; Rev 3:14), and possibly also in Smyrna, Pergamum, Thyatira, Sardis and Philadelphia (Rev 2:8,12,18; 3:1,7).

Ephesus was a centre for some of the pagan religions of the region (Acts 19:35). This meant that the Christian converts came from a society where superstition and false religious ideas were widespread (Acts 19:18-19,26-27), and Paul knew that sooner or later the church in Ephesus would be troubled by false teaching (Acts 20:17,29-30). He knew also that a society with false religious beliefs usually has low moral standards, and his letter to the Ephesians deals with the sorts of problems that arise when a church is planted in such a society.

Purpose of the letter

It seems that Paul wrote this letter during the time of his first imprisonment in Rome, when he was under house arrest for two years (Acts 28:16,30; Eph 4:1; 6:20). Tychicus was about to go from Rome to Colossae with letters from Paul to the Christians there, so Paul thought it worthwhile to send this more general letter, which Tychicus could pass on to Ephesus and other churches of the region (cf. Eph 6:21-22; Col 4:7).

A kind of false teaching was spreading around the region and creating much confusion among Christians. It was an early form of Gnosticism, a religious philosophy that regarded Jesus Christ as neither fully human nor fully God, but as a sort of semi-angelic being. This teaching asserted that, although Jesus Christ was superior to the Christians who followed him, both he and they needed help from unseen angelic powers if they were to reach perfection. Paul deals more specifically with this false teaching in his letter to the church in Colossae, a town not far from Ephesus. In that letter Paul shows that Christ is supreme over the universe, and needs no help at all from angelic beings. Christians, being already complete in Christ, likewise need nothing to be added to them. (For further details see introductory notes to Colossians.)

In his letter to the Ephesians, Paul repeats his assurances that Christ is supreme over the universe, and this includes all the angelic powers, good and bad. They can add nothing to him (Eph 1:20-21). There is no possibility that anything in the universe can fill up some lack in Christ. On the contrary he fills the universe (Eph 1:23; 4:10). By his death and resurrection he has triumphed over all the evil spiritual forces of the universe. Because of this, Christians likewise can have victory in their battle against evil (Eph 2:2-6; 6:12).

Paul considers not only Christians personally, but also the church as a whole. The church is the body of Christ, and it shares with him in his victory over all angelic powers (Eph 1:21-23; 2:6). The church does not have to humble itself before angels. Rather angels are humbled before the church, as they see in it an overwhelming demonstration of God's wisdom and power (Eph 3:10). All this is good reason for the Christians in and around Ephesus not to allow themselves to be persuaded by the clever, but wrong, ideas of the false teachers (Eph 5:6).

OUTLINE

1:1-23   A LIFE OF FULNESS THROUGH CHRIST

Praise for blessings in Christ (1:1-14)

In introducing himself, Paul reminds his readers that they are saints, God's holy people, who live their lives in union with Jesus Christ (1:1-2). He then offers praise to the triune God: in verses 3-6 on account of the Father who planned salvation; in verses 7-12 on account of the Son who made this salvation a reality; and in verses 13-14 on account of the Holy Spirit who guarantees salvation.

God's blessings, which believers receive because of their union with Christ, are not limited to the things of this world. They lift the lives of believers above everyday things so that now, in the present world, they can enjoy the spiritual blessings of the heavenly world (3). God planned his purposes for his people before the universe was created. In his love he chose them to be his children, his aim being that they should be holy and blameless, and so bring praise to him (4-6).

Through Paul, God now makes known more of his eternal plan. By calling it a mystery, Paul does not mean that he is going to tell people something to confuse or puzzle them. He means that he is going to tell them something they would not know unless God revealed it to them. God has, so to speak, a 'secret plan' (GNB), which he now reveals. Believers already know that people have forgiveness only through the grace of God and the blood of Christ, but a further truth is now made known. This truth is

that one day all the rebellion and confusion throughout the universe will cease, and unity between God and his creation will at last be restored through Christ. The universe will find its full meaning in him (7-10).

In choosing Jewish and Gentile believers to be united in one church as his people, God shows that he is already fulfilling his purposes for harmony and unity (11). Paul was a Jew, and his words 'we who first hoped in Christ' refer to the Jewish people who had waited for the coming of Christ for centuries. But most of Paul's readers were Gentiles. In the next sentence he therefore addresses them with the words 'you also', to emphasize that they too are now God's people, because of their response to the gospel. God gives the Holy Spirit to Jews and Gentiles without distinction. The Spirit is the guarantee that they are God's people now, and that one day they will receive all that God has promised them (12-14).

A prayer for understanding (1:15-23)

Paul's prayer for the Ephesians combines thanksgiving and praise with requests offered in true faith. Paul knows they are converts from paganism, but he expects them to develop a mature understanding of Christianity. He is not content that they should have a few basic Christian beliefs. He wants them to have true wisdom, based on a proper knowledge of God and a clear understanding of all the riches that are theirs through Christ, both in this world and in the next (15-18).

In addition Paul wants these converts to know the real power of God in their lives. This power is unlimited, as God has clearly shown by raising Jesus from the dead and placing him in the position of highest authority and honour. He is above all things, material and spiritual, now and for ever (19-21). As the head has control over the body, so Christ has authority over the church. At the same time he is inseparably united with it, for Christ and his church make up one complete whole. Because he fills the universe, Christ gives completeness to all things everywhere (22-23).

2:1-3:21   GOD'S PLAN FOR THE CHURCH

Sinners saved by grace (2:1-10)

In their natural state, all people are spiritually dead because of sin. Nothing they do can bring them back to life, because no matter how much good they try to do, they are still sinners. This is true of Jews and Gentiles alike. In body and mind they are under the control of Satan, and consequently are rebellious against God (2:1-3). Such rebels do not deserve God's love, but God loves them nevertheless. God does for sinners what they cannot do themselves. He gives them new life, and he does this on the basis of Christ's death and resurrection. By God's grace, Christ not only died to bear the penalty of human sin, but he rose to glorious life in the heavenly world so that repentant sinners can have a glorious new life in him (4-7).

This salvation is entirely God's work. Sinners cannot save themselves. Through faith they can only turn to God in their helplessness, and humbly accept the salvation that God offers. Good works cannot earn them salvation, but once they are saved their lives should be full of good works. When God gives people a new life, they must live a new life (8-10).

Jew and Gentile made one in Christ (2:11-22)

For centuries there had been bitterness and tension between Jews and Gentiles, mainly because of the way proud Jews looked down on Gentiles. Jews had circumcision as the sign that they were God's people; Gentiles did not. Because they were not God's people, Gentiles enjoyed none of Israel's privileges through the covenants and promises. They had no hope for a Messiah and no knowledge of God (11-12). The Jews, having been chosen to receive God's law, considered themselves close to God but the Gentiles far from him. They did not even allow Gentiles into the holiest part of the temple. It was as if a solid wall separated the two. But Christ, through his death, broke down this wall, abolished the offensive law and commandments, destroyed the hatred and made peace (13-16).

No longer are the 'near' Jews more privileged than the 'far off' Gentiles. In Christ there is no longer a distinction between Jews and Gentiles, for all who believe are God's people. All have equal status as citizens of God's heavenly city, all are members of his family, and all come into his presence through the one Spirit (17-19). The new temple in which God dwells is not a building like the old Jewish temple. It is a spiritual dwelling place. Apostles and prophets form the foundation, other believers form the main building, and all is built around and built into Christ (20-22).

God's wisdom and love displayed (3:1-21)

It was because Paul had taken the gospel to the Gentiles that he was imprisoned in the first place (Acts 21:27-36). Yet he feels humbled to think that God should graciously choose him for such a noble work (3:1-2). As a Jew he was once proud of his belief that only Jews were God's people. Even if some of the 'far off' Gentiles believed in God, they were still not God's covenant people in the sense that Jews were. Now God's special revelation shows Paul clearly that no longer is this so. Jewish and Gentile believers are united in one body, the church, and as God's people they share equally in all God's blessings (3-6).

Paul believes that only by God's grace could one as unworthy as he be given the work of taking the gospel to the Gentiles. He believes also that only by God's power will he be fruitful in that work (7-8). God's plan of uniting all believers in one church in and through Christ displays to people and to angels his great wisdom (9-11). This encourages Christians in their everyday lives, for if God is so wise and powerful, they know that they can enter into his presence at all times without fear or doubt. They therefore should not be discouraged, as some in Ephesus were when they heard that their apostle was in prison (12-13).

The one to whom Paul prays is the Father of all who believe, whether Jews or Gentiles. This one is the true Father. Everything in the universe has its origin in him. Even earthly fathers and their families exist only because there is a heavenly Father and his family (14-15).

Paul asks this heavenly Father that those who are his children might be strengthened inwardly through allowing the Spirit of Christ within them to control them. As they understand more of Christ's love, they will grow to be more like him in their lives (16-19). They should not think that this goal is too high to reach, for God is able to do far more than they think possible (20-21).

4:1-6:24 THE DAILY LIFE OF THE CHURCH MEMBERS

Unity in the church (4:1-16)

God's great purposes for his church should produce a new quality in the lives of the church members. The blessings that God gives should not lead the believers to pride. On the contrary, when they see that these blessings are an indication of the standard God expects, they will develop a new humility. When people or circumstances annoy them and try their patience, they will show love by being patient and helpful (4:1-2).

People in the church come from various racial, cultural and social backgrounds, but they must not allow these differences to spoil the unity that God has created in the church (3). After all, they hold all the important things in common. They are indwelt by the same Spirit, they own the same Jesus as Lord and they are children of the same heavenly Father. As fellow members of the same body, the church, they have experienced the same baptism, share the same faith and look forward to the same salvation (4-6).

Just as people in the church differ from one another, so the spiritual gifts that Christ has given for the functioning of the church vary from person to person (7). Christ is likened to a triumphant conqueror who has returned from battle and now divides the goods seized in battle among his people. In Christ's case he came down to earth where he conquered sin, Satan and all the other angelic powers of evil. He then returned to heaven, from where he shares out his gifts to his church (8-10).

These divine gifts are in fact people — apostles, prophets, evangelists, pastors and teachers. They are given to build up the Christians so that they also can do the work of God. This will help the Christians individually and the church as a whole to grow in maturity towards the perfection and fulness that is found in Christ himself (11-13).

Such Christians will not be like immature children who can be persuaded to believe almost anything (14). Mature Christians will be confident in their faith, though they will always act towards others in love. They will be under the control of Christ, as the parts of the body are under the control of the head. This will help them to maintain and develop strength in the church (15-16).

The old and the new standards (4:17-32)

Although believers have entered a new life through Christ, they still live in a society that does not know God and whose moral outlook is darkened by its ungodliness. The less Christian influence there is in the society, the lower the moral standards are. Christians, however, should not behave according to the commonly accepted practices of society. People without God, through repeatedly ignoring the warnings of conscience, can easily lose those feelings of guilt that conscience produces. They then live solely to please themselves, without thought for others (17-19).

Christians, by contrast, should act according to the teaching and example of Jesus (20-21). They must put off attitudes that belong to their former way of life, just as they would put off dirty clothes. They must put on fresh clean clothes; that is, they must have a new way of life, where their thinking is changed and they examine all practices in the light of their new life from God (22-24).

These instructions are not merely negative. As old practices go they must be replaced by new ones. For example, lying and deception must be replaced by openness in speaking the truth always (25). Christians may do well to be angry about sin, but when feelings of bad temper or revenge arise, they should put them out of the mind immediately. If not, Satan may use them to weaken their spiritual lives (26-27).

Instead of stealing, Christians should work honestly, both to help others and to look after themselves (28). The uncontrolled tongue, as much as any of the other bad habits listed here, saddens God's Holy Spirit. Therefore, bad habits of speech, especially in being angry with or talking about others, must be replaced by speech that is helpful to others. The lives of Christians should be characterized by love, kindness, compassion, understanding and forgiveness (29-32).

More about the new standards (5:1-20)

Just as children follow the example of their parents, so Christians must follow the example of their heavenly Father. Their love, then, will not be mere words, but will show itself by self-sacrifice, just as Christ's love did (5:1-2).

Converted pagans had a special problem in that many of the sinful practices they once engaged in were still widespread in the society in which they lived. One way to overcome the temptation to such practices was not even to speak about them. They should certainly not joke lightheartedly about them, because people who practise such things are enemies of God's kingdom (3-5).

Besides being careful about what they say, Christians should be careful about what they hear. They must examine what people say, whether concerning religion, morals or anything else, to see whether such people are on the side of Satan (darkness) or Christ (light). Only by careful testing will Christians know whether a thing is pleasing to God or not, whether it belongs to the light or to the darkness (6-10). If the lives of Christians are pure, they will show up the sins of others, just as light shows up dirt. Any who stir themselves from their moral laziness can be cleansed, if they allow themselves to be examined in the light of Christ (11-14).

Christians must be alert at all times. They must act wisely and display the worth of Christianity to a sinful world (15-17). In former days they might have tried to overcome depression or find enjoyment by drinking till they became drunk. Now that they are Christians, they should open their lives to God and allow God's Spirit to control them. They will find true joy in having fellowship with other Christians, singing praises together and giving thanks to God (18-20).

Christian relationships (5:21-6:9)

People can have good relations with one another only as they consider one another. When they insist on their rights without considering others, they only destroy harmony and fellowship (21).

In the next section Paul illustrates this principle in certain family and social relationships. In 5:22-33 he considers the the case of husbands and wives, in 6:1-4 the case of parents and children, and in 6:5-9 the case of masters and servants. In union with Christ, people within these various categories share the same spiritual status (Gal 3:28). But in the family and in society, people have different functions, and they must know how they should act towards each other.

If a family is to enjoy genuine contentment, it must have leadership, and this responsibility rests with the husband. As the church submits to Christ, so the wife is to submit to her husband (22-24). Christ's headship of the church, however, was shown not through the use of force, but through the sacrifice of himself for her, so that she might be pure and faultless (25-27). Likewise the husband's headship of the wife is shown not by forcing his authority upon her, but by treating her as equal with himself (28-29). There is unity between husband and wife, as there is between Christ and his church. This unity is the basis of the relationship (30-33).

Paul refers to the Ten Commandments to support his teaching that in the Christian family, children have a responsibility to obey and respect their parents. Although this is a duty, it will also bring a reward (6:1-3). Parents, on their part, must combine wise teaching with understanding discipline if they are to expect the children's respect and obedience (4).

Slavery was so widespread in the world of the first century that the social, political and economic order of the day could scarcely survive without it. Paul knew that he could not expect slavery to be abolished immediately, but he worked towards its abolition by encouraging new attitudes. In most churches there were Christian slaves and Christian masters, but their attitudes to each other had to change now that they were both 'in Christ'. The same principles can be applied to employers and employees in any society. Christians must work honestly and well for an earthly master, as if they were working for Christ (5-8). Christian masters must act with similar honesty and concern towards those who work for them. They must remember that, in the eyes of God, masters are servants and God is their master (9).

The Christian's warfare (6:10-24)

For Christians, life involves warfare, though the battle is not with earthy forces but with spiritual. They are involved in a struggle against hostile demonic powers who have rebelled against God and oppose his people. As ancient soldiers wore armour when they fought their battles, so Christians must prepare themselves for conflict. They receive their armour, as well as their strength, from God, but they themselves must fight the battle. Above all they must make sure that when the battle is over, they are still on their feet (10-13).

In putting on his armour, the Roman soldier first tied his under-robes together by a belt, then put on his breastplate and shoes, and finally took up his shield, helmet and sword. Christians likewise should be fully prepared to meet the enemy. They must secure the inner life through the truth, and protect the outer life by being morally upright (14). Their feet must be ready to take the gospel to any place at any time. A firm faith in God will provide them with a shield against the devil's temptations (15-16). The knowledge of their sure salvation will give them assurance of complete victory. As they increase their knowledge of God's Word, they will be able to use that Word when fighting the enemy. In addition they must pray constantly, both for themselves and for fellow Christians who are engaged in a similar battle (17-18).

Finally, Paul asks prayer for himself, not that he might escape prison, but that he might speak boldly for Christ as a good ambassador should (19-20). If the Ephesians want to know more about Paul's circumstances in prison, Tychicus can tell them when he delivers the letter. They can always be assured that God will be faithful to those who are faithful to him (21-24).

Philippians

BACKGROUND

At the time of writing this letter, Paul was being held prisoner (Phil 1:13), but the letter does not specify the location of his imprisonment. Over the course of his Christian service Paul was imprisoned many times (2 Cor 11:23), though the only places of imprisonment mentioned in the biblical record are Philippi (Acts 16:23), Jerusalem (Acts 22:23-30), Caesarea (Acts 24:23-27) and Rome (Acts 28:16,30). Paul could have written his letter to the Philippians from one of several places, but if that place was one of the cities mentioned above, the most likely is Rome. (See map located in the commentary on Acts.)

Paul and the Philippian church

Philippi was an important city in the province of Macedonia in the north of Greece. It was one of the select cities that the Romans established as colonies, which were centres of Roman life in a non-Roman world (Acts 16:12). Paul first visited the region during his second missionary journey, and the church in Philippi was the first church that he established in Europe (Acts 16:11-40). He visited it twice during his third missionary journey (Acts 20:1-6), and seems to have retained a special affection for it (Phil 1:8; 4:1,18).

After his third missionary journey and subsequent arrest in Jerusalem, Paul was sent to Rome to present his case to Caesar. He was imprisoned in Rome for two years (Acts 28:16,30), and possibly wrote his letter to the Philippian church towards the end of that time.

Paul was visited in his imprisonment by a Christian from Philippi called Epaphroditus, whom the church had sent as its representative to give Paul whatever help he needed. Epaphroditus brought news of the church in Philippi, together with a gift of money and goods from the Philippian believers (Phil 4:18). While with Paul, Epaphroditus became seriously ill. News of his illness travelled back to the Philippians, and news of their concern travelled back to Paul (Phil 2:25-27). With travel being slow in those days, this would have taken some time, indicating that Epaphroditus must have stayed with Paul several months.

The letter to the Philippians in our Bible is the letter that Paul sent back to Philippi, probably with Epaphroditus (Phil 2:28). Paul uses the letter to thank the Philippians for their gift, to put right some minor disorders that had arisen in the church, and to encourage the Christians to live the truly Christian life. A spirit of warmth and optimism runs through the letter.

Paul told the Philippians not to be discouraged because of his imprisonment, for he had plenty of opportunity to spread the gospel and teach believers (Phil 1:12-14). He enjoyed good fellowship with the Christians in Rome, and some Christians in the government service were able to visit him and help care for him (Phil 4:21-22). Timothy also was with him (Phil 1:1). Although execution was always a possibility (Phil 2:17), he was optimistic that he would be set free and so be able to visit the Philippians again (Phil 1:27; 2:24).

OUTLINE

1:1-26 PAUL'S EXPERIENCES DURING IMPRISONMENT

A prayer for the Philippians (1:1-11)

In greeting the church, Paul mentions in particular the church leaders, as these had probably been responsible for arranging the collection of gifts sent to him (1:1-2). He is thankful not only for the present gift, but for the many gifts they have sent him, from his first visit to their city to his current imprisonment. Through their prayers and gifts they have been true partners with him in spreading the gospel (3-5).

Paul prays that the work of God in their lives will continue to grow and develop till it reaches perfection in the day when they stand before Christ. Paul's feelings of joy towards them are but a reflection of Christ's feelings (6-8). As they learn more of God and his ways, they will learn how to act towards one another with genuine love. They will

534

also learn how to act in choosing what is spiritually helpful and rejecting what is not. Their lives will be filled with truly good qualities and will be pleasing to God (9-11).

Results of Paul's imprisonment (1:12-26)

Some of the Philippians were becoming down-hearted because Paul had been imprisoned so long. He tries to encourage them with the news that through his imprisonment he has been able to tell the good news of Jesus Christ to many people whom he could not reach otherwise. Among these were people such as Roman guards and government officials. His fearless example has encouraged the local Christians to evangelize more boldly (12-14).

Unfortunately, the local Christians are bold in different ways. Some are sincere disciples of Jesus Christ, and are more zealous for him because of Paul's example. Others, who are more interested in gaining status for themselves in the church, are jealous of Paul's influence and are glad to see him locked up. This enables them to pursue their selfish ambitions, knowing that Paul can do nothing to stop them (15-17). Paul, however, is not angry. He is glad that at least they are still preaching the true gospel, even if not from the best motives (18).

Paul believes that through the Philippians' prayers he will have added help from God's Spirit and so be set free. This will allow him to continue his work of spreading the gospel. But as he thinks also of the possibility of execution, his confidence is briefly shaken. He feels less certain that he will be released. Nevertheless, whether he will be released or executed, his aim is to bring honour to Christ (19-20). As for his personal desires, he does not know which he prefers. Life itself means to enjoy Christ, and death will only increase this joy; but if he is released he will have further opportunity to serve God in the world. His death will benefit him, but his life will benefit others (21-24).

At this thought Paul's original confidence returns. He expects that their prayers for his release will be answered. Apart from the joy this will bring to both Paul and the Philippians, it will increase their faith and lead to further progress in their lives for Christ (25-26).

1:27-2:30 TEACHING ABOUT HUMILITY

The need for unity and courage (1:27-30)

Signs of disunity were appearing in the Philippian church, and Paul seeks to correct the problem before it spreads. The believers must be careful of their conduct, particularly in their relations with one another. It is important that there be complete unity among the believers if the church is to withstand the attacks of the enemy (27).

Persecutors get an uneasy feeling of fear when they see the courage of those whom they persecute, and this fear is a warning to them of coming judgment. Christians, by contrast, get increased confidence when they withstand persecution, and this confidence is an assurance to them of coming salvation. As the Philippians suffer together for Christ's sake, they will be more firmly united with one another and with Paul (28-30).

Christ's example of humility (2:1-11)

Paul gives four reasons why Christians should have greater unity between them: the encouragement given them by Christ; the power of Christ's love working in them; the common sharing they have in the same Spirit; and the sympathetic kindness that God's children should show to each other. Although the Philippians bring Paul much joy, that joy will not be complete till there is genuine unity among them (2:1-2). They are not to be concerned solely with their own spiritual progress, for this can lead to self-satisfaction and pride. They must learn to look for and admire the good points in others (3-4).

If they are indeed 'in Christ Jesus', they should share his spirit of humility; and humility means denying self for the sake of serving others. Christ did not selfishly grasp for the supreme glory of heaven, even though it was his by right (for he was God). Rather he became a servant for the sake of sinful humankind. He became a man, and accepted the restrictions and hardships that human nature placed upon him. But, unlike all other members of the human race, he did not sin. He entered the world of human beings in order to save human beings from their sins. As a servant he spent his earthly life doing whatever his Father required, even though it meant that he suffered and eventually died on a cross (5-8).

Only after this humility, suffering and death was Christ raised to the place of supreme glory. The honour that he refused to seek by selfish ambition was given to him in even greater measure because of his humility and obedience. One day all people, angels and demons will acknowledge that he is Lord (9-11).

Putting belief into practice (2:12-18)

In view of Christ's example, the Philippians must remove all trace of pride and quarrelling, and show in their lives the nature of the salvation that God has given them. They must obey God's will as Christ did, and they will be able to do this because God works within them (12-13). They will then be like lights shining in darkness. They will be people of blameless conduct who take God's message to a spiritually and morally corrupt world. In this way they will fulfil God's purpose for them as well as please Paul (14-16). Their lives will be like a sacrifice offered on the altar to God; and if Paul is executed, his blood will be like an additional offering poured on top of their sacrifice. It will be a triumphant climax to Paul's life and a cause for rejoicing in praise to God (17-18).

Timothy and Epaphroditus (2:19-30)

For an example of self-denying humility and service, Paul refers them to Timothy. They will have a chance to meet Timothy again soon, as Paul is sending him to Philippi to help the church through its problems. Paul trusts that Timothy will return to him with the good news that the Philippians are united in love once again (19-20). Most people are too concerned with looking after themselves to stop and think how they can help others, but Timothy gives himself unsparingly to serve others for the sake of Jesus Christ (21-24).

Epaphroditus is another good example. He had been sent by the Philippian church to comfort and help Paul in his imprisonment. While there he fell ill and almost died, but far from looking for pity, he was upset to think that news of his illness had caused the Philippians anxiety (25-27). In being prepared to sacrifice his life for the sake of Paul, Epaphroditus gave an example of self-denying service for others. Paul himself is now another example, for he is about to sacrifice the valuable help of Epaphroditus just at the time when he needs it most. For the sake of the Philippians, Paul is going to send Epaphroditus back (28-30).

3:1-21 THE WAY TO PERFECTION

Paul's testimony (3:1-16)

At this point Paul repeats warnings that he gave the Philippian church some time earlier concerning Judaisers. He calls the Judaisers 'dogs' because they like to 'cut the flesh' of people; that is, they insist that they must circumcise Gentiles before those Gentiles can be saved. The true people of God, whom Paul calls the 'true circumcision', are not those who have carried out a ceremony to put a mark in their bodies, but those who have received new life from Christ through an inward spiritual change (3:1-3).

To support this statement, Paul refers to his own experience. He was born and circumcised a Jew and trained to be a zealous law-abiding Pharisee, but he found that trying to do good by keeping laws could not make the guilty sinner acceptable to God. Such things only prevented him from trusting in Christ (4-7). He has not only put aside religious ceremonies and national status, but he considers that all things in which he might boast are worthless. They cannot gain righteousness before a holy God. Righteousness is a gift that God gives to those who have faith in Christ (8-9).

But Paul does not stop there. Having died and risen with Christ, he wants to go on and experience in reality what this means — death to sin and selfish desires, and a new life of constant victory through the living power of the risen Christ within him. He is encouraged to keep moving towards this goal by his knowledge that final victory over sin, suffering and death is certain (10-11).

Paul knows that he will not reach perfection in this life. He will reach it only on the day when Christ returns and raises the righteous from death. But since he now belongs to Christ, he believes that perfection is the only goal he can aim at. Nothing less would be in keeping with such a high position. He therefore puts all his energy into his efforts to reach this goal, just as a runner strains every muscle to reach the finishing line and gain the prize (12-14).

Mature Christians will have the attitude to life that Paul has just outlined. Should any at present think differently, they will soon come to agree, if they allow God to teach them. Whatever the case, all should make sure that they do not slip back from the standard of practical holiness they have already reached (15-16).

A guide for behaviour (3:17-21)

Jewish false teachers tried to make the Philippians keep laws; other false teachers said they could do as they liked. Paul warns the Philippians to believe neither. They will learn the standards of Christian behaviour by following the example of Jesus and those who live like him. Those who allow themselves to follow the natural desires of their bodies and their minds are not disciples of Jesus Christ, but enemies (17-19). Christ's people are interested in things of spiritual and heavenly value. They will be careful how they live, knowing that the body they have now is the body in which they will meet Christ. When that time comes, Christ will change their bodies to be like his (20-21).

4:1-23 ENCOURAGEMENT AND THANKS

Concerning thoughts and conduct (4:1-9)

With words of warmest friendship, Paul encourages the Philippians to stand firm and not be shaken by problems that arise, whether inside the church or outside. He appeals to two women who had quarrelled to become friends again. The women had once worked with Paul, and no doubt they would be a help to the church if they were united. He asks a close friend in the church to do all he can to help these women forget their differences (4:1-3).

Above all, the Christians must at all times rejoice and be patient with one another. They must learn not to worry but to pray with thankful and believing hearts. God's peace will then protect them from unnecessary mental and emotional tension (4-7). By filling their minds with the things that are good and honourable, they will have conduct that is good and honourable. They must remember the example Paul has given them (8-9).

Thanks for the Philippians' gifts (4:10-23)

The Philippians thought constantly of Paul's needs, but were not able to send anything to him in his imprisonment until now. Paul's joy at receiving this gift is not because he has a greedy desire for money, because he has long ago learnt to be satisfied with whatever he has. His contentment comes not through money or possessions, but through the assurance that Christ enables him to meet every situation (10-13).

Paul repeats that his pleasure is not because of the personal profit he has gained through the Philippians' gifts, whether now or on previous occasions. Rather it is because of the profit they will gain through their sacrifice and generosity. Their gifts are like an investment with God, who, as their banker, will add interest to their account (14-17). Through their offerings, Paul has more than enough. They too will have more than enough, because God will repay them according to his abundant wealth in Jesus Christ (18-20).

On this joyous note Paul finishes his letter. Among the Christians who join him in sending greetings are a number of government officials. These people are of special interest to Paul, as they had probably been converted as a result of their contact with Paul at his place of imprisonment (21-23).

Colossians

BACKGROUND

The city of Colossae was in the Roman province of Asia (the western part of Asia Minor), inland from the important coastal city of Ephesus. It seems that Paul did not visit Colossae during his missionary travels recorded in Acts (Col 2:1; cf. Acts 16:6-8). The church there was probably established while Paul was in Ephesus during his third missionary journey, when converts from Ephesus took the gospel into the surrounding regions (Acts 19:8-10). The person chiefly responsible for founding the church in Colossae was Epaphras (Col 1:6-7).

However, the church had since been troubled by a very persuasive kind of false teaching and the leaders did not know how to deal with it. Epaphras therefore decided to seek Paul's help. By this time Paul was in Rome, where he was imprisoned for two years awaiting the outcome of his appeal to the Emperor (Acts 28:16,30; cf. 25:11-12; 27:1-2; Col 4:10,18). Upon hearing from Epaphras about the problem in Colossae, Paul wrote and sent off his letter to the Colossians (Col 4:12,16).

The messenger who carried the letter, Tychicus, also carried Paul's letter to the church in Ephesus, and probably his letter to the church in Laodicea (Eph. 6:21-22; Col 4:7-8,16). At the same time Paul wrote a short personal letter to Philemon, the man in whose house the Colossian church met (Philem 1-2,10,23-24; cf. Col 4:9). (For further details of Paul's writings of this time, see the introductory notes to Ephesians and Philemon.)

The false teaching in Colossae

One reason why false teaching arose in Colossae (and other churches of the region) was that certain people tried to combine Christian belief with pagan mythology. The teaching was an early form of Gnosticism, a heresy that created serious trouble throughout the church during the second century. The name Gnostic comes from the Greek *gnosis*, meaning 'knowledge'.

In Colossae the Gnostic-type teaching included ideas taken from Judaism, mainly in relation to religious ceremonies. Gnostic religions usually introduced their followers to a variety of rituals and regulations (Col 2:16,20-21). They also claimed to give their followers special knowledge of mysteries that people outside their group could not share (Col 2:4,18; 1 Tim 6:20). But the main problem centred

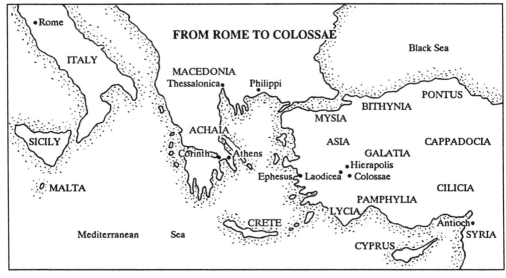

FROM ROME TO COLOSSAE

on a wrong understanding of Jesus Christ and the salvation that Christians receive through him.

The false teachers tried to reconcile things that they considered to be in conflict with each other, such as good and evil, spirit and matter, deity and humanity. They claimed that matter was evil, and that therefore a God who was holy could not come in contact with human beings who were sinful. This meant that Jesus Christ could not be both divine and human.

To solve this problem, the false teachers taught that the gap between God and the human race was bridged by countless beings who were part-spirit and part-matter (or part-divine and part-human). The first and highest of these sprang from God himself and was almost as great as God. The second originated from the first, the third from the second, and so on down the scale, so that those beings closer to God were more Godlike, and those closer to the human race less Godlike. Together these beings controlled the material universe, and people had to approach God through them if they wanted super-human protection against the world's evil forces. People climbed a ladder, so to speak, as they moved in worship from one angelic being up to the next, till finally they reached God (Col 2:8,18).

According to the false teachers, Jesus Christ was one of these part-divine part-human beings. Paul saw that if this were so, Christ was no longer the one mediator between God and humankind, and his death was no longer the one way to cleanse sinners and reconcile them to God. Paul asserted that Christ is God, and he is supreme over all things, whether seen or unseen. Christ did not originate from some intermediate being between God and humankind, but is himself the creator of all things, in both the spirit world and the material (Col 1:15-19; 2:9).

At the same time, Christ is the Saviour of sinful human beings and the conqueror of the powers of evil (Col 1:20-22; 2:15). Through him God entered the world of human existence and shares in a living relationship with his human creatures. As the head is united with the body, so Christ is united with his people, the church (Col 1:18; 2:19). This union means that believers can share Christ's victory over evil and that the character of Christ's life can be reproduced in them (Col 1:13; 3:3-5,10).

Practical outcome of the teaching

Because of the Gnostic belief that matter was evil, the false teachers in Colossae taught people to withdraw as much as possible from involvement in the material world. Among their teachings were

harsh treatment of the body and strict obedience to rules (Col 2:20-23; cf. 1 Tim 4:3). But in other churches, teachers who believed that matter was evil, encouraged the opposite sort of behaviour. They argued that since people live in material bodies in a material world, there is no way they can escape the evil associated with matter. The result of this teaching was a lack of self-control that produced much immorality (2 Tim 3:4-5; 1 John 3:4-10).

The false teachers claimed that their knowledge of heavenly mysteries raised them to a level of existence where the deeds of the body could not affect the spirit. The Christian response was that knowledge cannot be separated from behaviour. The true knowledge of heavenly mysteries is found only in Christ, and it always leads to right behaviour (Col 1:9-10; 2:2-4; 3:1-3; 1 John 2:4,29; 3:6,14-19).

OUTLINE

1:1-2:5 THE TRUE VIEW OF CHRIST

Paul's prayer for the Colossians (1:1-14)

The chief cause of Paul's thanksgiving is that the Colossians have accepted the gospel and come into union with Jesus Christ (1:1-3). This gospel, which they heard originally from Epaphras, is not just another of the many new religions of the day. It is the universal gospel that is preached everywhere and changes the lives of people of all nations and cultures. It proves its power in the new attitude of love that believers show to one another and to others (4-8).

Paul prays that in addition to having love, the Colossians will increase in knowledge. This know-ledge is not like the theorizing of the Gnostics, which leads only to feelings of superiority and self-satisfaction. It is a personal and practical knowledge of God and his will, which will produce a healthy spiritual life of fruitfulness for God. Right behaviour will only be possible as they have right knowledge (9-10). The power to live such a life with patience and joy comes from God alone. Through Christ he has saved them from the powers of evil and made them fit to share the good things that he has prepared for them in his kingdom (11-14).

Christ and his work (1:15-23)

Having completed his introduction, Paul begins immediately to correct the wrong ideas that had been taught. The teaching he gives in verses 15-23 provides a basis for what follows in the remainder of the letter.

Christ is not some part-angelic being, but God himself. God is invisible, yet people can see him and know him in Jesus Christ. Jesus is God and therefore was not created. He existed before creation, and is superior to all created things (15). In fact, he himself is the Creator. He is the source and controller of all things, seen and unseen, including the world of angelic beings that the false teachers liked to talk about. More than that, he is the goal of all creation; all things exist for his glory (16-17).

Because of his eternal godhead, Jesus is the source and the head of the physical creation. Because of his triumphant resurrection, he is the source and the head of the new creation, the church. As head, he is the sovereign ruler. He is not a mixture of God and angel, but has in himself the full nature and power of God (18-19). The only way that sinful creation, including men and women, can be reconciled to God is by Jesus Christ. Only through his death can people be brought back to a state of harmony with God (20).

The Colossians should know this, for they themselves have experienced his divine power in saving them from sin. Their salvation has been entirely by Christ, who took upon himself a physical body like theirs and, in that body, bore their sin. Angelic powers can add nothing to what Christ has already done. If the Colossians want finally to stand before God in the perfection of Christ, they must hold firmly to the truth that the work of Christ is complete and perfect. This truth is the foundation of the gospel wherever that gospel is preached, and it cannot be changed to suit human theories and philosophies (21-23).

Paul's service for Christ (1:24-2:5)

Some of the Colossians, confused by the clever arguments of the false teachers, might be tempted to accept their teaching. They might think that this teaching is more advanced, and therefore nearer the truth, than what they heard from Epaphras. Paul emphasizes that the gospel he and Epaphras preach is the only gospel. It has the authority of Christ, and its genuineness is proved in the experiences of those who preach it. Paul illustrates all this from his own life. The Gnostics appoint themselves teachers, but Paul was appointed by Christ. By enduring sufferings in the service of Christ, he is sharing in the sufferings of Christ (24-25).

Paul's message reveals to people the plan of God that had not been made known to previous generations. This secret plan is that Gentiles are to be his people, indwelt by Christ (26-27). (For the meaning of 'secret plan', or 'mystery', see notes on Ephesians 1:7-10; 3:3-6.)

Once the apostle has brought people to know Christ, he must teach and instruct them so that they might grow to spiritual maturity. Paul knows that much hard work is necessary in order to reach this goal (28-29).

Paul's concern for the churches in Colossae and Laodicea (churches that he has never visited) shows that his interest is not merely with churches that he himself has founded. He wants all churches to be strong, through the believers loving one another and having a full understanding of their riches in Christ. The hidden treasures of wisdom are found in him, not in Gnosticism (2:1-3). The Colossians must maintain the orderly fellowship and strong faith they have had in Christ from the beginning. They must examine all teaching carefully, and not allow themselves to be easily led astray by the arguments of the false teachers (4-5).

2:6-3:4 FALSE VIEWS LEAD TO BONDAGE

Freedom through Christ (2:6-15)

Again Paul reminds the believers that receiving Christ is only the beginning of the Christian life. There must be continual growth through building the life on him (6-7).

The Colossians know that God has freed them from the powers of evil (see 1:13). If, then, they turn and accept a religion powered by the unseen spiritual forces of evil, they are placing themselves in bondage once again (8). Christ needs no angelic powers to help him, for the fulness of God's nature exists in him in its totality. Those in Christ likewise need no angelic powers to help him, for they are already complete in him (9-10).

Paul gives an illustration that likens Christian salvation to the common Jewish rite of circumcision. Circumcision was literally a cutting away of the flesh. Salvation through Christ is also a cutting away of the flesh, though in this case 'flesh' refers not to part of the physical body but to sinful human nature. Christians have been freed from the power of the old nature (11).

A second illustration likens salvation to the rite of baptism. Union with Christ means the death and burial of the old life, and the rising again to new life (12). The Colossian believers had once been spiritually dead. Being Gentiles they did not even have the Jewish covenant sign of circumcision to

540

give them hope of better things to come. Yet God forgave them their sins (13).

The law of God shows up human sinfulness and demands death as the punishment. It is like a book that records sinners' debts, then demands their death because they cannot pay those debts. But God forgave the sins and wiped out the debts, because Christ paid the full penalty on behalf of repentant sinners. He destroyed the power of the law — as if he took that book with its record of sins and debts and nailed it to the cross with himself. Therefore, believers need no longer fear the power of the law (14). Nor need they fear the power of the spiritual forces of evil, for Christ has conquered them, taken away their power and displayed his victory over them (15).

Christian freedom in practice (2:16-3:4)

In view of the freedom that Christ has won for them, the Colossian believers must not listen to those who try to force them to obey the rules and regulations of the Israelite law. Practices taught in the law may be compared to shadows. They are not solid or permanent, but their existence enables the viewer to know that there is some real object that casts the shadows. That real object is Jesus Christ. Now that he has come, the shadows are of no further interest. The ceremonies of the law have no further use (16-17).

Neither should Christians listen to those who want to show their 'superior' knowledge by mixing their own philosophies with the gospel. Christian life and growth come from God through a direct relationship between the believer and Christ. There is no scale of angelic beings forming a ladder to link Christians with God (18-19).

Having been set free from the bondage of sin through Christ's death, Christians should not get into bondage again by becoming slaves of religious regulations that people want to impose upon them. To make laws to live by is the way of the worldly person, not the way of the Christian. No matter how clever and religious those laws may appear, they will not succeed in controlling the desires of the body (20-23).

Because they have died to sin, Christians are not in bondage to things of the world as the Gnostics are. Christians have been raised with Christ to new life in a higher world, where their desires and conduct are like Christ's (3:1-2). Through Christ they have life directly in God. In contrast to the Gnostics, they do not try to climb a ladder of countless intermediate spirit beings. Neither the Gnostics nor any other unbelievers can understand this life, because the life is 'in Christ' and therefore is hidden from their view. Its true character will be fully shown on the day when Christ's glory is revealed (3-4).

3:5-4:6 THE CHRISTIAN'S NEW LIFE

Old and new habits (3:5-17)

Not only do Christians believe that through Christ's death they have died to sin, but they must also show it to be true in their daily lives. They must make every effort to put away the old selfish habits that God hates, from obvious sins such as sexual immorality to hidden sins such as greed and other uncontrolled desires (5-7). They must control the tongue and discipline personal behaviour. This renewing of their lives is not something that happens only once. It must go on all the time, so that more of the old nature is conquered and the new person is more like God (8-10).

Since the goal of the Christian life is to become like Christ, there is no way that Christians can be divided into superior or inferior classes according to race, culture or social status. All are equal in him, united in him, and should strive to be like him (11).

Believers should put off old sinful habits as they would put off dirty clothes. They should put on new good habits as they would put on fresh clean clothes. They should have a new attitude, which thinks of others before thinking of self. It is as if the new 'clothes' they have just put on are bound together by love, so that their appearance is one of genuine beauty and completeness (12-14).

Within the church there are people of various personalities and social backgrounds, but they can all live together in harmony through allowing the peace-loving spirit of Christ to guide their actions. Through teaching and singing they can build one another up in the faith. At all times and in all places they should live and act as new people in Christ (15-17).

Life in the home and in society (3:18-4:6)

Harmony in the home depends on the husband's showing understanding love to his wife, and the wife's showing loyal submission to her husband (18-19). Children are to be obedient to their parents, but parents must treat their children with understanding and not be harsh or unreasonable (20-21). When slaves work for their masters as if they were working for the Lord Christ, they will produce work of good quality. Masters, on their part, must reward their slaves fairly, knowing that they too have a master, God, and he will treat them as they treat others (22-4:1).

Christians must be regular and persistent in prayer. They must keep alert as they pray, for they can be easily distracted (2). They should specifically pray for the servants of God with whom they are partners in the gospel, that God's messengers may have opportunities to make known his message, and that they may do so clearly (3-4). Besides praying for the activity of others, Christians should be careful of their own conduct, and make sure their speech is pleasant to listen to and sensible. In this way they will attract, and not repel, those who are not believers (5-6).

4:7-18 PERSONAL NEWS

Tychicus, who carried Paul's letter to Colossae, had the additional duty of telling the church how Paul was faring in his imprisonment. One person who accompanied Tychicus was Onesimus, a slave from Colossae who had escaped to Rome, met Paul and become a Christian. Paul wanted the Colossians to welcome Onesimus as part of the church (7-9). (Paul also wanted Onesimus's master, Philemon, to welcome him home and forgive him; Philem 10-20.)

With Paul during his imprisonment in Rome were three Jewish Christians: Aristarchus, who had travelled with him on the adventurous sea voyage from Palestine (see Acts 27:1-2); Mark, who had once helped him in the gospel and who was likely to visit Colossae soon (see Acts 12:25; 13:5,13; 14:36-39); and Jesus Justus (10-11).

Three other people with Paul were Gentiles: Epaphras, who had worked faithfully and prayerfully in and around Colossae (see 1:7); Luke, the writer of one Gospel and Acts, who also had travelled with Paul from Palestine to Rome (see Acts 27:1-2; 28:16); and Demas, who later deserted him (see 2 Tim 4:10) (12-14).

Paul also sends greetings to the church in the neighbouring town of Laodicea. The church there had likewise received a letter from Paul, and he asks that the Colossian and Laodicean churches exchange letters so that both may receive additional teaching (15-16). In closing, Paul encourages Archippus to carry out his work for God faithfully, and reminds the Colossians that he is still imprisoned and he needs their prayers (17-18).

1 Thessalonians

BACKGROUND

On his second missionary journey, Paul entered Europe for the first time when he crossed from Asia Minor to Macedonia, the northern part of present-day Greece. The first churches that he established in Europe were in the Macedonian cities of Philippi and Thessalonica (Acts 16:11-12; 17:1). Paul wrote his first letter to the Thessalonians only a few months after he established the church.

Growth of the Thessalonian church

Paul's initial work in Thessalonica brought fruit among the Greeks but violent opposition from the Jews. When the Jews created a public uproar, the city authorities tried to restore peace by getting rid of Paul. They made one of the local Christians deposit an amount of money with them, apparently as a guarantee that Paul would leave the city and not return (Acts 17:2-10; cf. 1 Thess 2:18). (Although Paul did not visit Thessalonica again on his second missionary journey, he may have visited it on his next journey; see Acts 20:1-2.)

From Thessalonica Paul went to neighbouring Berea and then on to Athens in the province of Achaia, the southern part of present-day Greece (Acts 17:10-15). From Athens he sent his fellow worker Timothy back to Thessalonica to help the young church (1 Thess 3:1-2). After a short time in Athens, Paul went across to Corinth, also in the south of Greece (Acts 18:1), and it was there that Timothy met him upon returning from Thessalonica a few weeks later (Acts 18:5; 1 Thess 3:6).

Timothy brought Paul news that the church in Thessalonica, though it suffered persecution, had grown strong. Within only a short time it had spread the gospel far and wide throughout the surrounding districts (1 Thess 1:6-8; 2:13-16; 3:3). Thankful at this news, Paul sent off the letter that we know as 1 Thessalonians. In this letter Paul also dealt with a number of matters that needed attention in the church. He defended himself against unwarranted accusations, instructed misguided believers about aspects of Christian behaviour, and cleared up mis-understandings about Christ's return.

OUTLINE

1:1-3:13   Relations with the Thessalonians
4:1-12   Teaching about marriage and work
4:13-5:11   Concerning Christ's return
5:12-28   Advice on other matters

1:1-3:13   RELATIONS WITH THE THESSALONIANS

Response to the gospel (1:1-10)

Paul gives thanks to God for the good news that Timothy brought back concerning the Christians in Thessalonica. Through their belief in Christ their lives have been changed, so that in everything they do their faith, love and endurance are clearly seen (1:1-3).

The Thessalonians have given proof that they are God's people by the way they have believed and stood firm for the gospel. They had seen how Paul was persecuted in Thessalonica and they knew that believing the gospel would bring suffering. But they also knew that the gospel operated by the power of God and they gladly accepted it, confident of its power to save them (4-6). Their conduct amid persecution has been an example to Christians throughout Macedonia and Achaia (7).

Much of Macedonia and Achaia had been evangelized as a direct result of the Thessalonians' zeal. Paul has no need to boast to others about this outstanding work, because Christians everywhere know about it already (8). Throughout the region people are talking about how readily the Thessalonians responded to the message Paul preached. No longer are they in bondage to lifeless idols. They have become servants of the living God, and they look forward to the climax of their salvation at the return of Jesus Christ (9-10).

Paul's work in Thessalonica (2:1-16)

In Paul's day there were some travelling preachers whose main aim was to make money, usually by crafty or dishonest methods. Certain people in the Thessalonian church, apparently angry that Paul had left them suddenly, accused him of being one of these untrustworthy travelling preachers. They said he was concerned only for himself, not for them. Paul replies that he has never used smooth words to deceive people or gain a following. His readers know that in both Philippi and Thessalonica he was so straightforward in preaching God's message that he suffered bodily harm (2:1-5).

Paul wanted neither praise nor money. As an apostle he had a right to be supported financially by those to whom he ministered, but he did not claim this right. Far from trying to make financial profit from the Thessalonians, he gave freely to help them (6-8). He worked at his trade to earn enough money to support himself, and spent the rest of his time preaching (9). The Christians in Thessalonica know that his conduct among them was without fault. It was a living example of the kind of life that Paul urged them to live, the life that pleases God and brings glory to his name (10-12).

The Thessalonians knew that the gospel they received was not something of human creation but was a message from God himself, and they were prepared to suffer for it. They were persecuted by the citizens of their own country, just as the Christians in Judea were persecuted by the Jews (13-14). Not only had the Jews crucified the Lord Jesus and rejected God themselves, but they were now trying to prevent the message of Jesus from reaching the Gentiles. In doing so they were building up a terrible divine judgment against themselves (15-16).

After leaving Thessalonica (2:17-3:13)

Having reminded the Thessalonians of his work and conduct while among them, Paul now outlines his thoughts and feelings for them since he left. In spite of what his opponents are saying, his failure to return does not mean that he has no interest in them. Several times he has tried to return, but each time something has stopped him (17-18). He wants to have joy, not shame, at Christ's return, and for

this reason he is eager to see his converts grow and develop in the faith (19-20).

Paul was faced with a difficulty. He was not able to return to Thessalonica, yet he was not able to rest if he did not return. He therefore did the next best thing and sent his fellow worker Timothy, even though it meant that Paul had to face alone the difficult task of preaching in Athens (3:1-2; cf. Acts 17:16-34). Timothy's task was to strengthen the Thessalonians' faith to withstand persecution. Paul did not want the good work already done among them to be destroyed through people turning away from Christ (3-5).

Timothy has now returned and Paul is overjoyed at the news he has brought. The believers in Thessalonica have progressed in their faith and love, and their longing to see Paul is as great as his longing to see them (6-8). He does not know how to thank God for such good news. He desires more than ever to revisit them, so that he can further help their growing faith (9-10). But he will return only if God wants him to. God is the one who guides their progress, and only he can make them strong. In view of Christ's return they should increase in love and holiness (11-13).

4:1-12 TEACHING ABOUT MARRIAGE AND WORK

God's will is that there be continual progress in the lives of believers, leading them to increasing holiness. As they try more to please God, they will become increasingly different from those who do not know God (4:1-3a).

For example, in relations between the sexes, Christians will not be uncontrolled as the pagans are, but will restrain their sexual passions (3b-5). If they commit immoral acts they shame themselves and harm others. They also sin against God, for God's purpose in calling people to himself is to make them holy. For this reason he gives his Holy Spirit to live within their bodies. When people fight against the holy purpose of the Spirit, they invite judgment (6-8).

The Thessalonians had love for each other as Christians, but apparently some used this as an excuse to become dependent on others instead of being ready to help others. If people love others they will work to support themselves, so that they do not become a burden to their friends. In addition, idle people are often guilty of being busybodies, and this is not a characteristic of love. The Thessalonians must correct faults such as these that have appeared in their church. This will prevent non-Christians from criticizing them, and prevent fellow believers from being unnecessarily burdened (9-12).

4:13-5:11 CONCERNING CHRIST'S RETURN

Those who have died (4:13-18)

Among the Thessalonians, some were worried that those in their church who had died would not share in the return of Christ and the final triumph of his kingdom. Paul assures them that they will share in his return just as they share in his death and resurrection. (13-14). Believers who have died, far from being at a disadvantage, will be raised to life first. Believers still alive will join them, and together they will meet Christ and be with him for ever (15-17). Christian faith should give people hope and encouragement. They should see death not as a tragic end but as a glorious entrance into something new (18; cf. v. 13b).

Those who are still alive (5:1-11)

Paul had already told the Thessalonians that no one knows when Christ will return. He will come as unexpectedly as a thief. His intervention in the affairs of the world will be as sudden as birth pains. His return will smash the non-Christian's sense of security with a destruction that none will escape (5:1-3). The life of the non-Christian is likened to a dark night of moral laziness and ill-discipline. The life of the Christian is likened to a bright day of watchfulness and self-control. Therefore, Christians of the 'day' should not act like non-Christians of the 'night', otherwise they will be both surprised and ashamed when Christ returns (4-7).

Just as soldiers must always be prepared for any eventuality, so Christians must always be prepared for Christ's return. They must be self-controlled in their behaviour, strong in faith and love, and confident in their salvation (8). Union with Christ means that they will escape God's wrath and enjoy salvation in its fulness. This is a further reason why they should live in a way that pleases God and encourages fellow Christians (9-11).

5:12-28 ADVICE ON OTHER MATTERS

Minor difficulties had arisen in the Thessalonian church, and the church leaders had the responsibility to see that these matters were put right. Paul therefore reminds the church members to respect those who have the duty of guiding the church, and not to be offended when the church leaders find it necessary to give corrective instruction (12-13). The leaders, on their part, must always act with patience and understanding (14).

All Christians should live in a constant attitude of helpfulness, joy, prayer and thanks (15-18). In all matters they need the unhindered help of God's Spirit. This is particularly so in being able to tell the difference between right and wrong, so that they do not despise Spirit-inspired messages as worldly, and do not exalt worldly attitudes as spiritual (19-22).

God alone can give the Thessalonians the necessary strength to put Paul's advice into practice. God wants his people to progress constantly towards greater holiness in every part of their lives and being (23-24). To this end Paul reminds the church leaders to read the letter to the church and to make sure that the believers understand it fully (25-28).

2 Thessalonians

BACKGROUND

Within a short time of sending off 1 Thessalonians, Paul received news that certain Christians in the Thessalonian church had misunderstood parts of the letter. He therefore sent off the letter known to us as 2 Thessalonians. Paul was still in Corinth (he remained there a year and a half; Acts 18:11), and his second letter may have followed his first by only a few weeks.

One misunderstanding of the Thessalonians concerned the return of Jesus Christ. Paul had said that Christ would return unexpectedly and suddenly, but some people thought this meant he would return immediately. There were even those who thought that if this were the case, there was no purpose in working any longer. As a result they became idle and a burden to others (2 Thess 2:1-2; 3:11). In writing to correct the misunderstandings, Paul gave additional teaching about the return of Christ, rebuked those who were idle, and gave further encouragement to those who were persecuted.

OUTLINE

1:1-2:12 CONCERNING CHRIST'S RETURN

A source of encouragement (1:1-12)

The Thessalonian Christians continue to grow in faith, love and endurance, in spite of the constant persecution they suffer; and Paul continues to talk about them as an example that should challenge others (1:1-4; cf. 1 Thess 1:3,6-7). He encourages them to keep moving forward, and points out that their suffering is proof of the genuineness of their faith. Their endurance shows that they are worthy to inherit the kingdom of God. In his righteous judgment God uses sufferings to bring his people to maturity, but by the same righteous judgment he will punish those who persecute them (5-6).

Christ's return will bring relief and rest to the persecuted believers (Paul here links himself with the Thessalonians), but it will also bring judgment to the ungodly. For the one it will bring glory, for the other eternal destruction (7-10). Paul prays that by God's power the Thessalonians will go on producing those qualities of Christian character that are fitting in those whom God has called. Such character will bring honour to Christ now and will reach its full expression in the age to come (11-12).

The day of the Lord (2:1-12)

Some of the Thessalonians thought that the final day of the Lord had already come. Paul states firmly that they did not get such an idea from any prophecy, preaching or letter of his (2:1-2). That day will not come until there is open and widespread rebellion against God, led by one known as the man of lawlessness (RSV; NIV) or the wicked one (GNB). This person will recognize no authority, Christian or otherwise, apart from his own, and will put himself in the place of God as the sole controller of human society (3-4).

The Thessalonians knew what Paul was talking about, because he had given teaching on these things while among them (5). They also knew what we do not, namely, what or who it is that prevents these things from happening now. One suggestion is that this restraining power is the system of law and government that to some extent can control evil in human society (cf. Rom 13:3-4). Evil is always at work in the world, but when the restraining power is removed, evil will reign unhindered till it reaches its fulness in the man of lawlessness. Then Christ will return and with terrible ease destroy him (6-8).

During his rise to power the man of lawlessness will be empowered by Satan to perform miracles. In this way he will deceive people who, having deliberately rejected God and chosen evil, give him their support and so fall under God's judgment. God will use the unrestrained work of Satan as a means of punishing a rebellious world (9-12).

2:13-3:18 PRESENT NEEDS IN THE CHURCH

Stability amid persecution (2:13-3:5)

From considering the terrible judgment that awaits the wicked, Paul turns to look at the bright future that awaits the Thessalonian believers. God will destroy the man of lawlessness and his followers, but the same God loves the Thessalonian believers. Their salvation is certain because God chose them as his from eternity, called them to himself through the gospel, and will in due course give them a share in Christ's glory (13-14).

In view of the security that is theirs through the gospel, the Thessalonians need not be frightened by persecution or worried about future events. If they hold firmly to the apostolic teaching given to them, they will find that God strengthens them with courage and hope (15-17).

Paul asks for prayer that his proclamation of the gospel in Corinth will bring the same fruitful results as it did in Thessalonica. He desires also that God will protect both him and the Thessalonians against the attacks of Satan (3:1-3). He is confident that they will continue to stand firm, and that they will obey the important instructions that he is about to give them (4-5).

Work to earn a living (3:6-18)

Thinking that Christ was about to return, some believers in Thessalonica stopped working for a living and were being supported by others in the church. Paul says that the church should not support such people. By their selfishness, these idlers are denying the teaching they have received concerning Christian brotherhood (6). They should follow Paul's example. As a teacher Paul had the right to be supported by those whom he taught, but instead he worked hard to earn his own living, so as not to be a burden to others (7-9).

If people refuse to work, others should not support them, because this only encourages them to remain idle (10). These people are not only an unnecessary financial burden, but because they have nothing to do, they become nuisances and busybodies. They must stop annoying others and start working to earn their own living (11-13). If any ignore these apostolic instructions and persist in their idleness, the believers should not show them sympathy. In fact, a brotherly warning might bring them to their senses (14-15).

In conclusion Paul prays that the Thessalonians, instead of being unsettled by misunderstandings concerning the return of Christ, may experience the calmness of God's peace among them (16). Paul then takes the pen from his secretary and, following his usual practice, writes a few words himself to prove the genuineness of the letter (17-18).

1 Timothy

BACKGROUND

Paul's letters to Timothy and Titus are commonly referred to as the Pastoral Letters. These letters show Paul's deep concern for the pastoral responsibilities he had entrusted to Timothy and Titus, and the warm relationship he shared with his two fellow workers. The letters belong to the final years of Paul's life, and give an indication of how church life had developed since the early days of Paul's missionary travels.

Paul's later travels

Although the book of Acts records many of Paul's travels, it does not record them all. It concludes at the point chosen by the author according to the purpose of his book, but it does not represent the end of the story of Paul. Paul was imprisoned in Rome for two years as he awaited the outcome of

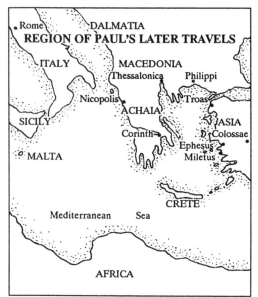

his appeal to Caesar (Acts 28:16,30), and the letters he wrote during that time showed that he hoped to be released. He even expected to travel to other countries and revisit some of the churches (Phil 1:25,27; 2:24; Philem 22). It seems certain that at the

end of two years Paul was released and went on further journeys, but since the book of Acts had by this time been completed, the only references to these journeys are in Paul's later writings.

Among the places Paul visited (accompanied, it seems, by Timothy and Titus) was the island of Crete. He soon found that the churches of Crete were in a state of serious disorder, mainly because they lacked the right leaders and were confused by false teachers. Paul gave whatever help and direction he could, but he had to move on to other places. He therefore left Titus behind to carry on the work and establish proper leadership in the churches (Titus 1:5,10-11).

Upon arriving in Ephesus, Paul found further problems of false teaching. Some years earlier he had warned the elders of the Ephesian church that he expected such problems to arise (Acts 20:29-30). Self-appointed 'experts' were causing much harm in the church with unprofitable teaching based on ancient myths, legends, laws and genealogies (1 Tim 1:4-7; 4:1-3; 6:3-5). Some of the teaching was so damaging that Paul decided the only way to deal with the offenders was to put them out of the church (1 Tim 1:19-20). But Paul could not stay in Ephesus indefinitely, as he wanted to visit churches in other regions. Therefore, when the time came to move on to Macedonia, he left Timothy behind to give further help to the church (1 Tim 1:3).

Letters to Timothy and Titus

In Macedonia Paul probably fulfilled his wish to visit the Philippian church (cf. Phil 2:24; 4:1), but he was concerned for Timothy and Titus whom he had left to deal with difficult church problems. He therefore sent to them the letters known to us as 1 Timothy and Titus.

The two letters are similar in many ways, though the letter to Timothy is longer and more personal. In both letters Paul encourages his fellow workers to be confident in carrying out the tasks entrusted to them (1 Tim 1:3,18; 4:6,11-12; Titus 1:5; 2:15). They are to establish order and leadership in the churches (1 Tim 2:1,8; 3:1-13; 5:17; Titus 1:6-9; 2:2-8), instruct people in Christian truth (1 Tim 3:14-15; 4:13-14; 6:20; Titus 2:1,7; 3:8), and avoid wasting time with arguments about senseless issues (1 Tim 4:7; 6:20; Titus 3:9).

OUTLINE

1:1-20	Warning against false teachers
2:1-4:16	Church leadership and teaching
5:1-6:21	Various kinds of people in the church

1:1-20 WARNING AGAINST FALSE TEACHERS

False and true (1:1-11)

The letter begins with a reminder to Timothy of the reason Paul urged him to stay at Ephesus. Timothy has to stop people wasting time and confusing others with senseless discussions that lead only to conflict and argument. Those responsible for this confusing teaching must learn to control their imagination. Instead of inventing fanciful stories based on Old Testament genealogies, they should concentrate on the kind of teaching that produces a sincere faith, a clear conscience and a pure heart (1:1-5).

Because these so-called teachers do not aim at building people up in faith and love, they are really false teachers. They want to have authority and prestige like the Jewish scribes, but they have no understanding of the Scriptures they so confidently try to explain. They only lead people away from the truth (6-7).

The false teachers, by using their imagination to interpret the law, try to establish a set of regulations by which Christians should live. The law, however, was not given for that purpose. It was given to sinful people to show them God's righteous standards. As a result it showed people their sinfulness, and in this way led them to God to ask his mercy. This is the way Paul uses the law in preaching the gospel (8-11; cf. Rom 3:19-20; 7:7-12).

Reminders from past experiences (1:12-20)

As soon as Paul mentions the gospel, he is reminded of the power and grace of God that he has experienced in his own life. God changed Paul, and turned the greatest of sinners into his special representative to take the gospel to the Gentiles. If God can do that, there must be no limit to his mercy, grace and love (12-15). No person is beyond hope. Christ's patience in dealing with the persecutor Paul should be an assurance to others that he will be merciful to them too. When repentant sinners are thankful for all that the Almighty God has done for them, they will respond by giving him honour and glory (16-17). Paul recalls the prophecy, given at the outset of Timothy's ministry, that indicated the kind of

ministry to which he was called. He trusts that as Timothy thinks over the words of that prophecy, he will find renewed courage to stand firm for what he knows to be right. A firm faith must be linked to a clear conscience (18-19a).

Hymenaeus and Alexander were two who had been guilty of serious wrongdoing because they separated their beliefs from their behaviour. They refused to change their ways and in the end were put out of the church. They were, so to speak, put out of the sphere where God's rule was acknowledged into the sphere where they were open to the attacks of Satan. But Paul hoped that the punishment would lead to correction, so that as they realized their wrongdoing they would turn from it (19b-20).

2:1-4:16 CHURCH LEADERSHIP AND TEACHING

Conduct in church meetings (2:1-15)

Teachers of the kind Paul has described in Chapter 1 are usually narrow in their outlook and pray only for those of their own group. Christians should avoid such selfishness. They should pray for all without distinction, for God wants all to be saved (2:1-4). This salvation comes through the death of Jesus Christ. Paul rejoices that God has appointed him an apostle and teacher to make known this good news to the Gentiles (5-7).

Paul then deals with two problems likely to arise when people participate in the public activities of the church. One concerns men, and the other concerns women. A tendency in men when leading a public gathering is to talk and act in a way that displays their abilities and so wins praise from others. A tendency in women is to dress in a way that attracts attention. Paul tells men to pray in a proper manner and to remember that the purpose of prayer is to speak to God, not to gain an advantage over others. He tells women that if they want to impress people they should do so by good deeds, not by extravagant dress (8-10).

On the subject of women's modesty, Paul adds that they should demonstrate this modesty in a quiet readiness to learn. He does not consider it their job to instruct and lead the church (11-12). Paul gives these restrictions because he believes women are more easily persuaded than men. Consequently, there is a greater risk that they will believe and teach what is false. He refers to the example of Eve to support this statement, and to show that from the beginning God designed each of the sexes to have its own particular place in the arrangement of human affairs (13-14). This does not mean that women have an unimportant place in God's plan. They will find their fulfilment, their 'salvation', their own unique honour, through having children and bringing them up in the ways of Christian faith, love and holiness (15).

Elders and deacons (3:1-13)

Churches of the New Testament era were self-governing bodies that were independent of each other and under the control of local elders. Elders were also known as shepherds, overseers, guardians, leaders and bishops, but these names represent only two words in the original Greek, *presbuteroi* and *episkopoi*.

These two Greek words refer to the same office and people. For example (in the words of the RSV), in Acts 20:17 Paul sent for the elders (*presbuteroi*) of the Ephesian church, but in verse 28 he called them guardians (*episkopoi*). Likewise in Titus 1:5 he told Titus to appoint elders (*presbuteroi*), then in verse 7 he called them bishops (*episkopoi*). Elders were like shepherds over the flock. Their responsibility was to lead, rule, guide, teach and care for the church (Acts 20:28; 1 Tim 3:5; 5:17; Heb 13:17; 1 Peter 5:1-3).

Early churches also developed an order of deacons, or church helpers. (The Greek *diakonos* was the common word for servant or minister.) It seems that deacons looked after many of the every-day tasks in the church so that the elders had more time for prayer and teaching (Acts 6:2-4; cf. Rom 12:6-8; Phil 1:1). However, deacons were not limited to routine affairs, and some were also preachers (cf. Acts 6:5,8-10; 8:5).

Most of the New Testament churches were founded in heathen cities, where many of the converts came from a background of low moral standards. Although some of these converts may have developed spiritually, they may also have retained disorders in their marriages, families and personal habits. These disorders, in spite of other-wise good qualities, would make such people a poor example to the church should they be in leadership positions as elders or deacons.

Paul therefore gave Timothy some guidelines concerning those who might hold office in the church. The qualities he lists are not qualifications in the sense that anyone who fulfils these requirements is an elder (for such a person may not have the elder-shepherd qualities outlined above). Rather they are minimum requirements that otherwise suitable people must fulfil if the church is to recognize them as elders or deacons.

Elders should maintain a quality of personal and family life that is a good example to others in the church. Their behaviour should be blameless and they should have some ability to understand and teach the Scriptures (3:1-5). They should not be recent converts, as time is necessary for spiritual character and gift to develop. They must each have a good reputation, not only among Christians but also among those who are not Christians (6-7).

Paul gives a similar list of qualities to test the suitability of deacons, both men and women. Although he does not require deacons to have an ability to teach, he does require them to have a sound understanding of basic Christian truth. He also gives a warning against gossip, since deacons are likely to know about the personal affairs of those who give to and receive from the church's finances (8-13).

The true church; the false teachers (3:14-4:5)

Timothy is urged to remind the believers that their behaviour should reflect the character of the church of God to which they belong. That church is not like a heathen temple occupied by some lifeless god, but is the dwelling place of the living God and the upholder of his truth (14-15). This living God (in the words of an early Christian song that Paul quotes) entered the world of human existence in the person of Jesus Christ, who died, rose from death, brought salvation to the world, and returned to heaven where he reigns in glory and is worshipped unceasingly (16).

Despite the greatness of God and his salvation, some abandon their faith. They claim to be following the true teaching of God, but actually they are following the deceitful teaching of evil spirits. They have ceased to teach that right moral behaviour is the natural outcome of true faith, and as a result their consciences have become dead (4:1-2). Instead of allowing the truth of God to mould people's minds and attitudes, they try to force people to obey laws. They teach, for example, that it is wrong to marry and to eat certain foods. But this teaching directly opposes God, who gave marriage and food for people's benefit (3-5).

(The false teaching that Paul and Timothy fought against at Ephesus was an early form of Gnosticism. It was a problem that Paul had dealt with in letters he wrote a year or two previously. For further details of this teaching see introductory notes to Ephesians and Colossians.)

Dealing with the false teachers (4:6-16)

Paul makes it clear to Timothy that good teachers do not waste time arguing about silly stories, but concentrate on teaching positive Christian doctrine.

This is the best answer to those who teach nonsense. By thinking and talking about the great truths of the Christian faith, teachers will build themselves up as well. They must not forget, however, to train themselves with the self-discipline that leads to spiritual fitness and lasting blessings (6-8). True servants of God persevere in all aspects of their work, whether in teaching others or in training themselves. They are assured that this will lead them to a fuller enjoyment of the salvation that God has given them (9-10).

Some older ones in the church may not be pleased to hear the younger man Timothy giving them instruction and perhaps correcting them. This is all the more reason why Timothy must make sure that he is blameless in his speech, conduct, love and faith (11-12).

God had given Timothy ability as a preacher and teacher. The elders of Timothy's home church, as well as Paul, had publicly acknowledged this by the ceremony of laying their hands on him when he first went out with Paul in the service of God (13-14; cf. 2 Tim 1:6; Acts 16:2). Nevertheless, Timothy must work hard to develop the gift God has given him. As a result of this combination of divine gift and human diligence, both God's servant and those among whom he works will enjoy salvation in its fulness (15-16).

5:1-6:21 VARIOUS KINDS OF PEOPLE IN THE CHURCH

The young, the old and the widows (5:1-16)

It may at times have been difficult for Timothy to deal with those who were older or those who were of the opposite sex. Paul therefore reminds him to be careful how he treats people, and always to show fitting courtesy and to act with moral uprightness (5:1-2).

The church must care for those of its members who are in need. But the church does not have a duty to support financially those elderly people who have children and grandchildren who can look after them. The church should support only the widows who are very poor and who have no one to whom they can turn for help except God (3-5). Other widows, who have found a means of support by turning to a life of pleasure, should be sternly warned, for they are killing their spiritual lives (6-7). Paul repeats that, wherever possible, the widows in the church should be looked after by their own families. Even unbelievers acknowledge they have a responsibility towards elderly parents (8).

Because of its limited finances, the church should limit the number of widows on its welfare list. It should include only those who are over the age of sixty, have been married only once, have promoted Christian standards in their families and households, have demonstrated the servant attitude in their manner of living and have a reputation for good deeds (9-10).

Younger widows should not be included on the church's welfare list. In past cases some have shown a tendency to remarry hastily and the results have been disastrous. Others have become gossips and busybodies. They would do better to remarry (to those who share their faith; cf. 1 Cor 7:39) and so have the responsibility of bringing up children and looking after the home (11-15). In summary, people should look for ways to provide for widows privately rather than to let them become a burden to the church (16).

Church elders and Timothy himself (5:17-25)

The church members should recognize the valuable service that the elders give and should reward them generously (17-18). Any accusation of wrongdoing against elders must be supported by witnesses. If they are shown to be guilty, they should be rebuked publicly, since their position as leaders in the church makes their sin the more serious (19-20).

Timothy is reminded not to show favouritism nor to act hastily in appointing people to positions of leadership in the church. Others will doubt his own purity if he appoints a person who is later shown to be a wrongdoer (21-22). The reminder to Timothy to keep himself pure does not mean he must no longer drink wine, for if he takes it in reasonable amounts it may help him enjoy better health (23). But (to return to the matter of appointing officers in the church) he must remember that not all the good or all the bad in a person can be seen at first. Sooner or later, however, it will become obvious. Therefore, it is wise not to accept or reject anyone too hastily (24-25).

The slaves (6:1-2)

Slaves had equal status with others in the church (Gal 3:28), but not in the households where they worked. Paul helped to raise the status of slaves, and eventually to bring an end to slavery, by encouraging Christian slaves to work with responsibility and dignity. They were not to think of themselves as mere tools of their masters. Paul assures them that if they act in a way that is fitting for those who are God's children, they will also bring honour to the name of God (6:1). Any who work for Christian masters should work all the better. In so doing they will bring added benefit to those who are their fellow believers in Christ (2).

Trouble-makers and God's servant (6:3-16)

The teaching of the false teachers differs from that of Christ, and their conduct likewise differs. Their kind of teaching arises out of pride and creates argument, which in turn leads to suspicious thoughts and insulting talk about others. Paul knows that their real reason for setting themselves up as Christian teachers is to become rich (3-5).

Christianity does make a person rich, but not in the way the false teachers think. Christians are rich when they learn to be satisfied with what they have, and are not always wanting more (6-8). Those whose chief desire is to build up their wealth are easily led away from God. They might gain the wealth they desire, but spiritually they finish in a state of terrible poverty. Their spiritual lives become ruined, their true happiness is destroyed, and their minds are full of worries (9-10).

Paul warns Timothy to beware of these dangers, and encourages him to concentrate on developing the Christian virtues. He must not give up the struggle. When he first committed himself by a public declaration to his work, he knew that this work would require much perseverance (11-12). He is encouraged by the example of Jesus who, when he was before Pilate, made a firm declaration in spite of the suffering he knew it would bring. Timothy likewise must be faithful to the end in spite of the hardships. His assurance is that he will then share in the triumph of that great day when Jesus Christ returns (13-16).

The wealthy (6:17-21)

One danger with wealth is that when people have financial independence, they may not trust God as they should. Instead of hoarding their riches, they should use them to help others. In this way they will be investing in something far more lasting than earthly wealth. They will be building a life far more enduring than earthly life (17-19).

Paul brings his letter to a close by reminding Timothy of two of its chief points. First, Timothy must preserve and pass on the true Christian teaching. Second, he must not waste time arguing with those who have replaced this teaching with their own foolish inventions (20-21).

2 Timothy

BACKGROUND

Some time after writing 1 Timothy and Titus, Paul left Macedonia. His exact route is unknown, but two of the places he visited were Corinth in the south of Greece and Miletus on the west coast of Asia Minor (2 Tim 4:20). He also visited Troas to the north, but it seems that he must have been forced to leave Troas in a hurry, for he left behind some of his most valued possessions (2 Tim 4:13). This suggests that Troas may have been the place where he was arrested. He was then taken to Rome, and from prison he wrote his final letter, 2 Timothy.

Last words to a fellow worker

When the government authorities in Rome laid their charges against Paul, he was deserted by friends that he thought would help him. But God rescued him from violence and enabled him to proclaim the gospel to his captors (2 Tim 4:16-17). Nevertheless, Paul did not have the optimism of his first imprisonment. Instead of expecting release, he expected execution (2 Tim 4:6-8).

With time running out, Paul wrote to Timothy to give him final encouragement and make some urgent requests. Because the church in Ephesus was still troubled by false teachers, Paul encouraged Timothy to persevere in giving wholesome Christian teaching and to avoid wasting time with senseless arguments (2 Tim 1:6-8; 2:14-16,23-25; 4:2,5). He also wanted Timothy to come to Rome quickly (2 Tim 4:9).

Paul was feeling cold and lonely in prison. He missed his friends, he needed warm clothing and he wanted his books (2 Tim 4:9,13,21). He felt particularly sad that Demas, who had been with him faithfully during his first imprisonment, had now deserted him (2 Tim 4:10; cf. Col 4:14). Some Christians visited him (2 Tim 1:16-18; 4:21), but others had gone to various places in the service of God (2 Tim 4:10,12). Only Luke was able to stay with him for any length of time (2 Tim 4:11).

The two people that Paul most wanted to come and be with him in his closing days were Timothy and Mark, the two who as young men had set out with him many years earlier on his missionary journeys. Mark was probably working in Colossae, not far from Ephesus, where Timothy was at the time (2 Tim 4:9,11; cf. Col 4:10). It is not certain whether Timothy and Mark reached Rome before Paul's execution. According to ancient writings, he was executed some time during the first half of the AD 60s.

OUTLINE

1:1-2:13 ENCOURAGEMENT TO TIMOTHY

Need for courage and faithfulness (1:1-18)

Paul recalls the time when he left Timothy behind in Ephesus, and remembers how Timothy wept as they parted. He longs to see him again (1:1-4). No doubt the quality of Timothy's faith, which so attracted Paul to him, was largely the result of a godly upbringing by those of sincere faith (5). At the beginning of Timothy's ministry Paul had shown publicly that he believed Timothy to be divinely gifted for his work. He encourages Timothy to keep working and not to become hesitant through fear of opposition (6-7).

Far from being timid, Timothy must be bold in showing himself of one mind with Paul in standing for the truth of Jesus Christ. True, this will result in suffering, but he will willingly bear such suffering when he remembers all that God has freely done for him (8). God saves sinners and makes them his people solely by his grace, not because of anything they have done. Before the world was made, God planned to give people eternal life, but this gift becomes theirs only through Christ's victory over death on the cross (9-10).

The imprisonment Paul suffers is not because he has failed in any way, but because he has steadfastly upheld the gospel. He has carried out the work God gave him to do. Therefore, his imprisonment neither causes him shame nor weakens his confidence. He knows that God will be faithful to him and will preserve the gospel, no matter how severe the persecution (11-12). Timothy also must stand firm and, with the help of God's Spirit, uphold the message of truth that God has entrusted to him (13-14).

Paul gives Timothy two examples of commitment, one bad the other good. The bad example concerns Christians from the province of Asia who apparently deserted Paul at the time of his arrest (15). By contrast another from Asia, Onesiphorus of Ephesus, went looking for Paul, in spite of the difficulties and risks involved. Paul prays that God will reward him with blessing on his family now, and mercy in the day of judgment (16-18; cf. 4:19).

Need for endurance (2:1-13)

Like Onesiphorus, Timothy must persevere for the sake of Christ and endure hardship. He must push on vigorously with his task of passing on the truth Paul has taught him. He should do this wisely and carefully, by instructing people who are trustworthy and have the ability to teach others (2:1-2).

In dealing with the difficulties in Ephesus, Timothy must realize that he is a soldier of Jesus Christ. He must expect suffering and endure it. A soldier is not concerned with civilian affairs, but concentrates on the battle before him. In the same way Timothy must give his full attention to the task before him (3-4). He must have the strict self-discipline of an athlete if he is to gain the heavenly prize (5). He must have the patient hard-working attitude of a farmer if he wants to see worthwhile results from his work (6). If he thinks carefully about these matters, he will understand more fully what is involved in working for God (7).

The example of the risen Christ is a source of encouragement to Christians. Christ endured even to death, but in the end he triumphed (8). No hardship is too great when it is the means of bringing blessing to those whom God has chosen (9-10).

Through their death with Christ, believers have new life. Because God is consistent in his character, he will be faithful to his promises and reward those who are loyal to him. But the same divine consistency of character means that he will show no pleasure to those who deny him (11-13).

2:14-4:5 AN APPROVED WORKER AND FALSE TEACHERS

Teach essentials; avoid quarrels (2:14-26)

Paul repeats the advice of his previous letter that Timothy should not waste time discussing fanciful theories (cf. 1 Tim 1:3-11; 4:6-10). Christian teachers build up their hearers by presenting the truth of God

clearly and honestly, not by allowing the imagination to control their preaching (14-16).

Foolish speculation and self-invented theories were what caused Hymenaeus and Philetus to depart from the faith. They denied the future resurrection of the body, apparently by asserting that the resurrection was the spiritual awakening experienced at conversion (17-18; cf. 1 Tim 1:19-20). But false teaching does not shake the firm foundation of God's truth. God protects those who belong to him, though they on their part must turn away from wrongdoing (19).

The presence of good and bad in the visible church is compared to the presence of many types of articles in a large house. Some articles are precious, but others are of little value and are unfit for honourable use (20). If believers are to be clean and fit for God's use, they must avoid sinful desires and foolish arguments, and seek instead the company of those who strive for the truly Christian virtues (21-23). By wise and patient instruction, the servants of God may be able to release wrongdoers from Satan's grip and lead them into the freedom that comes from knowing God's truth (24-26).

Warning of worse to come (3:1-9)

Timothy may be surprised that such evil should appear within the community of God's people. Paul warns him that worse is to follow. When people try to keep the outward form of religion but reject its inner power, the evil within them soon shows itself in their words and actions. The more they please themselves and reject God, the more wrong they do (3:1-5).

By cunning and deceit, people who call themselves Christians will gain entrance into private homes, where they will soon find people willing to listen to them. Women especially, being on the whole more aware of personal shortcomings than men, will be easily impressed by the words of these false teachers, and just as easily misled. Desiring to know the way to a better life, they will soon become captives of their evil teachers (6-7).

These teachers are like Jannes and Jambres, the Egyptian magicians who opposed Moses. Their words and actions are an imitation of the truth, and people who are easily impressed will readily believe them. But, as with the Egyptian deceivers, their true character will in due course be exposed (8-9; cf. Exod 7:8-12).

Preach the Word constantly (3:10-4:5)

Paul refers to his own experiences to illustrate the truth that the person who whole-heartedly follows

God must expect persecution. Timothy was well aware of this, even before he joined Paul in his work. In his own neighbourhood he had seen Paul suffer because of his devotion to Christ (10-12; cf. Acts 13:50; 14:5-6,19; 16:1-2). This shows in a clearer light the difference between the true teacher and the false. The latter gains a following only by turning away from the truth of God (13).

There is little likelihood that Timothy will be easily led astray by false teaching. From childhood he has been guided by the Scriptures, and his faith in those Scriptures gives him assurance in his salvation (14-15). He must maintain this confidence, knowing that the Scriptures are divinely given and that they are God's means of instructing people in right belief and right living. Those who are well instructed in the Scriptures will always be ready when an opportunity arises to do good (16-17).

Since God's servants must give him an account of their service, they should not miss any opportunity to teach the Scriptures, though they must always speak in a manner suited to the circumstances (4:1-2). Things will get worse as people turn away from those who teach the Scriptures, and listen to those who teach their own theories. This is a further reason why Timothy should endure hardship and not turn aside from the work God has given him (3-5).

4:6-22 PAUL'S LAST FAREWELL

Knowing that he has faithfully carried out the work God entrusted to him, Paul faces execution with confidence. He looks beyond death to the full enjoyment of salvation that will be experienced by all whose love for Jesus is the controlling force in their lives (6-8).

Before he dies, Paul would like Timothy to come and visit him. He is disappointed that Demas has preferred the safety and comfort of ordinary life to the danger and hardship of life with Paul. Others have left Rome because of urgent needs in distant places (9-10). Paul has valuable help and comfort from Luke. He desires also that Mark come to Rome with Timothy, and that on the way they call at Troas to collect the books and warm clothing that Paul had left with Carpus. Tychicus will provide some help in Ephesus while Timothy is absent on his trip to Rome (11-13).

Paul warns Timothy to beware of Alexander, a person who did him much harm, possibly as a prosecution witness (14-15). After his arrest, when the Roman authorities laid charges against him, Paul had stood alone. No one was willing to witness for him in his defence. But God did not fail him, and gave him the opportunity to proclaim the gospel fully to all present. Because God was with him, he was neither attacked nor silenced (16-17). He is therefore confident that God will remain with him through whatever lies ahead and bring him safely into his heavenly kingdom (18).

Among the Christian friends whom Paul greets in Ephesus are Priscilla and Aquila, the Jewish couple who were among the first to take the gospel to Ephesus. They had now returned to Ephesus after their second period of residence in Rome, and were no doubt of help to Timothy in his difficult task (19a; cf. Acts 18:1-4,18-26; Rom 16:3). Another who could help Timothy was Onesiphorus, who was apparently back in Ephesus after his visit to Paul in Rome (19b; cf. 1:16-18). Erastus and Trophimus could not yet help Timothy, as they were temporarily in other parts (20).

Some of the local Christians in Rome, though unable to stay with Paul, visited him occasionally. They join in sending greetings to Timothy. With a final note urging Timothy to come with all speed, Paul signs off for the last time (21-22).

Titus

BACKGROUND

For convenience in arranging the books in our Bible, Paul's two letters to Timothy have been kept together, followed by his letter to Titus. However, Titus was written some time before 2 Timothy, probably about the same time as 1 Timothy and for much the same reason. The background notes to 1 Timothy provide also the background to Titus, and should be read fully as an introduction to the study of Titus.

OUTLINE

1:1-16 THE NEED FOR ELDERS

God appointed Paul to be a preacher of the gospel, but Paul knows that this work involves more than merely the announcement of a message. God has chosen sinners to be his people, and Paul's first aim is to present the gospel in such a way that he can lead these people to eternal life. More than that, Paul wants to go on and instruct them in the Christian truth, so that they might develop practical godliness in their lives. His writing to Titus in Crete is in accordance with this wide-ranging responsibility (1:1-4).

Affairs in the churches of Crete were far from satisfactory, partly because the churches had no elders to provide the right sort of leadership. Paul was aware that time was needed for spiritual ability to show itself, and therefore he had been in no hurry to appoint elders during his brief time in Crete. Instead he left Titus to attend to this matter, while he himself moved on to other countries. He now writes to Titus from one of those countries and repeats instructions he gave earlier in Crete (5).

As in his letter to Timothy, Paul outlines certain minimum requirements for those who hold positions of leadership in the church. Such people must be blameless in conduct, firm in their understanding of Christian truth, and capable at both teaching truth and exposing error (6-9). (For fuller discussion on the character and responsibilities of elders see notes on 1 Timothy 3:1-13.)

Strong and suitably gifted elders are especially necessary because of the craftiness of false teachers, in particular the Judaisers. These false teachers move around private homes, where they soon gain people's interest through their unusual interpretations and clever arguments. In this way they make money, even though the things they teach are nonsense (10-11). They take advantage of what Paul sees as a weakness among the people of Crete in general, namely, their readiness to accept anything that appears to make life easier and more enjoyable, whether such things are true and wholesome or not (12-14).

The Judaisers were apparently insisting on ritual purity, but Paul asserts that if a person is spiritually and morally pure, ritual purity has no meaning. Wrong belief in relation to these things is a serious matter, because belief determines character. Wrong belief corrupts the mind, and the actions that follow are likewise corrupted. The false teachers and their followers do not know God as they claim, but in his sight are unclean and therefore unable to do anything good (15-16).

2:1-3:15 CHRISTIAN BEHAVIOUR AND ITS BASIS

Different people in the church (2:1-10)

The best way to resist wrong teaching is to give positive instruction in Christian doctrine and its moral application. This will produce spiritual growth and right behaviour in all groups alike, regardless of age or social background. Older men, for instance, should set an example of a well balanced Christian life (2:1-2). Older women also should be a good example. If their lives are free of such bad habits as gossip and social climbing, the younger women are more likely to benefit from their advice and learn how to carry out their responsibilities in the home (3-5).

In encouraging the young men to be self-controlled, Titus himself should be an example. By being careful in his behaviour and speech, he can prevent his opponents from finding any cause to criticize either him or his teaching (6-8). Slaves also can demonstrate the value of the Christian teaching by being obedient, cooperative and honest at all times, no matter how their masters treat them (9-10).

God's grace changes lives (2:11-3:11)

People are saved only by God's grace — that loving and merciful attitude of God that freely gives his immeasurable blessings to those who do not deserve them. When people accept the salvation that this grace brings, they learn that their most fitting response is to turn from their former sinful ways and follow the ways of God. They have a desire for holiness, and this desire is increased by their anticipation of Christ's return (11-13). Christ died not merely to save people from the penalty of sin, but to save them from all wickedness. He wants them to be pure in their everyday lives and eager to do good (14).

Titus must teach these truths vigorously. The Christian teacher must make it clear that God places moral responsibilities upon all who have faith in Jesus Christ (15).

Christians should be obedient to the civil authorities, and courteous and helpful to all. They should have a concern for the good of the society in which they live, and do all they can to promote peace and harmony in the community (3:1-2). Their new lives will be different from their former lives, because God in his grace has cleansed the past, made them new people, and poured out his Holy Spirit upon them. They are saved not because of anything they have done, but because of what God has done for them (3-6). God has declared them righteous, so that they are now acceptable to him. They have eternal life now, and can look forward to the full enjoyment of this life when Jesus Christ returns (7).

Titus must teach plainly this gospel which Paul has just summarized. He must emphasize that if people truly believe it, their lives will be changed. Although they are not saved by good works (see v. 5), they must now devote themselves to producing good works (8). Because of this positive approach to the Christian life, they must not waste time arguing about senseless topics. In fact, they should avoid people who specialize in such things. These teachings are not merely unprofitable, they are harmful, because they lead to quarrels and divisions (9-11).

Personal notes (3:12-15)

In his letter to Timothy written at the same time, Paul spoke of his desire to visit Ephesus (see 1 Tim 3:14), but in his letter to Titus he says nothing of any intention to go to Crete. Instead he will send Artemas or Tychicus to relieve Titus, so that Titus can go to meet him in Nicopolis in Achaia, where he intends to spend the winter (12).

Meanwhile certain people might visit Titus on their way through Crete, and Paul asks Titus to give them whatever help he can (13). All God's people should use all the opportunities available to them to help those in need. At the same time they should make sure that they themselves do not become a burden to others. The Christian life should be a useful life (14-15).

Philemon

BACKGROUND

Philemon was a Christian who lived in the city of Colossae and owned the house where the Colossian church met (Philem 1-2; see background notes to Colossians). He had a slave, Onesimus, who had stolen some of Philemon's goods and escaped to Rome in search of a new life of freedom. At that time Paul had just arrived in Rome for the first time, and was being held prisoner while he awaited the Emperor's decision on his case (Acts 28:16,30). In Rome Onesimus happened to meet Paul and was converted (Philem 10).

Onesimus knew that since he was now a Christian, he should correct the wrong he had done and return to his master, but he was understandably fearful. Paul, however, knew Philemon well, for Philemon also had been converted through the work of the apostle (Philem 19). Paul therefore wrote this letter to Philemon, asking him to forgive the runaway slave and receive him back as a brother in Christ. Not only was Philemon to welcome Onesimus back personally, but the church was to welcome him as a new and useful addition to its fellowship (Philem 17; Col 4:9).

It seems that the letters to Philemon and to the Colossian church were sent at the same time (cf. Col 4:10,12,14; Philem 23-24). With them Paul also sent his letter to the Ephesians (cf. Eph 6:21-22; Col 4:7-9).

CONTENTS OF THE LETTER

Paul greets Philemon, his wife Apphia, and the other believers who meet in their home. He also greets Archippus, who was possibly their son and who was serving God in that region (1-3; cf. Col 4:17). Paul rejoices because of what he has heard (probably from Epaphras and Onesimus; cf. Col 1:7-8; 4:9,12) of Philemon's strong faith in God and sincere love for God's people. This faith and love have been a source of strength and encouragement to the church in Colossae. Paul prays that Philemon will continue to share these blessings with others and so further build up the church (4-7).

Knowing Philemon's caring nature, Paul does not have to use his apostolic authority to command Philemon in any way. He knows he can depend on Philemon's generous spirit to forgive Onesimus and receive him back (8-9). Onesimus had once been a useless slave, but now his whole life has been changed. He has so lovingly helped Paul in prison that he has become like a son to Paul (10-11).

Although Paul would like to keep Onesimus with him, he feels that the right thing to do is to send him back to his original master, Philemon. No doubt Philemon would be happy to allow Onesimus to stay in Rome where he could continue to look after Paul, but that is a matter for Philemon to decide, not Paul. Whatever Philemon does, Paul wants him to do it willingly, not because Paul has forced him (12-14).

Perhaps it was God's will that Onesimus left Philemon briefly so that he might be saved eternally. No longer will he be a lazy and uncooperative slave, but a willing and helpful brother in Christ. Philemon should therefore treat him as a brother (15-16).

If Onesimus stole or damaged anything in making his escape, Paul will gladly pay the cost on Onesimus' behalf. However, Philemon should not forget the debt that he himself owes Paul, even his eternal salvation. But Paul's gladness will be much greater if Philemon freely forgives everything (17-20). Paul is confident that Philemon will act with generosity – maybe do even more than Paul suggests and give complete freedom to the slave (21).

Paul hopes to be released soon and pay a visit to Colossae. In the meantime, he and those with him send greetings to Philemon personally, in addition to the greetings they had sent to the whole church in the Colossian letter (22-25; cf. Col 4:10-14).

Hebrews

BACKGROUND

Since the title of this letter, 'To the Hebrews', is not part of the original writing, the Bible contains no direct statement to indicate to whom the letter was written. The title reflects an early and widely held belief that it was written to a group of Hebrew (i.e. Jewish) Christians. The contents of the letter support this belief.

Effects of persecution

During the reign of Nero (AD 54-68), persecution of Christians increased considerably. This caused some Jewish Christians to wonder if they had done right in giving up their Jewish religion and becoming Christians. They had believed, as Jesus and his followers taught, that the Jewish religion no longer served God's purposes, that the priesthood and the sacrifices would come to an end, and that the temple in Jerusalem would be destroyed. Yet, thirty years after Jesus' death and resurrection, the temple was still standing and the Jewish religion was still functioning.

With the increasing persecution, some of the Jewish Christians became discouraged. They began to doubt whether Christianity really was God's new and victorious way to the eternal kingdom. In their view, Judaism appeared to be as firm as ever, whereas Christianity appeared to be heading for disaster. Some had stopped attending Christian meetings and even given up their Christian faith and gone back to Judaism (Heb 10:25-31). The letter to the Hebrews was written to reassure the Jewish believers and prevent them from slipping back to their former religious practices (Heb 2:1-3).

The writer and his readers

Although the writer of this letter has not recorded his name, he was probably a well known Christian preacher of the time. Much of the letter is in the form of a sermon (Heb 13:22), and the beliefs that form its basis are the same as those taught by Stephen, Peter, Paul, John and other prominent preachers of the apostolic era. The writer was a Jew (Heb 1:1), though he wrote polished Greek and took his Old Testament quotations from the Greek version known as the Septuagint. Both he and his

readers heard the gospel from those who had personally heard Jesus teach (Heb 2:3).

The Jewish Christians who received this letter seem to have been a group within a larger church. There is little to indicate where their church was located, and suggestions vary from Jerusalem to Rome. They apparently knew Timothy, and may also have known the group of Italian Christians who sent them greetings by means of this letter (Heb 13:23-24). The writer hoped that he and Timothy would visit them soon (Heb 13:19,23).

In the meantime the writer wanted to reassure these discouraged Jewish believers that Jesus Christ was the true fulfilment of the Jewish religion. The Old Testament finds its completion in him. He is far above all prophets, angels, leaders and priests, and his sacrifice has done what all the Israelite sacrifices could never do. Nothing of human initiative or effort can add to God's way of salvation, for what Christ has done is final (Heb 10:12-13).

OLD TESTAMENT RELIGIOUS PRACTICES

Present-day readers sometimes find the book of Hebrews difficult to understand, because the writer refers repeatedly to the regulations and ceremonies of the ancient Israelite religion. His readers were familiar with what he was talking about, but readers today will find it helpful to refresh their knowledge of the Israelite religious system before starting to read Hebrews.

The old covenant

A covenant was an agreement between two people that carried with it obligations, and possibly benefits or penalties, depending on whether a person kept or broke it. But covenants between God and people differed from everyday covenants in that they were not agreements between equals. God was always the giver and people the receivers. Mere human beings could never negotiate an agreement with the almighty God or place conditions upon him. God's promises originated in his sovereign grace, and the people of his creation could do nothing but accept his favour and submit to his directions (Gen 15:18; 17:7-9).

These features are clearly seen in the covenant ceremony at Mount Sinai when the nation Israel formally became God's people. God, in his grace, had chosen Israel to belong to him, even though Israel had done nothing to deserve such favour. But if the people were to enjoy the blessings of the covenant relationship, they needed to do God's will. The people readily acknowledged this and promised to keep the law that God gave them through Moses. They swore that they would keep their part of the covenant (Exod 24:3,8; cf. 6:7; 19:4-6; Lev 26:3-13).

On account of this connection between the covenant and the law, people commonly speak of 'the old covenant' as a general term for the law of Moses. In some cases the expression is used to refer to Israel's entire religious system.

Though given by God, this old covenant was never intended to be permanent. Its purpose was to prepare the way for Jesus Christ (Heb 8:6-9,13). The writer of Hebrews wants to show that once Christ came, the old covenant was of no further use. His death on the cross did what all Israel's laws and ceremonies could not do. It brought cleansing from sin and the right to enter God's presence. Christ's death established a new covenant, one that is perfect and lasts for ever (Heb 9:15; 13:20).

Salvation under the old covenant

If the old covenant could not bring cleansing, how were people under that covenant saved? The answer is that they were saved by God's grace through their faith in him, which is the only way sinners have ever been saved. No one can be saved by keeping the law (Rom 3:20,27-28; Eph 2:8-9). Abraham lived before the old covenant was established, whereas David lived under the old covenant, but both were saved in the same way, by faith (Rom 4:1-16; Gal 3:17-18).

The old covenant was never intended to be a way of salvation. The law of Moses was not a means by which people could earn forgiveness. However, it helped them see their sin and God's holiness, and so encouraged them to turn in faith to God and ask for mercy (Rom 3:19; 5:20; Gal 3:19). When Christ came, he did what the law could not do, for by paying sin's penalty he made forgiveness possible for the repentant (Rom 8:3-4; Gal 3:23-25).

Although God saved people freely by his grace, the ceremonies of the law helped people see how it was possible for him to do so. They were a further stage in the revelation of God's purposes. God, before whom all things are eternally present, saw that those purposes would be fulfilled in Christ. It was on the basis of Christ's death that God was able to put sinners right with himself, even those who lived in Old Testament times (Rom 3:25-26; Heb 9:15).

The tabernacle

God's appointed place for the performance of Israel's religious duties was the tabernacle, or tent of meeting. The structure was of simple design, so that it could be easily put together, taken apart and transported. It was a mobile sanctuary, carried by the migrating Israelites on their journey from Mount Sinai to Canaan. Simply described, it consisted of a wooden box-like frame covered with a cloth and protected from the weather by a tent that covered the whole. All that people saw from the outside was a tent (Exod 26:1-30).

The wooden-framed structure under the tent had two rooms. The front room, which was entered through a curtain, was called the Holy Place and contained three pieces of furniture – a seven-headed lampstand, a table of sacred bread, and an altar for burning incense (Exod 25:23-40; 26:36-37; 30:1-10). A second curtain separated the Holy Place from the smaller rear room, which was known as the Most Holy Place or Holy of Holies. This room was the symbolic dwelling place of God. It contained the ark of the covenant (or covenant box), whose richly ornamented lid was the symbolic throne of God, known as the mercy seat (or grace throne) (Exod 25:10-22; 26:31-35).

Surrounding this tabernacle-tent was a rectangular court, whose perimeter was marked by a tall fence. In this court was an altar on which the priests offered all the animal and food sacrifices, and a laver (or large basin) in which the priests washed (Exod 27:1-19; 30:17-21). Outside the court were the tents of the Israelites, pitched in an orderly arrangement on the four sides, so that the tabernacle was in the centre of the camp (Num 2:1-34).

Priests and Levites

One tribe of Israel, the tribe of Levi, was responsible for the erection, maintenance and transport of the tabernacle. One man in this tribe, Aaron, the older brother of Moses, was Israel's first high priest, and his sons were the priests who assisted him (Exod 28:1; Num 8:14-19). The Old Testament priesthood is therefore sometimes called the Aaronic priesthood, sometimes the Levitical priesthood. Only the descendants of Aaron could be priests, and only members of the tribe of Levi could assist in the service and maintenance of the tabernacle (Exod 29:9; Num 3:1-10).

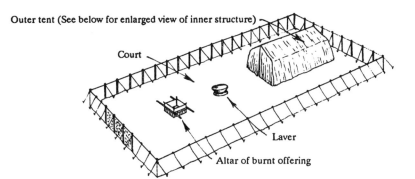

ABOVE: THE TABERNACLE AND ITS COURT

BELOW: ENLARGED CUTAWAY OF INNER STRUCTURE

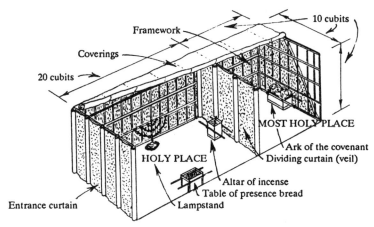

THE TABERNACLE

Priests were responsible to teach the law and to see that the Israelite people maintained God's standards of morality, holiness, cleanliness and justice (Lev 10:10-11; Deut 17:8-9; 24:8; 33:10). They offered sacrifices on behalf of those who brought them, and therefore were mediators between the people and God (Lev 1:4-9; 6:25-26). They also carried out daily functions in the tabernacle, such as tending the lamps and offering incense (Exod 27:20-21; 30:7-8).

Only priests could enter the Holy Place (Num 18:1-7; Heb 9:6), and only the high priest could enter the Most Holy Place. Even then he could do so only once a year, on the Day of Atonement. On that day he sprinkled the blood of the sacrificial animal on the mercy seat and approached God on behalf of the people to ask his mercy and forgiveness for their sins (Lev 16:2-3,11-15; Heb 9:7).

Sacrifices

People offered sacrifices (or offerings) to God as expressions of their devotion to him. Different sacrifices were appointed for different purposes, but all contained some element of atonement; that is, some part of the ritual symbolically dealt with sin's penalty so that the offerer could be restored to a right relationship with God.

In the sacrifice of an animal, for example, the worshipper may have presented it as a personal substitute, and, on the basis of the animal's death, asked God's forgiveness. The person knew that because death was the penalty for sin, there could be no forgiveness of sin apart from death. The sacrifice was the God-given means of expressing faith (Lev 17:11).

The sacrificial animal had to be healthy and free from defects. This was to symbolize perfection, as if the animal was not under condemnation and so was fit to be the substitute for the sinner (Lev 1:3,10). Forgiveness through blood meant, in other words, forgiveness through the death of a guiltless substitute (Heb 9:22).

Yet animal sacrifices could not take away sins (Heb 10:4). They were a temporary arrangement for Old Testament times that gave people a way to demonstrate their repentance, faith and obedience. They also taught people what their atonement involved. But whether people knew it or not, the sacrifice of Christ was the means by which God forgave them when they turned to him in faith (Rom 3:21-26).

The writer of Hebrews has a special concern for Jewish Christians who at one time had participated in the various rituals of Israel's religious system. He wants to impress upon them that although Israel's religious system prepared the way for Christ, it could never save guilty sinners. Jesus Christ is the only way of salvation.

OUTLINE

1:1-2:18 SALVATION THROUGH CHRIST

God speaks through his Son (1:1-4)

Israel prepared the way, but Jesus Christ brings God's plan of salvation to its fulfilment. In Old Testament times God spoke to people through Israelite prophets, but now he speaks more directly, for he speaks through his Son. In addition, his revelation is much clearer, for Jesus Christ is the exact expression of the divine nature. All things were created by him, are controlled by him, and one day will return to him as his rightful possession (1:1-3a).

Besides revealing God to needy sinners, Jesus brings needy sinners to God, by providing them with cleansing from sin through his death on the cross. Because of who Jesus is and what he has done, God has given him a position far above all things, angels included (3b-4).

Christ greater than angels (1:5-14)

According to Jewish beliefs, angels were beings of a high order who fulfilled an important role in the giving of God's law to Israel (Acts 7:53; Gal 3:19). The writer therefore shows from the Old Testament (which the Jews believed to be the Word of God) that Jesus Christ is greater than angels. His birth into the world as a man does not mean that he is inferior to angels. On the contrary, angels worship him, for he is God, inseparably united with his Father (5-6).

Angels are merely servants, and carry out God's commands through wind and fire. Christ is King, and is exalted by God to the highest place. He lived a life of practical righteousness, and God has given him an eternal kingdom (7-9). In contrast to created things, Christ is himself the Creator. Created things change and eventually pass away; Christ never changes and lives eternally (10-12). He was victorious in his work on earth and now awaits the final victory over all things. Angels, by contrast, are simply servants sent by God to help those who share in the victory Christ has won (13-14).

Warning against rejecting Christ (2:1-4)

God's law was announced to Moses by angels, but his salvation was made known to all humankind by his own Son. This is the more reason why people should not turn away from the gospel, but believe it (2:1-3a). Those who saw and heard Jesus Christ bore testimony to the divine origin of the gospel. Their testimony was confirmed by the miracles and other evidences of the Holy Spirit's power that accompanied the early apostolic preaching (3b-4; cf. Acts 2:43; Gal 3:5).

Christ's humanity and suffering (2:5-18)

Jews considered that human beings were inferior to angels. They therefore wondered how Jesus Christ could be superior to angels when in fact he was a man.

The writer points out that this human status of inferiority to angels is only temporary. God's original purpose was that human beings should rule over all things, but because of sin they lost this authority and are themselves in need of salvation (5-8). Jesus Christ, in order to save them, took their position of being temporarily lower than angels, so that he might accept sin's penalty on their behalf. He died in shame on a cross, but God exalted him to the highest place in heaven (9).

When Adam sinned, humankind lost its original God-given glory and suffered as a result. Jesus Christ therefore had to join in that suffering and bear it fully if he was to save a fallen race from the results of sin. Having suffered, Christ then entered his glory. Because he identified himself with the human race, those who now identify themselves with him have their sins removed and share his glory. Consequently, they can attain the position God originally intended for those he created in his image (10).

Three Old Testament quotations emphasize the union that exists between Christ and the men and women he has saved. He calls them his brothers and sisters, he trusts in God as they do, and he and these his children are God's new people (11-13).

Christ became a human being to save human beings, and he did so by living with them and dying for them. His death was a victory, not a defeat, for by it he set people free from the power of Satan. Those whom he saves are now free from the fear and bondage that sin brings (14-15). The reason Christ descended to a status lower than angels was that the people he wanted to save were lower than angels (16). By sharing their experiences of human life, he could be their representative in taking away sin. He could also be their helper in gaining victory over life's temptations (17-18).

3:1-5:10 GOD'S TRUE PEOPLE

Christ greater than Moses (3:1-6)

Moses was God's special 'apostle' to Israel, the chosen representative he sent to his people. Aaron was God's appointed high priest, the person who approached God on the people's behalf. Christ is greater than both (3:1). Christ was faithful in his work as Moses was in his. But Christ is far superior. Moses was but a servant in the house of God (i.e. the people of God), whereas Christ built the house and is head over it. That house (i.e. the people of God) is now the Christian church. It consists of all who hold firmly to Jesus Christ (2-6).

Warning against unbelief (3:7-4:13)

The writer warns his disheartened Jewish readers with some reminders from Israel's experiences in the wilderness (see Exod 17:1-7; Num 20:1-13; Ps 95:7-11). Those experiences show that people who appear to be God's people may be so unbelieving, bitter and complaining, that they cannot enjoy the inheritance God has promised (7-11). They should resist the tendency to unbelief and stubbornness, by encouraging one another to maintain their faith with

confidence to the end (12-15). They should bear in mind that many who shared in the deliverance from Egypt were refused entrance into the promised land because of their unbelief (16-19).

God's will was that the people of Israel, having been freed from bondage in Egypt, should find rest in Canaan, the land God promised them. In the same way God wants people everywhere to be freed from the bondage of sin and find rest in Jesus Christ. But, as with Israel, unbelief will exclude them from this promised rest (4:1-2). God's rest has been available from the time he created the world as a human dwelling place, but because of sin, people have not found this rest. It becomes theirs only through faith (3-5).

The Israelites who were disobedient under Moses did not reach the land or find the rest that God promised them. The Israelites who entered Canaan under Joshua were those of the generation that followed. However, long after the time of Joshua, David repeated God's promise of rest. This indicates that occupation of Canaan was not the complete fulfilment of God's promise (6-8; see Ps 95:7-8). The real rest that God promises is salvation through faith. Just as God rested after his work of creation, so people will find true rest when they stop working to try to earn salvation and trust in what Christ has done for them (9-10; cf. Matt 11:28).

People must make every effort to remove unbelief and all other hindrances to the enjoyment of God's rest. To help them in this, God has given them the Scriptures. His living Word penetrates into the heart, separates the merely natural from the truly spiritual, and exposes people as they really are before God (11-13).

A high priest for the faithful (4:14-5:10)

Because people were in danger of denying their Christian faith and going back to Judaism, they are reminded that Christ's priesthood is incomparably superior to Aaron's. Christ needs no tabernacle or temple, for he has passed through the heavens and into the presence of God. Through him, believers also may enter this presence, and ask God's help during their temptations. They can depend upon Christ, because being man he can sympathize with them, and being God he can give them super-human aid (14-16).

The Israelite high priest, since he acted on behalf of the people, needed to have a sympathetic nature and an awareness at all times that he too was a sinner who needed God's forgiveness. His high priesthood was an office to which he was appointed, not one he chose for himself (5:1-4). All this was true of Christ, except that he, having no sin, did not offer sacrifices for his own cleansing (see 7:26-28). He was God's Son, appointed by God to an eternal priesthood (5-6; for the priesthood of Melchizedek see 7:1-28).

Jesus Christ participated in the normal experiences of earthly life. In so doing he learnt the full meaning of obedience to his Father's will, even though it led to suffering and death (7-8; cf. Matt 26:36-46). Having fulfilled in practice God's ideal of human perfection, he is completely qualified to carry out his God-given work of saving and helping those who submit to him (9-10).

5:11-6:20 CHRISTIAN GROWTH AND PERSEVERANCE

Warning to the unstable (5:11-6:8)

The writer would like to say more about Christ's priesthood, but he feels his readers will not understand. Instead of being mature Christians they are spiritual babes, in spite of having received so much instruction in the Scriptures that by now they should be teachers themselves (11-12). They have not made the effort to study and understand the Word, and therefore are not able to apply its teachings to life's problems. Like children who have to be fed on milk, they have no ability to decide for themselves, but can only follow the lead of others. Mature Christians, by contrast, are like adults who can eat any food. They have trained themselves to discern between what is good and what is not (13-14).

Many Jews were of the childish kind just described. They said they were Christians, but they had made no progress. They seem to have merely added the name of Christianity to their former Jewish beliefs. Christianity, like Judaism, includes belief in sin, repentance, faith, cleansing, resurrection and final judgment, but Christianity involves more than mere acceptance of certain truths. If people do not progress beyond these basic beliefs, their Christian profession may soon be in danger. When persecution makes it uncomfortable for them to be known as Christians, they might give in to the temptation to go back to Judaism without changing their beliefs (6:1-3).

Christianity is not another name for Judaism. It completely replaces it, because Christ's death on the cross has made Judaism dead and useless. If people have joined in the life of the church and tasted the blessings that come through Christ's death, then deliberately renounce Christ, nothing is left for them but judgment. They have disowned and shamed

Christ by an action similar to that of the people who crucified him (4-6).

Just as all the earth receives rain, so all who meet in the church receive God's blessings. But as some soil later proves to be bad, so some in the church later prove to be without life. Those with true faith prove it by their perseverance (7-8).

Encouragement to sincere believers (6:9-20)

Although some who received this letter needed such solemn warnings, others had clearly shown by their changed lives that they were genuine Christians. The writer has no doubts about such people (9-10). He encourages them to keep up the good work. They are not to lose heart or become lazy, but persevere to the end (11-12).

Warnings of judgment need not unsettle the believers concerning their assurance of salvation. When God promises salvation he keeps his word. Moreover, he confirms his promise with his oath (or vow). Abraham's confidence in God gave him patient endurance so that he received what God promised (13-15). In legal affairs people swear oaths to confirm their statements. In his grace God does the same. He gives people double assurance of salvation by giving his promise and then adding his oath (16-18).

The security of believers is based on the work of Jesus Christ. That work is their guarantee that God will never cast them out. The Levitical high priest entered God's presence as the people's representative when he went through the curtain into the Most Holy Place. Jesus Christ, the great high priest, enters God's presence as the Christians' representative. More than that, he is their forerunner. He is the guarantee that one day they too will be permanently in God's presence (19-20).

7:1-10:18 CHRIST'S PRIESTHOOD AND SACRIFICE

The priesthood of Melchizedek (7:1-10)

Jesus Christ's high priesthood is far superior to Aaron's. Christ belongs to the priestly order of Melchizedek, a priesthood that existed before, and is far higher than, that of Aaron. (For the background concerning Melchizedek see Genesis 14:17-24 and Psalm 110:4.) Melchizedek was both a priest and a king, a combination not allowed in the Aaronic priesthood. In the Levitical order, people kept strict records of ancestry, birth and death, to confirm a person's right to be a priest (cf. Ezra 2:62-63; Neh 7:63-65), but no such records exist for Melchizedek. They are not necessary, because his priesthood is not limited by time or Levitical laws. This is clearly seen in Abraham's acknowledgment of Melchizedek as the representative of the Most High God long before the Levitical law was given. In all these things the priesthood of Melchizedek foreshadowed that of Christ (7:1-3).

Abraham was a great man, being the father of all Israel, but Melchizedek was greater, for he blessed Abraham. The one who blesses must be greater than the one blessed. Abraham acknowledged Melchizedek's superiority by giving him a tithe (one tenth) of his goods. Under the Levitical law ordinary Israelites paid tithes to the Levites, their religious representatives. But the Levites, being in Abraham (so to speak), paid tithes to Melchizedek. In this they acknowledged the superiority of his priesthood to theirs (4-10).

Christ, a priest like Melchizedek (7:11-28)

The necessity for a new priesthood under Christ shows that the Levitical priesthood (and with it the law of Moses) failed to bring perfection. Therefore, the new priest belongs not to Aaron's order but to Melchizedek's (11-12). Christ could not be a priest in the Levitical order, because he was not from the tribe of Levi. He was from Judah, a tribe that had no part in priestly affairs (13-14).

Laws concerning physical birth and age determined who could be Levitical priests and how long they could serve. The priesthood of Christ does not depend on human ancestry, nor, because of his indestructible life, can it be brought to an end (15-17). Christ has done what the Levitical system could not do. He has brought perfection and given people access to God's presence (18-19).

The Levitical priesthood lacked permanence and certainty, but not so Christ's priesthood. It is guaranteed by the oath of God (20-22). Christ is not like the Levitical priests, who needed others to take their place when they died. He lives on as a priest for ever, bringing people to God and giving them God's saving help (23-25). Because of the purity of his character, life and work, Christ is worthy of the place of highest honour. Levitical priests could not, with all the sacrifices they offered, make others perfect, because they themselves were sinners. Christ, God's sinless Son and great high priest, makes people perfect for ever by one sacrifice, the sacrifice of himself (26-28).

A new priest and a new covenant (8:1-13)

Only once a year could the Levitical high priest enter God's symbolic dwelling place (the Most Holy Place), but Christ the great high priest lives in the actual presence of God for ever (8:1-2). Levitical priests offered animal sacrifices, but Christ offered himself. He did not make this offering as a Levitical priest (for he was not of the family of Aaron), but the work of the Levitical priests pictured his work. The sacrifices they offered were a picture of Christ's sacrifice of himself (3-5).

The old priesthood failed along with the old covenant. Therefore, a new and greater priesthood is necessary for a new and greater covenant. The new priesthood is Christ's (6-7).

God never intended the old covenant to be permanent. It was given for Israel's benefit, but it failed to produce the promised blessings, because the people failed to obey its commandments. The new covenant cannot fail, because it depends not on people's obedience to a set of laws, but on God's grace in changing people from within. He gives them inner spiritual life that makes them loyal to him and enables them to do his will (8-10). Priests are no longer necessary to mediate between people and God, because all believers know God personally. They have direct fellowship with him, because he has taken away their sins (11-12).

Jeremiah made these statements about the new covenant more than six hundred years before the time of Christ (see Jer 31:31-34). This demonstrates that even in Old Testament times God showed that the old covenant was only temporary (13).

Priestly work under the old covenant (9:1-10)

Before discussing Christ's priestly work further, the writer describes the tabernacle and its furniture (see introductory notes). The golden altar of incense, though kept in the Holy Place, was connected with the ark of the covenant in the ritual of the Day of Atonement (see Exod 30:6; Lev 16:12-14,18-19). This may be why the writer mentions it as belonging to the Most Holy Place. He also mentions the three objects kept in the ark and the glorious creatures of beaten gold who spread their wings over the mercy seat (9:1-5).

Only priests could go into the Holy Place, and only the high priest into the Most Holy Place. He did this only once a year, on the Day of Atonement, when he sprinkled the blood of the sacrificial animal and asked forgiveness for himself and the people. This ritual, arranged by God, showed that under the old covenant people could not enter freely into God's presence (6-8).

Clearly, the sacrifices did not cleanse the worshippers of sin, because they were still kept at a distance from God. The sacrifices were a temporary arrangement for the era before Christ. They brought ceremonial cleansing, but not actual cleansing. Now that Christ has come and cleansed sin fully, they are of no more use (9-10).

Priestly work under the new covenant (9:11-14)

When the Jewish high priest entered the Most Holy Place, God's symbolic presence, he took the blood of the sacrificial animal with him. This was a sign that an innocent substitute had died for the guilty sinner, so that the barrier to God's presence through sin might be removed. Jesus Christ, the great high priest, offered himself as the sacrifice, and through his blood (i.e. by means of his sacrificial death) entered the presence of God, obtained eternal salvation from sin, and cleansed the sinner's guilty conscience. Ceremonial cleansing through animal sacrifices is replaced by actual cleansing through Christ's sacrifice (11-14).

Sacrifice under the old covenant (9:15-22)

Under the old covenant, repentant sinners offered sacrifices for their sins, but the sacrifices themselves could not bring forgiveness. They brought no more than ceremonial cleansing. The actual cleansing of those sins depended on the sacrifice of Christ. Whether sins were committed before the time of Christ or after, the death of Christ is the basis on which God forgives them. Through Christ, God has made a new covenant, and the inheritance he promises under this covenant is one of total and eternal forgiveness (15).

An inheritance can be received only after the death of the person who promised it. So also people can receive forgiveness of sins only through the death of Christ (16-17). Events at the making of the old covenant point to the necessity of Christ's death for the making of the new covenant. The old covenant was established with sacrifices, though the ritual of killing animals and sprinkling blood was more than just a dramatic way of swearing to keep the covenant. It signified also the removal of past sin, so that Israel entered the covenant cleansed (18-21; cf. Exod 24:3,6-8). The principle of cleansing through sacrifice was basic to the old covenant (22).

Sacrifice under the new covenant (9:23-10:18)

Levitical sacrifices were part of a material order and brought symbolic cleansing. Christ's death is concerned with the spiritual order and brings actual cleansing (23). The Levitical high priest entered the symbolic presence of God with the blood of a sacrificial animal, a ceremony that had to be repeated yearly. Christ entered God's *real* presence on account of his *own* blood, and he did so only *once*. His death is sufficient to remove completely the sins of the whole world, past, present and future (24-26).

People die once and face judgment. Christ died once and gained eternal salvation for those who trust in him. By his death believers are forgiven; their sins are taken away. They will enjoy the fulness of their salvation when Christ reappears, coming out of the heavenly tabernacle to be with them for ever (27-28).

The repeated offering of the Levitical sacrifices showed that they were unable to bring complete cleansing. They indicated that there must have been something better yet to come (10:1-4). God's plan was not that animal sacrifices be offered for ever, but that they prepare the way for Jesus Christ. As the man who came from God, Jesus spent his life doing God's will, even though it led him to offer that life in sacrifice. His death puts an end to all the old sacrifices, for it cleanses people from sin once and for all (5-10).

Israelite priests stood offering sacrifices day after day. Their work was never finished, because animal sacrifices could not remove sin. The great high priest offered one sacrifice (himself), took away sin for ever, then sat down in God's presence. His work of salvation is complete, and is available for those who want it. But there remains his work of judgment on those who refuse it (11-14). Under the new covenant a complete and permanent spiritual work is done in the lives of God's people. There is no need for further sacrificial offerings. God's work through Christ removes all sin and gives believers new life in the Spirit (15-18).

10:19-12:29 THE ENDURANCE OF GENUINE FAITH

The new covenant brings confidence (10:19-25)

Access to God's presence was limited under the old covenant. Only the high priest could pass through the curtain that closed the entrance to the Most Holy Place, and then only at certain times and under strict conditions. But now that Christ, by his death, has atoned for sin and opened the way to God, all God's people are able to come before him. They can do so confidently, yet with the reverence and purity that the old ceremonies symbolized (19-22). To fight against the tendency to lose heart, they must trust firmly in God's promises, help each other in everyday affairs, and meet regularly to encourage each other in the faith (23-25).

Warning against turning back (10:26-39)

Those who are tempted to go back to Judaism are reminded that apart from Christ's work there is no way of salvation. If they reject him, they can expect only judgment (26-27). Even under the old covenant rebellion met with death. How much worse will be the punishment of those who have experienced the grace of God through Christ, yet deliberately reject and disown it (28-31).

The writer encourages his readers not to forsake Christ, by reminding them of what they have suffered for his sake. They have persevered through insults, violence, imprisonments and robberies, because of their confidence of a lasting reward (32-35). Endurance is essential, since there must always be some waiting time before a promise can be fulfilled. For Christians the promised reward will be at Christ's return, when he judges between those who persevere in faith and those who turn back (36-39).

Examples of true faith (11:1-22)

In the previous chapter the writer asserted that people must join faith to perseverance if they are to enjoy the thing hoped for. He now supports this statement with illustrations from the Old Testament. If people have faith, it means they believe that things hoped for according to God's promises will be achieved and that unseen powers of God are real. Those with faith look beyond what they see. They know that they cannot explain the existence of the world solely by reasoning from the things that can be seen (11:1-3).

Abel's sacrifice, Enoch's daily life and Noah's obedience all pleased God because they arose out of faith. These men trusted in the unseen God and in his faithfulness to those who wholeheartedly sought him. God on his part rewarded them, but rejected those who showed no faith (4-7; cf. Gen 4:2-7; 5:21-24; 6:8-14).

Abraham's faith caused him to set out for a promised, yet unknown, earthly inheritance. More than that, it caused him to remain patient when he did not experience the fulfilment of the promise in his lifetime. By faith he looked beyond to a higher fulfilment of the promise (8-10; cf. Gen 12:1-5). His wife Sarah shared his faith. They trusted God's promise that they would have a son and through him a multitude of descendants, even though they were both past the age when they might normally expect to have children (11-12; cf. Gen 15:5; 18:11-13). Abraham and his family did not give up and go back to Abraham's home in Mesopotamia as soon as

difficulties arose. They looked beyond death for a greater fulfilment than they could experience in their earthly lives (13-16; cf. Gen 23:4).

When God told Abraham to offer up his son Isaac, Abraham's faith was tested, because Isaac was the person through whom God promised to give Abraham a multitude of descendants. Abraham had faith to obey, believing that God could bring Isaac back to life. In his willingness to go ahead with the sacrifice, Abraham did, in effect, offer up Isaac, but God intervened and Abraham received his son back, so to speak, from death (17-19; cf. Gen 22:1-18).

Isaac, Jacob and Joseph were all certain that the promise to Abraham would be fulfilled. This was why Joseph left instructions about his burial. He knew he would die in Egypt, but he instructed that his bones be buried in Canaan. In this way he declared his faith that one day his people would inherit the land God promised them (20-22; cf. Gen 28:1-4; 47:29-31; 49:1; 50:24-25).

More examples of true faith (11:23-40)

Moses' parents had faith to believe that God had chosen their child for a great purpose. Acting on this faith, they risked their own lives to preserve the life of the child (23; cf. Exod 1:22; 2:1-2). As Moses grew to adulthood, he too exercised faith, in spite of the sacrifice, hardship and danger that it brought. He endured because he was confident of the future reward and he trusted in the unseen God (24-27; cf. Exod 2:10-15).

Through faith the Israelites were protected at the time of the Passover judgment and delivered from the Egyptian army (28-29; cf. Exod 12:1-13; 14:21-31). Through faith they entered the promised land and conquered Jericho. Likewise it was through faith that Rahab was saved when others in Jericho were killed (30-31; cf. Josh 2:1-14; 6:15-25).

The writer finds that there are more examples of victorious and enduring faith than he can list. He selects certain people and achievements from the books of Judges, Samuel, Kings and Daniel to remind his readers of the triumphs of faith (32-34). People suffered terrible tragedies, extreme hardships and cruel tortures, but they held on in faith. They refused to give in to their persecutors or to forsake their trust in God (35-38).

These people could not receive the promised inheritance until Christ came. By his death he made complete salvation possible, so that God can accept believers as perfect in him. They will enjoy the fulfilment of their faith when believers of all eras are gathered together through Christ, and God reigns in love over all (39-40).

Discipline in the Christian life (12:1-11)

The examples of true faith that the writer has just given should encourage the Jewish Christians to face their difficulties with similar perseverance. They must remove the sin that hinders, and strengthen themselves to withstand defeat. They will be encouraged to endure as they consider the sufferings that Jesus endured and the heavenly reward that he now enjoys (12:1-2).

Whatever these Christians may have to endure, their sufferings are small when compared with those of Jesus Christ. At least their faith has not yet cost them their lives (3-4). God uses trials and difficulties to train, and sometimes chastise, his children, but this is no reason for them to become discouraged. Such discipline is proof of his love, for he loves them as a father loves a child. One who is not experiencing God's discipline is not a child of his at all (5-8).

Children submit to their parents' discipline. In the same way Christians should submit to their heavenly Father's discipline. His purpose is to use their trials to make them into the sorts of people that he, in his superior wisdom, wants them to be (9-10). Such experiences may be unpleasant at the time, but those who have learnt a right attitude towards their troubles will benefit in an increasingly fruitful Christian life (11).

Endurance without bitterness (12:12-17)

Christians must not allow life's trials to discourage them, but meet their difficulties with boldness and confidence (12-13). One way to help prevent people from turning away from Christ is to develop holiness among believers and to deal with those who show signs of bitterness. Such people can quickly have a bad influence on others (14-15). The story of Esau illustrates the hopelessness of the person who deliberately rejects God's promised inheritance for the sake of some temporary gain (16-17).

God's mercy and God's judgment (12:18-29)

There is no similarity between the experience of Israelite people under the old covenant and that of Christians under the new. Events that accompanied the giving of the law at Mount Sinai show that people saw the old covenant as something terrifying (18-21; cf. Exod 19:12-13; 20:18-19). By contrast, Christians see the new covenant as something joyful. They are not kept at a distance from God as the Israelites were at Mount Sinai, but come right into

his unseen heavenly presence. They are members of the community of God's people, where they are united with the faithful of all ages (22-23).

Because of Christ's blood, believers do not fear judgment. The death of Abel called for judgment on the murderer, but the death of Christ brings forgiveness for the sinner (24; cf. Gen 4:10).

The same God who spoke to Israel from Mount Sinai now speaks to all people from heaven. Those who refuse to listen to him will be punished as Israel was. God's voice shook the earth at Mount Sinai; one day he will shake the earth again, not literally but figuratively, for he will judge the whole creation (25-26). After this judgment, only that which is eternal will remain; the rest will pass away (27). In view of this fiery judgment from the holy God, Christians should be the more thankful that they belong to his heavenly kingdom, and respond with reverent worship (28-29).

13:1-25 MISCELLANEOUS INSTRUCTIONS

Hospitality, marriage and wealth (13:1-6)

Before closing his letter, the writer gives instruction on a variety of matters that need attention. First, Christians should act with love, not only towards those within their church, but also towards strangers. Some of these visitors may be messengers God has sent to them (cf. Gen 18:1-8; 19:1-3). They should also help fellow Christians who are imprisoned or in some other way suffering ill-treatment (13:1-3).

Second, Christians must remember that sexual relations are honourable only between husband and wife. God will deal severely with those who behave otherwise (4). Third, the desire to be wealthy shows a lack of faith, for God has promised to help and provide for his children. He will not leave them to face life alone (5-6).

Sacrifices, Jewish and Christian (13:7-16)

Some of the Jewish members of the church had an additional misunderstanding concerning the offering of animal sacrifices, and as a result faced a further temptation to return to their old religion. Misguided Jewish teachers had apparently taught them that because they no longer offered animal sacrifices, they no longer received the special benefit that came through eating the food of those sacrifices. The writer bluntly warns his readers not to listen to such teaching, but to follow the teaching of those who first taught them the gospel. The gospel has not changed, and Jesus Christ whom their leaders follow has not changed. He is the same now as he was when they first believed, and he will still be the same in the future (7-9).

Sacrificial feasts belong to the old Israelite religion and cannot be introduced into Christianity. If people join in eating sacrifices offered on the Jewish altar, they cannot join in receiving benefits from the sacrifice offered on the Christian 'altar', meaning the death of Christ (10).

In those Israelite sacrifices where the blood was brought into the tabernacle, the remains of the sacrifice were not eaten, but were burnt outside the camp (Lev 4:5-7,11-12; 6:30). The writer sees this as a picture of Jesus who was crucified 'outside the camp' (i.e. outside Jerusalem), and whose blood was used to bring forgiveness and cleansing of sin (11-12). Those Jews who still wish to be members of the earthly Jerusalem (i.e. the old Jewish religion) cannot belong to Christ and his heavenly kingdom. They must come out of the 'camp' of Judaism and share the shame of Christ through being insulted by their fellow Jews as Christ was (13-14). The sacrifices they then offer will not be dead animals, but sincere praise to God and practical kindness to their fellows (15-16).

Personal messages (13:17-25)

The writer repeats that the Christians must not be turned from the faith by these strange ideas. Rather they should follow the teaching given to them by their leaders, and so encourage the leaders in their difficult task (17). In asking the believers to pray for him, the writer emphasizes that he has written this letter out of a genuine desire to help their faith. He hopes to return to them soon (18-19).

Meanwhile he prays that God, who has established the new covenant through Christ's sacrificial death, will help his people to enjoy the blessings of that covenant (20-21). He trusts that they will gain encouragement from his letter, and from the news that Timothy has just been released from prison. Some Christians from Italy join him in sending greetings (22-25).

569

James

BACKGROUND

The letter of James was possibly the first New Testament letter to be written. It seems to have been addressed mainly to Jewish Christians — not those of a specific local church, but Jewish Christians in general. Like God's people in later Old Testament times, these Christians were scattered throughout the region of the Bible's story (James 1:1). Further indications of the Jewish background to the book are the writer's reference to the Christian meeting as a synagogue (James 2:2), and his references to the law of Moses (James 1:18; 2:8-11; 5:4).

Author of the letter

From early Christian times it has been understood that the person named James who wrote this letter was James the brother of the Lord Jesus (James 1:1; cf. Mark 6:3). During Jesus' earthly life, James and his brothers did not believe him to be the Messiah (John 7:3-5), but by the time of his ascension they had become believers (Acts 1:14). This suggests that Jesus' special appearance to James after the resurrection may have helped turn him and his brothers from unbelief to faith (1 Cor 15:7).

James later became the most prominent leader in the Jerusalem church (Acts 12:17; 15:13; Gal 1:18-19; 2:9,12). Although most of the Jews in the Jerusalem church still held to former beliefs and customs, James was not in bondage to the law. He constantly encouraged his fellow Jews to be more tolerant of others (Acts 15:13,19). The common people respected him for his sincere faith and called him James the Just.

Purpose of the letter

Jews who became Christians had the advantages of a long-established belief in God and a moral outlook moulded by the law of Moses. But these advantages could also become a hindrance. Some Christians were so devoted to the law that they became coldly legalistic and their Christianity lacked vitality. Others erred in the opposite direction. Now that they were released from the law's restrictions, they thought they were free to join in whatever practices were common in the society around them. As a result their behaviour became unchristian.

James dealt with these problems by giving teaching on the nature of Christian faith. Faith is not obedience to a set of rules, nor is it mere intellectual belief. It is something that is living, and it expresses itself in right behaviour. It does not give people the right to do as they like, but directs them towards a greater love for God and for others. Christian faith changes people's thinking and behaviour, and is relevant to the problems of daily life. It enables Christians to live positively for God in an ungodly society, without accepting the ungodly standards of that society. This applies not to Jewish Christians only, but to all God's people.

OUTLINE

1:1-18 LIFE'S TRIALS AND DIFFICULTIES

James' readers are scattered over the area of the early church's expansion (1:1), but no matter where they live, they share the same responsibilities as Christians everywhere. One of these responsibilities requires them to do something that by nature is very difficult, namely, face the trials of life with joy. This joy comes through the knowledge that trials help believers to develop endurance and so strengthen their Christian character (2-4).

When faced with problems, believers often do not know what to do for the best. God understands and gladly gives wisdom to those who ask for it, so that they can make the correct decisions (5). However, he does not give it to those who have confidence in their own wisdom, who doubt his ability to help, or who have no desire for the character that he wants to produce (6-8).

In the churches to which James wrote, some were rich, others poor. James assures them that there will be no problem of mixing with each other in true fellowship if all realize that through Christ they have equal status before God. The poor as well as the rich have a high position in Christ; the rich as well as the poor must humble themselves in coming to Christ. People are foolish to seek eagerly after financial status, for it has no lasting value (9-11).

Those who meet trials in the right attitude will grow in their understanding and enjoyment of the life God has given them (12). It is important to recognize the difference between the outward trial and the inward temptation. When people are experiencing trials, they can easily be tempted to do wrong and then blame God for their failure. God can neither tempt nor be tempted, because he is holy (13). Giving in to temptation prevents people from experiencing the sort of life that God intended for them. In the end it brings disaster (14-15).

Far from tempting to do evil, God is the source of all good. The light from the sun, the moon and the stars varies from hour to hour, but God who created them never changes. Likewise in matters concerning his children he never varies. He never desires evil, but always desires good (16-17). He wants them to be perfect, the finest creatures in all his creation, just as the grain that the Israelites offered was the finest in all their fields (18).

1:19-2:26 PUTTING BELIEF INTO PRACTICE

The Bible and everyday life (1:19-27)

A tendency in human nature is for people to become ill-tempered, especially in times of difficulty or stress. Christians must not excuse their ill-temper by claiming that they are defending God's honour. Such attitudes have no place in the Christian life. They must be replaced by new attitudes that arise from studying God's Word and putting its teachings into practice (19-21).

Christians must not merely read God's Word, but must do what it says. The Word is a 'law' that they must obey, but it is a law that sets them free, not one that makes them slaves. It is a law of liberty. Christians obey it not because they are forced to, but because they want to. When a person looks in a mirror and sees dirt on his face, he is not forced to wash his face, but it is natural that he should want to (22-25).

While some people thought their new religion meant that they could ignore the commands of the Bible, others thought that it required them to be stricter in obeying laws than they were before. This latter group prided themselves that they were very religious because of their law-keeping. James points out that the truly religious people are those who

control their speech and express their faith in acts of kindness. At the same time they are careful not to copy the wrong behaviour of the society in which they live (26-27).

Favouritism destroys love (2:1-13)

Standards of judgment in the church are not the same as those in the society round about. People ought not to be given important places in the church merely because they have important places in the society. Likewise poor people should not be ignored (2:1-4). God welcomes people into his kingdom regardless of wealth or social position, and gives his riches to them equally. James notes how strange it is that the Christians should show special favour to the rich, because the rich are from the class that oppresses Christians most cruelly (5-7).

In their dealings with others, the rule for Christians is 'Love your neighbour as yourself' (8). Those who show favouritism break that rule. They would, under Moses' law (where the rule was first taught; Lev 19:18), be considered law-breakers, no matter what other good they may have done. For example, they may not commit adultery, but if they kill they are still law-breakers (9-11).

Christians are not in bondage to the law of Moses, but God's 'law of liberty' within them should cause them to love others. If they show no mercy to the poor, God will show no mercy when he judges them. But if in mercy they refrain from harsh judgments, God will refrain from harsh judgment of them (12-13).

Proof of genuine faith (2:14-26)

The Christian faith is not merely a mental belief, but something that is practised. Those who say they have faith must give evidence of it by their behaviour. In the case of the poor Christians just referred to, it is useless to talk sympathetically to them but not give them food and clothing. A professed faith must produce a corresponding change in behaviour, otherwise it is dead and useless (14-17).

Genuine faith will prove itself by good deeds. The simple belief that God exists is not enough. Even demons have such a belief, but it will not help them escape God's judgment (18-19).

Abraham also had a belief in God, but it was a belief that completely changed his life and actions. True, Abraham was justified by faith when he wholeheartedly trusted God, even though he did not know how God could possibly fulfil his promise (Gen 15:6; Rom 4:1-3,16-25). But that is not the incident James is talking about here. He is talking about the incident thirty years later, at the time of Abraham's offering of Isaac (20-21; cf. Gen 22:1-18). Abraham not only said he believed in God, but he proved it by being willing to sacrifice Isaac on the altar. He believed that God could fulfil his promise of giving Abraham a multitude of descendants through Isaac, by bringing Isaac back to life (cf. Heb 11:17-19). Genuine faith is demonstrated not simply by the set of beliefs a person holds, but by the actions that those beliefs produce (22-24).

As with Abraham the friend of God, so with Rahab the prostitute, faith expressed itself in actions (25; cf. Josh 2:1-21). Faith and good deeds are as inseparable as body and spirit (26).

3:1-5:6 WORLDLY AMBITION AND CHRISTIAN FAITH

Control of the tongue (3:1-12)

James warns his readers not to be too ambitious to be teachers in the church, because if they instruct others and then fail themselves, they will receive greater judgment. This places teachers in particular danger, because they cannot avoid making some mistakes (3:1-2). A person who can control his tongue can control the whole self. Just as the bit controls the horse and the rudder controls the ship, so the tongue controls the person. Small as it is, the tongue can do great damage when uncontrolled, just as a tiny flame in dry grass can burn down a whole forest (3-5).

All the wrong within a person shows itself through the uncontrolled tongue. With the help of Satan, the tongue spreads evil through people's lives like a destructive fire that burns out of control. The more they speak evil, the more their behaviour becomes evil (6). People are able to tame wild animals, but they are unable to tame their own tongues (7-8). Three examples from nature illustrate the inconsistency of using the same tongue to bless God and curse people (9-12).

Spiritual and worldly wisdom (3:13-18)

Christians must distinguish between spiritual wisdom and worldly wisdom. Some people are undoubtedly skilful in laying plans and using circumstances to achieve their goals, but their actions are often characterized by jealousy, selfishness and dishonesty. This is worldly wisdom. It comes not from God but from Satan, and results in wrong actions. It contrasts sharply with spiritual wisdom, which is characterized by humility and uprightness (13-16).

In addition, those who act according to spiritual wisdom will consider the well-being of others before their own. They will be free of any trace of deceit or dishonesty (17). The farmer who sows good seed can expect a good harvest. Similarly, Christians who sow peace by building good relations with others can expect to see a harvest of righteousness in their lives (18).

Worldliness and its results (4:1-12)

Continuing his teaching on the evil results of worldly attitudes, James explains why fights and quarrels occur. Selfish ambition fights against the more spiritual motives. Some Christians are constantly looking for more power, increased possessions and higher status. Because they want the wrong things, they do not pray. If they pray, they find their prayers refused, and so try to do things their own way (4:1-3). This is worldliness, and it is opposed to the ways of God. God has given believers the Holy Spirit to control their lives and he wants no rivals, such as the spirit of worldliness, to turn them away from him (4-5).

God opposes those who, in their pride, ignore him and act according to their own ambitions. He strengthens those who, in their humility, draw near to him and resist Satan's temptations to rely on worldly methods (6-8). Those who gain pleasure from ungodly attitudes are rejoicing in their own foolishness. They should rather be sad and repent (9-10).

One matter in which they should immediately begin to change is that of unkind talk about others. This is another example of worldly pride, for the offending person, instead of obeying the law, claims the right to judge others. This right belongs to God alone (11-12).

Personal advancement without God (4:13-5:6)

Another sign of worldliness appears when Christians arrange their lives as if God does not exist, as if they control the future. Christians should view life differently from non-Christians. They should not live as if their lives on earth are going to last for ever, but should consider the eternal purposes of God and arrange their affairs accordingly. Their chief consideration should be to do God's will, not to look for personal gain and advancement (13-16). If they know this is the way they should live, but do not put their knowledge into practice, they are guilty of sin (17).

Then follows a pronouncement of judgment on the greedy landowners. These people hoard wealth and goods that only perish with age and disuse, but show no interest in helping the poor and needy around them. They grow rich through oppressing and cheating their workers. But God takes notice of all this. They are only building up evidence against themselves, which will bring for them a heavier punishment (5:1-4). Like animals they are fattening themselves only to be slaughtered. Because of their wealth they have power to do as they wish, but all their achievements will not save them on the day of judgment (5-6).

5:7-20 THE NEED FOR PATIENCE AND PRAYER

Many Christians were poor and oppressed, some of them no doubt farmers who suffered because of the rich landowners. James encourages them to wait patiently for the Lord's return (which will bring them victory in the end), just as the farmer waits patiently for the rain that will bring his crops to final harvest (7-8). God is using these trials to teach them patience, so they must not fight against his purposes by grumbling. Some Old Testament examples show that those who cooperate with God's purposes experience the enjoyment of his love and mercy (9-11; cf. Job 1:20-21; 2:10). James further warns that swearing rash oaths will not help them bear their trials. He suggests that they would do better to speak and act normally (12).

When believers are going though times of trouble, they should not complain or swear, but pray. When they are happy they should not act foolishly, but sing (13). Christians should realize the power that is available to them through prayer. If they are sick they may ask the elders to pray for them. (The act of pouring oil would give the sick person a symbolic reassurance of the divine help being given.) In certain cases physical suffering may be the result of personal sin, in which case healing will assure the sufferer that the sin is forgiven (14-15).

If Christians confess their faults to each other, they can pray more intelligently for each other's needs (16). The example of Elijah is an assurance that God answers the prayers of his people (17-18; cf. 1 Kings 17:1; 18:1,42-46).

Christians should be concerned for all people, not just for those who meet regularly in the church. They should always be looking for opportunities to bring people to God, so that those people can have their sins forgiven (19-20).

1 Peter

BACKGROUND

Peter wrote the letter known as 1 Peter to Christians who lived mainly in the northern provinces of Asia Minor bordering the Black Sea (1 Peter 1:1). This was a region where Paul had not been allowed to preach (Acts 16:7-8), but where Peter later carried on an extensive evangelistic work. Two co-workers at the time he wrote this letter were Mark and Silas, both of whom had earlier worked with Paul (1 Peter 5:12-13; cf. Acts 12:25; 13:5; 15:36-40). A brief survey of events from the time of their work with Paul to the time of Peter's writing will provide a useful background for an understanding of 1 Peter.

Peter, Mark and Silas

Just before the start of Paul's second missionary journey, Barnabas parted from Paul and went on a missionary trip to Cyprus, taking Mark with him (Acts 15:39). From early non-biblical records we learn that after Barnabas and Mark finished their work in Cyprus, Mark joined Peter. The two then worked together for many years preaching and teaching throughout the northern regions of Asia

Minor, where they helped establish the churches addressed in this letter.

Further early records indicate that after this, Peter and Mark went to Rome for a period and taught the Christians there. When Peter left to go on further missionary travels, Mark stayed behind in Rome. The Christians in Rome asked Mark to write down the story of Jesus as they had heard it from Peter, with the result that Mark wrote the book that we know as Mark's Gospel. About this time Paul arrived in Rome as a prisoner for the first time. It seems that he was imprisoned for two years and then released (Acts 28:16,30; see background notes to 1 Timothy).

Later, Paul was imprisoned in Rome again and, believing he was about to be executed, asked Timothy and Mark to come and visit him (2 Tim 4:6,9,11). Whether they reached Rome before Paul's execution is not clear, but Mark seems to have stayed on in Rome and was still there when Peter visited the city again. In keeping with a common practice among Christians at that time, Peter refers to Rome symbolically as Babylon; for Rome, like

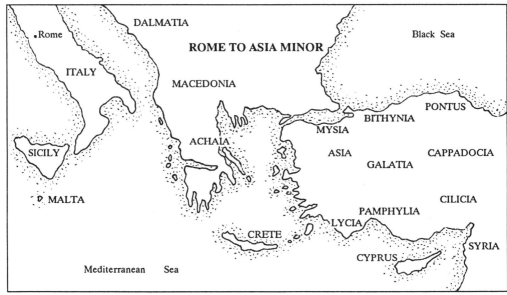

574

Babylon of Old Testament times, was the centre of society's arrogant opposition to God and his people (1 Peter 5:13). The secretary who wrote Peter's letter for him was his co-worker Silas (1 Peter 5:12).

Persecution of Christians

By this time Christians throughout the Empire were suffering increasingly severe persecution. Previously the Roman authorities seem to have regarded Christianity as a movement within Judaism. This meant that it was protected by law, for Judaism was a legal religion. But officials and common people alike were now becoming aware that there were vast differences between Judaism and Christianity.

When the Jews in Jerusalem killed the most prominent man in the church, James the brother of Jesus, everybody saw clearly that Christianity was not a movement within Judaism, but was plainly an illegal religion. (James was killed in Jerusalem about the same time as Paul was killed in Rome, the early AD 60s.)

Opposition to Christians intensified rapidly. People in general considered them to be anti-social because of their refusal to join in social practices that they considered idolatrous and immoral. To make matters worse, the Emperor Nero, who had begun a sensible reign ten years previously, had by now become senselessly brutal and anti-Christian. He blamed Christians for the great fire of Rome (AD 64), with the result that fierce persecution broke out.

It was probably just before the outbreak of this greater persecution that Peter wrote this letter to the persecuted Christians of northern Asia Minor. He wanted to assure them of their living hope and glorious future (1 Peter 1:3-9), and to encourage them to bear their persecution with patience, even if it meant death (1 Peter 2:20-23; 3:14-15; 4:12-19).

OUTLINE

1:1-2:10 HIGH STATUS FOR GOD'S PEOPLE

The character of salvation (1:1-12)

Peter's readers are 'God's scattered people', an expression that Peter uses with a wide meaning. In relation to their place of local residence, they are God's people scattered throughout northern Asia Minor. But in relation to heaven, they are God's people scattered in a foreign land. Their true homeland is heaven, and the foreign land is the world. They really belong to God. He chose them and cleansed them, with the aim that they be holy and obedient (1:1-2).

Through the death and resurrection of Christ, God gives believers new life and promises them eternal blessings. He also protects this life for them. They can therefore be assured that when the day of inheritance arrives at Christ's return, they will enjoy the promised blessings and so experience salvation in its fulness (3-5).

This assurance gives Christians joy amid the trials of the present life. Trials produce endurance, and endurance proves that faith is genuine (6-7). As faith grows stronger and joy increases, so their love for Christ is enriched. They experience in advance the greater fellowship that they will have with Christ when their salvation reaches its fulfilment at his return (8-9).

Old Testament prophets, who by God's Spirit foretold this salvation, tried unsuccessfully to find out when it would come about and who the great Messiah-Saviour would be. God showed them that their prophecies would be understood by a future generation. When Christ died and rose again, other messengers of God, guided by the same eternal Spirit, saw the real meaning of their prophecies and then taught others (10-12).

Fruits of salvation (1:13-2:3)

Now that Christians have received such a great salvation, they should discipline their thoughts and behaviour so that they will always be ready for the return of Jesus Christ (13). They should think and act not according to their former habits, but according to the ways of God. They should pattern their character not on the people of the sinful society around them, but on the holy God (14-16).

As Christians reverence God as their Father and Judge, they will want to be more holy in their daily lives (17). Their appreciation of what Christ has done for them will also make them want to be more holy; for his death, and nothing else, can set people free from the worthless manner of life passed down from one generation to the next (18-19). God planned salvation from eternity, and brought it to reality through the death of Christ. He showed it to be perfect by raising Christ from death, and sinners prove that it works when they put their trust in him (20-21).

Believers can show that they have received cleansing and been given new life, by acting with sincere love towards each other (22). This new life comes through accepting the gospel, and because the gospel is God's word, not man's, the new life is permanent. Things born of human origins die, but things born of God do not (23-25).

Since believers are to exercise love towards each other, they must remove from their lives all attitudes and actions that hinder love. They were born into this new life through the Word of God, and the only way to grow is through feeding on that same Word (2:1-3).

God's living temple (2:4-10)

People in general might see no worth in Christ and reject him, but God sees him as the chosen one through whom sinners have eternal life. Those who receive new life through Christ are likened to living stones who form a temple in which God is worshipped. They also form the priesthood that offers the worship (4-5).

Christ is the chief cornerstone in this living building, and those who believe in him will never be disappointed (6). The people of Israel, who were originally intended to build God a living temple, threw out the main stone when they rejected Christ. A rejected building stone lies in the way and becomes an obstacle to the builders, preventing them from doing their work as they should. In the same way Jesus Christ, whom the people of Israel rejected, becomes an obstacle to them, so that they cannot do what God requires of them. God has now taken this rejected stone and made him the chief cornerstone in a new living temple, the Christian church (7-8).

During the period of the Old Testament, Israel was God's people, God's chosen nation; but now all believers are God's people, regardless of race. They pass from the kingdom of darkness into the kingdom of light. They have received God's mercy, and their task now is to tell others about the great and merciful acts of God (9-10; cf. Exod 19:4-6).

2:11-3:12 CHRISTIAN RELATIONSHIPS

In society (2:11-25)

The present world is not the true home of those who have come into a living relationship with Jesus Christ. They are now God's people and they belong to the heavenly kingdom. But their higher status and greater citizenship do not give them the right to do as they like in the present world. They must discipline and control themselves. Negatively, they must not give in to the desires of the sinful nature; positively, they must maintain right behaviour in the

eyes of people in general. Their conduct should demonstrate to an unbelieving world the worth of the Christian life (11-12).

God desires life in human society to be orderly, and Christians should cooperate with God's purpose by obeying civil authorities. The civil authorities, on their part, should be just and fair in punishing those who do wrong and rewarding those who do good (13-14). Right conduct by Christians in this matter will prevent criticism from their opponents. It will also show that Christians, though they are free, know how to make the proper use of their freedom. They respect, love and honour people as true Christians should, and above all they reverence God (15-17).

Christian servants also must be cooperative, whether their masters are kind or harsh (18). Masters may be unreasonable and life may become difficult and painful, but those who follow Jesus must endure their sufferings patiently as he did (19-21). Jesus Christ did no wrong, but he had confidence that God would act justly on his behalf. Such confidence enabled him to endure unjust treatment silently (22-23).

What caused Christ's suffering, however, was more than the cruelty of his persecutors. It was the sins of Christians, the people who are now asked to suffer for his sake. It was *their* sins he bore on the cross. Through his death, sin's power over them is broken. They are cleansed, given new life, and brought under his loving care (24-25).

In the home and the church (3:1-12)

Another sphere where Christians should display the character of Christ is the home. Wives can display a Christlike character through an attitude of submission to their husbands, even though the husbands may be unbelievers. By the wives' good conduct and quiet spirit, the husbands may be won for God (3:1-4). Some women of Old Testament times, in particular Sarah, are good examples of a wife's conduct (5-6).

Christian husbands should not act thoughtlessly or harshly towards their wives, partly because women are physically weaker, but more importantly because women receive God's blessings equally with men. Tension between husbands and wives hinders their prayers (7).

In the church likewise believers must have consideration for one another. They must show love and kindness to all, even to those whom they find hard to like. Only as they act towards one another in love will they obtain the blessing that God desires for them (8-9). They will find true enjoyment in life as they turn away from insincere speech and hurtful actions, and concentrate instead on doing good and promoting peace. They will also find that such a life is assured of God's constant help (10-12).

3:13-4:19 SUFFERING FOR CHRIST'S SAKE

Example of Christ (3:13-22)

Persecution cannot really harm those who are eager to please God, because with such people persecution always results in greater spiritual blessing (13). Because they love what is right they may be persecuted by those who love what is wrong, but to suffer for such a reason is a cause for joy, not sorrow. If people are devoted to Christ and are always ready to give others an explanation for their devotion, they will not fear their persecutors (14-15). They should also try to avoid all forms of wrongdoing. Perhaps their enemies will see that they are persecuting without cause, and so feel ashamed of themselves (16-17).

As Peter thinks about those who suffer for doing good, he is reminded of the perfect example, Jesus Christ. The one who was perfect died for sinners to bring them to God. In his body he suffered the penalty for their sins — death. But he triumphed over death. His spirit, instead of being bound by those forces that lead to eternal condemnation, entered into fuller life. He then went to the place where evil spirits are imprisoned awaiting final judgment and announced his victory (18-19).

Those spirits had led people to rebel against God (as, for example, in the time of Noah; see Gen 6:1-8), but Christ has now conquered all sin and rebellion. God's saving of Noah and his family by means of the ark illustrates the salvation of believers. A corresponding illustration in the New Testament is baptism. Christ has died and triumphed over death, and therefore believers are, through him, cleansed from sin, made alive and brought back to God (20-22).

Changed lives of Christ's followers (4:1-11)

Christ's death dealt with sin once and for all. In that sense he has nothing more to do with sin. Christians are united with Christ in his death, and therefore they too should have nothing more to do with sin. They should live no longer to please themselves but to please God (4:1-2). Christians must have no more involvement with the disgusting practices of their former days, no matter how much their reformed behaviour brings jeers and insults from their former friends (3-4).

Ungodly people must one day face divine judgment and condemnation, but in the case of believers, Christ has already borne that judgment and condemnation. The only judgment of sin that they experience is the suffering of their present physical existence, which reaches its climax in death. Those believers who are now dead believed the gospel that was preached to them while they were still living (i.e. during their earthly lives). Therefore, although they experienced physical death as one of the natural consequences of sin, they now live spiritually with God (5-6).

The final great events of the world's history could begin at any time. Christians should be alert, but should not get over-excited. They should control themselves, pray, and act with love at all times (7-9). They should use their God-given abilities with diligence, whether in teaching God's Word or in giving practical help to others. Above all they must work in such a way as to bring praise and glory to God (10-11).

Joy amid persecution (4:12-19)

Christians should not be surprised when they have to suffer because of their faith in Christ. Their association with him means that they have to share his suffering now, just as they will share his glory in the future. They should be glad when they suffer for his sake, because it gives them added assurance that they are God's people. They know that God is testing and purifying their faith (12-14). They have no need to be downhearted because of persecution, provided such suffering is undeserved and not because of wrongdoing (15-16).

If present sufferings are, in a sense, God's judgment on his people for a good purpose, how great will be the sufferings of unbelievers when God acts in judgment against them! When believers know that they suffer because it is God's will for them and not because of any wrongdoing on their part, they will trust God to use these trials for their good (17-19).

5:1-14 LEADERSHIP, HUMILITY AND WATCHFULNESS

Church elders are to be sincere, understanding and hard-working in looking after the church that God has placed in their care. They are to be shepherds who care for the flock because they are interested in the flock's welfare, not because they want to make money (5:1-2). They must not use their authority to force people, but rather show by example how Christians should act. They must remember that they themselves are answerable to the Chief Shepherd, Jesus Christ, who will one day return and review their work (3-4).

Christian relationships should be characterized by a spirit of willing submission. This applies not just to the attitude of younger people to older people, but to attitudes in general. All Christians should submit to each other. God opposes the proud but helps the humble (5-6). God cares for his people, and they should confide in him. At the same time they must be careful how they live, for Satan will try to use any opportunity to make their lives useless for God (7-8). They must resist Satan, knowing that Christians everywhere suffer from his attacks. Yet God uses his people's sufferings to strengthen and perfect them, with the goal that they share Christ's glory (9-11).

Peter has used Silas to write this brief letter of encouragement. The church in Rome (figuratively referred to as Babylon, symbol of the world in its organized opposition to God) joins with Peter, Silas and Mark in sending greetings. The Christians who receive the letter should greet each other, and so encourage each other in love (12-14).

2 Peter

BACKGROUND

A year or two after writing his first letter, Peter wrote and sent off the letter that we know as 2 Peter. It appears to have been sent to the same group of churches as 1 Peter, namely, churches of the northern provinces of Asia Minor where he had carried out a widespread evangelistic and pastoral ministry (2 Peter 3:1; cf 1 Peter 1:1).

Reasons for writing

At the time of writing, Peter was in prison in Rome, probably awaiting execution (2 Peter 1:14). (According to tradition he was crucified in Rome during the latter half of the AD 60s.) He had heard of the activity of false teachers, and wanted to reassure the Christians of certain truths he had taught them (2 Peter 1:10-16).

The false teaching seems to have included ideas that became fully developed in the Gnostic heresies of the second century. Gnostics were people who claimed to have higher spiritual knowledge (see background notes to Colossians and 1 John), but this led to a separation between belief and behaviour. They argued that their knowledge placed them in a realm where the deeds of the body no longer affected the purity of the soul. Therefore, for people who possessed this higher knowledge, immoral practices were not wrong.

Peter announced God's punishment on those who taught such things, and urged true Christians to pursue holiness with greater diligence (2 Peter 1:5-8; 2:1-3). He also opposed those who mocked the Christians' belief in the return of Jesus Christ. Again he condemned the false teachers but reassured the believers (2 Peter 3:3-4,9-10).

Some illustrations and arguments that Peter used in this letter are similar to those found in the letter of Jude. This suggests that both writers used material that was in common use among those who opposed the false teaching.

OUTLINE

1:1-21 GOD'S POWER AT WORK IN BELIEVERS

The truly Christian character (1:1-15)

In his righteousness, God has given all Christians, from elderly apostles to new converts, equal blessing through the gospel (1:1-2). He has also given them everything they need to live lives of holiness in a world that is corrupt through uncontrolled passions. The lives of believers must be in keeping with the life of God that has been given them. God's promises are the assurance of his help in reaching this goal (3-4).

Faith that is genuine will produce lives of moral goodness, but only if believers apply some determination and effort. True Christians will want to increase in the knowledge of God, and this will teach them self-control and endurance, leading to godliness. As they know more of God and his ways, they will love others more (5-7). Those who eagerly seek these qualities will be useful for God, but those who neglect them are in danger of falling again under the power of sin from which they have been saved (8-9). By developing the truly Christian character, believers receive added assurance that they belong to God now and will enjoy his presence in the coming eternal kingdom (10-11).

Peter knows that he must continually remind Christians of their responsibilities, for even the mature can become lazy (12). By sending this letter to them now, he is making sure that they will have a constant reminder after he has gone. He expects that very soon he will face the execution that Jesus spoke of more than thirty years earlier (13-15; cf John 21:18-19).

Evidence of Christ's power and glory (1:16-21)

In speaking as he has concerning God's power to change lives, Peter has not been giving some theory out of his own imagination. He himself saw the power of God of which he speaks. He also saw something of the majesty and glory that will be revealed when Christ returns, for he was one of the three chosen disciples who were with Christ at the time of his transfiguration. Besides seeing the evidence of God's power, Peter heard the testimony that the Father spoke concerning his Son. What Peter speaks of is not a myth, but an actual event that happened at a certain place and a certain time in history. It cannot be denied (16-18; cf. Mark 9:2-8).

Apart from Peter's own witness of the power and glory of Christ, there is the witness of the Old Testament writings. Prophecies concerning Christ's first coming were fulfilled, and this gives assurance that those concerning his second coming will also be fulfilled. These prophecies are like a lamp in the night. They are useful and helpful until the full light dawns at the return of Christ (19).

It is important that Christians pay attention to these prophecies, for they are not stories that people have invented (cf. v. 16), but messages from God. They were given through God's Spirit, and people can understand them properly only with the help of the same Spirit (20-21).

2:1-22 WARNING AGAINST FALSE TEACHERS

Punishment of the ungodly (2:1-10a)

Having spoken about the purpose of prophecies, Peter now gives a warning to beware of those who will use prophecies to support their own teachings. History shows that there have always been false teachers who have tried to gain a following by the misuse of Scripture (2:1). The punishment of all such people is certain. They oppose Christ, give the church a bad name, lead people into sin and make financial profit from the Christians they deceive (2-3).

Old Testament examples show how God saves his people but punishes the ungodly. The angels who rebelled against God are imprisoned, awaiting the final judgment when all who oppose God will be condemned (4). The stories of Noah and Lot illustrate God's mercy on the righteous and his punishment of the wicked. In both cases he saved the righteous but destroyed the ungodly among whom they lived (5-8; cf. Gen 6:1-18; 19:12-25).

Christians who are troubled by false teachers should learn from these examples. If they trust more firmly in the overruling mercy and justice of God, their faith will withstand the attacks of the trouble-makers (9-10a).

Character of the false teachers (2:10b-22)

Being arrogant and self-assertive, the false teachers show no respect for anyone. They even insult angels, who hold a higher position than humans in the order of created beings. By contrast, the angels have such

reverence for God that they dare not use insulting language in his presence, even against those who deserve condemnation (10b-11).

The false teachers use neither their reasoning nor their willpower to control themselves. Like animals they simply follow their bodily appetites. They practise sexual immorality without any feeling of shame, and by their disgraceful gluttony they spoil the fellowship meals of the church. Because they act like animals, they will be destroyed like animals. Because they have made others suffer, they themselves will suffer (12-14). Like Balaam they would destroy God's people, both morally and religiously, because of their desire for personal gain (15-16; cf. Num 22:1-40; 25:1-9; 31:16).

By promising a new life of freedom, the false teachers deceive people. Like waterless springs and rainless clouds, they build up people's hopes only to disappoint by not giving the satisfaction they promised. By teaching that Christians are free to satisfy their bodily desires, they lead many new converts back into the sinful ways from which they have just escaped. But these misguided converts find not freedom but slavery, for a person becomes the slave of whatever defeats him (17-19). In turning from the ways of God, they are caught again by the deadly forces of sin. They are then led back into the sort of wrongdoing that they formerly practised as pagans. But because of what they have learnt of God's righteousness, their guilt is now greater. Their ultimate punishment also will be greater (20-22).

3:1-18 SIGNIFICANCE OF CHRIST'S RETURN

Assurance of his coming (3:1-7)

The activity of the false teachers is no reason for the Christians to panic or become confused. Peter's teaching has followed that of the Old Testament prophets and the New Testament apostles, both in helping develop pure faith and in warning those who would try to corrupt that faith (3:1-2).

Christians should not be discouraged by those who scoff at the idea of Christ's second coming. Such people argue that Christ will not return and that the natural course of events will continue uninterrupted as it has from the beginning (3-4). But these scoffers ignore some of the plain facts of history; for example, the flood in Noah's day. In the creation story, God made the land appear out of water, but he then interrupted what appeared to be the normal course of events by using water to cover the land and destroy the sinners (5-6; cf. Gen 1:6-7; 6:17). One day he will intervene in human affairs again, this time destroying the sinners by fire (7).

Reasons for the delay (3:8-18)

Some people may wonder why there is such a delay before Christ's return. The answer is that from God's point of view there is no delay, since he does not view time according to human standards. Eternity is not time carried on and on indefinitely, but is an entirely different order of things. If there seems to be a delay from the human point of view, it is because God is waiting as long as possible, so that people might realize the seriousness of their sins and turn from them (8-9).

When the day of God's intervention arrives, it will be as unexpected as a thief. Christ's return will bring all things to their destiny — destruction for all that is wicked, new life for all that is righteous. Christians should live in a state of constant readiness for that day by being holy in their conduct and dedicated to God in their manner of living (10-13).

This desire to be ready for the return of Jesus Christ is one reason why Christians should work energetically at developing their Christian lives. Only by determined effort will they be blameless in their behaviour (14).

Another reason why Christians should want to grow in holiness is their gratitude to God for his patience with them, for without such patience sinners could never be saved. Paul gave similar advice in his letters, but certain people twist the plain meaning of his words. Paul taught that sinners are saved by God's grace, not by their good deeds, but ignorant and mischievous people distort his teaching to mean that good deeds are not important. They therefore do as they like and so ruin their lives (15-16).

The best way for Christians to protect themselves against the destructive influence of such false teaching is to learn more about Jesus Christ. They should concentrate on developing within themselves the qualities that are found in him (17-18).

1 John

BACKGROUND

Almost from the time of their establishment, the churches in and around Ephesus had been troubled by false teaching. Paul had warned of such trouble (Acts 20:17,29-30), and his letters to Ephesus and Colossae show that major problems soon arose (Eph 5:6; Col 2:4,8,18). These problems increased over the decades that followed, and early records indicate that the person most concerned with correcting them was John, possibly the last surviving member of the original twelve apostles. John apparently lived in Ephesus, and wrote his Gospel and letters partly to deal with the false teaching of the Ephesus region (John 21:24; 1 John 2:26; 4:3; 2 John 7).

However, John was concerned with more than just opposing false teaching. A central purpose of his Gospel was to lead people to faith in Christ, so that they might experience the fulness of eternal life that Christ made possible (John 3:15; 6:27; 10:10; 20:31). A central purpose of his three letters was to reassure troubled believers of their possession of this eternal life, so that they might enjoy it fully in fellowship with God and with one another (1 John 1:3; 3:18-19; 4:13; 5:13; 2 John 5).

Teaching about Jesus Christ

John's reason for wanting to reassure the Christians was that many of them had become confused. False teachers were spreading ideas that were part of a developing Gnosticism, a destructive heresy that reached its full expression in the second century.

Gnosticism (from the Greek *gnosis*, meaning 'knowledge') tried to explain some of the mysteries of life by combining Christian belief with pagan philosophy. In particular, it was concerned with harmonizing things between which there appeared to be some tension, such as spirit and matter, body and soul, good and evil. This led to damaging false teaching in relation to the person and work of Jesus Christ and the salvation and behaviour of Christians. (For further discussion on Gnostic-type teachings of the region see background notes to Colossians.)

Because the false teachers believed that a perfectly good God could not come in contact with an evil world, they refused to accept that divinity and humanity were perfectly united in Jesus Christ. As a result they denied that the Son of God became a man and died on the cross. John saw this as an attack on the very basis of Christianity and he openly denounced the false teachers. He insisted that if they refused to accept either Christ's true humanity or full deity, they were not followers of Christ but enemies (1 John 2:18-19,22; 4:1-3).

Gnostic-type teachings also created problems in relation to everyday behaviour. The Gnostics asserted that those who accepted their teachings entered a spiritual realm that placed them above ordinary people. The evil of the material world could no longer affect the purity of the soul, and therefore people were free to express themselves without the need for self-control. The result was much immoral behaviour. This, said John, was further evidence that such people were not Christians, even though they mixed in Christian company (1 John 2:4; 3:6,8). True Christians were self-disciplined, obedient to God's commands, and considerate of other people (1 John 2:6; 3:3,17; 5:3).

OUTLINE

1:1-2:17 LIVING IN THE LIGHT

Fellowship with God (1:1-2:6)

In the opening few words of his letter, John states clearly certain facts about Jesus Christ that are basic to Christianity. Jesus Christ is the eternal God and he became a real man whom John and his fellow apostles have seen, heard and touched (1:1-2). John's joy will be complete if he knows that he and his readers share together in the eternal life that comes to them through Jesus Christ. This life unites them to one another as well as to the Father and the Son (3-4).

God is light, meaning that he is holy, true, pure and glorious. As darkness cannot exist with light, so sinful things can have no partnership with God (5). This means that although the life God gives believers is eternal, the fellowship that believers have with him can be broken because of sin. In three short sections John gives different advice to various people, to remind them of what is required if they are to have cleansing from sin and fellowship with God.

First, if people think they can sin as they please and still have fellowship with God, they are mistaken. But if they are careful to live righteously, they will enjoy unbroken fellowship with God and his people. God sees that they are living as he wants them to, and he graciously forgives those sins that they commit unknowingly (6-7).

Second, if people forget that they have a sinful nature and think that everything they do is right, they deceive themselves. But if, after honestly examining themselves, they become aware of their sins, they should confess those sins. God gives his assurance that he will forgive them and cleanse them (8-9).

Third, if people claim they never sin at all, they are really saying that God is a liar, because he has declared all people to be sinful. They must allow the light of God's truth to shine into their hearts and show them what they really are (10).

John is not saying all this so that people might think that sinning is normal behaviour for Christians, as if it does not matter if they sin. On the contrary he wants them *not* to sin. But it is inevitable that they will sin sometimes, and he wants them to be assured that when that happens, cleansing is available because of the atoning blood of Christ. On the basis of his death, Christ can ask the Father to forgive the sinner (2:1-2).

Those who know God will obey his Word. These are the true Christians. Their obedience results in assurance of salvation, greater love for God, and lives that become increasingly like the life of Christ (3-6).

Christian love in the present world (2:7-17)

The commandment to love one another is old because it is found in the Old Testament and was quoted by Christ (Lev 19:18; Matt 5:43-44; John 13:34). It is new because it belongs to the new age of 'light' that began with Christ, in contrast to the present world's age of 'darkness'. The work of Christ has given love a new meaning (7-8). The love shown by Christ is the love that Christians must show to others. If love determines their behaviour, they live in God's light. They see what they are doing and therefore they do right. If hate determines their behaviour, they live in darkness. They are spiritually blind and therefore they do wrong. If people claim

to be Christians but hate others, they only deceive themselves (9-11).

John does not want any to doubt their salvation unnecessarily because of what he just said, so he quickly reminds them of the grounds for their assurance. New believers may not yet have learnt a lot, but at least they know that they have a Father in heaven who forgives them. Elderly believers have the assurance that comes through their many years of knowing God. Believers in the energetic years of their Christian lives grow in confidence and strength as they see the power of God at work in defeating Satan (12-14).

Christians must not allow themselves to become affected by the attitudes and behaviour of the unbelievers around them. The ordinary people of the world belong to the age of darkness and make their decisions according to what they want for themselves, whether concerning possessions, activities, achievements, or status. Christians belong to the new age of light, the eternal kingdom where God's values rule and his will is done. They must make their judgments according to his standards, not the standards of the present ungodly world (15-17).

2:18-29 ENEMIES OF CHRIST

Those who claimed to have superior knowledge of Christian truth had left the church and tried to draw others away with them. By denying that Jesus Christ was at the same time fully divine and fully human, they denied a truth that was basic to the Christian faith. Far from being superior Christians, they were enemies of Christ. They showed that within them was the spirit of antichrist (18-19).

In contrast to these rebels, true believers are indwelt by the Spirit of God. This Spirit gives them added confidence that the teaching they originally accepted, which John is now repeating, is indeed the truth (20-21).

The Father and the Son are equally God and are inseparable. Therefore, if people reject Jesus as the Son of God, they also reject the Father. If they accept the Father, they must also accept the Son (22-23). People live in union with the Father through living in union with the Son, and the result of this union is eternal life (24-25).

As the indwelling Spirit confirms the truth of Christ to them, believers will learn to reject the teaching of the deceivers. They know what they have been taught by their teachers from the beginning. They do not need new (false) teachers to come and give them additional (false) teaching (26-27). As believers have a better understanding of God's character, they will have greater confidence in him and a clearer knowledge of how his children should behave. If they act upon this knowledge, they will have no cause for shame when they meet Christ at his return (28-29).

3:1-5:5 THE LIFE OF LOVE

Right behaviour for God's children (3:1-10)

John cannot find words to express his feelings when he considers the great love God has shown in making sinful people his children. They now think and act according to the nature of their heavenly Father, with the result that unbelievers, who think and act according to the world's standards, cannot understand them (3:1). God's children know little about the nature of life in the world to come, but they know at least that in some way they will be like Christ. This is good reason for them to become as much like Christ as possible in their present lives. They should be pure in thought and behaviour as he was (2-3).

According to the bold assertions of the false teachers, knowledge is all-important and behaviour does not matter. John contradicts this, pointing out that sin is the breaking of God's law. Therefore, if people deliberately carry on sinning, they know neither God who gave the law nor Christ who takes away sin. John is not saying that Christians cannot sin (he has already shown the impossibility of this in 1:6-10), but that they do not sin as they like. They may have failures and make mistakes, but they do not sin habitually (4-6).

The behaviour of people shows whether they belong to Christ or the devil. They cannot belong to both, as the two are opposed to each other (7-8). If they are true Christians, they will have a divine power within them fighting the devil so that they might not sin. If they sin habitually, it shows that they are not Christians (9-10).

God's children love one another (3:11-24)

Since Christians do what is right and refuse what is wrong, their lives will be characterized by love. But the world will not respond kindly to their goodness, just as Cain did not respond kindly to Abel's (11-12). When sinners are shamed by the uprightness of others, the outcome usually is that they hate them for it (13). Hate produces murder, and murder is obviously not a characteristic of the Christian (14-15).

Those who have genuine love, instead of taking the lives of others, would rather sacrifice their own. Self-sacrifice, even in the everyday things of life, is the chief characteristic of love. Love is proved by actions, not words, as Jesus Christ showed, and Christians must follow his example (16-18).

With such high standards before them, some Christians may feel guilty that they have failed to practise this love. They may even doubt their salvation. John assures them that they have no need for uncertainty. God knows their good intentions and sees even those acts of kindness of which they themselves are not aware. They must not doubt, but have confidence when they come into his presence (19-21). If they are obedient to his commands, they can be assured that he will answer their prayers. The indwelling Spirit reinforces this assurance and enriches their fellowship with God (22-24).

Truth and error (4:1-6)

Christians should examine carefully the teaching they receive, because not all teaching is correct, in spite of speakers' claims that they are speaking by God's Spirit. Wrong teaching about Christ may please those who do not want to believe that the Son of God is also a real man, but such teaching is from the devil (4:1-3).

There is no need for Christians to fear the false teachers, because those in whom God dwells can overcome those in whom Satan dwells (4). There will always be some people who listen to false teachers, because those with worldly minds like to listen to worldly ideas. God's people would rather listen to his truth (5-6).

The character of Christian love (4:7-5:5)

It is God's nature to love. Love in human nature has been spoiled by sin, but when people are born again by the work of God, they learn to love as God loves (7-8). The character of God's love is seen in his act of giving his Son to die for those who have rebelled against him. They are worthy of death, but Jesus died to bear the judgment of sin on their behalf. As a result they can now have life (9-10). People cannot see God, but they can see that he lives within Christians when they practise his love. They show this most clearly when they love those who do not deserve it (11-12).

Christians have increased confidence in God through their inward possession of the Holy Spirit and their outward acknowledgment of Jesus Christ as the Son of God and the Saviour of sinners. They know that they live in God and that God lives in them (13-15). This new relationship with God (who is love) enables them to practise love towards other people as Jesus Christ did. This gives them added confidence that they are saved eternally and need never fear God's judgment (16-18). In summary, if people love God they will love one another, but if they hate one another they cannot honestly claim to love God (19-21).

John repeats that people must believe in Jesus as the Son of God in order to be saved, and that love for God is inseparable from love for God's people (5:1). If believers genuinely love God they will also obey his commandments. They will do this not in a legalistic spirit, but in a spirit of joy and willingness, for they will want to do what pleases God (2-3). They will find strength to be obedient through their faith in Jesus as the Son of God. Because Jesus overcame the world's evil, the children of God who trust in Jesus can triumph also (4-5).

5:6-21 ASSURANCE OF ETERNAL LIFE
The basis of assurance (5:6-12)
Those who taught Gnostic-type theories did not believe that the person who died on the cross was Jesus Christ the Son of God. They claimed that 'the Christ' (i.e. God) descended on Jesus (the man) in the form of a dove after his baptism and empowered him to do miracles, but departed before his crucifixion. According to them, the Jesus who suffered and died was merely a man. He was not 'the Christ'. In other words, 'the Christ' came through water (his baptism) but not through blood (his death).

John emphatically denies this by saying that Jesus was the Christ, the Son of God, through both experiences. John quotes three witnesses as evidence to support this. The first is the water, for Jesus was already both God and man when he was baptized (cf. John 1:29-34). The second is the blood, for the person who died on the cross was both God and man (cf. John 20:26-31; Acts 2:22-24). The third is the Spirit, for Christ's indwelling Spirit is the one who

confirms this truth to the Christian (cf. 1 John 2:20; 3:24; 4:13). When the testimonies of three witnesses are in agreement, they must be accepted as evidence that cannot be disputed (6-8; cf. Deut 19:15).

If people accept the testimony of their fellow human beings, how much more should they accept the testimony of God. And God says that the one who died for the sins of the world was his Son. To deny the union of the divine and the human in Jesus is to call God a liar (9-10). God's Son is the source of eternal life, and those who accept God's testimony and believe in his Son have eternal life also (11-12).

Practical results of assurance (5:13-21)
When Christians know with assurance that God has accepted them and given them eternal life, they will have confidence to come to him with their requests. First, however, they must consider God's will, and not make requests from the wrong motives. They can then be assured that God will hear and answer their prayers (13-15). John encourages them to pray for one another, but he points out that there may be some cases where a person, through his sin, sets in motion a course of events that no amount of prayer can reverse. Christians must train themselves to see the difference between those cases where they should pray and those cases where they should not (16-17).

Sin is not a characteristic of Christians, because Christ keeps them from coming under the power of Satan. Since they belong to God, their lives are different from those of worldly people in general (18-19). John repeats that Jesus Christ, the Son of God who died for sinners, is the true God and he gives believers eternal life. The substitutes invented by the false teachers are false gods and must be avoided (20-21).

2 John

BACKGROUND

John wrote his Second Letter in relation to the same false teaching as he opposed in his First Letter (2 John 7). The teaching was a kind of Gnosticism, a heresy that distorted the truth of Christianity by trying to harmonize it with current philosophies. (For details of the false teaching see background notes to 1 John.)

This false teaching was not confined to the church addressed in the earlier letter, but was being spread around the region by travelling preachers. The short letter of 2 John was sent to a particular group of Christians, either a church or a large family, partly to encourage the believers and partly to warn them not to allow the teachers of false doctrine into their gathering (2 John 10-11).

CONTENTS OF THE LETTER

The 'elect lady' whom John mentions in his opening greeting could have been an individual known to John, but the expression seems more likely to refer to a church. If this is so, 'her children' would be the church members. Whoever they were, John addresses them in a way that shows the respect and love he has for them. They are united with John and with Christians everywhere through the truth of Christ that they hold in common and the love of Christ in which they all share. Truth and love are inseparable from the gospel by which they have been saved, and do not change to suit current trends and popular philosophies (1-3).

John is thankful that his readers have maintained their loyalty to the gospel, but he wants them to remember that they must also maintain their Christian love. Those who claim to live according to God's truth will show it in their love for one another and in their obedience to God's commands (4-6). In this way they will strengthen themselves and so will not be easily deceived by those who give wrong teaching concerning Christ. One error that some of the travelling preachers were spreading around was that Jesus Christ did not have a truly human body. John warns that if they are allowed to preach such things in the church, their erroneous ideas will soon destroy all the good work that the church has done (7-8).

The false teachers think that their teaching about Jesus is advanced, but actually it destroys all hope of salvation. By refusing to accept Jesus Christ as the Son of God who became a man, they are refusing God himself, for no one can have the Father without having the Son. Christians must not listen to such teaching nor give any encouragement or help to the teachers (9-11).

As John hopes to visit the believers soon, he will write no more at present. The group of Christians from which John writes (possibly the church in Ephesus) joins him in sending greetings (12-13).

3 John

BACKGROUND

In the letter known as 1 John, the apostle John opposed a kind of false teaching that seems to have been centred in Ephesus (1 John 2:26; 4:1). In 2 John he warned against travelling preachers who were spreading this teaching around other churches of the Ephesus region (2 John 7,10). However, not all travelling preachers were trouble-makers. Some were preachers of the true gospel, and 3 John was written to a church leader named Gaius, to encourage him to keep supporting such people, in spite of the difficulties he faced.

The letter does not state which church Gaius belonged to, but his difficulties were chiefly concerned with a man named Diotrephes who had worked himself into a position of power in the church. Diotrephes refused to receive the travelling preachers, claiming that they were representatives of the apostle John, whom he opposed. John's letter, therefore, in addition to giving encouragement to Gaius, gave advice concerning how to deal with Diotrephes (3 John 9-10).

CONTENTS OF THE LETTER

John is always glad to hear good news of Christians whom he has helped over the years. In particular, he is encouraged by the news he has heard about Gaius, namely, that he continues to grow in spiritual strength and remains faithful to the truth (1-4).

Besides being faithful to God in the things he believes and teaches, Gaius is helpful to the travelling preachers. He welcomes them to preach in the church and provides them with loving hospitality. This is true not just of those travellers who are his friends, but also of those who are strangers to him (5-6). By supporting such people, he is helping to preserve God's truth in a time of widespread false teaching. Others in the church should follow his example (7-8).

By contrast Diotrephes acts only out of selfish ambition. He opposes the authority of John (who was an apostle as well as an elder), refuses to pass on John's instruction to the church and makes false accusations against him. Harshly domineering and always self-assertive, he refuses to welcome the travelling preachers into the church and expels any who oppose him. If Gaius is unable to restore some harmony and order in the church, John himself may have to come and use his apostolic authority to punish Diotrephes (9-10).

John reminds Gaius of the need to stand firm for what is right and not to give in to wrongdoing merely for the sake of peace. He suggests that the respected Demetrius might be a reliable helper in this difficult time (11-12). John expects that he himself will visit Gaius soon, and this will give him the opportunity to talk over these and other matters at greater length. Meanwhile, he and his friends pass on their greetings to the church (13-15).

Jude

BACKGROUND

It is generally believed that the writer of this letter was Jude (or Judas), one of the brothers of Jesus (Mark 6:3). His older brother was James, a leading man in the Jerusalem church (Jude 1; cf. Acts 12:17; 15:13). Like James he was not a believer during the time of Jesus' public ministry (John 7:3-5), but he was among the disciples at the time of Jesus' ascension (Acts 1:11-14). It is believed that the resurrection had an impact on Jesus' brothers that helped turn them from unbelief to faith (cf. 1 Cor 15:4-7).

Jude seems to have later become a respected teacher in the church, though his letter does not indicate the region where he worked or the people whom he addressed. Nevertheless, the purpose of his letter is clear. He wrote to oppose a kind of false teaching that was doing great damage to Christianity through encouraging immoral behaviour (Jude 3-4).

The false teaching that Jude opposed was widespread during the second half of the first century. It was part of a developing Gnosticism (from the Greek *gnosis*, meaning 'knowledge'; see background notes to 1 John). The teaching claimed that self-control was not necessary for those who possessed a higher knowledge of spiritual things. In fact, immoral behaviour might even be a sign of spiritual maturity, as if people found true freedom through their higher knowledge. Jude pronounced God's certain punishment on those who taught and practised such a religion.

Parts of the letter of Jude are similar to parts of 2 Peter, particularly in the examples and illustrations that are used. The two writers opposed similar errors, and one may have borrowed from the other's letter. Alternatively, both may have used material that had become a widely accepted standard in dealing with the false teaching of the time.

CONTENTS OF THE LETTER

Condemnation of the false teachers (1-16)

Jude had intended to write about more general matters concerning the Christian faith, but when he heard of the activities of evil teachers he changed his mind. He now feels that it is more important to encourage the Christians to hold firmly to the truth they first heard and to fight against those who want to destroy it. Punishment is certain for those who distort the true teaching of the gospel in order to give themselves the freedom to practise immorality (1-4).

People may belong to a Christian community, or even be known as Christian teachers, but that is no guarantee of their salvation. If they do not truly believe, they will suffer God's condemnation. Three examples are given to illustrate this fact. First, all the people of Israel were delivered from Egypt, but those who did not believe were destroyed (5; cf. Num 14:26-35). Second, angels have high status, but those who rebelled met a terrifying judgment (6; cf. Gen 6:1-4). Third, Sodom and Gomorrah were great cities, but they were destroyed because of their immorality (7; cf. Gen 19:12-25).

Controlling neither their passions nor their words, these false teachers commit immoral sexual acts and insult both God and his angels. Yet the chief angel himself refused to condemn the devil with insulting words (even though he may have had good cause to), for he would not claim for himself the authority of judgment that belongs to God alone (8-9). (This story is taken from the apocryphal 'Assumption of Moses'. Apocryphal writings are certain recognized books written in the era of the Old Testament but not included in the Old Testament. They are grouped into two collections, the Apocrypha and the Pseudepigrapha.)

The ungodly teachers have no understanding of spiritual things, but act according to their physical instincts, like animals. They have Cain's jealousy, Balaam's greed, and Korah's spirit of rebellion against authority (10-11; cf. Gen 4:3-8; Num 16:1-50; 22:1-40; 25:1-9; 31:16). Their behaviour at Christian fellowship meals is a disgrace. Like rainless clouds they bring no good; like fruitless trees they are useless and should be destroyed; like the restless sea they are without control; like falling stars they will be swallowed up in the darkness, the darkness of God's eternal punishment (12-13).

Enoch's prophecy confirms the certain punishment of people characterized by such ungodliness. Whether they criticize or flatter, whether they grumble or boast, their actions are always motivated solely by what is going to benefit them personally (14-16). (The prophecy of Enoch is taken from the apocryphal 'Book of Enoch'.)

Encouragement to Christians (17-25)

The Christians are reminded of the words of the apostles. Years earlier they had warned that ungodly teachers would trouble the church, leading people into sin and causing divisions (17-19). The way to avoid their evil influence is to learn more of the Christian truth, to be more sincere in prayer, to grow in devotion to God, to hate sin in all its forms, and to help those affected by the false teachers to find new life in God (20-23).

Jude closes his letter on a note of magnificent praise to the only God and Saviour. God is supreme in majesty and authority, and the same power by which he saved Christians in the first place is still available to them. God is able to keep his people safe and pure amid the destructive corruption of the false teaching, and one day bring them triumphantly into his heavenly presence (24-25).

Revelation

BACKGROUND

As its name indicates, the book of Revelation reveals things that otherwise would remain unknown. The revelation originated in God and came from the risen Christ to the writer John, who then passed it on to a group of churches in the Roman province of Asia (in western Asia Minor). It was given towards the end of the first century and concerned things that were soon to happen (Rev 1:1,11).

The traditional view is that the person named John who wrote the book was the apostle John, though the book contains no statement that makes this identification certain. The writer had been arrested for his Christian faith and at the time of writing was imprisoned on the island of Patmos, off the coast from Ephesus (Rev 1:9-10). John the apostle seems to have lived in Ephesus during the latter part of the first century, and while there wrote his Gospel and letters (see background notes to

1 John). The churches with which John was concerned in his Gospel and letters were in the same region as those to whom the book of Revelation was sent.

By this time the churches of the region were well established. In fact, about forty years had passed since the region had been first evangelized (cf. Acts 16:6-10; 18:19,20-28; 19:1,8-10). Those parts of the book that are addressed to specific churches give us a picture of conditions in Asia Minor at the end of the first century.

The troubled church

Almost from its beginning, the church of the first century was persecuted. In the early days persecution came mainly from the Jews, but as the decades passed, government authorities also turned against the Christians. The main periods of official persecution came in the AD 60s under the Emperor Nero and in the AD 90s during the time of the Emperor Domitian. This latter period was the time

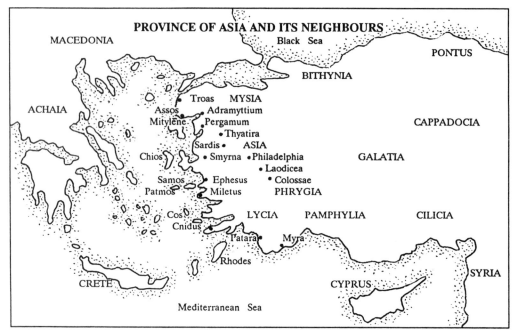

PROVINCE OF ASIA AND ITS NEIGHBOURS

of the revelation that the writer John has recorded in this book.

It was a testing time for Christians. Thousands were imprisoned, tortured, killed or put to work as slaves. Oppression increased, people in general became more anti-Christian, and the government enforced Emperor worship as a regular policy. To make matters worse, false teachers created trouble within the churches by encouraging Christians to cooperate with the pagan religions of the state by joining in practices that were idolatrous and immoral (Rev 2:10,13-14,20; 6:9-11).

Many Christians were discouraged and confused, and some had even renounced their faith. It seemed to them that Jesus Christ, the king they had expected to return in power, was either unable or unwilling to save them from the evil forces that were working against them. The real power appeared to be not in the hands of the Almighty God, but in the hands of the Roman Emperor.

Through John, Jesus reassured his suffering people that he was still in control, though he did not give them false hopes by promising them quick relief. On the contrary he prepared them for greater endurance, by revealing both the extent of the troubles yet to come and the eternal reward that awaited those who stood firm for him. He was still the ruler of the world and he was still in control. In God's time Jesus would return to punish his enemies, save his people, and bring in an age of eternal peace and joy (Rev 1:5; 12:10-11; 19:15-16; 21:1-4; 22:7).

Style of the book

The book of Revelation belongs to a category of literature known as apocalyptic that was common at that time. (The name comes from the Greek *apokalypsis*, the word translated 'revelation' in Revelation 1:1.)

In apocalyptic literature God gives revelations to people by means of strange visions that are usually explained by angels. These visions often feature fearsome beasts and mysterious numbers, and are mostly concerned with God's conquest of evil and deliverance of his people. God intervenes in world affairs to overthrow the wicked, give victory to the righteous, establish his kingdom, and introduce the era of the new heavens and new earth.

It is difficult to form mental pictures of these strange visions, even more difficult to draw them on paper, and impossible to join them all together in a continuous picture-story. But they were not intended for that purpose. The modern reader should not think of the visions as if they are photographs or videos of future events that the biblical writer has seen in advance. Details within the visions, whether in relation to times, places, objects or living beings, should not be understood as if they are descriptions taken from a news report or historical account. They are stylized and symbolic, and are often inconsistent with the realities of the natural world.

Features that have a particular meaning in one vision may or may not have the same meaning in another vision. Similarly, a particular truth may be symbolized by certain features in one vision, and by entirely different features in another.

Interpretation of the book

These characteristics make apocalyptic literature difficult for people of a different culture and era to interpret. Over the centuries various schemes of interpretation have appeared. Some people interpret Revelation as applying solely to the time of John, while others interpret it as applying solely to a time in the future when God will bring the present age to an end. Some interpret the book as a continuous history of the world from the time of John to the coming eternal age, while others see the book not as a description of historical events but as a presentation of the victory of the gospel in symbolic pictures. The variations in interpretation, whether of the book as a whole or of its separate parts and details, are considerable.

Some people attempt to solve the difficulties by choosing one scheme of interpretation and rejecting all the others. But this is not the best way to understand the book's message. Undoubtedly, the book had a meaning for the people of John's day, as it has for people today, and as it will have for those on earth at the end of the age. Readers should therefore be careful not to restrict the book's message or mould its meaning to fit their favourite scheme of interpretation.

A further precaution for readers is not to treat the book as a collection of puzzles. It was not given to amuse Christians in their spare time by giving them mysteries to work out. It was given to strengthen and guide Christians who were suffering intense persecution. There is little spiritual profit in finding the meanings of symbols while ignoring their relevance to personal experience.

The symbolic pictures in the book are taken mainly from life under Roman rule as John knew it, but the principles apply to Christians everywhere. In every era and nation those who suffer persecution for Christ's sake can find strength and encouragement as they see the relevance of the visions to their own experiences.

Anti-Christian persecutions and divine judgments on the persecutors have occurred repeatedly throughout the church's history, and they will continue to be repeated till Jesus Christ returns. From the first century to the present, Christians have triumphed over the forces of the antichrist through Christ's victory on the cross (Rev 12:11). But the ultimate victory will be when Christ returns to banish evil, save his people and bring in the eternal age of peace and joy (Rev 1:5-7; 19:13-16; 22:1-5,12-14).

OUTLINE

1:1-20 JOHN'S INTRODUCTION

Greetings to the seven churches (1:1-8)

Jesus Christ received this revelation from God and passed it on to John by a series of visions that an angel interpreted for him. John, in turn, was to pass this revelation on to God's persecuted people in Asia Minor, for it concerned events about to take place that would affect them. All who took notice of the book would be blessed, both the person who read it to the church and those who listened as he read it (1:1-3).

The writer greets his readers in the name of the Trinity — the eternal God, the ever-present Spirit and the faithful Son. This Son was a faithful witness through his sufferings and is still Lord of the kings of the earth. These include the Roman Emperor, their persecutor. Christians may share Christ's sufferings, but they also share his victory. Through him they have been cleansed from their sins and given the privilege of worshipping and serving him as a kingdom of priests (4-6). Christ's enemies thought they had conquered him, but he will return to conquer them, for he is almighty. Nothing existed before him and nothing will exist after him (7-8).

A vision of Christ (1:9-20)

One Sunday, the day of the Lord's victorious resurrection, John received this revelation in a series of visions. He knew of the sufferings of Christians, because he himself was imprisoned on account of his Christian faith. He carried a message for persecuted believers that he was to send to seven churches in the Roman province of Asia. The order in which the churches are listed is probably the order in which they were visited by the person who delivered the letters. From these churches the message would no doubt spread to the smaller churches round about (9-11).

The first vision that John sees is of the Lord of the church, Jesus Christ, walking among the churches (symbolized by lampstands; see v. 20). His appearance displays the greatness, majesty, wisdom and authority of God (12-15). He holds the churches (symbolized this time by stars; see v. 20) in the protective care of his right hand. At the same time he has the sword of authority to act against any in those churches who oppose his will (16).

John was so overcome with this vision that he collapsed. But Christ strengthened him, pointing out that he should be encouraged, not afraid, for Christ has authority even over death. Persecuted believers need not fear that death will separate them from him (17-18).

The revelations that John is about to receive will concern both his time and the future. The seven angels to whom he must address his letters are symbolic representatives of seven churches. This emphasizes that although John has a message for Christians in general, he has a specific message for each of the seven churches (19-20).

2:1-3:22 LETTERS TO THE SEVEN CHURCHES

Apart from occasional minor variations, the seven letters follow the same pattern. They begin with a greeting from the risen Christ (whose titles are mostly taken from the vision described in 1:12-16), followed in turn by a statement of praise and/or criticism concerning the current state of the church, a warning, an instruction and a promise. Although each church received the particular message for itself, it would also hear the messages for the other churches if the whole book was read in each church. Therefore, there is a note of warning for *all* to take heed: 'Let anyone who has an ear listen to what the Spirit is saying to the churches.'

Letter to Ephesus (2:1-7)

Over the years the church at Ephesus had been troubled constantly by false teachers, as Paul had warned (cf. Acts 20:17,29-30). The false teaching condemned in Paul's letters to Timothy and in the letters of John was centred in Ephesus. Later the church in Ephesus was troubled by the Nicolaitans, who taught that Christians could best demonstrate their freedom from rules and regulations by eating food that had been offered to idols and joining in immoral behaviour.

At the outset of his message, the risen Christ praises the Ephesians for their hard work and patient endurance in opposing the evil teachers (2:1-3). Unfortunately, in the process their love for Christ has lost its original warmth. They have become harsh, critical and self-satisfied. They are warned that if they do not quickly change and regain their original spirit of love, the one who rules over the churches (see v. 1; cf. 1:12-13,16) will act in judgment and bring the church to an end (4-6). Those who triumph, however, will enjoy the fulness of eternal life in the world to come (7).

Letter to Smyrna (2:8-11)

Poor materially, but rich spiritually, the Christians in Smyrna were also severely persecuted. The persecution came mainly from the Jews, who thus showed that they were not God's people, but Satan's (8-9). But worse is to come, for the Roman authorities are going to launch a fresh attack on the Christians. Many will be imprisoned and some martyred, but this fierce attack will last only a limited period. Their Saviour, the eternal one who has himself conquered death (see v. 8; cf. 1:17-18), will not allow death to touch their souls. Through him they have victory and eternal life (10-11).

Letter to Pergamum (2:12-17)

The difficulties of the church in Pergamum were mainly connected with the religious system known as Emperor worship, which in the province of Asia had its headquarters in Pergamum. Christians on the whole had stood firm and refused to join in the Emperor worship. At least one, Antipas, had been martyred (12-13).

But as at Ephesus, there were some who taught and practised Nicolaitan teachings. Like Balaam, they caused God's people to sin by joining in idolatrous feasts and practising immorality (14-15; cf. Num 22:1-40; 25:1-9; 31:16). The divine judge (see v. 12; cf. 1:16) is about to act against them with swift punishment. But those who refuse to join in the idolatrous feasts will be invited to join in God's heavenly feast. He will give each a special blessing known only to the giver and the receiver. This blessing is likened to the engraved white stone which, according to a custom of those days, was given to people invited to an important feast as evidence of their right of entry (16-17).

Letter to Thyatira (2:18-29)

There had been considerable progress in the church at Thyatira (18-19). Yet this church also had been corrupted by teaching that encouraged participation in idol feasts and their associated immorality.

In Pergamum the false teachers were men and were likened to Balaam. In Thyatira the teacher was a woman and is likened to Jezebel, whose false religion was similarly characterized by idolatry and immorality (20; cf. 1 Kings 16:31-33; 2 Kings 9:22). This false prophetess is now given a final warning, for the penetrating eyes of the righteous God see all that she is doing (see v. 18; cf. 1:14-15). If she does not turn from her sins, God will punish her and her followers with sickness, disease or death, according to the extent of each person's sin (21-23).

On the other hand, those who are faithful to the end will be rewarded when Christ returns (24-25). Victorious believers will share the royal rule of their victorious Lord. The 'night' of suffering will be over, and Christ the 'morning star' will be with them for ever (26-29).

Letter to Sardis (3:1-6)

The church in Sardis had so much followed the ways of the society around it that it was Christian in name only. Spiritually it was dead (3:1). The Lord of the church can give it new life through the Spirit (see v. 1; cf. 1:4,20), but first the believers must wake up, change their ways, and determine to follow the teaching of the gospel they first believed. If not, swift judgment will fall upon them (2-3).

Some in the church had proved the genuineness of their faith by refusing to alter their beliefs or behaviour to suit the majority. They had 'kept their clothes clean'. They will therefore join Christ in heaven in 'clothes' of greater purity; for he himself has cleansed them, made them his own and brought them into his heavenly Father's presence (4-6).

Letter to Philadelphia (3:7-13)

Smyrna and Philadelphia are the only churches that receive no blame from the Lord, but only praise and encouragement. Yet Smyrna was poor and Philadelphia was small. Also, both churches received their opposition from the Jews.

He who carries the key of David has the authority to allow people into or shut them out from the city of David, which here is symbolic of the new Jerusalem, the kingdom of Jesus Christ (7; cf. v. 12). The Jews claimed they were the people of God's kingdom and tried to shut the Gentiles out. But,

Christ points out, the small group of Christians who form the church of Philadelphia are the true people of God in that city. Christ has opened the door for these Gentile Christians, and no Jew is able to close it. In entering God's kingdom, Jews must follow the way of these Gentiles, not Gentiles follow the way of the Jews (8-9).

When God judges the ungodly, Christ will protect those who have remained loyal to him. He will reward them at his return (10-11). Each of the triumphant believers will be like a pillar in God's temple, secure in his presence for ever. Through Christ, who has the key to life and death (see v. 7; cf. 1:18), they will belong permanently to God, to the heavenly city and to their Saviour (12-13).

Letter to Laodicea (3:14-22)

Laodicea was an important commercial, educational and administrative centre whose citizens were secure and prosperous, lacking nothing. Sadly, the spirit of self-satisfaction among the people at large was found equally in the church. This church has no accusation of idolatry or immorality brought against it, yet it receives the strongest condemnation of all seven.

The Laodiceans not only thought they had all they needed, but they believed their prosperity had resulted from their spirituality. Actually, they were lacking in spirituality. Because of their reliance on material things, they could not exercise genuine faith in God. Nor could their lives witness to the total satisfaction that Christ brings. Christ introduces himself as the one who is faithful, the true witness, the creator with authority over all material things. He tells them plainly that he finds their comfortable spiritual pride repulsive (14-16). He urges them to see themselves as he sees them, as spiritually poor, blind and naked. They must realize that Christ alone can produce truly spiritual qualities in their lives, and he can do this only when they turn from their sins and humbly seek his help (17-19).

Christ still loves his people and asks them to welcome him into every part of their lives. Even if the church as a whole ignores his request, those individuals who open their lives to him will know the joy of constant fellowship with him. If they share their lives with him now, he will share his glory with them in the future (20-22).

4:1-5:14 A VISION OF HEAVEN

Vision of the throne (4:1-11)

Jesus has shown John the present state of the churches as he sees them. He now shows him, again from the divine viewpoint, certain things that are going to happen as God works out his purposes in the world. By means of a vision of heaven, John begins to have some understanding of how God sees the world's affairs. He is given a glimpse of the place where God, the possessor of absolute authority, reigns majestically in indescribable glory (4:1-3).

In this vision the throne on which the Almighty sits is in a large flat area that looks like a sea of crystal. The seven blazing lamps in front of the throne suggest the burning power of God's all-seeing Spirit, while the lightning and thunder coming from the throne create a feeling of overwhelming awe. Twenty-four elders seated on smaller thrones encircle the throne of the Almighty. They appear to be angelic beings that belong to one of the heavenly orders (cf. Isa. 24:23), but they cannot cross the sea of crystal to share God's throne. His position is unique (4-6a).

Between the elders and the throne of God are four 'living creatures'. These are probably heavenly beings of another order and resemble the cherubim of the Old Testament. Like the cherubim they appear to be guardians of the throne of God (6b-8; cf. 1 Sam 4:4; Ps 80:1; Ezek 1:4-28; 10:15-17).

The significance of the vision becomes clearer when the living creatures and the elders begin to sing praises and worship God. The vision's central meaning is that in heaven God is worshipped unceasingly. He is the Creator and Lord of the universe and he is always in control. The persecuted Christians need never doubt his power or his wisdom (9-11).

Vision of the Lamb (5:1-14)

In the hand of the Almighty is a scroll, which no doubt contains the revelation that John is to receive. Like most important documents it is sealed. In fact, it has seven seals, and these can be broken only by someone with the authority to do so. Since the scroll will reveal matters of worldwide importance, the person to break these seals must be one who has authority over the world's affairs. John weeps when it appears that no one in all creation can be found who is worthy to open the scroll (5:1-4).

Then one is found. Jesus Christ, the conquering Lion from the tribe of Judah, the Messiah from the family of David, is able to open the seals (5). He is all-powerful and all-knowing ('seven horns and seven eyes'), but he has the right to reveal God's purposes and carry out God's judgments only because of his submissive and sacrificial death as the Lamb of God (6; cf. v. 9).

Christ then takes the scroll from the Almighty, but before he opens it the living creatures and the elders break forth in fresh praise, this time directed to Christ (7-8). By his death he has brought people of all nations to God. These people already share in the victory he won at the cross, and as a kingdom of priests they represent him in the world. One day they will enjoy the fruit of this victory in its fulness (9-10).

Others join in the song of praise, till the countless angels of heaven are united in singing the praises of the Lamb (11-12). They are joined by creatures out of all creation, to praise both the Almighty who sits on the throne and the Lamb who has overcome the power of sin (13-14). In summary it might be said that in Chapter 4 God is worshipped as Creator, and in Chapter 5 he is worshipped as Redeemer. He is the Controller of the world and the Saviour of his people.

6:1-8:5 THE SEVEN SEALS

Much of the next part of the book records three series of judgment visions that John saw – the seven seals (6:1-8:5), the seven trumpets (8:6-11:19) and the seven bowls of wrath (15:1-16:21). John also saw another series of visions, the seven thunders, but God did not allow him to record them (10:3-4). This is a reminder that God has not given us all the information about what he is doing, and will yet do, as he brings his purposes in the world to fulfilment.

In the symbolism of Revelation, the number seven is used repeatedly. It seems to represent one complete unit, and may signify such ideas as wholeness, fulness, completion or perfection. In each of the first two series of seven there is an interval before the seventh vision, suggesting that God waits as long as possible before acting in judgment. He does not want any to be destroyed, but wants all to turn from their sins and receive the salvation he offers (cf. Rom 2:2-6; 1 Tim 2:4; 2 Peter 3:8-10).

The judgments that Jesus reveals to John are similar to, but more detailed than, those that he described to his disciples on the Mount of Olives. There is a similar emphasis on war, famine, death, earthquakes and persecution, but because of God's patience and forbearance, 'the end is not yet' (Matt 24:3-14). Nevertheless, one day the end will come. There will be no more delay; the judgment must fall (Matt 24:29-31).

In the book of Revelation, as in all prophetic and apocalyptic writings, there is a lack of exactness concerning the time that events will take place. This is because the writer sees everything from God's viewpoint in eternity, where time is not measured by human standards, and may even seem irrelevant. Certain events will take place; 'after this', other events. The person who sees the vision (and the person who reads of it) cannot tell whether the latter events take place immediately after or thousands of years after the former events.

From the words of Jesus himself, Christians are reminded that they do not know when the end of the present age will come. Moreover, God does not intend them to know. He does not satisfy their curiosity about the future, but reminds them of their responsibility in the present, which is to spread the message of salvation (Mark 13:32; Acts 1:7-8). They are to be ready at all times for God's final great intervention in human affairs, for Jesus Christ will return when they least expect (Matt 24:44; 1 Thess 5:2-8).

God gave his revelation to John not so that Christians might draw up a timetable of history in advance, but so that the persecuted might be encouraged. The certainty of God's judgment is an incentive to all Christians to be more holy and more dedicated to God (1 Cor 4:5; 1 Peter 4:18-19; 2 Peter 3:11-12).

First six seals (6:1-17)

The scroll was sealed in such a way that it had to be unrolled section by section. When the first seal was broken, the scroll could be unrolled only enough to reveal the first part of the revelation. Then the second seal was broken and the scroll was unrolled a little further; and so on till all seven seals were broken and the scroll was completely unrolled. An unusual feature was that as each seal was broken, instead of someone reading the scroll, a vision appeared. John now describes these visions.

As each of the first four seals is broken a horse appears. The first represents nations going out to conquer other nations. The second indicates the war and bloodshed that follow (6:1-4). The third shows the beginning of famine, where a shortage of basic foods results in rationing and high prices. The common people suffer most, for the rich can afford more expensive foods that are not yet affected (5-6). The fourth vision shows that the situation worsens. Widespread death results from the combined effects of war, famine and disease (7-8).

When the fifth seal is broken the scene shifts to heaven, where a vision shows that although God's judgments fall upon a sinful world, believers need not fear. Certainly, sinners will react against God by killing his people, but that is no reason to question

God's justice. Believers, not enemies, are the victors, a fact signified by the white robes given to them. Yet there will be more martyrs. The believers' prayers, though heard in heaven, do not bring an instant end to the suffering (9-11).

The vision of the sixth seal assures believers and unbelievers alike that God is still in control. He is righteous and at the right time his judgment will fall, accompanied by violent disturbances in the heavens and on the earth (12-14; cf. Matt 24:29-30). Sinners will not escape, no matter how powerful or rich they might be. He who carries out this judgment is the Lamb of God, the one who himself bore God's wrath so that sinners might escape it (15-17).

Interval before the seventh seal (7:1-17)

God gives John two additional visions before he reveals the vision of the final seal. He wants to reassure his people that he does not forget them during the difficult days when an ungodly world is preparing itself for judgment. God does not allow the winds of judgment to blow across the earth without thought for his people's security. He knows those who are his and marks them out for his special protection (7:1-3; cf. Ezek 9:4-6). The repetition of the number of people protected in each of the twelve tribes (symbolic of God's people on earth) emphasizes that God protects all his people. None is missed (4-8).

Having seen God's people on earth, John now sees the same people in heaven. They come from all nations and are more than anyone can count. They may have suffered persecution and even martyrdom on earth, but in heaven they are seen as conquerors, dressed in white and holding palm branches. The Lamb who died triumphed over death, and his victory is now theirs (9-10). Angels add their praise to that of the triumphant believers (11-12).

All this is explained to John, with special emphasis on the victory of the cross. Although the believers have been victorious in suffering persecution for Christ's sake, they are fit to stand in God's presence only because Christ died to give them cleansing and new life (13-14). As priests of God they will be permanently in his presence, where they will worship and serve him in true fellowship. No longer will they suffer, but the good shepherd, Jesus Christ, will protect them and care for them (15-17).

Seventh seal (8:1-5)

As the ungodly suffered the increasingly heavy judgments of the first six seals, they turned against the Christians with greater persecution. This had caused believers to ask God how long it would be before he dealt with those who were killing them (see 6:9-10). God is now going to answer that prayer. He has postponed judgment as long as possible, but now the time has come. All heaven waits silently. But when the seventh seal is broken, it reveals judgments so terrible that a new set of visions will be needed to explain them. The new visions will be announced by the blowing of trumpets (8:1-2).

Before seeing the new visions, John sees in picture form how the prayers of the persecuted Christians have brought about these judgments. He sees the prayers held by an angel in a golden container, then mixed with incense and burnt on the golden altar. As the smoke of the burning incense rises, it pictures the prayers going up to God (3-4). The angel then takes fire from the altar, puts it in the incense container, and throws the container to the earth. As soon as it hits the earth, terrible judgments break out. The whole vision is a dramatic way of showing how the prayers of God's people play an important part in his dealings with the ungodly world (5; cf. Matt 24:22).

8:6-11:19 THE SEVEN TRUMPETS
First four trumpets (8:6-13)

In the visions revealed by the breaking of the seals, the judgments arose largely from human sin. But in the judgments announced by the blowing of the trumpets, the judgments seem to come direct from God without the use of a human agency. The trumpet visions reveal another way of looking at God's judgment, but like the seal visions they build towards a climax.

The first trumpet announces widespread devastation on the land (6-7); the second, on the sea (8-9); the third, on the waters of the land (10-11); and the fourth, on the moon and stars (12). The destruction of the symbolic 'one third' is slightly more extensive than the 'one quarter' in the seal judgments (cf. 6:8), but is not a total judgment. It is a warning of what will happen if people do not repent. The three woes (GNB: horrors) announced by an eagle correspond to the three remaining trumpet judgments (13; cf. 9:1,12-13; 11:14-15).

Fifth and sixth trumpets (9:1-21)

Worse than the destruction by the forces of nature is the suffering brought by the forces of demons (fifth trumpet). These demonic forces are pictured in a strange and terrifying army of locusts. Though uncontrollable by any human power, they are not independent of the rule of God. He keeps them imprisoned in the abyss (RSV: bottomless pit), and even when he releases them he determines the extent of their activity (9:1-3).

The demons do not harm plant life (as ordinary locusts do), but harm people — though not God's people. They torment the ungodly with severe pain, rather like scorpions, but do not kill them. The vision shows how the ungodly become so tormented in mind and body by satanic forces that they wish to die, but they cannot. Just as a plague of locusts lasts for only a limited period, so does this attack by the forces of evil (4-6). John then describes the frightening appearance of this army of demons (7-10). He points out that they are led by a satanic leader whose name, whether in Hebrew or Greek, means 'destroyer' (11).

As the sixth trumpet sounds, a noise comes from the golden altar, giving a reminder that these judgments are a response to the prayers of the persecuted Christians (12-13; cf. 6:9-10). At that moment God allows wicked angels to be released and there is another outbreak of demonic activity. The locust-like demons were not allowed to kill people, but these demons bring widespread death to the human race (14-16). Again John describes the fearsome appearance of the demons. They are like an army of horses and riders equipped to bring suffering and death by the most frightful means (17-19).

God's aim is not merely to send his judgments upon the world, but to show people the seriousness of their sins so that they might repent and be saved. But no matter how severe his judgments, they continue in their sins (20-21).

Interval before the seventh trumpet (10:1-11)

During the lengthy interval before the blowing of the final trumpet, John has several other visions. First he sees a huge angel towering over land and sea, and holding a small scroll in his hand. The meaning apparently is that this angel is to make announcements that will affect the whole world. This results in a further series of visions, the seven thunders, but John is not allowed to record them (10:1-4). The angel announces that when the seventh trumpet is blown, it will introduce the final stage of God's plan (5-7).

John then eats the small scroll. Its contents must become part of him, so to speak, so that he can pass on its message with greater meaning and force. Because it is God's message he finds it sweet at first, but when he understands the judgments it reveals, he finds it unpleasant. He has no joy in announcing it (8-11; cf. Ezek 3:1-3; 2 Cor 2:15-16).

Two witnesses (11:1-14)

In Daniel 9:24-27 there is a prophecy that the enemies of the Jews would corrupt their city and their temple for three and a half years (which is the same as forty-two months, or 1260 days). This happened in 167-164 BC, when the ruler of the Syrian sector of the Greek Empire, Antiochus IV Epiphanes, conquered Jerusalem, killed Jews by the thousand and tried by every means to destroy their religion. His supreme expression of hate for God's people was to set up a Greek idol in their temple, build an altar, then take animals that the Jews considered unclean and sacrifice them to the Greek gods.

This event is now used as an illustration. Just as the Gentiles trampled the holy city and its temple for three and a half years, so for a time the ungodly world is allowed to trample the church. There is, however, a limit to the extent it can go. God's people in the world (compared in the vision to those in the outer courts of the temple) are persecuted and even killed; but from God's viewpoint they are eternally secure in his presence (compared in the vision to those worshipping within the temple). The message is one of encouragement to persecuted Christians. The church's task is difficult, but its triumph is certain. There may be martyrs, but God's church will not be destroyed (11:1-2).

Two messengers of God symbolize the church's powerful witness during this troubled period (3). This witness is likened to that of Zerubbabel and Joshua, who stood firm for God's truth in re-establishing the worship of God in Israel after the captivity in Babylon (4; cf. Zech 4:1-14). It is likened also to the witness of Moses and Elijah, to whom God gave his special power. As in the time of Moses, God saves his people from being destroyed by hostile rulers. As in the time of Elijah, he saves them from being destroyed by the corruption of false religion (5-6; cf. Exod 4:9; 7:1-12:51; 1 Kings 18:1-46; 19:1-21; 2 Kings 1:7-12).

But the more powerful the witness, the greater the opposition. Satanic power increases and large numbers of Christians are martyred (7). The world that killed Jesus Christ is now killing his followers. It is likened to a great city that is characterized by the wickedness of Sodom and the cruelty of Egypt (cf. Gen 19:1-24; Exod 1:9-16; 3:7). People rejoice when they get rid of those who expose their sin, and do all they can to bring the greatest possible shame upon the Christians (8-10).

The persecutors' apparent victory does not last long. They are filled with terror when they see that the church has not been destroyed but has received new life. The victory of Christ guarantees not only victory for believers, but also judgment for their opponents (11-12; cf. Phil 1:28). In John's vision the judgment is symbolized by an earthquake that brings extensive destruction upon the city and its citizens. The enemies of God at last give some recognition to his supreme authority and power (13; cf. 9:20-21). The third woe (i.e. the seventh trumpet) will now follow (14).

Seventh trumpet (11:15-19)

Having had an interval to consider the triumph of God's people, the revelation returns to the series of trumpet judgments. The climax of those judgments, announced by the blowing of the seventh trumpet, is the abolition of all human government and the establishment of God's everlasting kingdom under the rule of Jesus Christ (15). This brings with it the divinely appointed day of judgment for all people, when God rewards his servants and punishes sinners (16-18; cf. Acts 17:31; 2 Tim 4:1).

In a dramatic revelation, God then opens his heavenly temple and displays the ark, symbol of his covenant faithfulness. The significance of this is that through all his people's sufferings and trials, God has never forgotten them. The symbol of his faithfulness to them has always been before him in his heavenly sanctuary (19).

12:1-14:20 PICTURES OF CONFLICT AND TRIUMPH

The woman, the child and the dragon (12:1-17)

In this vision the woman who gives birth to a son seems to symbolize Israel who produced the Messiah, Jesus. But it is the true Israel, the true people of God, who are pictured here. The faithful of old Israel were those who began the Christian church, and in the church there is no distinction on the basis of nationality. All Christians are now God's people (12:1-2).

Then appears a dragon (identified in verse 9 as Satan) whose many heads, horns and crowns show his extraordinary power. He is hard to overcome. When apparently defeated in one place, he finds new energy in another. His conquest of a large portion of the angelic powers ('a third of the stars of heaven') is only a preparation for his main task, the conquest of the Messiah. He tried to destroy Jesus, from the day of his birth to the day of his death, but he never succeeded, not even at the crucifixion. Jesus Christ rose from the dead and returned in glory to his Father (3-5).

Unable to destroy Christ, Satan turns his attack on Christ's people. But God has foreseen this and he specially protects them and provides for them during this time. Persecuted Christians need not fear Satan. Their time of greatest trial (again represented by the symbolic figure of three and a half years; cf. 11:2-3) is their time of greatest blessing. They may be killed but they are not destroyed, for God saves them for his heavenly kingdom (6; cf. 2 Tim 4:6,18).

The battle between good and evil is fought in heaven as well as on earth. Believers can take courage when they learn that God's angels triumph, while the devil and his angels are thrown out of heaven (7-9). The heavenly conquest of Satan gives reassurance to Christ's people on earth that they too are conquerors of Satan. They share in the glorious victory of Christ's kingdom, and the basis of that victory is Christ's death. He was victorious through death, and those who are killed for his sake are likewise victorious (10-11). Satan responds viciously. Knowing that little time remains before Christ returns and captures him, he intensifies his attacks on God's people (12).

Returning to the picture of the woman, the revelation repeats that when Satan finds that he cannot destroy Christ, he tries to destroy Christ's people (13). It repeats also that the time of the Christians' intense suffering is the time of God's special protection (14; cf. 11:2-3; 12:6; 13:5). ('A time, times and half a time' means 'a year plus two years plus half a year', or three and a half years.) Satan tries every method he knows to destroy Christ's people but is not successful. God, by his supernatural power, preserves them (15-16). Unable to destroy them, Satan nevertheless does whatever he can to oppose and persecute them (17).

Beast from the sea (13:1-10)

Like the dragon of Chapter 12, the beast that arises out of the sea has seven heads and ten horns. If the dragon symbolizes Satan, the opponent of God in the spirit world, the beast out of the sea probably symbolizes the opponent of God in the world of humankind. As God took human form in Jesus Christ, so Satan takes human form in one called the antichrist (GNB: enemy of Christ), or man of lawlessness (GNB: wicked one). He combines cunning, strength, cruelty and ferocity (13:1-2).

Though always in the world, the spirit of antichrist expresses itself in different ways in various people, eras and systems (1 John 2:18). In John's time it expressed itself in the Roman Empire, but its fullest expression will be in the days immediately before Christ's return (2 Thess 2:3-10).

The antichrist tries to imitate Christ by giving an appearance of death followed by resurrection. He appears to lose his power, only to regain it and do greater and more horrible evil. People in general are impressed with his show of power and believe that none, not even God, can fight against him. They are overcome with a sense of awe, and gladly give their allegiance to the antichrist and his master, Satan (3-4; cf. 2 Thess 2:3-4,9-12).

Suffering Christians are encouraged to endure by the news that God has set a limit to the time of the antichrist's rule. But while he rules he curses God and demands that people worship him instead. All people give him homage except the Christians, and these he mercilessly attacks (5-8). Christians are given a special reminder that it is useless to resist when they are about to be captured or killed. They cannot establish God's kingdom in the world by force (9-10).

Beast from the earth (13:11-18)

With the appearance of the beast from the earth (who is identified as the false prophet; see 16:13; 19:20), the trinity of evil is complete. As the true Christ received his authority from the Father, so the antichrist receives his authority from Satan (see 13:2b; cf. John 8:28). As the Holy Spirit gives glory to the true Christ, so the false prophet gives glory to the antichrist (see 13:12; cf. John 16:14). The spirit of the false prophet is always in the world, for it represents false religion, or whatever philosophy people use in place of religion (Matt 24:24; 2 Peter 2:1). It too will have its most intense expression in the days immediately before Christ's return (2 Thess 2:11-12).

The false prophet tries to make himself look as harmless as a lamb, but his speech shows that he belongs to Satan (11). He has the same satanic power as the antichrist and cooperates with him. The meaning seems to be that religious power (represented by the false prophet) joins with secular power (represented by the antichrist) to establish anti-God rule throughout the world. The false prophet gains worldwide worship for the antichrist and builds a living image of him. False religion supports the ungodly system that controls human society. Any who refuse to give their support face death (12-15).

Since God marks his people with his seal (see 7:3), the antichrist marks his people. If any refuse to follow the anti-Christian system, they suffer social and economic discrimination. They are not able to buy even the basic necessities for living (16-17). But whereas the seal placed on God's people is that of the living God (see 7:2), the seal placed on the ungodly is that of the human rebel who fights against God. Its number, 666, is that of a man, not God. It is a human number, for it falls short of the perfect divine number, 777. The antichrist wants to be God, but he must fail, for he is only a man (18; cf. 2 Thess 2:3-4).

Song of the redeemed (14:1-5)

In 7:1-8 God's faithful people were seen on earth and in 7:9-17 in heaven. They are now seen with Christ in his kingdom. The reason why they alone can sing the new song is that only saved sinners can know the experience of redemption (14:1-3). Not only have they been cleansed by Christ, but they have kept themselves pure by not giving in to the temptations of the anti-God world. Like the first products of harvest, they belong specially to God (4-5; cf. Exod 23:19).

Angels and the harvest of the earth (14:6-20)

Three angels now make proclamations. The first reminds people of the good news of God's salvation, adding a warning of judgment and urging sinners to repent (6-7). The second announces judgment on Babylon, symbol of ungodly humankind who, in pride and opposition to God, has corrupted the world (8). The third announces judgment on all who have followed the antichrist (9-11).

John desires that these visions encourage the Christians to be faithful in enduring their sufferings for Christ's sake. Their sufferings are but temporary, whereas the sufferings of their persecutors will be eternal. Even if they suffer death, they can be assured of eternal rest with their Lord as a fitting reward for their faithfulness (12-13).

Evil has now reached its fulness. Angels have announced judgment, and more angels now carry out that judgment. The sinful world is compared to a harvest field ready for reaping, the reaping being God's great and final judgment (14-16). The horror of the judgment is further pictured in a grape harvest. As wine is squeezed out when workers tread grapes in a winepress, so the blood of sinners will run over the earth when God acts in his righteous anger (17-20).

15:1-16:21 THE SEVEN BOWLS OF WRATH

The many visions so far recorded in Revelation have pictured God's judgments in many ways, each time adding a little more detail as the climax approaches. The visions of the seven bowls of God's wrath (or the seven last plagues) repeat to some extent what has been said before, but they place more emphasis on the climax. The end has come. People have not heeded God's warnings, nor have they repented. All that remains for them now is the terrible experience of God's holy wrath.

Preparing to pour out the bowls (15:1-8)

Before describing the seven plagues, John has a vision of Christians who have triumphantly come through the time of suffering. Their deliverance from the forces of the antichrist is similar to, though far greater than, Israel's deliverance from Egypt in the time of Moses. In contrast to those who have been deceived and impressed by the miraculous deeds of the antichrist, Christians are impressed with the wonderful deeds of God, the one who is holy, just and true, the almighty King (15:1-4).

The scene returns to the place where the final trumpet vision concluded, God's heavenly temple (5; cf. 11:15,19). This indicates that just as the seventh seal led to the visions of the seven trumpets (see 8:1-2), so the seventh trumpet leads to the visions of the seven bowls.

Seven angels dressed in white come out of God's heavenly dwelling place to receive the bowls containing the judgments. This signifies that the judgments come from God, and whatever comes from him is pure and holy (6-7). While this work of judgment is going on, no one can enter God's presence to ask for his mercy. Judgment can no longer be avoided or postponed. It is certain (8).

Pouring out the seven bowls (16:1-21)

The bowl judgments are similar to the trumpet judgments, only much more severe. The judgments announced by the trumpets affected only one third of the various areas (see 8:7-12), but here the judgments are total and final. The first judgment brings disease on the earth, the second death in the sea, and the third death in the waters on the land (16:1-4). God acts justly by inflicting the persecutors with punishments suited to the evil they have done (5-6). The voice from the altar confirms that the judgments are God's answer to the prayers of his persecuted people (7; cf. 6:9-10; 8:1-5; 9:13-14; 14:18).

When the angel pours out the fourth bowl there is unbearable heat, but instead of repenting, people curse God all the more (8-9). The fifth plague brings darkness and pain, but people still will not change. Earlier, in the series of trumpet judgments, people had refused to repent (see 9:20-21), but now they also curse God, indicating an increasing hardness against him (10-11).

With the outpouring of the sixth bowl, demonic spirits from the satanic trinity entice the rulers of the world to make war with one another. What results is not just a battle between nations, but the great day of battle for the Almighty himself when he destroys his enemies (12-14). Without warning God acts. The unexpectedness of his intervention is good reason for believers always to be prepared, so that they are not ashamed when he comes (15-16).

As with the seventh seal and the seventh trumpet, so with the seventh bowl there are flashes of lightning, peals of thunder and an earthquake (17-18; cf. 8:5; 11:19). Like the great city Babylon, the ungodly world has become so proud of its achievements and power that it has chosen to ignore God and build a civilization solely to suit itself. Therefore, like Babylon, it is destroyed in a terrible judgment from the all-powerful and all-holy God (19-21). (This judgment will be described in greater detail in Chapters 17 and 18.)

17:1-19:10 BABYLON THE GREAT

The prostitute and the beast (17:1-6)

John's next vision is of a lavishly adorned prostitute. She is symbolic of Babylon (see v. 5, 18), which in turn is symbolic of human society organized independently of God.

In different eras and cultures Babylon shows itself in different ways. In John's day it stood for Rome, but its fullest expression will be at the end of the age as it heads for inevitable judgment. The picture is of the human race's pursuit of prosperity and power through collective effort. Rulers make decisions based on self-interest, and their people support them. Nations seek selfish gain through political and economic treaties, but such unions are likened to sexual relations with a prostitute. They are unions of shame and dishonour, for they ignore God's standards and oppose his authority (17:1-2).

An angel then carries John to a place where, looking from God's point of view, he sees the truth about the woman. She is supported by none other than the beast, the antichrist. An arrogant and defiant humanity seeks greatness, but the spirit that supports and directs it is anti-God (3; cf. 13:1). The woman looks splendid to the world, but John sees that she is full of wickedness. She delights in slaughtering the people of God, as a drunkard delights in drinking wine (4-6).

Power of the beast (17:7-14)

The angel now explains the meaning of the beast and the prostitute. The antichrist, empowered by

Satan, controls human society, using his power to fight against the authority of God. His attacks on God's people may die down for a period, but after he gains fresh life and strength the attacks will be renewed. In the end God will destroy him (7-8; cf. 13:3-4). (For believers of John's time this illustration was full of meaning. The calm that followed Nero's death was not permanent. Persecution was renewed under the Emperor Domitian, who appeared to the Christians to be a second Nero — Nero come back to life, so to speak.)

First century Rome, with its advanced civilization and organized opposition to God, was a clear expression of the anti-God spirit symbolized by the beast, the prostitute and Babylon. The seven heads of the beast, explained as representing both seven hills and seven rulers, symbolized the strength and stability of Rome. But in any age or society, as people's sense of collective self-sufficiency increases, they inevitably set themselves against God (9).

Interpreting the vision becomes more difficult when the angel gives further details of the seven rulers. Most of them already belong to the past. Only one is yet to appear, though he will be replaced by an eighth, who will display even greater satanic power than the previous seven. But God will destroy him. Again, events of the first century may have given this vision special meaning for Christians who experienced persecution under several emperors. No doubt the climax of evil at the end of the age will give the vision much fuller meaning. However, in any era Christians can look back on a line of ungodly rulers and look for relief in the future, even though the final ruler may embody the antichrist more than all who have gone before him. Rulers who become too harsh in their exercise of power usually bring about their own destruction (10-11).

There will always be rulers and nations who want to join forces with the antichrist. They see benefits for themselves in being part of the ungodly power system. They give wholehearted support to the antichrist, but their apparent success is only brief (12-13). In deciding to attack Christ, they guarantee their own destruction. Real power in the kingdoms of the world rests not with the beast (the antichrist) but with the Lamb (the true Christ) (14).

The beast destroys the prostitute (17:15-18)

In their pursuit of power and prosperity, people may develop international cooperation (15), but hatred and jealousy eventually bring disunity and conflict (cf. James 4:1-2). As the prostitute has relied on the beast to carry her, so the human race has relied on the forces of Satan to achieve stability, growth, wealth and power. But as the prostitute is killed by the beast that supported her, so the human race is destroyed by the very forces it has used to advance itself (16). People have a desire to build a society that is independent of God, and in the end God uses that desire to bring about their punishment (17-18).

Fall of Babylon (18:1-8)

The overthrow of human society in its worldwide opposition to God is announced as if it were the fall of the great and proud city of Babylon. The announcement, in the form of a funeral song, gives Christians a vivid picture of the world system in which they live. As they see the world as God sees it, they should want to avoid its dangers and live according to the principles of God's kingdom.

Once the commercial centre of the world, the city is now ruined and deserted, inhabited only by unclean spirits and foul birds. Human organization and commercial activity that ignore God lead in the end to destruction and death. They are likened to unlawful sexual acts, since they are guided by selfish lust without any thought for God's standards (18:1-3).

Christians, on the other hand, are guided by different values, ones that are based on their understanding of God. Their refusal to follow the ways of the ungodly may bring persecution and economic hardship (see 13:17), but at least it keeps them morally pure (4-5). In their proud self-satisfaction, the people of the world boast of their advanced civilization and impressive achievements. But their progress leads them only to assert a greater independence of God, and therefore will lead in the end to a greater punishment (6-8).

Reactions to Babylon's fall (18:9-19:5)

Those who grew prosperous through their commerce with the city weep and mourn at its destruction. The rulers of the nations stand afar off, watching the destruction but doing nothing to help the city in its distress (9-10). Merchants and businessmen mourn for the burning city, not because they have any love for it, but because they have no more market for their goods. Like the rulers they are guided by motives that are entirely selfish. They are distressed only because of their loss of profits (11-16). Shipowners and others who profit from international trade likewise mourn because their source of gain has suddenly been cut off (17-19).

Christians see the city differently. Because they stood firm for God and refused to follow the ways of the world, they rejoice that Babylon has been over-thrown. For them the occasion is one of victory (20).

With the destruction of Babylon, sinful human society exists no more. All activities cease, whether connected with recreation, work, or the everyday affairs of life. Merchants and businessmen are especially condemned, since they are the ones who, through their greed, corrupted the city (21-23). But the main reason for the city's destruction is that it attacked God's people (24).

The scene then shifts to heaven, where there is much rejoicing and praise. God's justice has been demonstrated in the fitting punishment of those who rebelled against his rule and persecuted his people (19:1-3). Although the Christians have triumphed, the one who has given them victory is God. He alone is the object of worship, whether offered by heavenly beings or his redeemed people (4-5).

Wedding feast of the Lamb (19:6-10)

God's rule has been clearly demonstrated in the destruction of the anti-Christian world system and the triumph of his persecuted people. That triumph is now pictured in a heavenly wedding feast in which the redeemed are seen as the bride of Christ. They are clothed in pure white to indicate their heavenly purity (6-8).

The symbolism then changes. The redeemed, though pictured collectively as a bride, are pictured individually as those invited to share the wedding feast with Christ. John, overcome by the vision, is tempted to worship the angel who explained it to him. He is reminded that Jesus, not the angel, is the source of all these revelations (9-10).

19:11-20:15 THE TRIUMPH OF GOD

Up till now the visions have mainly been concerned with the power of evil and the sufferings of believers. Persecuted Christians have been encouraged to endure their trials by the assurance that God is still in control. He guards his people, allowing the wicked to exercise their power only within the limits that he has set according to his eternal plan. Leaving behind the subject of the power of evil in the world, the visions now move on to their climax. They picture the final triumph of God over all enemies and his complete conquest of evil.

The holy war (19:11-20:3)

God's victory over a rebellious humanity and its satanic leaders is now pictured in a terrifying war (cf. 16:12-16). Jesus descends majestically to judge in righteousness and rule in power. His secret name indicates his unique authority (11-12). His blood-soaked robe signifies that his triumph has come through his death on the cross. Armies of angels are with him, but his conquest is not by armies or weapons. It is by the sword that goes out of his mouth. He is the living Word, the active agent of God who expresses God's will and carries it out. He speaks and it is done. As King of kings and Lord of lords he exercises God's rule over all humankind, and in divine wrath punishes the wicked (13-16).

An angel calls flesh-eating birds to prepare for a feast such as they have never had before, for the corpses on the battlefield will be beyond number (17-18). Once Jesus enters the battle, it is soon over. The antichrist and the false prophet are thrown into the lake of fire, signifying punishment from which there is no escape. Meanwhile the armies of the antichrist perish in battle (19-21).

With the antichrist and the false prophet destroyed, only the first member of the evil trinity remains to be dealt with, Satan himself. However, Satan is not yet destroyed. He is thrown into the abyss (see 9:1; 11:7; 17:8) where he is imprisoned for a long period, symbolized by a thousand years, so that he is no longer able to tempt the human race to rebel against God. At the end of this time he will be released for a short while (20:1-3).

Reigning with Christ (20:4-6)

Persecuted believers are now encouraged with a further revelation of their assured victory. Whereas Satan's brief time of apparent triumph is replaced by a lengthy imprisonment, the Christians' brief time of suffering is replaced by a lengthy reign with Christ. They may have been martyred, but now they are raised from death to share the resurrection life with Christ (4; cf. 1 Cor 15:51-57).

This raising of the believers is called the first resurrection. It is followed by the reign with Christ, symbolized by a thousand years. The believers share with Christ in the life of a new era where he rules as King, a position that the ungodly refused to acknowledge when he lived among them in the world. At the end of this reign with Christ there is a second resurrection, this time involving those who are not believers. Theirs, however, is not a resurrection to life, but a resurrection to damnation. They suffer that final punishment which John calls the second death (5-6).

Defeat of Satan (20:7-10)

At the end of the time of Christ's reign Satan is released, but he soon shows that he has not changed his ways. As usual he deceives people and incites them to rebel against God (cf. 16:12-16; Gen 3:1-6).

Rebels across the world unite against God and his people. As in a similar apocalyptic vision in the Old Testament, the anti-God leader is symbolized by a man called Gog who lives in the land of Magog. But, as in the Old Testament vision, Satan is allowed to draw all the rebels together so that God might destroy them all at the same time in one decisive act of judgment (7-9; cf. Ezek 38:1-9,16,18; 39:1-8). God then throws Satan into the lake of fire to join the antichrist and the false prophet. This is an imprisonment from which there is no release. It is the final punishment (10).

The last judgment (20:11-15)

When the rest of the dead are raised to life (see v. 5) the final judgment takes place. The one who carries out the judgment is the Lord of the universe, and he carries it out with absolute justice. At this judgment people face two independent witnesses. The first is the record of their works, according to which they will be judged. The second is the list of names in the book of life, which confirms whether or not they accepted God's offer of pardon (11-13). All people, in the end, share either the blessings of heaven or the horrors of the lake of fire. Finally, death and the world of the dead are made as powerless as all other enemies (14-15; cf. 1 Cor 15:26,55).

21:1-22:5 A NEW HEAVEN AND A NEW EARTH

In describing the state of things as it will be in eternity, John has to use the language of this world, for he has no other. He has to liken what he sees in the vision to things that his readers can see in the present world, for this is the only world they know. He has to use whatever language and illustrations he can find in an attempt to describe the spiritual quality of life in the eternal state.

John's visions symbolize spiritual realities. They are not pictures of the physical characteristics of the new heaven and the new earth. In fact, he makes it clear that the future state of things is vastly different from the present. The heavenly city is not an improved version of the present earthly city. Life as we know it in the present world is to be completely replaced by a new order.

God dwelling with his people (21:1-8)

Usually God is pictured as dwelling in heaven and people as dwelling on earth. In the eternal state no such distinction exists, because God now dwells with his people in an order of life never before experienced. It is an order that is holy and beautiful, where God and his people live together in the closest fellowship. All this is possible because the effects of sin in the previous order have now been removed (21:1-4).

This promise of a new life encourages persecuted believers. They need not fear the future, because God is always in control. As long as they feel their need of him, he will supply that need (5-6). Those who triumph through persecution and temptation prove the genuineness of their faith, and will enjoy a specially close relationship with God their Father. Those who deny Christ through fear of persecution prove that their faith is false, and will join their tempter in the lake of fire (7-8).

New Jerusalem (21:9-21)

God's redeemed people, who in a previous picture were seen as the bride of the Lamb (see 19:6-10; 21:2), are now symbolized by a holy city, the new Jerusalem. This city comes from God, for it was built by God. It is not something of human creation. People are saved by God's grace, not by their own achievements (9-10).

The city is glorious and indestructible, and the people who live in it are eternally secure. All believers, whether of the era before Christ or after, are united in one company. Those of the former era, the true Israel, are represented by the names of the twelve tribes. Those of the latter era, the Christian church, are represented by the names of the twelve apostles. Together they are God's people and they dwell in his heavenly city. In fact, they *are* the city (11-14).

An angel measures the city, apparently to assure its citizens that every part of it is protected by God. He finds that the city is a perfect cube, which no doubt confirms the citizens' assurance that everything God does is perfect. Although the realities pictured in the vision are real, the city is not like a literal city of the present physical world. (Where does one put a sixty metre high wall on a cubical city whose sides each measure 2400 kilometres?) The angel, realizing that ordinary human beings cannot imagine such a city, points out that he has used an ordinary human system of measurement to help illustrate a truth. And the truth is that the city is perfect, complete (15-17). Its worth and beauty are beyond measure – signified by its construction from the most costly and beautiful materials (18-21).

Life in the holy city (21:22-22:5)

No temple is needed in the city, because God is everywhere. Lights, whether natural or artificial, are unnecessary, because God's glory fills every place (22-23). Other cities close their gates at night to prevent possible enemy attacks, but this city never closes its gates, because there is no night and no enemy. People of all nations inhabit the city, adding colour and splendour, yet there is complete purity, because sin is excluded (24-27).

Although the original man and woman lost the first paradise, redeemed men and women now possess the final paradise (cf. Gen 2:9-10; 3:1-24). Having been healed from the curse of sin, they can now enjoy the blessings of the tree of life that God originally intended for them. The river that flows from God and the Lamb brings life, nourishment and enjoyment to people of all nations (22:1-2; cf. Ezek 47:1-12). Life in paradise is not spent in lazy idleness, but in the active worship and service of God. The redeemed see their God, bear his name, and share his glory (3-5).

22:6-21 CONCLUSION

John concludes his book by stressing that his visions have come from God and are trustworthy. They are given not to help people work out a timetable of future events, but to strengthen Christians so that they will be obedient and not forsake Christ simply to escape persecution (6-7). There is an added warning not to get over-excited because of the visions, but to respond by offering fitting worship to God (8-9).

A special word of advice is then given for persecuted believers. It is useless for them to fight against their persecutors. Rather they must leave such people to follow their evil ways, knowing that the wicked will meet swift punishment at Christ's return. Believers, on the other hand, must follow the ways of God. They must keep their Christian testimony pure, knowing that at Christ's return they will be rewarded (10-11).

The risen Christ, who is the eternal God and the judge of all people everywhere, gives a reminder that the climax of the world's history is approaching. He will return soon. Again this is not so that Christians might try to calculate the date of his coming, but so that they might be faithful to God and pure in their lives. When he comes he will reward people according to the way they have lived. The faithful will enjoy the blessings of life in the presence of God, but their opponents will be excluded for ever (12-15).

Christ, the promised Son of David, is like the morning star, whose coming signifies the dawn of a new day. The Holy Spirit, the universal church and individual believers join in urging him to return. At the same time they urge unbelievers to accept eternal life from him. The book has recorded much concerning judgment, but the invitation to accept God's salvation remains open to the end (16-17). John closes with a solemn warning to take heed to what he has written in the book and not to alter its contents or avoid its teachings. Jesus Christ is coming (18-21).